Windows® Server 2003/2000 Terminal Server Solutions, Third Edition

D0878918

Windows® Server 2003/2000 Terminal Server Solutions, Third Edition

Implementing Windows Terminal Services and Citrix MetaFrame Presentation Server 3.0

Todd W. Mathers

↔ Addison-Wesley

Upper Saddle River, NJ • Boston • Indianapolis
San Francisco • New York • Toronto • Montreal
London • Munich • Paris • Madrid • Capetown
Sydney • Tokyo • Singapore • Mexico City

The publisher offers discounts on this book when ordered in quantity for bulk purchases and special sales. For more information, please contact:

> U.S. Corporate and Government Sales
> (800) 382-3419
> corpsales@pearsontechgroup.com

For sales outside of the U.S., please contact:

> International Sales
> international@pearsoned.com

Visit Addison-Wesley on the Web: www.awprofessional.com

Library of Congress Number: 2004111393

This Book Is Safari Enabled

The Safari® Enabled icon on the cover of your favorite technology book means the book is available through Safari Bookshelf. When you buy this book, you get free access to the online edition for 45 days. Safari Bookshelf is an electronic reference library that lets you easily search thousands of technical books, find code samples, download chapters, and access technical information whenever and wherever you need it.

To gain 45-day Safari Enabled access to this book:

- Go to http://www.awprofessional.com/safarienabled
- Complete the brief registration form
- Enter the coupon code YHGA-0IJF-5NUN-2GF9-RBNK

If you have difficulty registering on Safari Bookshelf or accessing the online edition, please e-mail customer-service@safaribooksonline.com.

For information on obtaining permission for use of material from this work, please submit a written request to:

> Pearson Education, Inc.
> Rights and Contracts Department
> 75 Arlington Street, Suite 300
> Boston, MA 02116
> Fax: (617) 848-7047

Text printed on recycled paper
ISBN: 1-578-70276-3
1 2 3 4 5 6 7 8 9 10 MA 06   05   04   03   02
First printing, December 2004

For D

Contents

Preface

It has been almost 10 years since I first set eyes on the installation of a Windows server–based computing operating system, and it has been true love (in the traditional geek-loves-technology kind of way) ever since. My introduction to Citrix WinFrame was very much a life-altering (or at least career-altering) experience, expanding my interests far beyond the simple life of application development to one of systems architecture and the design and implementation of server-based computing solutions. Even back then I saw the potential for the technology, not only in revolutionizing the way companies delivered applications to their employees but also in how IT staff supported that environment. Coming from the world of application development, I had a true appreciation of how difficult it was both to develop the applications for an organization and to roll those products out to the myriad of desktop hardware and software configurations that existed within every company, regardless of its size.

Troubleshooting why the application installed and ran fine on one machine but not on another even though they appeared to be identical was truly a lesson in frustration.

Needless to say I was excited and intrigued by the concept of server-based computing and the potential benefits to be had from providing the end user with a centrally managed, secure, and—best of all—stable environment within which to run their applications. Delivering a consistent computing environment to the user, regardless of their local desktop hardware and software configuration, was like stumbling upon an oasis in the middle of the desert. I saw salvation.

After our project team used WinFrame 1.6 to build a 60-server load-balanced environment, spread across two distinct geographical locations, to successfully deploy a full desktop solution to over 2,000 call center and order processing staff, I was truly a believer. The fact that this little-known product from a small company named Citrix Systems had delivered so thoroughly on such a bold promise was truly remarkable. Considering the number of times we said, "Wow, it actually works," I'm sure people thought that was our team slogan.

Eight-plus years, three published books, and countless consulting hours later, I still am in love with this technology and continue to be impressed with the ways it can be used to deliver on the expectations of the companies that deploy the product and the end users who work within the environment. Certainly many things have changed since those early days—some good, some not so good—but one thing that remains the same is the truly impressed look on the faces of the IT staff when they see the technology work exactly the way it was promised. I'm pretty sure I had that same look back then, too.

Having said all that, I must also say that an undisputed truth about computers in general is that they do not deliver solutions all by themselves. I have yet to see a software package pop out of a box, jump into a server, and configure itself while the administrator sipped coffee and reviewed stock quotes. Until that day, the ultimate success of a project still is dictated by the people tasked with the job, not the software or hardware deployed.

Unfortunately, for every server-based computing project that succeeds, there is an equal number of projects that would be deemed far from successful. In most cases the list of problems are long and varied, but unfortunately—and whether justified or not—much of the blame falls on the administrators responsible for implementing the environment. Many administrators make the mistake of assuming that because they understand Windows and know how to administer a Windows environment, they're adequately qualified to deploy Terminal Services. Truly, such thinking is a recipe for disaster almost every time.

It doesn't have to be this way. With a bit of planning and a lot of patience, any Windows administrator can successfully implement a Windows server–based computing environment. My ultimate goal in producing this book is to provide the knowledge, insight, and guidance necessary to achieve delivering a robust, scalable, and stable server-based computing environment using Microsoft Windows Terminal Services (2000 or 2003) and Citrix MetaFrame Presentation Server 3.0.

Who Should Read this Book?

This book best serves the Windows administrator who wants to analyze, plan, test, and implement a server-based computing solution running Windows Terminal Services with or without MetaFrame Presentation Server 3.0. It focuses on the entire project life cycle, from properly assessing the needs of an organization and planning all aspects of the deployment (not just how to build a Terminal Server) right through to the actual implementation and support. The book is full of implementation examples, from server security to group policy creation and from patch management to client deployment. While I try to encompass all major aspects of a Terminal Server implementation, there are some areas where I provide only tertiary coverage and/or assume that you're already familiar with (or are readily able to learn) that area. These areas include the following:

- A basic knowledge of Windows Server 2000 and/or Windows Server 2003
- An understanding of Windows 2000/2003 Active Directory and how to use the provided tools, such as Active Directory Users and Computers
- Installation and use of Windows Internet Information Services (IIS)

In writing this book, my goal was to create a reference useful to administrators at a variety of skill levels related to the Terminal Server and MetaFrame technologies. What if you're completely new to the world of server-based computing? No problem. Working through this book from beginning to end will instill the knowledge necessary to successfully implement a Terminal Server/MetaFrame environment of any size. After reading this book, you will have the knowledge and understanding necessary to make smart choices about your new Terminal Server/MetaFrame implementation or about the changes necessary to better stabilize an existing environment that you've been tasked with managing and supporting.

What if you're an old-school Terminal Server/MetaFrame administrator who wants to update his or her knowledge on the latest and greatest technology from Microsoft and Citrix? Don't worry; I've got you covered as well. Key changes in the technology such as Microsoft's new licensing requirements for Windows Server 2003 Terminal Services, the Session Directory technology, and client drive and printer mapping support are all covered. And for all you MetaFrame 1.8 administrators who're finally looking to upgrade, configuring interoperability between MetaFrame 1.8 and MPS 3.0 is also discussed.

I know that the solutions discussed in this book work, because I've used them successfully, but I also know that not all environments are created equally, and creative solutions are the computer-world equivalent of duct tape. When discussing the various aspects of these technologies, I provide suggestions and recommendations on how these can be configured, but unless I explicitly say so, my suggestions should not be taken as the only solution that will work. I always encourage creativity (although it is best kept in the test environment and not in production), and playing around is still the best way to thoroughly understand the limitations of any computer system. One of the biggest differentiators between a good administrator and a great administrator is the ability to create, adapt, and develop solutions under a variety of conditions.

Organization of This Book

The book is divided into four parts. Part I provides an overview of both the Microsoft Terminal Services and Citrix MetaFrame Presentation Server technologies, describing the main features and functionalities of both. Many of the general questions about the similarities and differences between the two products are answered in this section, including details on exactly what the licensing requirements are, a topic commonly misinterpreted by many people.

Part II is a project manager's dream come true. In this section I cover the planning considerations of a Terminal Server/MetaFrame implementation, including topics such as client hardware and software planning, server hardware planning, and service pack and hotfix distribution planning.

Part III provides a detailed look at how to actually implement and support Terminal Server/MetaFrame, building on the planning discussed in Part II of the book.

Part IV consists of the appendixes, summarizing information such as the command line tools available with both Terminal Server and MetaFrame and providing detailed introductory information on areas such as file server and registry security.

Part I: An Overview of Windows Server–Based Computing

Chapter 1: "Microsoft Windows Terminal Services"

Looks at the functionality and features of Terminal Services, comparing both Windows 2000 Server and Windows Server 2003 Terminal Services. Differences in areas such as licensing are also reviewed.

Chapter 2: "Citrix MetaFrame Presentation Server"

Focuses on the MetaFrame extensions to Terminal Services and the functionality enhancements it provides. Changes in client licensing management in MPS 3.0 are also introduced.

Part II: Planning Your Terminal Services Implementation

Chapter 3: "Project Management Considerations"

Provides the project manager of a Terminal Services implementation with an introduction to many of the important tasks that need to be managed before and during the early stages of the project, including implementation requirements, business process management, and policies and procedures.

Chapter 4: "Network Planning"

Examines the importance of the network in your Terminal Services implementation. Printing considerations as well as dial-up and Internet access are also discussed.

Chapter 5: "Client Hardware and Software Planning"

Complete coverage of both the Microsoft RDP and Citrix ICA clients is provided in different deployment scenarios. I also look at the importance of proper client planning for a successful Terminal Services project.

Chapter 6: "Terminal Server Hardware Planning"

Discusses the two main considerations when planning the hardware requirements of a Terminal Server environment: the capacity-planning requirements and the appropriate hardware sizing to meet those requirements.

Chapter 7: "Server and Application Software Planning"

Examines the strategies for categorizing and planning the deployment of both the server and application software.

Chapter 8: "Server Installation and Management Planning"
Looks at planning the Terminal Server installation and the importance of developing a sound technical management plan in order to maximize scalability and stability of the Terminal Services environment. Common monitoring tools are discussed and a general guideline is provided, which can be used to benchmark different tools in order to find those providing the best fit for the implementation.

Chapter 9: "Service Pack and Hotfix Management"
Proper management of service pack and hotfix deployments are critical to ensuring a stable and secure environment. The final planning chapter looks at techniques for managing these requirements.

Part III: Implementing Terminal Services and Citrix MetaFrame

Chapter 10: "Installing Windows Terminal Services"
Details the steps involved in installation of Windows 2003/2000 Terminal Services. Features such as service pack integration with the base operating system installation and use of answer files are discussed.

Chapter 11: "Terminal Services Configuration and Tuning"
Provides a detailed walkthrough of configuring and tuning your Terminal Server for optimal operation. Performance and stability considerations are discussed.

Chapter 12: "License Server Installation and Configuration"
Terminal Services licensing is a critical component of any Terminal Server environment; its proper deployment is thoroughly covered in this chapter.

Chapter 13: "MetaFrame Presentation Server Installation"
Details the steps involved in installation of Citrix MetaFrame Presentation Server on a Windows 2003/2000 Terminal Server.

Chapter 14: "MetaFrame Presentation Server Configuration"
Configuration tasks specific to a MetaFrame server are discussed in this chapter. All configurable settings within the Management Console are reviewed here.

Chapter 15: "Group Policy Configuration"
Examines use of group policies in Windows Active Directory domain to establish a more controlled and consistent Terminal Services environment.

Chapter 16: "Terminal Server Security"
Focuses specifically on properly securing your Terminal Server implementation.

Chapter 17: "Terminal Server and MetaFrame Printer Management"
An important part of any implementation is the ability of the users to print. This chapter looks at configuration of the various printer features supported in Terminal Server and MetaFrame.

Chapter 18: "User Profile and Account Configuration"

Provides a detailed look at the role of the user profile in a Terminal Services environment and how to effectively manage these profiles. Leveraging centralization of Active Directory and DFS (distributed file system) are also discussed here.

Chapter 19: "RDP Client Installation and Configuration"

Looks at the steps for installation of the RDP client and provides more detailed examples of how you would configure the client based on the desired implementation scenario.

Chapter 20: "ICA Client Installation and Configuration"

Looks at the installation steps required for the Citrix ICA client. Configuration details on features such as the Program Neighborhood Agent and custom installations are also examined.

Chapter 21: "Application Integration"

Provides a detailed discussion of the special application support features available with Terminal Services, the tools and techniques that will assist you.

Chapter 22: "Server Operations and Support"

Looks at the shift in responsibility from implementation to operations and the tools that can be used to ensure availability of the production environment to the end user.

Part IV: Appendixes

Appendix A: "Terminal Services Command Reference"

Contains a complete list and explanation of Terminal Services–specific commands. Examples and common usage situations are also provided.

Appendix B: "MetaFrame Presentation Server Command Reference"

Describes the command line tools provided with MetaFrame. Examples and common usage situations are also provided.

Appendix C: "Network Primer"

Provides a general overview of networking and the OSI model.

Appendix D: "Terminal Server Tuning and Configuration Checklist"

A brief checklist that summarizes the settings discussed in Chapter 11.

Appendix E: "File System and Registry Security Primer"

Looks at Windows NTFS and registry security.

PART I

An Overview of Windows Server–Based Computing

CHAPTER 1

Microsoft Windows Terminal Services

What Is Windows Terminal Services?

Windows Terminal Services provides the multiuser capabilities that form the foundation of the material discussed in this book. This chapter takes a look at this architecture, including its history, how it is integrated into both the Windows server and the supported clients, and the new features that have been added to Windows Terminal Services since the initial Windows NT 4.0, Terminal Server Edition release, Microsoft's first official release of a Terminal Server product.

Conceptually, the idea behind Terminal Services is simple and will be familiar to anyone with experience accessing graphical environments such as X Windows, where most (if not all) application processing happens on a remote server, and only the visual input and output are handled on the client device. Terminal Services brings this same functionality to the Windows environment.

Windows Terminal Services lets multiple users simultaneously access applications that perform 100 percent of their processing on the centralized Terminal Server. Figure 1.1 shows a rather trivial yet effective example of this, with a Windows 2003 Terminal Services desktop session being accessed from within a Windows 2000 Professional desktop.

NOTE: When hearing about Terminal Services, many people immediately jump to the conclusion that this product provides remote access capabilities similar to remote presentation products such as VNC or pcAnywhere. While visually they appear to perform the same task, there is one fundamental difference. Terminal Services lets multiple users simultaneously establish their own distinct Windows session on a single Terminal Server, and load and run applications completely independent of other users also running on that same server. Products such as VNC or pcAnywhere let you remotely access the local desktop on a PC or server but do not provide the same robust, multiuser support.

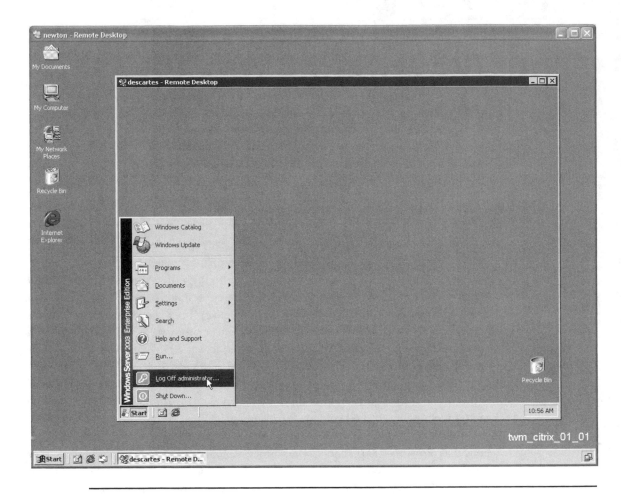

Figure 1.1 Client access to a Windows 2003 Terminal Server.

Application serving, server-based computing, and *thin-client computing* are all terms that have been used at one time or another to describe the use of Terminal Services to provide remote application support to users. On a Terminal Server you would find applications such as these:

- Microsoft Office (Word, Excel, Outlook, and so on)
- Mozilla Web browser
- Lotus Notes

Because Terminal Servers provide access to traditional desktop applications, they are commonly referred to as *application servers.*

The direct opposite of an application server is the traditional Windows server that supports standard or extended server system features such as

- File and print services
- Web services (Internet Information Server, Apache)
- Collaboration services (Microsoft Exchange, Lotus Notes)
- Database management services (Microsoft SQL Server, Oracle)

TIP: In the past, a standard Windows file server was sometimes called an *application server* if it contained application files that users accessed from across the network. This obviously differs from a Terminal Server in that the client still runs the application locally; only the application files are located on the central server. In this book, I use the term *application server* to refer only to Windows Terminal Server.

The fact that an application server and a standard Windows server are visually almost identical can have both a positive and a negative impact on your implementation and production management. On the plus side, the similarities let a skilled Windows administrator get up to speed quickly on how to install and maintain many of the Terminal Server components. This commonality can also have a negative side, however, as these skilled (and sometimes not so skilled) administrators may make assumptions about the configuration or operation of Terminal Server that are perfectly correct for a regular Windows server but not for a Terminal Server.

Before we continue this discussion and look more closely at the components that make up Windows Terminal Services, let us take a moment to review the history behind Terminal Server.

The History of Windows Terminal Server

Although Microsoft Windows Terminal Server has only been in existence since 1998, the technology behind it is not nearly so new. The Citrix MultiWin technology that was incorporated into Terminal Server was first conceived in the late 1980s by Ed Iacobucci. Iacobucci worked for IBM from 1978 to 1989, spending most of that time in the personal computer division, designing and architecting operating systems. When Microsoft and IBM set out to develop OS/2, Iacobucci was head of the joint design team. During this time, Iacobucci envisioned a way to let different types of computers on a network run OS/2 even though they weren't built to do so. The idea of MultiWin was born.

At the time, neither IBM nor Microsoft was interested in Iacobucci's idea, so he left to form Citrix Systems in 1989. Citrix developed the proposed technology (known as MultiView), and it worked. The problem with Citrix's new product was that it was based on OS/2, and the future of OS/2 was looking dim. In the fall of 1991, with Citrix on the verge of going under, Iacobucci turned to Microsoft. He was interested in rebuilding Citrix's technology based on Windows NT.

At the time, Windows NT's penetration into the market was slight, and Microsoft was confident that if Citrix could deliver this proposed product, it would help expand NT's market. Microsoft was interested enough to not only grant Citrix license to the NT source code required to make this work, but also to acquire a 6 percent stake in the company. In August 1995, Citrix shipped WinFrame, the first true application server version of Windows NT.

NOTE: Many of the most popular features of Windows Server 2003 Terminal Services, including local client printer and drive access, were originally developed and available with the WinFrame product.

In 1996, Citrix began working on WinFrame 2.0, which was to be the next major upgrade, based on the Windows NT 4.0 architecture. By early 1997, Citrix had WinFrame 2.0 well into beta. At that time, with NT sales booming, and fearing the possible fragmentation of NT into a UNIX-type operating system, Microsoft decided it was time to reclaim sole ownership of Windows NT. In February 1997, Microsoft informed Citrix that it was considering developing its own multiuser version of Windows NT. Shortly thereafter, Citrix made a public announcement explaining Microsoft's new position. The day after this announcement, Citrix's stock value lost 60 percent.

Over the next several months, during a time of intense negotiations between the two companies, the future of WinFrame remained uncertain until May, when Microsoft and Citrix came to an agreement. Much of the reasoning behind the agreement was Microsoft's desire to quickly become a player in the thin-client industry, something it had little chance of achieving if required to develop a new product from scratch.

Through this agreement, Microsoft licensed the MultiWin technology from Citrix to incorporate into future versions of Windows while letting Citrix continue development on its current WinFrame 1.x product and provide future extensions (Citrix MetaFrame Presentation Server) to Microsoft's Terminal Server product.

In July 1998, Microsoft shipped Windows NT Server 4.0, Terminal Server Edition, its first thin-client operating system. This was a special version of Windows NT Server 4.0, with the multiuser changes incorporated into it. While it looked exactly like regular NT 4.0, it was architecturally different and required its own special service pack and hotfix releases. Regular NT 4.0 fixes would not work with this special version, and very often the equivalent patch was weeks (even months) behind the standard NT server release.

With the release of Windows 2000 in February 2000, Microsoft consolidated the multiuser features of Terminal Server into its core server operating system, making these features available as services that could be installed on any Windows 2000 Server product. By merging this functionality, Microsoft made a huge leap forward in simplifying both the maintenance and availability of its thin-client product.

Now, with the release of Windows Server 2003, these multiuser features have been further enhanced, providing even more advanced and robust Terminal Server functionality.

Multiuser Support

The most obvious difference between a standard Windows server and an application server is the multiuser support. Until the introduction of WinFrame, and later Terminal Server, "logging on" to a Windows server meant one of three things:

- **Logging on at the local console**—An administrator or user is logging on using a keyboard, mouse, and monitor directly connected to the computer.
- **Remotely accessing a server resource**—A user accesses a resource on that server, such as a file or printer, the server's registry, or an extended server system service (Web server, database, or the like).
- **Remotely accessing the local console**—A user accesses the console remotely using a tool such as pcAnywhere, VNC, or the SMS Remove Control feature. In this case, you're either the only person logged on to the console (albeit remotely), or you're controlling the session of the person who is physically logged on at that console.

While multiple users can access a resource simultaneously (a Web server, for example), a standard Windows server can have only one person with an interactive console logged on at a time, as shown in Figure 1.2. This has been the standard operating behavior not only on Windows servers but also on Windows desktop systems and other PC-based operating systems, such as MacOS or OS/2.

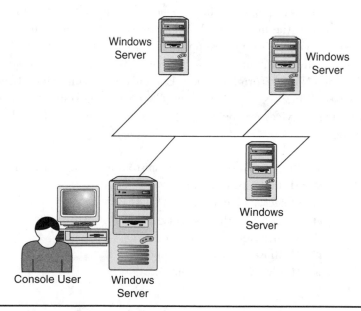

Figure 1.2   A traditional Windows system supports only a single console logon.

The introduction of server-based computing has ended the restriction that the console user is the only user with an interactive logon. Now there can be 2, 10, 50, or more users logged on concurrently in addition to the console user (see Figure 1.3).

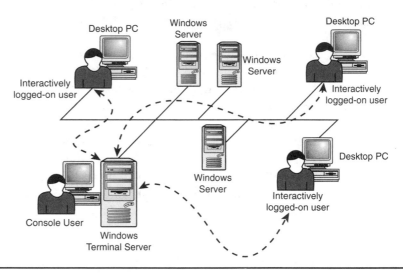

Figure 1.3   Terminal Server supports multiple interactive client sessions in addition to the console logon.

For Windows to support multiple concurrent interactive sessions, changes had to be made to a number of the underlying Windows operating system components to be able to manage each concurrent user's session. While the first release of Windows Terminal Services required the creation and maintenance of a completely separate operating system with Windows NT 4.0, Terminal Server Edition, these changes have been tightly incorporated into the base Windows Server 2003 and 2000 operating systems and are present whether or not Terminal Services are being used. Let's take a brief look at the following major areas of change:

- Remote Desktop for Administration versus Terminal Server mode
- Multiple-user desktops
- Object management
- Process and thread management
- Virtual memory management
- Multiuser application support
- Hardware requirements

Remote Administration Versus Application Server Mode

Windows 2003 Server and Windows 2000 Server both let you implement Terminal Services in one of two modes. The first is Terminal Server mode (called Application Server mode in Windows 2000), which provides the true Terminal Server features discussed in this book. This configuration must be specifically selected in order to be enabled on a Windows server. The other implementation mode is a special management mode known as Remote Desktop for Administration (Remote Administration mode in Windows 2000). This administration mode is installed by default on all Windows 2003 servers but must be explicitly enabled before it can be used (see Figure 1.4). On a Windows 2000 server, this component must be added through Add/Remove Windows Components.

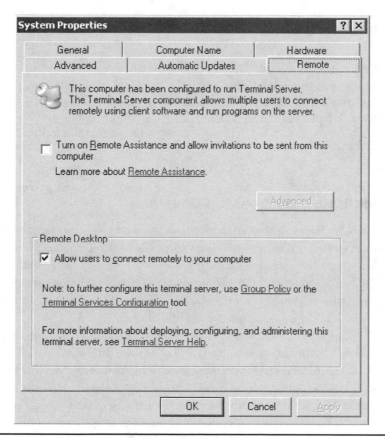

Figure 1.4   Remote Desktop for Administration can be enabled on any Windows 2003 server from under the Remote tab of System Properties.

As the name implies, Remote Administration is designed to let an administrator access *any* Windows server, even those not designated as true Terminal Servers, using a Terminal Services client strictly for administrative purposes. In addition to the console session, Remote Administration allows two concurrent client logons, without requiring any special Terminal Services licensing.

When Remote Administration is enabled, there is no change in the tuning or configuration of the server as there is when the Terminal Server mode is selected. All applications installed on the server prior to enabling Remote Administration are not affected in any way.

Enabling Remote Administration lets anyone with the Remote Desktop Protocol (RDP) client (Microsoft's Terminal Server client, discussed shortly) access a logon screen for the server. Because of this, you will need to ensure that good password practices are being enforced in your organization to prevent someone from guessing a password that would let them access the server.

TIP: Windows Server 2003 provides an enhancement to the Remote Administration feature, letting you remotely access the local console session (session 0) on a server and not just a remote desktop session. An overview of the RDP client is discussed later in this chapter, while detailed information on the installation of the client software is discussed in Chapter 19, "RDP Client Installation and Configuration."

Multiple-User Desktop Sessions

Probably the most obvious area of change is how the server handles each user session's graphical interface. With multiple interactive users, the Terminal Server needs to be able to differentiate the graphics data from each user session. The local (or console) session on a Terminal Server is exactly the same as on a regular Windows server. It contains the two standard windowstation objects (winsta0, Service-0x0-3e7$) and the standard desktop objects (default and winlogon) associated with winsta0.

The interactive windowstation (winsta0) contains a clipboard, a group of desktop objects, and the keyboard, mouse, and display device. This windowstation handles input from the user. The special windowstation 0x0-3e7$ is a noninteractive windowstation and is associated with the noninteractive services that use the LocalSystem account. One or more desktop objects are contained within a windowstation. A desktop object has a display area that contains windows, menus, and other user interface components. Only one desktop at a time can be active for a windowstation.

Remote Terminal Server sessions contain only the winsta0, windowstation, and three desktop objects: default, winlogon, and Disconnect. Disconnect is a special desktop that's made active when a user disconnects his or her Terminal Server session. Remote sessions don't require the Service-0x0-3e7$ windowstation, because all system services run under the local console context.

NOTE: When a user's session is disconnected, the link between the server and the client is terminated, but the session itself remains active on the server. A disconnected session will continue to process any running tasks, and if the user logs back on to that server, they will automatically be reconnected to that session.

Object Management

All operating system resources in Windows are represented by objects. The Object Manager, located in the NT Executive, is responsible for creating, modifying, and deleting these objects. Objects exist within what's called an *object namespace*. On a Terminal Services–enabled server, each interactive user session is assigned its own private object namespace, known as a user's *local namespace*. This allows multiple instances of the same application running on a server to create named objects that won't conflict with each other. Objects in one user's namespace are differentiated from the objects in another namespace by the unique name they are given. When creating a named object for a specific session, the Object Manager will append the user's unique session ID to the object name. An application cannot see objects in another user's namespace.

In addition to multiple user namespaces is the *system global namespace*. This namespace is visible to all sessions on the Terminal Server. Any services and all applications running on the local console execute within the system global namespace. Figure 1.5 depicts the multiple namespaces that exist in a Windows 2003 or 2000 Terminal Server.

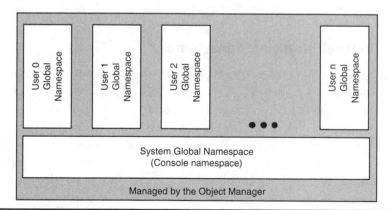

Figure 1.5   Object namespaces in a Windows 2003 or 2000 Terminal Server.

TIP: The context (user or system global) within which an application or one of its components operates can be controlled using the REGISTER command. For a complete description of this command, see Appendix A, "Terminal Server Command Reference."

Process and Thread Management

Just as with other components of Terminal Server, the Process Manager has been modified to recognize process and thread objects on a per-session basis. In addition, Microsoft has modified how Terminal Server handles task scheduling and prioritization as compared to a regular Windows server. On a regular server, the process scheduler allocates longer time slices to better support the background applications that typically run on a Windows server. These applications usually have very low user interaction on the console. On a Terminal Server, process scheduling is more like a Windows desktop operating system (Windows 2000 or XP Professional) in that user interaction and foreground tasks are more responsive. The time slices on a Terminal Server are much shorter than those on a regular Windows server. Thread priorities have been modified to maximize user responsiveness. Normally, new processes on Windows are assigned a lower priority than foreground tasks, but because multiple foreground processes exist on a Terminal Server, all starting processes have the same priority as foreground tasks. These changes in process priority and scheduling are what make Terminal Server a poor host of standard server services such as SQL Server or a domain controller.

Process and thread management changes are discussed in more detail in Chapter 11, "Terminal Services Configuration and Tuning."

TIP: When a Windows server has Remote Desktop for Administration enabled, the server remains in the traditional Windows processing scheduling configuration and is optimized for running standard server services, *not* Terminal Services.

Virtual Memory Management

Every process on a regular Windows server is assigned a virtual address space that's divided between the kernel and user address space. The kernel space is shared between all processes, and each process receives its own user space. User mode threads can access only the user space; kernel mode threads can access both the user and the kernel space. Within the kernel address space are the Windows subsystems and associated drivers. When multiple interactive Terminal Server sessions try to access this single kernel space, they introduce kernel-sharing issues. To resolve this problem, Terminal Server has introduced a new type of address space called the session address space. The session address space contains a private copy of the kernel space that's used by all processes within a session. This lets each session have its own Win32 kernel (also known as WIN32K.SYS, which contains the Windows Manager and Graphics Device Interface [GDI], display, and printer drivers).

Multiuser Application Support

In addition to the architectural changes just discussed, modifications to some of the standard Win32 API calls had to be made in order to more easily handle multiple interactive users accessing an application. Traditionally, Windows applications have been developed with the assumption that only one user at a time was running the application interactively on a computer. Many of these programs make improper use of configuration files in the Windows system root or in the system registry. Multiple users simultaneously accessing this information from a single location often introduce application conflicts.

Terminal Server attempts to deal with this problem by introducing a special method of registry and INI file monitoring so that changes made during an application installation can be properly recorded and reproduced for each user who runs the application. Installing an application using the Add or Remove Programs tool found in the Control Panel activates this special monitoring feature. When applications are installed on a Terminal Server in this fashion, the server is placed into *install mode*, so it can properly monitor and record system changes. If the application is not installed in this fashion, the server remains in what is known as *execute mode*, and any system changes made during the installation will be properly configured for only the person who installed the application. Figure 1.6 shows the Add or Remove Programs tool for Windows Server 2003.

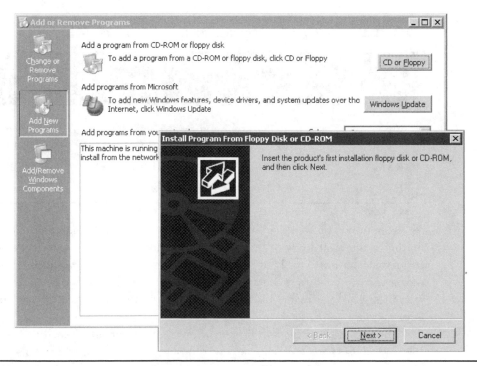

Figure 1.6 Use Add or Remove Programs to install applications on a Terminal Server.

TIP: A server can also be switched between install and execute mode from a command prompt using the CHANGE USER command. Details on this command are available in Appendix A, and a complete discussion of application installation and configuration is given in Chapter 21, "Application Integration."

Hardware Requirements

To support multiple interactive user sessions, a Terminal Server will usually have more substantial hardware requirements than the equivalent Windows server would need to support the same number of users through the traditional client/server scenario (file and print, SQL Server, or Web server, for example).

One thing that all Windows administrators learn is a standard set of guidelines for various Windows server hardware configurations. Many of the common server setups, such as a file and print server or a Web server, have minimum recommendations for a certain number of users. Table 1.1 shows a sample configuration for a Windows file server, an Internet Information Server (IIS) 6.0, and an Exchange 2003 server, all sized to handle 200 or more concurrent users.

Table 1.1   Standard Configuration for Common Windows Server Services

	Server Service Type		
Component	**File Server**	**Exchange 2003**	**IIS 6.0**
Processor	Single Intel Xeon, 2.4 GHz	Dual Intel Xeon, 2.4 GHz	Single Intel Xeon, 2.4 GHz
RAM	512MB RAM	512MB RAM	512MB RAM
Disk capacity	72GB+	72GB+	18GB+

Also common to these servers are hardware redundancy and other fault-tolerance features to maximize the availability of the server. For standard Windows servers, resources are sized based on the average (or better yet, the maximum) number of concurrent user requests that the server will need to process. Print, mailbox access, and Web page access requests are all examples. The user makes the request and then waits for the server to return the required information.

The hardware sizing for Terminal Server differs greatly from the preceding scenario. Because all users are accessing the server through interactive sessions, the server must be able to provide immediate feedback to any applications that users are currently running. This requires greater processor and RAM resources than those required by a standard Windows server. Table 1.2 shows a typical Terminal Server configuration to support 100+ average concurrent users. An average user typically is someone who runs 3–6 applications simultaneously.

These usually consist of a mail program, Word processor, and one or more line-of-business applications such as a host emulator or a client/server application. One or more applications may be 16-bit or DOS applications.

Table 1.2   Typical Terminal Server Configuration for 100+ Average Users

Component	Terminal Server
Processor	Dual Intel Xeon, 2.8 GHz
RAM	4GB RAM
Disk capacity	18GB+

NOTE: Please note that the configuration shown in Table 1.2 is just one example of a possible Terminal Server configuration to support 100 concurrent users and should not be taken as a representation of adequate hardware sizing under all circumstances. The results and requirements of this configuration may vary greatly depending on what environment the server must run in. Different applications react in different ways in a Terminal Server environment and may introduce significant load when simultaneously run by multiple users. Before deciding on a particular server size, it is always worthwhile to test out the configuration to ensure it will meet the needs of the business.

For a complete discussion of hardware requirements for Terminal Server, see Chapter 6, "Terminal Server Hardware Planning."

Compare the configuration in Table 1.2 to that of the standard servers in Table 1.1; none of those setups really comes close to the necessary requirements for 100+ concurrent Terminal Server users. Based on the memory configurations alone from Table 1.1, all three configurations would have insufficient memory to support the proposed user load.

In Chapter 6, I discuss in more detail the process of sizing a Terminal Server's hardware.

NOTE: The main limiting factor for concurrent users is the amount of physical memory in a Terminal Server.

Remote Desktop Protocol (RDP)

Remote Desktop Protocol (RDP) is Microsoft's distributed presentation services protocol, which controls the transmission of display and user input between the client and the Terminal Server. RDP has been adapted from the T.120 set of standards to meet the specific needs of the Terminal Server environment and continues to be updated with new features to improve the user's server-based computing experience. The following sections discuss the features available with RDP 5.0, which ships with Windows 2000 Terminal Services, and RDP 5.2, which ships with Windows Server 2003 Terminal Services. I begin by outlining the overall behavior of the RDP protocol.

RDP Basics

The transfer of RDP information between the server and the client can be broken down into two main components:

- Graphical data transmission
- Mouse/keyboard data transmission

Graphical Data Transmission

All graphical information that would normally be displayed on the console needs to be encoded and transmitted to the Terminal Server client so it can be displayed on the user's local desktop. As described in the earlier section "Virtual Memory Management," each user session has its own session address space that contains its own Win32 kernel and display and printer drivers. Each of these sessions uses a special RDP display driver that's responsible for receiving display commands from the GDI (just as a normal driver would) and passing this information to the kernel-mode Terminal Server device driver (termdd.sys). This driver encodes the input as RDP data and passes it on to the transport layer to be sent to the client. On reception, at the client, the RDP data is decoded and the display updated accordingly. Figure 1.7 illustrates the flow of graphical data between the server and the client.

Mouse/Keyboard Transmission

Every time a user generates an input message (keyboard or mouse), the information is captured by the RDP client, encoded as RDP data, and sent to the server. When input data is received by the Terminal Server device driver on the server, it's decoded and the actual mouse and keyboard input is sent to the Win32 kernel in the user's session address space, where it's processed as normal input. Figure 1.8 shows the flow of input data between the client and the server.

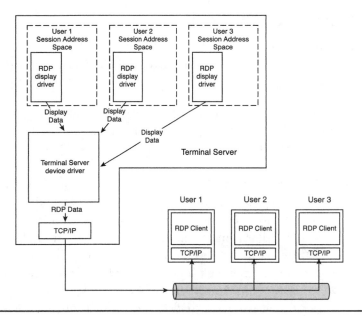

Figure 1.7   RDP graphical data flow between the client and the server.

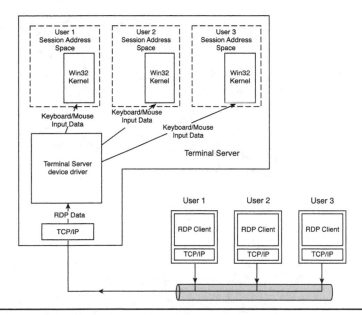

Figure 1.8   RDP mouse/keyboard data flow between the client and the server.

Microsoft RDP Clients

The actual RDP client application has continued to evolve since it was first introduced with Windows NT 4.0, Terminal Server Edition. Currently, three types of RDP clients are available:

■ **Terminal Services Client (RDP 5.0)**—This is one of the two RDP 5.0 clients that ships with Windows 2000 and provides a simple interface for connecting to a Windows Terminal Server. Primarily, the Terminal Services client (TSC) is used as a simple tool for establishing a connection to a Terminal Server. When TSC is launched, a dialog box appears (Figure 1.9), with the lower half of the dialog box listing all the Terminal Servers found in the current domain. To establish a connection, select one of the servers, choose the resolution size, and click the Connect button. The Server drop-down list shows a history of the servers you've previously connected to. If the server you want isn't in the list, you can type the name in the text box. Having the appropriate name service (DNS or WINS) configured in your environment ensures that all the valid Terminal Servers are displayed. Little configuration is involved in the TSC, and on its own it's not a very useful application to deploy to end users.

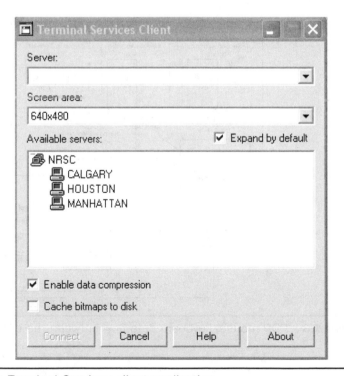

Figure 1.9 The Terminal Services client application.

■ **Client Connection Manager (RDP 5.0)**—This is the main RDP 5.0 client, and it provides a management tool for creating, configuring, and storing connections to different Terminal Servers. Figure 1.10 shows an example of what the main Client Connection Manager (CCM) application window looks like. The CCM lets you configure additional settings for the client that are not available with the Terminal Services client. Options include shortcut creation, saving connection configuration information, defining a specific application to launch from the Terminal Server, and even storing the user ID, password, and domain information to automate the user's logon process.

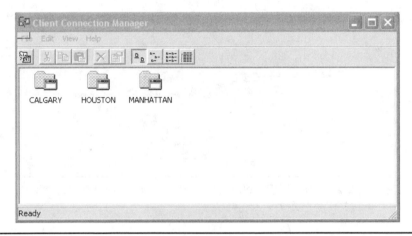

Figure 1.10 The RDP Client Connection Manager (CCM).

■ **Remote Desktop Connection (RDP 5.1 and higher)**—Originally introduced with RDP 5.1 and Windows XP, the Remote Desktop Connection application is the new RDP client interface being used with RDP versions 5.1 and higher. The latest version, 5.2, ships with Windows Server 2003. Figure 1.11 demonstrates the new interface given to the RDP client. In addition to supporting all the features available with the Client Connection Manager, the latest Remote Desktop Connection application supports additional features, which I discuss briefly in the "RDP Client Integration Features" section of this chapter. The Remote Desktop Connection application is fully backward compatible with all versions of Windows Terminal Server. Any client options selected in the RDC not supported by the host Terminal Server are simply ignored.

Figure 1.11   The RDP Remote Desktop Connection (RDC) client.

RDP Encryption

To ensure that data is transmitted securely between the client and the server, three encryption levels are available, from which you can choose based on your security requirements. All levels are encrypted using the RC4 encryption algorithm.

- **Low security**—Only data sent from the client to the server is encrypted; data from the server to the client is not encrypted. The encryption key is 56-bit for both Windows 2003 and 2000.
- **Medium security**—Uses the same encryption level as the low-security option, except that data is now encrypted in both directions, from the server to the client and from the client to the server.
- **High security**—The high-security option encrypts data in both directions, using a 128-bit encryption key.

NOTE: SSL encryption is expected to be available with the release of Service Pack 1 for Windows Server 2003.

RDP Client Integration Features

As mentioned, each new Windows Terminal Server release has introduced new client integration features that enhance the user's computing experience. Table 1.3 summarizes the features supported by the RDP 5.x clients, and what version of Windows Terminal Server is required to enable the feature. The latest RDP client (5.2) can be used to connect to older Terminal Servers (Windows NT 4.0, Terminal Server Edition; or Windows 2000 Terminal Server).

Table 1.3   RDP 5.x Features and Required Server Version

Feature	RDP Version 5.0	5.1	5.2	Terminal Server Version	Description
Local/remote clipboard integration	X	X	X	Both	Allows clipboard contents to be cut and pasted seamlessly back and forth between the active Terminal Server session and the user's local desktop.
Local/remote file copy and paste integration		X	X	Windows 2003 only	Allows the cut and pasting of entire file objects back and forth between the active session and the local desktop.
Local client printer redirection	X	X	X	Both	Printers that are configured on a local client can be made available automatically from within the user's Terminal Server session.
Network client printer redirection			X	Both	This allows for access to locally mapped network printers on the client desktop.
Session remote control	X	X	X	Both	Session remote control is the capacity for one person to remotely view and even control another user's active session.
Persistent bitmap cache	X	X	X	Both	The persistent bitmap cache is stored on disk so that it can be reused the next time a session is started. Version 4.0 allowed only in-memory caching.

Table 1.3   RDP 5.x Features and Required Server Version (continued)

Feature	RDP Version			Terminal Server Version	Description
	5.0	**5.1**	**5.2**		
Connection bar		X	X	Both	This allows you to still easily minimize a full-screen session without having to toggle the session between full screen and windowed using the Ctrl+Alt+Break key combination.
Automatic session reconnect			X	Both	If a network disruption causes your connection to a Terminal Server to be lost, the Remote Desktop Connection client will automatically attempt to reestablish that connection. If the connection cannot be reestablished, then after about one minute the client will give up and an error message will appear saying the connection has been lost.
Client drive redirection			X	Windows 2003 only	The automatic redirection of a client's local and network drives so they are accessible from within the Terminal Server session.
Client serial port redirection			X	Windows 2003 only	Redirection of the local serial ports.
Client audio redirection			X	Windows 2003 only	Audio is redirected from the Terminal Server session to the local client for output.
Smart card sign-on			X	Windows 2003 only	The user is able to provide their smart card to a local reader attached to their PC and have those credentials transmitted and authenticated on the Terminal Server.

Table 1.3 RDP 5.*x* Features and Required Server Version (continued)

Feature	RDP Version			Terminal Server Version	Description
	5.0	5.1	5.2		
Windows shortcut key support		X		Both Client must be running WinNT, 2000, XP, or 2003. Windows 98 or 95 operating systems don't support this feature.	Introduces support for the Alt+Tab and other Windows key combinations within the Terminal Server session.
Client time zone support		X		Windows 2003 only	Client time zone support lets the RDP client provide its own local time zone information to a Windows 2003 Terminal Server so that the server can automatically configure the user's session to reflect the same time zone information. A Terminal Server can support any number of users located in different time zones, and this feature lets the user maintain proper time and date information within his or her own session.
Direct Terminal Server console access		X		Windows 2003 only	This feature allows for the creation of a direct connection to the console and not a Terminal Server session. Applications that require direct console access will function within this special remote session. This feature is dependent on having a Windows 2003 Terminal Server.

More detailed information on each of these supported features is discussed in Chapter 5, "Client Hardware and Software Planning."

Microsoft RDP Clients

Table 1.4 summarizes the native Microsoft RDP client versions and the operating systems they support.

Table 1.4   RDP Client Versions and Their Supported Operating Systems

Operating System	RDP Client Version Supported	Notes
Windows 2003, XP, 2000, client are ME, 98, and NT 4.0	RDP 5.0 and higher	All versions of the RDP supported on all 32-bit versions of Windows, NT 4.0 or higher.
Windows 95	RDP 5.0 or 5.1 only	Microsoft does not officially support the RDP 5.2 (or newer) client on Windows 95.
Windows for Workgroups 3.11	RDP 5.0 only	Microsoft no longer supports this version of Windows with the new RDP client. Only the client that originally ships with Windows 2000 is available for the 16-bit version of Windows.
Macintosh OS X	Mac OS X RDP Client 1.0.2	This is currently the only RDP client that Microsoft produces for a non-Windows operating system.
Pocket PC 2002	PPC 2002 client	This special RDP client is designed specifically to run on Pocket PC 2002. It will not run on older versions of Pocket PC.
Windows CE	Handheld and CE-based terminals running CE 3.0 and CE.NET	Special versions of the RDP client can either be installed on a Windows CE client or come embedded with the CE operating system.

Third-Party RDP Clients

In addition to the RDP clients supplied by Microsoft, there exist clients created by other vendors to run on client operating systems not natively supported by Microsoft. Many of these clients support only a small subset of the functions available through the Microsoft RDP clients. Currently the only non-Windows operating system supported by Microsoft is Apple's Mac OS X. Table 1.5 lists some third-party RDP clients that are available.

Table 1.5   Examples of Third-Party RDP Clients That Are Available

Host Operating System Supported	Description
Platform-independent, Java-based client	HOBLink JWT, version 3.1, is a pure, Java-based RDP client that supports Windows 2003 Terminal Server features such as • Color depth up to 24-bit • Local client drive redirection • Local COM and LPT port redirection • Client audio redirection HOBLink also provides a number of additional features to extend the usefulness of Terminal Server to a Java-based client. HOBLink is developed by the German-based company HOB, and the client is available from http://www.hob.de/www_us.
Linux and DOS	Terminal-Services.net provides a commercial RDP client that runs on Linux and another that runs on DOS. The Linux-based client called LinRDP is fully compatible with the new RDP features available in the RDP 5.2 client and Windows 2003 Terminal Server: • Color depth up to 24-bit • Local client drive redirection • Local COM and printer redirection • Client audio redirection Evaluation versions of both clients are available for download from the Web site at http://www.terminal-services.net.

Table 1.5 Examples of Third-Party RDP Clients That Are Available (continued)

Host Operating System Supported	Description
UNIX OpenSource	An Open Source version of the RDP client is available from RDesktop.Org. Unlike the other two clients, this one provides only bare-bones connectivity at this time but is an option for those users who wish to have basic access from a Linux or UNIX desktop. Full source code is provided with this client.

Terminal Services Scalability

Terminal Services alone would be of little use without the ability to scale the environment to support users across more than one Terminal Server. Distributing concurrent user load across multiple Terminal Servers helps to mitigate the impact a server failure has on the environment and simplifies the task of growing the environment in the future to accommodate the growth requirements of your changing business. Microsoft provides scalability through Network Load Balancing (NLB), which is available with Windows 2000 (Advanced Server or Datacenter Server) and with all versions of Windows Server 2003.

Network Load Balancing

Microsoft's NLB is a component of Windows Clustering that allows for multiple servers to provide TCP/IP-based services to users through one or more IP addresses (cluster IP addresses). This setup improves both the availability and scalability of a particular service by allowing multiple servers to be grouped together and operate conceptually as a single entity. The primary use for NLB is to provide redundancy for Web-based services such as Web or FTP servers, but it can also be used to provide redundancy in a Terminal Server environment.

Once NLB has been configured for all participating Terminal Servers, then the RDP clients are configured to simply connect to the cluster IP or cluster hostname instead of a specific server. The connection is then routed to the appropriate Terminal Server in the cluster and serviced accordingly.

NLB runs as a network driver on the server and is completely transparent to the TCP/IP networking stack. Each Terminal Server that will participate in the NLB cluster is configured to enable this network driver. When implementing Windows 2000 Terminal Server, NLB must be configured on each individual Terminal Server that will participate in the NLB cluster.

Windows Server 2003 includes a new utility called the Network Load Balancing Manager, which can be found under Administrative Tools on the Start menu. This tool allows all aspects of an NLB cluster to be configured from a single point instead of having to configure options on each individual cluster member. Figure 1.12 shows the Network Load Balancing Manager with two Windows 2003 Terminal Servers in a test cluster.

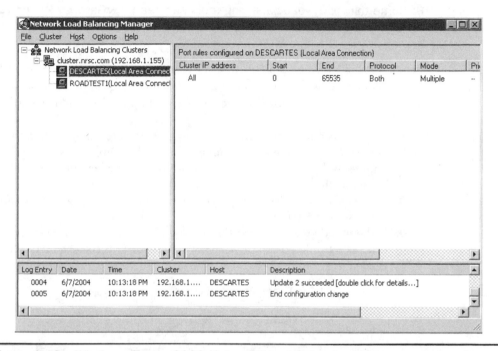

Figure 1.12   Windows Server 2003 Network Load Balancing Manager.

TIP: A user's Terminal Server session information is not maintained across multiple servers, as the term *clustering* might suggest. If a user is on a server that fails, his or her session and any information currently open within that session will be lost, and the user will have to log on to an alternate server in the cluster.

In Chapter 22, "Server Operations and Support," I look in detail at the steps required to configure NLB to function in your Terminal Server environment.

Windows Server 2003 Terminal Services Session Directory

Windows Server 2003 introduces a new cluster component called Terminal Services Session Directory, which can be used to further enhance the functionality of a load-balancing solution such as NLB by enabling support for reconnecting a user to a disconnected session within the load-balanced Terminal Server environment. Without such functionality, when a user disconnects an active Terminal Server session within a clustered environment it is likely that when the user reconnects, particularly from a different client, that user will be presented with a new Terminal Server session instead of reconnecting to their existing one.

TIP: Some third-party load-balancing tools such as WTS Gateway Pro provide their own session management components and do not require the use of Session Directory.

Figure 1.13 shows the components that exist when Terminal Services Session Directory has been implemented with Microsoft NLB. The following steps summarize how Session Directory integrates with a load-balancing solution to provide session accessibility.

1. The user contacts the Terminal Server cluster and is directed to Server A.
2. Server A contacts the server running the Session Directory service. This server queries its database to determine if this user already has an active but disconnected session in the cluster.
3. If no connection exists, then Server A continues the logon process and creates a new session for the user.
4. If the user does have an existing session (Server C, for example), then the logon process is handed off to Server C, where the user is reconnected to their existing session.

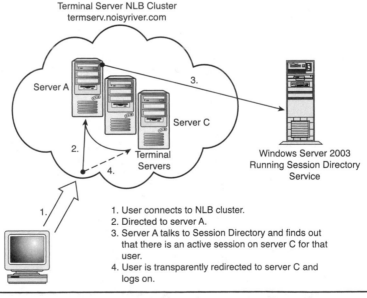

Figure 1.13   Terminal Services Session Directory components.

Terminal Services Management Tools

In addition to the standard administrative tools found on a Windows server, Terminal Server provides more tools for supporting the multiuser environment. The following tools provide Terminal Server–specific support features.

- **Terminal Services Client Creator**—Available only on Windows 2000, this utility lets you create client-installation diskettes for the Win32 or Win16 RDP 5.0 client.
- **Terminal Services Configuration**—Used to manage Terminal Server connection types, their transports, and their properties.
- **Terminal Services Manager**—Used to manage all active Terminal Servers, users, sessions, and processes.
- **Terminal Services Licensing**—Used to monitor and update Terminal Services licensing support.

Terminal Services Client Creator (Windows 2000 Terminal Server Only)

On a Windows 2000 Terminal Server, you have the option of using the Terminal Services Client Creator utility to generate installation diskettes for either the Win32 or the Win16 RDP 5.0 client. Figure 1.14 shows the main Client Creator dialog box. Use of the Client Creator tool is discussed in Chapter 19.

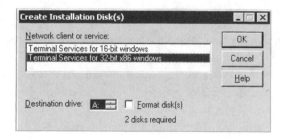

Figure 1.14   Windows Terminal Services Client Creator utility.

Terminal Services Configuration

Before a user can connect to a Terminal Server, the connections must be properly configured on the server. This is done using the Terminal Services Configuration tool, where you create the desired connection types and their associated network transports. Figure 1.15 shows a Windows 2003 Terminal Services Configuration application with the RDP connection type and the TCP transport. Properties such as access security, minimum encryption level, connection timeout options, or remote control options can be set for a connection type and will affect all users who access the server through the connection type. Currently, Terminal Server supports only two connection types, Microsoft RDP and Citrix ICA. When a Windows Server is configured as a Terminal Server, the RDP transport is automatically created with the default configuration. Connection security and proper configuration are discussed in Chapters 16, "Terminal Server Security," and 19, "RDP Client Installation and Configuration," respectively.

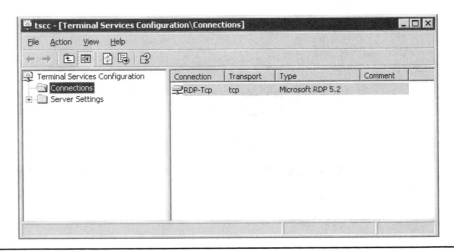

Figure 1.15   The Terminal Services Configuration tool.

Terminal Services Manager

The Terminal Services Manager is used to manage users, sessions, and processes on each Terminal Server from a single management console. Figure 1.16 shows a typical Terminal Services Manager session. Tasks such as remote control, which was discussed earlier in the "RDP Client Integration Features" section, are initiated from within this tool.

The management window is divided into two panels. The left panel contains a list of domains, Terminal Servers, and Terminal Server sessions on the network. The right panel contains a number of tabs with information pertaining to the object currently selected in the left panel. Notice the two idle RDP sessions in the left panel. The server initializes these sessions so that they're available immediately when a user connects to the server. This helps to speed up the client connection process.

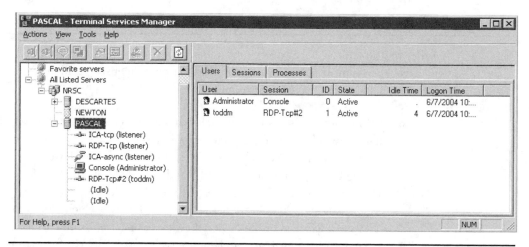

Figure 1.16 The Terminal Services Manager tool.

Terminal Services Licensing

The Terminal Services Licensing application is used to manage the Terminal Server licensing service. To run one or more Windows Servers in Terminal Server mode (Application Server mode in Windows 2000), you must have at least one license server running in your environment. A license server manages the licenses that are issued to clients when they connect to a Terminal Server. A client must have a valid Terminal Services client access license to log on to a Terminal Server. Figure 1.17 shows this utility. In Chapter 8, "Server Installation and Management Planning," I talk about planning the deployment of Terminal Services licensing, while in Chapter 12, "Licensing Service Installation and Configuration," I look specifically at the task of deploying a license server for your implementation.

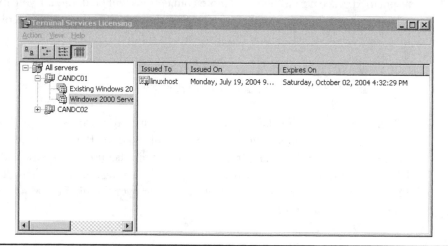

Figure 1.17 The Terminal Services Licensing tool.

Terminal Services Licensing Requirements

In order to utilize Terminal Services in your environment, you will be required to ensure that you have the appropriate server and client access licenses available. The following server and client access licenses are required:

- A Windows server license for each instance of Windows 2000 or Windows 2003 that you will be running in your environment.
- A Windows client access license (CAL) for each user or device that will be connecting to the Terminal Server. In Windows 2000 only the per-device license is supported, which grants one license for each device that is connecting. Windows Server 2003 introduces a per-user license, which allows for licensing of a user regardless of the device they are connecting from.
- A Windows Terminal Server client access license (TSCAL) for each user or device that will be connecting to a Windows Server and creating a Terminal Services session. This license is required in addition to the standard Windows CAL. Once again, Windows Server 2003 allows the TSCAL to be licensed either per-device or per-user, whatever is more appropriate for your environment.

Terminal Server client access license–compliance is enforced through use of a Terminal Services License Service, a special service that is required to run on a Windows Server in your environment. Whenever one or more Windows Servers are configured to run as Terminal Servers (Application Server mode in Windows 2000), a server running the Terminal Services licensing service is also required. A Windows server running Remote Desktop for Administration (Remote Administration mode in Windows 2000) does *not* require a license server.

A Windows Terminal Server will function without the existence of a Licensing Server for a specified grace period before remote connections will be denied. Even after the grace period has expired, logons directly from the console (not using a remote console session) will still be allowed. The grace period durations are as follows:

- Windows 2000 Server to 90 days
- Windows Server 2003 to 120 days

When a License Server does exist, until it is activated, it will issue only temporary TSCALS to the requesting clients, which are good for only 90 days. If a permanent license is not issued to the client within that time frame, the temporary license will expire and the client will no longer be able to connect to the server. The licensing server itself is activated through a Microsoft Clearinghouse, either electronically or over the phone. Details on this process are discussed in Chapter 12.

In the next chapter I provide an overview of Citrix's MetaFrame Presentation Server, an add-on component that provides a vast array of features and functionality specifically suited to deploying large-scale enterprise Terminal Server environments both through traditional Windows-based clients and through a Web browser.

The remainder of this book delves much deeper into all aspects of a Terminal Server project, either with or without MetaFrame, including planning, testing, and, of course, implementation.

CHAPTER 2

Citrix MetaFrame Presentation Server

What Is MetaFrame Presentation Server?

MetaFrame Presentation Server (MPS) 3.0 is the next generation of Citrix's server-based computing extension to Windows Terminal Services, building on major technological changes over previous versions of MetaFrame first introduced with MetaFrame XP 1.0. MetaFrame provides robust application server support for enterprise implementations of Terminal Server. The core technology behind MetaFrame is Citrix's own remote presentation protocol, known as Independent Computing Architecture (ICA). ICA is completely independent of Microsoft's Remote Desktop Protocol (RDP), which was discussed in Chapter 1, "Microsoft Windows Terminal Services." A number of RDP features are based on functionality previously available only with the MetaFrame ICA client; for example, client drive and audio mapping. Although Terminal Server with RDP provides a rich set of features and tools, some deficiencies become apparent when looking at a large-scale deployment of the product. MetaFrame overcomes these deficiencies at both the server and the client. Just a few key benefits to be realized with inclusion of MetaFrame Presentation Server in a Terminal Server implementation include the following:

- **Extended client support**—Citrix natively extends support for a number of computing platforms, including
  - Windows 2003, XP, 2000, NT, 95/98, Windows for Workgroups 3.11, Windows 3.1, Windows CE, and Pocket PC
  - DOS, Macintosh (OS X, PowerPC, M6800) and Linux
  - UNIX (Solaris [Sparc and i386], SunOS, SCO, SGI, HP/UX, Compaq Tru64, IBM, and AIX)
  - Web-based clients (Internet Explorer and Netscape) and Java
  - Not only does Citrix support these platforms, but the client software is much more than a bare-bones port to another OS with minimal supported features. Many key features found in Citrix's Win32 client can also be found in other client versions. For example, client drive and printer mapping—the ability to access a user's local disk drive or printers from within their MetaFrame session—is supported across *all* Citrix's clients.

■ **Desktop integration features**—These features provide integration with the user's local desktop through the concept of published applications and seamless windows support. In addition to delivering a complete set of local device-mapping support similar to that found in the Microsoft RDP client, Citrix introduces the idea of a published application, a means of delivering an individual application instead of a full desktop to the end user so this remote application can, as seamlessly as possible, integrate with the local desktop. Published applications are managed through the Management Console (see the fourth point in this list) and can be assigned to users based on their group membership. Figure 2.1 shows an example of Microsoft Word running seamlessly on a user's Linux desktop. Notice how the application integrates seamlessly with the local desktop; it appears as though Word is actually running on the Linux platform. Seamless windows support is available on Win32, Java, Linux, and most UNIX ICA clients.

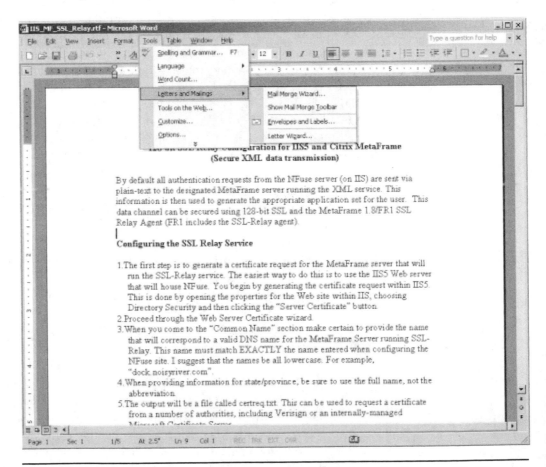

Figure 2.1   Citrix supports running seamless published applications on Win32, Linux, and most UNIX ICA clients.

- **Robust connectivity options**—MPS provides a number of access methods that can be tailored to suit the needs of any type of implementation. Beyond the traditional client software installed and configured directly on the client desktop, MPS provides Web-based and Web-managed clients such as its Program Neighborhood Agent and pure Web clients that allow for centralized configuration of the user's computing experience.
- **Centralized management capabilities**—MPS delivers on the idea of centralized management for a very large number of MetaFrame servers through the concept of a server farm. Server farms provide a layer of abstraction that delivers a simple, consistent means of managing any number of MetaFrame servers within the infrastructure. The Management Console for MetaFrame Presentation Server, also referred to as the "Presentation Server Console," (see Figure 2.2) is the tool used to manage the server farm. All aspects of the server farm and the MetaFrame servers contained within that farm are managed through this tool. Load balancing, application deployment, printer management, and resource management are just some of the features available, depending on the version of MPS you are running. The product versions available are discussed in the "MetaFrame Presentation Server Product Versions" section of this chapter. Although the tool is automatically installed on the server when you install MPS, it is not limited to running only on the server. The Management Console can also be installed as a standalone application on a separate desktop PC.

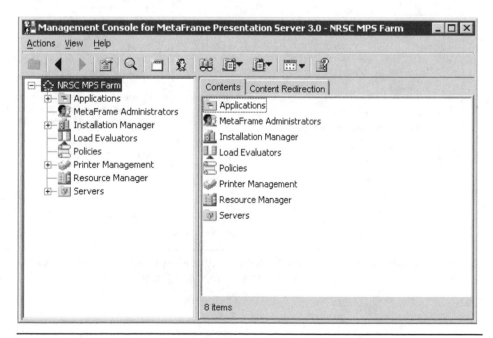

Figure 2.2   MetaFrame Presentation Server is centrally managed through the Presentation Server Console tool.

■ **Extensive security support**—Citrix has developed an extensive array of products and tools designed specifically for securing your MetaFrame implementation Secured-access infrastructure models such as the Secure Gateway for MetaFrame enable an administrator to design and implement a comprehensive and secure solution for their remote users. Figure 2.3 demonstrates the Web Interface for MetaFrame Presentation Server, the Web-based front end that lets users access their applications through a Web browser. Access to the Web Interface can be secured using the Secure Gateway for MetaFrame, making it possible for users to securely access their applications directly off the Internet.

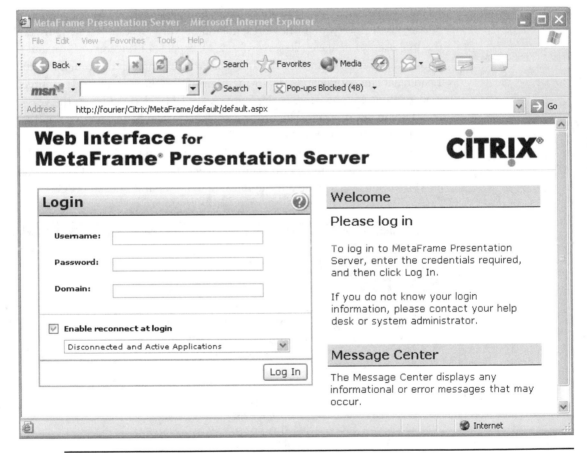

Figure 2.3   Web-based access to the MetaFrame server farm can be secured using the Secure Gateway for MetaFrame tool.

■ **True centralized printer management**—Historically, one of the biggest obstacles facing many Terminal Server administrators responsible for large server farm deployments was management of printers and the associated printer drivers. MPS provides a truly centralized method of managing and updating the appropriate printer information across all servers in a farm. No longer must an administrator manually update the printer and driver information or create custom scripts to automate the process.

■ **Centralized license management**—Gone is the traditional server/client licensing mechanism that has existed with only minor modifications since Citrix WinFrame 1.7. Citrix now provides a centralized license repository system very similar to Microsoft's Terminal Server Licensing service. Special reporting and alerting features are now also available, letting an administrator more proactively monitor the licensing requirements of their implementation.

If you are already familiar with MetaFrame XP (MFXP) 1.0, you will find that MPS 3.0 is similar in many ways; those of you coming from a MetaFrame 1.8 environment will find a significantly different MetaFrame product. MPS provides a number of improvements over MetaFrame 1.8, including the following:

■ **Expanded support for the server farm management metaphor**— MetaFrame 1.8 introduced the concept of a server farm; unfortunately, the actual management capabilities were very limited. MPS includes the Independent Management Architecture (IMA), both an architectural model for server management and the protocol used for communication between the servers in the farm. IMA was created for the sole purpose of supporting the management of the server farm.

■ **Implementation of a true database-hosted repository for server farm information including published application, load-balancing evaluator, and printer management information**—This replaces the registry-based server farm information maintained in MetaFrame 1.8 servers.

■ **Creation of a single management tool to consolidate the various MetaFrame management tasks**—The Management Console for MPS now exists, a single tool that provides nearly all management requirements and replaces different applications such as the Citrix Server Administration and Published Application Manager tools used in MF1.8. All farm management options are accessible from this management console.

■ **True per-seat licensing**—Instead of requiring the purchase of a server license and then additional client access licenses, Citrix has completely eliminated the per-server licensing cost and now bases pricing purely on the concurrent user load. For example, if you purchase 100 concurrent user licenses, the licensing cost is the same whether you deploy 2 or 10 servers running MPS.

NOTE: The preceding abbreviated list of features and enhancements is intended to give you an overall idea of the scope of the MetaFrame product and the type of management control it can provide. I realize that inundating you with a condensed list of features can be overwhelming and not necessarily understood or retained, particularly when first being introduced to the technology.

The purpose of this chapter is to provide an overview of the MetaFrame Presentation Server product and give you an idea of what can be achieved with this technology. Throughout this book, we look at how the tools that Citrix has provided can be used to meet the goals you set for your Terminal Server and MetaFrame implementation.

Citrix's latest marketing campaign touts its product suite as "Access Infrastructure for the On-Demand Enterprise," providing "anywhere, anytime, any device, any connection" access. Its goal is not only to provide users with the ability to easily access the necessary business applications, regardless of their location or the devices they may have at their disposal, but also to provide administrators with the tools necessary to manage such an infrastructure.

MetaFrame Presentation Server Product Versions

The following three versions of the MetaFrame Presentation Server product are available:

- **MPS Standard Edition**—This version provides the core feature set available with MetaFrame, including features such as
  - **Active Directory and NDS support**—Fully integrated support for authentication against these directory services products.
  - **Web Interface Console**—Allows for server farm management through a Web browser when IIS is also run on the MPS server.
  - **Complete printer management features**—Printer drivers and print servers can be centrally accessed, managed, and replicated through the printer management interface.
  - **Full support for all client device mapping**—All local device access now available in the latest iteration of the RDP client has been a standard part of the ICA feature set for a number of years.
  - **Client time zone support**—The local time zone information from the client session can be used to maintain the same time information from within the MetaFrame session as well, regardless of the local time set on the MetaFrame server. For example, if a MetaFrame server located in New York City had an actual time of 7:15 a.m. and a user in Singapore logged on to that server, the time displayed within their MetaFrame session would actually be 12 hours ahead at 7:15 p.m.

- **MPS Advanced Edition**—Advanced Edition contains all the features of Standard Edition, plus the following:
  - **Connection Control**—Lets you limit how many simultaneous connections a user has in the farm.
  - **CPU Prioritization**—Published applications can be assigned a priority level, letting an administrator perform "throttling" on those applications that may be ill behaved and consume large amounts of processor cycles.
  - **Load Management support**—Provides support for resource-based load balancing. Unlike Microsoft's Network Load Balancing (NLB), which is driven only by TCP/IP connections, Citrix's Load Management can be configured to manage load distribution based on a server's overall availability using criteria such as CPU load, available memory, and available disk space. Figure 2.4 shows a sample load evaluator screen where the desired load-balancing information is configured.

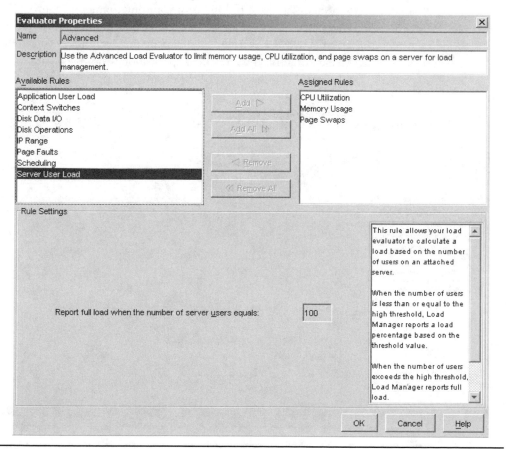

Figure 2.4 Load management in MPS Advanced Edition is configured using load evaluators.

- **MPS Enterprise Edition**—This edition of MPS contains all the Advanced Edition features, plus the following:
  - **Application Packaging and Delivery—This** tool provides centralized access to installation and removal of applications in the server farm, including service packs. Complete management capabilities help simplify an administrator's application deployment requirements in very large server farm implementations.
  - **Network Management features**—Support management through the SNMP standard as well as integration support into third-party network management tools such as Tivoli, HP OpenView, or Computer Associate's Unicenter.
  - **System Monitoring and Analysis**—Lets you monitor the status of the server farm directly within the Management Console. Complete reporting and real-time monitoring and alerting provide you with the necessary tools to remain on top of the status of your environment. Figure 2.5 shows the Watcher window with a warning event that has been raised for the DESCARTES server. Double-clicking the event takes you to the Resource Manager tab for the individual application, where you can find out more information on the status of the event.

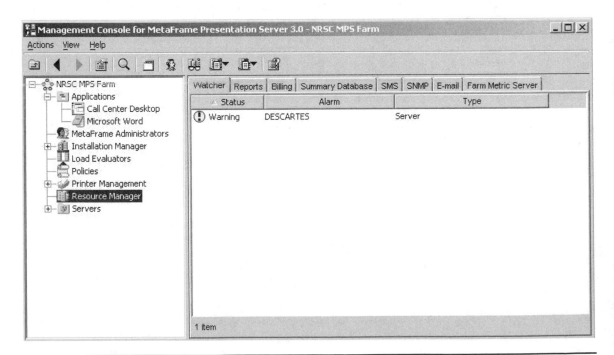

Figure 2.5   Events are raised by the system monitor when certain event thresholds are exceeded.

Independent Computing Architecture (ICA)

Even after Microsoft and Citrix agreed that Microsoft would license MultiWin for use in developing future versions of multiuser Windows (see "The History of Windows Terminal Server" in Chapter 1), Citrix retained complete ownership of its key technology, the Independent Computing Architecture (ICA) protocol. ICA is Citrix's presentation protocol used to deliver information back and forth between the MetaFrame server and the ICA client (also known as the MPS client). Figure 2.6 shows the general format of the ICA data packet.

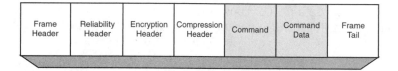

Figure 2.6   The ICA data packet.

The components that make up the packet are as follows:

- **Frame header**—The header for the framing protocol, used to frame the data for stream-oriented network protocols such as TCP/IP or SPX. The frame header contains a two-bit priority tag used to set the priority of the ICA data being transmitted. As of MetaFrame 1.8, FR1—the ICA protocol—supports a feature called ICA Priority Packet Tagging, which allows the data transmitted in an ICA session to be prioritized. For example, screen data can be prioritized over printer data.
- **Reliability**—The header for the reliability protocol, which is used when transporting data over an unreliable transport protocol such as IPX.
- **Encryption**—An encryption header is added if encryption has been turned on for the ICA session. When the encryption header is present, all the data that follows in the packet is encrypted.
- **Compression**—When compression has been enabled, a compression header is added to the data packet.
- **Command**—The command byte for the ICA packet. This is the only required component of the ICA data packet.
- **Command data**—The command byte is followed by optional command data.
- **ICA data**—The ICA data portion of the packet can consist of one or more command and command data packets. ICA packet data can consist of only a command byte; the command data is optional. Command data never exists without a preceding command byte.
- **Frame tail**—The tail for the framing protocol.

Data for an ICA packet is retrieved from an input buffer populated with data from an ICA virtual channel. *Virtual channels* are logical, bidirectional data streams from the various functional components of MetaFrame. These virtual channels include the ThinWire virtual channel—which is responsible for transmitting Windows display objects to the ICA client—the drive-mapping virtual channel, and the clipboard virtual channel.

Construction of an ICA packet begins with a single command byte followed by any command data necessary. The other data encapsulated in the packet (compression, encryption, and so on) is added based on the connection settings and the transport protocol being used. Finally, the packet is passed to the appropriate transport driver, where it is set across the network to the client.

TIP: An ICA data packet consist of data from only one virtual channel, and the maximum length of a single packet cannot exceed 2K (2,048 bytes).

Citrix MetaFrame Presentation Server Client (ICA Client)

Citrix provides four main ICA clients from which to choose:

- **Standard Citrix ICA client**—Traditionally known as the Remote Application Manager, this client provides basic connectivity support to a specific Citrix server or published resources in a Citrix server farm. This client type is available for most supported client platforms, including 32-bit Windows (as part of Program Neighborhood), CE, Mac OS X, Linux and other supported UNIX variants, OS/2, and 16-bit Windows. Figure 2.7 shows the Citrix ICA client for Linux running on SuSE Linux.

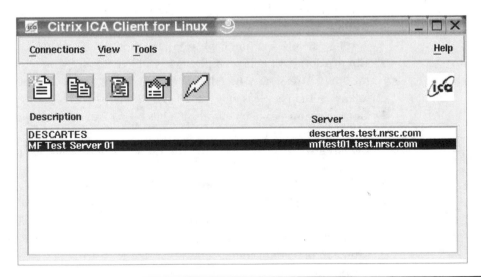

Figure 2.7 The Citrix ICA client for Linux.

■ **Program Neighborhood (PN)**—The traditional Citrix ICA client interface, PN is a full application environment from within which connections to various MetaFrame Presentation Servers or published resources (individual programs or other content made available on one or more MetaFrame servers) can be accessed. Most new implementations of MetaFrame do not deploy this full client to the end user but instead use the Program Neighborhood Agent or the Web client (both described later in this list) for regular user access. Administrators will likely want to have the full Program Neighborhood installed on their desktop for maximum flexibility in supporting their MetaFrame environment. Figure 2.8 shows the full Program Neighborhood main window.

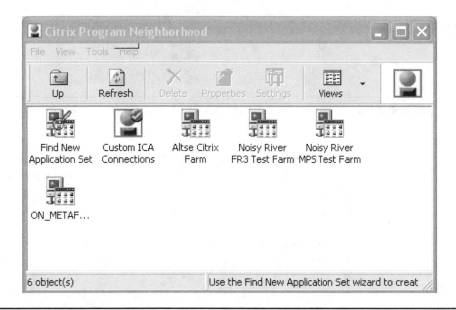

Figure 2.8   The Win32 Program Neighborhood ICA client.

■ **Program Neighborhood Agent (PN Agent)**—This client works in conjunction with the Web Interface for MetaFrame Presentation Server (discussed in Chapter 14, "MetaFrame Presentation Server Configuration") to provide a simple means of delivering published resources to the end user. Unlike the full PN, where all configuration changes must be performed locally on the client, configuration of the PN Agent is done centrally through the Program Neighborhood Agent Console and retrieved by the client via the Web Interface for MPS. Published resources are retrieved from one or more server farms and displayed on the user's local desktop by the PN Agent, based on the domain groups the user belongs to. The PN Agent does not have a full interface through which the user can create connections and access servers or resources. Certain options for the

PN Agent can be configured by right-clicking the PN Agent icon in the system tray (see Figure 2.9) and selecting the desired setting. You can also see the list of available applications from here, although they are usually configured to appear on the local desktop or Start menu.

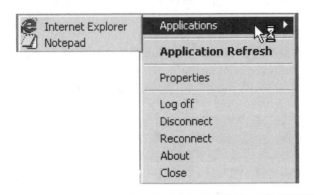

Figure 2.9   The Program Neighborhood Agent system tray properties.

- **Citrix Web client**—The smallest of the four client types, the Citrix Web client—available only for Windows 32-bit operating systems—provides access to published resources directly from hyperlinks on a Web page. The source of this Web page can be any of the following:

  - The Web Interface for MetaFrame Presentation Server
  - NFuse Classic, the previous iteration of the Web Interface product
  - A standard Web page with properly configured hyperlinks using a technique known as Application Launching and Embedding (ALE)

    For the Web client to function, you must be running Internet Explorer (5.0 or higher) or Netscape Navigator (4.78, 6.2, or higher). The Web client provides no separate user interface but instead retrieves the necessary configuration information directly from the source Web site and from the published application settings in the Citrix server farm. Figure 2.10 shows a sample Web page generated by the Web Interface for MPS, with Microsoft Word, Microsoft Excel, and a line-of-business application (Prophet 21 Commerce Center) available for access. Clicking any one of these application hyperlinks initiates a connection to the published application using the Citrix Web client.

Figure 2.10   The Citrix Web client is typically used to load applications accessed through the Web Interface for MetaFrame Presentation Server, NFuse Classic, or a custom Web page using ALE.

Two versions of the Citrix Web client exist. One provides the full set of ICA client features and is available both as a self-extracting executable and as a compressed Microsoft cabinet (.CAB) file. The other is known as the *minimal* Citrix Web client and is available only as a .CAB file. As the name suggests, this client is the smallest Win32 ICA client available, and in order to achieve this, certain features normally found in the other ICA clients had to be omitted. The Citrix Web client is discussed in more detail in Chapter 14.

TIP: Citrix provides a Java-based client also accessible directly from a Web browser and supports many features found in the full Win32 Web client. The ICA Java client is discussed in more detail in Chapter 14.

A thorough discussion on all the different ICA clients available, the features they support, and the deployments to which they are best suited is covered in Chapter 5, "Client Hardware and Software Planning."

ICA Encryption Support

All ICA clients, with the exception of the minimal Web client, provide full encryption support for the session logon and the session data itself. Citrix employs the RSA RC5 encryption algorithm and supports five encryption configurations:

- **Basic encryption**—Basic encryption employs a simple encryption algorithm using an encryption key less than 40 bits in size. This option should not be considered secure. Tools are readily accessible on the Internet that allow for network sniffing and decoding of Basic-encrypted ICA passwords.
- **128-bit encryption for logon only**—This option employs 128-bit encryption for the authentication process only, leaving the remainder of the session data to transmit with no encryption.
- **40-, 56-, and 128-bit encryptions**—For all these selections, the authentication process uses 128-bit encryption, and the remainder of the session data is encrypted using the selected encryption level.

TIP: In addition to the traditional encryption support for user authentication, Citrix employs Kerberos authentication in conjunction with the Security Support Provider Interface (SSPI) exchange mechanism for passthrough authentication with the 32-bit Windows 8.x or later client and MPS 3.0. When Kerberos is used, the client device, not the ICA client, is responsible for the user authentication, thus eliminating an avenue for a potential attack against the ICA client in order to try and gain access to the user's password. System requirements for Kerberos authentication and the steps on how to configure it are discussed in Chapter 20, "ICA Client Installation and Configuration."

Kerberos is an industry standard network authentication protocol that employs secret-key cryptography. Kerberos is built into Windows Server 2000 and Windows 2003 Server.

ICA Client Network Protocol Support

The ICA protocol is supported on four network transports: TCP/IP, IPX, SPX, and NetBIOS. Most of the ICA clients support only the TCP/IP protocol, but some clients, such as the Win32 and DOS clients, support all four types. For an ICA client to be able to connect over a particular network transport, not only must the client and the Terminal Server both be running the desired protocol, but the Terminal Server must also support Terminal Server connections over that particular protocol type. Table 2.1 summarizes the Terminal Server connection protocols supported by operating system type and presentation server protocol.

Table 2.1 ICA Client Network Protocol Connection Support

Windows Server Version	Supported ICA Connection Protocols	Comments
Windows Server 2003	TCP/IP only	Windows Server 2003 supports Terminal Server connections over only TCP/IP. Protocols such as IPX/SPX can be installed on the server for connecting to other systems such as Novell, but even when such protocols are present, a Terminal Server connection using that protocol is not supported.
		This change in protocol support over Windows 2000 Server can significantly impact the upgrade plans for an organization that wishes to move to this new operating system but currently supports ICA clients connecting over a protocol other than TCP/IP.
Windows 2000 Server	TCP/IP, IPX, SPX, and NetBIOS	Windows 2000 Server supports Terminal Server connections over all four of the protocols supported by ICA (TCP/IP, IPX, SPX, and NetBIOS).

TIP: Details on configuration of the ICA client to support a particular network protocol are discussed in Chapter 20.

ICA Client Integration Features

Table 2.2 summarizes the client integration features available with the Win32 and Linux ICA clients. A complete list of supported client operating systems and their available features can be found on the Citrix Web site (http://www.citrix.com). An X in a particular cell of the table means that client supports the corresponding feature. The letters *P* and *S* are used when showing what clients support the panning and scaling features. A complete description of the supported features is given in Chapter 5.

Table 2.2   ICA Client Features for the Win32 and Linux platforms.

Feature	Client Win32 8.*x*	Linux 8.*x*	Description
Text cut/paste clipboard integration	X	X	Allows clipboard contents to be cut and pasted seamlessly back and forth between the active Terminal Server session and the user's local desktop.
File cut/paste clipboard integration	X	X	Allows cut and pasting of entire file objects back and forth between the active session and the local desktop.
Local and network client printer redirection	X	X	Printers configured on the local client (directly connected or network mapped) can be accessed from within the user's MetaFrame session.
Universal printer driver support	X	X	A universal printer driver (UPD) can be designated as the driver to use when mapping client printers. The client must have a printer driver that supports the UPD.
Client disk drive redirection	X	X	A client's local and network drivers can be redirected and accessible within the MetaFrame session.
Client audio redirection	X	X	Audio from the server to the client is redirected by all clients, but client-to-server support is available only with the Win32, WinCE, and Linux clients.

Table 2.2   ICA Client Features for the Win32 and Linux platforms. (continued)

Feature	Client Win32 8.x	Linux 8.x	Description
Client serial port redirection	X	X	Allows redirection of the local serial ports.
Time zone support	X	X	Client time zone support lets the ICA client provide its own local time zone information to the MetaFrame server so the server can automatically configure the user's session to reflect the same time zone information.
Seamless windows	X	X	The seamless windows feature allows a published application to appear as if it were running locally on the user's desktop.
Panning and scaling	PS	P	When a session desktop is larger than the visible screen area, the ICA client lets you pan the desktop and, with certain clients, scale the desktop to fit within the visible session space.
SpeedScreen latency reduction	X	X	SpeedScreen latency reduction allows for echoing of text on the local client even if the information has not immediately been transmitted to the MetaFrame server due to latency in the network. This gives the impression to the end user that the session is more responsive than it actually might be.
Multimedia acceleration	X		Provides support for accelerating playback of streaming audio and video from Internet Explorer, Windows Media Player, and RealOne Player.
Web browser acceleration	X	X	Accelerates processing of images on Internet Explorer 5.5 or higher.

Table 2.2   ICA Client Features for the Win32 and Linux platforms. (continued)

Feature	Client Win32 8.*x*	Linux 8.x	Description
Automatic client reconnect	X	X	Lets the client automatically attempt to reconnect to a server when the connection has been unintentionally severed.
Roaming user reconnect	X	X	Lets a user connect to a MetaFrame server using one particular client, disconnect, and then reconnect from a different client. Cross-platform reconnection is supported with certain client versions.
Session reliability	X		Session reliability allows for continued display of a published application even if the actual connection to the server has been lost.
Workspace control	X	X	Lets a user quickly disconnect, reconnect, or log off all his or her currently open applications.
Automatic client update	X	X	Updates to the ICA client can automatically be deployed using the automatic client update feature. The MetaFrame server initiates automatic client updates when a supporting client connects.
Content publishing	X	X	Whereas application publishing makes individual applications on one or more MetaFrame servers available for user access, content publishing makes files such as Word documents or Web site URLs available for use. Content is distributed through the ICA client just as a published application would be.

Table 2.2 ICA Client Features for the Win32 and Linux platforms. (continued)

Feature	Client Win32 8.x	Linux 8.x	Description
Content redirection Server to client Client to server	X X	X X	Two types of content redirection are supported. The first is server-to-client redirection, which allows embedded URLs in a published application to be opened using the Web browser on the user's local desktop. The other is client-to-server redirection, which allows documents on the local client device to be associated with an application published on a MetaFrame server. The Win32 client supports client-to-server redirection only when using the PN Agent. Both the Mac and Linux clients support client-to-server redirection, but the desired redirection must be manually configured.
Program Neighborhood Agent	X	X	The PN Agent client allows for central management and distribution of client data using the MetaFrame Web Interface. Only a minimum-sized client is installed that has a limited local user interface.
Smart card support	X	X	The user can provide their smart card to a local reader attached to their PC and have those credentials transmitted and authenticated on the Terminal Server.
Novell Directory Services authentication	X	X	All the listed clients support authentication through NDS, Novell's alternative to Microsoft's Active Directory.
Passthrough authentication	X		This feature allows for the user ID and password provided within the local client on the PC to automatically be used to authenticate when connecting to a MetaFrame server. Only the Win32 client supports passthrough authentication.

Interoperability Modes

While many of you may be looking at MetaFrame and server-based technologies for the first time, there will be a number of readers looking to migrate their existing MetaFrame 1.8 server farms to an MPS 3.0 server farm environment. To facilitate this migration, Citrix lets the new MPS 3.0 server farm environment operate in one of two modes: MPS native mode or MPS mixed mode.

TIP: If you are implementing a new MetaFrame Presentation Server 3.0 environment and not migrating from an existing MetaFrame 1.8 environment, you need not be concerned with the material in this section. Never enable mixed-mode support unless absolutely necessary, as it will inhibit operation of certain native MPS features.

MPS Native Mode

The default operating mode for a new MPS installation is native mode, and when operating in this mode, the server farm can consist only of servers running MetaFrame XP 1.0 or higher. An MPS farm and a MetaFrame (MF) 1.8 server farm act completely independently of each other in this mode. This is because MPS uses the IMA protocol for server-to-server communications and the data store for managing farm information. MetaFrame 1.8, on the other hand, uses the ICA Browser service running on each server to perform server-to-server communications. In native mode, MPS completely ignores ICA Browser traffic. The components and operation of an MPS 3.0 server farm are reviewed briefly in the "Server Farms" section of this chapter.

MPS Mixed Mode

Operation of the server farm in mixed mode provides backwards compatibility with MF 1.8 and lets you transparently introduce new MPS servers into your existing MF 1.8 server farm. When the MPS farm is configured to enable mixed mode, you have access to interoperability features within the MPS Management Console. Figure 2.11 shows what features are available under the Interoperability tab. If you have experience administering an MF 1.8 environment, you will immediately recognize these settings from the old MetaFrame Administration tool.

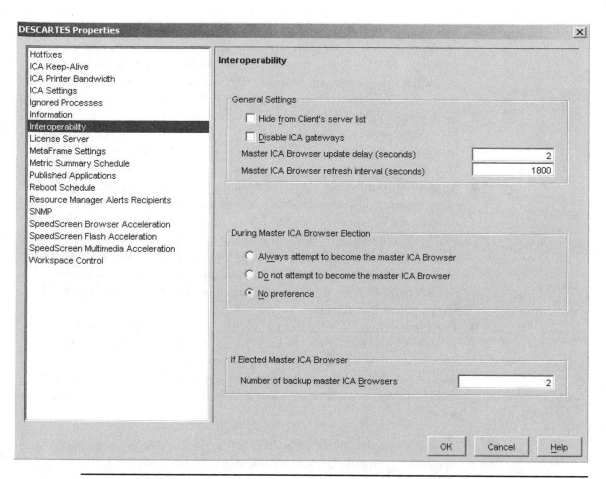

Figure 2.11   The Interoperability tab exists only when operating in mixed mode.

Some of the legacy features and support available in MetaFrame 1.8 are enabled in this mode and are summarized briefly in the following list. Details on these features and their limitations are discussed in more detail in Chapter 8, "Server Installation and Management Planning."

- **ICA Browser service**—Just as in a 1.8 environment, ICA Master Browser elections are supported in this mode along with the other standard ICA Browser service functionality. The standard election rules apply, but due to MPS 3.0's version number, it will always win an election over an MF 1.8 server.
- **ICA gateways**—ICA gateways are supported but must be managed from an MF 1.8 server. ICA license gateways are not supported in a mixed-mode environment.

- **License pooling**—MPS provides the ability to pool and share licenses when operating in mixed mode, although there are limitations to this. If you have implemented MF 1.8 license gateways to allow license pooling between subnets, they will no longer function when an MPS mixed-mode farm is introduced. The license division between these subnets is instead based on the settings under the Interoperability tab. Instead of having access to the entire license pool, the MetaFrame servers in each subnet will have access to only the 1.8 connection licenses available in their subnet and the available MPS licenses that have been allocated.
- **Application publishing**—While operating in mixed mode, the same application can be published between the two environments. For example, Microsoft Word could be published on both an MF 1.8 and an MPS server, and users would connect to the appropriate server based on the requested application and not based on a certain server version. Special steps must be taken to ensure that applications are published properly when operating in a mixed-mode environment. Application publishing considerations are discussed in detail in Chapter 21, "Application Integration."
- **Load balancing**—When a mixture of MF 1.8 and MSP servers are load-balancing applications, only the load-balancing features supported in MF 1.8 are available. Any new load-balancing features supported by MPS are not accessible. When determining what server to direct a user toward, if both an MPS and an MF 1.8 server have the same user load, the MetaFrame server is always selected.

An MPS 3.0 server is introduced into an existing MF 1.8 server farm by assigning the exact same farm name during installation. After the installation has completed, the 1.8 farm is detected and the two farms automatically establish the necessary relationship to coexist. You can enable and disable mixed-mode support after MPS has been installed by accessing the Interoperability option within Properties for the server farm. An existing 1.8 farm is detected only if it has the exact same name as the current farm you are modifying.

TIP: Mixed-mode support is intended as a migration mechanism only and not as a long-term solution for combining MF 1.8 and MPS 3.0 servers into a single farm.

Server Farms

The heart of any MPS deployment is the server farm. Whether you are deploying a single server or 45 servers, you are required to create a server farm within which the MetaFrame server(s) will reside. What exactly is a server farm? A server farm is a logical grouping of one or more MetaFrame servers that are then managed using the Presentation Server Management Console. Many of the settings managed from the root of the farm will be applied to all servers in that farm.

A thorough and proper server farm design is a key factor to the success of your MetaFrame deployment. An improperly designed server farm can result in poor or unreliable communications, not only between the clients and the servers but also amongst the servers themselves, whether located on the same physical network or distributed across multiple sites.

The most common farm implementation involves all MetaFrame servers deployed within a single server farm, and all co-located with other infrastructure servers at the same physical location. Local and remote users would then all connect into this central location in order to access their applications. Figure 2.12 shows this type of configuration, with all MetaFrame servers on the same network logically grouped into a single server farm. This is the configuration I use in this chapter to introduce and discuss the basic components of a server farm. A more detailed discussion on farm design and planning are undertaken in Chapter 8.

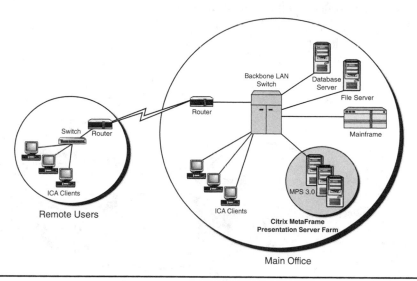

Figure 2.12 The most common MPS deployment has all servers in one location within a single server farm.

NOTE: Many administrators new to MetaFrame—or even those coming from a MetaFrame 1.8 environment—may feel intimidated by the idea of server farms and the apparent complexity of the MetaFrame Presentation Server implementation. The amount of planning and preparation required before actually deploying MetaFrame goes against the instincts (and desires) of most administrators in general (not just

Windows administrators), who want to get the software installed as quickly as possible and start playing around with it. In many respects, the best way to learn is to get your hands a little dirty, although "hacking around" with the software is not a substitute for proper planning.

Once you understand how the different components of an MPS 3.0 server farm interact with each other, you will be much better prepared to architect the server farm configuration that will work best in your environment.

Depending on the needs of your organization, a distributed MetaFrame environment may be best suited to deliver the applications to your end users. One example of such a configuration would have you maintain the common core set of applications and back-end data in a central location while still allowing access to other distributed applications or services located elsewhere for performance or security reasons. Figure 2.13, which is a modified version of the farm from Figure 2.12, still shows a set of MetaFrame servers in the main data center but remote resources have been co-located with their associated file and database servers in a remote office. All the servers in this scenario are still contained within a single server farm. Server farm membership is not restricted to only those MetaFrame servers located in one physical location.

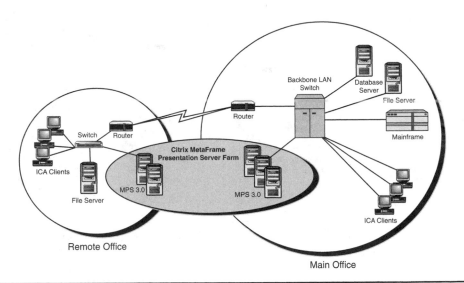

Figure 2.13   A single server farm still can be used to manage MetaFrame servers, even if they are distributed across a wide-area network.

Data Store

At the core of any MPS farm deployment is the data store repository. One master data store will exist in each server farm, although multiple replica data stores can exist if a distributed farm implementation is being created. The data store is where *persistent* information about the server farm is maintained, such as the following:

- **MetaFrame administration accounts**—Users who are able to administer a server farm are managed through the Management Console and maintained within the data store.
- **Farm configuration information**—Information such as the user connection limits, host license server, and general MetaFrame settings such as client time zone support and remote connection support for the local console are stored in the data store.
- **Server configuration information**—Server-specific settings such as client printer bandwidth throttling and reboot scheduling are also stored here. A number of options by default inherit the settings defined at the farm level, and unless absolutely necessary to do otherwise, I recommend always inheriting settings from the farm configuration instead of trying to maintain them on a server-by-server basis. Certainly this may introduce a bit of a learning curve for those administrators coming from a MetaFrame 1.8 environment, where most changes have to be done on each individual server.
- **Published application configuration information**—All aspects of a published application are maintained in the data store, including the MetaFrame servers hosting the application, Program Neighborhood client settings, and the access control list containing the users or groups able to launch the application.
- **Printer management**—The Printer Management module controls the behavior of auto-created client printers in the farm as well as managing driver replication and auto-created network printer assignments. Planning considerations for printer management in a Citrix server farm are discussed in Chapter 8, and installation and configuration of printer support are covered in Chapter 17, "Terminal Server and MetaFrame Printer Management."

All this persistent farm information is contained within a database management system (DBMS) and accessed via ODBC. MPS currently supports the following five DBMS repositories for the data store:

- Microsoft Access.
- Microsoft SQL Server 2000 Desktop Edition (MSDE)
- Microsoft SQL Server 2000 or 7.0 (with SP2)
- Oracle 9i Release 2 Enterprise Edition, Oracle 8i (8.1.6 or higher), Oracle 8 (8.0.6), and Oracle 7 (7.3.4) are all officially supported
- IBM DB2 Enterprise Edition 7.2 or 8.2

Microsoft Access and MSDE are most often used when there are 50 or fewer MetaFrame servers in the farm, less than 100 concurrent users, and less than 100 published applications. When you are selecting either MSDE or Access, the target database will need to reside on the first MetaFrame server created in the new farm. All other servers in the farm must then communicate with this server in order to access the data store (see Figure 2.14). This configuration is known as an *indirect* connection to the data store, since all other MetaFrame servers must go through the server housing the data store in order to access the farm information.

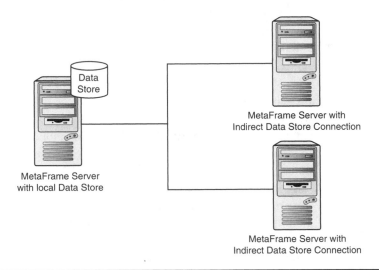

MetaFrame Server with Indirect Data Store Connection

MetaFrame Server with local Data Store

MetaFrame Server with Indirect Data Store Connection

Figure 2.14   MetaFrame servers indirectly connected to the data store depend on a single MetaFrame server to relay the necessary farm information to them.

WARNING: While MSDE does support up to five concurrent remote connections, configuring your MetaFrame server to directly connect to the MSDE instead of indirectly through the MetaFrame interface is not supported by Citrix. Because of the five-connection limit, exceeding this number can cause issues with one or more MetaFrame servers. Citrix recommends that the MSDE-based data store be accessed only through the indirect method, just as an Access database would be contacted.

Any one of the true enterprise database management systems (SQL Server, Oracle, or DB2) can be used when deploying a MetaFrame server farm of any size. In most situations, you would not use one of these systems in a small server farm unless you already had the DBMS functioning in your infrastructure and wanted to leverage the robust server support from the very beginning of your deployment, or you were planning on scaling the environment up in a relatively short period of time and did not want to have to worry about migrating from

Access or MSDE to a full DBMS package. Citrix does provide and support a migration path from Access and MSDE to any of the other DBMSs. Table 2.3 summarizes the general classification used by Citrix and others when describing MetaFrame server farm size.

Table 2.3 General MetaFrame Server Farm Size Classifications

	Small	Medium	Large	Enterprise
MetaFrame servers	< 50	25 to 100	75 to 200	> 150
Concurrent users	< 100	< 3000	> 2000	< 5000
				> 3000
Published applications	< 100	< 200	< 500	< 2000

Implementing a production environment with a data store server that has inadequate capacity to support the environment can adversely impact the start-up and performance of the IMA service on each server. The number of servers in the environment can also impact the speed of certain farm-based functions. Proper server farm sizing and data store selection are discussed in Chapter 8.

Zone Data Collectors

Zones are used to logically subdivide servers within a single server farm. Every server farm will have at least one zone, the default being the subnet in which the first MetaFrame server is created. During MetaFrame installation, in addition to being required to either create a new farm or direct the server to an existing farm, you are prompted to select a zone into which this server will be placed.

NOTE: A zone can have any name that you wish, but it cannot exceed 127 characters in length and should consist of only printable characters.

Within each zone there will exist one MetaFrame server designated as the *zone data collector*. Unlike the data store, which maintains persistent information about the farm, a zone data collector (ZDC) maintains dynamically updated information about all the servers in its own zone. The ZDC in each zone is responsible for providing information when requested to other ZDCs in the farm and to ICA clients that request information about servers or published applications. A ZDC maintains the following information:

- What servers exist in its zone and their current load level
- What applications are published on the servers in the zone
- What user sessions currently exist on the servers in the zone

NOTE: A ZDC collects and maintains only dynamic data about the servers in its zone. A ZDC does not replicate its data to a backup ZDC and does not save information that is reloaded at a later date. When a MetaFrame server is chosen as a ZDC, it always retrieves new information from the environment.

Whenever there is a change in status of any one of these settings on a MetaFrame server, the updated information is sent immediately to that server's ZDC. The information is not queued, and there is no way to adjust this update interval. Figure 2.15 shows the same network from Figure 2.13, showing two zones and a data collector in each. Even though all servers are part of the same farm there will be a separate ZDC for each zone. The ZDCs in each zone will share information with each other when requested.

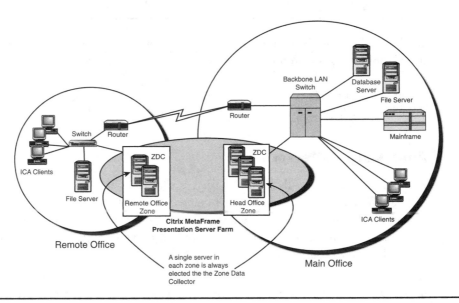

Figure 2.15   A single MetaFrame server in each zone is always elected as the zone data collector.

NOTE: In releases of MetaFrame prior to 3.0, the ZDC automatically stored information on all servers in the farm, not just servers in its own zone. By default, a ZDC now maintains information on only its own zone and dynamically queries other zones for information when necessary. Automatic storage of information from all other zones can still be re-enabled if desired.

By default, whenever a user requests a published application, the ZDC receiving that request automatically queries all other ZDCs in the farm to determine what MetaFrame server is available with the least load to satisfy this request. If an application is published on multiple servers located in different geographically distinct zones, it is very likely that a user will be directed across a WAN link to a least-loaded server in a remote location. Of course this is an issue only if you have the same application published on servers in the same farm located across a WAN link. Under certain conditions, you can utilize zone preferences and failover, a feature new to MPS 3.0 that lets you create zone preferences for users that will service all requests from that user and pass it off to an alternate zone only in the event of a failure. When a user has a zone preference defined, he or she is directed to the least-loaded server within that *zone*—even if a server has a lower load level in a different zone—and looks to a server in another zone only if no server can service the client's request.

The ZDC for a zone is chosen through an election process that will appear very similar to the Master Browser election process for those readers who have worked with MetaFrame 1.8 or earlier versions. A MetaFrame server can be assigned one of four priority levels that dictate the weighting assigned when a ZDC election is initiated. Figure 2.16 shows the four possible priority levels.

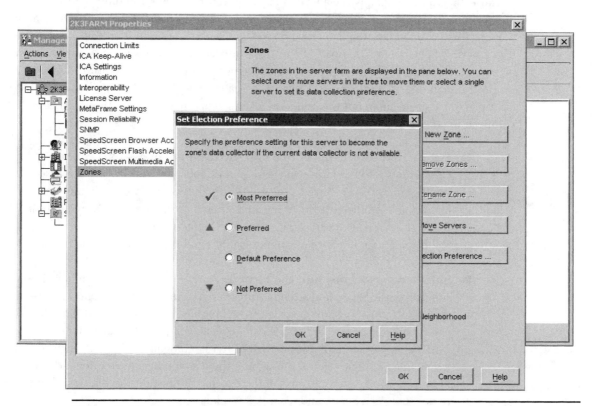

Figure 2.16 A MetaFrame server has four possible priority choices that dictate the likelihood that it will be elected the zone data collector.

These priority levels are

- **Most Preferred**—This is the default priority assigned to the first MetaFrame server added to the environment. A server with this setting is always the first choice to become the ZDC in an election. Best practices dictate that only one MetaFrame server in each zone be assigned this setting.
- **Preferred**—If the most preferred server is not available, the first server selected with this setting becomes the ZDC. Typically one or two servers designated as backup ZDCs should be assigned this priority level.
- **Default Preference**—This is the default setting for all MetaFrame servers in the zone, excluding the very first server. If no servers are found that match the first two criteria, the first server selected with a default preference becomes the ZDC.
- **Not Preferred**—Servers assigned this setting will not become the ZDC unless there are no other servers in the farm that have any of the three previous priority settings. Every server farm must have at least one ZDC, hence the reason why no MetaFrame server can be completely omitted from possibly becoming a ZDC.

Because the ZDC maintains the information required by clients to connect to published applications in the environment, performance issues with the ZDC result in delayed information retrieval or application launching on the client. It is important that the MF administrator periodically monitor the load of the ZDC in each zone to ensure it is not becoming overwhelmed servicing client requests and managing the server farm data for the zone.

A common rule of thumb is to establish a dedicated zone data collector when you exceed 50 servers in a single zone, but this is a loose estimate and in reality the threshold at which you need to consider a dedicated ZDC is based on the following:

- **Concurrent user connections into the farm or zone**—Total concurrent connections into the farm will affect all data collectors unless you have also implemented the Preferred zone policy for your users. By default, any user logon results in the corresponding ZDC querying all other ZDCs trying to find the least-loaded server to service the user's request. Instituting preferred zones will help contain inter-zone communications and reduce the load on the other ZDCs in the farm.
- **Simultaneous logons into the farm or zone**—When a large number of users simultaneously log on and attempt to acquire a connection to a MetaFrame server, this introduces a short-term load spike on the data collectors. If these logon counts are sufficiently large, they can noticeably impact the environment. If the work habits of the employees consist of frequent logons and logoffs instead of maintaining a single session throughout the day, you may encounter such jumps in processing at different times in the day and not just during the typical peak period, between 8 a.m. and 9 a.m. on weekdays.

■ **Total number of published applications and their distribution between MetaFrame servers**—This can also impact performance of the ZDC. Because the ZDC must account for all connection instances on all servers within the zone, it may receive frequent status updates from the different servers on the connection counts, server load, disconnections, and so on.

NOTE: Use of a dedicated ZDC is very similar to the idea of using a dedicated Meta-Frame Master Browser server in MetaFrame 1.8. Unlike the licensing model for Meta-Frame 1.8, where there was a separate cost for each MetaFrame server deployed, the MPS licensing model is solely based on concurrent users, allowing for as many server deployments as necessary to satisfy the needs of the environment. This allows for deployment of a dedicated ZDC without an additional MetaFrame server licensing cost. Of course there is still the required Microsoft server licensing cost.

When you are using a dedicated ZDC, Citrix suggests sizing a farm based on 500 MetaFrame servers per zone. This number is up significantly from the recommendation of 100 servers per zone with MetaFrame XP 1.0. While estimates can certainly be helpful in quickly determining what may be a suitable configuration for an environment, the configuration that will ultimately be implemented in your environment should be based on the results of your testing and monitoring. ZDC sizing and monitoring are discussed in Chapter 8.

A dedicated ZDC is simply a regular MetaFrame server without any user-accessible published applications. The server is part of the server farm and assigned to the zone for which it will collect data. See Chapter 13, "MetaFrame Presentation Server Installation," for notes on the ZDC installation.

WARNING: Citrix recommends that you not exceed 25 zones within a single server farm. Within a single corporate location this is not likely, but if a company has many remote offices, such a configuration may be a consideration. Look to either consolidate servers at fewer locations and reduce the zone count or create separate server farms.

Local Host Cache

In order to more effectively access information from the data store, each MetaFrame server in the farm maintains a subset of data store information in a special cache called the Local Host Cache (LHC). Information such as licensing is maintained in this cache, letting a MetaFrame server function for up to 96 hours without an active connection to the data store. The information in the LHC is updated in the following ways:

■ Whenever a MetaFrame server first boots, the necessary initialization information is retrieved from the data store and the LHC is verified to contain current information.

■ If a change is made to the data store through the Management console, all zone data collectors are notified and in turn responsible for notifying each MetaFrame server in their zone that their LHC needs to be updated.

■ By default, the MetaFrame server sends a query to the data store every 30 minutes to determine if changes have been made to the data store that are not reflected in the LHC. This allows for redundancy in LHC updates, protecting against a situation where a MetaFrame server misses an update request from the data store due to high server or network utilization. The update interval can be modified through the registry to adjust this interval up or down.

NOTE: In most situations I recommend against adjusting this update interval. If updates are being missed by a MetaFrame server, it may be signaling more significant issues that need to be addressed instead of simply attempting to counteract the problem through more frequent updates. Depending on the capabilities of your data store, frequent update requests from the LHC can cause performance issues. Adjustments to the LHC to troubleshoot high data store utilization are discussed in Chapter 22, "Server Operations and Support." The LHC can be manually refreshed or re-created using the DSMAINT command line utility. See Appendix B, "MetaFrame Presentation Server Command Reference," for details on use of this command.

Independent Management Architecture (IMA)

A discussion about the underlying components that make up the MetaFrame server farm is not complete without discussing Independent Management Architecture (IMA). As I mentioned near the beginning of this chapter, IMA is both an architectural model for server management and the protocol used for communication between the different components in the farm. Where the ICA protocol provides the presentation services transport between the MetaFrame server and the ICA client, the IMA protocol provides the communications vehicle for the MetaFrame servers as they pass farm information back and forth. IMA ties the components of the server farm together.

On each MetaFrame server you will find the Independent Management Architecture service, which listens on TCP port 2512 by default for server-to-server communications and listens on TCP port 2513 for incoming connections from the MPS Management Console. If the data store for the server farm is being maintained in an Access or MSDE database, then the MetaFrame server that is home to the database has what is called a *direct* connection with the data store. All other MetaFrame servers in the farm must talk to this server in order to retrieve data store information; this type of connection is known as an *indirect* connection with the data store. The IMA service on an indirectly connected server communicates outbound on port 2512 when talking with the data store.

TIP: If necessary, any of the TCP ports used by the IMA service can be modified using the IMAPORT command. Appendix B provides more information on this command.

MetaFrame Scalability

Considering that Citrix has architected an administrative framework capable of ensuring a maintainable environment regardless of how large it may grow, it shouldn't be surprising that Citrix also provides load management capabilities that easily scale to accommodate equally large user growth. This load management technology has been around since the days of WinFrame 1.6 (1996), when even in those early days it was proving to be an extremely capable technology. MetaFrame's Load Management support is included with the MPS Advanced and Enterprise Editions. The MPS Standard Edition does not include load management.

NOTE: The very first server-based computing installation I worked on was with WinFrame 1.6 in a load-balanced environment involving more than 30 servers in two distinct locations. At that time, the only documentation that even mentioned load balancing was a small Microsoft help file that explained how the feature could be enabled through a simple registry change.

In order to configure and leverage Citrix Load Management, two pieces of information are required:

- **The published application or desktop session to load-balance**—When you want to load-balance something in the MetaFrame environment, you begin by "publishing" it. You can publish an individual application, such as Microsoft Word, which users will run in combination with local applications on their client device, or you can publish a full desktop session. As the name implies, a *full desktop* means that the user is granted access to the entire Windows desktop on a MetaFrame server. The user's group membership dictates what privileges they actually have on the server. When an application or desktop is published on more than one server (see Figure 2.17), it is automatically set to load-balance.

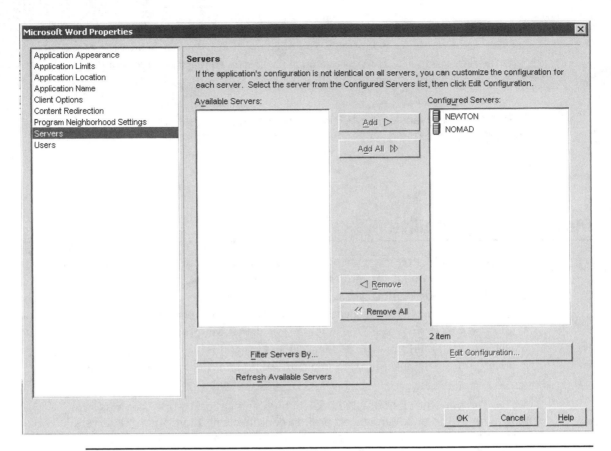

Figure 2.17   Load Management lets you publish an application on more than one server. Doing so automatically sets it up for load balancing.

- **A *load evaluator* specifying the calculations to be used to determine the actual load value for a server or application**—When deciding what server should service a user's request for an application or desktop, the load value that is calculated is compared with the load value of other servers and the least-loaded server is chosen. A load evaluator is automatically assigned to every server. This evaluator can be changed or modified. An evaluator can also be assigned to an individual application, letting you use different criteria for an application. When a user connects to that application, the application's load evaluator is also calculated. The higher value (server load evaluator or application load evaluator) is used as the actual server load. Figure 2.18 shows the load evaluation selection for a MetaFrame server. A complete discussion on load management, including configuration and use of load evaluators, is discussed in more detail in Chapter 21, as part of the application-publishing topic.

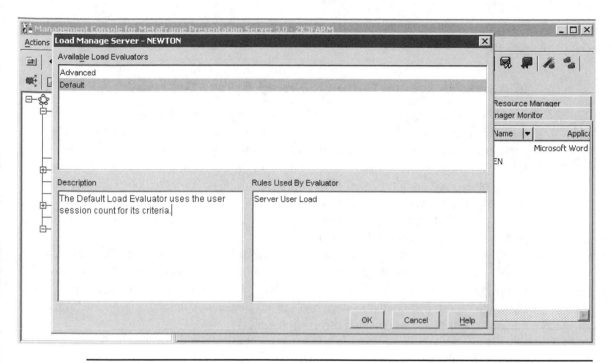

Figure 2.18   Citrix provides two default load evaluators that you can use or duplicate and modify to tailor as you see fit.

MetaFrame Server Licensing

We end this chapter by talking briefly about MPS 3.0 licensing and the introduction of the new MetaFrame Access Suite Licensing (MASL) infrastructure. MASL is Citrix's new strategy for centralizing client licensing across its entire suite of applications. Not only is MASL intended to provide license support for MPS, but it also eventually will support licensing for all Citrix's products. At the time of this writing, MetaFrame Conferencing Manager 3.0 is the only other product supporting this licensing infrastructure.

The introduction of MASL is a significant change from the licensing strategy of earlier versions of MetaFrame, which had licensing more tightly integrated with the application's functionality. The Citrix Management Console with MetaFrame XP had an integrated licensing module, and licensing information was maintained within the server farm's data store. Earlier versions of MetaFrame relied on the Citrix Licensing application to manage licensing, and the associated license information was maintained in the registry on each MetaFrame server. Ultimately, each change in the licensing strategy for Citrix has resulted in an improvement in management and allocation of client access licenses, but certainly MASL will be a major administrative change for those people already familiar with MetaFrame.

MetaFrame Access Suite Licensing Server Overview

MASL completely separates the licensing component of MetaFrame from the core functionality of the product by storing the licensing information in a database located on the server where the MASL product is actually installed, much like the Terminal Services Licensing service for Microsoft Terminal Server. While MASL can be installed on a server also running MetaFrame Presentation Server, ideally it should reside on a server whose primary function is not MetaFrame user sessions. Details on implementation planning of MASL are discussed in Chapter 8, while actual installation of the product is covered in Chapter 12, "Licensing Service Installation and Configuration."

Two methods exist for actually managing the MASL server. You can use either a Web-based management console (Figure 2.19) or a set of command line tools. Both methods let you perform the same basic license administration, but the Web console also lets you generate usage reports and configure alert mechanisms that can be helpful in proactively ensuring adequate licenses are available in the environment.

To use the Web-based console you must also have IIS installed on the licensing server, which can influence your decision on where to install MASL. My personal preference is to locate the Microsoft Terminal Server and MetaFrame licensing components on the same member server in a domain. Because MASL also requires IIS 5.0 or later to be installed in order to utilize a Web-based management console, I tend to avoid installing this product onto a domain controller unless the client is comfortable using the command line interface and the Web console can be omitted.

Two different operational grace periods exist for an MPS 3.0 server; the "start-up" grace period and the "fail-over" grace period.

Until a valid license file has been deployed on a license server, any MetaFrame server that is directed to this license server will operate in the "start-up" grace period mode. In this mode the following grace-period licenses are available:

- **Two non-administrative users**—96 hours (four days). When a non-administrative user connects they will be granted a temporary license that will be valid for four days. After this time the license will expire and the user will not be able to log on until a valid license file is placed onto the license server. A maximum of two non-administrative licenses will be issued per MetaFrame server.
- **Administrative user**—Indefinite. Administrative users will be able to connect indefinitely to the MetaFrame server, regardless of whether a license file is placed on the license server or not. Warning messages will appear during logon stating that client licenses are not available.

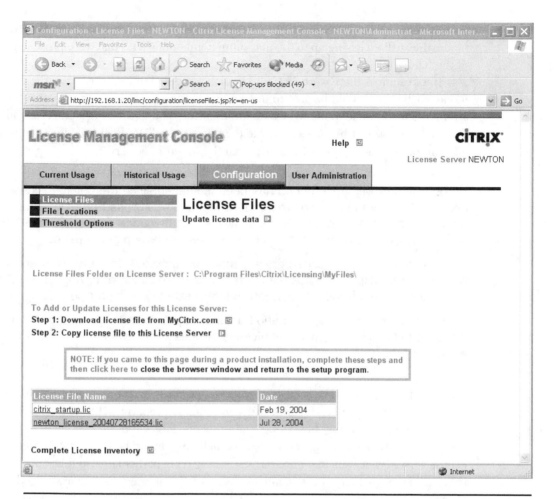

Figure 2.19 The preferred method of managing MetaFrame Access Suite Licensing is through the Web-based console. Command line tools are also provided with the product.

If a fully functional MASL server that has one or more license files installed, fails and becomes unavailable then all MetaFrame servers that were pointed to the license server will begin to operate in "fail-over" mode. In fail-over mode, a MetaFrame server will issue temporary licenses that are valid for a maximum of 30 days. If a valid license server does not become available within that time users will no longer be able to connect. MetaFrame servers do not share license file counts and do not pool licenses in the absence of a license server. Instead each MetaFrame server maintains their own separate copy of the current number of available CALS on a license server, and if they are forced to switch to fail-over mode, they will each issue up to the maximum number of CALS that were present at the time of the failure.

If for example, there were 25 CALS available and 6 MetaFrame servers, then in fail-over mode, each server would be able to independently issue up to a maximum of 25 CALS. No attempt is made while in fail-over mode to limit the total CALS allocated across all servers. Once a license server becomes available then licenses will automatically begin to be allocated from the license server, not directly from the MetaFrame servers.

NOTE: This fail-over grace period has been increased since the original license server documentation was released. The current MetaFrame Access Suite Licensing documentation available with MPS 3.0 still states that the grace period is only 96 hours (4 days) regardless of whether this is a fail-over or start-up grace period.

In order to utilize the extended grace period now provided with a fail-over scenario, you must have deployed a license file that was downloaded after August 19, 2004. An earlier license file will not support this new extended support period.

Also remember that this grace period does not apply to the start-up grace period. This grace period applies only when no license file has been downloaded and so, still remains at 96 hours.

The MASL server should be available *before* you install MPS 3.0, and an MPS 3.0 server must be able to access a MASL server in order to function properly. MPS 3.0 will install without the license server existing, but MetaFrame functionality will not be enabled and the server will periodically generate pop-up messages, including during boot-up, stating that the Citrix license server is not available. The start-up messages are particularly troublesome, as they can prevent remote ICA or RDP connections until the message is acknowledged from the console.

MetaFrame Client Access License Requirements

Unlike Microsoft Terminal Server licensing, which requires a unique license for each user or device that connects to the server, MetaFrame licensing is based strictly on concurrent user sessions (sometimes called *session-based licensing*). If for example you have 300 users who may connect to your MetaFrame server but only 125 are ever logged on at any given time, then you would be required to purchase only 125 MetaFrame client access licenses (CALs). No separate license is required for each MetaFrame server you wish to run; that cost is included in the per-session CALs. You can deploy as many MetaFrame servers as you wish, but you can have only 125 total concurrent users across all available MetaFrame servers.

When a user logs on to a MetaFrame server, the MetaFrame server is responsible for communicating with the MASL server and requesting the appropriate license for the user. If the request is approved, the license is assigned to the active user session and the CAL is considered to be checked out. The license remains checked out and in use until the user logs off his or her session, at which point the license is returned to the license server, available for use by someone else. If a user attempts to log on and there are no client licenses available, the logon is denied.

To make client access licenses available for use, the associated license code that came with your MPS product must be used to obtain a corresponding license file from Citrix's Web site. This file is generated by Citrix based on the name of your license server and is valid only when installed on that server. Once the file has been loaded and validated by the license server, the licenses are available for use by Citrix client sessions.

TIP: Probably the most common licensing question I'm asked is, "Since I'm going to be running MetaFrame Presentation Server, do I still have to purchase Windows Terminal Server client access licenses?"

The answer is, "Yes." Regardless of whether or not you will be using Citrix, you still must comply with Microsoft's licensing requirements for Windows Terminal Services (details of which were summarized in Chapter 1).

Consider the example I gave in the beginning of this section, where there were 300 total users and 125 concurrent users. Even though you would be required to purchase only 125 MetaFrame CALs, you still would be required to purchase 300 Microsoft Terminal Server CALs, 300 Microsoft Server user CALs, and a Microsoft Server product license for each Terminal Server you wished to run.

PART II

Planning Your Terminal Services Implementation

Project Management Considerations

Implementation Requirements

Although the material in this chapter is targeted mainly toward the project manager of a Terminal Server/MetaFrame implementation, I feel it's worthwhile for anyone involved in the project to have a clear understanding of the implementation requirements—not only what they are, but also why they're needed. Many technical people I've met feel this is really nothing more than "fluff" and has little impact on the "real" work they're required to do in order to drive the project to completion. While the technology is certainly important (or you wouldn't be reading this), without clearly outlining why it's being used, who will use it, and how it will be implemented, it's highly likely that the end product won't function as you or the business expected.

Poor planning leaves the door open for one of the most common project ailments, which is known as *project* or *scope creep*. This is the slow and continuous expansion of features and support that were never really a part of the initial project considerations but have somehow found their way into the list of requirements that must be met in order to consider the project a success. Many technical people fall victim to this. Some administrators agree to include something that is out of scope simply to get it out of their mind so they can concentrate on something else. Others often agree to do it simply to satisfy their ego in an attempt to prove that any expectation can be met and any requirement delivered, even if the possibility of meeting such a challenge is realistically impossible due to time constraints or other mitigating factors such as technical limitations.

As a result, most loosely defined and/or managed projects are beset with problems, some of the most common being the following:

- **Significantly over budget**—Poor planning and unforeseen difficulties require additional human and financial resources. While proper planning will not always protect against this, areas that are considered the most critical can be investigated and alternative solutions taken into consideration as part of the overall scope of the project.

NOTE: An odd offshoot of running a project over budget is being forced to manage a project that is confined to completely unrealistic budget constraints. Typically these have been imposed by upper management who adamantly insist that this is the cap that cannot be exceeded for the project. The unfortunate part of this is that this budget has usually been approved by the administrator's immediate supervisor based on sizing estimates that are completely unrealistic for the project at hand. The unlucky administrator in this situation is forced to make one of two choices.

- Try and acquire the hardware and software needed to successfully implement the project, while at the same time fitting it into a completely unrealistic budget.

- Argue the point that such restraints will surely result in an implementation that will not meet the needs of the business and as a result will be viewed as a failure by the end user community.

Obviously being able to argue the second point requires a clear understanding of what is required, as well as a realistic budget that will bring those requirements to life. Simply saying that there isn't enough money is not going to be very convincing.

The disappointing truth is that most administrators will opt for the first point and through shear determination hope to bring the project to life. The end result will likely be what you expect: an environment that is underpowered with second-rate equipment that will need to be upgraded or replaced within six months' time.

- **Late delivery**—A lack of thorough project planning and realistic time management will always impact the delivery dates.
- **Reduction of scope**—Either portions of the project that were originally in scope are omitted, or functionality that was originally planned has to be deferred or dropped completely. Many times a creep in the initial scope of the project can see the delivery of features or components not necessarily required, while other areas initially included end up being omitted.
- **Negative impact to the business**—This includes situations where the implementation introduces some major obstacles that require repeated rollbacks and redeployments to correct, affecting not only delivery dates and the project budget but also the user's confidence in the product. A poor impression by the end user community can be far more damaging not just to your reputation but also in the confidence that you can deliver on future requirements or changes. An issue on a Terminal Server can potentially be seen by and impact tens or hundreds of users, so taking the time to ensure a solid implementation is critical.
- **Failure to manage end users' and management's expectations**—Quite often people will read the hype surrounding Terminal Server and MetaFrame and feel they can deliver everything for nothing. This is not the case, and failure to manage users' expectations from the start will surely result in negative repercussions not only at the end but throughout the project.
- **Project cancellation**—The most drastic (and far more common than you might think) result of any of the problems described in this list, and usually a

combination of all of them, is the cancellation of the entire project. Not only is such a result incredibly demoralizing to you and your administrative team, but it also negatively impacts the user community, who quickly lose faith in their IT department to deliver the solutions required by the business.

While it has been argued that these difficulties happen more often than not and are simply a part of any project, I have yet to see a Terminal Server implementation encounter any of them when proper implementation planning and project management have occurred.

NOTE: Very often when I hear people complain about issues they have had with a Terminal Server implementation, the problems could easily have been avoided if the proper implementation planning had been performed.

One factor in minimizing potential problems arising during an implementation is to understand what I consider the five key implementation requirements:

- Documentation
- Leveraging desktop deployment flexibility
- Defining the scope of Terminal Server in your business
- Enlisting executive sponsors
- Not promising what you can't deliver

Documentation

The root issues with documentation are twofold:

- Traditionally, documentation has been very inconvenient to manage. There was no easy way to store documentation so it could be easily located, searched, or modified. Document management systems exist, but many organizations don't have the money to implement or resources to manage such an environment.

  The growth of the Internet as a business tool has greatly accelerated the development of products for authoring and managing Web-based information. The ease of use and availability of these tools, coupled with corporate intranets and extranets, has had an extremely positive impact on document management. Documentation can now be stored on an intranet Web site, easily accessible to anyone who's interested. Considering that Windows ships with both Web server and Web browser software, and that word processing tools such as Microsoft Word provide sophisticated capabilities for document creation and collaboration, including HTML creation, there are very few excuses for not having current, accessible documentation for your Terminal Server project. Even a page with links to the relevant Word documents can be a valuable tool in keeping the team members up-to-date with the necessary information.

Unfortunately it is the thinking of many managers and most technical staff that the time required to configure and manage a document library could be better spent working on the implementation itself. Even though a logical and simple folder structure could be created to centrally store the necessary documentation, convincing people that it is a worthwhile endeavor is another matter.

■ And of course, accessibility alone doesn't guarantee that documentation will actually be created. Time and resources must be available to ensure that the necessary documentation is written. Even if you're not responsible for managing the implementation, don't fool yourself into believing that you're saving time by not writing documentation. In fact, you're doing the opposite. Documentation is much like insurance, whose inherent worth becomes apparent only when it's needed. Documentation is the foundation for training, upgrades, and even disaster recovery of your Terminal Server environment. When your applications or systems are running smoothly, you don't think about documentation, but if disaster strikes, documentation can provide valuable information that might otherwise be forgotten.

NOTE: I can't even count how many times I've heard the statement that documentation will be written after the project is completed. Very rarely has this ever happened. By the end of the project, resources such as time and/or money have run out (because of a lack of documentation and planning, perhaps?) and another project is usually waiting to take its place.

Writing documentation makes you think about what you're doing and why you're doing it. It will help you uncover problems or deficiencies in your plan before they have the opportunity to affect your project.

As the project progresses through the implementation, documentation provides a clear footprint of where you've been and where you're going. This lets people new to the project be brought up to speed quickly, without misinterpreting the project's purpose, scope, and direction. Documentation also provides an audit trail, allowing you to review why certain decisions are made and greatly reducing the possibility of second-guessing a direction that was taken much earlier in the project's life.

While poor or nonexistent documentation may not doom your project to failure, having documentation that is current and accurately reflects the current and future state of your environment will go a long way to ensure its successful completion. Keeping a pad of paper readily available while you're working on your servers will allow you to quickly jot notes that you can refer back to later. It will certainly help you member tasks you've performed that you may later forget, particularly if you are extremely busy and become distracted troubleshooting some other problem.

Leveraging Desktop Deployment Flexibility

A Terminal Server implementation is a unique combination of client and server interaction that's unlike a traditional Windows server deployment. Although changes will be made to the client desktop, removing some or possibly all applications from the user's local control, the driving factor of the implementation is not the desktop. The desktop is simply the tool that you will use to deliver Terminal Server access to the user.

Terminal Server provides you with additional flexibility in your deployment that you wouldn't normally have in a traditional desktop upgrade project. Leveraging this flexibility will greatly reduce the impact on end users during the rollout. The goal is to introduce Terminal Server to them with minimal disruption to their work productivity.

Some areas where this flexibility can prove quite valuable are

- **Piloting**—Imagine being able to provide the user with two computers during a pilot. One contains the desktop that the user is piloting, and the other contains the user's original desktop. As soon as the user encounters a problem with the pilot computer, he or she simply returns to the original desktop until the problem is resolved. The Terminal Server client provides this same functionality. During piloting, the user can run in his or her new Terminal Server environment, returning to the local desktop if problems arise.

- **Testing validation**—One problem that continually arises when you are performing a desktop upgrade is that differences in the client hardware and software can pose compatibility issues for the applications you're deploying. What works fine on one desktop refuses to run properly on another desktop. The centralized nature of Terminal Server overcomes this problem and provides true validation for your piloting. Testing with a small group of users has greater value in a Terminal Server deployment because once the application is working properly for them, it will work for all users. Testing that Terminal Server is working properly doesn't require that you deploy it to a large number of users. By keeping the initial test groups small, you eliminate many problems early on while being able to quickly respond to users' issues as they arise. If Terminal Server isn't working for 5 users, it won't work any better for 50. Large-scale pilots add no value until you have validated the small test group. Don't fall into the trap of trying to do too much too quickly.

- **Training**—Terminal Server provides you with the ability to train a user on his or her Terminal Server session from any location, on any client device. Traditional training would involve sending users to a room to train on a generic computer with a configuration that usually didn't accurately reflect the user's personal computer setup. Terminal Server lets users see a familiar session, regardless of where they're physically located. Training is more consistent with how they'll actually be working. I've been involved in a couple of implementations in which a training room was established with Terminal Server accessible both to demonstrate the new environment and also to train administrative and support staff *prior* to initiating user testing. The ability to provide administrators and support staff with a look at the environment prior to having to assist users can be valuable in optimizing the time required to resolve an issue with a user.

- **Application migration**—It's very likely that not all users will have all their local applications moved to Terminal Server. This is an advantage of Terminal Server that isn't always apparent and in many cases is actually played down. Many references to Terminal Server imply that an implementation requires moving all local applications to the server. I feel that this thinking is tied too much to the traditional desktop upgrade, where all applications are moved to the new computer or reinstalled on the new operating system. Terminal Server provides the unique advantage of moving specific applications into the server-based computing environment while leaving other applications, such as those requiring special hardware, on the local computer. Too often I see issues arise in an implementation where a single application that's required by only a few users is holding up an entire deployment. See the next section for more details on this.

Defining the Scope of Terminal Server in Your Business

Human and financial resources and the types of applications in your current user environment will determine the scope of Terminal Server in your business. One of the decisions that will be made early on in the planning stage of your deployment is determining what the target user community will be. As mentioned in the preceding section, a common problem with many implementations is the misconception that all the user's applications must be moved off the desktop and onto the Terminal Server if any benefits are to be seen in the total cost of ownership (TCO). This simply isn't true. In fact, even moving only a subset of a user's applications can reduce TCO. The key is choosing the right software to move:

- Moving applications that have few support costs or are updated infrequently will show only a small reduction in TCO. Usually the benefits in this situation are not seen until the next major upgrade is required.
- Some prime targets to move are those applications that currently have large support or deployment costs. In most circumstances, the resulting move and standardization of the running environment to Terminal Server will help reduce many of the application issues and costs.

Terminal Server is not an all-or-nothing solution. All of the application migrations do not have to be planned to happen simultaneously, but can instead be staggered to happen when most appropriate for both the users and the administrator. Applications that don't fit within the scope of the project should be left to run on the user's desktop until a later date. If you want to have a successful deployment, clearly define the scope of the project from the beginning and deviate from it as little as possible. The two areas where I have most often seen a change in the scope of Terminal Server implementations are as follows:

- **Client scope**—Partway into the project, a decision is made to expand the client scope to include another user group that appears to be similar to the currently targeted users. Very often this includes adding applications required by these new users. In almost every situation where this has happened, hardware capacity or application issues have caused unexpected problems and delays in the implementation. Whenever possible, avoid modifying the client scope once you have moved beyond planning into piloting or the actual deployment. I discuss determining client scope in the later section "Developing the 'To-Be' Model."

- **Application scope**—Although you're likely to add and remove applications during the planning, testing, and even the pilot stage of you project, the deployment stage is not the time to be making application additions or modifications. Almost every project will encounter a situation in which an application will be discovered during deployment that would be a good candidate for inclusion in the project. Don't add these applications to your environment unless absolutely necessary. I would suggest instead that the information be inventoried so it can be reviewed and prioritized at a later time. Any unplanned modifications will almost always have a negative impact on the production environment, particularly if they haven't been part of any previous testing or piloting.

Enlisting Executive Sponsors

Every project must have three things in order to succeed:

- Leadership
- Money
- Human resources

To ensure that these elements are available for the duration of your project, you must enlist the support of one or more executive sponsors. An *executive sponsor* is a senior person within your business who can ensure that the changes you want to introduce are accepted and endorsed by the company from the top down. Top-down knowledge of the project ensures alignment with the company's strategic direction and is your only weapon in dealing with users and management who introduce resistance to your project for political or personal reasons. If you attempt to work in isolation without this top-down support, you will repeatedly have to justify your intentions and run the risk of losing access to one or more of the listed elements.

NOTE: I once was called in to consult for a company that was having issues with a Terminal Server implementation. They had deployed the product to approximately 200 users, and application problems were affecting the users' ability to work. After speaking with a couple of users, I found out that neither they nor their manager had received any prior notification that this change was even being made. Inadequate piloting and training had resulted in an unacceptable release situation.

Within a week the project was terminated, and all users were rolled back to their original desktops. The decision to deploy Terminal Server had come from the server support department without the official support of the end users' management. Even though the decision to deploy Terminal Server made sense both technically and from a business perspective, because the proper people had not endorsed it, the project was not allowed to proceed.

Don't Promise What You Can't Deliver

While it sounds simple, not delivering on promises is often the issue that causes the most problems. I don't know how many times I have heard someone promise things such as increased performance or greater stability without having any clear idea whether they could deliver this. If an application is slow or buggy on the local desktop, there's no guarantee that moving it to Terminal Server will eliminate either of these problems. It depends on whether the issues are due to the client desktop or the application itself. An application that leaks memory when run on the desktop will continue to leak memory when run on Terminal Server.

Make sure that you set realistic expectations for users. If you end up delivering more, all the better—but don't promise things you cannot deliver.

Business Process Management

An important part of managing a Terminal Server project is being able to manage the migration of the business processes effectively from the existing "as-is" model to the future "to-be" model. This migration is often called *business process reengineering* (BPR). When planning the BPR, there are two things you're trying to achieve:

- **Minimizing the change in how users must perform their work**—You want to integrate Terminal Server into their environment with as little disruption as possible.
- **Optimizing the process of managing the end user**—By implementing Terminal Server, you're looking to reduce the support requirements of the user and optimize the support that must still be performed. This includes support at the server as well as the client.

You need to consider the changes that you're introducing to the way in which these jobs have traditionally been done. For example, the existing activities required for maintaining a single desktop will be reduced or eliminated. Application support, hardware support, software upgrades, and training will all be affected. To maximize the benefits of your Terminal Server implementation, you must communicate these changes as effectively as possible. A clearly documented change in business processes will also minimize the uncertainty and misunderstanding around what exactly Terminal Server is bringing to your organization.

TIP: One common area with a large amount of uncertainty is the end-user support department. One of the key factors for introducing Terminal Server is the reduction in desktop support costs and hence a reduction in TCO. Most desktop support staff members equate the introduction of Terminal Server with the elimination of their jobs. While this is rarely the case, it is true that Terminal Server will affect how end-user support staff perform their jobs. By involving these support people early and making it clear what their support role will be once the implementation is complete, you'll have a much easier time with enlisting their cooperation to support you during the project.

To develop an effective BPR plan, you need to have an understanding of how the processes exist today and how they will work after the implementation. These are known as the "as-is" and "to-be" business process models, and together they form the roadmap for your Terminal Server implementation.

Developing the "As-Is" Model

The starting point for developing your BPR plan is determining what your business processes are today. This is commonly known as your "as-is" model. In an ideal world, a company would have an "as-is" model available with all the necessary information. In most cases, some form of a model will need to be developed. In forming this model, you need to concentrate on four areas:

■ **Users and user support**—Look at how the users work today: which applications they commonly use and which they don't. Before you begin, you will likely already have an idea as to what groups you will be targeting for the Terminal Server deployment. When preparing the "as-is" model, be sure to look for such things as one-off applications or other exceptions that will need to be flagged and accounted for when planning the implementation. Note what additional hardware users might use or access, particularly such things as file or print servers, scanners, modems, or even proprietary "dongles," cabling or other hardware-based licensing mechanisms required by certain legacy applications. Document concerns, issues, and suggestions that users may have about the existing environment. This will help in determining hardware requirements, pilot user groups, initial implementation groups, special needs' users, and exceptions that may need to be excluded from your Terminal Server deployment. Often, you'll be able to establish a group of users during this time that will be used to pilot and test the initial Terminal Server environment.

Another valuable user consideration is the establishment of measures for such factors as logon times, application speed, time to access network resources, and time required for switching between applications. You shouldn't spend a lot of time attempting to gather large amounts of detailed quantitative data, but some average times can be useful in flagging deficiencies in the infrastructure that may need to be addressed prior to a Terminal Server go-live. You may also be able to determine areas where Terminal Server can save time or boost performance of existing hardware. Often this is achieved by having the Terminal Server and one or more file servers located on the same physical network (see the next point). This proximity can dramatically enhance the performance of resource access and is usually noticed right away, particularly by the "power" users. Remember: Don't promise performance gains with Terminal Server until you're sure you can deliver them.

- **Network and network support**—The inclusion of the most accurate network infrastructure information available is a critical component of your "as-is" model. A network diagram should be available that includes all relevant client and server networks that will interact with your Terminal Servers. The types of networks and the supported protocols should also be included. A key piece of information is why servers have been placed in certain locations and if there are any issues with moving them. This is important when looking at where the Terminal Servers will be situated on the network. You'll need to co-locate them with whatever other servers users will need to access through their Terminal Server sessions. Knowing which servers can be moved and which can't will help in developing an accurate "to-be" model. A network support contact will be required not only to assist with any network issues that may arise but also as a resource for accurate information on network capacity and future direction.

- **Servers and server support**—You need to inventory which server hardware and associated operating systems are currently in production. Of particular interest will be those systems utilized by the end user, such as file and print servers. As complete a Windows domain diagram as possible, with the appropriate trust relationships, should be included if anything other than a simple forest/domain configuration is in effect. WINS, DHCP, DNS, and other network servers should also be noted, depending on the network protocols being used. As I mentioned, you will want to try and co-locate all the necessary servers accessed by the users with the Terminal Servers, if possible. If all your users will be accessing a particular file server, then it may be necessary to ensure that file server is placed on the same network as the Terminal Servers. A local domain controller will also be necessary to ensure timely authentication and logon script processing.

Determine what domain the Terminal Servers will reside in and what users are responsible for administering these domains. Terminal Server will require the creation of customized administrative groups in the domain to support the environment, so including the administrators in the planning process is critical. While in many environments the Terminal Server administrator is also a domain administrator, this is not always the case. Don't expect to have anyone's full cooperation if you spring your Terminal Server requirements on him or her at the last minute. A clear understanding of how Terminal Server will fit into the infrastructure is another key requirement to a smooth implementation.

- **Software**—Determine the current software standards within the organization, as well as any exceptions that should exist. Knowing the number of licenses that exist for software is important in determining how the software will be made available on a Terminal Server and whether access restrictions may be required. It's not uncommon to publish applications and manage their licensing by restricting access to members of a specific Windows security group or implementing restrictions on the total number of concurrent instances of a running application. When combining applications from different departments on a Terminal Server it is important to verify that all the applications can operate with the same version of software, such as the Microsoft Data Access Components (MDAC) or the Java Runtime Environment (JRE).

Developing the "To-Be" Model

I've always looked on the development of the "to-be" model as the creation of the answer to the question, "What are you trying to achieve?" The simple answer is that you're deploying Terminal Server and moving software off the local desktop to run on the server(s), but the complete answer is much more than that. Your "to-be" model will provide answers to the following questions:

- Who will be using Terminal Server?
- How were these people chosen?
- What software are you going to deploy?
- Which users will use what software?
- What deployment method will you use (desktop replacement, application replacement, and so forth?
- Where will the servers be located, and who will be responsible for supporting them?

The most common way to develop the "to-be" model is to work from the "as-is" model to determine the end state in each documented situation. For example, in your "as-is" model you will have noted existing user configurations along with the processes in place to support them. In your "to-be" model, you document how these setups would change to reflect the Terminal Server environment. The information doesn't necessarily need to be extensive but does need to clearly point out the changes that will be occurring. The changes in how the support staff handles client hardware issues might go something like this:

> If a user is having any hardware-related issue, then the desktop support person shouldn't attempt to repair the computer at the user's desk. The user should be directed to sit at an alternate desk if available and connect to Terminal Server through that machine until the first one has been repaired. If no alternate desk is available, a Windows terminal or backup PC should be provided temporarily, to let the user have Terminal Server access until a replacement machine can be delivered. Under no circumstances should the client hardware be disassembled or repaired while the user waits. Getting the user up and working again as quickly as possible should be the first priority.

Other examples might include the following:

- **Updating the network diagram to show the position of the Terminal Servers and any other new or moved hardware within the infrastructure**—A visual representation of your implementation is an excellent way to describe what is happening.
- **Developing Terminal Server–specific support procedures for your help desk so they can efficiently handle calls from your new users**—This would include training on how to use the remote control features of Terminal Server and accurately redirect calls to an application or Terminal Server administrator if necessary. The need to immediately deploy a support person to the user's desktop is not necessary in most situations.

To ensure that your "to-be" model is what's required by the business, take the time to describe the implementation clearly and note where you anticipate possible issues. Work closely with the appropriate contacts within the business to ensure that your goals are in line with both their requirements and yours. Afterward, you'll have a plan for implementing Terminal Server that's both clearly understood and accepted by the business.

Policies and Procedures

An important part of developing your "to-be" model is creating or modifying policies and procedures for both your clients and your servers. These will be used not only for managing and constructing the environment during implementation but also for continued management once in production. Create policies and procedures that will add value and lead to a more manageable environment—don't create them simply because you can. Before putting any policy or procedure in place, ask yourself these questions:

- Does the policy or procedure you want to introduce resolve or control an issue that exists today or is anticipated to exist in the near future? An example might be the establishment of disk quotas on personal file areas to resolve issues with exaggerated disk consumption by users with non-work-related data.
- Is this policy or procedure easy to communicate? Will it be understood easily by others?
- Is it simple enough that the people who are supposed to abide by it (users, developers, and administrators) will do so, or will they seek ways to circumvent it?
- What are the possible ramifications if these policies or procedures are not implemented?

Selecting Policies to Implement

Your company most likely already has a number of policies and procedures in place. They are most often implemented to protect the business from legal recourse, lost revenue, or tarnishing its public image. Some common examples include the following:

- A ban on the use of noncorporate or pirated software from home or the Internet. Many viruses and worms are introduced into a corporate network by users running pirated software they have acquired off of the Internet. Being caught with pirated software during an audit can be damaging to both the finances and the reputation of an organization.
- A ban on the viewing or possession of pornographic and other material (such as MP3s or pirated movies). The downloading of multimedia files of any kind can also place a large burden on a company's Internet or storage resources.
- Rules concerning storage of personal data such as personal tax information or children's projects on corporate computers.
- Rules against storing company information on a local PC instead of in an environment (such as a network) where the information is more secure, both from theft and loss through accidental or purposeful destruction.
- Taking suitable measures to protect against the theft or destruction of company property, including corporate "secrets."

Although each of these issues is important, all are behavioral policies and none are specific to the Terminal Server environment. The policies can exist without requiring Terminal Server, and Terminal Server can exist without these policies.

Terminal Server can be used to make the enforcement of these policies easier. For example, using Terminal Server as a complete desktop replacement and providing the user with only a diskless Windows-based terminal would greatly simplify enforcement of a policy concerning running pirated software or local storage of company information for these users.

When developing Terminal Server policies and procedures, concentrate on those that directly relate to its creation, administration, or support.

Many policies and procedures for Terminal Server are identical to those designed for the regular desktop environment. The key difference is in the amount of effort expended in enforcement. Enforcement of policies and procedures is inherently difficult when it must be taken out to each user's desktop. The most obvious reason is that it's nearly impossible to monitor or control what users are doing without a high level of maintenance.

These are some of the common areas where you may want to develop policies or procedures for Terminal Server:

- **Terminal Server system installation, configuration, and disaster recovery**— By developing a standard procedure for the creation of your Terminal Servers, you ensure that additional machines can be built at any time to augment the current environment or recover in a disaster situation.

- **Commercial software selection, installation, upgrades, and back-out plans**—A policy and procedure on how software that runs on Terminal Server is managed is very important. It lets you determine quickly whether a piece of software is suitable for running in the environment, along with guidelines for testing and implementing it into production.

- **Software developer guidelines**—This includes such things as documenting the software installation requirements for the applications in your environment. This is probably the most difficult policy to put into place in a large corporation. Because in-house developers move around frequently and new projects are born quickly, such a policy can be difficult to communicate and enforce in a timely fashion. Very often you'll encounter an application that needs to be deployed on Terminal Server but wasn't tested in such an environment through the proper development process.

  A well documented policy and procedure would need to exist to ensure that the Terminal Server administrator will not allow such an application to be deployed into the production environment without passing a set of minimum requirements, ensuring that its introduction does not impact the other applications or users on the system.

NOTE: Remember that most developers and their managers will know very little about Terminal Server and will most often completely ignore it until their application is complete. At this point, it can be difficult for them to make code changes if necessary to get their application to run in Terminal Server. This can mean that either the program will end up on the user's desktop, or you'll need to perform some workaround in Terminal Server to get the program to work. Easy accessibility to the necessary Terminal Server policies is key to ensuring that they're followed.

■ **In-house and custom-developed software management**—This includes unit testing, acceptance testing, piloting, production promotion, and "emergency" fixes due to software bugs. The proper process for moving these applications into production goes hand in hand with the need to ensure that applications are developed to run in Terminal Server.

Specific policies and procedures for clients, servers, networks, and applications are discussed in the next few chapters, where I talk in more detail about implementation planning for each component.

The centralized manageability and homogenous environment introduced by Terminal Server makes it very suitable for defining policies and procedures that can be enforced effectively. Terminal Server brings the user's desktop logically closer to the administrators of the environment, while still providing the required functionality to the user.

CHAPTER 4

Network Planning

Terminal Server and Your Network Infrastructure

By design, Terminal Server relies heavily on the network infrastructure of an organization to function effectively. The perceived stability of Terminal Server depends very much on the underlying stability and design of the network. A solid understanding of how to configure and deploy Terminal Server is only part of the criteria required for a successful implementation. If users are unable to maintain a reliable connection to the Terminal Server, the environment will be considered unusable from the perspective of both the users and the business.

NOTE: If you're unfamiliar with the general concepts of networking, see Appendix C, "Network Primer," where I provide an introduction to network communications protocols and physical and logical networks.

Of course, ensuring that adequate network resources are available for an application or system deployment is certainly not a new concept. In the past, when planning an application deployment into your company's existing network infrastructure, you would need to consider such things as the application's traffic patterns to ensure that the network was designed to meet the application's needs (or vice versa). In order to effectively access the impact of an implementation on your network, you need to be able to identify the strengths and weaknesses of your existing infrastructure and flag areas that may need to change in order to minimize bottlenecks or single points of failure.

Consider Figure 4.1, which represents the historical network design concept known as the 80/20 rule. In this design, the majority (80 percent) of the communications for local clients is handled by local file servers and never traverses other network segments. Most (if not all) local services would be lost in the event of a local file server failure. Twenty percent of the traffic would still be destined for other network segments. This traffic would most likely include e-mail or access to other shared resources or services. The main reason for this type of segregation was to minimize the impact of packet collisions on a segment due to a large number of host nodes.

Multiple subnets within a corporate LAN would be created in order to isolate one group of users from another. Servers most often used by a particular user group would be located on the same subnet as those users in order to minimize the traffic passing through the routers to other subnets.

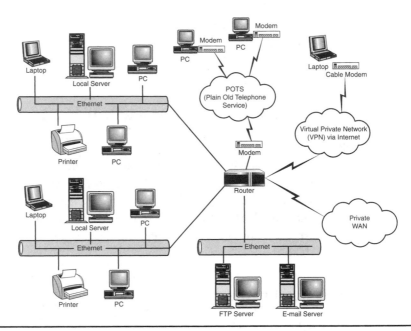

Figure 4.1 The 80/20 rule: 80 percent local traffic versus 20 percent remote traffic.

The increased complexity of today's applications and their demands on the network, along with changes in how corporations have traditionally worked, has made the 80/20 configuration unrealistic for most modern networks. This has necessitated the redesign of existing networks and development of new ones by network engineers that can satisfy these new requirements. Cross-functional teams not physically co-located, support issues, server clusters, application-specific file servers, and the introduction of new internetworking devices have all contributed to this need. Figure 4.2 shows the shift in design theory and the migration to flat networks, in which the main function of the router now becomes that of isolation rather than the interconnection of network segments.

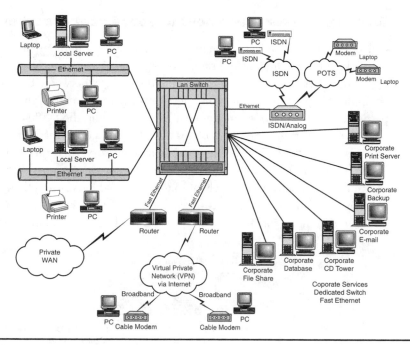

Figure 4.2 The changing demands of today's businesses have seen the migration to flat networks.

NOTE: As the number of nodes on a network increases, the logical layout of a flat network itself can become unusable, mainly because all these nodes are in the same broadcast domain. A significant amount of traffic can be generated because of this, ultimately impacting the network. Instead of segregating the network using routers, which themselves add latency, the use of switching implemented with VLANS (virtual LANs) allows for the separation of broadcast domains without the latency overhead created by the traditional router.

VLANs group together devices on different physical LAN segments, while allowing the different hosts on each network to communicate with each other as if they were all on the same physical (flat) LAN segment.

Terminal Server Placement in Your Local Area Network

One common mistake when planning a Terminal Server implementation is to assume that the network requirements are the same as for a traditional application deployment. Most network engineers won't intuitively know the differences between Terminal Server and a regular application deployment and may plan network infrastructure changes that aren't required, particularly if the existing environment is based around the 80/20 rule.

The way Terminal Server operates can allow for a continued return on investment (ROI) for existing networks. Unlike the traditional client/server relationships in which the desktop client communicates directly with the database server, Terminal Server creates an indirect communication path from the client to the Terminal Server and then from there to the destination database server. This is demonstrated in Figure 4.3, which depicts the data flow between the client, the Terminal Server, and the back-end database or file server.

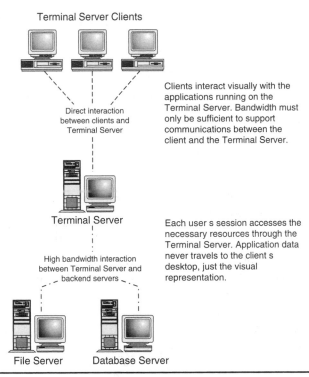

Figure 4.3   Data flow between Terminal Server clients and back-end servers.

As the figure shows, the database or file server is no longer in direct communication with the client. Instead, the communications occur between the client's Terminal Server session and the appropriate back-end server. This creates a situation where the high-bandwidth requirements exist only between the Terminal Server and the data or file server.

Understanding the data flow patterns and required resources for the applications that you'll be putting on Terminal Server will help determine the deployment strategies for your implementation. You need to ensure that bandwidth has been maximized between the Terminal Server(s) and the database/file server(s) that the applications will utilize. Very often this involves co-locating these servers onto a high-speed backbone to provide dedicated bandwidth, reduce latency, and improve scalability and fault tolerance.

NOTE: To sum up, good Terminal Server design dictates that Terminal Servers and back-end servers should occupy the same LAN segment whenever possible.

With the lower bandwidth requirements between the client and the Terminal Server (discussed further in the "Latency and Network Utilization on Client Performance" section of this chapter), local area networks (LANs) based on the 80/20 rule of the flat network model can often be used with a Terminal Server implementation without the costly requirements of an infrastructure change. Figure 4.4 illustrates how the network from Figure 4.1 might look after a Terminal Server implementation. The previously distributed servers have now been centralized on the same network as the Terminal Servers. This setup allows for fast local access to the required resource through Terminal Server. The existing client networks now have to support only the desired presentation protocol (ICA or RDP) traffic.

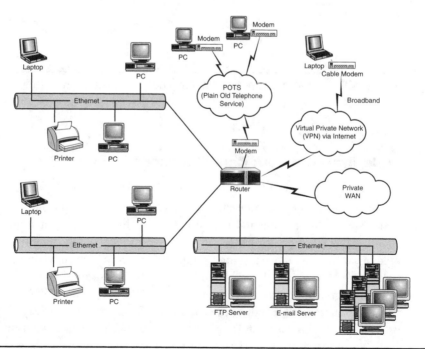

Figure 4.4   An 80/20 network after a Terminal Server implementation.

Figure 4.5 shows a similar configuration with a flat network implementation with Terminal Server. In most situations the centralized servers are connected via Fast Ethernet (100 Mbps) or Gigabit Ethernet (1000 Mbps), with shared client segments connected to a backbone router or switch.

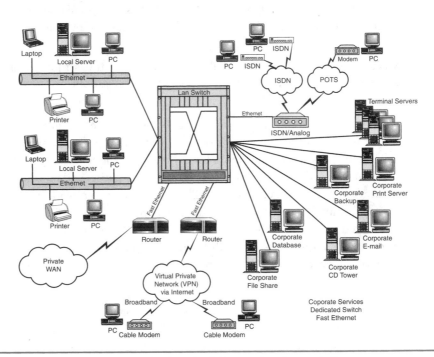

Figure 4.5   A flat network after a Terminal Server implementation.

Wide Area Network Considerations

The concepts discussed to this point with regard to Terminal Server and the LAN can be extended to include the wide area network (WAN). Today the more costly WAN lines are under siege from the amount of traffic that's being forced over them. Situations in which clients are accessing network resources located in a separate building—or sometimes even miles away in a separate city—are becoming more common. As a result, companies are forced to keep up by acquiring higher bandwidth connections through leases or other means.

Through the proper deployment of Terminal Server in a WAN configuration, RDP or ICA can help to greatly reduce the bandwidth requirements of the existing WAN and extend its ROI. To do this successfully, it's important to have a clear idea of the existing bandwidth available, possible latency issues, and the data flow requirements of the clients and their applications.

Figure 4.6 illustrates a not-so-uncommon mistake made when wide-area deployments of Terminal Server are being planned. The mistake is in co-locating the Terminal Servers with the clients instead of with the data servers. By placing the server local to the client, you're forcing the Terminal Server to cross a WAN connection in order to access the required resources, resulting in the same bandwidth requirements that existed prior to Terminal Server. On further inspection, it's clear that this isn't the optimal solution.

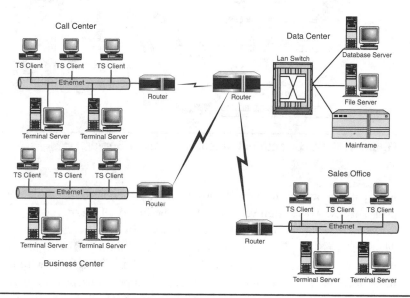

Figure 4.6   An incorrect deployment of Terminal Servers.

Figure 4.7 depicts resource allocation and deployment providing the best use of wide-area bandwidth. Using this deployment strategy, only the RDP and ICA traffic will traverse the wide-area connections. All the bandwidth-intensive processing requirements are at the same physical location as the high-speed switched backbone.

NOTE: In a scenario such as the one depicted in Figure 4.7, there may be an opportunity to reevaluate the current bandwidth requirements for the WAN links in light of the introduction of Terminal Server traffic and the removing of most other network traffic between sites. Of course most organizations are rarely interested in reducing their current bandwidth requirements but instead are more likely trying to find ways to avoid having to increase them.

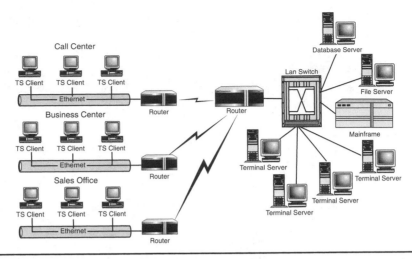

Figure 4.7   A correct deployment of Terminal Servers.

Figure 4.7 demonstrates what I consider an ideal scenario for implementing Terminal Server over a WAN. Most often you won't have the luxury of migrating all resources into one location, whether for resource or business reasons. In this situation you need to carefully review what resources can and can't be moved and position the Terminal Servers accordingly. You may also want to investigate dividing your Terminal Server environment between two or more locations. MetaFrame's server farm feature spans physical networks, allowing for a divided server environment with very little increase in administrative complexity. MetaFrame implementation planning is discussed in Chapter 8, "Server Installation and Management Planning."

Figure 4.8 shows an example of Terminal Servers divided between two locations. One set of Terminal Servers resides at the corporate head office, running a client/server application that accesses a database server, which is also at that location. These Terminal Servers are used solely by the sales office that's also on the same network (Sales Office #2). The data center contains the remainder of the Terminal Servers that make up the environment. This type of configuration lends itself well to MetaFrame's support for distributed server farms. You could also use RDP in this scenario, but the user would be required to maintain two separate desktops (one for each location) or would have to run the applications within RDP session windows.

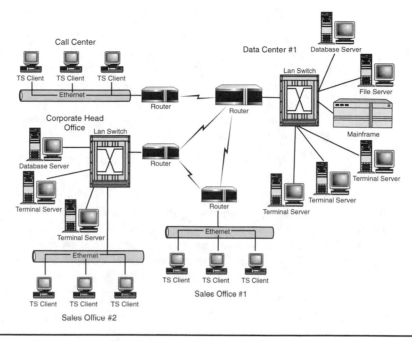

Figure 4.8   Multiple Terminal Server sites in a WAN configuration.

NOTE: Client configurations are discussed in Chapter 5, "Client Hardware and Software Planning."

Single Points of Failure

One issue that becomes immediately apparent with the centralization of the environment to support Terminal Server is the creation of single points of failure. Look again at Figure 4.8 in the preceding section. If the WAN link to the corporate office goes down, Sales Office #1 will not be able to access any published applications from that location. There are two ways that you can attempt to deal with this problem:

- Develop redundancy in the network to eliminate the single points of network failure. The addition of a WAN link directly from Sales Office #1 to the head office would provide a redundant link to protect against failure.
- Maintain a duplicate Terminal Server environment in a different location that's also accessible. If one site is lost, the other is still available to support user requests. By placing a set of Terminal Servers plus the database server at Sales Office #1, you would protect against all WAN failures.

In almost every situation, the first of these solutions is the preferred method, from both a cost and a logistics standpoint. Duplicating the Terminal Server environment would probably also require a means of replicating the information between the two database servers, which in turn would result in increased bandwidth requirements. The creation of a low-bandwidth redundant WAN link directly between the two sites would be much more cost effective and much easier to manage.

You should carefully evaluate the requirements for redundancy in your WAN and what risks are associated with each possible failure point. By highlighting the critical interconnections, you can then look to position the Terminal Servers so as to best minimize these redundancy requirements.

NOTE: In addition to single points of failure in your network infrastructure, you may have these vulnerabilities in your server layout itself. Dependencies on a single domain controller or file server can also be weaknesses in the planning and design of your environment. In Chapter 6, "Terminal Server Hardware Planning," I talk about identifying and accounting for those potential weaknesses in the environment.

Latency and Network Utilization on Client Performance

Although one of the highly touted features of Terminal Server is its ability to function well over low-bandwidth connections, it's still critical that reliable, sustained communication channels exist between the client and the Terminal Server. One of the most important network requirements for Terminal Server is minimizing the latency in the client connection to the server. Latency is critical because of the impact it can have on the user's perceived server or application performance. Latency manifests itself to the user as sluggish screen updates or unresponsive keyboard or mouse input.

NOTE: When latency is an issue in the environment, users encounter situations in which they can move the mouse pointer around the desktop but can't click anything or provide keyboard input to the Terminal Server session. This is because the local mouse tracking is handled by the client independently of data being sent to or received from the server.

High latency can also result in client disconnects from the Terminal Server. For optimal user interaction with the Terminal Server, latency should be kept under 100ms. At 150ms, users experience a decline in responsiveness, and anything over 300ms will usually result in severe client performance issues. If data packets are actually being lost between the client and the server, then it is likely that the user will experience a disconnection from the Terminal Server session. Keeping the average utilization in a network segment to less than 30 percent will help minimize latency on that segment.

TIP: A simple latency test is to use ping to gather average round-trip times between a computer on the client network and one on the server network. For example, on a Windows system the following command would ping the IP address 192.168.3.1 one hundred times with packets 1KB in size and pipe the output to a text file called out.txt:

ping –t –n 100 –l 1000 192.168.3.1 > out.txt

You can then average the round-trip times to get an idea as to the average latency in your network. While not exact, the results will certainly give you an idea as to whether potential latency problems may exist. The following example shows a sample output from a ping test that shows some high round-trip times and even a few time-outs, which would indicate that there could potentially be some speed and connectivity issues over this WAN link.

```
H:\>ping -t -n 100 -l 1000 192.168.3.1
Pinging 192.168.3.1 with 1000 bytes of data:
Request timed out.
Reply from 192.168.3.1: bytes=1000 time=109ms TTL=126
Reply from 192.168.3.1: bytes=1000 time=94ms TTL=126
Request timed out.
Reply from 192.168.3.1: bytes=1000 time=125ms TTL=126
Reply from 192.168.3.1: bytes=1000 time=93ms TTL=126
Reply from 192.168.3.1: bytes=1000 time=94ms TTL=126
Request timed out.
Reply from 192.168.3.1: bytes=1000 time=109ms TTL=126
Reply from 192.168.3.1: bytes=1000 time=94ms TTL=126
Request timed out.
Reply from 192.168.3.1: bytes=1000 time=109ms TTL=126
Reply from 192.168.3.1: bytes=1000 time=94ms TTL=126
Reply from 192.168.3.1: bytes=1000 time=94ms TTL=126
Request timed out.
Reply from 192.168.3.1: bytes=1000 time=109ms TTL=126
Reply from 192.168.3.1: bytes=1000 time=94ms TTL=126
Reply from 192.168.3.1: bytes=1000 time=94ms TTL=126
Reply from 192.168.3.1: bytes=1000 time=1188ms TTL=126
Reply from 192.168.3.1: bytes=1000 time=94ms TTL=126
Reply from 192.168.3.1: bytes=1000 time=110ms TTL=126
Reply from 192.168.3.1: bytes=1000 time=94ms TTL=126
Reply from 192.168.3.1: bytes=1000 time=1016ms TTL=126
Request timed out.
Reply from 192.168.3.1: bytes=1000 time=125ms TTL=126
Reply from 192.168.3.1: bytes=1000 time=78ms TTL=126
Reply from 192.168.3.1: bytes=1000 time=94ms TTL=126
Reply from 192.168.3.1: bytes=1000 time=188ms TTL=126
Reply from 192.168.3.1: bytes=1000 time=94ms TTL=126
```

```
Reply from 192.168.3.1: bytes=1000 time=78ms  TTL=126
Reply from 192.168.3.1: bytes=1000 time=94ms  TTL=126
Reply from 192.168.3.1: bytes=1000 time=94ms  TTL=126
Reply from 192.168.3.1: bytes=1000 time=94ms  TTL=126
Reply from 192.168.3.1: bytes=1000 time=94ms  TTL=126
Reply from 192.168.3.1: bytes=1000 time=109ms TTL=126
Reply from 192.168.3.1: bytes=1000 time=157ms TTL=126
Reply from 192.168.3.1: bytes=1000 time=110ms TTL=126
Reply from 192.168.3.1: bytes=1000 time=94ms  TTL=126
Request timed out.
Reply from 192.168.3.1: bytes=1000 time=109ms TTL=126
Reply from 192.168.3.1: bytes=1000 time=94ms  TTL=126
Reply from 192.168.3.1: bytes=1000 time=532ms TTL=126

Ping statistics for 192.168.3.1:
    Packets: Sent = 42, Received = 35, Lost = 7 (16% loss),
Approximate round trip times in milli-seconds:
    Minimum = 78ms, Maximum =  1188ms, Average =   144ms
```

Both RDP and ICA have similar utilization requirements, with an average of about 20Kbps per connected user session. The exact value depends on a number of factors, including compression, bitmap caching, client device-mapping features, and printing requirements. In many situations, 20Kbps is *above* the average requirement but can still serve as a marker for the upper threshold of concurrent user load—particularly over lower bandwidth connections such as 56K frame relay or ISDN.

A more accurate utilization assessment will require performing some analysis in a test environment running the applications that you intend to deploy. The applications that will be used have an impact on the overall utilization of the client. In general, highly graphical applications have higher requirements than simple word-processing applications, but in some cases this may not be true. For those users who are proficient typists, even text-based applications will appear to lag behind while they are typing.

TIP: Citrix has introduced features specifically designed to help mitigate the effects of latency on the user's computing experience. Collectively they are called SpeedScreen Latency Reduction features, and these will be discussed in Chapter 5.

Detailed data collection can provide some very realistic numbers on the expected bandwidth requirements, but the time required to prepare and implement such a test scenario is rarely a luxury that an administrator will have. Performing some initial estimates based on an average utilization between 12Kbps and 25Kbps will give an idea as to what load can be expected across a WAN link before latency will become a factor.

If, for example, you were trying to determine how much bandwidth would be required to support 45 users over a wide-area link, you would use the following calculation to evaluate this bandwidth requirement.

Let's assume that at the low end 12Kbps was the average utilization per client. In order to determine the necessary bandwidth you can't simply multiply 12Kbps by 45, which gives 540Kbps. Remember that keeping the average utilization under 30 percent will help minimize latency. So in order to take this into consideration we need to use the following formula to derive the proper bandwidth requirement.

$$B = (C \times A) / P$$

where

B = Total bandwidth required in Kbps

C = Number of client nodes

A = Average utilization per node in Kbps/client

P = Percentage utilization cap

So with an average utilization per node of 12Kbps, the desired number of client nodes at 45 and a utilization percentage cap of 30 percent (0.3), the necessary bandwidth is

$$B = (45 \times 12\text{Kbps}) / 0.3$$
$$= (540\text{Kbps}) / 0.3$$
$$= 1800\text{Kbps}$$

So in order to support 45 users with an average of 12Kbps and a percentage cap of 30 percent, you're looking at needing 1800Kbps (about 2 Mbps) of bandwidth—double that if you were to take the high estimate of 25Kbps per user.

The RDP and ICA Protocols

For the TCP/IP protocol, Table 4.1 lists the following well-known RDP and ICA ports:

Table 4.1 RDP and ICA Well-Known Installation Ports

Protocol	Function	Port Number
ICA	Listening port for client connections utilizing the session reliability feature.	TCP:2598
RDP	Listening port for client connections	TCP:3389
	Load balancing (using Microsoft Network Load Balancing)	UDP:2504
ICA	Listening port for client connections	TCP:1494
	Legacy ICA Browsing (TCP/IP)	UDP:1604
	HTTP server farm listening port	TCP:80
	HTTPS Citrix SSL Relay listening port	TCP:443

TIP: It is expected that Microsoft will introduce support for RDP via SSL with the release of SP1 for Windows Server 2003, in which case the RDP protocol would also support access via TCP port 443.

The various Citrix listening ports (except for the UDP port) can all be modified from their default by using the appropriate command. The client connection port is modified using the ICAPORT command (or the Management Console if using session reliability), the HTTP port is modified during the MetaFrame installation or using the CTXXMLSS command, while the HTTPS port is modified using the Citrix SSL Relay control application on the appropriate MetaFrame server. Whenever a port number is modified from the default, the ICA client must be updated to point to this alternate port. Port redirection settings are discussed in Chapters 5, "Client Hardware and Software Planning," and Chapter 20, "ICA Client Installation and Configuration." Please see Appendix B, "MetaFrame Presentation Server Command Reference," for more information on the ICAPORT and CTXXMLSS commands.

The RDP client connection listening port can also be modified, but this must be done by altering the registry on the Terminal Server and modifying the connection file on the client. There is no GUI tool available to manage this function.

Supported Network Protocols

As mentioned in Chapters 1 and 2, the following network protocols are supported by the RDP and ICA presentation protocols:

- ICA supports TCP/IP, IPX, SPX, and NetBEUI on Windows 2000 but only TCP/IP on Windows Server 2003.
- RDP supports only TCP/IP on both Windows 2000 and Windows Server 2003.

Regardless of which client or protocol is used to connect to a Terminal Server, once the user session has been established on the server, that user can access any available network resources using any of the network protocols installed on the Terminal Server.

For example, a user could use the RDP client to connect via TCP/IP to a Windows 2000 Terminal Server that's running both TCP/IP and the NWLink IPX/SPX protocol. Once connected, the user could use IPX to connect to any valid NetWare file server. The user session would communicate with the NetWare server using IPX, while Terminal Server and the client session communicate using TCP/IP.

Printing Considerations

An important requirement for almost any user is the ability to print. With Terminal Server, you need to pay particular attention to both the location of printers and how clients will access them. Figure 4.9 shows a typical WAN scenario with printers situated locally on each client network. When a user in this scenario wants to print to a local printer from the Terminal Server session, the print job has to traverse the WAN to reach the desired printer.

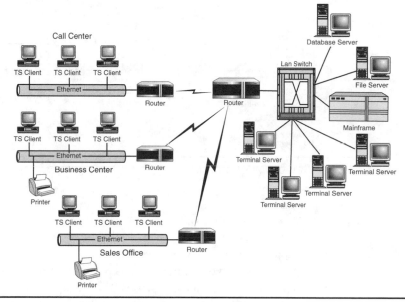

Figure 4.9   Typical WAN configuration with network printers.

All printing requires additional network bandwidth. The exact amount depends on how often users are printing and what they're printing. The larger or more complex the print job, the more bandwidth required. One thing you can do is distribute clients, Terminal Servers, print servers, and printers in such a way as to minimize the amount of network travel required to get the print job to the printer. There are three common scenarios for providing a client access to printers from within Terminal Server:

- Remote WAN print server
- Local (or remote) LAN print server
- Redirected client printing

The following sections look at each of these scenarios in more detail.

Remote WAN Print Server

In this configuration, a print server is located on the same network as the user. When the user prints from within Terminal Server, the server sends the print job directly to the print server. I usually refer to this configuration as "remote WAN print server" because the print server is located across a WAN link from the Terminal Server and the print job is destined for the remote network, as shown in Figure 4.10. This is a common configuration for an existing Windows implementation, since the print server is most often located on the same network as the printers it's supporting.

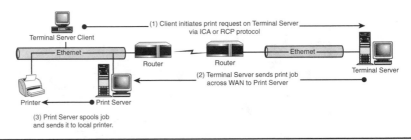

Figure 4.10   Remote WAN print server.

When a print job is initiated on the Terminal Server, the data normally is not spooled on the Terminal Server but instead passes immediately to the remote print server, where it's spooled for printing to the appropriate printing device.

The Remote WAN print server configuration is preferred if users on the remote network will need access to print from their local desktops. For example, if you're making Office XP available through Terminal Server, but users will continue to run AutoCAD locally, they still need to be able to print from AutoCAD to their printer. This configuration ensures that local printer traffic isn't unnecessarily crossing the WAN. Remember, print jobs that are initiated from within Terminal Server are crossing the WAN only once, on their way from the Terminal Server to the print server.

If users need to run completely from within Terminal Server with no local printing requirements, consider the next scenario, Local LAN print server.

Local LAN Print Server

In this configuration, the print server is located on the same network as the Terminal Server (see Figure 4.11). Print jobs are sent from the Terminal Server to the print server, where they're spooled and then sent to the physical printer located either on the LAN or across a WAN link. I refer to this as the "Local LAN print server configuration" because the print server is located on the same network as the Terminal Server. Jobs in this configuration are destined for either the local network or the remote network, depending on where the printer resides.

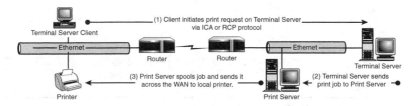

Figure 4.11 Local LAN print server.

Local LAN print server is the standard configuration when both clients and servers are situated within a single flat network, such as the one shown earlier in Figure 4.2, or possibly an 80/20 LAN configuration as shown in Figure 4.1, since no WAN links exist.

When clients are separated from the Terminal Servers by a WAN link, this scenario is valid only if all remote clients are performing all processing from within Terminal Server and don't require the ability to print directly from their local client device. If local printing was required, the user's print job would traverse the WAN twice to print: first from the client to the print server and then back again from the print server to the physical printer.

Redirected Client Printing

The third scenario involves users printing directly to a printer configured on the local client device. There are two ways that this can be done:

- Use regular Microsoft Networking to create a network printer share on the client device so that it can then be reached from within a Terminal Server session. Of course, this is only valid for Windows-based clients (excluding most non-Windows-based terminals).
- Use the automatic client printer-mapping feature available with both the RDP and ICA clients. Client printer mapping allows any printer that has been configured on the local client (either locally attached or through a network share) to automatically be configured and available from within the user's Terminal Server session.

Figure 4.12 demonstrates the print job flow in the redirected client printer scenario when the client is situated across a router. The exact same steps will occur if the client is located on the same physical network as the Terminal Server.

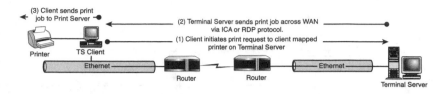

Figure 4.12 Redirected client printing.

While the specifics differ on how ICA and RDP handle client printer mappings, the general job flow is similar. The print job is processed on the Terminal Server and directed to the client, which then performs one of the following actions:

- If the printer is locally attached, the job is spooled on the client and sent to the printer.
- If the printer is a network printer, the job is redirected to the appropriate print server, where it's spooled and printed. When network printer redirection is occurring you need to be certain that the client is not redirecting the print job back to a network printer across a WAN link. If this is the case, you may need to look at using the local or remote LAN print server configuration. MetaFrame includes a customizable feature that will automatically route network redirected printers directly to the network-based print queue, bypassing the client completely.

Redirected client printing is most useful in two situations:

- **When clients have printers that are directly connected to their computers**—Client printer mappings provide a seamless way to access a locally attached printer without the user having to create a network share.
- **When used in conjunction with one or more published applications running in a seamless window**—When an application is in a seamless window, it appears to the user to be running locally. Client printer mapping enables the user to consistently access the same printer configuration regardless of whether the application is locally installed or accessed through a MetaFrame server. Seamless window functionality was discussed in Chapter 2, "Citrix MetaFrame Presentation Server."

Dial-Up Access

While high-speed Internet connectivity continues to become more readily available to the mobile and remote user (broadband access in hotels and mobile connectivity "hotspots" are just two examples), there is still a need in many organizations to either provide direct dial-up access or to at least attempt to accommodate those users who may be able to access the office remotely only by using a dial-up connection (landline or cellular-based).

The low-bandwidth requirements of Terminal Server make it well suited to providing remote users with access to applications and data within your environment. This can have great appeal to many organizations because the data itself never has to leave the internal network—only the visual representation is sent to the client.

Citrix's WinFrame product, the first multiuser-based version of Windows NT, was originally developed and marketed as a dial-up solution, allowing dial-up users to have LAN-like access to Windows applications such as Microsoft Mail. While the latest generation of this product contains many new features and enhancements, the basic advantages of accessing the product over a dial-up connection still exist. Referring once again to Figure 4.1 or Figure 4.2, notice the typical dial-up configuration in an environment with Terminal Server.

From a network-planning standpoint, very little needs to be done to provide dial-up access to a Terminal Server environment, and there are multiple configuration scenarios that can be implemented:

- Users dial up to their local ISP, establish an Internet connection, and then connect into the Terminal Server environment through the Internet. Internet-based connectivity is discussed in the next section.
- Users dial directly into a remote access solution, typically a bank of modems that then let the user establish a presence on the network, allowing the user's remote PC to become a host on the internal network. Once this connection has been established, the user can use either the RDP or ICA client to access the Terminal Server. Most of the remote access solutions will let the client use either the TCP/IP or NetBEUI protocols. If you intend to use the RDP client or are running Windows Server 2003, you must implement TCP/IP support for the dial-up connection. ICA running on Windows 2000 will support the NetBEUI protocol.
- A third dial-up option is to directly access the Terminal Server using either Microsoft's RAS solution installed on the Terminal Server or using the ICA client dial-in option available on a per-connection basis with MetaFrame. Figure 4.13 shows an asynchronous ICA connection entry that was created in the Terminal Services Configuration utility. Direct dial-up ICA connections can be created only on Windows 2000 MetaFrame servers. I recommend one of these strategies only for very small Terminal Server implementations, as they don't provide the same robust network support that dedicated dial-up products can provide and place extra resource requirements on the Terminal Server itself.

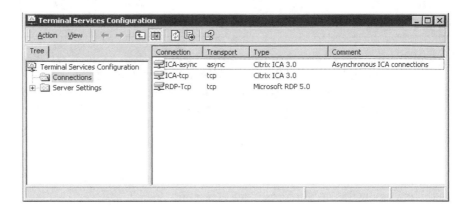

Figure 4.13 You can create direct ICA dial-up connections using Terminal Services Configuration on Windows 2000.

Internet Access

Today, many organizations are leveraging the availability of the Internet to provide connectivity between remote offices or mobile users and corporate data centers. This is particularly appealing for small- to medium-sized corporations that don't have the resources to acquire dedicated WAN links between remote offices. In Chapter 14, "MetaFrame Presentation Server Configuration," I talk in detail about configuring Web-based access to MetaFrame Presentation Server.

NOTE: Over the past few years a new service industry known as the application service provider (ASP) has emerged that leverages the Web-based technology available with Terminal Server, MetaFrame, and other products such as Tarantella. As the name suggests, an ASP provides its customers with access to a set of applications through a thin-client solution. Instead of the client purchasing the software and installing it on the local computer, the client leases or rents access to the applications and disk space to store data. This lets organizations such as law or accounting firms have access to the latest software without the requirements of an in-house information technology (IT) department. A low monthly fixed cost, usually bundled with support, is one of the key selling points of an ASP.

You can find out more about ASPs by visiting the Citrix Web site at http://www.citrix.com or other sources such as ASP News at http://www.aspnews.com.

Providing connectivity to Terminal Server via the Internet has its own set of challenges that must be considered carefully. The two areas of focus are security and connectivity.

Security

The number-one issue with providing access to your Terminal Server environment over the Internet is security. Simply stated, your goal is to let only authorized users access your environment. The type and extent of security you implement will depend on the size of your organization, what services you want to provide through Terminal Server, and the money you have available to spend. There are three main configurations you can implement to provide access to Terminal Server:

- Placing Terminal Server within a demilitarized zone (DMZ)
- Accessing Terminal Server over a virtual private network (VPN)
- Accessing Terminal Server directly and using high encryption with the presentation protocol to secure the session

Most other Internet configurations are simply a variation on one of these configurations. I suggest that if you're not familiar with firewalls or Internet security you enlist the assistance of someone who is. There's very little room for error when establishing a secure presence on the Internet.

The Demilitarized Zone

Figure 4.14 shows a typical topology for implementing Internet security. In addition to the obligatory firewall, there is what's called the *demilitarized zone* (DMZ). A DMZ is a network that's either sandwiched between two firewalls, as shown here, or in some situations sits out in the open directly off of the router. In either situation, the DMZ exists as a location where resources that need to be accessed by clients on the Internet can be placed. Access to an external resource doesn't automatically grant them access to the internal network. This way, if a malicious attack compromises the security of an external resource in the DMZ, it doesn't mean that your internal security has been compromised. Without a DMZ, your internal network would be at risk.

The DMZ shown in Figure 4.14 is commonly referred to as a *single-stage* or *one-hop DMZ*, because there is only one stage of restriction between the Internet and the internal network. There is also what is known as a *two-stage* or *double-hop DMZ*. Figure 4.15 provides an example of this, where less secure services such as FTP are placed in the outer stage, and more secure or restrictive services are placed in the inner stage.

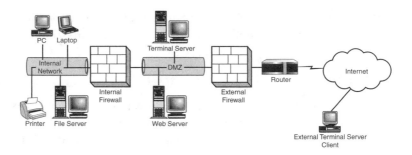

Figure 4.14   Terminal Server access through a DMZ.

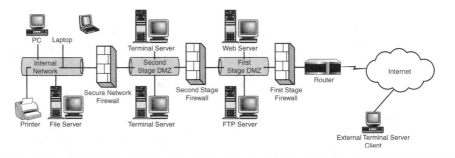

Figure 4.15   Terminal Server access through a two-stage DMZ.

One of the drawbacks to the DMZ configurations shown in Figures 4.14 and 4.15 is that there usually are many access points open from the DMZ into the internal network, particularly Windows network-related ports for file access, SQL Server access, and so on. The potential dangers of opening such ports will usually outweigh such a configuration, limiting its usefulness as an access method for remote user connectivity into the internal network. In the past this would usually mean that either a VPN-based solution or direct Terminal Server access, both described shortly, would be implemented instead.

Fortunately, alternatives exist that will allow the deployment of a proxy-based server into the DMZ that is responsible for connecting and rerouting incoming external clients through the firewall and into the appropriate server on the internal network. Figure 4.16 shows an updated, conceptual, single-stage DMZ diagram showing these servers in place. Citrix provides what is known as the Secure Gateway for MetaFrame Presentation Server, a security solution that allows for a secure method of access and authentication for users wanting to access the secured internal network from the Internet.

NOTE: A couple of issues can arise when relying on access to a Terminal Server/MetaFrame environment through a firewall:

- When firewalls are configured to perform some types of deep-packet inspection, they can introduce a small overhead in the communications pathway between the client and the server. This additional latency must be taken into consideration when evaluating the responsiveness of the Terminal Server environment in this scenario.

- The firewall can also introduce a single point of failure into your connectivity pathway if redundancy and fail-over provisioning has not been implemented. If you are going to rely on a firewall's availability in order to provide remote access to your production users, you will need to be certain that any load-balancing or failover support has also been implemented.

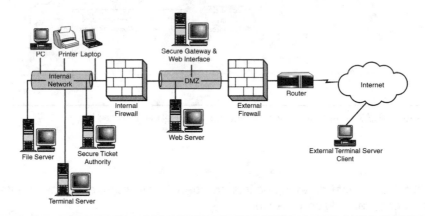

Figure 4.16 Secure Gateway for MPS provides secure access from the Internet to internal MetaFrame servers.

TIP: The configuration and use of Secure Gateway for MPS and Web-based access to your MetaFrame server farm are discussed in detail in Chapter 14.

Virtual Private Networks

One alternative to placing Terminal Servers into a DMZ is to implement a virtual private network (VPN) solution. VPNs have become increasingly popular as the technology has become more stable and secure on the Microsoft platform. A VPN can be thought of as a special case of dial-up access through the Internet. A client on the network establishes a connection to a corporate VPN server visible on the Internet. The VPN encapsulates all data sent between the two points within encrypted packets that hide the actual communications going on between the client and the server. Figure 4.17 shows a VPN between a client on the Internet and a Terminal Server located within the internal network.

VPNs are also used to create extranets. An *extranet* is two or more private networks connected through an unsecured (public) network such as the Internet. A VPN connection exists between the private networks, allowing them to talk securely with each other.

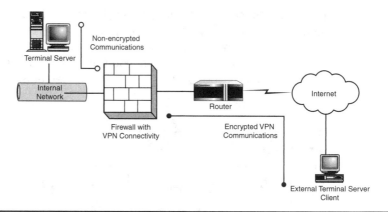

Figure 4.17 Terminal Server access through a VPN.

TIP: Today, most firewall products provide VPN services, either as an integrated feature or as an add-on package.

Direct Terminal Server Access

Although I use the term *direct,* in a direct Terminal Server access setup, the Terminal Servers themselves are not directly connected to the Internet but are accessed through a firewall that has the required ports open only to the specific Terminal Server IP addresses. Figure 4.18 shows this configuration, which is similar in appearance to the VPN example in the preceding section. The one difference is that the security is enforced through the high encryption (either RDP or ICA) of the Terminal Server connection and not through the VPN.

The biggest weakness in this configuration is the passwords used by the users. Unless strong passwords are enforced, a hacker with the necessary ICA or RDP client has only to guess an account and password to gain access to your environment. Additional policies and restrictions on the firewall can help reduce an unauthorized person's ability to reach the logon prompt and allow access only if the user is coming from a static location or using additional client-side firewall security settings.

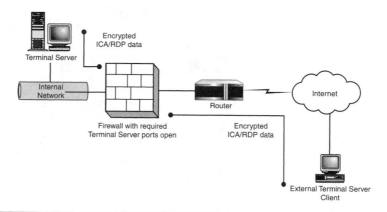

Figure 4.18 Terminal Server access through a high-encryption client.

Direct Terminal Server connectivity is best implemented as an alternative to the VPN solution when there are only a few remote users requiring access to your Terminal Server environment. For most other situations, I would look to using some form of Web interface that has been secured with SSL for the corresponding Terminal Server client deployment.

Connection Availability

The final point to touch on in this chapter is the importance of remembering that whenever you're utilizing a public network such as the Internet, you're not in control of latency, bandwidth, or overall stability. All these factors must be taken into consideration when you are trying to determine how your remote users will connect into the main Terminal Server environment. When you have mobile or roaming users, their options are fairly limited. The user can establish an Internet connection from their current location using high-speed (or dial-up) and then connect through via the Internet, or they can perform a direct dial into the environment where the Terminal Servers are located.

When connecting a remote office, if your users require a very high level of uptime due to the critical nature of the applications, you may need to forgo the use of an extranet client running over the Internet and instead look at the use of dedicated connectivity between the sites over leased lines in order to ensure a predefined quality of service (QOS) is being met.

In most cases, if your remote users will be establishing an Internet presence through the same ISP as the one your business is using, connectivity is more reliable than if the user were connecting through a different ISP. Terminal Server is much less forgiving about changes in bandwidth than other Internet applications such as FTP or a Web browser, so it is extremely important that a minimum acceptable baseline is developed.

CHAPTER 5

Client Hardware and Software Planning

Planning for the Proper Thin-Client Configuration

No matter how powerful and robust your server or how well you have architected your environment, in the end, success of the project is measured by usability of the client. Underestimating the importance of a proper client deployment to the success of your project greatly increases the odds of its ultimately being perceived as a failure. Management and senior executives will care very little about the great environment you created if users are not satisfied with the end result. Understanding what will be most important and noticeable to your users will take you a long way in helping your deployment succeed.

When first planning your client deployment, it is important to understand how to best integrate Terminal Server into this environment. A Terminal Server client deployment can be classified in one of three broad categories:

- Desktop replacement
- Desktop integration
- Application replacement

The exact features and functionality available within each category depend on the client that's implemented. Before discussing the pros and cons of specific clients in more detail, I look at the similarities and differences between these deployment categories.

Desktop Replacement

As the name suggests, desktop replacement involves moving all the applications that a user is running on his or her local desktop to run completely from within a Terminal Server session. No applications are running on the client's local device other than the Terminal Server client. When people talk about Terminal Server and thin clients in general, the desktop-replacement scenario is the configuration that usually springs to mind. Figure 5.1 shows a simple example of this with a Windows 2000 Terminal

Services desktop session running on a local Windows 2000 desktop. While Figure 5.1 shows the Terminal Server desktop as a window on the local desktop, normally you would run this as a full-screen session to hide the local desktop from view.

Figure 5.1   Desktop replacement has all the user's programs running from within their Terminal Server session.

Two main types of client devices are used to deliver desktop replacement to the end user:

- **Thin-client terminals**—This is the preferred device when a desktop-replacement project is being considered because of its total cost of ownership (TCO) advantages. A thin-client terminal, also known as a Windows-based terminal (WBT), is conceptually the same as an X Windows or 3270 terminal. Very little local processing or storage is normally provided. Most thin clients have a very small footprint, providing only a monitor, mouse, and keyboard for the user. Additional support features such as audio output, COM, LPT, or USB ports and centralized device-management tools are also available, depending on the terminal manufacturer. Thin clients are discussed in more detail in the later section "Thin-Client Terminals."

NOTE: All the main thin-client terminal manufacturers provide a full range of products designed to meet a customer's thin-client needs. The specific features available with each client vary from manufacturer to manufacturer, but typically there are three categories of thin clients:

- **Entry-level clients**—These provide support for connecting to a Terminal Server using the ICA and/or the RDP protocol. These solid-state devices should support flash upgrades of the embedded OS and the presentation protocols.

- **Mid-range clients**—A mid-range client has all the features of the entry-level units but usually includes support for multiple concurrent server connections and other terminal emulation protocols such as X Windows, 3270, and other mainframe and UNIX terminal emulations. Some mid-range units also include an embedded Web browser, normally based on Internet Explorer.

- **High-end clients**—These clients usually run an embedded operating system such as NT4 or Windows XP and may include storage devices such as CD-ROMs or even a hard drive. These units typically resemble more of a PC than a thin-client terminal but usually are much more task-focused than a standard PC.

Most thin-client devices are solid state and run an embedded operating system such as Windows CE, CE.NET, Linux, or Windows XPe. Some vendors such as Wyse also provide a proprietary embedded OS for certain entry-level products. When considering use of thin clients in your organization, it is always worthwhile to evaluate three to four models from different manufacturers in the price range you are interested in. Key factors are centralized manageability, flash-ROM upgrade support, presentation protocol support, and fast, crisp graphics reproduction. Graphics are vitally important to the end user. There can be no flicker or other visible anomalies, or users will not be satisfied with the product. User satisfaction should be the deciding factor, not simply cost, when comparing different thin-client devices.

- **Reduced-function personal computer**—In this scenario the PC is functioning as a terminal by providing access to the user's Terminal Server session only, without maintaining local storage or applications. The PC most often contains only the minimum required software and networking services, so it can establish the session connection, and usually has local security policies to prevent the end user from modifying the PC configuration. Many companies that use PCs to deliver desktop replacement do so in order to reduce their TCO by reusing existing hardware that otherwise would have to be replaced as part of the typical corporate hardware lifecycle.

PCs can have a higher TCO than thin clients, particularly if desktop restrictions have not been implemented to prevent users from manipulating the PC's configuration or maintaining local applications or data. Older desktop hardware such as Pentium II, Pentium Pro, and even Pentium-class machines make ideal PC terminals, as they typically have sufficient power to support a 32-bit operating system (Windows 98, Windows 2000, Linux, and so on) and the RDP or ICA client.

Desktop replacement is most often targeted at the type of user known as a *task-based worker*. The task-based worker is someone who performs a very specific job function with a common set of applications. A customer service or order desk call center is an excellent example of a group of task-based workers. The key to their productivity is access to the required applications. Desktop replacement allows a consistent environment to be available to users at any time and from any client device. Such configurations are well suited for call centers that may be distributed across multiple geographical locations or even within a large, centralized office that may want to group users differently based on operating hours and staff scheduling.

While desktop replacement is by no means restricted to only task-based workers, I've found that these users are much easier to migrate into a desktop-replacement scenario because of their common application usage and specific job roles. More diversified user groups such as technical support or application development staff typically use a much broader range of applications and, as a result, can be much more difficult to move completely to a desktop-replacement environment. For these types of users, an application-replacement scenario (discussed in the "Application Replacement" section of this chapter) usually works best.

Desktop Integration

Desktop integration is very similar to desktop replacement, except that instead of the client running completely within a remote desktop, the user is accessing a Windows-based desktop via Terminal Server while still accessing certain applications locally. In most situations, the local client operating system is non-Windows-based.

For example, a user with a Macintosh or UNIX workstation may use Terminal Server to gain access to a Windows desktop. This setup lets an organization standardize on Windows-based applications without requiring users to either switch to a Windows desktop or acquire an additional Windows computer to go with their non-Windows system.

This scenario is most common with users who require very specific client hardware to perform their main job function but also need to run one or more Windows applications. Examples might be engineers or architects who use UNIX-based graphical workstations or desktop publishers who use Macintosh computers. Figure 5.2 demonstrates a Windows 2000 desktop accessed from within a Linux desktop using the Citrix ICA client.

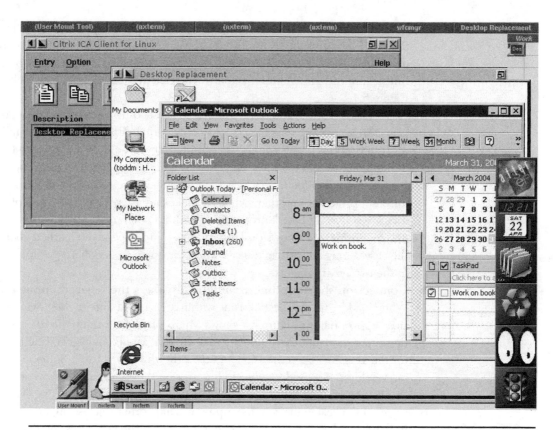

Figure 5.2 A desktop integration example showing a Windows 2000 desktop within a Linux desktop session.

Application Replacement

While desktop replacement is often the envisioned solution for a Terminal Server implementation, it's not always the most practical. Another common implementation scenario is application replacement. The idea behind application replacement is simply to remove the application from the user's local desktop and make it available from within Terminal Server, while leaving other applications in the user's local control. Application replacement allows for a much broader user base to be included in a Terminal Server implementation, since the only requirement is that users need to access the application that will be served by Terminal Server. The affected users are no longer restricted to a particular department or functional group. Application replacement is typically delivered in one of three ways:

- **Terminal Server desktop containing the common applications**—This configuration requires the user to work in two desktops simultaneously: the local desktop and the Terminal Server desktop. Instead of running a desktop session full screen, the configuration actually looks like the example shown back in Figure 5.1.

   I feel that this configuration should be avoided unless working with power users. Most regular users have a lot of conceptual difficulty working simultaneously in two desktops. While such a configuration is almost identical to the desktop integration example with Windows on Linux, there seems to be a difference in perception in that situation, likely because Windows and Linux are different products, and that somehow makes it easier for users to accept what they are seeing and work productively with it. When users work with a Windows desktop inside a Windows desktop, they seem to become concerned about what they are seeing and struggle more with being able to negotiate the applications in the two environments.

- **Connection shortcut that automatically loads the desired application**—When loaded, the application runs within a Terminal Server client window that's sized appropriately. Figure 5.3 shows Microsoft Word running in this configuration using the RDP client. Notice that the program contains two title bars: one for the Terminal Server session and the other for Word itself. Some user training would be required to educate the user on the differences between the two and how to properly close the session instead of simply disconnecting. Most users are used to clicking the X in the top right-hand corner to close an application, but in this case, doing so closes the client and leaves the active session disconnected on the server. I should mention that if the user clicks the Minimize button on the Word title bar in this example, Word minimizes within the session window boundary. Also, as soon as Word is exited, the Terminal Server session also ends.

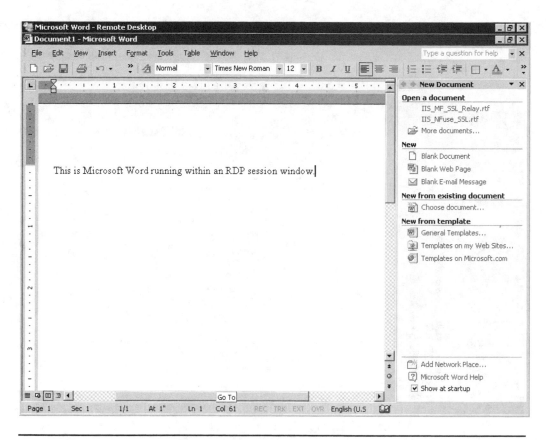

Figure 5.3   A single application can be launched within an RDP session window, but some users have difficulty working with the dual title bars that still appear.

■ **An ICA seamless window session**—Launched through a variety of ICA client options, a seamless window application appears to the user as if it's actually running locally. ICA seamless windows support is available using the Win32, Java, Linux, or UNIX clients. Figure 5.4 shows an example of Microsoft Word running in a seamless window on a Linux desktop. Notice that the application appears to be completely integrated into the Linux desktop and does not contain the dual set of title bars noticeable in Figure 5.3. A seamless windows application can be resized, maximized, minimized, and otherwise manipulated just as any other locally running application.

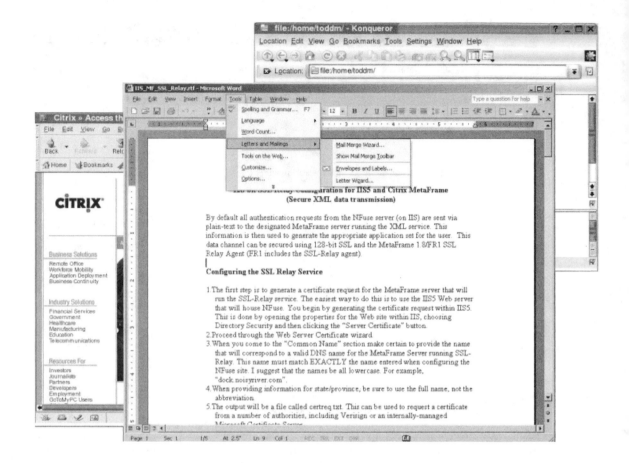

Figure 5.4 ICA seamless windows support lets a remote application appear as if it is running locally on the client's desktop.

Because application replacement involves a combination of programs running both locally and from a Terminal Server, a thin-client terminal is typically not a practical solution unless you're using a device containing an embedded operating system that supports locally installed applications. It's more likely that you'll want to let users continue to use their existing hardware and operating system, while providing support for these remote applications.

Client Operating System Selection

Often, one of the deciding factors in going with a server-based computing solution is the promise of an extension in the life of the antiquated hardware currently sitting on the user's physical desktop. The goal of reusing this hardware is to increase its return on investment (ROI) and reduce your total cost of ownership (TCO). Attempting to extend the life of the existing client hardware will ultimately influence your decision on what client operating system to use. The key is being able to find the right balance of hardware cost savings and client operating system support costs.

Unfortunately, it's not always as simple as picking the proper client to match the existing operating system and hardware. Other considerations need to be evaluated, including the following:

- What is the current support available for the existing operating system?
- What is the expected longevity of the existing hardware?

Existing Operating System Support

Microsoft maintains only a finite period of support for its operating system products before they are considered end-of-life. While this may not seem like much of a concern, the key part of this to note is that this also includes issuance of critical security patches for the product. In the last couple of years it has become clear to every Windows administrator that timely patching of known security vulnerabilities is a key requirement to ensuring a functional and stable environment. Turnkey tools and source code samples that exploit announced vulnerabilities appear very quickly on the Internet, making the window of time between the issue notification and proven exploit very small. Considering that numerous worms exploit these vulnerabilities, it is irresponsible for today's administrator to ignore these threats and maintain a desktop operating system that cannot be properly patched. While you may be able to continue to utilize your existing desktop hardware without the patches, to ensure a secure environment you may need to consider an upgrade to the client operating system.

TIP: While Microsoft has announced extended support for both Windows 98 and Windows Millennium Edition (ME) through June 30, 2006, this represents paid incident support only.

Microsoft no longer publicly releases security hotfixes for Windows 98 or Windows ME. Potential security issues are investigated and possibly patched, but a request must be made for such a fix through Microsoft's On-Demand Security Hotfix support.

In addition to available patch support from Microsoft, implementing Windows 2000 or XP Professional opens the possibility of implementing superior policy-based desktop security. If you have implemented or will implement an Active Directory domain, moving to one of these operating systems will let you use group policy objects to centrally manage the options and features locally available to your users. Use of group policy objects is discussed in Chapter 15, "Group Policy Configuration."

Hardware Longevity Expectations

When desktop hardware is on a three to four year lifecycle, most machines do not encounter hardware-related failures unless they happen almost immediately after implementation. Hardware longevity in a physical sense is rarely a concern. More often, the issue has to do with the capacity to support the new software being released. When the operational life of a desktop PC is extended to five or six years (or even more) as a result of a Terminal Server implementation, the probability of a hardware failure increases significantly. In order to minimize the impact of these types of failures on your users' productivity, you need to anticipate how you will deal with these issues and have mechanisms in place to respond quickly to resolve them.

Your recovery procedures will depend on the type of implementation (desktop or application replacement or desktop integration) you have deployed. The easiest situation to recover from is the desktop-replacement scenario. Because there are no other local applications or data, you can simply replace the damaged desktop computer with an alternate machine with the Terminal Server client properly configured and ready to go. Swap out the old machine with an alternate that has been preconfigured, and the user can be back up and working in a short period of time.

If the user has an application-replacement or desktop-integration scenario, a preconfigured PC with the Terminal Server client lets the user get back into their Terminal Server–based applications quickly, but recovery of local applications and data can take significantly longer. At the least, you should try to ensure that only the minimum amount of data, if any, is stored on the user's local desktop. Applications can be reinstalled, but local data may never be recovered if it is not backed up properly.

TIP: When looking to choose replacement hardware to have available, one consideration is the thin-client terminal hardware mentioned earlier.

Client Access Licensing

When planning your client hardware and software configuration, it is a good idea to carefully document and review expected licensing requirements for the environment. Ensuring that adequate licensing be available to support your production environment is critical to avoiding connectivity issues down the road. When sizing your client deployment, keep the following licensing points in mind:

- In addition to a server license and the standard Windows client access license (CAL), a Microsoft Terminal Services client access license (TSCAL) is required for each user or device that establishes a Terminal Server session.
- TSCALs are not concurrent licenses, so a unique license must be assigned to each user or device that will connect to the Terminal Server. For example, if you have 200 total users but only 125 on the system at any given time, you must still purchase 200 TSCALs.
- When deploying Windows 2003 Terminal Services, you need a license for all clients, even if they are running Windows XP Professional. This is a change from the Terminal Services licensing support in Windows 2000, which allowed Windows 2000/XP Professional desktops to connect to the Terminal Server without requiring an additional TSCAL. Transition TSCALs are available for those companies that owned licensed copies of Windows XP Professional prior to April 24, 2003. More details on this transitional information can be found at the following Web site: http://www.microsoft.com/windowsserver2003/howtobuy/licensing/overview.mspx#transition
- If you are also deploying Citrix MetaFrame Presentation Server (MPS), you need to take licensing for the ICA clients into consideration as well. Unlike Terminal Server, which is licensed based on total devices or users, Citrix MetaFrame is licensed based on concurrent users. For example, if you have 200 total users but only 125 on the system at any given time, you are required to purchase only 125 licenses. By the same token no additional server-based license is required for MPS, only the individual client licenses.

Having a clear idea as to the number of required licenses will also help you in planning your licensing server requirements. Both Microsoft Terminal Server and Citrix MetaFrame Presentation Server require existence of a licensing server responsible for managing distribution of CALs to users accessing the system. Even though the two licensing components are completely independent of each other, they can be combined to run off the same server. Knowing your total user load and the distribution of users will help to ensure that the licensing server is properly sized and located in the area where it will be able to service the majority of client requests. Licensing server hardware requirements are discussed in Chapter 6,

"Terminal Server Hardware Planning," while the appropriate license server location is covered in Chapter 8, "Server Installation and Management Planning."

NOTE: A mistake I have witnessed a Terminal Server administrator make on more than one occasion is deferring planning and purchasing of adequate Terminal Services CALs until *after* the implementation is complete. The administrator leverages the grace periods that exist with Windows Terminal Services licensing to operate the environment with insufficient CALs for all clients.

Ignore for a moment the fact that such actions violate the end-user license agreement and note that what often happens is the administrator completely forgets about the need to install and activate the permanent CALs until the expiry notices begin to appear on users' desktops. At this point, mad panic ensues as the administrator tries to acquire the necessary CALs before temporary licenses expire and users are unable to log on.

As an administrator, always ensure that you have the necessary Terminal Services licensing available *before* you go live.

RDP Client Support

If you have decided to implement a Windows Terminal Server–only solution (no Citrix MetaFrame), then even though to some extent your choice of which RDP client to use depends on the version of Terminal Server you will be deploying, realistically you will likely implement the latest RDP client version available. Newer RDP versions are fully backwards compatible with previous versions, although certain functionality may not be available based on your Terminal Server version and the client operating system being used. For example, some features supported in the RDP 5.2 client are available only when deployed on a PC running Windows NT, 2000, or XP (not on a PC running Windows 98) and accessing a Windows 2003 Terminal Server. In this section, we take a detailed look at the RDP client and the features it supports.

Windows-Based RDP Client Types

As mentioned in Chapter 1, "Microsoft Windows Terminal Services," the three main Windows-based RDP clients currently existing are:

- **Terminal Services client and Client Connection Manager**—These two combine to form the RDP 5.0 client. A 16-bit and a 32-bit version of the RDP 5.0 client first shipped with Windows 2000 Terminal Services.

■ **Remote Desktop Connection**—The RDP 5.1 and later client is now known as the Remote Desktop Connection client and first shipped with Windows XP. The RDC is available only as a 32-bit Windows client.

Terminal Services Client (RDP 5.0)

The Terminal Services client (TSC) really serves two functions. Primarily, it can be used as a simple tool for establishing a connection to a Terminal Server. When TSC is launched, a dialog box appears, similar to the one shown in Figure 5.5. The lower half of the dialog box lists all the Terminal Servers found in the current domain. To establish a connection, select one of the servers, choose the resolution size, and click the Connect button. The Server drop-down list shows a history of the servers you've previously connected to. If the server you want isn't in the list, you can type the name in the text box.

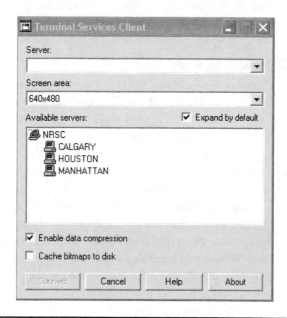

Figure 5.5   The Terminal Services client application.

Having the appropriate name service (DNS or WINS) configured in your environment ensures that all the valid Terminal Servers are displayed. Little configuration is involved in the TSC, and on its own it's not a very useful application to deploy to end users. Requiring the user to select a server (and desired resolution) every time he or she connects is not only unnecessary but also may cause problems if users shouldn't be connecting to some servers in the environment, such as test or development servers. A better solution is to provide users with shortcuts that they simply double-click to establish Terminal Server connections. These shortcuts are created using the Client Connection Manager (CCM), discussed next.

In addition to allowing a quick method of accessing a Terminal Server, the TSC works in combination with the CCM application to allow creation of shortcuts to sessions configured in CCM. The following command line would launch TSC and automatically have it run the client connection labeled ORCA in the CCM. MSTSC.EXE is the executable that launches the Terminal Services client.

```
"C:\Program Files\Terminal Server Client\MSTSC.EXE"  "ORCA"
```

Client Connection Manager (RDP 5.0)

Figure 5.6 shows an example of what the main Client Connection Manager (CCM) application window looks like. The CCM provides the following RDP client capabilities:

- Create and save connection configurations for specific Terminal Servers.
- Create shortcuts to these connections on the desktop.
- Specify connection properties such as window size, whether to open in a window or full screen, and connection speed.
- Configure a connection to launch a specific program automatically. When connecting in this way, the user is immediately presented with the application after he or she logs on and doesn't have direct access to a Windows desktop. This isn't the same as accessing a published application with the ICA protocol. With the RDP client, you must hard-code the path and application name on the client. With ICA published applications, this information is managed within the server farm, not on the client.
- Store user ID, password, and domain information that is automatically provided when the user connects. This allows the session to be logged on to a Terminal Server automatically.

NOTE: Allowing users to automatically log on to a server with cached ID and password information is a definite security concern and something I do not recommend. A Terminal Server can easily be configured to require that users always provide a password, regardless of the information they have stored on the clients. I describe how this is done in Chapter 16, "Terminal Server Security."

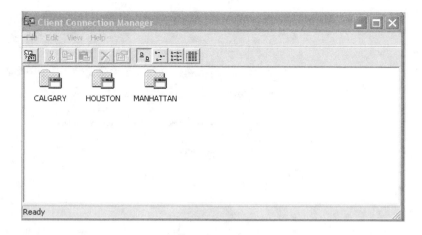

Figure 5.6 The RDP Client Connection Manager (CCM).

Both the Terminal Services client and the Client Connection Manager support only a limited set of client configuration options. They provide support for the following:

- Defining the screen resolution (640x480, 800x600, 1024x768, 1280x1024, full screen)
- Enabling data compression
- Enabling caching of bitmap information
- Providing a logon credential that can be saved for any given application; and
- Defining a program located on the Terminal Server that will launch automatically

Remote Desktop Connection (RDP 5.1 and Higher)

With release of RDP 5.1, Microsoft changed the name of its RDP client to Remote Desktop Connection (RDC) and introduced a new interface, as shown in Figure 5.7.

In addition to supporting all the features available with the Client Connection Manager, the latest Remote Desktop Connection application supports additional features that I discuss in the "Windows RDP Client Feature Support" section of this chapter. The Remote Desktop Connection application is fully backwards compatible with all versions of Windows Terminal Server. Any client options selected in the RDC that are not supported by the host Terminal Server are simply ignored.

Figure 5.7 The RDP Remote Desktop Connection (RDC) client.

Supported Windows Operating Systems

Table 5.1 summarizes the Microsoft RDP client versions and the Windows-based operating systems they support.

Table 5.1 RDP Client Versions and Supported Windows Operating Systems

Operating System	RDP Client Version Supported	Notes
Windows 2003, XP, 2000, ME, 98, and NT 4.0	RDP 5.0 and higher	All versions of the RDP client are supported on all 32-bit versions of Windows, NT 4.0 or higher.
Windows 95	RDP 5.0 or 5.1 only	Microsoft does not officially support the RDP 5.2 (or newer) client on Windows 95.

Table 5.1   RDP Client Versions and Supported Windows Operating Systems (continued)

Operating System	RDP Client Version Supported	Notes
Windows for Workgroups 3.11	RDP 5.0 only	Microsoft no longer supports this version of Windows with the new RDP client. Only the client that originally ships with Windows 2000 is available for the 16-bit version of Windows.
Pocket PC 2002	PPC 2002 client	This special RDP client is designed specifically to run on Pocket PC 2002. It will not run on older versions of Pocket PC.
Windows CE	Handheld and CE-based terminals running CE 3.0 and CE.NET	Special versions of the RDP client can either be installed on a Windows CE client or come embedded with the CE operating system.

The features supported by the Pocket PC and Windows CE client running on a handheld device are limited in comparison to the Windows desktop and Windows CE thin-client terminals. Handheld devices also have the obvious limitation of available screen real estate to deal with. Custom Terminal Server–based applications have been developed specifically for viewing and operating through RDP-based handheld devices, and unless you are looking to employ such an application, I would not recommend providing Terminal Server access via a handheld device to anyone other than an experienced administrator-level user. The typical end user will undoubtedly struggle with the complexity of trying to operate a Windows desktop within the confined space of the handheld's display.

NOTE: The 16-bit RDP client is available in version 5.0 only and ships with Windows 2000 Terminal Services. It is not available as a download. This version provides the exact same client options as the 32-bit 5.0 client, having both a Terminal Services client and a Client Connection Manager. The 16-bit version is single-threaded, which means that it must handle processing of user interface information as well as sending and receiving of data. This can result in reduced responsiveness in comparison to the 32-bit client.

I do not recommend use of the 16-bit client as a solution for a new Terminal Services implementation. If the only hardware available cannot run a Windows 32-bit operating system, I would consider looking at alternatives such as thin-client or PC upgrades to hardware that will support a 32-bit Windows operating system, or even a Linux-based system. While native Microsoft support does not exist for a Linux RDP client, third-party offerings are available and are discussed in the next section.

Windows RDP Client Feature Support

Table 5.2 summarizes the supported features by RDP version (5.0, 5.1, or 5.2) and the version of Terminal Server required (Windows 2000 or Windows 2003) in order for a user to utilize these features. More detailed information on each of the features is discussed immediately following the table.

Table 5.2 RDP Client Features and Required Server Version

	RDP Version				
Feature	5.0	5.1	5.2	Terminal Server Version	Description
Local/remote clipboard integration	X	X	X	Both	Allows clipboard contents to be cut and pasted seamlessly back and forth between the active Terminal Server session and the user's local desktop.
Local/remote file copy and paste integration		X	X	Windows 2003 only	Allows cut and pasting of entire file objects back and forth between the active session and the local desktop.
Local client printer redirection	X	X	X	Both	Printers that are configured on a local client can be made available automatically from within the user's Terminal Server session.
Network client printer redirection			X	Both	Allows for access to locally mapped network printers on the client desktop.
Session remote control	X	X	X	Both	Session remote control is the capacity for one person to remotely view and even control another user's active session.

Table 5.2 RDP Client Features and Required Server Version (continued)

Feature	RDP Version			Terminal Server Version	Description
	5.0	5.1	5.2		
Persistent bitmap cache	X	X	X	Both	The persistent bitmap cache is stored on disk so it can be reused the next time a session is started. Version 4.0 supports only memory-based caching.
Connection bar		X	X	Both	Allows you to easily minimize a full-screen session without having to toggle the session between full screen and windowed using the Ctrl+Alt+Break key combination.
Automatic session reconnect			X	Both	If a network disruption causes your connection to a Terminal Server to be lost, the Remote Desktop Connection client automatically attempts to reestablish that connection. If the connection cannot be reestablished, after about one minute the client gives up and an error message appears saying the connection was lost.
Client drive redirection			X	Windows 2003 only	Automatic redirection of a client's local and network drives so they are accessible from within the Terminal Server session.
Client serial port redirection			X	Windows 2003 only	Redirection of the local serial ports.
Client audio redirection			X	Windows 2003 only	Audio is redirected from the Terminal Server session to the local client for output.
Smart card sign-on			X	Windows 2003 only	The user can provide their smart card to a local reader attached to their PC and have those credentials transmitted and authenticated on the Terminal Server.

Table 5.2   RDP Client Features and Required Server Version (continued)

Feature	RDP Version			Terminal Server Version	Description
	5.0	5.1	5.2		
Windows shortcut key support			X	Both	Client must be running WinNT, 2000, XP, or 2003. Windows 9x operating systems don't support this feature.
					Introduces support for the Alt+Tab and other Windows key combinations within the Terminal Server session.
Client time zone support			X	Windows 2003 only	Client time zone support allows the RDP client to provide its own local time zone information to a Windows 2003 Terminal Server so the server can automatically configure the user's session to reflect the same time zone information. A Terminal Server can support any number of users located in different time zones, and this feature lets the user maintain proper time and date information within his or her own session.
Direct Terminal Server console access			X	Windows 2003 only	Allows for creation of a direct connection to the console and not a Terminal Server session. Applications that require direct console access function within this special remote session. This feature is dependent on having a Windows 2003 Terminal Server.

Local/Remote Clipboard Integration

This feature allows clipboard contents to be cut and pasted seamlessly back and forth between the active Terminal Server session and the user's local desktop. For example, text copied to the clipboard from Notepad running on the local desktop could immediately be pasted into Microsoft Word running on the user's Terminal Server session. Only graphics and text can be transferred back and forth between the client and the server. Files and other objects cannot be cut and pasted between the two environments. The integrated Clipboard feature is optional and can be enabled or disabled at the connection level using the Terminal Services Configuration tool.

Local/Remote File Copy and Paste Integration

This feature extends support of the local/remote clipboard integration available in all RDP clients to include support for copying and pasting files between the local desktop and the RDP session. This feature requires the Remote Desktop Connection client and Windows Server 2003.

Client Printer Redirection

Client printer redirection allows printers configured on a local client to be available automatically from within the user's Terminal Server session. The default printer on the local desktop can also be set automatically as the default printer from within Terminal Server. This feature allows a more seamless integration of the Terminal Server client with the local desktop. It also means that, in most circumstances, a user has access to a consistent set of printers, including those otherwise inaccessible directly from the Terminal Server. One such example might be a user at a remote office connecting over the Internet to a Terminal Server at the head office. The Terminal Server would have no way of allowing a direct connection back to the remote office printer, but through client printer redirection, the user could access it. There are some restrictions on behavior of the client printer mappings, however:

- Client printers are automatically mapped only when using the 32-bit RDP client. The 16-bit RDP clients must have their local printers configured manually.
- The corresponding printer driver must already exist on the Terminal Server for the automatic mapping to take place. If the driver doesn't exist, the printer won't be mapped. A message will be generated in the server's event log.
- Bidirectional printing is not supported.
- Network-based client printers will be mapped only when using the RDP 5.2 client on either a Windows 2000 or 2003 Terminal Server. If the RDP 5.0 client is being used, only printers directly connected to the local PC will be available.

Any printers automatically mapped for a client are visible to only that client. No other user on that server can use those printer connections. Figure 5.8 shows the Printers folder for a user with client-mapped printers. Automatic client printer mapping is also optional and can be managed at both the connection level and the user level. At the connection level, you can either allow individual user account settings to take effect or override these and enable or disable printer mappings for all users.

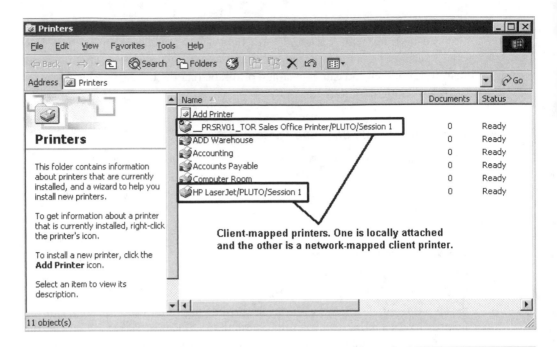

Figure 5.8 Redirected client printer example on a Windows 2000 server from an RDP 5.2 client.

TIP: Terminal Server and MetaFrame printing are both discussed in detail in Chapter 17, "Terminal Server and MetaFrame Printer Management."

Session Remote Control

Session remote control, first introduced with RDP 5.0, is the capacity for one person to remotely control another user's active session. With remote control, a user with sufficient security privileges can either passively view another person's session or interact with the session using the mouse and keyboard. This feature provides a tremendous benefit to both administrators and the support staff who may need to interact with another user's session in either a support or training capacity.

Remote control has the following characteristics:

■ A remote control session cannot be initiated directly from the console. The console also cannot be remotely controlled, although it can be accessed remotely on a Windows 2003 Terminal Server.

- To remotely control another user's session, your session must be operating in the same or higher video mode (resolution and color depth) as the desired target session.
- You must have the Remote Control privilege in order to remotely control another user's session. This privilege is managed at the connection level through the Terminal Services Configuration utility.
- The Terminal Server can be configured so a user receives a confirmation prompt prior to the remote control initiating (this is the default), or the remote control can start without any user notification. This is manageable at both the connection and the individual user level.
- Only one-to-one remote control is currently supported. You cannot have multiple people all controlling the same user (many-to-one). You also cannot have one person remotely controlling multiple people simultaneously (one-to-many).
- You are not required to be logged on to the same Terminal Server as the user whose system you want to control. You can remotely control a user located on a different Terminal Server than yourself. Figure 5.9 shows an example of how a remote control session can be initiated using the Terminal Services Administration tool on a Windows 2003 Terminal Server. In this example, the controller is requesting to remotely control a user located on a different server.

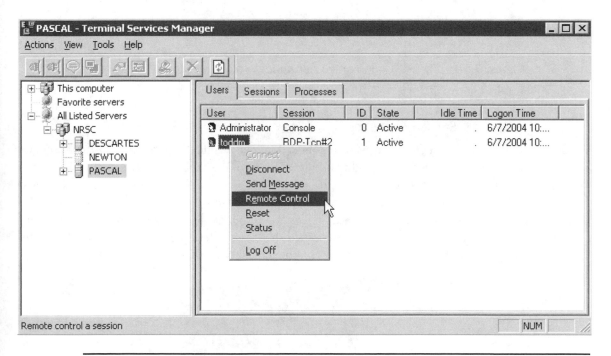

Figure 5.9   Remote control is most often initiated through the Terminal Services Administration tool.

Persistent Bitmap Caching

RDP 5.0 first introduced the persistent bitmap cache. Prior to this, RDP 4.0 provided only a RAM-based bitmap cache that was lost when the client connection to the server was terminated. The persistent bitmap cache is stored on disk so it can be reused the next time a session is started. This helps prevent retransmission of bitmap data sent in a prior session or earlier in the current session.

When a connection is made to the Terminal Server, the client transmits to the server a list of bitmap keys corresponding to its current cache contents. The server then knows that it's not required to transmit the bitmap contents the first time it wants the client to display those graphics. It can immediately start sending the bitmap key. The persistent cache uses 10MB of disk space; this size cannot be modified. Checking the Bitmap Caching option enables caching.

Connection Bar

RDP 5.2 now provides a connection bar made available when running an RDP session in full-screen mode (see Figure 5.10) on any version of Windows Terminal Server. It lets you still easily minimize a full-screen session without having to toggle the session between full screen and windowed using the Ctrl+Alt+Break key combination.

Figure 5.10   The RDP connection bar appears along the top of a full-screen RDP session.

Automatic Session Reconnect

If a network disruption causes your connection to a Terminal Server to be lost, the Remote Desktop Connection client automatically attempts to reestablish that connection. While the client is attempting to reconnect to the Terminal Server, the desktop becomes grayed out and a flashing disconnect symbol appears in the upper right-hand corner, as shown in Figure 5.11. If the connection is reestablished, the session automatically reappears and the icon disappears. If the connection cannot be reestablished, after about one minute the client gives up and an error message appears saying the connection was lost.

Figure 5.11   A flashing network disconnect icon appears while the RDP client attempts to reestablish the connection with the Terminal Server.

Client Drive Redirection

The RDC client and Windows 2003 Terminal Server allow automatic redirection of a client's local and network drives so they are accessible from within the Terminal Server session. Mapping is controlled globally through the RDP connection configuration or on a user-by-user basis through the user's domain or local account. Local drives are visible through My Computer as special drive mappings, as shown in Figure 5.12. These drives are not assigned standard drive letters, and if you wish to access them from a command prompt on the Terminal Server, they must be mapped to an actual drive letter using either the Map Network Drive GUI or the command prompt to map to the desired drive under the \\TSCLIENT UNC path. For example, mapping G: on the server to the local C: drive on the client could be done from a command prompt by issuing this command:net use G: \\TSCLIENT\C.

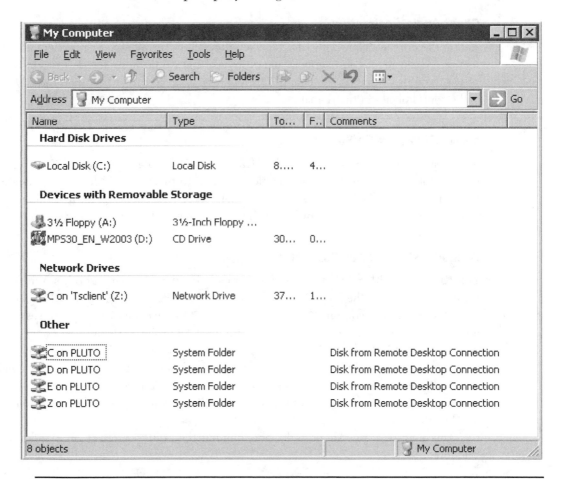

Figure 5.12   Local drives are now directly accessible from within a Windows 2003 Terminal Server session when using the RDP 5.1 or later client.

Client Port Redirection

In addition to supporting LPT port redirection, the Remote Desktop Connection client and Windows 2003 Terminal Server support redirection of the USB and COM ports on the local client by default. Port redirection can be managed through the RDP client or using Group Policy in the Active Directory. In addition to managing client port redirection, Group Policy in a Windows 2003 domain lets you control all aspects of data redirection. The data redirection features specifically for Terminal Services can be found under Computer Configuration in the following policy folder:

Administrative Templates\Windows Components\Terminal Services\Client/Server data redirection

Client Audio Redirection

Another feature available with RDC and Windows 2003 Terminal Server is client audio redirection. Audio redirection support allows sounds that would normally be processed on the server to be processed on the client. This feature can be controlled through the RDP client and Group Policies in the domain.

Smart Card Sign-On Support

Smart card sign-on support is available with Windows 2003 Terminal Server, letting a user provide their smart card to a local reader attached to their PC and have those credentials transmitted and authenticated on the Terminal Server. The client operating system must be able to read the smart card in order for this authentication to work properly.

Windows Shortcut Key Support

The RDP 5.1 and later clients introduce support for the Alt+Tab and other Windows key combinations within the Terminal Server session. Previous versions of the RDP client supported alternate key combinations that would have to be used within an RDP session so as not to conflict with the client keys. For example, Alt+Page Up would work the same as Alt+Tab in an RDP session. Now the user can simply use the familiar Alt+Tab combination to perform the desired task. By default, these shortcut keys override the local key combinations only when running a full-screen session. The RDC client can be configured to provide this key support within a windowed session if explicitly configured in the client to override the default.

This feature is not supported when running the RDP 5.x client on Windows 95 or Windows 98.

Client Time Zone Support

Client time zone support lets the RDP client provide its own local time zone information to a Windows 2003 Terminal Server so the server can automatically configure the user's session to reflect the same time zone information. A Terminal Server can support any number of users located in different time zones, and this feature lets the user maintain proper time and date information within his or her own session. Without this feature, all Terminal Server users would be forced to work within the time zone of the server, possibly creating a situation where a user in one time zone was forced to send and receive information based on time in a different time zone.

Client time zone support is not enabled by default and must be configured using a group policy. Figure 5.13 shows the policy Allow Time Zone Redirection, listed under the Client/Server Data Redirection folder.

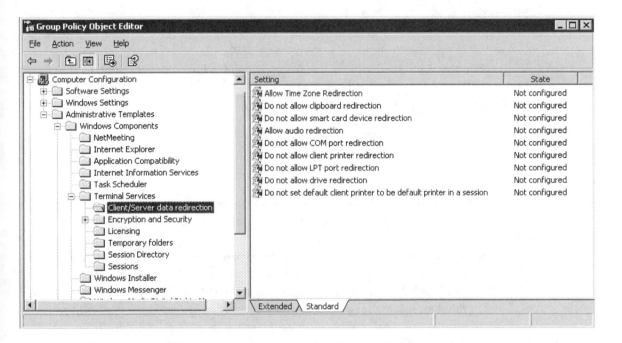

Figure 5.13 Client time zone support can be enabled only by configuring a group policy object.

Direct Terminal Server Console Access

Using the latest RDP client (5.2), you can connect directly to the console session (session 0) on a Windows 2003 server, running either in Terminal Server mode or Remote Desktop for Administration mode. To connect to the console session you must launch the Remote

Desktop Connection client with the /console parameter appended to the end of the executable used to launch the program. For example, the following will load the RDC and let you establish console sessions on Windows 2003 servers:

```
%windir%\System32\mstsc.exe /console
```

Unfortunately this feature is not supported with Windows 2000 Server.

Non-Windows RDP Clients

In addition to Microsoft's own Windows-based RDP clients, there exist non-Windows clients created by both Microsoft and other vendors to run on client operating systems not natively supported by Microsoft. Many of these clients support most, if not all, features supported in the Win32 RDP 5.2 client. Currently the only non-Windows operating system supported by Microsoft is Apple's Mac OS X. The Mac OS X client can be downloaded from http://www.microsoft.com/mac/Download/Misc/RDC.asp. Table 5.3 lists some non-Windows RDP clients that are available, along with the features they support.

While these RDP clients make it possible for users implementing non-Windows desktops to successfully connect to a Terminal Server using the RDP protocol, there are still some things that must be taken into consideration:

- **Terminal Services client access licensing**—Regardless of the RDP client used (Windows or not), you're still required to have the proper Terminal Services client access licenses purchased, installed, and activated on the Terminal Services Licensing Server.
- **Client software licensing**—Most third-party clients require an additional per-user cost specifically for the client software, which is above the cost for licensing Windows and Terminal Server.
- **Limited support**—Introducing a third-party client also means you will need to look to a non-Microsoft vendor that may provide only limited support for its product. While Microsoft now licenses the RDP protocol so other vendors can develop and expand on the existing client, Microsoft will not support third-party clients connecting to the Terminal Server. If issues arise with the Terminal Server when you are implementing a third-party client, you must be certain that the issue can be reproduced with a Microsoft client before Microsoft will provide any kind of support assistance.
- **Possible client stability issues**—Depending on how well the client was written and how thorough the RDP implementation, a third-party client may suffer from client-side or server-side issues resulting in unexpected downtime.

Table 5.3 Examples of Non-Windows-based RDP Clients Available

Host Operating System Supported	Description
Macintosh OS X	Microsoft's Mac OS X RDP Client 1.0.2.
	This is currently the only RDP client that Microsoft produces for a non-Windows operating system. It supports most features available in the Windows RDP 5.2 client, with one noticeable limitation in that it supports running only a single instance at a time. You cannot connect simultaneously to multiple (or even the same) Terminal Servers.
Platform-independent Java-based client	HOBLink JWT, version 3.1, is a pure Java-based RDP client that supports Windows 2003 Terminal Server features such as the following:
	■ Color depth up to 24-bit
	■ Local client drive redirection
	■ Local COM and LPT port redirection
	■ Client audio redirection
	HOBLink also provides a number of additional features to extend the usefulness of Terminal Server to a Java-based client. HOBLink is developed by the German-based company HOB, and the client is available from http://www.hob.de/www_us.
Linux and DOS	Terminal-Services.net provides a commercial RDP client that runs on Linux and another that runs on DOS.
	The Linux-based client, called LinRDP, is fully compatible with the new RDP features available in the RDP 5.2 client and Windows 2003 Terminal Server:
	■ Color depth up to 24-bit
	■ Local client drive redirection
	■ Local COM and printer redirection
	■ Client audio redirection
	Evaluation versions of both clients are available for download from the Web site at http://www.terminal-services.net.
UNIX OpenSource	An OpenSource version of the RDP client is available from RDesktop.Org. Unlike the other two clients, this one provides only bare-bones connectivity at this time, but is an option for those users who want basic access from a Linux or UNIX desktop. Full source code is provided with this client.
	RDesktop is available from http://www.rdesktop.org.

RDP Deployment Scenarios

Now that you have had the opportunity to review the various RDP client types available, let's look at how the RDP client could be used to satisfy the three deployment scenarios discussed earlier.

Desktop Replacement

The RDP client is configured for desktop replacement simply by defining the appropriate server or load-balanced cluster name and specifying other configuration options, specifically configuring the remote desktop size to full screen, as shown in Figure 5.14. A shortcut can then be created on the desktop or added to the Startup folder. Typically, desktop replacement clients are configured to run in full-screen mode to hide the local operating system desktop from the user. When utilizing the latest Remote Desktop client (version 5.2), users can continue to use their familiar Windows shortcut keys (ALT+TAB, ALT+ESC, and so on) by default when the client is operating in full-screen mode. This is a significant improvement over earlier versions of the RDP client, which did not support this feature, forcing users to learn alternate key combinations to perform these familiar tasks.

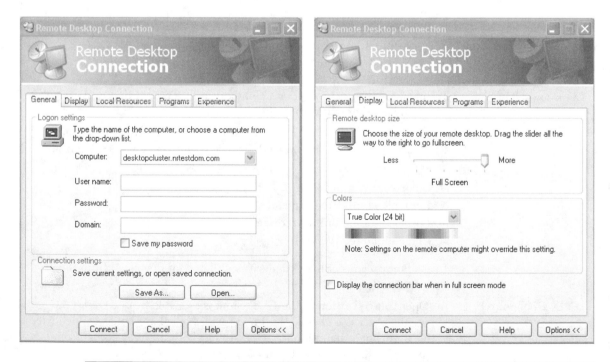

Figure 5.14   Configuring the RDP client options to launch a full-screen Terminal Server desktop.

While it may not appear to be that significant a feature, the 5.2 client's support for the Windows shortcut keys makes it a good candidate for use in a desktop replacement environment. The ability to capture these key combinations greatly enhances the user's computing experience and lets you more easily hide the local desktop from the user. When the connection bar is disabled in full-screen mode, many users do not even recognize that they are not accessing their applications locally. Figure 5.15 shows an example of a full-screen RDP session with the connection bar visible. This can be configured within the settings for the Remote Desktop Connection client, as shown back in Figure 5.14.

Figure 5.15 When implementing a desktop-replacement scenario using the RDP client, you likely will want to disable the connection bar.

Desktop Integration

When you want to utilize an RDP client in a desktop-integration scenario, you'll find Microsoft's support for non-Windows-based operating systems limited to their Macintosh OS X client. For other desktop operating systems, you will need to look to non-Microsoft clients such as the LinRDP client for Linux or HOBLink's pure Java-based RDP client, which will run on a number of desktop operating systems that support Java, including Windows, Mac OS (8.1 or later), Mac OS X, AIX, Solaris, HP-UX, and Linux.

Of course the other alternative is Citrix MetaFrame Presentation Server, which provides native ICA support for a number of non-Windows desktop operating systems, including DOS, OS/2, Macintosh, Linux, and UNIX. We look at Citrix's ICA client support in the next section.

Application Replacement

An RDP client is configured to use specific applications in one of three ways. The first is to configure the client's Programs tab, as shown in Figure 5.16. This screen shot shows an RDP client being configured to launch Microsoft Word from the D: drive of the specified Terminal Server.

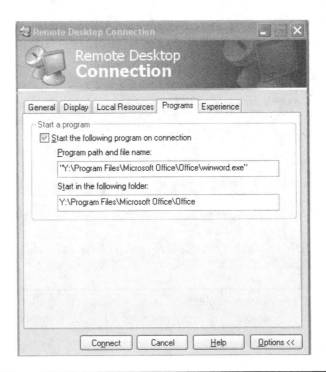

Figure 5.16   Preparing an RDP client to launch Microsoft Word.

The second option is to configure the application you wish to launch from directly within the user's domain account (Figure 5.17), thereby forcing the user to run this particular application whenever he or she logs on to a Terminal Server. When this option is configured, it automatically overrides any options set on the RDP client. The disadvantage to this, of course, is that this program executes regardless of the Terminal Server the user authenticates against. If there is at least one server upon which the user needs to run a different application, this option cannot be selected.

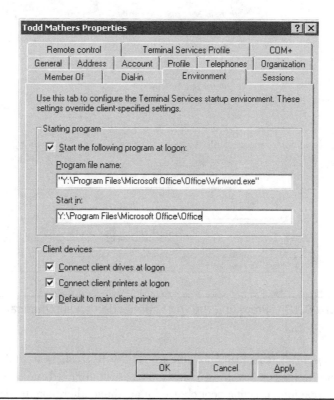

Figure 5.17 Preparing a user's account to launch Microsoft Word.

The final option is to configure the application settings at the connection level on the Terminal Server, as shown in Figure 5.18. When the application is configured here, it overrides any settings both on the local client and in the user's account. Of course when configured at the connection level, it applies to all users that connect to that server using the RDP client, even administrators. Typically you will not set application-launching options at the connection level.

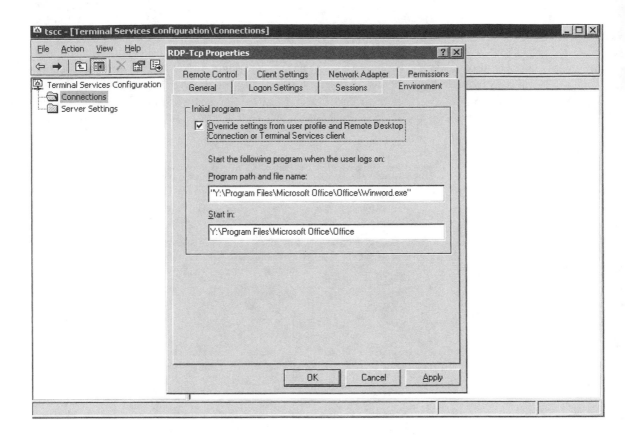

Figure 5.18 Preparing the RDP connection to automatically launch Microsoft Word.

Although it is technically possible to use the RDP client to deliver application replacement, the limitations on how these connections are configured and how they appear to the end user, in my opinion, make it a poor choice for anything other than the desktop-replacement scenario. Because the application is forced to run within the confines of the RDP session boundary defined by the connection settings, any other applications opened by the primary application, such as a Web browser, would also be contained in that window. Figure 5.19 demonstrates this behavior. This is certainly not what the end user would expect and can be extremely difficult to work with, not to mention the added support burden it will certainly introduce to the user support department.

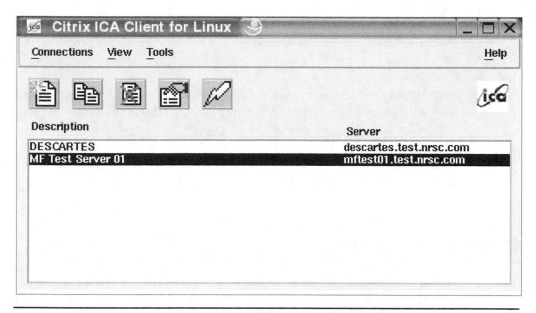

Figure 5.19   Preparing the RDP connection to automatically launch Microsoft Word.

Hardware Support

Assuming you will be implementing an RDP-based client solution, the next task is to determine what hardware changes may be necessary in your environment to accommodate the needs of the client. In the majority of new and existing Terminal Server implementations, you must account for a mixture of existing client operating systems. Usually there will be a combination of Windows 98 and Windows 2000 Professional desktops, with possibly some Windows 95 or NT 4.0 workstation machines still in use. Table 5.4 provides a summary of the minimum hardware requirements for the supported Windows operating systems. These requirements would be sufficient when you want to implement a desktop-replacement scenario, since only the RDP client is running locally on the desktop.

Table 5.4   Minimum Windows RDP Client Hardware Requirements

Client Operating System	Client Type	Minimum RAM	Minimum CPU
Windows XP, Windows 2000	32-bit (5.2)	64MB	Intel Pentium II or higher
ME, 98, and NT 4.0	32-bit (5.2)	32MB	Intel Pentium 133 or higher
Windows 95	32-bit (5.1)	32MB	Intel 486/66 or higher
Windows for Workgroups 3.11	16-bit (5.0)	8MB	Intel 386 or higher

As I mentioned earlier, maintaining a client operating system no longer supported by Microsoft could put you in a position where a known vulnerability exists that could affect one of these obsolete operating systems, potentially jeopardizing stability of the company's network infrastructure.

Microsoft no longer provides publicly released security patches for Windows ME, 98, or earlier versions. Because of this I recommend that you implement Windows 2000 Professional as the minimum desktop operating system version. You must determine if Windows 2000 will run on any existing hardware currently running an older Windows version; if the hardware will not support an operating system upgrade, you need to consider upgrading or replacing the hardware with something that will.

ICA Client Support

When implementing Citrix MetaFrame Presentation Server (MPS), you have a number of client options from which to choose. Your choices are dictated not only by the user's local desktop operating system but also by the implementation scenario (desktop replacement and so on) you choose to employ. At the time this book was being completed, a number of the Citrix MPS clients had been updated to version 8.x, including some such as the Linux client that had not been available when MPS 3.0 was initially released. I recommend that you consult the download section of the Citrix Web site to determine if a newer client version is available for your platform before you begin to perform the client deployment in your organization.

ICA Client Types

I begin this section by quickly reviewing the four main ICA client types supported by Citrix (first mentioned in Chapter 2, "Citrix MetaFrame Presentation Server"):

- **Standard Citrix ICA client**—Traditionally known as the Remote Application Manager, this client provides connectivity support to a specific Citrix server or published resources in a Citrix server farm. This client type is available for most supported client platforms, including 32-bit Windows (as part of Program Neighborhood), Windows CE, Mac OS and OS X, Linux and other supported UNIX variants, and OS/2. Figure 5.20 shows the Citrix ICA client for Linux running on SuSE Linux.
- **Program Neighborhood (PN)**—This is the traditional Win32 Citrix ICA client interface, providing a full application environment from within which connections to various MetaFrame Presentation Servers or published resources (individual programs or other content made available on one or more MetaFrame servers) can be accessed. Most new implementations of MetaFrame do not deploy this full client to the end-user but instead use the Program Neighbor-

hood Agent or the Web client (both described later in this list) for regular user access. Administrators will likely want to have the full Program Neighborhood installed on their desktop for maximum flexibility in supporting their MetaFrame environment. Figure 5.21 shows the full Program Neighborhood main window.

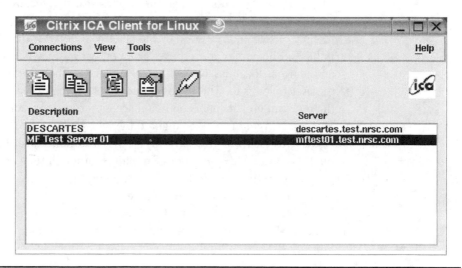

Figure 5.20   The Citrix ICA client for Linux.

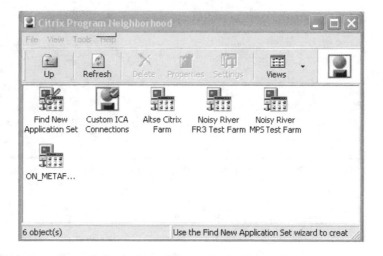

Figure 5.21   The Win32 Program Neighborhood ICA client.

■ **Program Neighborhood Agent (PN Agent)**—This client works in conjunction with the Web Interface for MetaFrame Presentation Server (discussed in Chapter 14, "MetaFrame Presentation Server Configuration") to provide a simple means of delivering published resources to the end user. Unlike the full PN, where all configuration changes must be performed locally on the client, configuration of the PN Agent is done centrally through the Program Neighborhood Agent Console and retrieved by the client via the Web Interface for MPS. Published resources are retrieved from one or more server farms and displayed on the user's local desktop by the PN Agent based on the domain groups that the user belongs to. The PN Agent does not have a full interface through which the user can create connections and access servers or resources. Certain options for the PN Agent can be configured by right-clicking the PN Agent icon in the system tray (see Figure 5.22) and selecting the desired setting. You can also see the list of available applications from here, although they are usually configured to appear on the local desktop or Start menu.

The PN Agent is the recommended way to deploy the ICA client on platforms that support this client. Currently the PN Agent is supported on Win32, Windows-based terminals running WinCE, CE-based handheld PCs, Linux, and Sun Solaris.

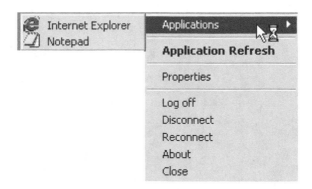

Figure 5.22   The Program Neighborhood Agent system tray properties.

■ **Citrix Web client**—The smallest of the four client types, the Citrix Web client, available only for Windows 32-bit operating systems, provides access to published resources directly from hyperlinks on a Web page. The source of this Web page can be one of the following:

■ The Web Interface for MetaFrame Presentation Server
■ NFuse Classic, the previous iteration of the Web Interface product

■ A standard Web page with properly configured hyperlinks using a technique known as Application Launching and Embedding (ALE)

In order for the Web client to function, you must be running Internet Explorer (5.0 or higher) or Netscape Navigator (4.78, 6.2, or higher). The Web client provides no separate user interface and instead retrieves the necessary configuration information directly from the source Web site and from the published application settings in the Citrix server farm. Figure 5.23 shows a sample Web page generated by the Web Interface for MPS, with Microsoft Word, Microsoft Excel, and a line of business applications (Prophet 21 Commerce Center) available for access. Clicking any one of these application hyperlinks initiates a connection to the published application using the Citrix Web client.

Two versions of the Citrix Web Client exist. One provides the full set of ICA client features and is available both as a self-extracting executable and as a compressed Microsoft cabinet (.CAB) file. The other is known as the *minimal Citrix Web client* and is available only as a .CAB file. As the name suggests, this client is the smallest Win32 ICA client available, and in order to achieve this, certain features normally found in the other ICA clients had to be omitted. The Citrix Web client is discussed in more detail in Chapter 20, "ICA Client Installation and Configuration."

TIP: Citrix provides a Java-based client that is also accessible directly from a Web browser and supports many of the features found in the full Win32 Web client. The ICA Java client is discussed in more detail in Chapter 20.

Figure 5.23 The Citrix Web client is typically used to load applications accessed through the Web Interface for MetaFrame Presentation Server, NFuse Classic, or a custom Web page using ALE.

Operating System Support

The Citrix ICA client is currently supported on a number of operating systems and computing environments. Table 5.5 summarizes the supported operating systems and the latest available client version.

The ICA client is capable of utilizing the TCP/IP, IPX, SPX, and NetBEUI protocols when supported by the underlying operating system. Windows 2000 supports installation and use of any one of these protocols. Windows Server 2003 supports only the TCP/IP protocol, regardless of whether or not any of the other network protocols are installed on the server.

Table 5.5 ICA Client-Supported Operating Systems and Client Versions

Operating System	Latest ICA Client Version
Windows 2003, XP, 2000, ME, 98, and NT 4.0	8.0
Windows for Workgroups 3.11 and Windows 3.1	6.20
Windows CE—Windows-based terminals	8.0
Windows CE—Handheld PCs (including PocketPC)	7.23
DOS (32-bit)	4.21
OS/2 Warp	6.0
Macintosh OS X	6.30
Macintosh PowerPC and M6800	6.20
Linux	8.0
UNIX (AIX and HP UX)	6.30
UNIX (Sun Solaris/SPARC)	7.0
UNIX (Sun Solaris/i386, Sun OS, Compaq Tru64, and SCO)	3.0
UNIX (SGI)	6.0
Java	8.0
EPOC/Symbian	2.01
Web client (part of the Win32 client)	8.0

Just as with the RDP client, your decision on what client operating system/ICA client combination to use will depend on the hardware currently available or designated for your users and what ICA client version is available for that hardware/operating system combination.

One advantage of ICA over RDP is the robust support for heterogeneous computing environments. This allows for much more flexibility in what client will be used, particularly in application-replacement or desktop-integration scenarios, the two areas where RDP provided only average support. In many situations, the ICA client can be introduced with little or no change to the user's existing client OS. Because Citrix natively supports these non-Windows operating systems, there is greater confidence in the software functioning as expected, and all support for MetaFrame, either on the desktop or the server, is directed to a single source.

Table 5.6 summarizes the features available with the most common ICA clients (expanding on the table first presented in Chapter 2. A complete list of supported client operating systems and their available features can be found on the Citrix Web site in its ICA Client Feature Matrix (http://download2.citrix.com/files/client_features.xls). An X in a particular cell of the table means that client supports the corresponding feature. An Xy designates a client that supports client-to-server audio support, such as the use of a microphone. The letters P and S are used when showing what clients support the panning and scaling features. A complete description of the supported features is discussed next.

Table 5.6   ICA Client Features by Common Client Platform

Feature	Client Win32 8.x	WinCE 8.0	Mac OS X 6.30	Linux 8.x	Java 8.0	Description
Text cut/paste clip board integration	X	X	X	X	X	Allows clipboard contents to be cut and pasted seamlessly back and forth between the active Terminal Server session and the user's local desktop.
File cut/paste clip board integration	X	X	X	X		Allows cut and pasting of entire file objects back and forth between the active session and the local desktop.
Local and network client printer redirection	X	X	X	X	X	Printers configured on the local client (directly connected or network mapped) can be accessed from within the user's MetaFrame session.
Universal printer driver support	X		X	X	X	A universal printer driver (UPD) can be designated as the driver to use when mapping client printers. The client must have a printer driver that supports the UPD.
Client disk drive redirection	X	X	X	X	X	A client's local and network drivers can be redirected and accessible within the MetaFrame session.
Client audio redirection	Xy	Xy	X	Xy	X	Audio from the server to the client is redirected by all clients, but client-to-server support is available only with the Win32, WinCE, and Linux clients.

Table 5.6   ICA Client Features by Common Client Platform (continued)

Feature	Client					Description
	Win32 8.x	WinCE 8.0	Mac OS X 6.30	Linux 8.x	Java 8.0	
Client serial port redirection	X	X	X	X		Allows redirection of the local serial ports.
Time zone support	X	X	X	X		Client time zone support lets the ICA client provide its own local time zone information to the MetaFrame server so the server can automatically configure the user's session to reflect the same time zone information.
Seamless windows	X			X	X	The seamless windows feature allows a published application to appear as if it were running locally on the user's desktop.
Panning and scaling	PS	S	P	P	P	When a session desktop is larger than the visible screen area, the ICA client lets you pan the desktop and, with certain clients, scale the desktop to fit within the visible session space. Scaling is available with only the Win32 and WinCE clients. Panning is not supported with the WinCE client.
SpeedScreen latency reduction	X	X	X	X	X	SpeedScreen latency reduction allows for echoing of text on the local client even if the information has not immediately been transmitted to the MetaFrame server due to latency in the network. This gives the impression to the end user that the session is more responsive than it actually might be.

Table 5.6 ICA Client Features by Common Client Platform (continued)

Feature	Client Win32 8.x	WinCE 8.0	Mac OS X 6.30	Linux 8.x	Java 8.0	Description
Multimedia acceleration	X					Provides support for accelerating playback of streaming audio and video from Internet Explorer, Windows Media Player, and RealOne Player.
Web browser acceleration	X	X		X	X	Accelerates processing of images on Internet Explorer 5.5 or higher.
Automatic client reconnect	X	X		X	X	Lets the client automatically attempt to reconnect to a server when the connection has been unintentionally severed.
Roaming user reconnect	X	X	X	X	X	Lets a user connect to a MetaFrame server using one particular client, disconnect, and then reconnect from a different client. Cross-platform reconnection is supported with certain client versions.
Session reliability	X	X				Session reliability allows for continued display of a published application even if the actual connection to the server has been lost.
Workspace control	X	X		X	X	Lets a user quickly disconnect, reconnect, or log off all his or her currently open applications.
Automatic client update	X		X	X		Updates to the ICA client can automatically be deployed using the automatic client update feature. The MetaFrame server initiates automatic client updates when a supporting client connects.

Table 5.6 ICA Client Features by Common Client Platform (continued)

Feature	Client Win32 8.x	WinCE 8.0	Mac OS X 6.30	Linux 8.x	Java 8.0	Description
Content publishing	X	X		X	X	Whereas application publishing makes individual applications on one or more MetaFrame servers available for user access, content publishing makes files such as Word documents or Web site URLs available for use. Content is distributed through the ICA client just as a published application would be.
Content redirection:						Two types of content redirection are supported. The first is server-to-client redirection, which allows embedded URLs in a published application to be opened using the Web browser on the user's local desktop. The other is client-to-server redirection, which allows documents on the local client device to be associated with an application published on a MetaFrame server.
Server to client	X	X		X	X	
Client to server	X	X	X	X		

The Win32 client supports client-to-server redirection only when using the PN Agent.

Both the Mac and Linux clients support client-to-server redirection, but the desired redirection must be manually configured.

Table 5.6 ICA Client Features by Common Client Platform (continued)

| Feature | Client | | | | | Description |
	Win32 8.x	WinCE 8.0	Mac OS X 6.30	Linux 8.x	Java 8.0	
Program Neighborhood Agent	X	X		X		The PN Agent client allows for central management and distribution of client data using the MetaFrame Web Interface. Only a minimum-sized client is installed that has a limited local user interface.
Smart card support	X	X		X		The user can provide their smart card to a local reader attached to their PC and have those credentials transmitted and authenticated on the Terminal Server.
Novell Directory Services authentication	X	X	X	X	X	All the listed clients support authentication through NDS, Novell's alternative to Microsoft's Active Directory.
Passthrough authentication	X					This feature allows for the user ID and password provided within the local client on the PC to automatically be used to authenticate when connecting to a MetaFrame server. Only the Win32 client supports passthrough authentication.

Some features such as session remote control (shadowing), persistent bitmap caching, high resolution (1280x1024), high color (24-bit), and strong encryption (128-bit) have been omitted from the list because they are supported by all the client versions, with the exception of the minimum ICA Web client.

Clipboard Integration

The ICA client and MetaFrame provide complete integration of the MetaFrame session's clipboard and the local desktop clipboard. Using the standard cut-and-paste functions (menu command and hotkeys only), you can move data (text, graphics, and files) between the two environments as if you were moving it between local applications. Dragging and dropping data between the client and a MetaFrame session is not supported. You must use the cut-and-paste menu and hotkey commands.

WARNING: Synchronization of large clipboard contents between client and server can have a significant impact on performance over a low-bandwidth connection. In this situation, it may be desirable to turn off the clipboard mapping features.

Local and Network Printer Redirection

Citrix has provided support for local client printer redirection for quite some time, and stability of the feature has continued to improve dramatically. Printer redirection allows printers configured on the local client to be accessible from within the MetaFrame session. This seamless access to the client's printing devices improves the user's computing experience, particularly when operating in an application-integration scenario where the MetaFrame-based application is interacting with the user's local desktop. Redirected printing also makes it possible to access a printer otherwise inaccessible through a direct connection from the MetaFrame server. A user's home printer when accessing MetaFrame through a corporate VPN connection is one example. There is additional information you should know about redirected client printers:

- Client printers are automatically mapped only through the Win32 client. Other ICA clients must initiate client mapping manually.
- If a matching printer driver is not found on the MetaFrame server, either a substitute can be manually configured on the server by an administrator and automatically used or a suitable Citrix universal printer driver (when supported) can be used instead. The universal printer driver is discussed shortly.

Any redirected client printers are visible to only the user they belong to and any administrator who may log on to that MetaFrame Server. No other user can see or use those printer connections. Figure 5.24 shows the Printers folder for a user with client-mapped printers. Client printer redirection can be controlled at the connection or user account level. It can also be managed through MetaFrame policies, discussed a little later in this section.

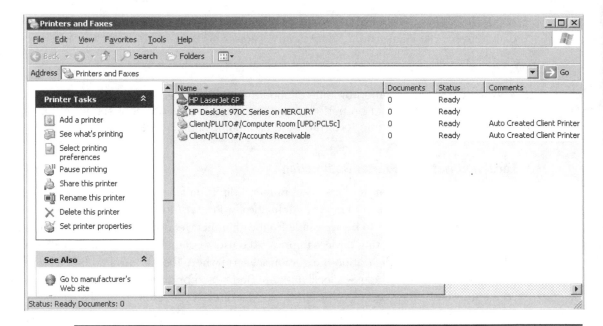

Figure 5.24 A user can access their Citrix client-mapped printers from within their MetaFrame session, just as with any other Windows printer.

Universal Printer Driver Support

To redirect a client's printer, a corresponding printer driver for that printer must exist on the MetaFrame server. If no such driver exists, the printer mapping cannot complete successfully. In order to account for this situation and provide a mechanism allowing mapping to continue successfully, Citrix provides a set of generic drivers called *universal printer drivers* (UPDs). Three UPDs are provided with MetaFrame:

- **PostScript (PS) Language**—Provided to support PostScript printers and printer emulators running on UNIX. UNIX clients running version 7.0 or later can utilize this driver.
- **Printer Control Language (PCL) 4**—Provided for backwards compatibility with older MPS clients and originally shipped with MetaFrame XP Feature Release 2. The PCL4 UPD supports monochrome printing up to 300 DPI.
- **PCL5c**—Supported only by Win32 MPS clients and Macintosh clients 6.2 or later.

When a client printer is auto-created and a universal printer driver is used, a prefix identifying this printer as a UPD printer is appended to the end of the printer's name. In Figure 5.24 you can see that the Computer Room printer has the text [UPD:PCL5c] at the end of the name. This identifies this printer as using the PCL5c universal driver.

By default, if a native driver cannot be used to automatically create the client-mapped printer when the user logs on, MetaFrame attempts to use a UPD instead. This behavior can be modified depending on how you want your environment to use the universal drivers. Configuration and use of the UPD are discussed in Chapter 17.

Client Drive Redirection

To further integrate the MPS client into the user's local desktop, MetaFrame provides client disk drive redirection functionality. This allows for easy transfer of data between the client device and the MetaFrame session. When enabled, local client disk drives are automatically mapped and made available within the remote session. Local network connections are not mapped automatically but can be mapped manually using either the NET USE command or selecting the Map Network Drive option from the Tools menu in Windows Explorer. Figure 5.25 shows the My Computer window for a MetaFrame client session on a Windows 2003 Terminal Server with MetaFrame Presentation Server 3.0 and locally redirected client drives.

In Figure 5.25 you can see that the local client drives C:, D:, and E: are mapped to the drive letters V:, U:, and T: on the MetaFrame server. This demonstrates how MetaFrame allocates available server drive letters to redirected client drives when the server drive letters were not reassigned during installation.

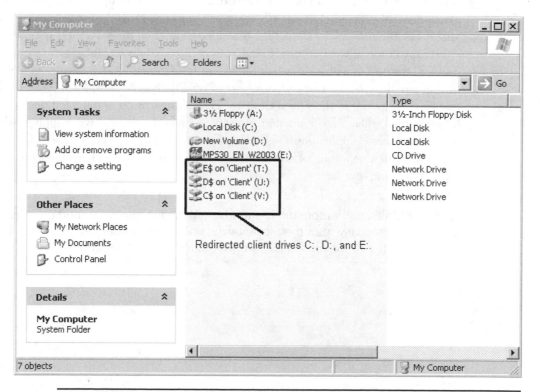

Figure 5.25   Redirected client drives with an ICA client.

By default, MetaFrame first attempts to match the client drive letter to a corresponding available server drive letter. So if the server had local drives reassigned prior to MetaFrame installation to begin at X:, and the server drives C:, D:, and E: were unused, the drive list for My Computer would appear as follows:

C$ on 'Client' (C:)	Network Drive
D$ on 'Client' (D:)	Network Drive
E$ on 'Client' (E:)	Network Drive
Local Disk (X:)	Local Disk
New Volume (Y:)	Local Disk
MPS 30 EN W2003 (Z:)	CD Drive

TIP: Server drive letters can be reassigned prior to MetaFrame installation using the drive reassignment tool DriveRemap.exe, found in the root of the installation CD. Use of this tool is discussed in Chapter 13, "MetaFrame Presentation Server Installation."

If the server drives have not been reassigned, as was the case in Figure 5.25, then MetaFrame maps client drive letters starting with V: and working backwards through all available drive letters; hence the reason why C: on the client appears as V: on the server, D: as U:, and E: as T:.

If any of the drives between T: and V: were already in use, MetaFrame would skip over it to find the next available drive letter. It's clear from this setup that having client drives map to alternate drive letters can certainly be confusing to the end user. Most users would expect that C: corresponds to their local C: drive. This is why it is recommended that server drives be reassigned when a large number of users will rely on client drive mappings when using MetaFrame-based applications.

Automatic remapping of client drives can be turned on or off at either the connection level or on a per-user basis.

WARNING: Although automatic client drive redirection can be turned off, clients are still able to manually map their local drives unless additional security steps are taken. Chapter 16 discusses client drive redirection and security.

Client Audio Redirection

MetaFrame supports redirection of server audio to the client with all versions of the MPS client that run on client hardware that supports audio. The reverse, client audio redirection to the server through input devices such as a microphone, is supported only when using the Win32, WinCE, or Linux clients.

Client Serial Port Redirection

MetaFrame also supports client serial port redirection. This allows devices attached to a local client's COM port, such as serial printers, card reader devices, or barcode scanners, to be accessible during a MetaFrame session. Unlike printer or disk drives, COM ports are not mapped automatically during a user's logon. COM ports can be mapped using the NET USE or CHANGE CLIENT command. Client COM ports would be referenced as \\Client\COMx: where x is the COM port number. See Appendix A, "Terminal Services Command Reference," for more information on the CHANGE CLIENT command.

Time Zone Support

This feature lets the MetaFrame server automatically configure the user's session to display the date and time based on the user's current time zone instead of defaulting to display the server's date and time. For example, if a MetaFrame server is located in New York City, it is 11:30 a.m. on June 15, and a client is connecting using a client from Singapore, where the current time is 11:30 p.m. on June 15, the MetaFrame server can display the proper time and date for that user from Singapore instead of showing them the New York City time. This feature can be very important to users, particularly if they are utilizing applications such as Outlook, which can rely heavily on the proper date and time.

Seamless Windows

Earlier in the chapter when discussing the application-replacement scenario, I mentioned the ICA seamless window feature. Seamless windows let a published application appear to the end user as if it were running on their local desktop. Seamless windows support is available with Win32, Java, and Linux or UNIX clients. Figure 5.26, which is the same as Figure 5.4 from earlier in the chapter, demonstrates this by showing Microsoft Word running as an integrated application on a Linux desktop.

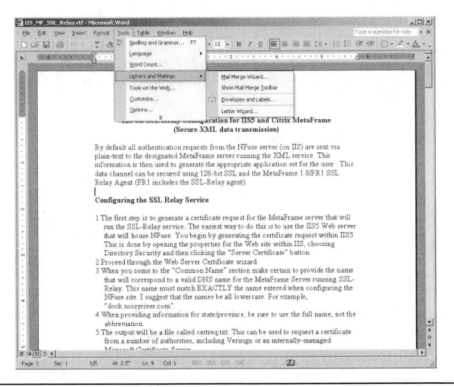

Figure 5.26   ICA seamless windows support lets a remote application appear as if it is running locally on the client's desktop.

Panning and Scaling

When a MetaFrame session desktop is larger than the visible screen area on an MPS client, the panning feature provides scroll bars that can be used to move different parts of the remote desktop into view. For example, a 1024x768 desktop viewed from a client running at 800x600 would require you to scroll around in order to view the entire contents of the screen. Figure 5.27 shows an example of this, where you can see the scroll bars used to navigate the larger MPS client window size.

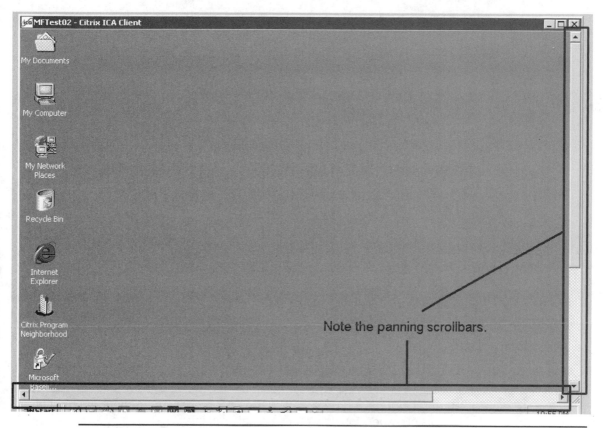

Figure 5.27 Panning lets you scroll and view a desktop session running at a higher resolution than your MPS client.

Scaling lets you shrink or expand the current session window to accommodate the change in screen resolution. The options to scale the session window can be found in the Control menu, located by clicking the icon in the upper-left corner of the session window. Figure 5.28 shows the Options menu visible when you request a change in size of the current MPS session window. Scaling is supported on only the Win32 and WinCE clients.

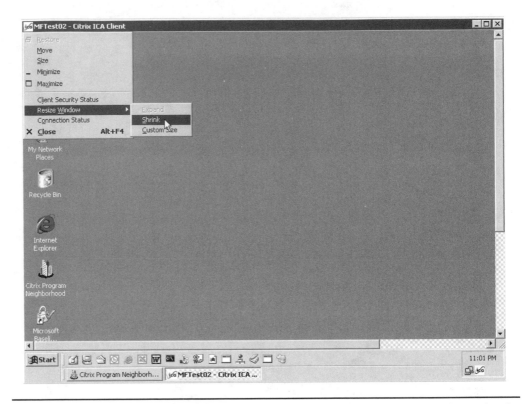

Figure 5.28   Scaling lets you resize a larger desktop session so more information is visible when forced to use a smaller display.

SpeedScreen Latency Reduction

A main inhibitor of a pleasant and productive MetaFrame (and Terminal Server in general) user experience is network latency. Lapses in network speed can cause a MetaFrame session to appear sluggish and unresponsive. Users immediately notice when a mouse click fails to generate a response or if multiple keystrokes appear out of time with typing on the keyboard. Citrix provides a suite of options collectively know as SpeedScreen, which are intended to help connection speed and session responsiveness. The first option is known as *latency reduction,* and as the name suggests, the purpose of these settings is to reduce the impact of latency on a MetaFrame session. Two latency reduction options exist:

- **Mouse-click feedback**—When a user clicks the mouse within a MetaFrame session, the mouse pointer automatically changes from the regular pointer arrow to an hourglass. This gives the impression that the system is busy processing the user's request and the user should wait for it to finish. Most users understand that, when the hourglass appears, they should wait for it to finish before continuing to click other applications or links within the MetaFrame session. Mouse-click feedback is enabled by default on the client and the MetaFrame server.

- **Local text echo**—If the network link is suffering from high utilization, users immediately feel the effects of the resulting latency on how quickly text they are typing appears on the screen. When text is entered, the information is sent to the MetaFrame server, where it is processed and then sent back to the client as a screen update. Any delay in transmission of data in either direction manifests itself as a very slow screen update.

  The local text echo option is intended to mask these latency issues by providing immediate feedback and displaying locally the text that has been entered, while the actual information is transmitted to the server and returned. When the actual update finally returns from the server, it is updated on the local client's display. Local text echo is disabled by default on both the client and the server. Under most circumstances I recommend that this feature not be enabled.

By default, the mouse-click feedback option is enabled while the local text echo option is disabled on both the client and the server. On the MPS client, these latency reduction features are configured for each custom connection or application set created. Figure 5.29 shows these settings for an application set's default options.

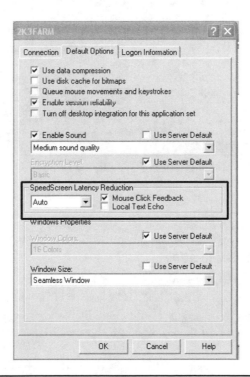

Figure 5.29   Latency reduction options are set for each custom connection or application set defined in an MPS client.

When the latency reduction options are configured to Auto instead of On or Off, they are enabled only if a certain threshold is exceeded and it is detected that latency issues may exist. As soon as the latency issue falls back below a minimum threshold, the latency reduction features are turned off. These thresholds are configured using a tool called the SpeedScreen Latency Reduction Manager, located under the Citrix\Administration Tools folder on the Start menu. Using this tool, you can define the thresholds on a server-by-server basis. You can also set latency parameters per application through this tool if you wish. Figure 5.30 shows the server-wide properties accessible within this tool.

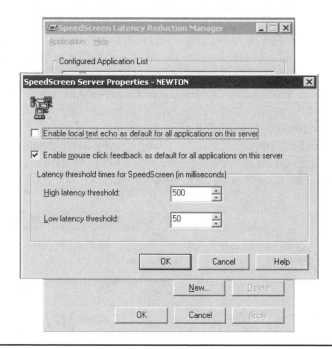

Figure 5.30   The SpeedScreen Latency Reduction Manager controls per-application and server-wide settings for the latency reduction options.

Multimedia Acceleration

MetaFrame provides multimedia acceleration features intended to optimize playback of multimedia content through an ICA session. Content playable through Internet Explorer, Windows Media Player, or the RealOne Player is streamed in its original compressed format through to the client device, which is then made responsible for decompressing and playing the content.

This process has two advantages over how such content would originally be processed on a MetaFrame server. First, by streaming the compressed content to the client, the bandwidth is much smaller than it would be if the content were decompressed on the MetaFrame server and then passed through to the client. Second, delegating the client to perform decompression and playback completely frees the MetaFrame server of such CPU-intensive tasks, ensuring that server resources are available for other user requirements.

Technically, any codec (Compression/decompression software for audio and video playback) compatible with Windows Media Player or RealOne Player can be used to stream multimedia content through to the client. The client must be able to process this content in order for a user to see it.

Multimedia acceleration is enabled at the farm level but can be defined on a per-server basis. Figure 5.31 shows the properties for a farm with multimedia and other visual SpeedScreen acceleration features.

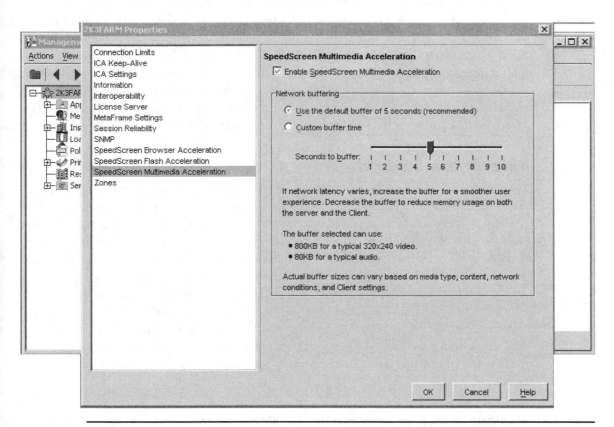

Figure 5.31 The multimedia acceleration features can be defined at the farm level.

Web Browser Acceleration

The browser acceleration feature supports accessing and interacting with Internet Explorer, Outlook Express, and Outlook while images for a particular site are downloaded in the background. This way you can continue to work instead of being forced to wait for all the data to become available. This basic browser acceleration feature is enabled by default for the entire farm (Figure 5.31) and can also be set on a server-by-server basis.

Another browser acceleration option not enabled by default is automatic compression of JPEG images (accessed from within one of the three listed applications). Compression allows for shrinking of JPEG files to increase available bandwidth while sacrificing some image quality. JPEG images processed by any other application are not subject to the browser acceleration logic.

Macromedia Flash Acceleration

A common multimedia component of many Web sites is Macromedia Flash. Rendering and playback of Macromedia Flash content suffer from many of the same problems encountered with other audio and video data. Unlike the multimedia accelerator, which streams content to the client, SpeedScreen Macromedia Flash acceleration is responsible for actually throttling rendering of Flash content on the server. Instead of allowing Flash to be rendered in the highest quality, which is the default, Flash is forced to render in a lower quality mode, reducing the size of each data frame and improving responsiveness to the client. The Macromedia Flash SpeedScreen option is also enabled by default.

Automatic Client Reconnect

The automatic client reconnect (ACR) feature lets an MPS client automatically detect a broken session connection and attempt to reestablish a connection with that session using cached credentials. These cached credentials, along with session information, are stored in a session cookie on the client when the MetaFrame connection is first created. As long as these credentials have not expired, the user is not required to reenter their password and the existing session automatically reappears once the connection can be reestablished.

Note that an intentional disconnect initiated by the user is not automatically reconnected. Only when a session disconnect is caused by a network connectivity or client issue (a PC crash, for example) is an automatic reconnect attempted. The reconnect attempt continues until the session is reestablished or the user cancels the reconnect process. Figure 5.32 shows this reconnection dialog box. As with many options, this feature is enabled by default at the farm level.

WARNING: If you have configured the TCP ICA connection settings to reset or end a broken or timed-out connection instead of forcing it into a disconnect state, the automatic reconnect feature always establishes a new connection to the server farm if the connection is lost. This option can be set using the Citrix Connection Configuration tool or within the Terminal Services Configuration tool (see Figure 5.33)

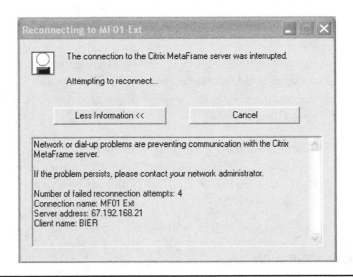

Figure 5.32   The automatic reconnection dialog box appears if a broken connection is detected.

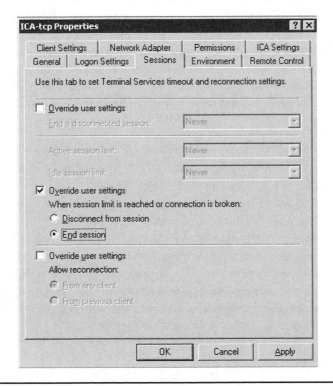

Figure 5.33   Forcing a broken connection to end or reset causes the automatic reconnect feature to always create a new session, since the old one is automatically cleared.

Roaming User Reconnect

This feature is one that most administrators (and some users) expect to be available, so it rarely comes as a surprise when people are told this option is supported. Roaming user reconnect lets a user connect to a MetaFrame server from one client type, disconnect, travel somewhere else, and then reconnect using a different device. There are certain limitations and restrictions on this support:

- When using HTTP browsing, roaming user reconnect is supported with the Windows, UNIX, Linux, and Mac OS X clients (version 6.30 or later).
- When using the legacy UDP broadcast browsing, roaming user reconnect is supported only with the Windows client.

Session Reliability

The session reliability feature keeps the MetaFrame session visible on the screen during an interruption in network connectivity. The session remains visible until the connection is reestablished, or it remains down for the default time-out period of three minutes. During the interruption, the mouse pointer changes to an hourglass and the session remains visible but inaccessible. When connectivity is restored, the MPS client automatically reconnects to the server. The user is not required to reenter his or her credentials.

Without session reliability, when a broken connection is detected, the client window closes and the user must then manually reconnect to the server in order to restore session connection. The session reliability feature is available only with the Advanced and Enterprise editions of MPS 3.0, and then only when using the 8.x version of the Win32 MPS client.

Workspace Control

The workspace control feature is available to only those users accessing a server farm using either the Web Interface for MPS or the Program Neighborhood Agent. Workspace control lets a user quickly log off or disconnect from all running applications with the click of a single button. When sessions are disconnected, they can quickly be reconnected from the same or a different client location. Workspace control is intended to let you quickly open and access your commonly used applications in your MetaFrame environment.

Workspace control can also be configured to automatically connect to a user's active applications running on other client devices when reconnecting or logging on from a different location. For example, if a user accidentally left a published application running on the desktop computer in his or her main office but now needs to connect from a satellite office, workspace control can automatically disconnect the session in the main office and reconnect it from the computer in the satellite office.

Workspace control is enabled in the farm by default and is fully configurable through the Web Interface Console or the Program Neighborhood Agent Console both of which are discussed in Chapter 20.

Automatic Client Update

Within a large MetaFrame environment, upgrading the MPS client can be a major project in itself and have a direct impact on two of the benefits of Terminal Server in general: centralized management and reduced maintenance costs. Citrix's solution to this problem is the ICA Client Update Configuration utility and the automatic client update feature of the MPS client.

This utility provides the ability to automatically update the Citrix MPS client on a user's desktop when he or she logs on to a MetaFrame server, pulling the latest client files from a centrally managed database. The administrator can schedule the automatic download and installation of the client software to the user's device when that user next logs on to the MetaFrame server. This provides a simple solution to keeping the version of the MPS client up-to-date and configured properly. Client Update Configuration enables you to fully configure how various clients are updated, including whether the update is visible or transparent to the user and whether only older clients or all clients are updated. Client installations can be preconfigured with all the necessary client settings, such as server locations and published application or server lists. In Chapter 20, "ICA Client Installation and Configuration," I walk through the process of configuring and using the Client Update Configuration application.

Content Publishing

Citrix not only provides access to applications through the delivery mechanism known as *publishing* but also expands this concept beyond applications to include support for what is known as *content publishing*. Content publishing provides the end user with access to specific files (HTML, Word, Excel, PDF documents, and so on) in much the same way the end user can access a published application. Figure 5.34 shows an example of the Web Interface for MPS containing an icon for a published desktop, a published application (Microsoft Word), and published content (the Web site link called Web Site).

Exactly how published content is processed depends on the type of content redirection being employed. Content redirection is discussed next.

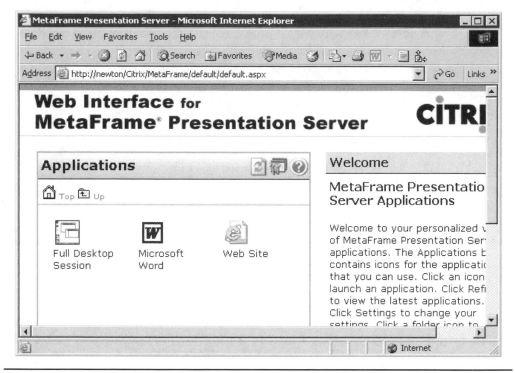

Figure 5.34   Citrix provides users with access to published content as well as published applications.

Content Redirection (Server to Client and Client to Server)

Content redirection lets an administrator dictate how a client device manages not only launching of published content but also management of local and remote documents, media files, and Web links. Basically, content redirection dictates what application launches what file and from where. Content redirection works in two directions, either from server to client or client to server, but the capabilities differ depending on which direction you are going.

- **Client to server**—This is the more robust of the two redirection configurations. When enabling client-to-server redirection, you can configure association of local documents so they are launched by applications published in the Citrix server farm. For example, if you had a Word document on the local desktop, you could configure client-to-server redirection so Microsoft Word published in a farm would launch if a user attempted to open the local file. Client-to-server redirection is supported on the Win32 platform only when using the Program Neighborhood Agent.

■ **Server to client**—This configuration lets a user open Web or multimedia content from within an application running on a MetaFrame server and have the content processed with a media player running on the user's local desktop. This configuration is part of the multimedia acceleration feature of SpeedScreen, discussed earlier.

Program Neighborhood Agent

The Program Neighborhood Agent (PN Agent) client allows for central management and distribution of client data using the MetaFrame Presentation Server Web Interface. Only minimum client-side configuration is supported. Behavior of the PN Agent is managed through the Program Neighborhood Agent Console, shown in Figure 5.35. Deployment and configuration of the PN Agent is covered in Chapter 20.

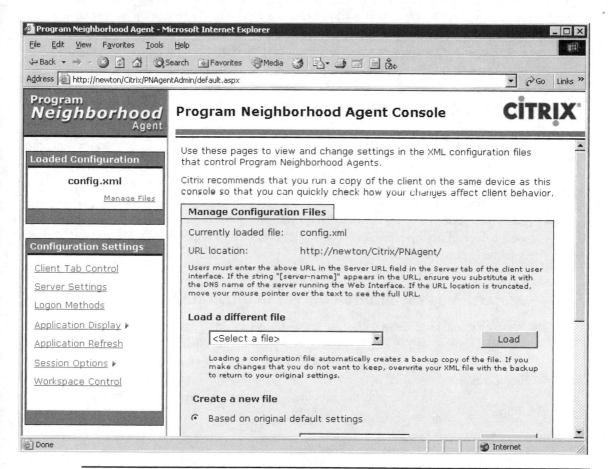

Figure 5.35   The PN Agent is configured using the Program Neighborhood Agent Console.

Smart Card Support

Citrix provides support for smart card authentication. A *smart card* is a physical card that provides a means of implementing a secure authentication mechanism using public-key encryption. Embedded logic and/or processing on the card is read using a smart card reader and then passed on to the MetaFrame server, where it is used to authenticate the user's session. Smart card readers are typically connected physically to the client device; MetaFrame supports smart card use with Win32, Linux, and WinCE (embedded in a Windows-based terminal) MPS clients.

Novell Directory Services Authentication

Citrix provides support for Novell Directory Services (NDS), letting users in this environment log on to a server (or server farm) using their NDS credentials. NDS is one alternative to using Microsoft's Active Directory services for user account management and authentication. By default NDS support is disabled, but it can be configured at the server farm level. If you open the properties for the server farm and then select MetaFrame Settings, you find a field called Novell Directory Services Preferred Tree. Entering the desired NDS tree in the space provided makes it available for use within the farm.

Passthrough Authentication

Passthrough authentication allows the user ID and password entered during logon of the local client to be automatically used to authenticate when connecting to a MetaFrame farm or server. For example, if a user logging on to their local Windows XP Professional desktop provides their Active Directory domain credentials, when they attempt to connect to an application in the farm the local Windows XP credentials can be automatically passed to the MetaFrame Server and processed. To be available, passthrough authentication support must be enabled during installation of the MPS client. Only the Win32 MPS client supports passthrough authentication.

MetaFrame Presentation Server Configuration Policies

Similar to policies defined within an Active Directory, MetaFrame supports farm-based policies that can be used to configure various session options that can then be applied to users, user groups, server groups, IP addresses, and client names. The application options have been expanded over earlier versions of MetaFrame, which supported only users and user group assignments. Through these policies you can configure the session options listed in Table 5.7.

Table 5.7   ICA Session Connection Policy Options

Policy	Description
Bandwidth—Session Limits: Audio Clipboard COM Ports Drives LPT Ports OEM Virtual Channels Overall Session Printer	For all these options you can set the maximum bandwidth allocated in kilobits per second (Kbps).
Bandwidth—SpeedScreen: Image acceleration using lossy compression	Lets you tailor the image compression used with SpeedScreen. By default image compression is set to High, but you can override this and use Medium or Low. You can also define a bandwidth threshold that enforces the specified compression only if bandwidth falls below the given Kbps value.
Bandwidth—Visual effects: Turn off desktop wallpaper Turn off menu animation Turn off window contents while dragging	These policies let you override the behavior of Windows and enforce disabling of certain visual effects that can consume unnecessary bandwidth and impact the user experience over low-bandwidth connections.
Client devices—Maintenance: Turn off auto client update	Disables automatic detection and deployment of client updates. Auto client update is discussed in Chapter 20.
Client devices—Resources: Audio	Control certain options specific to audio mapping.
Microphones	Microphones enables/disables use of a client-side microphone for audio input.
Sound Quality	Sound quality controls quality of the sound and, hence, the bandwidth used in transferring server-side audio to the client.
Turn off speakers	Turn off speakers disables audio mapping to the client.
Drives: Connections	Connections enables or disables client drive redirection.
Mappings	Mappings lets you control what client-side drives are actually mapped. From here you can disable mapping of floppy drives, local hard drives, CD-ROMs, and network drive mappings.

Table 5.7 ICA Session Connection Policy Options (continued)

Policy	Description
Local Printers:	
Auto creation	Auto creation turns on or off auto creation of client printers at logon. When enabled, you can specify all printers, the default printer only, or only local, not network client printers. This does not completely disable client printer mappings. Even if the printers are not mapped at logon, a user could still manually map them afterward.
Default	Default controls whether the local default printer becomes the default printer in MetaFrame.
Drivers	Drivers lets you select what server drivers will be used. You can allow only the universal printer driver, only native drivers, or the UPD only if no native driver is found.
Turn off client printer mapping.	Turn off client printer mapping completely disables access to local client printers.
Network Printers:	
Print job routing	Controls how the MetaFrame server routes print jobs for client-mapped network printers. The job can be routed either through the client device to the target printer or directly from the server to the printer.
	Selection depends on where the client is located and whether or not the network printer is directly accessible by the MetaFrame server. For example, users connecting via a VPN who have network printers available on their network would want to receive jobs through the client device, since the printer would not be directly available to the MetaFrame server.
Other:	
Turn off clipboard mapping	Simply enable or disable the listed option.
Turn off OEM virtual channels.	Disabling OEM virtual channels does not affect native Citrix functionality, but third-party applications that may utilize other channels will not function properly.
Ports:	
Turn off COM ports Turn off LPT ports	Enable or disable access to local ports on the client device.

Table 5.7   ICA Session Connection Policy Options (continued)

Policy	Description
Security—Encryption: Secure ICA encryption	Allows enforcement of the minimum required encryption level by the client. If the client device does not meet the specified minimum security level, the connection is denied.
User Workspace—Connections: Limit total concurrent sessions Zone preference and failover	Lets you control the maximum number of concurrent sessions a user can be running at one time. From here you can also specify the zone preference and failover priority for a user. Multiple zones must exist in your farm for this option to be available.
User Workspace—Content Redirection: Server to client	Enables or disables server-to-client content redirection.
User Workspace—MetaFrame Password Manager: Central Credential Store Do not use MetaFrame Password Manager.	Applies only if your environment has also implemented MetaFrame Password Manager (MPM). In this case, the MPM agent must also be installed on the MetaFrame server. The first policy dictates where the MPM store is located, while the second enables or disables use of MPM.
User Workspace—Shadowing: Configuration Permissions	Control behavior of shadowing for the affected users. Note that these policies affect how other users shadow the users affected by these policies and not how users of these policies shadow others. Configuration allows enabling or disabling of shadowing, whether notification is enforced, and if the shadower can provide input to the shadowed session. Permissions lets you specify a list of users or groups who will have permissions to shadow the users affected by this group. Typically these permissions are defined
User Workspace—Time Zones: Do not estimate time for legacy clients Do not use clients' local time	Control how client-side time zone support is implemented. The first policy determines whether MetaFrame will try and estimate the user's local time for those clients that do not provide local time zone feedback. The second policy enables or disables use of local time zone support.

Policy creation is straightforward, and once you have defined the desired settings to be applied to each policy, you can set the appropriate priority. Policy priority goes from bottom to top, with number one (1) having the highest priority. A setting higher in the priority list overrides one lower down if a user is assigned to more than one priority group. Figure 5.36 shows a simple example with two policies defined, one for Sales and the other for Customer Service.

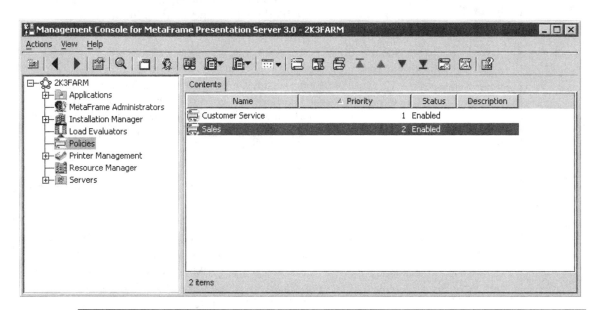

Figure 5.36   Policies are easily created from within the Management Console for MPS 3.0.

There are certain rules as to how policies are applied and when one rule overrides another. When a user logs on to a MetaFrame server, all applicable MetaFrame policies are applied from bottom to top and remain in effect until the user logs off. Connection policies have the following override rules:

- Connection policies override equivalent settings defined for the farm, for a specific server, or within the user's MPS client.
- The one exception to the preceding rule is the encryption level and shadowing restrictions. Higher encryption levels always override lower ones, regardless of where they are defined; the most restrictive shadowing permissions work the same way.
- Microsoft group policy objects also override MetaFrame connection policies, if they are more restrictive.

Figure 5.37 shows the policy settings for the Secure ICA encryption and demonstrates layout of the MetaFrame connection policies. Creation and implementation of these policies are discussed in Chapter 15.

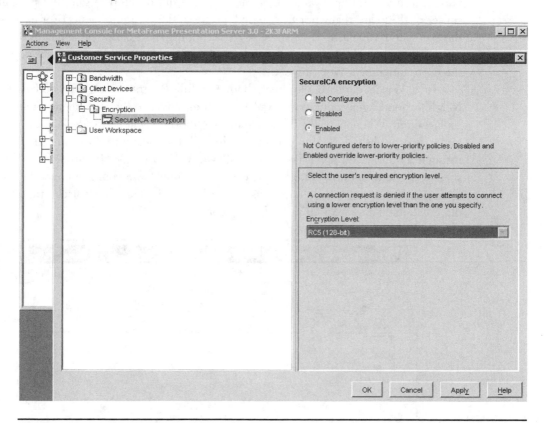

Figure 5.37   Individual settings within a policy are easy to configure. When a folder shows an exclamation mark (!), it signals that a setting has been defined within that folder.

ICA Deployment Scenarios

Now that we've had the chance to review the various ICA client properties in detail, we can look at how the ICA client can be used to satisfy the three deployment scenarios discussed earlier.

Desktop Replacement

When you are implementing MetaFrame and the ICA client in a desktop-replacement scenario, there are multiple ways a user can initiate a full desktop session, but typically only a subset of these are really practical, based on the desktop requirements. For example, while the Web client can easily provide access to the published desktop that launches the full desktop session, you will likely want to implement a more integrated method not dependent on the user launching a Web browser.

In a Win32 client deployment, both the full Program Neighborhood and Program Neighborhood Agent options are available as alternatives to the Web client for a full desktop replacement. When using the full Program Neighborhood client, the desktop can be accessed either as a published desktop connection through the Custom ICA Connection or as a link through a configured application set, as shown in Figure 5.38. In either case, the need to specifically have users go into the ICA client to initiate the connection can be avoided by making a shortcut available on the user's local desktop. This shortcut can then be used to directly launch a new MetaFrame desktop connection.

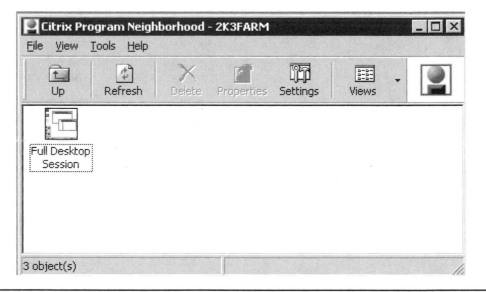

Figure 5.38   The full desktop-published application can be copied as a shortcut to the user's local desktop or directly into their Startup folder so it launches automatically when they log on to their PC.

Desktop Integration

As mentioned earlier, RDP support for non-Windows operating systems is limited to the Microsoft Macintosh client and other third-party products. On the other hand, the ICA protocol's robust client support allows for integration of Windows applications into non-Windows environments. Availability of native clients for Macintosh, UNIX, Linux, OS/2, and so on allows for Terminal Server access on the majority of non-Windows computing systems available today. Because all MPS clients support published applications, the interface for configuring a client connection is nearly identical for all clients. Shortcuts can be added to most non-Windows desktops, simplifying the process of establishing a MetaFrame desktop session from these clients.

Application Replacement

The MPS client has two modes of operation with regard to the application-replacement scenario. The first is identical to that supported by RDP, in which the desired application runs within the confines of a Terminal Server session window. The other method is through a seamless window available with the Win32, Linux, and Java clients. Seamless window support is the preferred method on the operating systems in which it is supported.

One of the main benefits of seamless window support is noticed when an auxiliary application is launched from within the main application, such as a Web browser. This application also runs from the MetaFrame server and appears as its own independent application, not restricted to the confines of the session window. Figures 5.39 and 5.40 show the same two applications, one within the confines of an RDP session window and the other working independently as a pair of published applications.

There are also certain limitations on how the seamless windows application can interact with the local desktop. Features such as drag and drop are not supported, although cut and paste are.

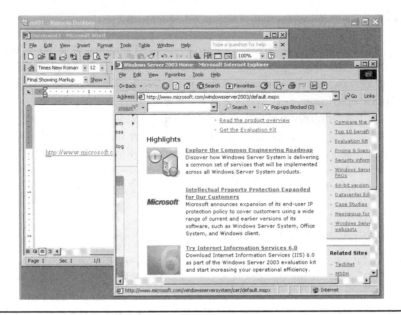

Figure 5.39 Multiple applications within a single RDP session boundary.

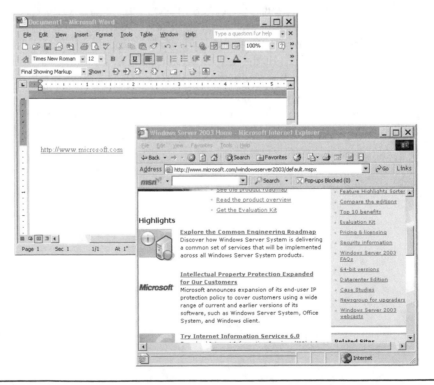

Figure 5.40 Multiple applications launched as seamless windows on a Win32 desktop.

Hardware Support

Just as with the RDP client discussed earlier in the chapter, you need to determine what hardware changes may be necessary in your environment to meet the needs of the ICA client. Unlike the RDP client, which is best suited for a desktop-replacement implementation, the ICA client is tailored toward providing robust support for application-replacement implementation as well as desktop-replacement and desktop-integration scenarios. In the application-replacement configuration, the local desktop resources would of course be required in order to support any applications that would remain running locally. Typically when sizing the hardware to support an ICA client, you would look at the minimum hardware requirements for the target operating system. For example, SuSE Linux has the following basic requirements:

- Intel Celeron or higher, including EMT64
- AMD K6 or higher, including Athlon 64
- Minimum 128MB of RAM for graphic mode installation
- Minimum 2GB of hard disk space

A machine meeting these requirements would be sufficient to support use of the MPS client.

If you're going to provide a full desktop-replacement scenario, the minimum hardware requirements in the preceding list would also apply for the MPS client. Table 5.8 provides a summary of the minimum hardware requirements for the supported Windows operating systems. These requirements would be sufficient when you wanted to implement a desktop-replacement scenario, since only the MPS client is running locally on the desktop. These are the same requirements listed back in Table 5.4 for the RDP client.

Table 5.8   Minimum Citrix MPS Client Hardware Requirements for a Desktop-Replacement Scenario

Client Operating System	Client Type	Minimum RAM	Minimum CPU
Windows XP, Windows 2000	32-bit (5.2)	64MB	Intel Pentium II or higher
ME, 98, and NT 4.0	32-bit (5.2)	32MB	Intel Pentium 133 or higher
Windows 95	32-bit (5.1)	32MB	Intel 486/66 or higher
Windows for Workgroups 3.11	16-bit (5.0)	8MB	Intel 386 or higher

As I mentioned earlier, maintaining a client operating system no longer supported by Microsoft could put you in a position where a known vulnerability existed that could affect one of these obsolete operating systems, potentially jeopardizing stability of the company's network infrastructure.

Microsoft no longer provides publicly released security patches for Windows ME, 98, or earlier versions. Because of this, I recommend that you implement Windows 2000 Professional as the minimum desktop operating system version. You need to determine if Windows 2000 will run on any existing hardware currently running an older Windows version. If the hardware will not support an operating system upgrade, you will need to consider upgrading or replacing the hardware with something that will.

Thin-Client Terminals

As with other traditional terminals (3270, VT220, and so on), the goal of the thin-client terminal, also commonly referred to as a Windows-based terminal (WBT), is to provide a fast, low-cost, and reliable way to access a Windows Terminal Server/MetaFrame environment. Thin clients have been around since the early days of Citrix WinFrame, and just as the server operating system has matured and grown in popularity, so has the thin-client device.

Thin clients fall into four main categories:

- **Windows CE devices**—These terminals run the Windows CE operating system and most often support both the ICA and RDP protocols.
- **Embedded Linux devices**—One category that has increased significantly in the last few years has been use of embedded Linux thin clients. These devices can also support both the ICA and RDP presentation protocols.
- **Proprietary OS devices**—Any non-CE or non-Linux device is usually considered to be a proprietary thin client. Most of the early thin-client manufacturers, such as Wyse, developed their products around these types of terminals and have now expanded their product lines to include both CE, Linux, and proprietary terminals. Proprietary devices are typically positioned at a lower price-point than CE or Linux devices and lack some of the advanced features such as integrated browser or support for alternative terminal connections such as 3270 or X Windows sessions.
- **Hybrid embedded operating system devices**—Some manufacturers such as Neoware provide thin clients containing embedded operating systems that run either on solid-state flash storage or standard hard drives. These terminals also allow limited installation of local applications and can be thought of as limited personal computers or network computer devices. Neoware provides a thin client running Windows XP embedded.

When the concept of a thin-client device for Terminal Server first came to fruition, a large number of thin-client manufacturers sprang onto the scene. Over time those vendors that provided truly robust devices (combined with a bit of luck and good marketing, I suspect) managed to survive, with other vendors either going out of business completely or being bought and assimilated into one of the surviving companies. Today, two big players in the thin-client market are Wyse and Neoware/NCD. Neoware and NCD work together, with NCD providing product distribution outside North America, while Neoware provides distribution inside North America only. Other vendors exist, and Web sites such as http://www.windowsfordevices.com provide general information on a variety of thin-client vendors available.

Determining whether you should use thin clients in your implementation, and if so what vendor to choose, can be a major undertaking in itself. Each vendor touts its product as the fastest and most robust thin-client solution, but you should evaluate at least three vendors' products to decide which product best suits your requirements. Never make your decision based solely on marketing information or even suggestions from your peers. You won't know for certain which terminal will meet your needs until you've had the opportunity to use one.

When evaluating thin-client terminals, look for the following features and capabilities:

- **Performance**—This is something that can vary greatly from one terminal to another. Screen updates, mouse and keyboard response, and printing in particular are all areas where a thin client may not meet the needs of the end user.
- **Centralized management**—For the terminal to be truly cost-effective, it must be manageable from a central location after it has been deployed to the user's desktop. Flash upgrades, asset tracking, or configuration changes should not require physical access to the unit. Multiple units should be configurable with a single command and shouldn't require management on a unit-by-unit basis. If you have 2,000 terminals deployed in your organization, you want to be able to deliver changes to all of them simultaneously instead of individually.
- **Administration security**—Coupled with centralized management should be security features to protect against unauthorized changes being made to the terminal units, either by the end user or by someone with access to the remote management software. At the least, an administrative password should be required to implement any changes.
- **RDP and ICA support**—Even if you require only RDP access today, it's a worthwhile investment to have a terminal that also includes ICA support or allows for a flash upgrade to add this support in the future, if necessary.
- **Support for advanced ICA features**—Beyond supporting standard ICA connections to a MetaFrame server, an ICA thin client must also support the load-balancing and published-application features of MetaFrame. An embedded operating system should also ideally support server farm access and Program Neighborhood, as well as other advanced features such as the PN Agent component.
- **Encryption support**—At one time this was a limitation of many devices, but all thin clients on the market today support strong encryption of the presentation

protocols. If you're looking to deploy legacy devices, be certain that they support higher than the minimum or basic encryption.

- **Point to Point Protocol (PPP) dial-up support**—Many companies have looked to thin clients as an alternative to providing employees with notebook computers simply for remote access from home. Many terminals now support PPP dial-up so users can connect directly into a company's network or dial up their local ISP and connect to a Terminal Server over the Internet. If you want to use terminals within your company, the ability to support PPP could provide further cost savings in areas such as telecommuting. Of course, for those home users who already have some form of high-speed access such as broadband or DSL, a dial-up solution is not a requirement.

- **Screen resolution and color depth**—One of the most common complaints about thin clients when they first came on the market was their relatively low screen resolution, color support, and refresh rates. Today, most terminals provide resolution and color capabilities that meet even the highest resolution and color depths supported by the ICA and RDP protocols.

- **Additional terminal or browser support**—In addition to ICA and RDP support, many terminals today also support additional terminal emulation modes such as 3270, VT100, X.11, Java, and Web browsing. The ability to use your terminal as a multiaccess device may be a valuable option, particularly if the business requires redundant access to certain critical business functions or you want to maintain certain applications, such as Web browsers, outside your Terminal Server environment. As you might expect, the cost of one of these multipurpose units is usually higher than the equivalent terminal without the support, so unless there's a business need to include these features, you could save money by omitting them.

NOTE: One market where thin clients have garnered a lot of attention is as a replacement to the mainframe dumb terminal sector (affectionately known as the "green screen"). This includes both true green-screen terminals and PCs used primarily as dumb terminal emulators. For many companies, the cost of switching from these terminals to a Windows environment is quite prohibitive, yet they are forced to make these changes simply to remain competitive. Thin clients are a cost-effective alternative to the PC as a dumb terminal replacement. The company can maintain the centralized manageability and reduced maintenance costs of dumb terminals and, at the same time, provide users access to the latest Windows software.

Such an environment could be built and tested without any impact to users. In fact, the multiple-terminal support of some thin clients might let you swap out your legacy terminals with thin clients that could continue to provide terminal support until the Terminal Server environment was ready to implement, at which time you could begin to use these terminals as true Windows thin clients.

CHAPTER 6

Terminal Server Hardware Planning

The Assessment Process

Two of the most common questions I receive from people interested in implementing Terminal Server are

- How many users can I expect to run on a single server?
- What are the server requirements in order to support x number of users (where x might be 20, 50, 100, 400, or more)?

Unfortunately, there's no easy answer to either question—for a number of reasons. Some of those reasons are the following:

- **Your server requirements will be influenced heavily by the applications you plan to implement**—Server requirements for running Microsoft Word by itself are very different from those required for concurrently running Word, Excel, SAPGui, and a custom-developed client/server application. Different applications stress a server in different ways. One application may have high memory requirements, for example, while another has high processor requirements.
- **Users with different skill levels and job functions utilize server resources in different ways**—For example, data entry workers typically introduce a smaller load on a server than a power user who's performing advanced Excel calculations.
- **Even users within the same job classification work within the Terminal Server environment in different ways**—One user may open all his or her applications immediately after logging on and then switch between them as necessary throughout the day. Another user may open and close the applications only as required.

So how do you go about sizing a Terminal Server environment? To properly size the hardware requirements for your implementation, you must take the time to work iteratively through a process of estimating and then fine-tuning to meet the expectations of the project. Don't expect to come up with a sizing solution simply by estimating user and memory requirements, performing some calculations, and then extrapolating the results. To properly size your environment, you need to develop a proposed sizing, perform some real-user testing with the applications against the estimated size, and from the results, determine what should be a reasonable expectation for the number of servers and users per server.

Figure 6.1 shows the process I typically follow when sizing requirements for an implementation. While the steps seem trivial, the actual work performed during each step varies, depending largely on the implementation requirements determined in Step 1.

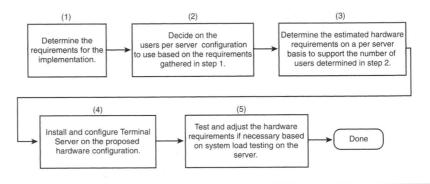

Figure 6.1   The server-sizing life cycle.

The remainder of this chapter focuses on working through the steps involved in the process illustrated in Figure 6.1.

Determining the Requirements

To properly size your Terminal Server environment, you first need to understand exactly what will be required and expected by both the users and the business. These requirements must be taken into consideration when making your sizing decisions. In general, there are four areas to consider when determining environmental requirements:

- User-capacity requirements
- Application requirements
- System availability
- Risk tolerance

The following sections describe in detail the considerations for each of these areas.

User-Capacity Requirements

There are two things to consider when looking at user-capacity requirements. The first is the maximum number of concurrent user sessions in the environment, as well as the total user base that will be receiving the ICA or RDP client. Accurate assessments of these numbers are important not only for sizing the necessary hardware but also for knowing how many user licenses will be required. Remember that Microsoft requires licensing for the total size of the user base, while Citrix requires licensing equal to only the total concurrent user count.

Once I have the total number of expected concurrent users, I typically add 10–15 percent to this estimate as a buffer. For example, say I'm sizing an environment that will need to support 400 concurrent user sessions in a desktop-replacement scenario, with a total client deployment of 600. So, even though I have 400 concurrent connections, theoretically there could be 600 if all users decide to connect at the same time. To the 400 concurrent user sessions, I add my 15 percent buffer to get a total of 460. The idea will be to size the environment to support 460 concurrent users.

TIP: Remember, at this point we're simply trying to determine the total user capacity; we're not interested quite yet in how many servers we will need to support the configuration.

If you will be publishing individual applications, you may need to calculate the total concurrent user distribution in your environment differently than you would when publishing a full desktop. Say, for example, you are planning to publish two applications (AppA and AppB) instead of a full desktop. Examining the applications individually, you then determine that the current sessions for each application are

- **AppA**—150 concurrent users
- **AppB**—450 concurrent users

Totaling both together you end up with 600 concurrent users, but this value can be deceiving. There are two factors that will directly influence the actual number of concurrent users in the environment:

- If, for some reason, the two applications will be completely segregated from one another on two different machines, you will have to size the two applications independently.

  AppA will need to be sized to support 150 concurrent users, while AppB will have to support 450 concurrent users. Each application should be treated as a separate deployment and the hardware sized independently by following the steps in Figure 6.1. Even if the same user will be accessing both applications, because the user will require a distinct *session* on each server, they will need to be treated separately.

■ If the two applications will be deployed on the same server, you will want to size the environment based on a true concurrent load of between 450 and 600 users.

If the users that run AppA are also all users that access AppB, your load will be 450 users. If, on the other hand, the user base is completely distinct for the two applications, you will have 600 concurrent users. More likely, you will have a mixture of some users who run both applications and some who run only one or the other.

TIP: When publishing multiple applications on multiple MetaFrame servers, the method by which a user is assigned to a server is not strictly based on the server with the lowest load level.

For example, say you deploy three servers in a Citrix server farm (ServerA, ServerB, ServerC), and all three servers are publishing both applications (AppA, AppB). Now, if a user is already connected to a server (ServerA) running AppA and attempts to launch the other published application (AppB), MetaFrame automatically directs the user to the same server (ServerA) on which the first application is already running. Because the user already has an active session that can run the desired application, MetaFrame does not waste resources establishing a session on another server to run this other application.

In addition to sizing the number of concurrent user sessions, you need to categorize the computing requirements of each user. Table 6.1 lists how users are typically divided, depending on whether it's an application-replacement or desktop-replacement scenario.

Table 6.1 Common Terminal Server User Types

User Type	Desktop Replacement	Application Replacement
Light user	Usually runs two or three applications—a line of business app plus host access or e-mail. Processing is typically light, and server downtime has little impact on the user's productivity. The published application is not usually directly related to the user's main job function.	Typically performs consistent and repetitive operations such as data entry or item lookup.

Table 6.1   Common Terminal Server User Types (continued)

User Type	Desktop Replacement	Application Replacement
Medium user	Runs between three and six applications, consisting of two or more client/server apps in addition to office or business productivity tools such as Microsoft Word or Microsoft Project.	Usually performs a specific task or job function as part of a business work flow. Overall processing requirements are higher than those of a light user, plus they're typically more dependent on availability of the environment. If the Terminal Server is down, users' jobs are affected. A call center or order desk employee typically fits into this category.
Heavy user	Runs more than six applications and utilizes advanced functionality such as charting, graphics, or numerical calculations.	When the published application is extremely process-intensive and/or memory-intensive, users are grouped into this category. Job productivity is severely affected if the Terminal Server is down.

Ideally you'd like to be able to determine the number of user sessions in each category that will make up the total concurrent user load, but rarely is this calculation easily achievable.

When publishing individual applications, I group all users into the medium-user category unless one or more of the applications in question is memory- and/or processor-intensive. If the implementation involves desktop replacement, I usually group it as 80 percent medium users and 20 percent heavy users.

Sometimes this approach yields an overestimate in the hardware requirements (although, surprisingly, not often), but any additional capacity resulting in such an overestimation is always available to provide failover support or room for short-term growth.

If you prefer to perform a more detailed breakdown of the user sessions, I suggest you look at the total user base instead of concurrent connections and establish a percentage of the users who fall into each category.

For example, I might have the following breakdown of my 600 total users for the desktop-replacement example:

- 25 light users (4 percent)
- 250 medium users (42 percent)
- 325 heavy users (54 percent)

Using these percentages, I can divide my 460 concurrent desktop-replacement users as follows:

- 18 light users (460 × 4 percent)
- 194 medium users (460 × 42 percent)
- 248 heavy users (460 × 54 percent)

We use these numbers when discussing the server sizing and users-per-server estimates in the next few sections of this chapter.

Application Requirements

Now that you have an estimate as to the number and types of users who will access your environment, the next step is to categorize the types of applications you'll be serving and whether they're 32-bit, 16-bit, or legacy DOS. It's particularly important to flag any 16-bit or DOS applications, because they introduce additional resource requirements (sometimes substantial). Chapter 7, "Server and Application Software Planning," talks in more detail about application considerations.

In general, all applications of the same type can be grouped together when you perform the sizing calculations, so calculations based on an application-by-application basis are usually unnecessary. What this means is that you can classify Word, PowerPoint, and Internet Explorer as 32-bit applications instead of looking at them individually.

Based on the information you gather, you should create a listing similar to the one shown in Table 6.2. Here I list each of the user categories and estimate how many instances of each application type would be running for a given user type. For example, a light user in my environment will typically run two 32-bit applications and one 16-bit application.

Table 6.2   Application Distribution Based on User Types

User Category	32-Bit Apps per User	16-Bit Apps per User	DOS Apps per User
Light users	2	1	0
Medium users	4	0	0
Heavy users	6	1	0

So at any given time, I could expect the following application distribution in my Terminal Server environment for all 18 of my "light users."

- 36 instances of a 32-bit application (18 × 2; 32-bit apps)
- 18 instances of a 16-bit application (18 × 1; 16-bit app)

Remember that these numbers represent my entire Terminal Server environment, not necessarily just a single server.

It's usually easier to simply base your estimates on medium or heavy users instead of dividing the applications into individual user categories. When doing this, you can usually base your calculations on the applications that would be run by the majority of the users or the applications run by your heavy users, whichever is greater. In my desktop-replacement example, I could assume that all 460 concurrent users were heavy users running six 32-bit applications and one 16-bit application. Multiplying 460×6 would give a total of 2,760 instances of a 32-bit application and 460×1 instances of a 16-bit application running in my Terminal Server environment.

System Availability

Another area of consideration very often completely overlooked during Terminal Server sizing is the business requirement for system availability. Does your environment need to be accessible 24×7 or only during local business hours? Expected time of availability for your Terminal Server environment will have a large bearing on your final sizing considerations. Be sure to provide sufficient capacity so you can take servers offline for maintenance or upgrade while minimizing impacts on system availability.

For my sizing example, I assume that my environment needs to be available 24×7, with a peak concurrent user load occurring between 8 a.m. and 6 p.m. Then from 6 p.m. to 8 a.m., the concurrent user load drops from 400 to 150. Using my 15 percent rule, I size this off-peak load at approximately 175. Table 6.3 summarizes this information.

Table 6.3 Estimated Concurrent Usage Based on System Availability Requirements

| | Concurrent User Load | |
Hours of Operation	Estimated	Plus 15% Overhead
8 a.m. to 6 p.m.	400	460
6 p.m. to 8 a.m.	150	175

I take this information into consideration during my system sizing and plan an environment in such a way that I can take certain servers offline after 6 p.m., while keeping others online to support the 175 concurrent-user load for the second shift.

NOTE: As you might expect, because the concurrent load is lower during off-peak hours, it is easier to accommodate taking one or more servers offline during this time than it would be if the load was consistent (400) during all hours.

Risk Tolerance

The final area of consideration is the level of risk tolerance your business has for downtime. While you would ideally never have a Terminal Server go down, the reality is you'll have an unexpected server failure at some point. Your goal in designing and implementing your environment is to minimize these outages and their impact on users.

Your company's level of risk tolerance will have the most significant bearing on your final decision as to the number of users you'll have per server. The reason is actually quite simple: The more users you have running on a single Terminal Server, the more users affected if the server goes down. The amount of risk tolerance is often dependent on the types of applications that will run in the Terminal Server environment and how critical they are to the business. A mission-critical application will likely have a much lower tolerance level than office productivity tools such as word processing or mail readers.

NOTE: Of course, some organizations consider office productivity applications such as e-mail to be mission critical, so be certain you have a clear understanding of what the business *must* have available in order to continue working, even if productivity is somewhat impaired by an outage.

Given the choice, most organizations would like to minimize risk as much as possible, but realistically the costs of doing this can make it impractical. A compromise must be reached between risk and cost when determining the user-per-server ratio.

The easiest way to do this is to provide a simple table containing different percentages of the total concurrent user count (not including the 10–15 percent overhead) and solicit feedback from the business (whenever possible) as to how many users can acceptably be affected by a server outage. Ideally you (or your supervisor) will discuss this with a representative from the different departments to be affected by the implementation.

Table 6.4 gives an example based on my sample environment of 400 concurrent users. The table contains calculations ranging from 5 percent to 60 percent, representing the percentage of concurrent users on each server. I omit 0 simply because it's impossible to have an outage without affecting at least some users. I also do not go higher than 55 percent (220) in this example due to a limitation in the page pool size in Windows 2000, which limits maximum size of the registry, which in turn limits the number of concurrent users on a server. In practice, the upper limit on concurrent connections per Terminal Server (Windows 2000 Server only) is around 200. This limit does *not* exist with a Windows 2003 Terminal Server.

Table 6.4 An Example of Users per Server Percentage Breakdown for 400 Total Concurrent Users

5%	10%	15%	25%	50%	55%
20	40	60	100	200	220

NOTE: Details on this registry limitation are discussed in Chapter 11, "Terminal Services Configuration and Tuning."

From the table select two numbers representing the business's acceptable and maximum risk-tolerance factors. For example, say that out of the 400 concurrent users, your business would be most comfortable having only 60 users affected by a server outage but could tolerate an impact of up to 100 users before it would have a significant affect on the business. Taking these values and adding the 10–15 percent overhead, you have the target range for determining the number of users per server. This is not necessarily the maximum capacity the servers will support, but it is the range you'll initially size for.

In my example, adding the 15 percent overhead would get a user count between 70 and 115. I record these numbers as U_L (for lower users per server) and U_H (higher users per server). This range is used along with the other information gathered during the requirements phase to develop a plan for the hardware requirements of the Terminal Server environment.

NOTE: Of course, the estimated number of users per server is by no means final. It's likely that you'll make at least some minor adjustments once you've decided on the hardware for your environment and have had the opportunity to perform some actual load testing.

Hardware Sizing

Now that you have an estimate of the number of concurrent users per server, the next step is to determine the hardware requirements that will support this environment. It's important to remember that this information should be used as a guideline in developing your hardware configuration but shouldn't be treated as the final word on the subject. The only way to ensure that the calculated estimates meet your requirements is to perform some load testing once you have Terminal Server installed on the proposed hardware.

Having said that, I want to make it clear that it is certainly to your benefit to try and determine as accurately as possible a server configuration that meets your expectations since in most cases, once the hardware has arrived, it is rarely returned for something different.

NOTE: I highly recommend that you consult the Microsoft Windows Server Catalog, formally known as the Hardware Compatibility List (HCL), prior to selecting any type of hardware if you are unsure as to its support of the target operating system (Windows Server 2003 or Windows 2000 Server). You don't want to have to worry about the server hardware causing unexpected stability or performance issues. You can find this information on the Microsoft Web site at http://www.microsoft.com/whdc/hcl/default.mspx.

Processors

One of the most important factors when looking at your Terminal Server's processor configuration is deciding on the *number of processors* that each server will have, not their maximum clock speed. While Microsoft describes a single-processor server as the minimum configuration for a Terminal Server, I recommend that you never plan to implement a single-processor server in a production environment, except possibly in the smallest of environments.

Using the data from Table 6.5, which summarizes the average number of users supported per processor, you can estimate the average processor requirements for each of your servers based on your user types. The Pentium 4 has been included in this table as a reference only. Intel does not provide support for a multiprocessor Pentium 4 configuration. Instead, the equivalent Pentium 4 multiprocessor support is delivered through the Intel Xeon processor family.

Table 6.5   Average Supported Users per Processor

Processor Type	Light Users	Medium Users	Heavy Users
Intel Pentium III Xeon 1 GHz	70	53	29
Intel Pentium 4.2 GHz	113	86	47
Intel Xeon 3 GHz	142	108	59

NOTE: The benchmark for processor performance is always being raised as manufacturers continue to deliver faster and more powerful processors. Coupled with this fact are additional processor options such as increased cache size, bus speed, and other performance-enhancing features; for example, hyper-threading technology. The users-per-processor estimates in Table 6.5 should be treated as nothing more than a starting point for estimating the size of your servers. During the load-testing phase, you can establish a more realistic users-per-processor ratio specific to your environment. I usually don't take the clock speed of the processor into consideration unless it's a change of at least 25 percent. When this is the case, I usually adjust the users-per-processor estimate by about half the percentage change in processors. So a 25 percent increase in clock speed would translate into a 10–15 percent increase in concurrent user support.

Realistically, when recommending what type of processor to use, I typically say the current low- or mid-level processor. For example, a hardware manufacture may offer four processor types, as follows:

- Intel Xeon 2.8GHz with 1MB cache and 800MHz front-side bus
- Intel Xeon 3.06GHz with 1MB cache and 800MHz front-side bus

- Intel Xeon 3.2GHz with 1MB cache and 800MHz front-side bus
- Intel Xeon 3.4GHz with 1MB cache and 800MHz front-side bus

The performance increase from the lowest process to the highest is only about 20 percent, but the additional cost can be upwards of $800 or more. In this situation, I would go with the low-end process and use the cost savings toward additional memory for the server. Memory requirements are discussed in the "Memory" section of this Chapter.

Now let's look at a couple of examples of how you could use the data from Table 6.5 to estimate the processor requirements for your server. Returning to our earlier example of 460 concurrent users, we have the proposed lower and upper estimates for the number of users per server at 70 and 115, respectively. Using the data from Table 6.5 and assuming that all users are classified as heavy users, we could calculate the number of processors per server as shown in Table 6.6.

Table 6.6   Estimated Number of Required Processors Required to Support the Concurrent User Load per Server

Processor	Calculation	Notes
Pentium III	70 divided by 29 heavy users = 2.414 = 2 CPUs 115 divided by 29 heavy users = 3.966 = 4 CPUs	When the result is not a factor of 2, I round the number to the nearest power of 2 unless it's a single processor, in which case I round it to 2.
Xeon	70 divided by 59 heavy users = 1.19 = 2 CPUs 115 divided by 59 heavy users = 1.95 = 2 CPUs	This is rounded to 2 because I will not run single-processor Terminal Servers.

Based on these processor calculations, the adjusted users-per-server estimate would now be as shown in Table 6.7.

Table 6.7   Adjusted Users-Per-Server Estimate Based on Type and Number of Processors

Processor Type	Original Estimate	New Estimate
Intel Pentium III Xeon 1 GHz	70 (dual processor)	$2 \times 29 = 58$
	115 (quad processor)	$4 \times 29 = 116$
Intel Xeon 3 GHz	70 (dual processor)	$2 \times 59 = 118$
	115 (dual processor)	$2 \times 59 = 118$

There are a couple of things to note in Table 6.7. First, I assumed that if one processor will support 29 users, two processors will support twice as many (58 users). This assumption is not strictly true, as increasing the number of CPUs in a server does not equate to a truly linear increase in performance. One reason that I assume a linear increase to be valid is that my estimates are based on the assumption that these users are continuously working, which in most environments is not strictly true. A fair percentage of users are either idle or introducing only minimal load on the server at any one time, so based on how my calculations average out, I've found that these estimates remain fairly close to the acceptable sizing values for a server.

Secondly, don't be alarmed by the fact that the users-per-server estimate for the Pentium III has dropped off from 70 to 58 to accommodate the new processor estimate. Remember, these numbers will be used only to size the server you'll use to perform load testing. It's not necessarily the final configuration that you're going to implement. Only after completing testing can you determine the final users-per-server total and from there decide on the actual number of servers to make up the environment.

The third thing you will notice is that the actual supported number of users on a dual Xeon 3GHz is well above the original estimate of 70 users. In this configuration a dual processor configuration supports either setup, so there is no reason to even consider a quad-processor system.

We return to these numbers in the "Determining the Number of Required Servers" section of this chapter, where the number of servers required to meet our implementation needs will be discussed.

NOTE: In most situations I don't believe there should ever be a need to deploy quad-processor Terminal Servers. While the configuration is certainly impressive from a technical standpoint, a pair of dual-processor servers will accommodate the load just as well and provide the server redundancy that a single-quad processor machine will not.

While arguments against the additional licensing costs for a second server have merit purely from a budgeting standpoint, I believe these additional licensing costs can easily be offset by the reduced cost of dual-processor hardware and the load distribution provided by a multiple-server configuration.

Memory

No matter how many processors you have or how fast they are, without sufficient memory your server cannot adequately service the needs of multiple simultaneous Terminal Server users. The most common cause of a Terminal Server failure is inadequate memory to support the number of concurrent users on the system.

There are three areas to consider when calculating the amount of physical RAM required on the server:

- **Operating system requirements**—The operating system requires a certain amount of memory in order to function. I recommend the following based on the Terminal Server version:
  Windows 2000 Terminal Services   150MB
  Windows Server 2003 Terminal Services   200MB
- **Per-user requirements**—A certain amount of RAM is required to support each user's session on a Terminal Server. In general, there are two ways to approach estimating the RAM requirements for each server. The first method is to look at the individual requirements based on the type of users running in the environment. Usually you can allocate memory as follows:
  Light user   15MB
  Medium user   20MB
  Heavy user   30MB

  These requirements may seem high in comparison to some recommendations from other sources, but I've always found that providing a slightly higher estimate on memory requirements helps to ensure that the server functions as robustly as possible. Using these numbers, you can then calculate the user RAM requirements for your implementation. As with the processor calculations, you can either calculate memory requirements based on the percentage breakdown of the different user types that will be accessing the server or simply base the calculations on the assumption that all users are either medium or heavy users. You then multiply the number of users per server by the allocated memory requirements: 20MB for medium users and 30MB for heavy users. This can result in an overestimate of the memory requirements for the server, but typically this results in a slightly higher users-per-server ratio than you originally anticipated.
- **Additional application memory requirements**—I've found that if users will be running *three to four* or fewer applications, memory sizing based on the per-user requirements listed in the preceding point of this list is sufficient without augmenting the memory totals. If users will run more than three or four applications, you'll need to perform additional calculations to take into consideration the memory requirements of those applications beyond three or four. Memory calculations for the different application types are summarized as follows:
  - **DOS apps**—2MB RAM per DOS application.

■ **16-bit apps**—4MB RAM per Windows on Win32 (WOW32) session plus 2MB for each additional 16-bit application running within the same WOW32 subsystem session.

■ **32-bit apps**—4MB–10MB RAM per application on average is usually fair for most Windows applications, although special care must be taken when estimating the size of database-driven client/server applications. These types of applications are notorious for consuming large amounts of RAM, particularly if they are left running for an extended period of time. Don't be surprised if you encounter such application consuming 50MB or more of RAM. A more realistic estimate of the memory requirements of an application can be gained by examining the application's behavior when running in a test Terminal Server environment or even when running on a regular Windows 2000 or Windows XP workstation computer. Figure 6.2 shows an example of Windows Task Manager running on a Windows 2000 Terminal Server, listing all running processes by memory used. The highest memory-consuming server in this example is a SQL Server–based client/server application.

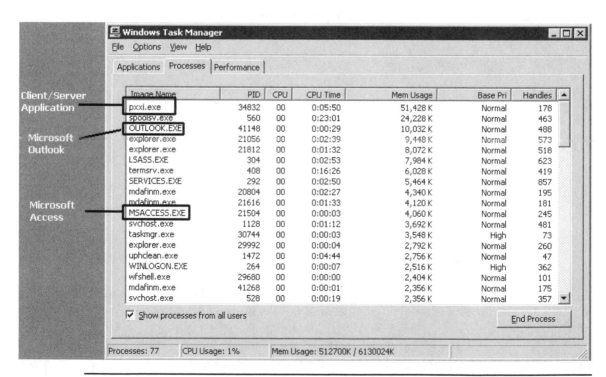

Figure 6.2   Memory-consumption example on a Windows 2000 Terminal Server.

Using my adjusted users-per-server estimate from the "Processors" section, I would calculate my environment's memory requirements as follows:

1. First I get the amount of RAM required for my operating system. I'll be implementing Windows Server 2003 Terminal Services, so I need approximately 200MB of RAM for the server.

2. Next I calculate the per-user memory requirements. For completeness, I calculate for both the processor types described previously. First I assume that all users are heavy users, so on a server with 58 user sessions, I would calculate this total RAM requirement:

     58 users × 30MB/user = 1740MB

   And for my 70 user sessions I would have this amount:

     70 users × 30MB/user = 2100MB

   Now, if I break down the user totals into the percentage of user types (4 percent light, 42 percent medium, and 54 percent heavy), my calculations for the 58 users per server would be as follows:

     (58 × 4 percent × 15MB) + (58 × 42 percent × 20MB) + (58 × 54 percent × 30MB)

     = 34.8MB + 487.2MB + 939.6MB

     = 1461.6MB – 1.5GB

   So using the more detailed calculation, you can see that I am still within a couple of hundred MB of the RAM estimate based on all heavy users on the system.

3. Now I calculate the additional RAM required to support the additional applications in the environment. If I assume that all users are heavy users, I calculate the requirements for all of them to run two additional 32-bit applications. Remember, I'm assuming that three to four 32-bit applications are already included in the base-size estimate for the per-user memory requirement. There is also the memory requirement of the one additional 16-bit application. I'll assume 8MB as the estimate for memory requirements in this situation for 32-bit applications.

   The application memory requirements for 58 users per server would be as follows:

     (58 × 2 × 8MB) + (58 × 1 × 4MB)

     = 928MB + 232MB

     = 1160MB

   And for 70 users per server:

     (70 × 2 × 8MB) + (70 × 1 × 4MB)

     = 1120MB + 280MB

     = 1400MB

4. Now all that's left is to total the memory requirements for each Terminal Server. For my 58 users-per-server example, I get the following total:

   Server RAM + Per-user RAM + Application RAM

     = 200MB + 1740MB + 1160MB

     = 3100MB

     = 3GB

   From this I can estimate that I would need around 3GB of memory per server in order to support 58 heavy users concurrently accessing six 32-bit applications and one 16-bit application.

For my 70 users-per-server example, I would have this total:
200MB + 2100MB + 1120MB
= 3420MB
= 3.5 to 4GB

Therefore, I can estimate that I need approximately 3.5 to 4GB of memory per server in order to support 70 concurrent heavy users accessing the same six 32-bit and one 16-bit applications.

Disk Subsystem

Your decision on which disk subsystem to use for your servers is based on a standard recommendation instead of a calculated per-user value. In a properly sized environment, you should encounter no bottlenecks (beyond the standard disk limitations) as a result of high disk utilization. It's much more likely that you'll first become memory- or CPU-bound.

The following issues should be considered when deciding on your disk configuration:

- Always use SCSI disk drives in conjunction with SCSI or RAID controllers.
- Divide your disk requirements into three areas: operating system, pagefile, and application files. When possible, configure your environment to service the operating system and pagefile with one controller and the application files with the other. If you want to provide disk redundancy in your environment, place the OS and pagefile onto a set of mirrored (RAID 1) drives and not within a RAID 5 configuration. The application files can be run from a RAID 5 configuration, although RAID 1 is usually sufficient, particularly if a hot spare configuration is supported.

NOTE: My preference is not to introduce RAID 5 unless the environment is configured in such a way that a server cannot be offline for an extended period of time (server uptime must be maximized). Because there's no permanent user data being stored on the Terminal Server, a high level of redundancy isn't necessarily required on the server. If a server happened to lose both disks in a mirror configuration, the server could be recoverable fairly quickly based on a standard server cloning and build process (see Chapter 22, "Server Operations and Support," for a discussion of server imaging). In most situations, having a small stock of spare drives on hand or configured as hot spares provides the necessary redundancy at the disk level for your server.

Network Interface Cards

Chapter 4, "Network Planning," talks about the requirements for planning a network configuration that supports your Terminal Server implementation, and the overall importance of network performance and availability in your Terminal Server environment. If network connectivity is unavailable, all the processing power in the world won't help your users. When deciding on the network interface card to use in your server, take the following into consideration:

- Select a card from a well-known and supported manufacturer. The de facto standard in many Terminal Server implementations is the Intel 8255*x* family of Fast Ethernet or 8254*x* family of Gigabit Ethernet controllers, or an equivalent from the server hardware vendor (such as the Broadcom NetXtreme Gigabit Ethernet controller supplied with many Dell PowerEdge servers).
- Choose an adapter that has current drivers for your OS and supports advanced features such as adapter fault tolerance (AFT) or hot swapping to increase server uptime and network availability.

NOTE: Because of the relatively low cost of network adapters, I usually recommend that dual NIC cards be implemented with some form of teaming or fault tolerance to improve availability. When you want to implement card teaming, always use well-known and supported hardware such as Intel or HP's Compaq. Poor hardware or outdated driver support can cause stability issues with NIC teaming.

Server Hardware Versus Workstation Hardware

Today, with the availability of high-performance and multiple processors in workstation computers, the performance gap between them and the server in many cases is practically nonexistent. The only difference between many high-end workstations and low-end servers is usually disk drive capacity (workstations may support only dual internal SCSI drives), onboard RAID support, hot-swappable components (power supplies or disk drives), and rack-mount support.

In many Terminal Server configurations, the workstation computer fits the role of a small to medium server, with a lower cost per user than true server hardware. The main limitations that exist in many workstations are their limited support for multiple processors (usually two) and RAM (2–4GB).

The workstation hardware is a viable option because, in most Terminal Server implementations, the servers contain no user data. Couple this with a plan for redundancy at the server level, and there's no longer the requirement for system redundancy such as RAID arrays or swappable power supplies. Of course, some features such as dual NIC cards are still available, although the fault tolerance in the environment is handled by the presence of multiple redundant Terminal Servers. If you lose a Terminal Server, no problem—there are still *x* number of other Terminal Servers in the environment that users can log on to.

NOTE: In situations where server uptime must be maximized, server-class hardware may be the only option to minimize downtime due to hardware failure. This simply means the introduction of hardware redundancy features, not necessarily an increase in the number of processors, RAM, or other components.

Load Testing

After gathering and analyzing your requirements and developing a sizing estimate for your server hardware, the next step is to perform some baseline testing on this configuration with your applications to determine what adjustments need to be made in order to best satisfy the requirements of your implementation. For example, you may determine that one of the applications you plan to deploy is very processor-intensive, forcing you to decrease the anticipated user load per server or increase the processing power of each server. This is the type of thing you want to know before you buy all the hardware for your implementation.

NOTE: Depending on whether you're introducing new applications or migrating them from the local desktop, you may already have a good idea as to the behavior of the applications and their typical memory and CPU resource requirements. You should still test these in a Terminal Server environment before committing to one hardware configuration or another.

Many big-name hardware vendors will be happy to provide you with an evaluation machine configured to your specifications for a limited demo or trial period, particularly if you make it clear that you also will be trying a competitor's configuration.

Plan to test your proposed hardware configuration as early in the project as possible and have this configuration finalized prior to the beginning of the proper server build and user testing. If you leave this testing until after you've started the user testing and piloting, the chances of your actually being able to switch to an alternate server configuration are pretty slim. What will likely happen is that you will be forced to deploy the hardware configuration you wanted to test, leaving you to hope it is sized close enough to the needs of the business that changes will not be necessary.

Typically, two types of server load testing are available. The first involves testing with a small set of test users. The second involves performing some automated testing to develop results based on high user-connectivity scenarios.

User and Application Testing

The first phase occurs after you have installed the base operating system (Terminal Server and MetaFrame) and a core set of applications that represent the majority of the usage in your environment. Don't spend too much time tweaking and tuning the system, since you're looking for only a reasonable expectation of how the hardware and software will perform. Get a few users (possibly only the members of your project, at this point) to log on to the system in a controlled fashion while monitoring some standard performance counters (see Table 6.8 for a list of some standard counters to monitor). During this testing, you will be monitoring the servers looking for unexpected changes in such things as memory or processor utilization.

Plan to monitor the system with one user, then two, then four, and try to estimate how you think the system should react to the increase in users. What you're looking for is some indication that the user sessions and their application usage will scale in a reasonably linear fashion. For example, moving from two users to four users should double (or less than double) the resources currently in use in the environment. This will help to validate that you've sized your servers correctly. A drastic change in resource consumption with a small change in user load could indicate a poorly behaved application or some other issue that may force you to adjust your server requirements or dedicate more time to adjusting and tuning the offending application.

NOTE: You may have noticed that I've omitted any network counters from Table 6.8. While issues with your network may severely hamper your users' computing experience on the Terminal Server, there's little in the way of server configuration you can do to correct this problem. As I mentioned in the "Network Interface Card" section, I recommend going with a network card–teaming strategy to introduce redundancy in the network cards and also provide a small performance improvement. If there are issues with your network, they need to be addressed separately. See Chapter 4 for a discussion of this topic. I have yet to see a server sized in such a way that it encounters a network utilization bottleneck prior to developing a system bottleneck in another area such as memory.

Table 6.8   Sample Performance Monitor Counters to Capture During Load Testing

Object	Counter	Comments
Processor	% Processor Time Instance = _Total	Monitors the total percentage of processor usage for all processors combined. A sustained usage of 85% or higher indicates that the server is either underpowered or possibly low on memory (if the percent of pagefile usage is also high).

Table 6.8 Sample Performance Monitor Counters to Capture During Load Testing (continued)

Object	Counter	Comments
System	Processor Queue Length	Measures the number of threads currently waiting in the processor queue for execution time. All processors on a server share a single processor queue. A sustained queue length of 15 or greater usually indicates that the server is operating at its user capacity.
Memory	Available KBytes	Represents the total amount of virtual memory (VM) that's currently available for use. A continuous decline in available kilobytes may indicate an application that's leaking memory and will eventually lead to exhausted memory resources. The virtual memory manager attempts to maintain a minimum amount of available physical memory for use (around 4MB), so as consumption of available bytes increases, the VM tries to swap more information to the pagefile. A sustained availability of less than 5MB (5, 242,880 bytes) indicates that all physical memory is in use, and pagefile usage will increase.
		Depending on the amount of memory in your server, you may want to select Available MBytes instead.
	% Committed Bytes in use	Represents the ratio of committed memory to the total available memory of the system (physical and pagefile). When this percentage is over 90 percent, the system is getting dangerously close to exhausting all available memory.
	Pages Input/sec	Monitors the number of pages read from the pagefile that weren't already in memory when referenced. When this counter rises above 65 pages per second, the system is performing too much paging and a continued increase will almost certainly result in a system crash. A steady increase in this counter is an indication that you have insufficient memory in the server to handle the current user load. it may also indicate an application is running that's leaking memory.
Paging File	% Usage Instance = _Total	Measures the percentage of the page file currently in use with information paged from physical memory. A steady increase in the percentage used indicates that the server has insufficient physical memory available to service the current user load. A usage above 85 percent usually indicates that the server will run out of virtual memory. You must increase the virtual memory, the physical memory, or both.

Table 6.8 Sample Performance Monitor Counters to Capture During Load Testing (continued)

Object	Counter	Comments
Physical Disk	Current Disk Queue Length Instance = _Total	This counter includes both waiting requests and requests being serviced by the disk at the time of the data capture. To calculate the number of requests currently outstanding, subtract the current queue length from the number of spindles on the disk. Multi-spindle drives service multiple requests simultaneously. A queue length consistently over 2 usually indicates a disk subsystem bottleneck.
	% Disk Time Instance = _Total	Indicates the percentage of time the disk is busy servicing read and write requests. An average percentage that's consistently in the 70–80 percent range is a good indication of a disk performance problem. Don't take % Disk Time as the only factor, however, since it's possible that a long queue may be developing while the percentage of disk time remains below the maximum.

Figure 6.3 shows an example of Performance Monitor running with the listed counters on a test Windows 2000 Terminal Server.

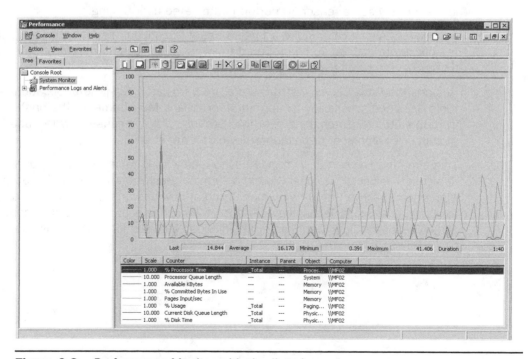

Figure 6.3 Performance Monitor with the listed counters.

Automated Server Load Testing

After performing initial testing with a small set of users, you may also want to develop some rough estimates on how you should expect the server to behave in a situation with an increased user load. One way to do this is to perform some automated server load testing, using a load-testing tool.

Two tools are available to help you do this. The first is the Capacity Planning Tool provided as part of the Windows 2000 Server Resource Kit, or as a link from within the Microsoft document "Windows 2000 Terminal Services Capacity and Scaling." This document includes some detailed information on capacity and scaling tests performed using this tool.

Citrix also provides a tool called the Citrix Server Test Kit (CSTK), free from the Citrix Developer's Network (CDN). The CDN can be accessed from the Developers link on the main Citrix Web site or directly at http://apps.citrix.com/cdn. Citrix includes documentation on how to configure and use this tool, along with sample scripts for use with Microsoft Office products.

Automated testing is usually done simply to validate that the server sizing is in the ballpark with regard to the system requirements and to get an idea as to how the server will behave under heavy user loads. Of course, automated testing can never fully replicate the behavior of real users.

NOTE: Unless you have concerns about the results of your configuration after the initial user testing, or you want some additional validation based on very large user loads, I rarely see a reason to perform automated user testing.

Automated testing can require a large amount of configuration in order to generate truly accurate results, so be prepared to invest a significant amount of time in order to acquire the results you're interested in.

Besides the Citrix Server Test Kit, there are third-party load- and application-testing tools designed specifically for Terminal Server and MetaFrame. In the past, such tools were ill suited for automating user load testing, either because they ran poorly in the multiuser environment or because they didn't run at all.

This situation has certainly changed. Now load-testing tools exist that have been designed specifically for operating in a Terminal Server environment. For example, Mercury Interactive (http://www.mercury.com) now has a product called LoadRunner for Citrix, and Scapa Technologies (http://www.scapatech.com) has its Scapa StressTester for Citrix MetaFrame. Downloadable evaluation software is available from both companies.

Determining the Number of Required Servers

Once all the sizing and load testing are finally complete, you should be able to comfortably predict the number of users a server in your environment will be able to support and, hence, determine the number of servers required in your environment.

To perform the calculations, you'll need the total number of concurrent user sessions including the 10–15 percent overhead, in addition to your estimated number of users per server.

If S is the number of servers, U_c is the number of concurrent users, and U_s is the number of users per server, the calculation is simply this:

$$S = U_c/U_s$$

We now take one last look at my example and the estimated number of users per server. Let's assume I'm interested in deploying only dual-processor servers and, after performing my load testing, I determine that the dual-processor configurations for the two types of servers actually can support more users than I originally anticipated. The actual supported loads are as follows:

- Dual Intel Pentium III Xeon: 78 concurrent users supported instead of the expected 58.
- Intel Xeon 3 GHz: 129 current users supported instead of the expected 118.

Based on these values, the number of servers I would need to support this number of users per server with a total of 460 concurrent users would be the following for a P3 processor:

$$S_{P3} = 460/78$$
$$= 5.90$$

This value I would round up to 6 (six) for the Pentium III configuration.

On a Xeon processor, the number of servers needed would be calculated as follows:

$$S_{Xeon} = 460/129$$
$$= 3.57$$

This value would be rounded up to 4 (four) servers for the Xeon configuration.

So it would seem that I would need six Pentium III or four Xeon-based servers in order to support the totally concurrent load of 460 users. But we're not quite finished. These calculations represent the number of servers required when all are operating at 100 percent and don't take into consideration the requirements for system availability in my environment. If for some reason there's a server failure, the environment won't have sufficient capacity to allow those users who were kicked off the failed server to log back on to the environment. To ensure environment availability, I should augment the calculated number of servers by approximately 25 percent.

So increasing my server count of six by 25 percent, I would end up increasing the number of servers to 8 in total, resulting in a reduced average number of users per server from 78 to around 57 but having sufficient capacity to be able to lose 2 servers and still support the entire concurrent user load.

Increasing the Xeon server count by 25 percent would increase it from 4 to 5 and reduce the average number of users from 129 per server to around 92.

NOTE: Don't be fooled by the assumption that fewer servers will directly result in reduced administration requirements. In a properly configured environment, the additional overhead required to support 10 servers versus 5 is very small, particularly when also implementing MetaFrame and leveraging the centralized management tools it provides. The increased availability of the 10-server configuration usually results in greater administrative flexibility, allowing you more time to troubleshoot or perform maintenance on a server without affecting the user community.

One final thing to note is how many servers are available for maintenance during peak and off-peak hours (refer to the "System Availability" section). In my example, even during peak hours, one to two servers could be offline without affecting the environment. During off-peak hours, when my concurrent user load drops to only 175 users, I can take more than half the available production servers offline.

Other Infrastructure Hardware Planning

In addition to assessing and planning for the Terminal Server hardware in your environment, there are a number of other servers that will be required in order to deliver the full set of services necessary for your Terminal Server implementation. I finish this chapter by taking a brief look at these servers, the services they provide, and what category of hardware would typically be required.

Terminal Server Licensing Server

The licensing requirements for Microsoft Terminal Server were discussed briefly in Chapter 1, "Microsoft Windows Terminal Services." When deploying Terminal Servers with or without Citrix MetaFrame, you will need a server upon which to run the Terminal Services Licensing service. Where exactly this service runs will depend on a couple of factors, which are summarized in Table 6.9.

The Windows Terminal Services Licensing service requires only minimal server resources and introduces no noticeable load increase on the server on which it is installed. The disk space requirements are only about 1KB for each assigned Terminal Services client access license (TSCAL).

One location where I *don't* recommend installing the Terminal Services Licensing service is on a Terminal Server. This is not so much because of the additional load it can introduce on the Terminal Server as it is because this would then create a dependency on that Terminal Server being available. When deploying Terminal Server, I always recommend trying to keep all data off the Terminal Server so scheduled backups of the server are not required. If the server is lost due to a failure, you do not want to have to worry about restoring data that may have existed on the server.

Table 6.9 Terminal Services Licensing Service Location

Windows Version	Without MetaFrame	With MetaFrame
Windows 2000	On a domain controller in a Windows 2000 Active Directory domain.	On a domain controller in a Windows 2000 Active Directory domain.
	On any member server in a work group or NT4 domain.	On the same member server as the MetaFrame Access Suite Licensing server in a workgroup or NT4 domain.
Windows 2003	On a domain controller in a Windows 2003 Active Directory domain.	On a member server in a workgroup or NT4 domain.
	On a member server in a Windows 2000 Active Directory domain. On the same member server as the MetaFrame Access Suite Licensing server in a workgroup or NT4 domain.	On the same member server as the MetaFrame Access Suite Licensing server in a Windows 2003 or 2000 Active Directory domain.

NOTE: From Table 6.9 you can see that when deploying MetaFrame I prefer to group the Windows Terminal Services Licensing service on the same server as MetaFrame Access Suite Licensing (MASL). My only exception to this is when Terminal Server licensing is running on a domain controller. I personally don't recommend running MASL on a domain controller, mainly due to the need to run IIS on the server in order to use the Web-based management tools. I discuss the MASL hardware requirements in the next section of this chapter.

Citrix MetaFrame Access Suite Licensing Server

MetaFrame Access Suite Licensing (MASL), discussed in Chapter 2, "Citrix MetaFrame Presentation Server," has completely different requirements from licensing for earlier versions of MetaFrame. MASL requires the following minimum software and hardware requirements:

- **Windows 2000 Server**—Regular server as well as Advanced or Datacenter server. All require Service Pack 3 or higher.
  OR
  Windows 2003 Server—Standard, Enterprise, or Datacenter Edition.
- **IIS 5.0 or higher**—This must be installed on the server before installing MASL and is required in order to run the License Management Console, an optional Web interface that allows access to some reporting features not available through a command line interface.
- **Intel Pentium III, 1GHz with 512MB RAM**—This is Citrix's recommendation and is more than adequate in most situations to support both the Citrix and the Microsoft licensing components.

Requirements for the licensing server are straightforward, and a standard configuration for a Microsoft file server will be more than sufficient to support both the Microsoft TSCAL service and Citrix's MetaFrame license server.

My recommendation when implementing Citrix MetaFrame Presentation Server is to install MASL onto either a dedicated server used solely to run Terminal Server and MetaFrame licensing or an existing file and print server running IIS. MASL will not impose a significant load unless you are implementing a large environment, in which case you will want to almost always use a dedicated licensing server. Microsoft Terminal Services Licensing and MASL should reside on the same server unless you are operating in a Windows 2000 domain and so Terminal Services Licensing must reside on a domain controller. In this case MASL should go onto a member server in the domain and reside separately from Terminal Services Licensing. I do *not* recommend running IIS on a domain controller.

TIP: Currently the MASL service is only a single-threaded application, which means that on a multi-processor computer, Citrix licensing will not be able to take advantage of the additional processor power. The application will run entirely off one CPU or the other but not simultaneously off both.

User Profile and Home Drive Server

An important part of a Terminal Server implementation is the file server upon which the user profiles and home folders will be stored. Whether these tasks will be managed by the same server or divided between multiple servers, the file server should have sufficient capacity to accommodate simultaneous connections equal to the total concurrent user load in your Terminal Server environment. Each Terminal Server user will connect to this server to retrieve their user profile and access their home folder. For example, if your environment has 450 concurrent users, the file server should be able to accommodate this without degraded performance. The main resources required for this are memory and disk access. A file server caches frequently accessed files in memory, so having sufficient physical memory in the server will ensure the system cache size is maximized. Both Windows 2000 Server and Windows Server 2003 have a maximum virtual cache size of 960MB on an Intel 32-bit processor server. This limitation is due to the 32-bit addressing space and not a coded limit imposed by Microsoft. The Microsoft support article "About Cache Manager in Windows Server 2003" (http://support.microsoft.com/default.aspx?scid=kb;en-us;837331) provides a summary of the cache manager and applies to both Windows 2000 Server and Windows Server 2003. A fast disk subsystem will also help speed up disk read and write operations, the relatively most expensive operation performed by the file server.

Specific details on sizing and deploying a file server are outside the scope of this book, but more information on this can be found on the Microsoft Web site. Information on tuning a Windows 2003 Server, including tuning for the file server role, can be found at the following URL: http://www.microsoft.com/windowsserver2003/evaluation/performance/tuning.mspx

CHAPTER 7

Server and Application Software Planning

Software Planning Overview

A final task to complete before beginning the actual process of planning your server installation and post-implementation management is selecting and categorizing all the software you plan to deploy on the Terminal Servers. This includes not only the applications you want to deliver to your users but also any server support software you'll use to manage the environment.

After developing the two application lists, you need to prioritize the order in which the applications will be installed. I usually arrange applications for installation as follows:

1. **Common application components**—These usually consist of low-level middleware components such as ODBC drivers or SQL drivers (Sybase, Oracle, and the like) that are required by the applications, the administrative utilities, and possibly the server software itself (MetaFrame, for example). The Microsoft Data Access Components (MDAC) application is a good example of an application installed during this step.

NOTE: MDAC 2.5 ships with Windows 2000 Server, while MDAC 2.8 ships with Windows Server 2003. The version appropriate for your implementation will depend on your application needs and any security updates that may have become available. For example, Service Pack 3 for MDAC 2.5 is currently available and a recommended update for a Windows 2000 deployment if you are not going to a newer MDAC version. This update would include bug fixes as well as patches for any known security issues. Find out more about MDAC on the MSDN Web site: http://msdn.microsoft.com/data/default.aspx.

2. **Administrative support software**—Next I install the necessary support software to be used by administrators. This usually includes tools such as the Server Resource Kit and any third-party resource management tools such as Microsoft Operations Manager (MOM) or NetIQ.

3. **Common-user-application software**—Next comes the common-user-application software that will be installed on all Terminal Servers, along with any software required for one or more other applications. In most cases this includes office productivity tools, Adobe Acrobat Reader, and so on. Alternate Web browsers such as Opera or Mozilla could be installed during this phase so they are available if required.

4. User applications—The final installation step handles remaining applications to be used by the user. Microsoft Office, Lotus Notes, and custom client/server applications are examples.

Chapter 21, "Application Integration," discusses the steps involved in installation and configuration of applications on Terminal Server.

Administration and System Support Software

Administration and system support tools are an important part of software planning, but their need in the environment is often overlooked until near the end of the project or when an issue arises requiring these tools. I always recommend that administrative support tools be identified early on, so any additional hardware or software requirements can be addressed and resolved prior to the project entering any form of piloting or testing phase. Some components, such as service packs or hotfixes, need to be addressed even before you begin the operating system installation, so you have a clear and documented idea of how the server should be built.

TIP: During the investigation of your planned support software, maintain a list of all the common components and additional resources they may require. For example, Citrix's Resource Manager, a component of MetaFrame Presentation Server Enterprise Edition, requires existence of a Microsoft SQL Server or Oracle database server to store historical application and server metrics.

Multilingual and International User Support

Many organizations look to leveraging the management features of Terminal Server to centralize their operations. A requirement of this may involve support of users who require access to non-English versions of software. Through use of the Multilingual User Interface (MUI), you can configure a Windows Terminal Server to support simultaneous users configured to access the Windows desktop in the language of their choice. Language selection can be configured by the user through the Regional Settings option on the Control Panel or defined within a group policy object.

To utilize this feature, you must purchase the MUI version of Windows Server 2003 or Windows 2000 Server. After installing the base English version of the server OS, the desired MUI components are installed on the server to enable access to those language options. You can find out more information about Windows MUI on the Microsoft Web site at http://www.microsoft.com/globaldev/DrIntl/faqs/MUIFaq.mspx.

Service Packs and Hotfixes

Both Microsoft and Citrix periodically release service packs, hotfixes, and security patches for their products. Considering how quickly tools and source code are created and distributed on the Internet that take advantage of a known exploit in an operating system, particularly a Microsoft operating system, it is the responsibility of every administrator to ensure that their servers are properly secured. I strongly recommend that you keep up-to-date on these patches as they become available. Chapter 9, "Service Pack and Hotfix Management," discusses in detail the process and steps to managing this patching process.

WARNING: Patch management is an ongoing part of your server maintenance, not just something performed when the server is first installed and then forgotten.

Load-Balancing Software

Microsoft and Citrix provide load-balancing solutions specific to their environments, which I discussed briefly in Chapter 1, "Microsoft Windows Terminal Services," and Chapter 2, "Citrix MetaFrame Presentation Server." Microsoft has its Network Load Balancing (NLB) component of Windows Cluster and Citrix has its Load Manager. If your deployment involves anything other than a single-server implementation, I recommend that you plan to include the appropriate load-balancing solution. Load balancing lets you better utilize existing resources by automatically distributing users across all available servers and providing a means of allowing users to quickly reconnect to the environment if a server becomes unavailable. It also eases support by letting you schedule removal of hardware for servicing without having to modify the clients. Through load balancing, users simply connect to the environment and log on to one of the remaining available servers.

Even if your current environment contains only a single server, planning to support a load-balanced environment now can make the transition much smoother in the future. For example, referencing the server using an alias that has been defined in the DNS for the environment instead of the actual host name can make switching to a cluster name with NLB much easier. Or publishing all applications on your MetaFrame server and not having users connect directly to the server name will mean that client changes will not be required when moving to a load-balanced MetaFrame environment. Chapter 22, "Server Operations and Support," provides details on implementation of Microsoft NLB and Citrix Load Management.

Cloning and Server Replication

One key to successful management of a large-scale implementation is being able to build a server quickly from a standard image. This functionality is important for two reasons. One, it provides a means of establishing an effective disaster-recovery plan that lets you quickly re-create your exact environment, given the proper hardware and supporting infrastructure. Second, it lets you expand the environment easily or roll back to a previous configuration in a consistent fashion.

A number of means exist for cloning a server. Utilities such as Symantec's Norton Ghost let you capture an entire snapshot of a drive and save it to a file that can be imaged onto another machine. Other methods of cloning involve use of backup software in conjunction with a second operating system installation used to restore the backup server image onto the new hardware. The exact process depends on the software used.

I've found cloning to be an invaluable process for managing a Terminal Server environment. Using cloning, a Terminal Server can typically be built from an image in 30–60 minutes. The result is a completely functional server containing all applications installed prior to creation of the image. Details on the planning and process of server cloning are discussed in Chapter 8, "Server Installation and Management Planning."

NOTE: Issues have been raised in the past about a lack of support on Microsoft's part for cloning of Windows 2000 or 2003 servers. Foremost is the question of *SID* uniqueness on the cloned server. When Windows is installed, a unique security identifier (SID) is generated for that machine. This SID plus an incremented value known as the *relative ID* (RID) are used to create local security group and user SIDs. If an image of this server is cloned onto another computer, that second computer will have the same computer and account SIDs that existed on the first computer, introducing a potential security problem in a workgroup environment. The local SID is also important in a Windows 2000/2003 domain, as it uniquely identifies a computer in the domain.

Fortunately, Microsoft does *support* a technique for cloning complete installations of Windows from one server to another. Using a utility available for free download from the Microsoft Web site called Sysprep, you can prepare a Windows Terminal Server for replication and have a unique SID automatically generated on the target server when it reboots. Sysprep doesn't perform the actual imaging but prepares a server to be imaged. Once Sysprep is run, any imaging tool can be used to create and distribute the server clone.

Application Deployment

Depending on the size of the Terminal Server environment you plan to deploy, you may want to consider use of application deployment tools to assist in timely and consistent delivery of applications to all your Terminal Servers. The key consideration here is consistency. In a small environment (two to five servers), you have a fairly good chance of being able to perform manual installations of an application on each of the servers and maintain a consistent configuration. But if you have a medium or large Terminal Server environment (10, 20, or more servers), odds of making a mistake on at least one of these machines during application installation goes up dramatically.

In these types of environments, it can be advantageous to look at developing an application deployment process involving use of some form of automated tool. Examples of tools that can be used include the following:

- **SysDiff**—Provided as part of the Resource Kit, the SysDiff tool is used to generate what's called a *difference* file, which contains information on an application installation that can then be applied against another machine to reproduce the exact installation. There are several steps to using SysDiff: Generate a base snapshot of the server before the application is installed, install the desired application, generate the difference file based on the snapshot and the current state, and then use the difference file to install the application on another machine. You can also use SysDiff to generate a list of differences in only registry and INI files if desired.

- **Citrix Installation Manager**—The Installation Manager (IM), provided as part of the Enterprise Edition of MetaFrame Presentation Server, provides the ability to install an application on a single MetaFrame server and have that application automatically installed on any other MetaFrame servers in the server farm. Conceptually it works similarly to SysDiff in that it generates what's called a *package*, containing the information on how an application was installed on the server. The difference between SysDiff and IM is that IM then pushes that application installation to target MetaFrame server(s) and is integrated as part of Citrix's published application metaphor.

- **Wise Solutions' Wise Package Studio**—Provides robust support for centralized package creation and distribution. Conceptually similar to Citrix's Installation Manager. For more information, see http://www.wise.com.

- **Altiris Software's Delivery Solution**—An advanced software distribution solution, this product allows for centralized distribution of software packages to remote systems. For more information see http://www.altiris.com.

Automating deployment of applications within a Terminal Server environment can take significant planning in order to properly develop and configure the environment. Thorough documentation on installation and configuration of the application is a key requirement to ensure the application is prepared properly for deployment. Chapter 21 provides details on these planning and implementation processes.

TIP: Due to permission restrictions and the simple fact that Terminal Server is a multiuser environment, the Windows Installer feature of Intellimirror is not available to users running on a Terminal Server. You can still create MSI or custom transformation files (when supported) so you've preconfigured an installation that can simply be run without any intervention by an administrator, but you need to make sure that all necessary components of an application are installed—not just the installation points. One area where Intellimirror can be utilized is with deployment of Terminal Services or MetaFrame clients.

Registry and File Replication

After implementation, there likely will be times when you will want to perform a change to the registry or file system on each of your Terminal Servers. Need for consistency is as important here as it is with an application installation. Many tools and scripting languages exist that you can use to automate replication of file or registry changes out to all your servers.

For example, the ROBOCOPY (Robust Copy) utility from the Windows Server Resource Kit provides an automated way to maintain an identical set of files between two servers and, because of the logging functionality it provides, is an excellent aid for developing scripted tasks. Another option is to use XCOPY, which is included with all versions of Windows and can be used to script replication of files from a source to a target server.

Using the REGDMP and REGINI utilities from the Resource Kit, you could extract the desired registry changes from one server's registry and then import those changes into another. Scripting languages such as VBScript or JavaScript, which provide robust registry editing support, can also be used to create customized scripts to replicate the necessary changes out to the remote servers. An example of use of these utilities is discussed in Chapter 20.

NOTE: A number of commercial products also exist that provide file and/or registry replication features. An excellent example is Tricerat Software's (http://www.tricerat.com) Reflect replication tool, which provides support for replicating both registry-based and file-based data.

Server Monitoring and Health Checking

Being proactive about the overall health and stability of your Terminal Servers before a system failure occurs is an important part of Terminal Server administration. Unfortunately, I've seen many implementations of Terminal Server in which inadequate consideration has been given to the tools and processes that would aid in managing the environment. Reacting to problems *after* they've brought down a server is far too common.

Numerous tools exist that have been specifically designed to run on a Terminal Server. The following list describes some key considerations for choosing a monitoring tool:

- **Terminal Server– and MetaFrame-"aware" tools**—These tools tend to be well tuned to operate in a Terminal Server environment without introducing too much additional overhead. They also usually have default configurations better suited for monitoring a Terminal Server than for monitoring a regular Windows server.
- **A robust notification system**—A monitoring tool is of little use if there's no way to configure it to send a notification to one or more administrators when a system problem is detected. At a minimum, it should support SNMP (Simple Network Management Protocol) and SMTP (Simple Mail Transfer Protocol).
- **Proactive error-correcting logic**—Some of the more robust monitoring tools can react to problems by attempting to correct them. An excellent example is a situation where a service fails and the monitoring software automatically tries to restart the service. A little-known feature of Windows 2000 and 2003 is the ability to configure a service to automatically attempt to restart or perform some other action when a failure is detected. While the functionality is somewhat limited, this is an example of proactive error correction. Figure 7.1 shows the Recovery tab for a service on a Windows 2000 server.

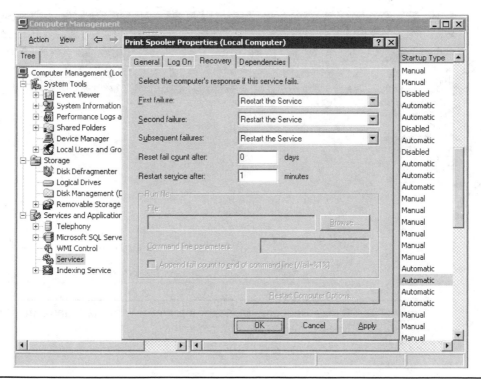

Figure 7.1 Windows 2000 and Windows 2003 support configuration of basic recovery logic for individual services.

- **Report generation**—Reports should be easily producible based on the performance data collected. This information is helpful not only for troubleshooting but also for trend analysis and future capacity planning.

Two common tools I've used are Citrix's Resource Manager (CRM) and NetIQ's AppManager. AppManager is a robust systems management and application management product that provides support for both Terminal Server and MetaFrame. It provides all the functionality summarized in the preceding list in addition to a number of other features, such as event log monitoring, automatic resetting of Terminal Server sessions, and the ability to push tasks out to each server where it's run. Using such a feature, you could have maintenance or application scripts scheduled to run at a given time locally on a server. NetIQ's AppManager is discussed in Chapter 22, "Server Operations and Support."

The Citrix Resource Manager, another component included as part of the Enterprise Edition of MetaFrame, provides detailed information on the health of a MetaFrame server as well as information such as which applications have been run, how often, by whom, and what resources they consumed (percent of CPU, RAM, and so on). CRM integrates into the Management Console for MetaFrame Presentation Server, letting you quickly monitor the status of the servers in your farm; see the example in Figure 7.2.

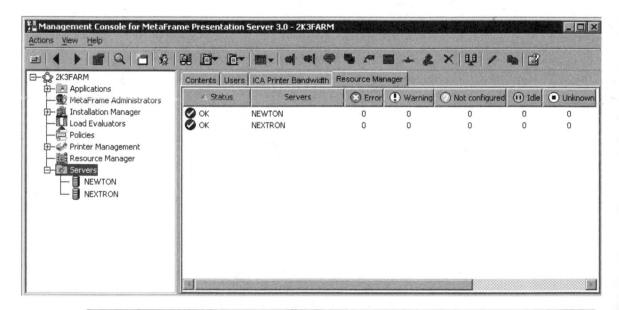

Figure 7.2 Citrix's Resource Manager integrates into the Management Console for MetaFrame Presentation Server.

A common requirement of most resource-monitoring tools is a database management system (DBMS) to store the collected data. The size and type of DBMS supported depends on the product being used. For example, Citrix Resource Manager requires a Microsoft SQL Server or Oracle database to store its information.

Make sure that such requirements are flagged early and tasked in your project plan. It's likely you'll need to engage assistance of a database administrator so the necessary tables can be created and available for populating by the monitoring product.

Antivirus Software

With the proliferation of computer viruses, particularly the continued exploitation success of e-mail–born viruses, desire for an antivirus solution as part of a Terminal Server implementation is growing stronger. While a properly locked down Terminal Server prevents a regular user (non-administrator) who accidentally comes across an infected file from introducing a problem onto a Terminal Server, there's still the problem of the user's personal files or user profile potentially becoming infected and in some fashion interrupt or impair the user's ability to work.

Fortunately, as popularity of Terminal Server grows, so does support from antivirus software manufacturers for the Terminal Server environment. The impact on server performance is a major factor in selecting the right antivirus solution. A poorly configured antivirus program can easily consume huge amounts of system resources, particularly when live scanning is enabled. Trend Micro's ServerProtect is one example of an antivirus software package fully supported on a Terminal Server. When looking for an antivirus product to use, always make sure it is supported on Terminal Server. Trend Micro's Web site is http://www. antivirus.com.

When testing an antivirus product on a Terminal Server, always try to work with the latest version available. Older product versions are more likely to produce issues that can ultimately result in system downtime or impaired performance. Look only at solutions that provide integrated security that prevents users from being able to modify the configuration or otherwise make changes that affect performance on the entire server. After the antivirus software has been installed, spend some time collecting performance data to get an idea as to the overhead the program introduces. Practically all antivirus product companies provide some form of limited trial download, so you should be able to evaluate a few products to get a fairly good idea of which product will work best in your environment.

Windows Server Resource Kit

I've found the Windows Server Resource Kit to be one of the most valuable tools to assist in administration of a Terminal Server environment. Tools such as SysPrep (for use with server cloning) or REGDMP and REGINI (registry changes and replication) are just a few examples of what's available. Many of these tools are downloadable at no charge from Microsoft's Web site.

A number of tools are designed specifically for Terminal Server. This list describes a few tools available with the Windows 2000 and 2003 Resource Kit Tools:

- **LSView and LSReport (Windows 2003)**—These tools provide the ability to query for Terminal Services licensing information in your environment. Their use is discussed in Chapter 12, "License Server Installation and Configuration."
- **RDPClip (Windows 2000)**—The RDPClip tool adds file-copy functionality to the Windows 2000 Terminal Services clipboard. On its own, Windows 2000 supports only text and graphics cut-and-paste between the server and the client. With this tool you can now also cut and paste files. This is not required with Windows Server 2003, which includes support for file cut-and-paste.
- **TSCTst (Windows 2003)**—This tool will dump all the Terminal Services license information stored on a client. This lets you see what temporary and permanent licenses may have been assigned.
- **TSReg (Windows 2000)**—This tool allows very granular tuning of sections of the RDP client's registry, which pertain to bitmap and glyph caching. Using this tool, you can modify settings such as the cache size.
- **Winsta (Windows 2000)**—This simple GUI tool provides a list of users logged on to the Terminal Server where the tool is run. It provides a simple way of quickly seeing who may be on the server. It's similar to the QWINSTA command line tool that's part of the Terminal Server command set, but it doesn't allow you to query information on a remote server.
- **Terminal Services Scalability Planning Tools (tsscaling.exe)**—Slightly different versions of these tools exist for both Windows 2000 and Windows 2003.

    This self-extracting executable contains utilities and scripts used to simulate the load on a Terminal Server. Additional documentation relating to Windows 2000 can be found at the following URL:

    http://www.microsoft.com/windows2000/library/technologies/terminal/tscaling.asp

Scripting Tools

Scripting can play an important role in the development and management of your Terminal Servers, particularly when deploying a large number of applications across multiple servers. Scripting is particularly important for the creation of domain or machine logon scripts, as certain per-user options can be set to assist in the smooth operation of an application. A number of scripting languages are available, and the decision of which to use is really a matter of personal preference and familiarity on the administrator's part, since you need to be able to manage and update these scripts as necessary. Here are some of the supported features you should look for in a scripting language:

- **Registry manipulation**—This is a very useful feature when creating customized application-compatibility scripts.

- **File read and write**—The ability to read and write to a text file can be very useful for such tasks as information logging or application-file configuration.
- **Structured programming**—Basic programming features such as IF…ENDIF and LOOP structures are important for developing robust and useful scripts.

In addition to third-party scripting languages such as KiXtart or Perl, Microsoft provides robust scripting support through its Windows Script Host (WSH). WSH is language independent and includes support for both VBScript and Jscript. Using VBScript with WSH, you can produce robust scripting solutions, including development of your own custom COM objects. Details on scripting are beyond the scope of this book, but a number of excellent resources exist both on the Web and in print. The best place to start is on the Microsoft Scripting Web site: http://www.microsoft.com/scripting.

Application Software

While the exact number and type of applications you'll be deploying is dependent on the requirements of your project, a standard methodology can be applied to capture the required information, making scheduling and actual implementation of the applications more manageable. When planning to install an application, gather the following information:

- Are any customization tools available for the application to automate installation and/or lock down the user's access to certain components that may not be suitable for Terminal Server?

  Two such utilities I commonly use are the Internet Explorer Administration Kit (IEAK) and the Microsoft Office Resource Kit. Both allow customization of their respective products prior to or post installation. Certain features such as the animated Office Assistant or the Internet Connection wizard can be turned off. Customized group policy object templates can also be used to provide granular control over the appearance and functionality of Internet Explorer and Microsoft Office. Chapter 15, "Group Policy Configuration," provides more details about group policies.

- How is user-specific information for the application maintained?

  Applications can maintain user-specific information in a number of different areas. In the registry, through INI files, or through other cusotmized or proprietary files. Depending on the original specifications for the application, it may assume that only one user can run the program at a time and not maintain per-user information. These types of applications, usually custom-built applications or commercial applications originating from smaller companies delivering vertical market solutions, can be troublesome in a Terminal Server environment. Understanding how this user information is managed will help in the assessment of how well the application can be expected to function in the Terminal Server environment.

- What additional drivers does this program need?

    Components such as ODBC drivers, the Borland database engine, or Oracle SQLNet drivers are a few examples. Collect this information so you can develop a list of common components you will install on the server prior to installing the application.

- Are any other applications dependent on this program? Are certain configuration features assumed to be available?

    The most common scenarios involve Web browsers or office productivity tools such as Microsoft Excel or Microsoft Access. When an application has been custom built for your organization, either internally or contractually, requirements on external components are not uncommon. Custom-built applications may interact with programs like Excel for displaying data results or creating graphs. These dependencies need to be flagged so these applications can be installed first on the Terminal Server. If multiple applications depend on a common component, this information will help to ensure that the requirements of one don't conflict with the requirements of another.

After collecting the necessary information, arrange and prioritize installation of each component, ensuring that all dependencies have been accounted for. From the results, you can schedule dates and times for installation of each component. This method can be extremely valuable, particularly if additional human resources must be scheduled to assist in the application installation. Table 7.1 shows a sample prioritization for a project. The numbers in the "Dependencies" column refer to any other listed applications an application is dependent on. For example, the Custom Visual Basic Client/Server application is dependent on application numbers 1, 2, and 3.

Table 7.1   Sample Application Installation Priority List

No.	Application	Dependencies
1.	Microsoft Data Access Components (MDAC) 2.7 with Service Pack 1	None
2.	Custom Forms Management package	1
3.	Internet Explorer 6 with latest service packs	None
4.	Microsoft Office Professional 2003	None
5.	Custom Visual Basic Client/Server application	1, 2, 3

Application Installation Standards

Although the actual process for application installation is covered in Chapter 21, one area that should be flagged during the planning stage is a standard on the location of installed application files.

Many commercial Windows applications default to installing in the %systemdrive%\ Program Files directory. My standard Terminal Server configuration involves use of two drives (or partitions), one containing the system/boot partition and the other containing the applications and static data available to the user. Whenever possible, all applications are installed onto this dedicated application volume.

Depending on the number of custom or in-house applications being maintained, a custom installation folder can be designated resulting in the following target folders. Note that the Y: drive represents my application volume.

- **Y:\Program Files** for commercial applications such as Microsoft Office.
- **Y:\Custom Program Files** for custom-developed applications specific to your company. I like to use this name because the eight-character short name will be custom~1, something easy to remember.

All associated administrators involved in the project should also clearly understand these standards, to help eliminate accidental deployment of an application on the system/boot drive. Unless an administrator is told otherwise, they will most likely install an application using the default target folder, which in most cases will be Program Files on the system/boot drive. Here are a couple of other application-related settings to consider:

- **Hard-coded target folders**—Be aware that some applications (most often, custom-built in-house applications) may have been hard-coded to expect to find their application files in a specific location, usually a folder under the C: drive. This is an obvious problem when you have separated your system/boot partition and your application partition, because the program will continually want to reference your system/boot drive. This can be even more troublesome for a Terminal Server administrator, especially if you have remapped your drives using the MetaFrame DriveRemap utility located on the root of the installation CD-ROM. In this configuration, there is no local C: drive on the Terminal Server, meaning that an application depending on this specific drive will fail unless a network drive mapping or the SUBST command are used to make it available.
- **Changes to the system path**—Pay particular attention to updates to the system path. Many in-house developed applications assume their specific application directory will be listed in the system path. In a Terminal Server environment, you should avoid this whenever possible. By keeping the system path size to a minimum, you reduce the chances of a misplaced DLL or other application file affecting functionality of another program. This also reduces overhead of directory searches, which are performed on all entries in the path when the system is searching for a file.

TIP: Make certain that these standards are conveyed to *all* development teams working on applications targeted for your Terminal Server environment. While hard-coded paths and the like are poor programming practice, proactively making development teams aware of this will help reduce the time required for the teams to fix it or for you to find ways to work around it in your implementation.

Change Management

As part of your software planning, you should also develop change and release management procedures. A critical part of maintaining a stable Terminal Server environment is having the proper software testing and validation procedures in place that must be completed prior to the software's deployment. System downtime as a result of a poor software deployment is completely avoidable in a Terminal Server environment.

NOTE: I once encountered an incident that serves to reiterate the need to develop change and release management procedures. A custom-developed application was presented to me for deployment into a production environment. I informed the project team that the application would have to go onto a test server before it would even be scheduled for deployment into production. Even though the developers were adamant about the fact that the program was very small and had caused no problems on the desktop, I wouldn't allow a production deployment without the new application going onto a test server first. I informed them that desktop validation was not a substitute for Terminal Server validation.

After installation on a test server, the program was working perfectly. Only a short time later, however, I discovered that a number of other applications had stopped functioning properly, including a mission-critical application for the organization. The reason was that the install program for the new application had placed a database driver file in the SYSTEM32 directory that was being picked up by the new application (and others), instead of the file from the standard database driver directory on the Terminal Server. This was a simple mistake made by the programming team while creating the install program and hadn't been picked up during testing on the desktop (since they hadn't run the other applications). To correct the problem, I just moved the database driver file into the new application's working directory, where it would be available to only this application.

Luckily, this problem was detected on a test server, and I was able to correct it before the actual production deployment, which went without incident. This certainly wouldn't have been the case had I not insisted on the testing in the first place. A simple change-management process helped me avoid impacting my production users and saved me the grief of having to troubleshoot the problem while under the added pressure of trying to recover a downed production environment. The main rule of change management is, "Test before you release."

Planning for Testing and Pilot Users

An area where you should start planning early is in selection of your test and pilot users. Choosing the right users for this task is an important ingredient in implementing an application successfully. These users are not the same ones you might employ to do some load testing prior to deployment. These are the veteran users who will become involved in the early days of your implementation. They'll be key in validating the acceptable level of performance and functionality for an application and will help pave the way for success of the software implementation. Choose these people with careful consideration. A suitable pilot user should have the following qualifications:

- **Advanced user of the application**—An advanced user can recognize immediately any variances from the normal operating behavior of an application. When looking for the advanced user, talk with both the desktop support staff who serve these users and the manager and other staff in that department.
- **Comfortable with change**—You may find that many advanced users are resistant to change. Such people don't make good pilot users. In many cases, they know how to do their jobs very well but are unable to adapt well to new situations. They've learned their jobs through repetition more than through knowledge.
- **Calm under pressure or stress**—There are times when testing a new environment or application can become very stressful, particularly when trying to perform production-type work. Querying data, accessing a Web site, running a report, or printing information are all examples of tasks that may require additional tweaking to correct minor problems. If a user is trying to operate in the new environment and continuously encounters these problems, potential for becoming discouraged is high. A calm disposition can be valuable for overcoming these types of problems. Obviously your goal is to avoid these problems as much as possible, but attempting to provide some protection in case problems do arise is certainly smart planning.

WARNING: No matter how tempting it may be, don't make false promises to solicit cooperation of an advanced user who is uncomfortable with change. He or she will expect you to live up to those promises. More specifically, don't promise better performance unless you can deliver it. I say this because it's done so often that it's almost cliché. Always be honest about why you're doing something and set realistic expectations. It is much better to say there will be chances of downtime so the user is at least prepared for it than having them surprised and annoyed if an application continuously fails to start.

- **Positive attitude toward success of the project**—The user needs to have a clear idea as to why the project is being undertaken and must believe in the benefits it will bring, regardless of the problems that may arise in getting there. Because this user will most likely be well known and respected among his or her peers, you can't have this person complaining loudly to anyone who will listen about problems he or she may have encountered during testing. This is a surefire way of planting seeds of resistance to your Terminal Server implementation. At the same time, positive feedback may increase the desire to move to the new environment. If it appears that your test user is operating in a "superior" environment, then very quickly his or her peers will want to get involved. Any negative experiences from your test user need to be dealt with quickly to reassure them that things are being resolved in a timely fashion.
- **Excellent listener and communicator**—Not only must pilot users be able to relay accurately any problems they may be having, but they also must be able to follow instructions given to them.

Don't hesitate to drop or replace a pilot user who hasn't measured up to your expectations. This is not to say that he or she should be removed just for being critical of the system. On the contrary, objective criticism can be beneficial in delivering a robust environment. Users who provide little or no feedback or who abuse the testing privileges should be prime candidates for immediate replacement.

Software Testing

Software testing and deployment in your Terminal Server environment will go through two distinct phases. The first is during the Terminal Server implementation, and the second is once you've gone into a production mode:

- **Terminal Server implementation phase**—During this phase, you'll be migrating one or more applications from the user's desktop into the Terminal Server environment, as well as introducing new applications. The key difference between this phase and the next is that the Terminal Server environment, being new, is more open to change now than it will be later. Until Terminal Server is rolled into production, its configuration is very malleable. This provides you with the flexibility to ensure not only that the environment is robust and stable but also that whatever is required to get the applications working is done properly. The biggest benefit is that you have some room for error. You can make some mistakes and not bring the world crashing down with you. Use this opportunity to its fullest potential. Take the time to understand what's happening and experiment with more than one solution to a problem. When your Terminal Server environment goes live, you'll no longer have this luxury.

- ■ **Production maintenance phase**—At this point you're running a production Terminal Server environment with many users running key applications. The number-one priority now is to maintain stability. Any changes you introduce must not have a negative effect on the existing users. You need to have a process in place for testing new software before it gets near the production environment. Production won't be the place for doing testing or last-minute changes. A set of one or more non-production Terminal Servers should be available for testing all changes.

The actual approach you take to implement software is the same in both phases, and Figure 7.3 outlines the process of adding and testing software in the Terminal Server environment. Details on the individual tasks are described in the next sections.

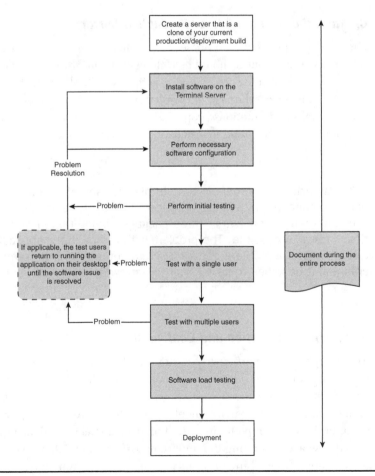

Figure 7.3   The software installation and testing procedure on Terminal Server.

NOTE: An important part of every step is proper documentation of what was done to configure an application to run on Terminal Server. Even if the installation was straightforward and without any issues, you should mention this somewhere so that, if the software ever needs to be installed again, someone can look up this information and quickly re-create the installation.

I've worked with some organizations that develop detailed "build books" that include information on all components of the server build, including the individual applications. While this may appear to be substantial work upfront, the benefits of having such information available can be invaluable if the server ever needs to be re-created at some point in the future.

Creating the Terminal Server Production Mirror

During the implementation phase the production mirror will not necessarily be a clone of a production server, but it should be a clone of the most recent build you're currently working with. See the earlier section "Cloning and Server Replication" for more information.

By using a cloned image of your latest "production" server, you ensure that if the application installs and functions properly, it will work in the production environment. Testing a new application on a generic installation of Terminal Server is not sufficient to guarantee its stability in *your* production configuration.

TIP: It's certainly reasonable to use this test server to test more than one software package concurrently, although I suggest that you handle this with care. It's best if you can keep to only two or three packages being tested on a single server at a time—fewer, if possible. The problem with having many applications being tested at once is that if a problem occurs, such as intermittent performance degradations or crashes, it becomes more difficult to narrow down the actual culprit.

Application Installation and Configuration

Many applications, particularly custom applications or older 16-bit or 32-bit applications, need to be configured differently or augmented with scripting to get them to function properly or to resolve performance issues when run on Terminal Server. Installation and configuration of applications in your environment will usually take up the majority of the project time. See Chapter 20 for a complete discussion on installing and configuring applications.

It is worth reiterating the importance of documentation, particularly during installation of your applications, since it's unlikely that you will remember subtle changes made to an application or that such changes can be easily re-created by someone else.

Initial Application Testing

After you have the software installed on your test server, you should do some initial testing. You'll be better able to examine general-purpose applications such as Microsoft Word than custom applications developed for a specific department. Depending on the sensitivity of the data within an application, you may not be able to test much more than the logon screen. Although you may not be able to run the application, when possible you should attempt to verify connectivity to back-end database systems such as SQL Server prior to having the test user become involved.

TIP: One additional test you can perform, especially if this application may be scheduled for an update or replaced in the near future, is to verify that the uninstall works properly. Be aware that when an application is installed from a network location, it may refer back to this location to perform the software uninstall. If that network point does not exist in the future, the software uninstall may fail.

Single-User Testing

Before you can run, you need to learn to walk. This is why initially you should introduce only *a single user* to the software on Terminal Server. Make sure that the process of switching back and forth between Terminal Server and the desktop is clear to the user (when implementing a desktop-replacement scenario). This will minimize the impact if the application in Terminal Server is not working properly. I highly recommend that you demonstrate the back-out procedures to anyone who may have concerns with downtime, such as a tester's manager. The ability to quickly roll back to the original desktop application is another benefit to software deployment during the Terminal Server implementation.

WARNING: If an application is being migrated from a user's desktop, don't remove the user's desktop version of the application until the Terminal Server version is in production. During testing, the desktop software will be the user's immediate back-out if there are problems on Terminal Server.

A frequent question is, "How long should I test with one user?" My response is typically, "Until you're comfortable that multiple users could work in the same environment with the same or fewer issues than the single user." If a single user is having frequent problems, there's no reason to believe that adding more users will make the problem disappear. More likely, multiple users will start to exhibit the same problem, and you will have succeeded only in increasing your support responsibilities. This is not usually what a busy Terminal Server administrator wants to do. Testing with a single user will very often eliminate the majority of the issues that would also be encountered by multiple users.

TIP: When performing your application testing, be sure you're replicating how the application will be run in the production environment. If users will be accessing a full desktop, make sure they're working in a full desktop session. If the application will run in a seamless window, test in a seamless window. This will help eliminate surprises later on and ensure that your testing results are actually a valid representation of the production environment.

Multiuser Testing

When the application is working properly for the single test user, the next step is to increase this to two or three users. The reason is to ensure that the software continues to function when multiple instances are being run on the same computer (the Terminal Server). A classic problem area is in applications that create temp files or user files in a location not unique for multiple users on a Terminal Server. The hard-coded folder C:\Temp is a common shared location where this problem occurs. Instead of an application using the %TEMP% environment variable, which is unique for each Terminal Server user, C:\TEMP is used instead.

An application's binary folder can also be a trouble spot, but you'll normally discover this when testing with a single user since he or she should not have write access to the folder by default. Don't let yourself fall into the trap of trying to add too many users too quickly. Always start out slowly when performing your initial testing. The more users you have testing, the more work required to ensure they are working properly and to provide any required user support.

Another potential problem area is the registry, where the software may place user-specific application information in HKEY_LOCAL_MACHINE instead of HKEY_CURRENT_USER. All users can then access the same information, causing problems in the application. Again, if access to the registry is being controlled, this problem will be uncovered during single-user testing. This issue is becoming less and less of a concern as most Windows-based applications have been certified to run on at least Windows 2000. In order to pass certification, certain minimum standards must be met. One of these standards is that user-specific information be maintained in the HKEY_CURRENT_USER registry hive and *not* in HKEY_LOCAL_MACHINE.

NOTE: Unfortunately, many software manufacturers can provide only minimal (if any) support for their product when run on a Terminal Server. You'll have much more success if you can describe the problem specifically for the manufacturer. For example, if a software package insists on writing a temporary file into a specific location and this is causing conflicts on Terminal Server, ask the vendor if there's a way to modify the location of this file. This will be more easily answered than why the program won't run on Terminal Server.

In a number of situations, I haven't revealed to the support people that I'm attempting to use their product on Terminal Server. When I do, the response is usually, "Sorry, we don't support our product on that platform," even though the issue usually has to do with a user having more restrictive access and not with the host operating system itself.

Because of the increased possibility of problems when you first begin testing with multiple users, don't add too many users during initial testing. "Too many" usually means more than five. With five or fewer users, ideally located in the same geographic area, the support responsibilities are manageable by a single support person. More than five, and your testing group may become much more difficult to support.

WARNING: *Never* put an application into production on a Terminal Server if you have done testing with only a single user.

Software Load Testing and Terminal Server

After the application has gone through multiuser testing successfully, the only outstanding task is to examine the load that the software will introduce to the Terminal Server. This can actually be started during single-user testing because severe performance problems may be noticed immediately. Performance Monitor is one tool that can be used to capture performance data for a specific application as well as the server. Even using only Task Manager, you can get an idea of the typical processor and memory utilization of an application. See Figure 7.4.

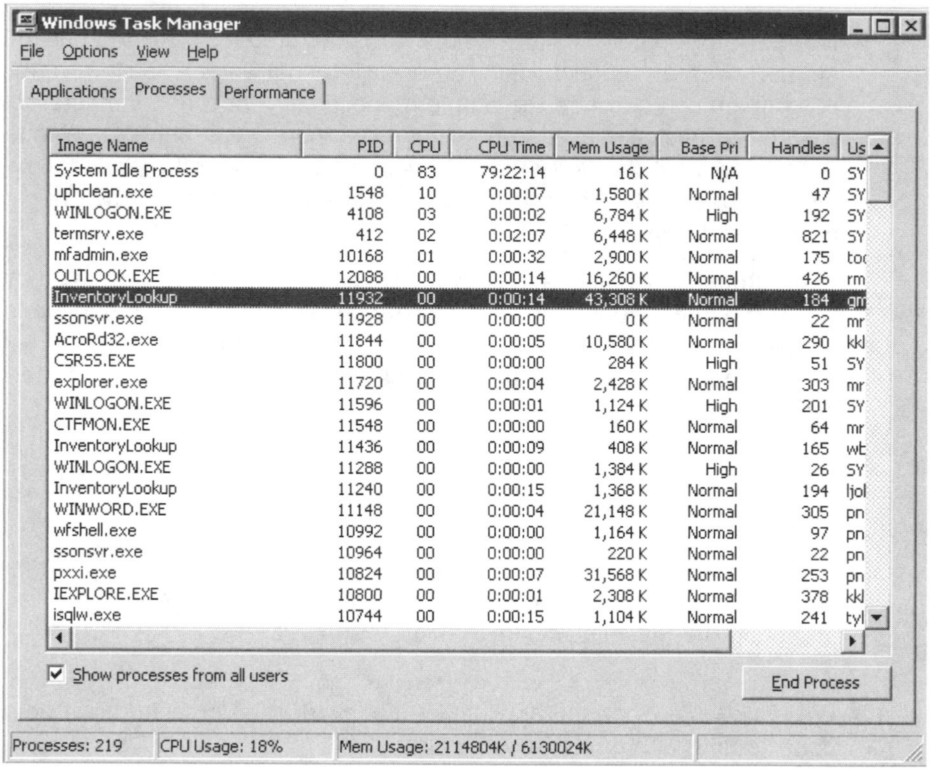

Figure 7.4 Task Manager can be used to retrieve basic information on the processor and memory utilization of an application.

Deployment

The final step is the actual deployment. By the time you're ready to deploy, there should be no doubt as to whether the application will work. Deployment should be no more than a formality.

Release Management

As part of the development of your change-management procedures, document the process that application developers and others need to follow if they want to have a program implemented within the Terminal Server environment. Regardless of which release procedures exist today, you need to establish a guideline that everyone will have to follow. Otherwise you run the risk of allowing releases to be scheduled before they've been properly tested. Figure 7.5 describes the release management process that I commonly implement.

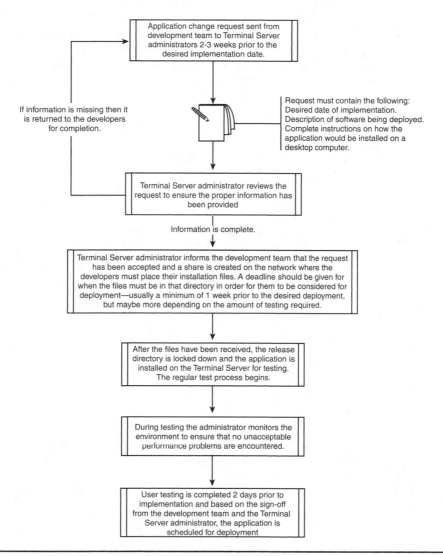

Figure 7.5 An example of a possible Terminal Server release management process.

A key requirement is insisting that the development team clearly document exactly how the application should be installed. You shouldn't necessarily expect that the documentation clearly explain how to deploy the application onto Terminal Server, but it should explain how the development team would normally install it on a desktop. You can then review this procedure and make any necessary adjustments to accommodate your Terminal Server requirements.

WARNING: *Never* let a development team install an application onto your environment without your direct involvement, ideally with you at the controls. Unsupervised access to install any application on your Terminal Server is an almost certain invitation to trouble.

CHAPTER 8

Server Installation and Management Planning

Before You Begin

Properly planning installation and management of your Terminal Server/MetaFrame deployment is extremely important to the overall success of the project. Going into a project with the belief that you can "wing it" and implement an environment driven by last-minute decisions and an "I think that will work" attitude is both idealistic and very likely to fail. At the least, you would manage to cobble together a configuration that worked but was far from an optimal solution for the target environment. Large amounts of time and energy would be spent modifying or re-engineering the solution to account for some unexpected requirement that would not exist had the time been taken to properly plan the configuration from the beginning.

The purpose of this chapter is to summarize the main implementation and management tasks and provide more detailed information to assist in solidifying your deployment strategy. I assume that you already have a pretty clear idea of the type of environment you're planning to implement and at least a general answer to questions such as the following:

- Are you implementing MetaFrame or only Terminal Services?
- What type of load balancing (if any) will you employ?
- How many and what type of licenses do you require?
- Will you use third-party monitoring tools such as Microsoft Operations Manager or NetIQ AppManager?
- What are the target client operating systems?

Those readers already managing a production environment may find information that will help improve and streamline their own management processes. If you currently operate a legacy environment, you may find this chapter helpful in planning your migration strategy.

The chapter has been divided into two main sections. The first covers topics relevant to installation and deployment of Terminal Services, while the second looks at those environments also running MetaFrame Presentation Server (MPS). Of course, since Terminal Services is a necessary component for running MetaFrame, material pertaining to Terminal Services is still relevant to those of you who will deploy or manage an MPS environment.

Microsoft Terminal Server

At this point in the book, planning your Terminal Services implementation is nearly complete. You have a general idea of what your environment will require and how it will look. Figure 8.1 provides an overview of the main components that make up a typical Terminal Server environment.

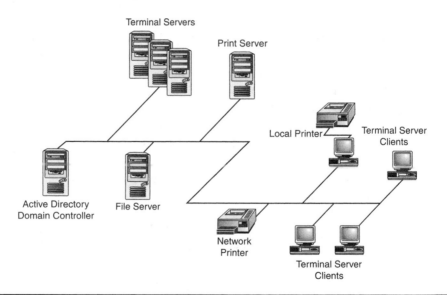

Figure 8.1 A network diagram representing a typical Terminal Server implementation.

Part III of this book focuses on the actual implementation of Terminal Services with and without MetaFrame Presentation Server. Table 8.1 summarizes the servers shown in Figure 8.1, along with the tasks performed and/or roles serviced by those servers and the corresponding chapter or chapters in Part III that explain how that task/role is implemented or configured.

Table 8.1   Components of a Terminal Server Implementation and Chapter Cross-Reference

Server Type	Implementation Task/Role	Corresponding Chapter
Terminal Server	Application/desktop serving	Chapter 10, "Installing Windows Terminal Services" Chapter 11, "Terminal Services Configu-ration and Tuning" Chapter 16, "Terminal Server Security" Chapter 17, "Terminal Server and MetaFrame Printer Management" Chapter 21, "Application Integration" Chapter 22, "Server Operations and Support"
Active directory domain controller	Terminal Services Licensing service Group policy objects Terminal Server home and profile folder definition Per-user Terminal Server settings Logon scripts	Chapter 12, "License Server Installation and Configuration" Chapter 15, "Group Policy Configuration" Chapter 18, "User Profile and Account Configuration"
Print server	Network printer queues	Chapter 17, "Terminal Server and MetaFrame Printer Management"
File server	Terminal Server home folders Terminal Server profile folders	Chapter 18, "User Profile and Account Configuration"
Terminal Server client	RDP client Local printer host	Chapter 17, "Terminal Server and MetaFrame Printer Management" Chapter 19, "RDP Client Installation and Configuration"

To prepare for moving on to the implementation section of this book, there are a few additional planning considerations to review.

Upgrades versus Clean Installations

If you currently run a Citrix WinFrame; Windows NT 4.0, Terminal Server Edition; or Windows 2000 Terminal Server (with or without MetaFrame) environment; you may be considering upgrading to a newer version of Terminal Server instead of performing a clean installation, in order to preserve any system, application, and security settings you already have in place. Table 8.2 summarizes available upgrade options based on your existing operating system.

Table 8.2   Upgrade Options for Terminal Server

Existing OS	Target OS Support	Comments
Citrix WinFrame 1.x	NT 4.0, Terminal Server Edition only	An upgrade directly from WinFrame to Windows 2000/2003 is not supported. You must first upgrade to Terminal Server Edition (TSE) 4.0 and then upgrade again to Windows Terminal Services 2003.
OEM WinFrame	Not supported	Upgrading from OEM versions of WinFrame such as NCD's WinCenter are not supported.
NT Server 3.51/4.0	Not supported	Upgrades from a standard NT or 2000 server to Terminal Server are not supported because any applications on the server will not be properly configured to run in a multiuser session environment after the upgrade. Because Terminal Servers aren't performing a typical server role, a clean installation in this situation is required.
Windows 2000 (not running Terminal Services)		
NT 4.0, Terminal Server Edition Server	Windows 2000/2003 Terminal Server	If you wish to upgrade to Windows 2003, you must ensure that Service Pack 5 (SP5) or higher has been installed on the TSE 4.0 server.
		Upgrading to either 2000 or 2003 Terminal Server is fully supported.
Windows 2000 Terminal Server	Windows 2003 Terminal Server	An in-place upgrade from Windows 2000 Terminal Services to Windows Server 2003 Terminal Services is fully supported by Microsoft.

In most cases, I recommend that you perform a clean installation instead of an upgrade. While an upgrade may initially save you time regarding application installation and configuration of the Terminal Server, you may find that troubleshooting a problem can be extremely difficult because you are not certain whether the problem is with the new OS installation or a remnant of the old environment. There is always the question of whether the problem is because of the upgrade. If you ever require support from either Microsoft or Citrix, one of the first questions the support person will typically ask is whether you have been able to duplicate the problem on a clean server installation.

Some common scenarios in which I suggest a clean installation include the following:

- You inherited an existing Terminal Server environment in which you do not have a clearly documented history of exactly what was installed, how it was installed, and any other changes that have been made to the server.

  Without knowing how the current environment was built, it can be extremely difficult to support the system once it has been upgraded.

- You will implement new or updated software not supported on the current Terminal Server version.

  Almost exclusively, this scenario involves an existing Windows NT 4.0, Terminal Server Edition environment that must be upgraded to support a company's new or upgraded major line-of-business application. In my opinion, upgrading the existing NT 4.0 Terminal Server to Windows 2000 or 2003, followed by installation or upgrading of the new application simply carries too much baggage from the old configuration into the new environment. If issues arise with either the operating system or the application, the first area in question will be the upgraded environment. A clean Terminal Server build followed by application installation eliminates this legacy environment from being a factor to consider if issues do arise. It simplifies troubleshooting and creates a more stable foundation for future application growth.

- The current Terminal Server is already an upgrade from a previous operating system.

  Multiple versions of DLLs and other system files are a common problem in this scenario, but thankfully these situations are actually quite rare as the hardware has typically become obsolete and will not support the system requirements of 2000/2003.

- The existing Terminal Server environment is suffering from stability problems such as random server or application crashes and poor server performance.

  You would be surprised how often I have been asked if upgrading a server's operating system will resolve any of these problems. The answer is almost always no. In most situations, if an application is behaving poorly in the current configuration, upgrading the server likely will not eliminate the problem. The problem may not manifest itself in exactly the same way, and the new OS may actually have safeguards that dilute the program's impact on the server, but the problems will still exist. Whenever possible, try to determine the root cause of the issue and work with the developers or vendor to come up with a true solution to the problem.

Having said all that, I must also say the one situation where I feel an upgrade may be a suitable course of action is when you are currently running a stable Windows 2000 Terminal Server environment and wish to upgrade to run Windows 2003 Terminal Server (to leverage support for expanded client device redirection or greater users per server, for example). While Windows 2003 Terminal Server does provide additional functionality compared to that of Windows 2000 Terminal Server, architecturally, the operating systems are very similar and as such should not pose major upgrade issues.

Even though the operating systems themselves support a clear upgrade path, you need to be certain that any of the applications currently on the Windows 2000 server are supported on Windows 2003. It would certainly be disappointing to successfully upgrade to a new operating system only to find that the required applications did not function properly.

TIP: When performing an upgrade for the first time, always make sure to take a backup or drive image of the server before you begin so you can easily recover in case of problems. Whenever possible, perform your initial upgrade on a test or development server before upgrading a production server. The basics on drive imaging are discussed in the "Server Cloning" section of this chapter, and an example of how it is actually performed is given in Chapter 22.

Installation Methods

Table 8.3 outlines the installation methods supported by Windows 2000 and 2003 servers. It is worth pointing out that Windows Server 2003 *does not* support an installation initiated by booting from floppy diskettes.

Table 8.3   Supported Installation Methods for Windows 2000 and 2003 Servers

Installation Initiation Method	Supported Operating Systems	Upgrade Installation?	Clean Installation?
Booting from floppy diskettes	Windows 2000 only	No	Yes
Booting directly from the CD-ROM	Both	No	Yes
Running WINNT from a DOS prompt	Both	No	Yes
Running WINNT32 from a 32-bit Windows OS	Both	Yes[1]	Yes

[1] The upgrade option is available only if WINNT32 is run from within one of the supported Windows server versions listed in the earlier section "Upgrades versus Clean Installations."

If you wish to reformat or repartition your existing boot drive during the installation, you must either boot from floppy diskette (Windows 2000 only) or from CD-ROM. The other two installation options (WINNT or WINNT32) won't let you reformat or repartition the drive on which the temporary installation files have been copied. In this situation you would need to partition and format the drives through DOS or another supported OS before running WINNT or WINNT32. This is one of the main reasons I prefer to boot directly from the CD-ROM when performing a clean Terminal Server installation.

TIP: If you have an enterprise agreement or Software Assurance Membership licensing agreement with Microsoft, you have access to use its Windows Pre-Installation Environment (WinPE), a special minimized boot environment based on Windows XP Professional that you can use to perform a Windows operating system setup. One of the reasons why this tool exists is to replace the need to boot a system in DOS in order to perform a customized installation. More information on WinPE can be found by searching the Microsoft site for the text "Windows PE" or reviewing Microsoft knowledgebase article 303891, which describes how to create a custom-bootable CD-ROM to launch WinPE.

Service Pack and Patch Management

One of the most important tasks required by a system administrator today is timely and thorough patching of all servers in the environment (test, development, production). Service pack and patch management is an ongoing process that does not end with deployment of the Terminal Server. Delinquency in application of patches in your environment could potentially result in a system compromise based on an available and well-published exploit of the Windows operating system.

Details of deployment and management of service packs and hotfixes are discussed in the final chapter of Part II of this book (Chapter 9, "Service Pack and Hotfix Management").

License Server Location

Chapter 1, "Microsoft Windows Terminal Services," provided a brief summary of licensing requirements for Terminal Server implementation. I now expand on this briefly from a planning perspective, leaving actual implementation details until Chapter 12.

When deploying a Windows Terminal Server (not a server running Remote Desktop for Administration), at least one server in your environment *must* run the Microsoft Terminal Services Licensing service. This service is responsible for allocating a valid Terminal Services client access license (TSCAL) the first time a user logs on in order to validate that the user is in fact licensed to use the Terminal Server.

Before deciding where to install the licensing service you should determine what scope the license service will have. There are two scope types available to choose from during installation:

- **Domain or workgroup scope**—This option limits the scope of the license server to the workgroup or domain within which it is a member. Terminal Servers from other domains or workgroups cannot request licenses from this server. This is the only option available when deploying a Terminal Server in a workgroup or an NT 4 domain configuration.

   By default, a domain license server services license requests from all license servers in a domain, regardless of their location. It is possible in this scenario to have a Terminal Server request a license from a domain license server located across a WAN link.

- **Enterprise scope**—When deploying a license server in a Windows 2000/2003 domain, you also have the choice of specifying that it will service licenses for all Terminal Servers across all domains in your enterprise. This is known as an *enterprise license server,* and by default it services license requests for all Terminal Servers within the same site, regardless of domain membership. Servers located in a different site will not request licenses from this server unless explicitly configured to do so. Servers within the same site will find the license server by querying the active directory for the name of the enterprise license server for their site. Figure 8.2 shows the enterprise license server entry for a given site in an active directory.

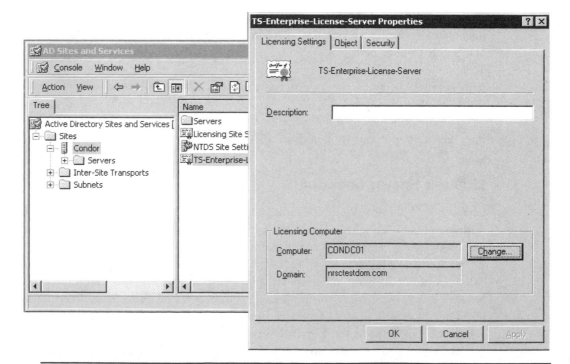

Figure 8.2   A Terminal Server enterprise license server object's properties for an active directory site.

Of the two scope types, my preference is to designate all license servers as enterprise license servers unless there is a particular need to segregate them for a specific domain. Once you've decided on the license scope to implement, you must decide where you will actually install the licensing service. Table 8.4 summarizes my preference based on the details of the implementation.

Table 8.4   Terminal Server Installation Location Based on Implementation Details

Terminal Server Version	Domain Configuration	Using MetaFrame?	License Service Location
Windows 2000	Active directory	Yes or no	Domain controllers
Windows 2000/2003	Workgroup or NT4 domain	Yes or no	Member servers
Windows 2003	Active directory	No	Domain controllers
Windows 2003	Active directory	Yes	Member servers

One factor that carries a lot of weight in my decision on where to host the license service is whether or not MetaFrame Presentation Server will also be run in the environment. When MPS will be used, I like to couple the two licensing services (MetaFrame and Terminal Server) together onto a single member server that may or may not be performing other tasks such as file and print or additional Web services. The one exception to this is when deploying Windows 2000 Terminal Services, in which case the licensing service must reside on a domain controller.

License Server Redundancy

Multiple license servers can be configured and deployed to provide redundancy and distribute the license request load. No special configuration must be performed other than dividing the licenses among the available servers. Microsoft does not support license pooling, since licenses are assigned to each valid user or client device on a "permanent" basis.

Once a license server is discovered, the Terminal Server continues to use this same server unless it becomes unavailable. Availability of this license server is confirmed by the Terminal Server once every hour. If the license server cannot be located, the query for an alternate license server is immediately initiated.

Redundancy is inherently supported by license servers because they are "aware" of each other and can communicate to share license information. If a license server does not have any permanent Terminal Server device tokens available for issuance to a requesting Terminal Server, it queries the other license servers in the domain to see if any of them have an available token. If a token is available on another server, the first license server requests that token from the other license server and then passes it on to the requesting Terminal Server. If no permanent tokens are available, one of two things happen. If the client does not currently have an expired temporary token, a temporary token is assigned and the user can log on. If the user has a temporary token that has expired, the user's access to log on to the Terminal Server is denied.

Full details on installation and configuration of Terminal Services licensing can be found in Chapter 12.

NOTE: A Terminal Services client access license assignment is not truly permanent because licenses unused for a maximum of 89 days are reclaimed by the server and made available for redistribution.

End-User Printing Support and Management

One measurement of the success of many Terminal Server implementations is the ability of the end user to successfully print to their desired printer through their Terminal Server session. Many companies depend heavily on timely and reliable printing to drive the success of their business, and recurring issues in this area can overshadow all other successful project deliverables. For example, inability of a manufacturing or distribution company to print out packing slips and invoices for its customers in a timely manner can easily result in lost business that ultimately impacts the success of the project.

A common mistake made by many novice Terminal Server implementers is to assume that the printer configuration and management will be a straightforward task in the overall project, and as a result they allocate insufficient time for planning or implementation. The majority of printing issues that occur once a Terminal Server implementation goes live can be avoided simply by understanding what printing options are available and taking the time to plan and implement them properly.

WARNING: Do not expect Terminal Server to miraculously solve any printing issues that may already exist in your current environment. Without taking specific action as part of your implementation to address these issues, they will surely reappear after your Terminal Server implementation is complete.

Printer Driver Selection and Management

Every printer in a Windows system requires an associated printer driver, and Terminal Server is no exception. From a user's perspective, printing is straightforward: The user's application sends a print job to the desired print queue, which in turn sends the print job to the target printer. Of course we know there is much more happening under the covers to deliver the print job from the application to the physical printer. Figure 8.3 demonstrates the conceptual flow of information through the logical components that play a part in the printing process.

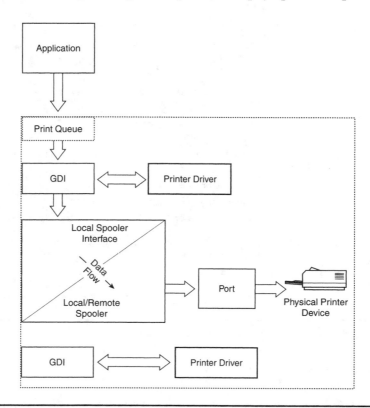

Figure 8.3   Information flow through the Windows printing subsystem.

An application sends the print request to a print queue, which is a logical graphical interface to the underlying spooler and printer. The print request is processed by the Windows graphical device interface (GDI), which communicates with the printer driver to determine how the print job will be spooled. This stage would represent the interaction with the printer driver located on the Windows Terminal Server.

The print job is next sent to the spooler's local interface, which then passes the print job either to the local spooler, if the printer is locally attached, or to the spooler on a print server via remote procedure calls (RPC). The file is then spooled until it is ready to print, at which time it is passed once again to the GDI, which uses the printer driver to create the actual data sent to the printer.

The current driver associated with a printer can be determined by opening the Properties page for the printer and selecting the Advanced tab. An alternate printer can be selected from the drop-down list, as shown in Figure 8.4. All drivers currently installed on the server are available for selection.

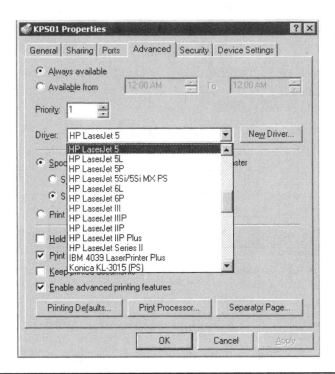

Figure 8.4   Printer driver assignment.

NOTE: There are actually two types of printer drivers supported by Windows 2000/2003: the traditional full printer driver and what is called a printer *mini-driver*. A mini-driver works in conjunction with the Windows Universal Printer Driver (WUPD) to perform actual printing to the physical device. Because a printer driver must interact with the GDI, it must provide a standard set of interfaces that the GDI expects to be available. A mini-driver provides what are called *stubs* to these interfaces but actually relies on the WUPD to deliver most of the functionality. The mini-driver provides only the information unique to that particular printer.

The alternative to a mini-driver is the *full printer driver,* which delivers all required GDI interfaces and does not use the WUPD in any way. Full printer drivers are much more complicated to develop than mini-drivers but can also provide more robust printing features and functionality.

Typically, the mini-driver can be much more stable than a full printer driver, because most GDI-based interaction is through the WUPD, which has already been thoroughly tested. This is the main reason why I recommend implementing a mini-driver whenever possible in a Terminal Server environment.

Ideally all printer drivers work flawlessly in a Terminal server environment, but unfortunately this is not the case, so care must be taken when deciding what drivers will be installed and available on your Terminal Servers. To be able to effectively make decisions on what drivers are good candidates for Terminal Server and which are not, it is important to understand why historically printer driver issues have existed with Terminal Server and how the introduction of Windows 2000 and now Windows 2003 have helped reduce these problems.

After the introduction of Windows NT 4.0, Terminal Server Edition, it was quickly discovered that a number of available printer drivers caused rather severe stability problems in the environment. These drivers became notorious for causing system STOP errors resulting in the Blue Screen of Death (BSOD) system crash. Of course a large part of the problem existed because of inherent issues in design of the drivers and how they functioned in a multi-user environment such as Terminal Server. But another part of the problem was the result of how Microsoft implemented operation of printer driver code in NT 4.0. In this version of Windows, the printer drivers run in what is known as *kernel mode,* a privileged operating level reserved for low-level "executive" services such as the Security Reference Monitor and the Virtual Memory Manager. Any fatal errors encountered by a program running in kernel mode are considered to be severe and compromise the stability of the environment. As such the system immediately halts all processing and generates a BSOD. Because the printer drivers run in this privileged mode, any issues with printing that generated a fatal error in the printer driver would immediately result in the server's terminating with the blue screen.

To counteract this problem and improve overall stability of Windows, Microsoft changed the execution mode of the printer drivers from kernel mode to *user mode* in Windows 2000 and later versions. From a user's perspective this change causes no difference in how the printer appears to work, but from a system perspective the change is significant. When a fatal error occurs in a program running in user mode, only that particular process fails. The rest of the system is typically *not* impacted and continues to function normally. In the specific case of Terminal Server printing, a fatal error with a printer driver now causes a failure only in the spooler process, not the entire system.

While this architectural change is certainly an improvement by reducing the number of blue screens resulting from printing issues, it does not actually fix the problem of poorly written printer drivers causing issues on a Terminal Server. Because a faulty driver can still cause the spooler process to crash, thereby preventing users from printing, it is still important to use due diligence when determining what printer drivers you will implement in your production environment. The following list summarizes the guidelines I recommend you follow when evaluating and planning what printer drivers will be included in your production Terminal Server environment:

- **Use only native Windows 2000/2003 drivers**—While Windows 2000/2003 support NT 4.0 printer drivers (Windows Server 2003 blocks them by default), these drivers will still operate in kernel-mode and can potentially impact the server's stability. If this is the only driver type available for this printer, make sure you have performed thorough testing before introducing it into production. You can determine the type of printer driver by opening the Printers and Faxes folder, opening Print

Server Properties from the File menu, and selecting the Drivers tab. The right-hand column lists the printer driver's version. Figure 8.5 shows an example of Windows 2000/2003 and Windows NT printer drivers installed on a Terminal

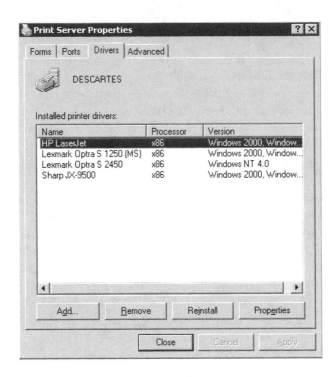

Server

Figure 8.5 Windows NT printer driver identification.

- **Use a printer mini-driver when available**—Sometimes two versions of a printer driver may be available from a printer manufacturer: The full printer driver and the mini-driver. In this situation, the mini-driver should be used on a Terminal Server. Because the mini-driver leverages most printing functionality through the Windows Universal Printer Driver (WUPD), it can be much more stable than a full-function printer driver. If additional functionality is required and there is a business need to use the full-featured driver, be sure to perform thorough testing before implementing it in production.
- **Use a Terminal Server–specific driver if available**—Sometimes a printer manufacturer will make a Terminal Server–specific driver available for its product. This driver should always be used on a Terminal Server over all other drivers available. An example of this can be found on the Hewlett Packard Web site (http://www.hp.com), where a Terminal Server–specific driver for the DeskJet 970Cse is available (see Figure 8.6).

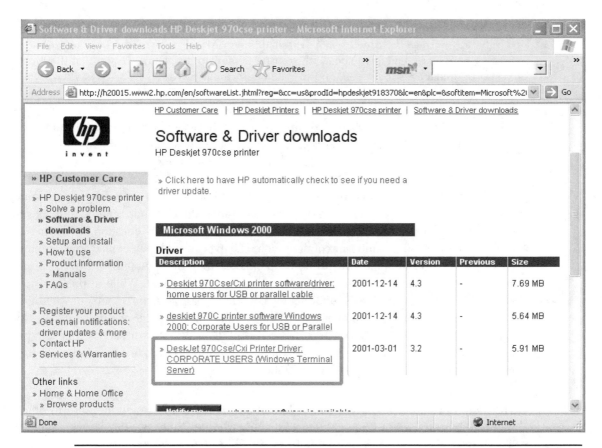

Figure 8.6   When provided, a printer driver designed specifically for Terminal Server
should be used.

- **Run the same version of the printer driver on both the Terminal Server and
  the print server**—Printer manufacturers usually ask you to run the same version of
  printer driver on both your printer client and print server when troubleshooting a
  printer
  driver problem. As a result, it is usually good practice to have a consistent driver
  version across your Terminal Servers and on any print servers you may be accessing.
- **Use the Windows-provided printer drivers when available**—If a compatible
  printer driver shipped with the Windows operating system, this is the preferred
  driver to use unless the vendor supplies a version providing additional functionality
  that you require. For example, Windows ships with a number of digitally signed
  Lexmark PCL drivers that are certified to work properly with Windows, including
  Terminal Server. If one of these drivers suits your printing requirements, it should
  be used over a vendor-provided driver, particularly if that driver was not digitally
  signed by Microsoft.

■ **Search for known issues with the printer driver**—Before adding the printer driver, take the time to scan Terminal Server/MetaFrame newsgroups to see if users have had any issues with your particular printer. Here are some of the most popular sites for keeping up-to-date on Terminal Server:

  ■ The Thin.net: http://www.thethin.net
  ■ Citrix knowledgebase and support groups: http://support.citrix.com/forums
  ■ Microsoft Terminal Services community: http://www.microsoft.com/windows2000/community/centers/terminal/default.mspx

Of all of the tasks in the preceding list, the most important to plan for is simply performing some concurrent user printing using the proposed printer driver. While sending some of your own test printouts is important, this will not answer the most basic question of whether the driver will hold up in a multiuser configuration. Having two to three people (users, administrators, whoever) simultaneously print documents of different types and sizes to the printer will help to determine if it can handle some concurrency and load. While testing on such a small scale will not introduce substantial load, it will at least give you an idea of whether or not the driver will fail even under light usage. A failure at this point certainly indicates the driver is ill-suited for a Terminal Server environment. Even after the driver has gone into production, be sure to monitor the server's stability very closely over the first few days or so, looking for signs of print spooler or server instability.

TIP: When developing your printer implementation and support plan, be sure to document all the printers currently in use and verify whether there are any known issues with any of these printers operating in a Terminal Server environment.

Terminal Server Printer Support

One of the reasons why printer support can sometimes seem overwhelming to a new Terminal Server administrator is simply because the administrator doesn't have a clear understanding of the options available and how they are best utilized in a Terminal Server environment. Printer support for Terminal Server falls into three categories:

■ Network printer shares
■ Local server printers
■ Local client printers

Network Printer Shares

Probably the most common printer access configuration and the one most familiar to a Windows administrator is use of one or more print servers that centralize access to various printers within the organization. These printers are all made available as network printer shares on the print server. Figure 8.7 gives an example of a number of printers shared off of a Windows print server and listed in an active directory.

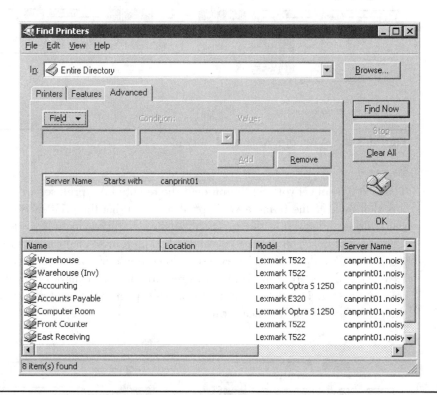

Figure 8.7   Printer shares for a print server listed in a Windows active directory.

As I mentioned in Chapter 4, "Network Planning," use of network printer shares will depend on the needs and physical distribution of your clients, the layout of your infrastructure, and the location of the printers that the users are required to access.

Three types of network configurations were discussed in Chapter 4; each of which is a different variation of the network printer sharing scenario. The first is the "Remote WAN Print Server" configuration shown in Figure 8.8, which has this name because the print server and shared printer reside on the same network as the client, and across the wide area network (WAN) from the Terminal Server. This is a common configuration in an existing Windows environment with remote offices, since the print server is most often located on the same network as the printers it's supporting. If a user still requires the ability to perform printing to this printer outside of Terminal Server then this is the appropriate configuration to use.

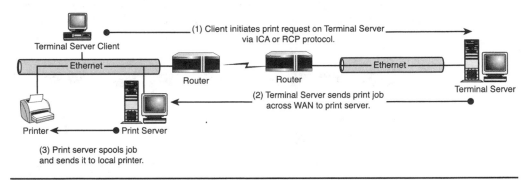

Figure 8.8 A remote WAN print server.

The next type of network configuration is the remote LAN print server (Figure 8.9). This differs slightly from the Remote WAN print server in that the print server itself resides on the same physical network as the Terminal Server yet still services clients located across a wide area network link. This scenario is valid only if all remote clients are performing all processing from within the Terminal Server and don't require the ability to print directly from their local client device. If local printing was required in this scenario, the user's print job would traverse the WAN twice to print: first from the client to the print server and then back from the print server to the physical printer.

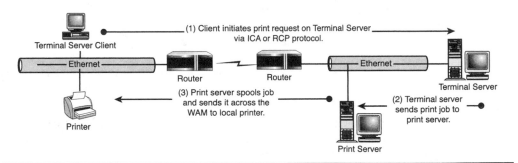

Figure 8.9 A remote LAN print server.

The final network configuration discussed in Chapter 4 was the local LAN print server and is almost identical to the remote LAN print server, except that with the local LAN print server all Terminal Server clients and printers are located on the same local area network as the Terminal Server. No print or presentation protocol data traverses a wide area network.

TIP: When providing access to network printer shares in a Terminal Server environment, note the current network layout and flag any changes that may be necessary to end up with the environment optimal for your deployment. Make sure to document the reasons why you chose to implement a particular configuration.

Shared printer resources are typically accessed in one of two ways: automatically through a logon script, or manually mapped by the user using the Add Printer wizard. Of the two, I prefer implementing logon scripts to automatically map the appropriate printers based on the user's group membership. This provides a means of transparently delivering the appropriate printers without interaction from the user. If printer assignments are left up to the user, you need to be sure users understand how to locate and map the printer properly using the Add Printer wizard. Inexperienced users can easily become confused and either map to the incorrect printer or fail to map the necessary printers at all. Either way, they are almost guaranteed to end up calling for support to try to resolve the problem.

When properly configured, logon scripts can provide a reliable and effective way to manage printer mappings for your users. While lack of programming skill will certainly limit the extent to which you can customize and modify scripts to suit your environment, the configuration steps involved are fairly straightforward, and the sample scripts I include can be customized to function in your environment with some minor changes. A simple logon script configuration can be created in a couple of steps.

Details on actual creation of a logon script to automatically map a printer are provided in Chapter 17.

NOTE: I once audited a Terminal Server environment where the administrator responsible for managing the environment was manually configuring printers for each and every Terminal Server user in the company (approximately 75 users). He logged on as the user, manually mapped the desired printers using the Add Printer wizard, logged out, and then did the same with the next user.

A thorough review of the environment followed by some assistance in implementing a logon script to manage printer assignments greatly reduced the amount of time required by the administrator to configure printers for the users in his environment.

Local Server Printers

Another printer configuration technique available on a Terminal Server is use of one or more local server printers. As the name suggests, this configuration involves setup of printers locally on the server, much like setting up a local printer on a Windows workstation. This configuration is common in smaller environments where only one or two Terminal Servers exist with limited supporting hardware (file servers, print servers, and so on) and a relatively small user community with only light printing needs. In larger environments, printers are usually configured on a central print server and shared out for access by Terminal Server users.

There are two types of local server printers: those directly connected to the server via a physical cable and those connected through a logical port that is redirected to a printer located on the network. Printers physically connected to a Terminal Server are rare, since most implementations have the Terminal Server located in an area not accessible by the end user. Use of a logical port is much more common than the direct physical connection, particularly when a TCP/IP port or a print manufacturer's custom printer port is used. Figure 8.10 shows an example of the Ports tab accessible from a printer's Properties dialog box. All ports that have been configured on the server (whether in use or not) are listed, and from here you can redirect the current printer to any given port if desired. The steps to configuring a local printer are straightforward and are discussed in Chapter 17.

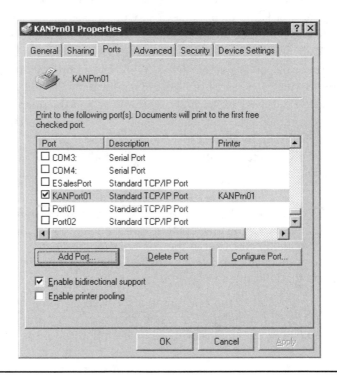

Figure 8.10 The local server printer port properties.

NOTE: Logical TCP/IP ports are commonly used on a print server to connect to an IP-based printer or print-serving device. The print server is connected to the printer through the logical port and then shares out access to the print queue using the traditional Windows printer share.

Local Client Printers

With the release of Windows 2000 came support for accessing a locally attached client printer from within a Terminal Server session. Previously this feature was supported only with the addition of Citrix MetaFrame. This feature, known as *printer redirection,* greatly enhances a Terminal Server's ability to more tightly integrate with the user's local desktop. To summarize, local client printer redirection provides the following features and functionality:

- Print jobs originating from within a user's Terminal Server session can be redirected to a printer on the user's local desktop.
- When connecting to a Windows 2000 or 2003 server using the RDP 5.1 or higher client, you can connect to either physically connected local printers or local network-mapped printers. Both versions of Windows Terminal Server support this feature in conjunction with the RDP 5.1 or higher client.
- The print job traffic is completely contained within the Terminal Server client's session data, utilizing a virtual channel between the client and the server to deliver the print job. No other network connectivity needs to exist between the client and the server.
- Client printers are mapped only if a suitable driver exists on the Terminal Server.

NOTE: Much confusion and misinformation currently exist, even in some documentation available on the Microsoft Web site, indicating that network-mapped client printers cannot be redirected through a Windows 2000 Terminal Server but only through a Windows 2003 Terminal Server. This is simply not true.

From a server's perspective, the logic behind redirecting a network-mapped printer is no different from the logic for a locally attached printer. It is the responsibility of the RDP client to enumerate the local print queues and pass the necessary information through to the Terminal Server. This information is then used to construct the corresponding printer queue on the server.

To integrate redirected network-mapped printer support into the RDP 5.0 protocol (used by Windows 2000), Microsoft developed the RDP 5.1 client so that it constructs the information delivered to the Windows 2000 Terminal Server in such a fashion that it still conforms to the older protocol's specifications. Figure 8.11 shows an example of a redirected network printer in an RDP session on a Windows 2000 Terminal Server.

The first printer in the list is the redirected network printer. Notice that the queue name has been constructed from the original mapped printer name, with the backslashes (\) converted to underscores (_). The last printer in the list is a redirected local client printer.

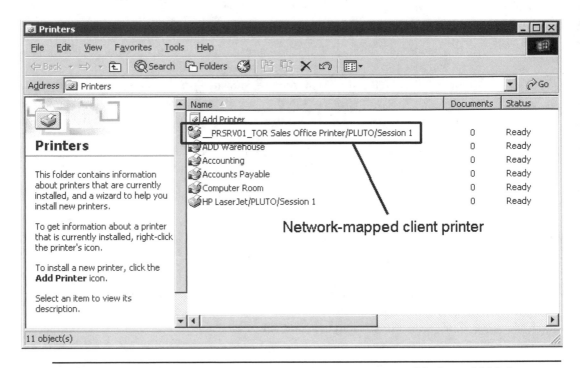

Figure 8.11 A redirected client network printer example on Windows 2000 from an RDP 5.1 client

By default, the Terminal Server tries to automatically map local client printers so they are available in the user's Terminal Server session. For this redirection to be successful, you must ensure that the Terminal Server is configured so this option is enabled at both the RDP connection level and the individual user account level. Details on this are provided in Chapter 17.

When local client printer redirection is enabled, the Terminal Server attempts to automatically connect all the printers available on a user's local desktop whenever the user logs on to the server. The process for automatically connecting and redirecting the client printers is as follows:

1. The RDP client establishes a connection with the Terminal Server and the user is authenticated.
2. During the logon, the RDP client enumerates all the client's local printers and sends the local queue name and complete driver name to the Terminal Server.
3. For the redirection to occur, the Terminal Server must take the client's driver name and find a corresponding driver on the server with the exact same name. For example, if the client machine has a driver called "hp deskjet 970c series," the server must have a driver with an *identical* name (same punctuation, same case, same everything) for the redirection to occur. If the names do not match or a driver cannot be found, an event ID 1111 (see Figure 8.12) is created in the server's system log and

the printer mapping silently fails. No error message is displayed to the user. If the corresponding driver has been installed and the mapping still fails, it is likely because the driver names differ between the client and the server. Details on correcting this issue are discussed in Chapter 17.

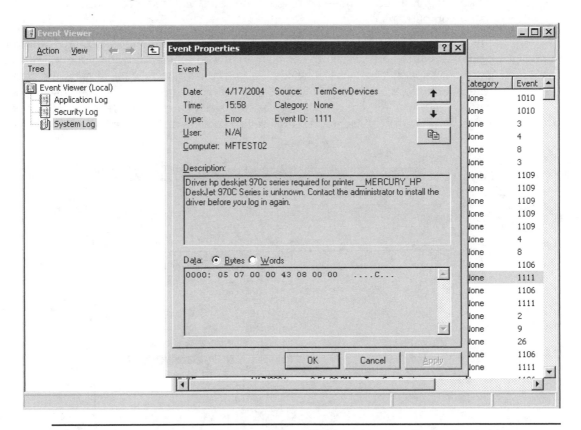

Figure 8.12 The event ID 1111 message displays when a client printer driver cannot be found on the Terminal Server.

4. If a matching driver is found, the Terminal Server creates a server-based queue for the client's local printer using this naming convention:

<full client printer queue name>/<client host name>/
Session <RDP session number>

If the client queue name is network based, any back-slashes (\) in the name are converted to underscores (_) when building the name.

TIP: If manually adding a printer on a Terminal Server using the Add Printer wizard, you may notice that, under the list of local printer ports, a number of special ports exist with the prefix TSxxx, where XXX is a three-digit number as shown in Figure 8.13. As you might suspect, these ports are associated with redirected local ports for the listed computer name.

I highly recommend that you not manually create a local printer associated with one of these printer ports. While the configuration may appear to work properly, Microsoft does not support it because of issues that may arise with how these ports are cleared when a user logs off. Normally the Terminal Server purges all redirected client ports when a user logs off, but because the server is not "aware" of these manually created ports, they will not be cleared and will remain on the server unless manually removed.

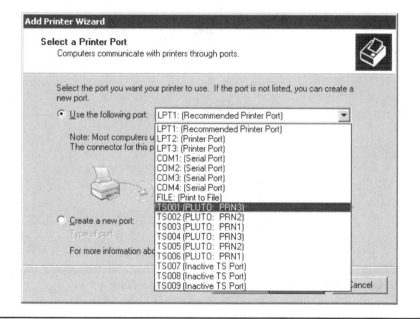

Figure 8.13 Terminal Server client-mapped printer ports.

Windows Terminal Server provides some highly robust printing support, particularly when it involves accessing redirected local client printers. With a clear understanding of what printer options are available, the Terminal Server administrator finds the task of selecting and planning the most appropriate configuration for printer support greatly demystified.

Even so, when preparing to implement a large-scale Terminal Server environment, you may need to consider the advanced printer support options available with Citrix MetaFrame.

These options were created specifically to help centralize and ease management of printer support in a large-scale environment. MetaFrame-specific printer support is discussed in the "End-User Printing Support with MetaFrame" section later in this chapter.

Terminal Server Load Balancing with Microsoft Network Load Balancing

As mentioned in Chapter 1, implementation of Terminal Services alone would be of little use without the ability to scale the environment to support users across more than one Terminal Server. Distributing the user load across multiple Terminal Servers helps mitigate the impact a server failure has on the environment and simplifies the job of scaling the environment when necessary to accommodate growth requirements. Microsoft provides scalability through Network Load Balancing (NLB), which is available with Windows 2000 (Advanced Server or Datacenter Server) and with all versions of Windows Server 2003.

NLB, which is a component of Windows Clustering, allows for multiple servers to provide TCP/IP-based services to users through one or more "clustered" IP addresses. The servers are "grouped" together and operate conceptually as a single entity. NLB was developed primarily to provide redundancy for Web-based services such as Web or FTP servers, but the same functionality can be used in a Terminal Server environment.

In an NLB environment, all RDP clients are configured to connect to a cluster host name or IP address and not to a specific server name. When a connect request is made to the cluster, all Terminal Servers in the cluster receive the incoming request, and based on the distribution algorithm, one client accepts the connection request while all others discard it. Distribution is coordinated between cluster members through periodic exchange of heartbeat messages. When a new host is added, removed, or fails to respond to a set number of heartbeat messages, the cluster enters a state known as *convergence*. During convergence, cluster membership is verified and client load redistributed accordingly. During this time, all cluster connections for the available hosts are serviced, but any requests destined for a failed host continue to fail until convergence is complete and an alternate host has been selected to handle those requests. The default heartbeat interval is one second and the threshold for missed heartbeats is five. Both values can be modified by editing the following registry keys on all cluster members. Under the key

HKEY_LOCAL_MACHINE\SYSTEM\CurrentControlSet\Services\WLBS\
Parameters

you find the values

AliveMsgPeriod: The default value is 1,000 milliseconds (1 second).

AliveMsgTolerance: The default value is 5, for five missed heartbeats.

Figure 8.14 demonstrates a Terminal Server client connecting to the host name termserv.noisyriver.com, which represents the NLB cluster containing three Terminal Servers. The user is directed to server A, B, or C depending on the current load distribution.

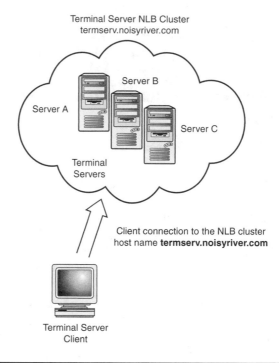

Figure 8.14   An NLB client connection example.

TIP: When NLB is used, a user's Terminal Server session information is not simultaneously maintained across multiple servers, as the term clustering might suggest. If a user is active on a server that fails, their session and any information currently open within that session are lost. If the user reconnects, they automatically are directed to an alternate server in the cluster that is still active.

NLB operates as a network driver on each server participating in an NLB cluster (Figure 8.15). Properties for the driver are configured in order to specify how the cluster will behave.

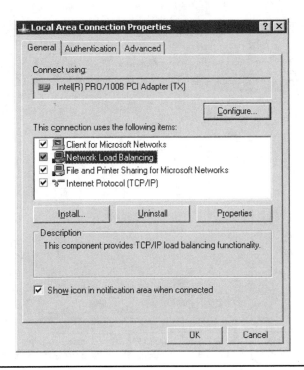

Figure 8.15   NLB is a special network service associated with a TCP/IP connection. No other connection type is supported.

The NLB settings are configured in one of two ways:

- By selecting the properties for the NLB driver on each server participating in the cluster. This is the only configuration option supported by Windows 2000 Server.
- By using the Network Load Balancing Manager tool provided as part of Windows Server 2003.

In an environment with only a few servers (typically 10 or less), I would consider configuring NLB directly on each server to be manageable. For larger Terminal Server environments, however, not only does this become much more time consuming to manage, but also the chance of errors in configuration of one or more servers increases. Dependency on this per-server configuration with Windows 2000 limits its usefulness in large Terminal Server environments.

Windows Server 2003 includes a new utility called the Network Load Balancing Manager, which can be found under Administrative Tools on the Start menu. This tool allows all aspects of an NLB cluster to be configured from a single point instead of having to configure options on each individual cluster member. Figure 8.16 shows the Network Load Balancing Manager with two Windows 2003 Terminal Servers in a test cluster.

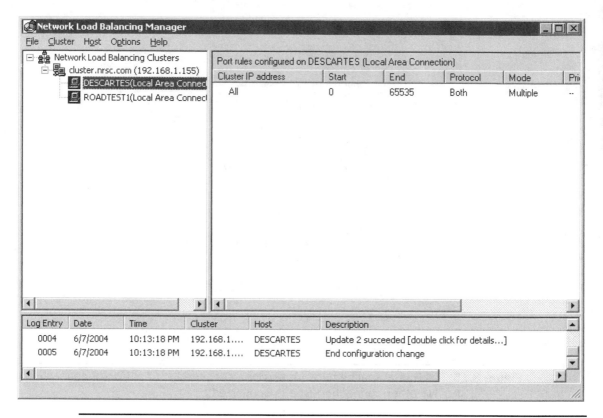

Figure 8.16 The Windows Server 2003 Network Load Balancing Manager.

Before you begin to configure and implement an NLB cluster in your Terminal Server environment, there are some hardware and configuration considerations that should be finalized. Figure 8.17 summarizes the main cluster parameters that need to be defined when creating the NLB cluster. These settings are

- **IP address**—This is the main IP address for the cluster. Ensure that this address will not be assigned to another server or PC and that it has been excluded from any DHCP servers that may exist. This address will be the same for all hosts in your NLB cluster. You can define additional cluster IP addresses later in the installation wizard or by modifying the cluster properties.
- **Subnet mask**—The subnet mask for your cluster IP address.
- **Full Internet name**—This is the fully qualified domain name for the cluster.

- **Network address**—This is the media access control (MAC) address for the cluster interface. The value cannot be directly manipulated but will be set based on the operation mode selected for the cluster. This is the "virtual" MAC address that is assigned to the cluster and advertised using the address resolution protocol (ARP). ARP is used to map the IP address of the cluster to the MAC hardware address, which is used by the data link protocol to actually transmit data over the physical network. See Appendix C, "Network Primer," for more information on the OSI model and the data link protocol layer.

- **Cluster operation mode**—These settings define how the cluster interfaces with the network adapter on the server and what type of MAC address will be assigned. The default configuration is *unicast* and, in this mode, the MAC address for the cluster overwrites the physical MAC address assigned to the network card on each server in the cluster. Because all hosts in the cluster share the same MAC address, no intra-host communications other than NLB-related communications are possible unless a second network adapter is present on each server. This includes use of the Network Load Balancing Manager. When a single network interface card (NIC) exists on each server and the cluster is operating in unicast mode, the NLB Manager cannot be used from one server in the cluster to manage another. Unicast mode does have the advantage of working in all routing situations, although switch-flooding can result when all hosts in the cluster are directly connected to a switch. *Switch-flooding* occurs when a unicast or multicast packet is received by a switch and sent out on all switch ports.

  Alternatively, multicast mode can be selected instead of unicast. Multicast mode adds the virtual MAC address of the cluster to each server's network card but allows each card to still retain its own physical MAC address. In this configuration, host communications are still possible between servers in the cluster when only a single network card is used. Multicast mode may not be supported in your network environment, depending on the router hardware in place. The router hardware must support mapping the single IP address of the cluster to the multicast MAC address, or the multicast mode cannot be used. Static ARP entries may also be required on routers that do not accept ARP responses that give a multicast MAC address for a single IP address.

  When multicast mode is selected, you have the option of enabling IGMP multicast. IGMP stands for Internet Group Membership Protocol, and when supported by the network switches in your environment, limits switch-flooding.

- **Allow remote control**—When enabled, cluster operations can be controlled remotely using the NLB command line tool. For security reasons, Microsoft highly recommended that this option not be enabled.

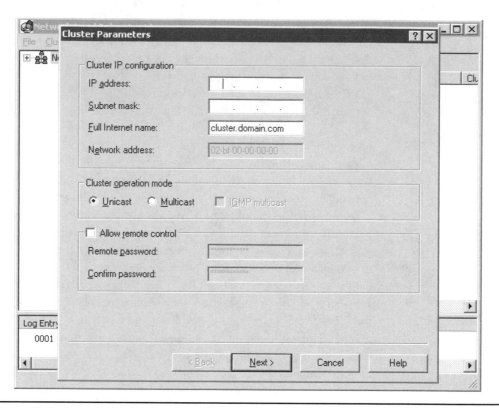

Figure 8.17 NLB cluster parameters.

I recommend that the operating mode for your NLB cluster be selected as follows:

- Whenever possible, have two network cards in your Terminal Server so that one can be dedicated for NLB and the other can be used for intra-host communications in the cluster. Select the unicast operating mode in this configuration.
- If your Terminal Servers have only a single network card and you must deploy NLB, then attempt to run in multicast mode whenever possible. With a single NIC, choose unicast only if your network infrastructure does not support the multicast operating mode. In multicast mode, verify from your network administrator whether IGMP multicast is supported or not and enable it when appropriate.

Once you have decided on the operating mode for the cluster, you should plan the specific port rules that will be load balanced in the cluster. Figure 8.18 shows the Port Rule dialog box, where you define the various port rules to be enforced in the NLB cluster. When configuring NLB for your Terminal Server environment, you would define a port rule for your RDP connections, which initiate a server connection over TCP port 3389.

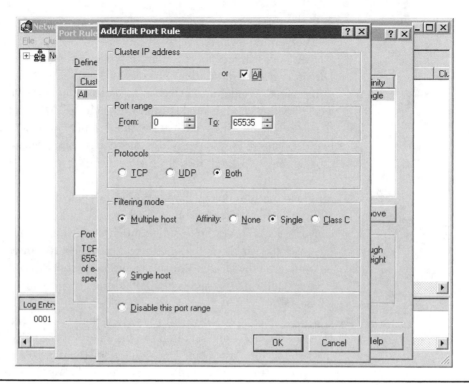

Figure 8.18 NLB cluster port rules.

The parameters for a port rule are

- **Cluster IP address**—If you have defined multiple IP addresses for your cluster, you can associate a single cluster address for this port rule or use the default selection of All.
- **Port range**—This refers to the range of port numbers associated with this rule. The default is all valid TCP/UDP ports (0 to 65535). If you wanted to define a rule only for RDP, you would enter the address 3389.
- **Protocols**—This refers to the corresponding protocol to associate with the port.
- **Filtering mode**—Three options are available. The default mode is Multiple Host and specifies that multiple hosts in the cluster will service this port rule. This is the mode you choose when configuring load balancing for Terminal Services. With this selection, you can choose from the following three client affinity options. Affinity controls how servers in the cluster manage multiple connection requests from the same client.
    - *None*—Allows multiple connections from the same client to be serviced by different cluster members. If a user connects to the cluster, logs out, and then reconnects an hour later, he or she will not necessarily be directed to

the same server. This can pose a problem if a user has a disconnected session on a server in the cluster. With affinity option None, there is no guarantee that the user will reconnect to that disconnected session unless the Session Directory feature of Windows Server 2003 is also used (discussed in the next section). Windows 2000 has no mechanism for automatically associating a client with a disconnected session in the cluster. Microsoft recommends that Terminal Servers in a cluster with an affinity of None be configured so that disconnected sessions are terminated and not maintained on the server, thus helping to prevent sessions from remaining unclaimed and consuming server resources.

- *Single*—Specifies that all connection requests from the same client IP address are always serviced by the same host (at least until the next cluster convergence). This is the default configuration and, when implemented, increases the likelihood that a user will reconnect to a disconnected session on a server in the cluster. For this to be successful, the user must connect from a client with the same client IP address that originally initiated the connection.

- *Class C*—Similar to single affinity except that, instead of directing a single IP address to the same server, it directs an entire class C address range to the same server. This option is best suited for Internet-based connects, which are typically distributed across a wide range of class C networks. Class C affinity should not be selected when servicing local area network users, since they will likely all be from the same class C network, resulting in all connects being serviced by a single host in the cluster.

Besides the Multiple Hosts mode, there is the Single Host filtering mode. The Single Host option specifies that a single host in the cluster will be selected to service this port rule. The same server manages all requests for this port until it fails or convergence selects a new server to take over this role. Single Host is not appropriate for most Terminal Server–based NLB implementations.

The final filtering option is Disable This Port Range, which blocks all traffic into the cluster for the given port rule.

Figure 8.19 demonstrates a sample port rule specifically for Terminal Services. Note that the Multiple Host mode has been selected, requiring either that Session Directory be implemented in Windows Server 2003 to manage disconnected sessions or that retention of disconnected sessions be disabled through the RDP connection settings. Details on configuring RDP connections are provided in Chapter 19. A step-by-step walkthrough on setting up RDP load balancing is covered in Chapter 22.

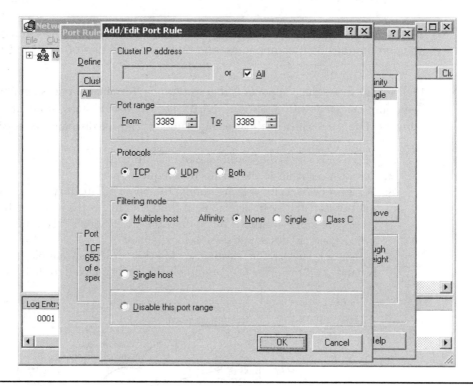

Figure 8.19   A sample configuration demonstrating an NLB cluster port rule for RDP connections.

TIP: A network load-balancing cluster can contain a maximum of 32 nodes (servers).

Windows Server 2003 Terminal Services Session Directory

Windows Server 2003 extends usability of NLB as a load-balancing solution for Terminal Services with the introduction of the new cluster component called Terminal Services Session Directory (TSSD). TSSD can be used to enhance functionality of load-balancing solutions such as NLB or DNS (domain name service) round-robin by enabling support for reconnecting a user's disconnected session within a load-balanced Terminal Server environment. As I described in the previous section, without such functionality, when a user disconnects an active Terminal Server session within a clustered environment it is highly likely that when the user reconnects, particularly from a different client, they will be presented with a new Terminal Server session instead of reconnecting to their existing one.

TIP: Some third-party load-balancing tools such as WTS Gateway Pro provide their own session management components and do not require use of Session Directory.

Figure 8.20 shows the components that exist when Terminal Services Session Directory has been implemented with Microsoft NLB. The following steps summarize how Session Directory integrates with a load-balancing solution to provide disconnected session accessibility.

1. The user contacts the Terminal Server NLB cluster.
2. Server A responds to the connection request.
3. Server A contacts the server running the Session Directory service. This server queries its database to determine if this user already has an active but disconnected session in the cluster. If no connection exists, Server A continues the logon process and creates a new session for the user.
4. If the user does have an existing session (Server C, for example) the logon process is handed off to Server C, where the user is reconnected to their existing session.

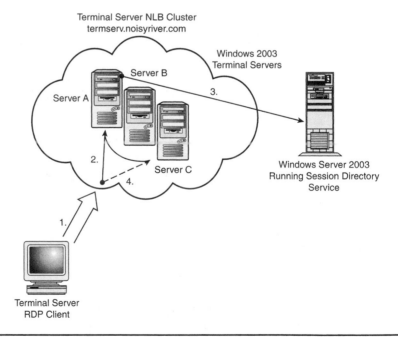

Figure 8.20 Windows 2003 Terminal Services Session Directory provides the ability to reconnect to disconnected sessions in a Microsoft network load-balancing cluster.

To implement TSSD, your environment must meet the following requirements:

- It must be running Windows Server 2003, Enterprise or Datacenter Edition.
- The Session Directory service must be enabled and running on a server in the environment. This server does not have to be running Windows Terminal Services, and in fact it is recommended that it not be a Terminal Server. The Session Directory service is installed on all Enterprise and Datacenter Edition servers but must be manually enabled and started through the server's Services properties, as shown in Figure 8.21.

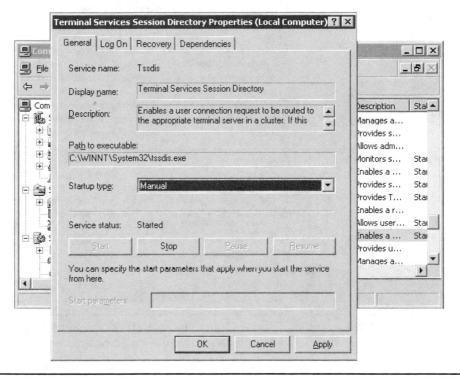

Figure 8.21   The Terminal Services Session Directory service needs only to be enabled and started to be accessible on a Windows 2003 Enterprise or Datacenter Edition server.

- All Terminal Servers that will participate in Session Directory must have their computer account added to the local group Session Directory Computers, which is automatically created the first time the Session Directory service is started on a server. Figure 8.22 shows an example of this security group created on a Windows Server 2003 member server. Terminal Server domain computer accounts must belong to this group in order to be able to join the Session Directory. If the

Session Directory service is subsequently stopped and disabled, this local security group is *not* deleted.

■ The servers must be in a Windows 2000 or 2003 Active Directory domain. Session Directory is not supported in a Windows NT 4.0 domain.

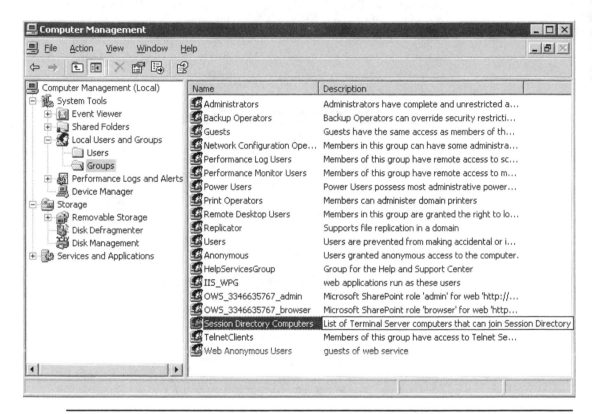

Figure 8.22 Terminal Servers must belong to the local Session Directory Computers group to be able to join a Session Directory.

Once these requirements have been satisfied, you can add your clustered Terminal Servers to the Session Directory server. Terminal Servers are added either through a domain group policy or from within the Terminal Services Configuration tool. Figure 8.23 shows the main dialog box in the Terminal Services Configuration tool, where Session Directory membership is configured. Details on joining and managing a Session Directory server are discussed in Chapter 22.

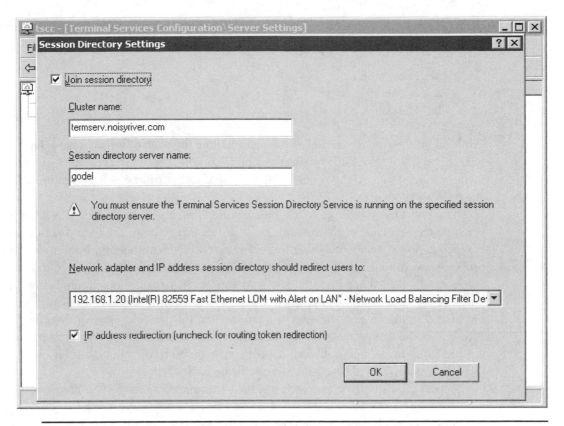

Figure 8.23 Terminal Servers can be manually added to a Session Directory through the Terminal Services Configuration utility, but best practices dictate that domain group policies be used instead.

Profile and Home Folder Access

An important part of proper deployment and management of your Terminal Server environment is establishing a location where each Terminal Server user's profile and home folders can be stored. In planning for this it helps to have a clear idea of the profile and home folder configuration you will implement and where this information will be stored.

User Profiles

Every user of a Windows 32-bit operating system (workstation or server) has what is known as a *user profile*. A user profile contains a combination of the user's desktop settings such as icons, screen colors, window positions, and user-specific information such as network or printer connections, Internet favorites, and e-mail preferences. A user profile also contains a copy of the contents of the HKEY_CURRENT_USER registry key, which is automatically loaded into the registry when the user logs on and unloaded when the user logs out. This registry key contains application and session information specific to that user. Windows supports three types of user profiles:

- Local profiles
- Roaming profiles
- Mandatory roaming profiles

While all profile types manage the same information, the main differences between the three types are the extent of the profile's accessibility and the amount of control the user has over saving changes back to the profile so that these changes can be accessed later or from an alternate location.

The first time you log on to a Windows computer, a *personal profile* is created for you when you save a copy of the computer's local default profile to the hard drive of the local computer. Any changes you make to your desktop or environment are then saved to this profile when you log off. The next time you log on to that specific computer, this profile is automatically loaded and appears exactly as you left it. Because this profile is saved locally onto the server it is commonly referred to as a *local profile*, and because it is local to that machine, logging on to a different computer does not present you with the same profile. Either a profile that previously existed for you on that other machine is used, or a new one is created from the default profile on that computer. If you travel around and log on to a number of computers, you'll have a distinct profile on each of them.

A local profile behaves the same way on a Terminal Server. The first time a user logs on to a Terminal Server, he or she is presented with a default profile, which the user can freely customize. The next time the user logs on to that same server, the user's profile is picked up automatically, along with any of the changes instituted by the user in the previous session. As you may have guessed, if the user logs on to a different Terminal Server, he or she won't pick up the local profile that was saved on the other server. It is clear to see that this can certainly cause problems for the end user in an environment composed of multiple Terminal Servers. If the desktop configuration is not uniform across all servers, the user will quickly become confused when things appear to change at random from one session to the next.

Local profiles are the default profile type used unless a roaming profile (regular or mandatory) has been defined for a user. Local profiles for both Windows 2000 and 2003 Terminal Servers are stored in this folder:

%SystemDrive%\Documents and Settings

Figure 8.24 shows an example of the Documents and Settings directory on a Windows 2000 Terminal Server. Notice that it contains folders for a number of users, including the local administrator, the default user, and even a folder called All Users, which contains common profile information for all users who log on to the server.

TIP: Only administrators, SYSTEM, and the associated user have access to a profile folder. By default, a user cannot access another user's profile folder.

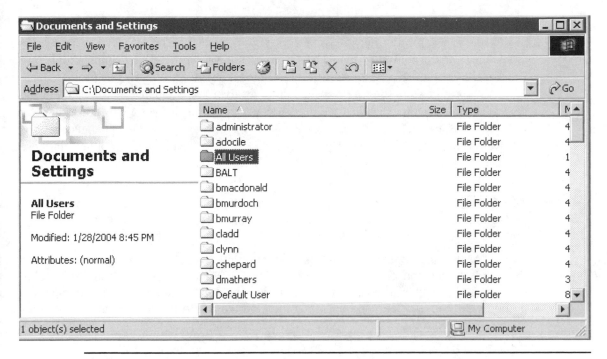

Figure 8.24   The Documents and Settings folder on a Windows 2000 Terminal Server.

Microsoft recommends that you not directly manipulate the profile folders located under Documents and Settings but instead use the User Profiles tab from the System applet in the control panel. In addition to finding summary information on the existing profiles (name, size, type, last modified), you can perform some basic profile manipulation from here.

For the reasons just outlined, local user profiles are not a suitable option for a Terminal Server implementation when anything more than a single server is used. As soon as a user can move between multiple Terminal Servers, the local profiles on each server quickly begin to differ from each other. Desktop settings seem to appear and disappear as the user logs on to different servers in the environment.

TIP: If left unchecked, user profiles can become extremely large as the number of temporary Internet files grows and users save objects directly onto their desktops instead of into a server-based folder.

Details on implementation of user profiles, including profile manipulation and size management, are discussed in Chapter 18.

One way to resolve this issue is to have a single profile available regardless of what server the user logs on to. This is where the roaming profile comes into play. The *roaming profile* is a user profile that is centrally stored in a network location and represents the master copy of the user's local profile. Regardless of what server a user logs on to, his or her profile is accessible from this central location. Details on accessing and processing roaming profiles are provided in Chapter 18. For the purpose of planning, it is sufficient to say that changes made to a user's profile while the user is logged on to a server are compared and updated in the centrally stored roaming profile when the user logs off. These changes are then available the next time they log on, regardless of what Terminal Server they access. Certain update logic is followed if multiple user logons exist and changes are being made to the profile from more than one location; this too is discussed in Chapter 18.

TIP: One thing worth noting now has to do with issues that can arise when a user's profile is not unloaded properly during logoff. In the past this was a common problem, and a number of tools have been developed to help counteract the issues.

As part of the user logoff process, the system normally unloads the registry portion of the user's profile and saves it back to the NTUSER.DAT file, located in the profile folder. If the registry fails to unload, the profile reconciliation process does not complete properly and the user can end up with a local profile and a roaming profile that are no longer synchronized.

When this happens, what the user experiences depends on the Terminal Server version they are running on. Windows 2000 users experience an extremely slow logoff process, with the process appearing to hang with the Saving Settings message for the default period of 60 seconds. This is because the server is retrying once every second for 60 seconds to successfully unload the profile. After 60 seconds, the server gives up and simply logs the user off. No profile synchronization happens in this situation.

Windows 2003 users are logged off immediately, and the system uses a copy of the current registry keys to complete the profile synchronization. The orphaned registry keys that could not be unloaded remain in memory until the system is restarted.

In either case, events are logged to the application event log on the Terminal Server stating that the registry could not be unloaded because it was in use by another process and access was denied. Figure 8.25 shows an example of this on a Windows 2000 Terminal Server.

When a user's profile fails to unload properly, this can result in issues the next time the user attempts to log on; for example, profile changes not being saved or error messages saying the roaming profile itself is not accessible are two of the most common side effects.

In the past, this type of problem could be resolved only by tracking down the offending application(s) and getting the vendor to correct its code. The main issue with doing this was simply the time required to get back a fix. Until the correction was available, the problem continued to occur and affected the user's computing experience.

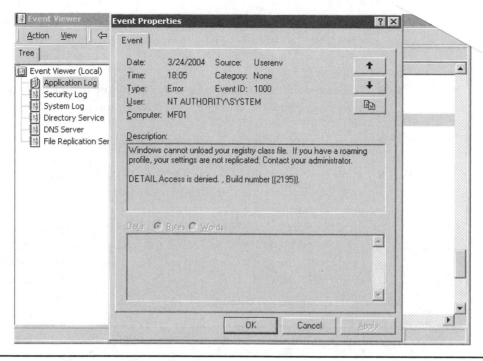

Figure 8.25 An application event log error is generated because a registry key could not be unloaded.

Microsoft now provides a special service that can be installed on a Terminal Server (or any other Windows machine) and monitors active users to ensure that the registry and profile are properly unloaded when a user logs off. This tool is called the User Profile Hive Cleanup Service (UPHClean, for short) and can be downloaded from the Microsoft downloads page at http://www.microsoft.com/downloads.

UPHClean is supported on Windows NT 4.0, Windows 2000, and Windows 2003. Installation is straightforward, requiring no special configuration. Once installed the service automatically starts and immediately begins monitoring the system for "stuck" profile issues. While UPHClean does not require a reboot, it is a good idea to perform an initial reboot once the product is installed to remove any existing registry entries that may have remained behind. I recommend that you include UPHClean as a standard part of your server installation.

Although a roaming profile provides the user with a consistent desktop regardless of which Terminal Server he or she uses, this can still introduce a number of administrative challenges:

- Giving users the ability to modify and control their own desktops and application settings can cause the type of support calls you intended to reduce (or eliminate) with the introduction of Terminal Server.

■ An additional user support requirement is immediately created because you must now work to ensure that the user's roaming profile is available when necessary. A loss in application or other desktop settings will most likely result in a support call from the user.

■ Roaming profiles introduce additional complexity in how updates to the application or other registry settings are effectively propagated to all users.

There are two ways to approach solving these problems:

■ Apply the necessary group policy settings to the Terminal Server organizational unit (OU) in the active directory to restrict the user's access to the desktop as much as possible.

Both Windows 2000 and 2003 provide a vast number of policy settings that can be used to control what changes the user can make to their desktop. In Chapter 15, the process of group policy creation and management is discussed. Figure 8.26 shows an example of some of the settings that can be configured to manage user profile accessibility.

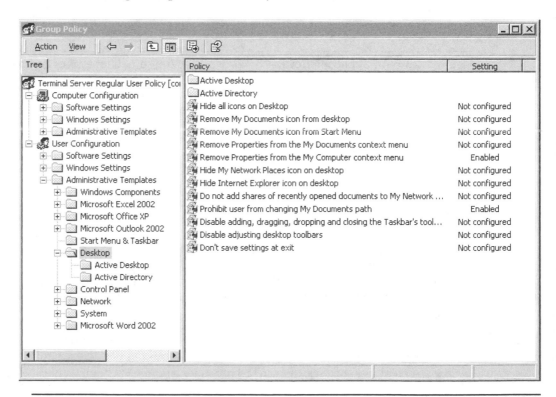

Figure 8.26 An example of Windows group policy object settings that allow configuration of a user's profile.

- **Use a mandatory roaming profile—**

  A mandatory roaming profile behaves exactly like a standard roaming profile, with one exception: Changes made by the user during a session are not saved to the profile stored on the server when the user logs off. The next time the user logs on, he or she once again receives the original profile from the server. Removing the user's ability to save profile changes gives you the capacity to assign the same profile to multiple users and, as a result, provides a single location where profile changes will automatically be updated for all associated users. This approach is most common in a situation where a number of task-based workers perform the same job function (a call center, for example) and you want to ensure that they all have a consistent user interface. This helps to simplify not only support but also issues such as training. It can also help reduce the amount of time users spend customizing their environments with such features as custom icons or wallpaper.

NOTE: In a Terminal Server environment, a mandatory roaming profile can provide an easy way to quickly implement a static profile in which a user can't make any changes. Creating and managing mandatory roaming profiles are discussed in Chapter 18.

With three profile configurations to choose from, you must make the important planning decision of how you will manage user profiles. You should ensure you have covered the following requirements:

- **Determine the different profile configurations that will be used—**If you're unsure, assume that you will implement roaming profiles with the plan of including mandatory profiles if the need arises. Do not consider use of local profiles except in the smallest of implementations where available server resources are minimal.

- **Establish a share location on a Windows file server that will house the roaming user profiles—**While most user profile information would not be considered critical, per-user application settings, registry entries, and possibly documents stored directly on the desktop are things you may not want to have to re-create. For this reason, a target profile server should be a Windows file server that has followed best practices for redundancy and availability. At this point you need to have only a location and share defined. I usually recommend TSProfiles as the share name on the host computer.

- **Plan to implement the UPHClean utility as a precautionary measure against hung user profiles in the registry—**There is no intricate installation plan required, but noting the need for this application ensures it is installed as part of the base server build.

Home Folders

Besides establishing a location for user profiles, you also need to decide on a network-based location for each user's home folder. A home folder serves two purposes in a Terminal Server environment. First, it provides the default working folder location when one has not been specified for an application, and second, it provides a location for user-specific application and system information within the Terminal Server. If a home folder location is not specified for a user's account, the default setting to use is the profile folder. This is not a desirable location, particularly for roaming profiles, because the contents of the home folder will likely grow quite large, increasing the time required to both download and upload the profile changes. This can further exacerbate disk space issues for the Terminal Server boot/system drive, where local profiles reside by default.

Traditionally the Terminal Server home folder path is configured for a user in their user account properties, as shown in Figure 8.27. Details on different methods of creating the home folders, including group policy objects in a Windows 2003 domain, are discussed in Chapter 18. When planning for use of home folders, the two key questions to answer are

- Where is the network share going to be located that will provide the access point into the user's home folder?

  It should be a proper Windows file server whose configuration follows best practices for maximizing server availability.
- What drive letter will be used to map the home folder?

  Most organizations have a standard set of drives consistent for all (or at least most) users. Typically, drive letters such as H:, U:, or P: are used to map the home folder. Be certain that the drive letter chosen does not conflict with any existing drive letters that a user might have for other applications or data access.

A common configuration I like to use in a Terminal Server environment is to map the My Documents folder for each user into their personal home folder location. This consolidates all the information into one location and not only makes it easy for the user to find documents they save but also simplifies configuration of data backups in the environment.

By default, the My Documents folder points into the user's profile folder, which is rarely a desirable setup in a Terminal Server environment. By redirecting My Documents, you can also avoid having to teach users to save data onto a specific drive letter, such as H:, in order to ensure the data is going onto a centralized file server. The My Documents metaphor is easily understood by most users. My Documents can be redirected through a group policy object; details are covered in Chapter 18.

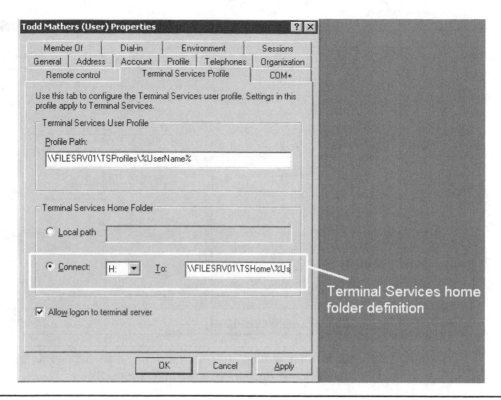

Figure 8.27 An example of the Terminal Services home folder path entered for a user.

TIP: When defining a user profile and home folder location, you have the option of configuring settings for Terminal Services that are different from those for regular Windows desktops and servers. Figure 8.28 shows the user profile and home folder entries for both Terminal Services and regular Windows logons.

Microsoft does provide a hierarchy that dictates the order in which these settings are applied. When a user logs on to a Terminal Server, Windows first looks to see if the Terminal Services home and profile settings are defined and uses those if available. If either of the Terminal Server settings are blank, Windows attempts to use the standard Windows home/profile paths to map the corresponding folder in the Terminal Server. If these paths are also not defined, the default local home and profile paths are used.

When logging on to a regular Windows desktop or server, the Terminal Server–specific profile and home settings are never queried or used.

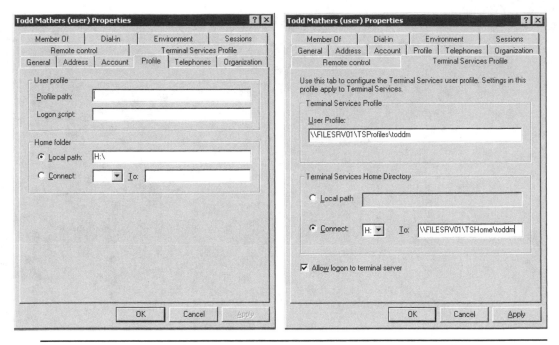

Figure 8.28   User profile and home folder entries can be defined for both Terminal Services and regular Windows logon sessions.

Home and Profile Mappings with Microsoft's Distributed File System

Traditionally, home and profile folders are mapped directly to resources shared on servers in the domain. For example, a user's profile folder could be mapped to a share called TSProfiles on a server called FILESERVER01, as shown:

\\FILESERVER01\TSProfiles\LindaH

While there is nothing technically wrong with this configuration, there are a couple of support issues that can arise and subsequently impact the uptime of the environment:

- If the hosting server goes down or must be taken offline, the users can no longer access their profile or home drive information, likely resulting in the users being unable to work in the Terminal Server until the hosting server is once again online.
- If there is ever a requirement to move the resources off the current file server and onto a different server, all references will need to be updated to reflect the change. Depending on how many Terminal Server users need to be updated, this task can be extremely time consuming.

An effective way to mitigate the risk of this type of issues is to implement your shared resource access via Microsoft's Distributed File System (DFS). DFS lets you access files shared on one or more servers in your network through a single virtual share reference. For example, a DFS share could be created called \\nrsc.com\DFSRoot, and from this location you could access both the TSProfiles and TSHome shares without ever actually including a reference to the physical server sharing these folders. The two folder references in this case would be

\\nrsc.com\DFSRoot\TSProfiles

\\nrsc.com\DFSRoot\TSHome

I provide more details on configuration and use of DFS in Chapter 18. If your current infrastructure has already implemented DFS, you may want to consider informing the appropriate DFS administrator that you may be requesting their services to assist in defining DFS entries for your Terminal Server profile and home shares.

More information on DFS can be found on the Microsoft Web site in the articles "Overview of DFS in Windows 2000" (knowledgebase article 812487) and "Simplify Infrastructure Complexity with Windows Distributed File System" (http://www.microsoft.com/windowsserver2003/techinfo/overview/dfs.mspx).

I highly encourage use of this technology as a means of delivering a layer of abstraction to the home and profile folder mappings and eliminating dependency on a specific server name for these mappings.

Scheduled Server Reboots

Issues with an application's stability or resource requirements on the desktop are quickly amplified when run on a Terminal Server. Problems such as memory leaks can have a significant impact on availability of a Terminal Server as the leaks slowly (or quickly, as the case may be) consume the available resources, eventually resulting in Low on Virtual Memory errors and system crashes. The only reliable way to ensure that issues like this do not impact your server environment is to establish a server reboot schedule.

The frequency with which reboots are performed depends largely on how many applications are being served and the overall stability of the environment during your testing and pilot phases. Using some of the load-testing criteria discussed in Chapter 6, "Terminal Server Hardware Planning," you can monitor your servers to determine the extent of resource issues (most often, memory) during piloting and plan any necessary reboot scheduling that may be required.

Whenever discussions of the reboot requirements for a Terminal Server implementation arise, the first reaction is almost invariably one of disbelief. Comparisons between the average uptime of a SQL Server or IIS Server are common but not valid. It's like comparing apples and oranges: same general shape but not really the same thing at all. Possibly a better comparison would be to look at the average uptime of a Windows desktop running the same suite of applications targeted for a Terminal Server.

It is not a question of whether or not you will schedule automatic reboots but more a question of how frequently reboots will be done and whether the process will be a manual or automated. The frequency and sophistication of this schedule depends on the applications in your environment and the system behavior you observe during testing and piloting.

The requirements for a reboot schedule should be included as part of your installation and management plan. Make note of any special environmental requirements that may impose restrictions on a reboot schedule. For example, if a call center accessing the Terminal Servers operated 24 hours a day, Monday through Friday, your reboot window would have to be sometime over the weekend to minimize impact on production users.

Various mechanisms exist for scheduling and managing server reboots; these are discussed in Chapter 11. The most common method is scheduling the reboot using Scheduled Tasks and a batch script with the TSSHUTDN command. If you're implementing MetaFrame Presentation Server, Enterprise Edition, the resource management components provide support for reboot scheduling directly within the Management Console.

NOTE: As Terminal Services has matured from the days of Windows NT 4.0, Terminal Server Edition, through the latest incarnation in Windows Server 2003, I've noticed a significant increase in average server uptime between reboots. Reboot intervals of 21–35 days or more are not uncommon. Frequency of required reboots has greatly diminished since the days of NT 4.0, Terminal Server Edition, but can still be valuable in maximizing server uptime and availability.

Server Cloning

Typically when implementing multiple Terminal Servers, the natural tendency of an administrator is to treat each server as an individual management entity built and supported independently of all others. If a new server is required in the environment, it's built from scratch (hopefully, using a set of documented guidelines to ensure it's configured properly). This process of management is a result of the natural progression of learning when the Terminal Server environment is first created. As you progress through the iterations of building the Terminal Server as desired, you develop a documented approach that can be followed to reproduce the environment you've created. After you move on to adding and testing the desired applications, the document continues to grow to include this new knowledge until eventually you have a complete history of how you progressed from start to finish.

While having thorough server build documentation is important, every time you manually build a new server or install an application using this documentation it is not only time consuming but also causes you to run the risk of introducing subtle configuration differences that can result in application or server anomalies. Always having to question the consistency of the production environment adds an additional layer of complexity when attempting to troubleshoot a production problem. Reliance on a manual build process introduces a constraint on the scalability of the environment.

One suggestion I often hear for overcoming the difficulty of managing an increasing number of servers is simply to upgrade the existing hardware to support an increased user load per server. As discussed in Chapter 6, the acceptable ratio of users to servers is more dependent on the risk tolerance of the business and less on the management load of the administrator. If a server goes down and users are affected, do you think the business will be understanding of the fact that the number of users affected was based on the need to reduce the workload required by the administrator to manage the environment? Obviously, an alternate strategy is needed to increase reliability in the build process while minimizing impact on the user.

The final Terminal Server–related planning topic I discuss in this chapter is the process of using server cloning to accelerate building and deployment of Terminal Servers while at the same time increasing reliability and consistency of the environment.

The concept of server cloning is straightforward. The idea is that you have a Terminal Server you have built and tested, and from this you create an exact replica of the hard drive containing the operating system and applications. You then place this replica onto a second server, thereby duplicating the configuration of the first. This process is repeated as required in order to build up an environment of servers all having the same configuration. The advantage of cloning quickly becomes apparent in a large server deployment scenario, since one or two servers can be used during installation and testing of the operating system and software. When the time comes to test the configuration on multiple servers, you simply place the cloned server's image onto the other hardware, and voilà, you have a multiple-server environment. While alternatives exist, such as scripted installations, I will always prefer cloning. It is fast, reliable, and straightforward. Cloning can be ideal in a disaster-recovery situation to get an environment back online as quickly as possible.

Figure 8.29 demonstrates how server imaging can be integrated into the build process for the Terminal Server environment. Of course, the environment could be created without the imaging step, but if a problem is encountered, it's likely you will need to start over from the beginning to rebuild the server. If you've been maintaining server images, you can easily roll back to the point where you had a stable server configuration. The process can be a valuable time-saver, even in a small Terminal Server implementation.

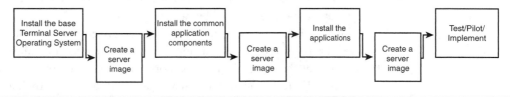

Figure 8.29   Integrating server cloning into the build process for a Terminal Server implementation.

NOTE: When using the cloning technique to build multiple Windows 2000/2003 servers, the first question is almost always regarding security identifier (SID) uniqueness on the cloned server. When Windows is installed, a unique SID is generated for that machine. This SID plus an incremented value known as the relative ID (RID) are used to create local security group and user SIDs. If an image of this server is cloned onto another computer, that second computer has the same computer and account SIDs that existed on the first computer, introducing a potential security problem in a workgroup environment. The local SID also plays a much greater role in a Windows 2000 or 2003 environment than it did in NT 4.0.

Fortunately, Microsoft supports a technique for cloning complete installations of Windows from one server to another. Using a utility called SYSPREP available for download free from the Microsoft Web site, you can prepare a Windows Terminal Server for replication and have a unique SID automatically generated on the target server when it reboots. SYSPREP doesn't perform the actual imaging but prepares a server to be imaged. Once SYSPREP is run, any imaging tool can be used to create and distribute the server clone. The process of server cloning is discussed in Chapter 22.

Here are a couple of guidelines I follow when planning installation and management of my Terminal Server environment that can aid in the cloning process:

- Maintain two separate partitions on the server, one for the boot/system drive and the other for the application drive.

    This configuration was first discussed in Chapter 6. Not only does this provide a clean division between where applications are located and where the operating system itself resides, but it also helps to facilitate cloning by letting the operating system partition/drive be cloned without requiring inclusion of the application files. This reduces the size of the boot/system image and subsequently speeds up the cloning process. A full clone of all partitions can be created when duplicating a server, while only the boot/system drive can be cloned to facilitate a speedy server recovery.

- Plan to have the latest SYSPREP tool available for use when creating a server image that will be used to build new servers.

    SYSPREP is not required if you're creating a backup image that is going to be used strictly to recover an existing server in the event of a failure. Because the purpose of this image is just to restore the existing server and not to create new servers, there is no issue with having a duplicate SID in the clone. If a server is rebuilt from this image, it is expected that the original server is no longer available.

Different cloning products exist, but my personal preference has always been Norton Ghost, which has provided excellent disk and partition cloning support for a number of years. I provide a demonstration of the server cloning process in Chapter 22.

Citrix MetaFrame Presentation Server

By now the makeup of the Terminal Server portion of your MPS implementation should be taking shape, and at least from a high-level the components summarized in Figure 8.1 should all have been accounted for. Figure 8.30 has the main components that make up a typical MetaFrame Presentation Server environment overlaid with the necessary Terminal Server components from Figure 8.1.

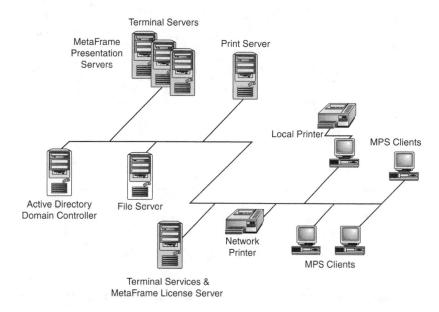

Figure 8.30   A network diagram representing a typical MetaFrame Presentation Server implementation.

Part III of this book also looks at implementation of MPS, and Table 8.5 summarizes the MetaFrame components listed in Figure 8.30 along with the tasks performed and/or the roles serviced by those components and the corresponding chapter or chapters that explain how the component is implemented or configured.

Table 8.5   Components of a MetaFrame Implementation and Chapter Cross-Reference

Server Type	Implementation Task/Role	Corresponding Chapter
MetaFrame Presentation Server	Application/desktop serving	Chapter 13, "MetaFrame Presentation Server Installation" Chapter 14, "MetaFrame Presentation Server Configuration" Chapter 16, "Terminal Server Security" Chapter 17, "Terminal Server and MetaFrame Printer Management" Chapter 21, "Application Integration" Chapter 22, "Server Operations and Support"
Terminal Services and MetaFrame License Server	License distribution and management	Chapter 12, "License Server Installation and Configuration"
Print server	Network printer queues	Chapter 17, "Terminal Server and MetaFrame Printer Management"
MPS client	MPS client	Chapter 17, "Terminal Server and MetaFrame Printer Management" Chapter 20, "ICA Client Installation and Configuration"
	Local printer host	

Most of the planning and preparation for a MetaFrame implementation will focus on the server farm and proper selection and distribution of the key components. This is where we begin our discussion of MPS installation and planning.

General Server Farm and MetaFrame Presentation Server Distribution Planning

In Chapter 2, "Citrix MetaFrame Presentation Server," I introduced the concept of an MPS server farm and described the key role it plays in any MPS deployment. Figure 8.31 shows a typical MPS implementation with all servers deployed within a single server farm and located at the same physical location.

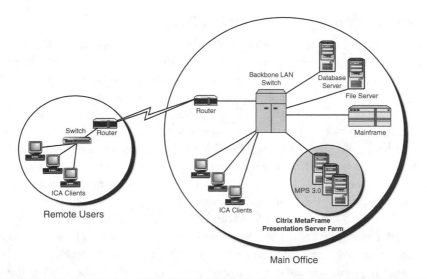

Figure 8.31 The most common MPS deployment has all servers in one location within a single server farm.

Before you begin actual installation of the MPS software, you should at least have an idea of how you would answer the following two questions:

- Will all your MetaFrame servers be centralized in one location or distributed across multiple sites?

  For many administrators, particularly those migrating from an existing MetaFrame 1.8 or XP environment with co-located resources, the physical server layout shown in Figure 8.31 will closely match their infrastructure. For others, particularly those with distributed users and resources across multiple sites, a more distributed MetaFrame server deployment may be necessary.

- Will you be required to implement more than one server farm?

  In most cases the answer to this question should be no, but certain situations may dictate the need for multiple server farms. Before deciding to implement multiple farms you should carefully consider what options exist and how each option may impact the ICA client you plan to deploy.

MetaFrame Presentation Server Distribution

In Chapter 4, I discussed how one of the design goals for optimizing the MetaFrame environment was to try whenever possible to co-locate the MetaFrame servers with the majority of the resources they are required to access. For example, if you have a client/server-based application you wish to run in MetaFrame, and this application accesses a Microsoft SQL Server, you should try to position the MetaFrame and SQL servers so they are operating on the same physical network in order to optimize the bandwidth available between these servers.

Always keep in mind that MetaFrame client connectivity is optimized to operate over reduced bandwidth. For this reason, when necessary, client bandwidth should take second priority to ensuring optimal bandwidth between MetaFrame and the necessary support servers (database, file, print, and so on).

Figure 8.32 shows a simple before-and-after diagram demonstrating positioning of a pair of MetaFrame servers relative to the SQL Server and the end users. A mistake commonly made by novice Terminal Server administrators is to attempt to locate the Terminal Servers close to the end users, assuming that maximizing session connectivity is the first priority for a successful Terminal Server environment.

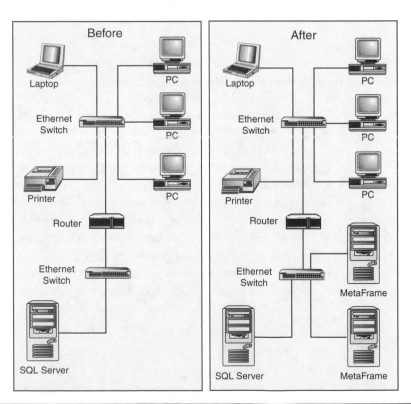

Figure 8.32   Always try to position MetaFrame as close as possible to the necessary support servers.

At this point in the planning stage you should have a clear idea of the applications being targeted for MetaFrame and what back-end infrastructure is associated with these applications. Network diagrams should be available that provide a visual layout of where these resources reside, and from this you should have developed the "as-is" layout of the environment.

When reviewing and planning distribution of the MetaFrame servers there is a standard process I work through, which is described next. Figure 8.33 shows the layout of a typical medium-sized company with a head office and two remote sites, which is used to demonstrate the planning steps I follow when determining distribution of the servers and server farm layout for a MetaFrame deployment. Assume that the following scenario exists:

> The environment depicted in Figure 8.33 represents a company that currently operates with traditional desktop-based applications in a semi-independent environment. The company wants to move to a MetaFrame solution to deliver a new line-of-business application to replace a group of antiquated applications it is using today. In addition, it wants to run all other Office productivity applications through MetaFrame so it can eliminate dependency on running local desktop applications at the Orlando office. The Seattle office must retain access to some local applications specific to marketing and advertising development. These applications are graphic intensive and not appropriate for a MetaFrame environment.

> Note that an NT 4.0 Terminal Server exists in the Orlando office to let users at the other two sites access an application running in that office, called Application Alpha. Application Alpha will not be replaced. There is also a SQL Server at the head office in New York City that houses the data for the company's main application. The Orlando and Seattle sites have only limited access to this data right now, but introduction of the new MetaFrame environment is supposed to make this information easily accessible to all users.

The following steps provide one method of evaluating and positioning MetaFrame servers in your infrastructure.

1. Begin by flagging the resources in the infrastructure that applications *and* end users in your MetaFrame environment will need to access, such as the following:

   - Database management systems such as SQL or Oracle servers
   - File servers where user or application data resides
   - Printers and print servers that will be accessed through MetaFrame

   Using Figure 8.33 as an example, we would flag the file and print servers and the printers in all three locations. We would also flag the NT 4.0, Terminal Server Edition server at the Orlando site and the SQL Server at the New York City site.
   Based on this, we have resources at all three locations that must be accounted for when assessing the MetaFrame server needs.

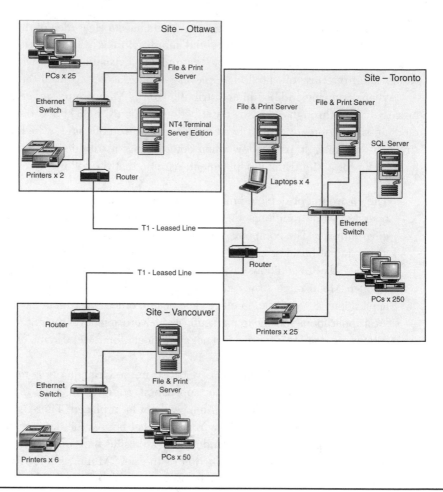

Figure 8.33 An example of the infrastructure for a medium-sized company that wants to migrate to a MetaFrame environment.

2. The next task is to determine which resources must remain in their current locations and which can be relocated to a central location. Unless there are specific requirements dictating that the resources remain in their current locations for failover or other reasons, plan on moving these resources to a central location.

In our example, there are some resources that can be relocated to the main office:

- NT 4.0 Terminal Server: This can be flagged for relocation and an upgrade (assuming that the existing application will run on Windows Server 2003). Because the objective is to have the Orlando users running 100 percent from MetaFrame, we do not want to have server dependencies existing at that location. Centralizing this will ease backup requirements and ensure the application is still accessible by the Seattle and New York users.
- File and print server in Orlando: This too can be relocated to New York, since there is no longer a requirement that it remain local to the Orlando users. The print server needs now will be managed in New York and the appropriate jobs streamed and sent to the printers, which will remain in the Orlando office.

The file and print server in Seattle will not be moved to New York. Portions of data may move to accommodate centralization of certain functionality, but the server must remain in order to service the graphical applications that will continue to run locally in that office.

3. Next, provide an updated network diagram showing centralization of the appropriate resources, including any resource consolidation that might be appropriate. Resources migrating from the remote sites should be evaluated to determine if the function they perform can be integrated into an existing server in the new location. Resource consolidation can help in allowing you to

- Reduce complexity by minimizing the number of servers required. This simplifies administrative tasks such as backups.
- Redeploy or decommission aging or obsolete hardware. If resources can be centralized on newer hardware, the older hardware can be reallocated or completely removed before failures impact the production environment.

Figure 8.34 shows the transitional infrastructure with the flagged resources now centralized at the head office in New York City. Because the entire file and print server itself is not being moved from Seattle, the resources on the server that are moving must be integrated into a file and print server located in the New York office. The target server in this case has been noted in the diagram.

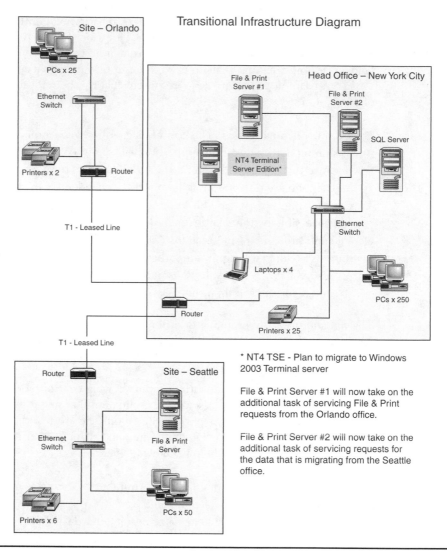

Transitional Infrastructure Diagram

Figure 8.34 Create a transitional infrastructure diagram showing flagged resources in their new location.

4. With the transitional infrastructure diagram complete, it is now time to pencil in MetaFrame servers at each of the locations containing resources that will need to be accessed through MetaFrame. A MetaFrame server is not located at a site unless a MetaFrame session must access a resource in that environment. Note that right now you are not specifying how many servers are required, just that at least one server may be positioned at that location. Details on sizing the environment were discussed in Chapter 6. Figure 8.35 represents the next iteration in our transitional infrastructure diagram, showing MetaFrame servers tentatively planned for the New York and Seattle offices.

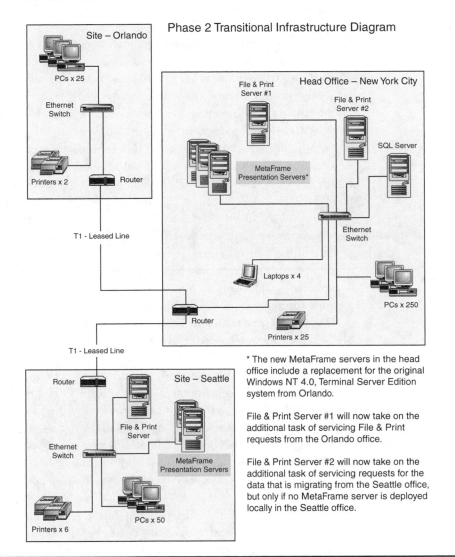

Phase 2 Transitional Infrastructure Diagram

Figure 8.35 The next iteration of the transitional infrastructure diagram should include where MetaFrame servers may be located in the new production environment.

5. With Figure 8.35 now in hand, a decision must be made about whether the current MetaFrame server distribution is appropriate for the environment or if further consolidation is necessary. Advantages and disadvantages exist for both types of configurations and are summarized as follows:

- Distributed servers provide advantages such as mitigating the impact of a failure at one site on another site. If one site is down due to connectivity or other failure, it is expected that at least partial access is still available to servers located at other sites. Full business continuity may not be possible and will depend on the amount of information and the applications available at different locations. With a distributed server configuration, you also set up an environment where administration of the servers at different locations can be delegated to local administrators. This doesn't fit in with the current example illustrated in Figure 8.35, but if we had a situation where two full data centers were being maintained in locations such as Los Angeles and Hong Kong, you would likely want to delegate full administrative authority at each of these locations but not necessarily the equivalent access from one site to another.

  One of the main disadvantages of a distributed server environment is the need to possibly replicate data between sites. Some of the most common data to replicate includes domain information (group policies, user accounts, and so on.), user account profiles, and user data.

  Distributed servers also introduce the requirement for intra-server MetaFrame communications between sites.

- The most obvious advantage to a centralized MetaFrame server environment is centralization of the administration and support of not only the servers but also the applications in the environment. Server-to-server bandwidth is maximized, user account and data management tasks are simplified, and server maintenance is streamlined. The bandwidth requirements to the remote sites are also reduced since data transmissions consist of MetaFrame presentation data, print jobs, and any client/server applications that must continue to function outside MetaFrame.

  Centralizing all these resources does introduce a single point of failure, at this location. If connectivity to this site is lost, remote users may not have an alternate means of accessing their data, necessitating introduction of additional fault tolerance into the environment to minimize chances of downtime between locations.

  In relatively smaller environments, unless significant concerns exist about the uptime of the data link between locations, try to centralize your deployment whenever possible. Additional resources can be focused on providing redundancy in the central location instead of spending resources trying to manage servers distributed across multiple locations.

  As environments become substantially larger, it may become necessary to maintain a number of distributed servers to support local access to large banks of data storage that cannot be centralized in an alternate location.

In the case of the environment illustrated in Figure 8.35, one or more MetaFrame servers are not required in the Seattle office for a couple of reasons:

- Because of the special needs of the Seattle office, most of its applications will remain local, with only its access to the specific line-of-business application managed through MetaFrame. Because all users from all three locations will access this same application and data, maintaining a local replica of the data in the Seattle office is not practical. Without a local set of data, it does not make sense to consider running the application locally.
- In addition to the local copy of the data, additional supplementary servers such as a domain controller would be required.

In this situation, it simply makes more sense to centralize all MetaFrame servers at the head office and migrate the necessary data from Orlando and Seattle to accommodate the environment.

NOTE: If the requirements for the Seattle office differed slightly from those in my example, a case could be made for deploying one or more MetaFrame servers at that location. Consider the scenario where the Seattle users would be running Microsoft Office and most other applications from MetaFrame, with the exception of advertising-specific applications. The decision on where these servers would reside would depend mainly on whether the graphical applications had any kind of dependency on or interaction with Microsoft Office. If so, it could be advantageous to have the Office data and associated applications physically close to the graphical applications and their data.

Even with a MetaFrame server located in that site to support the Office applications, the main line-of-business application could still be located at the main office and accessed remotely by the Seattle users. This type of "MetaFrame-within-MetaFrame" access utilizes the MetaFrame passthrough client. I talk further about this feature in Chapter 20.

If it has been determined that maintaining servers at more than one site is a requirement, always attempt to plan the environment in such a way that it minimizes administrative requirements. If you think you will require servers at four locations, review your decision to see if servers at only three locations would satisfy the business's needs. In most situations, even a reduction in sites from four to three simplifies administration.

Determining How Many Server Farms Should Be Deployed

It seems that as soon as I begin to discuss the concept of a Citrix server farm and the role it serves, someone asks whether Citrix supports multiple farms and, if so, how many should be used in a typical production deployment.

The answer to the first question is yes. Citrix supports deployment of as many concurrent server farms within an environment as desired. Multiple server farms usually exist for one or more of the following reasons:

- **A test or development farm has been segregated from production—** Many large MetaFrame deployments have additional farms that exist to facilitate development and/or user testing. These are typically created to mirror a production environment and consist of one to two servers that are exact replicas of production, allowing for simulation of production conditions without impacting the production users.
- **Separate farms have been created independently of each other by different de-partments or computer services groups**—*containing applications required by the end user.* In very large organizations with department-based computer services groups, this is not uncommon. Typically such a scenario dictates that administrators of one farm do not have the ability to administer any of the other farms.
- **MetaFrame servers have been distributed across multiple sites to co-locate these servers with their main data source, but the network connectivity between the sites is limited or unreliable**—In this case, separate farms can be instituted to eliminate server-to-server communications across the WAN, minimizing WAN traffic between remote offices. Essentially, the only traffic traversing the WAN is the users' ICA session traffic.
- **Highly secured departments within a single physical location have separate server farms on protected networks that restrict inbound and outbound traffic**— Communications that would otherwise take place between the MetaFrame servers is completely protected within the secured network.

While multiple farms are supported for most MetaFrame Presentation Server deployments, a single production MetaFrame server farm is the most appropriate choice for implementation. Administration and support features built into MPS 3.0 simplify management of large farms, helping avoid the situation where administrators feel they must separate the environment into smaller farms in an attempt to reduce complexity of a single large farm. Unless you're completely familiar with the functionality and requirements of MetaFrame and the MetaFrame server farm, introducing additional server farms (excluding test or development farms) can have the opposite effect of the one you want by increasing complexity of supporting the environment. I highly recommend that whenever possible you try to implement only a single production server farm.

In summary, server farms have the following characteristics:

- A farm must contain at least one MetaFrame server.
- A MetaFrame server can belong to only one server farm at a time. MetaFrame servers can be moved from one farm to another.

- Communications between servers in a server farm occur via the Independent Management Architecture (IMA) protocol, which uses port 2512. If a firewall or routing device separates servers in a farm, you must ensure that communications via this port are not blocked.
- Citrix's load balancing, available with the Advanced and Enterprise editions of MetaFrame, is supported only between MetaFrame servers in the same farm. Load balancing is not available between servers in different farms.
- Each server farm consists of a single database called the *data store,* within which all the persistent farm, server, application, and user configuration information is stored. Details on the data store are discussed in the next section, "Planning for the Server Farm Data Store."
- When the underlying database management system (DBMS) for the data store supports replication (SQL Server and Oracle both support this), the MetaFrame server farm itself can be configured to support a replicated data store. When MetaFrame servers in a single farm are distributed across one or more WAN links, a replicated data store can be used to localize the intra-farm communications to each individual LAN.
- Each MetaFrame server communicates directly with the data store to retrieve persistent configuration information.
- Servers within a single server farm, regardless of their locations, are organized into logical units called *zones.* The planning considerations for server farm zones are discussed in the section entitled "Zone Data Collector Planning Considerations."

Planning for the Server Farm Data Store

Each distinct MetaFrame server farm contains a single master data store repository, with possibly one or more replica data stores if a distributed farm implementation has been created. The data store is where *persistent* information about the server farm is maintained; for example:

- **MetaFrame administration accounts**—Users with access to administer a server farm are managed through the Management Console and this list of administrators is maintained within the data store.
- **Farm configuration information**—Information such as the user connection limits, host license server, and general MetaFrame settings such as client time zone support and remote connection support for the local console are stored in the data store.
- **Server configuration information**—Server-specific settings such as client printer bandwidth throttling and reboot scheduling are also stored here. A number of options by default inherit the settings defined at the farm level, and unless absolutely necessary to do otherwise, I recommend always inheriting settings

from the farm configuration instead of trying to maintain them on a server-by-server basis. Certainly this may introduce a bit of a learning curve for administrators who have come from a MetaFrame 1.8 environment, where most changes had to be done on each individual server.

- **Published application configuration information**—All aspects of a published application are maintained in the data store, including the MetaFrame servers hosting the application, the Program Neighborhood client settings, and the access control list containing the names of users or groups able to launch the application.

- **Printer management**—The Printer Management module controls the behavior of auto-created client printers in the farm, as well as managing driver replication and auto-created network printer assignments. Planning considerations for printer management in a Citrix server farm are discussed later in this chapter, in the "End-User Printing Support with MetaFrame" section. Installation and configuration of printer support are covered in Chapter 17.

All this persistent farm information is contained within a database management system (DBMS) and accessed via ODBC. MPS currently supports the following five DBMS repositories for the data store.

- Microsoft Access.
- Microsoft SQL Server 2000 Desktop Edition (MSDE).
- Microsoft SQL Server 2000 or 7.0 (with SP2).
- Oracle 9i Release 2 Enterprise Edition, Oracle 8i (8.1.6 or higher), Oracle 8 (8.0.6), and Oracle 7 (7.3.4) are all officially supported.
- IBM DB2 Enterprise Edition 7.2 or 8.2.

These five repositories can be further divided into two categories:

- **Indirect-access data stores**—Both the Microsoft Access and MSDE databases can physically reside on the first MetaFrame server created in the new farm. All other MetaFrame servers then added to the farm access the data store by communicating with the host MetaFrame server and not directly with the data store. This method of data store access is known as the *indirect-access* method, and Figure 8.36 provides a visual example of this.

    Microsoft Access and MSDE are most often used when there are 25 or fewer MetaFrame servers in the farm, less than 100 concurrent users, and less than 100 published applications.

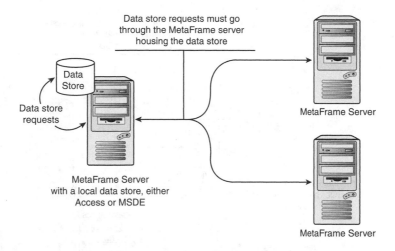

Figure 8.36   MetaFrame servers indirectly connected to the data store depend on a single MetaFrame server to relay the necessary farm information to them.

TIP: While Citrix supports both Access and MSDE databases operating in indirect-access mode, Citrix recommends that all new installations falling into the "small farm" category use MSDE instead of Access. Of the two, MSDE provides much better performance, particularly when there are five or fewer simultaneous connections to an MSDE database.

- **Direct-access data stores**—The true enterprise DBMSs (SQL Server, Oracle, and DB2), as well as MSDE (see the following tip for details on this), allow MetaFrame servers to establish *direct-access* connections. This means that each MetaFrame server is responsible for connecting to the database using ODBC and performing the necessary database querying. Figure 8.37 shows an example of this that helps illustrate the difference between direct and indirect connections.

    The three enterprise DBMSs are suitable for use when deploying a Meta-Frame server farm of any size, although the cost may be prohibitive in a small server farm unless you already had the DBMS functioning in your infrastructure and wanted to leverage the robust server support from the very beginning of your deployment. Smaller environments use MSDE as their direct-access data store (see the following tip for more details on this). Citrix does provide and support a migration path from Access and MSDE to any of the other database systems.

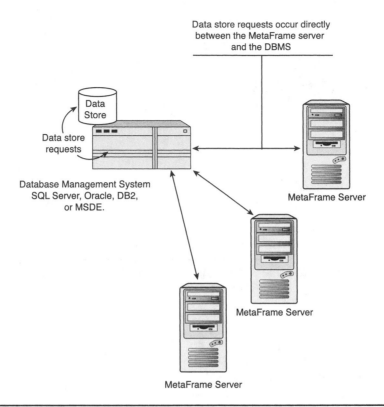

Data store requests occur directly
between the MetaFrame server
and the DBMS

Data
Store

Data store
requests

Database Management System
SQL Server, Oracle, DB2,
or MSDE.

MetaFrame Server

MetaFrame Server

MetaFrame Server

Figure 8.37 MetaFrame servers directly connected to the data store have no
dependency on another MetaFrame server to ensure their data store
access.

TIP: Contrary to what you may have read or heard, the MSDE database can be used
as a source for *direct,* as well as indirect, data store access. While Citrix does not
support this MSDE configuration, I've had success deploying it, with the largest production farm containing 10 MetaFrame servers.

Many people believe that MSDE has a hard limit of five concurrent connections, something stated in the Citrix administration documentation, but in reality this limit is not
on connections but on performance. To limit usefulness of MSDE as an alterative to
running the full Microsoft SQL Server product, Microsoft placed a hard-coded performance cap on MSDE that lets it scale exactly like SQL Server up to and including five
concurrent connections. Beyond this, MSDE no longer scales like SQL Server but

instead begins to mirror similar performance found when using a Microsoft Access database with a similar connection load. Connections beyond the fifth are not refused but simply throttled in their responsiveness.

MetaFrame servers contact the data store when they first start, if changes are made to the environment using the Management Console, and once every 30 minutes to retrieve any changes to the environment that need to be reflected in their local host cache (LHC). The LHC was first discussed in Chapter 2; it exists on every MetaFrame server and contains a subset of the data store information. Because servers do not maintain an active connection to the data store indefinitely, farms containing more than five servers can utilize the benefits of a centralized data store served up by MSDE. To date, the largest deployment with a centralized MSDE data store I have worked with contained 10 MetaFrame servers, an average of 200 concurrent users, and four published applications.

Implementing MSDE in a direct-access configuration requires you to modify the default installation parameters that would normally be used to install MSDE locally on a Meta-Frame server. The specifics on this modified installation are discussed in Chapter 13.

Table 8.6 summarizes the general classification used for describing MetaFrame server farm size. These numbers generally match those used by Citrix, with a couple of modifications based on experiences I've had in different environments. Typically, the Microsoft Access or MSDE database engines are used for implementing a small server farm, while any of the other three DBMS systems are used for implementing a medium-sized or larger farm.

Table 8.6   General MetaFrame Server Farm Size Classifications

	Small	Medium	Large	Enterprise
MetaFrame servers	< 20 to 25	25 to 100	75 to 200	> 150
Concurrent users	< 100	< 3,000	> 2,000	> 3,000
		< 5,000		
Published applications	< 100	< 200	< 500	< 2,000

Implementing a production environment with a data store server that has inadequate capacity to support the environment can adversely impact start-up and performance of the IMA service running on each MetaFrame server. The following are basic guidelines to consider when determining the DBMS to use for a MetaFrame implementation:

- If an enterprise DBMS (SQL Server, Oracle, DB2) already exists in the environment, plan to implement your data store on this server regardless of your projected MetaFrame farm size.

While a case can be made for using Access or MSDE when only one or two MetaFrame servers exist, if there are any plans to expand this environment in the near future, then leveraging the enterprise DBMS right from the beginning will ease this growth.

■ If an enterprise DBMS does not exist or is not an option for your project, the following are some suggestions to consider:

■ For small environments, an MSDE data store in a direct-access configuration should be considered since it provides the benefits of a centralized, directly accessed repository without the budget requirements of a full enterprise DBMS package.

Ideally this configuration will have a non-MetaFrame server assigned to host MSDE. One option is to host the MSDE-based data store on the same server as both the Microsoft Terminal Services licensing service and the MetaFrame license server. I have run such a configuration without issue. Performance monitoring should be reviewed to ensure that this server can adequately support both Terminal Server and MetaFrame licensing as well as the demands placed on the data store by the servers in the farm.

NOTE: Judging from the testing I have performed to this point, I can say that implementing MSDE in a direct-access configuration does not result in a noticeable performance degradation compared to a configuration that indirectly accesses MSDE or Access. While my tests with this MSDE configuration have not yet moved beyond 10 total MetaFrame servers, I speculate that MSDE can support at least 15 to 20 servers before moving to an enterprise DBMS becomes necessary. Part of my reasoning is based on the realistic maximum for an Access data store of around 20 MetaFrame servers.

Citrix does not support this configuration and actually discourages its use in the company's MPS Administrator's Guide. My suggestions are based solely on the results I have observed during implementations I have worked on. Before implementing MSDE in a direct-access configuration, be certain that it will adequately support the needs of your production environment.

Citrix does support migrating from an Access database to MSDE using the MigrateToMSDE tool available on the installation CD. Citrix also supports migrating from MSDE to SQL Server, Oracle, or DB2 using the DSMAINT command.

■ If the target environment is small and the available resources are limited due to budget constraints, then MSDE or Access operating in the indirect access mode are the choices for data store host. For one or two servers Access is still a suitable option, even though many people will suggest that Access should be disregarded completely over MSDE. There are a few reasons why Access is still a suitable choice. First, it is very simple to deploy. You simply select Access as the target host when setting up the first MetaFrame server, and it is installed and configured. There is no need to perform a separate database installation. Second, the Access data is completely contained within a single file and is easy to back up and restore. Transferring the data store to another server is also a fairly straightforward process. And third, for one or two servers, Access will not produce a noticeable performance hit.

■ For environments with three or more servers that still fit in the "small" category, I recommend deploying MSDE in indirect-access mode. While the installation requirements are still a bit involved, they are not that difficult, and the necessary data can be backed up and migrated to another server if necessary.

TIP: Data store backup and migration are discussed in Chapter 14.

■ When the number of servers in an environment grows beyond 20, you will need to consider deploying an enterprise DBMS instead of Access or MSDE. In particular, I have found that Microsoft Access begins to present a noticeable bottleneck on performance of the IMA service running on each server when the farm contains more than 20 servers.

■ When choosing an enterprise DBMS to implement, if you are planning to create an environment that includes replicated data stores at multiple locations, you can use DB2 only if the replicas will not be updateable. This means that all the replicas created are read-only, and updates are performed on only the main data store. This limitation exists because Citrix stores farm data in DB2 in binary large object (BLOB) format, and DB2 does not support use of BLOB data with updateable replicas. If updateable replicas are desired, you must use SQL Server or Oracle.

TIP: There is a final note to consider regarding selection of the data store and placement of MetaFrame servers in the environment. Citrix knowledgebase article CTX064157 describes the typical communication bandwidth requirements for a MetaFrame XP server as a function of the number of servers, published applications, and printer drivers that exist in the farm. These same numbers can be used when estimating bandwidth requirements for an MPS implementation. Based on internal testing performed by Citrix, the following function estimates the number of kilobytes (KB) read by a MetaFrame server on start-up:

Total KB = 275KB + (5KB × Servers) + (0.5KB × PubApps) + (92KB × PrnDrivers)

In the equation:

Servers is the number of servers in the farm.

PubApps represents the number of applications published in the farm, including published full desktops.

PrnDrivers is the number of printer drivers replicated in the farm.

If the bandwidth between a MetaFrame server and the data store is such that it imposes a bottleneck on transmission of the start-up data, you can experience significant slowness in starting of the IMA service and even messages stating that the IMA service failed to start properly.

Often this type of problem is misdiagnosed as an issue with the type of data store database being used instead of an issue with the bandwidth between the data store and the server. When planning the environment layout, be sure to keep this in mind.

When reviewing the knowledgebase article, keep in mind that behavior of the zone data collector (ZDC) has changed with MPS 3.0 versus MetaFrame XP 1.0. ZDCs no longer maintain load-balancing information for all other zones in the farm, which reduces the amount of update "chatter" between data collectors. Zone data collectors are discussed in Chapter 2 and reviewed in this chapter in the section "Zone Data Collector Planning Considerations."

Zone Data Collector Planning Considerations

Zones logically subdivide servers within a single server farm into functional groups within which summary information on all the servers in that zone is centrally maintained. Every server farm will have at least one zone, with the first zone created during installation of the first MetaFrame server in the farm. During creation of the farm, you are prompted to provide the name for the zone, with the default name being the network subnet in which the MetaFrame server resides. Multiple zones are usually created when MetaFrame servers are distributed across multiple locations, with one zone defined for each distinct location. Multiple zones are also used to group MetaFrame servers in large server farm environments, details of which are discussed later in this section.

NOTE: A zone can have any name you want, but it cannot exceed 127 characters in length and should consist of only printable characters.

Within each zone there will exist one MetaFrame server designated as the zone data collector. Unlike the data store, which maintains persistent information about the farm, a zone data collector (ZDC) maintains dynamically updated information about all the servers in its own zone. The ZDC in each zone is responsible for providing information when requested to other ZDCs in the farm and to ICA clients that request information about servers or published applications. A ZDC maintains the following information:

- What servers exist in its zone and their current load level
- What applications are published on the servers in the zone
- What user sessions currently exist on the servers in the zone

---

NOTE: A ZDC collects and maintains only dynamic data about the servers in its zone. A ZDC does not replicate its data to a backup ZDC and does not save information that is reloaded at a later date. When a MetaFrame server is chosen as a ZDC, it will always retrieve new information about the zone from the environment.

Whenever there is a change in status of any one of these settings on a MetaFrame server, the updated information is sent immediately to that server's ZDC. The information is not queued, and there is no way to adjust this update interval. Figure 8.38 shows an example of a server farm with MetaFrame servers at two locations (remote and main office) and two separate zones (Remote Office Zone and Head Office Zone), with a ZDC defined for each zone. The zone data collector in each zone will share information with the zone data collector in the other zone when requested.

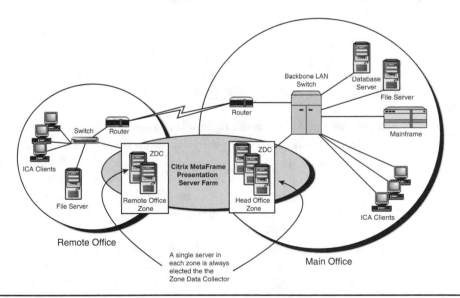

Figure 8.38 A single MetaFrame server in each zone is always elected as the zone data collector.

NOTE: In releases of MetaFrame prior to 3.0, the ZDC automatically stored information on all servers in the farm, not just servers in its own zone. By default, a ZDC now maintains information on only its own zone and dynamically queries other zones for information when necessary. Automatic storage of information from all other zones can still be enabled if desired. The details on this are discussed in Chapter 14.

When planning your MPS deployment, there is some basic zone and zone data collector planning you need to perform:

- Determine the number of zones that will be used, what servers will belong to those zones, and the naming convention that will be used.
- Designate the preferred zone data collector in each zone based on memory and processor capabilities.
- Determine if a dedicated zone data collector is appropriate for your environment.
- Configure the Zone Preferences and Failover option if necessary to manage how a ZDC directs a MetaFrame client to a requested published application.

The next three sections discuss these planning tasks in more detail.

Determining How Many Zones to Implement

While the purpose of a zone is to logically group servers together within a geographical location, as with most things, moderation is the best strategy when determining how many zones to implement. Create only the zones necessary for the implementation, avoiding the temptation to over-complicate the deployment with too many zones. In general, zones should be created using the following guidelines:

- **Create a distinct zone for each remote location that will have one or more MetaFrame servers in the same farm**—Figure 8.38 gives an example of this with the remote and main office locations each having MetaFrame servers. A zone is created at each location to reduce WAN traffic since all servers in each zone will talk to their local ZDC. If a single zone were created, additional WAN traffic would be generated as MetaFrame servers send update information across the WAN to the elected ZDC.
- **Within each site, begin by designating only a single zone for all MetaFrame servers unless the number of MetaFrame servers will exceed 500**—While a single zone can support more than 500 servers, Citrix recommends using 500 as the planned cutoff size for a single zone. This number is up significantly from the 100 servers recommended with MetaFrame XP 1.0. If you plan to have more servers in your farm, split the size and create two or more zones with around 250 to 300 servers in each. Multiple zones can exist on the same subnet if necessary. The only requirement is that they have a unique zone name.

When you are deciding on a naming standard, I do not recommend using the default subnet names suggested by the MetaFrame installation. Instead create names that provide information on the site location of the zone. For example, if your head office is located in Salt Lake City, you might have a zone name based on the city or possibly the state if remote sites belonging to the same farm exist across the country. A zone name might be something like UTZone01 or UT-Salt Lake City, or maybe UT-Head Office.

As I mentioned, a zone name can be whatever you wish as long as it is less than 127 characters in length and contains only printable characters. Zones can be renamed if necessary through the MPS Management Console.

WARNING: Citrix recommends that you not exceed 25 zones in a single server farm. Within a single corporate location this is not likely, but if a company has many remote offices such a configuration may be possible. Either consolidate servers at fewer locations and reduce the zone count or create separate server farms.

Designating a Preferred Zone Data Collector

The ZDC for a zone is chosen through an election process that will appear very similar to the master browser election process for those readers who have worked with MetaFrame 1.8 or earlier versions. A MetaFrame server can be assigned one of four priority levels that dictate the weighting assigned when a ZDC election is initiated. Figure 8.39 shows the four possible priority levels.

These priority levels are as follows:

- **Most Preferred**—This is the default priority assigned to the first MetaFrame server added to the environment. A server with this setting is always the first choice to become the ZDC in an election. Best practices dictate that only one MetaFrame server in each zone be assigned this setting.
- **Preferred**—If the most preferred server is not available, the first server selected with this setting becomes the ZDC. Typically one or two servers designated as backup ZDCs should be assigned this priority level.
- **Default Preference**—This is the default setting for all MetaFrame servers in the zone, excluding the very first server. If no servers are found that match the first two criteria, the first server selected with a default preference becomes the ZDC.
- **Not Preferred**—Servers assigned this setting do not become the ZDC unless there are no other servers in the farm with any of the three previous priority settings. Every server farm must have at least one ZDC, hence the reason why no MetaFrame server can be completely omitted from possibly becoming a ZDC.

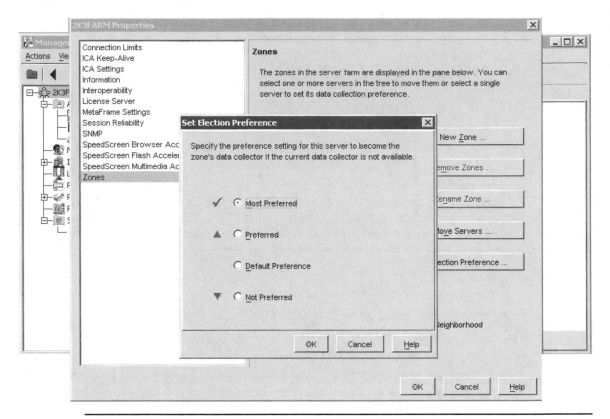

Figure 8.39   A MetaFrame server has four possible priority choices dictating the likelihood that it will be elected the zone data collector.

Because the ZDC maintains the information required by clients to connect to published
applications in the environment, performance issues with the ZDC result in delayed information
retrieval or application launching on the client. It is important that the MF administrator
periodically monitor the load of the ZDC in each zone to ensure it is not becoming overwhelmed servicing client requests and managing the server farm data for the zone.

The two key measures of ZDC performance are processor and memory. When selecting
the preferred ZDC for a zone, select the server with high CPU and memory capabilities
or a server that will service a reduced number of concurrent MetaFrame sessions allowing
additional resources to be dedicated to managing the zone. In large zones, you may want to
consider selecting a server whose sole purpose is to act as a dedicated ZDC and not to service any MetaFrame client sessions.

TIP: When upgrading the MetaFrame servers in your farm to a newer release of MetaFrame, always upgrade the server designated as your zone data collector first. By running the ZDC on the latest release, you ensure not only that it will support the MetaFrame servers still running the previous release but also that it will support changes in zone logic that may be introduced when a zone member is updated.

Creating a Dedicated Zone Data Collector

A common rule of thumb for creating a dedicated zone data collector is to establish the dedicated ZDC when you exceed 50 servers in a single zone, but this is a loose estimate. In reality, the threshold at which you need to consider a dedicated ZDC is based on the following:

- **Concurrent user connections into the farm or zone**—Total concurrent connections into the farm will affect all data collectors unless you have also implemented the preferred zone policy for your users, which I discuss in the "Establishing Zone Preference and Failover" section. By default, any user logon results in the corresponding ZDC querying all other ZDCs trying to find the least-loaded server to service the user's request. Instituting preferred zones helps to contain inter-zone communications and reduce the load on the other ZDCs in the farm.

- **Simultaneous logons into the farm or zone**—When a large number of users simultaneously log on and attempt to acquire a connection to a MetaFrame server, this introduces a short-term load spike on the data collectors. If these logon counts are sufficiently large, they can noticeably impact the environment. If employees' work habits consist of frequent logons and logoffs instead of maintaining a single session throughout the day, you may encounter such jumps in processing at different times in the day and not just during the typical peak periods in the morning and after lunch during the work week.

- **The total number of published applications and their distribution between Meta-Frame servers**—This can also impact the performance of the ZDC. Because the ZDC must account for all connection instances on all servers within the zone, it may receive frequent status updates from the different servers on the connection counts, server load, disconnections, and so on.

- **Implementation of Resource Manager**—When deploying Resource Manager into a MetaFrame environment, a server must be designated as the Farm Metric Server (FMS). Citrix recommends that the FMS be only lightly loaded and ideally also be the data collector for a zone. When you implement Resource Manager in your environment, I recommend that you give serious consideration to defining a dedicated ZDC/FMS server with few (if any) client connections, regardless of the size of your server farm. If you also plan to implement a Resource Manager Summary Database, then a dedicated ZDC/FMS can also be assigned the role of Database Connection Server (DCS). The DCS acts as the intermediary between the servers in the farm and the actual summary database.

A dedicated ZDC is simply a regular MetaFrame server without any user-accessible published applications. The server is part of the server farm and assigned to the zone it will collect data for. See Chapter 13 for notes on installation of MetaFrame. Chapter 14 discusses the minor configuration steps to configure a MetaFrame server as a dedicated zone data collector.

NOTE: Using a dedicated ZDC is very similar to the idea of using a dedicated MetaFrame master browser server in MetaFrame 1.8. Unlike the licensing model for MetaFrame 1.8 where there was a separate cost for each MetaFrame server deployed, the MPS licensing model is based solely on concurrent users, allowing for as many server deployments as necessary to satisfy the needs of the environment. This allows for deployment of a dedicated ZDC without an additional MetaFrame server licensing cost. Of course, there is still the required Microsoft server licensing cost.

Establishing Zone Preferences and Failover

Whenever a user requests a published application, the ZDC receiving that request automatically queries all other ZDCs in the farm to determine what MetaFrame server is available with the least load to satisfy this request. If an application is published on multiple servers located in different geographically distinct zones, it is very possible that a user will be directed across a WAN link to a least-loaded server in a remote location. Unless the network capacity of the WAN link was sufficiently large, most administrators would prefer to have the user's request serviced by a local server and look to a server located in a different zone only if no server in the current zone could honor the request.

One of the new features available with MPS 3.0, Enterprise Edition, is an option called Zone Preferences and Failover, which allows for just such a configuration. Using Zone Preferences and Failover you can define a preferred zone for a user that will service all requests from that user and pass a request off to an alternate zone only in the event of a preferred zone failure. When a zone preference is defined, a request is directed to the least-loaded server *within that zone*, even if a server located in a different zone has a lower load level.

Zone Preferences and Failover is supported only when the client is connecting through the MetaFrame Web Interface or the Program Neighborhood Agent. Other client connection methods are not supported by this configuration and function using the traditional farm-wide load evaluation.

Zone Preferences and Failover settings are defined as a MetaFrame policy rule in the MPS Management Console. Within this rule, you define the following settings:

- **Primary Group**—Zones listed in this group are queried simultaneously to find the least-loaded server to satisfy the client request. If no zone in the primary group responds, MetaFrame fails over to Backup Group 1.
- **Backup Groups (1 to 10)**—These 10 groups are prioritized from 1 through 10, and each group is checked one after the other until a server responds to the application request. Zones within the same group are queried simultaneously, and the next group is queried only if the previous one contained no response. Backup groups let you define multiple failover groups based on priority and location.
- **No Preference**—This is a list of zones queried only after none of the MetaFrame servers in the primary group or any of the 10 backup groups responded to the request.
- **Do Not Connect**—Zones that are members of this group are never queried by MetaFrame for a requesting application. Only in rare circumstances would you need to populate this group.

When servers are being grouped together, make certain that zones located across low-bandwidth connections are positioned in a lower priority group and not mixed with zones accessible from higher bandwidth connections. Citrix does not process group members one at a time but instead sends an application request simultaneously to all zones in the group. It waits for responses from all zones before selecting the least-loaded server to service the application request.

Zone Preferences and Failover should be configured only when you have multiple zones spread across a WAN link and the same application is being published in more than one zone. A deployment with only one zone does not even have this feature enabled for use. Details on configuration of MPS policies and the Zone and Preferences Failover settings are discussed in Chapter 14.

Server Drive Letter Reassignment

One of the product installation selections available with the MetaFrame Presentation Server 3.0 installation media is the "Remap drives" tool. "Remap drives" allows you to configure how drives will appear to users while they're logged onto the MetaFrame server. Table 8.7 demonstrates how client drives would be assigned within a client session on a MetaFrame server that has the standard server drive letters of C:, and D:.

Table 8.7   Default MetaFrame Server Drive Letter Assignments

Local Drive Letter Assignments	MetaFrame Presentation Server Drive Letter Assignments
A: (local floppy on client device)	A:
C: (local hard drive on client device)	V: (mapped client drive)
D: (local hard drive on client device)	U: (mapped client drive)
E: (local hard drive on client device)	E: (mapped client drive)
C: (local hard drive on MetaFrame server)	C: (server drive)
D: (local hard drive on MetaFrame server)	D: (server drive)

What this table is demonstrating is that from within a user's MetaFrame session, the C: drive would correspond to the C: drive on the server itself. The user's local C: drive on their PC would be available through the drive letter V: on the MetaFrame server.

If a client drive letter doesn't conflict with a drive letter on the MetaFrame server, it will keep the same drive letter, as the E: drive demonstrates in Table 8.7. Client drive letters that conflict with server drives are mapped to drive letters starting with V: and working *backwards*. The one mapping exception is server floppy drives, which are never available to client sessions.

In Table 8.7, the client floppy drive would map to the same drive letter in the MetaFrame session, whereas the client hard drives (C: and D:) would map to V: and U:, respectively. This is because the server drives are also labeled as C: and D:. By reassigning the server drive letters you can avoid this conflict.

Table 8.8 demonstrates what happens when the server drives are remapped to higher drive letters. In this example, the primary drive mapping starts at X: on the MetaFrame server. As you can see the client drives are now accessible from within MetaFrame using the same drive letter as the local drive assignment on the client device.

Table 8.8   Remapped MetaFrame Server Drive Letter Assignments

Local Drive Letter Assignments	MetaFrame Presentation Server Drive Letter Assignments
A: (local floppy on client device)	A:
C: (local hard drive on client device)	C: (mapped client drive)
D: (local hard drive on client device)	D: (mapped client drive)
E: (local hard drive on client device)	E: (mapped client drive)

Table 8.8 Remapped MetaFrame Server Drive Letter Assignments (continued)

Local Drive Letter Assignments	MetaFrame Presentation Server Drive Letter Assignments
X: (local hard drive on MetaFrame server)	X: (server drive)
Y: (local hard drive on MetaFrame server)	Y: (server drive)

When deciding whether or not to remap the server drives, consider the following:

■ Has the server been configured to use dynamic disks?
  MetaFrame drive remapping cannot be performed on a dynamic disk, so there is no need to even consider this option in this situation.

■ Are the majority of users going to be running a full desktop within MetaFrame?
  Full desktop sessions typically don't require a client drive mapping, so if there is no need to support the remapping of C: back to the local desktop, then there really isn't a need to implement alternate drive associations.

■ Are the majority of users accessing published applications and still performing the majority of their work on their local desktop?
  In this case, it is likely that the users will want to have access to a consistently labeled set of local drives. In this case expect that the drives will be remapped. I recommend that you start your drive mapping at the letter X:, as it is out of the way of most of the drive letters that are defined for a user's local desktop session.

While I have had a lot of success implementing MetaFrame servers that have had their drives remapped to X:, Y: and Z:, I would still caution you on think carefully about the decision to remap drives. Although rare, there are still situations where an application may run into issues when pointed at X: instead of C:. The remap utility can be used to reset drive letters back to C:, but the more applications that have been installed and are operating on the server, the greater the probability that something will fail when trying to set this value back. The process of remapping server drives is discussed in Chapter 13.

Resource Manager Implementation Considerations

Resource Manager is a component of MPS Enterprise Edition that allows for management of resources on one or more MetaFrame servers. Resource Manager enables an administrator to perform a number of performance- and monitoring-related tasks, including the following:

■ Capture details about system performance, including things such as application processor utilization and overall CPU and disk usage, as well as a number of other performance metrics.

- Monitor current system activity and generate reports based on both real-time and captured historical data.
- Generate billing reports based on calculations generated from captured data and costing information stored in what are called *fee profiles.*
- Generate alerts when monitored server metrics fall outside predefined limits.
  Server metrics are measurements of certain system characteristics such as "% Disk Time," which provides information on how busy the disk subsystem on the server is. Custom thresholds can be defined for all the Resource Manager metrics, letting you control when the appropriate alarm is raised. Any Windows Performance monitoring counter can be defined as a metric that can be monitored in Resource Manager.
- Receive special alerts when a MetaFrame server cannot establish a connection to a defined Citrix Access Suite license server.

More information on configuration and use of resource management is given in Chapter 22. Any plans you have to deploy resource management will not necessarily affect planning for your MetaFrame implementation, but there are a couple of considerations that, if provisioned for now, will ease the task of deploying resource management.

Designating the Primary and Backup Farm Metric Servers

Earlier when discussing the situations in which you might designate a dedicated zone data collector (ZDC), I mentioned the need for a Farm Metric Server (FMS) when implementing Resource Manager and how Citrix recommends that this server be deployed onto a ZDC.

The role of the Farm Metric Server is to receive and process metrics that apply to the entire MetaFrame server farm. Metrics such as total application counts or server-down events would fall into this category. These farm-wide metrics are routed from the MetaFrame servers in the farm running Resource Manager to the FMS through the zone data collector. This is why Citrix recommends that the Farm Metric Server and the zone data collector reside on the same physical server. Assigning the FMS is discussed in Chapter 22.

By default, the first MetaFrame server on which Resource Manager is installed is automatically assigned as the primary FMS. The second server on which Resource Manager is installed becomes the backup FMS. The designated primary and backup FMSs can be changed to a different machine after installation.

Designating the Database Connection Server

Another component of Resource Manager is the Database Connection Server (DCS). This component is required only if you will be implementing the summary database portion of Resource Manager in your environment. The DCS acts as the liaison between the server farm and the Resource Manager Summary Database. Neither the Farm Metric Server nor any other MetaFrame server running Resource Manager talks directly to the summary database besides the DCS.

Citrix recommends that this server be a relatively lightly loaded MetaFrame server with Resource Manager installed. Designating the Farm Metric Server as the DCS is a common implementation practice, particularly when the FMS, DCS, and zone data collector functions are all grouped together onto a centralized, dedicated server that does not allow regular interactive user sessions.

Provisioning for the Summary Database

To maintain historical information collected by Resource Manager, you must implement what is known as a *summary database.* Citrix supports either of the following enterprise database management systems for deploying a summary database:

- Microsoft SQL Server 7 or 2000
- Oracle 7, 8i, or 9i

A third option, not officially supported by Citrix but that works in smaller environments, is to utilize Microsoft SQL Server 2000 Desktop Edition (MSDE) as the repository for the summary database. If you are considering deploying Resource Manager and wish to implement the summary database, you will need to ensure that a dedicated server has been provisioned on which you will run one of these database systems.

Planning for the MetaFrame Access Suite License Server

I ended Chapter 2 with a brief discussion on the new MetaFrame Access Suite Licensing (MASL) infrastructure and the actual licensing requirements for MetaFrame. MASL is fundamentally different from earlier licensing implemented with MetaFrame, the most obvious difference being that there is now a requirement to have a separate licensing component installed and configured on a Windows server *before* you install your first MetaFrame Presentation Server. While MPS 3.0 will install without a license server present, no MetaFrame functionality will be available and pop-up messages will be generated stating that a license server could not be found. The most troublesome of these messages can appear when the server starts after a reboot. The pop-up message that appears prevents a remote RDP or ICA session from being accepted until the message is acknowledged from the local console.

To function properly, MPS 3.0 must be able to access an MASL server. As long as the license server is present (without client access licenses) the following grace-period licenses are available:

- Two non-administrative users: 96 hours (4 days)
- Administrative user: Indefinite

TIP: In the event that a production license server fails, all MPS servers continue to operate with full functionality for 30 days. If a license server has not been made available after 30 days, user connections are no longer accepted. This 30-day grace period is an extension to the 4 days originally implemented when MPS 3.0 was released. As of August 19, 2004, all license files downloaded from MyCitrix.com support this new extension to the grace period. This extension does not apply to the license grace period available before client access licenses are installed on the license server. This time frame remains unchanged at 4 days (96 hours).

While MASL can be installed on a server that is also running MetaFrame Presentation Server, ideally it should reside on a server whose primary function is not MetaFrame user sessions. The choice on where MASL will reside is dictated by a couple of factors:

- The first factor is the method with which you will manage the licensing server. Two methods are supported, one Web based and the other command line based. Of the two, the Web-based interface is the most common and recommended for those who are new to MPS 3.0 and the new MetaFrame licensing model (see Figure 8.40). To utilize the Web interface, you must run IIS 5.0 or later on the Windows server where MASL resides. Because of this requirement I usually recommend that MASL *not* be installed on a domain controller but instead be installed on a Windows member server.

- The second factor is the operating system on which you will run Terminal Services. A common deployment scenario that I implement has both the Terminal Services Licensing Service and MetaFrame Access Suite Licensing on the same server. One exception is in a Windows 2000 Terminal Services environment, since the Microsoft licensing service must reside on the domain controller. In this scenario, Terminal Services licensing would be installed on the domain controller while MASL would be installed on another member server along with IIS. In a Windows 2003 Terminal Server environment (or a Windows 2000 environment in a workgroup, not a domain), I always try to couple Microsoft and Citrix licensing on the same dedicated server, a server *not* providing MetaFrame client sessions.

Before you begin the process of implementing Terminal Services and MetaFrame, make certain you have clearly defined what server will host the MetaFrame Access Suite Licensing components. Also keep in mind the requirements for running IIS. Details on installation of MASL are covered in Chapter 12.

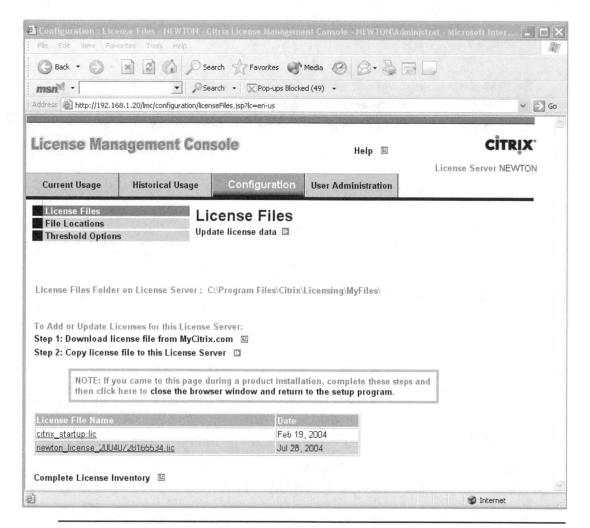

Figure 8.40   The preferred method of managing MetaFrame Access Suite Licensing is through the Web-based console. Command line tools are provided with the product.

Upgrading from MetaFrame 1.8 or XP to MetaFrame Presentation Server 3.0

If you are currently administering a production MetaFrame 1.8 or XP environment, you may be considering upgrading to MPS 3.0 instead of performing a clean installation of Windows and MetaFrame in order to maintain your current server configuration. Table 8.9 summarizes the supported upgrade options for MetaFrame Presentation Server 3.0. MetaFrame upgrades are supported only when the underlying Windows operating system remains unchanged, so if the original server version is Windows 2000 Server, the upgraded server version must remain Windows 2000 Server. Upgrade strategies differ slightly depending on the version of MetaFrame you are upgrading from.

Table 8.9 Upgrade Options for MetaFrame Presentation Server 3.0

Existing MetaFrame Version	Target MetaFrame Version
MetaFrame 1.8 with SP3 for Windows 2000 Server	MPS 3.0 for Windows 2000 Server
MetaFrame XP 1.0, FR1, FR2, or FR3 for Windows 2000 Server	MPS 3.0 for Windows 2000 Server
MetaFrame XP FR3 for Windows Server 2003	MPS 3.0 for Windows Server 2003

Upgrading from MetaFrame 1.8

To ease the transition from a MetaFrame 1.8 server farm to an MPS 3.0 server farm, Citrix integrated a feature into MPS 3.0 known as *interoperability* (or *mixed*) *mode*. While functioning in this mode, a MetaFrame 1.8 server farm can interoperate with an MPS 3.0 server farm of the same name. Details on interoperability mode are discussed in the "MetaFrame 1.8 Interoperability with MetaFrame Presentation Server" section, later in this chapter. To facilitate migration from 1.8 to 3.0, the basic steps listed next must be performed. Make certain that you perform your initial upgrade during off-peak work hours so as to minimize the impact on production users.

1. Install and configure the MetaFrame Access Suite Licensing server along with the necessary licenses for MPS 3.0 (see Chapter 12).
2. If you will be implementing a centralized DBMS (SQL Server, Oracle, DB2, or MSDE), ensure that this is configured and ready for the MPS installation (see Chapter 13).
3. When installing the first MPS 3.0 server, install it either on a new server or on an existing MetaFrame 1.8 server *not* currently designated as the ICA master browser. You can determine the current 1.8 master browser by issuing the QUERY SERVER command from a command prompt and looking for the server with the "M" designation beside it.

   When prompted, make certain that you select the option to create a new server farm and assign it the *exact* same name as the existing 1.8 server farm.
4. When the new MPS 3.0 server restarts, it comes up in interoperability mode and automatically forces a master ICA browser election with all other mixed-mode MPS 3.0 and MetaFrame 1.8 servers. An MPS 3.0 server always wins the browser election versus a 1.8 server, so once start-up has completed, rerun QUERY SERVER to verify that the new server is in fact operating as the new ICA master browser.

5. If the new MPS 3.0 server was previously a 1.8 server, you can verify that any published applications have been upgraded properly by consulting the summary output log displayed when the installation completed. Log files are stored in the %ProgramFiles%\Citrix\System32 folder.

6. Additional servers can now be upgraded to MPS 3.0. When performing the update on the remaining servers, be certain to select the existing farm name created when the first server was added. All subsequent servers in the 1.8 farm must be migrated before interoperability mode can be disabled and MPS 3.0 can function in full native mode.

Once all remaining 1.8 servers have been migrated to MPS 3.0, the farm can be switched from interoperability mode back to full MPS 3.0 native mode.

Upgrading from MetaFrame XP

The migration path from MetaFrame XP to MPS 3.0 is fully supported, but implementation requirements differ from those presented for MF 1.8. To upgrade an existing XP farm to MPS 3.0, you must ensure that certain servers and supporting applications are upgraded in a particular order to minimize issues that may arise. What complicates the upgrade of an existing server farm in general is the fact that a number of distinct components must interact with each other, and in order to preserve those interactions, the components must be upgraded in such a way as to ensure that the latest version is working in a backwards compatible way. A newer version of a data consumer can always process data from an older version of a data producer, but the opposite is rarely true.

When upgrading an existing MetaFrame XP server farm, you need to perform the following tasks:

1. Install and configure the MetaFrame Access Suite Licensing server along with the necessary licenses for MPS 3.0 (see Chapter 12).

2. If you will be implementing a centralized DBMS (SQL Server, Oracle, DB2, or MSDE), ensure that this is configured and ready for the MPS installation (see Chapter 13).

3. Provide all clients running earlier versions of the Citrix Management Console with the latest version available on the MPS installation media. Previous versions of this console are not supported with the new version of MetaFrame. Instances of the Management Console running on a MetaFrame server are automatically upgraded when the MetaFrame server is upgraded, so these servers can be omitted when determining what clients must be updated.

4. Before you begin to upgrade any of the MetaFrame servers in your farm, if you are also running MetaFrame Conference Manager (MCM), this component must be upgraded first. The MCM upgrade is performed by inserting the Components CD and selecting MetaFrame Conference Manager from the main dialog box.

5. Next, if there are any servers running the Web Interface for MetaFrame (previously known as NFuse) that are not also running MetaFrame, they should be upgraded to the latest version provided on the MPS installation CD. If you are running the Web interface on the same server as MetaFrame, you do not need to upgrade this component yet; it is automatically upgraded when MPS 3.0 is installed.

6. If you are running an older version of Resource Manager (XPe only) and will implement the latest Resource Manager version with MPS Enterprise Edition, then before upgrading any other servers, upgrade the Farm Metric Servers. Upgrading any other MetaFrame server first results in inconsistent data being sent to the older FMSs, causing incorrect collection of farm metrics.

7. Next, upgrade all MetaFrame servers designated as zone data collectors. These servers should always be running the latest MetaFrame version prior to other servers to ensure that all necessary information for a zone is being collected and managed properly.

8. Once you reach this step, you are finally ready to perform the MPS upgrade on all remaining MetaFrame XP servers in your farm.

When the last server has been upgraded, the farm is fully upgraded to MetaFrame Presentation Server 3.0.

WARNING: Never attempt to perform a MetaFrame Presentation Server installation through a Terminal Services or MetaFrame session, including using the remote console supported with Windows Server 2003. During the installation, certain files are upgraded that can render remote connections unavailable and make the server completely inaccessible until you can physically access it from a local console.

MetaFrame Presentation Server Service Pack and Feature Release Packages

Since release of the first service pack for MetaFrame 1.8, Citrix has consistently coupled its product enhancements, known as *feature releases*, with their service pack installations. When the service pack is installed on the server, the code enhancements to support the changes available with the feature release are also installed, but their functionality is not available unless an associated feature release license has been purchased and added to the license database.

While the feature release (FR) version numbers typically correspond to the service pack numbers, this is not always the case. For example, you may have installation files for Service Pack 4 and Feature Release 4, or you may have Service Pack 4 with Feature Release 2. Whatever the latest FR version is, that is typically bundled with the latest service pack.

If you plan to deploy a particular feature release with your MPS implementation (as of this writing, there are no feature releases available for MPS 3.0), you need to ensure that you purchased the necessary feature release licensing as well. Any special considerations that may exist for a particular service pack or feature release will be noted in the accompanying documentation. Make sure you clearly understand what changes will be introduced before deploying a service pack or feature release into an existing production environment.

Many service pack/feature release packages have a required installation order similar to that given for an upgrade from MetaFrame XP to MPS 3.0. A general rule of thumb is to apply service pack/feature release packages to all Farm Metric Servers, followed by zone data collectors, and finally any other MetaFrame servers in the farm.

WARNING: Always consult the documentation for the service pack/feature release before installing it on any server in your production environment.

End-User Printing Support with MetaFrame

Earlier in the "Terminal Server Printer Support" section of this chapter, when discussing planning considerations for a Terminal Server implementation, I stressed the importance that many organizations place on the ability to print to the desired printer from within their Terminal Server sessions. Timely and reliable access to printing can be a critical part of a company's business. These considerations apply with equal importance when determining implementation requirements for a MetaFrame deployment. Properly planning and accounting for the printing needs of a deployment go a long way toward ensuring that printing issues are minimized.

While MetaFrame Presentation Server supports all the printer options available with Terminal Server alone, MPS also includes advanced support in the following areas:

- **Printer driver management**—MetaFrame provides a centralized method of administering printer drivers on all servers in the Citrix server farm. The drivers need to be installed on only one MetaFrame server, and then replication can be configured so all other servers in the farm receive these same drivers.
- **Advanced network printer share support**—In addition to the standard network printer support available with a Terminal Server, MetaFrame expands this functionality by providing the ability to auto-assign network printers listed in the server farm to MetaFrame users based on user account or domain group membership, providing an easier way to manage printers than through logon scripts.
- **Advanced local client printer support**—Much like the client printer support provided by a Terminal Server, MetaFrame also automatically redirects a client's local printers so they are accessible from within a MetaFrame session. MetaFrame expands the support available for client-mapped printers by providing a number of customization features, including the ability to map printers using

a set of universal printer drivers that can compensate for a missing or ill-behaved native driver for the printer when used on a MetaFrame server. MetaFrame also provides the ability to throttle the amount of bandwidth a client-mapped printer consumes in the ICA presentation services data stream between the server and the client.

TIP: Complete details on configuration of MetaFrame to support end-user printing are discussed in Chapter 17.

Advanced Printer Driver Management

Just as with a Terminal Server alone, before any user can print from within their MetaFrame session, an appropriate printer driver must be available on the MetaFrame server. The process of driver installation is exactly the same as described in the "Printer Driver Selection and Management" section, earlier in this chapter. What MetaFrame does provide is an advanced mechanism for managing these printer drivers once they are installed on the Terminal Server. Figure 8.41 shows the Drivers tab for the Printer Management module in the MPS Management Console. The list of available drivers in this example represents the sum of all drivers across all servers in the farm. It is quite possible that all servers do not have all the listed drivers unless printer driver replication has been enabled in the farm.

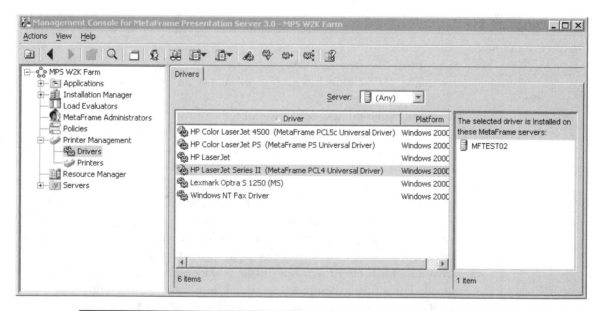

Figure 8.41   The Drivers tab for Printer Management in the MPS Management Console.

Figure 8.41 shows six listed drivers:

- HP Color LaserJet 4500 (MetaFrame PCL5c Universal Driver)
- HP Color LaserJet PS (MetaFrame PS Universal Driver)
- HP LaserJet
- HP LaserJet Series II (MetaFrame PCL4 Universal Driver)
- Lexmark Optra S 1250 (MS)
- Windows NT Fax Driver

Of these six drivers, you can see that three have descriptions that indicate they are universal printer drivers provided with MetaFrame. These universal printer drivers (UPDs) are provided to allow client printers to be mapped that otherwise would fail to map properly due to driver compatibility issues. I discuss the MetaFrame UPDs in more detail in the "Advanced Local Client Printer Support" section, later in this chapter.

TIP: Although the names are misleading, the MetaFrame universal printer driver differs from the Windows Universal Printer Driver (WUPD) discussed in the "Printer Driver Selection and Management" section, earlier in this chapter. The WUPD is a component of Windows that works as an interface between the graphical device interface (GDI) and a printer mini-driver. MetaFrame's UPD is a generic printer driver that can generate spooled printer data that can be interpreted and processed by the native driver that resides locally on a client device.

This list of drivers is kept up-to-date by the Independent Management Architecture (IMA) service, which polls the MetaFrame server at regular intervals to determine if new printer drivers have been installed or existing ones removed and if the status of a driver changes, the updated information is sent to the data store. Figure 8.42 shows an updated Drivers tab with two additional printer drivers added to the MetaFrame server. Immediately to the right you can see the list of drivers installed on the server.

In addition to simply presenting a centralized view of the installed drivers in the server farm, you can configure printer driver replication so the drivers installed on one MetaFrame server can be replicated to all other desired servers in the farm. MetaFrame supports two types of replication: You can either set up replication between specific servers, or you can configure auto-replication, which will replicate drivers to all servers in the farm running the same platform.

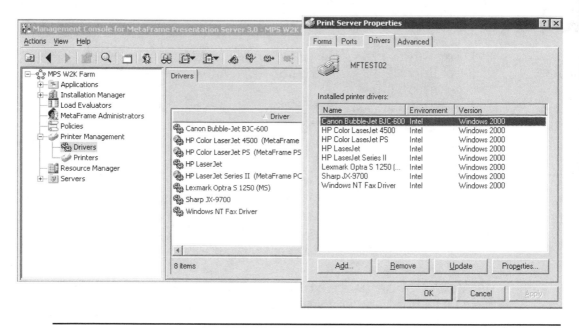

Figure 8.42 When drivers are added or removed from a MetaFrame server, the information in the data store is automatically updated.

Advanced Network Printer Share Support

Earlier in this chapter when discussing printing considerations for a Terminal Server, I mentioned how network printer shares were available to Terminal Server users through either a logon script or manually connected using the Add Printer wizard. MetaFrame expands on this functionality by letting you assign printers available in the server farm to any MetaFrame user based on their user ID or group membership. All available printers in the farm are listed under the Printers object in the Printer Management module of the MPS Management Console. Within a new server farm, only those printers currently being shared off MetaFrame servers in the farm appear automatically in this list. Figure 8.43 shows an example of this with one printer listed, which has been shared directly off a MetaFrame server (MFTest02). Many sources refer to these types of printers as "local printers," but I've found that people find this name rather misleading because the printer is actually local to only those users logged on directly to the MetaFrame server sharing the printer. I prefer to call this class of printer a "local server farm printer."

NOTE: While sharing a printer directly off a MetaFrame server is a convenient way to make it available within the farm, doing so introduces additional overhead on the server that can impact any active client sessions.

One way that Citrix recommends avoiding this additional overhead is to dedicate a MetaFrame server solely as a print server. This configuration has the server running MetaFrame and sharing out one or more printers to the farm but not allowing any ICA or RDP user logons. There is no additional MetaFrame licensing cost, since MetaFrame licensing is based on concurrent users and not on total active servers. There is of course still the appropriate Microsoft licensing cost for the server.

Additional overhead is introduced onto a print server also running MetaFrame, but with sufficient resources this should cause little impact, and it provides additional integration support compared to printers loaded off print servers outside the farm, as I discuss shortly.

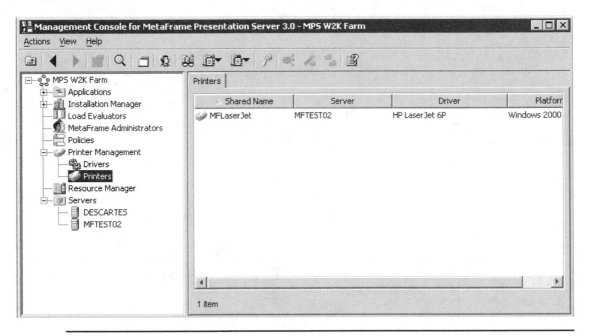

Figure 8.43 Printers shared off MetaFrame servers in the farm automatically appear in the Printers list.

Any printers shared off a print server not also running MetaFrame must be manually imported into the server farm. This is a straightforward process, and once the contents of the print server have been imported, the server appears in the Network Print Servers tab in the Printer Management module of the Management Console. Any changes to the print server are not automatically reflected in the Printer Management module; you need to update this information using the Update Network Print Server option.

Once the printers from a print server have been imported, they appear in the Printers list alongside any printers shared off servers within the farm ("local server farm printers").

Imported printers do not display all the information available for local server farm printers, as you can see in Figure 8.44. There is also added support for driver replication directly from a print server running on a MetaFrame server in the farm to any other "regular" production MetaFrame server in the environment.

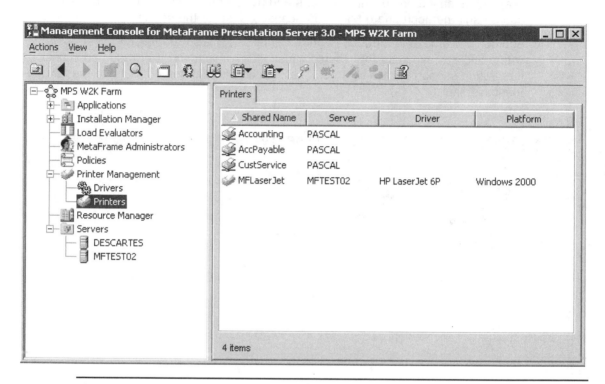

Figure 8.44   Imported printers do not provide all the information available from local server farm printers.

Any printer visible within the server farm can be assigned to a user ID or group so it is auto-created and available when the user logs on to a MetaFrame server.

Advanced Local Client Printer Support

In the "End-User Printing Support and Management" section earlier in the chapter, I discussed Terminal Server support for redirection of local client printers so they are accessible via printer queues directly off the Terminal Server. MetaFrame provides a nearly identical service with its ICA protocol. Here are some of the key features the two implementations have in common:

- Both require that a suitable printer driver exists on the MetaFrame/Terminal Server.
- Printer driver selection is determined by comparing the full printer driver name on the client with the corresponding printer driver name for the server.
- Any mismatches in driver name or in no driver being found result in the client printer mapping silently failing.

In addition to these common features, MetaFrame includes advanced support and management options specifically for client printer mappings, including the following:

- Complete centralized management of the drivers and printers pertaining to client printer redirection, including enabling or disabling of drive-mapping support.
- Support for a universal printer driver (UPD) that can be configured to be used if a suitable native driver match cannot be found.

By default, a MetaFrame server is configured to automatically attempt to use a UPD if the corresponding native printer driver cannot be found when attempting to automatically map a client printer.

TIP: MPS 3.0 provides a feature that allows for automatic installation of signed Windows (2000 or 2003) printer drivers on a MetaFrame server if they are not already available when a user attempts to establish a client-mapped or network-mapped printer. This option will install only the native drivers that ship with Windows. It cannot be used to install custom third-party drivers; these must still be installed manually and then replicated.

When a client printer is being mapped, the printer driver name on the client is compared to the driver name on the server. If the names do not match exactly, the mapping will not be generated. MetaFrame provides a graphical interface where any necessary cross-reference entries can be added without your having to make registry changes or modify text files. From here you can add any required client/server printer driver cross-references. Earlier in the "Terminal Server Printer Support" section I used the examples of the client and printer drivers "hp deskjet 970c series" and "HP DeskJet 970Cse," respectively. Entering this information in this dialog box would produce an entry similar to the one shown in Figure 8.45.

Once this option is set, whenever a client provides the server with the driver name "hp deskjet 970c series," the client queue is created but the driver "HP DeskJet 970Cse" is used instead.

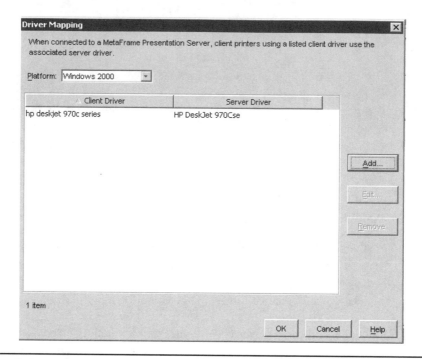

Figure 8.45 Printer driver mapping cross-reference information can be easily managed in MetaFrame.

Client-Mapped Printer Naming Convention

The final feature to look at in this section is the naming convention used by MetaFrame to name client-mapped printers created on the server. A client-mapped printer has the naming

Client\<Client name>#\<Printer Name>

where "Client" is a constant used to show that the mapping is a client printer. "Client name" is the name assigned to the client device during installation of MetaFrame. And finally, the printer name corresponds to the full printer name on the client device.

For example, if I have a local printer called HP LaserJet and I log on to a MetaFrame server configured to support this client mapping, I would expect to have a client printer mapping with the name

Client\TODDPC#\HP LaserJet

Where "TODDPC" is my client name. Similarly, if I had a network-mapped printer on my local PC with the mapping of

\\PrintServ\HP DeskJet 970C Series

then when I next logged on to the MetaFrame server, my client name would automatically become

Client\TODDPC#\\\PrintServ\HP DeskJet 970C Series

The extra backslashes in the name are not a concern because they are ignored and have no affect on actually attempting to print to that client-mapped printer.

Citrix Load Manager Considerations

For deploying MetaFrame Presentation Server Advanced Edition or Enterprise Edition, support for Citrix Load Manager is available with the product. There are no special planning considerations required for deploying load management beyond noting the following:

- Citrix Load Manager is an integrated part of the published application concept of MetaFrame. If an application is being published, then the application is automatically available for load balancing simply by publishing it on more than one MetaFrame server in a farm.
- For load balancing between two or more servers, both must belong to the same farm. Cross-farm load balancing is not supported.
- All MetaFrame servers that support load balancing are automatically assigned the default load evaluator, which dictates that the server will report that it is 100 percent loaded when there are 100 users logged on to the server. Load evaluators are completely customizable and can be updated at any time.
- Citrix Load Manager requires no additional server hardware or configuration planning beyond the standard MetaFrame server installation and application publishing processes.

Details on configuration and use of Citrix Load Manager are discussed in Chapter 22.

Scheduled MetaFrame Server Reboots

The comments I made earlier in this chapter in the section entitled "Scheduled Server Reboots" also apply for a Terminal Server running MetaFrame Presentation Server. The same application issues that plague a Terminal Server unfortunately still plague a MetaFrame Server.

If you plan to deploy MetaFrame Presentation Server, Enterprise Edition, one thing to note is that there is support available directly from within the MPS Management Console to configure the reboot schedule for MetaFrame servers in the farm. To access this feature you must also be running Resource Manager. Figure 8.46 shows the reboot schedule properties for a MetaFrame server. Once the reboot schedule has been set on an individual server, the settings can be applied to other servers in the farm by selecting the Apply to Other Servers button. This presents a list of all servers in the farm from which you can check the ones you wish to have automatically reboot. An option on this screen lets you flag the reboots to be staggered over a specified time interval.

When defining the reboot schedule for MetaFrame servers in your farm, I recommend that you stagger the server reboots to occur over the course of an hour or two, depending on the number of servers in the farm. Because a large amount of data is transmitted between the data store and a MetaFrame server when it first starts, it is not recommended that you configure multiple servers to restart simultaneously. Doing so would place a large burden on the data store and delay proper start-up of the IMA service on all these servers.

TIP: When you have MetaFrame servers localized in different time zones, the assigned reboot schedule is applied based on the local time of the server. So if you specify 11 p.m. as the reboot time for three MetaFrame servers, all in different time zones, the servers will not reboot simultaneously but in fact will restart when their local time is 11 p.m.

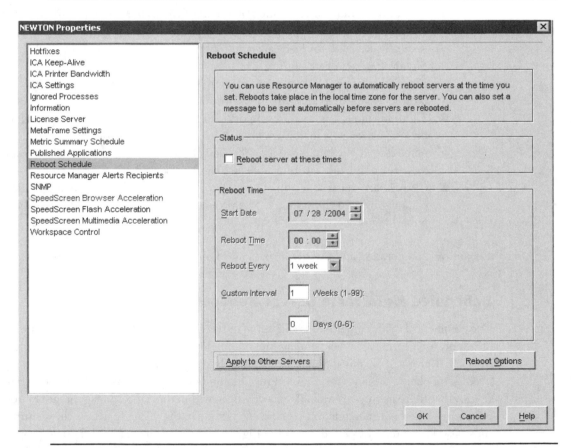

Figure 8.46 The resource management component of MPS Enterprise Edition lets you centrally manage reboot scheduling of MetaFrame servers.

MetaFrame 1.8 Interoperability with MetaFrame Presentation Server

In Chapter 2, I provided an overview of the interoperability modes supported by MPS 3.0 and of how it could coexist with MetaFrame 1.8 servers in an MF 1.8–based server farm. In this section I briefly review the considerations to keep in mind when planning the upgrade of an existing MF 1.8 farm. The actual upgrade steps were covered earlier in this chapter in the section entitled "Upgrading from MetaFrame 1.8 or XP to MetaFrame Presentation Server 3.0."

To facilitate migration from MetaFrame 1.8 to MPS 3.0, Citrix lets the new MPS 3.0 server farm environment operate not only in MPS native mode but also in MPS mixed mode.

NOTE: If you are implementing a new MetaFrame Presentation Server 3.0 environment and not migrating from or interoperating with an existing MetaFrame 1.8 environment, you need *not* be concerned with the material in this section. You should never enable mixed-mode support unless absolutely necessary, as doing so will inhibit operation of certain native MPS features.

MPS Native Mode

The default operating mode for a new MPS installation is *native mode,* and when operating in this mode the server farm can consist of only servers running MetaFrame XP 1.0 or higher. An MPS server farm and an MF 1.8 server farm will act completely independently of each other in this mode.

MPS Mixed Mode

Operation of the server farm in *mixed mode* provides backwards compatibility with MF 1.8 and lets you transparently introduce new or upgraded MPS servers into your existing MF 1.8 server farm. When the MPS farm is configured to enable mixed mode, the Interoperability tab becomes visible when you look at the properties for an MPS server in the Management Console, as shown in Figure 8.47.

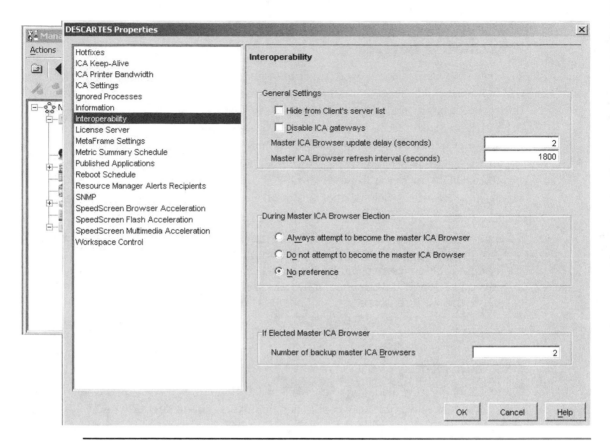

Figure 8.47   The Interoperability dialog box is familiar to anyone who has administered a MetaFrame 1.8 environment.

Legacy features and support available in MetaFrame 1.8 are enabled in mixed mode, for example:

■ **ICA browser service**—In MetaFrame 1.8, this service is responsible for maintaining and communicating status information about the MetaFrame server on which it is running to the elected ICA master browser. Just as in an MF 1.8 environment, the ICA master browser elections are still supported along with the other standard ICA browser service functionality. The standard election rules apply, and due to the fact that an MPS 3.0 server has the highest MF version, an MPS 3.0 server always wins an ICA master browser election over an MF 1.8 server.

- **ICA gateways**—An MPS mixed-mode server supports use of and can be selected as an ICA gateway, but this must be done from an MF 1.8 server. I do not recommend enabling an MPS server as an ICA gateway. ICA license gateways are not supported in a mixed-mode environment (this is discussed further in the next bullet point).
- **License pooling**—MPS provides the ability to pool and share licenses when operating in mixed-mode, although there are some limitations. Unlike MPS in native mode, which maintains one pool of licenses for all servers in the farm, connection license pooling in mixed mode will not span subnets. Instead, available connection licenses are divided between all subnets with MPS servers. All MF 1.8 and MPS licenses are pooled and available for use on those subnets. When MPS connection licenses are being divided, they are split evenly between all available subnets. Division of pooled licenses can be modified and should be reviewed from the Interoperability dialog box for the *server farm,* as shown in Figure 8.48. This figure shows pooled connection licenses divided between two subnets.

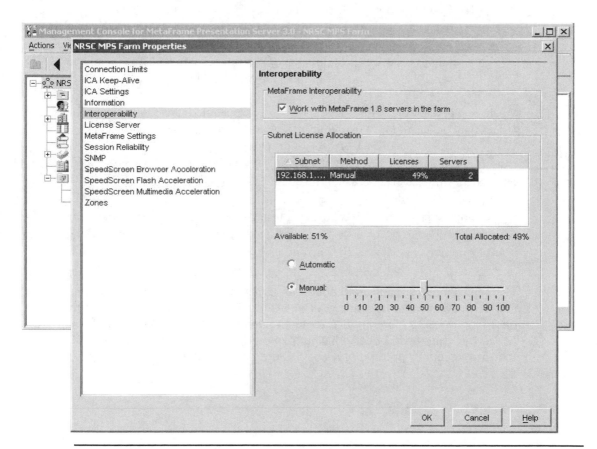

Figure 8.48 License pooling in a mixed-mode environment will not span subnets, so licenses must be manually divided as required between the subnets.

If you implemented MF 1.8 license gateways to allow license pooling between subnets, these license gateways will no longer function when an MPS mixed-mode farm is introduced. The license division between these subnets is instead based on the settings on the Interoperability tab. Instead of having access to the entire license pool, the MetaFrame servers in each subnet will have access to only the MF 1.8 connection licenses available in their subnet and the available MPS licenses that have been allocated.

■ **Application publishing**—While operating in mixed mode, the same application can be published between the two environments. For example, Microsoft Word could be published on both an MF 1.8 server and an MPS 3.0 server, and users would connect to the appropriate server based on the requested application and not based on a certain server version. Special steps must be taken to ensure that applications are published properly when operating in a mixed-mode environment. Application publishing considerations are discussed in detail in Chapter 21.

■ **Load balancing**—When a mixture of MF 1.8 and MPS 3.0 servers are load-balancing applications, only the features supported in MF 1.8 are available. Any new load-balancing features supported by MPS are not accessible. When determining what server to direct a user toward, if both an MPS 3.0 and an MF 1.8 server have the same user load, the MPS 3.0 server is always selected.

While conceptually the MPS and MF 1.8 servers appear to belong to the same farm, in actual fact they belong to two separate farms, both of which are assigned the same farm name. When you install your first MPS server and are prompted to create a new farm, you will provide the exact same name as the one currently used by the MF 1.8 farm. Once the new MPS farm's data store has been created, the existing MF 1.8 farm is detected and the two farms automatically establish the necessary relationship to coexist. You can also enable and disable mixed-mode support after MPS has been installed by enabling MetaFrame interoperability under the Properties tab of the server farm. An existing MF 1.8 farm will be detected only if it has the exact same name as the current farm you are modifying.

TIP: Mixed-mode support is intended as a migration mechanism only and not as a long-term solution for combining MF 1.8 and MPS servers into a single farm. While operating in mixed mode, native features such as Zone Preferences and Failover or Active Directory–based user principal name (UPN) entries (for example, todd@nrsc.com) supported only by MPS are not available.

CHAPTER 9

Service Pack and Hotfix Management

Before You Begin

An inevitable part of any system administrator's job is the testing and implementation of service packs, security patches, and other hotfixes. To many Windows administrators, the steady increase in publicized (and exploited) security vulnerabilities has served as a wake-up call to the importance of effective patch management as part of a secure server environment. Unfortunately, while most administrators and security professionals do acknowledge the importance of system patching, more often than not, this task is improperly managed or completely overlooked as part of an administrator's regular duties.

The most common complaints I hear from an administrator include the following:

- It is difficult to keep track of which fixes are actually required and which are optional. Many of the vulnerabilities announced by companies such as Microsoft apply only to specific software configurations and may not be required on all servers in an environment.
- It is also difficult to track which servers have what fixes already applied.
- The installation of multiple patches can result in multiple reboots of a server. This is not only time consuming but also can be difficult to schedule in a large server environment.

In general, it is perceived that it simply takes too much time to manage patches efficiently. Fortunately, resources and utilities are available that can directly address all these complaints. In this chapter I describe in detail how you can use them to develop a process for managing service packs and hotfixes in your Terminal Server environment.

NOTE: If you are or will be running Citrix MetaFrame Presentation Server (MPS) in your environment, you will have to take into consideration the deployment of MetaFrame-related service packs and hotfixes. The concepts of patch management discussed in this chapter will also apply to MPS, and any Citrix-specific patching information will also be covered here.

Service Pack Selection and Installation

The first decision you make regarding your patch inventory should be what service pack (if any) you will be installing on your Terminal Server and then, based on your Terminal Server environment, how that service pack will actually be deployed.

Deciding When to Install a Service Pack

When a new service pack becomes available, a common reaction by many administrators is to immediately begin installing it on the servers in their environment. While this may not be such a bad idea under most circumstances, when dealing with an existing production Terminal Server environment, thorough consideration of the potential consequences must be weighed before proceeding. For a new Terminal Server installation I recommend the latest service pack, since you are much less likely to run into problems when applying a service pack to a new server installation than you might with a system already in production.

TIP: If you are building a new Terminal Server environment and will be applying the latest service pack to all your servers, it may be worthwhile to look at integrating the service pack directly into the Windows installation files. The process is known as slip-streaming, details of which are discussed in Chapter 10, "Installing Windows Terminal Services."

For a Terminal Server environment already in production, I normally use the following guidelines:

- If the latest service pack (SP) has been available for at least two to three months, I install it followed by any post-SP hotfixes that may apply to my environment (I talk about hotfix selection later in this chapter).
- If the latest service pack is less than two months old, I stick with my current service pack level unless there is a specific bug fixed in the service pack that I need and cannot resolve with an existing hotfix for my current SP level.

For example, if a new service pack for Windows Server 2003 was released last week, then as long as my current environment was functioning normally I would *not* install this new SP right away. Once this service pack had "matured" for about two months I would look at applying it to my environment along with any other corresponding hotfixes for that service pack that might also be required. I would not install a service pack just because it had become available unless there was a specific reason, security or otherwise, that I should do so.

While it can be correctly argued that a service pack is an important requirement in maintaining a stable and secure Windows server, I still consider it to be a major software update that must follow the same change-management procedures as any other update. While it is true that a service pack undergoes much more thorough testing than the individual hotfixes themselves, a service pack is still a collection of multiple fixes, which have a greater potential for introduction of an error than a couple of individual hotfixes might. Only after thoroughly testing a service pack in your existing environment should you consider deploying it to all your production servers. For more information on planning a software release management process, please refer to Chapter 7, "Server and Application Software Planning."

TIP: It is always worthwhile to monitor newsgroups and mailing lists for other people's feedback regarding a newly released service pack or hotfix, particularly in reference to stability in a Terminal Server/MetaFrame Presentation Server environment. Places such as the following are all excellent resources for information on existing updates and how they may affect the stability of a Terminal Server/MetaFrame environment:

- Microsoft Terminal Server Community: http://www.microsoft.com/windowsserver2003/community/centers/terminal/default.mspx

- Citrix Support Forum: http://www.support.citrix.com/forums

- The Thin.net: http://www.thethin.net

Service Pack Considerations with MetaFrame Presentation Server

Even though MetaFrame is technically an add-on to Windows Terminal Server, the tight integration with the Terminal Services infrastructure means that special care must be taken when deploying a Microsoft service pack onto a MetaFrame server. When running MPS you must be careful to ensure that a service pack installation does not impair or completely break any of the MetaFrame functionality. I recommend that you search the Citrix knowledgebase using the text "service pack x," where x is the service pack number. Specifically, you're looking for any service pack–related issues. The knowledgebase can be found at http://support.citrix.com/kb/homepage.jspa

For example, searching the knowledgebase using the string "service pack 4" will return a number of articles, including one specifically discussing known issues with Windows 2000 Server and Service Pack 4.

If both a Microsoft and a Citrix service pack are available for deployment, I always give the Microsoft service pack precedence over the Citrix service pack. I feel that operating system changes should take priority over any other service packs, and in many cases, corrections to the operating system can help troubleshoot or resolve issues with other applications on the server, including MetaFrame.

Since the first service pack for MetaFrame 1.8, Citrix has consistently coupled its product enhancements, known as *feature releases,* with its service pack installation. When the service pack is installed on the server, the code enhancements to support the changes available with the feature release are also installed, but their functionality is not available unless an associated feature release license has been purchased and added to the license database.

The actual installation steps for a MetaFrame service pack/feature release (SP/FR) are as straightforward as for a Terminal Server service pack, but the appropriate planning and testing steps must still be considered before upgrading all the servers in your environment. Deploying a MetaFrame service pack without proper testing can easily cause instability in your environment.

When installing a MetaFrame SP/FR, I recommend the following guidelines:

- Apply the desired Windows service pack (if applicable) prior to adding a MetaFrame service pack/feature release. All security and non-security patches should be applied after all service packs have been installed.
- Whenever possible, install the MetaFrame SP/FR onto a test server that is located in a different server farm, and ideally a different network subnet, from your production MetaFrame servers. Changes in the behavior of the ICA or IMA protocols could cause this updated server to somehow impair the stability of the other servers in the environment. This is particularly true if you are currently running in a mixed-mode configuration where both MPS 3.0 and MetaFrame 1.8 servers coexist in the same farm. Mixed-mode support was discussed in Chapter 8, "Server Installation and Management Planning."
- When deploying an SP/FR into production, the MetaFrame servers should be updated in the following order:
    1. **Farm metric servers**—If you are running Resource Manager and your farm metric servers are different from your zone data collectors (ZDCs), then these servers should be updated first. Because these servers interpret Resource Manager data from other MetaFrame servers in the farm, if one of these servers is updated first it may attempt to provide data to the farm metric server that it cannot interpret properly. Typically, the farm metric server and the zone data collectors are deployed on the same server.

2. **Zone data collectors**—For reasons similar to those for updating the farm metric servers, because the zone data collectors gather data from all other MetaFrame servers in their zone, if another MetaFrame server is updated first, it may pass information to a ZDC that it cannot interpret properly. For this reason all ZDCs should be updated before other servers, with the exception of the farm metric servers.

3. **Non–data store MetaFrame servers**—All other non–data store MetaFrame Presentation Servers should be upgraded next.

4. **Jet or MSDE-based data store**—If you are running a Jet or MSDE data store database, this server should be upgraded last to the latest service pack/feature release level.

Detailed information on the various components of MetaFrame Presentation Server and the recommended implementation planning steps are discussed in Chapter 2, "Citrix MetaFrame Presentation Server," and Chapter 8.

WARNING: Never deploy a Windows or MetaFrame service pack into a production Terminal Server environment unless you have first tested it in a development or test environment.

NOTE: A common question I'm asked is whether or not the Microsoft Software Update Services (SUS) tool can be used to manage deployment of service packs. With the release of Service Pack 4 for Windows 2000, SUS now supports deployment of service packs for both Windows 2000 and Windows Server 2003, in addition to supporting critical updates, security patches, and update rollup packages.

Third-party patch management tools such as St. Bernard Software's UpdateEXPERT (http://www.stbernard.com) provide robust alternatives to SUS for managing both service packs and hotfixes.

Microsoft's next iteration of SUS, officially called Microsoft Windows Update Services (WUS), is expected to become available near the end of 2004 and promises to be a large improvement over the current SUS product.

While it appears that these types of tools could greatly simplify deployment of a service pack, particularly in a large and/or geographically dispersed Terminal Server environment, there are still risks involved in automating an SP installation. An SP installation should be considered a major upgrade to your server environment, and as such, be monitored closely. While the process can be tedious, interactively monitoring the SP installation provides the best way to ensure a successful and stable upgrade of your environment, at least until you are certain the deployment will proceed without a problem. Before you can even consider how you might automate the installation process, you must still be sure that the service pack or hotfix you are planning to deploy has been thoroughly tested.

I discuss patch management tools such as SUS in the "Security Hotfix Analysis and Management Tools" section, later in this chapter.

Hotfix Notification

In order to effectively manage service packs and hotfixes, you need to have a mechanism in place to receive timely notification of any new fixes that may become available, particularly security-related fixes. If you wish to ensure that your environment remains secure, it is critical that you keep current on what security updates have been released for your server configuration.

While regular (non-security-related) hotfixes are typically sought out only when a problem arises on a server, security-specific hotfixes need to be proactively pursued. You obviously want to have the latest pertinent security updates on your server *before* they have been exploited.

Security-Related Update Notification

One way to ensure the reception of timely security information is via e-mail notification. Probably the one mailing list that every Windows administrator should belong to, whether they are managing Terminal Server or not, is Microsoft's Product Security Notification service. This is a free Web-based resource that automatically sends you e-mail notifications of security bulletins affecting Microsoft products. Instructions on how to subscribe, as well as additional information on this service, can be found at http://www.microsoft.com/technet/security/bulletin/notify.mspx

You can also subscribe to receive an e-mail notification when new updates are available for SUS by selecting the Sign Up for E-Mail Notification link on the SUS homepage at http://www.microsoft.com/windowsserversystem/sus/default.mspx

And finally, an up-to-date list of security patches organized by product and service pack is available for browsing and searching at http://www.microsoft.com/technet/security/current.aspx. For example, a list of security patches available for Windows Server 2003 can be searched as shown in Figure 9.1.

Instinctively, many administrators download and install all listed security patches without necessarily reviewing the details of each fix to ensure it is required in their environment. One of the flaws in this approach is that these fixes have been created to resolve specific system exploits that may not apply to a Terminal Server environment. For example, a fix designed specifically for an Active Directory domain controller would have no relevance on a Terminal Server unless that server was also a domain controller.

Considering that each distinct fix may introduce stability issues with the server, the goal of any administrator is to maximize the security of the Terminal Server while minimizing the actual number of security patches required. Later in this chapter I look more closely at selecting the appropriate patches to install on your Terminal Server.

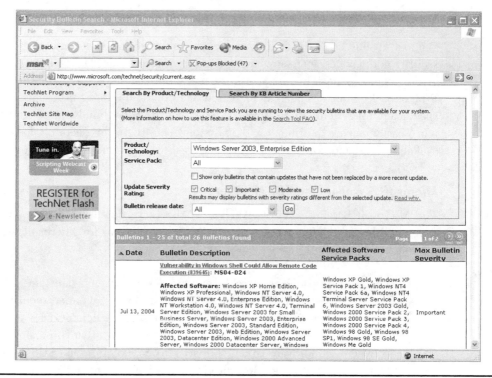

Figure 9.1 Windows Server 2003 security update list.

NOTE: In addition to Microsoft's security site, many other security resources exist on the Internet, for example:

- CERT: http://www.cert.org
- SANS Institute: http://www.sans.org
- NTBUGTRAQ: http://www.ntbugtraq.com
- Hacking Exposed: http://www.hackingexposed.com
- PatchManagement.org: http://www.patchmanagement.org

Each site provides information not only on Microsoft-specific security issues but also on issues with other operating systems and products. I look more closely at Terminal Server security in Chapter 16, "Terminal Server Security."

Security Hotfix Analysis and Management Tools

While a mailing list or Web site can provide you with up-to-date information on the latest security notifications, manually having to reviewing and track such a list is both tedious and error-prone. Fortunately, one of the results of Microsoft's ongoing Strategic Technology Protection Program has been an increased focus on (and interest in) security tools designed specifically for system administrators—tools that provide administrators with the means to more easily manage and monitor their system security. In this section I look at a few tools available and demonstrate how they can be used to streamline the hotfix detection process.

Microsoft Baseline Security Analyzer

The Microsoft Baseline Security Analyzer (MBSA), version 1.2, is a free, GUI-based tool developed by Shavlik Technologies (http://www.shavlik.com) for Microsoft, which supports the following features:

■ Compares the fixes currently applied to your system against an XML database (MSSECURE.XML) and generates a list of recommended security fixes for your server. The XML database can be either the default database available from Microsoft or a database of approved updates that you maintain via the Microsoft Software Update Services (SUS) tool. I discuss SUS in more detail later in this chapter. Specifically, MBSA will scan for security updates for a number of Microsoft products, including the following:
  ■ Windows NT 4.0, XP, 2000, or 2003
  ■ Microsoft Office 2000 and higher
  ■ Internet Explorer 5.01 or higher
  ■ Microsoft Virtual Machine
  ■ Windows Media Player 6.4 or higher
  ■ IIS 4.0 or higher
  ■ SQL Server 7.0 or higher
  ■ Exchange Server 5.5 or higher
  ■ Microsoft Data Access Components (MDAC) 2.5 and higher
■ Provides a brief description and a link directly to the corresponding "knowledge-base article" article for each hotfix that is missing on the system. This provides a convenient way to quickly determine whether a fix may apply to your particular configuration or not.
■ Scans for additional Windows vulnerabilities such as Guest account status, Administrators group membership, or weak local account passwords. It won't scan domain controllers for weak domain account passwords.
■ Maintains a history of previously run reports that can be quickly reviewed.

It should be noted that MBSA provides only the mechanism for reporting on what security deficiencies one or more servers in your environment may have. It does not provide a means of retrieving and deploying those missing security updates to the affected servers. Unless you are utilizing a tool that provides such support (discussed later in this chapter), you will still need to manually retrieve and install the desired updates on your server based on the information returned by MBSA.

You can download MBSA from the Microsoft Web site at www.microsoft.com/technet/security/tools/tools/mbsahome.asp.

You can install MBSA directly on your Terminal Server, or you can install it on a desktop computer running Windows NT, 2000, or XP Professional and from there perform distributed security scans of all your other machines. In order to perform these remote scans, you must be logged on using an account that has administrative privileges on the remote system.

TIP: Only users with administrative privileges can perform a security scan with MBSA. While regular users are able to load the application (this can be restricted through NTFS permissions, if desired), attempting to perform a scan without admin privileges will always result in the appearance of the message "No computers were found." Regular users also won't be able to load any previously generated reports that may exist on the server.

Figure 9.2 shows the main window displayed in MBSA when selecting a computer to scan. Notice the available options, which are all selected by default. At least one option must be selected before you can actually perform a system scan.

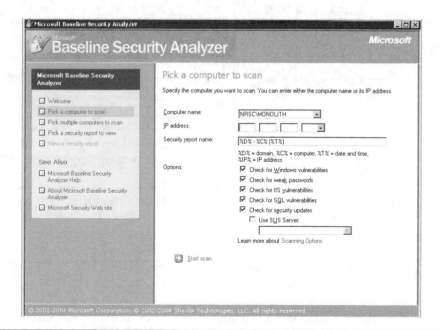

Figure 9.2   The MBSA Pick a Computer to Scan window.

You may be wondering how the MBSA utility performs its analysis to determine if a hotfix is present or not. Contrary to what many people may think, it does more than simply check in the registry to see if a particular hotfix reference exists. It also performs a validation of the file's checksum, comparing what has been installed on the server with what should be available with a particular patch. A discrepancy indicates that the patch either does not exist on the system or the installation is incomplete.

Once a scan has completed, MBSA generates a security report similar to the one shown in Figure 9.3. This scan was performed against a Windows 2000 Terminal Server with SP4 (no hotfixes) and Internet Explorer 6.1 (SP1) installed. By default, the report is saved as an XML file in a folder called SecurityScans under the profile folder of the user who initiated the scan. For example, if user "Todd" ran MBSA, the report would appear in the following folder: C:\Documents and Settings\Todd\SecurityScans

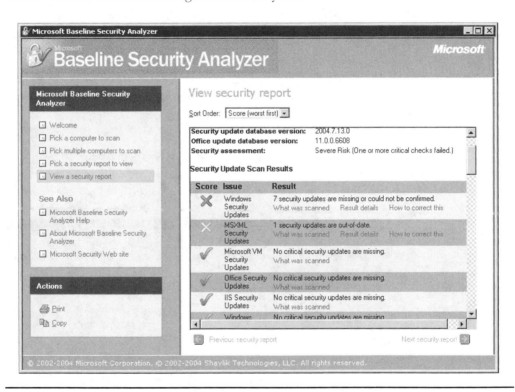

Figure 9.3 MBSA security report example for a Windows 2000 Terminal Server with SP4 and IE 6.1 SP1.

In the first row of the scan results you will see the issue labeled Windows Security Updates. By clicking the "Result details" link in the Results column you'll see a list of all of the missing Windows security updates for the scanned server. If updates are being compared against the MSSECURE.XML database obtained from the Microsoft Web site, then all available security updates are compared. If you are using an SUS server, then only approved updates are compared. The list is ordered by security bulletin number, and clicking on any one of these bulletins will link directly to the article the Microsoft Web site.

TIP: You can also initiate an MBSA scan directly from a command prompt using the mbsacli.exe executable. This tool supports two modes of scanning. The first method generates an XML output file in the same SecurityScans folder that the GUI-based MBSA tool does. The GUI tool can then be used to view these scan results.

The second method generates output directly to the console (STDOUT) and is known as the HFNetChk-Style scan mode. Prior to version 1.1 of MBSA, Shavlik (on behalf of Microsoft) actually provided two distinct tools. One was MBSA, with the GUI interface, and the other was HFNetChk, the Network Security Hotfix Checker, which provided the command line interface. Both tools referenced the same XML database managed by Microsoft. As of version 1.1, Shavlik combined the HFNetChk support directly into the MBSA tool. The old-style command line switches were preserved to allow for backwards compatibility with previous versions of HFNetChk.

You can see a full list of the available command line switches by running

    mbsacli.exe /?

The MBSA help file also provides a complete description on use of the available switches.

One advantage to providing a command line interface is that the process of scanning can be fully scripted, allowing for a completely automated process of creating security reports for your servers.

Microsoft Windows Automatic Updates and Software Update Services (SUS)

First introduced with Windows XP and now a standard feature in Windows 2000 (with SP3 or higher) and Windows Server 2003, the Windows Automatic Update (WAU) service is a tool provided by Microsoft to allow for automation of security update retrieval and installation on a Windows-based desktop or server computer.

When enabled, the WAU service allows a computer to periodically query a Microsoft Windows Update Web site (or a SUS server, discussed shortly) to determine if there are any new security updates available that may be required by the host machine. If it is determined that new security updates are available, one of three things can happen, depending on how the WAU client has been configured:

- The update is automatically downloaded and installed on the computer. If a reboot is required to complete the installation, it is automatically performed.
- The update is automatically downloaded but is not installed until a user confirms that the installation should be performed.

■ The user is notified of the update, but neither the download nor the installation is performed until confirmation has been given by the user.

The WAU client is configured by accessing the Automatic Updates applet from the Control Panel, as shown in figure 9.4.

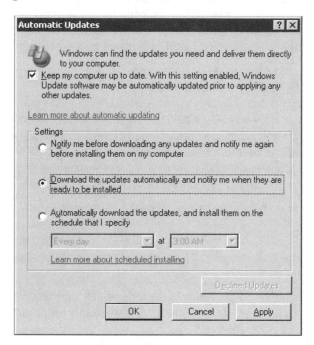

Figure 9.4   The Automatic Updates applet in the Control Panel.

In more than one case I have witnessed Terminal Server environments where WAU was used to automate the process of keeping production Terminal Servers current with the latest critical and security-related updates. Unfortunately there are limitations to using WAU, particularly in a Terminal Server environment; for example:

■ All security updates published by Microsoft to the Windows Update site are queried by WAU, even if the update does not specifically apply to the server's configuration. If the automatic download and installation of updates has been configured for a server, all these updates will be applied. In this configuration, an administrator is unable to filter whichever updates they wish to apply to a server. With use of SUS, discussed shortly, you can provide update filtering.

■ If WAU has been configured to notify an administrator when updates are available or when they have been downloaded and are ready to install, the administrator must still log on to each Terminal Server to review the available updates and select the ones to install, as shown in figure 9.5. In a large Terminal Server environment, this quickly becomes a time-consuming task.

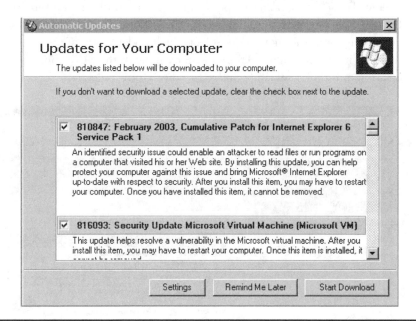

Figure 9.5 Update selection in the Windows Automatic Updates tool.

■ Because WAU runs independently on each Terminal Server, every time an update is required, each server downloads its own personal copy of the update files. This can introduce a large amount of bandwidth overhead in a large Terminal Server environment.

■ When there are multiple users with administrative privileges in the Terminal Server environment, it is possible that if a notification message appears it could be accepted without your knowledge.

TIP: Automatic updates that have been declined will not appear again the next time a notification is given. In order to have declined updates once again appear, you will need to select the Declined Updates button on the WAU configuration dialog box shown in Figure 9.4.

In order to provide an administrator with more centralized control over the use of WAU, Microsoft created Software Update Services (SUS). SUS is a free, downloadable tool that allows for the creation of an Internet Information Services (IIS) Web server within your intranet that provides the same back-end functionality as Microsoft's own update servers that are queried by default by WAU.

A SUS server periodically polls the main Microsoft update servers for any new updates that have become available and displays this list of updates within a Web-based interface that an administrator can then use to select which updates are "approved" for distribution within their environment. Figure 9.6 shows an example of the SUS Approve Updates screen. I discuss the criteria for selecting hotfixes in the "Hotfix Selection" section, later in this chapter.

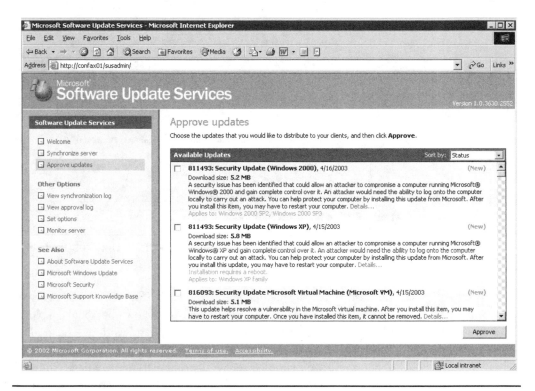

Figure 9.6 Update approval within Microsoft SUS.

TIP: As mentioned earlier, you can have Microsoft automatically e-mail you when new updates become available for SUS. This ensures that you are able to test and approve updates as quickly as possible for your environment.

Sign up for automatic e-mail notification from the main SUS Web page at www.microsoft.com/windows2000/windowsupdate/sus/default.asp.

On the client side, a special "SUS-aware" version of the WAU client is installed that can be configured to periodically poll the SUS server instead of the standard Microsoft update server for available "approved" updates. Only the approved updates will be available for download and installation.

A "SUS-aware" version of the WAU client is available as part of the base Windows 2003 server installation. If you are running Windows 2000, I recommend installing the updated WAU client in one of two ways:

- Install Windows 2000 Service Pack 3 or later. The updated WAU client is included as part of SP3.
- Use the MSI installation package available directly from the SUS Web site.

Once installed, the updated client behaves almost exactly the same as the standard WAU client. By default it will query the Microsoft update servers for available updates, and the configuration of the client is managed through the Automatic Updates Control Panel applet. In order to have the WAU client query a SUS server, it must be configured using either Group Policy (locally or in an Active Directory) or directly via the registry on the client machine. Figure 9.7 shows an example of the Group Policy used to set where WAU will query for updates. Once you have configured WAU via Group Policy, the options in the Automatic Updates Control Panel applet will be disabled for all applicable servers.

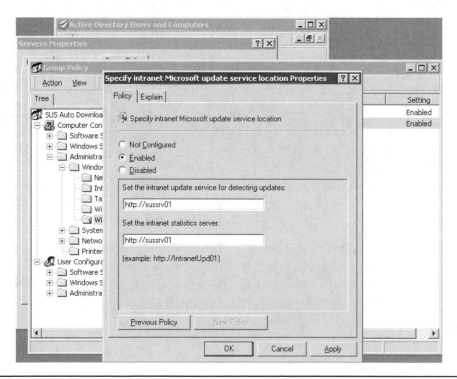

Figure 9.7   Configuring the SUS location for WAU update queries.

When updates are applied to a host by the WAU client, information is written to the client's system event log and back to the SUS server to track what is being done. Figure 9.8 shows an example of an event created by Automatic Updates. This event lists the updates that have been downloaded and are ready to be installed on the Terminal Server. Additional associated events are generated if a restart is required (Installation event ID 22) and once the updates have been successfully installed (Installation event ID 19). A complete list of the events that can be generated by Automatic Updates can be found in the SUS Deployment Guide, available from the SUS homepage on the Microsoft Web site at http://www.microsoft .com/windowsserversystem/sus/default.mspx

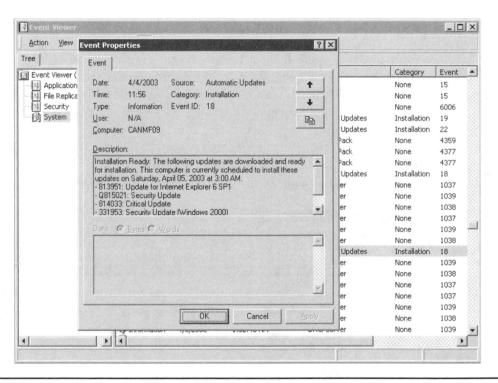

Figure 9.8 System event generated by WAU when updates are ready to be installed.

While the Windows Automatic Updates service alone may be suitable for a small Terminal Server environment (one to five servers), if you are considering using WAU in a larger implementation, then I recommend that you also consider SUS as an additional component to assist in the automation of your security and critical patch management.

When you are looking to implement SUS in a Terminal Server environment, I recommend the following:

- **Create a test environment consisting of a SUS server and at least one test or limited production Terminal Server.** Figure 9.9 illustrates a simple environment consisting of both a test and production SUS server configuration. As new updates are made available on the Windows update servers, the test environment can be used to validate the approval and installation of these updates on the test Terminal Server(s). Only updates that have passed validation on the test SUS server are approved for production. At the very least, this configuration could be used to ensure that the installation of a critical update does not prevent a server from restarting properly. If such an update were to go unchecked across all Terminal Servers in a production environment, the results could be disastrous.

  A separate production SUS server is then used to approve updates that will be deployed into production. Two separate SUS servers must be used because the current version of SUS (1.0, with SP1) cannot function in both roles, as there is no way to approve updates for only a subset of the available WAU clients.

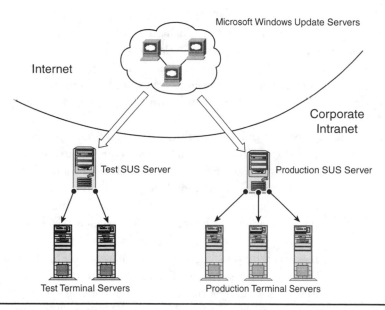

Figure 9.9 A simple SUS implementation consisting of both a production and a test SUS server.

■ **Schedule your updates to be installed during nonproduction or off-peak hours.** A weekly installation schedule early every Saturday or Sunday morning is a standard setup for most environments that operate with a typical Monday to Friday, 8:00 a.m. to 6:00 p.m. workday. If an environment must support extended business hours, then a more detailed installation schedule must be developed.

One suggestion might be to create two or more installation schedules and divide the servers between them to ensure that not all servers are being updated and possibly rebooted simultaneously. For example, one half of the servers could be updated on Saturday morning, while the other half was scheduled for updates on Sunday morning. Special scripting could also be introduced to force users off the server prior to the scheduled update time or disable user logons to the server a few hours prior to the scheduled updates to minimize the number of active users that might be on the server.

It is recommended that you review the deployment guide for Software Update Servers prior to implementing SUS in your environment. Complete SUS documentation is available from the Microsoft Web site at http://www.microsoft.com/windowsserversystem/sus/default.mspx

Shavlik HFNetChkPro

The developers of the original HFNetChk and MBSA tools for Microsoft have their own advanced patch-scanning and deployment tool available. The latest version of Shavlik Technology's (http://www.shavlik.com) flagship product, HFNetChkPro (version 4.3), delivers an advanced GUI-based interface that provides not only superior patch-scanning capabilities over MBSA but also a far more robust and feature-rich patch deployment tool compared to Microsoft's SUS. Some key features found in HFNetChkPro include the following:

■ **Extensive patch-scanning support**—Scanning can be performed against an individual machine, a group of machines within a managed group, all the machines in a domain, or all the machines on a network. All the scan types can be configured to run immediately or on a recurring schedule.

■ **Detailed scan reporting**—A patch scan will produce a summary report detailing information on what patches are installed, which ones are missing, and what the associated Microsoft and TruSecure threat ratings are. For example, an unchecked buffer vulnerability may have a Microsoft rating of Moderate and a TruSecure rating of High. These ratings are relative and provide a guideline for how you should treat the number of updates being issued. Figure 9.10 shows the results of a scan performed against a Windows 2000 Terminal Server with Office XP installed. The right pane lists all the patches and whether they are present or not. The lower pane provides a summary for the currently selected machine.

Figure 9.10 Patch scan results in HFNetChkPro for a Windows 2000 Terminal Server with Office XP.

■ **Configurable patch-rating system**—All patches and service packs can have a custom criticality rating assigned to them. This is a rating system that you can use to group patches in a way that is appropriate for your environment. Five ratings exist: Critical, High, Medium, Low, and Ignore. You can use these ratings to filter what is viewed on any of the patch screens in the application.

■ **Centralized patch deployment**—Any required patches can be deployed using Shavlik's PatchPush technology. PatchPush provides a powerful deployment tool that allows for full control over the scheduling and deployment of these patches to the target machines. Unlike SUS, which requires that an updated version of the WAU client be installed, HFNetChkPro requires no client-side component. It also provides instant validation on the status of a deployment so you can easily track and verify the current state of all your pushed patches. Figure 9.11 shows an example of the PatchPush Tracker window with a few deployment events listed.

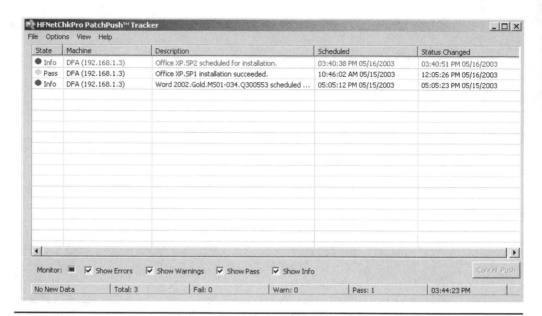

Figure 9.11   HFNetChkPro's PatchPush Tracker.

TIP: Considering the wide selection of robust tools available, there is really no reason why you shouldn't be able to develop a manageable process to ensure that your environment remains current with the latest relevant security patches, regardless of the number of Terminal Servers in use.

While dedicating the time required to properly configure such an environment, particularly early on in a project, may seem difficult to justify, the end result will be an environment that maximizes your responsiveness to the latest security threats while minimizing the time required to perform the necessary corrective action. Postponing such a configuration until after the Terminal Server implementation may quite possibly leave you scrambling to react to a situation that has already occurred instead of proactively minimizing the risks to your environment.

Non-Security-Related Patch Notification

Now that I've thoroughly covered a number of the tools and procedures available for the notification, searching, and scanning of security-related patches, the next task is to locate resources to aid in determining what non-security-related fixes exist for Terminal Server and whether any may be required as part of your implementation.

The most appropriate starting point for this type of information is Microsoft's Service Pack Web page. From this site you can quickly navigate to all the available service packs and associated hotfixes for the different Microsoft products. The Web site can be found by going to http://support.microsoft.com, selecting Downloads and Updates from the left-hand frame, and then selecting Product Service Packs. Figure 9.12 shows a portion of this Web page.

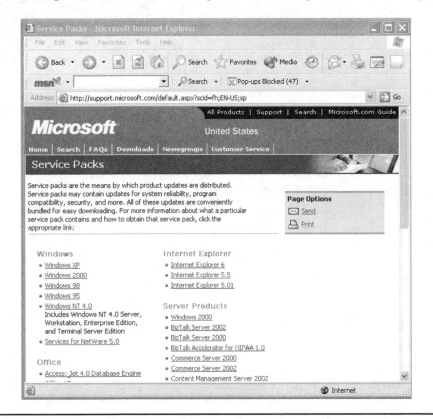

Figure 9.12   Microsoft Service Packs Web page.

Clicking the appropriate Windows version (Windows 2000, for example) will take you to the Web page containing not only information on the latest available service pack but also links to any post–service pack hotfixes that may be available, as well as any previous service packs that may have been released. Figure 9.13 shows a portion of the Post-SP4 Hotfix page for Windows 2000.

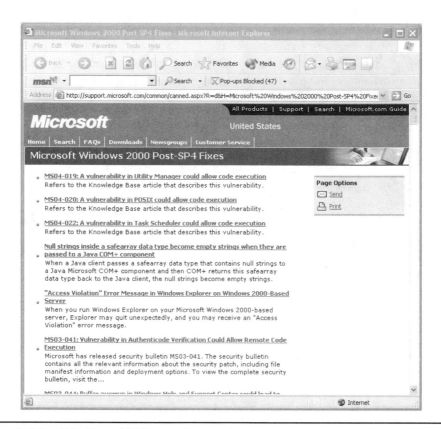

Figure 9.13   Windows 2000 Post-SP4 hotfixes.

NOTE: Unfortunately, unlike security updates, Microsoft does not provide a mailing list for notification of any new non-security-related fixes that are released. While at first this may appear unusual, there is actually a logical reason why this is so. Non-security-related fixes are released to resolve specific issues that only certain Windows implementations have experienced. In most cases, the majority of the companies running a production Windows environment never encounter these problems.

As a result, no automated process for notifying people of these fixes exists, mainly to prevent users from feeling that they "should" install them even if it doesn't actually pertain to their environment. Microsoft advises people against installing these hotfixes unless absolutely necessary and even goes so far as to restrict download access to most of them unless a call is first made to Microsoft's Support Center.
If it is determined that the fix will resolve the problem, download access will be granted and any support charges that would normally be incurred are waived. Users who receive access to these patches are then tracked so they can be advised by Microsoft of any issues discovered with the patch or if a newer iteration of the update becomes available.

Hotfix Selection

With a complete list of the available security and non-security-related fixes in hand, your next task is to determine what hotfixes should actually be installed on your Terminal Server and what criteria should be used when evaluating any future hotfixes for possible deployment. Before installing any hotfix, you need to be sure to weigh the risks of implementing it versus not implementing it. Don't feel that just because a fix exists you must install it on your server. If you're not experiencing the specific problem, or running a component that is vulnerable to a security issue, then the safest course of action is to not apply the fix at all. Fortunately many (but not all) hotfixes for Windows 2000/2003 Server can easily be uninstalled through Add/Remove Programs, if necessary.

Choosing the Hotfixes to Install

When it comes time to review the list of available patches, I recommend dividing the task into two phases. The first phase involves selecting the necessary security patches to be installed in your environment. If you're using a scan and deployment tool such as SUS or HFNetChkPro (both discussed earlier in this chapter), you will be able to approve the patches that will be deployed by the tool; otherwise, you will need to note the desired patches and manually download the installation files from Microsoft.

The second phase involves selecting any non-security-related patches to apply to your server. I recommend looking specifically for Terminal Server fixes that have been released and ignoring all other existing patches unless searching for a solution to a specific problem you are currently experiencing. Don't apply a patch just because you "think" you might experience that problem someday.

Security Hotfix Selection

When selecting the security updates for you Terminal Server environment, the following general rules should be followed:

- Unless access to Internet Explorer has been completely restricted for both users *and* administrators, you should always include the latest available updates for Internet Explorer (IE), regardless of whether you are using IE as the default Web browser on your Terminal Server or not. Considering that IE is a prime target for security exploitation, and a number of Web sites function best with IE (such as Microsoft), then even if only administrators are using the browser, running with the latest security updates should be part of the standard patch process.
- Similar updates should be applied to any of the other core applications included with Windows 2000/2003. This includes applications such as Outlook Express and Windows Media Player. Of course, if access to these applications has been removed, then the installation of these updates is not necessary.

■ Select only the security updates for your operating system that apply to your particular configuration. For example, if there is a patch available that fixes a known vulnerability in the SNMP service, but you're not running SNMP on your Terminal Server, then you do not need to install this update.

TIP: This section focused on security patches for the operating system and "core" components, such as Internet Explorer. If you're already running a production Terminal Server, then be sure to include any of the required patches for all the applications you are currently running in production.

Non-Security Hotfix Selection

Before we can say that our hotfix installation list is complete, we must review the list of all non-security-related post-SP hotfixes that Microsoft has issued, looking specifically for Terminal Services hotfixes that may be required. The easiest way to do this is to search the appropriate post-SP hotfix Web page for all fixes pertaining to Terminal Services. For example, from the Windows 2000 Post-SP4 Hotfixes page, you can search for the strings "Terminal Serv" and "RDP," using Ctrl+F or the menu item "Edit-Find(On this page)." Searching specifically using the phrase "Terminal Server" or "Terminal Services" may not return all results, as both names may be used in separate knowledgebase articles. You can also try searching for "MetaFrame" or "Citrix," as some patches may exist specifically to resolve issues that occur when operating with MetaFrame Presentation Server. Figure 9.14 shows an example search result on the Windows 2000 Post-SP4 Hotfixes page.

After searching the list you will likely find that most (if not all) Terminal Server–specific fixes are available for download only if you first contact Microsoft support. As I've mentioned, unless you are experiencing the problem described in the knowledgebase article, there is no need to acquire and install any of these non-security-related updates.

You should now have a complete list of the patches you will need to install when completing the build or update to your Terminal Server environment. Actual installation of hotfixes, including streamlining of multiple hotfix installations and integration of service pack files included with the base server installation files, is discussed in Chapter 10.

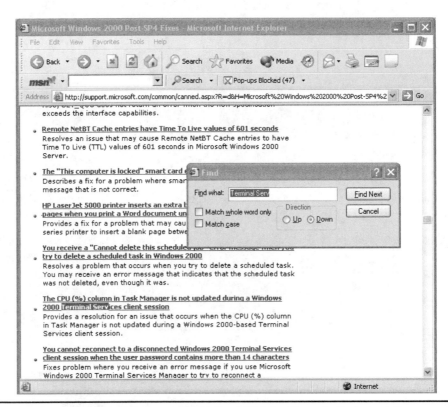

Figure 9.14 Searching Windows 2000 Post-SP4 hotfixes for Terminal Server–related patches.

Implementing Terminal Services and Citrix MetaFrame

CHAPTER 10

Installing Windows Terminal Services

Before You Begin

This chapter discusses installation of Terminal Services on a Windows 2000 or Windows 2003 server. The post-installation configuration and tuning for a Terminal Server is discussed in Chapter 11, "Terminal Services Configuration and Tuning." Before getting into the step-by-step details on the actual installation process, I review some of the pre-installation planning and preparation you should perform. In the last section of this chapter, "Automating the Terminal Services Installation," I discuss use of the unattended installation support in Windows to more quickly and consistently build a base Terminal Server.

NOTE: The server hardware configuration I am using to demonstrate the Terminal Server installation in this chapter is as follows:

- Dual Intel Pentium III processors at 1GHz
- 1GB RAM
- Dual 18GB SCSI hard drives in a RAID 1 configuration. This will be used to store both the system and application partitions.
- Single 9GB SCSI hard drive. This drive will be used to store the system pagefile.

For a complete discussion on choosing the appropriate hardware configuration for you Terminal Server, please refer back to Chapter 6, "Terminal Server Hardware Planning."

General Installation Guidelines

Here are some general guidelines I feel are worth reviewing *before* you begin the actual operating system installation:

1. *Take an inventory of your server hardware before you begin the operating system installation.* Use this inventory to verify that there are no hardware incompatibilities with your Windows server. You also need to determine whether you will need to use updated or new drivers provided by the manufacturer instead of those included with Windows, particularly if you are using a disk array controller. It is worthwhile to note things such as server type (Proliant, PowerEdge, and so forth), physical RAM size, and disk size, as well as NIC, disk controller, and video card types present in the system. The latest Windows hardware compatibility list can be found on the Windows Hardware and Driver Central Web site at http://www.micro soft.com/whdc/hcl/default.mspx

---

TIP: If you are going to be installing Windows Server 2003 and the server hardware currently has an operating system on it that is upgradeable to 2003, you can run the Check System Compatibility test provided on the server installation CD to quickly verify if your hardware is supported by Windows Server 2003. When started either via the Autorun feature or by running SETUP.EXE from the CD, the Welcome dialog box appears, and clicking on the Check System Compatibility option lets you either automatically check the compatibility or redirects you to the Microsoft Web site, where you can perform a manual verification. The automated check will compare your system against the latest installation files, which are automatically downloaded directly from Microsoft if necessary. Any incompatibilities will be listed in a summary report presented at the end of the system check.

---

2. *Take note of all other servers (Terminal Server or otherwise) on the subnet where you will be introducing your new Terminal Server.* Verify that your server name and IP address are unique and be sure to note any production Terminal Servers that may be on the same subnet. Ideally, you will try to keep your new server on a separate subnet until you are ready to move it into production, but if this is not possible, you will need to be sure to notify the appropriate people in charge of those servers (if they are not yourself) so they are not surprised to see a new Terminal Server appear. Even if you will be operating the server in a test domain, the physical presence of the server on the network could be a concern, particularly if there is a MetaFrame 1.8-based farm present and you are planning to install MetaFrame Presentation Server on this machine. The topic of MetaFrame interoperability is discussed in Chapter 8, "Server Installation and Management Planning."

When the Terminal Server is ready for deployment into production, for performance reasons it is recommended that this server be placed into the same subnet as other servers that are frequently accessed from the Terminal Server. The servers containing the home directories and profiles or a domain controller are both examples of servers that would be good candidates. Server co-location strategies were discussed in Chapter 4, "Network Planning," and in Chapter 8, "Server Installation and Management Planning."

3. *Always format all Terminal Server drives and partitions as NTFS, not FAT.* Many Windows administrators commonly suggest formatting a server's system partition as FAT for performance and recovery reasons and because share permissions provide sufficient security across a network to protect these drives from unauthorized access. When implementing Terminal Server, share permissions are inadequate for protecting the file system from regular users, since these users are logging on *locally*. For security reasons you should never format any of your Terminal Server drives as FAT. I recommend not doing this even in a test or development environment. If you can't properly simulate the different access rights that users will have in production, you have no way of knowing whether more restrictive permissions will cause application issues or invalidate any of your testing or development results.

TIP: A common Windows tuning tip is to increase the cluster size of an NTFS partition when it is being formatted, to realize a small gain in disk performance. An NTFS hard disk is organized into clusters, which represent the smallest space that can be allocated for a file on the disk. For example, if you have a file that is 16KB in size, then it would occupy four clusters of 4KB, or 32 clusters of 512 bytes. By storing files in larger cluster sizes, you can decrease the time required to retrieve that data. Of course additional space on the disk can be wasted if you are storing a large number of files that are smaller than the cluster size. For example, files less than 4KB in size would still occupy the entire 4KB cluster.

When the boot partition is formatted during a Windows Server 2003 or Windows 2000 Server installation, Windows automatically assigns the appropriate cluster size based on the drive size. For any drives over 2GB in size, the cluster size defaults to 4KB, which is an appropriate cluster size for a Windows server boot partition. You will not need to worry about adjusting this setting.

---

4. *Segregate the system files from the application files.* As discussed in Chapter 6, my preference is to create two partitions on the main disk, one designated as the main system/boot partition for Windows, and the other designated for the application files. In Chapter 6 I also discussed the following calculation used to estimate the size of the system/boot partition.

```
(OS Disk Space) + Physical Memory + (Total Users * 15MB) +
2GB
```

- "OS Disk Space" is 1.5GB for Windows 2000/2003.
- "Physical Memory" is the actual memory that has been installed in the server.
- The "Total Users" calculation represents the estimated disk space consumed by the user profiles. By default, user profiles are stored in the Documents and Settings folder located on the boot partition and can easily consume a substantial amount of disk space, depending on how profiles have been configured and what data users are maintaining in their profile folder. Chapter 15, "Group Policy Configuration" looks at use of policies to limit what data is stored in the user's profile. The Documents and Settings folder can also be moved to an alternate location, but this can be done only through an unattended installation script. Use of these scripts is discussed in the "Automating the Terminal Services Installation" section, later in this chapter.
- The additional 2GB is used as a buffer to provide room for growth and protect against unexpected disk consumption issues such as a runaway print spooler file.

The resulting calculated size assumes that the server's pagefile will be stored on a *separate* disk. If you are planning to store the pagefile on the system drive, make sure to multiply the Physical Memory by 2 (Physical Memory $\times$ 2). For example, if I wanted to install Terminal Server on a system with 1GB of physical memory to support 120 total users, and I wanted to store the pagefile on the system drive, I would need to calculate the system/boot partition as follows:

```
1.5GB + (Physical Memory x 2) + (120 * 15MB) + 2GB
= 1.5GB + 2GB + 1.8GB + 2GB
= 7.3GB
```

So a partition of 7.5GB or larger would be sufficient for this configuration to support both the pagefile and the estimated user profile space. Of course you are free to select a larger partition size if you wish, and it is certainly not uncommon for administrators to allocate 9GB or more for the system/boot partition regardless of whether they are going to be keeping the pagefile on the same drive or not.

Even if the pagefile will be on its own drive, you will need to ensure that the system partition has enough free disk space to accommodate a full system dump if one is ever required. This free space must equal the amount of physical memory in the system. The system/boot size calculation already takes this into consideration.

NOTE: When performing a typical Windows Server installation, the boot and system files will reside on the same partition or volume. The boot partition contains the hardware-specific files necessary to initiate the startup of the Windows operating system. On Intel x86-based systems, this partition must reside on Drive 0. The specific files that make up the system partition are NTLDR, NTDETECT.COM, NTBOOTDD.SYS (SCSI drives only), and BOOT.INI.

The system partition contains the Windows operating system files. Unless stated otherwise, I will assume that both the boot and system partitions for the Terminal Server installation reside on the same partition/volume. If you have set up a multiboot server for testing (multiboot systems are not recommended for production), you will find that only one copy of the necessary system partition files exists, while boot partition files exist for each copy of Windows that is installed on the server.

5. *Designate your Terminal Server as an application server only.* Whenever possible avoid adding additional services or roles to your Terminal Server, such as a domain controller, Web server, file and print server, or even SQL Server. While it may seem like a good idea to consolidate these resources onto a single server, not only will they impact Terminal Server users by consuming additional system resources, but the changes to system tuning for a Terminal Server will also have a detrimental effect on how these other services may perform. Except in very small environments, competition for available resources can be avoided by limiting, or completely eliminating, all non–Terminal Server–related roles found on a Terminal Server.

6. *Make sure you understand the licensing requirements for your Terminal Server.* In particular, remember that you have 120 days (90 days for Windows 2000) after the installation of Terminal Server before you must have a Terminal Services licensing server installed and working. After that you still have 90 days in which the licensing server will distribute temporary licenses until your Terminal Server client access licenses (TSCAL) must be added to the activated Terminal Services License Server. One of the most common mistakes I see when people install Terminal Services for the first time is that they think they must install the Terminal Services licensing service at the same time and on the same server. Refer back to Chapter 1, "Microsoft Windows Terminal Services," for a detailed look at Terminal Services licensing.

TIP: Even though Microsoft has included provisions that allow a Terminal Server to function for a limited period of time without client access licenses, implementing a Terminal Server environment and enabling access to that environment without having purchased the required licenses violates the End-User License Agreement (EULA).

Terminal Services Operating Modes

Both Windows 2000 Server and Windows Server 2003 support two distinct modes of operation for Terminal Services. Table 10.1 summarizes these modes and the different terminology used in the two Windows versions. These operating modes were discussed in Chapter 1.

Table 10.1   Terminal Services Operating Modes

Windows Server 2003 Terminology	Windows 2000 Server Terminology	Description
Remote Desktop for Administration	Remote Administration Mode	This mode is enabled by default on all Windows Server 2003 variants, while it must be explicitly installed for all versions of Windows 2000 Server. This operating mode lets an administrator remotely connect to the server and perform any required administrative tasks. A maximum of two concurrent sessions can be active on the server, and no additional Terminal Services licensing is required. This operating mode does not change the configuration of the server to support multiple concurrent user sessions. It simply allows remote desktop logons to the server with only minimal impact to the server's performance.
Terminal Services	Application Server Mode	This operation mode enables the server to function as a true Terminal Server, allowing multiple concurrent user sessions running one or more applications. All versions of Windows 2000 Server support this mode, while only Windows Server 2003 Standard Edition and higher allow enabling Terminal Services. The Web Server edition of 2003 supports only Remote Desktop for Administration.
		This option requires Terminal Services licensing to be accessible within 120 days on Windows 2003 and 90 days on Windows 2000.

Windows Component Selection

One noticeable difference between a Windows Server 2003 and a Windows 2000 Server installation is that you are not presented with the Windows Components dialog box during a 2003 installation. Instead, adding or removing any components, including Terminal Services, must be done *after* the 2003 installation has completed (Figure 10.1). The exception to this is if you are performing an unattended installation, where components can be selected for addition during the installation. I discuss this further in the "Automating the Terminal Services Installation" section, later in this chapter.

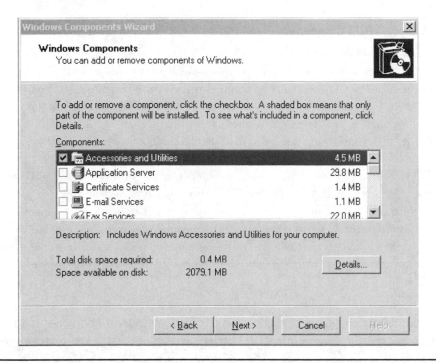

Figure 10.1 Windows Server 2003 Components dialog box, accessible only after 2003 has been installed.

Windows Server 2003 Components

During a 2003 installation (Standard Server version and higher), only the following two components are installed by default:

- **Accessories and Utilities**—Most of these components are installed, with the exception of Document Templates, Mouse Pointers, and HyperTerm.
- **Updated Root Certificates**—This component enables Windows Server 2003 to automatically download the most current root certificates when necessary. If a user receives a certificate and that certificate authority (CA) is not currently trusted by the server, Windows will automatically contact the Windows Update Web site to determine if a root certificate is available for this CA. If there is one available then it is downloaded and added to the list of trusted CAs.

Once the operating system installation has completed, you can assign the Terminal Server role, at which time the Terminal Services component is automatically added to the server. Details of this are discussed later in the chapter.

Windows 2000 Components

During a Windows 2000 Server installation, you will be presented with the Components dialog box, where you can select any components you want to install on the server. The one thing to remember is that every service you add will consume resources that would otherwise be allocated to Terminal Server–specific processes or user sessions. Unless the service is vital to the operation of your Terminal Server, I recommend that you not install it. Table 10.2 summarizes the components available for installation, along with a brief description of whether or not they should be included in your Terminal Server installation.

Of course, the one component you want to make sure you install is Terminal Services, located near the bottom of the list. This service is required in order to provide multiuser access to your application server. The other service, Terminal Services Licensing, *should not* be selected at this time. In Chapter 12, "Licensing Service Installation and Configuration," I discuss installation requirements for this service, depending on the configuration of your Windows domain. Specifics on the requirements for Terminal Services licensing are covered in Chapter 1.

Table 10.2   Suggested Windows 2000 Terminal Server components to install.

Component	Comments
Accessories and Utilities	Deselect the subcomponents Communications, Games, and Multimedia. These are typically not required on a Terminal Server.
	Under Accessories, deselect Desktop Wallpaper, which can add unnecessary bandwidth and processing requirements, since the data needs to be transmitted to the client. All other options can be selected/deselected as you wish.
Certificate Service	Deselect.
Cluster Service	Deselect.
Indexing Service	Deselect.
Internet Information Service	Deselect.
Management and Monitoring Tools	Deselect. If necessary, specific components such as SNMP can be added later.
Message Queuing Service	Deselect.
Networking Services	Deselect.

Component	Comments
Other Network File and Print Services	Deselect.
Remote Installation Services	Deselect.
Remote Storage	Deselect.
Script Debugger	Deselect.
Terminal Services	Select. This is the service that provides multisession connectivity to the Windows 2000 Server.
Terminal Services Licensing	Deselect. I discuss installation requirements for this service in Chapter 12.
Windows Media Services	Deselect.

Permission Compatibility for Terminal Services

Both versions of Terminal Services support a feature known as Permission Compatibility, which dictates the level of security imposed on the registry and file system. A more loosely restricted configuration can be enabled in order to provide backward compatibility with legacy applications that may not function properly when forced to run in an environment that more tightly limits the privileges granted to a non-administrative user. While both versions provide the same functionality, they are labeled differently and accessed at different stages in the Terminal Server setup and configuration.

Windows 2000 Terminal Server Application Compatibility Permissions

During the installation of Windows 2000 Terminal Services, you will be presented with the dialog box prompting you to choose the desired application compatibility permissions for Terminal Services, shown in Figure 10.2.

As you can see, this dialog box contains two options:

- **Configure permissions compatible with Windows 2000 users**—This option provides for a more secure Terminal Server environment by enforcing more restrictive security on the registry and file system. These restrictions limit users to read-only access to the majority of the system, allowing for write permissions only on personal and temporary data locations. Depending on the applications you plan to implement, it may require greater effort in order to configure them to function properly in the environment. All applications that have been certified to run on Windows 2000 or 2003 should have no problem functioning in this permission configuration. This is the default option for Windows 2000 Terminal Servers, and I recommend that you always select this option as it provides for a much more secure Terminal Services environment.

■ **Configure permissions compatible with Terminal Server 4.0 users**—This setting configures the server with the same permissions found on an NT 4.0 Terminal Server. These permissions grant users write access to portions of the registry and file system not accessible in the Windows 2000 permission scenario. While selecting this option may reduce the effort required to get many legacy applications working on your Terminal Server, it grants elevated privileges in both the file system and registry for regular users, and as a result, introduces potential security concerns.

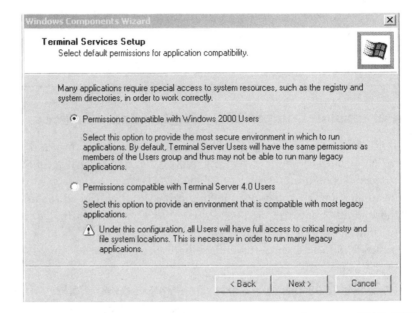

Figure 10.2   Windows 2000 application compatibility permissions selection during Terminal Services setup.

Windows 2003 Terminal Server Permission Compatibility

On a Windows 2003 Terminal Server, the permission compatibility options are as follows:

■ **Full Security**—This is the default configuration for all 2003 Terminal Servers and cannot be modified during the server installation (unless you are performing an unattended installation, discussed later in this chapter).

■ **Relaxed Security**—Lets the Terminal Server operate in a less restrictive security configuration. Permissions on the file system and registry are adjusted to allow users to have elevated access to certain areas in order to make the integration of legacy applications less of a concern.

Just as with Windows 2000, this option can be modified after installing Terminal Server by running the Terminal Services Configuration application (under Administrative Tools on the Start menu) and selecting Permission Compatibility under the Server Settings folder, as shown in Figure 10.3.

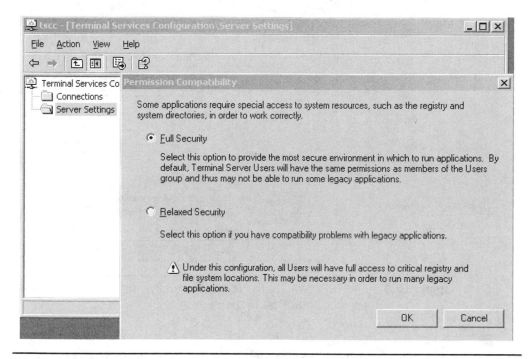

Figure 10.3 Windows 2003 Terminal Server Permission Compatibility.

TIP: When a Terminal Server is configured to operate in the more relaxed security mode (NT4-compatible), there are no actual modifications made to the existing security access groups on the server. Instead, the Terminal Server automatically assigns users who log on to the Terminal Server to a special user group called TERMINAL SERVER USER. This group cannot be found as a local group on the server, nor in the domain. It is a dynamically created group that is assigned additional permissions on the server, so members automatically receive these additional access rights. Figure 10.4 shows the permissions for the SOFTWARE key under HKEY_LOCAL_MACHINE in the registry. You can see that the TERMINAL SERVER USER group is listed in the access control list.

If the server is switched from the "relaxed mode" back to the more secure operating mode, then users are no longer assigned to this group at logon and the permissions are effectively revoked. You cannot manually modify this group membership, but you can modify or revoke the permissions assigned to this group.

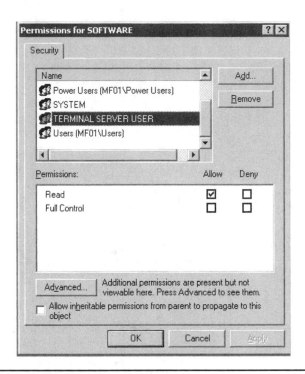

Figure 10.4   The TERMINAL SERVER USER group is automatically assigned to the access control list in the registry.

Unfortunately, increased security rarely comes without a price, and this situation is no exception. Some legacy applications may have issues running in these more restrictive security modes and, until the application has been installed and tested, there is really no way to know for certain if you will experience these security-related issues or not. In Chapter 21, "Application Integration," I discuss how to recognize, troubleshoot, and resolve security-related issues.

NOTE: While it may be tempting, do not simply look to take the easy way out and go for the more lax security permissions. Weak security leaves a Terminal Server susceptible to both accidental and intentional modification. Unless you take the time to properly implement the stronger security from the beginning, it is unlikely that you will implement it once your servers have moved into production.

Windows Terminal Server Installation

Now that the pre-installation preparation is complete, we are ready to perform the actual installation. This section provides a step-by-step walkthrough for installing Terminal Services on either a Windows Server 2003 or a Windows 2000 Server. These steps are based on the assumption that the installation is initiated by booting from the server CD-ROM. If you are initiating the installation through another method (floppy diskettes, WINNT32 executable, and so forth), then the initial startup sequence will differ slightly, although the main installation steps will remain unchanged. The supported installation methods for Windows 2000 Server and Windows Server 2003 were discussed in Chapter 8.

TIP: If you're performing an upgrade, much of the installation is completely automated and you will not have the opportunity to select the same options that you would during a clean installation. A discussion regarding an upgrade versus a clean installation of Windows Terminal Services was discussed in Chapter 8.

Part 1: Beginning the Windows Server Setup

The installation begins by booting the server with the operating system CD-ROM in the CD-ROM drive:

1. During the system boot up, you will see the words "Press any key to boot from CD" appear for approximately five seconds on the screen. Press any key to initiate booting from the CD-ROM.
2. The text-based portion of the installation begins, and the necessary drivers are loaded from the CD-ROM. A message will appear along the bottom of the screen prompting you to press F6 if you are required to install a third-party SCSI driver. Unless specifically requested by the hardware vendor, you typically will not be required to select this option. Most often this is necessary if you are using a RAID controller much newer than the operating system and a compatible driver is not included with the OS. Once this has completed, the Windows Server 2003/2000 Server Setup Welcome window will appear with the options to Setup, Repair, or Quit. Press Enter to continue the installation.

TIP: An installation initiated by running WINNT.EXE or WINNT32.EXE will require that files be copied to the local file system and the system be rebooted before the Welcome screen will appear.

---

3. Next you will see the End-User License Agreement. After reviewing it, press the F8 key if you accept the terms of the agreement, to continue with the installation.

4. The next screen prompts you to select and configure the boot partition. You don't need to worry about setting up any other partitions or drives (application or page-file) right now; you can do this by running Computer Management after you've completed the Windows installation. I talk more about post-installation configuration in Chapter 11.

If you have not already done so, I recommend that you review the "General Installation Guidelines" section, earlier in this chapter, before deciding how you will partition and format your Terminal Server. My preference is to maintain the boot files and application files on separate partitions.

Once you have configured the desired target boot partition, highlight it on the screen and press Enter to proceed.

WARNING: If you're going to be deleting an existing partition in order to create more free disk space, then any information on the partition you are deleting will be permanently lost. Make sure to double-check that you are absolutely certain that the data on the partition is no longer required before you delete it.

---

5. If this is a newly created partition, you will need to format it before it can be used. Make sure the NTFS file system type has been selected and then proceed with the format. Never format any Terminal Server drives using the FAT file system. If necessary, you can refer to the earlier section "General Installation Guidelines" for more information on why this should never be done.

6. Immediately after completing the format, the setup program will automatically begin copying the necessary files to this system drive. Once all files have been copied, the setup program automatically reboots the server and proceeds with the GUI portion of the installation.

TIP: If the partition you selected was already formatted as FAT, then Setup will ask whether or not you would like to convert the drive to NTFS. If you are not going to reformat the drive, make sure you select the NTFS conversion option before proceeding with the installation. The conversion is actually done once the files have been copied and Setup reboots.

You can manually perform the conversion once the operating system installation has completed, but I prefer to have the NTFS format completed as part of the installation process. This helps ensure that this configuration step isn't accidentally forgotten, leaving the server with a completely insecure file system.

Part 2: The GUI Setup Wizard

After the server has restarted, the GUI Setup Wizard will start:

1. The Setup Wizard begins with the Plug and Play detection phase and installs the necessary drivers for your hardware. Depending on your hardware configuration, this step may appear to pause for quite a while before completing. You may also notice that your video display will flicker while the appropriate video drivers are selected.

2. After the necessary drivers have been loaded, the Regional Settings dialog box opens. Here you can specify the appropriate settings for such things as number, currency, time, and date formats. Once you've selected the desired options, press Next to continue.

3. You will now provide the name and organization information. This is used simply to show who has licensed the software. Press Next to continue.

4. Next you will need to provide the product key for your Windows Server. This key is usually located on the back of the CD jewel case.

5. The next dialog box prompts you to select the appropriate client access license (CAL) mode. This *isn't* the client license for Terminal Server but is instead the client license required to let a user or device access the Microsoft server itself. Both Windows and Terminal Server CALs are required in order to properly license a Terminal Server. The appropriate licensing option for your server will depend on the requirements of your organization. For complete information on Terminal Server licensing, see the "Terminal Services Licensing" section of Chapter 1. After selecting the appropriate licensing mode, click Next to continue.

NOTE: Installation and configuration of Terminal Server client access licensing are covered in Chapter 12.

---

6. Next you're prompted to provide both a name for the server and the local administrator's password. Select something that's not easily guessed and, ideally, contains a combination of upper- and lowercase letters, symbols, and numbers. If necessary, write down the password and store it in a safe place. Click Next. I look more closely at Terminal Server security in Chapter 16, "Terminal Server Security."

7. (Windows 2000 Servers only.) In a Windows 2000 Server installation, the Components dialog box appears next. Here you can select which additional components should be installed along with the base operating system, including Terminal Services itself. Refer to the section "Windows Component Selection," earlier in this chapter, for a list of all available components and suggestions on which ones should or shouldn't be installed on a Terminal Server. The one thing to try and remember is that you want to minimize waste of resources on use of components not vital to the operation of your Terminal Server. After selecting the appropriate components (don't forget to select Terminal Services), click Next to continue.

8. When asked to confirm the date, time, and time zone, enter the appropriate values and then click Next to continue.

9. (Windows 2000 Servers only.) On a Windows 2000 installation, the next dialog box prompts you to select the desired Terminal Services configuration for your server. In order to let multiple users concurrently run applications on this server, you will need to select Application Server Mode and click Next. You would select Remote Administration if you were setting up a regular Windows server (File and Print, SQL Server, and so forth) and wanted to allow administrators remote console access to manage the server via the RDP client. Remote Administration is automatically installed with all 2003 servers. For more information on the Remote Administration mode, see Chapter 1.

10. (Windows 2000 Servers only.) The next dialog box, Application Compatibility Permissions for Terminal Services, will provide two options: Configured as permissions compatible with Windows 2000 users, or with Terminal Server 4.0 users. See the "Windows 2000 Terminal Server Application Compatibility Permissions" section earlier in this chapter for more information on this. The discussion of application integration in Chapter 22 assumes that you have implemented the Windows 2000 User Permissions.

TIP: The default configuration for a 2003 Terminal Server is Full Security, which is the equivalent of the Windows 2000 User Permissions option. More information on these settings can be found in the earlier section on application compatibility permissions.

---

11. Once network services have started, you're prompted to choose either Typical or Custom network settings. The Typical option assumes that you want to use DHCP for TPC/IP addressing, client for Microsoft networking, and file and print sharing. The Custom option gives you complete control over configuring the server's networking. In order to provide a static IP address, you must click the Custom radio button. If you wish, you can allow a DHCP assignment during the installation, but be certain to correct this once the server build is complete. Terminal Servers (and Windows servers in general) should not be assigned dynamic IP addresses. In order to ensure consistent addressing you should statically-assign these values before allowing user access.

12. If you selected Custom for network services, the next screen lets you view and modify the properties for the default network components that will be installed. Once you have finished configuring the desired network information, click Next to continue.

13. At this point, you must decide whether the server will participate in a domain or workgroup. My preference is to leave it in a workgroup until the installation is complete and then add it into the desired domain as one of the final steps in the configuration process.

After you select the domain or workgroup, Setup installs the necessary components and performs the final tasks required to complete the installation.

NOTE: The following steps (14 and 15) apply only for Windows Server 2003. Windows 2000 Terminal Server installations are complete after Step 13.

14. (Windows Server 2003 only.) Once the 2003 server has rebooted, you will need to log on as the local administrator in order to complete the Terminal Services installation. After logging on, you will see the Manage Your Server window. Click Add or Remove a Role, and the Configure Your Server Wizard will appear. On the next screen you will see the Server Role options, as shown in Figure 10.5. Select the Terminal Server role from the list and click Next. After verifying your selection, the necessary components will be installed and the server will automatically restart.

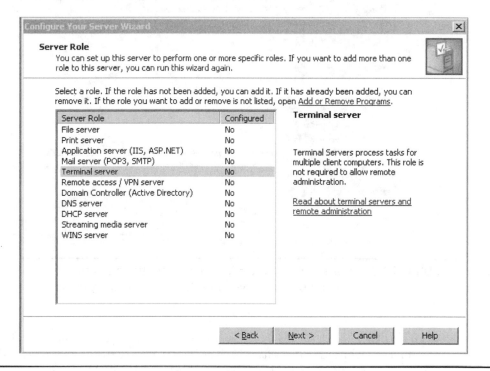

Figure 10.5 Defining the Terminal Server role for a Windows 2003 server.

15. (Windows Server 2003 only.) The next time you log on to the server you will receive a confirmation that the Terminal Server was successfully configured, as shown in Figure 10.6. A help file listing common Terminal Server tasks also will open. After you click Finish, the Manage Your Server (MYS) window reappears, updated with the information for your new Terminal Server. For now you can close the MYS application. Terminal Server is now installed on your Windows Server 2003.

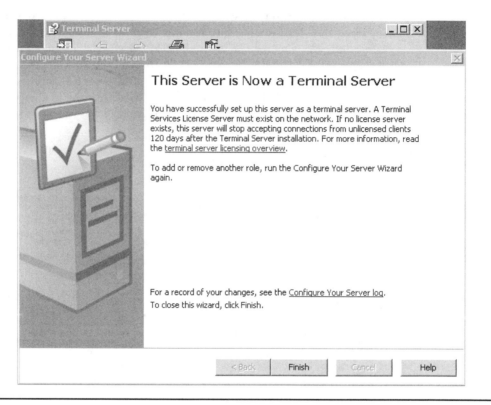

Figure 10.6   The Terminal Server installation confirmation message will appear in Configure Your Server after the installation is complete.

Once Terminal Server installation is complete, the next step is to make sure that the necessary service packs and hotfixes have been applied to ensure that the server is both secure and functioning properly. In Chapter 9, "Service Pack and Hotfix Management," I looked at the task of managing service pack and hotfix updates on your Terminal Servers, including selection of appropriate service packs and hotfixes for your new or existing implementation. Service pack and hotfix installations are discussed in Chapter 11.

TIP: If you are also planning on installing Citrix MetaFrame Presentation Server, make sure that MetaFrame has been installed *before* you install any applications on your server. See Chapter 13, "MetaFrame Presentation Server Installation," for more information on this.

Automating the Terminal Services Installation

One very effective way to streamline installation of a Terminal Server is to utilize Windows support for automating the installation. Automating the installation provides the following benefits:

- Installation automation creates a consistent server configuration that is guaranteed to be the same every time. You do not need to rely on a list of steps that have to be followed every time a server is installed.
- Shortens the time required to perform the installation. Since the options are preselected you can simply start the installation and walk away (or at the very least provide minimal input), returning when it is complete.
- The answer file is essentially self-documenting. With the answer file, an administrator can quickly see what options have been chosen for an installation and verify it for correctness.

A single answer file that is read during the initialization of Windows setup drives the entire automation process. We continue by looking first at how an answer file is structured and how it can be created and modified. I end this chapter by providing a sample answer file that I use with both my Windows 2003 and Windows 2000 Terminal Server installations.

The Answer File Structure

Those of you familiar with INI files will immediately recognize the structure for the installation answer file. A portion of a 2000/2003 server answer file may look as follows:

```
[Data]
    AutoPartition=1
    MsDosInitiated="0"
    UnattendedInstall="Yes"

[Unattended]
    UnattendMode=DefaultHide
    FileSystem=ConvertNTFS
    OemSkipEula=No
    OemPreinstall=No
```

```
    TargetPath=\WINNT

[GuiUnattended]
    ; uncomment to have the admin password automatically set to
"password"
    ;AdminPassword=password
    OEMSkipRegional=1
    TimeZone=35
    OemSkipWelcome=1

[UserData]
    FullName="Todd W. Mathers"
    OrgName="Noisy River Software Corp."
    ComputerName=*
```

As you can see, this is simply a plaintext file that is divided into multiple key and value sections containing answers to the questions normally presented during the server installation. A complete reference of all options available for the unattended installation file can be found in the Deploy.cab file on the Windows Server CD under the \Support\Tools folder. Double-clicking on this file will let you view the contents. You can then drag and drop the desired files into a folder where you can view them.

On the Windows 2000 Server CD, the unattend.doc file contains the relevant information, while the equivalent information can be found in the deploy.chm help file on the Windows Server 2003 CD.

Creating the Answer File

While it is possible to create an answer file from scratch using a text editor such as Notepad, Microsoft provides a tool that lets you quickly create a file with most of the options automatically generated based on the input you provide to a wizard. This tool is called Windows Setup Manager and can be found in the same Deploy.cab file as the documentation. It is a single file (setupmgr.exe) that you can simply extract from the Deploy.cab file and run.

TIP: The configurable options in Setup Manager for Windows 2000 are nearly identical to those found in the 2003 version of Setup Manager. The main difference between the two products is the order and presentation of the individual configuration screens.

Using the Windows Setup Manager from the Windows Server 2003 CD, you can create an answer file as follows:

1. Start the Setup Manager and click Next after you see the Welcome screen.
2. Select Create New and click Next.
3. Select Unattended Setup as the target for this answer file. Click Next.
4. Now select the appropriate Windows Server target (Web, Standard, or Enterprise) and click Next.
5. The next screen (see Figure 10.7) lets you select the user interaction level. Clicking on the different radio buttons will show the corresponding description. I normally select Hide Pages, since this allows me to keep certain pages visible if there is input I would rather provide manually instead of through the answer file. An example of this might be the administrator's password or the product key. If answers have been provided in the answer file, the corresponding page is automatically suppressed.

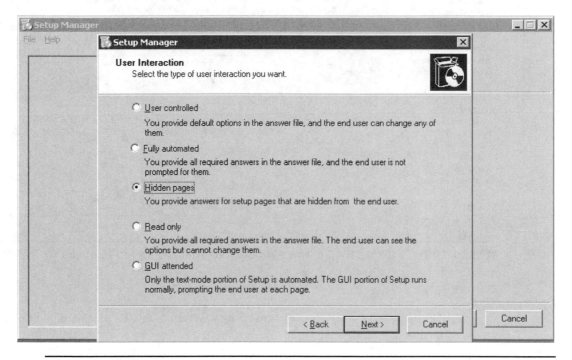

Figure 10.7   Setting the User Interaction level in the Windows Setup Manager application.

6. Next you can specify whether this answer file is for a custom distribution or for an installation directly off the server CD. For now, select Install from CD. Later in this chapter I discuss creating custom distributions for 2000/2003 installations when I talk about slipstreaming service packs in with the base installation files (the "Integrating Service Packs with Server Installation Files" section).

7. If you are running the Windows Server 2003 version of Setup Manager you will see the main options window (see Figure 10.8), where you can configure the desired options that will automatically be answered during the server installation. Once all the desired options have been set, click the last entry in the list, Additional Commands, and then click Finish.

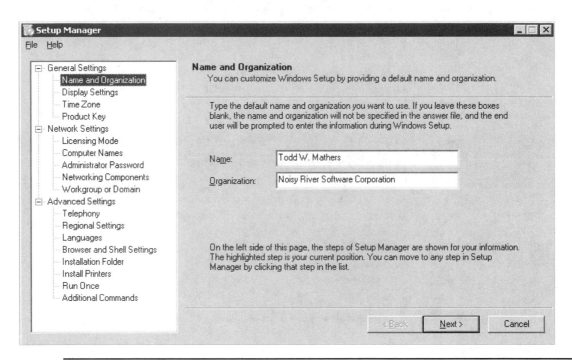

Figure 10.8   Entering the answer file data into Windows Setup Manager for Windows Server 2003.

8. The final input screen lets you specify the target file to save to. The default name is unattend.txt.

As you may have noticed while working through the wizard, there is one piece missing that would truly automate the installation of the Windows Terminal Server: the option to select what components are actually installed during setup.

While the Windows Setup Manager does not let you select the components to add or remove, you can manually enter these options into the unattend.txt file. The documentation provided with the Deploy.cab file lists all the options that can be included in this unattend.txt file. The specific file is ref.chm. Components are configured by added a [Components] key to the file and then specifying the desired components with either an On or Off value. "On" means the component should be installed, while "Off" means that it shouldn't be installed. For example, the following would explicitly exclude all options under Accessories and

Utilities except for Calculator, Character Map, and Microsoft WordPad when installing Windows Server 2003.

```
[Components]
     ; Specifies which components are installed (or not)
     ; Any component not explicitly listed uses its default behavior

     ; Accessories and Utilities
     accessopt=Off
     calc=On
     charmap=On
     chat=Off
     clipbook=Off
     deskpaper=Off
     hypertrm=Off
     mousepoint=Off
     mswordpad=On
     paint=Off
     templates=Off
```

TIP: See the "Sample 2000/2003 Terminal Server Answer File" section at the end of this chapter for a complete answer file with the recommended components excluded for a Terminal Server installation.

Using the Answer File

Once the answer file has been created, using it is very straightforward, although it does differ slightly depending on whether you are booting directly from a CD or initiating the installation by running WINNT or WINNT32:

- **Booting from a Windows server CD**—If you are planning on booting from a CD to install Windows, you will need to copy your unattend.txt file onto a floppy diskette and rename it to WINNT.SIF. During boot up, as soon as you see the Press Any Key to Boot from CD message appear, insert the diskette and press any key. One of the first things that setup will do is read the contents of the diskette and use the WINNT.SIF information to automate the installation.
- **Running WINNT.EXE**—The following syntax will force the unattend.txt file to be read during setup:
  winnt.exe /u:unattend.txt /s:d:\i386

If unattend.txt is not in the folder where winnt.exe is being run, make sure to include the full path to the file. Also, the /S: parameter is required and points to the source installation files. In this example I've used D:\i386, but you can edit this to point to the appropriate location for your install.

■ **Running WINNT32.EXE**—The syntax for WINNT32 is very similar to that for WINNT and looks as follows:

winnt32.exe /unattend:unattend.txt /s:d:\i386

Just as with winnt.exe, if necessary make sure to include the full path to unattend.txt, and make sure the source folder location is correct.

TIP: In addition to generating the unattend.txt file, the Windows Setup Manager will generate a sample unattend.bat file that is configured to run winnt32.exe with the appropriate parameters for the corresponding unattend.txt file.

Sample 2000/2003 Terminal Server Answer File

The following is a complete sample answer file that I use for both Windows Server 2003 and Windows 2000 Terminal Server installations. I included additional comments in the file to document settings specific to one operating system or the other. I also included information on options you should modify to correspond to your specific environment, such as the default time zone (Eastern Standard Time, in this file), regional settings, personal information, and the server product key. This file can be loaded into the Windows Setup Manager so you can modify any of the general settings if you wish. You cannot edit any of the component settings through the Setup Manager. These must be modified using a text editor, such as Notepad.

As it is, this sample unattend.txt file is not completely automated. There are a few options where you will be prompted to enter information unless you modify the file accordingly. You will be prompted to do the following:

■ Select and configure the target system partition, unless the hard drive is already partitioned.
In this situation Setup automatically selects the first partition with suitable space and installs the Windows server there. If the partition is FAT, it will automatically be converted to NTFS.
■ Accept the End-User License Agreement (EULA).
■ Provide your full name and organization name.
■ Enter the server product key.
■ Set the administrator's password.

All other options, such as the network settings and system components, are automatically selected and configured in the answer file.

TIP: This sample answer file can be downloaded from this book's Web site at http://www.awprofessional.com/title/1578702763.

```
;SetupMgrTag

; Windows 2000/2003 Terminal Server Installation Answer File
; This answer file performs a standard Terminal Server installation.
; Created by Todd W. Mathers
; Version 1.4

[Data]

    AutoPartition=1
    MsDosInitiated="0"
    UnattendedInstall="Yes"

[Unattended]
    UnattendMode=DefaultHide
    OemSkipEula=No
    OemPreinstall=No

    ; the default target on a 2003 server is \Windows, not \WINNT
    TargetPath=\WINNT

    ; 2003 Only
    CrashDumpSetting=0
    WaitForReboot=No

[GuiUnattended]

    ; change the timezone to correspond to your location if you are
not
    ; in the Eastern Standard timezone (US and Canada)
    TimeZone=35

    OemSkipWelcome=1
    OEMSkipRegional=1

[UserData]

    ; Uncomment these and enter your personal information
    ;FullName="Todd W. Mathers"
    ;OrgName="Noisy River Software Corp."
```

```
     ; The * means to randomly generate a computer name
     ; You can enter a specific name here if you wish instead of *
     ComputerName=*

     ; You can uncomment this and add the appropriate product key so
that it
     ; is entered automatically during the install
     ;ProductID=xxxxx-xxxxx-xxxxx-xxxxx-xxxxx

;2003 only
[LicenseFilePrintData]
     AutoMode=PerSeat

[Identification]
     JoinWorkgroup=WORKGROUP

[Networking]
     InstallDefaultComponents=Yes

[Components]
     ; Specifies which components are installed (or not)
     ; Any component not explicitly listed will follow the default
     ; behavior defined for the operating system (may or may not be
installed)

     ; Accessories and Utilities
     accessopt=Off
     calc=On
     cdplayer=Off
     charmap=On
     chat=Off
     deskpaper=Off
     dialer=Off
     freecell=Off
     hearts=Off
     hypertrm=Off
     media_blindnoisy=Off
     media_blindquiet=Off
     media_clips=Off
     media_jungle=Off
     media_musica=Off
     media_robotz=Off
     media_utopia=Off
     minesweeper=Off
     mousepoint=Off
     mplay=Off
     mswordpad=On
     netcm=Off
```

```
netcps=Off
objectpkg=On
paint=Off
pinball=Off
rec=Off
solitaire=Off
spider=Off
templates=On
vol=Off
zonegames=Off

; Certificate Services
certsrv=Off

; Cluster Service
; This is always installed on 2003
cluster=Off

; Fax Service (2003 Only)
fax=Off

; Indexing Service
indexsrv_system=Off

; Internet Explorer Shortcuts (2003 Only)
IEAccess=On

; Internet Information Services
; Some components apply to 2000 or 2003 only
fp_extensions=Off
iis_common=Off
iisdbg=Off
iis_doc=Off
iis_ftp=Off
iis_htmla=Off
iis_inetmgr=Off
iis_nntp=Off
iis_nntp_docs=Off
iis_smtp=Off
iis_smtp_docs=Off
iis_www=Off
iis_www_vdir_printers-Off

; This is the Terminal Services ActiveX client
; Shouldn't be installed by default on a Terminal Server
iis_www_vdir_terminalservices=Off
netcis=Off

; Message Queuing Service
msmq=Off
msmq_Core=Off
```

```
    ; MSN Explorer (2003 Only)
    msnexplr=Off

    ; Network Optional Components
    netoc=Off

    ; Remote Installation Services
    reminst=Off

    ; Remote Storage
    rstorage=Off

    ; Script Debugger
    iisdbg=Off

    ; Terminal Server Client Install Files (2000 Only)
    TSClients=On

    ; Terminal Server Web Client (2003 Only)
    TSWebClient=Off

    ; Enable Windows 2000 Terminal Services
    ; This setting will enable Terminal Services on a W2K server
    TSEnable=On

    ; Enable Windows 2003 Terminal Services
    ; This setting will enable Terminal Services on a W2K3 server
    TerminalServer=On

    ; Terminal Services Licensing Service
    LicenseServer=Off

    ; Windows Media Services
    wms=Off
    wms_admin_asp=Off
    wms_admin_mmc=Off
    wms_server=Off

[TerminalServices]
    ; ApplicationServer applies only to W2K
    ApplicationServer=1

    ; Applies to both 2000 and 2003
    ; Set to  0 = Windows 2000/2003 permissions (Full Security mode)
    ;         1 = NT4 TSE permissions (Relaxed Security mode)
```

```
PermissionsSetting=0
; These settings apply to 2003 only
; Select the appropriate license mode (PerDevice or PerUser) for
; this connection to help it from happening again.
; Chpt 1. in book describes the differences in these license
modes.
LicensingMode=PerDevice
```

Integrating Service Packs with Server Installation Files

A useful feature that can help in streamlining both the installation and future maintenance of Terminal Server (and Windows in general) is the ability to integrate the latest service pack directly into the base server installation files. This process is also referred to as *slipstreaming*.

A common administrative mistake is to add a component to a server at a later date but forget to reapply the corresponding service pack and hotfixes, thereby possibly introducing a security or stability risk. By slipstreaming the service pack into the core installation files, the necessary service pack files are automatically updated if a component is added.

The process of slipstreaming a service pack is not complicated but in order for it to work properly you must perform the slipstream build operation on a Windows 2000/2003 machine. The creation steps are as follows:

1. Begin by copying the contents of the 2000/2003 Server CD into a folder on your computer. For this example I will use the folder D:\W2KCD.
2. If you have not already done so, download the full network version of the latest service pack. Save this into a separate folder on your computer.
3. Now traverse into this folder and extract the entire contents of the service pack file by running

   "<service pack name> /x"

   For example, SP4 for Windows 2000 would be

   "w2ksp4.exe /x"

When prompted, enter a temporary folder where the files can be extracted, as shown in Figure 10.9.

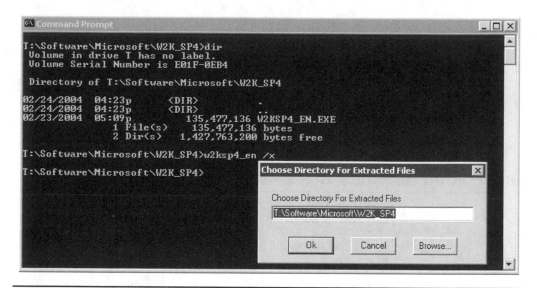

Figure 10.9 Selecting where the service pack files will be extracted.

4. Once the extraction is complete, from a command prompt traverse into the i386\Update folder within the service pack folder and execute the following command:

> update.exe –s:<Server folder>

where <Server folder> is the folder where you copied the contents of the Windows Server CD. This should be the parent folder for the i386 folder, *not* the i386 folder itself. For example, if the contents of the Windows 2000 Server CD are in the D:\W2KCD folder, you would run the command

> update.exe –s:C:\W2KCD

5. Once the update has completed, the server CD folder will contain the completely integrated service pack installation files.

TIP: While being able to create a folder containing an integrated installation is fine if you're performing network-based installations, slipstreaming is really most useful in conjunction with creating an updated, bootable Windows server installation CD. Some excellent resources exist on the Internet that provide detailed information on how to create customized bootable Windows CDs. A couple of different sites are

- http://www.bink.nu/bootcd/
- http://www.windows2000faq.com/Articles/Index.cfm?ArticleID=13914

The same instructions used to create a bootable Windows 2000 CD apply to creating bootable 2003 CDs. The only difference is in the identification files that must exist in the root of the CD in order for Windows Server 2003 to boot properly. These identifier files are simply text files that contain the word *Windows*. The different 2003 files are

- **WIN51**—2003 CD identifier. This must exist on all Windows Server 2003 CDs.
- **WIN51IS**—Standard Server 2003.
- **WIN51IA**—Enterprise Server 2003.

These files can be copied off of your original Windows Server 2003 CD.

I've had people ask me if it is also possible to integrate hotfixes with a slipstreamed service pack to make a completely up-to-date Windows server installation. The short answer is yes. Microsoft provides information on how this can be done in the Installation and Deployment Guide for the service pack. This file can be downloaded from the service pack's Web site. For example, the Deployment Guide for Windows 2000 SP4 can be found on the following site: http://www.microsoft.com/windows2000/downloads/servicepacks/sp4/spdeploy.htm

Personally, I don't bother trying to integrate the individual hotfixes into an installation source since new hotfixes are frequently released and/or updated.

I prefer to create an integrated installation CD with the latest service pack and manage application of the appropriate hotfixes using either an automated deployment tool or scripting, whichever meets the needs of the implementation.

CHAPTER 11

Terminal Services Configuration and Tuning

Before You Begin

In this chapter, I review many of the Terminal Server changes that need to be implemented *prior* to installing any applications or letting any users access the system. It has always been my preference to implement these changes first, perform the necessary testing to ensure stability, and then move on to add the desired server extensions (such as MetaFrame) and applications. I have found that issues are much easier to troubleshoot when following this approach.

TIP: MetaFrame-specific configuration and tuning options are discussed in Chapter 14, "MetaFrame Presentation Server Configuration."

Performing Systematic Changes

One of the most important things you should remember when configuring your server is to perform systematic changes. Always know what changes are being made and why. Document these changes to ensure that not only you but also anyone else who may become involved in the project knows and remembers exactly what has been done. As part of a complete change management strategy, the importance of this cannot be stressed enough.

I recommend that you review this entire chapter before you begin to make any changes to your server. This will give you an idea as to what changes are appropriate for your deployment and let you decide which ones you will implement. *Don't* simply proceed from the beginning of the chapter to the end, applying every listed change. Many changes need to be made only in certain situations and others only if certain issues arise when you begin to test your implementation. For example, if your Terminal Server environment involves only local users connecting over a 100MB local area network, you likely will not need to modify the default TCP/IP KeepAlive option.

NOTE: In response to feedback from readers of the previous edition of this book, I've included a summary checklist of all the changes discussed in this chapter, which you can use as an easy reference for tracking what changes you have made to your Terminal Server. Not only does this list the suggested changes, but it also flags whether the change is "recommended" or "optional" and if it applies to Windows 2003, Windows 2000, or both. You will find this checklist in **Appendix D, "Terminal Server Stability and Tuning Configuration Checklist."** An electronic version of this checklist can be downloaded from the Web site for this book at http://www.awprofessional.com/title/1578702763.

Restricting Client Connectivity

While performing any kind of configuration change, you likely will not want to allow users access to your Terminal Server. If the server you are configuring is not yet in production, this should not be an issue and you will not need to worry about modifying any connection options.

If the machine is or was recently a production server, you may need to take some extra precautions to ensure user connections are properly restricted. While the easiest way to ensure this is to perform your configuration changes outside normal business hours, this is not always possible depending on the nature of your business. The restrictions that need to be implemented will depend very much on how users are accessing your server. In general, users can access a Terminal Server in one of three ways:

- **By directly connecting to the server using the Terminal Server RDP or Citrix MetaFrame Presentation Server Client**—In this configuration the client is hard-coded to point to a specific Terminal Server.
- **By connecting to a Terminal Server via Microsoft's Network Load Balancing service**—The client is assigned the address of the cluster, not the individual Terminal Server, and connectivity is determined based on connection load.
- **By establishing a connection via a MetaFrame Presentation Server published application**—The client requests access to a published application, and MetaFrame determines what server will actually service the request.

TIP: The different connectivity options available are discussed in Chapter 5, "Client Hardware and Software Planning." Specific installation information can be found in Chapter 19, "RDP Client Installation and Configuration," and Chapter 20, "ICA Client Installation and Configuration."

Restricting Direct Terminal Server/MetaFrame Connections

Direct connections are most common in one or two server implementations where no load balancing is being performed to dictate what servers are available to service a connection request. Direct connections are also commonly used by an administrator when they need to service a specific Terminal Server.

If you'll be performing your entire configuration directly from the server's console (which I normally recommend), you can disable these direct RDP or ICA connections using the Terminal Services Configuration tool, found under Administrative Tools on the Start menu. Under the Connections folder, you will see all installed connection types. If you right-click the desired connection, select All Tasks, and then choose Disable Connection, you will prevent *all* users, including administrators, from connecting remotely.

Please note that *all* active user connections via this protocol will be immediately terminated when you disable a connection type. Figure 11.1 shows the disabling of RDP connections on a Windows Server 2003 Terminal Server. Anyone attempting to connect to a Terminal Server using a protocol that has been disabled will receive an error message stating that the specified protocol type may be disabled or that the server itself is unavailable. Once disabled, a connection protocol will remain disabled until it has been explicitly re-enabled. A server reboot will not change the protocol's current state.

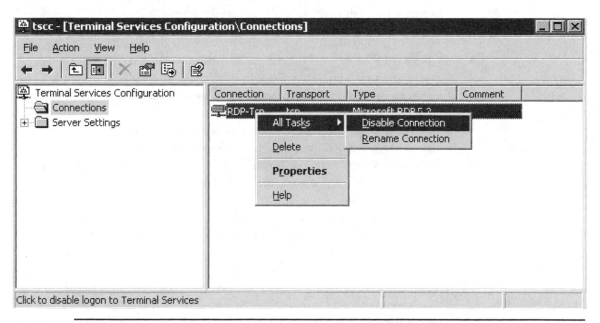

Figure 11.1   Disabling RDP connections on a Windows 2003 Terminal Server.

TIP: This behavior differs from the CHANGE LOGON command, which disables logons only until the next time the server is rebooted, or until they are once again enabled. It is also worth noting that disabling logons using CHANGE LOGON *won't* automatically terminate any active users currently on the server but will prevent any new connections from being made. New logons are disabled by issuing the command

```
change logon /disable
```

They are once again enabled either by rebooting the server or issuing the command

```
change logon /enable
```

The CHANGE LOGON command is also discussed in Appendix A, "Terminal Services Command Reference."

If you want to perform at least some of your server configuration through a remote client connection, then disabling remote connections obviously is not an option. Alternatively you can restrict the connection permissions, thereby limiting who can establish a Terminal Server connection. The process by which you can do this differs slightly between Windows 2003 and Windows 2000:

- If you have a Windows 2003 Terminal Server (or a Windows 2000 Terminal Server configured with a local Remote Desktop Users group), you can simply remove any users or groups that you don't want accessing the server from the local Remote Desktop Users group.
  By default, in order for any non-administrator to log on to a Windows 2003 Terminal Server, they must belong to this local security group.
- On a Windows 2000 Terminal Server with the default connection permissions, you will need to manage the security within the Permissions tab of the appropriate connection protocol.
- From the Terminal Services Configuration utility, right-click the desired connection (RDP or ICA) and select Properties; then select the Permissions tab. You can either remove the desired non-administrative groups from here or modify the group memberships as required. Figure 11.2 shows the RDP permissions for a Windows 2000 Terminal Server. If you're running MetaFrame Presentation Server, be sure to verify the security of all available connection types (RDP and ICA) when restricting connection permissions to a Terminal Server. On more than one occasion I've seen a server where the administrator has the ICA protocol locked down, but the RDP protocol has been left with its default permissions.

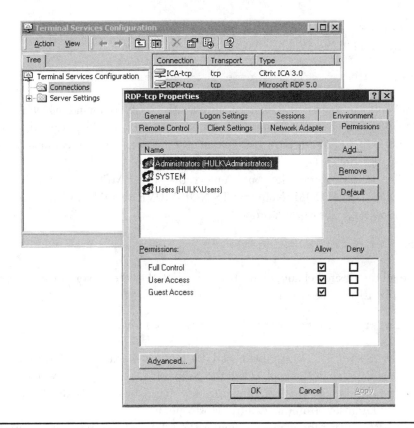

Figure 11.2 Windows 2000 Terminal Server RDP connection permissions.

TIP: I discuss security in detail, including protocol connection permissions, in Chapter 16, "Terminal Server Security."

Restricting Network Load-Balanced Connections

If you have implemented Microsoft Network Load Balancing (NLB) to distribute client connections amongst multiple Terminal Servers, you will want to remove any machines you will be servicing from the load-balancing cluster prior to making any system changes.

The preferred method of removing an active host from an NLB cluster is to place the host into "drainstop" mode. Drainstopping allows the host to continue to service existing connections, while preventing any new connections originating from the cluster to be serviced by this host. Drainstopping will not prevent direct connections to the Terminal Server from still being allowed. In order to prevent direct connections, you will need to disable or restrict connection access as described in the previous section of this chapter.

Drainstopping can be initiated directly from a command prompt. The following syntax will work on either a Windows 2000 or 2003 NLB cluster:

```
wlbs drainstop <cluster name | ip address>:<host>
```

On a Windows Server 2003, you can also use the NLB command, which is exactly the same as WLBS. If you have configured your NLB cluster to require a password, then you will need to append the /PASSW <password> parameter to the end of your command in order to properly manage the cluster.

The following example would remove the server MF03 from the NLB cluster called TS.NOISYRIVER.COM. Note that TS.NOISYRIVER.COM must resolve to an IP address within DNS for this to work properly.

```
wlbs drainstop ts.noisyriver.com:mf03 /passw password
```

Once all the desired changes have been completed to the server; it can be reassigned to the cluster by issuing the command

```
wlbs start <cluster name|ip address>:<host>
```

Windows Server 2003 also provides a GUI tool for managing an NLB cluster. Figure 11.3 shows an example of this tool, called the Network Load Balancing Manager. You can drainstop hosts (and entire clusters) using this tool simply by right-clicking the desired object and selecting Drainstop from the Control Hosts menu.

Whether using the command line or the GUI tool, you need to be sure to wait for the convergence process to complete and all existing connections to terminate before taking the server offline.

NOTE: An overview of Network Load Balancing and load management with Windows Terminal Server is discussed back in Chapter 1, "Microsoft Windows Terminal Services." More detailed information on the actual implementation of Network Load Balancing is covered in Chapter 22, "Server Operations and Support."

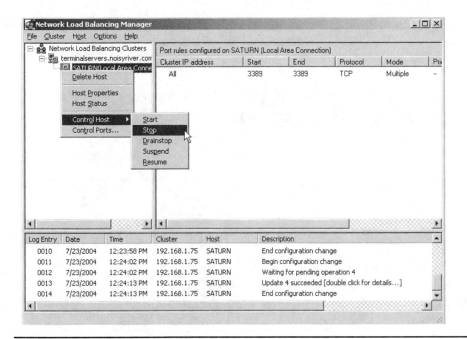

Figure 11.3 Windows Server 2003 Network Load Balancing Manager.

Restricting MetaFrame Presentation Server Published Application Connections

When running MetaFrame Presentation Server, you likely are providing your users with access to the server via one or more published applications instead of through a direct, server-specific connection. In this situation, disabling or restricting access at the connection level, as described earlier, will not alter how MetaFrame directs users to the desired published applications. What can result is that the user is still directed by MetaFrame to the Terminal Server you are servicing, but they fail to gain access to the published application because of the connection restrictions. They will then receive an error message, which likely will initiate a call to your help desk.

Instead of trying to restrict access at the connection level, you should manage the server access through the Citrix Management Console (CMC). One way to temporarily restrict access to a server is to completely disable remote logons from within the CMC. Figure 11.4 shows the settings for the MetaFrame XP server Toronto. This is accessed by right-clicking the appropriate server within the CMC and selecting Properties. Click MetaFrame XP Settings, and the settings will appear on the right-hand side. You will see the Control Options group box, where the Enable Logons to This Server checkbox exists. When logons have been disabled (unchecked), no one can remotely access the server, either via a published application or through a direct connection to the server (RDP or ICA). This includes administrators.

While existing connections are not affected, unless you have access to the server's local console, you likely will not run the risk of locking yourself out of the server by using this approach.

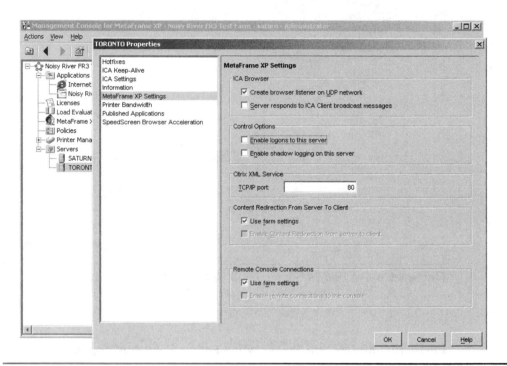

Figure 11.4 Disabling remote logons for a server with the Citrix Management Console.

Restricting access in this manner is identical to using the

```
CHANGE LOGON /DISABLE
```

command from a command prompt. As a consequence, if the server is rebooted, logons will automatically be re-enabled.

TIP: When connections have been disabled in this manner, MetaFrame Presentation Server is aware of this configuration change and automatically omits that server from participating in any application publishing. This can easily be verified by running the following command from a command prompt:

```
QUERY FARM /APP
```

This command will display a list of all applications that are published, what servers they are available on, and what their current server load level is. If a server's logons have been disabled, the server should disappear from all application-publishing lists.

Instead of disabling logons, another option to consider is simply stopping the Citrix Independent Management Architecture (IMA) service on the Terminal Server. Once stopped, this server will no longer be able to participate in any Citrix-based services, and it will appear in the offline list when the following command is run:

```
QUERY FARM /OFFLINE
```

It may take a few minutes once the service has stopped for the server farm to be updated with this information, but once the update has occurred, the server will no longer service any published application *or* direct server connection requests until the IMA service is restarted. RDP connections are in no way affected by the IMA service and will continue to function normally.

When the IMA service is eventually restarted, the server will once again appear in the online server list, and all previously published applications will automatically become available again for use on this server. No additional configuration steps are required.

NOTE: One option that is commonly considered is revoking the server's participation in all applications published. This is performed on an application by application basis in the Management Console, as shown in Figure 11.5. One of the biggest drawbacks to this approach is that you need to be certain you have properly recorded all published application associations so they can all be restored when the server is returned to production. While this approach may work well if there are only a couple of applications published on the server, if the application count is large, the restoration job can become very time consuming and prone to error. In this situation I recommend choosing one of the other options for disabling access.

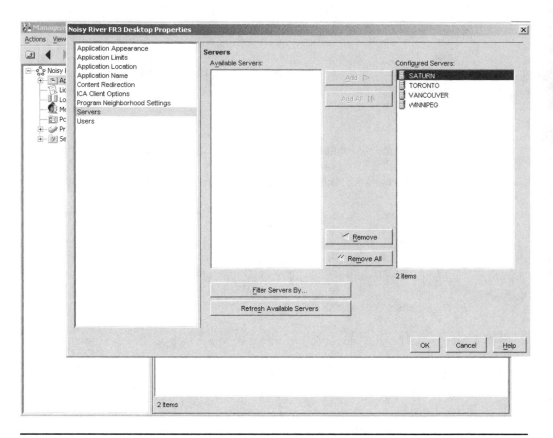

Figure 11.5   Managing the properties for a published application from within the Citrix Management Console.

Windows Service Pack and Hotfix Installation

In Chapter 9, "Service Pack and Hotfix Management," I discussed selection, installation, and management of service packs and hotfixes in your Terminal Server environment. One of the first configuration tasks you need to perform will be installation of the desired service pack. If you have not yet reviewed Chapter 9, I recommend doing so before proceeding with service pack and hotfix installation.

Installing a Windows Service Pack

If this is a new Terminal Server installation, you likely will want to install the latest available service pack, as discussed in Chapter 9. The installation itself can be performed a couple of ways:

- **Download, or order on CD-ROM, the full installation (known as the Network Installation) directly from the Microsoft Web site.** This download is typically around 125MB or more in size. The installation can be performed from a CD-ROM, directly from a network share point, or even "pushed" out to target machines using Windows Installer and Group Policy in a Windows 2000/2003 Active Directory domain.

TIP: Information on deploying a service pack using Windows Installer and Group Policy can be found in the corresponding Installation and Deployment Guide for the service pack, available on the Microsoft Web site or directly on the service pack CD-ROM.

- **Perform an express installation directly from the Microsoft Web site.** An express installation will detect the components installed on your server and apply only the necessary updates. While the total amount of data downloaded during an express installation will typically be less than that of a full network installation, if you are planning to apply the service pack to multiple servers, repeated installations using the express installation method will be more time consuming. The express installation method is best suited for personal computers in a small office or home environment, not for a production Windows Terminal Server environment.

When managing or building even a single Terminal Server, I recommend that you download the full network installation and store it locally on your network. This not only makes it easier to apply (or reapply, as the case may be) the service pack to one or more servers, but it also is required if you wish to integrate the service pack directly into the base OS installation. See the "Integrating Service Packs with Server Installation Files" section in Chapter 10, "Installing Windows Terminal Services" for more information on this.

The service pack installation is straightforward. Once you have initiated the installation, you are presented with the service pack setup wizard. As you proceed through the setup wizard, you eventually are given the opportunity to archive any files that might be required to uninstall the service pack at a later time.

Be aware that this backup process will *only* archive the current system files. If you perform a reinstallation of the same service pack at a later date, the archive option will attempt to overwrite the original backup with a backup of the most current system files on the server. The setup wizard will warn you if this situation does arise and ask for confirmation before proceeding.

Once the service pack installation has completed, you are required to reboot the server before the changes take effect.

Hotfix Installation

The hotfix installation is also straightforward. If you're using an automated deployment tool (Windows Update, SUS, HFNetChkPro, and so forth), you simply need to select the desired updates to deploy and then the tool manages the installation and any reboots required.

If you're manually installing the necessary updates, you will need to download all the patches and run them on the desired Terminal Server. The necessary files are extracted and updated, and then you are prompted (in most cases) to reboot the server in order to complete the install. For example, if you wanted to apply the patch for knowledgebase article Q816093, an update to the Microsoft Virtual Machine (VM), you would download the file Q816093_W2K_SP4_X86_EN.exe and execute it on your Terminal Server. After the installation completed, you would be required to reboot the server for the changes to take effect.

Obviously the need to reboot after the installation of each hotfix becomes completely unacceptable if you are installing more than a couple of fixes on a server. In a situation where you needed to apply multiple hotfixes to a Terminal Server, it would be nice if there were a way to install all the patches at once with a single reboot at the end.

Streamlining Multiple Hotfix Installations

When you are looking to streamline the manual installation of multiple hotfixes, the most common solution is to create a batch script that runs the hotfix installation files one after the other. Once this is completed, you can either reboot the server manually or have it reboot automatically as part of the script.

The one problem you have to be concerned with is the order in which the hotfixes are installed. For example, if you install hotfix A followed by hotfix B, and they both update the same file (with A's version being more recent), you may end up with B's version of the file on the system, which is not the desired result.

To address this problem, Microsoft originally developed a tool called QChain, which lets you install multiple hotfixes (in any order) with only a single reboot and ensures that only the most recent version of the files actually get installed on the server. For this to work properly, the QChain command had to be executed once all the desired patches were applied.

All patches released since December 2002 have the QChain functionality integrated directly into the installation file, so QChain is not required when chaining any of these hotfixes together. While patches released between May 2001 and December 2002 also were supposed to include this functionality, a bug was found that could cause these to fail in certain situations. Because of this, Microsoft recommends that QChain be used whenever chaining together patches released prior to December 2002.

TIP: The QChain utility, along with a detailed knowledgebase article explaining the tool's functionality (with examples) can be found by searching the Microsoft Web site for article number 296861.

Automated deployment tools such as Microsoft Software Update Services (SUS) or HFNetChkPro include the necessary QChain functionality so multiple patches can be applied to a target machine with only a single reboot.

Once you've completed the patch installations and rebooted the server, I recommend that you perform another security patch scan to ensure that they all have been properly applied. Your server should now be up to date with the desired service pack and hotfixes.

TIP: In certain situations you will find that your patch scan tool is unable to determine whether a particular security update is actually installed or not. For example, Figure 11.6 shows the Microsoft Baseline Security Analyzer (MBSA) results window with a number of security updates that it could not confirm as being installed. You will need to perform a manual confirmation, details of which are described in knowledgebase article 306460, for each of the listed updates. The MBSA tool was discussed in Chapter 9.

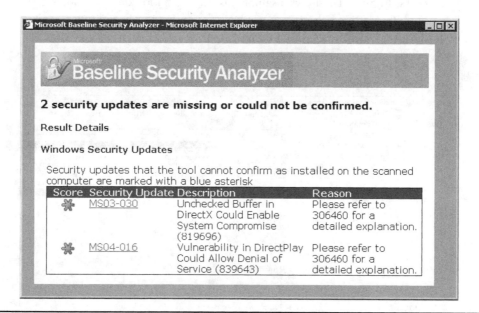

Figure 11.6   MBSA results window showing unconfirmed security updates.

Basic Configuration Tasks for Stability and Availability

There are a number of changes that should be made to a Terminal Server in order to improve its overall stability and availability. Most, in one way or another, modify the default configuration of the Windows server to better suit the multiple concurrent user sessions existing on a Terminal Server. With each iteration of Microsoft's Terminal Server offering, more and more multiuser configuration requirements are finding their way into the default Terminal Server configuration. This is one of the reasons why typically you will find there are more configuration changes suggested for a Windows 2000 Terminal Server than for a Windows 2003 Terminal Server. A similar trend existed when comparing a Windows 2000 Terminal Server to a Windows NT 4.0, Terminal Server Edition, server. In this chapter, unless otherwise stated, all change suggestions apply to both Windows 2000 and Windows 2003.

Partition and Format Non-System Drives

If you have not already done so, now is a good time to partition and format the remaining disks on your system using the Disk Management snap-in. You can access this by clicking My Computer, selecting Manage from the pop-up menu, and then selecting Disk Management from under the Storage folder. You should format both your application volume and pagefile volume (if applicable) as NTFS. Remember, you do not want to use the FAT file system on any of the drives on your Terminal Server, since you will have no way of restricting user access. Figure 11.7 shows a sample disk configuration on a Windows 2003 Terminal Server. When formatting a drive, you will have the option to select a quick format.

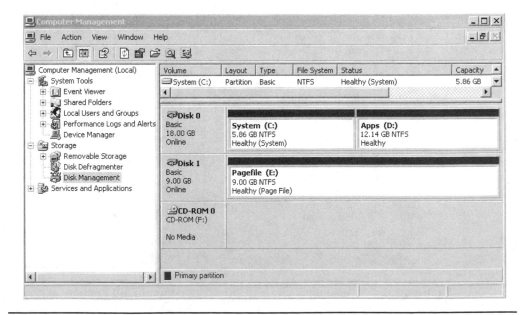

Figure 11.7   Sample disk configuration on a Windows 2003 Terminal Server.

TIP: A common Windows tuning tip is to increase the cluster size of an NTFS partition when it is being formatted to realize a small gain in disk performance. An NTFS hard disk is organized into clusters, which represent the smallest space that can be allocated for a file on the disk. For example, if you have a file that is 16KB in size, then it would occupy four clusters of 4KB, or 32 clusters of 512 bytes. By storing files in larger cluster sizes, you can decrease the time required to retrieve that data. Of course additional space on the disk can be wasted if you are storing a large number of files smaller than the cluster size. For example, files less than 4KB in size would still occupy the entire 4KB cluster.

When formatting an NTFS drive, if the allocation unit size is left as Default, any drive over 2GB in size will have the cluster size default to 4KB, which is the optimal cluster size for a Windows NTFS disk partition. I do not recommend that you adjust this size from the default.

TIP: Many people have asked what the difference is between a regular disk format and the Perform a Quick Format option. A regular or full disk format purges the volume of all files and then performs a check to determine if the drive has any bad sectors or not. A quick format performs only the file purge and skips the bad sector check. The process of scanning for bad sectors is what takes the majority of time during an NTFS disk format. I recommend that you always perform a full disk format the first time you format any drives in your Terminal Server.

Configure the Pagefile

While the pagefile could technically be considered a performance factor, the importance of a properly configured pagefile on a Terminal Server is the reason I have chosen to discuss it now. Configuring the pagefile now is particularly important if you're planning to set it up on a partition where other data or files will exist. This helps ensure that the pagefile occupies contiguously allocated space on the disk.

As I discussed in Chapter 6, "Terminal Server Hardware Planning," the ideal location and size for the pagefile is

- On a single drive or partition other than the system partition
- On a non-fault tolerant drive configuration
- As close as possible to the beginning of the physical disk
- Occupying a contiguous space on the physical drive
- Approximately 1.5 to 2 times the physical memory on the server

The pagefile configuration screen can be found under the System properties dialog box as follows:

1. Right-click My Computer and select Properties from the pop-up menu.
2. Click the Advanced tab and then click the Settings button under Performance. On a Windows 2000 Server, the button will be labeled Performance Options instead of Settings.
3. (Windows Server 2003 only.) Select the Advanced tab on this dialog box.
4. Click the Change button under Virtual Memory to open the Virtual Memory dialog box, shown in Figure 11.8. While the Virtual Memory screens differ slightly between Windows 2003 and Windows 2000, the basic pagefile configuration remains the same.

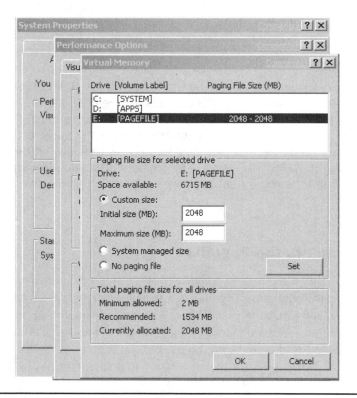

Figure 11.8 Windows Server 2003 Virtual Memory dialog box.

When you first open this dialog box, the default configuration has an initial size of 1.5 × physical memory and a maximum size of 3 × physical memory. You are going to need to change this to optimize your pagefile configuration.

5. Highlight each of the volumes that will *not* contain a pagefile and set the initial and maximum pagefile size to zero (or simply click No Paging File, on a Windows 2003 server). A message appears warning you that debug information can't be created if a STOP error occurs. As I discuss in more detail shortly, by default we are not going to have the server perform full system dumps, so select Yes if prompted.

6. Now select the drive where you maintain your pagefile. Enter the initial and maximum size for this pagefile, making sure they are set to the *same* value. This will "lock" the pagefile at the designated size and help ensure it occupies a contiguous space on the disk. For example, on my test server with 1GB of RAM, I would create a 2GB (2 × physical memory) pagefile on my dedicated pagefile drive (E:).

7. Click Set to store the change and then click OK. You will be required to reboot the server in order for the change to take effect.

NOTE: On a Windows 2003 server you will see there are two additional paging file options: System Managed Size and No Paging File. The No Paging File is equivalent to setting your initial and maximum pagefile to zero on all drives. The System Managed Size tells Windows 2003 to choose the best paging file size for you. This simply causes Windows to use the defaults of 1.5 × physical memory for the initial size and 3 × physical memory for the maximum size.

Verify the Registry Size

This change applies only to Windows 2000 Servers.

Depending on the number of concurrent users you expect your Terminal Server to support, you may need to look at increasing your server's registry size limit (RSL) from the default. Typically each user hive loaded into the registry takes approximately 0.8 to 1.5MB of space. An initial RSL calculation would be something like

0.8MB × (number of concurrent users) = RSL

For example, if you expected to have 120 concurrent users on the server, your initial registry size would be

0.8MB × 120 users = 96MB

You will want to monitor the growth of the registry during testing and piloting to see if you need to increase the registry size further.

While it may seem reasonable to simply set the registry size to an arbitrarily large value, Windows 2000 does have an upper limit on the registry size. Windows 2000 restricts the size of the registry to be no more than 80 percent of the paged pool size, which itself has a maximum size. The paged pool size is set dynamically by Windows based on the amount of physical memory in the server. Table 11.1 shows the maximum possible paged pool size and the corresponding maximum registry size that can be set for Windows 2000 without making special system kernel modifications.

Table 11.1   Maximum Paged Pool and Registry Size for Windows 2000

Maximum Paged Pool Size	Maximum Registry Size Limit
370MB	296MB

If you attempt to set the RSL to greater than 80 percent of the current paged pool size on the server, you'll receive a message similar to the one shown in Figure 11.9. Clicking OK causes Windows to do two things:

- Increase the maximum size of your pagefile as required.
- Increase the paged pool size (up to the maximum listed in Table 11.1) so that it is 20 percent greater than the RSL value you specified. This paged pool size is then hard-coded into the registry. Once this value is hard-coded, Windows no longer dynamically adjusts the paged pool size based on the physical memory in the system.

If you attempt to set the RSL greater than the maximum value listed in Table 11.1, Windows ignores your value and simply uses the listed maximum. For a Windows 2000 Server with 512MB or more RAM, the maximum paged pool size will automatically be used, so your maximum registry size limit will be 296MB. For more information on the actual paged pool calculations, see the Microsoft knowledgebase, article 124594.

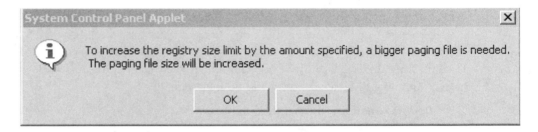

Figure 11.9   When attempting to set the RSL to greater than 80 percent of the current paged pool size on a Windows 2000 Server, you receive this message.

NOTE: Through special kernel modifications, an upper maximum of 400MB for the paged pool size (320 for the RSL) can be attained if space is taken away from the System Page Table Entry (System PTE) memory area and assigned to the paged pool. Details on performing this nontrivial operation can be found in the Microsoft knowledgebase, article 247904. I highly recommend that additional hardware be considered instead of trying to tweak the kernel in order to squeeze an additional 10 to 20 users onto an existing server.

If we took the estimate of around 1MB per user of registry usage, this would limit a Windows 2000 Terminal Server with a nontuned kernel to around 300 concurrent users (or less), regardless of how much physical memory was actually in the server. The Microsoft document "Windows 2000 Terminal Services Capacity and Scaling" provides an example where a limit of 350 script-controlled user sessions was encountered due to the page pool size limitation on a server *with* a tuned kernel. You can find the complete document at the following address:

http://www.microsoft.com/windows2000/techinfo/administration/
terminal/tscaling.asp

The registry size on a Windows 2000 server is modified in the same Virtual Memory dialog box as the paging file. Figure 11.10 shows the Windows 2000 Virtual Memory dialog box.

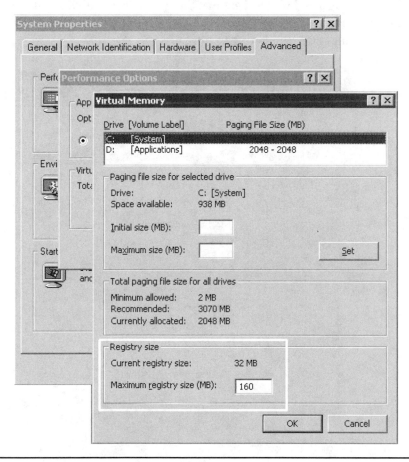

Figure 11.10 The registry size is modified in the Virtual Memory dialog box on a Windows 2000 server.

NOTE: With the release of Windows Server 2003, the registry contents are no longer contained in the paged pool but instead are mapped into the system cache space. This change effectively removes the limits previously existing for the maximum registry size and eliminates the need for an administrator to manually manage a proper size configuration. As a result, the Virtual Memory dialog box on a Windows 2003 server no longer provides an option where an administrator can adjust the registry size.

Set Server Startup and Recovery Options

Windows lets you configure the startup and recovery options for your server, which dictate how it will respond in the event that the system halts with a STOP error, also known as the infamous Blue Screen of Death (BSOD). Figure 11.11 shows the default configuration for these settings on a Windows 2003 Terminal Server.

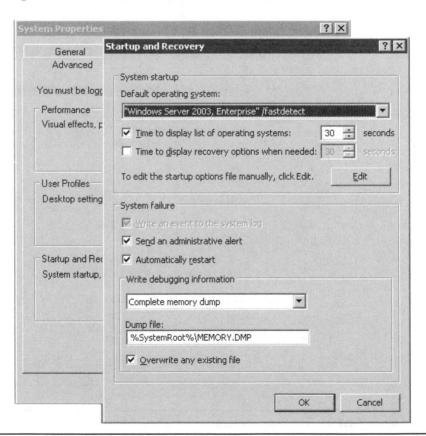

Figure 11.11 The default server startup and recovery options on a Windows 2003 Terminal Server.

The number of production Terminal Servers, the requirements for availability, physical accessibility to the servers, and personal preference will all play a large part in influencing your decision on how these settings will be configured. Basically there are two configurations from which to choose. The first configures the Terminal Server to halt when a STOP error is encountered, and the server remains inaccessible until it is physically restarted by an administrator. The other configuration instructs the Terminal Server to automatically recover in the event the system halts with a STOP error. Here are some of the questions you will want to consider:

- **Do you have enough capacity in your environment to continue functioning if a Terminal Server were to unexpectedly go offline?** If you are load-balancing multiple Terminal Servers, then ideally you will have sufficient capacity to continue supporting your concurrent user load even if one (or possibly two) of the servers were to go offline. In this situation you may have the ability to allow a server with a STOP error to remain offline until you or another administrator has had time to review the STOP message displayed on the screen. If you are working in a one or two server configuration, you will likely not be able to allow the server to remain down, so you will need to configure the server to automatically attempt to restart on a system failure.

- **Do you employ system monitoring that will alert you if a Terminal Server goes offline due to a STOP error?** Regardless of the size of your environment you should have some form of monitoring in place that will alert you to the situation where a server has become inaccessible. In a large-scale production environment this is an essential part of effective server management. Without proper monitoring, a stopped server could remain down for an extended period of time before you would even notice. If adequate capacity exists this may be acceptable, but you will likely want to configure the server to automatically reboot to ensure server uptime and availability.

- **Are you physically able to access your Terminal Servers, or are they located in a remote office that requires travel time to access?** If your Terminal Servers are physically located in a remote location that you cannot quickly access, they will have to remain hung until you can arrive to access them, or some form of hardware-based remote access will need to be employed to allow you to restart the machine. You likely would want to configure the servers to automatically restart, and you would have to rely on event log monitoring, in addition to user feedback, to alert you when a server had crashed.

When you have decided on the appropriate configuration for your environment, you can modify the settings by opening the properties for My Computer, selecting the Advanced tab, and then choosing the settings for Startup and Recovery. I suggest the following steps:

1. I recommend that you begin by reducing the display time for the operating systems list from the default of 30 seconds down to 5 seconds. This speeds up booting of the server but allows enough time to select an alternate OS or recovery option if desired.

2. If you're not using Windows alerts, you can deselect Send an Administrative Alert. Chapter 22, "Server Operations and Support," discusses configuration of Windows alerts.

3. Now choose whether to enable or disable the Automatically Restart option.

4. Finally, choose the desired level of debugging information to record. The default option of Complete Memory Dump will save a complete copy of all memory contents to the specified dump file. It can take a significant amount of time to write this file, depending on how much memory is in the server. A full memory dump will also consume disk space equal to the amount of physical memory plus 11MB. My preference is to select (none) and adjust this only if a BSOD occurs more than once on the server, although the small memory dump option will record additional crash information without consuming too much space or taking up too much time.

On a Windows 2000 server, you are required to reboot the server before these changes take affect. A Windows 2003 server does not require a reboot.

TIP: Although you can change the location of the dump file, Windows 2000/2003 will always write the debug information to a pagefile on the %systemroot% partition first and then move it to the location you have specified. If you want to enable the complete memory dump, you must have sufficient space on your system partition to accommodate creation of a pagefile equal to the amount of physical memory on your server plus 11MB.

Add the Recovery Console to the Startup Menu

While adding the Recovery Console to the startup menu is not necessarily essential to the stability of the server, I've found that having the Windows Recovery Console added to the list of options on the startup menu can be invaluable if you ever find yourself in the situation where the server will not boot properly. Even though you can access the Recovery Console by booting from a setup CD-ROM or a floppy diskette, it is certainly more convenient to have it already configured on the server.

Adding the Recovery Console to the server is straightforward. Simply place the Windows Server CD into the drive, traverse into the i386 folder from a command prompt, and run the following command

```
winnt32.exe /cmdcons
```

A Windows setup wizard appears, letting you install the Recovery Console. During the installation, Microsoft's Dynamic Update tool attempts to download the latest versions of the installation files. You can cancel Dynamic Update and continue the installation with the existing files by pressing the Esc key.

Once installation has completed, the next time you reboot your server you will see the Recovery Console as an option on your startup menu. An entry containing the Recover Console information is added to the boot.ini file located in the root of the system drive. The specific entry added is

C:\CMDCONS\BOOTSECT.DAT="Microsoft Windows Recovery Console" /cmdcons

For details on functionality and use of the Windows Recovery Console, see the Microsoft knowledgebase article "Description of the Windows Recovery Console," article number 229716.

Configure the Event Log Sizes

An area often overlooked during configuration of any Windows server (not just a Terminal Server) is the proper sizing of the event logs. Proper log sizing is even more important on a Terminal Server, where many extra log events (particularly security events) can be generated as users work on the system. While both Windows 2000 Server and Windows Server 2003 have default log settings, these settings are not the same. Table 11.2 summarizes the default settings for the two operating systems.

Table 11.2 Default Event Log Properties for Windows Server 2003 and Windows 2000 Server

	Operating System	
Log	**Windows 2000**	**Windows 2003**
Application	Maximum size = 512KB Overwrite events older than 7 days.	Maximum size – 16384KB Overwrite events as needed.
Security	Maximum size = 512KB Overwrite events older than 7 days.	Maximum size = 16384KB Overwrite events as needed.
System	Maximum size = 512KB Overwrite events older than 7 days.	Maximum size = 16384KB Overwrite events as needed.

As you can see, the default log sizes for Windows Server 2003 are quite a bit larger (16MB as opposed to 0.5MB) than the Windows 2000 Server default sizes. While I would consider the 2003 default settings much more appropriate for a Terminal Server, Table 11.3 lists my recommended configuration for both 2003 and 2000 Terminal Servers.

Table 11.3   Recommended Event Log Sizes for Both Windows Server 2003 and Windows 2000 Server

Log	Maximum Size	When Maximum Log Size Is Reached
Application	16384KB	Overwrite events as needed.
Security	65536KB	Overwrite events as needed.
System	16384KB	Overwrite events as needed.

The Event Viewer can be found in the Computer Management snap-in or launched directly from a command prompt by executing eventvwr.exe. Individual properties for each log can be accessed by right-clicking and selecting Properties, as shown in Figure 11.12.

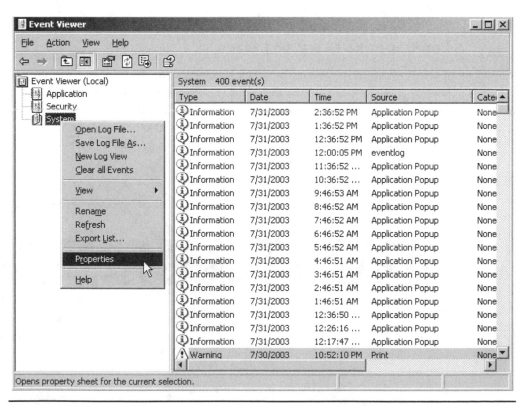

Figure 11.12   The properties for each log are accessed by right-clicking and selecting Properties.

Of course, event logging is pointless unless there is actually a mechanism in place where entries are reviewed and logs cleared on a regular basis. A number of simple tools exist that can be used to schedule the automatic archiving of the event log data. Once again, SysInternals (http://www.sysinternals.com) provides an excellent tool that not only allows for contents of both local and remote event logs to be dumped but also automatically clears a log once the information has been retrieved. The tool in question is called PsLogList and is available free as part of the PsTools suite of utilities.

This is the preferred way of dealing with event logs, as it provides a way to preserve past log information without having to resort to maintaining event logs with large maximum sizes and then having to manually review and clear the contents on a regular basis.

TIP: I provide more detailed information on event log management, including examples of use of PSLogList in Chapter 22.

Modify Printer Event Logging

The default print spooler configuration on a Terminal Server can result in a large number of informational print events being logged to the System event log, particularly when client printer connections have been enabled. Figure 11.13 shows a portion of the System event log with printer-related entries generated when logging on to and off of a Windows 2003 Terminal Server with MetaFrame Presentation Server.

The log information generated by printer events can be managed through Print Server Properties, which is found under the File menu of the Printers and Faxes (just "Printers" on Windows 2000) folder. In Figure 11.14 you can see this dialog box with all event options deselected except for logging of spooler error events. This is the configuration I use unless I suspect there may be an issue with client printer mappings. If that is the case, I re-enable the appropriate logging options to assist in troubleshooting the issue. Once the problem has been resolved, I once again revert back to my default configuration.

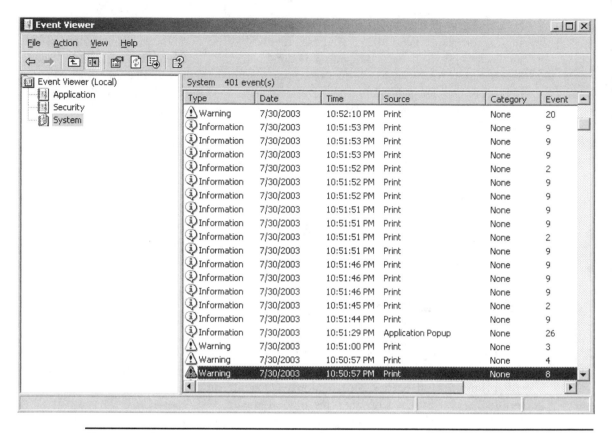

Figure 11.13 System event log entries generated by client printer connections.

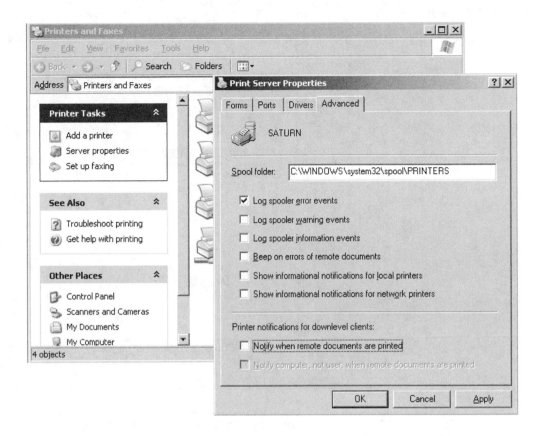

Figure 11.14 Suggested printer event-logging settings.

Turn Off Network Interface Card Auto-Detect

Another recommended change is to verify that the network interface card (NIC) on the server has been configured specifically for the appropriate speed and duplex as opposed to having it set to auto-detect these features. Most network administrators agree that this is preferred, particularly in a switched environment.

The exact interface for making this change depends on the NIC manufacturer, but in general the change is made by selecting Network Connections from under the Control Panel, double-clicking the appropriate local area connection, and then clicking the Properties button. The top portion of the dialog box shows the NIC information along with a Configure button. Clicking this button brings up the properties for the NIC. Figure 11.15 shows an example of the properties for an Intel PRO/100B card. The property changes you make here take effect immediately and don't require a reboot.

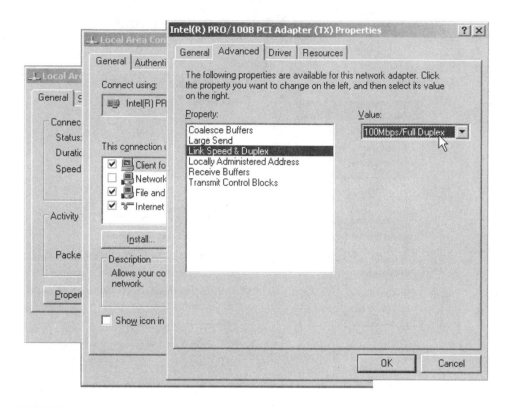

Figure 11.15   Configuration settings for an Intel PRO/100B network interface card.

WARNING: Make sure you configure the NIC to match the specifications of the network. Improperly configuring the NIC can result in severe network performance degradation. If you are unsure of the network configuration, I recommend leaving the NIC in auto-detect mode until you can confirm the proper settings with a network administrator.

Disable Automatic Updates

The default configuration on a Windows 2003 server has the Automatic Updates option enabled with the settings shown in figure 11.16. While the purpose of Automatic Updates is to ensure timely delivery of critical security and system patches, without proper testing, the introduction of a change into your production Terminal Server environment could result in stability issues on the server. In an environment with multiple administrators, allowing

Automatic Updates to download and prompt for installation confirmation can easily result in a patch being applied without proper consideration for the implications it may have to the environment.

The Automatic Update settings on Windows Server 2003 are accessed under the System Properties for My Computer. On Windows 2000 Server they are found under Automatic Updates on the Control Panel. In order to have access to the Automatic Update feature on a Windows 2000 server, you must be running Windows 2000 Service Pack 3 or later.

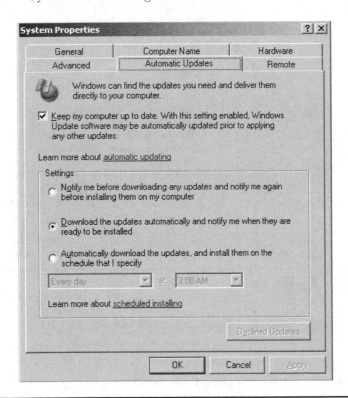

Figure 11.16   Default Automatic Update settings for Windows Server 2003.

TIP: For a thorough treatment of patch management, refer to Chapter 9.

Modify the Folder Options View

This is a change I've become accustomed to making on all Terminal Servers I've worked with and is more of a usability and convenience issue for the administrator than anything else. This change won't help improve the stability of your server, but from an administrative standpoint, some of the default options are unnecessarily restrictive. Folder Options can be found in Control Panel; the specific tab we are interested in is the View tab, shown in Figure 11.17.

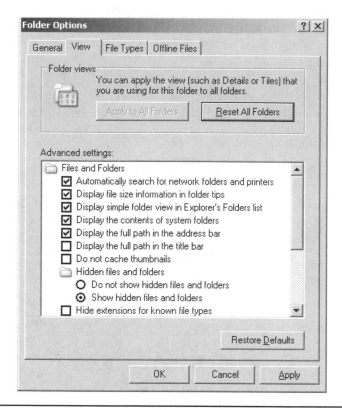

Figure 11.17 The Folder Options View tab.

Table 11.4 summarizes my suggested settings for the View tab. If an option is not listed, you can assume that it can be set as desired.

Table 11.4 Suggested Folder Option View Settings

Checked	Option	Notes
Yes	Display the full path in the address bar.	This can be handy if, for example, you want to cut and paste the path into a command prompt or application.
Yes	Show hidden files and folders.	This makes finding files and folders easier through Explorer.
No	Hide extensions for known file types.	As an administrator you should always be aware of what type of file you are accessing. This helps you avoid falling for the trick of double-naming a file with two extensions; for example: CheckItOut.jpg.exe.
No	Hide protected operating system files. (Recommended.)	Through Explorer, the only way to see files that have their hidden and system file attributes set is to deselect this option.

Disable the Manage Your Server Wizard

The very first time a user with administrative privileges logs on to a 2000/2003 server they are presented with the Manage Your Server ("Configure Your Server," on Windows 2000) wizard. While some people may find this wizard helpful, I feel it is a tool better left on the Start menu and accessed only when required.

You can disable automatic startup of this tool by modifying the registry as follows:

1. From a command prompt, open REGEDT32.EXE.
2. Select HKEY_USERS and then, from the Registry menu, click the Load Hive option. In the Load Hive dialog box load the file
   c:\Documents and Settings\Default User\ntuser.dat

   This is a hidden folder, so if you haven't enabled Show Hidden Files and Folders as discussed earlier, you can still type the above path into the File Name field and hit Enter.
3. You can enter any name you wish for the key name, but I suggest using "Default User."
4. Navigate into the key
   HKEY_USERS\Default User\Software\Microsoft\Windows NT\CurrentVersion\ Setup\Welcome and change the value for srvwiz from 0x1 to 0x0.
5. Now click the root of your loaded hive (Default User) and select Unload Hive from the Registry menu. Manage Your Server will no longer load the first time an administrator logs on to the Terminal Server.

TIP: You can launch the Manage Your Server wizard on Windows Server 2003 simply by clicking the Start menu and selecting the option from the top of the menu.

On Windows 2000 Server, Configure Your Server is found under Administrative Tools on the Start menu.

Disable the Internet Connection Wizard

This change applies only to Windows 2000 Servers.

Probably the most annoying thing that happens the first time you log on to a Windows 2000 Server and try and access an Internet resource is being presented with the Internet Connection wizard (ICW). Contrary to what some people may think, the ICW is *not* required to access the Internet, and disabling it will not impact your connectivity.

The ICW can be disabled in one of two ways. The first is to implement the change using group policies. If you're deploying your Terminal Servers in an Active Directory, using a group policy is a straightforward means of manually changing a number of configuration settings for your users. The specific policy to disable the ICW is called Disable Internet Connection Wizard and is located under
   User Configuration\Administrative Templates\Windows Components\Internet Explorer

For more information on group policies, see Chapter 15, "Group Policy Configuration."
The other method of disabling the ICW is to modify the registry settings for the default user, similar to how the changes to Manage Your Server were done earlier.

1. Begin by running REGEDT32.EXE.
2. Select HKEY_USERS and then, from the Registry menu, click the Load Hive option. In the Load Hive dialog box load the file

   > c:\Documents and Settings\Default User\ntuser.dat

   This is a hidden folder, so if you haven't enabled Show Hidden Files and Folders as discussed earlier, you can still type the above path into the File Name field and hit Enter.
3. You can enter any name you wish for the key name, but I suggest using "Default User".
4. Now navigate into the key
   HKEY_USERS\Default User\Software\Microsoft\Windows\Runonce
   and delete the value ^SetupICWDesktop. This prevents the ICW icon from being created on the desktop.
5. Next create the key "Internet Connection Wizard" under
   HKEY_USERS\Default User\Software\Microsoft\
   and add a value to this key with the label "Completed" a type REG_DWORD and a numeric value of 0x1. This prevents ICW from appearing when you try and run applications such as Internet Explorer.
6. Finally, click the root of your loaded hive (Default User) and select Unload Hive from the Registry menu. The Internet Connection wizard no longer appears the first time you try to run an application such as Internet Explorer.

NOTE: The Internet Connection wizard is not included with Windows Server 2003.

Disable Dr Watson

Very few people have not encountered the good doctor at least once during their use of Windows. Dr Watson is the default application debugger in Windows that's automatically launched to trap all unhandled application errors. Most often, these are memory exception errors that occur when an application attempts to access a memory location that hasn't been allocated for it by the operating system.

When the exception is raised, Windows automatically starts Dr Watson to gather information about the application error. This usually involves writing a crash dump file and a log file containing information such as the application's stack and symbol table contents. While this is similar to the behavior of a system STOP error (Blue Screen of Death), the two are not the same, and their configuration options are completely distinct from each other.

The current options for Dr Watson on your Terminal Server can be viewed anytime by running DRWTSN32.EXE from a command prompt. The default configuration for Dr Watson is the same in both 2003 and 2000, with the only exception being that Windows Server 2003 allows for the selection of an alternate crash dump type instead of a full dump. The options managed by this application are stored in this registry key:

> \\HKEY_LOCAL_MACHINE\Software\Microsoft\Dr Watson

Note that this key won't exist until the first time you actually run DRWTSN32.EXE.

Unless you're debugging a recurring application problem, I suggest completely disabling use of Dr Watson. Windows looks in the following registry location to determine what debugger it should run in the event of an application error:

> HKEY_LOCAL_MACHINE\Software\Microsoft\Windows NT\CurrentVersion\ AeDebug

The particular value in question is Debugger. After a clean Windows installation, the value usually contains the following text:

```
drwtsn32 -p %ld -e %ld -g
```

To disable Dr Watson, simply delete this registry key. You can also delete the Dr Watson key mentioned earlier, which is located under the key

> \\HKEY_LOCAL_MACHINE\Software\Microsoft\DrWatson

If you ever want to restore the Dr Watson registry values, simply run DRWTSN32 –I from a command prompt.

TIP: Dr Watson will default to writing crash dump and log file information to the following folder, based on the specific operating system:

- Windows 2000: %ALLUSERSPROFILE%\Documents\DrWatson

- Windows 2003: %USERPROFILE%\Local Settings\Application Data\Microsoft\ DrWatson

As you can see, Windows Server 2003 will write dump information into each user's personal profile folder, while Windows 2000 attempts to write dump information for all users to the same common folder.

If you're debugging a user's problem on a Windows 2000 Terminal Server, you'll probably want to edit this entry so the user is pointed to a location where they are sure to have write access. The easiest way to do this is to run DRWTSN32 and change the file paths to use the user's home or root drive setting (H:, for example) instead of the All Users profile path. I talk more about use and configuration of the root drive a little later in this chapter.

Suppress Hard Error Messages

Under certain conditions, if the operating system or an application encounters a critical error, they may display what is known as a *hard error* message. Hard error messages remain on the screen and typically prevent an application from completely terminating until acknowledged by the user. A common example of this is the display of an exception error such as the following:

```
Application popup: Excel.exe - Application Error
The instruction at "0x100ff373" referenced memory at "0x04310f30".
The memory could not be "read".

Click on OK to terminate the application
```

In this situation, the application will not properly terminate until the user clicks the OK button. In most situations, if a user encounters this problem, they click OK and restart the application or possibly contact their help desk to report the problem.

Where real problems can develop is if these messages appear on the console because a running service has generated a hard error, or if a user logs off while a hard error is being displayed. In the first scenario, the service will remain hung until an administrator acknowledges the error pop-up message from the console. In the second scenario, a user's profile may fail to unload properly because the server is delayed in completing the logoff of their session. Hard errors rarely prevent a Terminal Server session from completely resetting, but they can cause issues with unloading and saving profile information.

Microsoft does provide a way to control how hard errors are processed through modification of a registry key. You can control display of hard errors by modifying the *ErrorMode* REG_DWORD registry value, located under the following registry key:

HKEY_LOCAL_MACHINE\SYSTEM\CurrentControlSet\Control\Windows

The three possible values for ErrorMode are

0	(Default.) All error messages are displayed and handled normally.
1	Application-generated hard errors are displayed normally, but all system-generated hard errors are suppressed. An error event is written to the system log for system-generated hard errors only.
2	All hard errors are suppressed from the screen, but an error event is written to the system log regardless of the error's source (application or system).

I recommend that hard errors be suppressed only after all desired applications have been installed on your Terminal Server and you have completed at least your preliminary application testing. Suppressing visual notification of hard errors may make it more difficult to troubleshoot application issues.

TIP: See Microsoft knowledgebase article number 128642, "How to Change Hard Error Popup Handling in Windows NT," for a brief discussion on hard error pop-up handling.

Customizing the My Computer Text

When managing multiple Terminal Servers, very often an administrator needs to quickly verify which server they are currently logged on to. While this question can be answered by opening the Computer Name properties for My Computer, it is a cumbersome way to retrieve this information. I prefer to modify the actual text portion of the My Computer icon to include the name of the server (and sometimes the user ID).

Quick and consistent access to this information also makes it easy for a user to provide information on what server they are currently on when attempting to resolve an issue with support staff. Figure 11.18 shows an example of the My Computer icon on a Windows 2003 server customized to include the server name in parentheses.

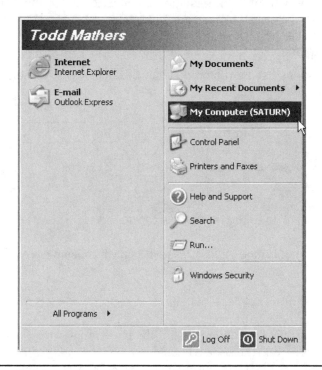

Figure 11.18   Customized My Computer text on a Windows 2003 Terminal Server.

The registry location where this information is modified is the same on both a Windows 2003 and a Windows 2000 server. The registry key in question is

HKLM\Software\Classes\CLSID\{20D04FE0-3AEA-1069-A2D8-08002B30309D}

The specific value that controls the My Computer name is LocalizedString. On a Windows 2000 server, this value must be deleted and replaced with a value with the same name but of type REG_EXPAND_SZ. On Windows 2003, you simply need to delete the current text and replace it with the desired My Computer name.

The text assigned to LocalizedString to produce the result shown in Figure 11.18 was

My Computer (%COMPUTERNAME%)

The REGINI script shown in Listing 11.1 updates this registry key to include the server name in parentheses after the My Computer text on either a Windows 2000 or 2003 server.

WARNING: Be sure to back up the information stored in LocalizedString prior to making this change so you can revert back to the original configuration if desired. The easiest way to back up this information is to launch the REGEDIT utility and then traverse to the registry key under HKLM\Software\Classes\CLSID listed above, being sure to highlight the key you wish to back up. Now select Export Registry File from the Registry menu. You can now save the file as a .REG file.

The settings can be restored simply by double-clicking the file from within Explorer. This automatically writes the registry information stored in the file back to the registry.

Listing 11.1 A REGINI File to Update the Registry Key

```
HKEY_LOCAL_MACHINE\Software\Classes
   CLSID
     {20D04FE0-3AEA-1069-A2D8-08002B30309D}
         LocalizedString = DELETE
         LocalizedString = REG_EXPAND_SZ My Computer (%COMPUTERNAME%)
```

The script in Listing 11.1 is executed simply by opening a command prompt and running the command

```
REGINI <script file name>
```

This script provides an example of the types of information you could display with the My Computer icon. The user ID could also be displayed by using the %USERNAME% environment variable. The file containing this script (MyComputerUpdate.2000_2003.ini) can be downloaded from the Web site for this book at http://www.awprofessional.com/title/1578702763.

Schedule Automatic Reboots

As discussed in Chapter 8, "Server Installation and Management Planning," it is not so much a question of whether or not you will schedule automatic reboots as it is a question of how frequently you will do so. Frequency and sophistication of this schedule depend on the applications in your environment and the system behavior you observe during testing and piloting.

I recommend that the reboot scheduling not be implemented until you've performed at least some preliminary testing with the applications on your Terminal Server. Only then can you determine the requirements for your reboot schedule. The stability of your environment will dictate whether reboots need to be performed nightly, weekly, monthly, or at even longer intervals.

NOTE: As Terminal Services has matured from the days of Windows NT 4.0, Terminal Server Edition, to the latest incarnation in Windows Server 2003, I've noticed a significant increase in the average server uptime between reboots. Reboot intervals of 21–35 days or more are not uncommon.

Conveniently, Windows 2000/2003 come with a command line tool called TSSHUTDN, which can be used in conjunction with the Scheduler Service and the AT command (or Scheduled Tasks) to automate shutdown and restart of your server. The full syntax of the TSSHUTDN command is described in Appendix A. The simplest implementation is as follows:

```
tsshutdn /reboot
```

This command shuts down and restarts the Terminal Server 60 seconds after being executed. Immediately after starting, it issues a message to all users on the Terminal Server, stating that the system will restart in 60 seconds. It sends another message at the 30-second mark and then restarts the server. For example, to schedule a Terminal Server to automatically reboot at 11 p.m. every Saturday with a 2-minute wait period, you could issue the following AT command:

```
at 23:00 /every:S "tsshutdn 120 /reboot"
```

The same task could be scheduled using the Scheduled Tasks tool, located under the Control Panel in both Windows 2000 Server and Windows Server 2003.

Configure Windows Time Service

In a Windows domain, the Windows Time Service (WTS) is automatically enabled and configured to retrieve the time settings for the local machine from a domain controller in the Active Directory domain. The purpose of WTS is to ensure that the system time on the local computer is synchronized with an external time source (in this case, the domain controller), which is assumed to be maintaining accurate time itself.

If your Terminal Server is or will be in an Active Directory domain, you have nothing further to do. WTS will be configured automatically. If your servers will not participate in a domain and instead will run in a workgroup, you may want to configure this service to ensure your Terminal Servers maintain accurate time. This can be performed using the w32tm command line tool. Issuing the following command forces the Terminal Server to synchronize its time with the provided WTS name(s).

```
w32tm /config /syncfromflags:manual /manualpeerlist:<"local or remote
time service>"
```

Performance Considerations

Once the basic stability and availability options have been configured, you can move on to apply a number of (sometimes subtle) changes to Terminal Server to help boost its overall performance. The same things apply here as for the stability and availability changes. Make sure you have a clear idea as to which changes are appropriate for your environment before you begin to actually implement the changes.

Disable Active Desktop

On a Windows 2000 Terminal Server, the Active Desktop feature is enabled by default, while on a Windows 2003 Terminal Server it is not. I recommend disabling the Active Desktop, as it can consume unnecessary resources and doesn't add any real value to use of applications on the server. To disable the Active Desktop, launch Terminal Services Configuration from the Administrative Tools option on the Start menu. Next click the Server Settings folder and then double-click the Active Desktop option and disable it, as shown in Figure 11.19.

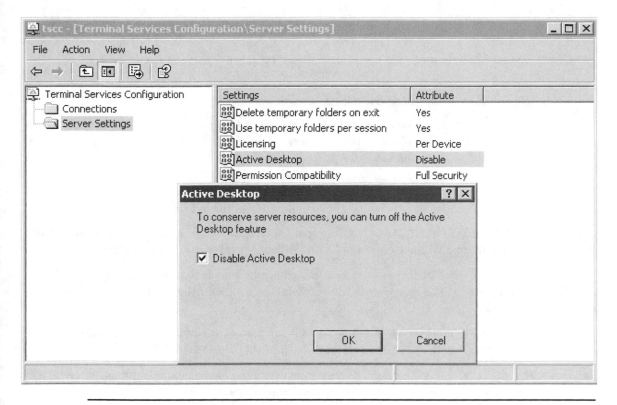

Figure 11.19 Disabling the Active Desktop option.

Minimize Windows Visual Effects

Windows provides a number of visual effects that, while attractive, can have a negative impact on the perceived speed and usability of a Terminal Server session. Even on a local area network, animated windows and menus may appear choppy and sluggish through an ICA or RDP client session. Through a combination of registry, profile, and policy changes, not only can you effectively eliminate (or minimize) all these visual effects, but you can also prevent your users from modifying these settings. The end result is a much smoother and perceptually faster user experience.

NOTE: Regardless of the changes you make in order to optimize performance of your Terminal Server, the only way most users will measure the speed of your system is through the responsiveness of the graphical interface. Even the slightest delay in how their remote session responds to their input can have the user complaining about how "slow" the system appears.

For now, I concentrate on the visual effects controlled through registry changes. Details on the associated profile and policy changes are discussed in detail in Chapter 15, "Group Policy Configuration," and Chapter 18, "User Profile and Account Configuration."

Define WinStation User Overrides

Terminal Server provides a registry key you can use to override the desktop and application behavior settings for all users who remotely log on to the Terminal Server. Any information that would normally appear under the registry key

HKEY_CURRENT_USER\ControlPanel\Desktop

can be overridden by placing the appropriate value in the following key:

HKEY_LOCAL_MACHINE\System\CurrentControlSet\Control\TerminalServer\Win Stations\<Winsta Connection Name>\UserOverride\Control Panel\Desktop

where <Winsta Connection Name> is the connection name that appears in Terminal Server Configuration. For example, the default RDP connection name is RDP-Tcp, so the corresponding registry key would be

HKEY_LOCAL_MACHINE\System\CurrentControlSet\Control\TerminalServer\Win Stations\RDP-Tcp\UserOverride\Control Panel\Desktop

Figure 11.20 shows the RDP-Tcp registry key with the recommended options defined. Many of these settings are equivalent to the default values found under HKEY_ CURRENT_USER\Control Panel\Desktop but are duplicated here to ensure that a user does not try and change them. Table 11.5 lists these recommended settings along with a brief description of what they do.

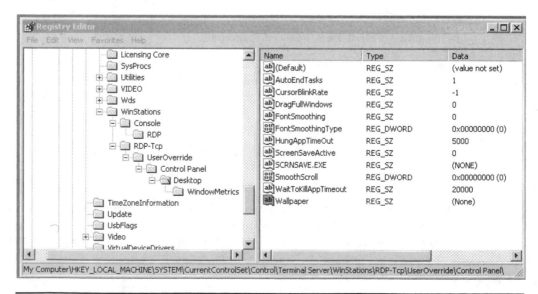

Figure 11.20 Recommended WinStation overrides for RDP-Tcp connections.

Table 11.5 Recommended WinStation Overrides

Key/Value Name	Value		Description
AutoEndTasks	REG_SZ	1	Automatically closes down any tasks that are "not responding." The wait time before these tasks are terminated is defined by WaitToKillAppTimeout.
CursorBlinkRate	REG_SZ	−1	The default value of 1200 sets the cursor to blink once every 1.2 seconds. Setting the value to −1 completely stops the blinking cursor. The value is in milliseconds.
DragFullWindows	REG_SZ	0	When set to 0, dragging a window will show only the outline instead of all contents.
FontSmoothing	REG_SZ	0	Turns off smooth edges for screen fonts.
FontSmoothingType	REG_DWORD	0x0	The specific smoothing type employed.
HungAppTimeout	REG_SZ	5000	This is the final amount of time that Windows will wait after it has decided to terminate an application before it actually does. The value is in milliseconds.
ScreenSaveActive	REG_SZ	0	Flags whether the screen saver is active or not.
SCRNSAVE.EXE	REG_SZ	(NONE)	The default screen saver for the user.
SmoothScroll	REG_DWORD	0	Turns off Smooth Scrolling in Windows. This does *not* disable Smooth Scrolling in Internet Explorer. That will be discussed in Chapter 15.
WaitToKillAppTimeout	REG_SZ	20000	The time that Windows will wait to see if a process will honor a shutdown request before it is considered to be "not responding."
Wallpaper	REG_SZ	(NONE)	This is the default for both 2003 and 2000. Users will not have a desktop wallpaper.
\WindowMetrics\ MinAnimate	REG_SZ	0	Turns off window animation when minimizing and maximizing.

Once these settings have been applied, the next time a user logs on using the corresponding connection type (RDP-Tcp, in this example), these settings automatically override any settings already set in the user's profile. If there are any users logged on when you make these changes, they will not pick up the settings until the next time they log off and back on.

TIP: If you will be installing Citrix MetaFrame, you will have to repeat this configuration for the ICA-Tcp WinStation connection.

Visual Effects in Windows Server 2003

While we are on the subject of Windows visual effects, it is worth discussing briefly the Visual Effects properties on a Windows 2003 server. Under the Advanced\Performance settings on the System Properties dialog box, you will find the new Visual Effects tab for Windows Server 2003 (see Figure 11.21). This tab allows you easy access to fine-tune the appearance and behavior of the Windows 2003 desktop. Some of the options discussed in the previous section ("Define Winstation User Overrides"), are also listed here.

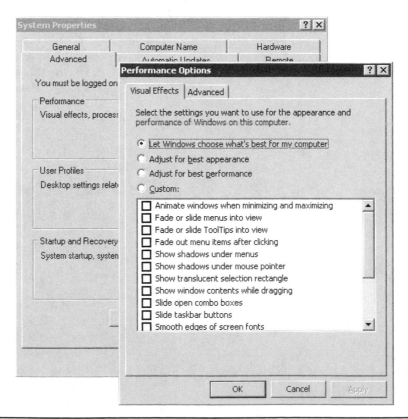

Figure 11.21 Explorer Visual Effects on Windows Server 2003.

The default option Let Windows Choose What's Best for My Computer recognizes a Terminal Server configuration and disables all but one of the visual effects listed on this screen. Although it may not be immediately clear, any changes made within this dialog box will affect *only* the user who is making the change. No other users are affected by any changes made here. Managing configuration and access to these settings for all users will require the use of group policies and user profiles, both discussed in detail in Chapters 15 and 18, respectively.

Optimize Memory Usage

The memory in a Windows 2000 or 2003 server is divided between the file system cache and the individual process working sets. The file system cache is used to store recently accessed data from the file system for quick retrieval. A working set is the portion of memory allocated by a process currently accessible in physical memory. If a process attempts to access memory currently not in physical memory, one of two things happens:

- A soft-page fault occurs if the page of memory being sought was recently reclaimed by the virtual memory manager but was not yet reallocated. Soft-page faults are processed relatively fast, although there is still a delay while the page is reallocated to the working set.
- A hard-page fault occurs if the memory must be retrieved from the pagefile. This impacts performance since the process must wait for the page to be retrieved from disk and assigned to the working set before it can be used.

The default configuration for both Windows 2000 and 2003 is to allocate more space to the *system cache*. This configuration is optimal when the server's role is that of a file and print server, since file system data can be retrieved quickly and there are a low number of processes running on the server. This is *not* the desired configuration for a Terminal Server. Instead of allocating the additional memory to the system cache, you want to maximize the available memory that can be used by process working sets, and thereby minimize the occurrence of hard-page faults.

The system cache allocation is controlled through the single registry value entitled LargeSystemCache, which is located in the registry key

HKEY_LOCAL_MACHINE\System\CurrentControlSet\Control\SessionManager\ Memory Management

While this value can be modified directly, both Windows Server 2003 and Windows 2000 Server provide a GUI interface that can modify this value appropriately.

Memory Usage on Windows Server 2003

The memory usage on Windows 2003 Server is controlled on the Advanced Performance Options screen, located under System Properties (see Figure 11.22). The recommended option is to select Programs versus selecting System Cache. Setting the memory usage option to Programs will set the LargeSystemCache value to 0. A reboot is required before this change takes effect.

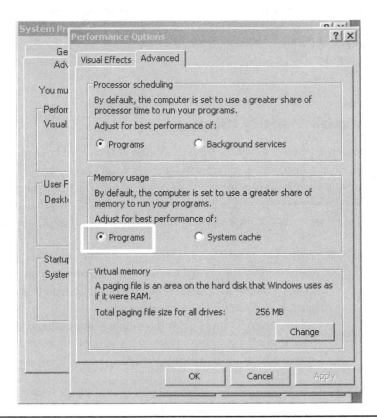

Figure 11.22   Managing System Cache allocation on Windows 2003 Server.

Memory Usage on Windows 2000 Server

On Windows 2000 Server there is no obvious Memory Usage dialog box. Instead you need to look in the most unlikely place, which is under the properties for File and Printer Sharing for Microsoft Networks. You can get to this dialog box by first opening Network and Dial-Up Connections, next opening the properties for Local Area Connection, and finally opening the properties for File and Printer Sharing for Microsoft Networks. Figure 11.23 shows the default option for Windows 2000 Server, while Table 11.6 summarizes how the different File and Printer Sharing properties affect the state of the LargeSystemCache registry entry.

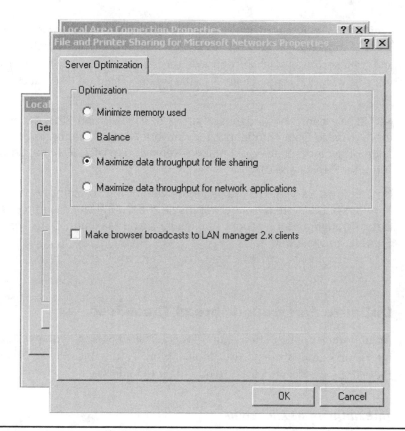

Figure 11.23   The File and Printer Sharing properties for Microsoft Networks is where the system cache setting is managed.

Table 11.6   LargeSystemCache State Based on File and Printer Sharing for Microsoft Networks Option

Optimization Setting	LargeSystemCache State
Minimize memory used.	Off
Balance.	Off
Maximize data throughput for file sharing.	On
Maximize data throughput for network applications.	Off

While conflicting information exists about whether Minimize Memory Used or Maximize Data Throughput for Network Applications is the ideal Optimization selection for a non–file and print server, I have had continued success selecting the latter. The Windows 2000 Server must be restarted before changes to the system cache will take effect.

NOTE: Microsoft knowledgebase articles 308186 and 228766 both discuss selecting the Maximize Data Throughput for Network Applications option to optimize performance of systems that would make extensive use of TCP/IP-based connections (as Terminal Server would).

On Windows Server 2003, toggling between the two Memory Usage options Programs and System Cache will toggle the Optimization setting between Maximize Data Throughput for Network Applications and Maximize Data Throughput for File Sharing, respectively.

Optimize Foreground Thread Timeslices

An important configuration option for a Terminal Server is the optimization of the timeslicing for foreground thread execution. Before getting into the details on the configuration, there are some details I feel are important to understand.

Thread Quantum Allocation

As you know, Windows 2000 and 2003 Server are preemptive multitasking operating systems, whose thread execution is priority-based. This means that the highest priority thread that is in the ready state will always be the next to access the processor.

Once a thread has been selected to run, it has a maximum *timeslice* in which it is allowed to execute. This timeslice is measured in *quantums*. A thread's quantum is decremented by the system at specific intervals during the thread's execution. Once the thread's quantum has been reduced to zero, if there is another thread at the same priority level, then the current thread enters a wait state and the other thread is allowed to execute. If there are no other threads at the current priority level, the thread is assigned a new quantum value and allowed to immediately return to the processor.

I should mention that any higher priority threads that become ready to execute are immediately able to preempt a lower priority thread and begin execution on a processor. Once that higher priority thread has completed, the preempted thread is the first to be able to resume processing.

A thread's quantum is in no way associated with the priority of the thread. Regardless of a thread's priority it will receive the same initial quantum length as any other thread. When a thread is created it will inherit the base priority of its parent process, but unlike a process its priority may be temporarily increased by the system in order to service a request that needs immediate attention.

In order to see the current priority of a process's individual threads you will need to use Performance Monitor. Figure 11.24 shows an example of the base and current priorities for a Microsoft WordPad process and its associated threads. You can clearly see the temporarily elevated priority of 12 assigned to a thread as it responds to mouse activity and keyboard input, followed by a decline back down to the base priority of 8 as the boost is decremented by the system.

After receiving a priority boost, a thread will run at that priority level for one quantum unit, at which time the thread will drop back down one priority level. This continues until the thread is once again at its base priority. Looking again at Figure 11.24 we clearly see the priority decrementing, indicating the thread has expended quantum units of processing. You may notice threads that seem to run at an elevated privilege for quite a while before being decremented. This is actually because the thread is awaiting some input and is not running. Until it returns from the wait and consumes a quantum, it remains at the same priority level.

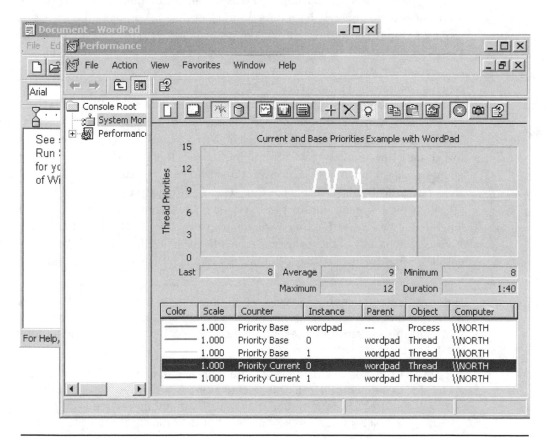

Figure 11.24 An example of a thread's priority temporarily elevating during execution.

You are probably wondering: Then, how many quantum units does Windows assign to each thread? Table 11.7 lists the default quantum units assigned to a thread for Windows 2000/XP Professional and for a Windows 2000/2003 server prior to its beginning execution.

Table 11.7   Default Quantum Units Assigned to a Thread Based on the Operating System

Operating System	Starting Quantum Value
Windows 2000/XP Professional	6
Windows 2000/2003 server	36

The number of assigned quantum units is set higher by default on a Windows 2000/2003 server in order to try and give a thread sufficient time to complete the execution of a client request before its quantum expires and it is forced to relinquish execution to another thread. On Windows XP or 2000 Professional, shorter quantum values are assigned in order to make applications more responsive to user input and also to allow more threads to be serviced in a timely fashion.

In addition to using the shorter quantum values, 2000/XP Professional also institutes quantum boosting for foreground applications versus background applications. Initially all threads are assigned the same quantum length of 6, but when an application is running in the foreground (the window that currently has focus), the system will immediately boost the quantum values for all of that process's threads to be 1 to 3 times the base quantum length. By default, this boost will triple the thread's current quantum from 6 to 18.

Boosting the quantum for the foreground threads provides more favorable access by lengthening the processing time without adversely affecting the execution of other threads. Because the priority of these threads has not been changed, other background processes still get their opportunity to execute, but just not as much time as the foreground threads.

Note: A common question asked is, "So how long is a quantum?" A quantum is not an actual unit of time. Quantum units are consumed based on different execution states in the system. Some examples under which quantum are consumed include the following:

- During each clock interval the currently running thread has its quantum decremented by 3. This occurs even if the thread has not run for an entire interval. So one thread may have its quantum reduced after running for only 2 milliseconds (ms), while another may run for 9 ms before it loses 3 quantum units.

- When a thread goes into a wait state, its quantum is typically (but not always) decremented by 1.

Because quantums are decremented by 3 during every clock interrupt, they are usually treated as being equal to one-third of a system's clock interval. The clock interval is dependent on the server's hardware, but typically it is 10 milliseconds on a uniprocessor Intel x86 system and 15 milliseconds on a multiprocessor x86 system.

Configuring Thread Quantum Values

On a Windows 2000/2003 server you have the option of switching the server to favor applications over background processes. This is done on the Advanced tab of the Performance Options dialog box, which is accessed through the properties for My Computer, shown in figure 11.25. Changing this option will *immediately* affect the quantum assignments for all threads on the server. You are not required to perform a reboot. When a Windows 2000/2003 server is configured as a Terminal Server, the Programs option (labeled "Applications" on Windows 2000) is selected by default, and the server is configured to use the same quantum configuration settings as a Windows 2000/XP Professional installation.

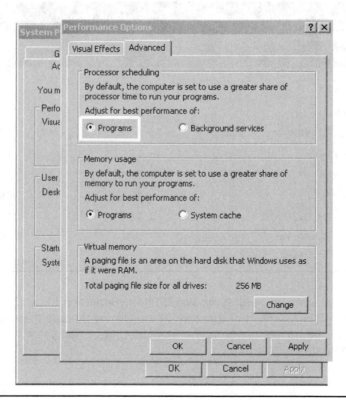

Figure 11.25   Configuring processor scheduling on a Windows 2003 Terminal Server.

TIP: Changing between the Programs option and the Background Services option will update the registry value Win32PrioritySeparation located in this registry key:

HKEY_LOCAL_MACHINE\System\CurrentControlSet\Control\PriorityControl\

The numeric value stored here specifies the default quantum value assigned to all threads as well as the boost that should be applied to the foreground applications on the server. This two-digit hexadecimal value is used to create an index into an in-memory quantum table, where the appropriate quantum information to use is stored. By changing this registry entry you can affect how quantum values are assigned. Table 11.8 summarizes the different values for Win32PrioritySeparation and how these affect the default quantum value for all processes, as well as the boosted value for foreground processes. The value 0x26 corresponds to the Programs option, while 0x18 corresponds to the Background Services option.

Table 11.8   Default and Boosted Quantum Values Based on the Win32PrioritySeparation Value

Win32PrioritySeparation Value (Hexadecimal)	Default Thread Quantum	Boosted Foreground Thread Quantum
0x24	6	6
0x25	6	12
0x26 (Programs)	6	18
0x14	12	12
0x15	12	24
0x16	12	36
0x28, 0x29, 0x2A	18	18
0x18 (Background Services), 0x19, 0x1A	36	36

So, for example, setting the Win32PrioritySepartion to 0x15, would assign all threads the default quantum of 12, and all foreground threads the boosted quantum of 24. When the boosted value is the same as the default value, this means that no boost is actually assigned.

The information I have touched on here is only the tip of the complete story on how Windows 2000/2003 manages thread scheduling and priority assignment. For more detailed information on this subject, including a more thorough treatment on exactly how the values for Win32PrioritySeparation are derived, please see the following:

- Description of performance options in Windows—Microsoft knowledgebase article number 259025.
- Win2K quantums, system internals—http://www.sysinternals.com/ntw2k/info/nt5.shtml.
- "Inside the Windows NT Scheduler"—*Windows* and *.NET Magazine*, instant doc #302, http://www.winntmag.com.
- *Inside Microsoft Windows 2000, Third Edition*—David A. Solomon and Mark E. Russinovich. Probably the ultimate Windows architecture reference.

Recommended Thread Quantum Settings

Now that you have a clear understanding of how thread timeslicing works and how quantum values are assigned, we can look at what settings are appropriate for a Terminal Server. Table 11.9 summarizes my suggested settings based on a couple of Terminal Server configurations. Under almost all circumstances, the Performance Options setting of Programs is appropriate for a Terminal Server.

Table 11.9   Suggested Quantum Tuning for Different Terminal Server Configurations

Terminal Server Configuration	Suggested Setting	Comments
Dedicated Terminal Server providing only user sessions and running no additional services.	Programs setting under the Performance Options dialog box. Equivalent to setting Win32PrioritySeparation to 0×26.	This configuration is appropriate for most standard Terminal Server installations. Uses a default and boosted quantum of 6 and 18, respectively.
Small Terminal Server deployment running both user sessions and additional services such as IIS.	Win32PrioritySeparation set to 0×15 or 0×16.	This raises the default quantum setting from 6 to 12, which will benefit background processes while still boosting foreground apps to minimize the impact on user sessions.

Note: In the past, many people (including myself) have configured Terminal Servers to use Background Services as the preferred configuration, with the assumption that this would even the playing field for all processes and prevent any kind of backlog of boosted foreground sessions waiting for access to the CPU that might result from using the Programs option. At least for myself, part of this reasoning was a result of the false assumption that foreground tasks were actually receiving a priority boost, not just a quantum boost.

In actual fact, all this change was doing was lengthening the default quantum assigned to all threads on the system (up to 36 from 6). In most situations there was no discernible difference to the users, since they typically ran Office-type applications such as Word or Excel, and no additional processor-intensive background applications were running on the server. So even though background processes were running with a longer quantum, most were simply waiting for user input while the foreground task was running. The thread scheduling on Windows ensured that applications still responded in a timely fashion by boosting the priority of a process when necessary.

Where this change may have caused problems was if poorly behaved applications were looking to acquire processor time even while in the background. The longer quantum value would permit this application to hog the processor for longer periods of time before having to relinquish execution.

Disable Error Reporting

This change applies only to Windows Server 2003.

A new feature available with Windows Server 2003 is the Error Reporting service. This tool monitors the system for any user-mode or kernel-mode exception errors that may occur. When a user-mode error occurs, the service displays a dialog box (see Figure 11.26) asking the user choose between Send Error Report and Don't Send. Clicking Send Error Report immediately sends the error report anonymously to Microsoft via the Internet, using SSL.

When a kernel-mode exception occurs (Blue Screen of Death), the next time the system boots up and you log on, a dialog box appears prompting you to provide an explanation as to why the system shut down unexpectedly. The Error Reporting service then generates a report that can be sent to Microsoft. While the kernel-mode feature might be useful in troubleshooting a recurring problem, I suggest that this feature not be enabled by default. Not only does the service provide additional overhead, but also you may end up with users sending reports to Microsoft concerning internal application issues.

This feature can be configured on the Error Reporting screen, located at the bottom of the Advanced tab on the System Properties dialog box, as shown in figure 11.27. Select the Disable Error Reporting option. If you check the option But Notify Me When Critical Errors Occur, a user will still see the exception error message displayed, but minus the Send/Don't Send options.

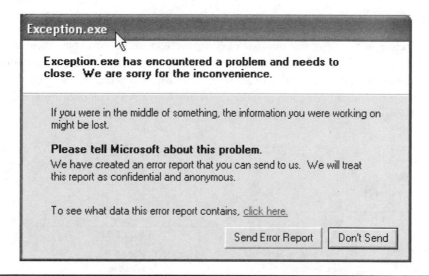

Figure 11.26 User-mode exception errors will prompt the user to choose whether to report the problem to Microsoft or not.

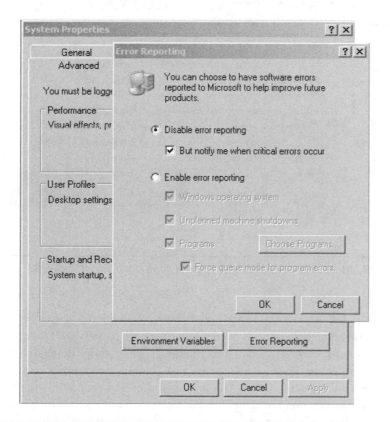

Figure 11.27 The Error Reporting configuration screen in Windows Server 2003.

Stop Unnecessary System Services

Even after minimizing the number of components installed on your Terminal Server, there still are a few additional services that can be stopped in order to free up additional processor and memory capacity. You can quickly view the list of running services by right-clicking My Computer, selecting Manage, and then selecting the Services icon located under Services and Applications, as shown in figure 11.28.

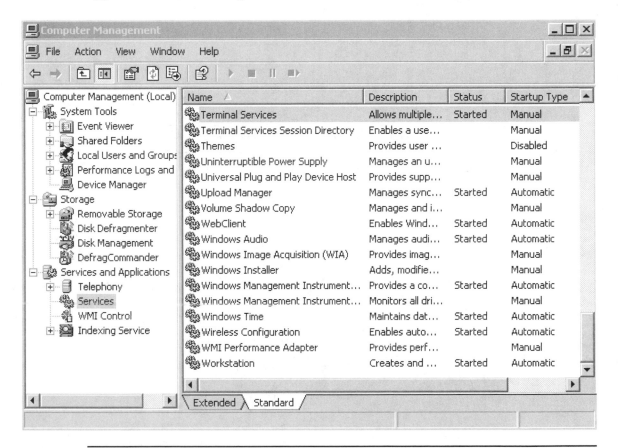

Figure 11.28 Example of the running services on a Windows 2003 Terminal Server.

Table 11.10 summarizes the services that will typically be running after a standard Terminal Server installation and are good candidates for being stopped. Make sure that you verify that a service is not required in your configuration before you decide to stop it.

When stopping a service, make sure that you also configure it to have a startup type of either Manual or Disabled. My suggestion would be to select Manual the first time you have stopped the service and check upon reboot to see whether it has been enabled again or not. If it has restarted, there may be another service or application that is dependent on this service in order to run. If this is the case, you may not be able to stop this service. To change the startup type for a service, simply right-click the service, select Properties, and then go to the General tab.

Table 11.10 Services to Consider Stopping on a Terminal Server

Service Name	Description
Alerter	If you are not using administrative alerts, you can stop this service. This service is disabled by default in Windows 2003.
Automatic Updates	Enables downloading and installing Windows updates. Even if you have turned off Automatic Updates, this service will run. Depending on how you are managing critical updates to your server, this service may not be required. See Chapter 9 for details on properly managing updates in a Terminal Server environment.
DHCP Client	Unless your server is using DHCP to acquire an IP address, you can stop this service.
Distributed Link Tracking Client	This service is responsible for gathering link source information and transmitting any changes back to the distributed link-tracking server, which would run on a domain controller. This service is not required on Terminal Server and can be disabled.
Error Reporting	(2003 only.) Even if you have disabled error reporting, this service continues to run. If you are not using the Error Reporting features of this service, it can be disabled. You will not be able to immediately stop this service, but setting it to Manual prevents it from starting on a reboot.
Help and Support Center	(2003 only.) This persistent service is a core component of the new Help and Support option available from the Start menu on Windows Server 2003. Even if you have stopped and disabled this service, it immediately restarts the next time anyone runs Help and Support. The only way to stop this for good is to hide the Help option through use of a group policy and then stop this service. In a production Terminal Server environment, you probably will not want to run the Help and Support Center service.
License Logging	This service monitors and records client access license usage on the server. It does not manage Terminal Server client access licenses, only the traditional Windows access licenses. This service also automatically replicates license information to the licensing service on a domain controller. Disabling this service halts license monitoring but *not* license enforcement.

Table 11.10 Services to Consider Stopping on a Terminal Server (continued)

Service Name	Description
Messenger	Messenger is responsible for transmission of "net send" and Alerter service messages. Stopping this service will not affect usage of the Terminal Server MSG function. See Appendix A for a complete description of the MSG messaging command. This service is disabled by default on Windows 2003.
Portable Media Serial Number	(2003 only.) Retrieves serial numbers from connected portable music devices. Not needed on a Terminal Server.
Remote Access *Auto* Connection Manager	This service becomes active when there is no network connection and offers to make connections to dial-up or VPN networks if necessary to establish connections with a remote address. Not normally required on a Terminal Server. *Don't* attempt to disable the other similarly named service, Remote Access Connection Manager, as this is a required component of the Network Connections folder.
Remote Registry	Allows remote users to modify the registry settings on this server. Definitely a good candidate to be stopped, not only to conserve resources but also as a security consideration. This service is disabled by default on Windows 2003.
Shell Hardware Detection	(2003 only.) Handles the detection and notification of AutoPlay events. Disabling this prevents the standard AutoPlay of CDs from occurring.
SSDP Discovery	(2003 only.) Allows for discovery of UPnP (Universal Plug and Play) devices on your network. Not a service that is necessary on a Terminal Server.
Wireless Configuration	(2003 only.) This is part of the wireless zero configuration support for wireless devices by Microsoft. Unless you are running an 802.11 wireless adapter in your server, you will not require this service.

Remove Unnecessary User Startup Applications

Many applications today add one or more entries to the registry during installation so that instances of certain processes are running every time a user logs on to the system. What happens is that you have multiple users all running instances of the same application, which typically is not necessary and ultimately results in waste of system resources.

For each of the following registry keys, you should examine the entries and remove any not required for your configuration. Fortunately, both Windows 2000 and 2003 do not have any entries in these locations after a base installation.

The most common location where applications are defined to run during a user's logon is this registry key:

HKLM\Software\Microsoft\Windows\Current Version\Run

Applications defined in this location will be launched for every user who logs on to the Terminal Server. The associated registry location to examine is

HKLM\Software\Microsoft\Windows NT\CurrentVersion\Terminal Server\Install\Software\Microsoft\Windows\CurrentVersion\Run

This location is where any Run entries created on a per-user basis are added during an application installation. Removing them from here ensures that they are not replicated into the user's profile the next time they log on. In Chapter 21, "Application Integration," I talk in detail about application installation and how Windows handles the necessary file and registry replication.

After a base Windows 2000/2003 installation, a couple of registry locations will contain startup entries that should not be modified. First, the registry key HKLM\Software\ Microsoft\Windows NT\CurrentVersion\WinLogon\AppSetup will contain the entry UsrLogon.cmd, which is the main Application Compatibility Script (ACS). This entry should not be changed unless you wish to completely disable the ACS feature. If you have installed MetaFrame, you will also find the entry cmstart.exe. This executable is responsible for launching the various client device-mapping processes.

The final location to review is

HKLM\Software\Microsoft\Windows NT\CurrentVersion\WinLogon\UserInit

Normally there should be only one entry here. This is %SystemRoot%\System32\ userinit.exe. This entry is responsible for launching the Explorer shell when a user first logs on. It is not a common location to add startup processes, so you may want to view any entries here with some suspicion.

TIP: A good habit to get in to is reviewing these registry keys on a regular basis to ensure that there are no applications launching within your user sessions that you're not aware of. I normally review these keys immediately after installing a new application onto a Terminal Server, particularly an application I'm not already familiar with.

Disable NT Executive Paging

On Terminal Servers with large amounts of physical memory, you can provide a response boost to the server by forcing drivers (user-mode and kernel-mode) and system code to remain in memory, even if they were written to be "pageable." Even on large memory systems, these pageable components may be swapped out to disk unless this option is set. The following registry key handles this option:

HKEY_LOCAL_MACHINE\SYSTEM\CurrentControlSet\Control\Session Manager\Memory Management

The REG_DWORD value to modify is DisablePagingExecutive. Setting this value to 0×1 will turn off the paging of these drivers and system code to disk.

WARNING: This option consumes additional physical memory, so you should ensure that your server is not operating at full physical memory utilization under regular user load before configuring this setting. Doing so will result in less physical memory being available for the user sessions and increased pagefile usage. Enabling this option on a server with insufficient physical memory can result in an unstable server.

Disable Last Access Time Update on Directory Listings

By default, Windows updates the last access time on each directory when traversed. You can provide a slight disk-read performance increase by disabling this option, since users on a Terminal Server will mostly be performing file reads on the server. You can turn off this default behavior. For the registry key

HKLM\System\CurrentControlSet\Control\FileSystem

add the new value:

```
NTFSDisableLastAccessUpdate REG_DWORD
```

and set it to 0×1. A reboot is required in order for this change to take effect.

Manage Disk Fragmentation

Over time, as files (and folders) are created and deleted on a disk volume, the files tend to become fragmented. When a file is fragmented, it does not occupy a single contiguous space on the disk but instead is broken down into multiple pieces (clusters) that are spread out across the disk. The result is the need for multiple disk reads in order to retrieve all the information for a file. Fragmentation is also a problem with write operations. As files are deleted, small "holes" of free space develop on the disk. When a new file is written, the file system attempts to fill these holes with the contents of the file. If the file is too large to occupy the first hole, a portion of the file's contents are written to the first hole, and the remainder is written to the next available hole(s).

As a volume becomes more and more fragmented, the performance of the server can be adversely impacted, particularly when a large amount of read and write operations are occurring. Typically, file servers are the most susceptible to high amounts of fragmentation as users read, write, and delete files. On a Terminal Server, the amount of fragmentation is usually lower, since users have limited access to perform write and delete operations on the server.

Even so, each of the separate disks and partitions on your server should be examined individually to determine its defragmentation requirements:

- **System volume**—This is where the majority of fragmentation usually occurs, since each user's profile and temporary folders are stored here. Typically I suggest performing a defragment on the system volume once every month or so, although the schedule frequency for your environment will depend on your fragmentation reports. Ideally you should schedule the defrag to occur either when the server is out of production or during off-peak times so as not to affect users.
- **Pagefile volume**—Typically, very little file fragmentation will occur when the pagefile is located on its own physical disk. If the pagefile is maintained on a volume with other data or applications, fragmentation can be more of an issue. The pagefile and other system files such as the registry hives or event logs cannot be defragmented during normal server operation, as these files are in use. These files can be defragmented only during system startup. I discuss this further in the "Manage Pagefile and Registry Fragmentation" section of this chapter.
- **Application volume**—Very little fragmentation should occur on the application volume, since users should have no (or only minimal) write or delete access. Normally I suggest that you defragment the application volume after you have completed installation and configuration of all the applications on your Terminal Server. A scheduled defrag is not normally required.

Defragmentation Software

Software solutions are available to remedy the situation of fragmented volumes. Windows 2000 and 2003 ship with a tool called Disk Defragmenter, which is a limited version of the full commercial product called Diskeeper from Executive Software. To start Disk Defragmenter, open Administrative Tools from the Start menu and then select Disk Defragmenter after opening the Computer Management application. A dialog box appears, similar to the one in Figure 11.29.

Before defragmenting a disk you should analyze the drive to determine whether a defrag is required. Simply select the drive you want to analyze from the top portion of the Disk Defragmenter tool and then click the Analyze button located near the bottom. A pop-up box indicates whether the volume should be defragged; if you want to continue with the defrag, click the Defragment button to begin.

While the Disk Defragmenter tool that's included in Windows 2000/2003 is useful, there are a few limitations (see Table 11.11), particularly with the Windows 2000 version.

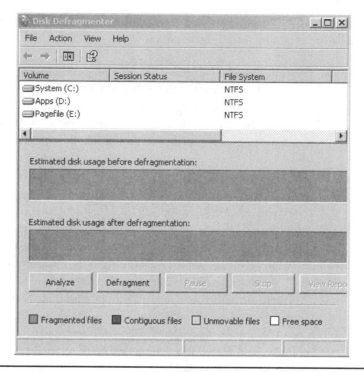

Figure 11.29   Disk Defragmenter in Windows Server 2003.

Table 11.11   Limitations in Windows Disk Defragmenter

Limitation	Windows 2000	Windows 2003
Can defragment only local volumes.	*True.*	*True.*
Can defragment/analyze only one volume at a time.	*True.*	*True.*
This includes the command line version, which can have only one running instance at a time.		
Cannot be scheduled.	*True.*	*False.*
The command line version of Disk Defragmenter can be scheduled using the task scheduler.		
Cannot be configured from a command prompt.	*True.*	*False.*

Windows Server 2003 ships with a command line version of Disk Defragmenter called DEFRAG.EXE.

Windows Server 2003 Disk Defragmentation

The addition of the command line version of Disk Defragmenter in Windows Server 2003 lets you schedule the unattended defragmentation of volumes on a Windows 2003 Terminal Server without the need to buy third-party software. For example, the following would schedule the automatic defrag of the C: drive every Sunday morning at 1:23 a.m.

```
at 1:23 /every:Su defrag c:
```

The only thing you won't get with this is an output report summarizing what was done. The solution to this is to schedule a batch file containing DEFRAG.EXE, as shown in Listing 11.2, instead of scheduling DEFRAG.EXE directly.

Listing 11.2   Using the RUNDEFRAG.CMD File to Capture DEFRAG.EXE Output

```
ECHO OFF
REM ** Pipes the DEFRAG.EXE output to a file that can then be examined
REM ** to ensure the scheduled job ran properly. The output goes into
REM ** the c:\DefragReport folder.

defrag.exe c: > c:\DefragReport\defrag.output.txt
```

The batch is scheduled by running:

```
at 1:23 /every:Su RUNDEFRAG.CMD
```

If the batch file is not located in the SYSTEM32 folder, you will need to include the full path in the AT scheduler command.

Windows 2000 Disk Defragmentation

The lack of support in Windows 2000 for scheduling, either through the GUI or the command prompt, is what limits this tool's effectiveness in a Windows 2000 Terminal Server environment. In order to defragment a volume, you need to log on to the Terminal Server, launch the tool, and then perform the defrag one at a time on each desired volume. In order to schedule disk defragmentation, you need to look at third-party tools. Two products I have used in the past on Terminal Server are

- **Defrag Commander (Winternals Software)**—A simple yet effective tool that provides all the key features missing from the Windows Disk Defragmenter. From within a single MMC snap-in you can configure and schedule defragmentation jobs on all your servers without having to install any client software on them. The number of remotely manageable servers is dependent on the number of licenses purchased. A 30-day trial version is available from http://www.winternals.com.

■ **Diskeeper (Executive Software)**—The full version of Diskeeper provides a number of enhancements over the basic version that ships with Windows 2000/2003, including boot-time defragmentation of the pagefile, movement of directories to the front of a volume, and multiple simultaneous volume defragging. A licensed version of Diskeeper must be installed on each server. A 30-day trial version is available from http://www.diskeeper.com.

Manage Pagefile and Registry Fragmentation

As I alluded to briefly in the previous section, system files such as the pagefile or the registry hives cannot be defragmented during normal system operation and must be processed during system startup. To ensure that fragmentation is kept to a minimum, I recommend periodic defragmentation of these files (either manual or automated). While Windows 2000/2003 provides no built-in mechanism for compacting these resources (Windows Disk Defragmenter is not able to defragment the pagefile or registry files), alternate solutions are available:

■ **Diskeeper (Executive Software)**—In addition to this full-featured commercial product's supporting standard file defragmentation, it is able to automatically defragment the pagefile during system startup. A 30-day trial version is available from http://www.diskeeper.com.

■ **PageDefrag (SysInternals)**—This freeware utility lets you view the current state of fragmentation in the registry hive files, event log files, and pagefile and provides the option of automatically scheduling a defragmentation either during the next restart or after every future restart. Figure 11.30 shows the main window for PageDefrag. This utility is available free from http://www.sysinternals.com.

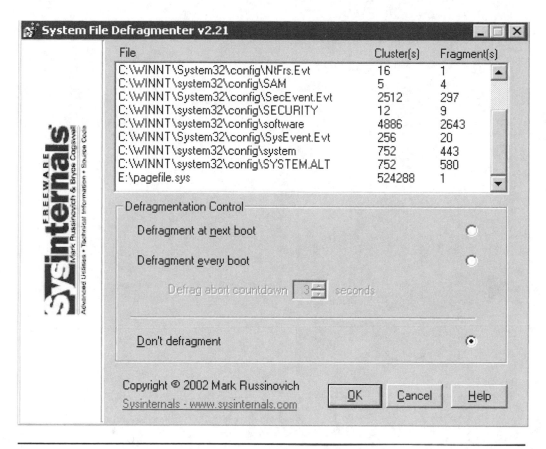

Figure 11.30 SysInternals' PageDefrag utility.

CHAPTER 12

Licensing Service Installation and Configuration

Before You Begin

This chapter looks at the installation and configuration of the client access license (CAL) management services for both Terminal Server and MetaFrame Presentation Server. In order to run these products, a separate licensing service must be installed and configured for each product to enforce proper user access license compliance. A grace period is provided by each vendor (these durations are discussed shortly) before the corresponding licensing service must be "activated" and purchased licenses installed for client use. These grace periods exist to allow an administrator time to test out the proposed implementation and make any necessary changes without having to worry about reactivating the required licenses. Before getting into the details of the installation and configuration, I quickly summarize the licensing requirements and behavior of Terminal Services and MetaFrame.

Windows 2000 and 2003 Terminal Services Licensing Requirements Summary

Licensing requirements for Windows 2000 and 2003 Terminal Server are compared and summarized in the two following lists. More detailed information on Terminal Server licensing was discussed in Chapter 1, "Microsoft Windows Terminal Services."

License Server Requirements

- Whenever one or more Windows servers are configured to run as Terminal Servers (Application Server mode, in Windows 2000), a server running the Terminal Services licensing service is also required. A Windows server running Remote Desktop for Administration (Remote Administration mode, in Windows 2000) does *not* require a license server.
- A Windows Terminal Server will function without a licensing server for a specified grace period before remote connections are denied. Even after the grace period, logons directly from the console (not using a remote console session) will be allowed. The grace period durations are as follows:

  - Windows 2000 Server: 90 days
  - Windows Server 2003: 120 days

- Where the Terminal Services licensing service can actually reside will depend on what Terminal Server version is being used, as well as within what domain configuration the Terminal Server resides. Table 12.1 summarizes the host options for the licensing service.

Table 12.1   Terminal Server Licensing Service Host Options

Windows Terminal Server Version	Windows Domain/ Workgroup	Notes
Windows 2000 or 2003	Workgroup or NT 4 domain	The licensing service can reside on any Windows server, including the Terminal Server itself.
		A Terminal Server will check the LicenseServers (DefaultLicenseServer, in Windows 2000) registry key and, if that does not exist, it will broadcast on the network looking for all available license servers. One is then chosen at random to use.
Windows 2000	Windows 2000 or 2003 domain	The license server must reside on a domain controller within which the Terminal Server resides.
		The Terminal Server will first check the DefaultLicenseServer registry key and, if that doesn't exist, will query all domain controllers for available licensing servers. One is chosen at random from the list returned.

Table 12.1   Terminal Server Licensing Service Host Options (continued)

Windows Terminal Server Version	Windows Domain/ Workgroup	Notes
Windows 2003	Windows 2003 domain	If no license servers are returned for the same domain as the Terminal Server, the Terminal Server will query the Active Directory for an Enterprise License Server.
		Note that a Windows 2003 Terminal Services License Server can service license requests from a Windows 2000 Terminal Server. The licensing service obeys Windows 2000 rules for license allocation when receiving a license request from a Windows 2000 Terminal Server.
		The Windows 2003 Terminal Server will first query the LicenseServers registry key for a list of specified license servers. If no entry is listed, the Terminal Server next attempts to locate an Enterprise License Server by querying the active directory.
		Failing that, the Terminal Server queries all domain controllers within the same site and, if still no license servers are found, finally queries all domain controllers.
		From all the domain controllers returned for a specific method, one is chosen at random.
		The Windows 2003 Terminal Services licensing service can reside on a member server in the domain, but in order for the Terminal Server to find it, an entry must be added to the LicenseServers registry key. One exception to this is if the license service on a member server is installed as an Enterprise License Service. In this scenario, an entry is added to the Active Directory that allows a Terminal Server to locate it properly.
		Note: A Windows 2000 Terminal Services licensing server can service only Windows 2000 Terminal Servers. It will not allocate or manage license requests from Windows Server 2003 Terminal Servers.

TIP: Adding an entry to the registry specifying the desired license server will override the normal discovery process. If a license server is listed in the registry but is unavailable, the Terminal Server will not attempt to find a license server using an alternate method. Populating the appropriate registry key is discussed a little later in this chapter.

■ The license server maintains license information within a Microsoft Jet database that exists locally on the license server. The license file itself is called TLSLic.edb and is located in

   %SystemRoot%\System32\LServer

On average the storage requirements for each assigned license are less than 1KB, so an allocation of 1500 licenses would be expected to consume less than 1.5MB of total disk space.

■ During installation the license service can be defined as an Enterprise License Server, allowing it to automatically service client licenses to Terminal Servers residing in different domains within the same forest.

■ Once a license server has been discovered, the Terminal Server continues to use this same server unless it becomes unavailable. Availability of this license server is confirmed by the Terminal Server once every hour. If the license server cannot be located, the query for an alternate license server is immediately initiated.

■ If a license server has no permanent Terminal Server device tokens available for issuance to a requesting Terminal Server, it queries the other license servers in the domain to see if they have an available token. If a token is available on another server, the first license server requests that token from the other license server and then passes it on to the requesting Terminal Server.

Terminal Services Client Access Licensing Requirements

■ Any client connecting to a Terminal Server requires a valid Terminal Server Client Access License (TSCAL), issued by the Terminal Server licensing server.

■ Until activated, the Terminal Services licensing server issues only temporary TSCALs, good for only 90 days to the requesting clients. If a permanent license is not issued to the client within that time frame, the temporary license expires and the client is no longer able to connect to the server. The licensing server itself is activated through a Microsoft clearinghouse; this process is explained in the "Activating a Windows 2000 Terminal Services License Server" and "Activating a Windows 2003 Terminal Services License Server" sections of this chapter.

■ The exact type of client license required varies based on the version of Terminal Server being implemented and is summarized in Table 12.2 and Table 12.3.

Table 12.2 Supported Windows 2000 Terminal Server Client Access Licenses

Available License Types	Notes
Per Device licensing	Only one type of client licensing is supported with Windows 2000 Terminal Services; this is known as *Per Device licensing*.
	With Per Device licensing, a separate TSCAL must be purchased for each device that will be connecting to the Terminal Server with the exception of devices running Windows 2000 Professional or Windows XP Professional. Devices running one of these operating systems are issued *built-in* client access licenses by the licensing service. A built-in license is automatically available for use and never expires.
	All other devices such as Windows 98, Windows ME, Linux, and so on must acquire a permanent license that was purchased and installed on the license server. Purchased Terminal Server CALs must also be activated through the Microsoft clearinghouse. If no purchased licenses are available for these devices, the server issues a temporary license to the client that is valid for 90 days. If no purchased license is available within that time frame to replace the temporary license, the device is no longer able to connect.
	Client devices retain and use the same permanent client device license they were issued the first time they successfully logged on to the Terminal Server. This license is not relinquished when the user logs off. Because of this, the pool of available licenses diminishes as devices connect and licenses are allocated by the server.
	In order to facilitate the recovery of licenses that may have accidentally been assigned to the wrong device, an expiry date between 52 and 89 days is assigned to the license token when issued. If no validation occurs within 7 days of the expiration date, the license server automatically recovers the license and makes it available for re-use. This automated recovery feature was not present in the original Windows 2000 Server release but was added as a hotfix and eventually incorporated into Service Pack 3. As long as you are running Service Pack 3 or later for Windows 2000, this feature will automatically be included and available.
Internet Connector License (ICL)	Windows 2000 also supports a special type of licensing called Internet Connector Licenses. These licenses are used to allow up to 200 concurrent anonymous non-employee connections to the Terminal Server. If a Terminal Server is configured to request ICLs, it will not process regular Terminal Services licenses. Any user connecting to this Terminal Server will be assigned an ICL and automatically be logged on using the special TSInternetUser account.
	The ICL is installed on the Windows 2000 license server, and then the Terminal Servers that will utilize this license must each be configured within the Terminal Services Configuration tool, as shown in Figure 12.1.

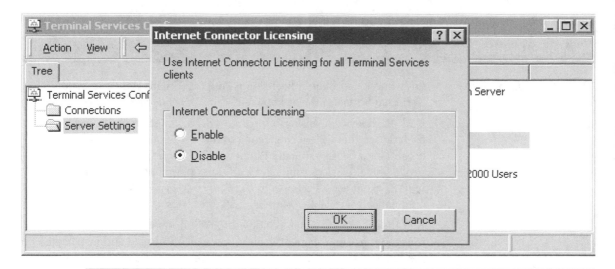

Figure 12.1 Enabling the Internet Connector License on a Windows 2000 Terminal Server.

Table 12.3 Supported Windows 2003 Terminal Server Client Access Licenses

Available License Types	Notes
Per Device licensing	Windows 2003 Terminal Services licensing also supports Per Device licensing, which is almost identical to the support for Per Device licensing in Windows 2000. The main difference is that Windows Server 2003 no longer provides support for built-in licenses.
	For operating in Per Device mode, a separate TSCAL must be purchased for each device that will connect to a Windows 2003 Terminal Server, including clients running Windows 2000 Professional, Windows XP Professional, or later Windows client operating system versions. Unlike Windows 2000 licensing, Windows Server 2003 will not issue built-in licenses to clients connecting to a Windows 2003 Terminal Server. A 2003 license server *will* honor the original licensing model and issue a built-in license to a valid client connecting to a Windows 2000 Terminal Server that is using a 2003 license server. Windows Server 2003 supports five types of Per Device licenses:
	■ Temporary Windows 2000 TSCAL ■ Temporary Windows 2003 TSCAL ■ Permanent Windows 2000 TSCAL ■ Permanent Windows 2003 TSCAL ■ Existing (built-in) Windows 2000 TSCAL

Table 12.3   Supported Windows 2003 Terminal Server Client Access Licenses (continued)

Available License Types	Notes
Per User licensing	A new Terminal Services licensing model has been introduced with Windows 2003; this is known as Per User licensing. Per Device licensing ties the license to the device, regardless of the user on that device. Per User licensing ties the license to the user, regardless of what device they are connecting from.
	Unlike Per Device mode, Per User licensing is currently unmanaged. License compliance in this mode must be enforced by the Terminal Services administrator.
	A Terminal Server will default to being in Per Device licensing mode, but you can change this after Terminal Services has been installed through the Terminal Services Configuration tool; this is discussed later in this chapter.
External Connector License (ECL)	Windows 2003 has replaced the Internet Connector License in Windows 2000 with the External Connector License. This licensing configuration supports unlimited connections to a Terminal Server, unlike the 200-user limit imposed with the original ICL.
	In order to use an ECL license, it must be installed on the Windows 2003 licensing server, and then the Terminal Servers that will utilize this licensing mode must be configured for Per User licensing. There is no longer an Internet Connector License option within Terminal Services configuration as there was with Windows 2000.

MetaFrame Access Suite Licensing Requirements Summary

In conjunction with the release of MPS 3.0, Citrix introduced the new licensing model for MetaFrame known as MetaFrame Access Suite Licensing (MASL). Central to this is the requirement for a separate licensing server responsible for storing and issuing licenses when requested. MASL not only provides license support for MPS but also will eventually support licensing for the entire suite of Citrix products. At the time of this writing, MetaFrame Conferencing Manager 3.0 was the only other product supporting this licensing infrastructure. Following is a brief summary of the licensing requirements for the licensing server and MetaFrame client access licenses. A complete discussion on licensing requirements for MetaFrame Presentation Server is discussed in Chapter 2, "Citrix MetaFrame Presentation Server."

License Server Requirements

- When deploying one or more MetaFrame Presentation Servers, you are required to have a Citrix license server, where the MetaFrame client access licenses will be centrally stored and allocated to users connecting to an MPS 3.0 server.
- The new MetaFrame Access Suite Licensing is not backwards compatible with previous versions of MetaFrame. It cannot manage licenses for earlier MetaFrame versions such as MetaFrame XP.
- In order for an MPS 3.0 server to function, a license server must be present and accessible. As long as the license server is present, the following grace-period licenses are available:

  - Two non-administrative users: 96 hours (4 days)
  - Administrative user: Indefinite

  The Citrix licensing service should be installed and functioning *before* installing MPS 3.0.
- You will need to decide whether the license server will reside on a dedicated server or on a server that has also been assigned other roles (Terminal Server, file and print server, and so forth). There are two factors that directly influence the load exerted on the license server:

  - The number of MetaFrame servers that have been configured to point to the license server.
  - The number of user connections per MetaFrame server.

  As each user logs on to a MetaFrame server, the server contacts the licensing server to check out or check in a client access license. Only under extremely high usage situations should you ever expect to see a significant load on the license server. Having said all that, I must add that Citrix does have some recommendations regarding whether or not to create a dedicated license server:

  - If you currently have or are expecting to have between 50 and 500 MetaFrame servers, you should have a dedicated license server.
  - If the number of servers is expected to exceed 500, it is recommended that you create multiple license servers to divide the load.

  If you also currently have or will be implementing other Citrix products that utilize the new licensing server, you will need to include them in the total server count. When more than one license server exists in an environment, they do not communicate in any way and licenses on one server cannot be automatically transferred to the other server. If you must use more than one server because of multiple Citrix products, try to segregate them so that all the licenses for a product remain on the same server. For example, all MPS licenses go on one server and all Conferencing Manager licenses go on the other.

■ You should look into placing your license server on the same network as the majority of your MetaFrame servers. This keeps the license traffic on the local network, reducing chances of a wide area network (WAN) issue causing any problems.

■ If you have MetaFrame servers spread between two or more geographic locations, you may want to run a license server in each location.

■ Multiple license servers can also be employed when segmenting licensing into different departments for management or security reasons.

■ Multiple instances of the licensing server cannot be run on the same Windows server. If you require two distinct license servers, they must be located on separate machines.

■ Hardware selection for the license server was discussed in Chapter 6, "Terminal Server Hardware Planning."

NOTE: My personal preference is to combine the Windows 2003 Terminal Services licensing and MPS licensing onto the same member server in the domain (something Citrix supports), regardless of the number of MetaFrame servers that will be implemented. Unless absolutely necessary, I try to avoid adding critical services such as licensing or the data store to a MetaFrame server.

In a Windows 2000 domain I do not recommend that you run the Citrix licensing service on a Windows 2000 domain controller. I suggest trying to find another server in your environment that could host the licensing service.

■ The licensing server can be managed either from the command prompt or using the License Management Console (LMC). The LMC is a Web-based service that must reside on the license server and requires IIS 5.0 or later. The license server itself is *not* dependent on IIS. In order to view the license reporting that is available, you will need the LCM.

■ The licensing server currently runs only on all Windows Server versions (2000 or 2003), except for Windows Server 2003, Web Edition.

MetaFrame Client Access License Requirements

Unlike Microsoft Terminal Server licensing, which requires a unique license for each user or device that connects to the server, MetaFrame licensing is based strictly on concurrent user sessions. If for example you have 300 users who may connect to your MetaFrame server, but only 125 are ever logged on at any given time, you would be required to purchase the following licenses:

■ 300 Terminal Server CALs
■ 125 MetaFrame CALs

When a user logs on to a MetaFrame server, the MetaFrame server is responsible for communicating with the Citrix licensing server and requesting the appropriate license for the user. If the request is approved, the license is assigned to the active user session and the CAL is considered to be checked out. The license remains checked out and in use until the user logs off his or her session, at which point the license is returned to the license server, available for use by someone else. If a user attempts to log on and there are no client licenses available, the logon will be denied.

In order to make client access licenses available for use, the associated license code that came with your MPS product must be used to obtain a corresponding license file from Citrix's Web site. This file is generated by Citrix based on the name of your license server and is valid only when installed on that server. Once the file has been loaded and validated by the license server, the licenses will be available for use by Citrix client sessions.

Now that we have completed a quick summary of the characteristics of the Microsoft and Citrix client access license management systems, we can move on to look at the actual installation and configuration steps for these products.

Windows 2000 Terminal Services Licensing Installation

TIP: If you are considering running the licensing service on a Terminal Server, keep in mind that although the overhead is relatively small, this service will consume additional resources that would otherwise be available to your end user. If alternate member servers are available in your workgroup or NT 4.0 domain, I recommend that you consider using them as the host for your licensing service instead of a Terminal Server.

Installing Windows 2000 Terminal Services Licensing

When you are ready to implement a Windows 2000 Terminal Services licensing server, the installation steps are as follows:

1. Log on to the server that will host the licensing service and open Add or Remove Programs from the Control Panel.
2. Click the Add/Remove Windows Components button, scroll to the bottom of the list, and select Terminal Services Licensing, as shown in Figure 12.2. Click Next to continue.

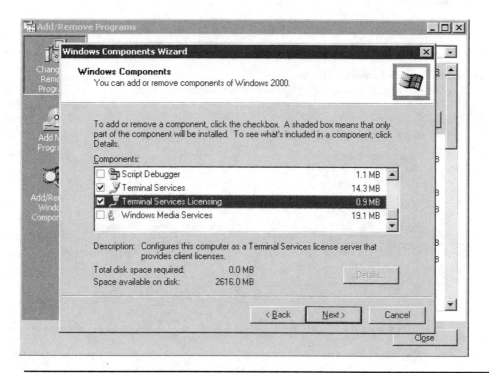

Figure 12.2   Installing the Terminal Services licensing component.

3. If you have Terminal Services installed on the server (Application or Remote Administration mode), the Terminal Services setup dialog box will appear. Make sure the correct mode has been selected and then click Next to continue.

4. The Terminal Services Licensing Setup dialog box appears (Figure 12.3). Here you can define the scope of this license server's role in your domain or workgroup. When you are installing the license service on a server in a workgroup or NT 4.0 domain, only the Your Domain or Workgroup option is available. When installing the licensing service on a Windows 2000 domain controller, you will also have the option of defining this licensing server as being available to "Your entire enterprise." An enterprise license server will service TSCAL requests from all Terminal Servers on the same physical site, regardless of their domain membership. Based on your implementation plan (discussed in Chapter 8, "Server Installation and Management Planning") you should already know what choice of license server you will deploy. Once you have selected the appropriate scope for your license server, provide the location where you would like to store the license database information. The default location is suitable for most implementations.

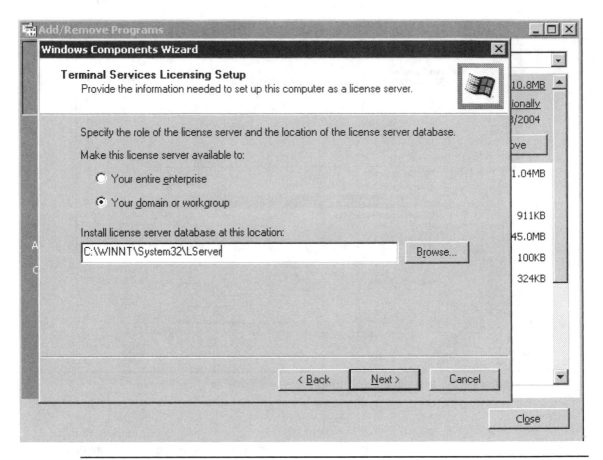

Figure 12.3 The Terminal Services Licensing Setup dialog box.

5. After you click Next, the necessary licensing service files are copied to the server and the installation completes. The licensing service becomes accessible immediately; you are not required to reboot the server.

Now that the licensing service has been installed, the next step is to activate it through the Microsoft clearinghouse. Until the licensing service has been activated it will not allocate Terminal Services licenses, and purchased CALs cannot be added to the server.

TIP: After its installation has completed, the Terminal Services licensing service should automatically start. The most common reason for its failing to start is that you installed it onto a member server in a Windows 2000 domain instead of onto a domain controller. In this situation, an error is logged in the system event log stating, "Terminal Services Licensing can only be run on Domain Controllers."

An undocumented feature does exist allowing you to configure this service to run on a member server even in a Windows 2000 domain. You simply update the ImagePath registry value for the TermServLicensing registry key and add the parameter -nodc. Once this has been done, the service starts properly. In order for a Terminal Server to locate this license server, the DefaultLicenseServer registry key must be populated on the Terminal Server (this will be described in the "Common Terminal Services Licensing Configuration Tasks" section of this chapter). This undocumented feature *is* supported by Microsoft and was originally created to assist customers who were unable to deploy the licensing service on a domain controller. I recommend against using this feature unless absolutely necessary. I have deployed Terminal Services licensing on a number of domain controllers and never had an issue with it affecting the stability or performance of that domain controller.

Activating a Windows 2000 Terminal Services License Server

The new Terminal Services licensing service is activated using the Terminal Services Licensing application, located under Administrative Tools on the Start menu. While starting up, this tool queries for all available license servers and lists those it finds. In the right pane it displays whether the licensing service has been activated or not. Clicking on a specific server will display what licenses exist, which are available, and how many are in use.

TIP: If a license server that you know exists does not appear in the list, you can manually add it by right-clicking All Servers, selecting Connect, and then entering the name of the license server when prompted. You need only provide the name of the server, *not* the UNC name with the leading double backslashes (\\).

The status of each server is listed (activated or not). If you click a specific server, the right pane displays which licenses exist, which are available, and how many are in use (see Figure 12.4).

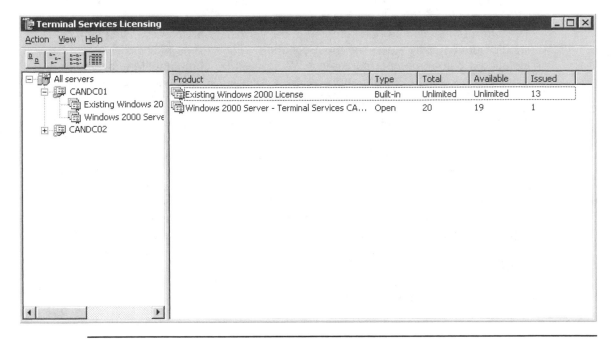

Figure 12.4 License allocation can be viewed by clicking on a server in the Terminal Services Licensing tool.

To activate a server, simply right-click the server name and select Activate Server. The Licensing Wizard launches and begins the following activation process:

1. After the welcome screen, you are provided with the four methods of activation listed in Table 12.3. The two recommended methods, Internet and Web activation, require the least amount of time and provide almost immediate access to the activation code.

Table 12.3 Terminal Services Licensing Activation Options for Windows 2000

Activation Method	Description
Internet	This option establishes a direct connection with the Microsoft clearinghouse.
Word Wide Web	Information is manually entered on Microsoft's Terminal Server Licensing Web site at https://www.activate.microsoft.com, and the provided key is used to activate the server.

Table 12.3 Terminal Services Licensing Activation Options for Windows 2000 (continued)

Activation Method	Description
Fax	This option lets you generate a form that is then faxed to Microsoft for processing. If you select this option, you are presented with a list of countries from which to choose an appropriate fax number for sending the necessary information.
Telephone	Information is provided to a customer service representative who gives you the necessary activation information. A call to customer service may also be required if you need to have your client licenses re-issued due to a licensing server failure, migration to another license server, or other licensing issuance problem. This option presents the same list of countries provided with the Fax option. Select the appropriate country, and a customer service clearinghouse number will be provided. Call this number to receive your required activation code.

2. Selecting the Internet option and clicking Next will immediately initiate a connection with the clearinghouse. If the connection is successfully established, you will be asked to choose the appropriate licensing program under which to request the license activation (Figure 12.5).

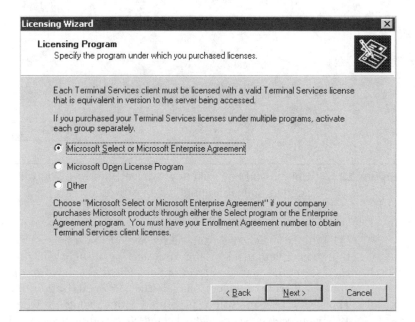

Figure 12.5 Choosing the appropriate licensing program to activate your client licenses.

3. After choosing the desired licensing program, click Next. You are then asked to provide company information such as name, contact name, phone number, and so on. Provide the required information and then click Next.

4. Reenter your e-mail address to verify it is correct. The activation code will be sent to this account, so be certain it has been entered properly.

5. Provide the remainder of the requested company information. After you click Next, the activation server is once again contacted and the request is prepared to be sent.

6. The next screen prompts you with the three options shown in Figure 12.6. Unless you wish to wait until the PIN arrives via e-mail, select the middle option: Postpone Completion of the Process Until the PIN Arrives. Clicking Close completes this process, and the status of the license service will then change from "Not activated" to "PIN needed to complete activation."

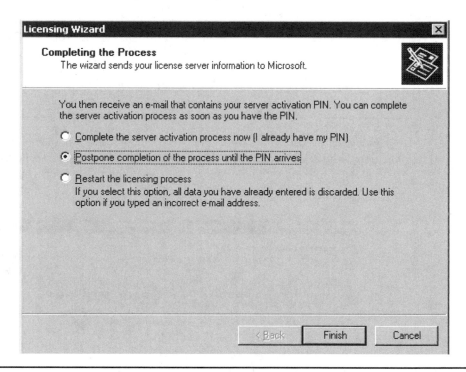

Figure 12.6   Unless you have already received the PIN, you will want to postpone the license activation until it has arrived.

7. When the e-mail arrives you will receive a PIN, which you must enter into the system to complete the activation. You once again right-click the server to activate and then select the Activate Server option. The dialog box from Figure 12.6 once again appears. This time select Complete the Server Activation Process Now (I Already Have My PIN). You will be presented with a dialog box where you paste in the PIN you received via e-mail. Clicking Next completes the activation.

After activating the Terminal Services License Server, you're ready to install the Terminal Server client access license packs. These licenses are required for all Terminal Server clients other than those running Windows 2000 Professional or Windows XP Professional.

NOTE: The activation PIN provided by Microsoft is generated specifically for the server from which you initiated the activation process. You cannot take this PIN and use it to activate a different license server. The PIN is specifically for the server's product ID, which is displayed on the first screen that appears when the server activation process is initiated.

Adding Windows 2000 Terminal Server Client Access License Packs

Client access licenses are installed on activated license servers by right-clicking the server name in the Terminal Services Licensing tool and selecting Install Licenses. The Licensing wizard is similar to the one used to activate the license server itself. With each client license pack comes a license and/or activation code that is sent to Microsoft; in return, you receive an activation code to be used to make the TSCALs available for distribution. The Licensing wizard requests the following information in this order when processing an Internet-based activation:

1. When the Licensing wizard starts, it displays the activation information for the license server including connection method, licensing program, and product ID. The activation method used to activate the server is automatically used to activate client licenses.
2. The next dialog box prompts you to provide the necessary client licensing information. Figure 12.7 shows an example of the information that would be requested with the Microsoft Open Licensing program. All this information should be available on the license information sheet that accompanied the purchased licenses. Enter all the information requested for your particular licensing program. If the information provided is correct, then after you click Next the information will be processed and the requested licenses will be added and activated on the Terminal Server.

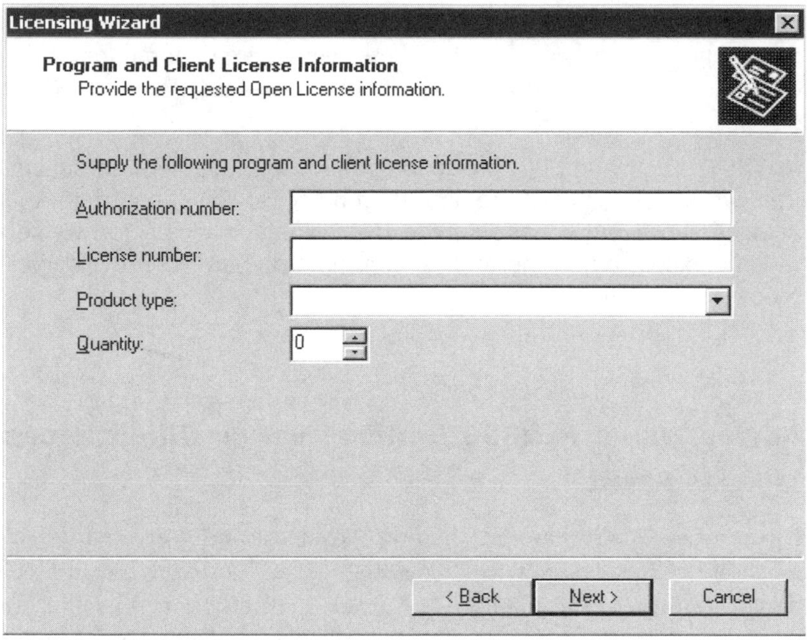

Figure 12.7   The information requested will correspond to the licensing program you selected when activating your Terminal Services Licensing module.

Windows 2003 Terminal Services CAL Downgrade Rights

With the release of Windows Server 2003, Microsoft discontinued the sale of Windows 2000–specific Terminal Services CALs. Instead, if you are required to purchase licensing for a Windows 2000 Terminal Server environment, you must purchase Windows Server 2003 Terminal Services licenses and then take advantage of the downgrade rights granted by Microsoft to apply these licenses to a Windows 2000 environment. A summary of the Windows Server 2003 downgrade rights appear on Microsoft's Web site at http://www. microsoft.com/windowsserver2003/howtobuy/licensing/downgrade.mspx.

The process of downgrading to Windows 2000 TSCALs is not automated. You must contact the Microsoft clearinghouse and acquire a Windows 2000–equivalent license key that you can then apply to your Windows 2000 Terminal Services License Server. You cannot directly install a Windows Server 2003 TSCAL package on a Windows 2000 Terminal Services License Server.

To acquire the downgrade license, you will need to call the appropriate clearinghouse for your country and explain that you wish to downgrade the licenses from Windows 2003 Terminal Services to Windows 2000 Terminal Services. You will then receive a valid license key you can use to complete activation of the Windows 2000 TSCALs, as outlined in the previous section.

TIP: If you will be deploying a Terminal Services License Server on a Windows 2003 server, you are not required to explicitly downgrade your existing Windows 2003 Terminal Services licenses in order to support Windows 2000 Terminal Servers. If a Windows 2000 Terminal Server requests a license from a Windows 2003 license server and there are no Windows 2000 TSCALs available, by default the license server will issue an available 2003 license in its place. This behavior can be modified by using a group policy and is discussed in the "Licensing Group Policy Objects" section of this chapter.

Windows Server 2003 Terminal Services Licensing Installation

The steps for installing and activating a Windows Server 2003 Terminal Services licensing server are similar to those for a Windows 2000 licensing server. One of the main differences is the eligibility of a member server in a Windows 2003 domain to host the licensing service. As mentioned in Table 12.1, if a member server is configured as a domain license server, the Windows 2000/2003 Terminal Servers in the domain must have the license server listed as a preferred server. My recommendation regarding where to place the licensing service in a 2003 environment depends on whether or not you will be running MetaFrame Presentation Server:

- **Windows 2003 Terminal Services only**—Unless you are running in a workgroup or NT 4 domain, place the licensing service on a domain controller. The overall load introduced by a license server is relatively low, and placing it on a domain controller ensures that all your Terminal Servers can locate the license service even if you forget to hard-code the server location.
- **Windows 2003 Terminal Services with MetaFrame Presentation Server 3.0**—In this scenario, I prefer placing both the Microsoft and Citrix licensing servers on a dedicated or at least non-domain controller server. I do not recommend running the MPS license server on a domain controller, mainly due to the IIS requirement in order to use the management console.

NOTE: I do not like running the licensing service on a Terminal Server, except in very small environments. As much as possible I recommend not having any data on a Terminal Server that must be backed up, even if it is only the license database.

Installing Windows Server 2003 Terminal Services Licensing

When you are ready to set up a Windows Server 2003 Terminal Services licensing server, the installation steps are as follows:

1. Log on to the server that will host the licensing service and open Add or Remove Programs from the Control Panel.
2. Click the Add/Remove Windows Components button, scroll down to the bottom of the list, and select Terminal Services Licensing. Unless this server is also a Terminal Server, you are *not* required to enable the Terminal Server option when adding the licensing service.
3. The Terminal Services Licensing Setup dialog box appears (Figure 12.8). Here you define the scope of this license server's role in your domain or workgroup. The option you choose will depend on the number of domains in your forest and the licensing distribution your environment is implementing. License server distribution is discussed in Chapter 8. For most environments, the Your Domain or Workgroup option is appropriate. Once you have selected the appropriate scope for your license server, provide the location where you want to store the license database information. The default location is suitable for most implementations.

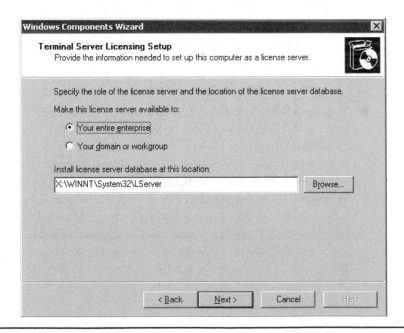

Figure 12.8 The Terminal Server Licensing Setup dialog box.

4. After you click Next and provide the Windows Server 2003 CD-ROM if prompted, the necessary licensing service files are copied to the server, and the installation completes. The licensing service becomes available immediately; you are not required to reboot the server.

The next step is to proceed with activating the license server with Microsoft's clearinghouse.

Activating a Windows 2003 Terminal Services License Server

Once the license server is installed, you are required to activate it with Microsoft's clearinghouse before it can provide anything other than temporary licenses. It is activated using the Terminal Services Licensing application, located under Administrative Tools on the Start menu. This tool must be run from the server on which you installed Terminal Services licensing. When loading, this tool queries for all available license servers and lists those it finds. If a server is not listed, it can be manually added by right-clicking All Servers and selecting Connect. In the dialog box, type the name of the server you wish to add.

The status of each server is listed (activated or not). If you click an existing server, the right pane displays which licenses exist, which are available, and how many are in use. Figure 12.9 shows how this would look immediately after installing Terminal Services licensing on a Windows 2003 domain controller. The only licenses available by default are the existing built-in Windows 2000 tokens, which are included to provide backwards compatibility with the Windows 2000 Terminal Services licensing.

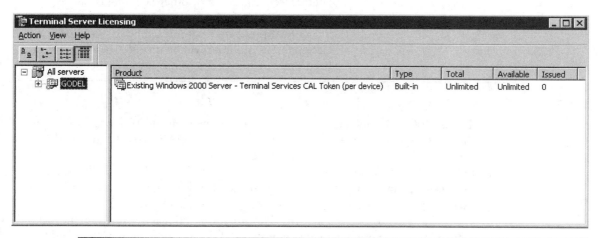

Figure 12.9   The Terminal Server Licensing management tool.

To activate a server, simply right-click the server name and select Activate Server. The Licensing wizard will launch and begin the following activation process:

1. After clicking Next to move past the welcome screen, you are provided with three methods of activating, which are listed in Table 12.4.

Table 12.4   Terminal Services Licensing Activation Options for Windows Server 2003

Activation Method	Description
Automatic connection	Establishes a direct connection with the Microsoft clearinghouse.
Web browser	Information is manually entered on Microsoft's Terminal Server Licensing Web site at https://www.activate.microsoft.com, and the provided key is then used to activate the server.
Telephone	Information is provided to a customer service representative who then gives you the necessary activation information. A call to customer service may also be required if you need to have your client licenses re-issued due to a licensing server failure, migration to another license server, or other licensing issuance problems. This option presents a list of countries. Select the appropriate country, and a customer service clearinghouse number will be provided. Call this number to receive your required activation code.

The two recommended methods, automatic connection and Web browser, require the least amount of time and provide immediate access to the activation code. For this example, we will choose automatic connection.

2. Select Automatic Connection and then click Next. The application will attempt to establish a connection with the clearinghouse. If this is successful, you will be asked to provide your name, company's name, and country.

3. On the next dialog box you are asked to provide additional information, including your e-mail address and a mailing address. All this information is *optional* and can be left blank. After you click Next the application establishes a connection with the clearinghouse and automatically activates the license server. With the Automatic Connection option, there is no need to wait for an e-mail response as you would with a Windows 2000 license server.

After activating the Terminal Services License Server, you're ready to install the Terminal Server client access license packs. On a Windows 2003 license server, you can install both Windows 2000 and Windows 2003 Terminal Server client access licenses. Depending on what version of Terminal Server a user connects to, the license server will issue the appropriate license to that user.

Adding Windows 2003 Terminal Server CAL Packs

Client access licenses can be installed only on activated license servers. This is done by right-clicking the server name in the Terminal Services Licensing tool and selecting Install Licenses. The Client Licensing wizard is very similar to the one used to activate the license server itself. With each client license pack comes a license and/or activation code that must be provided during the activation; in return, you receive an activation code to be used to make the TSCALs available for distribution. When the Terminal Services CAL Installation wizard is launched, the first dialog box displays the license server settings, including the installation method (defaults to the one used when activating the server) and the licensing program. If any of the displayed information needs to be changed, you can cancel the license installation, right-click the server name, and then choose Properties from the pop-up menu. From here you can also modify any of the information you may have entered when activating the server.

Automatic license activation would proceed as follows:

1. After confirming the settings on the Welcome dialog box, click Next to begin.
2. You are now requested to choose the appropriate license program for your environment. You are presented with eight options:

   - License Pack (Retail purchase)
   - Open License
   - Select License
   - Enterprise Agreement
   - Campus Agreement
   - School Agreement
   - Services Provider License Agreement\
   - Other agreement

   When an option is selected, the description at the bottom of the dialog box updates to reflect that selection, and an example of the license code format required is also shown. Choose the option that most closely matches your current license program with Microsoft and then click Next.
3. You are now required to enter all the desired licenses that you wish to install on this license server, as shown in Figure 12.10.

Figure 12.10   You are presented with a dialog box asking you to provide one or more license codes to add to the license server.

4. Once you have added the desired license codes, click Next. Each valid code is sent to the clearinghouse and processed, and the corresponding license is installed on the license server. When the process is completed, a Summary dialog box appears listing all the installed licenses.

All installed licenses are now available for distribution when requested by a Terminal Server.

Configuring the Desired Windows 2003 Terminal Services License Type

If you have not already done so, I suggest you configure your Terminal Servers to use the appropriate license configuration for your Terminal Server environment, either Per Device or Per User. This option is configured on the Terminal Server by running the Terminal Services Configuration utility, selecting Server Settings, and then choosing the licensing mode as shown in Figure 12.11. This option must be explicitly set on each Terminal Server. It currently cannot be set using a group policy object in an Active Directory domain.

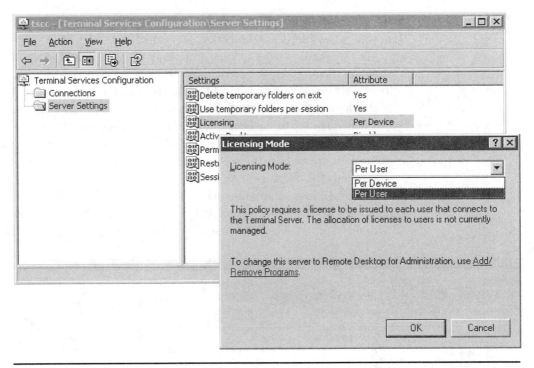

Figure 12.11   The type of licensing method is assigned on a per–Terminal Server
basis.

Licensing Group Policy Objects

Windows Server 2003 Active Directory introduces a number of additional group policy
objects (GPO) tailored specifically for Terminal Services. Included in this set are two
Computer Configuration policies specifically created to dictate the behavior of the Terminal
Services licensing service. These policies can be found in the following folder within the
GPO editor: Computer Configuration\Administrative Templates\Windows Components\
Terminal Services\Licensing

The two policies are

- **License Server Security Group**—This policy allows you to limit what
  Terminal Servers and other license servers can request licenses from a 2003
  Terminal Services License Server. By default, a 2003 license server will grant
  licenses to any requesting Terminal Server (2000 or 2003) or other license server. When this policy is applied to a 2003 license server, a local security group is
  created on the server called "Terminal Server Computers." The license server
  will then issue licenses to only a requesting Terminal Server or license server if
  it is a member of the local security group. Initially when this policy is applied,

the group is created without any members, so until Terminal Servers are added to this group the license server will not issue licenses to any server.

The standard practice of local group membership should be applied in this situation. Begin by creating a domain group called something like "Authorized Terminal Servers," and into it add all the Terminal Servers and license servers in the domain that you want to be authorized to request TSCALs. Now assign this domain group to the local group on the license server. If the license service is running on a domain controller, this will be a domain local group. Once the domain group has been added to the local group, you need to manage membership in only the domain group in order to control the list of authorized servers. Figure 12.12 shows this group, which was automatically created on my domain controller when I enabled this GPO. In this example I have a Windows 2003 Terminal Services license service running on this test domain controller.

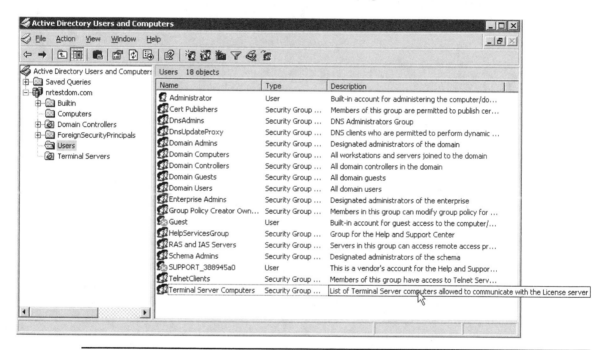

Figure 12.12   The Terminal Server Computers local security group was automatically created when the License Server Security Group policy was enabled.

■ **Prevent License Upgrade**—The other GPO dictates whether or not the license server will substitute an available Windows 2003 TSCAL when a Windows 2000 Terminal Server requests a Windows 2000 TSCAL but none are available for issuance on the license server. The default behavior is to allocate a Windows 2003 TSCAL if there are no Windows 2000 TSCALS available. By enabling this GPO, you prevent this substitution and instead force the Terminal Services License Server to issue a temporary license if there are no full TSCALs available.

TIP: Use of group policies to manage a Terminal Server implementation is discussed in detail in Chapter 15, "Group Policy Configuration."

Transitional CALs for Windows XP Professional Clients

One of the major changes in licensing between Windows 2003 and Windows 2000 is the elimination of the built-in license for the most recent version of the Windows desktop operating system, commonly referred to as "desktop equivalence." Windows 2000 Terminal Services licensing exempts users running Windows 2000 Professional or Windows XP Professional from requiring an additional license to access a Windows 2000 Terminal Server. A license is automatically provided by the licensing service for clients running one of these operating systems. The license in this case is drawn from an infinite pool of built-in Windows 2000 licenses.

Windows 2003 Terminal Services eliminates this exemption and requires that a license be provided for all clients, regardless of the desktop operating system they are using. In order to provide some compensation to those users who may have anticipated that desktop equivalence was going to continue to be supported, Microsoft is offering a Windows Server 2003 TSCAL for each Windows XP Professional license purchased prior to April 24, 2003 (the official date of Windows Server 2003's launch). These transitional licenses are being offered on a one-to-one basis, and if you also have Software Assurance or Upgrade Advantage coverage as of that date, that coverage will automatically carry over to this new license as well. More details on these transitional licenses as well as the form letter required to request a license can be found athttp://www.microsoft.com/windowsserver2003/howtobuy/licensing/tsletter.mspx.

Common Terminal Services Licensing Configuration Tasks

Now that the Terminal Services licensing server has been installed, there are some additional tasks you may wish to perform based on the needs of your implementation, either now or sometime in the future. Because many of these tasks differ only slightly between operating system versions, I've grouped them together in this section.

Hard-Coding the Default License Server

The Terminal Services license discovery process can be overridden by hard-coding the desired license server in a Terminal Server's registry. By hard-coding the server name, you force the Terminal Server to go to only that server to request client licenses. If this target server is not available, the Terminal Server will not attempt to locate an alternate server.

A common scenario in which the license server is hard-coded is when you have Terminal Servers from different domains all located at the same site and you would like them to all share the same license server instead of creating a separate license server for each domain. By default a Terminal Server will attempt to find and use a license server in its own domain, even if that server is located across a wide area network (WAN) link. For example, a Terminal Server would choose this remote server over a local license server simply because the remote server is located in the same domain as the Terminal Server and the local license server is not.

The specific registry location where the default license server is defined differs between Windows 2000 and Windows 2003. For a Windows 2000 Terminal Server, in order to designate a specific license server to talk to, you must traverse to the following registry key on every participating Terminal Server: HKLM\SYSTEM\CurrentControlSet\Services\TermService\Parameters.
and add the value DefaultLicenseServer: REG_SZ: <Server Name>, where <Server Name> is the NetBIOS name of the server hosting the licensing service.

For a Windows 2003 Terminal Server, the parent registry key is the same: HKLM\System\CurrentControlSet\Services\TermService\Parameters, but under this key you must then create another key called LicenseServers. For each license server you wish to add, create a new *key* (not a value) and assign it a name representing the target license server. Unlike the Windows 2000 Terminal Server, where the name must be the NetBIOS name, the 2003 Terminal Server lets the registry key have any one of the following types of names:

- The NetBIOS name of the license server (HERCULES)
- The fully qualified domain name of the license server (hercules.nrsc.com)
- The IP address of the license server (192.168.1.1).

For this registry change to take effect, the Terminal Server must be restarted.

TIP: Microsoft recommends that the name of the license server be hard-coded on each Terminal Server to minimize issues that might arise with standard Terminal Services license discovery.

Terminal Services CAL Recovery

When a Terminal Services CAL is issued to a client, it is stored in the registry of the client device and then presented whenever requested by the Terminal Server to verify that a valid license has been assigned. As I mentioned earlier, when running either Windows 2000 with Service Pack 3 or later or Windows Server 2003, an issued client license will automatically be recovered within 52–89 days of assignment. No other automated mechanism exists for recovering a client license that may have been allocated to the wrong device.

You can remove the license that has been stored *locally* on the client device by deleting the registry keys under HKLM\Software\Microsoft\MSLicensing\Store.
All keys under here represent Terminal Services client access licenses (see Figure 12.13). By deleting the existing keys you will eliminate the license from the local client, but you are not modifying the allocation reference from the Terminal Services License Server.

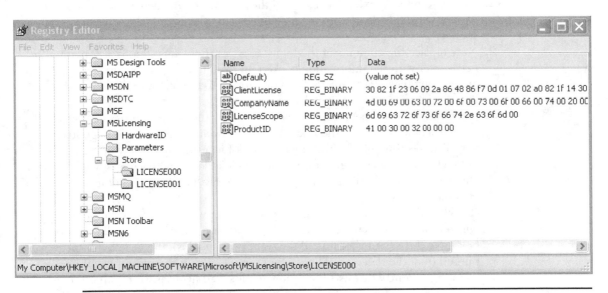

Figure 12.13 Terminal Services client access license certificates are stored in the local registry on Win32 devices.

In order to recover licenses that may have been erroneously allocated or lost due to a license server failure, you must contact the Microsoft clearinghouse and request a replacement license key. This key is then activated on the existing or new license server to make the client access licenses available. If this key is added to an existing license server, it will simply appear as another set of CALs in the license manager. There is no special designation for replacement license keys.

Migrating Client Access Licenses Between License Servers

No automated mechanism exists for migrating the currently allocated and available CALs from one Terminal Services licensing server to another. If you are recovering from a failure of the license server, and you have a full backup of the original license server that includes the registry and the license server files located under %SystemRoot% \system32\LServer, then the recovered server will maintain all information on currently issued and available Terminal Server licenses.

If you had to restore the license database onto a new Windows server, or if you wished to migrate the licenses from one Windows server to a completely different server, you would need to do the following:

1. Install Terminal Services licensing on the new server and activate it as described earlier. Once it is up and running, manually stop the Terminal Services licensing service.

2. Now replace the contents of the folder %SystemRoot%\System32\LServer on the *new* server with the information backed up from the original license server. If you are copying these files directly from one server to the other, be sure to stop the licensing service on the original server as well.

3. Once the files have been copied, you can restart the service on the new server. The service should start up without any errors, and you should be able to go in and view licenses through the Terminal Services Licensing tool. You will immediately notice that only assignments for the built-in Windows 2000 licenses will have actually been imported. All other license references will be lost, including any installed client access licenses.

   When the licensing service on the new server was restarted, it immediately recognized that licenses were present in the database, but since they did not originally belong to this server (because of different product IDs), the installed licenses were purged from the database. These actions are logged in the system event log, including an entry that lists how many unallocated licenses were purged. Figure 12.14 shows the two event log entries generated when a foreign database is detected and when any unassigned licenses are purged.

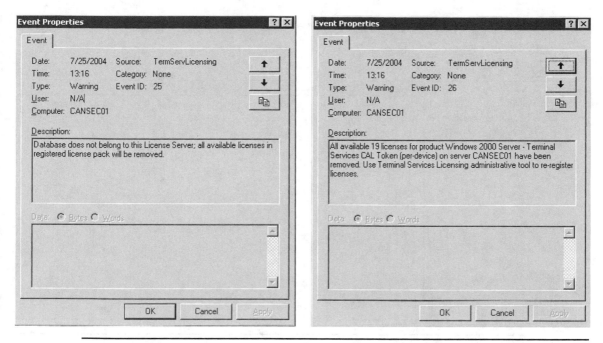

Figure 12.14 When a database from a different license server is detected, installed licenses are automatically purged, including any allocation references. Unallocated licenses are counted and reported.

4. In order to restore the missing licenses, you will need to contact the Microsoft clearinghouse and explain what was done; the Clearinghouse will issue you a new license code that can be activated on the new license server to restore the missing client access licenses.

I recommend that you stop the licensing service on the original server but do not uninstall or rebuild the server for a few days, at least until you have verified that the new licensing server is functioning properly.

Monitoring Terminal Services CAL Usage

There are three different tools readily available that you can use to monitor the Terminal Services client license usage. The first tool is Terminal Services Licensing, which we have used to add and activate the license server and TSCALs. This tool provides an interface where you can quickly see how many licenses have been allocated and how many remain. It also lets you view who has been assigned a license and what their expiry date is, if applicable. Figure 12.15 shows an example of this, with a Terminal Services device CAL assigned to a host named linuxhost. You can see that the expiry date for this token is Saturday, October 2, 2004, at 3:32:29 p.m. If linuxhost does not log on sometime within a week of the expiry date, the CAL will be reclaimed by the license server to be issued to someone else.

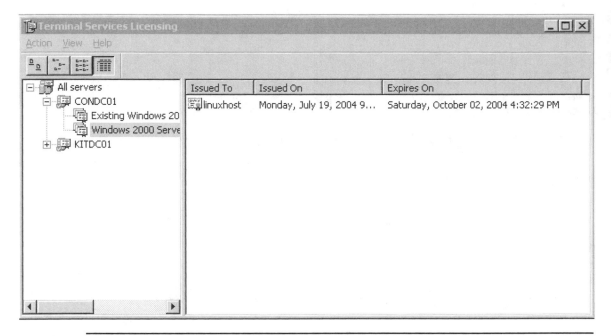

Figure 12.15   The Terminal Services Licensing tool can be used to view the current license allocations and how many CALs are still available for use.

Another tool is the Terminal Services License Reporting tool, available for both the Windows 2000 and 2003 Resource Kits. This simple command line tool will output the information from the Terminal Services license database to a text file with tab-delimited formatting. This file can then be viewed or manipulated using software such as Excel.

The tool is launched by issuing the command lsreport.exe from a command prompt. Without any parameters, the tool will query the domain controller to acquire a list of license servers and then query those servers for the license information. The output from this will be written by default into the current folder with the name lsreport.txt. Running this command with the /? parameter outputs the usage for the tool.

The final tool is also provided as part of the Windows Resource Kit. This tool, the License Server Viewer (LSView), simply queries the network at regular intervals (every five minutes, by default) looking for available Windows Terminal Server licensing servers. The utility uses the same discovery process as the Windows 2003 Terminal Server, so running this tool directly off a Terminal Server will indicate whether the license server is visible or not. Figure 12.16 shows the main display for this utility with a couple of license servers detected. LSView can be a useful tool in troubleshooting license server connectivity problems.

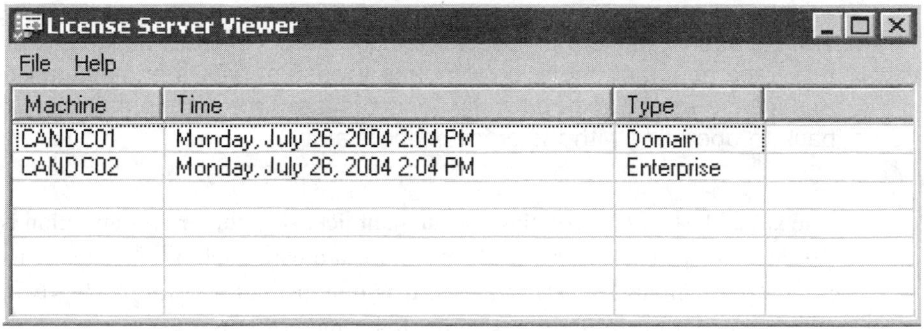

Machine	Time	Type	
CANDC01	Monday, July 26, 2004 2:04 PM	Domain	
CANDC02	Monday, July 26, 2004 2:04 PM	Enterprise	

Figure 12.16 The main window of the LSView utility lists the license servers that have been discovered on the network using standard Terminal Services license server acquisition methods.

Configuring Terminal Services Licensing for High Availability and Fail-Over

You are likely wondering what happens if a license server is unavailable due to some type of failure, whether it be hardware or software related. If a Terminal Server is operating past its grace period and any of the following situations are true for a user attempting to connect to a Terminal Server, and the Terminal Services licensing server is inaccessible, the user will be denied access to log on to the Terminal Server:

- It is the first time the user is trying to connect, and they currently have no Terminal Server license. Because there is no license server available to issue even a temporary access license, the user's connection is refused. If the Terminal Server was still operating in its grace period, the user's connection would be accepted.
- A user is trying to connect to the Terminal Server but their temporary or permanent TSCAL has expired. If a user's CAL has expired, there is no license server available either to renew the existing license or attempt to allocate a permanent license from its pool. In either case the Terminal Server has no choice but to reject the connection and prevent the user from logging on.

License verification is currently enforced only with Per Device licensing. Beyond the Terminal Server being able to contact a license server after its grace period has expired, there is no actual interaction with the licensing server when dealing with Per User licensing.

TIP: As soon as a Terminal Server is successfully able to connect to a license server, the grace period of operation without a license server is immediately terminated. If the license server goes down five minutes later, the Terminal Server will not revert back to operating with the grace-period status.

The actual task of constructing a redundant licensing server configuration is straightforward. Because licensing servers already communicate with each other in order to attempt to satisfy any permanent TSCAL requests, it is only a matter of deploying two or more license servers in your environment using the following criteria:

- Configure all license servers to be Enterprise License Servers. This will allow for their discovery by any Terminal Server within the same site regardless of what domain the Terminal Server resides in.
- Divide your available permanent licenses between the different license servers. For example, if you have three license servers you could activate one-third of the licenses on each server. If one server happens to have allocated its entire set of permanent licenses, it will still query other servers in an attempt to provide a requesting Terminal Server with the appropriate license.

When two or more license servers are deployed in this fashion, they will provide high-availability support for your Terminal Services implementation.

MetaFrame Access Suite Licensing Server

During installation of MetaFrame Presentation Server, you will be prompted to provide the server name and port number of the server running your MetaFrame Access Suite Licensing (MASL) server (Figure 12.17). As a consequence, the MASL server is typically installed and configured *prior* to installation of the MPS software itself.

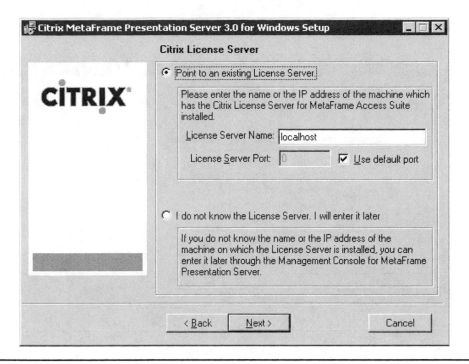

Figure 12.17 The MetaFrame Access Suite Licensing server location is requested during the MPS installation.

Installing MetaFrame Access Suite Licensing

Installation steps for the MASL server are as follows:

1. Log on to the server that will host the Access Suite Licensing and then launch the Autorun feature from the installation CD-ROM.

2. When the Setup window appears, select MetaFrame Access Suite Installations and then click Install MetaFrame Access Suite License Server.

3. Once you have moved through a couple of informational dialog boxes, you arrive at the Select Components dialog box, where all the MPS components are listed (see Figure 12.18). Ensure only the license service option has been enabled and then click Next. The Windows Installer component for the license server immediately begins.

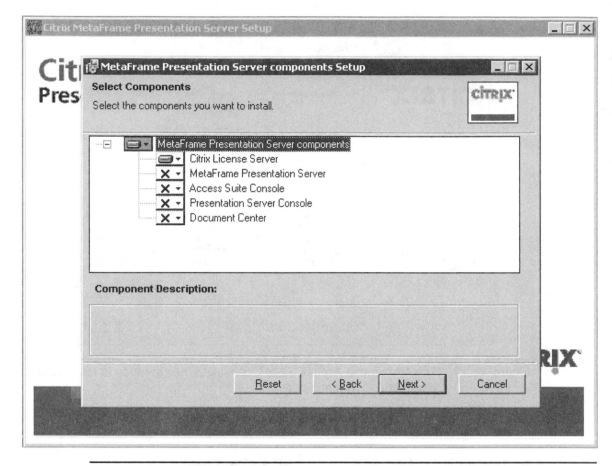

Figure 12.18 MetaFrame Presentation Server Components Setup dialog box.

4. Next the Welcome to the Citrix MetaFrame Access Suite Licensing Installation Wizard dialog box appears. Click Next to move past the screen and be presented with the MetaFrame license agreement. If you agree with the terms of the agreement, click the appropriate radio button and then click Next to proceed.

5. Choose the desired destination folder for the application and then click Next.

6. You are now presented with the Select Features installation dialog box for the licensing setup. If you do not have IIS installed on your server, the License Management Console Web Service option will not be enabled. The license server itself does not require IIS in order to install and function properly. Select the desired options to install and then click Next to continue.

7. You are prompted to specify a folder where the license files that are received from Citrix will be stored. In order to install licenses with MPS 3.0, you must now fulfill the license entitlement on the Citrix Web site (http://www.MyCitrix.com) and then download the generated license file for your server. This process is discussed shortly in the "Managing and Assigning Citrix Licenses" section. In most cases the default license file location is appropriate. Click Next to proceed.

8. If you will be installing the Web interface, the next dialog box will require you to authorize the restart of the IIS service in order to complete the installation. The installation cannot complete successfully until this service has been restarted. Make certain that a service stoppage will not affect any production users.

9. Once the IIS service has been restarted (if applicable), the installation completes. An installation summary is presented at the end of the setup listing all the possible components that can be installed along with the status of their installation attempt. After you click Finish, the licensing server is available for use. You can now assign licenses and provide this server's information when required during the MetaFrame Presentation Server installation (discussed in Chapter 13, "MetaFrame Presentation Server Installation").

TIP: You can verify that the licensing service has been installed and started properly by viewing the status of the CitrixLicensing service through Computer Management or issuing the NET START command from a command prompt (see Figure 12.19).

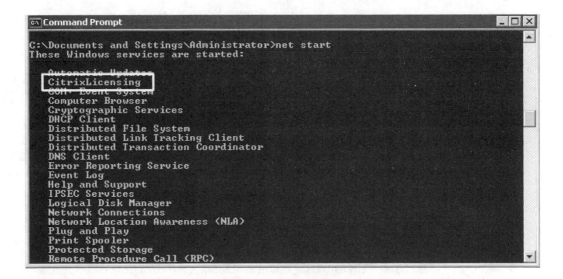

Figure 12.19   You can verify that the license service is running by looking for CitrixLicensing after running the NET START command.

The Citrix License Management Console

If installed on your Citrix license server, all license server management can be done through the License Management Console (LMC), which is accessed by pointing a Web browser at http://<server name>/lmc/index.jsp, where <server name> is the name of the server where you installed the licensing service and management console. Alternatively, you can select the License Management Console from the Citrix folder on the Start menu of the license server. Figure 12.20 shows the main welcome screen for the License Management Console.

Figure 12.20   MetaFrame Access Suite License Management Console.

This menu provides four selections:

■ **View Current Usage Data**—Displays the current license usage as reported by the LMC, including any special alerts. Information on this screen does not update automatically and must be manually refreshed.

- **Generate Historical Reports**—Lets you generate reports based on the license usage data logged by the license server.
- **Configure License Server**—Lets you manage all aspects of the licensing server, including the Citrix licenses.
- **User Administration**—Lets you manage the user access to your license server via the LMC.

From within any of these menus you can access any other menu simply by clicking the appropriate toolbar across the top of the screen.

Managing and Assigning Citrix Licenses

The first task you will want to complete is assignment of the appropriate licenses to the license server so they are available to the MetaFrame servers in your environment. In order to install the licenses on your license server, you need to do the following:

1. Go to Citrix's Web site (http://www.citrix.com) and complete the entitlement process for your specific licenses.
2. Acquire the associated license files that are generated as part of the entitlement process.
3. Install the license files onto the license server.

Acquiring the License Files

To acquire the license files necessary for your implementation, you must log on to your MyCitrix portal session (http://www.mycitrix.com) and process the desired license entitlement. The license file acquisition process can be completed as follows:

1. You can go directly to the MyCitrix site from your Web browser or from within the LMC, select the Configuration menu, and then select Download License File from Citrix Web Site. When prompted, log on to your MyCitrix session.
2. From the Licensing menu, select the Fulfillment submenu and then Fulfill Eligible Products. Select the appropriate license to fulfill and then complete the wizard. You will then receive a license code that you will use to perform the license activation and receive your license file.
3. Select Activate *or* Allocate Licenses and enter the license code you just received. You then see a Web page listing the product(s) you are eligible to fulfill (see Figure 12.21). Select the checkbox next to the product(s) that should be fulfilled and then enter the actual license quantity to fulfill. You are not required to fulfill the entire license quantity at once. You will be required to provide the host name of your Citrix license server.

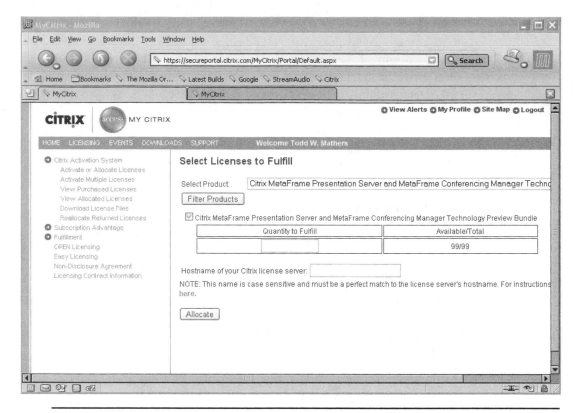

Figure 12.21 Performing license fulfillment in the My Citrix portal.

When entering the host name of your Citrix license server, you will need to be certain that you match the spelling exactly. This includes any capitalized letters. You can find the host name by right-clicking My Computer and loading the system properties. On the Computer Name tab you will find the full computer name shows the proper spelling of the host name. Provide only the host name, not the fully qualified domain name.

4. Once you have entered the correct information, click the Allocate button. When you have reviewed the information on the confirmation page and found it to be correct, click the Confirm button to complete the fulfillment. If the fulfillment is processed correctly, you are presented with the option to download the license file, as shown in Figure 12.22. Click Download License File and save the file onto the license server, or a network-accessible folder if you are not actually performing the download from the license server.

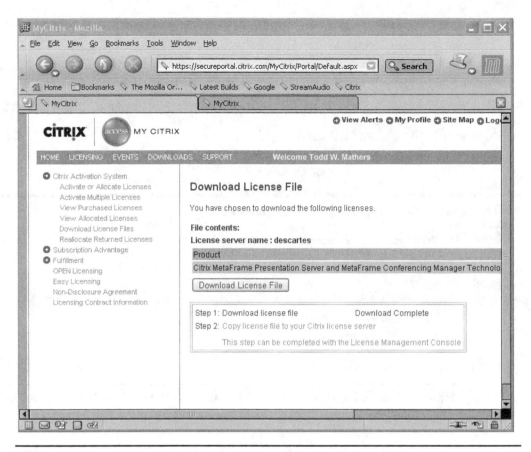

Figure 12.22 The Download License File web page.

5. Once you have the file, you need to make sure it is copied onto the license server. You can do this from within the LMC by selecting Copy License File to License Server from the Configuration menu. You can also do this directly from the download page of MyCitrix, as shown in Figure 12.22.

   The second step on this page, Copy License File to Citrix License Server, is actually a link directly to http://www.<license server>/lmc/configuration/upload LicenseFile.jsp. If you click this link and provide the valid credentials, you will be taken to the appropriate page within the LMC automatically.

6. On the Upload License File page of the LMC (see Figure 12.23), browse to the location where you saved the license file and then select the Upload button. The license file is then uploaded and added to the license server. You should now be able to go to the Current Usage page of the LMC and see the licenses you just added. You may need to select the Refresh button or even close and reopen your browser for the new license information to appear properly.

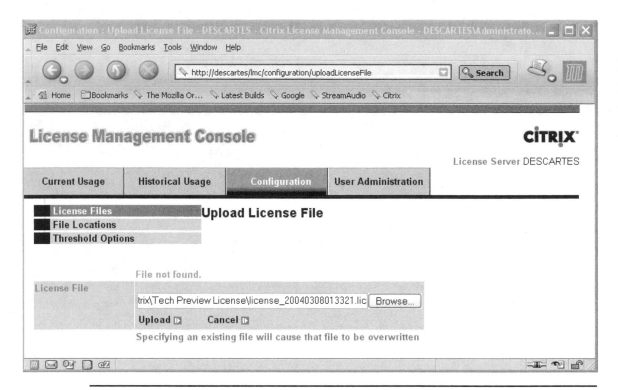

Figure 12.23 The Upload License File page of the License Management Console.

TIP: License Management Console needn't be present in order for you to perform many of the necessary administration tasks. License files can be retrieved and loaded into the license server using either the command line tools or a Windows-based GUI for these command line tools.

First, you can still download the appropriate license file to your server through the MyCitrix portal (Steps 1 through 4 in instructions for installing licenses on your license server). Once the file has been downloaded from Citrix, copy it into the license location folder that you defined when installing the license server. The default location is

C:\Program Files\Citrix\Licensing\MyFiles\

Once the license file has been copied into this folder, you must tell the license server that a new license file is available. All the command line tools for the license server are located in the following folder, by default:

C:\Program Files\Citrix\Licensing\LS

Open a command prompt and traverse into this folder. You can now force a reread of all license files by issuing the command

lmreread "<license folder path>"

For example, using the default license folder, the command would look as follows:

lmreread "c:\program files\citrix\licensing\myfiles"

If the reread is successful, you will see a message stating this.

An alternate tool that can be used is called LMTOOLS. Launching this executable opens the GUI program that provides a front end to some of the tools. I highly recommend that you do not change any of the settings within this tool, or you may render the license server unusable. If you select the Stop/Start/Reread tab, you can then click the ReRead License File button, and it will reread the licenses in the corresponding license folder (see Figure 12.24). The current folder will be listed along the bottom of the dialog box. You can also view the current setting by clicking the Config Services tab. Among other things, it shows the current path to the license files.

Please note that this tool is not documented in the Citrix literature and as such is not necessarily supported by Citrix. I recommend that you use the command line tool (LMREREAD) instead unless you are working in a test or development environment that will not impact production users.

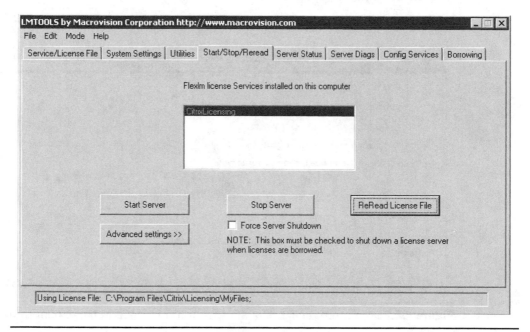

Figure 12.24   The undocumented LMTOOLS utility can be used to reread an imported license file.

Monitoring License Usage

License usage is tracked through the Current Usage page of the License Management Console. From here you can quickly see the following licensing information:

- The product and types of licenses currently available for issuance.
- The total number of licenses available for distribution.
- The number of licenses currently issued, the number remaining, and the usage percentage. Details on who has been issued what license can be viewed by clicking the small red box next to the In Use count, shown in Figure 12.25.

In addition to the current usage statistics, the Current Usage page issues alerts based on threshold settings under the Configuration menu. Figure 12.25 shows a "% in Use" warning that was tripped when the license usage exceeded a defined threshold. In this case, I set the threshold to issue a warning when the license usage exceeded 15 percent. As you might expect, warnings appear in yellow and critical alerts appear in red.

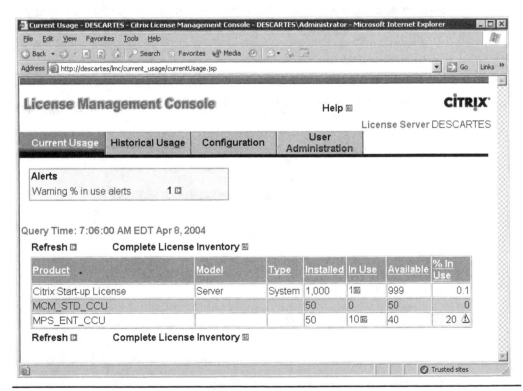

Figure 12.25   Current usage statistics from the License Management Console.

As I mentioned, the license alert thresholds are maintained from the Thresholds page under the Configuration menu; see Figure 12.26, which also shows the default values defined upon installation. The three categories of thresholds are

- **License Usage**—The warning and critical levels are assigned based on the percentage of total licenses in use.
- **Subscription Advantage Date**—These values represent the days remaining before Subscription Advantage must be renewed.
- **Expiration Date**—These values indicate the number of days prior to the expiration date of a license.

In each situation, the actual values appropriate for your implementation will depend on the length of time your organization takes to procure licenses. If the turnaround time is very short, you can raise the alert thresholds so you are not being alerted to license or date values prematurely. For example, warning levels for license usage could be raised to 80 percent for warnings and 95 percent (or higher) for critical warnings. Of course it is always better to know sooner than later that you have impending license issues, but typically when notifications appear too early, they are dismissed by the administrator and forgotten until dates expire or license usage reaches 100 percent.

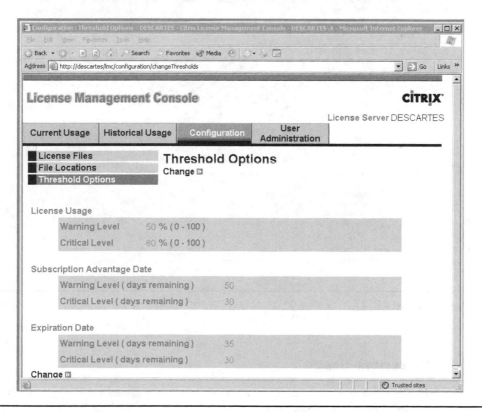

Figure 12.26   Thresholds are configured for different types of data from under the Configuration tab.

TIP: You can monitor license usage and find out information on available and in-use licenses by running the command line tool LMSTAT. After traversing into the C:\Program Files\Citrix\Licensing\LS folder that contains the command line tools, issuing the following command returns rather detailed information about the number of server licenses and their allocation, as well as the number of user licenses installed and their current allocation.

```
lmstat -a -c "C:\Program Files\Citrix\Licesing\MyFiles"
```

From within the LMTOOLS utility you can access this same feature from the Server Status tab. Figure 12.27 shows the results of a status enquiry immediately after installing the license server.

Of course this output is not as condensed as the Web GUI, nor is there support for alert notification, but this option does allow for some general license server querying.

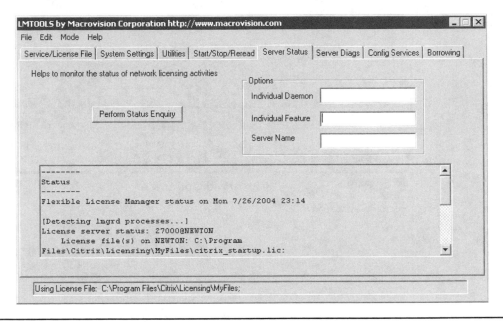

Figure 12.27   Status information for the license server can also be queried from the LMTOOLS utility.

Historical Usage

The Historical Usage tab lets you generate reports based on the data logged in the usage report. The usage report is generated automatically by the license server as it processes license requests. The default usage report file name and location are

C:\Program Files\Citrix\Licensing\LS\reportlog.rl

From the Historical Usage window, you need to select the Usage Logs button and add the desired logs to the list included in the historical report. After adding the desired logs and returning to the main screen, the logs should automatically appear in the usage logs list (see Figure 12.28). As long as there is at least one log available, you can select either Product Reports or Summary Reports and generate reporting information based on the available logged data. When generating a report you have the option of selecting additional criteria to fine-tune the output of the report.

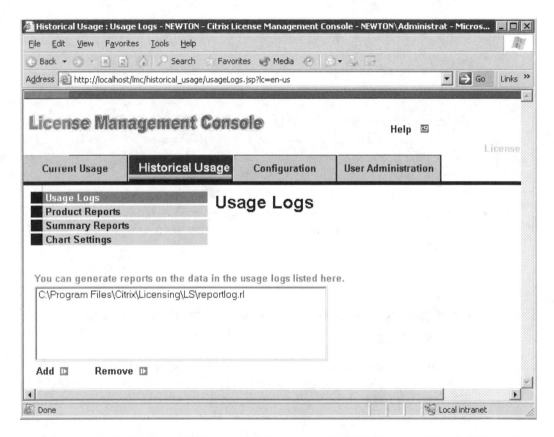

Figure 12.28   You must manually add the desired usage logs to the list in order to generate historical reports against these logs.

Administrative Delegation

By default the administrative account used to install the license server is automatically added to the list of administrators with full access to manage the configuration of the license server. Additional user accounts can be granted access to the management console by selecting the User Administration option. When this page opens, you see a list of the currently assigned users along with the privileges they have been granted. The access privileges correspond to the four menu options available:

- Current Usage
- Historical Usage
- Configuration
- User Administration

You can add a new user to the list by clicking the Add New User link. This opens a new page where you can add the desired users and define their access privileges. Existing accounts can also be modified by selecting Change Existing User Access Privileges. The list of existing users is then displayed, and you have the option to select or deselect the appropriate privilege.

TIP: Because the information stored in the license database is sensitive and critical to the proper function of MetaFrame, you should keep the list of users with access to this server as small as possible.

Configuring MetaFrame Licensing for High Availability and Fail-Over

Currently the Citrix license server does not support any form of real-time high availability or fail-over. The main factor impeding this is that all license files in this new licensing model are driven by the name of the license server, and you cannot have two machines operating with identical computer names on the network. There are a few options available that can be implemented to reduce the recovery time in the event of a catastrophic license server failure:

- **Maintain a backup copy of all license files in an alternate location that can be used to rebuild a new license server with the current license configuration**—This only needs to have the same computer name in order to use the existing license files. This name must match the original server's name exactly.

- **Maintain an image of the current license server**—This option uses any one of a number of popular drive-imaging software products, such as Symantec's Ghost, to store a complete image of the license server for quick recovery. This approach works best if you can use hardware as close as possible to the same as that of the original hardware.
- **Maintain a second license server with the exact same name but kept offline**—This approach, while effective, can be costly. Effectively, you are maintaining a hot spare of the license server that can quickly be brought online if the current production server fails.

Unfortunately none of these configurations is ideal, but I feel the first option is adequate in most situations. Very little is required to bring up a Windows server with a matching server name and perform the basic license server installation. Even if IIS is not available, the command line tools let you perform the necessary administration to get the new server up and running. A MetaFrame Presentation Server will function for 96 hours without active license server connectivity, which under normal circumstances should allow enough time to get even a very basic server up and running to keep the environment functioning until a permanent replacement can be put in place.

NOTE: Many people suggest running multiple license servers with different names and dividing the licenses between these servers, much like you could load-balance the Terminal Services License Server. Unfortunately this configuration works only if you have an environment where you can divide your MetaFrame servers in such a way that they can point at different license servers and there exists no overlap of user sessions between these server groups. If you have a user who requires access to two different servers, each pointing to a different license server, that user will consume two licenses.

In this chapter, we looked in detail at installation and configuration of both the Microsoft and the Citrix license server components. Once you have these license servers up and running properly, you are ready to proceed with installation of MetaFrame Presentation Server (if applicable) and then the remainder of the Terminal Server/MetaFrame environment configuration.

CHAPTER 13

MetaFrame Presentation Server Installation

Before You Begin

While I do not consider the actual installation steps for MetaFrame Presentation Server (MPS) to be much more complex than with previous versions of MetaFrame, the success of an MPS installation and deployment is much more dependent on the amount of implementation planning and preparation work done prior to actual installation of the first server.

Unlike MetaFrame 1.x, where all core environmental data (load balancing, application publishing, server farm membership, and so on) is maintained within the registry, MetaFrame Presentation Server now manages all this information in an actual database management system (DBMS). As a result, a number of configuration requirements may need to be satisfied before you can begin the actual MPS installation. For example, if you will be managing your MetaFrame data store from within a SQL Server database, the appropriate DBMS configuration must be done prior to initializing this data store with the first MetaFrame server installation.

This chapter looks not only at the installation steps for MetaFrame Presentation Server on Windows 2000/2003 but also discusses the steps required to configure these external components. During these discussions, I am assuming that you have already completed the necessary planning for your MetaFrame implementation. In particular, you should already know the following:

- Where your data store will reside and what DBMS you will implement.
- What connection type (direct or indirect) your MetaFrame servers will use to access this data store.
- Whether or not you will reassign the server drive letters.
- If you are creating a new server farm, you will need to know the name you will assign to your farm as well as the primary zone within which the initial server will reside.

- If you're joining an existing farm, then you will need to know the connection information for the system that is hosting the data store. This will either be the credentials for the DBMS or the name of the MetaFrame server that is hosting a local data store.

- If you're upgrading an existing MetaFrame 1.8 environment, you'll need to have decided whether you'll run your MetaFrame XP servers in mixed mode or in a completely separate parallel environment running in native mode.

NOTE: If you are not yet clear on your planned MetaFrame architecture, I highly recommend that you review Chapter 8, "Server Installation and Management Planning," prior to continuing your MetaFrame server installation. All the MetaFrame configuration suggestions discussed in this chapter are covered in detail in Chapter 8.

When Should MetaFrame Be Installed?

A commonly asked question is, exactly when in the server build process should MetaFrame Presentation Server be installed? In Chapter 8, "Server Installation and Management Planning," I provide a recommended order for configuration of a Terminal Server both with and without MPS. Here is an abbreviated list of steps I follow when building a MetaFrame Presentation Server (corresponding chapters containing more information on the particular step are shown in parentheses):

1. Install the base Windows operating system (Chapter 10, "Installing Windows Terminal Services").
2. Apply the appropriate service pack and/or hotfixes (Chapter 11, "Terminal Services Configuration and Tuning").
3. Perform the base Terminal Server stability and tuning configuration (also Chapter 11). If applicable to the implementation, I typically take a full backup image of the server at this point. Server imaging is discussed in Chapter 22, "Server Operations and Support."
4. If appropriate for your environment, reassign the server drive letters (Chapter 13, this Chapter).
5. Install and configure MetaFrame Presentation Server (Chapters 13 and 14).
6. Configure the base group policy objects and define the system security for the environment (Chapter 15, "Group Policy Configuration," and Chapter 16, "Terminal Server Security").

While it can be reasonably argued that MetaFrame can be installed prior to performing the stability and tuning configuration, I always recommend that all the necessary Windows service packs and hotfixes be applied before MPS is installed. Once the base MPS server has been built, the remaining server configuration and application installation steps can be performed. Chapter 8 provides details on these additional tasks.

General Installation Guidelines

When preparing to install MPS on your Terminal Server, the following installation guidelines should be observed:

- *Reassign server drive letters first.* If you have decided to reassign the server drive letters as part of your MetaFrame implementation (C: and D: become X: and Y:, for example), I recommend performing the Remap Drives option available on the main MPS installation screen (see Figure 13.1) prior to installing the MPS software or any of the dependent components, such as the Microsoft SQL Server 2000 Desktop Engine (MSDE) if this is the DBMS you will be using for your farm data store.

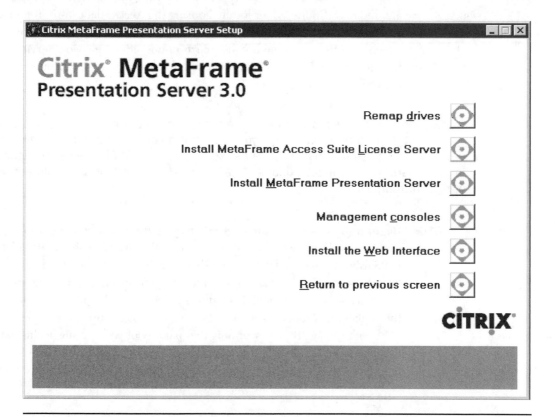

Figure 13.1 The Remap Drives option in the MPS installation dialog box lets you remap server drive letters.

NOTE: Server driver letter reassignment cannot be performed on a disk volume that has been converted to a dynamic disk using the Disk Management utility. If you want to reassign drive letters on your MetaFrame server, you must leave the disk volume configured as Basic.

- *Perform the MetaFrame installation prior to adding any applications to your Terminal Server*—Because MPS is so tightly integrated with operation of the server environment itself, it is always my preference to have MetaFrame installed, configured, and validated prior to introduction of any user applications onto the server. I find this helps simplify troubleshooting of any issues that may arise during either MPS installation or application installation phases.

- *Run consistent service pack/hotfix levels across all MetaFrame servers in the farm*—When deploying a service pack/feature release (along with any hotfixes), remember you need to ensure that you are running a consistent service pack/hotfix level across all servers in your farm, particularly the data collectors and the MetaFrame server locally housing the Access data store (if applicable). Fixes from Citrix typically involve corrections to the ICA or IMA components, which sometimes can modify their current operating behavior. Service pack/ feature release deployment is discussed in Chapter 14, "MetaFrame Presentation Server Configuration."

NOTE: One of the reasons why I like to remind administrators about the importance of consistent Citrix service pack deployment is that a common tendency when building a new server is to simply install the latest service packs without necessarily considering whether this may affect existing MetaFrame servers and/or users already working in the environment.

- *Begin testing your production infrastructure as early as possible*—Most experienced Windows administrators will likely perform a simple installation of MPS using an Access database and then start casually testing the features to see how they work. While this helps you to get up to speed with the features and functionality of the product, it shouldn't be considered a substitute for testing the actual infrastructure you expect to deploy. For example, if you plan to run MPS with Oracle, then performing the majority of your testing against an Access data store will not provide you with a good indication of how your production environment will behave. Plan to have your production infrastructure available as early as possible so you have adequate time to perform proper testing.

NOTE: If you're creating a MetaFrame server that will act as a dedicated zone data collector (discussed in Chapter 8), then it is not necessary to remap the server drive letters or install client software such as Microsoft Office.

It *is* still extremely important that you retain consistent MetaFrame versioning amongst all of the MetaFrame servers, including any dedicated zone data collectors that might have been built. The specific configuration options for a dedicated ZDC are discussed in Chapter 14.

Upgrades Versus Clean Installations

Another commonly asked question is whether an existing MetaFrame server should be upgraded to MetaFrame Presentation Server, or if a clean installation of the operating system followed by MetaFrame is preferable. Table 13.1 provides a summary of the migration suggestions I discussed in Chapter 8.

Table 13.1 A Summary of Migration Options for MetaFrame

Current Configuration	Target Configuration	Comments
MetaFrame 1.8 or XP 1.0 on Windows NT 4.0, Terminal Server Edition	MetaFrame Presentation Server on Windows Server 2000 or Windows 2003 Server	I recommend that you perform a clean installation of the Windows server followed by installation of MetaFrame. Performing an upgrade will not let you take advantage of the tighter registry and file system security features of Windows Server 2000 or 2003. All existing security settings will simply be inherited from the existing NT 4.0 Terminal Server environment.
MetaFrame 1.8 or XP 1.0 on a Windows 2000 Terminal Server	MetaFrame Presentation Server on Windows Server 2000 or Windows 2003 Server	A clean installation of the operating system is normally *not* required unless you have concerns about the stability of your current environment. If there are issues, it is highly *unlikely* that an upgrade will resolve them. You should either correct the current problems before upgrading or consider starting with a clean server build.

Table 13.1 A Summary of Migration Options for MetaFrame (continued)

Current Configuration	Target Configuration	Comments
		If you plan on upgrading the existing MetaFrame 1.8 server, *don't install MPS directly over the top of it.* Instead, stop publishing any of the applications on the server and uninstall the current MetaFrame version. Next, upgrade to Windows Server 2003 if desired and follow that with an installation of MetaFrame Presentation Server.

Remapping Server Drive Letters

If you will be reassigning your server drive letters (C: to X: and D: to Y:, for example), it is recommended that you perform this remapping operation before proceeding with any other MetaFrame installation task. MetaFrame server drive remapping lets you configure how server and local drives will appear to users while they're logged on to the MetaFrame server. Figure 13.2 shows the main system drive reassigned from the traditional C: to X:. The section titled "Server Drive Letter Reassignment" in Chapter 8 discusses in more detail the features and purpose of client drive reassignment and Citrix's support for client drive mapping. If you have not yet made a decision as to whether you will reassign local drive letters, please review this section in Chapter 8 before continuing.

NOTE: It is not absolutely required that you perform the server drive remapping prior to installing MPS, but from a complexity standpoint, the earlier in the server configuration process the remapping is done, the greater the probability that it will complete without issue. Because remapping the server drives involves updating such system components as the registry and shortcut links, the more applications installed on the server, the greater the likelihood that something will be missed and begin to fail once the drive letters have changed. Because of this, it is generally suggested that the remapping process be one of the first tasks performed when installing MetaFrame Presentation Server.

Server drive reassignment is initiated in one of two ways: Either click the Remap Drives option from the Citrix MetaFrame Presentation Server Setup dialog box, or double-click the DriveRemap.exe located in the root of the MPS Setup CD-ROM. Once the utility has started, you are presented with the dialog box shown in Figure 13.3.

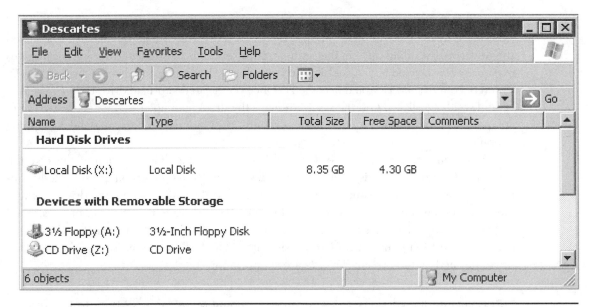

Figure 13.2   The system drive reassigned to X: from C: on a Windows 2003 Terminal Server.

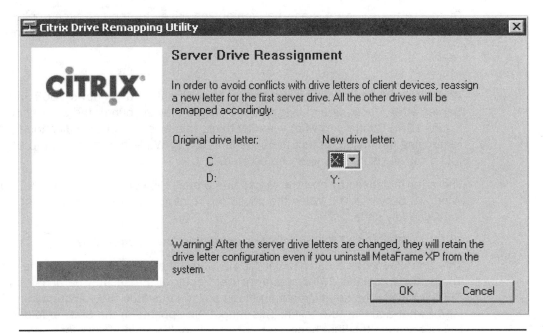

Figure 13.3   The Citrix MetaFrame Server Drive Reassignment dialog box.

To reassign the server drive letters, simply select the alternate drive letter on the right-hand side of the dialog box. All other physical drives on the server will automatically be assigned the next corresponding drive in the sequence. For example, if you had three physical drives on your server labeled C:, D:, and E: and you selected the remapped drive to be X:, then D: would become Y: and E: would become Z:. Once the desired alternate drive has been selected and you have clicked OK, the system remaps the drives and updates the necessary system components. You will be required to restart the server in order to complete the remapping operation.

As I mentioned earlier in the "General Installation Guidelines" section of this chapter, you cannot perform a reassignment on any disk volume that has been configured as a dynamic disk volume. When a volume has been configured as dynamic, running the drive reassignment program will not generate an error, but only those drive letters that can be reassigned will be displayed. This usually means that only the CD/DVD-ROM drive is listed as being able to convert to the new drive letter assignment. The system/boot partition and any other drives defined on the dynamic volume are simply ignored.

TIP: Unlike earlier versions of MetaFrame, including MetaFrame XP prior to Feature Release 3, server drive remapping is no longer a one-way operation. You can rerun the DriveRemap utility as often as required to change the drive letter assignments.

Of course the same rules as when remapping drives for the first time apply. You should still remap drives prior to installing any other MPS component or application.

WARNING: When performing the drive reassignment on a Windows 2003 Terminal Server, after rebooting and logging back on you may encounter the error shown in Figure 13.4. Contrary to what you may think, this error is not an indication that the remapping has failed. In fact the secedit.INTEG.RAW file that exists in the Startup folder for All Users can safely be deleted.

The error is caused by how the remapping process is currently implemented for Windows Server 2003. When the drives are remapped, an entry is added to the RunOnce key under

HKEY_CURRENT_USER\Software\Microsoft\Windows\CurrentVersion

This entry launches a batch script the next time that user logs on after the reboot. The script automatically initiates a recover/repair of the security database called SECEDIT.SDB. The resulting output file is called secedit.INTEG.RAW and contains a log of what actions were taken. This output file appears in the Startup folder for All Users because this just happens to be the default working folder for entries in the Run and RunOnce keys.

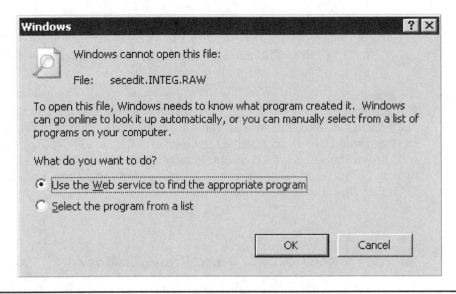

Figure 13.4 An error message that may appear after remapping drives on a Windows 2003 Terminal Server.

IMA Data Store Installation Prerequisites

At the beginning of this chapter I mentioned how important it is to have determined what type of database management system (DBMS) you will be using to house your MetaFrame server farm data store *before* performing the actual installation of the MPS software. In this section, I look at configuration requirements for the five supported database management systems:

- **Microsoft Access**—Available by default as a component of Windows Server 2000 or Windows 2003 Server.
- **Microsoft SQL Server 2000 Desktop Engine (MSDE)**—Included on the Citrix MetaFrame Presentation Server CD-ROM in the Support folder or free of charge directly from the Microsoft Web site. Citrix supports running MSDE only in *indirect* mode (direct and indirect modes were discussed in Chapter 8), although MSDE can be implemented in a direct-mode configuration for small MetaFrame environments.
- **Microsoft SQL Server**—SQL Server 2000 or SQL Server 7.0 (with SP2 or higher) are both supported.

- **Oracle**—Oracle9i Release 2 Enterprise Edition, Oracle 8i (8.1.6 or higher), Oracle 8 (8.0.6), and Oracle 7 (7.3.4) are all officially supported.
- **IBM DB2**—DB2 Enterprise Edition 7.2 and DB2 8 are both supported.

NOTE: You should know not only what DBMS you will use but also where it will reside. Aside from the Microsoft Access and MSDE solutions, no other supported database system should be run on a MetaFrame server. SQL Server, Oracle, and DB2 all require a dedicated server on which to run. In large deployments where you will implement Access or MSDE, you may also want to have a dedicated data store server. This configuration was discussed in Chapter 8.

Microsoft Access Data Store Prerequisites

Microsoft Access is by far the easiest data store to configure for your MetaFrame server farm. The default ODBC drivers available with both Windows Server 2003 and Windows 2000 Server are suitable for connecting to an Access-based MetaFrame data store. As a result, there are no additional configuration steps required before you can install MPS. During MPS installation you are prompted to create the Access data store.

Microsoft SQL Server 2000 Desktop Engine Prerequisites

The Microsoft SQL Server 2000 Desktop Engine (MSDE) can be deployed in one of two ways:

- The first requires MSDE to be installed onto the first MetaFrame server in the environment. This is the only method currently supported by Citrix.
- The second involves installing MSDE onto a separate database or file server and configuring MSDE to allow remote network connections, much like a traditional Microsoft SQL Server. The limitations on this approach are discussed below.

Indirect MSDE Access Prerequisites.

If you plan to use MSDE as your server farm's indirect data store, you will need to install it on the first MetaFrame server in your farm *prior* to installing MPS itself. Before installing MSDE, remap the server drives if desired. If you wish to access MSDE in direct mode, please follow the installation instructions in the "Direct MSDE Access Prerequisites" section. MSDE for indirect access can be installed as follows:

1. Place the server into install mode by issuing the following command from a command prompt:

```
change user /install
```

2. Now run the SetupMSDEForMetaFrame.cmd batch script located in the \Support\MSDE folder on the MPS Setup CD-ROM. This batch script installs MSDE with an instance name of CITRIX_METAFRAME, which MetaFrame will look for when using an MSDE-based data store.

3. Once installation completes, the MSDE setup dialog box closes, and the service labeled MSSQL$CITRIX_METAFRAME is created and set with a start-up type of "automatic." The service is *not* initially started by the setup program, so you will have to either reboot the server or manually start the service. Once installation completes, place the server back into execute mode:

```
change user /execute
```

4. You can start the service a couple of different ways: using the Computer Management MMC snap-in or using the SQL Server Service Manager. The SQL Server Service Manager automatically launches the next time you log on to the server; the short cut can be found in the Startup folder under Programs on the Start menu. When the program is launched, an icon appears in the system tray; double-clicking it brings up the SQL Server Service Manager, shown in Figure 13.5. Make sure that the service labeled SQL Server appears in the Services field, and then click the Start/Continue button. Once the service has started, you are ready to continue on to the final pre-installation configuration steps before MetaFrame Presentation Server installation using the MSDE-based data store.

Figure 13.5   The SQL Server Service Manager application.

Direct MSDE Access Prerequisites.

In Chapter 8 I briefly discussed how MSDE could be implemented as either a directly or an indirectly accessed database management system. When operating in a direct-mode, MSDE access is identical to that of Microsoft SQL Server. Citrix does not official support this configuration because of the performance throttling that automatically initiates when there are 5 or more concurrent connections to the database system. When this is exceeded, Microsoft throttles the performance of MSDE to mirror similar performance from a Microsoft Access database under similar load. Even when artificially loaded, MSDE will continue to function properly, continuing to accept connections, contrary to what most people may think.

When implementing a direct-access MSDE data store, the prerequisites are identical to those for a full Microsoft SQL Server data store, including support for Windows authentication. The SQL Server data store prerequisites are discussed in the next section.

Before you can configure MSDE access, the software must first be installed on the host server. Even if another instance of MSDE is already running on the host server, you will need to install a new instance of MSDE on the server specifically for the Citrix MetaFrame data store. The easiest way to do this is to utilize the MSDE installation files that are provided on the MPS CD-ROM media. The installation steps are as follows:

1. Log onto the server that will host the MSDE database and run the SetupMSDEForMetaFrame.cmd batch script located in the \Support\MSDE folder on the MPS Setup CD-ROM. This batch script installs MSDE with an instance name of CITRIX_METAFRAME. You can change this instance name by modifying the batch command file. In order to do this you will have to copy the contents of the MSDE folder to the server's local hard drive.

2. Once installation completes the MSDE setup dialog box closes, and the service labeled MSSQL$CITRIX_METAFRAME is created and set with a start-up type of "automatic." The service is *not* initially started by the setup program, so you will have to either reboot the server or manually start the service.

3. You can start the service a couple of different ways: using the Computer Management MMC snap-in or using the SQL Server Service Manager. The SQL Server Service Manager automatically launches the next time you log on to the server; the short cut can be found in the Startup folder under Programs on the Start menu. When the program is launched, an icon appears in the system tray; double-clicking it brings up the SQL Server Service Manager, shown in the previous Figure 13.5. Make sure that the service labeled SQL Server appears in the Services field, and then click the Start/Continue button.

Once the service has started, you will need to review the Microsoft SQL Server data store prerequisites in the next section to ensure your environment is ready to utilize an MSDE-based data store accessed in direct mode.

Microsoft SQL Server Data Store Prerequisites

If you plan to use Microsoft SQL Server to house the data store for your MetaFrame server farm, there are a few configuration tasks you need to complete prior to performing the actual MetaFrame installation. In particular:

- If you are going to use Windows authentication on the SQL Server, you need to create the appropriate domain account.
- You need to create the database and configure security so the MetaFrame setup program can create the data store tables.
- You need to install and configure the ODBC SQL Server drivers on your Terminal Server.

Windows Authentication Requirements

Microsoft SQL Server supports two methods of authentication. The first is native SQL Server authentication, which validates users based on user IDs and passwords that are managed from within the SQL Server Enterprise Manager. These accounts are valid only within the SQL Server and cannot be used for authentication outside this scope. The second method is Windows authentication, which grants (or denies) access to objects in SQL Server based on the user's Windows domain credentials, not a local SQL user ID. Figure 13.6 shows the New Login dialog box within SQL Server 2000. You can see the option for selecting the desired authentication type (Windows or SQL Server) for this login ID.

While use of SQL Server authentication simplifies installation of a MetaFrame data store, many organizations have configured their production SQL Servers to support only Windows authentication. This authentication mode is Microsoft's recommended security mode and is the default for SQL Server 2000.

NOTE: MSDE also supports both authentication methods, although only Windows authentication is enabled by default. The steps to utilize Windows authentication with MSDE in direct mode are identical to those for SQL Server.

MetaFrame Presentation Server *does* support use of Windows authentication within Microsoft SQL Server, but some configuration work must be done both before and after installation of MetaFrame in order to ensure everything is working properly. For now I focus on the steps that must be done *prior* to installing MPS in order to support Windows authentication. The post-installation steps are discussed in the section "Post-Installation Tasks," later in this chapter. The following steps must be performed if you wish to use Windows authentication with your data store:

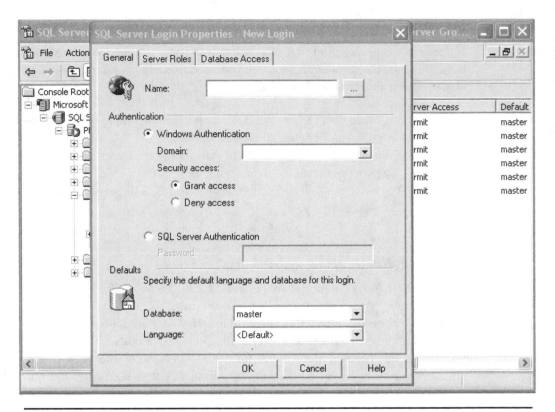

Figure 13.6 The authentication options available within Microsoft SQL Server.

1. First, the Terminal Server must belong to a Windows domain that is accessible by the SQL Server. If your Terminal Server is not yet in a domain, you need to join one prior to installing MetaFrame.

2. Next, you need to create an account in the domain that will be used by all Meta-Frame servers when connecting directly to the SQL Server data store. This account doesn't require administrative privileges on either the domain or the SQL Server and ideally should be configured with as limited access as possible.

   I recommend that you also create a global domain security group, such as "Citrix Data Store Access," whose sole member (at least initially) will be your new domain account. The domain user account should be excluded from all other groups, including domain users. Figure 13.7 shows the Members Of tab for a domain account that I created (called CitrixDSUser). Note that this account belongs only to the global group Citrix Data Store Access, which is used nowhere else in the environment to assign permissions.

   Make certain that a strong password is used for this account. Even though it will have limited privileges, every effort should be made to ensure the account remains secure. If you ever modify the password for this account, you must remember to make the corresponding change on *all* MetaFrame servers that use this account to connect to the data store; otherwise, the IMA service will continue to try to authenticate using the old password. This will not only cause the IMA service to fail on start-up but also may cause the user account to become locked out.

You can change the password used by the IMA service to access the data store by running the DSMAINT command. See Appendix B, "MetaFrame Presentation Server Command Reference," for details on use of this command.

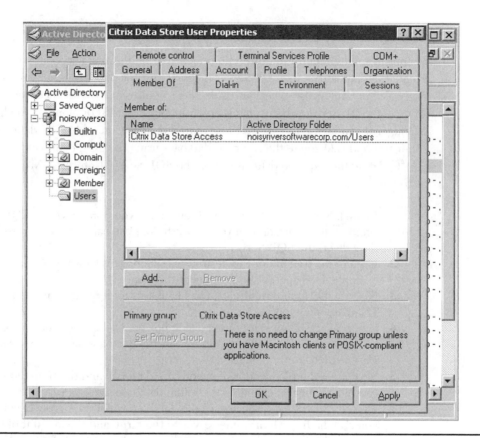

Figure 13.7 The Members Of tab for the special Citrix Data Store user account.

3. The final requirement is that your newly created domain account (or the domain group it resides in) be temporarily added to the local Administrators group on the Terminal Server where you will be installing MPS. Otherwise, the MetaFrame installation will fail when it tries to start the IMA service. Once installation is complete you can terminate this user's membership in the local Administrators group. I remind you of this step in the "Post-Installation Tasks" section of this chapter. Before you can begin installing MetaFrame you must first ensure that a database exists on the SQL Server (or MSDE server) into which the data store information will be written. This is discussed in the next section.

NOTE: While the steps in this section provide a walkthrough for preparing a SQL Server for installing a Citrix data store, unless you are intimately familiar with installation and management of SQL Server, I recommend that you enlist the services of a SQL Server database administrator (DBA) to ensure that your server is optimally configured for performance and availability.

SQL Server Data Store Creation

Before installing MetaFrame Presentation Server on the first server in your farm, you must create the database on the SQL Server that will host the data store. One method is to use the SQL Server Enterprise Manager. This tool requires you to be licensed to run the full Microsoft SQL Server product and is not available with MSDE alone. If you have Enterprise Manager it can be used to create the required database on an MSDE database as well. The other method is to create the required database using the SQL command line tool OSQL.

Creating the required database using the SQL Server Enterprise Manager is performed as follows:

1. Launch SQL Server Enterprise Manager. If you don't have the SQL Server management tools installed on your workstation, you can run Enterprise Manager directly off the SQL Server.
2. Expand the tree under the desired SQL Server, as shown in Figure 13.8. In this example, I expanded the contents of the local SQL Server.
3. Next, highlight and right-click the Databases folder and then select the New Database menu option.
4. When the Database Properties dialog box opens, enter the desired database name for the data store. In this example I use the database name Citrix_DataStore (see Figure 13.9).
5. Verify that the file locations for both the database and the transaction log are correct. I also suggest changing the initial database size from 1MB to somewhere around 25 to 50MB. The size of the database will always grow beyond 1MB once you add the first MetaFrame server to the farm, and the amount of growth to be witnessed will depend on factors such as number of published applications, number of printer drivers being replicated, and number of servers in the farm. Setting the database to a relatively large initial value is not going to impact the data store itself, but it can waste server drive space because the requested size is pre-allocated by the SQL Server. In general I use 2MB per server as a guide and ensure that the database is configured to grow as required. The transaction log can be left at the default value of 1MB. Click OK to create the database.

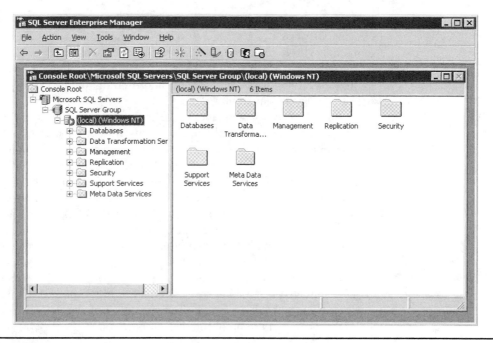

Figure 13.8   SQL Server 2000 Enterprise Manager.

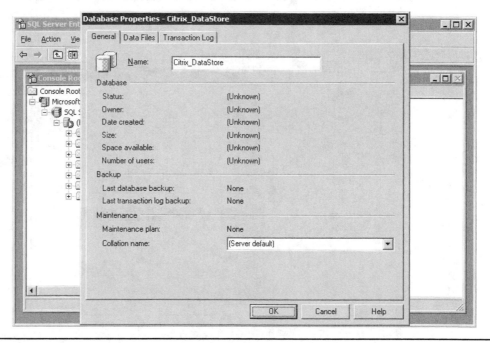

Figure 13.9   Creating the SQL Server database for the Citrix data store.

6. Now that the database has been created, a user account must be assigned permissions to this database so it can be used to set up the necessary tables during MetaFrame installation. This account will also be used by the IMA service on all MetaFrame servers within the server farm that will be *directly* connecting to the data store. Begin by expanding the Security folder and then right-click Logins and select New Login from the pop-up menu.

7. Before entering the new login name, select the desired authentication method. If you have chosen Windows authentication, enter the appropriate domain name in the Domain drop-down list box. Alternatively you can enter the domain name as part of the login name. For example, if I had a domain called NRSC and the account CitrixDSUser, I would enter NRSC\CitrixDSUser in the Name field.

   If you're using SQL Server authentication, in addition to entering the user name, make sure to enter a password in the Password field. Both the user name and the password will be required during MetaFrame installation.

8. Next, make sure to modify the default database for the user to match the one you just created.

9. Now click the Database Access tab (along the top of this dialog box) and select the check box next to the database you just created. In the lower list box, make sure the check box next to db_owner is also selected, as shown in Figure 13.10.

10. Click OK to complete setup of the data store account.

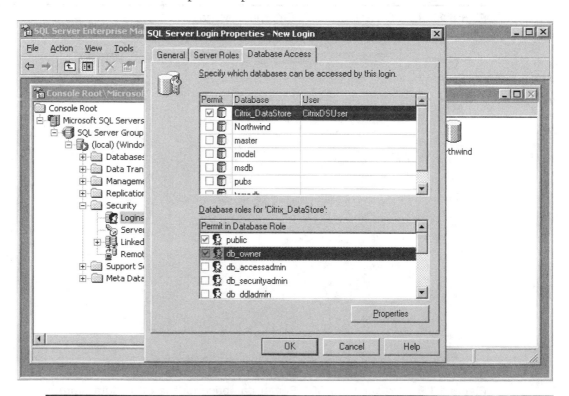

Figure 13.10   Assigning access to the Citrix_DataStore database.

If you're using MSDE or don't wish to use Enterprise Manager, you can create the required database using OSQL. If you have already created the database using the Enterprise Manager then you do not need to perform this manual step. The database is now ready to be populated.

While you can enter individual commands from the OSQL command prompt, I prefer to prepare a SQL script that can then be called from within OSQL to perform all of the necessary tasks. The following script, (available on the Website for this book) will create a database called Citrix_DataStore and assign ownership to an account called NRSC\CitrixDSUser. You will have to modify this file to use your Windows domain account or local SQL Server account.

Listing 13.1   Sample script to create the Citrix data store database in a SQL Server or MSDE server.

```
CREATE DATABASE Citrix_DataStore
GO

USE Citrix_DataStore
GO

exec sp_grantlogin N'NRSC\CitrixDSUser'
exec sp_defaultdb N' NRSC\CitrixDSUser ', N'Citrix_DataStore'
GO

EXEC sp_grantdbaccess N' NRSC\CitrixDSUser ', N'Citrix_DataStore'
GO
```

1. While this task can be performed remotely, I prefer to log on locally to the server running SQL Server or MSDE.
2. Open a command prompt on the server and execute the command

   ```
   OSQL -E -S <server>\<database instance>  -i <path to
   script file> -o <path to output file>
   ```

   If you're accessing a single instance on a SQL Server then omit the <database instance> name. If you're accessing MSDE then make sure that it has been included. For example, if my server name is TURING, and I've performed a default MSDE installation, then my full OSQL command would be:

   ```
   OSQL -E -S turing\Citrix_MetaFrame -i c:\createdb.sql -o
   c:\output.txt
   ```

3. The script will then be executed and the output redirected to the output.txt file.

The SQL Server (or MSDE) data store is now ready to be populated during installation of the first MetaFrame Presentation Server in your farm.

TIP: If you plan to implement multiple MetaFrame data stores, note they can be maintained on the same SQL Server. Furthermore, the same logon account can be used for all direct data store connections. You can specify an alternate database for the logon account during MPS installation. This database is then used every time the MetaFrame server connects to the SQL Server.

Grouping multiple data stores on a single SQL Server introduces a single point of failure, and such risk needs to be suitably mitigated to satisfy the business. In most cases, hardware redundancy such as RAID disk drives or multiple power supplies coupled with a sound backup and recovery process are sufficient to ensure that the SQL Server is available to support the hosted server farms.

SQL Server ODBC Driver Requirements

To access a Microsoft SQL Server data store, your Terminal Server must have version 3.70.08.20 or higher of the SQL Server ODBC driver installed. A supported version of this driver ships with both Windows Server 2003 and Windows 2000 Server. You can determine the current version of your driver by running Data Sources (ODBC), located under Administrative Tools on the Start menu. Under the Drivers tab, you will find the SQL Server driver listed with its version number, as shown in Figure 13.11. With the appropriate ODBC drivers available, you are ready to proceed to the final pre-installation configuration steps before MetaFrame Presentation Server installation.

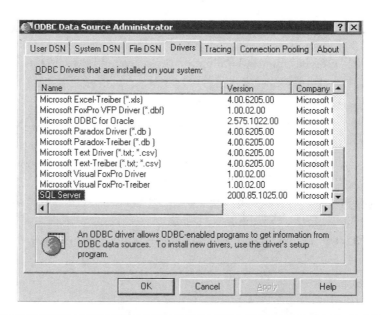

Figure 13.11 Find the SQL Server driver version using the ODBC Data Source Administrator dialog box.

Oracle Data Store Prerequisites

If you are going to use Oracle as the data store repository for your MetaFrame server farm, then, just as with Microsoft SQL Server, there are a few tasks you must perform prior to actual installation of the MetaFrame Presentation Server software:

- Create a new database and the associated tablespace that will contain the data store information. While Citrix documentation suggests using the default database, I prefer creating a completely separate database for this purpose.
- Create the user account that will access these tables.
- Install the Oracle client on the Terminal Server and configure the ODBC Oracle driver.

TIP: While Oracle does support Windows authentication when the DBMS is run on a Windows server, Citrix currently doesn't have a mechanism to support using this authentication method to connect to an Oracle-based data store. Native Oracle authentication is the only authentication option currently supported.

NOTE: The steps in the following section provide a walkthrough for preparing an Oracle server for installation of a Citrix data store, but unless you are intimately familiar with management of an Oracle server, I recommend enlisting the services of an Oracle database administrator (DBA) to ensure that your server is optimally configured for performance and availability.

Oracle Data Store Creation

Before you can install MetaFrame on the first server in your farm, you must create the database on the Oracle server that will host your farm's data store. The following steps summarize how this is done on an Oracle9i server.

1. Begin by launching the Database Configuration Assistant, located under the Programs->Oracle–OraHome90->Configuration and Migration Tools folder on the Start menu. Click Next to proceed past the Welcome dialog box.
2. Select the Create a Database operation and then click Next.
3. Now select the New Database radio button shown in Figure 13.12 and click Next. If you do not see the Includes Datafiles column, you can resize the dialog box to bring this column into view.

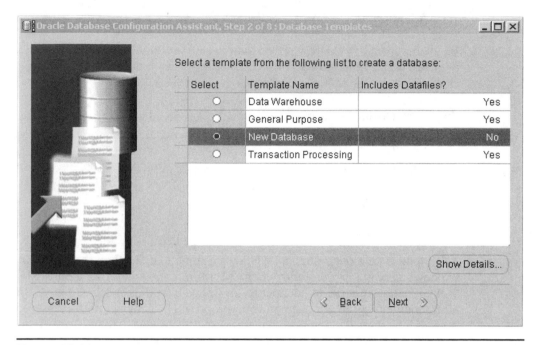

Figure 13.12   Selecting a template for your new Oracle database.

NOTE: As you work through the Database Configuration wizard, I suggest that you review each dialog box carefully to ensure that all information is actually displayed and not cut off because a dialog box was inappropriately sized.

---

4. In the next dialog box, provide a global database name. On an Oracle 8i server, this name must be eight characters or less. The SID field will automatically be populated with the same name information. For example, you might use CITRIXDS as your global database name.

5. Next you are presented with the Database Options dialog box. You can deselect the Example Schemas check box, since these are not required for your data store. When deselecting the sample schemas you may be presented with the option to delete any associated tablespaces. Deleting these will not affect your database creation. Click Next to continue.

6. Step 5 of 8 is the Database Connection Options dialog box (see Figure 13.13). Here you select the operation mode for your database. The Shared Server Mode is an appropriate configuration for the data store, as it allows access to more tuning options and features such as load balancing.

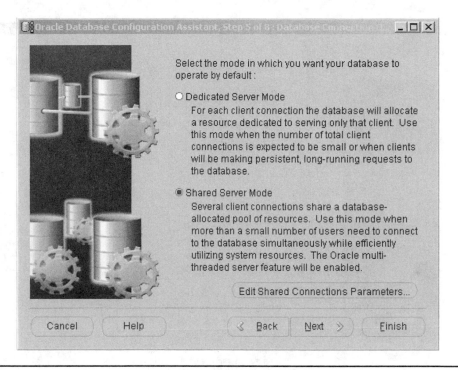

Figure 13.13   The Oracle Database Connection Options dialog box.

7. Next you define the initialization parameters, as shown in Figure 13.14. Select the Typical radio button and then enter the number of servers you expect to be directly connected to the data store in the concurrent connected users text field. For example, if you will have five servers in your farm, you can enter a value between 5 and 10. You can modify this value at any time to reflect changes in your farm configuration.

The default memory percentage of 70 percent should not be adjusted unless this server is going to provide other services in addition to the Oracle data store. Reducing the memory allocation will impact performance of the database if not managed properly. If the value is set too low, the actual database creation step later in the wizard will generate an error message and prevent you from completing the installation.

The Database Type drop-down list box should be changed from Data Warehousing to Online Transaction Processing (OLTP). Once these options have been set, click Next to continue. The remaining parameters don't need to be modified for a typical Citrix data store.

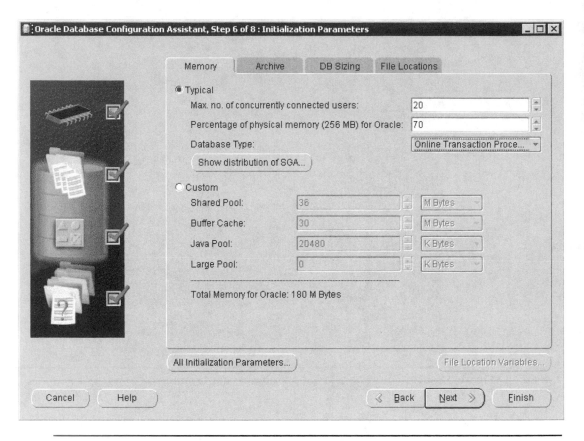

Figure 13.14   The initialization parameters for Oracle9i database installation.

8. Although the Database Storage dialog box lets you add or delete objects (such as tables) from the listed folders, I recommend that you delay any such adjustments until after the database creation is complete. Click Next to proceed to the final dialog box.

9. Here you can specify the final options before the actual database is created. At the very least, make sure that the Create Database check box is selected and then click Finish to begin the actual database creation process. Once the creation has completed, a summary message for the new database should appear. Do not exit this dialog box yet; we have one more step to accomplish.

10. Click the Password Management button located on the bottom right of the dialog box. You must manually unlock each of the locked accounts by clicking the checkmark and then enter a new password to replace the default password assigned. The SYSTEM password will remain as "manager."

11. Finally, click Exit to complete the database creation.

Now that the database exists, the next task is to create a separate tablespace to manage all the Citrix data store objects. A *tablespace* is a logical storage unit in an Oracle database and is typically used to simplify administration by grouping an application's objects together into one location. The tablespace is created as follows:

1. Begin by running the Enterprise Manager Console located under the Oracle-ORAHOME90 folder on the Start menu. If you don't have an Oracle management server in your environment, select Launch Standalone when prompted.
2. The console opens and should look similar to Figure 13.15. If the new database is not listed, you can right-click the Databases folder and add it to the list.

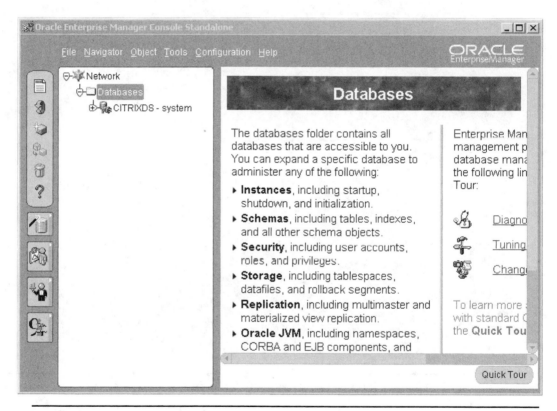

Figure 13.15   The Oracle Enterprise Manager Console.

3. Click the plus (+) sign next to your data store to expand the tree. When prompted, provide a user ID and password. For example, use the SYSTEM user ID and "manager" password. If you receive an error such as "ORA-12154:Could not resolve service name," run the Net Configuration Assistant (under Oracle-ORAHOME90 on the Start menu) first and define a new Local Net Service Name configuration for your database service.

4. With your data store name highlighted, select Create from the Object menu. A window opens listing the objects that can be created. Scroll down until you see Tablespace, highlight it, and then click the Create button.

5. The Create Tablespace dialog box now appears. Begin by assigning a name to the tablespace, as shown in Figure 13.16. For this example I use CITRIXDSTS. The corresponding file name is automatically entered.

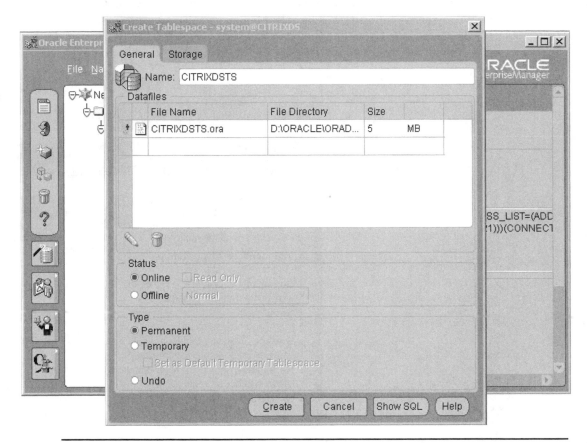

Figure 13.16   The Create Tablespace dialog box for the Citrix data store.

6. Next double-click the datafile name to open the Create Datafile dialog box. Select the Storage tab and then select the Automatically Extend Datafile When Full (AUTOEXTEND) option. The increment value can be set to 5000KB (5MB). The maximum size should be set to Unlimited. Click OK to close the dialog box and then click Create to create the new tablespace. The corresponding SQL to generate this tablespace looks as follows:

```
CREATE TABLESPACE "CITRIXDSTS"
LOGGING
DATAFILE 'D:\ORACLE\ORADATA\CITRIXDS\CITRIXDSTS.ora' SIZE 5M
AUTOEXTEND ON NEXT 5M MAXSIZE UNLIMITED EXTENT MANAGEMENT LOCAL
```

7. Now you need to create the associated user account that the MetaFrame servers will use to connect to the data store. Once again select Create from the Object menu, but this time select the User object. The Create User dialog box appears.

8. Provide a name for this account, for example, CitrixDSUser, and then enter the account's password. Make sure the password is suitably complex so it cannot be easily guessed. Make sure to record this information, as you will need it during MetaFrame Presentation Server installation.

9. Change the default tablespace from USERS to the tablespace you created earlier (CITRIXDSTS). The temporary tablespace entry can remain unchanged. Figure 13.17 shows what this information might look like.

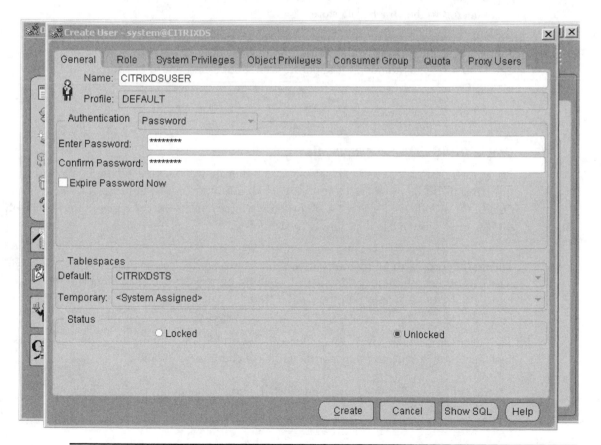

Figure 13.17 The Create User dialog box for the CitrixDSUser account.

10. Now select the Role tab and make sure this account is granted the CONNECT and RESOURCE roles. The Admin Option should not be selected for either account. No other options need to be modified, so you can click the Create button to add this new user to the system. The corresponding SQL to create this user would look similar to the following:

```
CREATE USER "CITRIXDSUSER" PROFILE "DEFAULT"
IDENTIFIED BY "password" DEFAULT TABLESPACE "CITRIXDSTS"
ACCOUNT UNLOCK;
GRANT "CONNECT" TO "CITRIXDSUSER";
GRANT "RESOURCE" TO "CITRIXDSUSER";
```

Once the user account has been created, you are ready to proceed with configuring the appropriate Oracle ODBC drivers on any soon-to-be MetaFrame servers that will be directly connected to the Oracle data store.

> **TIP:** Multiple MetaFrame data stores can reside within the same Oracle Server, but each must be maintained in a separate tablespace and use a separate Oracle logon account.

Oracle ODBC Driver Requirements

For your MetaFrame server to be able to communicate with an Oracle-based data store, you must install the appropriate ODBC driver. MetaFrame Presentation Server requires the Oracle ODBC driver, version 8.1.55 or later. MetaFrame does not support the Microsoft ODBC driver for Oracle that ships with Windows.

> **TIP:** You can determine the current version of your driver by running the Data Sources (ODBC) tool located under Administrative Tools on the Start menu. All currently installed drivers are listed on the Drivers tab.

The necessary Oracle installation files can be added by running the Oracle Universal Installer. Basic installation steps for the Oracle9i client are as follows:

1. Place the Terminal Server into install mode by opening a command prompt and running the command

```
change user /install
```

2. Launch the Oracle Universal Installer by running Setup from the Oracle installation media and selecting the Install/Deinstall Products option.

3. After clicking Next to move past the Welcome screen, enter the desired destination folder and Oracle Home name.

4. After you click Next, the Available Products screen loads, as shown in Figure 13.18. Select the Oracle9i Client option and click Next.

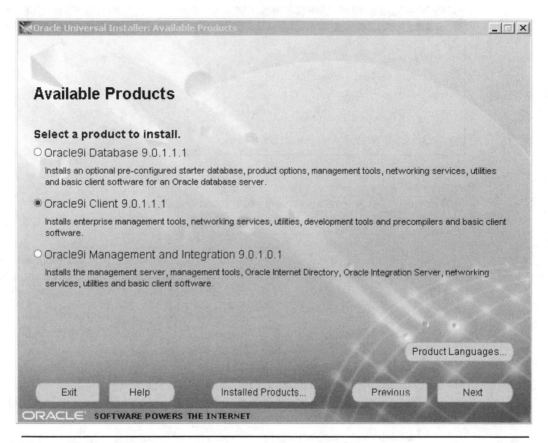

Figure 13.18 The Available Products screen for Oracle9i.

5. The 9i client provides three installation options: Administrator, Runtime, and Custom. While Runtime provides the necessary ODBC files, it also installs a number of additional options normally not required on a Terminal Server. Options such as the Oracle HTTP Server (Apache) are installed by default with the Runtime option. Table 13.2 summarizes the options that should be selected if you elect to go with the Custom option, which I recommend instead of Runtime. Aside from these options, all other components can be deselected. Begin by deselecting the Oracle HTTP Server component, as a number of dependent components cannot be deselected before this one. After selecting the components to install, click Next to continue.

Table 13.2 Custom Components Required to Connect to an Oracle-Based Citrix Data Store

Component to Install
Oracle Programmer 9.0.1.1.1
Oracle ODBC Driver 9.0.1.0.1
Oracle Net Services 9.0.1.1.1
Oracle Universal Installer 2.0.1.6.0
Oracle9i Windows Documentation 9.0.1.0.1

NOTE: Both the Oracle9i and 8i clients automatically install the Java Runtime Environment. This option cannot be deselected.

6. After entering the desired destination for the non-OracleHome components (Oracle Universal Installer and Java Runtime Environment), click Next to continue.

7. The Oracle9i Summary dialog box appears. After verifying your selections, click the Install button to perform the actual installation.

Once client installation is complete, the Oracle Net Configuration Assistant automatically launches (Figure 13.19). This tool lets you perform some basic client configuration and verify connectivity to the Oracle database. I recommend completing this step, as it ensures you can communicate properly with the database server prior to installing MetaFrame Presentation Server.

The Oracle Net Configuration Assistant can be configured as follows:

1. Begin by ensuring the Perform Typical Configuration dialog box *isn't* selected and then click Next. This allows more granularity in the configuration of your Oracle connection.

2. If a centralized directory server is configured for use with Oracle, you can select Yes on the next screen to configure this client to utilize those services. (Use of these services is beyond the scope of this book, but more information is available in the Oracle documentation provided with the installation media or online at http:// www.oracle.com.) Here I assume that no directory service is being used by Oracle and select "No, I want to defer this configuration to another time."

3. Next you are asked to select the methods used to locate and connect to a remote database service. The default option of Local is appropriate for a MetaFrame Presentation Server data store connection.

4. After selecting the correct Oracle database version, you are asked to provide the database's service name (see Figure 13.20). This is the name that was defined when the database was created. In the "Oracle Data Store Creation" section earlier in this chapter, I used the service name CITRIXDS.

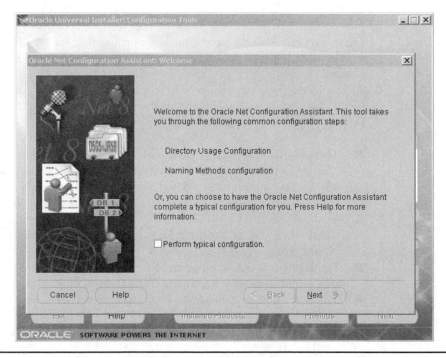

Figure 13.19 The Oracle Net Configuration Assistant.

Figure 13.20 Providing the service name for your Oracle database.

5. On the next screen, select TCP as the network protocol. After clicking Next you are asked to provide the host name and port number for the Oracle database server. The default port should be appropriate unless you provided an alternate during database creation.

6. After clicking Next you are asked to test your connectivity to the Oracle database. Click "Yes, perform a test" and then click Next. If the connection fails, this is likely due to one of the following reasons:

- The user name and password used to perform the test was invalid. Click the Change Login button and enter alternate credentials. For example, you should use the user account you created when setting up the tablespace for the data store. In the "Oracle Data Store Creation" section earlier in this chapter, I used the user ID CITRIXDSUSER. If the proper credentials have been provided, when you click OK the Details window should change to display "Connecting... Test successful."

- The host name could not be resolved. Make sure the name you entered is correct and, if necessary, make sure it is a fully qualified domain name.

- The port number is incorrect. You can verify the listening port number by running the Enterprise Manager Console on the Oracle server and selecting the database you created. The port number is listed in the General Properties tab for the database.

7. Once the connection has been tested successfully, the final configuration screen asks you to choose a name for this net service. After clicking through the final few screens, you are returned to the Oracle Universal Installer and receive the message that the installation was successful.

8. After exiting the installer, place the server back into execute mode by issuing the command

```
change user /execute
```

9. Unfortunately we are not quite finished. You now need to modify the SQLNET.ORA file to disable NT authentication support for the Oracle client. Citrix does not currently support this authentication mode for data store connectivity. Unless this option is disabled, the MetaFrame connection to the Oracle data store will fail. The SQLNET.ORA file is located in the following folder:
<Oracle_Base>\<Oracle_Home>\Network\Admin

For example, on my test server the path is
D:\Oracle\ora90\network\ADMIN

Edit the SQLNET.ORA file with a text editor such as Notepad and remove the (NTS) option so the variable simply looks like this:
SQLNET.AUTHENTICATION_SERVICES =

You can now save the file and exit from the editor.

10. The final configuration step, even though you are not prompted to do so, should be to reboot the Terminal Server prior to installing MetaFrame. Otherwise, the MetaFrame setup may fail when attempting to connect to the Oracle data store.

Once the server has rebooted, you are ready to proceed with configuration of the Java Runtime Environment (see the "Java Runtime Environment Installation" section, later in this chapter) before performing the actual MetaFrame Presentation Server installation.

NOTE: Those of you who have experience with earlier versions of MetaFrame XP and Oracle 8i or 9i clients are aware that there was an issue with the MFXP installation's not detecting the Oracle client after it had been installed on the server. This is no longer an issue with MetaFrame Presentation Server, and any Oracle 8i or later client is now properly detected by the MetaFrame installation.

IBM DB2 Data Store Prerequisites

If you will be using IBM DB2 as the data store repository for your Citrix farm, you will need to ensure that the following configuration tasks have been addressed prior to performing the MetaFrame server installation:

- Create a database on the DB2 server where the MetaFrame setup program can create the required data store tables.
- Install the DB2 runtime client with FixPak 5 or higher on each Terminal Server that will be directly connected to the DB2 database.

NOTE: While the steps in this section provide a walkthrough for preparing a DB2 server for installing a Citrix data store, unless you are intimately familiar with installation and management of IBM DB2, I recommend enlisting the services of an IBM DB2 database administrator (DBA) to ensure that your server is optimally configured for performance and availability.

DB2 Data Store Database Creation

Before installing MetaFrame on the first server in your farm, you must create the database on the DB2 server that will host the data store. This is done as follows:

1. From under the DB2 program folder on the Start menu, load the DB2 Control Center and traverse to the instance on the system where you will create the target database for your Citrix data store (see Figure 13.21).

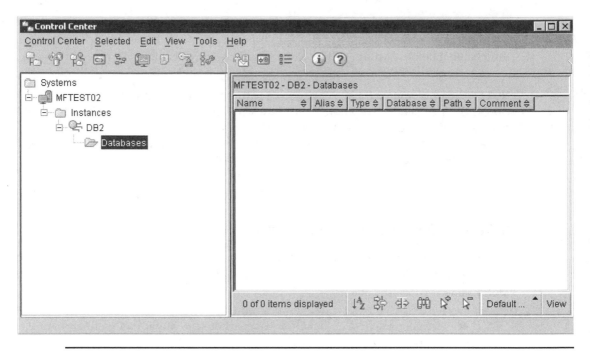

Figure 13.21   The DB2 Control Center application.

2. Right-click the Databases object and select the menu option Create -> Database Using Wizard.

3. The wizard begins by prompting you to select the desired name for your new database. I typically use a name such as CITRIXDS. The Alias and Comment fields can be left blank.

4. The next three dialog boxes prompt you to specify where you want to store the user tables, system catalog tables, and system temporary tables. You have the option of letting the system select a location, or you can manually specify the location yourself. Based on the data store load you expect to experience, select the storage location and method appropriate for your implementation. The Low Maintenance option is suitable for most implementations. If no containers are specified with this option, the system automatically creates one. Figure 13.22 shows the dialog box prompting where to store the user tables.

5. Depending on your server configuration, the next dialog box lets you tune performance of the database. Unless you are familiar with how these changes can affect the server's performance, I recommend that you not change any of the settings.

6. Next, configure the locale of your database based on your country or region and the requirements of your infrastructure.

7. The final screen summarizes the actions that will be performed to create the database. If everything appears correct, click the Finish button to initiate the creation sequence.

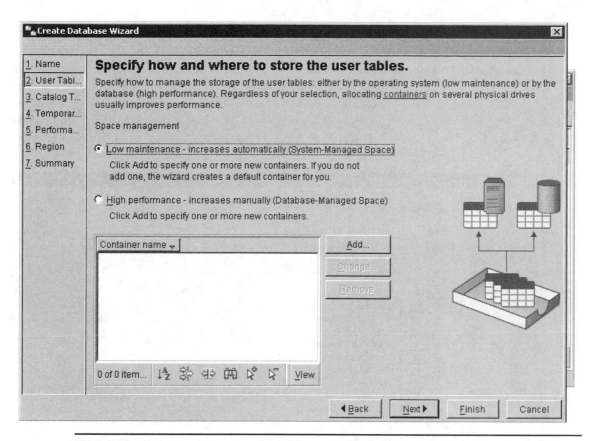

Figure 13.22   The dialog box for DB2 user tablespace management.

8. Once the database has been created, you are given the option to run the Configuration Advisor to tune the database. This utility can be run at any time simply by right-clicking a database in the Control Center and selecting Configuration Advisor from the pop-up menu.

TIP: If you plan to implement multiple MetaFrame data stores, note that they can be maintained on the same DB2 server. Furthermore, the same logon account can be used for all direct data store connections. You can specify an alternate database for the logon account during MetaFrame installation. This database is then used every time the MetaFrame server connects to the DB2 server. The specific change is pointed out in the "MetaFrame Presentation Server Installation Walkthrough" section of this chapter.

DB2 ODBC Driver Requirements

To access a DB2-based data store, your Terminal Server must have the DB2 ODBC runtime client installed prior to installing MetaFrame. The necessary client files can be installed using the DB2 installation media and selecting only the necessary client support features. Figure 13.23 shows an example of some of the options selected when installing the client files off the DB2 Enterprise Server Edition CD, and Table 13.3 shows a summary of the options that must be selected for the ODBC client. All other installation options not listed can be omitted.

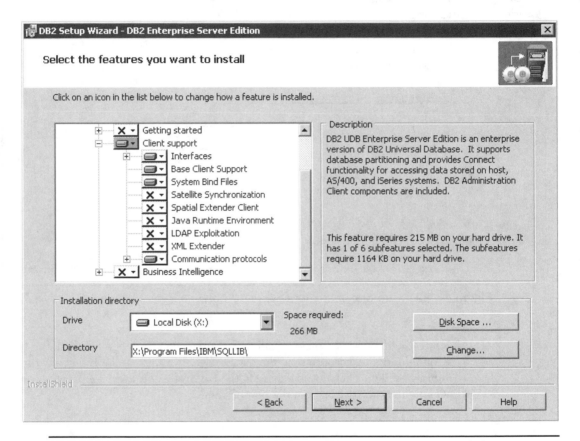

Figure 13.23   DB2 options for installing ODBC support.

Table 13.3 DB2 Client Installation Requirements for Allowing MetaFrame Database Access

ODBC Client Installation Requirements
Administration Tools\
Client Tools
Configuration Assistant
Client Support\Interfaces\ODBC Support
Client Support\Base Client Support
Client Support\Communication protocols\TCP/IP

Once installation has completed, you should verify that the ODBC driver has been installed by opening the Data Sources (ODBC) utility and looking for the driver labeled "IBM DB2 ODBC DRIVER" under the Drivers tab. If the driver is not present, then from within Add or Remove Programs, select Change for the DB2 application entry and verify that the necessary components listed in Table 13.3 have been selected. After confirming the existence of the DB2 ODBC driver, restart the server before continuing.

After the server has rebooted, configure the ODBC data source entry *prior* to starting the MPS installation as follows:

1. Open the Configuration Assistant application located under IBM DB2\Setup Tools on the Start menu.
2. Now select Add Database Using Wizard from the Selected menu, as shown in Figure 13.24.
3. The first screen asks you how you would like to set up your new connection. Select the Search the Network radio button and click Next. This option lets you specify a known server or scan the network for available DB2 servers.
4. If you know the name of the server that will host your data store, click the Add System button and then enter the server name when prompted. If you don't know the server name, you can double-click the Other Systems folder; the network will be searched and known DB2 servers will be listed.
5. The desired server should appear in either the Known Systems folder or the Other Systems folder. From here, drill down into the server until the target DB2 database you created is displayed, as shown in Figure 13.25. Highlight the database and then click Next.

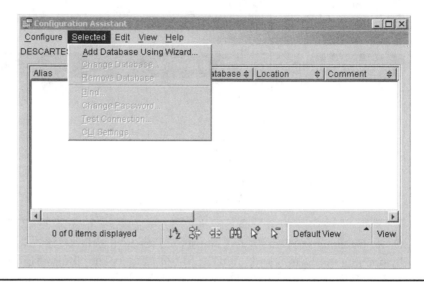

Figure 13.24 Adding a new database connection entry using the Configuration Assistant.

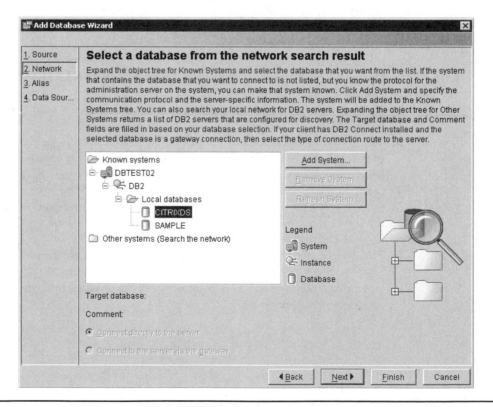

Figure 13.25 Selecting the target DB2 database for the Citrix data store.

6. Assign an alias to this database if you wish and then click Next.

7. You are presented with the option of registering this database as an ODBC data source. Begin by selecting the check box "Register this database for ODBC." Then configure this as a system data source and assign it a name. This is the name you will use to reference it when you install MetaFrame. Leave the optimization option set to None and then click Finish.

8. The test connection dialog box appears. Make sure the ODBC connection type has been selected and that you enter the user ID and password that your MetaFrame servers will use to connect to the data store (see Figure 13.26). Click Test Connection, and a successful connection message should appear.

You are now ready to proceed with configuration of the Java Runtime Environment, the final configuration task before performing the actual MetaFrame Presentation Server installation.

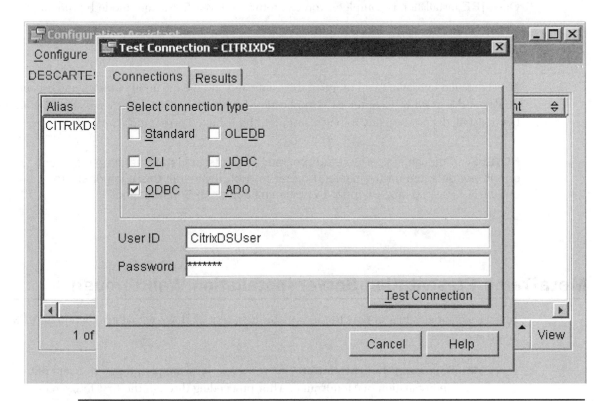

Figure 13.26 Testing the DB2 ODBC connection.

Java Runtime Environment Installation

With the necessary data store configuration tasks completed, there is only one task remaining before you can finally begin the MetaFrame installation: ensuring that the Java Runtime Environment (JRE) version 1.4.1_02 or higher is running on the server. The latest JRE version can be obtained directly from http://www.java.com, or you can install version 1.4.1_02 off the MPS installation CD-ROM. The installation files are located in the \Support\JRE14102 folder. You can determine the current JRE version on your server simply by running the command java –version from a command prompt.

Prior to installing JRE, make certain that the server is running in installation mode. The easiest way to set this is to open a command prompt and issue the following command:

```
change user /install
```

Once JRE installation is complete, you can return the user to execute mode by running the command

```
change user /execute
```

More detailed information on usage of this command and the meaning of install and execute modes is discussed in Chapter 21, "Application Integration." Once the necessary JRE has been installed, you are ready to begin setup of MetaFrame Presentation Server.

NOTE: Even though the MPS setup program attempts to install the supplied JRE if one is not detected on the server, I prefer to explicitly install this component to ensure it is set up properly prior to beginning actual MPS installation.

MetaFrame Presentation Server Installation Walkthrough

To try to maintain a logical flow to the walkthrough, I break down actual installation of MPS into three parts:

- **Beginning the installation**—Here you perform simple preparation and initiate installation of MetaFrame. After proceeding through the first few screens, you are asked to select the server farm in which this server will reside.
- **Server farm selection**—Here you either create a new farm or join an existing server farm. Installation steps for all four currently supported data stores (Access, Microsoft SQL Server, Oracle, and DB2) are discussed.

■ **Completing the installation**—After farm configuration is complete, remaining server installation steps are reviewed, including configuring shadowing functionality on the server and setting the XML TCP/IP listening port.

Beginning the Installation

To install MetaFrame Presentation Server, perform the following steps:

1. Log on at the Terminal Server's console using an account with administrative privileges. If you will be creating a new server farm and using Windows authentication on a Microsoft SQL Server, make sure to log on using the domain account you've created specifically for data store access. This account should also have temporary administrator privileges on your Terminal Server. Details on this are discussed in the "Microsoft SQL Server Data Store Prerequisites" section, earlier in this chapter.

After logging on, make sure that no users are logged on to the system. Unless you are 100 percent certain that no one will be logging on during the installation, I recommend also disabling client logons. My preference is to issue the following command from a command prompt:

```
change logon /disable
```

This disables Terminal Server logons for all client sessions (except the local console), ensuring that users can't log on while you're performing MetaFrame installation. Anyone attempting a remote connection receives a message stating that remote logons are currently disabled. This command will *not* automatically log off any users currently on the server. For a complete description of the CHANGE LOGON command, see Appendix A, "Terminal Services Command Reference." Once the server reboots at the end of MetaFrame installation, logons automatically are re-enabled.

Alternatively, you can disable connections using the Terminal Services Configuration tool, found under Administrative Tools on the Start menu. If you right-click a connection and select All Tasks, you see the option to disable connections. Disabling connections using this method immediately logs out any remote users currently logged on the system, and connections remain disabled even after a reboot.

WARNING: I recommend that you always perform MetaFrame Presentation Server installation directly from the console, particularly when installing MPS on the first server in a farm. I've experienced problems with the IMA service failing to start after performing the installation via a remote connection, including the remote console feature supported by Windows Server 2003.

---

2. Insert the MPS CD-ROM into the drive on your server. The main setup dialog box should appear. Click the MetaFrame Access Suite Installations icon, and then click Install MetaFrame Presentation Server to begin the installation. If the CD-ROM doesn't Autorun, or if you're performing the installation across the network, you can also initiate the installation by running AUTORUN.EXE from the root of the installation folder.

3. The MetaFrame License Agreement dialog box appears. You must accept the terms of this agreement before you can install MetaFrame. After you click the I Agree option, the Product Edition Selection dialog box appears, as shown in Figure 13.27. Make certain you have selected the product version you are licensed for and then click Next.

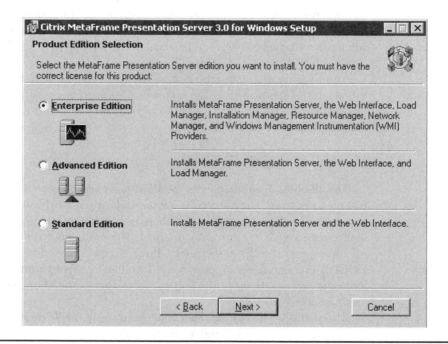

Figure 13.27   The MetaFrame Product Edition Selection dialog box.

4. You now have the choice of what components you will install on your MetaFrame server. Of course, the specific choices available depend on the product version you chose. Make sure you choose the components appropriate for your implementation based on the planning discussed in Chapter 8.

5. The next dialog box (Figure 13.28) prompts you to select whether or not to enable passthrough user authentication for the ICA Win32 passthrough client on the MetaFrame server. This setting dictates how the Win32 client on the MetaFrame server will behave, not how a local client on a user's desktop computer will authenticate. The passthrough client on a MetaFrame server lets you establish an ICA session from one MetaFrame server to another and was also discussed in Chapter 8.

Normally I recommend setting this option to Yes. Choose whether or not to enable passthrough authentication for the passthrough client and then click Next. If you wish to change your selection once MetaFrame has been installed, you must reinstall the passthrough client.

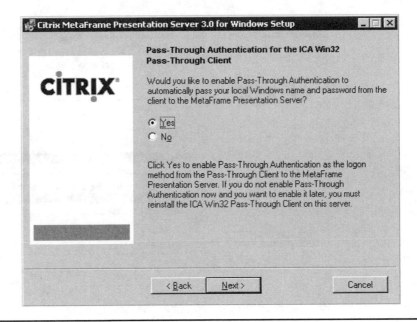

Figure 13.28   The passthrough authentication selection dialog box for the ICA Win32 client.

6. MetaFrame presents you with the Create or Join a Server Farm dialog box. You have two options on this screen: Either join an existing server farm or create a new farm. If this is the first MetaFrame server in your farm, you must select "Create a new server farm." If you are adding a server to an existing farm, you can jump directly to the "Joining an Existing Server Farm" section, later in this chapter.

Creating a New Server Farm

If you're adding your MetaFrame server to an existing farm, proceed to the section "Joining an Existing Server Farm"; otherwise, select "Create a new server farm" and click Next. You are asked to decide whether to use a local data store (Microsoft Access or SQL Server 2000 Desktop Engine [MSDE]) or a third-party database management system (Microsoft SQL Server, MSDE in direct mode, Oracle, or DB2). Figure 13.29 shows what the Create a Server Farm dialog box looks like. You should already have a clear idea as to which data store is appropriate for your implementation. Criteria for selecting the appropriate data store repository are discussed in Chapter 8. After selecting the desired data store, click Next to continue.

NOTE: If you are going to be accessing MSDE in direct mode, make sure that you select SQL Server and not MSDE. The MSDE selection on this screen will configure MSDE locally on this MetaFrame server.

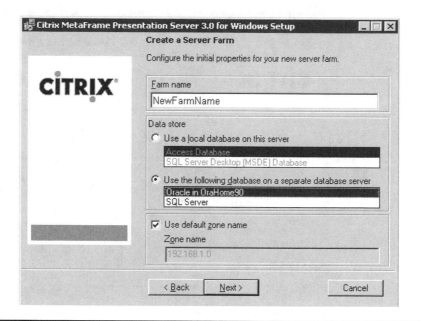

Figure 13.29   The MetaFrame Create a Server Farm dialog box.

The uppermost data entry field is where you will provide the name for your server farm. When entering a farm name, remember it can be no more than 32 characters in length and is case sensitive. For example, MetaFrame considers the farm names "Test Farm" and "Test farm" to be different. If you plan to run this server in interoperability mode, the farm name must match the MetaFrame 1.8 server farm name you plan to interoperate with.

In the lower section of this dialog box, you will see the zone name configuration option, with the default zone name automatically selected. If you decide to use the default zone name, MetaFrame generates a name based on the subnet address within which the server resides. For example, if the IP address for the MetaFrame server is 192.168.1.50 with a subnet mask of 255.255.255.0, then the zone name will be 192.168.1.0. I recommend providing your own unique zone name that represents either the geographical location of the zone or the zone's division in relation to other zones in the farm. Zone names can be changed after the installation through the Management Console. Once you've entered the desired zone name for this MetaFrame server, click Next to continue setting up the selected data store. You can now proceed to the appropriate following data store section for more information on setting up your farm to use the desired database management system.

Microsoft Access Data Store

No additional steps are required when using Microsoft Access to house your data store. From here you can move on to the "Completing the Installation" section, later in this chapter.

Microsoft SQL Server 2000 Desktop Engine Data Store

Just as with the Microsoft Access data store, there are no additional steps required when using MSDE to house your data store. The required configuration was performed when the MSDE component was installed on the server. From here you can move directly to the "Completing the Installation" section, later in this chapter.

Microsoft SQL Server Data Store

If you selected SQL Server as the database server, then when you click Next, a Wizard launches that guides you through creation of a new ODBC data source name (DSN) for SQL Server. This will be a file-based DSN called MF20.DSN. This file name cannot be changed. The first dialog box lets you enter a description and the name of the SQL Server that will house the data store, as shown in Figure 13.30. If the SQL Server you configured to contain the data store does not appear in the drop-down list, you can type the name in the appropriate field.

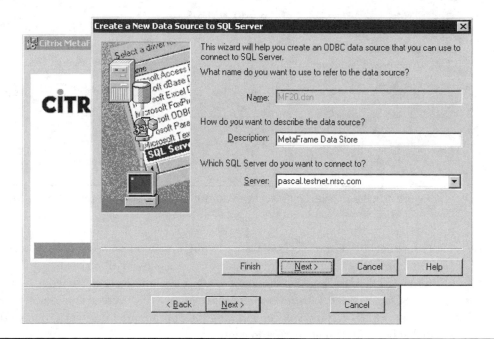

Figure 13.30   Creating the SQL Server ODBC data source.

After clicking Next, you are asked to select the appropriate authentication method for SQL Server (Windows or SQL authentication). Select the authentication type that you wish to implement. Prerequisite information on Windows authentication was discussed in the "Microsoft SQL Server Data Store Prerequisites" section, earlier in this chapter. If you selected SQL Server authentication, make sure to enter the corresponding login ID and password at the bottom of the dialog box shown in Figure 13.31.

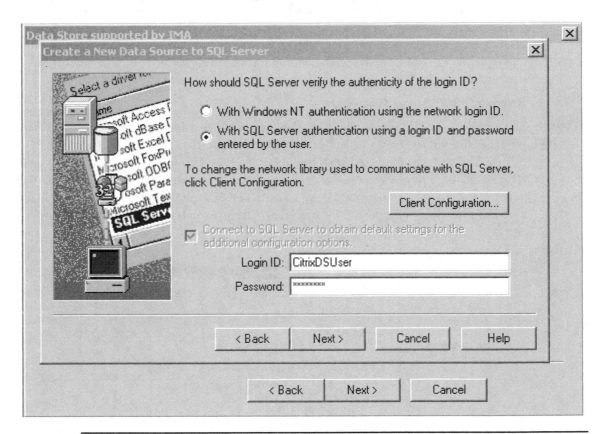

Figure 13.31   Selecting the desired authentication type for the SQL Server.

Before clicking Next, select the Client Configuration button. This opens the Network Library Configuration dialog box. Verify that the correct network library is being used to connect to your SQL Server. The default selection of Named Pipes may not function, depending on how the SQL Server has been configured. Typically the correct configuration will be either Named Pipes or TCP/IP. After selecting the appropriate information, click OK to close the dialog box and then click Next to continue.

If the correct network library and user account information have been entered, you will see a dialog box where you can modify certain connection defaults, including the default database. Verify that the listed default database matches the one that you want to use as the data store for this server farm. As I mentioned in the SQL Server prerequisites section, you can use the same user authentication account to access more than one data store on a SQL Server. It is here that you would change the target database from the default for this user account. No other options need to be changed on this screen, so click Next to continue.

The final screen contains some additional configuration settings. You normally will not need to modify these options. Click Finish to complete setting up the ODBC data source and bring up the confirmation screen. From here you can click the Test Data Source button to verify that the connection information you entered is correct. I recommend that you always select this to verify your settings. If you receive a TEST FAILED! message, click OK and then click Cancel to return to the previous dialog box where you can then scroll back through the setup wizard and verify your user account, password, and network library settings. Typically a failure indicates that the incorrect network library was selected.

Because of how the Data Source wizard caches information, you may need to actually cancel the wizard, which will return you to the ODBC Driver setup screen where you can restart the Data Source wizard. Once you have successfully tested your data source, click OK to finish. If you previously had MetaFrame installed on this server, you may already have an existing MF20.dsn file. If prompted, click Yes to overwrite this file.

Once the DSN has been created you are returned to the MetaFrame installation wizard, where you are prompted to provide the data store access credentials (Figure 13.32). These credentials are used by MetaFrame to access the data store. If you are using SQL authentication, you enter the SQL user information, but if you are using Windows authentication, you enter the Windows domain account. The user name must be prefixed with the domain name, as follows:

```
<domain name>\<username>
```

For example, if my domain was called NRSC, I would enter NRSC\CitrixDSUser as my user name. Once you click Next, the SQL Server data store configuration is complete and you can proceed to the "Completing the Installation" section of this chapter.

TIP: Citrix's Data Store Access dialog box currently doesn't support Microsoft Active Directory's Universal Principal Naming (UPN) for user accounts. So, for example, the user name NRSC\CitrixDSUser would be valid, while CitrixDSUser@NRSC.COM would not.

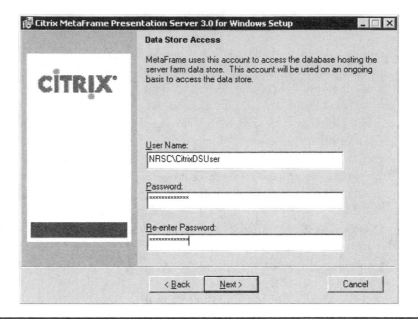

Figure 13.32   The Data Store Access dialog box.

Oracle Data Store

After selecting the Oracle database and clicking Next, you are presented with the Oracle ODBC Driver Connect dialog box, which requires you to provide the service name, user name, and password to connect to the Oracle database. This information should match exactly the options you chose when creating the Oracle database. See the "Oracle Data Store Prerequisites" section, earlier in this chapter, for details on this. Figure 13.33 shows an example of the information I would enter corresponding to the Oracle database setup that I used in the "Oracle Data Store Prerequisites" section in this chapter. If MetaFrame was previously installed on this server, you are prompted to overwrite the existing ODBC data source. Click Yes to overwrite this file and continue. Once you click Next, the Oracle data store configuration is complete and you can proceed to the "Completing the Installation" section of this chapter.

TIP: If during installation you receive a message saying the IMA service failed to start, it is most likely because you haven't disabled NT authentication support in the Oracle client. Refer to the "Oracle ODBC Driver Requirements" section, earlier in this chapter, for details on disabling NT authentication support.

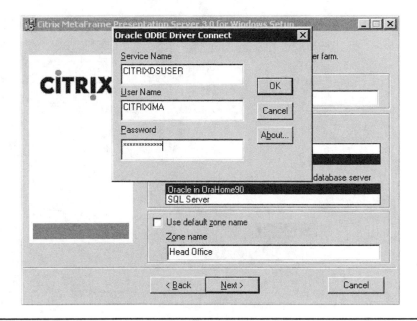

Figure 13.33   The Oracle ODBC Driver Connect dialog box.

DB2 Data Store

After selecting the DB2 ODBC database driver and clicking Next, you are presented with the Connect to DB2 Database dialog box. Click the drop-down list box next to the Add button and select the database alias that you created earlier when setting up the DB2 ODBC connection (see Figure 13.34).

Enter the user ID and password for the data store connection, ensure Share is the selected connection mode, and then click OK to continue. If MetaFrame is unable to establish the connection with the given user ID and password, you receive an error message; otherwise, the connection is successfully established and you can proceed to the "Completing the Installation" section of this chapter.

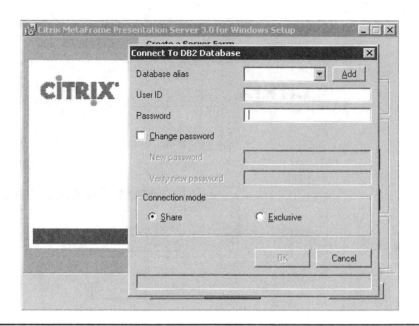

Figure 13.34 The Connect to DB2 Database dialog box.

Joining an Existing Server Farm

If you already have an existing server farm and you want to add this server to that farm, select the Join an Existing Data Farm option and click Next. You then have one of two options to choose from (see Figure 13.35):

- *Connect directly to the database using ODBC*—To use this option, the data store must reside on a Microsoft SQL Server, an Oracle server, or a DB2 server. You must also have the necessary ODBC driver installed. See the corresponding prerequisite sections for the database management system (SQL Server, Oracle, DB2) earlier in this chapter for more information on these requirements.
- *Connect to a database on this MetaFrame Presentation Server computer*—This connection method must be used when the server farm's data store resides in an Access or MSDE database. ODBC drivers are not required on an indirectly connected MetaFrame server. The only information required is the name of the MetaFrame server containing the data store and the associated port number. You will not need to change the default port number unless you changed the IMA listening port (see the IMAPORT command in Appendix B).

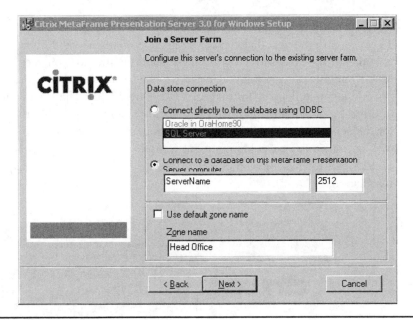

Figure 13.35   Join a server farm.

On the lower half of the dialog box, you need to enter the appropriate zone name for this server. Just as with creation of a new server farm, the default zone name MetaFrame generates is based on the subnet address within which the server resides. For example, if the IP address for the MetaFrame server is 192.168.1.50 with a subnet mask of 255.255.255.0, the zone name will be 192.168.1.0.

If you're adding this MetaFrame server to an existing zone, make sure to enter the correct zone name. If you make a mistake or decide to move this server to a different zone, you can do this after the installation through the Management Console. Once you've entered the desired zone name for this MetaFrame server, click Next to continue connecting to the existing server farm.

Direct Database Connection

Depending on the target database you selected on the previous screen, you are now presented with the same ODBC Data Source wizard that appeared during installation of the initial MetaFrame server in your server farm. For specific information on the ODBC wizards for SQL Server, Oracle, and DB2, refer to the "Creating a New Server Farm" section, earlier in this chapter.

Database Connection on a Remote MetaFrame Server (Indirect Connection)

To proceed to the next dialog box, you need to enter the valid MetaFrame server name that is home to the data store. If the server name is invalid, you receive an error stating the MetaFrame server could not be located. Once a valid server is entered, you are prompted to provide login credentials for that server (Figure 13.36). These credentials must correspond to those for an administrator who has already been set up within the Management Console for the server farm. Typically the local Administrator account on the target server is set up with permissions for the Management Console. Enter the appropriate credentials and then click Next. You can now proceed to the next section in this chapter, "Completing the Installation."

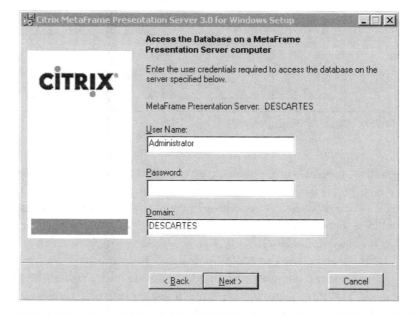

Figure 13.36 Prompting for Administrator login credentials for the MetaFrame server containing the data store.

Completing the Installation

The final few dialog boxes presented during MetaFrame Presentation Server installation are the same regardless of the database management system used to house the Citrix data store. The first couple of dialog boxes presented appear only when creating a new data store:

1. (New data store only.) You are asked to provide the name and domain that will be assigned as the first administrator for the farm (Figure 13.37). This user will have the ability to manage the farm through the Management Console, including assigning additional administrators to the farm if desired.

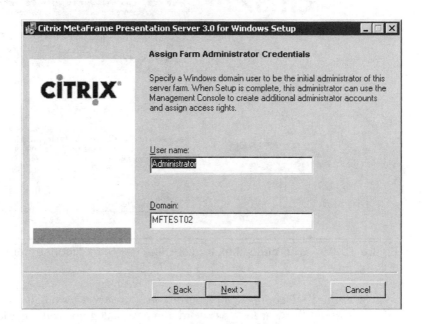

Figure 13.37 The Assign Farm Administrator Credentials dialog box.

2. (New data store only.) The next dialog box prompts you to provide information on the MetaFrame Access Suite Licensing server in your environment (Figure 13.38). When installing the first MetaFrame server in a new farm, you are asked to provide the location of the License Server. Details on installation and configuration of the Citrix License Server can be found in Chapter 12, "License Server Installation and Configuration." If you have an existing License Server, enter the server name and port number (if different from the default port). If you do not have the License Server information available, it can be configured after the installation has completed through the Management Console. Until the License Server has been configured, the MetaFrame services will not be available and a service failure message will appear when the server starts up, saying, "There is no license service configured for this MetaFrame server."

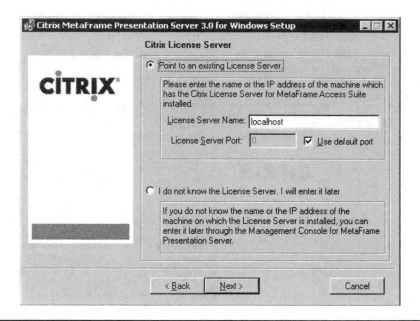

Figure 13.38   The dialog box for selecting the Citrix License Server.

3. If the RDP connection properties on your server have been configured to always prompt the user for a password, the next dialog box you see asks if you want to turn off this feature. Selecting Yes still requires users to provide a password when using the Web interface, but they will not be prompted for a password every time they open an application.

4. Next is the Shadowing Setup screen (see Figure 13.39). This is where you can configure the shadowing options that will be explicitly available or prohibited on your MetaFrame server. By default, all shadowing features are installed and available for use. Access to this feature can be restricted based on individual user or group accounts once installation is complete.

Any options explicitly prohibited on this screen *won't* be available to any users (including administrators) on the MetaFrame server and cannot be changed without uninstalling and reinstalling MetaFrame. I recommend that you select the default "Allow shadowing of ICA sessions on this server" and restrict permissions to the appropriate users unless you will run applications on your server that require explicit security precautions to prevent sensitive data from possibly being viewed by a third person. Human resources or accounting applications may fall into this category.

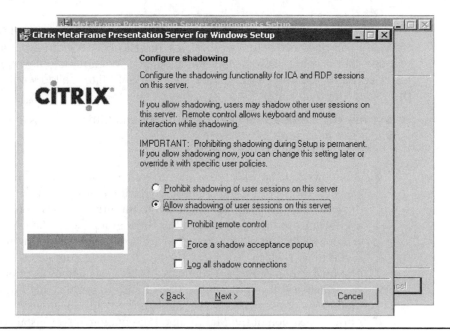

Figure 13.39 The Configure Shadowing dialog box.

WARNING: Prohibiting ICA shadowing options during setup won't affect RDP remote control options in any way. Even if ICA session shadowing has been completely disabled, users connecting via RDP (and having sufficient privileges) can still shadow other RDP sessions. RDP remote control restrictions must be managed through permissions set within the Terminal Server Configuration tool.

5. Next you are asked to select the desired TCP/IP listening port for the Citrix XML service. If IIS is also installed on your Terminal Server, the default option is to share port 80 with IIS. If IIS is not installed, the only available option is to use a separate port for the XML service, with the default being set to port 80.

   All MetaFrame servers in a farm must have the XML service running on the same port, so if you already have servers in your farm be certain to use the same port number. If this is the first server in your farm I recommend leaving the XML service on port 80. This listening port can easily be changed at a later date if you decide that an alternate port number is preferred. See the CTXXMLSS command in Appendix B for more information on changing the XML listening port.

NOTE: When the XML service is configured to "share" port 80 with IIS, the XML Service itself does not actually run. If you run NET START from a command prompt, you see that it is not listed as a running service. What is actually happening is that IIS is servicing the Citrix XML requests via an ISAPI filter called wpnbr.dll located in the folder \InetPub\Scripts.

Use of the XML service in conjunction with IIS and Citrix's other Web-based solutions is discussed in Chapter 20.

---

6. (Windows 2003 only.) If there are currently no users assigned to the local Remote Desktop Users group, you are prompted with a dialog box asking if members of the local users group should be added to this group. Unless a non-administrator user belongs to the Remote Desktop Users group, he or she cannot log on to a Windows 2003 Terminal Server. You are not required to add members to the group at this time. You can do so once the installation has completed.

7. The final screen provides a summary of your installation selections and asks for confirmation before proceeding. Click Finish to begin actual installation of MetaFrame Presentation Server based on your specifications.

8. At the conclusion of the MetaFrame Presentation Server installation, you have the option of launching the ICA Client Distribution wizard. This lets you update the system with the latest ICA client files. Specifically, three areas are updated:

- The ICA client update database—This database maintains an inventory of the client files available for automatic client distribution.
- The associated ICA client installation images—The actual images used to deploy the ICA client through automatic distribution.
- The ICA passthrough client—This is the special version of the ICA client that is run directly off the MetaFrame server. I talk more about the passthrough client in Chapter 20, "ICA Client Installation and Configuration."

  You are not required to perform the ICA client update now. Once MetaFrame server installation has completed, the ICA Client Distribution wizard is added to the Citrix program group on the Start menu. My preference is to update the client files after MetaFrame installation is complete. See the "Automatic ICA Client Distribution" section in Chapter 20 for details on using the ICA Client Distribution wizard.

  If you do decide to install the ICA client files now, click "Launch the ICA Client Distribution wizard" before clicking the Close button.

9. The final screen simply informs you that a restart is required in order to complete MetaFrame Presentation Server installation.

Post-Installation Tasks

Once MetaFrame installation is complete and the server has restarted, there are a couple of additional tasks you should perform as part of the final installation cleanup.

SQL Server Windows Authentication Cleanup

If your data store resides on a SQL Server and you have implemented Windows authentication, then once the server reboots, you need to log on as an administrator (but not using the account created for accessing SQL Server) and perform some account cleanup. My preference is to log on as a domain user with administrative privileges on the MetaFrame server and then perform the following cleanup steps:

1. Begin by removing the SQL Server domain authentication account from the local Administrators group on your MetaFrame server. This is done through Computer Management under Administrative Tools on the Start menu.
2. Next you need to make one file permission change so the IMA service starts properly now that your data store account is no longer in the Administrators group. This account needs to have access to read the DSN information for the data store in order to connect to the SQL Server using Windows authentication. You must provide the user account with read permissions to the following folder and all files and subfolders:

   %SystemDrive%\Program Files\Citrix\Independent Management Architecture

   By default, only SYSTEM and Administrators have access to this folder. For example, if my domain account for accessing the data store was NRSC\CitrixDSUser, I would add read privileges for this user to the aforementioned folder and its contents. A CACLS script that would assign the appropriate permissions might look as follows, assuming that X: is the system drive on the MetaFrame server:

   ```
   cacls "X:\Program Files\Citrix\Independent Management
   Architecture" /E /T /G NRSC\CitrixDSUser:R
   ```

   Once these permissions have been set, shut down and restart the MetaFrame server to ensure that all the necessary services start properly. If the Independent Management Architecture service starts, you know it was able to communicate properly with the SQL Server data store using Windows authentication.

Changing the Access Data Store Password

When implementing a Microsoft Access data store, I suggest that the password for the Access database be changed from the default blank value. Even though only administrators and SYSTEM are granted permissions to the folder containing the Access database file (%SystemDrive%\Program Files\Citrix\Independent Management Architecture), assigning a non-blank password does provide an additional (although somewhat small) level of security. The password is changed by doing the following:

1. First stop the Independent Management Architecture service. Accomplish this either by using the Services application found under the Administrative Tools folder on the Start menu or by issuing the following command from a command prompt:

   ```
   >net stop "Independent Management Architecture"
   ```

2. Now, using the DSMAINT command line tool, run the following command from a command prompt:

   ```
   >dsmaint config /pwd:<password>
   ```

   where <password> is the new password. You should see a message stating that the configuration was successfully changed.

3. You can now restart the IMA service. From a command prompt, you can issue the command

   ```
   >net start "Independent Management Architecture"
   ```

You do not need to perform any other configuration changes. The DSMAINT utility automatically configures the IMA service to use the new password when accessing the Access database file.

Installing the Citrix Support Tools

The Citrix MetaFrame Presentation Server CD includes a suite of tools that can be used by an administrator to both troubleshoot and monitor their MetaFrame server farm. These tools can be found in the following folder on the corresponding setup CD:

> \support\debug\W2K for Windows 2000 MPS
>
> \support\debug\W2K3 for Windows 2003 MPS

I normally copy the tools from the CD into one of the following folders, based on the Windows version being used. Make sure to copy the contents of the Resource folder into the same directory, or attempts to launch one of these applications will fail. Do not delete the Resource folder if it already exists.

> "%SystemRoot%\System32\Citrix\IMA" on Windows 2000
>
> "%ProgramFiles%\citrix\system32" on Windows 2003

I use one of these folders because it keeps the tools with other related Citrix components and, because it is added to the system path during MetaFrame installation, commands can be run easily from an open command prompt. These tools are typically only required when there are issues in the MetaFrame environment, but I prefer to have them readily available instead of having to chase down an MPS installation CD and add these tools if they are ever required. The specific support tools added are the following:

- DSVIEW.EXE — A tool that provides an administrator with the ability to view the contents of the MetaFrame data store and the local host cache. The goal of this tool is to provide a means of troubleshooting farm issues by viewing the actual data store contents.
- FTACLN.EXE — When the Program Neighborhood Agent is installed, client file type associations may be updated to associate with server-side applications on the MetaFrame server. As part of the client installation the original associations are backed up and can be restored by running this utility directly on the client (or wherever the PN Agent is causing problems). Client file type associations can be cleaned using this utility.
- MSGHOOK.EXE — A utility for collecting IMA traffic data. This is a debugging tool to help Citrix support identify specific customer issues with MetaFrame.
- QPRINTER.EXE — QPRINTER serves two purposes. First it allows an administrator to view the status of currently pending printer driver replications. Second it allows you to import file-based printer cross-reference information into the data store. The most common use for this is to import a pre-existing file from a MetaFrame 1.8 or standalone Terminal Server environment. Details on why printer drive cross-reference information is necessary is discussed in Chapter 17, "Terminal Server and MetaFrame Printer Management."
- QUERYDC.EXE — Allows for querying the data collector (DC) for a give zone. You can also force a new DC election with this tool.
- QUERYDS.EXE — Provides a means of querying the memory-based information stored in the current local zone data collector. Only the DC for the current zone can be queried.
- QUERYHR.EXE — Displays information about the MetaFrame servers (host records) in the server farm.

WARNING: Special care should be taken when modifying any MetaFrame server farm data using any of these commands. Improper use could render a server in the farm or the farm itself unusable, requiring a reinstall of the MPS software.

MetaFrame Presentation Server Configuration

Before You Begin

Once you finish installation of MetaFrame Presentation Server (MPS), there are some standard configuration changes you will want to make to tailor the server to the needs of your deployment. In this chapter we review the suite of tools provided by Citrix to manage the environment and the options that can be configured through each tool. I also discuss the list of changes I perform as a standard for each MPS build and provide suggestions based on different implementation scenarios.

Once installed, MPS provides a number of management and configuration tools. Table 14.1 summarizes these tools, providing a brief description of each and where in this book I provide more information on the use of the tool. All the MPS tools can be found on the Citrix menu under the Start menu.

Table 14.1 MetaFrame Presentation Server Management Tools

Administration Tool	Description	Chapter/Section Reference
Access Suite Console	The MetaFrame Access Suite Console is a Microsoft Management Console (MMC) snap-in that allows for centralized management of all components of your Access Suite deployment. There are currently four products that make up the MetaFrame Access Suite: MetaFrame Presentation Server, MetaFrame Conference Manager, MetaFrame Password Manager, and MetaFrame Secure Access Manager.	The Access Suite Console is discussed in the "Using the MetaFrame Access Suite Console" section of this chapter.

Table 14.1 MetaFrame Presentation Server Management Tools (continued)

Administration Tool	Description	Chapter/Section Reference
Presentation Server Console	Also known as the Management Console for MetaFrame Presentation Server, this is the tool you will use to perform most of the MetaFrame server and farm configuration.	An extended discussion on configuration and use of this tool can be found in the "Configuring and Using Management Console for MetaFrame Presentation Server" section of this chapter.
Program Neighborhood Agent Console	The Program Neighborhood Agent (PN Agent) Console is a Web-based interface used to configure the settings downloaded and used by the Program Neighborhood Agent MetaFrame client. PN Agent is a small-footprint client that reads applications and configuration information from a server running the Web Interface and allows an administrator to centrally control the behavior of the client. PN Agent is the preferred client for deployment in most situations.	Configuring PN Agent clients using the Console is discussed in Chapter 20, "ICA Client Installation and Configuration."
Web Interface Console	The Web Interface Console is another Web-driven interface used for managing configuration settings for the Web Interface. Options such as MetaFrame server communications, Secure Gateway interaction, and user authentication support are only some of the settings configured through this interface.	Configuring the Web Interface using this console is discussed in the "Web Interface" section of this chapter.
Citrix Connection Configuration tool	ICA connections for the MetaFrame server are managed through this utility. Options configured through this tool apply to all users who connect to the Citrix server.	See the section "Configuring ICA Connection Properties" later in this chapter.
Citrix SSL Relay Configuration Tool	The SSL Relay tool is used to enable secured communications between a MetaFrame server and a Web server hosting the Web Interface (formerly known as NFuse Classic).	Details on use of this tool are provided in the "Citrix SSL Relay Configuration" section of this chapter.

Table 14.1   MetaFrame Presentation Server Management Tools (continued)

Administration Tool	Description	Chapter/Section Reference
ICA Presentation Distribution wizard	This tool is used to update the following three types of client files: ■ *ICA client images*—These image files are used by the ICA Client Creator utility, a program found only on Windows 2000 Servers with MPS. The ICA Client Creator is used to create installation diskettes for the DOS or Windows ICA clients. This tool is not supported on Windows Server 2003, so these image files are not updated on a 2003 server. ■ *ICA Client Update Database images*—The distribution wizard will also update the client image files used by the Auto Client Update feature of MetaFrame. Auto Client Update allows for the automatic update of client files when a client connects to a MetaFrame server. ■ *ICA passthrough client files*—The passthrough client is a version of Program Neighborhood or Program Neighborhood Agent that is installed and runs directly off the MetaFrame server. This client lets the user access published applications from within a MetaFrame server session. The distribution wizard will also upgrade this client to the latest version. This client is simply a delivery mechanism, relying on the appropriate client files to be accessible on a CD or a network location.	Details on the ICA Client Distribution wizard can be found in Chapter 20.
ICA Client Printer Configuration tool	This is actually a tool that a MetaFrame user would run to establish connections to client printers. Primarily, this tool is used by someone accessing the MetaFrame server using a DOS or CE client that supports client-mapped printers but cannot automatically establish client printer mappings.	Use of this tool is discussed in Chapter 17, "Terminal Server and MetaFrame Printer Management."

Table 14.1 MetaFrame Presentation Server Management Tools (continued)

Administration Tool	Description	Chapter/Section Reference
ICA Client Update Configuration tool	This is the tool you would use to manage the automatic client update feature of MetaFrame. From here you can manage options such as the ICA client types maintained in the update database as well as configure client update specifications.	See Chapter 20 for information on configuration and use of the ICA Client Update Configuration tool.
ICA toolbar	This is the customizable toolbar that appears down the right-hand side of the screen whenever an administrator logs on to a MetaFrame server for the first time. This toolbar remains until explicitly closed and disabled from automatic start-up. This toolbar provides quick access to the most common MetaFrame tools. The list of accessible tools can be fully customized; this is managed by right-clicking and choosing the Customize option.	A brief discussion on configuration of this tool is given in the "Configuring the ICA Toolbar" section of this chapter.
Shadow taskbar	This tool provides the ability to centrally shadow one or more user sessions simultaneously, even when run from a MetaFrame console session.	Using the Shadow taskbar to manage user sessions is discussed in Chapter 21, "Server Operations and Support."
SpeedScreen Latency Reduction Manager	Citrix provides a special feature known as SpeedScreen Latency Reduction, which is a collection of features intended to help improve the computing experience of a user connected to a MetaFrame server over a high-latency connection, such as a WAN or dial-up connection. Latency reduction features can be defined at the server and individual application levels. These settings help dictate what latency reduction measures a client will take as requested by the MetaFrame server.	Details on configuring the environment using this tool are provided in the "Managing SpeedScreen Latency Reduction" section, later in this chapter.

Before getting into the details on use of these tools, an appropriate place to begin our post-installation discussion is with management and deployment of MetaFrame service packs and hotfixes.

MetaFrame Service Packs and Hotfixes

As with most other applications or operating systems, Citrix periodically releases hotfixes and service packs for its MetaFrame product. All hotfixes, security related or otherwise, for all of Citrix's products can be found on their Web site at http:// support.citrix.com/hotfixes.jsp

Figure 14.1 shows an example of this Web page. This site provides a good starting location for finding out information on the latest patches available for MetaFrame. A number of pieces of information are displayed on this page, and the three main areas to discuss have been boxed in this figure.

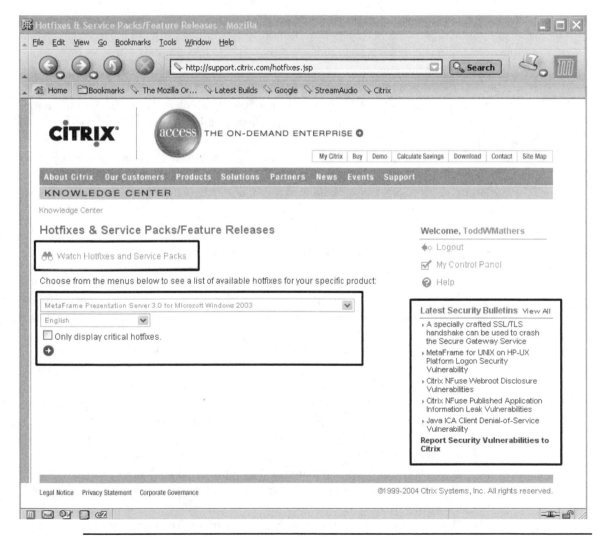

Figure 14.1   Hotfixes and service packs for all Citrix products can be found on the Hotfixes and Service Packs/Feature Releases Web site.

If you are logged on to the Citrix site with a valid MyCitrix account and are not using a Guest account, you will see an option labeled "Watch Hotfixes and Service Packs" in the upper left-hand side of the page. Citrix provides "watch" capabilities for a number of areas on its site. When a watch is enabled, then depending on how you configured your account, you can receive e-mail notifications whenever any changes are made to the watched material. Watch settings are managed through the My Control Panel link.

Immediately under the watch settings is where you can perform the query to retrieve available hotfixes and service packs for the desired product. You begin by selecting the appropriate product from the first drop-down list and then choose the desired language from the second list. The Only Display Critical Hotfixes check box lets you filter the list of hotfixes to show only fixes that have been deemed critical by Citrix. Critical fixes are either related to a security vulnerability that has been found or an issue in the product that can cause system failures or erratic behavior. When the list is retrieved, you have a number of ways from which to choose how the information is sorted. By default the newest fixes are listed first.

On the right-hand side of Figure 14.1 you can see a list of the latest published security bulletins. Selecting the View All link takes you to the main bulletins page, where all security bulletins for all Citrix products are listed. You can enable a watch on this page as well, allowing you to be immediately notified when new security bulletins are released. I recommend that this feature be enabled, because it is the easiest way to ensure you're receiving notification of potential security vulnerabilities that have been discovered. You can link directly to the list of all bulletins via this URL: http://www.support.citrix.com/latestsecurityall!execute.jspa

Reviewing Available Hotfixes and Service Packs

In Chapter 11, "Terminal Services Configuration and Tuning," I discussed planning and deployment of hotfixes and service packs, in particular some general guidelines to follow when deciding on what hotfixes and service packs to deploy. In summary, they are as follows:

- *Deploy the latest service pack with a new installation of MetaFrame*—Include the latest service pack in a new server deployment but include associated hotfixes only if specifically recommended by Citrix.
- *Deploy a service pack in an existing production environment only after performing extensive testing in a test or pilot environment*—Deployment may be expedited if a fix exists in the release that is critical to the stability of your environment. Typically, I plan to deploy a new service pack one to two months after it has been publicly released and after reviewing any known issues that were discovered from other administrators or from personal work with the release in a test environment.
- *Deploy a hotfix only if it resolves an issue you're currently experiencing in production*—Never deploy a hotfix simply because it is available. In many cases the testing performed on a hotfix is minimal and localized only in the code area that contains the issue. Hotfixes may potentially introduce a new issue not

anticipated by the development team. Even when building a new MetaFrame server, never include a hotfix unless recommended by Citrix. Instead, closely monitor the environment during testing and piloting for issues that would facilitate the need to include a particular hotfix.

MPS 3.0–related hotfixes all have names that follow the structure MPSx300W2Kyzzz, where x is the language for the hotfix (E for English, F for French, G for German, S for Spanish, J for Japanese); y is blank for Windows 2000 fixes and the number 3 for Windows 2003 fixes; and the zzz suffix is the incremented hotfix number. You will not necessarily find all hotfixes (starting at 001) on the Web site. Older fixes may be rolled into a newer release if the same components are modified to resolve another issue. It is common for Citrix to roll three to four fixes within a single hotfix installation if all these fixes are related to the same MetaFrame component (DLL, system driver, and so on).

As of this writing, the following seven fixes are available on the Citrix Web site specifically for MetaFrame Presentation Server 3.0 and Windows Server 2003:

- **MPSE300W2K3001**—Contains fixes for print spooler, client drive mapping, and audio playback under certain conditions.
- **MPSE300W2K3005**—Resolves an issue with connecting to the MetaFrame License Server if the license server's IP address was changed.
- **MPSE300W2K3006**—Resolves an issue where MPS servers in a farm would intermittently experience a fatal STOP error in the WDICA.SYS driver. Additional issues in the WDICA.SYS driver are also resolved in this hotfix.

  This fix is an example of a fix that would be flagged as a likely candidate for inclusion in a MetaFrame environment (existing or new) based on results of testing, particularly load testing. In many cases, this type of STOP error is exacerbated by higher user load. Because a STOP error immediately causes all users on the server to lose their session and all unsaved work, it is likely that this type of hotfix would need to be added to the server.
- **MPSE300W2K3007**—Contains a number of seamless-window-related fixes. One resolved issue deals with an unresponsive seamless application preventing access to other seamless applications also running on the desktop. This fix may be important for certain deployments; the environment should be monitored to see if this problem arises during testing and requires this fix to resolve. All these fixes are grouped within this hotfix because they all pertain to code within the same pair of DLLs.
- **MPSE300W2K3008**—Resolves an issue with intermittent failing of installing or uninstalling MetaFrame in a large server farm. This fix need be installed only on an existing server if you're planning on uninstalling MetaFrame and you're running in a large server farm. Use of pre-installation fixes was discussed in Chapter 13, "MetaFrame Presentation Server Installation."

- **MPSE300W2K3011**—Resolves issues with generation of disconnected session alerts and time zone–related issues in the Access Suite Console.
- **MPSE300W2K3012**—Resolves an issue in the MPS Management Console where the content-redirection file type associates could become corrupted. This fix should be applied only if the specific issue is being experienced in your environment.

After installing MPS, it is recommended that you review the available hotfixes and service packs and note those fixes that may apply to your environment. Often I find that this helps to plant ideas about the types of issues I may encounter while piloting.

Service Packs and Feature Releases

In Chapter 9, "Service Pack and Hotfix Management," I briefly discussed Citrix's standard practice of coupling its service packs with special feature upgrades called *feature releases*. Since the first service pack for MetaFrame 1.8, Citrix has consistently coupled its product enhancements with its service pack installation. When the service pack is installed on the server, the code enhancements to support the changes available with the feature release are also installed, but their functionality is not available unless an associated feature release license has been purchased and added to the license database. Unless a feature release license is present on the license server, only the fixes included in the service pack are available to the MetaFrame server.

A service pack automatically includes all fixes found in earlier released service packs in addition to new fixes that may or may not have previously appeared as hotfixes. The list of all included hotfixes is usually found in the Readme file that is available from the Service Pack/Feature Release download page.

As of this writing, no service pack/feature release has been made available for MetaFrame Presentation Server 3.0 on Windows 2000 Server or Windows Server 2003.

Hotfix and Service Pack Installation Considerations

Installation steps for either a hotfix or a service pack/feature release are straightforward, but appropriate planning and testing steps must still be considered before applying the changes to any production servers in your environment. I recommend the following guidelines for installing hotfixes or service packs on a MetaFrame server:

- Make certain there are no active user sessions on the server when you begin the installation process.

    I like to perform a reboot of the server *prior* to starting any patch or service pack installation. This way, I'm certain that any hung processes have been terminated and any leaked memory resources have been reclaimed. While the chances that this might impact the update are slim, it is usually better to be safe than sorry.

- Apply the desired Windows service pack (if applicable) prior to adding a MetaFrame service pack/feature release.

    All security and non-security patches should be applied after all service packs have been installed.
- When first testing, try whenever possible to install the MetaFrame service pack/feature release onto a test server that is located in a different server farm, and ideally a different network subnet, from your production MetaFrame servers.

    Changes in behavior of the ICA or IMA protocols could cause this updated server to somehow impair the stability of the other servers in the environment. This is particularly true if you are currently running in a mixed-mode configuration where both MPS 3.0 and MetaFrame 1.8 servers coexist in the same farm. Mixed-mode support was discussed in Chapter 8, "Server Installation and Management Planning."
- When deploying an update into production, the MetaFrame servers should be updated in the following order:

    1. *Farm Metric Servers*—If you are running Resource Manager and your Farm Metric Servers are different from your zone data collectors (ZDCs), these servers should be updated first. Because these servers interpret Resource Manager data from other MetaFrame servers in the farm, if one of these servers is updated first it may attempt to provide data to the Farm Metric Server that it cannot interpret properly. Typically the Farm Metric Server and the zone data collectors are deployed on the same server.
    2. *Zone data collectors*—For reasons similar to those for updating Farm Metric Servers, because the zone data collectors gather data from all other MetaFrame servers in their zone, if another MetaFrame server is updated first, it may pass information to a ZDC that it cannot interpret properly. For this reason, all ZDCs should be updated before other servers, with the exception of Farm Metric Servers.
    3. *Non–data store MetaFrame servers*—All other non–data store MetaFrame Presentation Servers should be upgraded next.
    4. *Jet- or Microsoft SQL Server 2000 Desktop Engine (MSDE)-based data store*—If you are running a Jet or MSDE data store database in indirect mode, this server should be upgraded last to the latest service pack/feature release level.

Citrix releases its hotfixes as Microsoft Installer (MSI) files, which can be deployed using the application deployment support found as part of the IntelliMirror technology of Windows Active Directory or by using Citrix's own Installation Manager utility. More information on the software installation and management features of IntelliMirror can be found on the Microsoft Web site (http://www.microsoft.com). This URL is a good starting point:

http://www.microsoft.com/windows2000/techinfo/howitworks/management/
intellimirror.asp

Before you even consider automating deployment of a hotfix, make certain that it is functioning properly through the standard installation method and that the automated process has been properly tested in a non-production environment. An automated deployment into production can easily produce unexpected results, impacting the stability of the environment and even rendering your servers unusable. Because of the number of users who can potentially be impacted by a server outage, extra caution should always be exercised when planning any kind of server update, automated or not.

Installing a MetaFrame Hotfix

Installing a MetaFrame hotfix is straightforward. After downloading the desired patch from the Citrix Web site and launching the installation file, you are presented with the introduction screen for the hotfix installation wizard (Figure 14.2). Verify that this is indeed the hotfix you wish to install and then proceed through the prompts presented by the wizard.

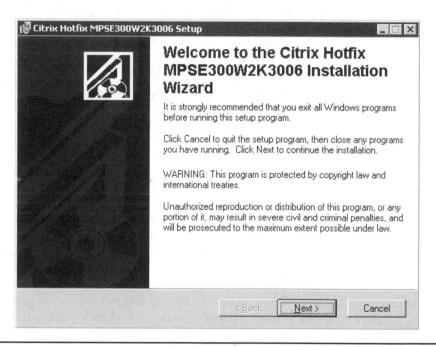

Figure 14.2   MetaFrame hotfixes are MSI installation files, which display an installation wizard introduction screen when installation is initiated. Always verify the hotfix number before proceeding.

WARNING: Most MetaFrame hotfixes and service packs require a server reboot before the changes take affect. Always schedule a server upgrade to occur during off-peak hours, when there are no active user sessions on the server.

Viewing the Installed Service Pack and Hotfixes for a MetaFrame Server

From within the Management Console for MPS you can quickly view the current list of hotfixes and the service pack for a MetaFrame server. Under the Server tab, right-click a server and select the Properties context menu. This opens the Properties dialog box for the server (see Figure 14.3). The Hotfixes tab lists all the hotfixes for both Citrix and Microsoft that have been applied to the server. All MetaFrame hotfixes are prefixed with the characters *MPS*. You also are provided with additional information such as who installed the hotfix, on what date, and at what time. Microsoft hotfixes show only the associated knowledgebase article pertaining to the hotfix.

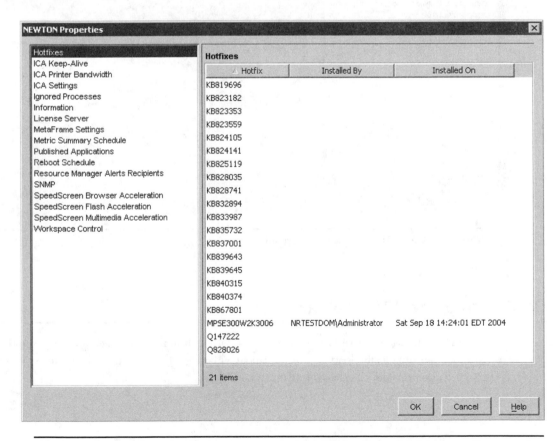

Figure 14.3 All MetaFrame hotfixes have the MPS prefix and full information on who installed the hotfix, on what date, and at what time.

General information on the server setup—including the installation date, host operating system version, and current MetaFrame service pack version—can be viewed under the Information option (Figure 14.4).

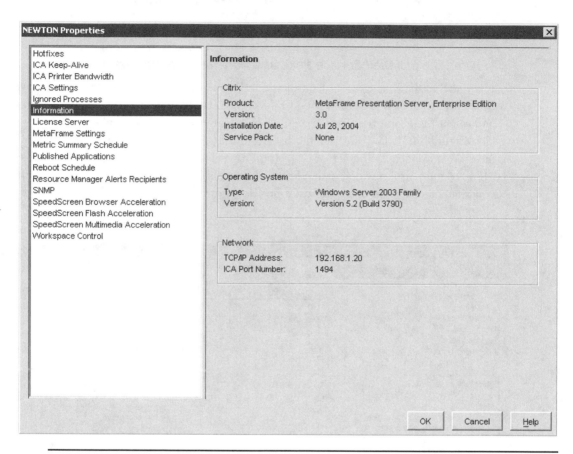

Figure 14.4   Service pack information can be found under the Information option.

Configuring the ICA Toolbar

When you first log on to a MetaFrame server with an administrative account, you see the ICA toolbar automatically load up and appear attached to the far right-hand side of the MetaFrame desktop, as shown in Figure 14.5.

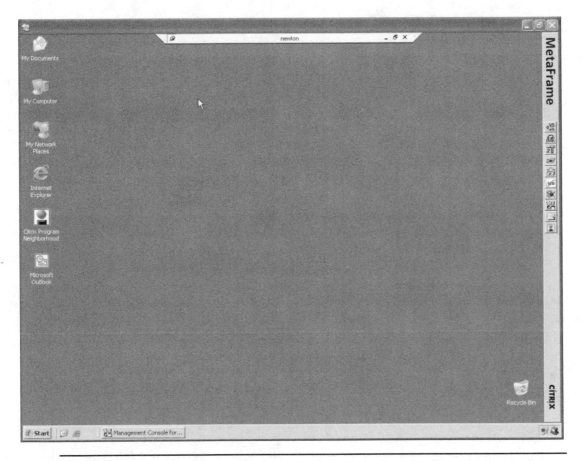

Figure 14.5   The ICA toolbar provides a quick way to launch administrative tools on a MetaFrame server.

As with other Windows toolbars, this toolbar can be dragged and anchored to any of the four corners of a desktop session. It can also float freely on the desktop. The toolbar is fully customizable by right-clicking anywhere on the toolbar and selecting the Customize option. From here you can add or remove any of the listed Citrix tools and reorder them as you wish. Other executable and batch files can be added to this menu, allowing you to centrally access all your tools from one convenient location.

I prefer not to use the toolbar. It can easily be removed by right-clicking, selecting Exit, and then responding No when asked if you'd like the toolbar to appear every time you log on. You can also permanently prevent the toolbar from starting up for any user by launching the REGEDIT tool, traversing to the registry key

HKEY_LOCAL_MACHINE\Software\Microsoft\Windows\CurrentVersion\Run

and deleting the IcaBar entry.

Connection Configuration Settings

The Citrix Connection Configuration (CCC) tool is Citrix's utility for managing both ICA and RDP connection properties. The CCC tool provides access to the entire set of connection configuration features found in the Terminal Services Configuration utility as well as allowing configuration of a couple of important ICA protocol features that cannot be configured from within the Terminal Services Configuration tool, with the main one being setting of the minimum required encryption level for the ICA connections. When MetaFrame is installed, additional connection features specifically designed for MetaFrame clients become available. Figure 14.6 shows the main CCC application window.

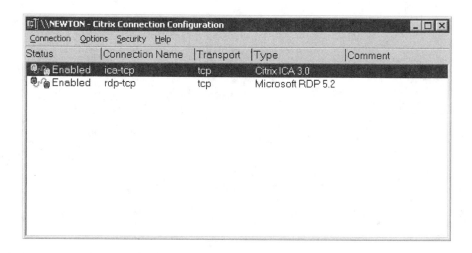

. Figure 14.6   The Citrix Connection Configuration tool can be used to configure both ICA and RDP connections.

Using the CCC tool to configure both ICA and RDP connections is a matter of personal preference. When configuring ICA connections, you should use the CCC tool to ensure that the desired minimum connection encryption level is set, unless you will be using MetaFrame user policies (discussed in the "Managing ICA Connection Settings Using MetaFrame User Policies" section of this chapter).

Unlike the Terminal Services Configuration tool, which provides a wizard to guide you through creation of a new connection, the Citrix Connection Configuration tool simply provides the Properties dialog box where you can modify the settings as required. Even when using the Terminal Services Configuration tool wizard, ICA security features are not available for editing.

If you intend to allow non-administrative users to access a Terminal Server via the RDP protocol in addition to supporting ICA connections, you need to use the CCC tool to modify the RDP properties to allow direct connections to the server instead of to only published application connections. Details on this are discussed in the "Allowing Direct ICA and RDP User Connections to a MetaFrame Server" section of this chapter.

Managing Connection Configuration Settings via Group Policies

When deploying Windows 2003 Terminal Servers in a Windows 2003 Active Directory domain, many of the features manually configured using the Citrix Connection Configuration or Terminal Services Configuration tools can be defined using a group policy. Employing group policies lets you easily define different connection settings depending on the user's access level. When connection settings are defined within a group policy, they override any settings in either the Citrix or Microsoft configuration tools.

TIP: Unfortunately, group policy–based connection configuration is not supported with Windows 2000 Terminal Services. In this environment your only choice is to implement settings using the CCC and Terminal Services Configuration tools, unless you're also deploying MetaFrame Presentation Server, in which case MetaFrame user policies are available that can be used to manage many of the ICA-specific connection settings. MetaFrame user policies are not applied to RDP connection. I discuss actual configuration of MetaFrame user policies in the "Managing ICA Connection Settings Using MetaFrame User Policies" section, later in this chapter.

Details on actual implementation of group policies are provided in Chapter 15, "Group Policy Configuration." In the meantime I provide a brief outline of the location of the group policy settings and some details on where these policies would best fit into a Terminal Server implementation. Before actually configuring these policies, I highly recommend that you review Chapter 15 and ensure you have the core organizational unit structure configured and base policies in place for the environment.

Terminal Services Group Policies

New with the introduction of Windows Server 2003 are a number of group policy settings specifically related to Terminal Services. When editing the properties for a policy using the Group Policy Object Editor, you see that Terminal Services information can be found in both the Computer Configuration folder and the User Configuration folder (see Figure 14.7). A number of these settings can be found in both locations, including session and connection settings discussed in this section; when settings have been defined for both, precedence is always given to those settings defined in the Computer Configuration folder.

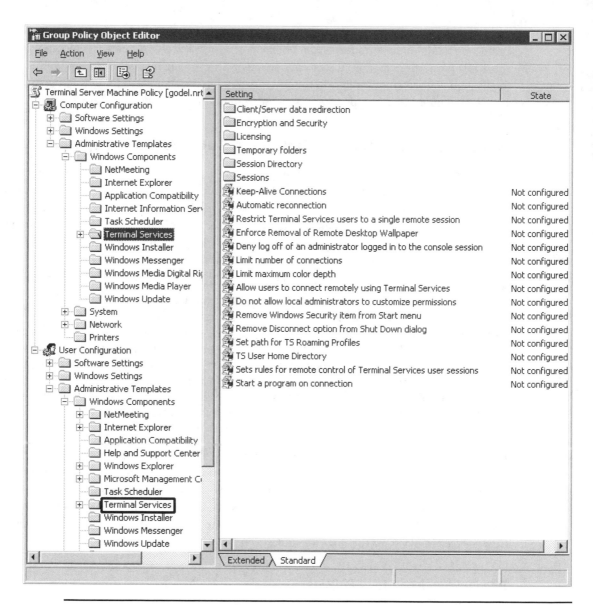

Figure 14.7   Services group policy settings are a new feature introduced with Windows Server 2003.

As I mentioned, specifics on structure of the organizational units in the active directory and layout of the group policies are discussed in Chapter 15. For now it suffices to summarize with the following suggestions and information on implementing connection and session settings via group policy objects.

- Base connection and session settings that should apply to all users connecting to the Terminal Server can be applied either to the Terminal Server Machine policy or to the Terminal Server All Users policy. If the settings will go into the Machine Policy, they should be configured within the Computer Configuration section; if applied within the All Users Policy they should be defined within the User Configuration section.
- Any restrictions that apply specifically to non-administrator users should go into the User Configuration section of the Terminal Server Regular Users Policy.
- In most situations, group policies will affect both RDP and ICA connections. Make certain that any GPOs you define are appropriate for both RDP and ICA connections to the server.

MetaFrame User Policies

MetaFrame Presentation Server provides you with the ability to define and apply different user policies to manage various MetaFrame-specific connection and session options. These policies are applied using filter rules that can be assigned based on any of the following criteria:

- Server or domain user name or group
- Client IP address
- Client name
- Server name or IP address

MPS user policies are managed using the Management Console within the Policies object (see Figure 14.8). I look at configuration of MetaFrame user policies in detail in the "Managing ICA Connection Settings Using MetaFrame User Policies" section of this chapter. If you're new to MetaFrame, I recommend that you take the time to review the settings configured using the CCC and Terminal Services utilities prior to looking at implementing MetaFrame user policies. I find this makes it far easier to visualize the connection settings that are managed through the MetaFrame policies.

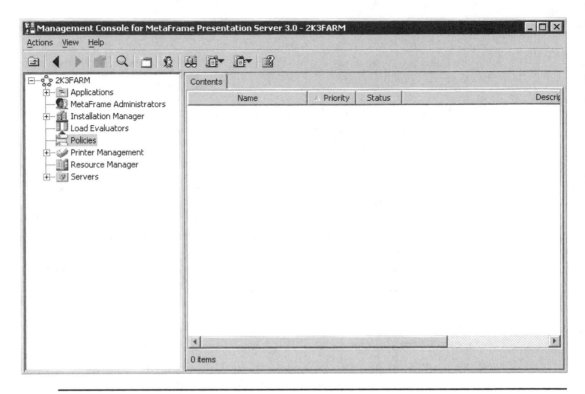

Figure 14.8 MPS user policies are defined and managed in the Policies object of the Management Console.

Configuring ICA Connection Properties

The following few sections summarize the information found in the CCC utility and demonstrate how an ICA connection can be configured once the base MetaFrame server software is installed. These same steps can be applied when configuring an RDP connection using the CCC tool. For each of the settings discussed, I also note whether or not it can be managed via a group policy. ICA (or RDP) connections on a MetaFrame server can be modified using the CCC utility. In this section, I use ICA as the example protocol.

Edit Connection Settings

After launching the CCC tool you see the TCP connections for both the ICA and RDP protocols. Begin by highlighting the ica-tcp entry, right-clicking the line, and selecting Edit from the context menu that pops up.

The main Edit Connection dialog box appears, as shown in Figure 14.9. The two main options to configure on this screen are the adapters on which this transport is configured and the maximum number of supported connections. Unless the server has multiple adapters and you want the ICA protocol to be accessible on only one adapter, you can leave the LAN Adapter setting as "All network adapters configured with this protocol." This setting cannot be configured through a group policy.

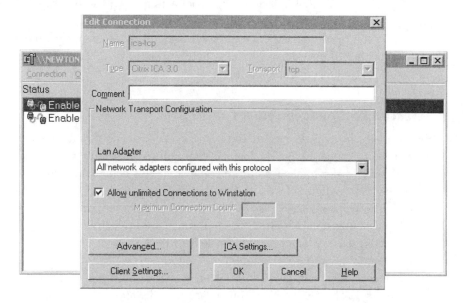

Figure 14.9   The Edit Connection dialog box is the main dialog for managing ICA connection properties.

The default setting for the maximum number of supported connections allows for an unlimited number of client connections to the current WinStation type. I recommend that this option be changed from an unlimited maximum to a fixed value equal to the maximum number of users you have sized your server to handle. For example, if the maximum workable concurrent user load on a server were expected to be 125, you would deselect the Allow Unlimited option and enter the value 125 in the provided field. In the event that there were too few servers available to service all user connection requests, this setting would ensure that the load on a server was capped, allowing those users already on the server to continue to function without the risk of the server becoming overloaded with user connections and itself eventually failing. The end result is that some users might not be able to log on, but the environment as a whole would continue to operate, even if it was at a reduced capacity. This option can be configured using a group policy, and the associated setting can be found only under the Computer Configuration portion. Specifically:

> Computer Configuration\Administrative Templates\Terminal Services\

and the value is called "Limit number of connections". This setting should be configured as part of the Terminal Server Machine Policy.

Once you finish making the desired changes on this screen, click the Advanced button to move to the Advanced Configuration Settings dialog box. Most of the session connection information can be configured on this screen.

Advanced Configuration Settings

Figure 14.10 shows an example of the typical ICA connection configuration settings for a production MetaFrame server. The logon option in the upper-left corner of the dialog box must be enabled in order to allow a user to connect via this connection type. This specific option is not directly configurable via a GPO, but you can enable or disable all connections to a Terminal Server using the "Allow users to connect remotely using Terminal Services" property. Typically this option is not managed through a GPO but instead is controlled for specific servers through the Management Console for MetaFrame.

Located immediately below the Logon setting are the Connection Timeout, Disconnection Timeout, and Idle Timeout settings (all three of which are configurable via group policy). The Connection Timeout setting dictates how long a session is connected before it is automatically timed out and terminated by the server. This option is rarely enabled for most implementations but can be useful if you enforce a maximum amount of time that someone can be logged on. Kiosk or Internet café implementations are examples where this could be useful.

Next is the Disconnection Timeout option. This controls how long a disconnected session remains active on the MetaFrame server before it is automatically logged out. Defining no timeout allows disconnected sessions to remain on the server until either manually terminated by an administrator or the server is shut down and restarted. A typical disconnection timeout value is usually something between 30 and 60 minutes, depending on how long you want to provide a user the opportunity to reconnect to their active session.

The Idle Timeout setting controls how long an active user session can remain idle on the server before it is either disconnected by the server or immediately terminated. As a security feature this setting should always be enabled. Idle sessions should not be allowed to remain active indefinitely unless the organization is enforcing locking of either the MetaFrame session or the local client in order to prevent a user from being able to simply walk up and start accessing another user's idle session. Deciding on the appropriate timeout value depends on the behavior of the workers. If a worker can walk away from a device for 30 minutes or more but require immediate access to an active application, a timeout needs to be set to something such as 60 or 90 minutes.

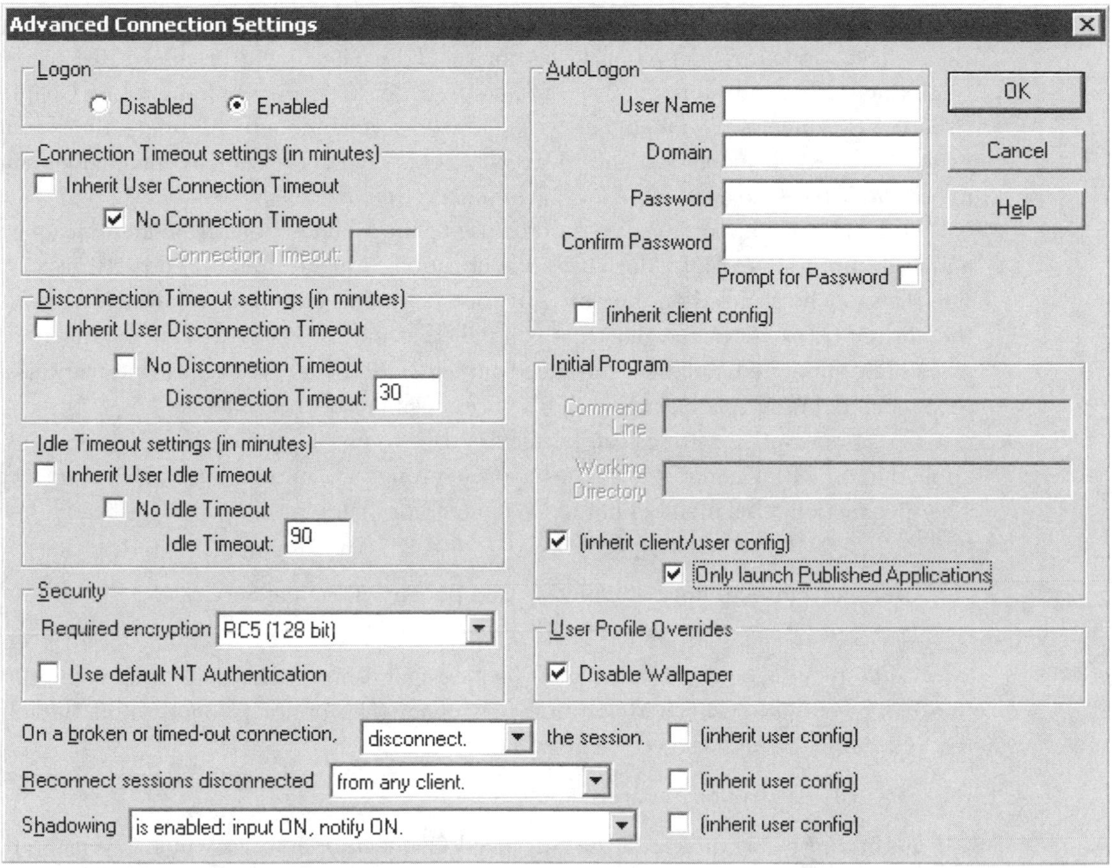

Figure 14.10   Most of the ICA settings are configured in the Advanced Connection Settings dialog box.

The various timeout settings can be found under both the Computer folder and the User Configuration folder for a GPO. Where you define these properties depends on whether you're going to set these timeout values the same for all users or maintain different timeout values for different classes of users (administrators and regular users, for example).

NOTE: I use the following guidelines when configuring timeout values for a MetaFrame server. If all users will share the same timeout values, I define this single set of values within the Computer Configuration folder in the Terminal Server Machine Policy. If administrators will have different timeout values than regular users, I prefer to define the administrative values in the All Users Policy and then introduce the more restrictive timeout values within the Regular Users GPO.

The Security setting lets you set the minimum encryption required by the connecting client. The supported encryption levels for the ICA client were discussed in Chapter 2, "Citrix MetaFrame Presentation Server," and the RDP client encryption levels in Chapter 1, "Microsoft Windows Terminal Services." I always recommend enforcing the strongest encryption possible for all ICA and RDP connections. Do not leave ICA connections configured to use the Basic encryption level. This encryption level is not secure. The Use Default NT Authentication option lets you enforce use of the Windows graphical identification and authentication (GINA) DLL for user authentication, instead of any third-party authentication that may be installed on the server. If you enable this option, it will override the use of the custom Citrix GINA (ctxgina) that is installed as part of MPS. Basic Citrix functionality will still be supported, but some advanced authentication features such as automatic session reconnect and user principal name (UPN) logon will not be available.

Client encryption settings can be managed with a group policy, but these settings are applied to only RDP connections. These policy settings are ignored by the ICA connections. The specific policy is a member of the Computer Configuration section only. It can be found under

Administrative Templates\Windows Components\Terminal Services\
Encryption and Security

While ICA encryption levels cannot be managed using a Microsoft group policy object, they can be enforced using a MetaFrame user policy. This option is found within the following folder, which is also shown in Figure 14.11:

Security\Encryption\SecureICA Encryption

Returning to Figure 14.10, the Advanced Connection Settings window, you see three options located at the very bottom of the dialog box. The first, labeled "On a broken or timed-out connection," determines how the server reacts when a session connection is either broken due to an interruption in network connectivity or disconnected because of an idle timeout.

If Reset is chosen, a broken or timed-out connection is immediately terminated by the server, ending any active applications in that session. The Disconnect option leaves the user session active on the server (all applications continue running) but disconnects it from the current client device. When the session is disconnected in this fashion, any timeout rules that have been defined still apply. This option can also be controlled through a GPO setting. The following location exists under both the Computer and User Configuration sections of the GPO:

Administrative Templates\Windows Components\Terminal Services\Sessions

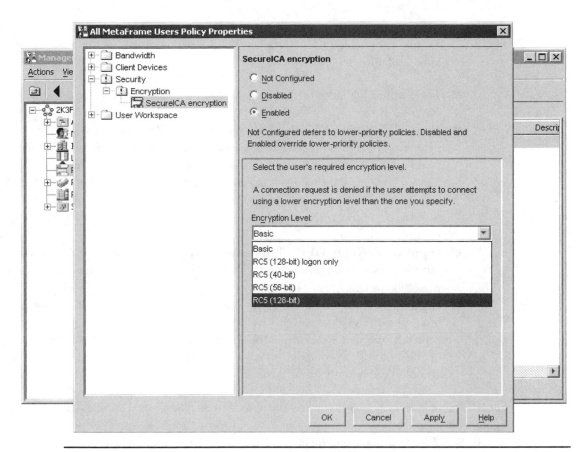

Figure 14.11   The minimum allowed ICA encryption level is managed through a MetaFrame user policy.

The specific property that controls this setting is called "Terminate sessions when time limits are reached."

The second option is called "Reconnect sessions disconnected"; this allows you to select whether a disconnected session can be reconnected from any client or from only the client that disconnected the session in the first place. If your users roam from desk to desk and require the ability to reestablish a disconnected session, make sure the From Any Client option is chosen. Remember that these connection settings also apply to administrators, so if you want to be able to remotely connect to a session you disconnected from in the office, this setting must be defined with the From Any Client value. This value can also be managed through a GPO and can be found in both the Computer and User Configuration modules. The specific location is

Administrative Templates\Windows Components\Terminal Services\Sessions

The property for this setting is called "Allow reconnection from original client only."

The final setting at the bottom of the dialog box determines how shadowing will function. If shadowing was enabled when installing MetaFrame, you can modify these settings; four choices are available:

- **Is Disabled**—Shadowing has been disabled for the corresponding connections on this server.
- **Input ON, Notify ON**—The shadower can control the mouse and keyboard of the person being shadowed. When the shadow is initiated, the person being shadowed must accept the request before remote control can be established. This feature prevents someone from shadowing another user without that user's knowledge and possibly acquiring access to information the shadower normally couldn't see. An administrator shadowing someone in the payroll department would be an example of this.
- **Input OFF, Notify OFF**—The shadower has view-only access to the session, but the person being shadowed is given no message indicating that someone is remotely watching his or her actions.
- **Input ON, Notify OFF**—The shadower has the ability to take control of the other person's session, and that user is given no indication that they are being remotely watched and possibly controlled. I recommend that this option not be enabled unless the company is very clear on the possible ramifications and has accepted the potential risks involved.

Shadowing (known as *remote control* in Windows Terminal Services) can be managed through group policies in both the Computer and User Configuration settings. The specific setting is called "Sets rules for remote control of Terminal Services user sessions" and is found in

Administrative Templates\Windows Components\Terminal Services

Wording for the three options differs slightly in the GPO, but the options in the GPO provide the same characteristics as those described in the preceding list. Table 14.2 lists the permissions in the GPO next to the corresponding permissions in the CCC.

Table 14.2 Shadowing/Remote Control Rules Comparison

Windows 2003 GPO Settings	Citrix Connection Configuration Settings
No remote control allowed.	Is Disabled.
Full Control with user's permission.	Input ON, Notify ON.
Full Control without user's permission.	Input ON, Notify OFF.
View Session with user's permission.	Input OFF, Notify ON.
View Session without user's permission.	Input OFF, Notify OFF.

In the top right-hand corner of the Advanced Connection Settings dialog box is the AutoLogon setting. You can define a user ID and password that are automatically used by everyone to log on to the Terminal Server (including any administrators). The limited flexibility of this configuration makes it applicable in only very limited deployments. A typical Terminal Server/MetaFrame deployment should not modify this connection. This AutoLogon setting cannot be configured through a group policy.

The Prompt for Password setting forces the user to provide credentials regardless of the passthrough authentication settings that may have been defined elsewhere. Enabling this option can play havoc with clients attempting to launch applications through a Web interface or portal that uses passthrough authentication. The GPO property is called "Always prompt client for password upon connection" and is located in

> Administrative Templates\Windows Components\Terminal Services\
> Encryption and Security

When accessing a Terminal Server with passthrough authentication, be sure that this option has not been enabled.

Immediately under the AutoLogon setting are the Initial Program settings, which, when defined, can affect all users who log on to the server via this connection type. As with the AutoLogon setting, this option is normally not configured for an ICA connection; instead the (inherit client/user config) option is enabled. Hard-coding a specific application, either at the connection level or on a per-user basis, is rudimentary and not recommended, particularly when more advanced application publishing features are available. The program selected to launch can be defined in the "Start a program on connection" GPO property and exists in both the Computer and User Configuration sections in the following location:

> Administrative Templates\Windows Components\Terminal Services

By default, when MetaFrame is installed, the (inherit client/user config) option is automatically enabled and the "Only launch published applications" setting is checked. The purpose of this setting is to enforce use of published applications as the sole connection mechanism to a MetaFrame server by preventing all non-administrators from being able to directly connect to a MetaFrame server by providing only an IP address or the server name.

This option cannot be configured through a group policy (Windows nor Citrix) and instead must be set manually from within the CCC tool.

The final option on the Advanced Connection Settings screen is the Disable Wallpaper setting, which overrides any setting in the user's profile and prevents display of the desktop wallpaper if defined. Preventing display of the desktop wallpaper helps speed up redrawing of the user's desktop session and can make a noticeable difference in responsiveness over a high-latency connection. By default a Windows 2003 Terminal Server does not display the background wallpaper for any user while in the Terminal Server session. This option can be set within a GPO and the property is called "Enforce Removal of Remote Desktop Wallpaper". It is found only in the Computer Configuration portion of the group policy, within this folder:

> Administrative Templates\Windows Components\Terminal Services

This policy can also be set within the MetaFrame user policies. These policies are located under Bandwidth\Visual Effects, and the property in question is called "Turn off desktop wallpaper."

Once all the Advanced settings have been defined, click the OK button to close the dialog box and save the changes.

Configuring Client Settings

Now that you once again are back on the Edit Connections dialog box, click the Client Settings button to access the dialog box shown in Figure 14.12. Here you can enable or disable any of the client device mapping features, including overriding specific mapping options such as audio and LPT port mapping. All unnecessary mappings such as audio or COM should be disabled to conserve bandwidth and other resources.

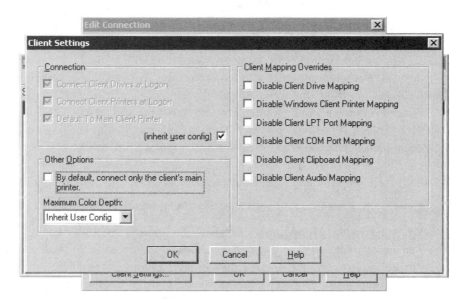

Figure 14.12 The Client Settings dialog box is where you specify what client features will be available for these connections.

The Connection options in the upper left-hand side of the dialog box determine whether or not client drives and printers are automatically mapped. By default, settings maintained in each user's personal user account are inherited and used. Deselecting that (inherit user config) check box enables these three items for editing. If client-mapped printers are not being used by anyone connecting to the server, these settings can be disabled. All three of these settings can be defined within a Windows GPO but are set at the computer level and not on a per-user basis. These settings are found in this folder:

Administrative Templates\Windows Components\Terminal Services\Client/ Server data redirection

Under this folder you find a number of settings that control redirection of client devices, all of which relate to the options listed in the dialog box from Figure 14.12.

Citrix also provides the ability to manage these options through MetaFrame user policies. These policies can be defined on a more granular level, since different settings can be assigned to different groups of user connections. The MetaFrame policies also provide far more options for fine-tuning behavior of the client connections. Figure 14.13 demonstrates some of the options available for client drive mappings.

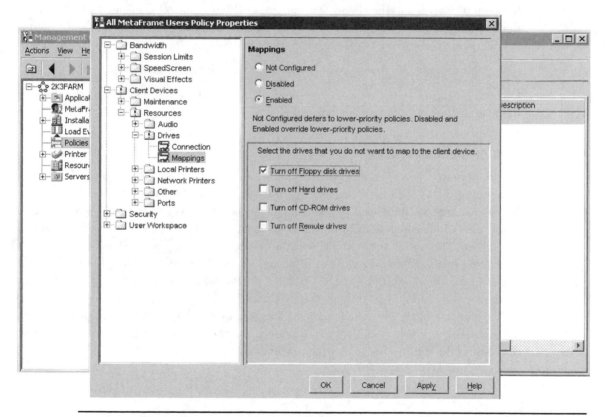

Figure 14.13 Besides enabling client drive mappings, you can specify what type of drives to include and exclude from the mapping process.

Down the right-hand side of the Client Settings dialog box are the client mapping overrides. These allow you to explicitly disable certain components of client device mapping. When an option is disabled on this screen or within a GPO, it affects all users, whether they are an administrator or not. All the options listed in this dialog box can be managed through the Client Devices\Resources section of the MetaFrame user policies.

The lower left-hand side of Client Settings has a pair of additional options. The first, when enabled, forces MetaFrame to connect and map only the client's local default printer through to the MetaFrame session. Any additional printers are not automatically mapped. Enabling this option conserves resources and speeds up the time required to map all existing client printers.

The final option lets you define the maximum supported color depth for these connections. Reducing the color depth reduces the bandwidth required to transmit screen information between the server and the client. This option can also be controlled through a GPO and has the property name "Limit maximum color depth." It is located only in the Computer Configuration section and is specifically in this folder:

Administrative Templates\Windows Components\Terminal Services\

Once all the desired client settings have been defined, clicking the OK button returns you to the main Edit Connection dialog box.

Configuring ICA Settings

The final button on the Edit Connection screen is the ICA Settings button. Clicking this brings up the ICA Settings dialog box with a single entry that controls the client audio quality. Depending on the selection you choose, the accompanying text updates to provide a description of the capabilities of the client audio choice. Figure 14.14 shows the contents of this screen. This option is not available within a Microsoft GPO, but a MetaFrame user policy setting exists for this option and is located under the Client Devices\Resources\Audio folder and labeled "Sound Quality." Besides the MetaFrame user policy, the only other method of managing this is through the CCC tool.

After deciding on the default audio quality, you are returned to the Edit Connection dialog box. Clicking OK here either creates a new connection (depending on what you're doing) or modifies the settings for an existing connection.

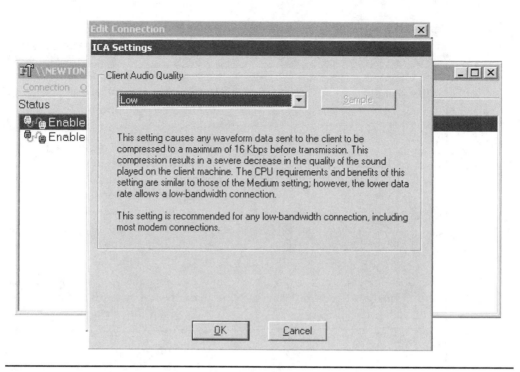

Figure 14.14 The lowest audio quality should always be chosen unless a higher quality is required. A lower quality helps minimize bandwidth requirements.

Managing ICA Connection Settings Using MetaFrame User Policies

The MetaFrame user policies described in the preceding section are accessed through the Policies object in the Management Console for MPS. Using these policies, you have the ability to define and apply different user policies to manage various MetaFrame-specific connection and session options.

MetaFrame User Policy Options

MetaFrame user policies let you configure a number of different user-connection-related settings. Table 14.3 summarizes all the options that can be configured with user policies in MetaFrame Presentation Server 3.0.

Table 14.3 MetaFrame User Policy Summary

Policy Property	Description
Bandwidth	All policies under this category are related to bandwidth optimization.

Session Limits
     Audio
     Clipboard
     COM Ports
     Drives
     LPT Ports
     OEM Virtual Channels
     Overall Session
     Printer
	By configuring the options under this folder you can assign the maximum bandwidth that particular channels in the ICA data stream can consume. All bandwidth caps are assigned a value in kilobits per second (Kb/s). Settings under here are rarely assigned based on a user ID but more often are assigned based on the Client device name or IP address.

SpeedScreen
     Image acceleration using
     lossy compression
	SpeedScreen-related settings are managed under here. Currently the only setting available under here dictates behavior of the lossy compression for image acceleration.

	Lossy compression is enabled by default and set to High in order to maximize the compression used and minimize the bandwidth consumed. You can adjust the default compression as well as set the bandwidth threshold in which lossy compression is automatically enabled.

Visual Effects
     Turn off desktop wallpaper
     Turn off menu animations
     Turn off window contents
     while dragging
	This option controls what Windows visual effects are available to the users. When these options are enabled they consume additional bandwidth.

Client Devices	These rules dictate behavior of server-to-client connectivity.
Maintenance	These options control maintenance of client connections.
Turn off Auto Client Update	The one option controls whether or not the Auto Client Update feature is enabled for a particular client. MetaFrame supports the automatic update of a number of client types. Details on configuration and use of Auto Client Update are provided in Chapter 20.

Table 14.3   MetaFrame User Policy Summary (continued)

Policy Property	Description
Resources	The Resources option controls availability and relative resource impact of client devices.

Audio
  Microphones
  Sound quality
  Turn off speakers
	Audio settings allow for enabling or disabling certain audio-related mapping options.

Drives
  Connection
  Mappings
	The Drives option controls whether client drives are mapped or not, as well as allowing control over whether certain drives, such as the local floppy or CD-ROM drives, are excluded from being mapped.

Local Printers
  Auto creation
  Default
  Drivers
  Turn off client printer mapping
	Local Printers settings manage how client printer mapping is performed, what printers are mapped, how the default printer is defined, and what drivers (native, universal printer driver, or both) are used. The printer options normally managed at the connection level can be managed here and assigned to various group members.

Network Printers Print job routing	Network Printers manages settings that relate only to network printers. Currently the print job routing setting is the only option that exists; it allows you to specify whether a print job destined for a network printer will always be sent through the client device to the printer or directly from the server to the printer. When sent via the client the information is compressed, which consumes less bandwidth but is slower. A direct send to a network print queue from the server consumes more bandwidth but is faster than going through the client first.

Other
  Turn off clipboard mapping
  Turn off OEM virtual channels
	The Other option contains settings for turning off clipboard mapping as well as OEM virtual channels. Disabling OEM channels does not affect any of the native Citrix MetaFrame functionality but prevents third-party applications that utilize ICA virtual channels from functioning properly.

Table 14.3 MetaFrame User Policy Summary (continued)

Policy Property	Description

Ports
   Turn off COM ports
   Turn off LPT ports
	The final option, Ports, allows you to turn off COM and LPT port mapping.

Security
   Encryption
      SecureICA encryption
	Security-related options are managed under the Security folder. Currently the only option found under this heading is the SecureICA encryption option, which is where you define the minimum encryption level required by the client to connect to the server. Enforcing the strongest encryption available is my recommended setting for all production MetaFrame deployments.

User Workspace	The User Workspace policies refer to some of the general settings that determine configuration of the MetaFrame environment in which the user runs his or her applications.

Connections
   Limit total concurrent sessions
   Zone preference and failover
	Under Connections, there are two options. The first places a limit on the total number of concurrent sessions (unique client connections) that a user can have in the server farm.

	A user running multiple published applications, all published on the same server, would consume only a single connection. If any of the applications required a logon to a different server, this would be considered a unique connection and would consume an additional license.
	The other Connections option is the zone preference and failover setting. This option lets you define the preferred zone for one or more connections. Details on zone preferences and failover were discussed in Chapter 8.
Content Redirection Server to client	The Content Redirection option contains only one setting, which lets you enable or disable redirection of server content to the client. By default Web URLs are processed using Web browsers and multimedia players running on the server, but enabling this option causes the local Web browser or multimedia player to process the URL. This option is supported only by the MetaFrame Win32 and Linux clients. Other clients ignore these options.

Table 14.3   MetaFrame User Policy Summary (continued)

Policy Property	Description
MetaFrame Password Manager Central Credential Store Do not use MetaFrame Password Manager	The MetaFrame Password Manager option lets you configure certain settings if the Citrix MetaFrame Password Manager application is also being used in the environment.
Shadowing Configuration Permissions	The Shadowing options are used to define who can shadow the recipients of this policy (Permissions) as well as what shadowing capabilities they will have (Configuration). The biggest point of confusion with this policy has to do with the Permissions tab. Any user account added on this screen is granted permission to shadow any user who is assigned this policy.
Time Zones Do not estimate local time for legacy clients Do not use Clients' local time	The final set of MetaFrame user policy options have to do with managing how MetaFrame interprets the local time zone of the MetaFrame client. The first option disables the server's default behavior of attempting to estimate the local time zone for those ICA clients that did not provide time zone information. If users are receiving inaccurate time information this is likely the cause, and either this policy should be enabled or the MetaFrame client upgraded. The last option controls whether the client provides time zone information or the local time of the MetaFrame server is used instead.

Creating MetaFrame User Policies

A new policy is easily created by right-clicking the Policies object and selecting Create Policy from the context menu. You can also quickly access this option using the Alt+P keyboard combination or clicking the Create Policy icon on the main toolbar in the Management Console. A dialog box opens, prompting you to provide the name of your new policy. Figure 14.15 shows an example of this, with one other policy already visible in the policy contents.

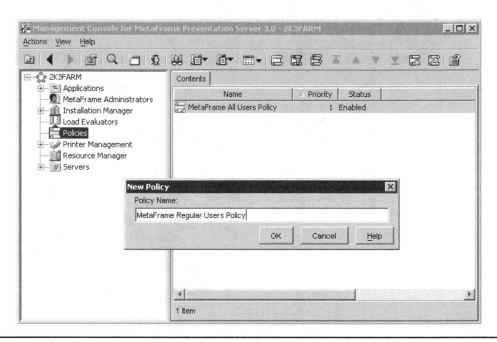

Figure 14.15   A policy name is the only prompt required when a new policy is created.

When creating a policy structure for your MetaFrame environment, always keep it as simple as possible. Unless there is a need to implement a particular policy, do not create policies simply for the sake of being able to do so. When there is a need for MetaFrame user policies in a deployment, I typically begin by creating a MetaFrame policy structure containing the following two policies:

- **MetaFrame All Users Policy**—Into this policy I place settings that should be applied to all MetaFrame users in the farm, regardless of whether or not they are administrators. Settings such as visual effects restrictions or enforcing a minimum SecureICA encryption level are commonly set for all users.
- **MetaFrame Regular Users Policy**—These policies are applied against all regular MetaFrame users, excluding the Administrators group. Restrictions include such options as disabling access to the local floppy or CD-ROM driver.

Additional user policies should be created only when options must be defined that are not appropriate for either of the more general policies. One example of this is use of the zone preferences and failover option, which is most often used in large environments where different groups of users require access to different preferred and failover zones. Typically special policies are created and applied to a range of IP addresses corresponding to the site that requires the zone configuration. Details on policy assignment are discussed shortly, in the "Assigning MetaFrame User Policies" section. Such policies should have a name that clearly defines the special role it is performing. With such policies I suggest using a descriptive name such as "MetaFrame <site> Zone Policy", where <site> corresponds to a descriptive site name such as New York HQ or Seattle Sales Office.

Defining Settings for a MetaFrame User Policy

Once a policy has been created it appears in the contents pane, but specific properties must be set before it will actual do anything. The properties for a user policy are accessed by right-clicking the desired policy name and selecting Properties from the context menu. You will then be able to define the desired options as listed earlier in the "MetaFrame User Policy Options" section. Once applied the options are saved with the policy into the target data store.

Assigning MetaFrame User Policies

After defining the desired options, the policies are applied using filter rules. Until a filter rule has been applied to a policy it is not applied to any user, client, or server in the farm. Filter rules are applied by right-clicking a policy and selecting the Apply This Policy To option. The Policy Filters dialog box appears, as shown in Figure 14.16.

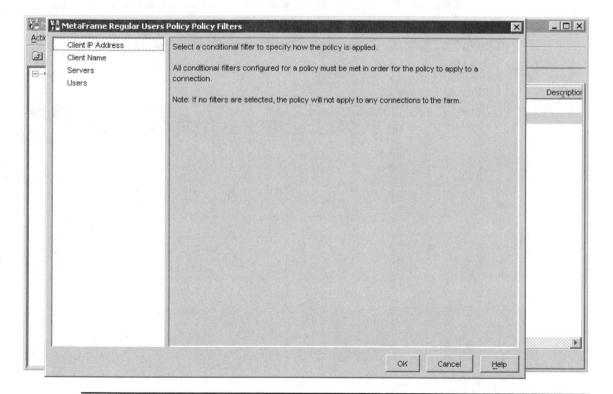

Figure 14.16   At least one filter rule must be applied to a policy before the policy is applied.

Policy rules are assigned based on any of the following criteria:

- **User or group name**—One or more individual users (explicit or anonymous) or groups can be assigned to a policy. When assigning the desired user object, you have the option of allowing or denying application of that policy. When you want to ensure that a particular user or group is never assigned a particular policy, include them in the filter but set their assignment to Deny.
- **Client IP address**—A policy can be applied to all client IP addresses, specifically listed IP addresses, or one or more ranges of addresses. Ranges can also be assigned Allow or Deny, as shown in Figure 14.17.
- **Client name**—You can provide a list of one or more client names to which the specified policy will be applied. Client names must be entered manually but are not case sensitive. You must ensure that you enter the correct name, because there is no validation that can be applied when entered. Note that the client name policy filter is not applied when a user connects using the Web Interface. Users connecting using the Program Neighborhood Agent client can process these client name filters.
- **Server name**—Filters can be applied for any MetaFrame server within the server farm. The server must appear in the farm list in order to be selectable as a potential filter candidate. Server names or IP addresses cannot be manually entered.

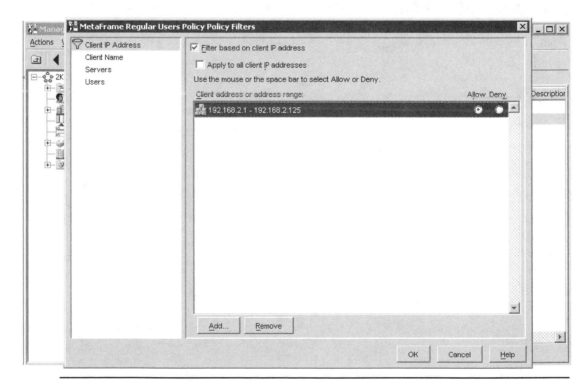

Figure 14.17 A range of client IP addresses is just one filter criterion available for a MetaFrame user policy.

TIP: When a policy is applied against a user, it is done during the connection logon. If changes are made to a policy, those changes are not reflected in a user's session until the next time that user logs on.

Managing MetaFrame User Policy Priority

To ensure that policies are applied properly, they are assigned a priority in which they are applied. As policies are applied, any change in settings overrides a setting defined in an earlier policy, so care must be taken to ensure that the desired order is appropriate for your environment. Priority levels work from highest to lowest, so the priority level of 1 (one) is the highest priority; policies defined here override any policies set earlier. You can adjust the priority of a policy by dragging it to the desired position or by right-clicking and choosing the desired action from the Priority menu. If you're implementing the All Users Policy and Regular Users Policy I discussed earlier, you should implement them in the following order:

1. MetaFrame Regular Users Policy
2. MetaFrame All Users Policy

This way, the All Users Policy settings are applied first, because of priority 2, and then the Regular Users Policy settings are applied.

ICA Connection Security Settings

Security on an ICA or RDP connection is a critical part of ensuring that only authorized users actually have access to log on to the Terminal Server/MetaFrame server. The connection permissions can be configured using either the CCC tool or the Terminal Services Configuration tool. Figure 14.18 shows the same permissions for the ICA connection displayed in both the CCC tool and the Terminal Services Configuration tool. The default permissions for the ICA connection depend on the options you chose when installing MPS and the version of Windows you are implementing. Details on the recommended permissions and a walk-through on how this is done are provided in Chapter 16, "Terminal Server Security."

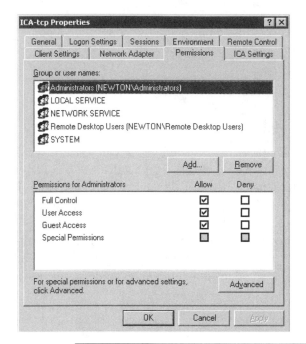
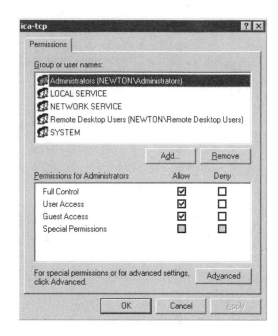

Figure 14.18   ICA or RDP connections can be configured using either one of the connection management tools.

Allowing Direct ICA and RDP User Connections to a MetaFrame Server

A common problem that arises after MetaFrame has been installed is that a regular user (non-administrator) receives the error message shown in Figure 14.19 and his or her access to the server is denied. The same message appears regardless of whether the user is connecting over an ICA or RDP connection and can be particularly confusing if the user was able to create a direct RDP connection immediately before MetaFrame was installed.

Figure 14.19   Users attempting to directly connect using an ICA or RDP client may encounter this error message immediately after MetaFrame is installed.

The reason for this is because when MetaFrame is installed it automatically configures both ICA and RDP connections to accept only connections originating from a published application request and not a direct connection to the server. The option itself is accessible only with the CCC tool and cannot be configured via group policies. Figure 14.20 shows where this setting is configured on the Advanced settings. When only published applications can be launched, which is the default set when MetaFrame is installed, regular users cannot directly log on to the MetaFrame server.

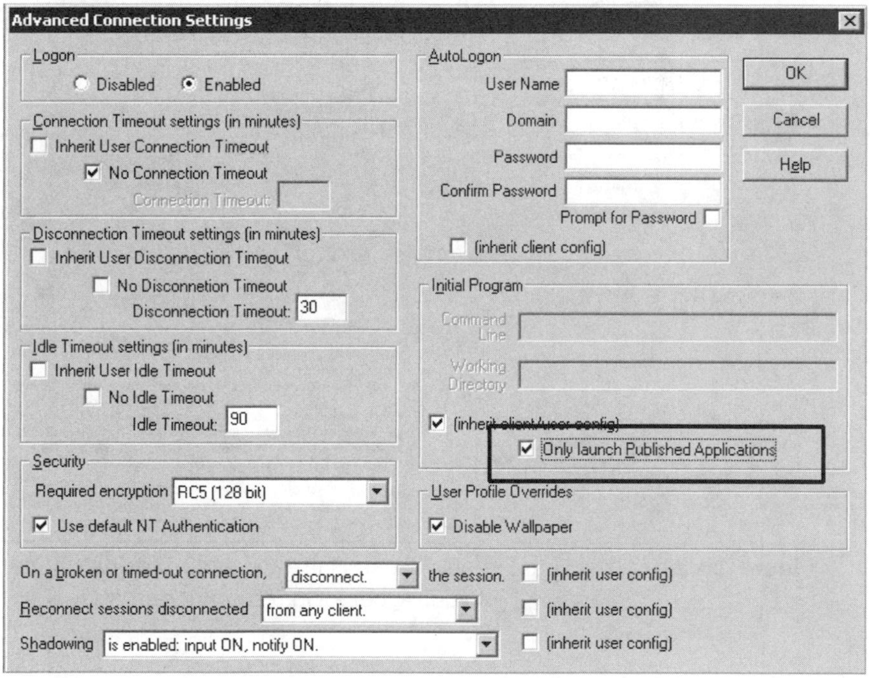

Figure 14.20   When only published applications can be launched, a non-administrator cannot directly log on to a Terminal Server.

Using the MetaFrame Access Suite Console

The MetaFrame Access Suite Console (MASC) is a Microsoft Management Console (MMC) snap-in that allows for centralized monitoring and management of all components of your Access Suite deployment. There are currently four products that make up the MetaFrame Access Suite: MetaFrame Presentation Server, MetaFrame Conference Manager, MetaFrame Password Manager, and MetaFrame Secure Access Manager. Figure 14.21 shows the main MASC window. In this section we focus on management of MetaFrame Presentation Server, which as of this writing is the only product that can be managed using the MASC. The other three objects are currently only placeholders for future management support features.

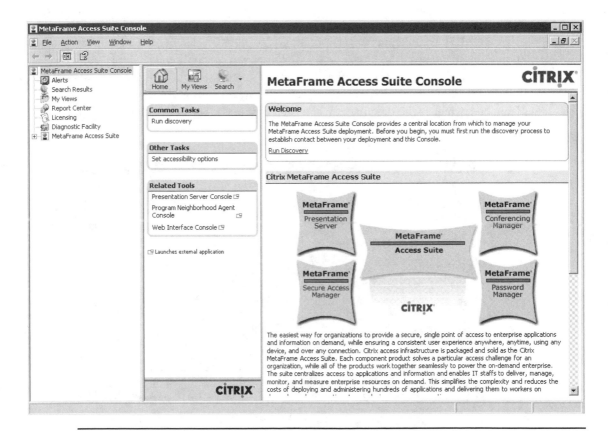

Figure 14.21 The MetaFrame Access Suite Console provides a means of centrally managing all your Access Suite components.

The Access Suite Console can be launched directly off a MetaFrame server or from any machine on which it has been installed. The first time it is launched, the main console window shown in Figure 14.21 appears. This demonstrates the general layout of the MASC and how information is viewed and processed. In this view, the four supported modules are visible as links that can be selected. As I mentioned, in this section we concentrate on the MPS-related management available in the MASC.

Discovering Your MetaFrame Server Deployment

Before you can begin to perform any management tasks, you must run the Discovery task in order to link the MASC with your MetaFrame deployment. You can launch Discovery from the welcome message shown in Figure 14.21 or select it from under the MetaFrame Access Suite submenu.

When Discovery is launched, a simple dialog box appears (Figure 14.22) asking you to provide the name of at least one server in each farm that you wish to manage. If you're running MASC on a MetaFrame server in the farm, you can click the Add Local Computer button; otherwise, click the Add button and enter the name of the MetaFrame server. Make certain that the name you're entering can be resolved by the computer on which you are running the Access Suite Console. Provide a fully qualified name if necessary or an IP address. If the name entered cannot be found, the discovery process eventually fails.

After the discovery process has successfully located the server farms you wish to monitor, they appear in the Deployment Status grid in the lower right-hand corner of the main window for the MASC. A status of OK appears if the server farm is reachable by the Access Suite Console.

The Presentation Server for Windows module under MetaFrame Access Suite now also shows the names of all discovered farms. Figure 14.23 shows this information in the highlighted box.

At this point you can drill into the specific server farm to view more detailed information on the existing applications, servers, and zones.

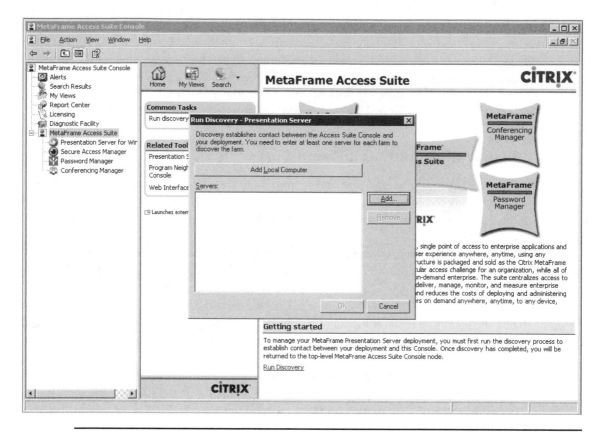

Figure 14.22 The MetaFrame Access Suite Console presentation server Run Discovery dialog box.

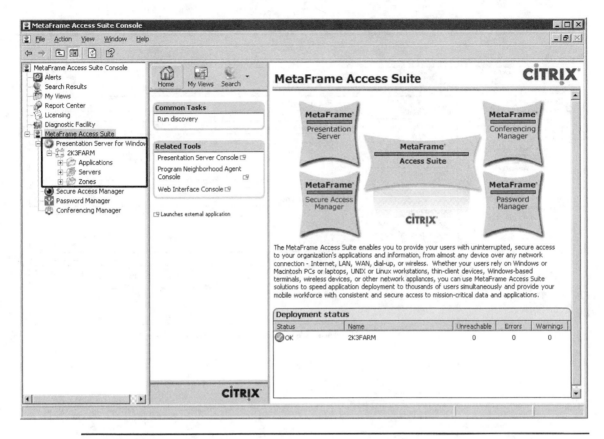

Figure 14.23 Once discovered, the MetaFrame server farms appear under the Presentation Server for Windows object.

Presentation Server for Windows Farm Management Overview

Once you select a desired server farm, you are presented with the main farm view shown in Figure 14.24. There are a number of options on this screen, which I describe briefly in the next few sections.

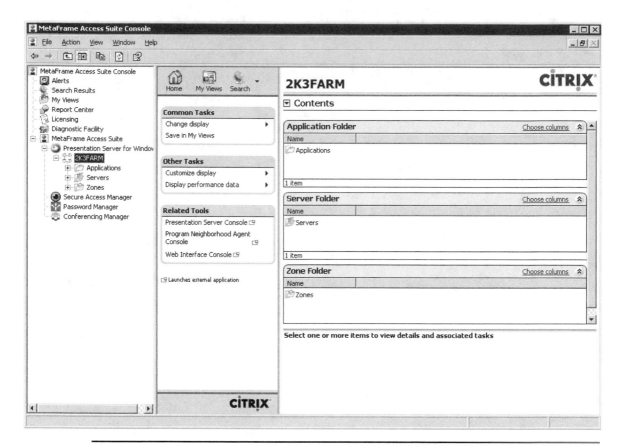

Figure 14.24   The main farm view within the Access Suite Console shows details of the farm content.

Common Tasks

The Common Tasks grouping has two options available. The first is Change Display, which lets you modify the current information view for the server farm. Four view choices are available:

- **Contents**—Summarizes the contents of the server farm, broken into applications, servers, and zones. Double-clicking any of these items immediately takes you to the main page for that farm object type. I look at the properties of each of these areas in more detail shortly.
- **Information**—Shows you summary information including the number of currently active sessions, the number of servers in the farm, the number of published applications, the number of published desktops, and the amount of published content.

- **Alerts**—Shows any alerts generated by Resource Management. To receive alerts, you must be licensed for MPS Enterprise Edition and have configured Resource Management.
- **Sessions**—Displays all the active sessions (RDP or ICA) on any of the servers within the farm.

The other option within Common Tasks is the Save in My Views task. Clicking this option allows you to add the current view to the My Views folder located in the root of the MASC display. From here you can access the most commonly used views and quickly jump to the desired information.

Other Tasks

When currently viewing the contents of the farm, the Other Tasks option lets you select how the contents are displayed (large icons, small icons, details) and also view performance data for the selected item. For performance data to be accurately displayed, you must have Resource Manager installed and configured to monitor your farm environment. Unless the Resource Manager is functioning properly, access to the performance data dashboard is available but information is not visible when requested.

Related Tools

Whenever the Related Tools view is available, it lets you quickly launch an associated tool to access additional information or manage a specific component. Depending on the tool selected, you are prompted to provide additional information to use to establish a connection with that tool.

MetaFrame Presentation Server Farm Information Review

From Figure 14.24 you can see that the contents of a server farm, at least as far as the Access Suite Console is concerned, are made up of applications, servers, and zones. For each of these choices, you can click the object's name and see additional planning and configuration information. General information can be quickly reviewed, but most modifications require launching and authenticating against the appropriate management tool.

Applications View

The Applications view lists all the applications currently published within the farm, their status, their connection type, and the minimum required encryption level. Figure 14.25 provides a visual summary of the application information available from the MASC. From the Applications view you can disable any of the listed active applications.

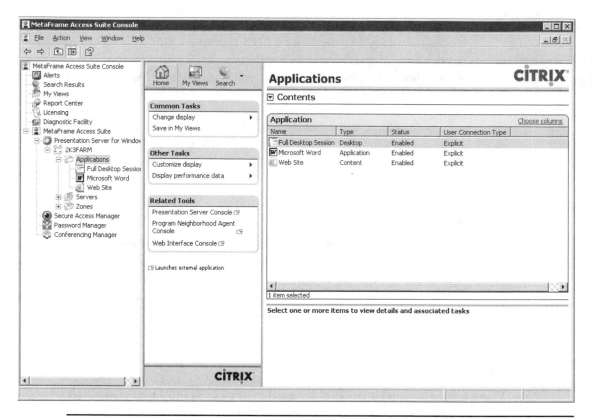

Figure 14.25 The Applications view lists the applications currently published within the farm.

In addition to the Contents view are the Information view, which displays a link to run the Presentation Server Console, and the Alerts view, which shows any alerts for the given applications.

Servers View

The default display for the Servers view is shown in Figure 14.26. The Contents view lists all the servers currently in the farm as well as a summary of useful information about those servers, such as the current service pack level, the number of active sessions, and the server's IP address. Additional columns can be added or existing ones removed if desired.

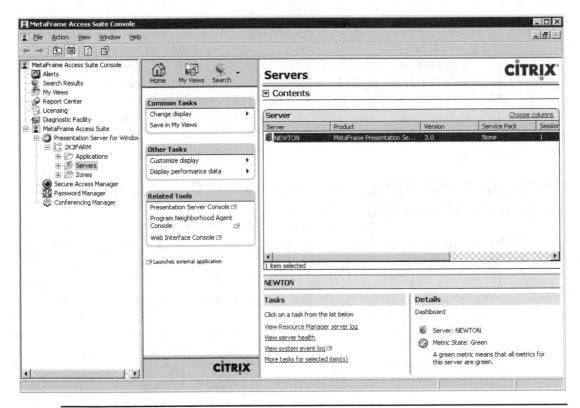

Figure 14.26   The Servers view lists the servers currently in the farm.

When a server is selected a number of resource management tasks become available, such as reviewing of logs specific to that server from within the Resource Manager or accessing the server's system event log.

Another option is the Sessions view, which lists all the active sessions for the corresponding servers in the farm. If a specific session is highlighted, all the standard tasks supported by an active connection become available, such as resetting, logging off, or shadowing an active session.

The two remaining display types are Information, which displays a link to the Presentation Server Console, and Alerts, which displays any generated alerts for the servers.

Zones View

The final farm member that can be selected from the Access Suite Console is labeled "Zones." Zones refers to groupings of MetaFrame servers, usually distributed across one or more wide area network links. Aside from being able to view all the zones defined for a server farm, you cannot perform any maintenance on those zones.

> **NOTE:** While there certainly are some useful management options accessible from within the Access Suite Management Console, I feel there still are fundamental updates that need to be made to the software before it becomes a truly useful tool to consolidate management of the environment. Until that time I prefer to continue to simply use the Management Console for MetaFrame Presentation Server.

Configuring and Using the Management Console for MetaFrame Presentation Server

Almost all the configuration of your MetaFrame server farm will be performed using the Management Console for MetaFrame Presentation Server. This tool is also referred to as the Presentation Server Console (PSC) and can be found under the Citrix menu on the Start menu of any MPS 3.0 server or on any computer where the PSC has been installed.

When logging on to the tool, you are prompted to provide the name of a server in the farm and then enter the credentials of a user who has been delegated permission to administer the farm. If this is the first time you are logging on, provide the name of the default administrator you defined when installing MPS. Figure 14.27 shows the main PSC logon screen. When validating your logon, the chosen MetaFrame server is used to communicate with the data store to verify that your credentials match those of a user who has been granted access to administer the MetaFrame server farm.

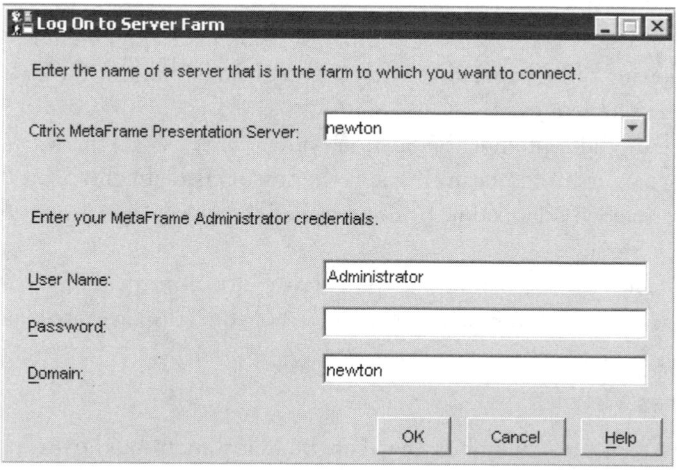

Figure 14.27   The main logon screen for the Presentation Server Console uses the MPS server selected to communicate with the data store.

Once you have been authenticated, the PSC loads and you are presented with the main application interface shown in Figure 14.28. From here you can control configuration of the main components of the server farm and the servers within that farm. For the remainder of this chapter we review the main administrative configuration changes you would typically make after completing installation of your MetaFrame server farm.

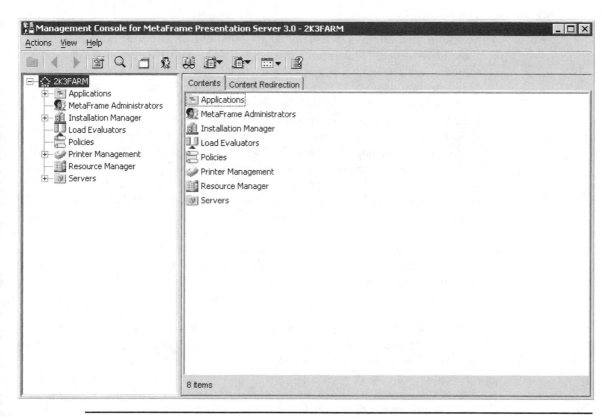

Figure 14.28   The Presentation Server Console is where most of your server farm configuration will be performed.

Delegating Administrative Authority

One of the first tasks you will want to perform is ensuring that the appropriate users have been delegated administrative authority in the server farm. This is done by right-clicking the MetaFrame Administrators icon in the PSC and choosing Add MetaFrame Administrator from the context menu. You are then presented with the Add MetaFrame Administrator wizard, the first screen of which prompts you to choose the appropriate user or group to assign administrative authority. The appropriate groups should be chosen based on the planning decisions discussed in Chapter 8. I usually recommend that only the Terminal Server Administrators group be delegated full administrative authority to the server farm. Additional delegations are discussed a little later in this section.

Once the desired administrative group or groups are chosen, the remaining wizard steps are as follows:

1. The next dialog box that appears prompts you to provide alert contact details for the delegated administrators. When defining a group of administrators this information should consist of general information monitored by multiple administrators. A shared e-mail account is a common setting that is used. To send alerts, the Resource Manager component of MPS Enterprise Edition must be installed and configured properly. Once you have entered the desired information, click Next to continue.

2. Next you are asked to select the privileges for the delegated administrator, as shown in Figure 14.29. The Full Administration option should be chosen when configuring your main administrators. The View Only privilege lets the delegated users have read-only access to the entire farm. The third choice is to create custom privileges for this delegated group. When this option is chosen the Finish button changes to Next, and you can define the specific areas in the PSC that these users will have access to as discussed in Step 3. If you're not creating custom privileges, click Finish to complete the permission delegation.

3. If you're creating custom privileges, click Next to proceed to the permissions selection dialog box shown in Figure 14.30. From this screen you select the component you wish to grant access to and then choose whether the users will have read-only access or if additional permissions will be granted. A common use for these custom privileges is creation of special access for the Terminal Server Operators or Terminal Server User Support groups. The suggested custom privileges for these groups are shown in Table 14.4. Basically, the Server Operators group can view the majority of options in the farm and change a select few. The User Support group has read-only access to a select portion of the farm plus the ability to manipulate session connections in order to help support the users. The extent to which operators and user support personnel can actually make changes to the farm depend on your comfort level with their abilities. Minimizing the number of people who can actually manipulate the farm helps protect against some unexpected change negatively impacting the environment. Once you complete selecting the desired permissions, click Finish.

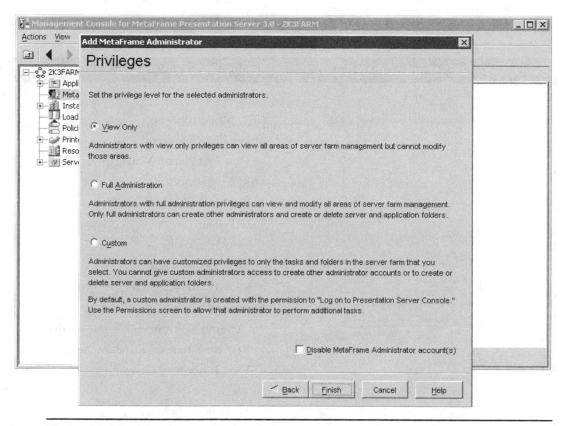

Figure 14.29 You are required to define the privileges that the delegated administrators will have to the server.

Table 14.4 Suggested Custom Permissions for Server Operators and User Support Groups

Terminal Server Security Group	Permissions
Terminal Server Operators	Applications
	Published Applications
	View Published Applications and Contents
	Resource Manager
	Receive Application Alerts
	View RM Applications and Content

Table 14.4 Suggested Custom Permissions for Server Operators and User Support Groups (continued)

Terminal Server Security Group	Permissions
	Sessions
	All Permissions
	Installation Manager
	View Installation Manager
	Load Evaluators
	View Load Evaluators
	User Policies
	View User Policies
	Printer Management
	View Printers and Printer Drivers
	Resource Manager
	Generate Current and Summary Reports
	Receive Summary Database Alerts
	View Resource Management Configuration
	Servers
	Published Applications
	Assign Applications to Servers
	Resource Manager
	Receive Alerts from Servers
	Servers
	Terminate Processes
	View Server Information
	Sessions
	All Permissions
Terminal Server User Support	Applications
	Published Applications
	View Published Applications and Contents
	Resource Manager
	Receive Application Alerts

Table 14.4 Suggested Custom Permissions for Server Operators and User Support Groups (continued)

Terminal Server Security Group	Permissions
	Sessions
	Disconnect Users
	Log off Users
	Send Messages
	View Session Management
	Load Evaluators
	View Load Evaluators
	Printer Management
	View Printers and Printer Drivers
	Resource Manager
	Generate Current and Summary Reports
	Receive Summary Database Alerts
	Servers
	Sessions
	Disconnect Users
	Log off Users
	Send Messages
	View Session Management

Once the delegation is completed, you can return to the MetaFrame Administrators object at any time to adjust these permissions if necessary to change the access that certain administrative users have to the Presentation Server Console.

TIP: You can also edit the permissions of the different components of the PSC by right-clicking the component and selecting Permissions from the context menu. You can then immediately adjust the permissions for any of the existing delegated users or groups.

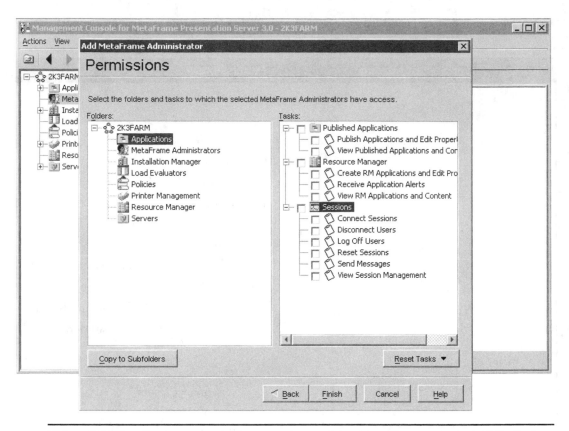

Figure 14.30   Custom permissions can be assigned to allow support staff limited access to the Presentation Server Console.

Configuring Server Farm Properties

Once the administrative privileges to the server farm are delegated, it is time to begin actual configuration of the farm. The most common place to begin is with configuration of the properties for the entire farm itself. The properties for the server farm are accessed by right-clicking the server farm name and selecting Properties. The main Properties dialog box shown in Figure 14.31 appears.

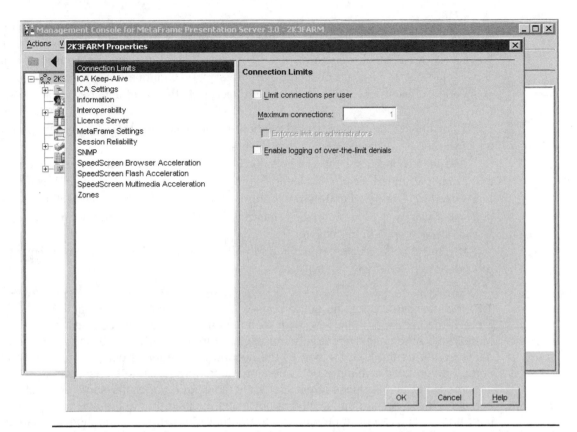

Figure 14.31 Adjusting settings for the server farm is good place to start the general configuration of the MetaFrame environment.

In the next few sections I discuss the common configuration settings for the various server farm properties.

Connection Limits

You can use the Connection Limits property to configure the maximum number of concurrent connections users can have in the farm at one time. By default users can have an unlimited number of connections into the farm. Enforcing a connection limit helps not only to conserve system resources, including licenses, but is also a good security practice, since it can discourage sharing of user passwords by preventing multiple distinct logons from being active in the farm at one time. Use caution when enabling this feature because it could inadvertently prevent users from being able to access all the applications in the farm. When deciding on the maximum number of connections to support, take into consideration the number of published applications that are run on distinct MetaFrame servers.

For example, if you have a main grouping of servers that published all the applications in the farm but also have a pair of servers designated to share only one particular application, you need to ensure that users can have a connection limit of two, one for the main group of servers and one for the pair of special-purpose servers. Granting access to only one active connection prevents users from being able to access both sets of applications at the same time.

You can have attempts to exceed the limit set automatically logged in the system event log of the server where the action was attempted.

Although connection limits can be enforced on administrators, I do not recommend this as it can impair the administrator's ability to properly support the environment. If connection limits need to be assigned to different groups of users, I recommend using MetaFrame user policies, which were discussed in the "Managing ICA Connection Settings Using MetaFrame User Policies" earlier in this chapter.

If connection limits are defined in user policies, whatever limit is more restrictive takes precedence.

TIP: If a user already has an active connection to a published application on a MetaFrame server, and then the user launches a second published application, MetaFrame automatically redirects the user to run that second application on the same server as the first, as long as the second application is being published on the same server. Load levels are not taken into consideration in this case, and it is assumed that all the user's applications should be run under the same connection if possible. If the second application is not being published on the same server, the user has no choice but to be directed to another MetaFrame server, hence creating another connection in the farm.

ICA Keep-Alive

If users are accessing the MetaFrame environment over WAN connections or across unreliable connections such as the Internet, what can happen is that the user is disconnected from a MetaFrame server, but the server itself does not detect that the session was terminated, so it remains in an active state on the server for an extended period of time. If the user reconnects, then unless they are using the new Workspace Control features discussed in Chapter 20, the user is give a new connection and their existing one remains orphaned on the server.

To prevent these sessions from remaining active indefinitely on the server, you can enable the ICA Keep-Alive option. When enabled, this option configures the MetaFrame server to send periodic "ping" requests to the client to verify that it is still available. If a client does not respond, the server places the user's session into a disconnect state. The Keep-Alive interval does not need to be enabled unless your environment is experiencing these types of issues.

The default refresh interval is 60 seconds, but this may have to be adjusted depending on your network configuration. When trying to minimize unnecessary network traffic, increase the refresh interval until you exceed the effective threshold and then drop the interval back by 10 to 15 seconds.

TIP: If users will access your server farm through the Secure Gateway for MetaFrame Presentation Server, you need to configure Keep-Alive values in the Secure Gateway, as it will intercept keep-alives originating from MetaFrame servers, preventing them from reaching remote clients.

When the ICA Keep-Alive option is enabled, it overrides any Keep-Alive values set in Active Directory group policy objects. The setting can be found in the following location in a GPO:

Computer Configuration\Administrative Templates\Windows Components\
Terminal Services

and the property is called Keep-Alive Connections. More information on group policy objects can be found in Chapter 15.

TIP: The Keep-Alive setting also ensures that idle sessions remain active on the server and are not disconnected by network devices that may automatically close idle connections.

ICA Settings

The ICA Settings property page (Figure 14.32) lets you fine-tune some of the ICA display settings to optimize bandwidth and improve the visual responsiveness of the MetaFrame session. I do not recommend modifying any of the default ICA Display properties unless you're experiencing an issue that may be resolved by changing a setting. If you want to enforce an upper limit on the amount of memory allocated to each user session to manage the display properties, you can modify the maximum memory allocation. The Degradation Bias option is used only if the maximum memory allocation for a user session has been reached and either color depth or screen resolution must be reduced to fit within the allotted memory. The default of 5MB is more than sufficient in most implementations. The maximum memory required for a user session is calculated as follows:

Memory in bytes = Color Depth in bits per pixel (bpp) / 8 × horizontal pixels × vertical pixels

So if a client wishes to run with 24bpp color at 1024 × 768, the memory required would be

$(24bpp / 8) \times 1024 \times 768 = 2,359,296$ bytes = 2.3MB

From this you can see that the default of 5MB will support most requested client color and resolution requests.

TIP: Even though the default maximum memory allocation is 5MB, MetaFrame does not pre-allocate this amount. It allocates only the amount required to support the requested color depth and screen resolution.

Auto Client Reconnect is a feature of the ICA client that allows it to automatically reconnect to a disconnected MetaFrame session. Normally the client caches the user's logon credentials and uses them to automatically log back on to a disconnected session. If the required user authentication option has been checked, cached credentials are not used and the user is required to provide authentication information in order to reconnect to a disconnected session. Enabling this option overrides the "Always prompt client for password upon connection" GPO setting in a Windows active directory. This setting can be found in

Computer Configuration\Administrative Templates\Windows Components\ Terminal Services\Encryption and Security

If logging is enabled, the reconnection attempts are logged in the system event log on the MetaFrame server. A high number of reconnection attempts may indicate an issue with either the local network or a WAN link. When I'm suspicious of the reliability of a remote link, I will enable this feature to log automatic reconnect attempts. Recall that automatic reconnect attempts are initiated only when a client enters a disconnect state that was not initiated by the user. These are typically caused by network latency or client device issues.

Information

The Information property page provides the following summary information:

- **Connection Information**—The current number of active user sessions and the total number of servers in the farm.
- **Published Resources**—Displays the current subtotals for published applications, desktops and content along with a total of the number of published resources that exist in the farm.
- **Zone Information**—The active zones in the server farm a listed along with their corresponding zone data collector.

Aside from being a convenient location to quickly review some high-level information about the farm, there are no functional changes that can be made from here.

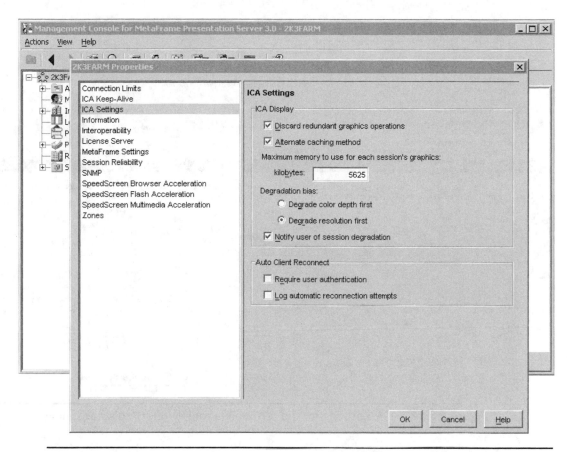

Figure 14.32   ICA Settings for the farm focus mainly on ICA display tuning.

Interoperability

MetaFrame 1.8 interoperability is enabled and disabled from this page by selecting or deselecting the Work with MetaFrame 1.8 servers in the farm option. MetaFrame 1.8 interoperability was first discussed in Chapter 2, "Citrix MetaFrame Presentation Server," and then reviewed in more detail in Chapter 8, "Server Installation and Management Planning." If you're enabling interoperability mode, the warning message shown in Figure 14.33 will appear. This service disruption will likely manifest itself to the end user as an error message when attempting to connect to a published application. Because of this potential for disruption to the production environment, changes to the interoperability mode should not be performed during production hours.

   When interoperability mode is enabled, the Interoperability configuration tab becomes available in the properties for each MPS 3.0 server in the farm.

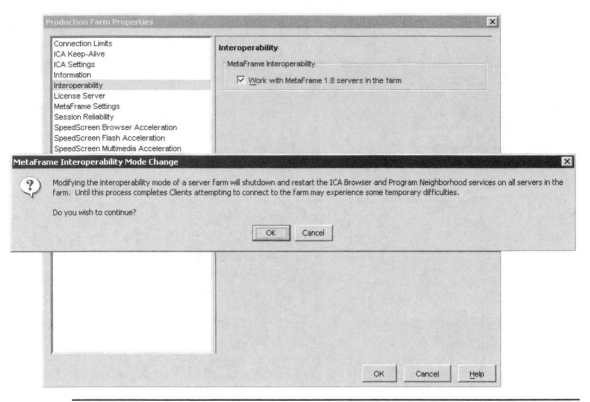

Figure 14.33 ICA Settings for the farm focus mainly on ICA display tuning.

TIP: Mixed-mode support is intended as a migration mechanism only and not as a long term solution for combining MF 1.8 and MPS servers into a single farm. While operating in mixed mode, native features such as Zone preferences and failover or Active-Directory-based user principal logon name (UPN) entries (todd@nrsc.com) supported only by MPS 3.0 are not available.

License Server

The farm-wide license server setting is configured from this tab. All MetaFrame servers in the farm that are configured to use the farm-wide setting (the default), will use the MetaFrame Access Suite License Server entered here. If this setting has not been modified since the creation of the farm, then it will match the MetaFrame Access Suite License Server name that you provided during the initial MetaFrame server build. More detailed information on the MPS licensing is discussed in Chapter 12, "License Server Installation and Configuration."

MetaFrame Settings

The MetaFrame Settings pane (Figure 14.34) is where you can modify some general farm-wide settings that affect both servers and clients within the farm. The available settings on this page are:

- **Broadcast Responses**—These settings allow you to specify what types of Meta-Frame servers in your farm will respond to broadcast requests from ICA clients. The default configuration has both options in this grouping enabled by default. The first configures the elected data collector for each zone to service client broadcast messages. In order for a data collector to service broadcast requests there cannot be any MetaFrame 1.8 servers on the same subnet. This is because the MPS 3.0 data collector could inadvertently process broadcast requests in-tended for a MetaFrame 1.8 server farm. MPS 3.0 will attempt to detect a MetaFrame 1.8 server on the network, and if successful, this option is automatically disabled. Enabling zone data collectors to respond to ICA broadcasts by default is a change from MetaFrame XP, where this option was disabled by default. The data collector setting will also be overridden if a server in the farm has been configured to respond to broadcast requests. By default servers are not configured to do this.

  The other broadcast response option enables MetaFrame servers that are also running the remote access service (RAS) to respond to client broadcast messages. This behavior remains unchanged from MetaFrame XP.

- **Client Time Zones**—Basic support for estimating each connected client's time zone (discussed in Chapter 2) is managed here. By default, local time zone support is enabled, but support for estimating the local time zone for legacy clients is disabled. Typically estimating the client time zone does not produce accurate results so is disabled by default. The client time zone setting is managed only through the server farm properties and automatically applies to all MetaFrame servers in the farm. Depending on your configuration you may need to disable this feature in order to provide uniform time displays for all users.

- **Enable XML Service DNS address resolution**—While this setting may seem innocuous, enabling it without fully understanding the consequences can produce unpredictable client behavior, most often resulting in users being unable to connect to the server farm. By default, when ICA clients request server information, that information is returned in the form of an IP address that the client can directly access. When the Enable XML Service DNS address resolution option is enabled, those clients requesting server information via the Citrix XML Service (client protocols TCP/IP+HTTP or SSL/TSL+HTTP) will receive the fully qualified domain name (FQDN) for a MetaFrame server instead of the direct IP address.

Unless a client is able to reliably resolve all FQDN entries corresponding to all MetaFrame servers in the farm, inconsistent issues with MPS connectivity can result. In this situation, leaving this option disabled, and working with the default behavior involving the server IP address is recommended. In a typical MetaFrame deploy you will not be required to enable this option.

- **Novell Directory Services Preferred Tree**—When an NDS tree name is specified here, it is used by MetaFrame servers in the farm for account authentication.

- **Enable Content Redirection from server to client**—Enabling this option allows users running the Win32, WinCE, Java, or Linux MPS client to access Web-based content originating within a MetaFrame session through a Web browser running directly on the local client device. The normal behavior is to open such Web-based content using a Web browser that also runs on that same MetaFrame server. Unless you have a specific requirement to allow server to client content redirection then this option should remain disabled.

- **Enable remote connections to the console**—Enabling this option allows an administrator to connect directly to a Windows 2003 MetaFrame server console using an ICA client (Windows 2000 Server is not supported). Regardless of how this option is set, direct console sessions are still available using the RDP client (see Chapter 19 for details on this). This setting can be overridden on a server-by-server basis, but by default all servers in the farm will use this setting.

A common question is exactly how can you access the console via an ICA client once it has been enabled? Console sessions are initiated from within the Management Console by right-clicking on the MetaFrame server whose console you wish to directly connect to, select the Launch ICA Session option, then select the menu option labeled Connect to Server's Console. This will bring up the local console logon for that server.

In order to log directly on to the console you must be a member of the local Administrators group on that server.

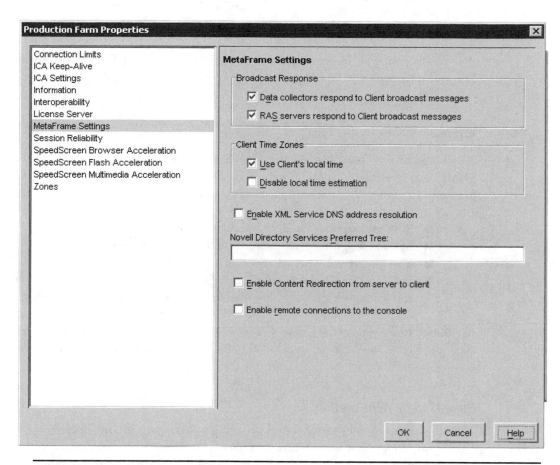

Figure 14.34 ICA Settings for the farm focus mainly on ICA display tuning

Session Reliability

Session Reliability is a MetaFrame feature designed to provide the end user with a sense of continuity even during interruptions in network connectivity. This feature was first described back in Chapter 5, "Client Hardware and Software Planning." During a disruption in network connectivity, session reliability will keep the MetaFrame session visible on the screen. The session will remain visible until the connection is reestablished or it remains down for the default timeout period of three minutes. This timeout value is configured on this screen along with the port number used for this service (2598 by default).

During the interruption, the mouse pointer changes to an hourglass and the session remains visible but inaccessible. When connectivity is restored, the MPS client automatically reconnects to the server. The user is not required to reenter his or her credentials.

Without session reliability, when a broken connection is detected, the client window closes and the user must then manually reconnect to the server in order to restore their session connection. The session reliability feature is available only with the Advanced and Enterprise editions of MPS 3.0, and then only when using the 8.x version of the Win32 MPS client.

SNMP

When running the Enterprise Edition of MPS, the SNMP farm option is available. When the SNMP agent is enabled, all MetaFrame servers in the farm by default will issue SNMP traps for the listed events. Traps are automatically issued when any of these events occur:

- **Session Logon**—Each time a user logs onto a server.
- **Session Logoff**—Each time a user logs off of a server.
- **Session Disconnect**—Every time a user session is disconnected.
- **Session Threshold Exceeded**—Whenever the number of user sessions on a server exceeds the value specified in the Session Limit Per Server field.

In addition to supporting the issuance of these basic traps, enabling the SNMP agent will also allow the MetaFrame servers to respond to SNMP events sent from the Network Manager plug-in.

SpeedScreen Acceleration

The three SpeedScreen acceleration features are all part of the SpeedScreen Latency Reduction support that was discussed in Chapter 5. The three acceleration features are all managed on the farm-level by default, but individual servers can be configured to override these settings. When implementing MetaFrame I keep the default settings for these features unless there is an implementation requirement to either modify their behavior or disable them. The three acceleration features are:

- **SpeedScreen Browser Acceleration**—Figure 14.35 shows the settings available on this property page. This feature supports accessing and interacting with Internet Explorer, Outlook Express, and Outlook (accessed as published applications) while images for a particular site are downloaded in the background. This way the user can continue to work instead of being forced to wait for all the data to become available. Another browser acceleration option, which is not enabled by default, is automatic compression of JPEG images. Compression allows for shrinking of JPEG files to increase available bandwidth while sacrificing some image quality. JPEG images processed by any other application are not subject to this browser acceleration logic.

When running MPS, Enterprise Edition, a third option exists labeled Determine when to compress. Enabling this option causes Enterprise Edition MetaFrame servers to dynamically compress JPEG images based on their size and the available bandwidth. When sufficient bandwidth exists no compression is performed.

You should note that if Macromedia Flash content exists on a page and Flash is enabled (see the next setting) then Browser Acceleration will not work. In order to ensure that Browser Acceleration is enabled for all sites, Flash support should be disabled, which is not the default configuration.

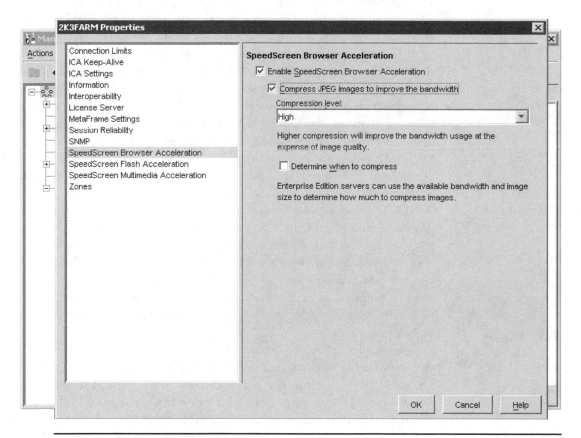

Figure 14.35 Browser acceleration currently applies only to Internet Explorer, Outlook Express, and Outlook.

- **SpeedScreen Flash Acceleration**—A common multimedia component of many Web sites is Macromedia Flash. Rendering and playback of Macromedia Flash content suffer from many of the same problems encountered with other audio and video data. Unlike the multimedia accelerator (described in the next bullet), which streams content to the client, SpeedScreen Macromedia Flash acceleration is responsible for actually throttling rendering of Flash content on the server. Instead of allowing Flash to be rendered in the highest quality, which is the default, Flash is forced to render in a lower quality mode, reducing the size of each data frame and improving responsiveness to the client.

From this property page you can force MetaFrame to disable the playing of Macromedia Flash content completely, or enable support but enforce the optimization of Flash content as described in the previous paragraph. By default Flash content is enabled, but optimized for restricted bandwidth connections, which Citrix marks as any connection with bandwidth under 150Kbps. Higher bandwidth connections are enabled to run Flash at the full default resolution.

If you are planning on utilizing browser acceleration then you may want to disable support for Macromedia Flash content. Web pages containing Flash content are not optimized using the browser acceleration feature.

- **SpeedScreen Multimedia Acceleration**—The multimedia acceleration features are intended to optimize playback of multimedia content through an ICA session. Content playable through Internet Explorer, Windows Media Player, or the RealOne Player is streamed in its original compressed format through to the client device, which is then made responsible for decompressing and playing the content.

  This process has two advantages over how such content would originally be processed on a MetaFrame server. First, by streaming the compressed content to the client, the bandwidth is much smaller than it would be if the content was decompressed on the MetaFrame server and then passed through to the client, which is how Flash content is managed. Second, delegating the client to perform decompression and playback completely frees the MetaFrame server of such CPU-intensive tasks, ensuring that server resources are available for other user requirements.

  Technically, any codec (Compression/decompression software for audio and video playback) compatible with Windows Media Player or RealOne Player can be used to stream multimedia content through to the client. The client must be able to process this content in order for a user to see it. Like the other acceleration options, multimedia acceleration is enabled at the farm level but can be defined on a per-server basis. Figure 14.36 shows the multimedia acceleration properties. The default buffer settings should not be modified unless you're required to ensure a certain level of multimedia support. Increased buffer settings will introduce additional CPU and memory load on both server and client, and should be monitored closely if increased to ensure that the impact to the servers in the farm is acceptable.

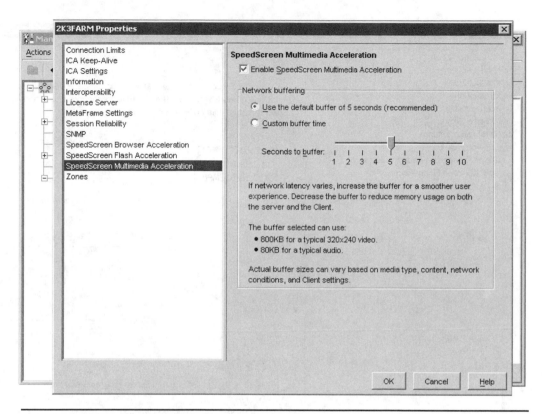

Figure 14.36 The multimedia acceleration features can be defined at the farm level.

Zones

The final configuration option for the server farm is the Zones property page (Figure 14.37). Zones logically subdivide servers within a single server farm into functional groups within which summary information on all the servers in that zone is centrally maintained. Every server farm will have at least one zone, with the first zone created during installation of the first MetaFrame server in the farm. A complete discussion on server farm zones was covered in Chapter 8, including the planning of how many zones to implement and the selection of a preferred zone data collector. This property page is where those planning considerations are implemented.

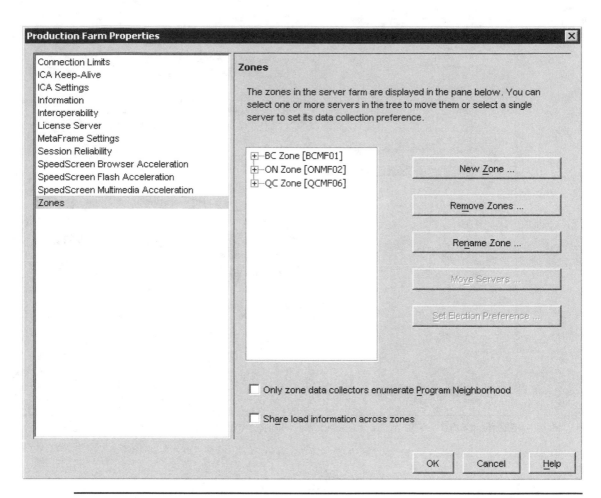

Figure 14.37   The Zones property page is where all zone data collector configuration for the farm is performed.

TIP: Zones are a server farm management construct, and so do not have any configurable settings at the individual server level.

From under the Zones property page there are some basic zone-related functions that can be performed. First, this page allows you to quickly see what zones are known in the server farm and which server in that zone is currently the active zone data collector. Expanding the tree for a zone will list all active servers in that zone along with an icon representing their current zone election preference. Selecting an individual server will enable the Set Election

Preferences button, which brings up the Set Election Preferences dialog box (Figure 14.38). From here you simply choose the appropriate election settings for that server and click OK to save those changes. The very first MetaFrame server created is automatically assigned the Most Preferred data collector setting, while all subsequent servers added to the farm are assigned the Default Preference. You will want to adjust these only if you have configured an environment in which a dedicated zone data collector (ZDC) has been implemented, or there is a specific MetaFrame server, other than the current default, that you wish to be the preferred ZDC. Chapter 8 provides a detailed discussion on configuring the appropriate election preferences.

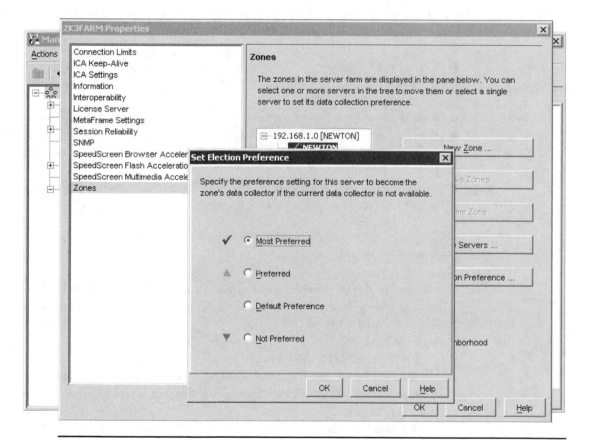

Figure 14.38   Election settings for a server are set from within the Set Election Preferences for that server.

TIP: Changing the data collector election preferences will not automatically force a data collector election. Aside from rebooting the currently designated ZDC, you can force an election by issuing the following command from a command prompt.

```
querydc -e
```

The utility will appear to hang while the election is initiated but once completed a message will appear that says Force Election Completed. The querydc command is discussed in Appendix B, "MetaFrame Presentation Server Command Reference."

In addition to assigning the election preferences you can also do the following from this property page:

- **Create a new zone**—The zone will appear immediately in the list, but before you leave this page you must move at least one server into that zone. Empty zones cannot be saved.
- **Delete an existing zone**—A zone can only be deleted if it contains no servers.
- **Rename an existing zone**—Renaming the zone has no affect on the servers in that zone or the users accessing resources in that zone. It is purely an administrative function.
- **Move servers between zones**—Once the last server is moved out of a zone it must be deleted, or another server must be moved into that zone.

Two options at the bottom of this screen allow you to defined global settings for all data collectors in the farm. These options are:

- **Only zone data collectors enumerate Program Neighborhood**—This setting controls whether all servers in the farm will enumerate applications for Program Neighborhood (the default), or if only zone data collectors should perform this task.

     For standard MPS deployments I recommend leaving this option deselected, allowing any MetaFrame server in the farm to enumerate applications for Program Neighborhood. This will minimize the wait time for the user's application list to appear.

     The most common reason for restricting PN enumeration to only the zone data collectors is to ensure that MetaFrame servers in the farm that users are not authorized to access do not attempt to service client enumeration requests. In order for a MetaFrame server to enumerate applications for a user, the user must have the log on locally user rights assignment. If a user has not been granted this user right then the enumeration will fail.

This user rights assignment is required regardless of whether the user is accessing a Windows 2000 or Windows 2003 Terminal Server. The Windows 2003 "Allow log on through Terminal Services" user right is not sufficient for PN application enumeration to succeed.

- **Share load information across zones**—As I first mentioned back in Chapter 8, zone data collectors in releases of MetaFrame prior to 3.0 (MetaFrame XP) would automatically store information about all servers in the farm, not just servers in their own zones. The default behavior was modified with MPS 3.0 so that a ZDC would store information only about servers within its own zone. The main advantage to this is a reduction in network "chatter" between data collectors as server loads move up and down within each zone.

  Instead, when a user requests a published application, the MPS 3.0 data collector receiving the request automatically queries all other ZDCs in the farm to determine what MetaFrame server is available with the least load to satisfy this request.

  Sharing load information across zones will reduce the server selection process, since each ZDC has full information on application loads in all other zones. Unless there is a large amount of available network bandwidth between zones, the overhead of transmitting updates between ZDCs may not justify the reduction in the time required to complete the server selection process.

  I would recommend that unless all of your zones are located across high bandwidth connections (LAN speed), then this option should not be enabled.

NOTE: If an application is published on multiple servers located in different geographically distinct zones, it is very likely that a user will be directed across a WAN link to a least-loaded server in a remote location. Unless the network capacity of the WAN link is sufficiently large, most administrators would prefer to have the user's request serviced by a local server and look to a server located in a different zone only if no server in the current zone could honor the request.

Support for this is available with the Enterprise Edition of MPS 3.0, and is called Zone Preferences and Failover. Details on this feature were discussed in the "Establishing Zone Preferences and Failover" section of Chapter 8.

Once you have completed the desired configuration changes (if any) to the zones in your farm, the basic server farm configuration is now complete.

Configuring the MetaFrame Server Properties

Next in your MetaFrame server configuration should be making any desired changes to the properties for each server in your farm. These changes are made under the Servers folder in the management console. Right-clicking on an individual server will bring up a menu similar to the one shown in Figure 14.39. The exact options available in the menu will depend on the edition of MetaFrame that you are running.

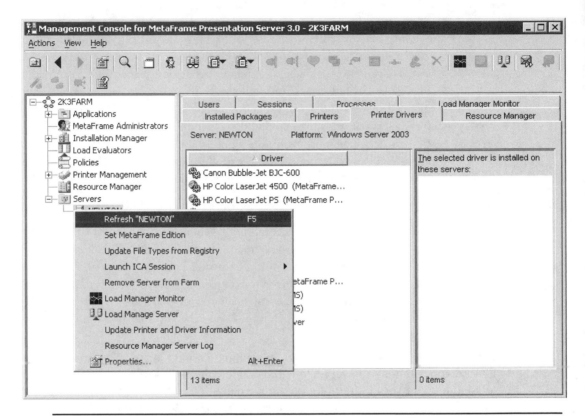

Figure 14.39 A number of tasks and tools are accessible by right-clicking on an individual server.

The menu options available when right clicking on a MetaFrame server are:

- **Refresh**—Simply refreshes the information for the given server.
- **Set MetaFrame Edition**—This option opens a dialog box where you choose the edition of MetaFrame that you would like this server to attempt to license. In order for the features associated with a particular edition to be available, the MetaFrame server must be able to acquire a corresponding license from the Access Suite License Server.

  You can simultaneously configure multiple MetaFrame servers by clicking on the main Servers folder, selecting the Contents tab from the right-hand pane and then highlighting the servers to be modified. Right-click on any highlighted server, select Servers from the popup menu and then choose Set MetaFrame Edition. The exact same edition selection dialog box appears, but any saved changes are automatically applied to all highlighted servers instead of just one.

- **Update File Types from Registry**—Selecting this option will initiate an update of the file type associations in the data store with those contained in this Meta-Frame server. Only those applications that are currently published in the farm will have their file type associations updated in the data store. These associations are available for selection when creating or modifying a published application. File type associations from multiple MetaFrame servers can be loaded into the data store at once by right-clicking on the farm name and selecting the Update File Types from Registry option. If the desired file type for an application is not available when you are publishing the application, performing this action will make that association available.

- **Launch ICA Session**—The Management Console provides this handy option for quickly connecting to a specific MetaFrame server in your farm. Three choices are available for selection:
  - *Connect to Server's Published Desktop*—Selecting this will generate an error if the server does not actually have a desktop published.
  - *Connect Directly to Server's Desktop*—Establishes a direct ICA connection to the server.
  - *Connect to Server's Console*—This choice is available only if you have enabled support for this within the server farm or for this specific server.

- **Remove Server from Farm**—The preferred method of removing a server from the farm is to uninstall MPS 3.0 from that server, but this menu option will perform the same task. I consider this to be more brute-force than performing a clean uninstall and would recommend that this be used only if issues with the server are preventing you from successfully uninstalling.

- **Load Manager Monitor**—On Advanced or Enterprise Edition MetaFrame servers you can select this option to display a graph showing load graphs for the overall load evaluator for this server and the individual rules that are calculated to create the overall load. Figure 14.40 shows an example of the Advanced load evaluator and the three rules associated with that evaluator, the page swaps, memory usage, and CPU utilization. The same monitor information can be viewed by selecting the Load Manager Monitor tab in the right-hand pane. The refresh interval for this monitor can be adjusted by left-clicking on the server, then selecting the Actions menu, and then Load Manager Settings from under the Load Manager menu option.

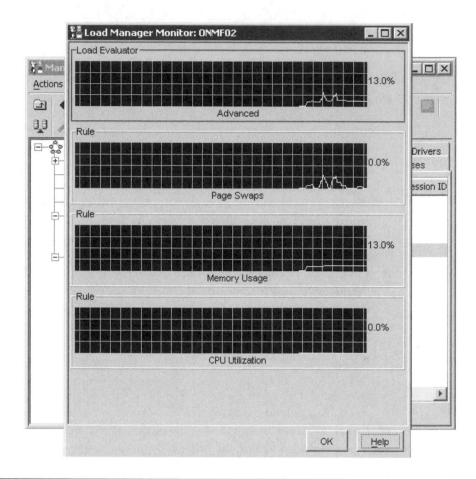

Figure 14.40 The Load Manager Monitor shows a real-time graph of the load evaluator and the load rules for a given server.

■ **Load Manage Server**—From here you can quickly choose the load evaluator to associate with a server. A dialog box will open listing all evaluators that have been created, the rules associated with each evaluator, and a brief description about the evaluator. New evaluators cannot be created here. They must be created from under the Load Evaluators object in the Management Console. Load evaluator creation and use is discussed in Chapter 22, "Server Operations and Support."

- **Update Printer and Driver Information**—Forces the MetaFrame server to send current printer and driver information to the data store. If a printer and/or driver have been added recently to the server and this information has not yet appeared in the Drivers or Printers section of the Printer Management module, this option will force the update to occur. You should be aware that there is no notification from the Management Console if this option succeeds or fails.

- **Resource Manager Server Log**—On an Enterprise Edition MetaFrame server, this option will be present. Selecting it will open a separate window containing the text-based Resource Manager Server log file, an example of which is shown in Figure 14.41.

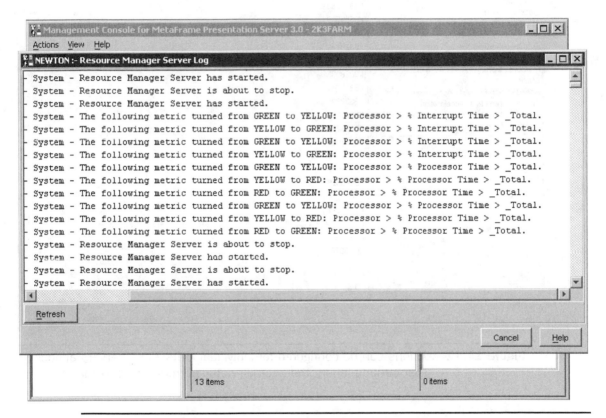

Figure 14.41   The MetaFrame server's text log from the Resource Manager Server is available for viewing when running the Enterprise Edition of MPS 3.0.

- **Properties**—The final option on the menu brings up the properties for the server. I will briefly discuss these settings in the following section. Figure 14.42 shows the available properties for a MetaFrame server. A number of these properties are identical to those described in the "Configuring Server Farm

Properties" section of this chapter. I have noted these but have not duplicated the detailed description given early. In most situations I recommend using farm-wide settings for all of the MetaFrame servers. This simplifies administration and the task of troubleshooting if there are issues.

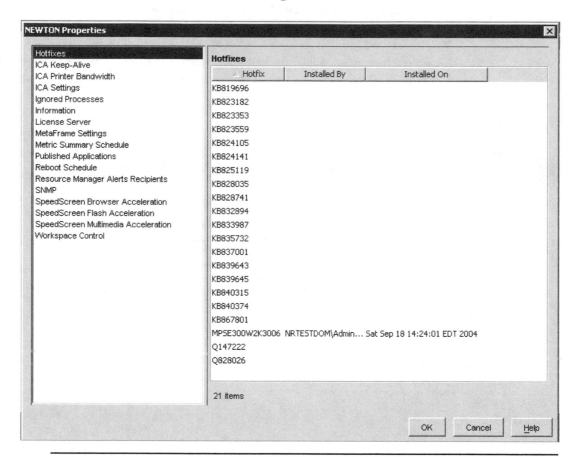

Figure 14.42 Options can be configured for individual MetaFrame servers although most options inherit their default settings from the server farm.

Hotfixes

This property displays a list of all Microsoft and Citrix hotfixes that have been installed on the server. Only MetaFrame hotfixes will display the name of who installed the hotfix and the installation date. Microsoft fixes will not display this information. Details on hotfix installation and management are discussed in Chapter 9, "Service Pack and Hotfix Management."

ICA Keep-Alive

The same settings are available here as are for the farm ICA Keep-Alive property. By default no option is selected for this property. Choose either the use the farm settings or define settings specific to this server option.

ICA Printer Bandwidth

This option allows you to limit the available bandwidth allocated to client print jobs originating from this server. The default option is unlimited, but you can provide an upper limit in Kbps. This setting is enforced on a per print job per client connection basis. So an upper limit of 15Kbps would mean that each client connection with an active print job would be limited to a maximum of 15Kbps. A more detailed discussion on client printer bandwidth throttle is discussed in Chapter 17, "Terminal Server and MetaFrame Printer Management."

ICA Settings

These exact options are also configurable at the server farm level, and all options on this screen are set by default to use the farm settings.

Ignored Processes

An MPS Enterprise Edition server has the Ignored Processes option (Figure 14.43), where you configure a list of processes that are ignored by the Resource Manager. These processes are not monitored, nor recorded in the summary database. A list of default processes is always present, but this list can be modified if desired. When the ignore system processes checkbox is selected, all system processes are automatically ignored and do not need to be added to this list. Processes are added simply by clicking the Add Process button and entering the executable name. The names are case-insensitive, but you must ensure the name matches exactly, including the .exe extension. All instances of that process are then ignored on the server.

Changes you make on one server can be replicated to other servers simply by clicking the Apply to Other Servers button. A list will then appear of all servers in the farm and you simply place a check beside the servers that you wish to update.

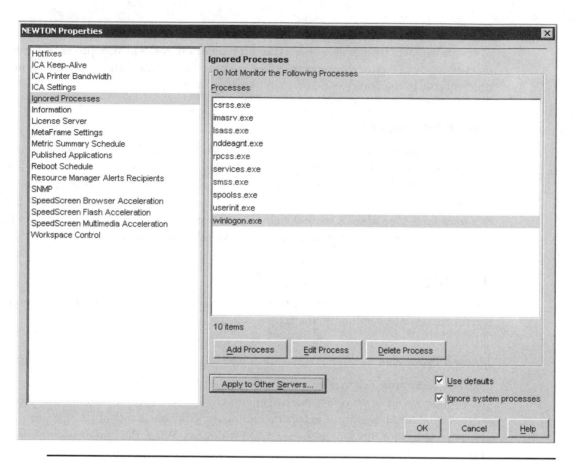

Figure 14.43 MetaFrame allows you to select processes that are completely ignored by the Resource Manager.

Information

Displays general read-only information about this server including MPS version, Windows operating system version, the IP address, and the active ICA listening port (default is 1494).

License Server

The same information as at the farm-level. MetaFrame servers inherit the farm setting by default and should only be modified if a particular server has specific license server requirements that dictate that it must be segregated from other servers in the farm. Details on MetaFrame licensing are discussed in Chapter 12.

MetaFrame Settings

The MetaFrame Settings for an individual server contain a combination of server-specific information and information that can be defined at the farm-level. Figure 14.44 shows the properties for this option. The options available on this page are:

- **ICA Browser**—These settings dictate how the MetaFrame server responds to various ICA browser requests. The "create browser listener" options configure the server to respond to ICA Browser network packets for the respective protocol and are enabled by default. Windows 2000 Server and Windows Server 2003 both support the UDP protocol, but only a Windows 2000 Server will support the IPX and NetBIOS protocols. These two options will not be available on a Windows Server 2003 server. A MetaFrame server can be configured to respond to client broadcast messages when the farm is operating in native mode (no mixed-mode with MetaFrame 1.8). By default MetaFrame servers do not respond to client broadcast requests. Instead the farm is configured so that only the elected data collector for a zone will respond to client broadcast requests.

- **Control Options**—Two options are part of this group. The first enables or disables logons to the server. When logons are disabled, access is only available from the server's console (locally or remotely). This option must be explicitly enabled. Unlike earlier versions of MetaFrame, this option remains disabled after the server is rebooted.

  The second option enables logging of shadow attempts to the System log. This is disabled by default, but I would recommend that this option be enabled in order to provide additional security logging. If you have configured shadowing so that users are not prompted when a shadow attempt is performed, then enabling this feature will also allow you to track whether someone may be abusing the shadowing capabilities. See the "Configuring ICA Connection Properties" section earlier in this chapter for details on how to configure the shadowing behavior for the server.

- **Citrix XML Service**—If IIS has also been configured on this server and the XML Service is sharing port 80 with IIS, this field will be read-only and you will see the text Sharing with IIS. Otherwise, this field is editable, showing the currently assigned port number for the Citrix XML Service, which is port 80 by default. You can modify the current port number for the XML Service using the CTXXMLSS command. Details on this are discussed in Appendix B.

- **Content Redirection From Server To Client**—This option defaults to inheriting the same setting from the farm level.

- **Remote Console Connections**—Also defaults to inheriting the same setting from the farm.

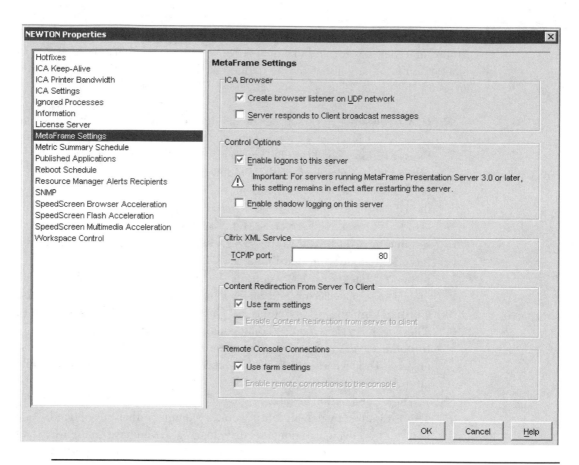

Figure 14.44   MetaFrame settings for a MetaFrame server have some server-only settings.

Metric Summary Schedule

Another Enterprise-Edition-only setting, this page is where you can specify when summary information should be gathered by Resource Manager and stored in the summary database. The default configuration is 24 hours a day, Monday through Sunday. You can specify what days and times the information should be collected. If your environment does not operate on a 24-hour basis, defining a more restrictive timeframe will reduce the amount of data logged.

Settings defined for one server can quickly be replicated to other servers by clicking on the Apply to Other Servers button.

Published Applications

This option provides a read-only summary of the applications currently being published by this server.

SpeedScreen Acceleration

All three acceleration settings (browser, Flash, multimedia) inherit their equivalent farm settings.

Workspace Control

The workspace control feature is available to users accessing a server farm using either the Web Interface for MPS or the Program Neighborhood Agent. Workspace control lets a user quickly log off or disconnect from all running applications with the click of a single button. When sessions are disconnected, they can quickly be reconnected from the same or a different client location. Workspace control is intended to let you quickly open and access your commonly used applications in your MetaFrame environment. Details on the configuration of Workspace Control are discussed in Chapter 20, "ICA Client Installation and Configuration."

The one option on this property page is labeled Trust requests sent to the XML Service and when enabled, allows connect, disconnect, and terminate requests sent to the XML service to be processed even though user credentials are not provided as part of the request. Personally I feel that the potential security risk that enabling this feature can create is not adequately conveyed simply by viewing this tab.

Under most MetaFrame deployment conditions there is no reason that this option should be enabled.

WARNING: Do not enable this option unless it is a specific requirement, and even then, only after you have performed the proper testing in a separate test environment.

In fact, this setting exists only to enable Workspace Control to function properly under the following conditions:

- Users are connecting to their applications through the Web Interface for MetaFrame Presentation Server and they are also authenticating with either passthrough authentication or smart cards. Users accessing applications using the Program Neighborhood Agent are not affected by this.
- These users need to leverage the Workspace Control features of MPS 3.0.

If your environment satisfies this criteria, then you will need to enable this setting in order for Workspace Control to function. In order to minimize the security risks associated with this setting, Citrix recommends the following steps be taken to protect your environment.

- Employ the IPSec feature of Microsoft along with any other technology such as firewalls to ensure that only trusted resources are able to communicate with the XML Service on any MetaFrame server with this option enabled. A quick search of the Microsoft Website for IPSec will uncover a number of resources that provide information on properly configuring IPSec on a Windows server.
- Limit the MetaFrame servers that have this option enabled to only those that are directly contacted by the Web Interface server. The list of server contacts is managed from within the Web Interface Management Console.
- If you're also running IIS on the MetaFrame server and IIS and the XML Service are sharing port 80, you can use IIS to restrict port access to only those servers running the Web Interface.

NOTE: The amount of additional work involved in securing the server when this feature is enabled makes it very difficult to justify its use. While the workspace control feature is certainly useful, there appear to be too many areas where an administrator can make a mistake in locking down the environment, making it possible for someone to exploit the XML Service when operating in this trusted configuration. It is very likely that many administrators will simply enable this feature and worry about implementing the necessary security at a later date.

If you are considering enabling this option then you need to be certain that you have performed the necessary due-diligence in your security assessment for the implementation.

With the desired changes implemented for the individual MetaFrame servers in your environment, the basic MPS farm configuration is now complete. Additional configuration from within the Management Console for MPS 3.0 will be discussed over the remaining few chapters of this book. Figure 14.45 shows the main Management Console window for an MPS 3.0 Enterprise Edition server farm. More information on the implementation details for the main objects shown can be found in the following locations:

- **Server Farm**—The "Configuring Server Farm Properties" section of this chapter.
- **Applications**—A walkthrough on the basic creation of published applications is discussed in Chapter 21, "Application Integration."
- **Installation Manager**—An overview of Installation Manager can be found in Chapter 22, "Server Operations and Support."
- **Load Evaluators**—Also discussed in Chapter 22.
- **Policies**—MetaFrame user policies were reviewed earlier in this chapter. See the section entitled "Managing ICA Connection Settings Using MetaFrame User Policies."

- **Printer Management**—All aspects of printer management within MPS 3.0 can be found in Chapter 17, "Terminal Server and MetaFrame Printer Management."
- **Resource Manager**—The Resource Manager is discussed in Chapter 22.
- **Servers**—Covered in the section we just completed, "Configuring the MetaFrame Server Properties."

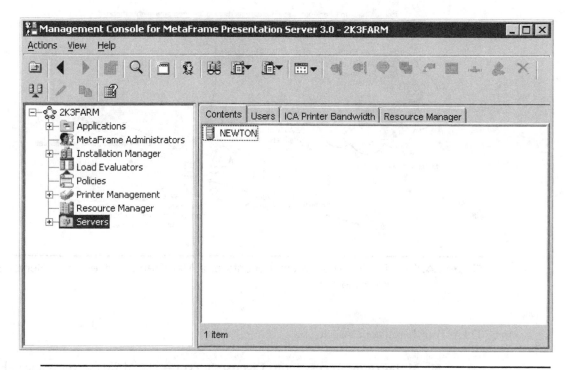

Figure 14.45   The Management Console for MPS 3.0, Enterprise Edition.

The Web Interface for MetaFrame Presentation Server

Since the introduced of Web-based application access for their WinFrame product, Citrix has continued to make the Web browser more of a central tool for not only accessing, but also managing a MetaFrame Presentation Server environment. Figure 14.46 shows a simple diagram that illustrates the various Web-based components that comprise an MPS 3.0 environment.

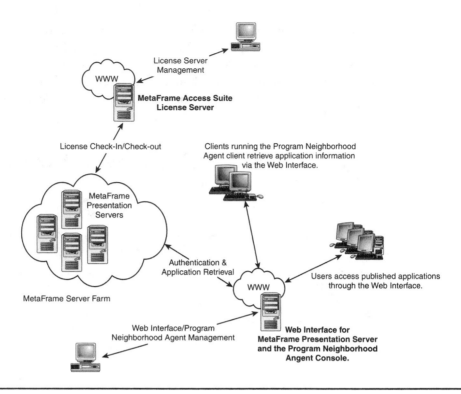

Figure 14.46 The Web-based components of a MetaFrame Presentation Server 3.0 environment.

These Web-based components are

■ **MetaFrame Access Suite License Server**—The MASL server is a mandatory component of any MPS 3.0 implementation, and while a set of command lines are available, Citrix encourages all administrators to manage the license server through the Web-based interface.

■ **Web Interface for MetaFrame Presentation Server**—The Web Interface for MPS is the collective name for a number of components that work together to deliver Program Neighborhood application set support to users either through a Web browser interface or in conjunction with the Program Neighborhood Agent. Applications published within a Citrix server farm scope are available through the Web Interface, just as they would be through the regular Program Neighborhood application.

Until the introduction of the Web Interface (originally called NFuse), Web-enabled applications were accessed only through statically created Web links. With the Web Interface, after a user is presented with an HTML logon page, the passed credentials are used to determine the application set to which the user has access. An HTML page is then generated with links to the individual applications within the set. Figure 14.47 shows both a sample logon page and the resulting application set page.

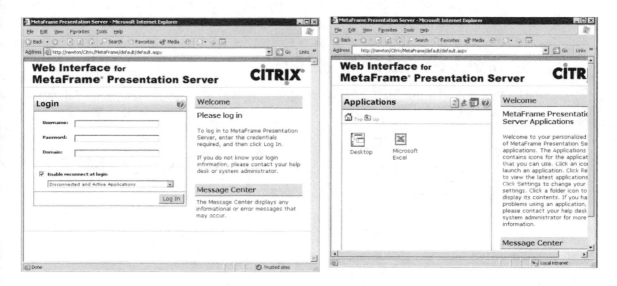

Figure 14.47   The Web Interface allows users to access their assigned published applications through a Web browser.

■ **Program Neighborhood Agent**—As part of the installation of the Web Interface, support for the Program Neighborhood Agent (PN Agent) is also installed. The PN Agent works in conjunction with the Web Interface to provide a simple means of delivering published resources to the end user. Unlike the full Program Neighborhood client, where all configuration changes must be performed locally on the client device, configuration of the PN Agent is done centrally through the Program Neighborhood Agent Console. The PN Agent encapsulates the access to the Web Interface, eliminating the need for the user to open a Web browser to retrieve their applications.

The published resources are retrieved from one or more server farms and displayed on the user's local desktop. The availability of these resources is dictated by the domain groups to which the user belongs. The PN Agent does not have a full interface through which the user can create connections and access servers or resources. Certain options for the PN Agent can be configured by right-clicking the PN Agent icon in the system tray and selecting the desired setting, but access to these features is centrally managed through the PN Agent Console. Details on the configuration and use of the PN Agent are discussed in detail in Chapter 20, "ICA Client Installation and Configuration."

Basic Web Interface Components

The Web Interface for MPS itself is actually comprised of three components, as shown in Figure 14.48.

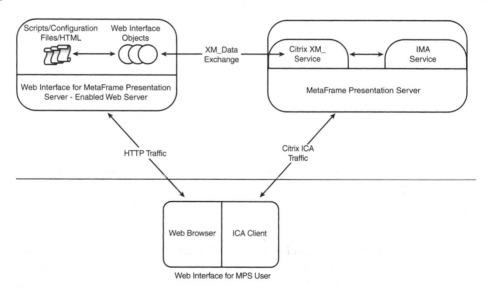

Figure 14.48 The basic Web Interface component diagram.

- **Citrix XML Service**—The XML Service runs on the MetaFrame servers in the server farms and is responsible for brokering communications between the Web Interface objects on the Web server and the Independent Management Architecture (IMA) service on the MetaFrame servers. Based on the authentication information received from the Web Interface, the XML Service returns the appropriate application set information.
- **Web Interface Objects**—The ASP.NET scripts and Java objects are responsible for processing the user's authentication information by passing it to the Citrix XML Service. In return, they receive the appropriate application set data that is used to generate the HTML page. When the user clicks an application link on the page, these objects create the corresponding ICA file. This file contains all the information required for the user's ICA client to connect and launch the desired published application.
- **Citrix ICA Client/Web Browser**—The user actually makes use of two separate applications. The first is the Web browser, which is used to display the appropriate Web Interface Web pages. The other is the ICA client, which the browser relies on to process the ICA files associated with the application link on the Web page.

The installation of MPS includes the Citrix XML Service, so no additional components are required to be installed on any of the MetaFrame servers in your farm in order to leverage the basic Web Interface functionality. Additional security requirements will be discussed in the "Web Interface Security Considerations" section of this chapter.

Deploying the Web Interface for MPS on Microsoft Internet Information Services

Citrix currently provides support for the installation of the Web Interface for MPS on the following platforms:

- Microsoft Internet Information Services (IIS) 6.0 on Windows Server 2003
- Microsoft IIS 5.0 on Windows 2000 Server with Service Pack 4
- Apache 1.3.x or 2.x with the Sun JDK 1.4.x or higher and the Tomcat 4.1.x servlet engine on Red Hat 8.x or 9.x
- Sun ONE 7.0 with the Sun JDK 1.4.x or higher and the Sun ONE 7.02 servlet engine on Sun Solaris 9
- IBM WebSphere 5 on Red Hat 9.x

This section focuses on the installation of the Web Interface on a Microsoft IIS server.

Securing Your IIS Server

A properly secured Web server is critical to ensuring that the Web Interface remains operational. Details on locking down an IIS Web server are beyond the scope of this book, but a good starting point is the Microsoft Web site where a plethora of information is available for both IIS 5.0 and IIS 6.0. Following are a couple of sources for further information:

- **A Guide to Securing IIS 5.0**—A white paper that discusses some key considerations to securing an IIS 5.0 server. The URL is http://www.microsoft.com/serviceproviders/security/iis_security_P73766.asp.
- **Managing a Secure IIS 6.0 Solution**—A technical reference that discusses the securing of an IIS 6.0 environment. The URL for this reference is http://www.microsoft.com/resources/documentation/IIS/6/all/techref/en-us/iisRG_SEC.mspx.

Once you have properly configured your IIS server, you need to prepare the environment for the installation of the Web Interface for MPS.

Before You Begin

You will need to perform two configuration tasks prior to setting up the Web Interface on your Web server:

- **Install the Microsoft .NET Framework 1.1 (Windows 2000 Only)**—This package can be installed a few different ways. You can install it as part of a Microsoft Windows Update. You can download the installation files directly from Microsoft's Web site (http://www.microsoft.com/downloads). Or you can use the .NET Framework installation files located in the Support folder of the MPS 3.0 installation CD-ROM.

    The .NET Framework should be installed *after* installing and securing IIS 5.0. This ensures that the ASP.NET components are properly registered within IIS. If IIS is installed after the .NET Framework then you need to either reinstall the framework or install the ASP.NET component and update the scriptmaps in IIS by opening a command prompt, traversing to the folder %SystemRoot%\ Microsoft.NET\Framework\v1.1.4322 and running the following command:

    ```
    aspnet_regiis.exe -i
    ```

    When installing IIS 6.0 on a Windows Server 2003 server, the ASP.NET component should be selected. If IIS 6.0 is installed as part of the Windows Server installation, then the ASP.NET components will automatically be included.

■ **Install the Visual J# .NET 1.1 components**—The redistribution package for Visual J# can also be downloaded from the Microsoft site, or you can use the redistribution package located in the Support folder of the MPS 3.0 installation CD-ROM.

Once you have installed these components on your IIS server, you are ready to install the Web Interface for MPS 3.0.

Installing the Web Interface for MPS

You can initiate the installation of the Web Interface directly from the Web Interface folder on the MPS 3.0 installation CD-ROM, or you can use the MetaFrame Presentation Server Setup that is launched by Autorun when the CD-ROM is inserted into the server. Within the MPS Setup program, the Web Interface setup is found under the "Install MetaFrame Presentation Server and its components" option. The option for the Web Interface will be available. All other components should be deselected.

The following steps walk through the Web Interface for MPS setup on the component select screen:

1. After clicking Next to continue past the introduction and accepting the terms of the license agreement, you are prompted to provide the name and port number of a MetaFrame server you designate as the Web Interface server with the published application information (Figure 14.49). Only one server can be provided at this point, but additional servers can be added after configuring the Web Interface in order to provide redundancy and access to different server farms.
2. Next you are asked to install the MPS client setup files on the Web server. In order for the Web Interface to be able to provide the users with the option of downloading and installing the appropriate MPS client, the setup files must be available. Unless the MPS client has already been deployed, or the Web Interface will be used strictly to deliver the Program Neighborhood Agent, you want to provide the client files on the Web server.

   Select the "Install the Clients from the Components CD-ROM" radio button and click the Browse button to locate the ICAWEB folder. This is found on the Components CD-ROM, available as part of the MPS 3.0 installation media. Swapping CD-ROMs to locate the client images will not cause a problem with the installation. After locating the ICAWEB folder, click Next to continue.
3. You are now presented with the opportunity to set the Web Interface login page as the default page for Web site. If this is not set, the full URL to the Web Interface page will be http://<Web server>/Citrix/MetaFrame/default.htm. Click next after making the desired choice.
4. The final dialog box confirms the Web Interface for MPS installation. After the installation has completed a restart of the server is not required before you can begin to test the Web Interface.

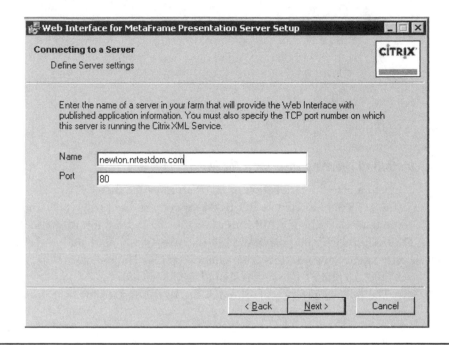

Figure 14.49   You are prompted to provide the name and XML port number of a MetaFrame server in your farm.

You can confirm that the Web Interface and Program Neighborhood Agent consoles have been installed by looking on the Start menu for the Citrix folder, and here you should see the Management Consoles folder.

The basic Web Interface installation is now complete. You are ready to perform the basic configuration necessary in order for users to be able to access applications in the farm through this Web site.

Verifying the Web Interface for MPS Functionality

Once the Web Interface installation is complete, it is immediately available for use. Pointing your Web browser at the Web server and providing the appropriate URL should bring up a page similar to the one shown in Figure 14.50. If credentials for a test user are provided then the Web Interface should process the authentication and present you with a generated HTML page showing any published applications assigned to that user.

WARNING: Even though the basic Web Interface setup is complete and the core functionality is available for use, the current configuration is not secure. User credentials are transmitted in plain text to the Web page requesting the credentials, and that information is then passed in plain text between the Web server and the MetaFrame server via the XML service. Do *not* put this server into production, until you have reviewed the "Web Interface Security Considerations" section of this chapter.

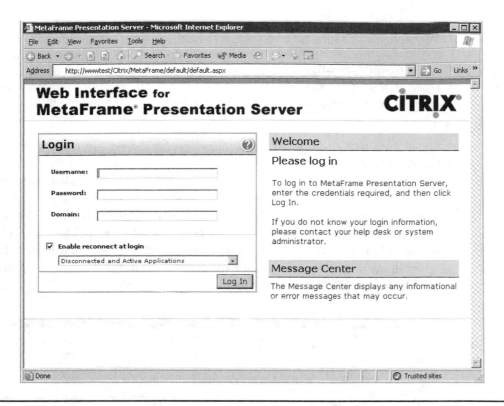

Figure 14.50   Pointing your Web browser at the Web server and providing the appropriate URL should bring up a page similar to this one

Configuring the Web Interface for MPS

When the Web Interface is hosted on a Microsoft IIS server, most MetaFrame administrators will perform the majority of their configuration through the Web Interface Console (WIC), a Web-based console access through the following URL: http://<web server name>/Citrix/MetaFrame/WIAdmin.

In order to access the WIC you must be an administrator. If your credentials cannot be verified or you are not an administrator you will be prompted to provide proper logon credentials with sufficient authority to administer the Web Interface. When proper credentials have been provided the WIC opens to the main page shown in Figure 14.51.

The WIC provides a visual representation (also referred to as an image map) of a Web Interface environment from the client all the way through to the MetaFrame server farms. The grouping of options down the left-hand side of the page offer alternate links to the same information found by clicking the hyperlinks in the image map.

TIP: Before navigating off of a page on which you have made changes, you must click the Save button, otherwise the changes will be lost. After clicking Save or Cancel you are automatically returned to the main WIC image map. After all of the desired changes have been made, they can be applied to the current system by clicking the Apply Changes button at the bottom of the screen on the main WIC image map.

An alternate method of editing the configuration for the Web Interface is to directly modify the WebInterface.conf file. This is the main configuration file for the Web Interface and allows editing of all the same information as the WIC, plus some additional information not available in the WIC. When hosting the Web interface on a non-Windows Web server, this is the only means by which the Web Interface can be configured. The WebInterface.conf file is located in the folder <Webroot>\Citrix\Metaframe\conf on an IIS server. <Webroot> is the location where the IIS webroot begins. This is usually C:\Inetpub\wwwroot. The following listing shows a portion of the default WebInterface.conf file. Within the file itself, the text does not wrap as it does in this listing.

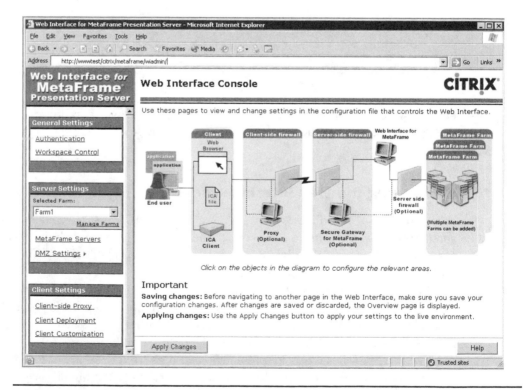

Figure 14.51   The Web Interface Console can be used to edit the configuration of the Web Interface when run on a Windows IIS Server.

Listing 14.1   A portion of the WebInterface.conf file.

```
# The UnrestrictedSessionFields property controls which session
fields can
# be set by user supplied data. All session fields can be made unre-
stricted
# by commenting out this property.
UnrestrictedSessionFields=NFuse_Application,NFuse_AppCommandLine,NFuse
_User,NFuse_Domain,NFuse_Password,NFuse_LogonMode,NFuse_ClientName,NFu
se_WindowType,NFuse_WindowWidth,NFuse_WindowHeight,NFuse_WindowScale,N
Fuse_WindowColors,NFuse_EncryptionLevel,NFuse_ICAAudioType,NFuse_Sound
Type,NFuse_VideoType,NFuse_COMPortMapping,NFuse_ClientPrinting,
NFuse_HostId, NFuse_HostIdType, NFuse_SessionId, NFuse_Template
SessionFieldLocations=PNAgent,Script,Template,Properties,Url,Post,Cook
ie
Timeout=60
Version=3.0
AlternateAddress=Off
CacheExpireTime=3600
SessionField.NFuse_TicketTimeToLive=200
AllowCustomizeWinSize=On
AllowCustomizeWinColor=Off
AllowCustomizeAudio=Off
AllowCustomizeSettings=On
AddressResolutionType=IPv4-port
OtherClient=default
#OverrideClientInstallCaption=[Place your text here]
Win32Client=default
Win16Client=default
SolarisUnixClient=default
MacClient=default
SgiUnixClient=default
HpUxUnixClient=default
IbmAixClient=default
ScoUnixClient=default
Tru64Client=default
LinuxClient=default
LoginType=default
#LoginDomains=[Place your domain here]
#RestrictDomains=Off
#HideDomainField=Off
#UPNSuffixes=[Place your UPN suffixes here]
#NDSTreeName=[For NDS logins place NDS Tree name here, and also
change LoginType to NDS]
```

In the following section, I will use the WIC to demonstrate the basic configuration changes and point out the associated changes that would need to be made to the WebInterface.conf file.

A third and final method of modifying the Web Interface configuration requires some Web development skills. Creating customized Web scripts using ASP.NET or JavaServer pages, you can fully customize the Web interface to suite your needs. For those readers who are so inclined, Citrix provides a PDF document titled "Customizing the Web Interface for MetaFrame Presentation Server 3.0," which can be downloaded from their Web site. The associated Citrix document ID is CTX103931.

Complete information on the Web Interface application programming interface (API) is included—an essential resource to anyone developing code to customize the Web Interface. Additional documentation notes and examples are included with the package.

Configuring Client Settings

When it comes to configuring the Web Interface, I usually start by making changes to the client settings. Details on the configuration of all client settings for the Web Interface are discussed in Chapter 20.

Server Settings

The Server Settings group is located on the left-hand side and has three options that can be modified. The first is the server farm selection dropdown list box. This contains a list of all server farms that have been configured for this Web Interface. The Web Interface supports the consolidation of a user's published applications from multiple farms. For each of the farms listed, unique values for the MetaFrame Servers and DMZ Settings can be stored. Before configuring those settings the first task is to configure the names for farms that you will be accessing.

Manage MetaFrame Server Farms

The Manage MetaFrame Server Farms page (Figure 14.52) is where you add, delete, and prioritize the server farms your users will access. One farm reference is automatically created when the Web Interface is installed and is called Farm1. Contrary to what you might think, the names that appear here do *not* have to match the actual names of the farms that will be accessed. The Web Interface uses the explicit MetaFrame servers listed for each farm created to communicate with the XML Service, which in turn makes information such as the farm name available. The farm names created here are simply placeholders so that you can define unique information for each farm that users will access. This is why you are able to log on to the Web Interface even though the WIC shows only the name Farm1.

From the Manage MetaFrame Server Farms page, add in all of the server farms that you want to access through the Web Interface. Once added, use the Up and Down buttons to set the desired priority. All farm communications from the Web Interface are processed in the order specified. For example, each farm is contacted in the order listed and all published application information is collected before the user is presented with their application Web page.

In the WebInterface.conf file, a record is added for each farm that is added. Each record is assigned the standard MetaFrame server default values. For example, if I added the farm Noisy River – West Coast, the following entry is added to the configuration file. Note that this entry does not wrap in the configuration file.

```
SessionField.NFuse_Farm1=localhost,Name:Noisy River - East
Coast,XMLPort:80,Transport:HTTP,SSLRelayPort:443,BypassDuration:60,Loa
dBalance:On,AdminToolEmpty:
```

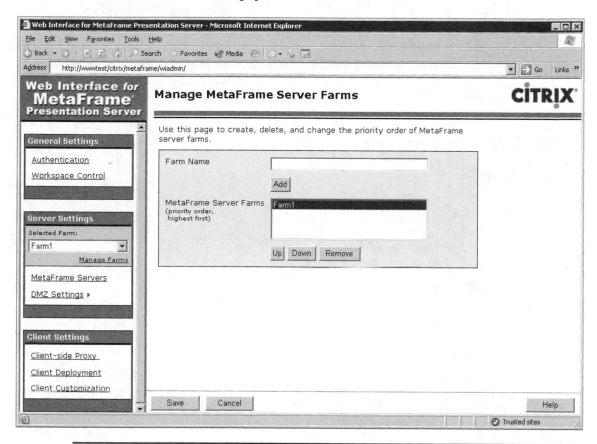

Figure 14.52   A unique farm entry must be created for each farm in which your users access published applications.

MetaFrame Servers

Once the desired server farms have been added, you are ready to define the list of servers that the Web Interface can contact to acquire published application information for that farm. This is done by selecting the desired farm from the Selected Farm listbox and then clicking the MetaFrame Servers hyperlink. The page shown in Figure 14.53 will now open. For each farm you must add at least one MetaFrame server that is running the Citrix XML service so that the Web Interface can pass logon credentials and receive application information back from that farm.

Begin by removing the default localhost entry, unless your Web Interface server also happens to be running MetaFrame.

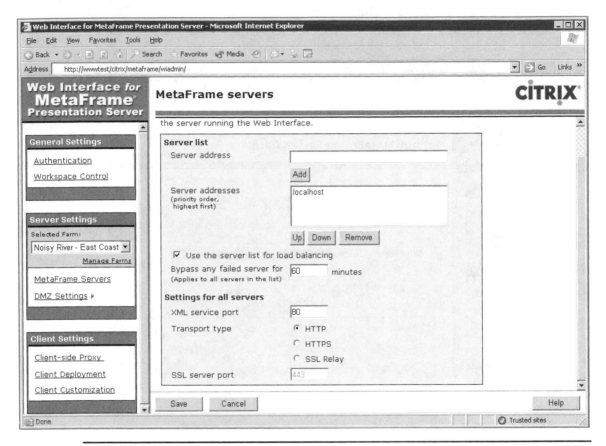

Figure 14.53 At least one MetaFrame server must be defined for each farm reference you have created.

To add a server, type in the name or IP address in the server address field, then click the Add button. Verify that the name can be resolved by the Web Interface server. If the Web Interface is communicating with the XML service via HTTPS or SSL, then you need to make certain that the server name matches exactly the name used on the certificate for that MetaFrame server.

The order in which you arrange the MetaFrame servers dictates the order in which they are contacted when implementing fault tolerance. If load balancing is enabled then the server order is not utilized.

When load balancing is enabled (the default), all listed servers are contacted evenly. If a server in the list fails, then it is omitted from further load balancing for the specified time frame, which by default is 60 minutes. When load balancing is disabled, the Web Interface operates in fault tolerance mode. In this configuration the first server in the list is used for all communications unless it fails, then the next server in the list is used. Communications are not attempted with the first server until the bypass time expires (60 minutes by default).

The last two settings determine how the Web Interface will communicate with the Citrix XML service running on all servers in the farm. The default port for the Citrix XML service is 80, and this will not need to be changed unless you have designated a different port for all servers in your list. There are three options available for the transport type, which determines how the Web Interface and the XML server will communicate. By default the transport is HTTP, which transmit clear-text XML data. This configuration is not secure. The other two alternatives (HTTPS and SSL Relay) will be discussed in the "Web Interface Security Considerations" section of this chapter.

DMZ Settings

DMZ (demilitarized zone) Settings has two separate pages of information that can be configured. The first is the Network Address Translation (NAT) link. If users will be accessing your MetaFrame servers across a firewall then you need to properly configure NAT to ensure that the users are able to connect to their published applications. Figure 14.54 shows a simple firewall implementation. On the internal side of the firewall there are the MetaFrame servers, the Web Interface server, and a client who connects to published applications in the farm. On the external side of the firewall there is another client who also wishes to access published applications in the farm.

If the external client attempted to access a published application with the Web Interface running in its default configuration, the attempt would fail. This is because the Web Interface would pass the internal IP address of the MetaFrame server to the external client. This address is of no use to this client, since the client has no way to route to that internal network address. It is because of this specific problem that the NAT configuration for the Web Interface exists.

Assume that the firewall has been configured to perform NAT using the external IP addresses shown in Table 14.2.

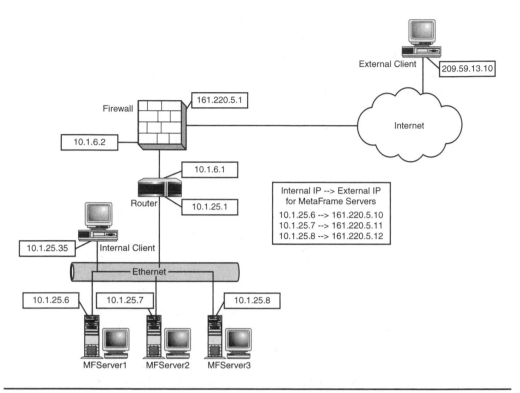

Figure 14.54 Simple firewall implementation requiring network address translation (NAT) in order to access the MetaFrame servers.

Table 14.2 Network Address Translation Examples

MetaFrame Server Name	Internal IP Address	External IP Address
MFServer1	10.1.25.6	161.220.5.10
MFServer2	10.1.25.7	161.220.5.11
MFServer3	10.1.25.8	161.220.5.12

In order for the external client to connect to an internal MetaFrame server, the client must be made aware of what the equivalent external address is for each MetaFrame server. The function of providing the proper external address to the client is performed by the Web Interface. Before this can happen, the Web Interface must know what the external versus internal IP address cross-reference is for each MetaFrame server. There are two ways that this information can be made available to the Web Interface.

■ The first is when the alternate addressing has been configured on the MetaFrame server. Using the command line tool AltAddr, an administrator can assign the corresponding external IP for each MetaFrame server in the farm. More information on the AltAddr command can be found in Appendix B, "MetaFrame Presentation Server Command Reference." In this configuration, the Web Interface must be configured to retrieve the alternate address from the MetaFrame server and pass it onto the client.

Figure 14.55 shows the upper portion of the Network Address Translation Settings page. By default, the address translation rule used is "normal address," which means that the true IP address of the MetaFrame server is always returned. Selecting the Alternate Address radio button will make the alternate address of a MetaFrame server the default IP address that is always presented to the MetaFrame Presentation Server client.

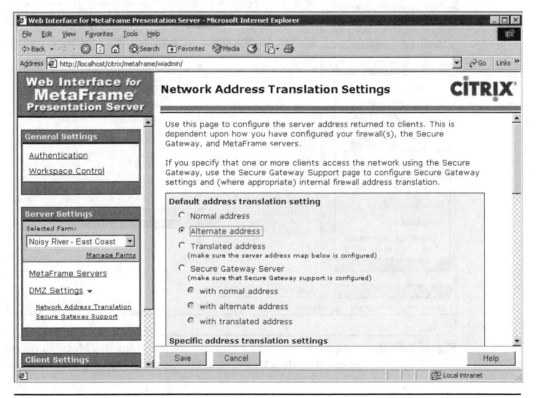

Figure 14.55 Set the default address translation choice to configure the IP address that the Network Interface server returns when requested by a client.

■ If alternate addressing has not been configured on a MetaFrame server, then it
will not be able to provide this information to the Web Interface if requested.
Instead, the alternate address cross-reference must be configured directly in the
Web Interface. The configuration for this begins with selecting the Translated
address radio button visible in Figure 14.55 (directly under the Alternate Address
option). Next scroll down to the bottom of the Network Address Translation
Settings page and enter the required server address and translated external
address mapping. Figure 14.56 demonstrates how this would look with two of the
three MetaFrame servers from my example entered into the translation map. The
port numbers were not modified in this example, since each server had its own
external address assigned and there was no need to change the default port. You
could use alternate ports and perform port translation using a single IP address.

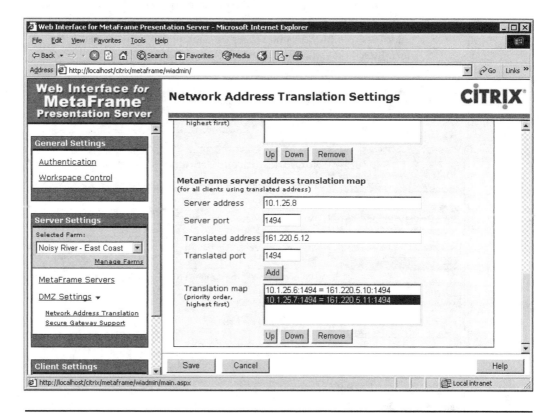

Figure 14.56   Internal and external address mapping for the MetaFrame servers can
be entered directly into the configuration for the Web Interface.

While both of these solutions properly provide alternate addresses to external Web Interface clients, they unfortunately provide the same alternate address to any internal clients that may request a published application. These configurations need to be modified slightly so that they continue to provide the normal address to internal Web Interface clients, while providing the alternate address to external clients. This is accomplished by adding an exception for the internal network, telling the Web Interface to provide the normal address whenever a device on the internal network requests one.

Scrolling down from the top of the NAT settings page you will see the section titled "Specific Address Translation Settings." With this option you define translation rules for specific networks or individual IP addresses. The internal network would be configured to use the normal server address by providing the internal network address, subnet mask, and the desired address option. Clicking Add adds the entry into the setting map listbox. Figure 14.57 shows the settings that would ensure both the internal and external clients could still access the published applications on the Web Interface.

The other DMZ Settings option is the Secure Gateway Support link. I will discuss the configuration of the Secure Gateway and the Web Interface later in this chapter.

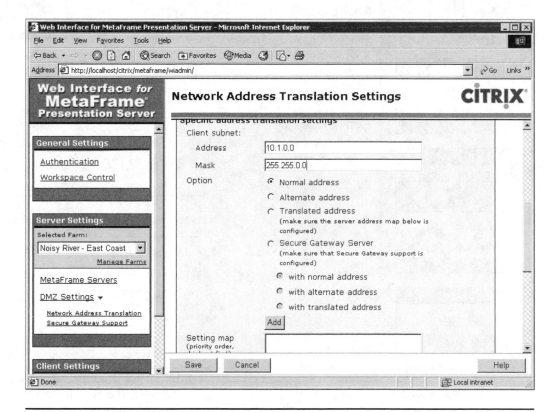

Figure 14.57   Specific address translation settings can be configured on a subnet by subnet basis.

General Settings

The two final options discussed exist in the General Settings section of the WIC. They are called Authentication and Workspace Control.

Authentication   The Authentication page (Figure 14.58) is where you manage the authentication methods available to your Web Interface users. When an option is enabled on this page, it becomes available as an authentication choice for the user, so it is important that you have provided access to only those options that you want your users to see. Providing unnecessary or inappropriate choices can easily result in the user selecting the incorrect authentication method and preventing them from successfully logging on to the MetaFrame environment.

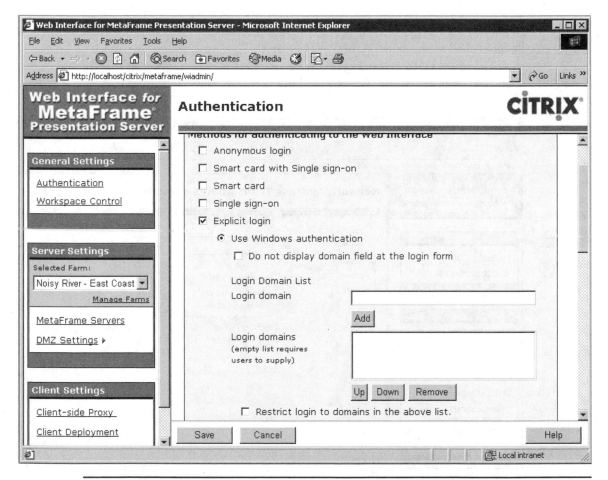

Figure 14.58   The authentication methods supported by the Web Interface are managed through the Authentication settings page.

The following are the five authentication methods that are currently supported by the Web Interface:

- **Anonymous logins**—An anonymous login allows a user to connect to the farm without providing a user ID or password. Anonymous users have access only to those applications that have been published specifically for anonymous users.
- **Smart card with single sign-on**—When the underlying client operating system has been configured to use a Windows-compatible smart card reading device, then enabling this authentication method allows the Web Interface to use the credentials directly from the local Windows client. The user is not prompted for the smart card access PIN (personal identification number) and is automatically logged into the MetaFrame environment.

    Smart card authentication is supported when running the Web Interface on Microsoft IIS. It is not supported with a UNIX-based Web Interface. Client requirements for smart card authentication are discussed in Chapter 20.
- **Smart card**—The same underlying smart card reading device is used, except that the Web Interface will prompt the user for the associated PIN number.
- **Single sign-on**—When this option is selected, the credentials that the user provided when logging on to his or her local Windows desktop are automatically used to log on to the Web Interface. Due to the sensitive nature of single sign-on through the Web Interface, special client-side configuration is required in order to use this feature.

    The full Win32 client must be installed by an administrator on the client's PC. Single sign-on is supported only with the Win32 client and because of a potential security issue when single sign-on support is enabled for the Win32 client via the Web Interface, an automated client installation of the Win32 client will not enable this feature.

    During the Win32 client installation, support for passthrough authentication must be enabled. Details on this are discussed in Chapter 20. Once that is completed, the user's personal Win32 client configuration file called AppSrv.ini must be edited. After launching the Win32 client for the first time, this file is created in the user's profile (%UserProfile%\Application Data\ICAClient"). Editing it with a text editor such as Notepad, you must add the following two entries to the [WFClient] section:

```
EnableSSOnThruICAFile=On
SSOnUserSettings=On
```

    This user will now be able to utilize single sign-on through the Web Interface.

WARNING: Enabling single sign-on via the Web Interface configures the Win32 client in such a way that when it is passed an ICA file requests that it send the local user credentials to the server, it will do so. By default the Win32 client will ignore this request. Honoring this request introduces the potential for the theft of the user's credentials if an attacker sends the client a properly configured ICA file requesting these credentials. Because of this it is recommended that single sign-on for the Web Interface be implemented only in secured environments.

- **Explicit login**—This option requires that the user provide credentials when prompted by the Web Interface logon screen. When the explicit login method is chosen, there are two main authentication methods to choose from: a Windows-based authentication or an NDS (Novell Directory Services)-based authentication method.

  When the Windows-based authentication is chosen, there are a few additional options that control exactly how those credentials will be requested by the Web Interface (Figure 14.59). The first set of options controls the available Windows domain information. One or more domains can be added to the list, making them available to the user for selection during logon. Otherwise the domain field is left blank and the user must provide the proper domain name. The domain can be hidden from view, requiring that the user provide a full user principal name (UPN) for logon, unless a domain has also been hard-coded. The security requirements of your implementation will dictate what options are configured and whether users will even be able to see what domains are being used for authentication. Besides managing the domain information, you are also able to dictate what UPN suffixes are supported when users attempt to logon using a full UPN name such as twmathers@noisyriver.com. Allowing only certain UPNs will ensure users can only access certain user authentication domains.

  NDS-authentication provides similar configuration features, allowing you to provide a context list for limiting what resources are performing NDS authentication.

  Two additional configuration choices can be found for explicit logins. The first controls whether users can modify their Windows password from within the Web Interface and if so, under what circumstances. The two choices are to allow password changes at any time, or to allow them only when a password expires.

  The final explicit login setting controls whether users are authenticating using 2-factor authentication or not. The two supported systems are SafeWord and RSA SecurID. Enabling 2-factor authentication will prevent the use of the Program Neighborhood Agent with the Web Interface. Details on the integration of SafeWord and the Web Interface can be found at http://www.securecomputing.com. Information on RSA SecurID can be found at http://www.rsasecurity.com.

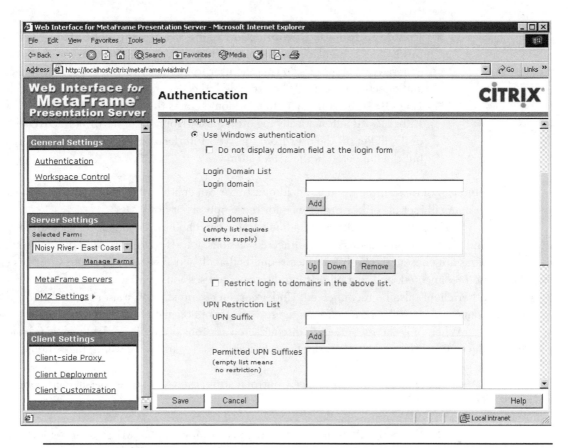

Figure 14.59   Windows authentication choices for explicit logins.

Workspace Control   Workspace Control, also referred to as "follow-me roaming" in certain Citrix literature, is a new feature of MPS 3.0. Workspace Control lets a user disconnect or log off all applications initiated from a device with the click of one button. It also lets all currently active and/or disconnected applications be reconnected either manually or automatically when a user logs on to the Web Interface. Three options are available on this screen:

- **Enable Automatic Reconnection at Log In**—When this option is enabled, the user's sessions are automatically connected when the user logs on to the Web Interface. You can specify whether only disconnected, or both active and disconnected sessions will automatically be reconnected when the user logs on. When this option is disabled, disconnected sessions must be manually reconnected using the Reconnect button.

- **Enable Automatic Reconnection Using the Reconnect button**—When this option is enabled, the Reconnect button choice will appear on the user's generated Web page, allowing the user to manually reconnect to disconnected and/or active sessions. When disabled, the Reconnect button is not available.
- **Log Off Behavior**—The final option dictates the behavior of the logoff button. Either it will automatically log off the user from all of his or her active sessions, or it will log off the user from the Web Interface only, leaving the sessions active but disconnected in the server farm.

For each of these three options, an administrator can control whether the user has the ability to manually set his or her preference for these options or not.

For the first two options, an administrator can choose to connect either existing active and disconnected sessions or disconnected sessions only. If both active and disconnected sessions are chosen, the Web Interface requests that all active sessions initiated from this client be reconnected, and that all existing disconnected sessions (initiated from this client or any other client) also be reconnected. Under certain circumstances, a user's session may be disconnected yet still appear active on the server. This option allows for recovery of these sessions.

When only the reconnect to disconnected sessions option is available, active sessions in the farm are ignored and only disconnected sessions (regardless of where they originated) are reconnected.

When enabling the Workspace Control feature, there are some special considerations to note:

- When the Web Interface is accessed from within an MPS client session, the Workspace control feature is automatically disabled. This protects against the reconnection feature accidentally disconnecting the user's current ICA session as well.
- The current version of the Web Interface supports Workspace Control when using single sign-on, smart card authentication, or smart card authentication with single sign-on, but only when you have enabled the trust relationship between the Citrix XML service on one or more MetaFrame servers in the farm and the Web Interface. Enabling this option was discussed in the section titled "Configuring the MetaFrame Server Properties," earlier in this chapter.
- If the user's HTTP Web Interface session times out because of inactivity, the Web page will return to the logon screen, but any active MetaFrame sessions will remain active on the servers. In this case, the user will not be able to reestablish a connection unless at least one of the reconnect features is configured to reconnect active sessions.

Similar workspace control features are available with the Program Neighborhood Agent and are discussed in Chapter 20.

CHAPTER 15

Group Policy Configuration

Introduction to Group Policies

With the introduction of Active Directory in Windows 2000, Microsoft provided an advanced policies implementation known as *Group Policy*. Although it is conceptually similar to the policy features originally available in Windows NT, Group Policy provides a much more robust and centralized way of managing Windows policies. Without a proper understanding of Windows Active Directory and Group Policy management, a Terminal Server administrator is greatly handicapped in his or her ability to successfully implement and effectively manage the production environment. It is important to have a clear understanding of the role policies play in configuration of your Terminal Server environment.

While a profile (which I discuss in Chapter 18, "User Profile and Account Configuration") is used to store the desktop and application settings for a user, it doesn't provide a mechanism for controlling which features are actually available to the user. This is where policies come in. Policies are used to control the features and restrictions for one or more users. For example, a policy may be implemented that removes the Shutdown option from the Start menu and replaces it with the Log Off option for all non-administrative users. A policy may also be used to redirect a user's My Documents folder to an alternate location on the network instead of storing it locally on the Terminal Server.

Policies are not simply about imposing restrictions but, more importantly, they provide a means to easily configure a Windows environment to function exactly as required, simplifying the user's workspace and allowing users to more easily focus on their designated tasks. Profiles and policies work together to provide the optimum environment in which your Terminal Server users will work.

WARNING: If you intend to implement policies, review the entire contents of this chapter before beginning your implementation. Unless implemented properly, a policy you create may affect a user's settings not only when the user is logged on to a Terminal Server but also when he or she is logged on to any other Windows desktop or server. Certain improperly applied policies can also effectively lock an administrator out of certain areas of a system.

Environment Preparation

Before getting into the details of how to create and manage policies, there is some preparation work to be done in order to maximize the effectiveness and organization of your policy implementation.

Group Policy Management Tools

Probably the best place to start is by summarizing the tools that can be used to manage and support the group policy objects (GPO) in the domain. A number of tools are provided by Microsoft for managing, monitoring, and troubleshooting group policies in an active directory; they are summarized here:

- **Group Policy Object Editor**—In Windows 2000 this tool was known simply as the Group Policy Console, and while the name has changed, the basic functionality remains. This Microsoft Management Console (MMC) snap-in is the tool commonly used to actually update the individual policies in a GPO. This tool is available on all Windows 2000 and Windows 2003 installations. It is accessed directly from a command prompt by running the command GPEDIT.MSC. When launched in this fashion, it automatically opens the Local Computer Policy for the computer upon which it is run. Both the Active Directory Users and Computers tool and the Group Policy Management Console tool launch this snap-in when an administrator edits a group policy object.

- **Active Directory Users and Computers**—This is the primary tool for managing all objects in an active directory (AD) and was the main tool for creation and management of GPOs in Windows 2000 Active Directory. Active Directory Users and Computers is one of the tools I use when demonstrating creation and editing of GPOs in this chapter. This tool is available for both Windows 2000 and Windows 2003 and is installed by default on a domain controller. It can be launched from a command prompt by executing DSA.MSC.

  While the Group Policy Management Console tool, which I discuss in the "Creating and Managing Group Policies" section of this chapter, lets you create organizational units (OUs), you cannot use that tool to modify OU membership. Active Directory Users and Computers is still the primary tool for managing OU membership.

- **Group Policy Result**—This is a command line tool provided with the Windows 2000 Server Resource Kit or available for download directly from the Microsoft Web site. This tool will generate a summary of the group policies in effect for both the user who runs the tool and the computer upon which the tool is executed. Group Policy Result was created to assist in troubleshooting issues with application of group policies. While this tool will run on Windows Server 2003, its functionality has been superceded by the new Group Policy Management Console.

- **Group Policy Management Console**—With the release of Windows Server 2003, Microsoft made available a new unified tool for managing GPOs, the Group Policy Management Console (GPMC). The GPMC is downloadable from Microsoft (details of which I discuss in the "Installing the Group Policy Management Console" section) and can be used to manage group policies in both Windows 2000 and 2003 Active Directory domains. GPMC will run only on Windows XP Professional or Windows Server 2003; it will not run on any earlier version of Windows. If you wish to use it to manage a Windows 2000 domain, you must have a computer *in the domain* running XP or 2003.
- **Resultant Set of Policy**—Another Windows 2003 tool, Resultant Set of Policy (RSoP) provides an administrator with the ability to determine the cumulative effects of multiple GPOs on any user or computer. It also generates information on how modifications to GPOs in a domain can impact objects in the network. Much of the basic functionality found in RSoP has also been integrated into the Group Policy Management Console, and this is the access method that Microsoft recommends for administrators. The RSoP utility can be launched from directly within the GPMC tool if advanced information is desired after reviewing the basic report.

When discussing management of policies in this chapter, I demonstrate the corresponding configuration option using both the Active Directory Users and Computers tool and the Group Policy Management Console tool. Because of the robust and centralized support provided by GPMC, I recommend use of this tool whenever you're implementing a Windows 2003 Active Directory or if you're implementing a Windows 2000 Active Directory and have access to either a Windows XP Professional desktop or Windows Server 2003 machine.

Installing the Group Policy Management Console

The first task to perform when preparing to configure GPOs in your environment is to download and install Group Policy Management Console. This tool is an invaluable aid for an administrator responsible for configuring and managing group policies in an Active Directory domain. I use this tool, along with Active Directory Users and Computers (ADUC), to demonstrate how to create and manage group policies in your Terminal Server/MetaFrame implementation.

TIP: Once you have installed GPMC on a server, group policies can no longer be managed using ADUC from that server. If the GPMC is uninstalled, GPO functionality is immediately reinstated to the ADUC tool.

The Group Policy in the Windows Server 2003 home page is an excellent resource for finding information on group policies in Windows 2003 Server, as well as accessing the link to download GPMC. The URL for that page is

http://www.microsoft.com/technet/prodtechnol/windowsserver2003/technologies/ management/gp/default.mspx

From this page you will find the link "Download the Group Policy Management Console" with Service Pack 1. After clicking this hyperlink, you are taken to the main download page where you can download GPMC. Save the MSI installation file into a convenient location on your network where it will be accessible from the machines on which you will install this tool.

After logging on to the server where you will install GPMC, locate the file you downloaded and double-click it to launch the installer. The installation is straightforward. After you agree to the license agreement, the snap-in is installed and a new shortcut entitled Group Policy Management appears under Administrative Tools on the Start menu. Before you can begin to use this tool, you need to ensure that you are logged on to the host computer using a domain account.

NOTE: When installing GPMC into an environment, I always add it to all the domain controllers. This is because most administrators establish a remote desktop session with a domain controller when they want to perform a domain configuration task such as managing group policies. Even if most administrators run this tool locally, it is a good practice to have it available on all domain controllers in case there is an issue and this is the only mechanism available for running the tool.

Domain Security Groups

If you have not already done so, you should create the base Terminal Server domain security groups that I discussed in Chapter 8, "Server Installation and Management Planning." In that chapter I discussed creation of these local security groups and the role they play in managing the file, registry, and connection security. Besides security, which I discuss further in Chapter 16, "Terminal Server Security," domain groups also play a key role in implementation of policies, as you will soon see. Table 15.1 describes the domain security groups I use in the examples in this chapter.

Table 15.1 Terminal Server Domain Security Groups

Domain Group Name	Description
Terminal Server Administrators	Members of this group have full authority to manage the Terminal Server environment, and as a result, membership in this group must be tightly managed.
Terminal Server Operators	Users with this privilege level have the authority to monitor the various system functions and perform such tasks as shutting down the server or terminating a process. They don't have the ability to make any system changes or perform application installations.
Terminal Server User Support	Members of this group can perform basic support functions such as shadowing another user's session or logging an active user off. They don't have the ability to restart a server or perform any other server maintenance operations.
Terminal Server Users	This domain group is used to grant basic user access to the production Terminal Servers in the environment. A member of this group can log on to a production Terminal Server and access all the generally available applications. The user has no administrative privileges of any kind.

Terminal Server Organizational Units

In an active directory, you'll need an organizational unit structure to which you can apply the desired group policies. Figure 15.1 shows the OU configuration I use to demonstrate creation and use of group policies in this chapter. This configuration allows assignment of group policies specific to Terminal Servers, without affecting other Windows servers.

NOTE: Please be aware that I'm using this OU configuration simply to demonstrate the steps involved in configuring group policies for your Terminal Server implementation and not necessarily as a recommendation on the best practices for an AD configuration.

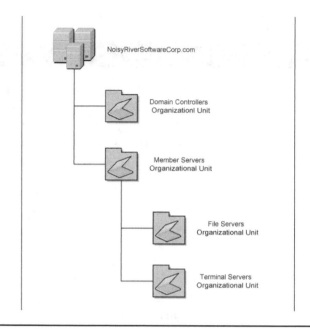

Figure 15.1   A Terminal Server organizational unit example.

Creating and Managing Group Policies

Each group policy definition created is made up of two components, computer configuration and user configuration, and can be applied to objects contained in a site, domain, or organizational unit. Figure 15.2 shows an example of the User Configuration options available within a group policy from within the Group Policy Object Editor.

Policies implemented higher in the Active Directory tree apply to all objects situated lower in the tree unless special override features have been put in place. For example, in Figure 15.3, if a policy is applied to the Member Servers OU, it affects all objects underneath it, including those within the Terminal Servers OU. On the other hand, if a policy is applied for the Terminal Servers OU, it applies only to the server objects contained within it and to no other objects within the active directory. A group policy applied to a child OU does not affect any objects "higher up" than itself (at the parent OU's level or higher).

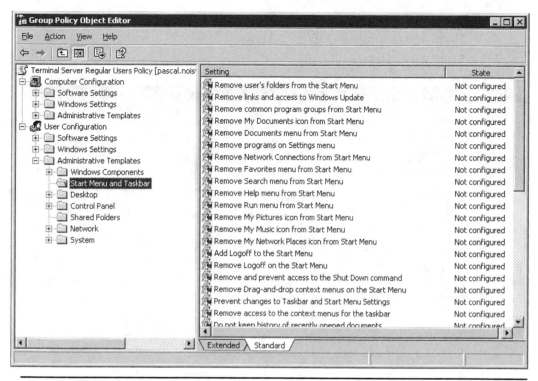

Figure 15.2   A Windows User Configuration group policy example.

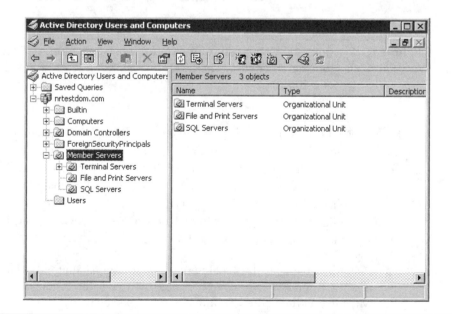

Figure 15.3   Policies applied to a parent OU are automatically applied to any child
OU unless explicitly overridden.

Figure 15.4 demonstrates how the same OU hierarchy configured using Active Directory Users and Computers (Figure 15.3) would appear from within Group Policy Management Console.

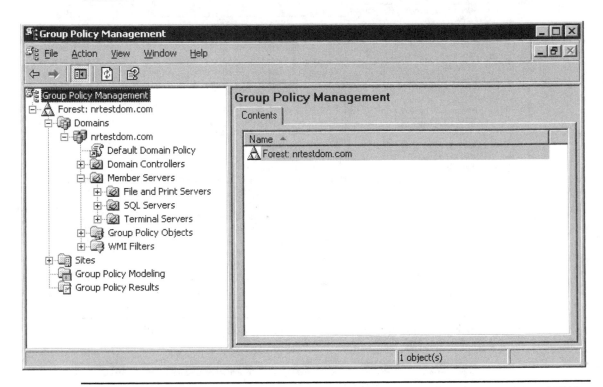

Figure 15.4   Once the OU structure is created, policies can be defined using GPMC running on Windows 2003 Server or a Windows XP Professional desktop.

All the policies I discuss in this chapter will be applied to the Terminal Servers OU and not any of the parent OUs in the tree. The main reason for this is that the policies are configured in such a way as to affect users only when they log on to a Terminal Server that is a member of this OU. When users log on to any other server, including Terminal Servers located in other OUs, these policies do not apply.

When configuring group policies for a Terminal Server environment, I suggest that you perform the following tasks in the order shown.

1. Begin by creating a "Terminal Server" organizational unit into which you will place all your Terminal Server computer objects. This is the container against which you will apply all the desired Terminal Server–specific policies.

2. Create the server-specific policies that will dictate configuration of the Terminal Server itself. Some server-specific settings include things such as clearing the page-file during shutdown, deleting cached copies of user profiles, or setting the refresh interval for applied policies.

3. Next, define the default policies that will apply to all users who log on to the Terminal Server, regardless of whether they are an administrator or a regular Terminal Server user. Policies that apply to all users include ones such as removing the shut-down command from the Start menu or defining an alternate location for the My Documents folder.

4. Next is creation of the user-specific policies. These policies are applied to users based on their group membership. You may define different policies here for administrators, server operators, helpdesk support staff, and regular Terminal Server users. User-specific policies typically dictate what Windows features and functionality are available to the users.

5. Once all the desired policies have been defined, the final step is to ensure that the proper priorities have been set so these policies are applied in the desired order.

In the next few sections of this chapter I focus on looking at each of the preceding steps in more detail.

Creating the Terminal Server Organizational Unit

Earlier in the "Terminal Server Organizational Units" section I discussed the OU that would be used to demonstrate creation of group policies (refer to Figure 15.1). The Member Servers OU is created by opening the Active Directory Users and Computers Microsoft Management Console (MMC) snap-in. This snap-in can always be found on any Windows 2000 or 2003 domain controller under Administrative Tools on the Start menu.

TIP: You can also load this tool onto a member server or Windows desktop by installing the AdminPak.msi file found on the Windows installation CD. This will add the Administrative Tools folder to the Start menu on the computer where it is installed. You can download the AdminPak for Windows Server 2003 from the Microsoft Web site. The Windows Server 2003 administrative tools will run only on a Windows 2003 Server or Windows XP Professional with Service Pack 1 or higher.

Once you have Active Directory Users and Computers running, you can simply right-click the domain and then select New and Organizational Unit from the Context menu. Similarly, you can create the Terminal Servers OU by right-clicking the new Member Servers OU, selecting New, and then selecting Organizational Unit.

Creating the Terminal Server Machine Policy

The first policy you create will be the Terminal Server Machine Policy, which will contain only those settings that directly affect the Terminal Server and, as a result, any users who log on to that server. No user-specific policies should be defined in this group policy. While technically there is no reason for avoiding this, from an administrative standpoint, differentiating server policies from user policies helps maintain some structure to the configuration. A poorly structured group policy implementation can quickly become overwhelming for an administrator.

The base Terminal Server Machine Policy is created as follows.

Creating the Terminal Server Machine Policy Using Active Directory Users and Computers

In a Windows 2000 domain in which you will not be running GPMC, you can use ADUC to manage your group policies. If you're using GPMC, skip ahead to the "Creating the Terminal Server Machine Policy Using Group Policy Management Console" section.

1. Launch the Active Directory Users and Computers MMC snap-in and drill down into the Terminal Servers OU. Right-click the OU and select Properties to open the Terminal Servers Properties dialog box.
2. Click the Group Policy tab (see Figure 15.5). This tab is available only if you have not installed GPMC on this computer. Here, you'll manage the group policies for all Terminal Servers in your environment. You now have three options:

   ■ Create a new group policy object (GPO).
   ■ Add an existing GPO that may be linked to another site, domain, or OU.
   ■ Enable the Block Policy inheritance option. This will prevent policies defined in parent objects from affecting objects in this OU, unless an override option has been enabled that forces these changes to occur. I normally enable this option, as it prevents policies that may not have been configured explicitly for Terminal Server from being applied accidentally.

3. Click the New button to create a new policy. Its name is automatically added to the GPO link list. Right-click the object, select Rename, and then change the name to "Terminal Server Machine Policy."

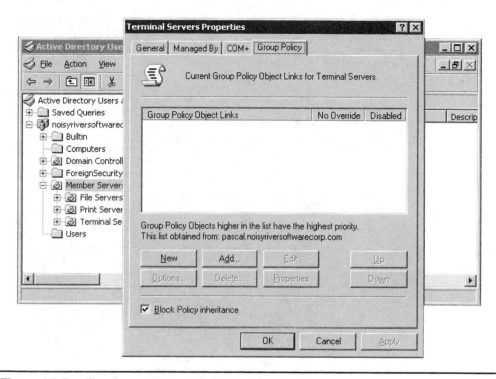

Figure 15.5 The Group Policy tab for the Terminal Servers organizational unit.

4. With the Terminal Server Machine Policy highlighted, click the Properties button. The general properties for this policy are set in the resulting dialog box. There are three tabs of information for a Windows 2000 Server, and four tabs of information for a Windows Server 2003 server:

■ The General tab provides a summary of the policy's creation and modification history and lets you disable the Computer or User settings. Because this will be the Terminal Server Machine Policy, click the Disable User Configuration Settings option (see Figure 15.6). This helps speed up application of the policy on a server by skipping all the user settings.

■ The Links tab shows which other sites, domains, or OUs are using this policy. Because the policy in this example is new, only the current OU has this policy assigned.

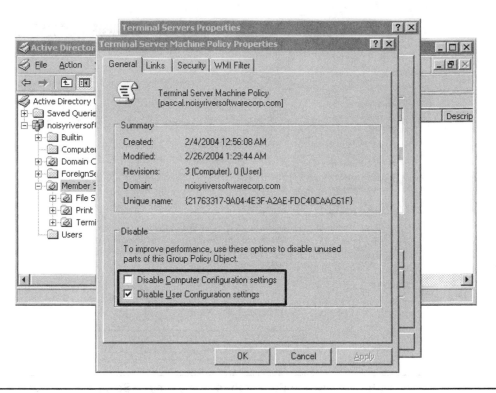

Figure 15.6   The general properties for a group policy.

- The WMI Filter tab (Windows 2003 only) lets an administrator define a WMI filter used to control whether a GPO is applied or not. The filter contains one or more scripts that must evaluate to TRUE in order for all settings in the GPO to be applied to the target machine. The Windows Server 2003 Deployment Kit available on the Microsoft Web site provides more detailed information on use of WMI filters and how they can be applied. WMI filters can be very slow to process, and because they are processed each time a group policy is applied, this can impact the time required for a user to log on. Under most circumstances you will not need to worry about utilizing WMI filters for your Terminal Server implementation.
- On the Security tab, you define who can access, manage, and apply these policies. This includes the Terminal Server computers themselves; unless they're authorized to apply a policy, the policy won't be applied to the server.

Figure 15.7 shows the adjusted list of user permissions I've set for this example. My list includes only three user permissions: Terminal Server Administrators, authorized to manage the policy; Authenticated Users, which ensures that all servers in the OU are able to apply the given policies; and the SYSTEM account.

Before changing your security, make sure that you're a member of the Terminal Server Administrators group, or you'll end up locking yourself out of the policy as soon as you close the dialog box. Table 15.2 shows the permissions that should be assigned to each of these groups.

WARNING: Make certain that you are a member of the Terminal Server Administrators group before you close the Security dialog box. If you are not a member of this group, you'll immediately lock yourself out of the policy as soon as you close the window.

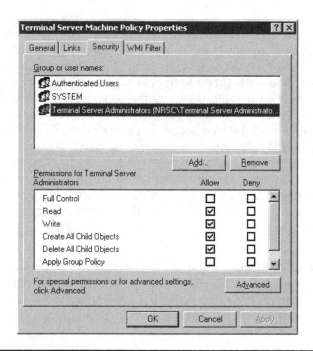

Figure 15.7   Terminal Server Machine Policy security properties.

Table 15.2   Suggested Terminal Server Machine Policy Security Permissions

Permissions	Authenticated Users	SYSTEM	Terminal Server Administrators
Full Control			
Read	Allow	Allow	Allow
Write		Allow	Allow

Table 15.2 Suggested Terminal Server Machine Policy Security Permissions (continued)

Permissions	Authenticated Users	SYSTEM	Terminal Server Administrators
Create Child Objects		Allow	Allow
Delete Child Objects		Allow	Allow
Apply Group Policy	Allow		

NOTE: You will notice in Table 15.2 that the Terminal Servers Administrators group has not been assigned the Apply Group Policy permission. When this permission is set to Allow for a user, any user group policies that have been defined are applied to the user. The Apply Group Policy permission need only be enabled in one of the groups that a user belongs to for the policy to be applied. For the Terminal Server Machine Policy this is not a concern, since only computer configuration settings are being applied. But if this policy also included user configuration options and I wanted to ensure that a member of the Terminal Server Administrators group would not have the policy applied, I would explicitly set the Apply Group Policy privilege to Deny. This is necessary because a member of the Administrators group is also a member of the Authenticated Users group, which does have this permission set and so would have the policy applied. Remember that Deny overrides any other permission setting from a different group.

5. With the permissions configured, you can now set the actual policy options. After closing the Properties dialog box, you return to the Group Policy tab in the Terminal Servers Properties dialog box. Now highlight the Terminal Server Machine Policy that you just created and click the Edit button. The Group Policy Object Editor window opens.

The Group Policy Object Editor is used for both ADUC and GPMC. See the later section entitled "Configuring the Terminal Server Machine Policy Using Group Policy Object Editor" for details on configuring this policy.

Creating the Terminal Server Machine Policy Using Group Policy Management Console

If you're using GPMC, creating the Terminal Server Machine Policy is slightly different from how it would be when using ADUC.

■ Begin by launching the Group Policy Management Console application from under Administrative Tools on the Start menu. Drill down into the desired domain until you locate the Terminal Servers OU you created earlier. Right-click this OU and select Create and Link a GPO Here. Immediately a dialog box opens, prompting you to provide a name for this new GPO.

■ Enter the name "Terminal Server Machine Policy" and click OK. The GPO is immediately created and appears in the right-hand pane, as shown in Figure 15.8. It also appears as a child object to the Terminal Servers OU in the left-hand pane.

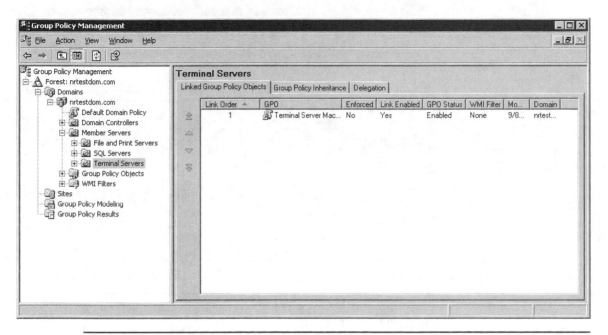

Figure 15.8   A group policy for the Terminal Servers organizational unit.

■ When a new GPO is created, it is not limited to being accessible by only our Terminal Servers OU. In fact the GPO is defined globally for the entire domain but linked to only our Terminal Servers OU. The GPO is applied nowhere in the domain except against objects in the Terminal Servers OU. If you expand the Group Policy Objects folder located immediately below our Terminal Servers OU folder (you can see this in Figure 15.8), you see our newly created GPO listed.

■ From under the Terminal Servers OU click the newly created policy. Because you are clicking a link to the GPO and not clicking the actual GPO itself, you will likely see a dialog box appear warning you that any changes you make to this GPO will immediately apply to all other instances where it has been linked. Click OK to proceed. You immediately see the contents of the right-hand pane change to reflect the properties for this policy, as shown in Figure 15.9.

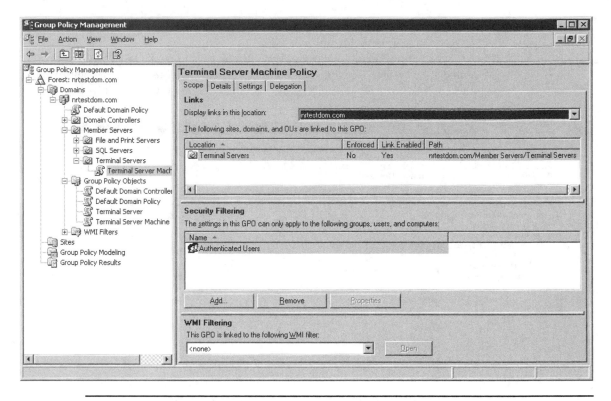

Figure 15.9   Terminal Server Machine Policy properties in the Group Policy Management Console.

The first tab, which is labeled Scope, provides a summary of the following information:

- **Links**—Lists where in the domain or forest this GPO is linked. For our purposes, this GPO will likely ever link to only the Terminal Servers OU.
- **Security Filtering**—Lists all the objects in the domain to which this policy will be applied. For an object to have this policy apply, it must first be a member of the OU. When actually applying GPOs, Windows looks to the security filter to see if the object in the OU fits the criteria for having this policy apply. For the Terminal Server Machine Policy you can leave this filter defaulting to Authenticated Users. Computers in the domain automatically fall into the Authenticated Users category, and we're going to have machines as members of only this OU.

    Another option is to create an alternate group in the domain called Terminal Servers, for example, add all your Terminal Server computer objects to this security group, and then replace Authenticated Users in the security filter with that Terminal Servers group.

■ **WMI Filtering**—Lists the WMI filter to which this GPO is applied. A WMI filter must already have been defined before it can be selected. A WMI filter can be used to control whether a GPO is applied or not. The filter contains one or more scripts that must evaluate to TRUE in order for all settings in the GPO to be applied to the objects listed in the security filter. The Windows Server 2003 Deployment Kit, available on the Microsoft Web site, provides more detailed information on use of WMI filters and how they can be applied. WMI filters can be very slow to process, and because they are processed each time a Group Policy is applied, this can impact the time required for a user to log on. Under most circumstances you will not need to worry about utilizing WMI filters for your Terminal Server implementation.

The second tab is labeled Details (see Figure 15.10); it provides a summary of the policy's creation and modification history and lets you select whether to disable the Computer or User settings or enable/disable the entire policy. Because this is going to be the Terminal Server Machine Policy, click the GPO Status drop-down list box and select User Configuration Settings Disabled. This helps speed up application of the policy on a server by skipping all the user settings.

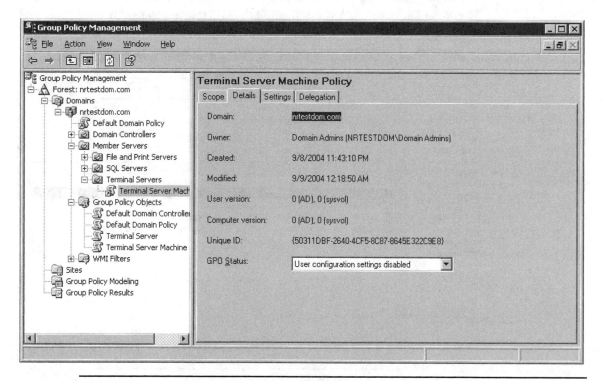

Figure 15.10 The Details tab provides a summary of the group policy and lets you disable sections of the policy that will not be applied.

The third tab is called Settings and automatically generates an HTML report that shows what settings within the policy have been defined. This is a powerful administrative tool that we review later in this chapter when I demonstrate how it appears once a number of policies have been defined.

The fourth and final tab is Delegation. This is where you will set who has access to manage this group policy. Any objects defined under Security Filtering on the Scope tab will appear here with a note appended stating that this permission is coming from a setup done on the Scope tab. Figure 15.11 shows the default delegation permissions for a GPO. You can see how the Authenticated Users entry came from the Scope tab, while the other settings are delegation entries setting who can actually manage the GPO. Depending on the requirements of the organization, you may want to restrict who can manage this GPO. Let's assume that only Terminal Server Administrators will manage this GPO. Click the Add button and then enter the group name when prompted. You are prompted to choose the permissions to assign. Click the drop-down list box and select Edit Settings, Delete, Modify Security and then click OK. The group should be added to the list with the appropriate permissions. If you're not going to let any other users modify this GPO, remove them from the list.

Make certain that you belong to the Terminal Server Administrators group, or you will immediately lock yourself out of the GPO when you modify the permissions.

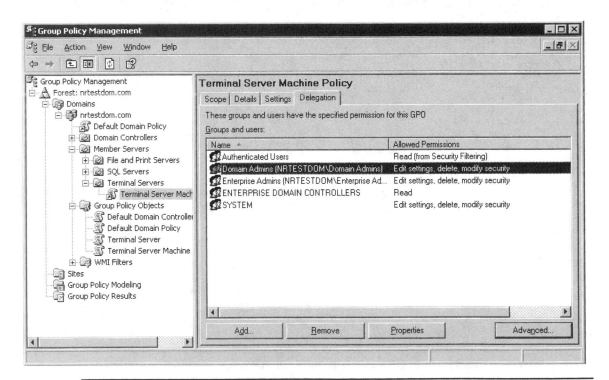

Figure 15.11   The GPMC tool does a nice job of separating delegation permissions from application permissions (security filtering), providing an intuitive interface for management.

■ Now that the properties for the GPO have been set, the next task is to actually configure the appropriate policy options. Open the Group Policy Object Editor by right-clicking the Terminal Server Machine Policy folder in the left-hand pane and selecting Edit from the Context menu.

The Group Policy Object Editor is used by both ADUC and GPMC when actually editing the policy. Details on this are provided in the next section, entitled "Configuring the Terminal Server Machine Policy Using Group Policy Object Editor."

Configuring the Terminal Server Machine Policy Using Group Policy Object Editor

A window similar to the one shown in Figure 15.12 appears when you begin to edit the Terminal Server Machine Policy. The first Terminal Server policy that must be created is required so any *user configuration* settings defined in other Terminal Server policies are applied to the users when they log on to one of the Terminal Servers located in the Terminal Servers OU. Normally when a group policy is created for an OU containing only computers (no user groups or accounts), only the computer configuration settings are applied to these machines, and any user configuration settings that are defined are simply ignored. User-related policy settings normally come from the OUs containing those user accounts and are applicable throughout the scope of Active Directory.

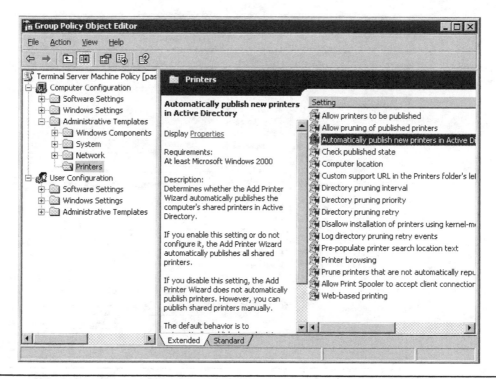

Figure 15.12 The Group Policy Object Editor configuration window.

When implementing a Terminal Server environment, you will usually want to modify this default behavior so user configuration settings can be defined within the Terminal Servers OU that are applied to users only when logged on to a Terminal Server—not when the user logs on to a regular (non–Terminal Server) computer. To modify the default behavior, the User Group Policy Loopback Processing Mode option (simply Loopback Processing Mode, on Windows 2000) must be enabled. This policy is found under

Computer Configuration\Administrative Templates\System\Group Policy

When you are enabling this policy you will see that there are two operating modes available to choose from, as shown in Figure 15.13. The two modes available are

- **Merge**—This option merges the policies defined for the Terminal Servers OU with any policies defined for the user in other OUs.
- **Replace**—This option replaces the policies defined for the user in other OUs with the policies defined within the Terminal Servers OU. Normally I use this option to ensure that only the appropriate policies are applied to the user while he or she is logged on to Terminal Server.

Once you have made your selection and clicked OK, the changes are immediately saved for the GPO.

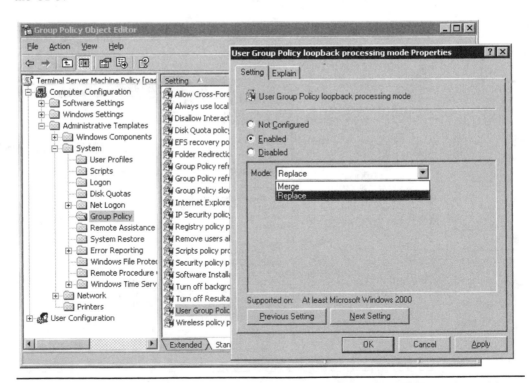

Figure 15.13 Enabling loopback processing mode for the Terminal Server Machine Policy.

After enabling the loopback mode, a couple of other options that I will typically set for the base Terminal Server Machine Policy are:

- **Delete Cached Copies of Roaming Profiles**—The location of this policy differs between Windows 2000 and Windows 2003. The policy location is

Windows 2003: Computer Configuration\Administrative Templates\System\User Profiles
Windows 2000: Computer Configuration\Administrative Templates\System\Logon

  Enabling this option ensures that all locally cached roaming profiles are cleared when the user logs off. This helps to conserve disk space on the Terminal Server, particularly if you have a large user base that may log on to your servers. If user profiles are very large, though, this setting increases the logon time because a new profile must be copied down to the server every time a user logs on.

- **Set path for TS Roaming Profiles**—In a Windows Server 2003 Active Directory domain with Windows Server 2003 Terminal Servers, this policy can be used to globally set the Terminal Server roaming profile property for all users. When set here, you are not required to populate the TS roaming profile setting within each user account. Details on user profiles will be discussed in Chapter 18, "User Profile and Account Configuration." This policy is located in:

  Computer Configuration\Administrative Templates\Windows Components\Terminal Services

After updating the desired settings, simply close the Group Policy dialog box. The changes are automatically saved as you edit them. This group policy is now applied automatically to any computers that exist within the Terminal Servers OU the next time they reboot, or at regularly scheduled intervals. By default, this update is done every 90 minutes plus at random intervals from 0 to 30 minutes. You can modify this refresh rate for the policy by updating the Group Policy Refresh Interval for Computers option, located under

  Computer Configuration\Administrative Templates\System\Group Policy

Windows also provides a command line utility you can use to immediately refresh a policy. The utility used differs between versions of Windows being run, as shown in Table 15.3. If the update fails, an entry is added to the server's Application event log.

Table 15.3 Group Policy Refresh Utilities by Windows Version

Windows Version	Group Policy Refresh Command	Comments
Windows 2003	GPUpdate.exe	Replaces the SECEDIT functionality provided with Windows 2000. Issuing the GPUpdate command by itself initiates a refresh of both the Computer and User policies. You can refresh the two configurations separately by using the /target: option followed by "computer" or "user".
Windows 2000	Secedit /refreshpolicy MACHINE_POLICY	Refreshes the computer configuration settings on the current computer.
	Secedit /refreshpolicy USER_POLICY	Refreshes the user configuration settings for the user account.

Creating the Terminal Server All Users Policy

After creating the base machine policy, the next step is to create the default policy that will apply to all users who log on to a Terminal Server, including Administrators. The steps to configure this are almost identical to those for setting up the Terminal Server Machine Policy:

1. Return to the Terminal Servers OU and add a new policy called Terminal Server All Users Policy.
2. This policy will apply only user settings, so disable the computer configuration settings. In ADUC this is done by opening the properties for the policy and selecting the appropriate check box. In GPMC you do this by opening the Details tab for the GPO and selecting Computer Configuration Settings Disabled from the drop-down list box for GPO Status (see Figure 15.14).
3. The permissions for the GPO should now be set. Using ADUC, you can set the permissions as shown in Table 15.4. As mentioned, my security configuration is made up of Authenticated Users, Terminal Server Administrators, and SYSTEM. This time the Administrators are explicitly set to apply this group policy. This is because this group policy will affect all Terminal Server users.

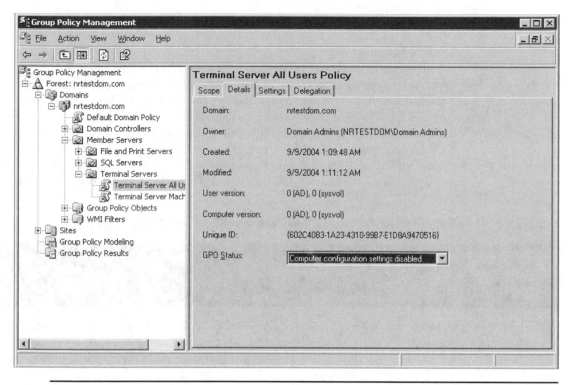

Figure 15.14 Computer configuration settings are disabled under the Details tab for a GPO in GPMC.

Table 15.4 Suggested Terminal Server All Users Policy Security Permissions for ADUC

Permissions	Authenticated Users	SYSTEM	Terminal Server Administrators
Full Control			Allow
Read	Allow	Allow	Allow
Write		Allow	Allow
Create Child Objects		Allow	Allow
Delete Child Objects		Allow	Allow
Apply Group Policy	Allow		Allow

When using GPMC, you will begin on the Scope tab with the security filter. This can remain unchanged with the default entry of Authenticated Users. This setting covers all users, Administrators or not.

The Delegation tab is where you will define who can edit this policy. I suggest that you set this up to have the same permissions as those you set for the Terminal Server Machine Policy.

4. After setting the appropriate permissions, open the policy for editing. Table 15.5 lists some of the common policies I implement that affect all users. All these options are set under the User Configuration\Administrative Templates folder. Unless stated otherwise, the individual policy names are the same for both Windows 2000 and 2003. If the names differ, the Windows 2000 name appears in parentheses. Be careful when configuring options within the Terminal Server All Users Policy. Remember that these options affect all users, *including* Administrators. Before enabling/disabling an option, make certain that you want this option to impact your Admini-strators as well.

Table 15.5   Example of Common Settings for Terminal Server All Users Policy

Location under User Configuration\ Administrative Templates\	Comments
Windows Components\ Windows Explorer	Enable *Do Not Track Shell Shortcuts During Roaming*. Normally Windows stores both a relative and an absolute path (UNC path) to a shortcut. If the file isn't found with the relative path, the absolute path is used. Enabling this option ensures that users are not trying to access a shortcut across the network to a remote computer if it is not found locally.
	Enable *Remove UI to Change Menu Animation Settings (Disable UI to Change Menu Animation Settings)*. Menu animation introduces additional traffic between the client and the server. Enabling this option ensures that users can't turn on animation.
Start Menu & Taskbar	Enable the options *Add Logoff to the Start Menu* and *Remove and prevent access to the Shut Down command (Disable and Remote the Shut Down Command)*. I like to set these options for all users so that even an administrator can't easily shut down a server. This helps reduce the chance of an accidental server reboot. An administrator can still shut down a server by using the TSSHUTDN command, even if the option on the Start menu is not available.
	Enable the option *Do not use the search-based method when resolving shell shortcuts*. Normally Windows attempts to do a comprehensive search of the target drive in order to find a shortcut if it cannot be resolved directly or by searching for the file ID (on NTFS only). Disabling this option prevents this exhaustive search behavior, and instead Windows simply says that the file could not be found.

Table 15.5 Example of Common Settings for Terminal Server All Users Policy (continued)

Location under User Configuration\ Administrative Templates\	Comments
	Enable the option *Do not use the tracking-based method when resolving shell shortcuts*. This option works in conjunction with the one listed previously and prevents Windows from attempting to search using the file ID (on NTFS only) when the shortcut cannot be resolved directly.
Control Panel\Display	The Display folder is where you will configure your screen saver options for your Terminal Server. Normally you should try to avoid running a screen saver at all on your Terminal Server sessions, but if the user's client machine does not provide a lockable screen saver option, then for security reasons you may want to enable this feature.
	By default, a Windows 2003 Terminal Server has the Windows Server 2003 screen saver enabled and is set to password-protect after 15 minutes of idle time.
	Whether the screen saver is active or not is set through the *Screen Saver (Activate screen saver)* policy. When enabled a screen saver can be defined, but if disabled no screen saver can be set and the option in the Display dialog box is automatically removed.
	When a screen saver is being used, the screen saver is set through the *Screen saver execute name* policy. I recommend that you use only the default screen saver: scrnsave.scr. This simply blanks out the screen and minimizes the bandwidth used. Do not use any of the graphical rendering screen savers because they consume way too much bandwidth and server resources.
	Screen saver timeout should be set to the desired time in seconds. The default is 900 seconds (15 minutes).
	Password protect the screen saver should always be set to ensure that the user's session is locked when idling for a long period of time.
System\Group Policy	The default refresh interval for applying user policy updates is every 90 minutes plus a random 0–30 minute increment. Policies are always applied when a user first logs on. When a policy is applied, the user's session flickers momentarily and any open menus close. While this isn't a problem, the relatively short interval can be disruptive in a production environment where policy updates should not be happening at regular intervals anyway. I prefer to enable the option *Group Policy refresh interval for users* and set the refresh interval to 720 minutes (12 hours).

Creating the Terminal Server Regular User Policy

Most configuration and restriction changes you implement will be placed within the Terminal Server Regular User Policy. All settings configured within this policy apply to only non-administrative users on the system. The steps to creating the policy are the same as for creating the policy for all users discussed in the previous section, except when it comes to setting the appropriate permissions.

Table 15.6 summarizes the permissions that should be configured when using ADUC. Notice that in this case the Administrators group has the Deny permission explicitly set on the Apply Group Policy setting. This ensures that these policies never apply to anyone in the Terminal Server Administrators group.

Alternatively, you could replace the Authenticated Users group with the Terminal Server Users group, but I still recommend that you enable the Deny option to ensure that if an administrator accidentally belongs to that group as well as the Administrators group, they do not get the user policy restrictions applied to them.

Table 15.6   Suggested Terminal Server Regular User Policy Security Permissions when Using ADUC

Permissions	Authenticated Users	SYSTEM	Terminal Server Administrators
Full Control			
Read	Allow	Allow	Allow
Write		Allow	Allow
Create Child Objects		Allow	Allow
Delete Child Objects		Allow	Allow
Apply Group Policy	Allow		Deny

When using the GPMC, you can choose to leave the security filter containing only the default Authenticated Users group, or you can replace this with the Terminal Server Users group. Once this has been set, you need to click over to the Delegation tab and modify the permissions for the administrative groups. Assuming that you have the Terminal Server Administrators group, you will want to ensure that a member of this group never has a regular user's policies applied to them. You can do this by clicking the Advanced button. A dialog box opens listing all the security users and groups for the policy, as shown in Figure 15.15. Highlight the desired group, scroll down until you see the Apply Group Policy permission, and then select the Deny check box. This ensures that the members of this group will never have this GPO applied to them.

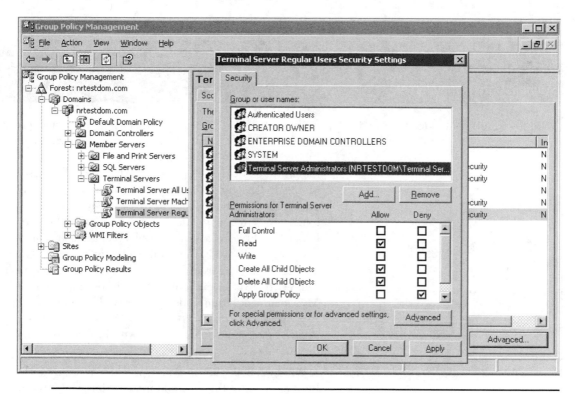

Figure 15.15 Denying the Apply Group Policy permission ensures that the policy is never applied to members of that group.

NOTE: Depending on the complexity of your environment, you may be required to create additional Terminal Server policies to accommodate different groups of users. For example, you may need to create a set of policies for your Terminal Server support staff. You might call such a policy something like Terminal Server User Support Policy.

Table 15.7 provides an example of some of the policy options I normally enable for regular Terminal Server users. All these options are located under the User Configuration folder.

Table 15.6   Example of Common Settings for Terminal Server Regular User Policy

Location under User Configuration\ Administrative Templates\	Comments
Windows Settings\Folder Redirection	An important part of configuring a user's Terminal Server environment is the redirection of certain folders to a centralized network location—in particular, the My Documents folder, which by default is contained as part of the user's profile. In Chapter 18, I discuss user profiles in more detail, but it's important to note here that the My Documents folder tends to become quite large over time. When this folder is redirected to a network location, only the network path is stored in the profile, greatly reducing its size and decreasing the user's logon and logoff times. I normally redirect the My Documents folder. To do this, right-click My Documents from under Folder Redirection and select Properties. From under the Target tab, select *Basic – Redirect everyone's folder to the same location* from the drop-down list.
	A Windows 2000 Group Policy provides you only with a location to enter the desired target folder location. For example, if I've created a distributed file system (DFS) share containing each user's home folder where My Documents will exist, then I would enter a target location as follows:
	\\nrsc.com\dfsroot\TSHome\%Username%
	A Windows 2003 Group Policy provides an additional drop-down list box from which you can select different methods of directing the target folder location, as shown in Figure 15.16. If I wanted to use the same DFS share just mentioned, I would select *Create a folder for each user under the root path* and then enter the following for the root path:
	\\nrsc.com\dfsroot\TSHome\
	The default options under the Settings tab can be left as-is.
	If you want to redirect folders to multiple locations, you can specify where to redirect the folders based on the user's group by choosing the Advanced setting instead of the Basic setting.

Table 15.6 Example of Common Settings for Terminal Server Regular User Policy (continued)

Location under User Configuration\ Administrative Templates\	Comments
	Note: In some cases this particular policy can be defined as part of the Terminal Server All Users Policy, so that even administrators have their My Documents folder redirected.
Administrative Templates\Desktop	In conjunction with folder redirection, the option *Prohibit user from changing My Documents path* should be set.
Administrative Templates\ Windows Components\ Windows Explorer	There are two options under this location that you'll probably want to enable for regular users. *Remove the Folder Options menu item from the Tools menu* prevents users from accessing the Windows Explorer properties while *Remove (Hide) hardware tab* removes the hardware option from the properties panel for all local devices as well as from the control panel.
Administrative Templates\Control Panel	One option commonly set here is *Prohibit access to the Control Panel (Disable Control Panel)*, which prevents users from being able to load the control panel or any applet. In some situations you may want to allow users access to a subset of the control panel applets, in which case you would use the *Show only specified control panel applets* policy and explicitly list which applets users can access. If you're unsure of what the file name for the applet is, you can search the Windows directory for files with the extension .CPL. Most have a descriptive name that either matches or is similar to the control panel applet name.
Administrative Templates\Control Panel\ Regional and Language Options	The one option here, labeled *Restrict selection of Windows menus and dialogs language* allows you to set what language the users will automatically start working with. On a Terminal Server that has multiple languages installed (the multilingual user interface version of Windows), you can use this policy to enforce different languages for different users. When multiple languages are being supported a separate policy is usually created to enforce a specific language such as German based on group membership.
Administrative Templates\System	The option *Disable Registry Editing Tools* is commonly set to prevent regular users from launching the registry editing tools REGEDT32 and REGEDIT.

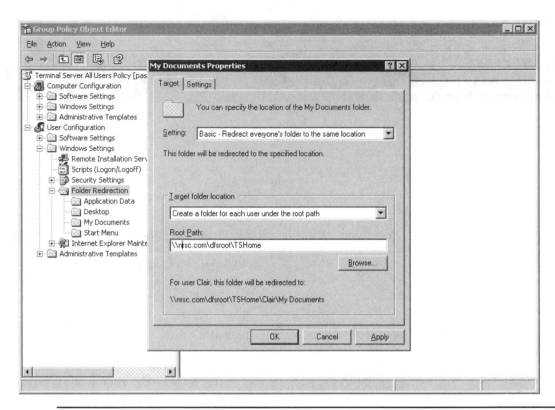

Figure 15.16   The Windows Server 2003 dialog box for folder redirection of My Documents.

As mentioned, this is not a comprehensive list of what options to enable in a Terminal Server configuration but rather a suggestion as to which ones you're likely to employ. While the number of group policy options available is extensive, it's certainly worth the time to review and employ the ones that will help ensure that you implement a manageable and secure Terminal Server environment. In Chapter 16, I look specifically at some of the security-related group policy settings you likely will want to deploy in your environment.

NOTE: When you configure the group policy settings, I recommend that you use caution and not implement a large number of settings simultaneously. A common mistake made by many administrators is to become slightly euphoric over the prospect of what can be restricted and proceed to implement a number of settings spread across many subfolders. The problems begin if there is an issue with one or more policies affecting a user's ability to work properly. Tracing back to the changes made and determining where the issue is occurring can be quite time consuming. There is really no substitute for patience and adequate testing when implementing group policies.

Setting Group Policy Priorities

After all the desired policies have been created, the final step is to establish an order of priority in which the policies are applied. Policy order is important because it determines what settings for a particular property are actually applied. If a policy setting has been defined in multiple GPOs, the one contained in the highest priority GPO determines how the setting is actually configured. Of course, the means by which you establish this priority differs between the ADUC and GPMC tools.

Group Policy Priority using Active Directory Users and Computers

When using ADUC, the policies are applied starting at the bottom and working up to the top. Figure 15.17 demonstrates how I normally order the three GPOs that were created in this chapter. The yellow exclamation marks exist to flag that either the user configuration or computer configuration settings have been disabled.

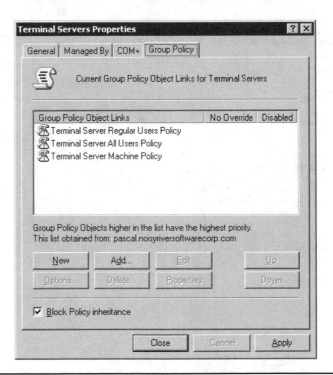

Figure 15.17   A group policy object priority example within ADUC.

The Terminal Server Machine Policy applies only to the servers themselves, and therefore can have the lowest priority. No other policy in the list should affect the computer settings in any way. Next comes the Terminal Server All Users Policy, which contains settings generally assigned to all users (including administrators). The third and final group is the Terminal Server Regular Users Policy, where most of the restrictions are applied. Any member of the Administrators group will not have any of these settings applied.

Group Policy Priority Using Group Policy Management Console

When using GPMC, the policies receive an actual number assignment that dictates the order in which they are applied. Numbers start at 1 and work their way up. The higher the number the higher the priority, so number 1 is actually the lowest. GPO priority is set in GPMC by clicking the OU and then selecting the Linked Group Policy Objects tab, as shown in Figure 15.18. This lists the policies with the exact same precedence as the ones in Figure 15.17, but of course they appear visually in reverse order.

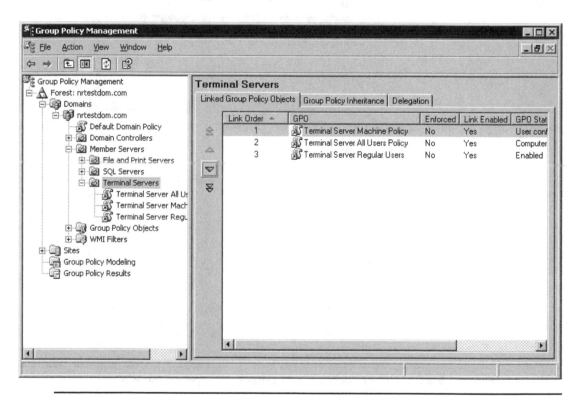

Figure 15.18   A group policy object priority example within GPMC. The higher the link order number, the higher the precedence. Lower ordered numbers are applied before higher ordered numbers.

In Figure 15.18, the Terminal Server Machine Policy applies only to the servers themselves and therefore can have the lowest priority (number 1). No other policy in the list should affect the computer settings in any way. Next comes the Terminal Server All Users Policy (number 2), which contains settings generally assigned to all users (including administrators). The third and final group is the Terminal Server Regular Users Policy (number 3), where most of the restrictions are applied. Any member of the Administrators group will not have any of these settings applied.

The final point to mention pertains to the Group Policy Inheritance tab within GPMC. This tab lets you see what linked and inherited GPOs apply to this OU. Unless inheritance has been blocked for the OU, it will pick up any GPOs that have been defined higher up in the structure. You can enable or disable inheritance by right-clicking the OU and selecting the desired option from the Context menu. If a policy is set to Enforced, it will always override the inheritance setting and be applied to any child OU.

Whether you disable inheritance or not for Terminal Server OUs will depend on the structure of the active directory and whether a large number of policies may be applied higher up. If you're unsure about what to choose, consider disabling inheritance until you are confident that a parent GPO won't negatively impact your Terminal Server configuration.

Group Policy Templates

You can import administrative template files into a Windows server group policy to allow for the addition of new policy options. The template files have the extension .ADM and are loaded from within the Group Policy Object Editor. You do this by right-clicking Administrative Templates and then selecting the desired template to load. The Office XP and Office 2003 Resource Kits provide .ADM files designed for use in an active directory; Figure 15.19 shows an example of the custom templates for Office XP loaded into a group policy. The .ADM files are typically located in the %SystemRoot%\INF folder. I always recommend the use of templates when available to centralize the configuration of an application on one or more Terminal Servers.

Once a template has been added then the associated policies can be configured just as any of the other policies discussed in this chapter have been configured. Be aware that many of these imported policies lack the detailed README information associated with the policies native to Windows 2000 Server and Windows Server 2003.

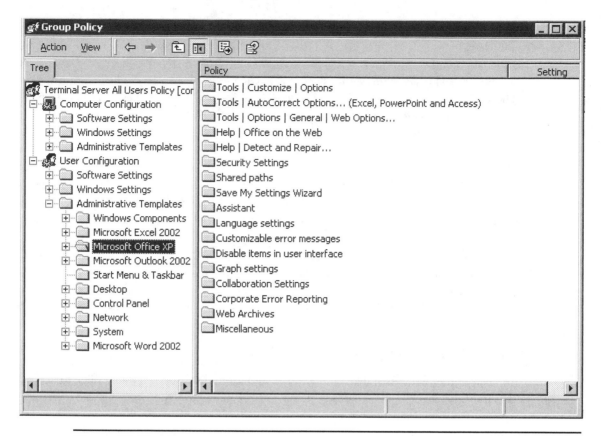

Figure 15.19 An example of Office XP administrative templates in a group policy.

CHAPTER 16

Terminal Server Security

Before You Begin

Regardless of the size of your Terminal Server environment, it is imperative that you take the time to properly assess the security requirements of your infrastructure. Unlike the typical Windows server, a Terminal Server lets users interact with the server in very unpredictable ways. You must provide a security mechanism that protects the Terminal Server both internally and externally. After the user has established a connection, he or she has an interactive presence on the server with direct access to the resources shared between all users, such as disk and memory. Actions of one user can have an impact on all other users on the system unless the proper steps are taken to protect against this possibility. This requirement covers *all* users, including system and network administrators.

Considering the multiuser nature of a Terminal Server environment, even with little risk of a malicious threat, an accidental change performed by a single user could affect every other user on the system. For this reason, the key to developing a suitable security configuration requires the right balance between mitigating risks while still providing an environment within which the end user can perform their dictated job function. While a server can be hardened to the point where it is extremely secure, the end result might be a configuration completely unusable from an end user's perspective. This chapter focuses on helping you decide and implement the desired level of security suitable for your Terminal Server implementation.

Most security settings discussed in this chapter are implemented using group policy objects (GPOs) in a Windows Active Directory domain. An overview of implementation and use of a GPO is provided in Chapter 15, "Group Policy Configuration." The information covered in Chapter 15 forms the foundation on which the security changes in this chapter are discussed. If you're unfamiliar with configuration of group policies in an active directory, I highly recommend reviewing Chapter 15 before proceeding. Figure 16.1 shows the sample organizational unit (OU) configuration I use to demonstrate the security changes discussed in this chapter. As you can see, this follows the suggestions outlined in Chapter 15, whereby an organizational unit called Member Servers exists off the domain root, and under here an OU exists for each of the subcategories of member servers. In this case, I have an OU for Terminal Servers, file servers, and print servers.

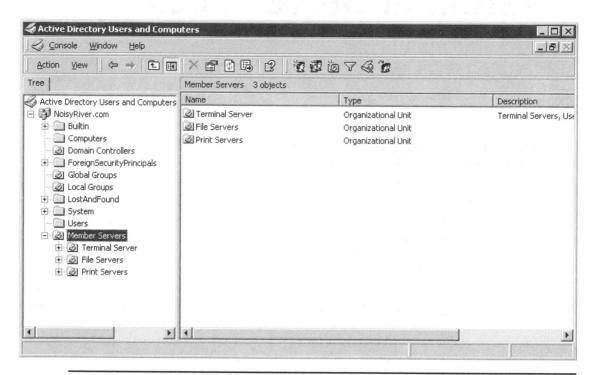

Figure 16.1 Sample "Member Servers" OU configuration containing Terminal Servers.

NOTE: Entire books have been written on the subject of Active Directory configuration, and details of such a configuration are beyond the scope of this book. For the purpose of this chapter I focus on configuration of the Terminal Server organizational unit in an active directory.

While most screen shots in this chapter come from a Windows 2000 domain controller, unless otherwise noted, the exact same steps can be performed against a Windows 2003 domain controller.

In Chapter 8, "Server Installation and Management Planning," I briefly discussed the eight areas of Terminal Server security that I recommend all administrators consider when developing a security implementation plan for their environment. Figure 16.2 shows a simple visual representation of these eight layers, which I discuss in more detail in the next few sections of this chapter.

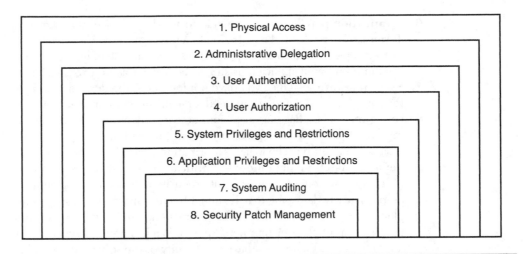

Figure 16.2 The eight recommended areas of review for Terminal Server security.

1. **Physical access**—Physical access to your Terminal Server (and associated server hardware) should be restricted as much as possible to only the people responsible for managing the Terminal Server environment.

2. **Administrative delegation**—Before any other security considerations can be addressed, a decision must be made as to who will have administrative authority over the Terminal Server OU and all servers that reside within this OU.

3. **User authentication**—Almost all Terminal Server implementations have some form of user authentication to verify that a user is who they declare themselves to be. The most common form of authentication is the combination of user ID and password. In most organizations, this is also typically the weakest and most vulnerable of the security layers.

4. **User authorization**—Unlike user authentication, which deals with verifying identity of a user, user authorization deals with regulating what users have access to log on and what server resources they can access. Just because a user is who they say they are does not necessarily mean they are authorized to access the resource they are attempting to use.

5. **System privileges and restrictions**—Once an authorized user has logged on to the Terminal Server, their ability to interact with objects on the server is managed through user rights, security restrictions, and administrative templates. These three components work in combination to limit a user's access to only those components of the server pertinent to their job function.

6. **Application privileges and restrictions**—Usually access to the applications on a Terminal Server should be restricted to a subset of users based on their job function. For example, administrative applications are available only to administrators, while accounting-related applications should be accessible only to the accounting staff.

7. **System auditing**—Once you have implemented the desired security configuration for your Terminal Servers, you need a means of monitoring effectiveness of the configuration and flagging suspicious activity when it occurs. System auditing is an important part of any secure environment but is of little use unless an effective means of monitoring the logged information is also implemented.

8. **Security patch management**—A critical part of any secure environment is the timely deployment of all appropriate security patches. Poor patch management can be particularly damaging to a Terminal Server environment, since many of the exploits released into the wild specifically target end users and impact common applications such as Outlook or Internet Explorer. While a properly secured server normally limits the effects a user can have on stability of the server, some exploits can specifically target privilege elevation, effectively granting administrative access to the user's session and allowing a malicious program to cause system-wide problems. In Chapter 9, "Service Pack and Hotfix Management," I discussed security patch management in detail.

Physical Access

Whenever possible, one of the first steps in securing your Terminal Server environment should be to establish a secure location to store the servers and all associated hardware. The goal is to limit physical contact to only authorized Terminal Server administrators. Surprisingly, physical security is not always practiced as diligently as might be expected. Once physical security has been compromised, an otherwise secured server is at risk to a number of threats. Aside from the obvious concerns such as theft, easy-to-use tools exist that can be used to reset an administrator's password simply by booting the server from a floppy disk or CD-ROM. Through this, code can easily be inserted onto the server allowing for further privilege elevation or data theft. Such physical attacks can completely bypass any other security and auditing measures that you may have in place. Aside from malicious threats, accidental interference is also a real concern. For example, a poorly placed server could be mistaken for a different piece of hardware and accidentally shut down.

NOTE: I once audited an environment where they had to leave a note taped to the server reminding users not to turn the machine off. The server was stored in a stationary closet accessible by all the employees in the branch location. The note was required because certain users were frequently powering the machine off and on in order to try to fix the application problems they were experiencing instead of first contacting a support person.

Physical security should also be a consideration in large corporate data centers. Many large companies have a single data center containing all the servers (file, print, e-mail, and so on) for the organization. In these types of environments there are usually a large number of people with access to this room, all of whom are responsible for administering a subset of these servers. In this situation you should consider investing in secured server racks that can be locked to prevent administrators of another system from accidentally tampering with one of your servers.

Here are the two basic guidelines to follow when physically securing your servers:

1. Store servers in a room closed off from general staff traffic and accessible only with some form of card or key authentication.
2. If necessary, lock the servers in their own rack or shelving device accessible only by valid Terminal Server administrators.

Administrative Delegation

It should be fairly obvious that granting a regular user administrative privileges to a Terminal Server will inevitably result in stability issues. It may not be quite so obvious that the exact same threat exists when legitimate administrators in your domain who are unfamiliar with managing a Terminal Server environment are also granted administrative access to your servers. In this situation, the administrator is just as likely as the regular user (if not more so) to cause server-wide problems based on a change made to the server or an application's configuration.

Historically it has been common to have only one administrative classification in a Windows environment without any further subdivision of privileges into more granular groupings. When someone requires administrative privileges to manage resources in a domain, they are likely added to the Domain Admins group, giving them full administrative privileges that span the entire domain. The result is an environment with multiple administrators with full control over all resources in the domain, yet they may lack the experience to properly administer many of the resources they have full control over. For example, someone skilled in maintenance of Windows file servers may not be qualified to manage Active Directory, a Microsoft SQL Server, or even a Terminal Server. While many argue that it is just "easier" to manage the resources with these privileges, allowing this practice in a Terminal Server environment can introduce a significant threat to your infrastructure's stability.

To help ensure a stable and secure Terminal Server environment, you must not give anyone administrative authority on your servers unless they are qualified to use it. The more Terminal Server administrators you have, the greater the risk of an undesirable change affecting your production environment.

Terminal Server Domain Group Creation

When configuring administrative delegations for your Terminal Server environment, a logical starting point is creation of the four global domain security groups listed in Table 16.1. These are the same groups discussed in Chapter 8 and used when demonstrating group policy object creation in Chapter 15. I review the specific roles of the Terminal Server Operators and User Support groups in more detail in Chapter 22, "Server Operations and Support."

Table 16.1   Terminal Server Administrative Domain Groups

Domain Group Name	Description
Terminal Server Administrators	This domain group is granted full control over the Terminal Server organizational unit and all Terminal Servers in the OU. Members of this group have full authority to manage the Terminal Server environment, and as a result, membership in this group must be tightly managed.
Terminal Server Operators	Users with this privilege level have the authority to monitor the various system functions and perform such tasks as shutting down the server or terminating a process. They don't have the ability to make any system changes or perform application installations.
Terminal Server User Support	Members of this group can perform basic support functions such as shadowing another user's session or logging an active user off. They don't have the ability to restart a server or perform any other server maintenance operations.
Terminal Server Users	This domain group is used to grant basic user access to the production Terminal Servers in the environment. A member of this group can log on to a production Terminal Server and access all the generally available applications. The user has no administrative privileges of any kind.

Delegating Organizational Unit Authority

Once the domain groups are created, you need to delegate administrative privileges for the Terminal Server Administrators group to the Terminal Servers OU. There are two ways you can accomplish this: Either utilize the Delegation of Control wizard, accessible by right-clicking the OU and selecting Delegate Control; or directly update the access control entries from the Security tab found under the properties for the OU, as shown in Figure 16.3. If the Security tab is not visible on the Properties page, you will need to select the Advanced Features option from the View menu.

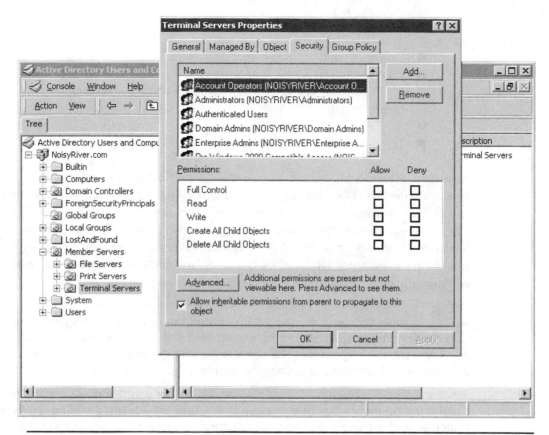

Figure 16.3   The Security tab for the Terminal Server organizational unit.

Once the Terminal Server Administrators group has been added, I suggest disabling inheritance of permissions from the OU's parent container. This ensures that permissions must be defined directly against the OU in order to affect delegation of authority, reducing the chances that an undesirable change performed in a parent container will negatively affect this OU's access control list (ACL).

Inheritance is disabled by deselecting the check box labeled "Allow inheritable permissions from parent to propagate to this object." In a Windows 2000 domain, this check box appears on the main Security tab (see Figure 16.3), while in a Windows 2003 domain, you must first click the Advanced button to bring up the dialog box containing this check box. When this option is deselected, you then must make a choice between whether you will keep a copy of inherited permissions or remove all inherited permissions and keep only permissions explicitly defined for the OU.

For this Terminal Server OU, I suggest removing all inherited permissions and keeping only those explicitly defined. In a typical Active Directory environment, your access control list would then look similar to the following:

- Account Operators
- Authenticated Users
- Domain Admins
- Print Operators
- ENTERPRISE DOMAIN CONTROLLERS (Windows 2003 Active Directory only)
- SYSTEM
- Terminal Server Administrators

Management of this OU should be restricted further by removing the Account Operators object and the Print Operators object from the ACL, leaving Terminal Server Administrators and Domain Admins as the two groups with full authority over the organizational unit. If you have any concerns that a member of the Domain Admins group might inadvertently modify properties of the Terminal Servers OU, you should consider restricting this group's access to the OU as well, either by completely removing the group from the ACL or by modifying the permissions to restrict activities the group can perform.

NOTE: On more than one occasion I've debated the reasons for granting or revoking Domain Admins group access to manage a Terminal Server organizational unit or server. Very often it is argued that the Domain Admins group simply *must* retain complete control over all elements of a domain, including the Terminal Server environment.

While in theory I agree that this should be the proper configuration, the one condition I feel must be met is that membership in the Domain Admins group be tightly controlled and only those users actually requiring administrative privileges in the domain belong to this group. If this group contains users requiring administrative access to a resource in the domain but not the entire domain itself, I would consider the administrative hierarchy in the domain to be "broken" and would advise against allowing the Domain Admins group to administer the Terminal Server environment. It is simply too risky to give users not familiar with, or responsible for, the Terminal Server environment the ability to modify a Terminal Server's configuration.

Managing Local Group Membership

Now that administrative permissions for the Terminal Server OU have been delegated accordingly, the next step is to create and populate the necessary local groups on each of your Terminal Servers. The idea is to use the local groups on a Terminal Server to assign all the necessary server privileges and then delegate these privileges by populating these groups with the appropriate domain groups. We begin by delegating administrative authority through these local groups and return later in this chapter to assign the appropriate user privileges.

When server security is implemented in this fashion it greatly simplifies administration by introducing a layer of abstraction between the domain and the server. When you know that all security on a server relates back to the local groups, you can verify who has access to what resources simply by viewing local group membership. If domain groups or individual users were directly assigned to the access control lists (ACL) of resources on the server, you would be required to trace back permissions from these resources to the appropriate domain group to ensure that security had not been compromised (intentionally or accidentally).

Before domain groups can be assigned to the local groups on a Terminal Server, we must ensure that these local groups exist. As I discussed in Chapter 8, I typically recommend that the following two additional local groups be created on a Terminal Server to allow for more granular delegation of administrative authority on a Terminal Server:

- **Terminal Server Operators**—Used to assign a subset of administrative privileges to those users responsible for managing the day-to-day operations of the Terminal Server. For example, members of this group would have the ability to terminate processes or restart the Terminal Server but would not have the ability to install/remove applications or modify configuration of the server.
- **Terminal Server User Support**—Used to assign privileges to those users who would perform typical user support functions. Among other privileges, members of this group would have the ability to shadow other users—something a regular user can't do.

While local groups can be added to a Terminal Server by manually creating them through the Microsoft Management Console (MMC) Computer Management snap-in, I prefer scripting their creation using the Net LocalGroup command. The script is run locally on a Terminal Server during the initial configuration phase to create the desired local groups. The following code sample demonstrates how these two groups could be created using a script:

```
@ECHO OFF
REM Create the desired local groups on the Terminal Server
net localgroup "Terminal Server Operators" /add
net localgroup "Terminal Server User Support" /add
```

Once the necessary local groups have been created, we are ready to assign the appropriate domain groups. The most common means of assigning a domain group to a local server group is directly through the MMC Computer Management snap-in, as shown in Figure 16.4. While easy enough, this method is still prone to error when the task must be duplicated across a number of Terminal Servers. Another option to consider is scripting the local group assignment, similar to what I suggested for creation of the local groups. Unfortunately this is really effective only if the local group memberships will remain static. In a production Terminal Server environment, it is likely that local group membership assignments will change over time. In a large Terminal Server environment it would not be practical to adjust and rerun a membership script on all servers. As a result, an alternative allowing more dynamic control over local group membership is necessary.

The preferred method of managing local group membership is through a group policy object (GPO) in an Active Directory domain. Through a single GPO we can define a local group membership standard that is consistent across all Terminal Servers in the domain. This method not only allows for consistent definition of the local group members but also provides dynamic control over the membership we are looking for.

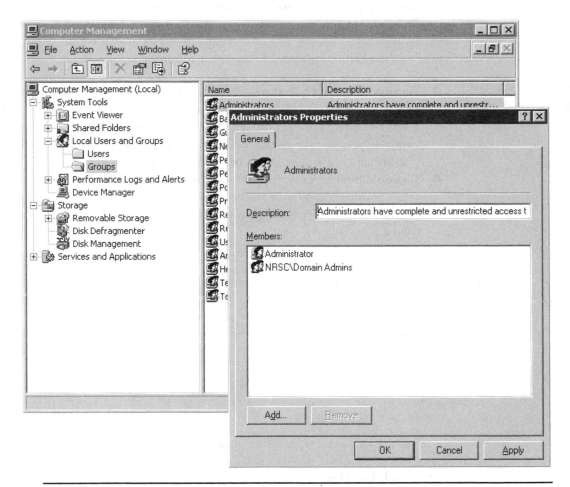

Figure 16.4 Assigning domain groups to a local group through the Local Users and Groups container.

To demonstrate how this is done, I use the "Terminal Server Machine Policy" created in Chapter 15. This GPO contains all the base computer configuration settings for all the Terminal Servers in the OU. There are no user configuration options defined in this GPO.

The local group membership is controlled from within the Restricted Groups policy, located under Computer Configuration\Windows Settings\Security Settings.

Managing the local group membership is a two-stage process. First the local groups that will be populated are added to the Restricted Groups policy, and then the desired domain members are added to each of these groups. The local groups are added to the policy by right-clicking Restricted Groups and selecting the Add Group menu option. The dialog box shown in Figure 16.5 opens, where you can enter the desired local group name.

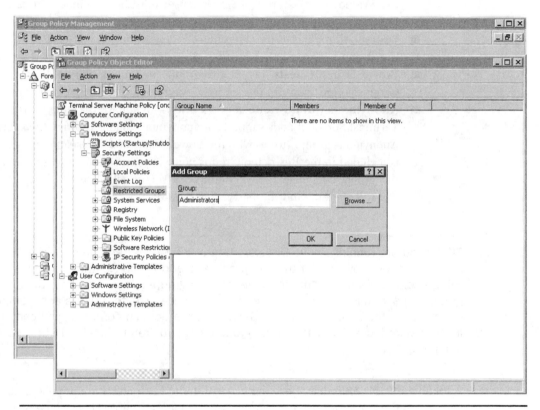

Figure 16.5   Accessing the "Terminal Server Machine Policy."

Note that there is no validation performed on any groups that you add to the Restricted Groups policy. If the group name you provide does not exist on the Terminal Server, the group name is simply ignored and is *not* automatically created by the GPO.

Typically I define the following local groups within the Restricted Groups policy:

- **Administrators**—Members of this group will have full administrative control over the Terminal Server. Because of this, access should be very tightly controlled.

- **Terminal Server Operators**—This group name is used to assign a subset of administrative privileges to those users responsible for managing the day-to-day operations of the Terminal Server.
- **Terminal Server User Support**—Those users responsible for performing typical user support functions such as shadowing or session logoffs would be members of this group.
- **Remote Desktop Users (Windows Server 2003 only)**—To remotely log on to a Windows 2003 Terminal Server, a user must be a member of this existing local server group.
- **Users**—All regular users who require access to run one or more applications on the Terminal Server are assigned to this local group.
- **Power Users, Guests**—These two groups are included in the Restricted Groups policy to ensure that no users are members of either of them.
- **Anonymous (MetaFrame servers only)**—When MetaFrame is installed on a Terminal Server, it adds support for anonymous logons through the special Anonymous group. Just as with the Power Users and Guests groups, this group is included in the Restricted Groups policy to ensure that no users belong to this group. Of course, if your MetaFrame server will allow this type of support you will need to omit this entry from the GPO.

TIP: If you are running Active Directory Users and Computers directly off a domain controller, then browsing for the group name to add to the Restricted Groups policy will present you with only the available domain groups. To be able to browse for local groups on a Terminal Server, you need to run Active Directory Users and Computers directly from the member Terminal Server. From a domain controller, you can still type in the desired local Terminal Server group name; you're just unable to browse for it using the GUI.

After all the local groups have been defined within the Restricted Groups policy, the next step is to assign the appropriate domain groups to these local groups. This is done by right-clicking the desired local group in the right-hand pane and selecting the Security option from the pull-down menu. The Configure Membership dialog box appears, as shown in Figure 16.6. By default this group contains no members and belongs to no other group. If these options are left as-is, then when the policy is applied to the server, all members who may have been manually added to the local group are removed. Domain groups are added by clicking the Add button on the upper half of the dialog box for the Members of This Group option. Since we're configuring only local groups on the Terminal Server, there is no need to modify the lower portion of the dialog box, labeled This Group Is a Member Of.

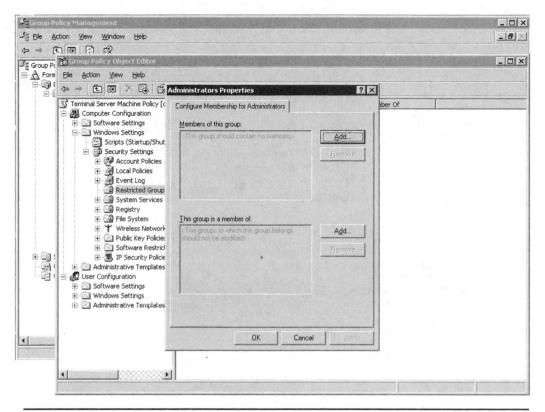

Figure 16.6 The Configure Membership dialog box for a listed Restricted Group.

Once the Add button has been clicked, an Add Members dialog box appears. This dialog box lets you type in the name of the domain group or click the Browse button to find the desired group within the domain. Multiple groups can be entered at once by separating them with a semicolon. When manually typing in the group name, be sure to precede it with the domain name and a backslash. For example, to add the domain group Terminal Server Operators of the domain called PRODUCTION, you would type the following:

PRODUCTION\Terminal Server Operators

When you have completed entering the desired domain groups for a given local group, click OK to close the Configure Membership dialog box. Each of the local groups listed in the Restricted Groups policy now appears in the Members column when the Details view is active (see Figure 16.7, which shows the defined groups in a Windows 2000 domain). When the GPO is applied to all servers in the Terminal Server OU, all the listed local groups are updated with the corresponding domain groups. As I mentioned, groups with no explicit memberships will have any existing memberships removed on the affected Terminal Servers.

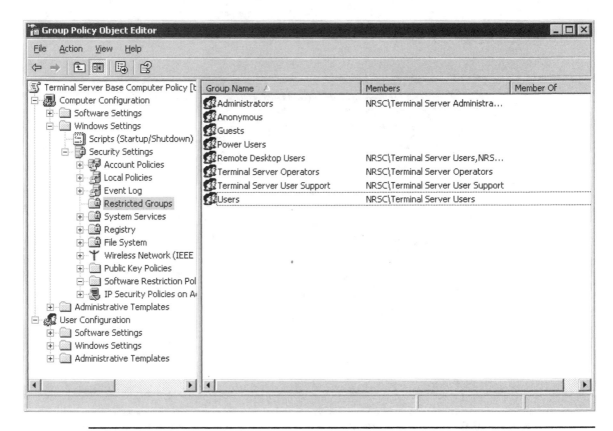

Figure 16.7   Viewing local groups in Restricted Groups.

Table 16.2 summarizes my suggestions for local group membership in a Terminal Server Restricted Groups policy. The domain groups listed in this table were discussed in the "Terminal Server Domain Group Creation" section, earlier in this chapter.

Table 16.2   Terminal Server Restricted Group Membership Suggestions

Local Terminal Server Group Name	Domain Group Membership Suggestion
Administrators	Terminal Server Administrators—Only administrators will have full authority on a Terminal Server.
Anonymous	Leaving this group empty ensures that the local group contains no user accounts.
Guests	Leave this group empty.

Table 16.2 Terminal Server Restricted Group Membership Suggestions (continued)

Local Terminal Server Group Name	Domain Group Membership Suggestion
Power Users	Leave this group empty.
Remote Desktop Users (Windows Server 2003 only)	Terminal Server Users, Terminal Server Administrators—For users to be able to log on via a Terminal Server session (RDP or ICA), they must belong to this group. This applies to a Windows Server 2003 Terminal Server only.
Terminal Server Operators	Terminal Server Operators.
Terminal Server User Support	Terminal Server User Support.
Users	Terminal Server Users—Users with standard access to a Terminal Server and its applications.

NOTE: I've found that managing security exclusively through the local security groups on a Terminal Server is also helpful when migrating a Terminal Server from one domain to another. I was once involved in a project where a number of Terminal Servers were being tested in a test domain that was an exact duplicate of production but completely segregated from the production domain. Once the testing and validation had been completed, the Terminal Servers were removed from one domain and added to the other. Once the Terminal Servers were in the production domain, the only change required was to assign the appropriate domain groups to the local groups on the Terminal Server. All other aspects of the servers remained unchanged, helping ensure that the configuration tested matched the final production deployment as much as possible.

User Authentication

Almost all Terminal Server implementations require that the users perform some form of authentication in order to verify that they are who they say they are. Exceptions to this rule would include kiosk-type implementations where anonymous users access a general-purpose Terminal Server session in order to utilize a specific application. Most corporate Windows environments utilize the familiar Windows logon dialog box (see Figure 16.8) to enforce use of a user ID/password combination for user authentication. While this is the most common form of authentication, it unfortunately is also typically the weakest and most vulnerable of the security layers.

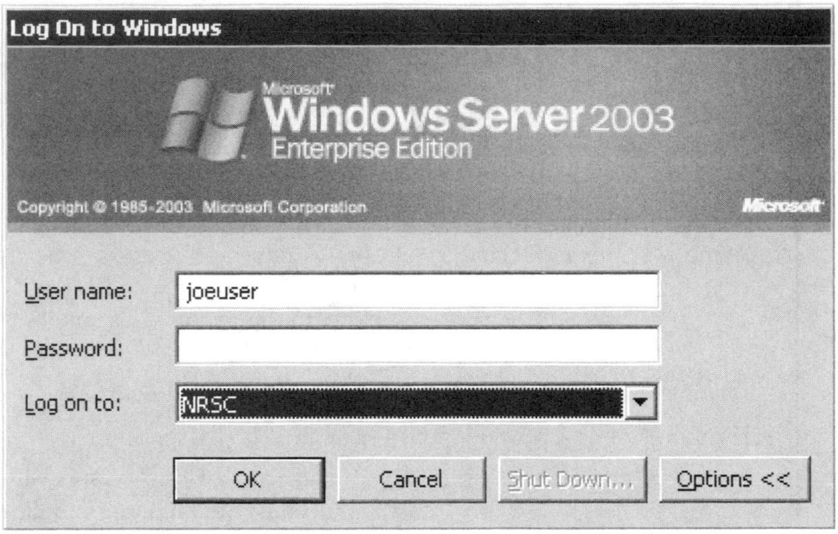

Figure 16.8   The Windows Server 2003 logon window.

The reason for this weakness is not simply technical but also educational. In most organizations, the user community lacks understanding regarding the importance of adequate password "strength" and the potential consequences of a compromised user account. Password-cracking tools are readily available and can easily be used to discover weak passwords in an organization.

TIP: The term *strength* is often used to describe the relative complexity of a password and its resistance to cracking through either manual or automated means. Some common weak passwords include the following:

- A blank password or no password at all.
- Some variant of the word *password.*
- A password based on the user's name, their spouse's name, or some other common dictionary word such as *bird, tree, snow, monkey, dog,* and so on.
- A password based on a user's phone number, home address number, birthday, an so on.

   Password-cracking tools attempt to exploit use of weak passwords and typically uïtilize a combination of three cracking strategies to achieve their goal:

- **Dictionary attacks**—Common words found in the dictionary are used to try to quickly match user passwords.
- **Targeted-word attacks**—A customized dictionary of specific words is used to try to determine the user password. Custom dictionaries are usually created based on information gathered either through social engineering or other means of personal information acquisition and typically target a specific user or group of users.

- **Brute-force attacks**—Every possible combination of characters is used to try to discern the password. In many cases the dictionary and brute-force attacks are integrated to try to find quick hits. With sufficient time, a brute-force attack will determine any password. Of course, the complexity and length of a password determine whether such an attack can discover a password in a realistically finite amount of time.

It is not difficult to see that these strategies would easily pick off passwords such as disney, porsche, or jennifer27, all of which are passwords I've encountered within large production Terminal Server environments.

A number of different password-cracking tools are readily available for most operating systems. A small sample of these include

- **LC5**—The latest version of the famous L0phtCrack password auditing and recovery tool. Different variants of this product are available to be purchased, with the high-end product offering a number of different password-cracking techniques such as brute-force, dictionary attacks and pre-computed password tables (also known as rainbow tables). Trial versions used to be available for the product, but at the time of this writing, the latest version did not offer a trial version. The Website is http://www.atstake.com/products/lc/
- **Cain & Abel**—A robust and powerful password recovery tool, Cain boasts an astounding array of features, including a number of different network packet filtering options. Best (or worst) of all, this tool is completely freeware. The product can be found at http://www.oxid.it/projects.html.
- **Sarca Rainbow Tables**—An online Web site that allows you to paste LanManager and NT password hashes onto the site and submit them for cracking using their generated rainbow tables. The site only processes hashes once per day but can crack a large number of passwords. Limitations on the actual processing are discussed on the site. http://sarcaprj.wayreth.eu.org

Not only are such tools a threat on their own, but when used in combination can very easily crack even relatively complex passwords. Of course certain conditions must be met, namely the potential cracker must be able to access the encrypted passwords. In most cases administrative privileges are required to access this information, but certain exploits may make such information available without directly acquiring these rights. Just another reason for keeping up-to-date with the available security patches for your environment.

My reason for listing these tools here is purely to demonstrate how readily up-to-date password-cracking and acquisition tools are available. Listing them here does not imply that I endorse the use of these tools for anything other than testing the strength of the passwords in an environment. I recommend caution when looking to use any password-auditing tool, particularly in production.

Please understand the risks involved in such endeavors. Use common sense when downloading and testing any software that may be coming from a suspect source.

While it is obvious that a "strong" password will be much more difficult to crack than a "weak" one, the added complexity can be a formidable obstacle during early stages of implementation, with the primary issue being simply that it is more difficult for the end user to remember a new, stronger password. In nearly every situation where I have been party to introduction of complex password requirements, the end user community in general has commented that the new passwords are "far too confusing," and "not necessary" for their organization or department. Without the proper education, users are unclear as to why they must use a complex password and as such become easily frustrated if the simple tasking of logging on is delayed enough to impact their ability to work. Failure to successfully introduce and enforce strong-password requirements in most cases is a result of the system administrator's inability to adequately manage the initial flood of demands from users requesting password resets or unlocking of a locked-out account in a timely fashion.

NOTE: Microsoft has tried to stress to administrators the idea of teaching users the concept of a "passphrase" instead of simply a password. While many users can struggle with trying to come up with and remember a seven-character password, a common phrase such as "I really love to drink coffee" can be easier to remember, easier to type, and stronger than a typical seven-character password. In an environment that is enforcing complex passwords, one way to ease password creation is to develop a passphrase that can then be used to "build" the password.

For example, a common technique I've used is to create a passphrase such as "Todd loves to spend money on his sports car." I then delete all but the first letter of each word and substitute the word *to* with 2 and *money* with $. The result is the password Tl2s$ohsc, which is suitably complex and also very easy to remember. I talk more about enforcing strong passwords in the next section of this chapter.

Account Password Policies

Unfortunately, education alone rarely ensures that all users in your organization use only a strong password. Most users, given the opportunity, try to use as simple a password as possible and recycle this password (or minor variations) over and over, if periodic password changes are required. As a general rule, an administrator should never leave it solely up to the end user to ensure that a sufficiently strong password is being used.

As a complement to user education, an administrator should leverage the security features available in Windows 2000/2003 to help enforce strong user password requirements. Both Windows versions support the same six password policies shown in Figure 16.9. A subset of these policies is enabled by default in a Windows 2003 domain; unfortunately the same cannot be said for a Windows 2000 domain, where none of these policies is enabled by default.

To modify the default password requirements in a Windows domain, these settings must be defined within the Default Domain Policy group policy object (GPO), located at the root of the domain. For example, in my noisyriversoftware.com domain, this GPO is found under the Group Policy tab for the noisyriversoftware.com object. If you wish to define these password settings for local accounts on a member server or PC, a GPO containing these settings must be created and assigned to an OU that contains the computers you want to update.

WARNING: Many organizations make the mistake of assuming that only those accounts with administrative privileges require strong passwords and that "regular" user accounts are not really as much of a concern. This is a dangerous misconception, particularly in an environment where regular patch management is not being performed. Frequently exploits are discovered that make it possible for a regular user to elevate their privileges beyond what they have been assigned and to gain full administrative control. Because of this, password security really must be enforced for all users in your environment and not only for those users with administrative privileges.

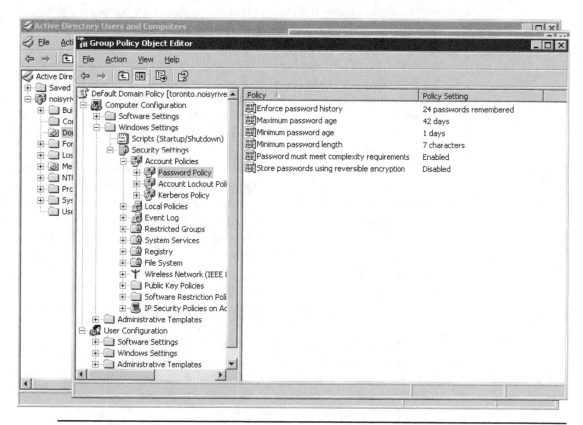

Figure 16.9   Windows 2000/2003 account password policies.

The six policies shown in Figure 16.9 provide the following functionality:

- **Enforce password history**—To counteract the tendency of users to reuse the same password (or small set of passwords) over and over, this policy ensures that a specific number of unique passwords are used before a user's oldest password can be reused. By default this option is set to the maximum of 24 passwords remembered in a Windows 2003 domain.

  A possible side effect of enforcing a lengthy password history is that users may start maintaining a paper record of their password to help them remember what they are currently using. The two most effective ways to counteract this are through the proper education of secure computing practices and the use of a suitably long maximum password age (described next) to allow the user time to learn the password before the system once again requires them to change it. My preference is to use the maximum value of 24 in all production Windows domains whenever possible.

- **Maximum password age**—The longer a user is allowed to retain the same password, the greater the chances that the account may be successfully cracked or accessed by someone who may already have the password to the account. Periodically forcing a user to change their password helps minimize these risks. A Windows 2003 domain has a maximum password age of 42 days, which most administrators find to be an optimal medium between frequent password change requirements and adequate password aging.

  Similar to enforcing a large password history, requiring users to change their passwords too often will likely result in at least some of the users keeping a paper record of their current password, often in an easily accessible location (taped to the monitor, under the keyboard, and so on). I highly recommend not setting the maximum password aging to zero (0) but instead using the default of 42 days.

- **Minimum password age**—Complimenting the maximum password age policy is the minimum password age policy. This policy defines the minimum number of days a user must use the same password before it can be changed. The main reason for this policy is to ensure that users do not attempt to quickly change their password multiple times in order to reuse a desired password, effectively circumventing the "Enforce password history" policy.

  Windows 2003 defaults to a minimum password age of one (1) day, meaning that a user can change their password only once per day. This policy does not prevent an administrator from resetting a user's password.

- **Minimum password length**—An adequate password length is critical to ensuring that user passwords remain secure by minimizing the effectiveness of brute-force attacks. Each increase in the minimum password length by one character exponentially increases the number of possible password permutations. Using only the standard characters on the keyboard, users have 94 possible characters to choose from when selecting their password. These 94 characters are comprised of 52 alphabetical characters (uppercase and lowercase), 32 additional characters (#, $, °, @, etc.), and 10 numeric characters (0, 1, 2, 3, etc.). When the minimum password length is 7, the user can choose from 94^7 (approximately 64,000,000,000,000) possible different passwords.

Of course, as the password length increases, so does the risk that a user will be unable to remember the password they are using. Windows 2003 defaults to a minimum length of seven characters, and I recommend that passwords use at least this many characters.

■ **Password must meet complexity requirements**—Even with all these password requirements in place, education alone will not ensure that the end user consistently selects a strong password. Without some means of ensuring that a minimum level of strength is being used, the users are likely to pick the simplest password possible that complies with the policies in place.

The "Password must meet complexity requirements" policy lets you enable your Windows environment to perform a complexity validation check whenever a user's password is changed. Here are the complexity requirements

---

Password must have a minimum length of six characters.

This requirement takes priority over the "Minimum password length" policy if the minimum length has been set to less than six characters.

The password must contain characters from at least three of the following categories:

- Uppercase characters "A" through "Z."
- Lowercase characters "a" through "z."
- Numeric characters 0 through 9.
- Non-alphanumeric symbols such as !, @, #, %, and so on.

The password cannot contain substrings of three or greater characters in length found in the user's full account name. When this requirement is validated, the user's full name is broken up into substrings using commas, periods, dashes, hyphens, underscores, number signs, and spaces as string delimiters. The password is then searched for substrings matching these tokens. If any matches are found, the password is rejected. Any substrings of three or fewer characters are ignored. For example, if a user has the name Steven Li Chan, it is broken into three substrings: "Steven", "Li", and "Chan". The name "Li" is dropped because it is less than three characters, while the other two tokens are used to search the password. If either "Steven" or "Chan" appears in the password, it is rejected. The searches are case insensitive, so "CHaN", "chan", and "ChaN" are all considered to be the same.

When a user's password is changed and it fails validation, a message similar to the one in Figure 16.10 appears. The Windows 2000 message differs slightly, providing a more verbose description of the password requirements. Invariably, when this policy is first implemented, users have a difficult time interpreting the password requirements. I've found that a separate description of the password requirements (including some password examples) made available to the user, either via an e-mail message or as a physical printout, can greatly ease transition pains associated with enforcement of complex passwords.

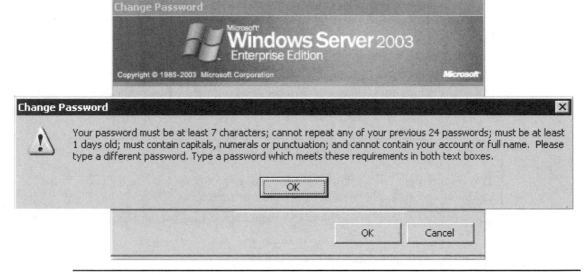

Figure 16.10   A Windows Server 2003 complex password requirements message.

TIP: Password validation requirements are provided as part of the passfilt.dll system file. When a password change request is made, the Local Security Authority (LSA) module of the Windows subsystem calls the password filters provided in this DLL to validate the password requirements. While the password requirements supplied with the default passfilt.dll file cannot be modified, a custom passfilt.dll file could be created containing customized password requirements for your organization. Details of such an undertaking are beyond the scope of this book, but if you are interested, you can find more information on the Microsoft Developers Network (MSDN) Web site at http://msdn.microsoft.com/library/default.asp?url=/library/en-us/security/security/strong_password_enforcement_and_passfilt_dll.asp

■ **Store passwords using reversible encryption**—In most situations, this policy should *never* be enabled because it forces Windows to store passwords in such a way that they can be decrypted. This is inherently much weaker than the standard method of one-way encryption and provides an attacker with an additional means of compromising one or more user accounts.

With proper use of these six security policies you can minimize the vulnerabilities traditionally found with ID/password user authentication.

Account Lockout Policies

In addition to enforcing use of strong passwords, another mechanism for increasing security of Windows user authentication is use of user account lockout policies. Essentially, these policies provide a means of temporarily disabling a user's account if a predefined number of unsuccessful user ID/password authentication attempts are performed within a given period of time. Figure 16.11 shows the three account lockout policies found in both Windows 2000 and Windows 2003. By default none of these options are enabled in either operating system.

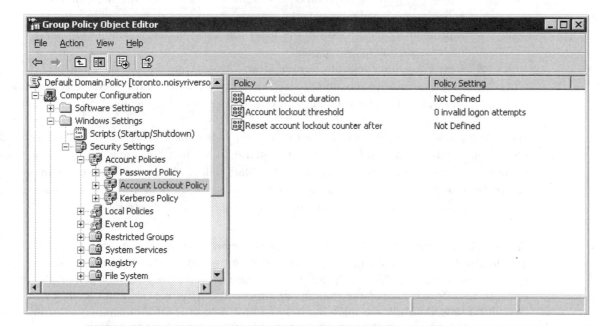

Figure 16.11   Windows Server 2003 account lockout policies.

The three policies shown in Figure 16.11 provide the following functionality:

■ **Account lockout duration**—This policy determines the amount of time a user's account remains disabled until it is automatically re-enabled by the system. I typically recommend that the duration be set to zero (0) in order to minimize the number of brute-force or dictionary-based attempts that can be performed against a user account before an administrator's intervention is required. When set to zero, an account remains locked until manually unlocked by an administrator.

The one thing to consider when setting the lockout duration to zero is that a user cannot log on until an administrator manually re-enables the account. To minimize the chances of a user legitimately locking themselves out, settings for the other two account lockout policies must be set accordingly, as discussed in the following points.

■ **Account lockout threshold**—The lockout threshold represents the number of incorrect password attempts allowed before a user's account is disabled. One factor influencing this value is the lockout duration you configured for your environment. If the duration is set to zero (0), the lockout threshold can typically be assigned a value of 10 to 15. In most situations a user is not likely to repeatedly try their password this many times within the account lockout reset interval (see the following point).

■ **Reset account lockout counter after**—This setting dictates the amount of time that must pass before the lockout counter is automatically reset to zero. A value of 30 minutes is usually appropriate for most environments.

When first implementing account lockout policies in your organization, it is not unusual to see a high number of account lockouts occur, particularly when first implementing strong password requirements. It will likely take a few days before the issues balance out to an acceptable level. At this time you may need to make minor adjustments to your configuration to reach a mutually agreeable configuration for both users and administrators.

WARNING: An unfortunate downside that exists when lockout policies have been implemented is that a malicious user could exploit this configuration to purposely lockout user accounts, effectively performing a denial of service (DOS) attack on the environment. This is one of the reasons why the administrator's account cannot by default be locked out. While there is no sure-fire way to prevent this, limiting external access to the environment as much as possible will at least help to contain such a threat to within the confines of the internal network.

Connection Authorization

While user authentication deals with verification of a user's identity, connection authorization deals with regulating what server resources a validated user is authorized to access. For example, you may have 500 users in your organization, all of which have access to resources in the Windows domain (printers, file servers, and so on) but only 100 of which require access to log on to and function within the Terminal Server environment. While it may appear easier from an administrative standpoint to simply allow all users access to the Terminal Server environment, this invariably results in users not supposed to be logged on to the environment in fact being logged on, either intentionally or by accident. In addition to the obvious security concerns this can raise is the issue of license and server resource consumption. If you have implemented a Terminal Server environment to support 100 concurrent users, you had better be certain that you have the mechanisms in place to ensure these resources are available for the intended users.

In the "Administrative Delegation" section earlier in this chapter, I discussed use of local security groups to delegate user permissions on a Terminal Server. We now leverage the local group configuration discussed in that section to manage the connection authorization for a Terminal Server. All properties for Terminal Server connections, including security, are managed through the Terminal Services Configuration application in the Administrative Tools folder on the Start menu. Figure 16.12 shows the Terminal Services Configuration application for a Windows 2000 Terminal Server supporting both RDP and ICA connections. The Windows 2003 Terminal Services Configuration tool has the exact same interface.

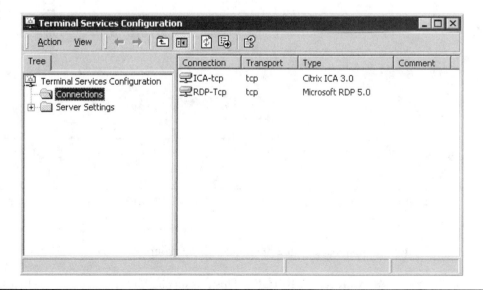

Figure 16.12   The Windows 2000 Terminal Services Configuration application.

Connectivity permissions for a Terminal Server are managed through the Permissions tab, found on the Properties page for each of the listed connection types, as shown in Figure 16.13. As with other access control lists in Windows, this tab lets you specify what groups have connectivity access to the Terminal Server and what specific privileges they possess. Table 16.3 shows both the default and recommended connectivity permissions for the RDP and ICA protocols. As you can see in the table, the default connection permissions differ slightly between the Windows 2000 (RDP 5.0) and 2003 (RDP 5.2) protocols.

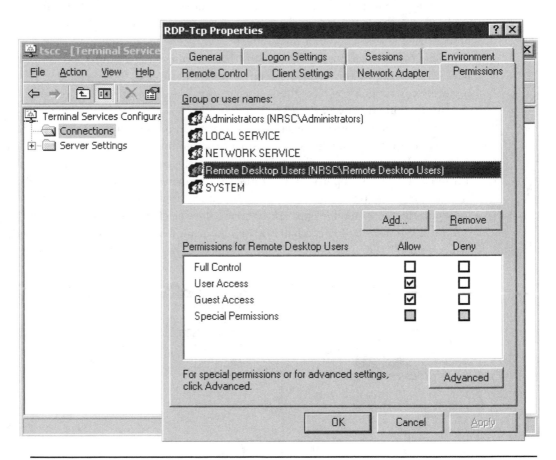

Figure 16.13   The default Windows Server 2003 RDP permission properties.

Windows Terminal Server 2003 utilizes three group/user objects not found in Windows 2000:

- **LOCAL SERVICE**—This is a special built-in user account that has the same privileges as a member of the local Users group. This account has very limited access to network resources, presenting only null session information with no user credentials when prompted by a remote system. This account exists to make it easier for an administrator to grant limited privileges to services that require only local access on a server. By default this account has permissions to send text messages to all RDP protocol users on a server.

■ **NETWORK SERVICE**—This built-in account also has privileges equivalent to a member of the local Users group. Where this account differs from the LOCAL SERVICE account is in the network privileges it has been granted. When prompted by a remote system for network credentials, this account sends the computer's account credentials.

■ **Remote Desktop Users**—By default, a user requires membership in this local group in order to log on to a Windows 2003 Terminal Server. The appropriate connection privileges and local user rights are all preconfigured for members of this group.

The main reason for creation of this group was to improve default security of a Terminal Server by negating the assumption that all members of the local Users group should be granted access to log on to a Terminal Server session. A common security problem in the Windows 2000 Terminal Server environment occurred immediately after the server was added into a domain, because a byproduct of domain membership is that the domain Users group is automatically added to the computer's local Users group. This resulted in granting all domain users connectivity privileges necessary to be able to log on to the Terminal Server remotely. An administrator needed to be aware of this situation and modify the connectivity permissions accordingly in order to negate this potential security issue.

Table 16.3   Default and Recommended Terminal Server Connection Permissions

Default RDP Settings (Windows 2000 and 2003)		Default ICA Settings (MetaFrame XP)	
Account/Group	**Access**	**Account/Group**	**Access**
Administrators (local)	Full Control	Administrators (local)	Full Control
SYSTEM	Full Control	Everyone	Guest Access
Users (local) (W2K only)	User Access Guest Access	Guests (local)	Guest Access
LOCAL SERVICE (W2K3 only)	Special—Message only	SYSTEM	Full Control
NETWORK SERVICE (W2K3 only)	Special—Message only	Users (local)	User Access Guest Access
Remote Desktop Users (local) (W2K3 only)	User Access Guest Access		

Table 16.3 Default and Recommended Terminal Server Connection Permissions (continued)

Recommended RDP and ICA Settings (Windows 2000)		Recommended RDP and ICA Settings (Windows 2003)	
Account/Group	**Access**	**Account/Group**	**Access**
Administrators (local)	Full Control	Administrators (local)	Full Control
SYSTEM	Full Control	SYSTEM	Full Control
Users (local)	User Access Guest Access	Remote Desktop Users (local)	User Access Guest Access

Terminal Server Operators (local)	User Access
	Guest Access
	Special
	   Allow Reset
	   Allow Remote
	      Control
	   Allow Logoff
	   Allow
	Disconnect
		Terminal Server Operators (local)	User Access
			Guest Access
			Special
			   Allow Remote
			      Control
			   Allow Logoff
			   Allow
			      Disconnect

Terminal Server User Support (local)	User Access
	Guest Access
	Special
	   Allow Reset
	   Allow Remote
	      Control
	   Allow Logoff
	   Allow
	      Disconnect
		Terminal Server User Support (local)	User Access
			Guest Access
			Special
			   Allow Remote
			      Control
			   Allow Logoff
			   Allow
			      Disconnect

		LOCAL SERVICE	Special— Message only
		NETWORK SERVICE	Special— Message only

When configuring the RDP connection permissions, you do not need to modify the default entries, but if you plan to utilize the local Terminal Server User Support and Server Operators groups discussed earlier in this chapter, you should configure their appropriate connectivity privileges. In Table 16.3 I configured these two groups with the same permissions, but you can make the User Support permissions more restrictive if desired.

Both these groups have been assigned the same User and Guest Access privileges assigned to normal Terminal Server users, but special privileges have been added to elevate their access for specific functions. The individual permissions are assigned by clicking the Advanced button on the Permissions tab and then highlighting and editing the desired permission entry, as shown in Figure 16.14. When the additional permissions are assigned, they grant the following privileges:

- **Reset (Windows 2000 only)**—This attribute grants the user the ability to reset any RDP connection to the server. A reset forces the connection to be terminated and the resources allocated to be immediately freed. Unlike the execution of the Logoff command (controlled using the Logoff privilege; see the third point in this list), this does *not* send the Windows logoff message to the session's running applications, allowing them to terminate. If a user has an application open and their connection is reset, any unsaved data is likely lost.

- **Remote Control**—This attribute grants the user the ability to remotely control (or shadow) another user's session. The specific remote control permissions are discussed in Chapters 19 and 20, where I discuss connection-specific settings for both the RDP and ICA clients.

- **Logoff**—This attribute lets a user log off another user's session just as if that target user had themselves selected Logoff from the Start menu. All running applications receive the Windows logoff message, allowing them an opportunity to cleanly shut themselves down before the user's session is terminated.

- **Disconnect**—Instead of being logged off, a user can also be disconnected. This simply terminates the presentation connection between the client and the server but leaves the running desktop session active on the Terminal Server. Any running applications continue to run and be available if the user reconnects before the session is terminated by an administrator or automatically logged off by the system. Maintaining disconnected sessions on a server for long periods of time is usually discouraged because maintaining the state information consumes additional server resources.

Unlike the default RDP permissions, the default ICA permissions are not as secure, providing connectivity permission entries for both the Guests and Everyone groups in addition to the local Administrators, SYSTEM, and local Users. These privileges are not secure and at the very least should be modified to remove the Guests and Everyone groups.

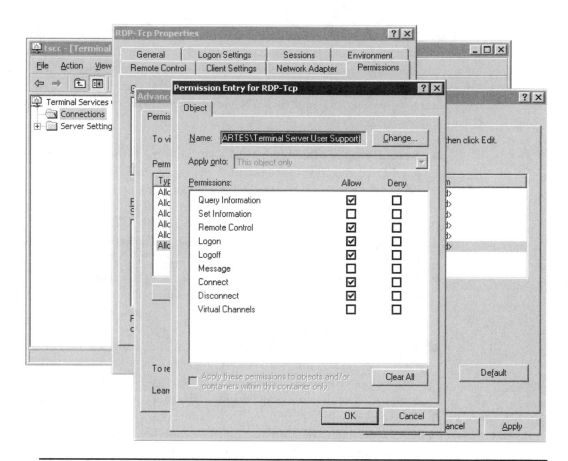

Figure 16.14   Permission entries for the Terminal Server User Support group on a Windows 2003 Terminal Server.

TIP: If a presentation protocol (RDP or ICA) is not going to be used in your environment, then one way to further secure the environment is to disable or completely remove the unused protocol entry. Removing a presentation protocol is not a permanent thing; in fact it can be re-added at any time if the requirements ever change. Another option is to further restrict the unused protocol by limiting access to only Administrators and SYSTEM. This makes the protocol available if an administrator ever requires it, while ensuring that users cannot use it to gain unauthorized (or uncontrolled) access to the environment.

For example, a common configuration when implementing Citrix MetaFrame is to make RDP connections available but limit their access to only two to four administrative accounts. This type of access can be valuable for an administrator, particularly if there are issues connecting using the ICA protocol.

In addition to the presentation protocols, when reviewing connection security other forms of potentially available connectivity should be examined. The number of running services should be minimized to limit the number of open ports on the server. The fewer network ports that are open, the fewer points of entry that are exposed. In Chapter 11, "Terminal Services Configuration and Tuning," I discussed stopping unnecessary services on a Terminal Server.

System Privileges and Restrictions

Once an authorized user has logged on to the Terminal Server, the security focus shifts from one of complete access prevention to one of access restriction. A user's ability to interact with objects in the system is managed through user rights, system security restrictions, administrative templates, and file and registry restrictions. The task of configuring these settings is further complicated by the need to ensure that adequate session security exists while still providing the functionality required by the users to perform their job.

As I discussed in the "Administrative Delegation" section of this chapter, whenever possible system privileges and restrictions should be managed using local user groups as opposed to individual user accounts or domain security groups. The idea is to then assign the desired domain group or user to the corresponding local group that is appropriate for their access level. Assignment of access rights on a Terminal Server should be kept as simple as possible. When the security requirements become too complex, this increases the likelihood that some setting may be missed. In most implementations this means dividing the users into two categories when delegating access rights. Either the user is a member of the Administrators group, with full rights to the entire server, or the user is a member of the Users group, with only limited access to the server's resources.

NOTE: With such a simplified division of access rights (Administrators group or Users group), care must be taken when the default Users permissions are not sufficient to let a user perform a particular job function. In most circumstances this occurs when an application does not operate properly under the limited privileges granted the Users group.

A common reaction to this type of problem, particularly under pressure from the user community to come up with a quick solution, is to assign regular users full administrative access. While this certainly resolves the application issue, it is critical that this *never* be allowed on a production Terminal Server. Such privilege elevation immediately brings the integrity of the Terminal Server into question since any mistake by a user can render the server completely unusable.

Assignment of privileges when pertaining to application integration is discussed in the "Application Privileges and Restrictions" section of this chapter.

User Rights Assignment

User rights are a special set of privileges that define which basic operating system functions a user or group of users can perform. While I recommend that you review the User Rights configuration on your server to ensure that the appropriate groups have been defined, under most circumstances you will not have to modify the default settings. Figure 16.15 shows the default User Rights Assignment policies for a Windows 2003 Terminal Server as viewed from within the Local Security Settings MMC snap-in. This utility is found under Administrative Tools on the Start menu for both Windows 2000 and 2003 and is used to view the settings currently in effect on the server.

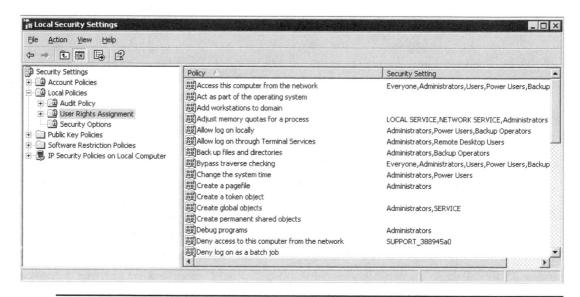

Figure 16.15   The default User Rights Assignment policies for a Windows 2003 Terminal Server.

While the Local Security Settings snap-in is used to review the current settings on a Terminal Server, if you wish to make changes to the User Rights Assignment policies, I recommend that they be performed within the Terminal Server Machine Policy defined in Active Directory and not within the Local Security Settings snap-in. This ensures consistency across all Terminal Servers in your domain, since all necessary policy settings are automatically applied once the policy has been added to the Terminal Servers organizational unit. Policies defined at the domain level always take precedence over those options set locally when a conflict occurs.

When assigning user rights within a GPO, make certain that you include all the groups that require access to that user right. Rights defined within a GPO override the local settings; they do not merge with them. Also be aware that because the GPO affects all servers within the organizational unit, you need to assign permissions based on the domain groups and not the local groups of a specific server. As I discussed in Chapter 15, this is an exception to the general rule of assigning permissions based on local groups. Because GPOs are defined at the domain level, domain-level groups must be used. Figure 16.16 shows an example of User Rights Assignment policies defined within a Terminal Server Machine Policy for the Terminal Servers OU in a Windows 20003 domain.

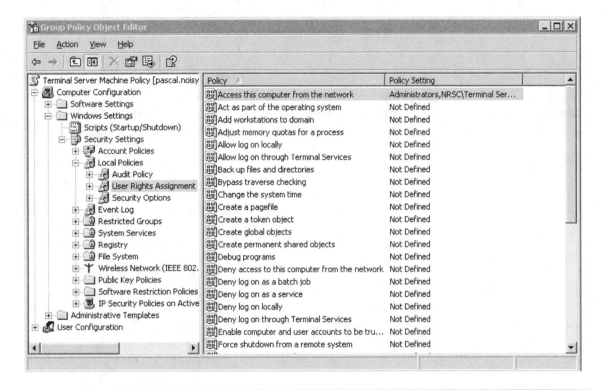

Figure 16.16 A User Rights Assignment policies example in a Windows 2003 Active Directory domain.

Table 16.4 lists the user rights for both Windows 2000 and 2003 that most directly pertain to a Terminal Server. A complete explanation of each of the Windows 2000 user rights can be found in the Group Policy Reference included in the Windows 2000 Resource Kit documentation. An explanation of the Windows 2003 user rights can be found simply by right-clicking the desired user right and selecting Help.

Table 16.4   Terminal Server–related User Rights Assignment Policies for Windows 2000 and 2003

Windows Server 2003	Windows 2000	Explanation
Access this computer from the network.	Access this computer from the network.	This right is not required for a user to be able to establish a Terminal Server session. This right is required only if you will be sharing folders or printers off the Terminal Server. The default group assignments can be limited to only Administrators if no file or print sharing is required.
Deny access to this computer from the network.	Deny access to this computer from the network.	Members of this group are explicitly denied access to network resources on this server. The Deny property overrides any other permissions that might be assigned.
Allow log on locally.	Log on locally.	This right is required for a user to be able to interactively log on to the server. On a Windows 2000 server this right is required to be able to log on to a Terminal Server session. On a Windows 2003 Terminal Server this right is required only when logging on directly from the server console. Omitting or denying this user right does not prevent a user from being able to establish a Windows 2003 Terminal Server session as long as they possess the "Allow log on through Terminal Services" privilege.
Allow log on through Terminal Services.	Log on locally.	To establish a Terminal Server session a user must have this user right. Without it a user receives the message "The local policy of this system does not permit you to logon interactively" immediately after providing their logon credentials.

WARNING: Use caution when modifying the default User Rights Assignment policy for a Terminal Server. Incorrectly restricting the rights can adversely affect server operability.

Local Security Options

Windows local Security Options policies allow an administrator to configure additional machine-specific security settings. As with local User Rights Assignment policies, it is recommended that changes to the local Security Options policies be performed within the Terminal Server Machine Policy and not directly on the individual Terminal Servers. Table 16.5 lists the changes I suggest making to local Security Options policies for your production Terminal Servers.

Table 16.5 Suggested Local Security Options Policies Changes for a Windows Terminal Server Environment

Windows Server 2003	Windows 2000 Server	Explanation
Accounts: Guest account status.	N/A	(W2K3 only.) Controls whether the local Guest account is enabled or disabled. While it is disabled by default, enforcing the disabled status for the Guest account is always a good security practice.
Accounts: Rename administrator account.	Rename administrator account.	Lets you define an alternate name for the local Administrators account. This simple change makes it more difficult for someone to guess the administrator's password, since they won't even know what the local administrator's account name is. Be sure to select an alternate name you can remember but is not immediately obvious to a would-be hacker. This option is disabled by default.

Table 16.5   Suggested Local Security Options Policies Changes for a Windows
Terminal Server Environment (continued)

Windows Server 2003	Windows 2000 Server	Explanation
Accounts: Rename guest account.	Rename guest account.	Even though it's disabled, renaming the Guest account to something more obscure is a good security practice.
Devices: Prevent users from installing printer drivers.	Prevent users from installing printer drivers.	Enabled by default on all Windows servers. On a Terminal Server in particular you do not want users to have the ability to arbitrarily install printer drivers when connecting to a network printer. While most Windows 2000/2003 printer drivers work without issue on a Terminal Server, it is still best if an administrator monitors what drivers are and are not available to the users. A single ill-behaved printer driver can easily cause a Terminal Server to crash with a STOP error (blue screen of death).
Interactive logon: Do not display last user name.	Do not display last user name in logon screen.	When an RDP session is initiated to a Terminal Server, the logon screen automatically displays the name of the last user to log on to that server from that particular client machine. Enabling this security option eliminates this behavior. The ICA client never displays the name of the last user to log on, and as such this option has no effect on the ICA client's behavior.

Administrative Templates

In Chapter 15, I discussed use of administrative templates and how they provide a centralized mechanism for applying behavioral changes and restrictions to both the target computers in the organizational unit and the users who log on to those computers. Both Windows 2000 and 2003 provide a set of standard administrative templates that include a number of security-related options. Windows Server 2003 includes new template options as well as updated naming for many of the options found in Windows 2000 Server. Because of this, I divide my policy suggestions into two separate tables. Table 16.6 lists suggested security settings for Windows 2000, while Table 16.7 lists my equivalent settings for Windows 2003. These suggestions have been subdivided based on the group policy object they should be applied in. The categories used are Terminal Server All Users Policy, Terminal Server Regular Users Policy, and Terminal Server Machine Policy. These tables list only Windows system-specific changes and no application-related settings that may pertain to a Terminal Server environment. These types of changes are discussed in the later section "Application Privileges and Restrictions."

TIP: As I discussed in Chapter 15, customized or third-party administrative templates can be added to the active directory, allowing for the centralized management of applications or additional Windows components. Applications such as Microsoft Office support extensive configuration via administrative templates. You can also create your own custom .ADM files. General information on creation of custom administrative templates can be found in Microsoft knowledgebase article 323639.

Table 16.6   Windows 2000 Administrative Template Security Suggestions

Administrative Templates Policy	GPO Affected	Explanation
Start Menu & Taskbar	Terminal Server All Users	
Add Logoff to the Start Menu.		This ensures that all users have the Logoff <UserName> option on the Start menu.
Disable and remove the shutdown command.		This option makes it more difficult for even an administrator to accidentally shutdown a Terminal Server. On more than one occasion I've witnessed an administrator accidentally select Shutdown instead of logoff and acknowledge the action before they even know they've done so. An administrator can still shutdown a server by using the TSSHUTDN command from a command prompt.

Table 16.6   Windows 2000 Administrative Template Security Suggestions (continued)

Administrative Templates Policy	GPO Affected	Explanation
Windows Components\ Windows Explorer	Terminal Server All Users	
Only allow approved Shell extensions.		This setting ensures that only those Shell extensions approved by an administrator are allowed to load when Explorer starts.
Windows Components\ Windows Explorer	Terminal Server Regular Users	
Hide the Manage item on the Windows Explorer context menu.		Removes the Manage item from Explorer and My Computer. If the MMC snap-in access has been prohibited (see Microsoft Management Console later in this table), this menu item has no effect on regular users, but I like to completely remove it as part of my standard configuration.
Hide Hardware tab.		This setting removes the Hardware tab from all local drives on the server, preventing users from being able to see what hardware is being used for hard drives, CD-ROM drives, and so on.
Disable DFS tab.		When a user has a drive mapping to a distributed file system (DFS) share, the DFS tab is available on the Properties dialog box. This option disables access to this tab, preventing users from seeing the available physical locations for the particular DFS share point.
Windows Components\ Microsoft Management Console\	Terminal Server Regular Users	
Restrict users to the explicitly permitted list of snap-ins.		Enabling this policy prohibits all regular users from accessing any MMC snap-in.

Table 16.6   Windows 2000 Administrative Template Security Suggestions (continued)

Administrative Templates Policy	GPO Affected	Explanation
Start Menu & Taskbar	Terminal Server Regular Users	
Disable and remove links to Windows Update.		Removes the link to Windows Update from the Start menu and prevents the users from accessing the Windows Update Web site.
Remove Network & Dial-up Connections from Start Menu.		Completely removes access to the Network & Dial-up Connections folder, preventing users from finding out specific details about the server's network configuration.
Remove Run menu from Start Menu.		Eliminating this option from the Start menu prevents users from quickly launching an application by name. This policy does not prevent users from starting applications present on the Start menu or double-clicking them through Windows Explorer.
Disable user tracking.		Windows enhances the user's work experience by tracking user-specific information such as what applications they commonly run, the documents they open, and so on. Disabling this option turns off this tracking feature.
Desktop	Terminal Server Regular Users	
Remove Properties from the My Computer context menu.		Disables access to the System Properties dialog box for the My Computer icon. This dialog box provides general access to information such as available memory, CPU type, and operating system version.
Prohibit users from changing My Documents path.		If you redirected the My Documents folder for your users, you must implement this policy. Normally users have the ability to change their My Documents path, and allowing such access could result in users storing sensitive documents in a location where they may be easily accessible by others or omitted from the regular backup process. Enabling this policy does not affect use of the folder redirection policy.

Table 16.6   Windows 2000 Administrative Template Security Suggestions (Continued)

Administrative Templates Policy	GPO Affected	Explanation
Desktop\Active Desktop	Terminal Server Regular Users	
Disable Active Desktop.		In addition to providing a performance improvement, this policy increases security by preventing Web-based content from being enabled directly on the user's desktop.
Control Panel	Terminal Server Regular Users	
Show only specified control panel applets.		If users require access to one or more control panel applets, only those specific options should be made available and all other entries suppressed. Usually I provide users with access to only the Display applet so they have access to make minor changes to their visual desktop experience. The specific applet file name is DESK.CPL.
Control Panel\Add/ Remove Programs	Terminal Server Regular Users	
Disable Add/ Remove Programs.		This option completely eliminates access for all regular users to the Add/Remove Program option.
Control Panel\Display	Terminal Server Regular Users	
Hide Screen Saver tab.		Very often, users try to run custom screen savers without realizing they not only consume available system resources but also can pose a security risk. Removing access to the Screen Saver tab prevents users from easily configuring and activating screen savers. It does not prevent a user from directly executing a screensaver file (*.scr) that he or she may have acquired through email or a Web site.

Table 16.6   Windows 2000 Administrative Template Security Suggestions (Continued)

Administrative Templates Policy	GPO Affected	Explanation
Network\Offline Files	Terminal Server Regular Users	
Disable user configuration of Offline Files.		Completely removes the user's ability to modify the Offline Files menu option. Offline files in general can pose a security risk by making files available in a location that may not be secure.
Disable 'Make Available Offline'.		Turns off the ability to make files or folders available offline.
Network\Network and Dial-up Connections.	Terminal Server Regular Users	
Prohibit access to properties of a LAN connection.		While users typically do not have access to modify the properties for a LAN connection, by default they can still view network configuration options. Enforcing this policy prevents access to this information.
Prohibit viewing of status statistics for an active connection.		Users do not require access to the statistics for a LAN connection. These statistics provide information such as link speed and connection uptime. The properties for the LAN connection are also directly accessible from here.
System	Terminal Server Regular Users	
Disable the command prompt.		Enabling this policy prevents users from directly launching a command prompt while still allowing scripts (logon, startup, and so on) to be processed.
Disable registry editing tools.		When enabled, this policy prevents users from being able to run the registry tools REGEDIT and REGEDT32. Users can still update the registry by directly running valid .REG files, but interactive traversal of the registry through either tool is not permitted.

Table 16.6   Windows 2000 Administrative Template Security Suggestions (continued)

Administrative Templates Policy	GPO Affected	Explanation
		To effectively limit what applications a user can run on a Terminal Server, the policy "Run only allowed Windows applications" should be enabled and configured. I discuss configuration steps for this policy in the later section "Application Privileges and Restrictions."
System\Logon/Logoff	Terminal Server Regular Users	
Disable Task Manager		Prevents users from viewing their running processes as well as seeing the current performance statistics for the server.

TIP: Windows Server 2003 administrative templates provide extensive support for many of the Terminal Services options normally configured through the Terminal Services Configuration utility. Unless otherwise stated, any Terminal Server client-related settings defined in a Windows 2003 administrative template apply to only RDP connections. Citrix ICA (MetaFrame) connections are not affected by most of these group policies.

Table 16.7   Windows 2003 Administrative Template Security Suggestions

Administrative Templates Policy	GPO Affected	Explanation
Windows Components\Internet Information Services	Terminal Server Machine Policy	
Prevent IIS Installation.		This policy is intended to prevent an administrator from installing IIS or any applications that require IIS.

Table 16.7   Windows 2003 Administrative Template Security Suggestions   (continued)

Administrative Templates Policy	GPO Affected	Explanation
Windows Components\ Terminal Services	Terminal Server Machine Policy	
Restrict Terminal Services users to a single remote session.		This policy limits a user to a single active Terminal Server session and is enabled by default on all Windows 2003 Terminal Servers. Note that it is applied on a perserver basis and does not restrict a user from having active simultaneous sessions on different Terminal Servers.
Limit number of connections.		This sets the maximum number of concurrent connections supported on the server. Enabling this policy in conjunction with the previous policy helps protect a Terminal Server against a crude denial-of-service attack performed by logging on to the server with the same user continuously until all server resources are exhausted. The maximum number of connections should be set to match the maximum number of users supported by your server-sizing estimate.
Sets rules for remote control of Terminal Services user sessions.		As I discussed in Chapter 8, remote control allows an administrator (or other authorized user) to connect into a user's session and interact with the environment. This policy lets you configure the rules for remote control on each Terminal Server. There are four choices available: ■ *No remote control allowed at all.* This feature is completely disabled. In highly secure environments where even an administrator should not be able to view a user's session, this option may be selected.

Table 16.7 Windows 2003 Administrative Template Security Suggestions

Administrative Templates Policy	GPO Affected	Explanation
		■ *Full control with user's permission.* I recommend this option for most implementations. A user must explicitly grant an administrator access before they can control the user's session. This ensures an administrator cannot remotely control a user's session without the user's knowledge. ■ *Full control without user's permission.* This option can introduce a security risk as an authorized user could shadow another user, manipulate their session, and then exit without the user even knowing. One way to counteract this would be to proactively monitor audit logs for shadowing. I do not recommend selecting this option for the remote control configuration. ■ *View session with/without user's permission.* Similar to the previous two entries except that the administrator shadowing the user cannot interact with the user's session in any way but can only view what the user is doing.
Windows Components\Terminal Services\Client/Server data redirection	Terminal Server Machine Policy	These policies control the behavior of various data redirection options supported by Windows 2003 Terminal Services. The requirements of your implementation will dictate what redirection options will be used. It is good practice to disallow all options not required. For example, if client drive redirection is not required, the associated policy "Do not allow drive redirection" should be explicitly enabled to prevent this client drive mapping for any remote user.

Table 16.7   Windows 2003 Administrative Template Security Suggestions (continued)

Administrative Templates Policy	GPO Affected	Explanation
Windows Components\Terminal Services\Encryption and Security	Terminal Server Machine Policy	
Always prompt client for password upon connection.		The RDP client supports entry and caching of a user's password so it can be automatically passed to the server to log the user on. Enabling this policy causes the Terminal Server to ignore any password passed by the client and instead always prompts the user to provide their password.
Set client connection encryption level.		The minimum encryption level required by an RDP client connecting to a Windows 2003 Terminal Server is set to High by default, but you can ensure this option isn't changed by enabling this policy and selecting High Level.
Windows Components\ Windows Explorer	Terminal Server All Users	
Allow only per user or approved shell extensions.		This setting ensures that only those shell extensions that have been approved by an administrator or run only for a single user are allowed to load when Explorer starts.
Start Menu & Taskbar	Terminal Server All Users	
Add Logoff to the Start Menu.		This ensures that all users have the Logoff <UserName> option on the Start menu.
Remove and prevent access to the Shut Down command.		This option makes it more difficult for even an administrator to accidentally shut down a Terminal Server. On more than one occasion I've witnessed an administrator accidentally select Shutdown instead of Logoff and acknowledge the action before they even know they've done so. An administrator can still shut down a server by using the TSSHUTDN command from a command prompt.

Table 16.7 Windows 2003 Administrative Template Security Suggestions (continued)

Administrative Templates Policy	GPO Affected	Explanation
Windows Components\ Windows Explorer	Terminal Server Regular Users	
Hide the Manage item on the Windows Explorer context menu.		Removes the Manage item from Explorer and My Computer. If the MMC snap-in access has been prohibited (see Microsoft Management Console later in this table), this menu item has no effect on regular users, but I like to completely remove it as part of my standard configuration.
Remove Hardware tab.		This setting removes the Hardware tab from all local drives on the server, preventing users from being able to see what hardware is being used for hard drives, CD-ROM drives, and so on.
Remove DFS tab.		When a user has a drive mapping to a DFS share, the DFS tab is available on the Properties dialog box. This option disables access to this tab, preventing users from seeing the available physical locations for the particular DFS share point.
Windows Components\ Microsoft Management Console\	Terminal Server Regular Users	
Restrict users to the explicitly permitted list of snap-ins.		Enabling this policy prohibits all regular users from accessing any MMC snap-in. Be aware that you may need to add specific snap-ins to the permitted list within Terminal Server User Support Policy.
Start Menu & Taskbar	Terminal Server Regular Users	
Disable links and access to Windows Update.		Removes the link to Windows Update from the Start menu and prevents the users from accessing the Windows Update Web site.
Remove Network Connections from Start Menu.		Completely removes access to the Network Connections folder, preventing users from finding out specific details about the server's network configuration.

Table 16.7 Windows 2003 Administrative Template Security Suggestions (continued)

Administrative Templates Policy	GPO Affected	Explanation
Remove Run menu from Start Menu.		Eliminating this option from the Start menu prevents users from quickly launching an application by name. This policy does not prevent users from starting applications present on the Start menu or double-clicking them through Windows Explorer. The ability to launch programs or navigate folders through the Internet Explorer address bar is blocked.
Turn off user tracking.		Windows enhances the user's work experience by tracking user-specific information such as what applications they commonly run, the documents they open, and so on. Disabling this option turns off this tracking feature.
Desktop	Terminal Server Regular Users	
Remove Properties from the My Computer context menu.		Disables access to the System Properties dialog box for the My Computer icon. This dialog box provides general access to information such as available memory, CPU type, and operating system version.
Prohibit user from changing My Documents path.		If you redirected the My Documents folder for your users, you must implement this policy. Normally users have the ability to change their My Documents path, and allowing such access could result in users storing sensitive documents in a location where they may be easily accessible by others or omitted from the regular backup process. Enabling this policy does not affect use of the folder redirection policy.
Desktop\Active Desktop	Terminal Server Regular Users	
Disable Active Desktop.		In addition to providing a performance improvement, this option increases security by preventing Web-based content from being enabled directly on the user's desktop.

Table 16.7   Windows 2003 Administrative Template Security Suggestions (continued)

Administrative Templates Policy	GPO Affected	Explanation
Control Panel	Terminal Server Regular Users	
Show only specified control panel applets.		If users require access to one or more control panel applets, only those specific options should be made available and all other entries suppressed. Usually I provide users with access to only the Display applet so they have access to make minor changes to their visual desktop experience. The specific applet file name is DESK.CPL.
Control Panel\Add/ Remove Programs	Terminal Server Regular Users	
Remove Add or Remove Programs.		This option completely eliminates access for all regular users to the Add/Remove Program option.
Control Panel\Display	Terminal Server Regular Users	
Hide Screen Saver tab.		Very often, users try to run custom screen savers without realizing they not only consume available system resources but also can pose a security risk. Removing access to the Screen Saver tab prevents users from easily configuring and activating screen savers.
Control Panel\Display\ Desktop Themes	Terminal Server Regular Users	
Remove Theme option.		Completely removes the Themes tab from the Display dialog box.
Network\Offline Files	Terminal Server Regular Users	
Prohibit user configuration of Offline Files.		Completely removes the user's ability to modify the Offline Files menu option. Offline files in general can pose a security risk by making files available in a location that may not be secure.

Table 16.7   Windows 2003 Administrative Template Security Suggestions (continued)

Administrative Templates Policy	GPO Affected	Explanation
Remove 'Make Available Offline'.		Turns off the ability to make files or folders available offline.
Network\Network Connections	Terminal Server Regular Users	
Prohibit access to properties of a LAN connection.		While users typically do not have access to modify the properties for a LAN connection, by default they can still view network configuration options. Enforcing this policy prevents access to this information.
Prohibit viewing of status statistics for an active connection.		Users do not require access to the statistics for a LAN connection. These statistics provide information such as link speed and connection uptime. The properties for the LAN connection are also directly accessible from here.
System	Terminal Server Regular Users	
Prevent access to the command prompt.		Enabling this policy prevents users from directly launching a command prompt while still allowing scripts (logon, startup, and so on) to be processed. While the stability of this option has improved over earlier versions of Windows Terminal Services, anomalies with certain applications that rely on access to a command prompt may exist. Proper testing is very important when this policy has been enabled.
Prevent access to registry editing tools.		When enabled, this policy prevents users from being able to run the registry tools REGEDIT and REGEDT32. Users can still update the registry by directly running valid .REG files, but interactive traversal of the registry through either tool is not permitted.

Table 16.7   Windows 2003 Administrative Template Security Suggestions (continued)

Administrative Templates Policy	GPO Affected	Explanation
		To effectively limit what applications a user can run on a Terminal Server, the policy "Run only allowed Windows applications" should be enabled and configured. I discuss configuration steps for this policy in the later section "Application Privileges and Restrictions."
System\Ctrl+Alt+Del Options	Terminal Server Regular Users	
Remove Task Manager.		Prevents users from viewing their running processes as well as seeing the current performance statistics for the server.

File and Registry Restrictions

Chapter 8 discussed the file and registry security configuration on a Windows 2000/2003 Terminal Server and how they are both more secure when the Permission Compatibility option is set to Full Security on a Windows 2003 Terminal Server and set to Permissions Compatible with Windows 2000 Users on a Windows 2000 Terminal Server. Figure 16.17 shows the Permission Compatibility dialog box from within the Windows 2003 Terminal Services Configuration utility.

File Security Permissions

In Chapter 8 I talked about the following four general rules for file server security:

1. *Divide the server's storage into at least two logical drives.* For my discussions in this chapter I assume that the server drives are X: for the system drive and Y: for the application drive.
2. *When assigning permissions, restrict access to read-only and then grant or revoke permissions as required.* When Permission Compatibility has been set to Full Security, as just discussed, the file system for the most part is already secure. There is one major change required on a Windows 2000 Terminal Server, which is discussed later in this section.
3. *Script security changes so they're reproducible.* File permission changes can be easily scripted using the CACLS command line file security utility that is included with both Windows 2000 and 2003.

4. *Be certain to implement all file security prior to installing any applications onto the Terminal Server.* I discuss suggested default security settings for the application drive immediately after the system drive discussion. Security-related issues with application installation and execution are discussed in more detail in Chapter 21, "Application Integration."

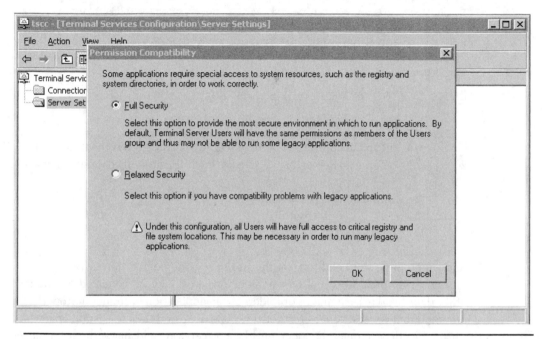

Figure 16.17 The Windows 2003 Terminal Services Permission Compatibility dialog box.

On a Windows 2003 Terminal Server the default file system permissions provided with the Full Security option provide a suitable security configuration for the system drive. No custom changes are necessary unless you want to be very restrictive in folders and executables accessible by your Terminal Server users. A Windows 2000 Terminal Server, even with the Permissions Compatible with Windows 2000 Users option set, requires one rather significant change to the permissions on the root of the system drive in order to properly secure the volume.

During installation of Windows 2000, the Everyone group is assigned Full Control access to the root of the system drive by default. On a Terminal Server this configuration is unacceptable because it lets a regular user add files or folders to the root of the system drive, which in turn can potentially cause stability- or security-related issues. This can be corrected by assigning the following permissions to the root of the system drive only:

- Administrators (Full Control)
- SYSTEM (Full Control)
- Users (Read)

These permissions should *not* be propagated to all subfolders but instead should be applied to only the root of the drive. The following simple CACLS script demonstrates how this type of configuration can be scripted for reuse on all Windows 2000 Terminal Servers in the environment.

```
@ECHO OFF
ECHO Setting security permissions on system volume. Please wait...

REM ** Grant local Administrators and SYSTEM Full Control
REM ** Grant local Users READ access to the root of the system
volume.

CACLS X:\ /c /g Administrators:F SYSTEM:F Users:R
```

Configuring the initial application-volume security permissions is the same for both Windows 2000 and 2003 Terminal Server. I always set the initial application volume permissions as follows:

- Administrators (Full Control)
- SYSTEM (Full Control)
- Users (Read)

As I mentioned, you need to treat this as the starting point when installing the applications into your Terminal Server. In some situations, you may be required to grant permissions other than Read to certain files or folders for an application to function properly. I always recommend that you start out as restrictively as possible and then loosen up only when required. Make sure that you clearly document these exceptions and place them into a script so the changes can be reapplied if necessary. The following script can be used to assign the default permissions on the application volume.

```
@ECHO OFF
ECHO Setting security permissions on application volume. Please
wait...

REM ** Grant local Administrators and SYSTEM Full Control
REM ** Grant local Users READ access to the entire volume.
REM ** Permissions should be adjusted on specific applications if
necessary.

CACLS Y:\ /T /c /g Administrators:F SYSTEM:F Users:R
ECHO y|CACLS Y:\* /T /c /g Administrators:F SYSTEM:F Users:R

REM ** Application-specific changes should be appended below.
```

NOTE: If you have implemented a separate pagefile drive on your server, you should assign the same default permissions to this volume as you've assigned your application volume, otherwise users will have unrestricted access to write data to this drive, which in turn can cause security or stability issues.

Registry Security Permissions

While the registry's security requirements are similar to those of the file system, the process of assigning security in the registry can be much more difficult. The problem is that in certain situations an application can have a legitimate reason for writing to the registry. Fortunately, most applications available today are adhering to the standard of writing machine-specific information to the HKEY_LOCAL_MACHINE key (normally done during installation) while maintaining user-specific information in the user's personal profile (HKEY_CURRENT_USER). By default, users have write access to their personal registry but not to HKEY_LOCAL_MACHINE.

If the Full Security option is not enabled, users gain additional write privileges within the registry that they normally do not have. These permissions have been granted to the special Terminal Server Users group, which is automatically assigned to Terminal Server users when legacy application support has been enabled by reducing the Terminal Server security configuration. As long as the Windows 2000 or 2003 Terminal Server is using full security, the default registry permissions do not need to be modified to support the multiuser environment.

Another part of proper registry security is restricting access to the Registry Editor tools (RECEDIT and REGEDT32). The group policy change that should be made to restrict access to these tools was discussed in the "Administrative Templates" section, earlier in this chapter. When this change is implemented, if a user attempts to launch a Windows registry tool a message similar to the one shown in Figure 16.18 appears.

Figure 16.18 The message that appears when Registry Editor tool restrictions have been implemented on a Windows 2000 Terminal Server.

Application Privileges and Restrictions

Application security can be broken down into two categories. The first deals with managing user access to only those applications they are required to use, and the second deals with controlling what options and functionality within an application are available to different users. The extent to which you need to manage both categories depends on the requirements of your implementation. If you run a large number of applications on your servers, it is likely you will need to limit access to one or more of these applications (or functionality within these applications) based on security, licensing, or performance requirements.

NOTE: Two separate Terminal Server audits I performed easily demonstrate how different organizations can view application security. In both cases, one finding was that all applications remained accessible to all users on the server.

For one administrator this came as no surprise and had been left as such simply because all Terminal Server users accessed the same group of applications, and highly sensitive data was not accessed through their Terminal Server implementation.

For the other administrator it was a completely different story. Application segregation was supposed to have been implemented prior to this team's inheriting the Terminal Server environment, and the lack of any proper controls was a major concern because sensitive sales and customer information was easily accessible to any user interested and determined enough to search for it.

Application Access Restrictions

In a Terminal Server environment, application access is usually managed in one of two ways:

- **Restricting application access**—The most common method of access management is to assume that all Terminal Server users have access to all applications on the server, and only those applications that require limited access are restricted through special application security groups.

  This implementation is commonly used simply because this is the default behavior of Windows. When an application is installed on a Windows Terminal Server, by default it is accessible to all users unless access restrictions are defined at the file system level, the application level, or both. For example, an inventory management system may be installed on a Terminal Server and all users can launch the application and reach the logon prompt, but only those users authorized to actually access the application have a valid user ID and password.

■ **Granting application access**—The alternate application access method assumes that users have no access to any of the applications on the server unless such access has been explicitly granted. Not only is this management method the more restrictive of the two, but it also takes much more work up front to configure properly and can quickly become cumbersome, particularly when a large number of applications are involved. One benefit to being so restrictive is that users are not automatically able to run new applications introduced onto the server; this as a result helps guard against rogue applications being introduced via e-mail or download.

While the second option is certainly more appealing from a security perspective, trying to manage multiple application access lists for different groups of users can quickly become overwhelming. The best approach to restricting application access is to implement a combination of the two access methods. By combining the two, you still enjoy the additional security benefits of explicitly defining what executables a user can run while minimizing the time required to manage such an implementation.

When combining the two, the first task is to establish a list of all applications users are authorized to run. Specific items on the list are then restricted further, accessible only to the subset of users authorized to run those specific applications. For example, a typical application access list for a Terminal Server user might look like the one shown in Table 16.8. A single application access list is created, but then only users belonging to the appropriate groups can access the Inventory Management or Customer Billing programs.

Table 16.8   A Windows Terminal Server Application Access List Example

Application	Notes
Microsoft Word Microsoft Excel Microsoft Outlook Custom Time-Tracking App	These applications are available to all users and not restricted based on group membership.
Inventory Management	This application is available only to members of the APP_Inventory_Mgr group.
Customer Billing	This application is available only to members of the APP_Cust_Billing group.

How you approach the restriction of application access will depend on the version of Windows that you are running and how tightly you wish to enforce these restrictions. The three different methods of locking down application access that I will discuss are:

- The "Run only allowed Windows Applications" group policy object. This GPO allows you to manage a list of allowed Windows applications that can be executed by users affected by the policy. Usually the policy is applied to all non-administrative users logged on to a Terminal Server. The one limitation of this policy is that it does not track applications based on their full path, only their application name. This creates the situation where a user could execute any desired application, simply by changing the application's name to be the same as an application that is authorized to run.

- The APPSEC security utility. This tool, available as part of the Windows 2000 Server Resource Kit allows you to define a list of allowed applications, much like the "Run only allowed Windows Applications" group policy. The three main differences between this utility and the GPO are:

  - All non-administrator users are affected by this application's restrictions. There is no way to limit the access based on a particular security group.
  - Only application executables that reside on a server's physical drive can be executed. Any attempt to launch a network-based executable will fail.
  - The listed applications must reside with the specific path specified for that application. Attempting to run a listed application from any other location will fail.

  These differences greatly increase the effectiveness of the APPSEC utility to more tightly secure an environment when compared to the "Run only allowed Windows Applications" GPO.

- Windows Server 2003 does not support the APPSEC security utility. Instead it has introduced the "Software restriction policies," a much more robust version of the "Run only allowed Windows Applications" GPO. This GPO allows for the following:

  - Determine whether the default behavior of the GPO is to allow applications to execute based on the access rights of the user, or to restrict access to all executables regardless of access rights.
  - Applications to be allowed or restricted can be identified by a binary hash that is calculated, a certificate or a file system path or Internet security zone. These choices allowing for the clear identification of the authorized executable while still allow flexibility in how it is located and run.
  - Entire folders can also be managed, allowing all applications within those folders to be assigned restricted or unrestricted application execution access.

I will now take a brief look at each of these three choices.

Run Only Allowed Windows Applications Group Policy Object

Through use of a group policy object, Windows provides the ability to limit a user's access to only those applications explicitly defined for that user. The specific GPO is located under

User Configuration\Administrative Templates\System

and is called "Run only allowed Windows applications." Typically this particular policy can be defined as part of the Terminal Server Regular Users GPO, so it is applied to all non-administrative users logged on to a Terminal Server. Figure 16.19 shows the dialog box for this policy in a Windows 2003 domain. The applications are added by clicking the Show button and entering the corresponding *executable name*.

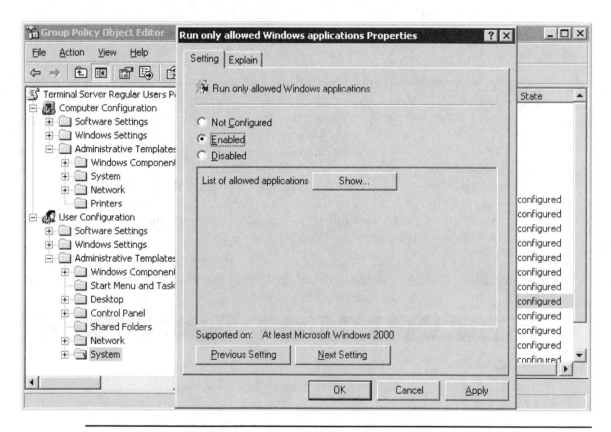

Figure 16.19 The Run Only Allowed Windows Applications Properties dialog box.

For a user to be able to properly work within a Terminal Server session, you must be certain that you include *all* the necessary executables the user will need to run. When a user attempts to run an application not included in the list, they receive an error message similar to the one in Figure 16.20.

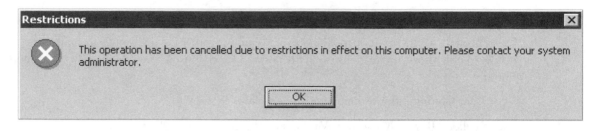

Figure 16.20   Attempting to access an application not authorized results in this message.

Contrary to what you might think, you are not required to list any of the core Windows components required for a user to be able to log on, such as winlogon.exe, wfshell.exe, or explorer.exe. This is because the application list applies only to launching programs through Windows Explorer. Applications launched directly from the system or through a command prompt are not controlled by this policy. If you restricted the user's ability to access the command prompt, they cannot circumvent Explorer to launch applications directly. If you enable this policy but include no applications in the list, the user still can log on to the server but once logged on cannot launch any applications.

Table 16.9 shows an actual executable list taken from a Terminal Server implementation where users were restricted to running only the listed applications. Note that this list also includes a batch script. If you provide users with an application shortcut that launches a batch script that in turn launches an executable, you must include the batch script name in the authorized application list or it will fail to launch. The name of the executable itself is not required because it is launched from within the batch script.

Table 16.9   Sample Listing of Allowed Application Executable Names Taken from an Actual Terminal Server Implementation

Executable Name	Application Name	Notes
Excel.exe	Microsoft Excel	
Iexplore.exe	Internet Explorer	

Table 16.9 Sample Listing of Allowed Application Executable Names Taken from an Actual Terminal Server Implementation (continued)

Executable Name	Application Name	Notes
Notes.cmd	Custom batch script to launch Lotus Notes	This batch script performs some configuration prior to starting Lotus Notes. Note that the script name is included in the executable list but not the actual Notes executable. This is because the executable is launched from within the CMD session initiated by the batch script and is not controlled by this application access list.
Osa.exe	Microsoft Office Startup Assistant	This is provided with Office XP and initializes a number of shared Office components for use. It is normally found in the Startup folder.
Outlook.exe	Microsoft Outlook	
PN.exe	Citrix Program Neighborhood	If you're going to allow users to access published applications available on different servers through a Terminal Server session, then PN.exe must be made available. This is required only when using the ICA passthrough client. If users are launching published applications directly from their local PC desktop, this executable does not need to be included in the list.
Powerpnt.exe	Microsoft PowerPoint	
Winword.exe	Microsoft Word	

Once the list of all allowable applications has been defined and implemented, access to these applications can be further restricted using security groups if necessary. For example, if access to Microsoft PowerPoint was to be limited to only a few individuals, then a group could be created (for example, APP_TS_PowerPoint_Users) and used to define security on the PowerPoint executable. Any users not belonging to this group who attempted to run PowerPoint would receive an access-denied message.

TIP: Whenever a Terminal Server implementation calls for restriction of access to one or more applications, it can be less confusing to the user if the Start menu has been organized in such a way that applications they cannot access are segregated and, ideally, not even visible. Common applications accessible by all users are usually located under the main portion of the Start menu, while restricted applications available to only a limited number of users are located in subfolders with labels such as "Customer Service Managers" and "Order Desk Sales Reps." The permissions on these subfolders are set to grant read access to only those users authorized to run the applications they contain, so when other users click the subfolder it appears empty, as shown in Figure 16.21.

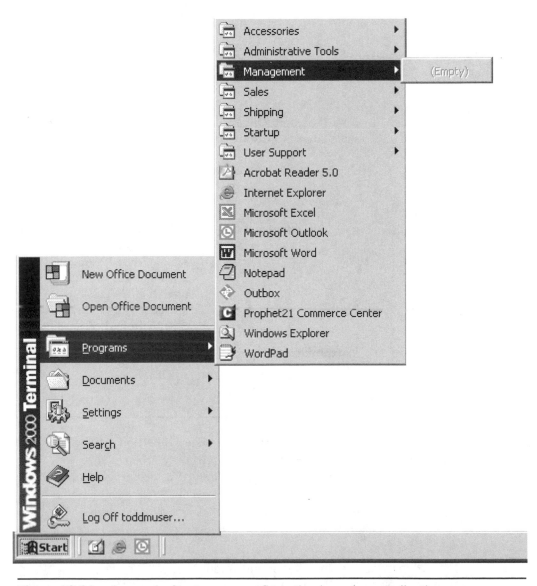

Figure 16.21   A sample Start menu configuration based on application access restrictions.

The APPSEC Security Utility

Before running the APPSEC utility you must download the appropriate installation files from the Microsoft Web site and install APPSEC on your Terminal Server. The version of APPSEC that ships with the Windows 2000 Server Resource Kit will not function properly as it is missing some necessary system files. The APPSEC.ZIP file can be downloaded from the Microsoft FTP site at: ftp://ftp.microsoft.com/reskit/win2000/

Once downloaded, extract the contents into a temporary folder and then run InstAppSec to install the tool.

The APPSEC security utility is launched by running APPSEC from a command prompt or using the Run command on the start menu. Once started, the main APPSEC application window will appear as shown in Figure 16.22. The application automatically includes a set of applications required for a user to be able to log onto the server. By default the APPSEC utility will be disabled until explicitly enabled by an administrator.

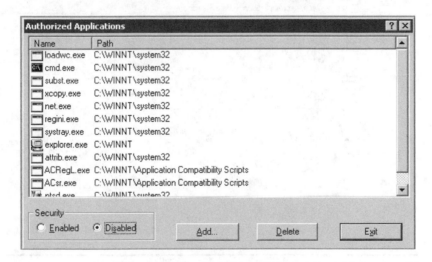

Figure 16.22   The APPSEC Windows 2000 application security utility.

Once APPSEC has been enabled, the settings will immediately be applied to any new user session logons. Users currently logged onto the server will not pickup these changes until they have logged out and back into the server. APPSEC settings apply only to regular users and will never restrict anyone with administrative privileges. When a user attempts to run an application not in the list they will receive an error message stating that "Access to the specified device, path or file is denied."

Adding and removing applications from the list are very straightforward and performed by selecting the desired option. When adding new applications to the list, there is an option available to "track" the results of running a particular application (Figure 16.23). Tracking allows an administrator to run an application while APPSEC monitors and adds any associated executables to the list. This helps to ensure that a particular program has all of the necessary components in order to work properly.

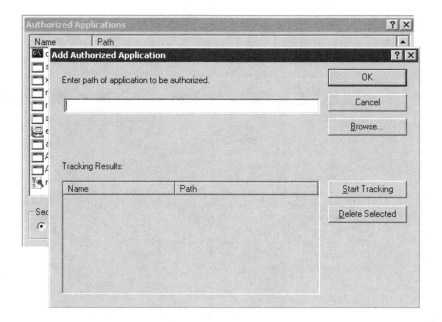

Figure 16.23 The APPSEC utility provides a means of tracking any associated executables for an application to ensure they are all added to the allowed application list.

While APPSEC provides a very rudimentary interface, it can be a very powerful tool for securing a Windows 2000 Terminal Server environment.

Windows Server 2003 Software Restriction Policies

Windows Server 2003 provides the specific GPO for Software Restriction Policies, which can be found under

Windows Settings\Security Settings\Software Restriction Policies

By default this policy is not enabled and must be created by right-clicking Software Restriction Policies and selecting New Software Restriction Policies (SRP). Once selected the appropriate settings for the policy are created and available to be set as shown in Figure 16.24.

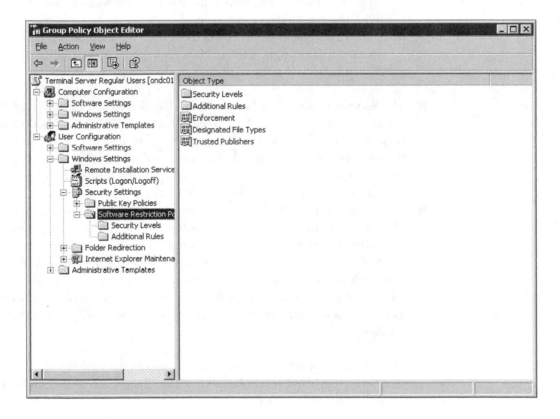

Figure 16.24 Software Security Policies in Windows Server 2003 replace the APPSEC tool.

The basic layout of the Software Restriction Policies is as follows:

■ Only one SRP is created for each GPO. After selecting New Software Restriction Policies, that option will no longer be available unless the existing SRP is deleted.

- Under the Software Restriction Policies folder, there are three attributes, which are

  - Enforcement—This setting dictates the general enforcement criteria for the policy. By default, it will restrict only executables (not executable libraries such as DLLs) and will apply to all users affected by the policy, including administrators.
  - Designated File Types—In addition to the standard executables files with the suffix EXE all of the file types listed here are assumed to represent executables and will be included in the software restrictions. File types can be added and removed on this screen.
  - Trusted Publishers—Defines whether or not the user has any control over what publishers will be trusted when presented with certificates that verify the authenticity of an application.

- The Security Levels folder has two items, Disallowed and Unrestricted. Only one of these items can be set as the default at any given time. When Disallowed is chosen, the policy enforces that no users will be able to run software, unless the software has been designed as an additional rule, which is discussed next. If the Unrestricted option is chosen, then all applications are accessible unless explicitly denied in the Additional Rules section.
- The Additional Rules folder is where the majority of the items will be managed. The purpose of this folder is to store either specific entries that are unrestricted or disallowed. Entries are added here simply by right-clicking and choosing the rule to define the entry. The four choices are Certificate Rule, Hash Rule, Internet Zone Rule and Path Rule. The most common select is Path Rule, allowing an administrator to provide an explicit path to a folder, executable file, or registry location. The security level for the rule dictates if the entry is unrestricted or disallowed.

In a Terminal Server deployment, the Software Restriction Policies are usually created within the Terminal Server Regular Users policy so that the changes are picked up by the non-administrative users in the environment.

Application Functionality Restrictions

In addition to allotting the desired application access to your various user groups, quite often you will want to control what options and functionality in an application are available to different users. The exact method by which these changes are performed (if they're even supported) will vary from application to application. Many provide their own integrated security based on a logon ID and password managed from within the program, while others such as Microsoft Office leverage functionality of group policy objects to allow customization based on group membership. When an application supports configuration changes using a GPO, the functionality is added into the active directory through what are know as *administrative template* files. Figure 16.25 shows the Add/Remove Templates submenu along with some of the Office XP templates already loaded into the Administrative Templates folder. Custom template files are usually stored in the WINNT\INF folder and have the extension ADM. More details on general installation and use of template files are provided in Chapter 15.

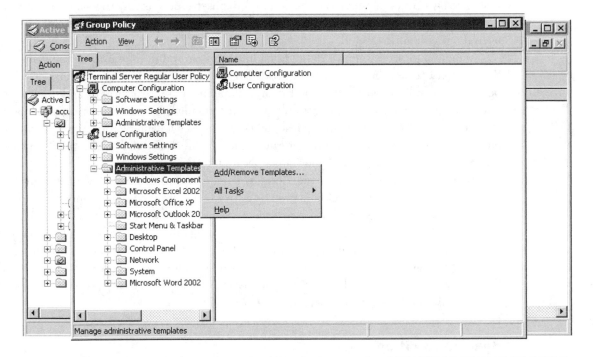

Figure 16.25   Custom and third-party administrative template files can be added to a group policy in the active directory.

As part of a complete security implementation, I recommend that whenever you have the opportunity to customize and/or lock down any of the applications you are implementing, you should do so. By pre-configuring options such as target data directories, turning off Web-based integration, or disabling automatic update features, you are simplifying the user's environment and reducing the exposed areas where potential security issues could develop. The fewer the number of customization options available to the end user, the less likely you are to have application-related issues in the environment. In Chapter 20, I look more closely at some of the configuration options available for Microsoft Office through administrative templates.

System Auditing

As I mentioned in Chapter 8, a secure environment not only consists of properly configured servers but also requires effective auditing to detect anomalies in application or user behavior. Auditing alone is of little value unless you also have a means of effectively monitoring these logs and flagging suspicious activity when it occurs. Unfortunately, most organizations are quick to implement the logging portion but rarely establish any effective method of monitoring these logs. As a result, the environment typically logs huge amounts of security information that is rarely ever even examined. The log files themselves are usually so small that information is quickly overwritten, eliminating any possibility of examining the security information even if a problem is detected.

Windows provides support for auditing in a number of different areas of the system; in this section I review these areas and provide suggestions on specific event auditing that can be useful to audit. Even if you do not plan to implement any real form of auditing in your environment (although I advise against this), understanding how auditing works can be an important tool when performing application integration (see Chapter 21 for more information on this) because it can help you to determine files or directories that may require modified security permissions in order to allow an application to function properly.

If you will implement security auditing, you need to consider carefully what events you actually want to audit. Although it is easy to simply configure your environment to audit all events, the resulting logs are difficult to review and manage, defeating the purpose of auditing in the first place. Finding the proper level of auditing for your environment requires a bit of work but is an exercise I highly recommend. My simple rule is if you are not planning on proactively monitoring an event, don't waste your time auditing it. People may disagree with this, but in most situations, by the time you discover there is a security problem, the pertinent log information very likely is gone.

System Auditing

Before you can begin to track audited events, you must enable auditing on the system itself. As with the other security options configured in this chapter, Terminal Server auditing should be enabled through a group policy object in the active directory. Alternatively you can configure the audit settings directly from the Local Security Settings application, but any options configured in the domain will override this. Figure 16.26 shows the Audit Policy folder containing the available policy properties, which are located in

Computer Configuration\Windows Settings\Security Settings\Local Policies\

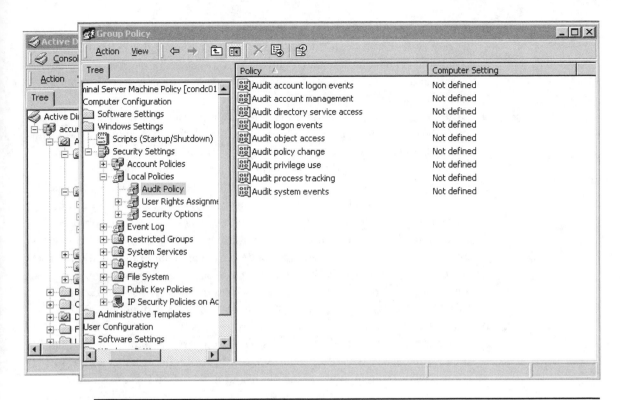

Figure 16.26 Audit policy settings for Terminal Servers should be defined in a GPO in the active directory.

The auditable events listed in the Audit Policy folder are described in the following list. Unless otherwise stated, these policies are not enabled for either Windows 2000 or Windows 2003 Terminal Server.

- **Audit Account Logon Events**—This audit policy should not be confused with the Audit Logon Events policy described later in this list. The purpose of this policy is to log an event whenever an account on *the* computer being configured is used to authenticate on this or any other computer. This option is typically enabled only on a domain controller and is not normally required on a Terminal Server. Windows Server 2003 has this option set to SUCCESS by default on all member servers.

- **Audit Account Management**—The result of a creation, deletion, or modification of a *local* user account or group is logged when this audit event is selected. I recommend tracking both success and failure.

- **Audit Directory Service Access**—Access to an active directory object that has its own system access control list (SACL) is audited using this policy. This audit policy is valid on only a domain controller and so does not need to be set on a Terminal Server. A group policy object is an example of an object in an active directory that has its own SACL.

- **Audit Logon Events**—Whenever a user attempts to log on or log off the Terminal Server, an event is written to the log. This differs from the Audit Account Logon Events policy, which generates a log entry on the server where the user account resides. The Audit Logon Events policy generates a log entry on the server where the logon was *attempted*. I recommend that you audit both success and failure. Successful logons let you audit the logon activities for users, and failures may indicate an attempt by someone to access a restricted resource. MetaFrame includes a command line tool called AUDITLOG, which generates output from the security event log based on the logon/logoff information in the security log. See Appendix B, "MetaFrame Presentation Server Command Reference," for more information on this. This event is enabled and set to track SUCCESS events on Windows 2003. It is not defined for Windows 2000.

- **Audit Object Access**—Access to standard objects that have their own SACL defined, such as files, folders, printers, or the registry, are audited using this policy. I recommend auditing failures since this will indicate users with insufficient privileges attempting to access a resource. Mapping successes offers little value except in isolated situations, because users can successfully access a large number of objects during a single Terminal Server session.

- **Audit Policy Change**—This setting covers any changes made to the security policies, which are composed of the user rights policies and the audit policies on a Terminal Server. Because of the sensitive nature of this security information and the fact that it should rarely change, both success and failure should always be audited.

- **Audit Privilege Use**—This audits use of a user right on the Terminal Server, such as taking ownership of an object or changing the system time. Failure should be tracked for this policy.

- **Audit Process Tracking**—This policy tracks actions such as process (including program) starting and stopping. Indirect object access would include tracking a process or thread from an application that manipulated an object in some way. Failures should normally be audited for this policy.

- **Audit System Events**—When a user attempts to restart or shut down a system, this policy is triggered. Any event that affects the system security or the security log is also tracked with this event. I recommend auditing both success and failure.

Auditing introduces additional performance overhead, so unless you are willing to actively monitor your audit logs and feel their use is necessary, you can provide a performance gain by not implementing auditing. Of course, the performance gains must be worth not having the auditing information available for review if necessary. I suggested some events to audit, but the ones you implement will depend on the information you're interested in tracking and what you feel is necessary. You should monitor your security logs carefully to see if there is extraneous information that can be eliminated.

NOTE: If the Shutdown command has not been removed from the Start menu using a group policy, do not be too surprised if you see restart and shutdown attempt failures made on your Terminal Servers shortly after you implement the new infrastructure. If your users have had previous experience with Windows, they may be accustomed to shutting down their computers when they finish working for the day. This will be common among users who use the Alt+F4 key combination to terminate Windows. Even on a Terminal Server, using Alt+F4 presents the user with the Windows Security dialog box where he or she has the option to shut down. Although regular users will have insufficient privileges to successfully complete this operation, the shutdown or restart attempt still will be logged.

File System Auditing

After enabling object access auditing, you can set up the desired file system auditing. If object access is not being audited (see the preceding section regarding system auditing), any file auditing you configure will simply be ignored. File auditing is enabled by following these steps:

1. Right-click a file object (drive, folder, or file) and select Properties.
2. Click the Security tab and then the Advanced button.
3. Here you find the Auditing tab. By clicking the Add button, you can add groups or users that will be audited based on the options you select. Figure 16.27 shows the auditing options available for both Windows 2000 and 2003, which correspond to the file system security attributes. More information on these specific attributes can be found in Appendix E, "File System and Registry Security Primer."

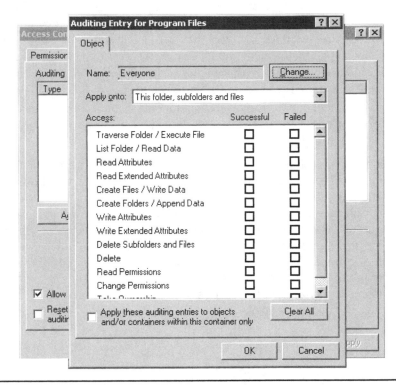

Figure 16.27   File and folder auditing options for Windows 2000 and Windows 2003.

Table 16.10 lists my suggested auditing settings for the system and application volumes on a Windows 2000/2003 Terminal Server. On the system volume, you may want to create separate audit settings for the profile directory (%SystemDrive%\Documents and Settings"), since users will continuously be writing, editing, and deleting information from that location.

Table 16.10   Suggested Windows 2000/2003 Terminal Server System and Application Volume Auditing Settings

Volume	Permission	Audit Setting
System/Application	Create Files/Write Data	Failure
	Create Folders/Append Data	Failure
	Delete Subfolders and Files	Success, Failure
	Delete	Success, Failure
	Change Permissions	Success, Failure
	Take Ownership	Success, Failure

Registry Auditing

Typically, registry auditing is enabled only on the HKEY_LOCAL_MACHINE hive and all subkeys. The auditable events are set similar to those shown in Figure 16.28.

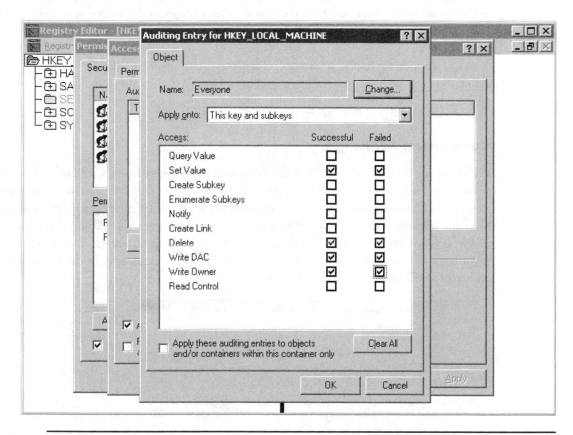

Figure 16.28   Registry auditing options for Windows 2000 and Windows 2003.

Registry auditing is enabled through the registry-editing tool (REGEDT32 on Windows 2000, REGEDIT on Windows 2003). Depending on the operating system, the Auditing dialog box is accessed as follows:

- Windows 2000: Open REGEDT32, select the Permissions menu, click the Advanced button, and select the Auditing tab.
- Windows 2003: Open REGEDIT, choose Permissions from the Edit menu, click the Advanced button, and select the Auditing tab.

Click the Add button to add the users or groups and then select the events to audit. You will need to select the Reset Auditing Entries check box to configure all child objects and enable propagation of inheritable audit entries.

You may receive a message indicating that all subkeys could not be updated. This is okay, as the update process will fail to update subkeys for which you don't have access, such as the HKLM\SECURITY or the HKLM\SAM\SAM key. Auditing on the relevant keys will be updated properly.

You shouldn't monitor success of either the Query event or the Enumerate Subkeys event, because both generate a large number of event entries very quickly and should be enabled only when attempting to troubleshoot or resolve a specific issue.

Connection Auditing

Both versions of Windows support connection auditing, which monitors actions that one user session performs against another or performs directly on the connection configuration. Actions such as modifying connection properties or remotely controlling a user's session can be monitored when connection auditing has been enabled. Figure 16.29 shows the Auditing dialog box for an RDP-TCP connection entry. The selected entries also represent my recommendations for the events to audit. Connection auditing simply tracks the success or failure of performing a particular connection action.

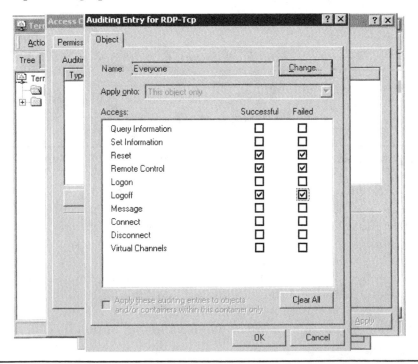

Figure 16.29   A connection auditing example for the RDP-TCP protocol.

Connection auditing is enabled as follows:

1. Open the Terminal Services Configuration tool located under Administrative Tools on the Start menu.
2. Right-click desired connection protocol (RDP or ICA) and select Properties.
3. From the Permissions tab, click the Advanced button and then select the Auditing tab, where you are presented with the familiar Audit dialog box.

Security Patch Management

Even if an administrator has been completely diligent in all aspects of securing their Terminal Server environment, failing to employ proper security patch management can still leave them vulnerable to attacks. In fact, even a cursory configuration of traditional security measures on a Terminal Server coupled with a diligent security patch implementation strategy can leave a server much more secure than one without proper patching.

Today, administrators have little choice but to ensure that their servers remain up-to-date with the latest patches. Because of this I've dedicated a complete chapter to this subject. Chapter 9 provides a thorough discussion on properly managing deployment of security patches in your Terminal Server environment.

Terminal Server and MetaFrame Printer Management

Before You Begin

In Chapter 8, "Server Installation and Management Planning," I provided a large amount of background material around properly planning implementation and support of printing in your Terminal Server/MetaFrame environment. The goal of this chapter is to successfully implement that plan and deliver a robust and reliable printing infrastructure for your Terminal Server/MetaFrame deployment.

We begin by discussing installation and management of printer drivers, which are required on the Terminal Server regardless of the printer access method used. Next, the three general categories of printer support provided by Terminal Server and MetaFrame are reviewed, after which focus shifts for the remainder of the chapter to how these scenarios are implemented and managed within both Terminal Server and MetaFrame, based on the appropriate network configuration (see Chapter 4, "Network Planning").

NOTE: The printing categories and features supported by both Terminal Server and MetaFrame were discussed in Chapter 8.

Printer Driver Management

One area discussed in Chapter 8 was the need to evaluate the printers required in your environment and ensure that you have the appropriate printer drivers available. Regardless of how your printers will be configured in your environment, every printer in a Windows system requires an associated printer driver.

Two types of printer drivers are supported by Windows 2000/2003: the traditional printer driver, and what is called a printer *mini-driver*. A mini-driver works in conjunction with the Windows Universal Printer Driver (WUPD) to perform the actual printing to the physical device. Because a printer driver must interact with the graphical device interface (GDI), it must provide a standard set of interfaces that the GDI expects to be available. A mini-driver provides what are called *stubs* to these interfaces but actually relies on the WUPD to deliver most of the functionality. The mini-driver provides only the information unique to a particular printer.

NOTE: The Windows Universal Printer Driver differs from the universal printer drivers provided with MetaFrame Presentation Server. I discuss more about the MetaFrame UPDs in the "MetaFrame Printer Support" section of this chapter.

The alternative to a mini-driver is the full printer driver, which delivers all the required GDI interfaces and does not use the WUPD in any way. Full printer drivers are much more complicated to develop than mini-drivers but can also provide more robust printing features and functionality.

Typically, the mini-driver can be much more stable than a full printer driver, since most of the GDI-based interaction is through the WUPD, which has already been thoroughly tested. This is the main reason why I will recommend implementing a mini-driver whenever possible in a Terminal Server environment.

WARNING: Deploying a printer driver on a production Terminal Server or MetaFrame server should always be taken very seriously. Ideally, the process is subjected to the same change management process as any other application or operating system update. Deploying an unstable printer driver into a production Terminal Server environment can introduce significant printing issues.

When deploying a new printer driver on a Terminal Server, always be sure to test, test, and test some more. One good test to perform is having multiple users concurrently sending jobs to the printer as opposed to one user sending multiple large jobs. Many Terminal Server printer failures occur when a printer driver is stressed under a heavy load resulting from concurrent user print requests.

The current driver associated with a printer can be determined by opening the Properties page for the printer and selecting the Advanced tab. An alternate printer can be selected from the drop-down list, as shown in Figure 17.1. All drivers currently installed on the server will be available for selection.

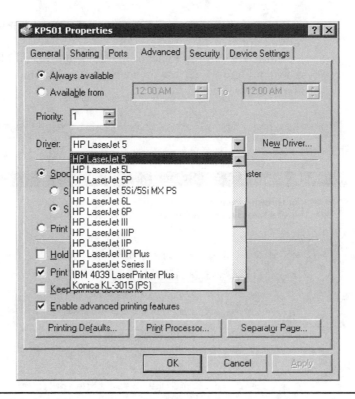

Figure 17.1 Printer driver assignment.

Before choosing a printer to install on your Terminal Server, make sure you have reviewed my list of recommendations regarding printer driver selection in Chapter 8. In this chapter I discussed the concerns about printer driver stability in a Terminal Server environment, as well as some of the reasons printer drivers fail and the impact they can have on a Terminal Server. The most severe printer driver issues can result in the system halting with a STOP error (the familiar blue screen of death). In an ideal world all printer drivers would work flawlessly, but unfortunately this is not the case and care must always be taken when deciding on the drivers to be installed on a Terminal Server. Whenever possible test the driver before deploying it into production.

Adding Printer Drivers to a Terminal Server

Printer drivers can be added to a Terminal Server in a couple of ways. The first, which will be familiar to Windows NT 4.0 Terminal Server Edition administrators, is using the Add Printer wizard under the Printers and Faxes folder and installing a "fictitious" local printer with the desired driver. This can be done as follows:

1. Launch the Add Printer wizard and select the Local Printer Attached to This Computer option.

   Be sure to *deselect* Automatically Detect and Install My Plug and Play Printer, as shown in Figure 17.2. You do not want Windows to try to detect a nonexistent printer on your server.

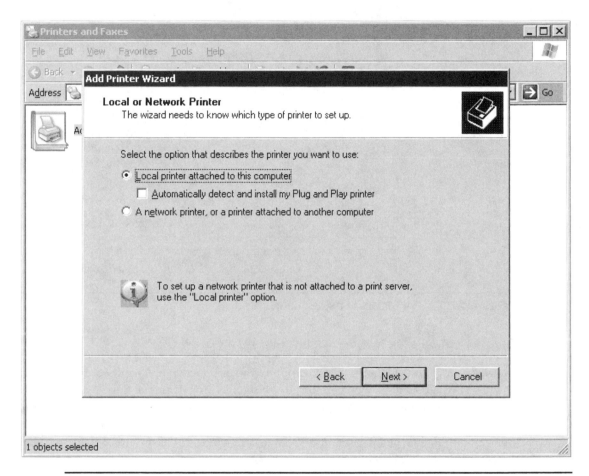

Figure 17.2   Adding a printer driver using the Add Printer wizard.

2. Select the desired port.

   It is best to choose a port not currently being used. I normally select LPT2.

3. Select the desired printer driver to install.

   If the driver is not listed, you need to download and install a driver provided by the printer manufacturer. Refer to the section, "Printer Driver Stability on a Terminal Server," in Chapter 8 for information on choosing the appropriate printer for your environment.

4. The default printer name is usually appropriate, but if you already have a large number of printers installed on your server, appending text such as "Delete-" to the beginning of the name will make it easy to find when it's time to remove the queue.

5. Make sure you do not share the printer, and do not try to print a test page.

   Unless the print queue is associated with an existing printer, the test page will, of course, fail.

6. Once the printer has been created, return to the Printers folder and delete this printer.

   Even when deleted, the associated printer drivers remain installed and available on the server.

A more straightforward method of adding a printer driver to your server is through the Print Server Properties dialog box. This is found by opening the Printers and Faxes folder and selecting Server Properties from the File menu. Under the Drivers tab, you find a list of all currently installed printer drivers (see Figure 17.3). You can also fully manage your drivers from this location by adding, deleting, updating, or viewing a driver's properties. Clicking Add launches the Add Printer Driver wizard.

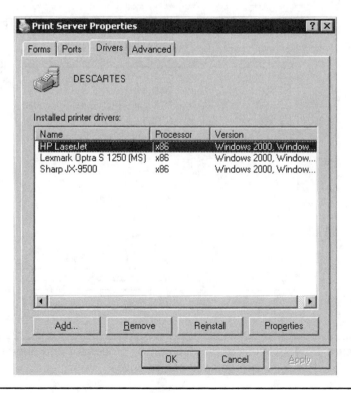

Figure 17.3   The Print Server Properties page.

The steps to install the printer driver are as follows:

1. After the introduction screen, the Add Printer Driver wizard immediately takes you to the printer driver selection dialog box. From here you can select an existing driver or choose a driver you downloaded separately by clicking the Have Disk button. If you have not already done so, you need to extract the necessary driver files into a temporary folder, where you can select the appropriate driver to install.
2. Once the driver is chosen, the next screen asks you to select the appropriate processor/operating system combination that will use this driver (Figure 17.4). Usually the default selection is appropriate.
3. The final screen simply asks you to confirm your selection before the driver is installed on the server. Once this step is finished, the newly installed driver appears on the driver installation list.

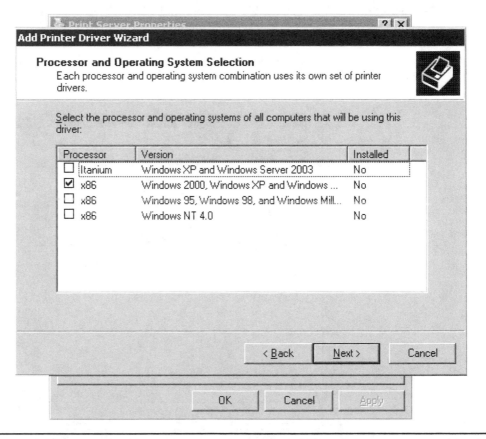

Figure 17.4 Selecting the appropriate processor and operating system combination for an installed printer driver.

The steps required to install a printer driver are fairly straightforward, but if you have a large number of Terminal Servers in your environment (5, 10, or more), having to manually install the necessary drivers on each server can become tedious, time consuming, and prone to error. A more effective method of distributing the desired drivers throughout the environment would certainly be desirable. In the next section, I look at printer driver replication techniques.

Printer Driver Replication

Microsoft provides a downloadable tool that can be used to simplify the task of replicating printer drivers from one server to another. Originally designed as a tool for backing up the printers on a print server, the Windows Print Migrator tool works very well at replicating printers and their drivers from one server to another. The Windows Print Migrator tool can be downloaded from the Microsoft Web site by going to http://www.microsoft.com/downloads and searching on "Print Migrator." The latest version at the time of this book's release was 3.1, and it supports both Windows Server 2000 and Windows 2003 Server. No installation is required for this product; it is simply downloaded into a folder and executed. The main window for Print Migrator is shown in Figure 17.5, with the currently installed printer driver list expanded.

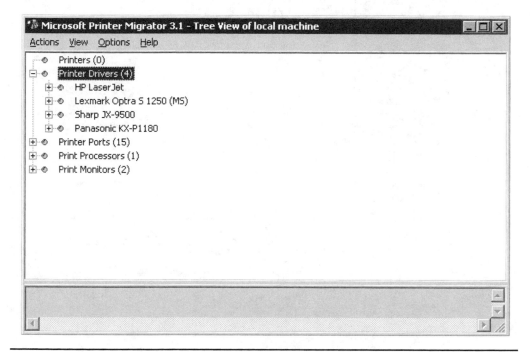

Figure 17.5 The main window of the Microsoft Print Migrator 3.1 migration tool.

Printer driver replication is performed in a two-step process. First, the current printer drivers on the source server are backed up by selecting Backup from the Action menu, selecting the Target source backup server if necessary, and providing the file name in which to store the printer information. This data is backed up into a Microsoft cabinet (CAB) file.

Once you have the printer driver information backed up into the CAB file, the next step is to restore it onto the target destination server. Select the Restore option from the Action menu. When prompted, provide the source CAB file and the target server where the printer drivers will be replicated, as shown in Figure 17.6. Click Open to begin the restore. The results of the restore are automatically logged to the file PM.LOG, located in the folder

%SystemRoot%\System32\spool\pm

If errors or issues are encountered during the restore, they will be logged in this file and you will receive visual notification at the end of the restore attempt.

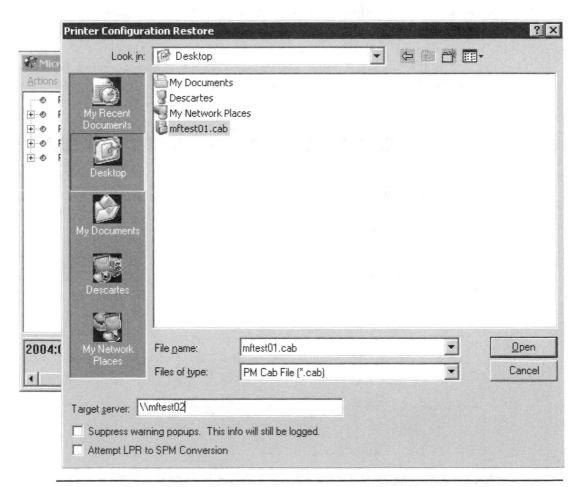

Figure 17.6   The Printer Configuration and Restore dialog box for Microsoft Printer Migrator.

TIP: If you will be implementing MetaFrame Presentation Server, you can leverage the advanced printer driver management and replication features that it provides. I look more closely at these features in the "MetaFrame Printer Support" section of this chapter.

Terminal Server Printer Support

The different types of printer support offered through Terminal Server were covered in Chapter 8. The three categories discussed were

- Network printer shares
- Local server printers
- Local client printers

Network Printer Shares

Probably the most common printer access configuration and the one most familiar to a Windows administrator is use of one or more print servers that centralize access to various printers within the organization. These printers are all made available as network printer shares on the print server. Figure 17.7 gives an example of a number of printers shared off a Windows print server and listed in the active directory.

Shared printer resources are typically accessed in one of two ways: automatically through a logon script or manually mapped by the user using the Add Printer wizard. Of the two, I prefer to implement logon scripts to automatically map the appropriate printers based on the user's group membership. This provides a means of transparently delivering the appropriate printers without interaction from the user. If printer assignments are left up to the user, you need to be sure they understand how to locate and map the printer properly using the Add Printer wizard. Inexperienced users can easily become confused and either map to the incorrect printer or fail to map the necessary printers at all. Either way, they are almost guaranteed to end up calling for support to try to resolve the problem.

When properly configured, logon scripts can provide a reliable and effective way to manage printer mappings for your users. While a lack of programming skill will certainly limit the extent to which you can customize and modify scripts to suit your environment, the configuration steps involved are fairly straightforward, and the sample scripts I include can be customized to function in your environment with some very minor changes. A simple logon script configuration can be created in a couple of steps.

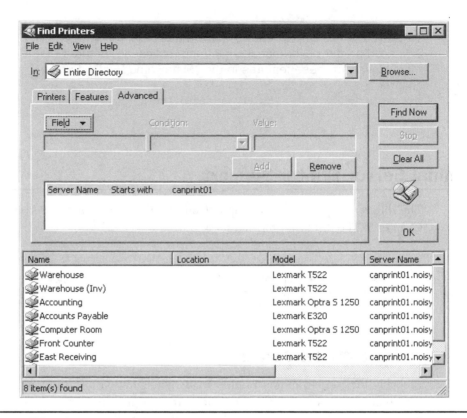

Figure 17.7 Printer shares for a print server listed in a Windows active directory.

Mapping Printer Shares Using Logon Scripts

The first task is to create a simple logon script that will map printers based on a user's group membership. The following code sample demonstrates how such a script could be created using Visual Basic Scripting (VBScript).

The logic for this script is straightforward. A global user group called PRN Accounting has been created in the active directory, and any users who should map to this printer are assigned to that group. The script looks to see if the user belongs to this group, and if so, the printer connection is established and set as the default. When a user is mapping the drive, a pop-up message briefly appears saying the drive is being mapped. This message closes either when OK is clicked or automatically after being displayed for three (3) seconds. I like to include this message not only as a visual confirmation to the user that the proper printer mapping is being initiated but also as a troubleshooting tool for an administrator if printer mapping issues arise.

Listing 17.1 Windows Logon Script Sample Demonstrating How to Script Mapping of Client
Printers

```vbs
'*********************************************************************
**
'*  ConnectPrinters.vbs
*
'*
*
'*  Connects the user's printers based on their group membership.
*
'*  Printers are assigned by the particular group's business function.
*
'*  For example, the accountants belong to the group "PRN Accounting".
*
'*********************************************************************
**
option explicit

'Define the printer groups that are being evaluated
'We use constants so that the code doesn't have to change if
'the printer name changes.
Const PRN_Accounting - "cn=PRN Accounting"

'Define the variables that will be used for mapping
dim wshNetwork, ADSysInfo, oCurrentUser
dim sPrinterPath, sPrinterDriver, sGroups
dim wshSysEnv, wshShell

'Initialize the variables and retrieve the necessary information
Set wshShell = CreateObject("WScript.Shell")

'system environment information
set wshSysEnv = wshShell.Environment("PROCESS")
Set WshNetwork = CreateObject("WScript.Network")
Set ADSysInfo = CreateObject("ADSystemInfo")

'retrieve the user's account information
Set oCurrentUser = GetObject("LDAP://" + ADSysInfo.UserName)
sGroups = LCase(Join(oCurrentUser.MemberOf))

'verify the user's domain group membership and map printers
If InStr(sGroups, LCase(PRN_Accounting)) Then
    wshShell.Popup "Mapping Accounting printer...", 3, "Mapping
Printer", 64
    wshNetwork.AddWindowsPrinterConnection "\\PRNServer01\Accounting"
    wshNetWork.SetDefaultPrinter "\\PRNServer01\Accounting"
End If
```

Once you have a simple script created, the next step is to define what logon script will be used and under what circumstances it will execute. Logon scripts can be initiated either through a group policy or from within the user's domain account on the Profile tab, as show in Figure 17.8. The entry in the user's profile is executed under all circumstances, whether the user is logging on to a desktop PC or a Terminal Server. If you wish to use the same logon script for all desktop environments, it can be defined here. If you prefer to configure logon scripts that apply only from within the Terminal Server environment, the script should be configured to start within a group policy defined for Terminal Servers only.

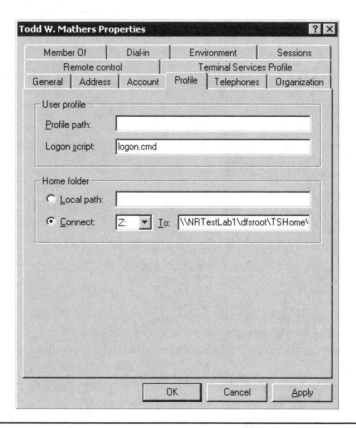

Figure 17.8   The logon script setting defined for specific user accounts.

In this example I use a logon script defined within the group policy called All Users Policy, as defined in Chapter 15, "Group Policy Configuration." This policy is applied to all users who log on to a Terminal Server that is a member of the Terminal Servers organizational unit. The specific policy to modify is located under

User Configuration\Windows Settings\Scripts (Logon/Logoff).

By double-clicking the Logon entry, you open a dialog box where you can list the logon scripts that will execute (see Figure 17.9). If multiple scripts are listed, they are processed in order from top to bottom. In order for Windows to process the desired logon script(s) during a user's logon, the script must be saved into the specific Scripts folder for the policy. You can quickly access this folder by clicking the Show Files button located on the lower left-hand side of the Logon Properties dialog box shown in Figure 17.9. This opens a Windows Explorer screen pointing into the proper script folder. The logon script you created earlier can now be copied into this folder.

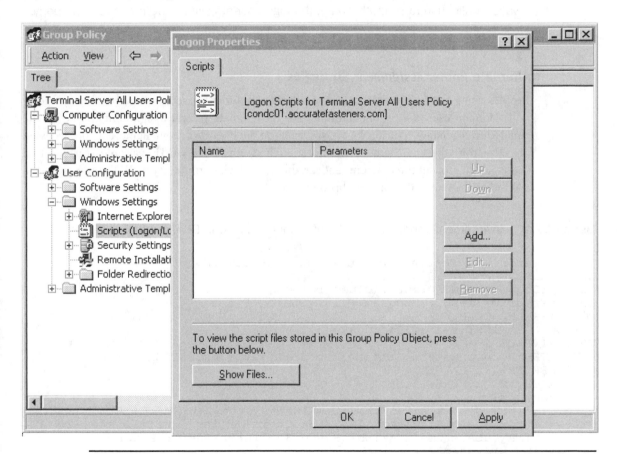

Figure 17.9   Logon scripts can also be defined in a group policy object.

Once all the desired scripts have been copied into this folder, close the dialog box and then click Add from the main Logon Properties screen. The Add a Script dialog box opens, and you can then click Browse to be taken into the Scripts folder where you can select the logon scripts to add to the policy. Once added, the scripts appear in the script list, and once the Logon Properties dialog box is closed by clicking OK, the scripts are configured and ready to execute.

You can now test out the script processing by logging on to your Terminal Server using a user account configured to process the corresponding group policy. If you used the same policy configuration as the one I discussed in Chapter 15, any Terminal Server user will process this logon script. If everything is configured properly, the desired network printers should automatically be connected and ready for use.

TIP: If you implemented the application restrictions discussed in Chapter 16, "Terminal Server Security," you need to include the script processor WSCRIPT.EXE as a valid application to run; otherwise, the logon scripts will not be processed properly.

Alternate Printer Assignment Strategies

Besides using the traditional method of printer assignment based on membership in one or more domain user groups, one alternative is to designate printer assignments based on the client device's name. During logon, information such as the client name can be accessed directly from the environment variables, such as CLIENTNAME variable. Listing 17.2 shows an example of the environment variables listed when running the SET command from a Windows Server 2003 command prompt.

Listing 17.2   Environment Variables Provide Information That Can Be Used to Assign Printers

```
C:\Documents and Settings\administrator.NRTESTDOM>set
CLIENTNAME=GLENROTHES
ClusterLog=C:\WINNT\Cluster\cluster.log
CommonProgramFiles=C:\Program Files\Common Files
COMPUTERNAME=OBAN
ComSpec=C:\WINNT\system32\cmd.exe
HOMEDRIVE=C:
HOMEPATH=\Documents and Settings\administrator.NRTESTDOM
LOGONSERVER=\\LAGAVULAN
NUMBER_OF_PROCESSORS=1
OS=Windows_NT
Path=C:\WINNT\system32;C:\WINNT;C:\WINNT\system32\WBEM; C:\Program
Files\Citrix\System32\Citrix\IMA; C:\Program Files\Citrix\System32
\Citrix\IMA\Subsystems;C:\WINNT\System32\Citrix\IMA;C:\Program
Files\Citrix\system32
PATHEXT=.COM;.EXE;.BAT;.CMD;.VBS;.VBE;.JS;.JSE;.WSF;.WSH
PROCESSOR_ARCHITECTURE=x86
PROCESSOR_IDENTIFIER=x86 Family 6 Model 8 Stepping 3, GenuineIntel
PROCESSOR_LEVEL=6
PROCESSOR_REVISION=0803
ProgramFiles=C:\Program Files
PROMPT=$P$G
SESSIONNAME=RDP-Tcp#8
SystemDrive=C:
SystemRoot=C:\WINNT
TCP_NODELAY=1
```

```
TEMP=C:\DOCUME~1\ADMINI~1.NRT\LOCALS~1\Temp\3
TMP=C:\DOCUME~1\ADMINI~1.NRT\LOCALS~1\Temp\3
USERDNSDOMAIN=NRTESTDOM.COM
USERDOMAIN=NRTESTDOM
USERNAME=Administrator
USERPROFILE=C:\Documents and Settings\administrator.NRTESTDOM
windir=C:\WINNT
```

Depending on how the client machines are named, you may be able to modify your logon scripts to assign printers based on the client and its location in the organization. This approach is one way to address the problem of users who roam to different computers in the organization and wish to print to the printer local to that particular printer, not just the printer they access normally. For example, if a user normally works in the Miami office but travels to the Orlando office for the day, that user would likely prefer to print to a printer in the Orlando office instead of defaulting to their normal printer back in the Miami office.

For such a logon script configuration to work effectively, the company would have to be sure to employ a naming standard based on physical site location, as well as possibly office location, if the site was large enough. While scripts could be created for each individual computer name, being able to break things down based on some general geographic region would expand the range of the scripting and simplify the management process.

For example, you could employ a client-naming standard such as

<SITE>PC-<FLOOR><REGION><COUNT>

where SITE is the actual PC site (MIA or ORL, for example). In the example,

PC- is a constant value.

FLOOR is the building floor where the PC is located (a fixed, two-digit number such as 01).

REGION is the region on the floor where the PC is located.

COUNT is the PC count for that location.

An example client name might be ORLPC-03WEST003.

With this information, you could create a logon script that would look at the SITE, FLOOR, and REGION information and assign a default printer based on this. While certainly more complicated than simply using a domain security group, this method can provide much more flexibility in how printers are managed.

NOTE: I once was involved in a large Citrix deployment to implement the strategy of assigning printers based on location of the client device and thereby reduce complexity of managing large numbers of domain user groups. The issue was that the client device names did not employ a naming standard based in any way on the geographical location of the device, so no algorithm could be derived from the name that would allow the associated printer to be easily deduced.

Maintaining a reference list based on the PC name and corresponding printer was simply out of the question, and the complications involved in trying to group PCs was also not a viable option. A solution had to be created that would make it easy for the user to manage the printers if necessary while remaining as simple as possible.

Instead, what I ended up doing was developing a simple custom application that provided the users with an interface that listed the available printers (based on a text file maintained by the administrators in a central location) from which the user could select the two they wished to connect to. One printer was set to be the default printer and the other to be a backup printer. This printer information was then stored in a central location and cross-referenced with the name of the client device.

After selecting and saving the choices, the application would automatically map the printers and set the default. To eliminate the requirement for the user to do this every time they wanted to map the printers, the application also generated a script that was stored in a well-known location with a name matching the client device. The next time anyone logged on from that machine, the script matching that client name was run to automatically reconnect to those printers.

This application achieved two goals. First, it allowed the default printers to be associated with the name of the client device. Second, it achieved this without having to place the full setup and support burden directly on the administrators. Because the users had access to a simple tool, they could easily adjust the printers if necessary, and when saved, the changes would automatically be associated with the client device, ensuring those changes were available the next time anyone logged on from that device.

Local Server Printers

This printer configuration technique involves setup of printers locally on the server, much like setting up a local printer on a Windows workstation. This configuration is common in smaller environments where only one or two Terminal Servers exist with limited supporting hardware (file servers, print servers, and so on) and a relatively small user community that has only light printing needs. In larger environments, the printers are usually configured on a central print server and shared out for access by Terminal Server users.

There are two types of local server printers: those directly connected to the server via a physical cable and those connected through a logical port that is redirected to a printer located on the network. Printers physically connected to a Terminal Server are rare, since most implementations have the Terminal Server located in an area not accessible by the end user. Use of a logical port is much more common, particularly when a TCP/IP port or a print manufacturer's custom printer port is used. Figure 17.10 shows an example of the Ports tab accessible from a printer's Properties dialog box. All ports configured on the server (whether in use or not) are listed, and from here you can redirect the current printer to any given port if desired.

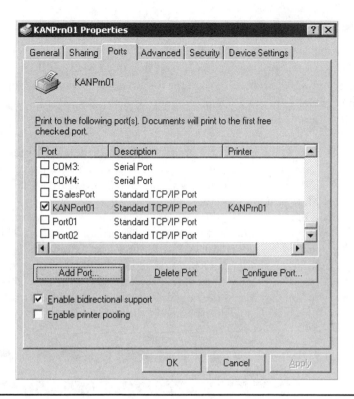

Figure 17.10   The local server printer port properties.

Configuring a local printer is straightforward and usually done with the Add Printer wizard but can also be set up using a third-party installation program, such as a Lexmark Network Port. These custom ports are typically used in conjunction with a network-enabled printer or a dedicated print server device that connects to the network and shares any printers physically connected to it. A TCP/IP port is used to connect to a network-enabled printer that supports TCP/IP printing or to a UNIX-based printer queue that uses the LPD print daemon.

WARNING: Some third-party custom port software, such as Lexmark Network Port, must be installed and configured from the local console; it cannot be managed through an RDP or ICA client session. Attempting to do so results in error messages such as "This operation is not supported." Using the remote console support in Windows Server 2003 resolves this issue in most—but not all—situations.

Of course, once these ports are configured, they can be the target of print jobs for Terminal Server clients without any issues. It is only the configuration that must be managed through the local console.

Installing a TCP/IP Printer Port

To install and complete configuration of the TCP/IP port, you need to know the TCP/IP address of the printer or print server, the protocol used (RAW or LPR), and the corresponding protocol setting (port number for RAW or queue name for LPR). Of the two, LPR is much more common. When using the Add Printer wizard, the steps for configuring a local TCP/IP port are as follows:

1. Begin by opening the Add Printer wizard under Printers and Faxes and then click Next until prompted to select a local or network printer. Choose "Local printer attached to this computer" and then be certain to deselect the "Automatically detect and install my Plug and Play printer" option.

2. On the next dialog box you are asked to select the desired printer port. Click Create a New Port and select the Standard TCP/IP Port option. This launches a new wizard called Add Standard TCP/IP Printer Port, where you are prompted to provide two things (see Figure 17.11): first, either the fully qualified domain name of the device or its IP address and, second, a name for the port. This is the name that will appear when viewing all the available ports on the Ports tab of a printer's properties. It does not have to match the name of the printer that will be assigned to the port.

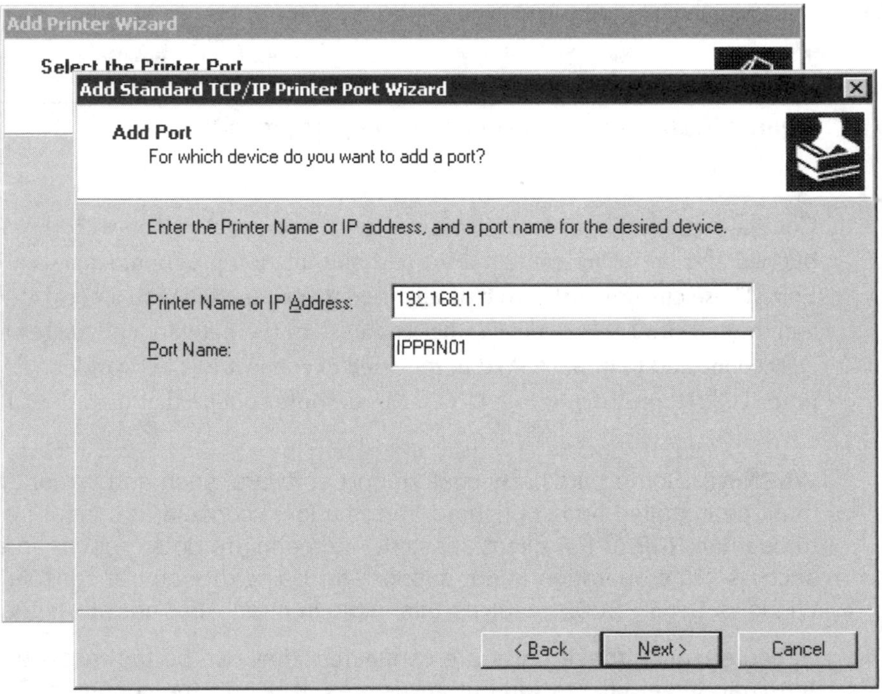

Figure 17.11   The Add Standard TCP/IP Printer Port Wizard dialog box.

3. Windows tries to detect the device type using SNMP (Simple Network Management Protocol). If the device cannot be detected, a dialog box appears prompting for additional information regarding the network device you are attempting to connect with.

4. Unless the desired device exists in the drop-down list, you need to select the Custom radio button and then click the Settings button to bring up the customization screen shown in Figure 17.12. Here you can define the proper settings for connecting the port to the network device. The default protocol option of RAW with port number 9100 will likely need to be changed to the LPR protocol and the proper queue name. The LPR Byte Counter option normally should not be enabled.

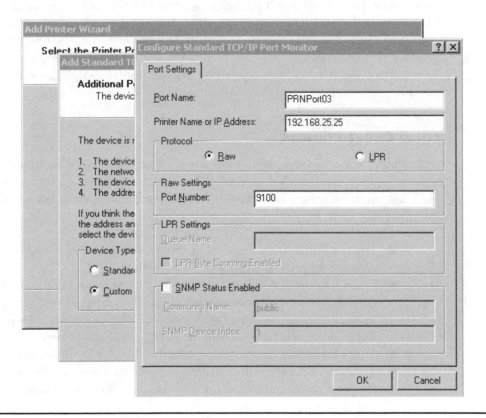

Figure 17.12   The Port Settings dialog box for the new printer port being created.

5. Once the custom settings have been configured as desired, you are returned to the previous dialog box requesting the additional port information. After clicking Next, you reach the final port creation confirmation screen and then are returned to the standard printer installation wizard.

6. Upon returning to the printer installation wizard, you are asked to provide the appropriate printer driver. Printer driver requirements were discussed earlier in this chapter, in the "Printer Driver Management" section.

7. Next you're asked to provide a name for the printer. Try to use a name both concise and descriptive. Ideally, it is something users can quickly recognize and determine as the right one for them.

8. The final two screens prompt you to configure printer sharing and attempt to print a test page. Enable printer sharing only if absolutely necessary, particularly when sharing off a Terminal Server.

9. When finished, print a test page to verify that the port and new printer are configured properly.

While the steps involved in setting up a local printer on the server are straightforward, take care when implementing such a configuration. Additional load is introduced because of the print server responsibilities this creates, which in turn diminishes the resources available to Terminal Server sessions. Local server printers are best suited for smaller, less loaded Terminal Servers that have the capacity to manage print server duties without noticeably degrading the user's Terminal Server experience.

Local Client Printers

As I mentioned in Chapter 8, the introduction of client printer mapping (printer redirection) support greatly enhanced a Terminal Server's ability to more tightly integrate with the user's local desktop. In summary, local client printer mapping provides the following features and functionality:

■ Print jobs originating from within a user's Terminal Server session can be redirected to a printer on the user's local desktop.

■ When connecting to a Windows 2000 or 2003 server using the RDP 5.1 or higher client, you can connect to either physically connected local printers or local network-mapped printers. Both versions of Windows Terminal Server support this feature in conjunction with the RDP 5.1 or higher client.

■ Print job traffic is completely contained within the Terminal Server client's session data, utilizing a virtual channel between the client and the server to deliver the print job. No other network connectivity needs to exist between the client and the server.

■ Client printers are mapped only if a suitable driver exists on the Terminal Server.

■ When local client printer redirection is enabled, an attempt is made by Terminal Server to redirect all client printers within the Terminal Server session. A subset of the desired printers cannot be selected, for example, only the local default printer can be selected. This type of functionality is available with MetaFrame Presentation Server.

In the remainder of this section, I describe how to properly configure your Terminal Server to support redirection of local client printers and methods of troubleshooting common printer redirection issues.

NOTE: A lot of confusion and misinformation exist, even in some of the documentation available on the Microsoft Web site, indicating that network-mapped client printers cannot be redirected through a Windows 2000 Terminal Server but only through a Windows 2003 Terminal Server. This is simply not true.

From a server's perspective, the logic behind redirecting a network-mapped printer is no different from the logic for a locally attached printer. It is the responsibility of the RDP client to enumerate the local print queues and pass the necessary information through to the Terminal Server. This information is then used to construct the corresponding printer queue on the server.

To integrate redirected network-mapped printer support into the RDP 5.0 protocol (used by Windows 2000), Microsoft developed the RDP 5.1 client so that it constructs the information delivered to the Windows 2000 Terminal Server in such a fashion to still conform to the older protocol's specifications. Figure 17.13 shows an example of a redirected network printer in an RDP session on a Windows 2000 Terminal Server.

The first printer in the list is the redirected network printer. You will notice that the queue name was constructed from the original mapped printer name, with the backslashes (\) converted to underscores (_). The last printer in the list is a redirected local client printer. I discuss queue naming for local client printer redirection in the "Enabling Redirection of Local Client Printers" section.

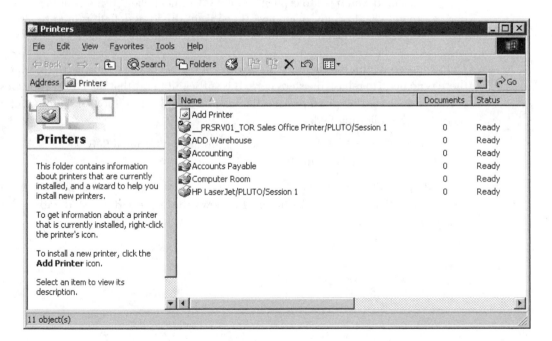

Figure 17.13   A redirected client network printer example on Windows 2000 from an RDP 5.1 client.

Enabling Redirection of Local Client Printers

For this redirection to be successful, you need to ensure that the Terminal Server is configured so it automatically attempts to map the client's printers when he or she logs on to the server. To do this, client printer redirection must be enabled at both the RDP connection level and the individual user account level. By default both methods are enabled, but you can verify or modify this option as desired. At the RDP connection level, you can configure this setting using either the Terminal Services Configuration tool or a group policy object, which is the preferred method in large deployments because it centralizes the management process and alleviates the need to log on to each server to set these options. If you want to use the Terminal Services Configuration tool, you can do so as follows:

1. Open the Terminal Services Configuration application located under Administrative Tools on the Start menu and then select the Connections folder.
2. Double-click the RDP-Tcp connection to open the Properties dialog box and then select the Client Settings tab (Figure 17.14).
3. Within the Connection group box, you have two available options. You can configure the properties for the RDP-Tcp connections to use the settings from the individual user accounts or to define the settings here that will affect all users who log on to the Terminal Server, including administrators. If you enable "Use connection settings from user settings," no other change needs to be made here. If this option is disabled, you need to explicitly enable "Connect client printers at logon" in order to get client printer mappings. If you want the local default printer to also be the default Terminal Server printer, enable "Default to main client printer."

Details on configuration and use of group policy objects were provided in Chapter 15, so there is no need to rehash the steps here. It is sufficient to say that the GPO properties directly related to managing printer redirection can be found within the Computer Configuration section in the following folder:

Administrative Templates\Windows Components\Terminal Services\
Client/Server data redirection

Any settings defined here override any set directly on the Terminal Server using the Terminal Services Configuration tool. Figure 17.15 shows these properties listed within the Group Policy Object Editor.

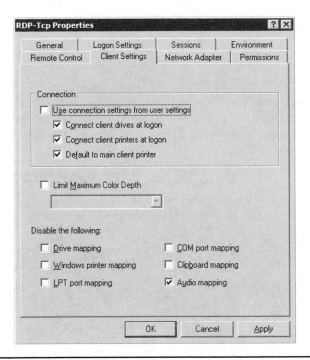

Figure 17.14   RDP connection properties for enabling or disabling client printer re-direction.

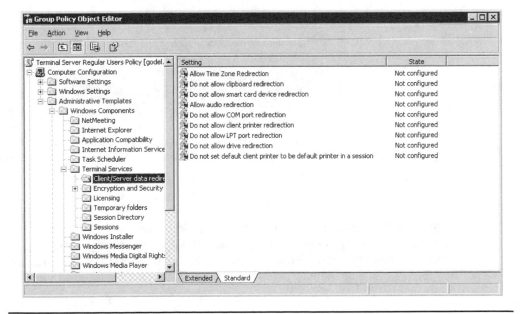

Figure 17.15   Printer redirection settings can be defined within a group policy object.

Client printer mappings for individual user accounts are managed as follows:

1. Open Active Directory Users and Computers for the domain and select the user account you want to manage.
2. Select the Environment tab; in the lower portion of the dialog box, you find the Client Devices group box, as shown in Figure 17.16. "Connect client printers at logon" must be enabled. If you wish to have the local default printer also set as the default printer in Terminal Server, you also need to select "Default to main client printer."

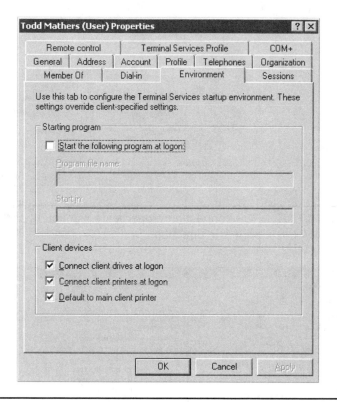

Figure 17.16   The client device properties for an individual user in an active directory.

TIP: As I discussed in Chapter 1, "Microsoft Windows Terminal Services," the RDP protocol can be expanded to support additional, customizable features using what are called *virtual channels*. Virtual channels are also used to drive RDP features such as clipboard mapping, client drive mapping, and local client printer redirection.

While it has been suggested that access to these features is dependent on whether the Virtual Channels permission for the RDP protocol is allowed or not, this information is false (see Figure 17.17). Local client printer redirection is in no way affected by the status of this connection permission. Even if Virtual Channels have been expressly denied, local client printer redirection still functions as designed.

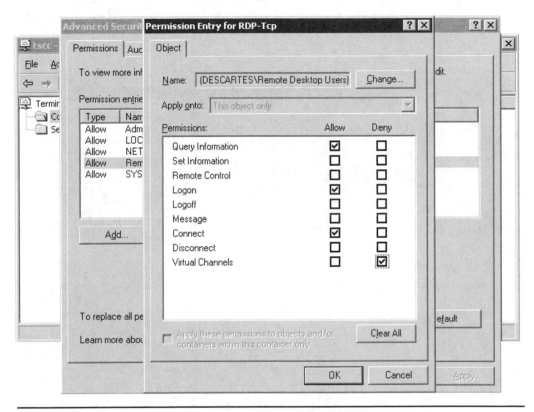

Figure 17.17 The Virtual Channel permission for the RDP-Tcp connection does not control whether or not client printer mapping is available.

When local client printer redirection is enabled, the Terminal Server attempts to automatically connect all the printers available on a user's local desktop whenever they log on to the server. Whether or not a client printer is successfully redirected within an RDP session depends on whether a suitable match between the client and the server printer drivers can be determined.

During the logon, the RDP client enumerates all the client's local printers and sends the local queue name and complete driver name to the Terminal Server. For this redirection to occur, the Terminal Server must take the client's driver name and find a corresponding driver on the server with the exact same name. For example, if the client machine has a driver called "hp deskjet 970c series", the server must have a driver with an *identical* name (same punctuation, same case, same everything) in order for the redirection to occur. If the names do not match or a driver cannot be found, an event ID 1111 (see Figure 17.18) is created in the server's system log and the printer mapping silently fails. No error message is displayed to the user. Driver installation is discussed in the "Printer Driver Management" section, earlier in this chapter. If the corresponding driver has been installed and the mapping is still failing, it is likely because the driver names differ between the client and the server. I discuss ways to correct this problem in the next section.

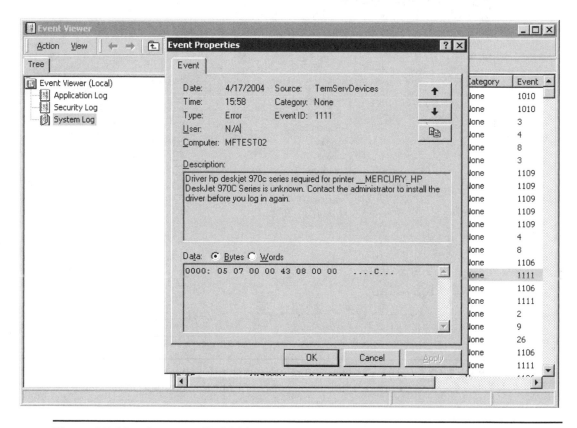

Figure 17.18   An event ID 1111 message is displayed when a client printer driver cannot be found on the Terminal Server.

NOTE: If a local client printer is using a local printer port that is labeled something other than LPT, COM or USB, then it will not automatically be redirected to the Terminal Services session. This is a common problem for multifunction printing devices, which very often use a DOT4 port. Because of this port name, the printer is not automatically available within the Terminal Services session.

The one exception to this is when the client device is running Windows Server 2003. Details on this issue along with a resolution can be found in the Microsoft Knowledgebase article 302361.

Driver Naming Requirements and Alternate Name Matching

When an event ID 1111 is generated, it is either because the driver names on the client and the server do not match or because a corresponding driver has not yet been installed on the Terminal Server. If the driver is not yet installed, it needs to be made available before you attempt the mapping. The earlier section entitled "Printer Driver Management" discusses in detail the criteria for managing printer drivers on your Terminal Server.

If a suitable server driver has been installed and the client printer mapping still fails, then the two drivers have slightly different names and a special cross-reference matching (also commonly called a mapping or substitution) file must be used to tell the Terminal Server that these two names do in fact reference the same drivers. For example, if we have a Windows XP client connecting with an updated version of the DeskJet 970c driver with the name

"hp deskjet 970c series"

and our Windows 2003 Terminal Server has the following driver installed:

"HP DeskJet 970Cse"

then when the mapping comparison is made, we see that these two drivers are certainly not identical, so the mapping is not created and an event ID 1111 is created. To remedy the problem of nonstandard driver names, Microsoft provides the ability (Windows 2003, and Windows 2000 post–Service Pack 2) to create a custom substitution file to handle these anomalies. The substitution file would then contain an entry such as

"hp deskjet 970c series" = "HP DeskJet 970Cse"

This entry tells the Terminal Server that whenever a client connects and provides the driver name "hp deskjet 970c series", the corresponding server driver "HP DeskJet 970Cse" should be used.

To use this custom substitution file, you must first make an addition to the system registry telling the Terminal Server what file to use and where within that file to find the custom substitution information. You can do this by opening REGEDIT, traversing to the following registry key:

HKLM\SYSTEM\CurrentControlSet\Control\Terminal Server\Wds\rdpwd

and adding the two values listed in Table 17.1 to the key.

Table 17.1 Registry Values Required to Enable an Alternate Driver Cross-Reference File

Value Name	Value Type	Description
PrinterMappingINFName	REG_SZ	The name and full path to the file that will contain the cross-reference file. You can use whatever name you wish. A common name for this file is ntprintsubs.inf
		Example: C:\WINDOWS\INF\ntprintsubs.inf
PrinterMappingINFSection	REG_SZ	The name of the section within the INF file where the cross-reference information resides.
		Example: Printers

The substitution file would then need to be created and placed in the proper folder. For example, my sample INF file for these DeskJet drivers would look like the one shown in Listing 17.3. You can list multiple driver substitutions within this file if necessary.

Remember that for the substitution to function properly, you must have the server-side driver installed on your Terminal Server. The driver will *not* automatically be installed by itself.

Listing 17.3 A Sample Substitution File Containing a Single Printer Driver Match

```
[Printers]
;
; Client Side Driver    |    Server Side Driver
;
"hp deskjet 970c series" = "HP DeskJet 970Cse"
```

> **NOTE:** Pay particular attention to the syntax of this custom file. If a mistake is made in the creation of this file, an event log entry (Event 1110) will be generated stating that the NTPRINT.INF file is corrupt. This is a misleading error, and actually pertains to a syntax error in this custom substitution file.

The Printer Driver Redirection Wizard

To assist users in making the necessary changes to a substitution file, Microsoft released a tool called the Printer Driver Redirection wizard, which is downloadable free from the Terminal Services Community Web site. The URL for this site is http://www.microsoft.com/windowsserver2003/community/centers/terminal/default.mspx

Both the Windows 2000 and 2003 communities point to the same home page. As you scroll down toward the bottom of this page, you see the link for the Printer Driver Redirection wizard. After downloading the file, simply extract it into a folder on your Terminal Server and double-click the TSPDRW.EXE executable. The redirection wizard will scan either a local or remote server for any existing event ID 1111 entries in the event log with the source "TermServDevices". Once completed, it provides you with an option screen where you either choose an existing printer driver to use as a substitution or manually add a driver. Figure 17.19 shows this utility prompting for the choice of the installed driver to be used to substitute for the "hp deskjet 970c series" entry that was found.

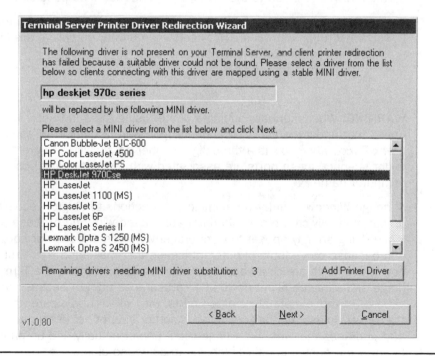

Figure 17.19   The Printer Driver Redirection wizard automates creation of the substitution file used to map printers with different printer driver names on their client and the MetaFrame server.

After choosing the appropriate file to create the substitution with, you can click Next and see the next driver found in the event log displayed. If you do not wish to create a substitution, you can select the (none) entry located at the bottom of the list.

Once the last driver is prompted, the tool displays a summary message stating what changes were made. On the very last screen you are provided with the name of the substitution file that was created or updated. The necessary registry entries to have MetaFrame read the contents of this file are also automatically set. If a reboot is required to complete the setup, you are prompted. If you say no, the updates are deferred until later.

TIP: As I discussed in the "Printer Driver Management" section earlier in this chapter, whenever possible you should try to use matching driver versions on both the client and the server. While the substitution feature does allow some flexibility in the drivers used, certain features may not be supported if an older or nonmatching server driver is being substituted. If exact driver matches cannot be implemented, use a Windows-certified driver as close to the same make and model as possible.

The Terminal Server substitution feature pertains to only client printer redirection. Driver substitution entries are not used when printer mappings are initiated through the Add Printer wizard or a logon script.

WARNING: When manually adding a printer using the Add Printer wizard, you may notice that under the list of local printer ports are a number of special ports with the prefix TSxxx, where xxx is a three-digit number as shown in Figure 17.20. As you might suspect, these ports are associated with redirected local ports for the listed computer name.

Although Windows will let you complete the action, it is highly recommended that you *do not* manually create a local printer associated with one of these printer ports. While doing so may appear to work properly, Microsoft does not support the configuration because of a couple of different issues that may arise. The first has to do with how these ports are cleared when a user logs off. Normally the Terminal Server will purge all redirected client ports when a user logs off, but because the server is not "aware" of these manually created ports, they will not be cleared and will remain on the server unless manually removed. Another side effect of this manual mapping is that print jobs that are sent to one client printer actually end up printing out on a different client printer, usually belonging to someone else.

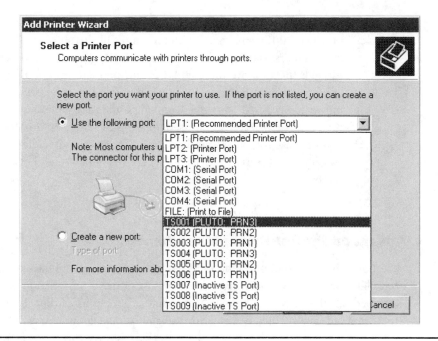

Figure 17.20   Terminal Server client-mapped printer ports.

MetaFrame Printer Support

While Terminal Server alone provides rather thorough printer support, there are some limitations that can become a factor in large-scale implementations. This is where MetaFrame Presentation Server's advanced printer support features become a valuable addition to the implementation. In addition to supporting all the same printer options as Terminal Server alone, MPS supports the following:

- **Advanced printer driver management**—MetaFrame provides a centralized method of administering printer drivers on all servers in the Citrix server farm. The drivers need be installed on only one MetaFrame server, and then replication can be configured so all other servers in the farm receive these same drivers.
- **Advanced network printer share support**—In addition to the standard network printer support available with Terminal Server, MetaFrame expands on this functionality by providing the ability to auto-assign network printers listed in the server farm to MetaFrame users based on user account or domain group membership, providing an easier way to manage printers than through logon scripts.

■ **Advanced local client printer support**—Much like the client printer support provided by Terminal Server, MetaFrame will also automatically redirect a client's local printers so they are accessible from within a MetaFrame session. MetaFrame expands the support available for client-mapped printers by providing a number of customization features, including the ability to map printers using a set of universal printer drivers that can compensate for a missing or ill-behaved native driver for the printer when used on a MetaFrame server. MetaFrame also provides the ability to throttle the amount of bandwidth a client-mapped printer consumes in the ICA presentation services data stream between the server and the client.

Advanced Printer Driver Management

Whether or not you're implementing MetaFrame, you must still have a suitable printer driver available on the Terminal Server. The process of driver installation is exactly the same as described in the "Printer Driver Management" section, earlier in this chapter. What MetaFrame provides is an advanced mechanism for managing these printer drivers once they have been installed on the server. Figure 17.21 shows the Drivers tab for the Printer Management module in the MPS Management Console. The drivers shown on this tab are dependent on the server selected from the drop-down list. When (Any) is selected, as it is in this example, all the drivers installed on the servers across the farm are displayed. The drivers listed may not actually be installed on all servers; clicking an individual driver brings up, in the right-hand side of the window, a list of the servers on which the driver resides. Changes in status of a printer driver (added, removed, updated) are automatically communicated back to the data store and are visible in the Printer Management Drivers folder. Through printer driver replication, which I discuss in the next section, you can ensure that all the necessary drivers are available on all servers in the farm.

Three of the six drivers are Citrix universal printer drivers (UPDs) and allow client printers to be mapped that otherwise would fail due to driver compatibility issues. UPDs are discussed in more detail in the "Advanced Local Client Printer Support" section, later in this chapter.

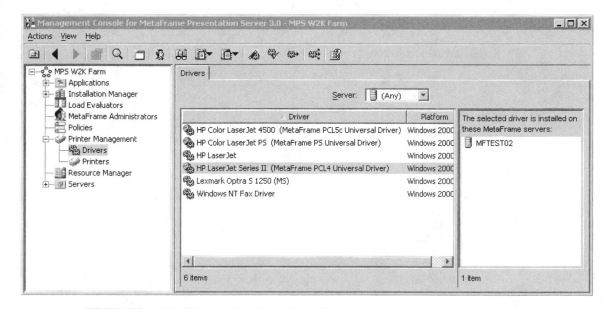

Figure 17.21 The Drivers tab for Printer Management in the MPS Management Console.

Printer Driver Replication

Two types of printer driver replication are supported by MPS: replication between specific servers, and auto-replication of printer drivers between all servers in the farm running the same operating system platform.

Replication between specific servers running the same Windows platform is configured as follows:

1. From under the Printer Management module, click the Drivers object and then select the desired drivers from the right-hand pane.

2. Now right-click and then select Replicate Drivers. This opens the Replicate Driver dialog box, shown in Figure 17.22. From here you can choose to replicate to all servers and add to the auto-replication list, or you can choose the specific servers to replicate the driver(s) to.

3. Click OK to complete the replication setup and queue up the drivers for replication. As the replication completes, events are written to the target server's system event log. Replication is performed on servers running the same platform operating system (Windows 2000 or 2003). Drivers are not replicated between different operating system versions.

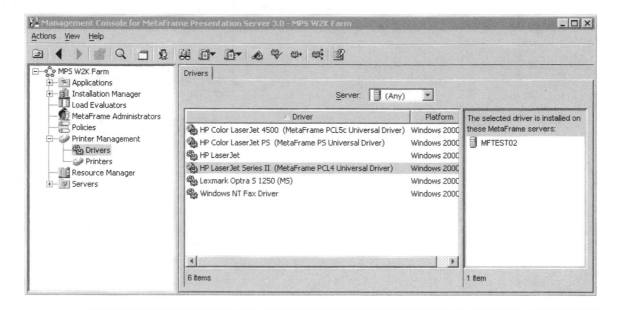

Figure 17.22   The Replicate Driver dialog box.

Auto-replication of printer drivers to all available MetaFrame servers in the farm is configured as follows:

1. From under the Printer Management module, right-click the Drivers object and select the Auto-Replication option.

2. The Auto-Replication dialog box opens, and any drivers configured for replication are displayed. To add one or more drivers, click the Add button to open the driver selection dialog box (Figure 17.23).

3. Select the desired server from the drop-down list. This should be the server you arbitrarily designated as the main printer driver replication source. Do not use the default option of (Any). Once you select the specific server, the driver list changes to show only the drivers installed on that server.

4. Highlight the drivers you want to replicate and then click OK. The selected drivers are then added to the Auto-Replication dialog box. Once you click OK on this screen, the drivers are automatically queued for replication to all other servers running on the same platform operating system (Windows 2000 or Windows 2003). As replication completes, events are written to the target server's system event log.

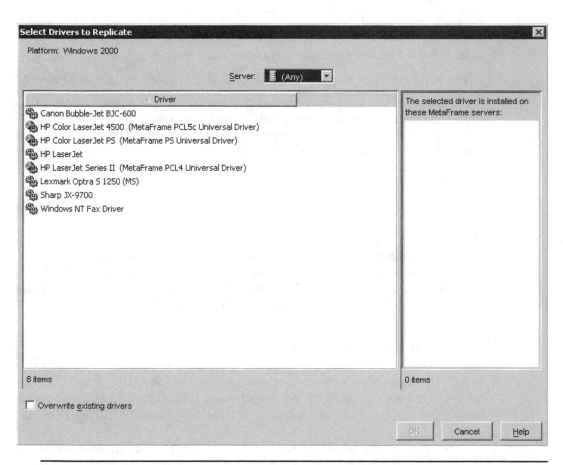

Figure 17.23   The auto-replication driver selection dialog box.

NOTE: While printer driver replication can be a valuable administrative tool, care must be taken when replicating a large number of printer drivers across a large number of MetaFrame servers. The data store maintains information on all printer drivers when auto-replication is being used, which increases the size of the data store. During replication, the server acting as the source for driver replication may experience a high CPU load. This can negatively impact the computing experience of users who may have user sessions on this source server. A few options are available for reducing possible negative effects of driver replication:

■ Establish the MetaFrame server acting as the source server as a dedicated print replication server. By eliminating user logons, you can allocate resources to the replication effort without fear of impacting the production users. Establishing such a printer configuration is one example of when a MetaFrame print server may be appropriate for the environment.

- Perform the replication when load on the farm is relatively light.

- Use scheduled replication instead of auto-replication.

- Implement the data store on a true DBMS database (SQL Server, Oracle, or DB2).

Performance of the replication itself is dictated by the size of the replication queue; this is the queue from which the printer drivers are pulled for replication. Citrix recommends that the queue itself not exceed 1,500 entries because beyond that, performance begins to degrade. At first glance this size seems more than sufficient, but considering how the queue size itself is calculated, this recommended cap could be quickly exceeded.

The queue size is easily calculated using the formula

QueueSize = (# printer drivers) × (# of servers)

So if you have 8 printers in your environment and want to replicate these to all 25 servers in your farm, the queue size will be 8 × 25, which calculates to 200. If the number of servers was much higher, say 50 servers and 20 printers, the queue length would be 1,000, which is much closer to the soft cap of 1,500.

The speed at which these entries are processed is a direct product of how busy the server is managing other tasks. Because the IMA service processes the queue entries with a low priority, if the server is busy with other things this process takes much longer. The number of servers that are the target of the driver replication also affects the replication speed. As the number of servers increases, the time it takes to replicate each driver to all servers also increases.

The QPRINTER utility can be used to help monitor and troubleshoot printer driver replication. The tool is located in the \Support\debug\<OS Version> folder on the Windows MPS installation CD. The OS version is W2K3 for Windows Server 2003 and W2K for Windows 2000 Server.

Advanced Network Printer Share Support

Earlier in the "Managing Printer Shares Using Logon Scripts" section of this chapter I discussed use of logon scripts as a method for assigning network printers to users when logging on to a Terminal Server. MetaFrame compliments this functionality by letting you assign printers available in the server farm to any MetaFrame user based on their user ID or group membership. All available printers in the farm are listed under the Printers object in the Printer Management module of the MPS Management Console. Printers can be added to this list in one of two ways:

- Printers shared directly off a MetaFrame server automatically appear in the printer list for the farm. Many people refer to these types of printers as "local printers," since they are local to a MetaFrame server, but I've found that many users and administrators find this name misleading because the printer is actually local to only those users logged on to the MetaFrame server sharing the printer. I prefer to call this type of printer a "local server farm printer."

■ If the printers reside on a print server not also a MetaFrame server, shared printers do not automatically appear in the farm printer list. These printers must be manually imported into the farm. This is done from within the Printer Management module, details of which are discussed in the next section.

Figure 17.24 shows a pair of printers listed in the 2K3FARM. The first printer, HPDJ970Cse, was imported from a print server that is not a MetaFrame server (or is a MetaFrame server in a different farm), while the second printer, MFLaserJet, was automatically added because it is currently being shared off the NEWTON server, which is running MetaFrame. Because the MFLaserJet printer is shared off a MetaFrame server, additional information about that printer is available within the Management Console.

Regardless of how a printer is added, once it is visible within the server farm, it can be assigned to a group (or specific user) so that when a member of that group logs on to a MetaFrame server in the farm, the corresponding printers are auto-created and available for use. This provides the MetaFrame administrator with an alternative to using logon scripts for printer assignment. I describe how to configure this printer auto-creation in the next section of this chapter.

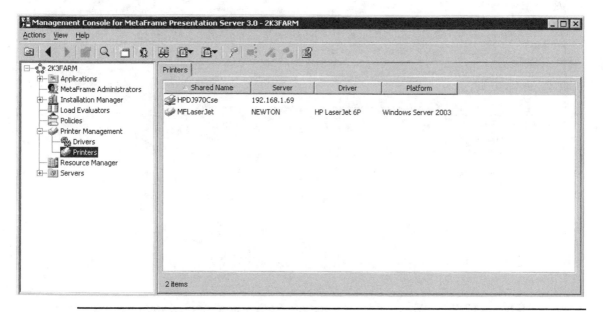

Figure 17.24   How printers are added to the farm depends on whether or not they are shared off a MetaFrame server.

NOTE: While sharing a printer directly off a MetaFrame server is a convenient way to make the printer available within the farm, doing so introduces additional overhead on the server that can impact any active client sessions.

One way Citrix recommends avoiding this is to dedicate a MetaFrame server solely as a print server. This configuration has the server running MetaFrame and sharing out one or more printers to the farm but not allowing any ICA or RDP user logons.

Importing Printers from a non-MetaFrame Print Server

Manually importing printers from a non-MetaFrame print server is a straightforward exercise executed by right-clicking the Printer Management module in the Management Console and selecting Import Network Print Server. You are then prompted to provide the name of the print server. Do *not* include the double-backslash that normally would precede a Windows server name; instead, just enter the server name. You then need to provide the credentials necessary to allow the connection with the server to be established. Figure 17.25 shows an example.

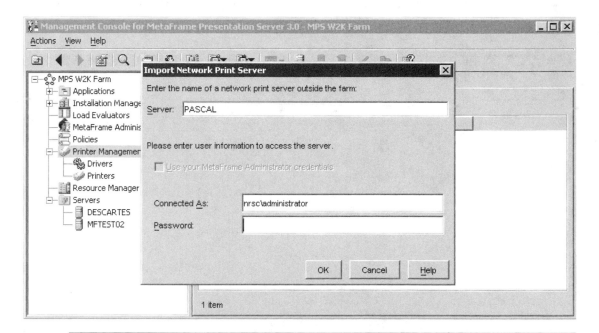

Figure 17.25 When importing printers from a print server, you must provide the server name and credentials for authentication.

Once the contents of the print server have been imported, the server appears on the Network Print Servers tab that is visible when you click the Printer Management module. The print server remains on this list indefinitely until manually discarded. If you add or remove specific printers from any of the listed print servers, you must manually update the printers in the data store by right-clicking the print server and selecting Update Network Print Server. You will need to provide valid credentials before the updated contents are read from the server. Once the printers from a print server have been imported, they appear in the Printers list alongside any printers shared off MetaFrame servers within the farm.

If at some point it is ever decided that printers from this print server are no longer required, they can all be removed simply by right-clicking on the print server and selecting Discard Network Print Server. The print server will be removed from the list and all associated printers under the Printers object will also immediately be removed.

With all the desired printers now listed in the server farm, you are ready to configure the network printer auto-creation so these network printers are automatically mapped to the appropriate users based on their user ID or group membership.

Network Printer Auto-Creation

Printer auto-creation assignment is performed by right-clicking the desired printer listed in the Printers object and then selecting the Auto-Creation option. You are then presented with a dialog box where you are expected to select the desired user ID or group to be assigned to this printer when they log on to any MetaFrame server in the farm (see Figure 17.26). When a user who belongs to this group logs on to a MetaFrame server in the farm, they have their associated printers automatically mapped for them.

If you wish to assign the same groups to more than one printer, you can duplicate an existing auto-creation configuration from one printer onto another simply by right-clicking the printer you wish to replicate and selecting Copy Auto-Creation Settings. You can then select one or more printers from the list and click OK. The auto-creation settings are automatically replicated for the selected items.

One configuration option exists that dictates whether or not a user can maintain personal configuration settings from one session to the next for an auto-created network printer. By default, a user can modify the settings for an auto-created network printer and have those settings persist from session to session. The option can be found by right-clicking the Printer Management icon and selecting Properties from the Context menu. From the Properties dialog box, select the Printers settings. You see the auto-created network printers setting at the bottom of the dialog box. I describe the settings that pertain to auto-created client printers in the next section.

Now that we've examined the advanced features MetaFrame provides for managing *network-mapped* printers in your environment, we look more closely at the features MetaFrame provides to enhance support for client-printer redirection.

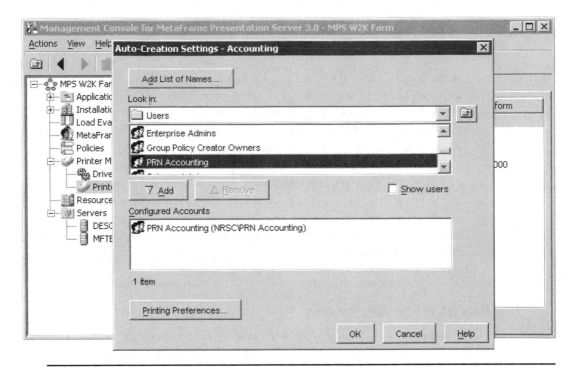

Figure 17.26   Printer auto-creation is best assigned to user groups instead of individual users.

Advanced Local Client Printer Support

Some of the key requirements that Terminal Services and MetaFrame have in common with regards to redirection of local client printers are

- A suitable printer driver is required to exist on the MetaFrame/Terminal Server.
- Printer driver selection is determined by comparing the full printer driver name on the client with the corresponding printer driver name for the server.
- Any mismatches in driver name, or no driver being found, result in the client printer mapping silently failing.

MetaFrame attempts to offset some of the time required to support printers in your environment by including advanced support and management options specifically for client printer mappings, including the following:

- Complete centralized management of the drivers and printers pertaining to client printer redirection, including enabling or disabling of drive-mapping support.

■ Support for a universal printer driver (UPD) that can be configured to be used if a suitable native driver match cannot be found.

In this final section of the chapter, I look at the options pertaining to MetaFrame's client printer mapping support and how they are configured. Most of the options pertaining to local client printer redirection on MetaFrame are managed from the Printer Management Properties dialog box, as shown in Figure 17.27.

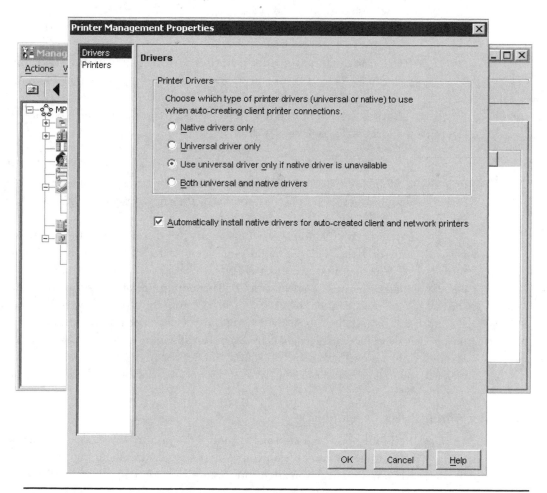

Figure 17.27   The Printer Management Properties dialog box contains most of the settings specific to client-printer mapping.

Printer Driver Support

The first group of printer management options available pertains directly to the logic employed by MetaFrame when attempting to establish a printer driver match between the client and the server. There are four options available:

- **Native drivers only**—The available universal printer drivers (UPDs) are never used; if a driver is not found that matches the client's driver, the mapping is never established.
- **Universal driver only**—Regardless of whether or not a native driver exists, a suitable UPD is used instead.
- **Use universal driver only if native driver is unavailable (Default option)**—The UPD for a printer is used only if the corresponding native driver cannot be found.
- **Both universal and native drivers**—A printer queue is created for both types of drivers. Even if a native driver exists, a universal printer driver is also created.

The default option of using the native driver and falling back on the UPD only if the native driver is not found is a suitable configuration under most circumstances, but there may be certain situations where you want to support only the native drivers. In this case, you need to modify the default printer driver action.

When the option "Automatically install native drivers for auto-created client and network printers" is enabled, the MetaFrame server automatically installs the signed drivers provided by Microsoft if they are not already available when a user attempts to establish a client-mapped or network-mapped printer. This option installs only the native drivers that ship with Windows; it cannot be used to install custom third-party drivers. Third-party drivers must still be installed manually and then replicated. Because the printer drivers being installed have been digitally signed by Microsoft, they are certified to work not only with Windows but also with Windows Terminal Services. I prefer not to enable this option, in order to maintain control over exactly what drivers are available on the MetaFrame servers.

Printer Driver Compatibility

Under certain situations you may want to control the printer drivers that are used to support client printers. You may wish to limit your MetaFrame environment to use only a specific set of printer drivers, or maybe you are having issues with only one particular printer driver and want to ensure that it is never loaded into your MetaFrame environment.

The drivers used by client printers are managed using the Printer Driver Compatibility tool, which is accessed by right-clicking on the Drivers object and selecting Compatibility from the context menu. This opens the Driver Compatibility dialog box shown in Figure 17.28.

The default behavior of MetaFrame is to allow all printer drivers to be used except for any that are added on this screen. You can add the drivers to exclude simply by clicking the

Add button and either typing in the driver name, which must match exactly, or selecting the driver from the listbox.

You can also configure MetaFrame so that all drivers are disallowed, except for those that are explicitly added to this list.

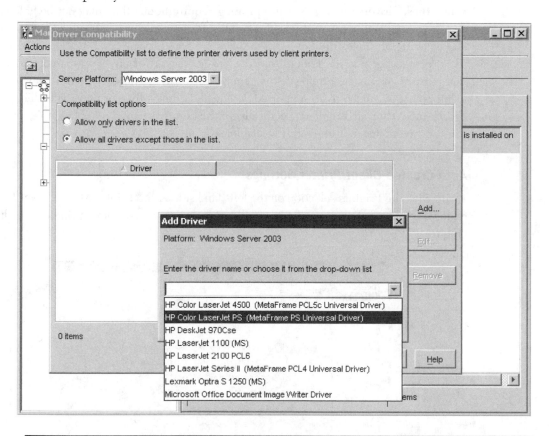

Figure 17.28   The Driver Compatibility dialog box allows you to control what printer drivers are used by client-mapped printers.

MetaFrame Universal Printer Drivers

Many people have asked why they should even bother with managing installation and replication of printer drives now that MetaFrame supports the different universal printer drivers (UPDs). Why not use the UPD for all client-mapped printing? While certainly the UPD helps ensure that most client-based printers are accessible through a MetaFrame session, there are some limitations to this approach.

The universal drivers by nature must be based on a generic printer driver that is most likely to be compatible with most of printers available. Citrix has deployed three flavors of its UPD, one for PCL5c based on the HP Color LaserJet 4500 driver, a PCL4 driver based on the HP LaserJet Series II, and a PostScript (PS) driver based on the HP Color LaserJet PS. While these drivers meet most basic printing requirements, they may not be able to access certain special features available with a printer; for example, special paper trays, output bins, and collating or duplex options.

I prefer to try to implement the true printer driver for any work-based client printers that must be mapped and relegate the generic universal drivers to support of any other client printers that may need to be supported. Home and home-office printers will fall into this category, since many are targeted specifically for the home user, and reliable, stable server-grade printer drivers may not be readily available.

Auto-Created Client Printer Settings

If you click the Printers selection on the left-hand side of the Printer Management Properties dialog box, the options specific to configuring auto-created client printers are displayed (Figure 17.29).

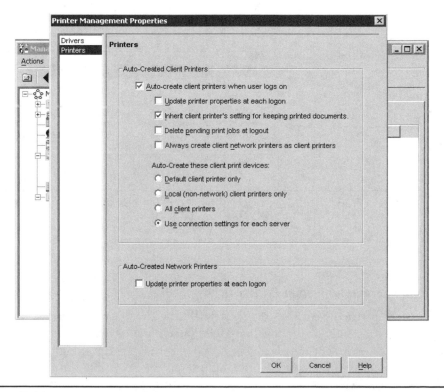

Figure 17.29 The Auto-Created Client Printer settings for the Printer Management Properties dialog box.

From this screen you can centrally manage the state of client printer redirection for the server farm. The default options are suitable under most circumstances, except that you may want to change the "Auto-create these client print devices:" setting from reading the individual connection settings on each server to following a single configuration option. The function of each property is described in Table 17.2.

Table 17.2   Auto-Created Client Printer Settings

Property	Description
Auto-create client printers when user logs on.	Controls whether client printers are mapped globally on all servers in the farm. If it is disabled here, it will be disabled on all servers in the farm.
Update printer properties at each logon.	Disabled by default, this option controls whether setting changes to be made on the local client's printer are applied to the client-mapped printer on the MetaFrame server at each logon. When disabled, changes made to the properties of the client-mapped printer within the MetaFrame session are retained and can differ from the settings on the client. If you want to retain the server-side settings, do not enable this option.
Inherit client printer's settings for keeping printed documents.	Enabled by default, this option dictates whether the client-side setting for retaining printed documents in the print queue is applied to the server-side printer as well. A kept document is retained in the print queue and not deleted once the print has completed. This setting can consume a large amount of disk space on the boot/system drive of the server, as all job files are retained in the %SystemRoot%\System32\Spool\Printers folder.
Delete pending print jobs at logout.	Normally if there are pending print jobs and a user logs off, the print queue is retained on the server and the jobs held until the printing has completed. When this option is enabled, the pending jobs are deleted without being printed and the client printer queue is removed.
Always create client network printers as client printers.	By default, if the client-mapped printer is a network printer and that printer is directly accessible by the MetaFrame server, the print jobs are sent directly from the MetaFrame server to the network printer, bypassing the client-side print queue. This results in faster printing of network printer–bound print jobs.

Table 17.2 Auto-Created Client Printer Settings (continued)

Property	Description
	This configuration results in degraded performance if the printer resides across a WAN link, in which case the full job is being sent across the WAN, consuming additional bandwidth. If this is the configuration for most of the farm users, this option should be enabled.
	When this option is enabled, the print job is always sent through the client device. This results in slightly slower printing but consumes less network resources because the client-server communications utilize the ICA protocol and data compression.
Auto-create these client print devices.	You can choose one of the four listed options, which dictate for all servers in the farm what type of client-side print devices are auto-created. The available choices are ■ *Default client printers only.* Only the default client-side printer is mapped through to the MetaFrame session. All other client printers are ignored. This option reduces the time it can take to map printers, particularly if the client has a large number of local printers. ■ *Local (non-network) client printers only.* This option maps only those printers directly connected to the client or configured through a local printer port. All mapped network printers are ignored. This option may be desirable if you want to provide network printer access only through the MetaFrame server itself. ■ *All client printers.* All printers on the client are mapped through to the MetaFrame session. ■ *Use connection settings for each server.* This option bases the client printer mappings on the settings defined for the ICA connections on each server. Management of the ICA connection properties was discussed in Chapter 14, "MetaFrame Presentation Server Configuration." Within a farm I prefer to manage the client printer settings centrally from here instead of allowing the individual settings on each client to be utilized. This ensures a consistent configuration across all servers in the farm.

Table 17.2   Auto-Created Client Printer Settings (continued)

Property	Description
Auto-Created Network Printers: Update printer properties at each logon.	This option pertains to any auto-created network printers, which were discussed in the "Network Printer Auto-Creation" section of this chapter. When this option is enabled, the printer settings that a user may define for an auto-created network printer are replaced every time they log back on. This option may be enabled if you want to ensure that a printer maintains a consistent configuration and do not want your users to be able to modify this configuration.

Printer Driver Cross-Reference Support

Earlier in the chapter, in the "Driver Naming Requirements and Alternate Name Matching" section, I explained that when a client printer is being mapped in a Terminal Server session, the printer driver name on the client is compared to the driver name on the server. If they do not match exactly, the mapping is not generated. MetaFrame provides a graphical interface directly within the Management Console where any necessary substitution entries can be added without having to make registry changes or modify text files. The specific dialog box is opened by right-clicking the Drivers object and then selecting Mapping from the Context menu. The Driver Mapping dialog box opens, listing all the existing mappings that have been created. A new substitution is added by clicking the Add button. The dialog box shown in Figure 17.30 appears. In the upper portion, enter the full client driver name exactly as it appears. The spacing and capitalization must match exactly, or the substitution will not function properly. For the server driver, you can either manually type in the name or select the name of an installed printer driver from the drop-down list box.

Once the information has been entered, click OK to save the changes. The information then appears in the Driver Mapping dialog box (Figure 17.31). Once entered, this information is applied to all servers in the farm. In this example, when a client provides the server with the driver name "hp deskjet 970c series", the client queue is created but the driver "HP DeskJet 970Cse" is used instead.

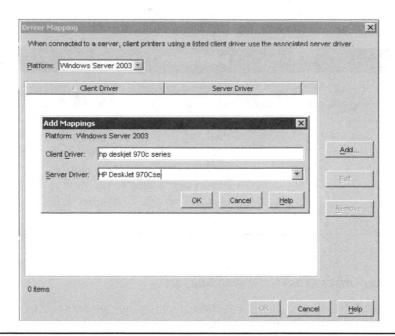

Figure 17.30   When you enter a mapping, enter the client-side drive name exactly as it appears on the client.

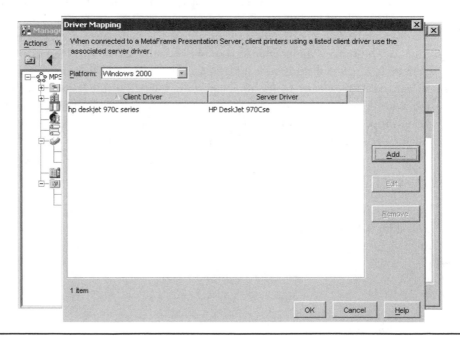

Figure 17.31   The Driver Mapping dialog box.

The Client-Mapped Printer Naming Convention

The final note to mention has to do with the naming convention used by MetaFrame for client-mapped printers. This was discussed in Chapter 8, but I review it quickly here. When mapped, a MetaFrame client-mapped printer has the following naming:

Client\<Client name>#\<Printer Name>

where "Client" is a constant used to show that the mapping is a client printer. "Client name" is the name assigned to the client device during installation of MetaFrame. And finally, the printer name corresponds to the full printer name on the client device.

For example, if I have a local printer called "HP LaserJet", and I log on to a MetaFrame server configured to support this client mapping, I would expect to have a client printer mapping with the following name:

Client\TODDPC\HP LaserJet

where "TODDPC" is my client name. Similarly, if I had a network-mapped printer on my local PC with the mapping of

\\PrintServ\HP DeskJet 970C Series

then when I next logged on to the MetaFrame server, my client name should automatically become

Client\TODDPC\\\PrintServ\HP DeskJet 970C Series

The extra backslashes in the name are not a concern because they are ignored and have no effect on actually attempting to print to that client-mapped printer.

Client Printer Bandwidth Throttling

When clients are connecting to a MetaFrame server over a limited bandwidth connection, the amount of bandwidth consumed by client printer jobs can directly impact the user's computing experience. To the end-user the impact manifests itself as sluggish screen updates and slow system response to keyboard and mouse input. In order to counteract this problem, Citrix provides the ability within MetaFrame to dictate the maximum bandwidth that all client print jobs on a server can utilize. This setting is accessed by clicking on the Printer Management icon in the Management Console and then selecting the Bandwidth tab as shown in Figure 17.32.

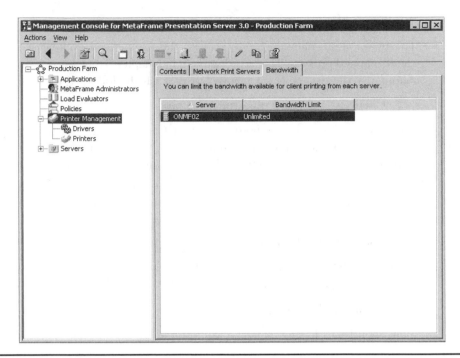

Figure 17.32   The bandwidth available for client printing can be set from within the Printer Management module.

By default all servers in the farm are automatically assigned no limit on the bandwidth that is consumed by client-mapped print jobs. A limit on bandwidth is set by right-clicking on the desired server and selecting Edit. A dialog box will then open allowing you to choose Unlimited or to set a limit by specifying a value in Kilobits per second (Kbps). This value has the following characteristics:

- The setting dictates the maximum bandwidth for print jobs only for the given server. If you have 10 servers in your farm you will need to define a maximum bandwidth on all MetaFrame servers that will allow connections over the link you're trying to manage.
- The bandwidth value represents the maximum bandwidth available per ICA connection on the MetaFrame server. So if you have 20 connections and a maximum bandwidth of 5Kbps, then 100Kbps of total bandwidth would be consumed on the server.
- The setting defined here is server-wide and affects all client connections. If you wish to manage client printing bandwidth for only certain users then create a MetaFrame policy specific to those users and set the client printing bandwidth within that policy. MetaFrame policies are discussed in Chapter 14, "MetaFrame Presentation Server Configuration."

In order to determine the per-connection client printing bandwidth you need to know how much available bandwidth there is over the link and then divide that by the total number of concurrent users that are operating across that link. Using this simple formula you can establish an initial estimate that you can then adjust up or down as necessary to maximize the configuration for your environment.

PrinterBandwidth = (Total bandwidth available – Total bandwidth utilized) / Total concurrent users

The specific parameters are

- **Total bandwidth available**—This is the total bandwidth for the network link. For example 1.54Mb for a T1 connection.
- **Total bandwidth utilized**—This is the total bandwidth that is being consumed. This value can be estimated or based on data gathered using network monitoring tools. An average over a few days will give a more accurate estimate of usage over time.
- **Total concurrent users**—The total number of concurrent user connections across all MetaFrame servers that need to be managed.

With this information you can generate some numbers that will give a starting point. For example, say I have a T1 connection (1540 Kb), a total bandwidth utilization of 80% or around 1232Kb, and 45 concurrent users that must access that link. The formula would generate a result of around 6.8Kb per connection. This means that you would then enter the value of 7Kb for the bandwidth limit. You can enter only integer values, so I have simply rounded the number 6.8Kb up to 7Kb.

I would recommend that after entering this value you monitor the network to see if the change has reduced the network load. With this information you can increase or decrease the value as necessary to fine-tune your environment.

When in doubt about the bandwidth available, you can simply start off by setting the value to 5Kbps and then slowly adjusting the value upwards until a noticeable degradation in performance occurs. At this point you will know that you have reached that threshold and need to throttle back a little.

NOTE: One important point to remember is that these limits on bandwidth apply only to client-mapped printers. This is because these print jobs are sent through a virtual channel in the ICA protocol, which can be directly managed by MetaFrame.

Print jobs sent to standard network-based printers are not throttled by this bandwidth setting, including client network printers that are being directly access via the network and are not being treated as client printers. This behavior is managed from within the Printer Management properties, which were discussed in the "Auto-Created Client Printer Settings" section in this chapter.

CHAPTER 18

User Profile and Account Configuration

Before You Begin

This chapter provides a complete review of the function of user profiles and their role in a Windows Terminal Server environment. In Chapter 8, "Server Installation and Management Planning," I provided an introduction to user profiles, what types are available, and how they function. In this chapter I focus on what implementation steps should be reviewed and performed in preparation for user profile implementation, and finally, what is involved in actually creating and managing your users' profiles in production.

Every Windows Terminal Server user (and Windows 32-bit OS user in general) has what is known as a *user profile*. A user profile contains a combination of the user's desktop settings such as icons, screen colors, or window positions and user-specific information such as network or printer connections, Internet favorites, and e-mail preferences. A user profile also contains a copy of the contents of the HKEY_CURRENT_USER registry key, which is automatically loaded into the registry when the user logs on and unloaded when the user logs off. This registry key contains application and session information specific to that user. The contents of the registry key are maintained in the file NTUSER.DAT, which resides by default in the profile folder. By default a local copy of a user's profile is maintained on a Windows 2000 or 2003 server in this folder:

%SystemDrive%\Documents and Settings

Figure 18.1 shows an example of the Documents and Settings directory on a Windows 2000 Terminal Server. Notice that it contains folders for a number of users, including the local administrator, the default user, and even a folder called All Users, which contains common profile information shared between all users who log on to the server. The contents of the All Users folder are read-only to non-administrators. Users cannot modify the information contained in this folder.

TIP: Only administrators, SYSTEM, and the associated user have access to a profile folder. A user cannot access another user's profile folder.

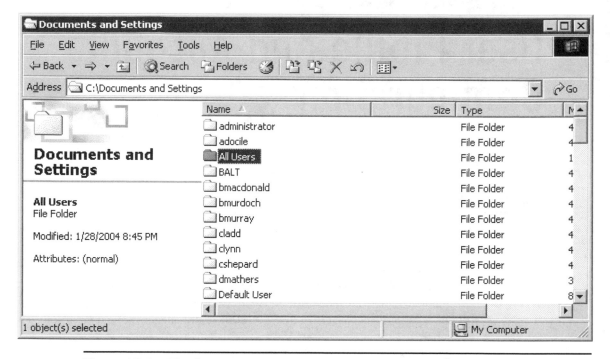

Figure 18.1   The Documents and Settings folder on a Windows 2000 Terminal Server.

The three types of user profiles first introduced in Chapter 8 are

- Local profiles
- Roaming profiles
- Mandatory roaming profiles

Local Profiles

The local profile is automatically created and maintained directly on the Terminal Server that the user logs on to. Information is maintained within this profile and is accessible from one logon to the next. Because this profile is managed locally on the server, if the user logs on to a different Terminal Server they will not have access to these same settings. The changes are retained only on the server where the profile was originally created. This configuration is certainly not desirable in a load-balanced Terminal Server environment, where users can be logged on to server A one day and server B the next. The local profile is the default type used unless a roaming profile has been defined within the properties of the user's account.

Local profiles are found under the Documents and Settings folder on the system drive, and just as with any other files on the system, you can traverse into the folder and modify the available files or folder structure. I recommend that direct manipulation of these folders be kept to a minimum, particularly if you wish to delete an existing local profile.

Instead of directly deleting the folder structure for a user, Microsoft recommends using the User Profiles tab in the System applet in the control panel. In addition to a view of the existing profiles on the server, you have the ability to use this dialog box to perform some profile manipulation. Figure 18.2 shows how the profiles list from Figure 18.1 would appear in the User Profiles tab.

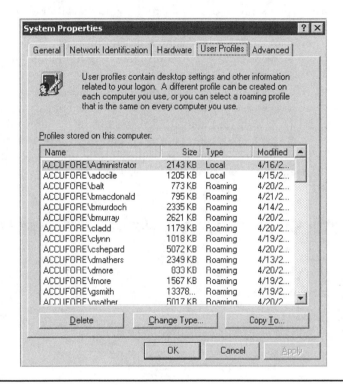

Figure 18.2   The User Profiles tab from the System applet on a Windows 2003 Terminal Server.

Roaming Profiles

As the name implies, a roaming profile travels with a user as they log on from one Terminal Server to the next. When a user logs on to a server for the first time, a copy of their network-based roaming profile is copied down to the server and used as a local profile. When the user logs off, any changes made to the profile are saved back to the network where they are accessible from whatever server the user next logs on to. Roaming profiles are processed in Windows as follows:

1. A user with a roaming profile logs on to a Terminal Server.
2. The Terminal Server checks whether the user has a local (cached) copy of his or her profile stored on the server. If so, the local copy is compared with the server copy to see which is newer (the comparison is based on a last updated timestamp). If the server copy is newer, the server profile is copied down to the local machine. If the profiles are the same, the local copy is used, and if the local copy is newer than the server copy, the local copy is once again used.
3. If the user has no cached profile on the local server, the network-based profile is copied to the local server. It remains on the local server until the next time it's updated, deleted manually by an administrator, or deleted automatically by the system (see Chapter 15, "Group Policy Configuration," for information on enabling this option).
4. After the appropriate profile has been placed on the local server, the registry information stored in the file NTUSER.DAT is loaded into the registry hive HKEY_USERS. Figure 18.3 shows this hive with a number of keys listed off the root. Each unique key pair represents one user currently logged on to the Terminal Server. The numbers listed represent the unique security identifier (SID) of each user. The default user's profile is also loaded, from the NTUSER.DAT file in the Default Profile directory.

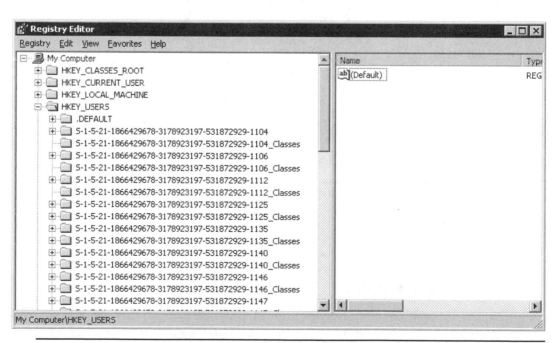

Figure 18.3   The HKEY_USERS registry hive showing active user sessions loaded into the registry.

5. Any desktop changes that occur to the profile are stored locally while the user is logged on. When the user logs off the Terminal Server, his or her information is unloaded from the registry and written back to the NTUSER.DAT file on the local computer. The individual files within the profile are compared with those in the profile on the server (see Figure 18.4 for a visual breakdown of the logic involved in the profile comparison mechanism).

The files are handled as follows:

- If a file exists in both the local and the remote profile, the file with the newer timestamp is kept. In Figure 18.4, File A in the local profile will overwrite File A on the server, while File B on the server is kept because it's newer than the one in the local profile.
- If a file exists in the local profile but not on the server, the timestamp of the remote profile is compared with the timestamp of the file. If the profile is newer, it means that the file was deleted in another instance of the profile on a different computer, so the file is deleted from this profile as well. If the file is newer, it's copied to the remote profile. File C in this example will be deleted from the local profile, because the server profile's timestamp is newer than the timestamp on the local file
- If the file exists in the remote profile but not in the local profile, the timestamp of the file is compared with the timestamp of the local profile. If the local profile is newer, the file must have been deleted from the local profile, so it's also deleted from the remote profile. If the file is newer, it must have been added in another instance of the profile on a different computer, so the file is kept in the remote profile. File D in this example will be deleted from the server profile, since its timestamp is older than the timestamp on the local profile, so Windows assumes that it was deleted from the local profile.

If you watch the HKEY_USERS registry hive when a user logs off, you'll see the user's associated registry keys disappear.

NOTE: I recommend that you avoid implementing a Terminal Server environment that allows production users to use local profiles. Even in a single-server environment, use of roaming profiles provides a number of benefits, including the following:

- Establishing a core infrastructure that does not require changing if an additional server is added in the future.
- Allowing for redirection of large folders off the local server, reducing the amount of disk space consumed by these profiles.

■ (In multiple-server implementations) Ensuring that users have a consistent desktop, regardless of the server they're on. If only local profiles are used, changes to the desktop will seem to "disappear" as a user logs on to different servers in the environment.

After reading this chapter you will see that the process to configure roaming profiles for your users is fairly straightforward.

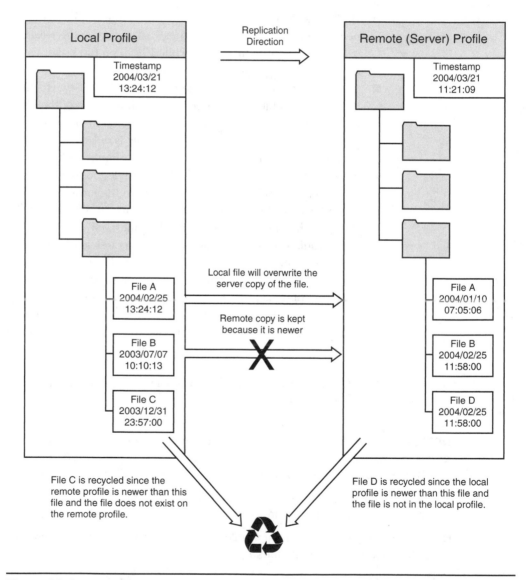

Figure 18.4 The Windows local and remote profile comparison mechanism.

Terminal Server Roaming Profile and Home Folder Settings

Chapter 1, "Microsoft Windows Terminal Services," talks about the Windows 2000/2003 Active Directory Users and Computers component for managing user account properties and how it contains profile configuration options specific to Terminal Server users, as shown in Figure 18.5. From this tab you can define a user profile and home directory that are specific to Terminal Server and separate from the standard Windows profile and home directory paths.

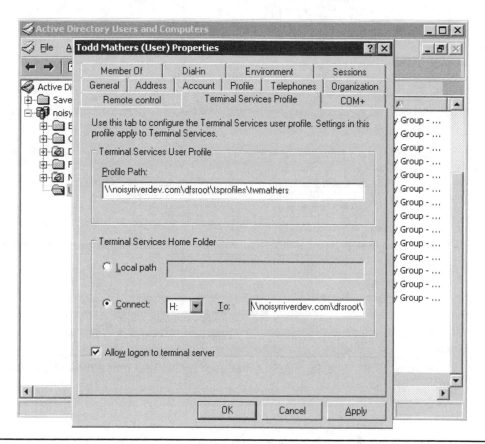

Figure 18.5   Windows Server 2003 Active Directory Users and Computers properties for configuring Terminal Server–specific profile information.

Figure 18.6 shows the process flow that Terminal Server follows when determining a profile and home directory to use. The decision process is repeated twice, once for the profile and once for the home directory, so it is possible to define only one option and not the other. Basically, if either the Terminal Server home directory or profile is left blank, the system attempts first to use the Windows home directory or profile path if they have been defined (see the Profile tab), and failing that uses the default local home directory and profile paths.

TIP: When a user logs on to a Windows workstation (2000 or XP), the Terminal Server profile information is never queried, only the standard profile information. The Terminal Services profile tab applies only to users when logging on to a Terminal Server.

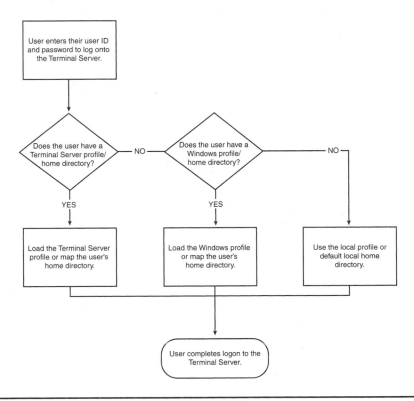

Figure 18.6 The Terminal Server user profile and home directory decision tree.

Mandatory Roaming Profiles

A mandatory roaming profile behaves exactly like a standard roaming profile with one exception: Changes made by the user during a session are not saved to the profile stored on the server when the user logs off. The next time the user logs on, he or she once again receives the original profile from the server. Removing the user's ability to save profile changes gives you the capacity to assign the same profile to multiple users, and as a result, provides a single location where profile changes are automatically updated for all associated users. This approach is most common in a situation where a number of task-based workers perform the same job function (a call center, for example) and you want to ensure that they all have a consistent user interface. This helps to simplify not only support but also issues such as training. It can also help reduce the amount of time users spend customizing their environments with such features as customer icons or wallpaper. Mandatory roaming profiles are processed in almost exactly the same way as regular roaming profiles:

1. A user with a mandatory profile logs on to a Terminal Server.
2. The Terminal Server checks whether the user has a cached copy of the profile on the server. If so, the cached copy is compared with the server-based profile to see if they're the same. If they are, the local copy is used. If they aren't, or no local copy of the profile exists, the server-based profile is copied to the Terminal Server and used. The cached profile remains until the next time the profile on the remote server is updated or until it's deleted from the Terminal Server either automatically or manually by an administrator.
3. The registry information, which in the case of a mandatory profile is stored in the file NTUSER.MAN, is loaded into the registry hive HKEY_USERS.
4. Any desktop changes made during the user's session are saved to the registry but are not written back to disk when the user logs off. When the user logs off, the registry information is simply unloaded. The profile is not written back to the remote profile share location.

Details on creation and use of mandatory profiles are provided in the "Creating and Assigning Mandatory Roaming Profiles" section, later in this chapter.

TIP: Windows Server 2003 provides a group policy object (GPO) setting that can be applied to easily configure a user's roaming profile to behave as a mandatory profile. This greatly simplifies implementation of a mandatory roaming profile, which is also discussed later in this chapter.

Environment Preparation

Before getting into the details of how to create and manage profiles, there is some preparation work that needs to be completed ahead of time. If you prefer, you can skip this section for now and return after you have reviewed the specifics on profiles and are ready to perform the actual implementation.

Domain Security Groups

If you have not already done so, you should create the appropriate Terminal Server security groups as discussed in Chapter 16, "Terminal Server Security." Table 18.1 summarizes these global security groups, which I use in the discussions on profile and home folder creation in the next two sections of this chapter.

Table 18.1 Terminal Server Global Domain Security Groups

Domain Group Name	Description
Terminal Server Administrators	Members of this group have full authority to manage the Terminal Server environment, and as a result, membership in this group must be tightly managed.
Terminal Server Operators	Users with this privilege level have the authority to monitor the various system functions and perform such tasks as shutting down the server or terminating a process. They don't have the ability to make any system changes or perform application installations.
Terminal Server User Support	Members of this group have the ability to perform basic support functions such as shadowing another user's session or logging an active user off. They don't have the ability to restart a server or perform any other server maintenance operations.
Terminal Server Users	This domain group is used to grant basic user access to the production Terminal Servers in the environment. A member of this group could log on to a production Terminal Server and access all generally available applications. The user would have no administrative privileges of any kind.

Profile Folder Share

Before you can implement roaming profiles in your Terminal Server environment, you need to establish a directory share location on the network where you will manage your profile information. Figure 18.7 shows a sample profile hierarchy for maintaining both roaming and mandatory roaming profiles. All mandatory profiles are normally maintained in a single directory since they're shared by multiple users, while each user must have his or her own personal profile folder for a regular roaming profile. You're not required to create each user's roaming profile folder; these are created automatically the first time a user attempts to access his or her roaming profile.

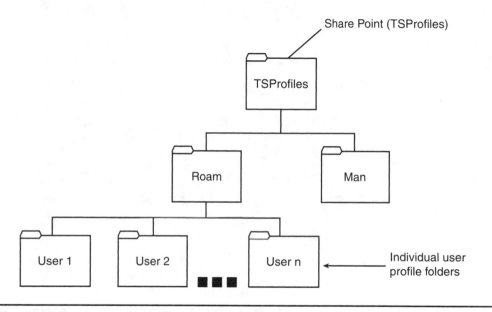

Figure 18.7 A sample profile share hierarchy.

Based on the hierarchy in Figure 18.7 and assuming that the share TSProfiles existed on the server FILESERV01, then a user's Terminal Server profile path for their user account would look like the example in Figure 18.8. Notice that the user's name is entered using the %UserName% environment variable. Microsoft supports use of environment variables when defining properties such as the profile path or the home folder path.

TIP: In Chapter 15, "Group Policy Configuration," I mentioned that a policy could be defined in the Terminal Server Machine Policy to automatically direct all users logged onto the Terminal Server to use a specific Terminal Server Profile Folder. The specific option is called "Set path for TS Roaming Profiles" and you specify the share path such as \\ServerName\ShareName, and Windows automatically appends the user ID to the end. When this policy is implemented you do not need to specify a Terminal Server profile in the user account. The specific policy location is found under Computer Configuration\Administrative Templates\Windows Components\Terminal Services.

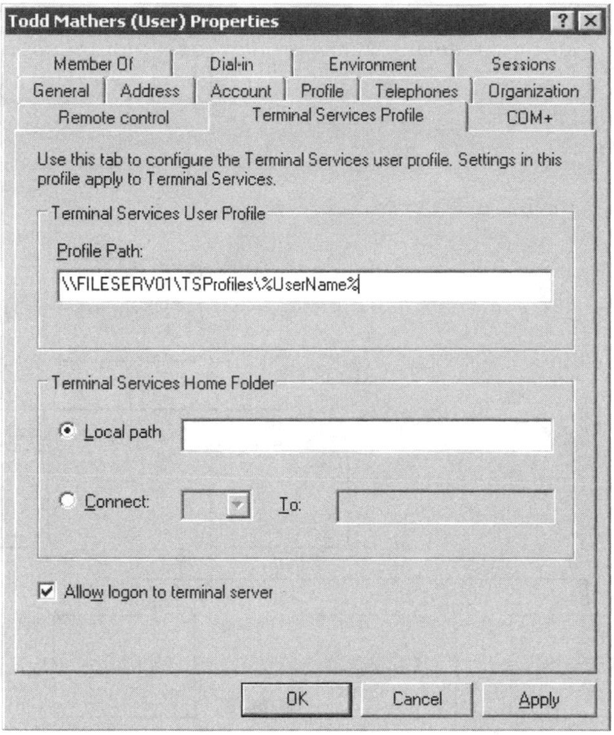

Figure 18.8   An example of the Terminal Server profile path entered for a user.

After the folder structure and shares have been created, assign the appropriate permissions to them. The permissions should be set as shown in Table 18.2. Note that the share and folder names correspond to those shown in Figure 18.7. This was done to keep the example simple. You are certainly free to use alternate names or directory structures on your system.

Table 18.2   An Example of the Permission Assignments for the Profile Hierarchy

Share/Folder Name	Permissions
Profiles Share	SYSTEM: Full Control
	Terminal Server Administrators: Full Control
	Terminal Server Operators: Full Control
	Terminal Server User Support: Full Control
	Terminal Server Users: Full Control

Table 18.2   An Example of the Permission Assignments for the Profile Hierarchy (continued)

Share/Folder Name	Permissions
Profiles folder	SYSTEM: Full Control
Man folder	Terminal Server Administrators: Full Control
Roam folder	Terminal Server Operators: Change
	Terminal Server User Support: Read & Execute
	Terminal Server Users: Read & Execute

When the personal profile folder is created for the user by the system, Full Control is assigned to the individual user and SYSTEM only. No other users (including administrators) will have access to these folders by default. So even though all users have Read access at the root of the Roam folder, they can't view the contents of another user's profile.

NOTE: For support reasons it may be desirable that the Administrators group has access to the user's profile folder. Because the default configuration grants only the user access to this folder, the administrator must take ownership of the folder and adjust the permissions in order to gain access to the information.

Alternatively you can modify this default behavior using a group policy to grant Administrators groups full access when a new profile folder is created for a user. This GPO addition should be made to the Terminal Server Machine Policy, since it is the responsibility of the machine on which the profile is first created to assign the correct security permissions. Figure 18.9 shows the specific policy under the Computer Configuration module. The policy location under Computer Configuration is

Administrative Templates\System\Logon

and the policy is "Add the Administrators security group to roaming user profiles." Enabling this option ensures that administrators have Full Control access to all users' roaming profiles. This policy is applicable to both Windows 2000 Server and Windows Server 2003.

For more information on configuring group policies, refer to Chapter 15, "Group Policy Configuration."

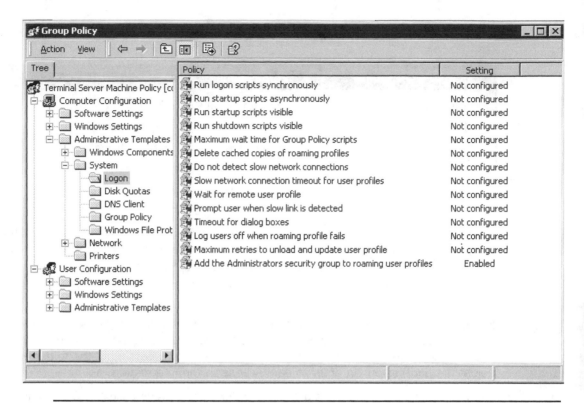

Figure 18.9 Windows group policy for granting administrators Full Control access to roaming user profiles.

Home Folder Share

In addition to creating a location for the user profiles, you should create a share to contain the home folder for each user. A unique home folder is required for each user in order to provide a location for user-specific application and system information within Terminal Server. If a home folder location is not specified for a user's account, the default setting is to use the profile folder. This is not a desired result, particularly for roaming profiles, because the contents of the home folder will likely grow quite large and increase the time required to both download and upload the profile changes. This can also introduce disk space issues on your Terminal Servers. Table 18.3 lists the recommended permissions for both the home folder share and the folder contents. Usually I use the share name TSHome when creating the home folder location.

Table 18.3   Share and Folder Permissions for the User Home Folder TSHome

Domain Security Group Name	Share Permissions	Folder Permissions
SYSTEM	Full Control	Full Control
Terminal Server Administrators	Full Control	Full Control
Terminal Server Operators	Full Control	Change
Terminal Server User Support	Full Control	Read
Terminal Server Users	Full Control	Read

Just as with user profiles, you do not need to create the individual user folders; they are created automatically when the user's account is configured to point to their personal folder. After the system creates the user's home folder, the user is assigned Full Control. The configuration of the user's home folder would look like the example shown in Figure 18.10. Just as the earlier example for the profile folder used the %UserName% environment variable, the same thing can be used here.

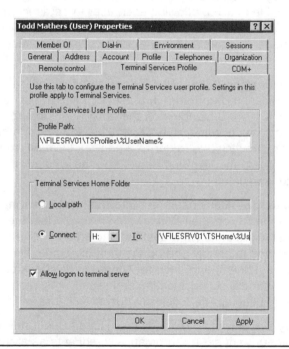

Figure 18.10   An example of the Terminal Server home folder path entered for a user.

Any desired drive letter can be used for the home folder drive letter, just be certain that it will not conflict with another drive assignment that may be in use. I typically like to use H: or U: as the home or user folder when available.

TIP: A common configuration I like to use in a Terminal Server environment is to map the My Documents folder for each user into his or her personal home folder location. This consolidates all the information into one location and makes it easy for the user to find documents saved.

By default, Windows points the My Documents folder into the user's profile folder, which is rarely a desirable setup in a Terminal Server environment. By redirecting My Documents, you can also avoid having to teach users to save data onto a specific drive letter, such as H:, in order to ensure it is going onto a centralized file server. My Documents has slowly become the standard location where most Windows users now maintain their document information.

My Documents can be redirected through a group policy object. This setting should be implemented in the Terminal Server All Users Policy. The specific policy location is under the User Configuration module in

Windows Settings\Folder Redirection\My Documents

Figure 18.11 shows the Properties dialog box for this policy, with an example of how the My Documents folder can be redirected. Once again the %UserName% environment variable is used, allowing each user to be directed properly to their home folder location. In addition to allowing redirection of the My Documents folder, additional folders normally contained in the profile can be redirected. The full list of supported redirects is as follows:

- **Application Data**—All Windows-certified applications are supposed to use the Application Data folder in a user's profile to maintain user-specific data for the application. Depending on the applications being used, the information in this folder can become quite large; 2MB to 3MB or more is certainly not uncommon. By redirecting this folder to a network location, you can reduce both the data stored on the Terminal Server and the amount of data copied around as the profile is updated.

- **Desktop**—Many users get into the habit of saving documents and creating folders directly on their Windows desktops. While the preferred process is to create only shortcuts on the desktop, most users have a hard time distinguishing the two and invariably end up creating the actual files on the desktop. All desktop icons, folders, and such are stored in the Desktop folder. Redirecting this folder to a central server location can significantly reduce the size of the user profile and speed up the logon and logoff processes.

- **My Documents**—(Already discussed.) Under this folder is also the My Pictures folder; if not set, it automatically redirects as a subfolder of My Documents. You can also define a separate location for My Pictures that is independent of My Documents.

■ **Start Menu**—The ability to redirect this folder is retained more to provide legacy support with Windows NT 4.0 than for any other reason. While you can use it to redirect the Start menu for users, Microsoft recommends that you manage the Start menu through other administrative group policy settings and avoid redirection of this folder.

I find that redirecting Application Data, Desktop, and My Documents to the user's personal home drive location significantly reduces the size of the user profiles.

In Figure 18.11 you can also see that the user's home folder is being accessed through a distributed file system (DFS) reference. In the next section I discuss how DFS can be used to create a layer of abstraction between the reference to the user's personal data and the actual pointer to its physical location.

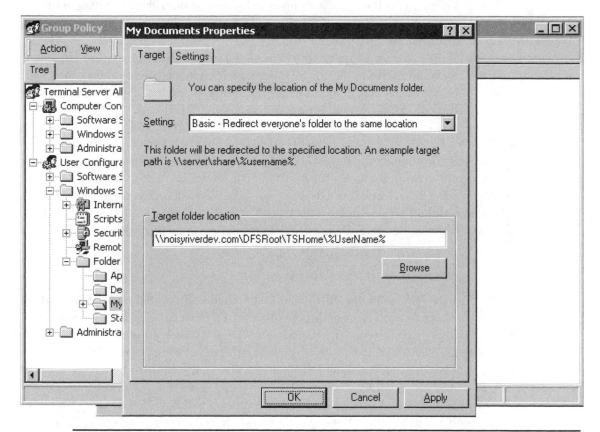

Figure 18.11 Redirecting the My Documents folder using a group policy object.

Using Microsoft's Distributed File System (DFS) for Profile/Home Folder References

Traditionally, home and profile folders are mapped directly to resources shared on servers in the domain. For example, a user's profile folder could be mapped to a share called TSProfiles on a server called FILESERVER01 as shown:

\\FILESERVER01\TSProfiles\%UserName%

While technically there is nothing wrong with this configuration, there are a couple of support issues that can arise and subsequently impact the uptime of the environment:

- If the hosting server goes down or must be taken offline, the users can no longer access their profile or home drive information, likely resulting in the users being unable to work in Terminal Server until the hosting server is once again online.
- If there is ever a requirement to move the resources off the current file server and onto a different server, all references must be updated to reflect the change. Depending on how many Terminal Server users need to be updated, this task can be extremely time consuming.

An effective way to manage these types of issues is to implement your shared resource access via Microsoft's distributed file system (DFS). DFS lets you access files shared on one or more servers in your network through a single virtual share reference. For example, a DFS share could be created called \\nrsc.com\DFSRoot and from this location you could access both the TSProfiles and the TSHome shares without ever actually including a reference to the physical server sharing these folders. The two folder references in this case would be

\\nrsc.com\DFSRoot\TSProfiles

\\nrsc.com\DFSRoot\TSHome

DFS is managed using the Distributed File System utility, found under Administrative Tools on the Start menu. The starting point of any DFS namespace is the DFS root. This is an actual Windows file system share hosted on a Windows server (either a member server or a domain controller). A Windows server can host only one DFS root. A new DFS root is created by right-clicking the Distributed File System folder in the utility and selecting New DFS Root. The wizard then guides you through creation of a new DFS root node.

Once the DFS root has been created you can begin to add DFS links, which represent logical access points to actual Windows file shares located on other servers in the domain. DFS links are created by right-clicking a DFS root and selecting New DFS Link. Each link created appears as a node under the DFS root, as shown in Figure 18.12. Once created, a link is accessible by using the full UNC path, beginning with the DFS root name and ending with the logical DFS link name.

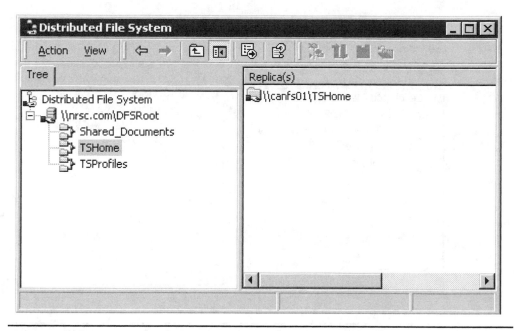

Figure 18.12   An example of a distributed file system topology.

DFS limits the risk of the two bullet points discussed at the beginning of this section as follows:

- First, DFS can eliminate the risk of a single point of failure introduced by the traditional file sharing by allowing you not only to define multiple shares for a single DFS link but also to leverage Microsoft's File Replication Service (FRS) to keep changes between these multiple shares synchronized. FRS can be fully managed for the DFS root through the DFS management tool. Figure 18.13 shows the properties for the TSHome DFS link with multiple replicas listed in the right-hand pane. In addition to establishing multiple replicas for a DFS link, you can create replicas for the DFS root, protecting against the main DFS root reference server's failing.
- The second issue is addressed by the fact that the DFS link names can remain constant while the underlying replicas for that link can change. Because of this, you are free to move the actual data from one server to another without having to change any of the user account references, which point to the DFS link and not the actual replica location.

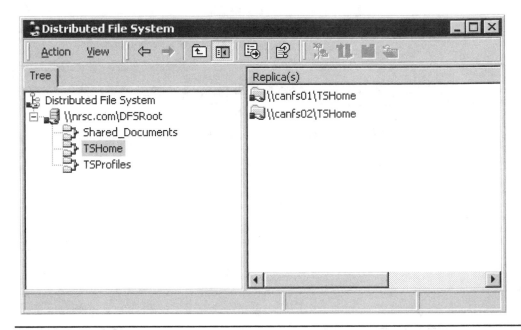

Figure 18.13   Multiple replicas can be defined for a single DFS link and automatic replication can be created.

TIP: Additional help on DFS can be found in the help file for the Distributed File System utility or on the Microsoft Web site in the article "Overview of DFS in Windows 2000" (knowledgebase article 812487) or the article "Simplify Infrastructure Complexity with Windows Distributed File System" (see the Word document at http://www.microsoft.com/windowsserver2003/techinfo/overview/dfs.mspx).

Creating and Managing User Profiles

When developing the user profiles for an implementation, I usually perform the following three steps:

1. Configure the default settings within the local default profile on the Terminal Server. This is important for two reasons:

   - First, this is the profile that every user loads the first time he or she logs on to a Terminal Server, unless the user has been set up with a mandatory roaming profile or a standard roaming profile has already been preloaded to the user's remote profile location.

■ It's also the default profile a user receives if, for whatever reason, his or her roaming profile is unavailable (the profile server is down, for example). In certain situations, a user may also receive this default profile if the mandatory profile is unavailable.

2. Create any custom roaming profiles that will be deployed to a user's personal roaming profile area prior to the user's first logon. This is a way to bypass the user picking up the default profile and instead forces the user to immediately use a customized profile you've created.

3. Create any required mandatory roaming profiles.

NOTE: An integral part of configuring roaming and mandatory profiles is implementation of a number of associated group policies, as discussed in Chapter 15. I recommend not undertaking final creation of profiles until you have reviewed both this chapter and Chapter 15 and have a complete understanding of the steps involved.

Because group policies provide such granular control over what options are and are not available to the user, if you proceed with creating a customized profile, you may be duplicating changes more easily managed through group policy objects.

Creating Template User Accounts

A common practice when creating and managing profiles is to use what I call "template user accounts." These are special user accounts created solely for the purpose of configuring a user profile. In most cases, these accounts have administrative privileges on the Terminal Server so all the necessary configuration options can be performed. Domain privileges may be required, depending on what's being configured. For security reasons, I recommend disabling any template accounts when they're not required. This ensures that the account cannot be used until it has been enabled by a valid administrator (an auditable event).

Typically I assign names to these template accounts so their function is immediately obvious. For example, a template account used to manage a mandatory profile for the accounting department may be named something like TS Template Accounting.

Configuring the Local Default Profile

If you have a common configuration that you want applied to *all* users, the first step is to configure the local default user profile so it contains this information that will be applied the first time the user connects to the Terminal Server. Unfortunately there's no way to specify a different default profile based on a user's group membership, so you must ensure that only common settings are placed within the default profile.

Settings you can define within the default profile include the following:

- Background color or default font
- Regional settings such as date, time, and currency formats
- Special per-user Start menu settings or application shortcuts

---

NOTE: If you need certain options to be set for a user based on his or her group membership, you can configure many of these options through scripting in the user's logon script. Options such as common folders or application shortcuts on the user's desktop can all be done from within the logon scripts.

To configure the default local profile, follow these steps:

1. Create a template account with a name such as TS Template Default. This account must have administrative privileges on the Terminal Server. Assign a standard Terminal Server home folder for the account (for example, \\FileServer01\Home\%UserName%), but leave the Terminal Server Profile field blank.

2. If this account already exists, make sure there's no local profile for this account on the Terminal Server by running the System applet under Control Panel and reviewing the User Profiles tab.

3. Log on to the Terminal Server with the template account. This assigns a copy of the current default profile to the user.

4. Now configure the session as you want it to appear for any user the first time he or she logs on.

5. After configuring the profile, log off as the template account and then log back on using another administrator's account (you can use the local administrator account if you want).

6. Open the System applet from Control Panel and select the User Profiles tab. You should see the local profile for the template account (see Figure 18.14).

7. Click the profile and select the Copy To button. The Copy To dialog box opens (Figure 18.15). Click the Change button in the lower part of the dialog box, under Permitted to Use, and select the Everyone group. You must do this to ensure that the users will have rights to access the registry component of the profile.

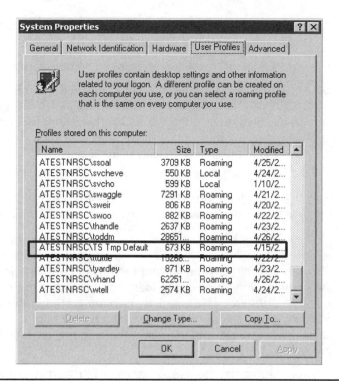

Figure 18.14   A template account profile in the User Profiles tab.

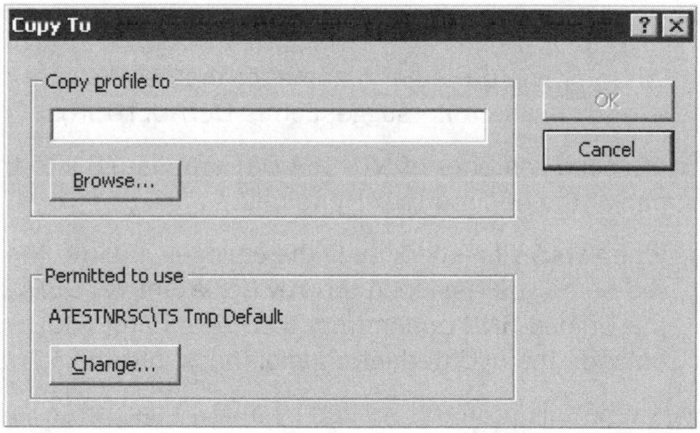

Figure 18.15   Copying the modified profile over the top of the existing default user profile.

8. Under the Copy Profile To section, enter the location where the current default profile is located on the Terminal Server. This would be

    %SystemDrive%\Documents and Settings\Default User

9. After the contents have been copied, delete the existing profile for the template account and then log back on with that account. You should now automatically receive the settings that are stored in the default user profile.

10. When you're confident that the settings have been saved properly, disable the template account until you're ready to use it again.

Now that the default profile has been configured, any user who logs on to this server for the first time automatically receives these settings as part of his or her newly created roaming profile.

TIP: You can also directly manipulate the registry settings for the default profile (or any user profile) without having to load, edit, and save the entire profile. The contents of the HKEY_CURRENT_USER registry hive are stored in the NTUSER.DAT file located in the user's profile folder. You can load the contents of this file into the registry, modify any desired settings, and then save the changes back to the file. The steps to do this are as follows:

1. Open REGEDT32 (Windows 2000) or REGEDIT (Windows 2003), select the HKEY_USERS hive, and click the HKEY_USERS text.

2. From the Registry (or File) menu, select Load Hive. When the dialog box appears, traverse to the default user's profile directory and select the NTUSER.DAT file, as shown in Figure 18.16.

3. When prompted, enter a name for the new key. Be sure to select a name not already in use (one suggestion is DEFAULTUSR).

4. After the contents of NTUSER.DAT are loaded into the registry, you can modify any of the desired registry values.

5. When you're finished, save the changes back to the NTUSER.DAT file, select the name you assigned the key (for example, DEFAULTUSR), and then choose the Unload Hive option from the Registry (or File) menu. This automatically unloads the updated information back into the NTUSER.DAT file.

The next time this profile is loaded by a new user, or an existing user if you modified their personal registry file, the updated registry information is automatically used.

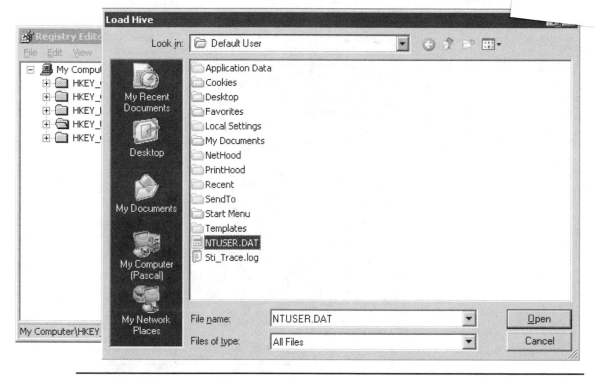

Figure 18.16   Loading the contents of NTUSER.DAT into the registry.

Assigning Roaming Profiles

Assignment of a roaming profile to a user is straightforward. All that's required is configuring the user's account to access a roaming Terminal Server profile. Figure 18.17 shows an example, with the user's profile location set as follows:

\\nrsc.com\DFSRoot\TSProfiles\%UserName%

Windows automatically resolves the %UserName% value to the corresponding user's ID. In Figure 18.17 it was resolved to my user ID, toddm.

After the roaming profile location has been set, the first time the user logs on to a Terminal Server, Windows checks the network location for the profile. If it doesn't exist, the default user profile on the Terminal Server is used to create the new profile. From that point on, the user retrieves his or her profile from the appropriate network location.

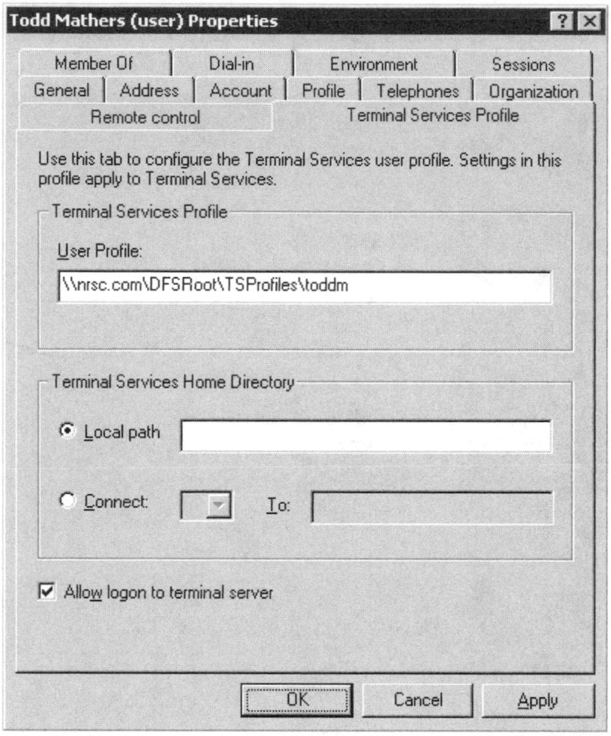

Figure 18.17   A roaming profile assignment in a user's account.

TIP: Normally when copying an existing user account in an active directory, common settings are copied over to the newly created account, shortening the time required to configure the account information. Unfortunately, when you copy an account, the settings on the Terminal Services Profile tab are not automatically copied for the new user. You must manually go into the copied account to properly configure the profile settings.

Managing Group-Specific Default Roaming Profiles

In many situations, you would rather assign a previously configured profile to a user or group of users than have the users load the default profile from a Terminal Server. There's no way to designate a default user profile based on a user's group membership. Because of this deficiency, a process must be developed where a user's profile is copied to the appropriate network location prior to the user logging on to a Terminal Server for the first time.

There are two steps in managing these customized default profiles:

- Creation of the profile
- Distribution to the appropriate network location

The following sections describe these steps.

Configuring the Custom Roaming Profile

The steps in creating a custom roaming profile are nearly identical to those for modifying the default user's profile:

1. Create a template account for managing this profile. For example, if you're creating a profile for users in the sales department, you could create a template account called TS Template Sales. This account must have administrative privileges on the Terminal Server. You should assign a standard Terminal Server home folder, but leave the Profile entry empty for now.
2. Log on to the Terminal Server with the template account and perform any desired profile configuration. After you've finished, log off the template account and log back on with a regular administrator account.
3. Open the System applet from the Control Panel and select the User Profiles tab. Click the profile and select the Copy To button. The Copy To dialog box opens.
4. Click the Change button and select the Terminal Server users group (in my case, it would be Terminal Server Users). You must do this to ensure that the users will have rights to access the registry components of the profile.
5. Now provide a destination for the profile copy. I recommend that you copy this to the network location where other roaming profiles are stored. For example, I might specify this location as the destination:

    \\nrsc.com\DFSRoot\TSProfiles\TS Template Sales

6. You need to make one other permission change to this profile so Terminal Server operators can deploy copies to users if necessary. Go to the profile folder on the server (or in the DFS root, if applicable) and add an operators group (Terminal Server Operators) with Read and Execute permissions.
7. The final step is to update the template account so it now uses the profile you copied to the server. This lets you make future changes to this profile simply by logging on as the template user, making the changes, and then logging off.

Deploying the Group-Specific Roaming Profile

Now that you have created the customized profile, the next step is to deploy the profile to the appropriate users prior to their logging on to Terminal Server. There are two steps in this process:

1. Copy the template profile to the user's profile folder.

2. Update the security permissions on the folder so the corresponding user has Full Control access.

For a few users, this can be done manually without too much effort. If you must do this for 50 users, however, it would obviously be very time consuming. It's much easier to script this change to create these profiles automatically.

The following is a sample batch script that takes the user ID as a parameter and performs the necessary folder copying and permission updates to create that user's profile. This script assumes that the profiles are stored under the \\nrsc.com\DFSRoot\TSProfiles share.

```
@echo off

REM Copy template profile to user profile
xcopy \\nrsc.com\DFSRoot\TSProfiles\TS Template Sales
\\nrsc.com\DFSRoot\TSPRofiles\%1 /E /I /H /K /X

REM Now update security
xcacls \\nrsc.com\DFSRoot\TSProfiles\%1 /E /G %1:F /Y
xcacls \\nrsc.com\DFSRoot\TSProfiles\%1 /T /E /G %1:F /Y
```

Managing Changes in a Roaming Profile

One of the more difficult tasks in managing roaming profiles is replicating a change to each individual profile. For example, suppose you have 500 users, each with his or her own profile, and they've been working in your Terminal Server environment for the past two months. You now want to install a new application onto the Terminal Servers and deploy it to a subset of these 500 users (say 200, for example).

You have two requirements for this deployment:

■ The necessary application registry entries need to be replicated to each user's profile so the user can launch the application.

■ A custom shortcut for this application needs to be added to the relevant users' desktops.

While the first requirement seems by far the most difficult, in fact Terminal Server provides an implementation feature that makes this step quite easy. I defer a complete discussion of application deployment until Chapter 21, "Application Integration," but in the meantime I'll mention here that Terminal Server provides a special mode of operation known as *install mode*. When in this mode, the Terminal Server records every HKEY_CURRENT_USER (HKCU) registry key change that's made using the standard API calls (direct updates to the registry through other means are not captured) and stores this information so it can be applied to each user who logs on to the Terminal Server when it's put back into *execute mode*. There are a few caveats, but in general that's how this feature operates. When a user logs on to the server, Terminal Server compares the last synchronize time of the user's HKCU registry with the last update time of the information stored on the server. If the server version is newer, the changes are automatically applied to the user's HKCU.

Unfortunately, management of the user's personal profile isn't quite as easy. Unless you have the luxury of being able to delete a user's roaming profile and assign the user a new default profile, you need to develop a way of making updates as required without affecting the user's current environment. If you're deploying an application to all users, there is very little work that needs to be done. You can simply add the shortcut to the Desktop folder under the All Users profile folder. When changes need to be made to the roaming profile for a subset of all users, a few options are available, depending on what needs to be updated:

- **Group policies**—Many applications support their own special set of group policy options that can be used to configure many of the settings within the application. Microsoft Office is one example that supports configuration through group policies in the active directory. Group policies generally aren't helpful when you want to manage shortcuts on the user's desktop.

- **Logon/startup scripts**—Logon or startup scripts can be very helpful when updating the Start menu or the user's desktop. The addition of an application shortcut to a user's desktop can be achieved easily through such a script. Typically, what I do is create a directory on the application volume of a server where I keep shortcuts that need to be deployed. Then I make a short addition to the startup script so that the shortcut is copied to the appropriate area, depending on the user's group membership. Following this list is an example script that demonstrates this by copying the Microsoft Project shortcut for only the appropriate users. Normally I place a call to any additional customization scripts at the end of the USRLOGON.CMD script, which runs for every user who logs on to the Terminal Server and is responsible for launching the necessary application compatibility scripts. This script is located in the %SystemRoot%System32 directory. Before you make changes to this script, however, review the "Application Compatibility Scripts" section in Chapter 21.

  In this example, for this script to work, users need Read access to the Y:\Shortcuts folder. Because the script is actually running as the user when he or she logs on, the user has access to update the files in his or her Desktop directory. I also make use of the %UserProfile% environment variable, which automatically points to the user's proper profile directory. Be sure to include the quotes around the copy parameters to ensure that any spaces are handled properly.

```
REM Sample script to update a user's desktop
REM with a shortcut when he or she logs on.
REM ifmember is a Windows 2000/2003 Server Resource Kit tool.
REM and can be downloaded free from the Microsoft Web site.
```

```
ifmember "Terminal Server Sales Users"
if not errorlevel 1 exit

REM User is a member of the Sales group if
REM we reach here, so update the profile
if exist "%UserProfile%\Desktop\MSProject.lnk" goto END
Copy "y:\shortcuts\MSProject.lnk"
"%UserProfile%\Desktop\MSProject.lnk"
:END
```

TIP: When implementing MetaFrame Presentation Server, you can leverage the published application technology and the ICA passthrough client, which is automatically installed on each server, to quickly deploy any application to a subset of the MetaFrame users. Once an application has been published, the passthrough Program Neighborhood or Program Neighborhood Agent clients can retrieve that information and display the program icon on the user's MetaFrame desktop. When the user double-clicks that icon to start the application, if the program is published on the same MetaFrame server the user is currently on, the program simply starts locally and doesn't attempt to create a new ICA connection. This is one of the powerful features of the passthrough client that is rarely mentioned or implemented. I discuss use of this client when I talk about deploying applications in Chapter 21.

Creating and Assigning Mandatory Roaming Profiles

Creation and assignment of the mandatory roaming profile is nearly identical to that of the standard roaming profile. These are the differences:

- The profile is assigned a standard name such as SALES or MARKETING instead of an individual user's name.
- The profile has a .MAN extension assigned to it.
- Multiple users are assigned the same mandatory profile since it can't be updated by a user. This means that you don't have to worry about one user making a change to the profile that is then picked up by the other users who have also been assigned that profile. It also means that any environment changes that the users make will be lost when they log off, and the original profile defaults reloaded the next time they log on.

Figure 18.18 shows a user account configured with a mandatory roaming profile called SALES.MAN.

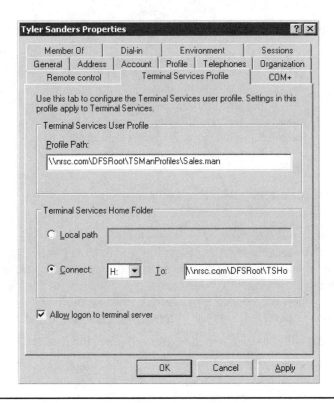

Figure 18.18   A mandatory profile assigned in a user's account.

Creating a Mandatory Roaming Profile

To create a mandatory profile, follow steps 1 through 7 in the earlier section "Configuring the Custom Roaming Profile." You should still save the new profile into the standard roaming profile. After creating the roaming profile, perform the following additional steps to configure it as a mandatory profile:

1. Copy the profile from the roaming location to the mandatory profile location you've created. For example, I have a mandatory profile location of \\nrsc.com\ DFSRoot\TSManProfiles. Make sure that you do this after you've copied the local profile from the Terminal Server to the network and updated the access permissions to include Terminal Server Users; otherwise, users won't be able to load the registry portion of the mandatory profile (see steps 3 through 5 in the procedure for creating the roaming profile).

2. Go into the mandatory profile folder where you copied the roaming profile and add the .MAN extension to the roaming profile folder.

3. Now go into the new .MAN template folder and rename the NTUSER.DAT file to NTUSER.MAN.

4. Validate that the proper permissions have been set on the mandatory profile folder. SYSTEM and Administrators should have Full Control, while the appropriate user group requires only Read and Execute permissions.

5. Assign this profile to the users who will be using it from within their user account, just as you would with a regular roaming profile. Because this is a mandatory profile, multiple users can be assigned to it. Don't forget to include the .MAN extension when specifying the profile name.

Now anytime a user who has been assigned a mandatory profile logs on, he or she always receives the same consistent user interface.

TIP: If you're implementing Windows Server 2003 Active Directory and Terminal Servers, you can take advantage of a new group policy setting that prevents users from saving changes to their roaming profile back to the network server, effectively turning their profile into a mandatory roaming profile. The policy setting in question is located under the Computer Configuration section in the following location:

Administrative Templates\System\User Profiles

The property is called "Prevent Roaming Profile changes from propagating to the server." Group policies are discussed in Chapter 15.

Managing Changes in a Mandatory Roaming Profile

In some ways, management of the mandatory profile is simplified by the fact that a single copy of the profile can serve any number of users. This makes changes such as the addition of a shortcut to the desktop or the Start menu very easy. Changes to the mandatory profile can be done simply by logging on as the associated template account—for example, TS Template Sales—and making the desired changes to the profile, which are then copied back to the template account's roaming profile on the network. This profile can then be copied to the mandatory profile location, and the folder and NTUSER.DAT file renamed accordingly. The next time a user who has been assigned the mandatory profile logs on, he or she picks up the changes you introduced. This is much simpler than trying to implement similar profile changes with a regular roaming profile.

Mandatory profile maintenance is even easier in a Windows Server 2003 environment, since you do not even have to adjust the NTUSER.DAT file settings; you simply need to make the changes using the template account, ensuring that it does not have the same policy restriction as regular users do when trying to update a roaming profile.

The major drawback to the mandatory profile is actually due to its major benefit, which is protection from any changes by the user. This is a problem when new applications are introduced into the environment or applications want to store user-specific information in the user's personal registry settings. For these applications to operate properly with a mandatory profile, much more work must be done during the application integration phase to ensure that the necessary registry entries are part of the mandatory profile. In many cases, this requires extensions to the application compatibility scripts that write user-specific information into the registry every time a user logs on to the Terminal Server. The registry capture features of the CHANGE USER /INSTALL command help to some degree, but customized configuration is almost always required.

NOTE: As Microsoft has continued to integrate more and more administrative control over a user's session into the group policy objects, it has become much easier to limit what a user can modify in their profile. This in turn makes it possible to allow the user to have a roaming profile, which simplifies management of certain application settings, while still minimizing what they can change, which reduces the support re-quirements of the administrator. The need for implementing a mandatory roaming profile has diminished significantly compared with that of earlier versions of server-based computing products such as WinFrame or even NT Server 4.0, Terminal Server Edition.

Roaming Profile Maintenance

Ideally the creation, loading, and unloading of user profiles is a flawless process that an administrator can simply configure and forget about, but unfortunately there are situations where proactive maintenance may be required to help minimize the issues that can arise from a large number of profiles being managed in a Terminal Server environment. Because you have many users concurrently working on a single Terminal Server, and all these users have their own personal profiles that must be managed by Windows, anything that can be done to help improve the stability of the system is worthwhile.

TIP: In Chapter 8 I discussed the benefits of implementing a reboot schedule for your Terminal Server environment. Regularly scheduled reboots can also help to limit issues with loading and unloading of roaming profile information from the registry.

Implementing the User Profile Hive Cleanup Service

As part of the user logoff process, the system normally unloads the registry portion of the user's profile and saves it back to the NTUSER.DAT file. If the registry fails to unload, the profile reconciliation process does not complete properly, and the user may end up with a local profile and a roaming profile that are no longer synchronized.

When this happens, what the user experiences depends on the Terminal Server version they are running on. Windows 2000 users will experience an extremely slow logoff process, where it appears to hang with the message Saving Settings for up to 60 seconds by default. This is because the server is retrying once every second for 60 seconds to successfully unload the profile. After 60 seconds, it gives up and simply logs the user off. No profile synchronization happens in this situation.

Windows 2003 users will be logged off immediately, and the system will use a copy of the current registry keys to complete the profile synchronization. The orphaned registry keys that could not be unloaded remain in memory until the system is restarted.

In either case, events are logged to the application log on the Terminal Server stating that the registry could not be unloaded because it was in use by another process and access was denied. Figure 18.19 shows an example of this on a Windows 2000 Terminal Server.

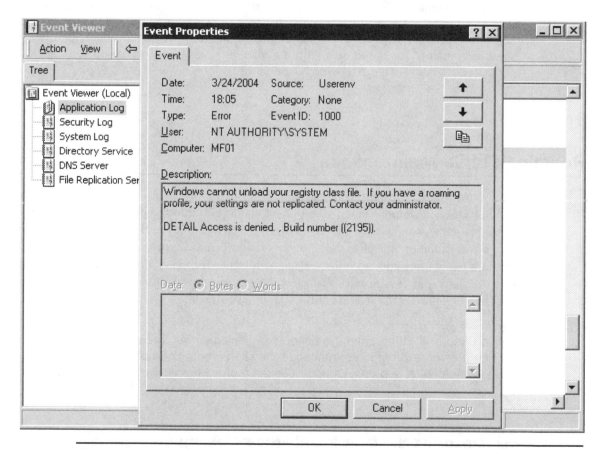

Figure 18.19   An application event log error is generated because a registry key could not be unloaded.

When a user's profile fails to unload properly, it can result in issues the next time the user attempts to log on; for example, profile changes not being saved or error messages saying that the roaming profile itself is not accessible are two of the most common side effects.

Previously, this type of problem could be resolved only by tracking down the offending application(s) and getting the vendor to correct its code. The main issue with this was simply the time required to get a fix back. Until the correction was available, the problem would continue to occur and affect the user's computing experience.

Microsoft now provides a special service that can be installed on a Terminal Server (or any other Windows machine) that monitors active users and ensures that the registry and profile are properly unloaded when a user logs off. This tool is called the User Profile Hive Cleanup Service (UPHClean, for short) and can be downloaded from the Microsoft downloads page at http://www.microsoft.com/downloads.

The installation is straightforward and requires no special configuration. Once installed, the service automatically starts and immediately begins monitoring the system for "stuck" profile issues. While UPHClean does not require a reboot, I recommend performing an initial reboot once the product has been installed to remove any existing registry entries that may have been orphaned from earlier issues. UPHClean runs on both Windows 2000 Server and Windows Server 2003.

Compressing the Registry File Using CProfile

Another useful utility that ships with both versions of Windows Server is the CPROFILE (Clean Profile) utility. This simple tool cleans out any wasted space from the NTUSER.DAT registry file for each user profile on a server. If per-user file accesses exist within the registry file, they are also removed. More information on the CPROFILE command can be found in Appendix A, "Terminal Services Command Reference."

Ideally, this utility is run against both the locally cached profiles on a Terminal Server and against roaming profiles stored on the network server. This command can be scripted to run on a schedule similar to that for a reboot schedule.

CHAPTER 19

RDP Client Installation and Configuration

Before You Begin

Chapter 5, "Client Hardware and Software Planning," discusses in detail both the ICA and the RDP clients, the various implementation categories that exist (desktop and application replacement, desktop integration), and the planning and support issues you must consider when planning a Terminal Server implementation. This chapter begins by providing a brief overview of the RDP clients available, followed by a discussion of how they are installed and configured to support the various client implementation categories, and finally finishes off with a brief look at the client distribution methods that exist.

NOTE: Actual installation of both ICA and RDP clients is very straightforward, but don't let this ease of installation lead you to believe that a formal implementation plan for your clients is not a necessity. "Easily installed" does not necessarily equate to "simple implementation."

Your choice in what version of the RDP client to deploy is dictated by where you access the client installation files. Table 19.1 summarizes the various client versions available and from where you would retrieve the appropriate installation files.

Table 19.1   RDP Client Installation Options

RDP Client Version	Description
RDP 5.0	RDP 5.0 ships with Windows 2000 and the installation files can be found in the
	%SystemRoot%\System32\Clients\tsclients
	folder on a Windows 2000 Terminal Server, by default. There are three folders provided: Net, Win16, and Win32. The Win16 and Win32 folders are used as the source for creation of client installation disks using the Client Creator program, while the Net folder allows network-based client installations.
RDP 5.01	RDP 5.01 is also known as the Terminal Services Advanced Client (TSAC). This version was found to contain a major security flaw and is no longer available for download. It was replaced by version 5.1 of the Web-based RDP client software.
RDP 5.1	This version of the RDP client ships with Windows XP with Service Pack 1 and is called the "Remote Desktop Connection" software. The installation files can also be downloaded from the Microsoft Web site at
	http://www.microsoft.com/windowsxp/pro/downloads/rdclientdl.asp
	This version provides an MSI file that can be used when performing client distribution with Active Directory.
	A Web-based ActiveX control is also available as a download from
	http://www.microsoft.com/windowsxp/pro/downloads/rdwebconn.asp
	Use of the ActiveX control and Web-based access to Terminal Server are discussed in the "Web-based Access with Terminal Services" section of this Chapter.
RDP 5.2	This version ships with Windows Server 2003 and can be found in the folder:
	X:\WINNT\system32\clients\tsclient\win32
	On Windows Server 2003, only the Win32 version is provided, and no Net or Win16 folders are available (as they are with Windows 2000). Just as with RDP 5.1, an MSI installation file is provided.
	A download link for both the Win32 client and the Web-based ActiveX control can be found on the Microsoft Windows Server 2003 Web site at
	http://www.microsoft.com/windowsserver2003/technologies/terminalservices/default.mspx

As I discussed in Chapter 5, your choice of what RDP client to deploy is driven by the version of Terminal Server you are implementing and the client-side functionality you want to support. Each new release of the RDP client delivers support for the new features and functionality available on the latest server product, while still providing full backwards compatibility with previous versions of Windows. For example, if you were deploying Windows 2003 Terminal Server to replace your existing Windows NT 4.0, Terminal Server Edition environment, you could deploy the latest RDP client knowing it would still allow all users to access the old environment during the transition. You would not have to worry about maintaining two separate RDP clients or leaving the client-side deployment until the very last minute during your cutover to the new Terminal Server environment.

TIP: When deciding on the client version to implement, always consider running the latest version available from Microsoft. The backwards compatibility ensures that you can continue accessing any legacy Terminal Servers that exist during or after your implementation.

Information on the RDP clients that shipped with Windows 2000 Server are included in this chapter for completeness and to ensure that the reference is available for any of those administrators who must support an environment that has these clients in production. For any reader who is looking to implement a new Terminal Services environment, I highly recommend that you run only the latest RDP client available.

RDP Client Types

In Chapter 5 I discussed the three RDP client types currently available. They are

- **Terminal Services client (TSC)**—This is one of the two RDP 5.0 clients that ship with Windows 2000 and provides a simple interface for connecting to a Windows Terminal Server. TSC serves two functions. Primarily, it can be used as a simple tool for connecting to a Terminal Server. It also works in combination with the Client Connection Manager (CCM) to allow creation of shortcuts to sessions configured within the CCM. TSC functionality is integrated into the latest RDP client, called the Remote Desktop Connection.
- **Client Connection Manager (CCM)**—This is the other RDP 5.0 client and provides a management tool for creating, configuring, and storing connections to different Terminal Servers. Specific options such as caching of logon information and launching of a specific program are available through this program.
- **Remote Desktop Connection (RDC)**—Originally introduced with RDP 5.1 and Windows XP, the Remote Desktop Connection application is the new RDP client interface being used with RDP versions 5.1 and higher. RDC supports all

the features available with the CCM client, as well as new features such as increased color depth, audio redirection support, and support for Windows keyboard combinations such as Alt-Tab. RDC is fully backwards compatible with all versions of Windows Terminal Server. Any client options selected in the RDC that are not supported by the host Terminal Server are simply ignored.

Don't let the name "remote desktop" fool you. The RDC client is used not only to connect to remote desktop sessions on a Windows XP Professional system, but is also the primary tool for connecting to a Terminal Server running Windows NT 4.0, Terminal Server Edition or higher. Microsoft has simply chosen to standardize on a new name for the RDP client software.

TIP: Full details on the features and functionality of each client type can be found in Chapter 5.

Installing the RDP Client

The actual installation steps for the different RDP clients are straightforward, so I have omitted the installation steps for the legacy clients and focus only on the Remote Desktop Connection client.

Installing the Remote Desktop Connection Software

Remote Desktop Connection installation is usually initiated by launching MSRDPCLI.EXE, which automatically extracts the associated MSI file and begins the setup wizard. The installation steps are as follows:

1. After clicking Next to proceed past the introduction screen, you are presented with the End User License Agreement (EULA). If you accept the terms of the agreement, you can click Next to proceed.
2. Enter the customer information and choose whether the application will be configured for all users on the server or only yourself. If you are installing this software on an end user's computer, select the All Users option.
3. After clicking Next, you are asked to confirm your desire to install the software. Once this is confirmed, the installation completes and the RDP client is available for use. A reboot is not required to complete either the install or the uninstall of the RDP client.

TIP: If you have any active drive substitutions created using the SUBST.EXE command, you need to temporarily delete them before beginning the Remote Desktop Connection client installation. Otherwise, the install will fail with a message stating that the substituted drive letter is invalid. This message is generated by the MSI installation package. For example, if you created a drive substitution:

SUBST D: = Y:\

then the installation would fail, saying that drive D: was invalid. Simply delete this substitution, using

SUBST D: /d

before proceeding with the installation.

Once the client has been properly installed, the next task is to configure it for your desired implementation scenario, which I discuss next.

RDP Client Configuration

In this section we look at how to configure the RDP client to support the three implementation scenarios discussed in Chapter 5. These scenarios are

- **Desktop replacement**—The users will be running all their applications from within a Terminal Server session.
- **Application replacement**—The users will be running a combination of Windows applications on their local desktops and on the Terminal Server. They run side by side on the local computer.
- **Desktop integration**—Users are running a non-Windows operating system and integrating access to individual applications or the full Windows desktop from this non-Windows client.

Regardless of what implementation scenario you use, the general installation steps remain the same. Before discussing how the clients are configured for each of the three scenario types, we look at the general steps for setting up an RDP connection.

Client Connection Manager Connection Setup

Creation of a new connection in the CCM is straightforward:

1. Launch CCM and then click New Connection on the File menu. This launches the Client Connection Manager wizard. Click Next to begin.

2. Figure 19.1 shows the initial screen in the wizard. Enter a description for the connection (you can include spaces). Also enter the name or IP address of the Terminal Server or network load-balanced environment. If you don't know the name of the server, click the Browse button to list all available Windows domains and then drill into the desired domain to see the available Terminal Server. You must have access to a domain to see its Terminal Servers. After entering the desired information, click Next to continue.

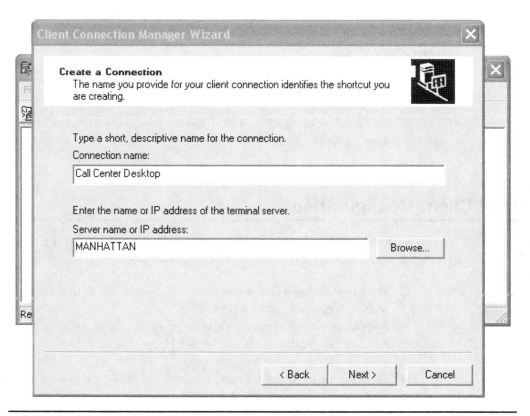

Figure 19.1 Entering the connection description and server name in the CCM wizard.

3. On the next screen, you can enter automatic logon information. If you do, you're required to provide all the information; for example, you cannot provide only the domain name. Because of the obvious security reasons, I don't recommend using this feature. If a Terminal Server is configured to always prompt for a password, any settings entered here are ignored.
4. In the next dialog box, select the screen options for the session (see Figure 19.2). Only screen sizes equal to or smaller than the client's actual screen resolution are available for selection.

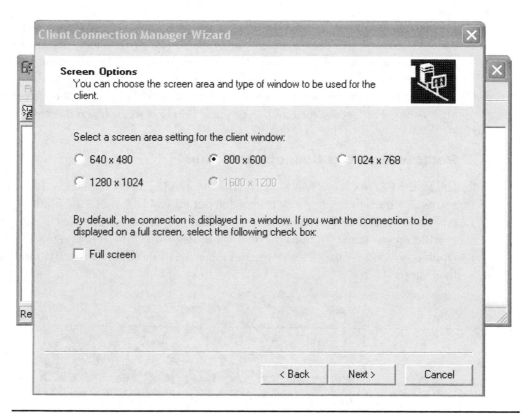

Figure 19.2 Setting the screen resolution option in the CCM wizard.

5. Next you can configure the compression and bitmap caching settings for the RDP client. If you'll be connecting over a slow dial-up or WAN link, I recommend selecting both options. If you're on a fast LAN connection, select only the Compression option. Compression will introduce only a small additional load on both the client and the server. In Chapter 4, "Network Planning," I demonstrate how the different client options can affect the average bandwidth utilization for both RDP and ICA. After selecting the desired options, click Next.

6. Now you can specify an application to start automatically after the user has logged on to the Terminal Server. This information is usually left blank unless you're creating an application-replacement connection.

7. The next screen lets you select the icon and folder to be used when CCM automatically creates the shortcut to this new connection. The default folder is the Terminal Services Client folder in the common Start menu. Enter the desired options and click Next.

8. The final screen presents a brief summary of the connection you've just created. Click Finish to complete the setup.

The icon for the newly created connection now appears in the CCM and in the folder that you selected in Step 7. You can modify the properties for this connection at any time by right-clicking the icon and selecting Properties. You can create a desktop shortcut for the connection by right-clicking the connection within the CCM and selecting Create Shortcut on Desktop. To test the connection, double-click the icon within the CCM or select it from the Start menu. The logon screen for the Terminal Server session should now appear.

Remote Desktop Connection Setup

Unlike the Client Connection Manager, the Remote Desktop Connection (RDC) client does not use a wizard to create a new connection but instead lets you configure the various property sheets with the desired information. When you first open RDC, you are prompted to provide only a target Terminal Server name. Begin the connection setup by clicking the Options button to make all the properties available, as shown in Figure 19.3, and then follow these steps.

Figure 19.3   Properties available in the Remote Desktop Connection client.

1. The General tab is where you enter the basic information about your connection and where you will return to save the connection you've configured. On this tab provide the name of the target Terminal Server. You can click the drop-down list to expand the list of known Terminal Servers; this includes all servers you've previously connected to. You can also click the Browse for More option in the list to scan the available domains for Terminal Servers. Once this information is complete, move on to the Display tab.

2. The Display tab is where you provide the remote desktop size, color depth, and connection bar options. You cannot configure either the desktop size or color depth to be greater than your current client settings. These options can be overridden by settings on the server.

3. The Local Resources tab lets you configure what client-side devices will be supported within the Terminal Server session (Figure 19.4). These options can also be overridden by settings on the Terminal Server.

Figure 19.4   The Local Resources tab in the RDC.

- **Remote computer sound**—This lets you configure whether server-side sound plays on the local client. The default is to enable this option and bring the sound to this computer. You can also turn this option off or have the sounds play on the Terminal Server.
- **Keyboard**—This lets you configure whether Windows key combinations will be captured by the Terminal Server session or the local desktop. Normally these key combinations are applied only when running in a full-screen (remote desktop) configuration.
- **Local devices**—This configures what local devices will be redirected through the Terminal Server session. Printers and COM ports are supported by both Windows 2000 and 2003, while disk drive support exists only in Windows Server 2003.

4. The Programs tab is where you would configure a specific application to automatically launch when logging on to the Terminal Server instead of the default desktop. When specifying the program and start-up folder, be sure to use the correct *server-side* path.

5. The final tab is the Experience tab (see Figure 19.5), where you can adjust what "experience-enhancing" options are enabled depending on the available connection bandwidth. The lower the bandwidth, the fewer the options that should be supported. You can either select the specific options available by selecting or deselecting the appropriate options or you can choose from the drop-down list the connection type that most closely matches your environment. Depending on the connection chosen, the appropriate options will be enabled or disabled. The available bandwidth choices are

- **Modem (28.8Kbps)**—Only bitmap caching is enabled.
- **Modem (56Kbps)**—Caching and themes are enabled.
- **Broadband (128Kbps to 1.5Mbps)**—All options except Desktop Background are enabled.
- **LAN (10Mbps or higher)**—All options are available.
- **Custom**—This option is displayed if you selected your own connection options.

The Remote Desktop Client (version 5.2) that ships with Windows Server 2003 has one additional option on the Experience tab. This property is called "Reconnect if connection is dropped" and it controls the automatic session reconnect feature. The details on this feature were discussed back in Chapter 5, "Client Hardware and Software Planning." Basically if a connection with the Terminal Server is dropped, the client will automatically attempt to log back onto the server using credentials that have been cached on the client. The client will retry for a maximum of 20 times at an interval of 5 seconds between each attempt.

Figure 19.5 The Experience tab in the Remote Desktop Connection utility.

The 5.1 version of the Remote Desktop client also supports this feature, but no checkbox exists to easily enable or disable the feature (it is enabled by default). Instead, this option must be managed in one of two ways. Either you modify the registry or modify the Default.rdp file that is automatically created in each user's My Documents folder and contains the default settings for the RDC.

The registry value is called fDisableAutoReconnect of type DWORD and when created will exist in the key:

HKLM\Software\Policies\Microsoft\Windows NT\Terminal Servers

If you wish to turn off automatic client reconnect then you need to create this key and set the value to 1.

Alternatively, you can directly modify the Default.rdp file located in the My Documents folder. This is a plaintext file and the contents will look similar to the listing shown in Listing 19.1. The entry labeled autoreconnection_enabled controls whether the auto reconnect feature is enabled or not. When the value is set to 0 (zero) the feature is disabled and when set to 1 (one), which is the default then it is enabled.

There is one value that must be defined within the Default.rdp file that cannot be set anywhere else. This value allows you to modify the maximum number of retries before the client gives up.

Listing 19.1   Default.rdp client settings

```
screen mode id:i:1
desktopwidth:i:1024
desktopheight:i:768
session bpp:i:24
winposstr:s:0,2,72,43,1104,845
auto connect:i:0
full address:s:10.100.128.12
compression:i:1
keyboardhook:i:2
audiomode:i:0
redirectdrives:i:1
redirectprinters:i:1
redirectcomports:i:0
redirectsmartcards:i:1
displayconnectionbar:i:1
autoreconnection enabled:i:1
username:s:Todd
domain:s:TEST
alternate shell:s:
shell working directory:s:
disable wallpaper:i:0
disable full window drag:i:0
disable menu anims:i:0
disable themes:i:0
disable cursor setting:i:0
bitmapcachepersistenable:i:1
```

Enabling Client Time Zone Redirection Support

Version 5.2 of the RDC also supports client time zone redirection when connecting to a Windows Server 2003 server, which means the client will pass local time zone information from the client session to the server, where it can be used to provide the user with local time settings from within the Terminal Services session. Time zone redirection was discussed in Chapter 5.

Support for client time zones must be enabled using a group policy. The specific property to set is called "Allow Time Zone Redirection" and is located under the Computer Configuration object in:

Administrative Templates/Windows Components/TerminalServices/Client/Server Data Redirection

If time zone redirection is enabled, then a user must log off and back onto the server before the change will take effect. Because this is a Computer Configuration policy, I would normally enable this as part of the Terminal Server Machine Policy. Details on group policies are discussed in Chapter 15.

Connecting Directly to a Windows Server 2003 Console

One of the new features supported with Windows Server 2003 and the Remote Desktop Connection client is the ability to connect directly to the console on the server (session 0). In order to do this you must start the RDC with the parameter /console. For example, if you were to open up the properties for a shortcut to the RDC, you could add the suffix /console to the Target executable name. It would look similar to the following:

```
%windir%\System32\mstsc.exe /console
```

When launched with the /console parameter, there is no special labeling that dictates that you are connecting to the server's console. One way to verify this is to run the Terminal Server command QUSER and note the user account currently accessing the console.

Saving Your Remote Desktop Connection Settings

Once you have completed configuration of your RDP connection, you can save these settings by returning to the General tab and clicking the Save As button. When the Save As dialog box opens, it automatically selects the file name Default.rdp from your My Documents folder. This file stores your personal default configuration options that will automatically load every time the Remote Desktop Connection application is opened. If you want the client settings you just configured to automatically load every time you launch the RDP client, save your settings to this file.

You can also save your settings to an alternate RDP file, which can then be directly launched to connect to a specific server. For example, if you configured your Remote Desktop Connection to connect to the server MANHATTAN and saved this file as Manhattan.rdp, you could save a shortcut to this file on your desktop and launch a server connection directly from this shortcut.

NOTE: When initiating a connection through Remote Desktop Connection and having enabled client disk drive or serial port remapping, you are presented with a dialog box warning you that these connections may be unsafe if the host Terminal Server is not "trusted" (see Figure 19.6).

This dialog box does not signal an error in the client but is simply an information message. Clicking OK allows the connection to complete successfully. If you select the option "Don't prompt me again for connections to this remote computer," this message will not appear the next time you connect to this host. You still are prompted with this message if you connect to a different server.

Figure 19.6   A security warning appears when client disk drive or serial port remapping is enabled.

Now that we have reviewed the basic configuration options for the different RDP clients, we can look more closely at how these clients would be configured to support the different client implementation scenarios.

Desktop Replacement

The desktop-replacement scenario is probably the most common configuration for an RDP connection; the steps to configure these options for the available RDP clients are listed in the next two sections. Typically, when employing a desktop-replacement scenario, you'll configure the local desktop to launch the RDP client automatically and initiate the Terminal Server connection when the user logs on or starts the local computer. This configuration usually works best when all the computers in a certain area are being employed merely as a form of Windows dumb-terminal. Call center or shop-floor implementations are both common examples, since all users of the computer are running completely from within a Terminal Server desktop and don't need access to the local desktop.

The exact method of launching the RDP session depends on the client operating system, but a simple example is to add the session shortcut to the All Users Startup menu, located in

%SystemDrive%\Documents and Settings\ All Users\Start Menu\Programs\Startup

Another option is to create a batch script that runs during the logon script or when the application compatibility scripts run on the server. Application compatibility scripts are discussed in Chapter 21, "Application Integration."

All values listed under this key are automatically executed whenever a user logs on to the Terminal Server. The following script (Listing 19.2) demonstrates how a Remote Desktop Connection could be scripted to automatically execute.

Listing 19.2   Remote Desktop Connection Launch Script

```
REM Launch a Remote Desktop Connection session
REM The specific session shortcut is called and is launched through
REM the Terminal Services association.

"C:\Documents and Settings\Todd Mathers\My Documents\CONFS01.rdp"
```

Configuring the Client Connection Manager for Desktop Replacement

When configuring a CCM connection for desktop replacement, the only options you need to configure are the Screen Area and the Connection Startup options. If you are creating a new connection, follow the steps outlined in the earlier "Client Connection Manager Connection Setup" section. When you reach Step 4, select the proper screen area and then select Full Screen. If you are modifying an existing connection, right-click the Connection icon in the CCM, select Properties, and then modify the screen information on the Connection Options tab (Figure 19.7).

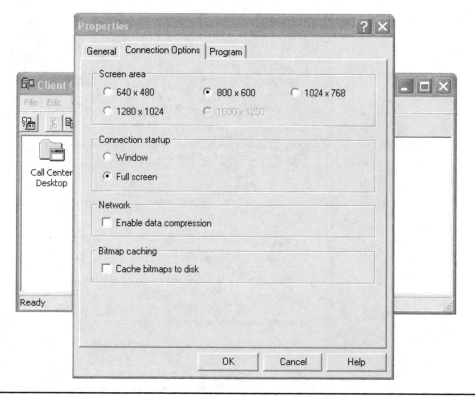

Figure 19.7   Modifying the screen properties for a CCM RDP connection.

TIP: For your RDP session to use the full screen, you must select the proper desktop screen resolution. For example, if you have a client with a screen resolution of 1024×768 and you select Full Screen but selected 800×600 as the screen area, the usable desktop space within the session will be only 800×600, and the remaining area will simply appear as a black border.

Configuring the Remote Desktop Connection for Desktop Replacement

Configuration of the Remote Desktop Connection to support the desktop-replacement scenario is similar to CCM configuration. The options to change are located on the Display and Local Resources tabs. From the Display tab, you need to select the Remote Desktop Size option and move the slider completely to the right to choose the Full Screen option (Figure 19.8). Unless you want your users to be able to access their local desktops, make sure that the "Display the connection bar when in full screen mode" option is not also checked. This removes the potentially distracting connection bar from the user's session.

Figure 19.8   Modifying the Display properties for a Remote Desktop Connection.

On the Local Resources tab, the one option that directly impacts the full-screen session is the Keyboard setting. Behavior of the Windows key combinations is dictated by this setting. In most situations you will want to configure this setting to be either "In full screen mode only" or "On the remote computer." When this is set, the Windows key combinations such as Alt+Tab or Alt+Esc are processed within the Terminal Server session and not on the local client desktop. This produces the most intuitive desktop scenario for the end user, since they do not need to learn any alternate key combinations to perform common tasks within Terminal Server, which they are required to do if they're using the CCM RDP client. I discuss these alternate key combinations in the next section of this chapter.

Windows Shortcut Key Support in an RDP Session

When running a full desktop session, users may wish to perform standard Windows key combinations such as Alt+Tab. While the Remote Desktop Connection client supports capturing and redirection of standard Windows key combinations through to the Terminal Server, the CCM client does not. So for a user running the CCM to access these key functions, alternate keys must used. Table 19.2 lists the standard key combinations and their Terminal Server equivalents. Both CCM and Remote Desktop Connection support these alternate keys.

Table 19.2 Windows Shortcut Key Support in an RDP Session

Local Desktop Shortcut Key	Terminal Server Session Shortcut Key	Desired Function
Alt+Tab	Alt+Page Up	Move forward between active programs.
Alt+Shift+Tab	Alt+Page Down	Move backward between active programs.
Alt+Esc	Alt+Insert	Cycle through programs in their start order.
Ctrl+Esc	Alt+Home	Display the Start menu.
Ctrl+Alt+Delete	Ctrl+Alt+End	Display the Windows security dialog.
Alt+Spacebar	Alt+Delete	Display the active window's Control menu.
Not applicable	Ctrl+Alt+Break	Toggle the client between a window and full-screen session.

Application Replacement

With the RDP client, the only option currently available to support an application-replacement implementation is to configure an RDP connection to include the application name and path. I mentioned this briefly when discussing the connection setup for the Client

Connection Manager (Step 6) and the Remote Desktop Connection (Step 4). Figure 19.9 shows a sample configuration of an RDP connection (using Remote Desktop Connection) that automatically launches Microsoft Word.

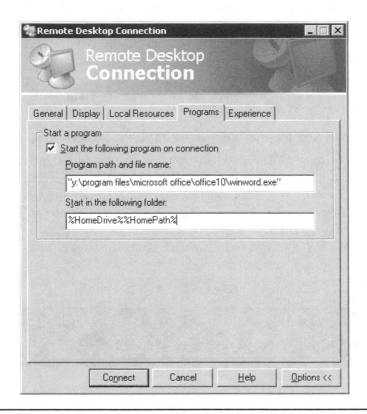

Figure 19.9   Configuring application replacement in the Remote Desktop Connection.

Notice that in this example the environment variables %HomeDrive% and %HomePath% have been defined as part of the application setup on the local client. These variables are not defined on the client but are defined on the Terminal Server. This is possible because the client passes the information to the server to execute the desired program. The server takes the variables and expands them before processing. I talk more about these environment variables and their use in application access in Chapter 20.

When a user launches a connection configured for application replacement, the user is presented with two title bars: one for the application (for example, Word) and the other for the RDP client (see Figure 19.10). This configuration can cause confusion for users not familiar with seeing dual title bars. The only way to overcome this problem is through education and training users to understand why there are two title bars.

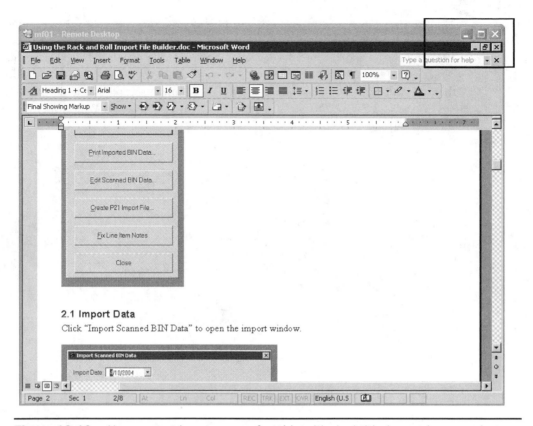

Figure 19.10   Users must become comfortable with dual title bars when running a
direct application session off a Terminal Server.

TIP: When setting up the RDP client to launch a specific application, no validation is
performed with respect to the application folder, working folder, or application file
name. Test a connection immediately after setting it up to ensure that it's working
properly. Otherwise, when run, the Terminal Server session will fail with an error message stating the application could not be found.

Configuring the Client Connection Manager for Application Replacement

Two options must be configured within the CCM in order to support application replacement. The first is defining the full path to the application executable and the starting folder.
These are set under the Program Tab for an existing CCM connection or in Step 6 when
defining a new RDP connection for the CCM (see section entitled "Client Connection

Manager Connection Setup"). Figure 19.11 shows the Program tab with the same Microsoft Word application that was configured earlier for the Remote Desktop Connection (Figure 19.9). Once the application information is provided, the final task is to define the associated screen area. In this configuration you will want to set the screen area to a window size less than the full-screen dimensions; 800×600 is a common setting, particularly when the client desktop size is 1024×768. Make certain that you also selected Window as the connection start-up setting.

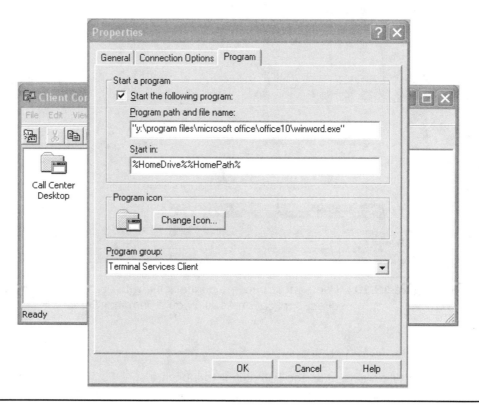

Figure 19.11 Configuring application replacement in the CCM.

Configuring the Remote Desktop Connection for Application Replacement

The same two settings must be configured in the Remote Desktop Connection (RDC) as would be configured in the CCM. First, define the full path to the application executable and the start-up folder under the Programs tab in the RDC (Figure 19.12). Next, define the appropriate remote desktop size. Just as with the CCM, you will likely want to define the desktop size as less than the full-screen dimensions. For example, 800×600 would be set for the application size when the local desktop was configured with a size of 1024×768.

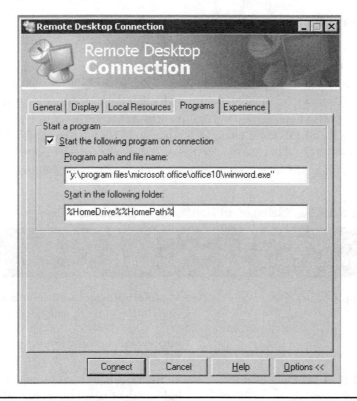

Figure 19.12 Configuring application replacement in the Remote Desktop Connection application.

For more information on planning the client portion of an application-replacement scenario, see the section "Planning for the Proper Thin Client Configuration" in Chapter 5. This section discusses some of the issues that exist with the RDP client when using it in an application-replacement scenario.

NOTE: Do not rely on configuring a user's client to launch only a specific application as a means of preventing the user from accessing other applications on the Terminal Server. If you want to grant access to only certain applications while denying access to others, implement the necessary security as discussed in Chapter 16, "Terminal Server Security."

Desktop Integration

Microsoft provides an RDP client for only one non-Windows operating system, the Apple Mac OS X. Using this client you can implement the desktop-integration scenario, allowing you to access a Windows session from within your OS X session. If you want to provide access to a Windows Terminal Server through other desktop operating systems, you need to look for third-party clients developed to support access to Terminal Server. Table 19.3 lists Microsoft's Mac OS X RDP client along with other non-Windows-based RDP clients that are available. As I mentioned in Chapter 5, Microsoft does not support any third-party clients connecting to a Terminal Server. Any support for these clients must go through the product's vendor.

Table 19.3 Examples of Non-Windows-Based RDP Clients

Desktop Client Operating System	Comments
Apple Mac OS X	Microsoft provides an RDP client for this operating system. It can be downloaded from http://www.microsoft.com/mac/DOWNLOAD/MISC/RDC.asp
Platform-independent Java-based client	HOB, a German-based company, provides a platform-independent Java-based client that allows access to a Terminal Server. Find it at http://www.hob.de/www_us
Linux and DOS	Terminal-Services.net provides one commercial RDP client that runs on Linux and another that runs on DOS. Find them at http://www.terminal-services.net
UNIX	RDesktop provides an open-source RDP client that runs on UNIX. Find it at http://www.rdesktop.org

RDP Client Distribution Methods

The RDP client supports a number of deployment options, which vary slightly based on the client version used. The main types of distributions supported are

- Client installation diskettes (RDP version 5.0 only).
- Network-based installation access point (all versions).
- Web-based installation access point (all versions).
- Distribution via Active Directory (all versions, although 5.1 and later include an MSI file, while 5.0 requires that you create one manually).

Client Installation Diskettes

Only Windows 2000 supports creation of RDP client installation diskettes using the Terminal Services Client Creator program located under Administrative Tools on the Start menu. When you start the program, the Create Installation Disk(s) dialog box opens (see Figure 19.13). Here you simply select the type of client floppy disks you want to create and then click OK to begin the process of copying the necessary files to the floppy disk. Two blank, formatted 3.5-inch floppy disks are required for the 32-bit client, or four if you want to create the 16-bit Windows client installation disks.

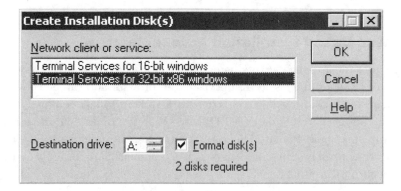

Figure 19.13 The Create Installation Disk(s) dialog box.

TIP: Make sure that the client diskettes are blank or that you select the Format option; otherwise, the Client Creator generates an error saying it couldn't copy the listed file. It never actually states that there was insufficient disk space.

Network-Based Installation Access Point

If you're considering setting up a network-based installation access point from which the appropriate client installation files will be available, I recommend that you create the share on a proper file server and not on the Terminal Server. Even though the setup files are available off the Terminal Server, it is best if Terminal Server–based file sharing of any sort is minimized as much as possible. Instead, delegate the task to a server properly configured to provide file-sharing services.

Access to the network-based installation point can be restricted to only administrators or it can be made available to end users as a set of read-only files. The choice depends on whether you will allow non-administrators to install and configure the RDP client. No special security configuration is required as long as all the installation files have Read and Execute access granted.

TIP: Microsoft's Distributed File System (DFS) can be used to provide a standard location where the RDP client files can be accessed. A share such as

\\nrsc.com\DFSRoot\Clients\TSClient

could be created in DFS that would let you centralize access of not only your Terminal Server clients but also any other client files you may use in your environment.

Web-Based Installation Access Point

Very similar to the network-based installation access point, the Web-based installation (as the name suggestions) is accessible via a Web browser and can be configured to provide a standard means of providing access to the RDP client installation files. The traditional client files can be set up either on an HTTP-based Web site or an FTP site for download. You can also implement the Remote Desktop Web Connection (Figure 19.14), from which the ActiveX RDP control is automatically downloaded and installed for use when a user attempts to connect to a Terminal Server.

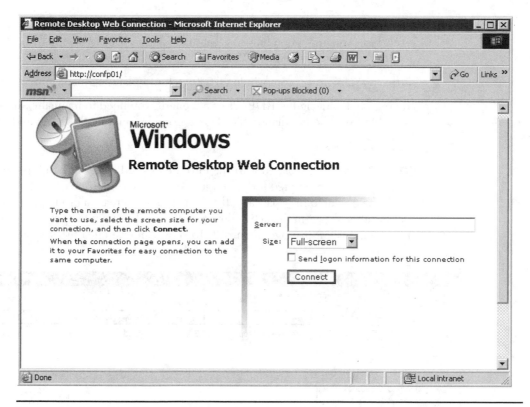

Figure 19.14 The Microsoft Remote Desktop Web Connection automatically downloads the ActiveX RDP client if necessary.

Distribution via Active Directory

If you want to deploy the RDP client to users running Windows 2000 or later in an active directory, you can utilize the Windows Installer component and group policy to automate this task. In general, creation and deployment of a client package would work as follows:

1. If you plan to deploy the RDP 5.0 client, you first need to create an MSI installation package that will be used to deploy the application. An MSI file is not provided with this client version as it is with versions 5.1 and 5.2. The Windows Installer (MSI) package is created on a clean workstation using the Veritas WinINSTALL

LE application, which ships with Windows 2000. Microsoft provides a very helpful Web-based document on how to create installation packages with WinINSTALL; it can be found at the following URL:

http://www.microsoft.com/windows2000/techinfo/planning/management/veritas.asp

If you are deploying the RDP 5.1 or 5.2 client, you need to manually extract the MSI file from the installation file. This is done by running the command

```
msrdpcli.exe /c
```

This extracts the associated MSI file into the desired folder. When this command is run you will be prompted for the target destination folder.

2. With the available MSI package, the next step is to create a group policy for an organizational unit in the active directory that will contain the users who should receive the client package. Figure 19.15 shows an example of this.

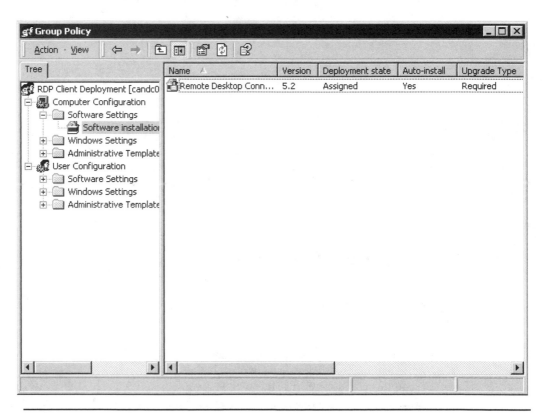

Figure 19.15 Assigning an installation package within a group policy.

3. Depending on how you've configured the package, you can have it auto-install, or you can simply make it available in the Add/Remove Programs utility under Control Panel.

NOTE: A discussion on use of group policies to deploy software is beyond the scope of this book, but detailed information is available in the Windows 2000 and 2003 Help files. Simply look for "Windows Installer" in the Help index.

Web-based Access with Terminal Services

Besides the traditional Terminal Services clients, Microsoft has also made the latest edition of their Web client available. This client is called the Remote Desktop Web Connection (RDWC) and is intended to provide a Web interface from which you can establish connections to Terminal Servers (or desktops running Windows XP Professional). The web client is an ActiveX control that provides almost all of the same functionality as the true Windows 32 client. The installation of RDWC is very straightforward and requires only Internet Information Server 4.0 or higher.

The installation software is downloaded from the Microsoft Website and can easily be found by searching downloads for "Remote Desktop Web Connection". Once you have downloaded the software make sure that it is accessible from your IIS server and initiate the installation TSWEBSETUP.EXE.

Once started the first dialog that will appear asks only to confirm that you want to install the RDWC application software. After accepting the end user license agreement the necessary files are copied to the server and the installation is complete. A reboot is not required in order to enable this software. At this point you are ready to test out the Web interface.

Accessing the Remote Desktop Web Connection

In order to test the RDWC client you will need to point your Web browser at the site where the Web page is being hosted. Typically this means using the following URL:

http://<web server>/tsweb

Immediately after connecting to the Web page a confirmation dialog box (Figure 19.16) will appear asking you to install and run the Remote Desktop ActiveX Control. After saying Yes, the ActiveX control is installed and you're presented with the connection screen.

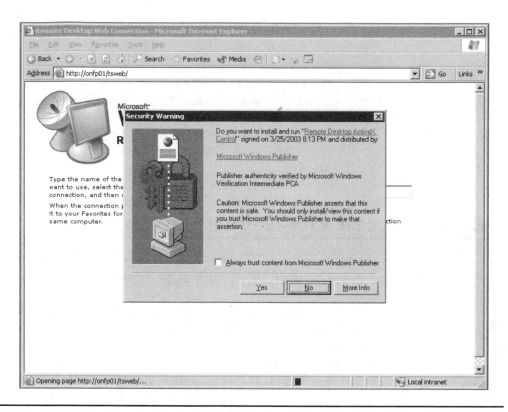

Figure 19.16 The Remote Desktop ActiveX control is required so that a Terminal Services session can be launched from within the Web page.

From the connection Web page the user is prompted to provide a server name, what size of client Terminal Services window will exist and whether or not to send logon information entered on the Web page through to the Terminal Server. For any window size selected other than full screen the new ICA session will be contained within the bounds of the Web page as shown in Figure 19.17.

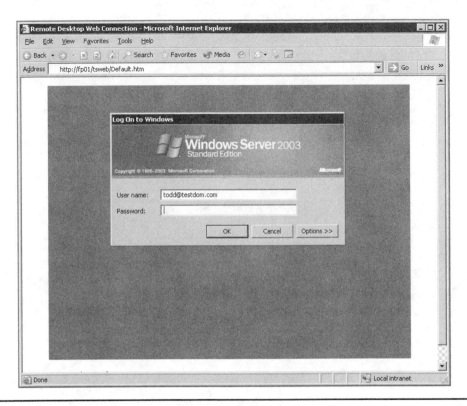

Figure 19.17 Selecting a Window size other than full screen will create a server session sized to fit in the displayed Web page.

CHAPTER 20

ICA Client Installation and Configuration

Before You Begin

Chapter 5, "Client Hardware and Software Planning," talks in detail about both the ICA and RDP clients and the planning and support considerations you must account for when planning your Terminal Server/MetaFrame implementation. The various implementation categories common to both protocols (desktop and application replacement, desktop integration) and those categories unique to a MetaFrame deployment (content publishing) are also discussed. This chapter focuses on the ICA client, beginning with a brief review of the main client choices available, which I first discussed in Chapter 2, "Citrix MetaFrame Presentation Server." This review is followed by a look at how these client choices are installed and configured to support the various client implementation categories available. The chapter concludes with a brief look at the ICA client distribution methods available.

NOTE: As mentioned in Chapter 19, "RDP Client Installation and Configuration," don't let ease of installation for the ICA and RDP clients lead you to believe that a formal implementation plan is not required for your client deployment.

On more than one occasion I have encountered poorly planned client installations that resulted in an inconsistency in configuration and choice of the ICA client application. Very often different choices and versions of the ICA client have been used for an implementation without any proper thought into how they should be configured.

One example is the differences in configuration of the keyboard mappings for the ICA client (these are not configurable in the RDP client), which can sometimes lead to conflict with another application running within the MetaFrame session. A conflict with a 3270 host emulator is a good example of this, since it requires certain PF and PA key combinations that often match the default keys for the ICA client. Unless this modification has been considered during the client planning and configuration phases, it likely will result in an issue that must be corrected either during or after the implementation.

The choice of what ICA client to use will depend on two main factors: what client operating system you will be supporting and what type of client configuration you want to implement. For example, if all your clients are running Linux, your choices will be to use either Citrix ICA client connections or the Program Neighborhood Agent component, both of which are contained within the same client application. If, on the other hand, your users will be running Windows XP, you will want to implement one of the three available Win32 ICA clients (Program Neighborhood, Program Neighborhood Agent, or the Web client).

TIP: With the introduction of MetaFrame Presentation Server 3.0, Citrix began to call its ICA client for both Java and the Win32 platform the MetaFrame Presentation Server client. Other clients continue to be called ICA clients. Throughout this chapter, when discussing the ICA client, I include the MPS clients for Java and Win32 unless explicitly stated otherwise.

In Chapter 2, I provided an introduction to the four main types of ICA clients available. The four types are

- **Standard Citrix ICA client**—Traditionally known as the Remote Application Manager, this client provides basic connectivity support to one or more specific Citrix servers or published resources in a Citrix server farm. This client type is available for most supported client platforms, including 32-bit Windows (as part of Program Neighborhood), CE, Mac OS X, Linux and other supported UNIX variants, OS/2, and 16-bit Windows.
- **Program Neighborhood (PN)**—Program Neighborhood is a full application environment within which connections to various MetaFrame Presentation Servers or published resources can be accessed. This client lets you create connections to application sets (groups of published resources available within a server farm) or specific custom ICA connections. ICA connections can be made directly to a MetaFrame server or to published resources. Most new implementations of MetaFrame do not deploy this full client to the end user but instead use the Program Neighborhood Agent or the Web client (both described later in this list) for regular user access. Administrators will likely want to have the full Program Neighborhood installed on their desktops for maximum flexibility in supporting their MetaFrame environment.
- **Program Neighborhood Agent (PN Agent)**—This client works in conjunction with the Web Interface for MetaFrame Presentation Server (discussed in Chapter 14, "MetaFrame Presentation Server Configuration") to provide a simple means of delivering published resources to the end user. Unlike the full PN, where all configuration changes must be performed locally on the client, configuration of the PN Agent is done centrally through the Program Neighborhood Agent Console (discussed later in this chapter) and retrieved by the client via

the Web Interface for MPS. Published resources are retrieved from one or more server farms and displayed on the user's local desktop by the PN Agent based on the domain groups the user belongs to. The PN Agent does not have a full interface through which the user can create connections and access servers or resources. Certain options for the PN Agent can be configured by right-clicking the PN Agent icon in the system tray and selecting the desired setting. You can also see the list of available applications from here, but the PN Agent is usually configured to place published application shortcuts directly on the local desktop or Start menu.

■ **Citrix Web client**—The smallest of the four client types, the Citrix Web client is available only for Windows 32-bit operating systems and provides access to published resources directly from hyperlinks on a Web page. The source of this Web page can be any of the following:

■ The Web Interface for MetaFrame Presentation Server
■ NFuse Classic, the previous iteration of the Web Interface product
■ A standard Web page with properly configured hyperlinks using a technique known as *application launching and embedding* (ALE)

For the Web Client to function, you must be running Internet Explorer (5.0 or higher) or Netscape Navigator or Communicator (4.78 or 6.2 or higher). The Web client provides no separate user interface and instead retrieves the necessary configuration information directly from the source Web site and from the published application settings in the Citrix server farm.

Two versions of the Citrix Web client exist. One provides the full set of ICA client features and is available both as a self-extracting executable and as a compressed Microsoft cabinet (.CAB) file. The other is known as the *minimal* Citrix Web client and is available only as a .CAB file. As the name suggests, this client is the smallest Win32 ICA client available, and in order to achieve this, certain features normally found in the other ICA clients had to be omitted. These missing features are summarized in Table 20.1.

Table 20.1   ICA Client Features Not Available with the Minimal Citrix Web Client

Feature
Client audio mapping
Client COM port mapping
Content redirection
Extended parameter passing

Table 20.1 ICA Client Features Not Available with the Minimal Citrix Web Client (continued)

Feature
Multiple monitor support
Novell Directory Services (NDS) support
Panning and scaling
Per-user time zone support
SecureICA encryption (RC5)
SpeedScreen latency reduction
Universal printer driver
User-to-user shadowing
Wheel mouse support

TIP: Citrix provides a Java-based client that is also accessible directly from a Web browser and supports many of the features found in the full Win32 Web client.

Installing the ICA Client

Once you have determined the ICA client you will implement, you need to thoroughly understand how this client is installed and what configuration options are available. This ensures that the client has been properly configured to maximize the end user's computing experience while minimizing the chances of issues arising while the user is working.

All the Citrix ICA clients available at the time of the MetaFrame Presentation Server 3.0 release are accessible from at least one of the following locations:

- Installation files can be found on the MPS Components CD included in the MPS media package. If Z: is the CD-ROM drive, the available client installation files can be found in one of two locations on the CD-ROM.

    The first location is Z:\icainst\<language>, where *language* is the appropriate language abbreviation; for example, *en* for English. This folder contains client installation files for Win16, Win32, EPOC/Symbian OS, 32-bit DOS, Mac OS X, Mac OS 9.*x*, OS/2, Windows CE, and the UNIX and Linux variants.

The other location is Z:\icaweb\<language>, which contains all the ICA clients that can be installed directly via the Web. These client installation files include Win16, Win32, Java, Mac OS 9.*x* and OS X, Windows CE, and the UNIX and Linux variants. As you can see, the Java client is accessible only from under the ICAWEB folder.

Currently, the following are the available language folders that can exist:

- de—German
- jp—Japanese
- en—English
- es—Spanish
- fr—French

- The latest version of the desired ICA client can be downloaded directly from the Citrix Web site (go to http://www.citrix.com/download and select the Clients hyperlink) free of charge.

In this section I focus on the installation steps for the two Win32 ICA clients that provide a local user interface (Program Neighborhood and Program Neighborhood Agent) and the ICA Linux client.

Installing the Citrix Program Neighborhood

The full Program Neighborhood client can be installed using any one of the three available setup files:

- MetaFrame Presentation Server (MPS) Client Packager (Ica32Pkg.msi)
- Self-extracting executable (Ica32.exe)
- Self-extracting cabinet file (Wfica.cab)

All these files can be found in the ICAWEB\<language>\ica32 folder on the MetaFrame Presentation Server Components CD.

Using the MetaFrame Presentation Server Client Packager

The MSI file is typically used to configure packages for automating installation of the desired ICA client using either the software installation feature of Active Directory or Microsoft Systems Management Server (SMS). This file can also be used to perform a standard installation of any one of the available 32-bit ICA clients. The general installation steps are as follows:

1. Begin by launching the Ica32Pkg.msi file and then click Next past the opening welcome screen.
2. After accepting the terms of the license agreement, click Next to continue.

3. You are prompted to select the desired client features to install. Click the button to the left of the Web Client and Program Neighborhood Agent options and select the option "Entire feature will be unavailable." A red X should appear beside each of these client choices, as shown in Figure 20.1. Click Next when you're ready to proceed.

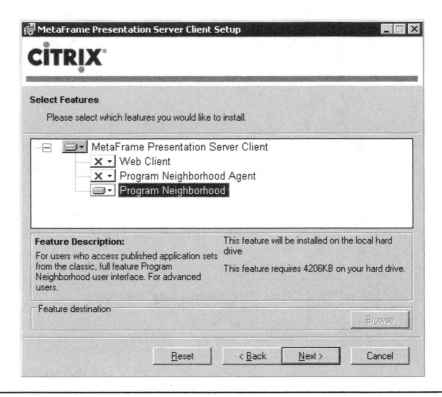

Figure 20.1   Select only the MetaFrame Presentation Server client you want to install.

WARNING: It is not recommended that you install both the full Program Neighborhood and the Program Neighborhood Agent on the same client machine.

---

4. Choose the desired program folder where the Program Neighborhood Start menu icon will appear.
5. Next choose the name for this ICA client. By default, the local computer name is used to assign the ICA client name. Unless you plan to implement some other unique naming convention for your ICA client connections, I recommend that you leave the default option selected.

6. The next dialog box prompts you to decide whether or not to enable and use local user passthrough authentication (Figure 20.2). If you plan to implement passthrough authentication at some point, you must select Yes now, or the option will not be available until you first reinstall the Program Neighborhood client.

Even though passthrough authentication is available on the client once selected, it must be explicitly configured for an application set or connection; it is not used by default. See the "Configuring the Program Neighborhood Client" section later in this chapter for more information on configuring this option.

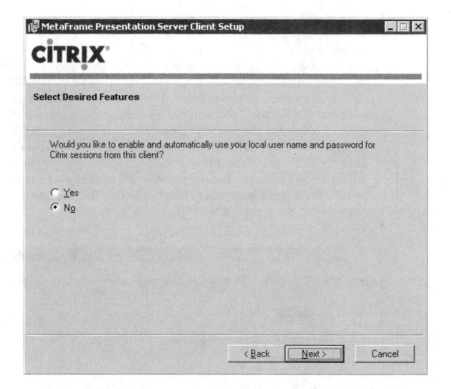

Figure 20.2 Passthrough authentication must be enabled during the client installation; otherwise, it is not available for use unless the ICA client software is reinstalled.

7. The final dialog box provides a summary of the features you selected. When you click Next, the Program Neighborhood installation finishes. You are required to reboot the client computer in order to complete the installation.

Once the client machine has rebooted, you can log on and perform the necessary client configuration.

Using a Self-Extracting Installation File

Unless stated otherwise, the installation steps using the self-extracting executable or cabinet file are nearly identical. When launching a Program Neighborhood installation from a self-extracting executable, you are presented with the InstallShield welcome screen. After you click Next to move past this welcome screen the actual client setup begins, and you see the actual ICA client setup welcome screen. From this point forward, both the executable and the cabinet-based installations are identical:

1. Click Next to proceed past the ICA client setup welcome screen.
2. You must accept the terms of the license agreement in order to continue past the license screen.
3. After selecting the destination location for the application files (the default is usually appropriate) and the location for the Program Neighborhood shortcut, you are prompted to decide whether to use your local user name and password for Citrix sessions (Figure 20.3). Although the installation dialog box wording is slightly different from that in the passthrough authentication prompt for the MSI installation package, the requirements are the same. If you do not enable this option now, you must reinstall the PN client if you decide to use this feature at a later date.

    After you choose the desired passthrough authentication configuration, the installation copies the necessary files to the PC. To complete the installation, you must reboot the client machine.

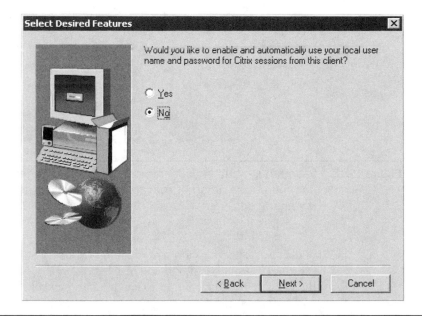

Figure 20.3 When using the self-extracting installation file, the prompt for enabling passthrough authentication is slightly different but produces the same results.

Once the client machine has rebooted, you are ready to proceed with completing configuration of the Program Neighborhood client.

Installing the Program Neighborhood Agent

Just as with the full Program Neighborhood client, the Program Neighborhood Agent (PN Agent) can be installed using one of the following two available setup files:

- MetaFrame Presentation Server Client Packager (Ica32Pkg.msi)
- Self-extracting executable (Ica32a.exe)

Both of these files can be found in the ICAWEB\<language>\ica32 folder on the MetaFrame Presentation Server Components CD.

WARNING: As I mentioned earlier, it is *not* recommended that you install both the full Program Neighborhood and the Program Neighborhood Agent on the same client machine.

The basic installation steps for the PN Agent are identical to those outlined for the full Program Neighborhood client with one main exception. As you progress through the installation wizard you will at one point be requested to provide the name of the Web Interface server. This server is queried by the PN Agent to determine the published application shortcuts to display on the user's desktop and what configuration settings to apply to the PN Agent client itself. You can provide either an HTTP or HTTPS URL. When providing the URL, I recommend providing the fully qualified domain name for the Web Interface server. For example, if my Web server PASCAL was serving up the Web Interface and I wanted to establish an SSL connection, I would provide the following URL:

https://pascal.nrsc.com

After this, the installation continues as normal, with requests for the subfolder where the PN application will be located and the desired name for the ICA Client, which by default is the local computer name.

You will be prompted to decide whether or not to enable and use local user passthrough authentication. If you plan to implement passthrough authentication at some point, you should select Yes now, or the option is not available unless you first modify the PN Agent installation.

Once the PN Agent installation is finished you must reboot the client computer to complete the installation. After rebooting the PN Agent will contact the Web server that was provided during the installation and retrieve the necessary configuration information. See the "Configuring the Program Neighborhood Agent" section, later in this chapter.

Installing the Citrix ICA Client for Linux

Two installation methods exist for version 8.x of the Citrix ICA client for Linux:

- Execute the installation script (setupwfc) found by first extracting the contents of the linuxx86.tar.gz file downloaded from the Citrix Web site.
- Install the client using the .RPM package file, also available from the Citrix Web site.

NOTE: My preference is to execute the installation script, but either method will produce the desired result.

Using the Linux Installation Script

Once you have extracted the contents of the linuxx86.tar.gz file (using a tool such as Ark) into a folder, the script file setupwfc must be executed from a shell console with root privileges. When the script file has executed, you are presented with the main selection menu shown in Figure 20.4.

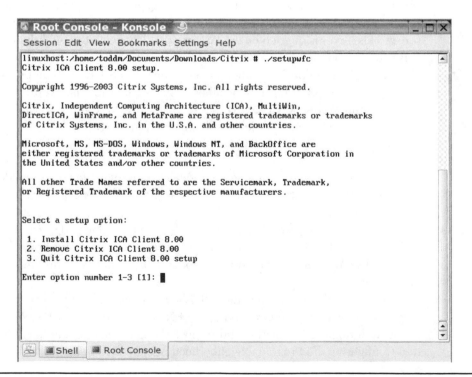

Figure 20.4   The setupwfc executable can be used to install the ICA client for Linux.

From here you have three possible choices:

1. Install Citrix ICA Client 8.00.
2. Remove Citrix ICA Client 8.00.
3. Quit Citrix ICA Client 8.00 setup.

Select choice number 1 and press Enter to begin the client installation. The remainder of the installation proceeds as follows:

1. You're prompted to provide the directory into which the client will be installed. The default location is

   /usr/lib/ICAClient

   Enter the desired target directory and press Enter to continue.
2. The client is now ready to be installed. You must enter the letter Y and then press Enter to continue.
3. The Citrix end user license agreement is displayed; scroll through this to the end and then decide whether or not to accept the terms. You cannot install the client unless you accept the terms of the agreement. If you accept the terms, type the number 1 and press Enter to continue.
4. The installation then begins to copy the contents to the hard drive. If you are using either the KDE or GNOME window managers, you are asked if you want to integrate the ICA client with the desktop; doing so adds a Citrix ICA client icon under *Internet* on the desktop menu, as shown in Figure 20.5. If you select N, you must manually add an icon for your users. You may need to refresh the desktop before the icon appears in the menu.
5. The client installation is now complete, and you are returned to the initial installation menu. Select 3 and press Enter to quit.

You are *not* required to reboot the PC in order to begin using the client and are now ready to complete the Linux client configuration. Begin by reviewing the following section, "ICA Client Server Location Configuration," and then proceed to the "Configuring the Citrix ICA Client for Linux" section, later in this chapter.

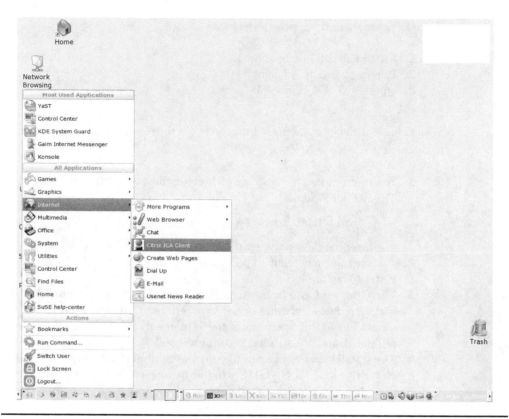

Figure 20.5   The ICA client installation for Linux integrates the client with either the KDE or the GNOME window manager.

Using the RPM ICA Client Package

An alternative to extracting the contents of the tar.gz file is to use the RPM package available on the Citrix Web site. Most Linux distributions support the RPM command, and the client can easily be installed by issuing the following command as root:

```
rpm -U -v -h ICAClient-8.0-1.i386.rpm
```

It is assumed that the command is issued from the directory containing the RPM package. The "-v –h" switches will run the package installation in verbose mode, allowing you to see the display of hash marks during the install. You are presented with no prompts other than a message saying whether or not the installation completed successfully. When the RPM package is used, there is no integration with the current windowing manager. You must manually add the ICA client icon to the desired menu or desktop. The files are installed by default into the directory /usr/lib/ICAClient and the executable file name is wfcmgr.

The first time this file is executed, it displays the Citrix end user license agreement, which must be accepted before the client can be run. The user is not presented with this agreement again once it is accepted.

As with the script, you are not required to reboot the PC before you can begin to configure the client for your implementation. Begin by reviewing the next section, "ICA Client Server Location Configuration," and then proceed to the "Configuring the Citrix ICA Client for Linux" section, later in this chapter.

ICA Client Server Location Configuration

For the Program Neighborhood and other ICA clients to locate a MetaFrame server farm, a published application, or even a server, it must have information on where to look to find the resource. Most ICA clients, with the exceptions of the Program Neighborhood Agent and the Web client, allow for configuration of a setting called Server Location. The Server Location property lets you configure a list of one or more MetaFrame servers that the client can communicate with in order to retrieve the necessary information about the MetaFrame environment. Typically this option can be found on any screen where you can configure a new connection to a MetaFrame resource. For example, Figure 20.6 shows the Server Location dialog box that is accessible when creating a new custom ICA connection in the Program Neighborhood client.

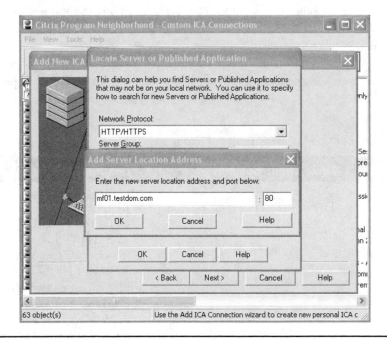

Figure 20.6 The Server Location property is accessible when creating a new custom ICA connection.

If server location information is not provided or incorrect information is used and the client is unable to locate a published resource or server, an error message similar to the one in Figure 20.7 appears.

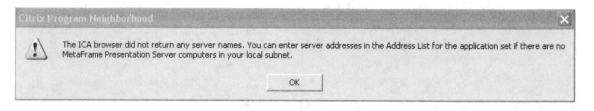

Figure 20.7   PN fails to retrieve server names and published applications if a MetaFrame server cannot be found to access Citrix farm information.

Server Location Configuration in the Program Neighborhood Client and ICA Client for Linux

In the Program Neighborhood client, there are four protocol groups to which you can assign unique server location information; these are listed in Table 20.2 alongside the corresponding protocol groups for the ICA client for Linux. The Linux client supports only three of the protocol groups, and they are arranged slightly differently, but the basic functionality remains the same.

If a protocol is not used in your environment, or at least not used for MetaFrame connectivity, there is no need to assign server location information to that protocol within the Citrix client.

Table 20.2   Server Location Network Protocol Groups

PN Client Setting	Linux Client Setting	Description
HTTP/HTTPS	TCP/IP+HTTP server location	Represents the server list used when either the TCP/IP+HTTP or SSL/TLS+HTTPS network protocols are selected for use. When providing addresses for the list, you should use fully qualified domain names (FQDN). For example, I would use the FQDN descartes.nrsc.com in my server list instead of just the host name "descartes".

Table 20.2   Server Location Network Protocol Groups (continued)

PN Client Setting	Linux Client Setting	Description
		When no entries are provided in the server list, the TCP/IP+HTTP network protocol attempts to retrieve farm information by querying the server named
		ica.<domain name>
		where <domain name> is the full TCP/IP domain name of the client machine. If your domain was nrsc.com, the fully qualified domain name queried would be ica.nrsc.com.
		If you're not planning to populate the server location list and you're using one of these protocols, you'll need to ensure that one or more alias records exist in your DNS that redirect the name ica to a MetaFrame server. You are not required to actually name one of your MetaFrame servers ica.
		Unless one of these settings is configured, Program Neighborhood is unable to locate a server farm using the HTTP/HTTPS protocol.
		Unlike the PN client for Windows, which groups HTTP/HTTPS server location information together, the Linux client separates these options. Aside from letting you maintain a separate server location list for these two protocol types, the information describing TCP/IP applies to this option as well.
TCP/IP	TCP/IP	The original method of communicating with the MetaFrame server is via the TCP/IP protocol, and the functionality of this protocol has changed very little. When no server list is associated with the protocol, the

Table 20.2 Server Location Network Protocol Groups (continued)

PN Client Setting	Linux Client Setting	Description
		client initiates a UDP broadcast on the local subnet using port 1604 and looks for a MetaFrame server to respond. When one or more servers are provided in the server list, a directed broadcast is performed to all listed servers simultaneously, and the first one to respond is used to retrieve the desired information.
IPX/SPX	N/A	Represents the server location list for both the IPX and the SPX network protocols. These protocols also perform broadcasts to find MetaFrame servers on the local network when no server names have been explicitly provided. IPX/SPX-based client connections are supported only on Windows 2000 servers. Windows Server 2003 does not support IPX/SPX connections.
NETBIOS	N/A	This protocol also performs a broadcast to find available MetaFrame servers when no servers have been listed and is supported only on Windows 2000. Windows Server 2003 does not support NETBIOS-based ICA client connections.

Up to three groups of five servers can be defined for each of the available network protocols that your clients will use to create MetaFrame server connections (Figure 20.8). By default, the groups are labeled Primary, Backup 1, and Backup 2, but you can rename them by highlighting the existing name and clicking the Rename Group button.

The client queries all servers in the Primary group for the necessary farm information; if no response is received within the given time interval, the client repeats the request with the Backup 1 group and finally the Backup 2 group, if necessary. If no response is received from any of the servers in any of the groups, the client fails with the message shown back in Figure 20.7.

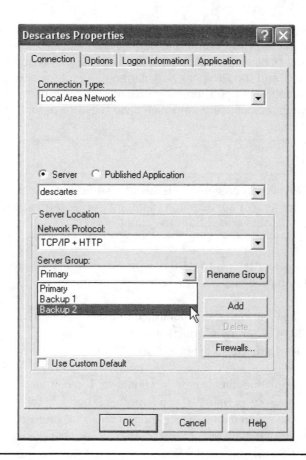

Figure 20.8   Up to three groups of five servers can be defined for a single network protocol.

The backup groups are most often used when a separate MetaFrame environment exists on a different network that would support users if the primary environment was unavailable. This feature is known as Business Recovery and is one component of Citrix's business continuity strategy for rapid disaster recovery and maximum server uptime.

TIP: There is sometimes confusion on the part of a new administrator between the entry of server location information and the management of the preferred and failover zone information that is maintained through MetaFrame user policies, which were discussed in Chapter 14, "MetaFrame Presentation Server Configuration."

Server location information is required in order to let the MetaFrame client locate at least one MetaFrame server that can provide information about the server farm.

Zone Preferences and Failover, an option supported with the Enterprise Edition of MetaFrame, lets you define the default and failover zones used when a user attempts to access published applications in the farm. This feature is available only with the Web client and the Program Neighborhood Agent, neither of which lets you provide a server location list. The preferred zone is where a user runs their applications unless this zone is inaccessible, in which case they are automatically redirected to the failover zone.

WARNING: When assigning MetaFrame servers to a server location list, make certain you do *not* assign servers from different server farms to the same list. Doing so causes unpredictable behavior in the client.

An ICA client attempts to retrieve information from the server farm when performing any of the following actions:

- Connecting to a published resource (application or content)
- Gathering information about a server farm
- Returning a list of available MetaFrame servers or published resources

When populating the server location list, I recommend that you specify at least two MetaFrame servers (more, if you have them) but only for the protocol(s) you're supporting. Do not bother populating the server location list for protocols you're not going to use. By providing multiple MetaFrame server entries, you provide redundancy in case one of the servers in the list becomes unavailable.

TIP: A common misconception is that in order to work properly the server list must include the name of the server that contains the data store. This is not true. The list needs to contain only the names of MetaFrame servers that are members of the appropriate server farm. Also, you cannot list Terminal Servers not running MetaFrame Presentation Server.

Firewall Settings

When assigning servers to any of the TCP/IP-based network protocols supported by the PN client (TCP/IP+HTTP, SSL/TLS+HTTP, TCP/IP), you will notice that the Firewalls button near the bottom right-hand side of the dialog box is enabled. Clicking this button brings up the dialog box shown in Figure 20.9.

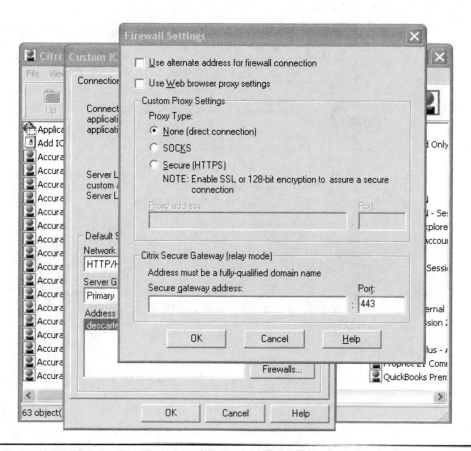

Figure 20.9 Firewall settings in the Program Neighborhood client.

The Firewall settings for the Linux client are accessed by selecting the Firewall Settings option, which brings up the dialog box shown in Figure 20.10.

The properties configured on this page exist to deal with the situation where the ICA client is located on one side of a firewall and the MetaFrame server is located on the other side. Table 20.3 explains the options available on this page.

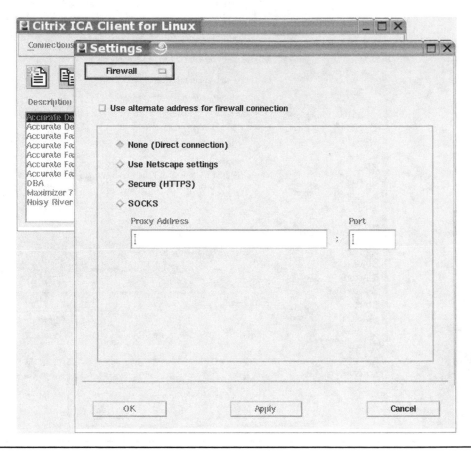

Figure 20.10   Firewall settings in the ICA client for Linux.

Table 20.3   Program Neighborhood and Linux ICA Client Firewall Settings

Protocol	Description
Use alternate address for firewall connection.	Normally when connecting to a published application in a server farm, the client is passed information on what MetaFrame server it should connect to in order to access the desired published application. When you are located on the same internal network as the server farm, you know how to route to the internal IP address provided.

Table 20.3 Program Neighborhood and Linux ICA Client Firewall Settings (continued)

Protocol	Description
	If, on the other hand, you are located externally (on the Internet) and must traverse a firewall in order to access the MetaFrame server, when you are passed the internal IP address of the target MetaFrame server, you cannot connect. This is because you need to be given an external address that the client can use that is translated and routed properly through the external interface, onto the internal network, and directly to the target MetaFrame server.
	To do this, the client must be able to tell the MetaFrame server that it wants to be given an external address to work with, not the standard internal address. This is the purpose of the "Use alternate address for firewall connection" option. Enabling this tells the client to request the alternate address from the MetaFrame server when it provides published application information.
	You are required to enable this option *only* if you're connecting from an external network that does not have a direct route to the internal MetaFrame servers.
	For the MetaFrame server to provide an alternate address, it must have an alternate address assigned using the ALTADDR command line tool. Use of this tool and more details on alternate addresses are discussed in Chapter 14.
Use Web browser proxy settings Program Neighborhood Client only	If you must go through a proxy server prior to connecting to a MetaFrame server and the proxy settings are managed through the Web browser, you can enable this option so the two servers share the configuration information. The Linux client manages access to these settings from the Custom Proxy Settings option.
Custom Proxy Settings PN Client options None SOCKS Secure (HTTPS)	You can also manage the necessary proxy information directly from here. The default option is to use no proxy (None) and connect directly to the target MetaFrame server. When accessing servers on the local network, this is the option to choose.

Table 20.3 Program Neighborhood and Linux ICA Client Firewall Settings (continued)

Protocol	Description
Linux Client options None Use Netscape settings Secure (HTTPS) SOCKS	If you must go through a SOCKS proxy server to access the MetaFrame server select SOCKS and provide the target proxy server address and port. The default SOCKS port is 1080 but may be different in your environment; consult your SOCKS proxy administrator to verify these settings.
	If you're going through a secure (HTTPS) proxy server, select Secure (HTTPS) and provide the target HTTPS server address and port. This default port is 8080 but can be changed if necessary. Again, consult the proxy administrator to ensure you are using the proper settings.
	If you must go through a proxy server prior to connect to a MetaFrame server and the proxy settings are managed through the Netscape Web browser (Linux only), you can enable this option so the servers share the configuration information.
Citrix Secure Gateway (relay mode) Program Neighborhood client only	Available only in version 1.x of the Citrix Secure Gateway product and no longer supported in newer versions, the relay mode of CSG acts as an SSL-based entry point into the MetaFrame server farm. If the client is connecting through CSG configured to run in relay mode, you must select this option and provide the fully qualified domain name of the secure gateway entry point. The default port is 443 (standard SSL port) and likely will not need to change unless modified in the CSG configuration.
	For more information on the latest version of Secure Gateway for MetaFrame, please see Chapter 16.

Properly configuring the firewall settings and the server location information in general ensure that your ICA connections function properly. Now that we've reviewed the basic requirements for the server location, we can move on to look at the configuration steps for some of the most common ICA clients in use.

Configuring the Program Neighborhood Client

Across all client platforms, the standard Citrix ICA client and the full Program Neighborhood client share a number of common properties. Before discussing how to configure the Program Neighborhood to support a particular implementation scenario, it is important to have an overall understanding of how the ICA client settings affect the behavior of one or more application connections. This knowledge can also greatly simplify the task of configuring ICA clients not explicitly discussed in this book, such as the Windows CE client or the Mac OS X client.

All the ICA clients (with the exception of the PN Agent, Web client, and Java client) provide a means of explicitly configuring connections to one or more published resources. Most of these clients also have two distinct kinds of settings that can be configured. The first is client-wide settings that are applied to all connections defined within the ICA client. Typically these settings pertain to options such as the ICA client name, the keyboard layout, bitmap caching, and the hotkey configuration—options that logically should apply to all ICA connections originating from the client.

Settings in the second group apply directly to the MetaFrame connections and either define default options that apply to all connections (unless overridden) or are settings specific only to an individual connection definition.

Client-Wide Program Neighborhood Settings

In the Program Neighborhood, the first level of global settings can be found by selecting ICA Settings from the Tools menu, as shown in Figure 20.11. Any changes to the ICA Settings property page are applied to all connections defined within the Program Neighborhood, whether they are custom ICA connections or applications within an application set.

The global settings for the Program Neighborhood client are divided into four tabs:

- **General**—Contains general settings that are applied to all ICA client connections.
- **Bitmap Cache**—Where the caching feature for the client is configured.
- **Hotkeys**—Where the alternate hotkeys are defined to access the standard Windows function keys such as Ctrl+Alt+Del, Alt+Tab or Alt+Esc.
- **Event Logging**—Where client-side event logging of information can be configured.

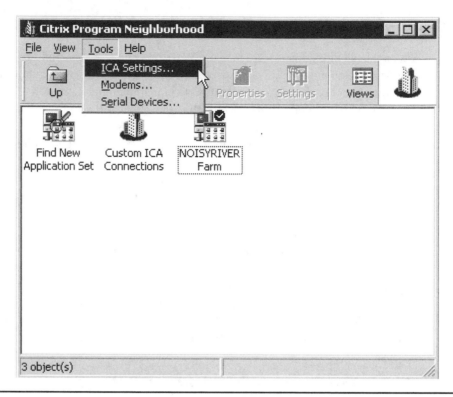

Figure 20.11 Any changes to ICA settings apply to all connections configured within Program Neighborhood.

General Tab

Figure 20.12 shows the General ICA Settings tab for the Program Neighborhood client, and Table 20.4 summarizes the settings on this dialog box.

Table 20.4 Program Neighborhood General ICA Settings

Setting	Description
Client Name Enable Dynamic Client Name	The client name is used to uniquely identify resources such as client printer or drive mappings. Enabling this option forces PN to match the ICA client name to the user's local PC (device) name. If the device name is changed, the ICA client name automatically changes. Normally, Enable Dynamic Client Name should be used.

Table 20.4   Program Neighborhood General ICA Settings (continued)

Setting	Description
Keyboard Layout Keyboard Type	These options let you define the keyboard layout and type used by the client device. This information is used by MetaFrame to properly configure your client session. The default settings of [User Profile] and [Default] are appropriate for most situations.
Display Connect To screen before making Dial-In Connections Display terminal window when making Dial-In Connections	These options apply only when performing a dial-in connection directly to a MetaFrame server. The first option, enabled by default, shows the Connect To screen during dial-in. The second option displays a terminal window during the dial-in connection. This is necessary only if there is some intermediary device that requires terminal input prior to allowing the connection to the MetaFrame server to be established. Direct dial-in connections to a MetaFrame server are supported on only Windows 2000, and their configuration is discussed in Chapter 14.
Allow automatic client updates	This option controls whether the client responds to a client-update request issued from a MetaFrame server. For a client to be properly updated, this option must be enabled. Unfortunately this option currently can't be overridden by anything on the server side. This means that if a user had sufficient privileges on the desktop, he or she could disable this option and prevent client updates from occurring.
Passthrough Authentication	If passthrough authentication was enabled during the client installation, this option is available for selection. Enabling this allows the ICA client to be configured to pass the user's credentials from the local desktop through to the MetaFrame server. Passthrough authentication works best when the local PC is a member of the same domain on which MetaFrame authentication is being performed and you wish to seamlessly allow access to published resources in the domain.

Table 20.4   Program Neighborhood General ICA Settings (continued)

Setting	Description
Use local credentials to log on	This option must be selected before the ICA client will pass the user information through to the MetaFrame server.

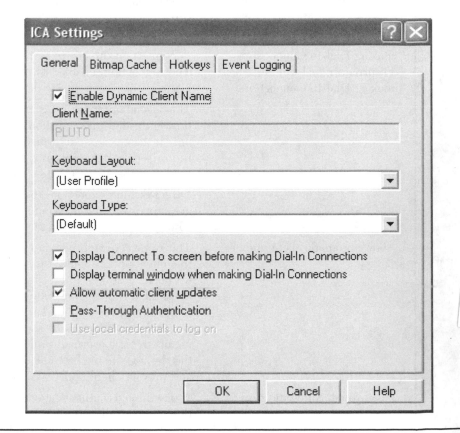

Figure 20.12   The General tab of the ICA Settings page in Win32 Program Neighborhood.

Bitmap Cache Tab

Most ICA clients provide the ability to modify the bitmap cache settings, including the size and location of the actual cache as well as the minimum bitmap size that will be cached (the default is 8K). On some clients the cache size is entered as a static value in kilobytes, while other clients display the value in megabytes and as a percentage of the total disk volume size where the cache is located. On a large volume, even 1 percent can be quite significant, so pay close attention to the bitmap cache configuration.

Hotkeys Tab

Because the standard key combinations such as Alt+Esc and Alt+Tab are in use on the local desktop, and the ICA client does not support capturing of these keys within the Citrix session, the ICA client lets you specify alternate key combinations to perform the same function from within a MetaFrame session (see Figure 20.13). A standard set of hotkey combinations should be developed that will not conflict with any of the applications the user may be running within MetaFrame. For example, many terminal emulation programs such as 3270 host emulators use keys such as Shift or Ctrl+F1 to represent traditional 3270 PA or PF key mappings. These key combinations (Shift+F1, Ctrl+F1) would be overridden by the corresponding Citrix client hotkeys unless the client keys were mapped differently.

Table 20.5 shows the key combinations that seem to introduce the least number of conflicts with other applications. I disable a number of hotkeys and utilize the ALT+ combination with all others; I've found that most users use key combinations such as Alt-Esc so rarely that few people even notice when it's not available. Of course, you need to provide a standard keyboard set that's suitable for your environment, and this should be finalized during the client planning phase prior to deploying any clients to the end user.

Table 20.5   Suggested ICA Hotkey Combinations

Keystroke Action	Suggested Hotkey Combination
Task List	[None]+[None]
Close Remote Application	[None]+[None]
Toggle Title Bar	Alt+F2
Ctrl-Alt-Del	Alt+F3
Ctrl-Esc	Alt+F1
Alt-Esc	[None]+[None]
Alt-Tab	Alt+Plus
Alt-BackTab	Alt+Minus
Ctrl-Shift-Esc	[None]+[None]
Toggle Latency Reduction	Alt+F5

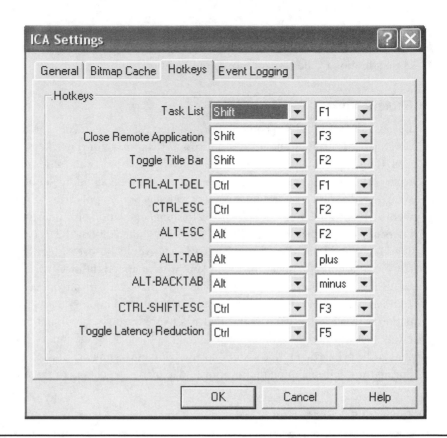

Figure 20.13   The Win32 Program Neighborhood Hotkeys tab.

Event Logging Tab

If you're encountering problems with a user accessing a MetaFrame server, you can configure event logging to record information about the user's session so you can review and debug it. When gathering data, select the option Append to Existing Event Log; otherwise, the log is overwritten every time the user logs on to a MetaFrame server. Normally you'll want to log only connections, disconnections, and errors. The other options, Data Transmitted, Data Received, and Keyboard and Mouse Data, would fill the logs very quickly. Never enable these other options unless actively debugging an issue, because they will have a large negative impact on the client's performance.

Custom ICA Connections

The Custom ICA Connection portion of Program Neighborhood is nearly identical to the functionality provided by the basic ICA clients supported by other non-Windows operating systems such as Linux and Macintosh. Within this portion of PN, you define connections to specific servers or published resources. When connecting to legacy applications published within a Windows NT domain scope and not a server farm, you must use a custom ICA connection to establish the connection. Before creating a connection to a server or published resource, you should review the default options automatically applied to all Custom ICA connections unless explicitly overridden within a connection's properties.

Default Custom ICA Connection Properties

Before I discuss the default options specific to custom ICA connections, you should know that the first setting you can adjust is what portion of Program Neighborhood opens automatically when the client is launched. When the PN client is launched for the very first time, it attempts to locate a server farm to which it can connect, prompting the user to provide their logon credentials. The resulting application set is then marked as being the default view, so the next time the user opens Program Neighborhood, they automatically are requested to provide credentials to log on to that farm. You can see what is currently set as the default view for PN by opening the Application Set Manager. The current view will have a small check mark in the right-hand corner of the icon. You can assign either custom ICA connections or an existing application set as the default by right-clicking the icon and selecting Set as Default, as shown in Figure 20.14.

Figure 20.14   You can change the default view by right-clicking and selecting Set as Default from the context menu.

You can also select no default view by deselecting the current default icon. When no default is selected the main Application Set Manager window opens, allowing you to choose what portion of Program Neighborhood you wish to use.

After selecting the desired default view, you are ready to proceed with configuring the default options for the custom ICA connections. These default options are accessed by right-clicking the Custom ICA Connections icon or from the File menu when the Custom ICA Connections folder has been opened. If you select the Custom Connection Settings option, the dialog box shown in Figure 20.15 opens.

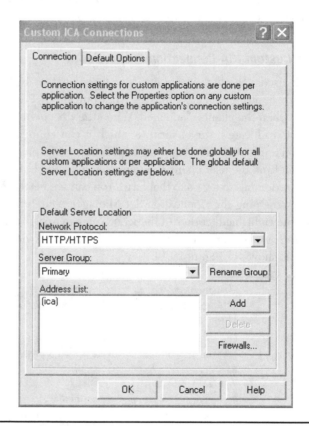

Figure 20.15 The Connection tab of the Custom ICA Connections dialog box.

Two tabs exist in this dialog box: the Connection tab and the Default Options tab. The Connection tab is where you configure any desired default server locations for the protocols your client will utilize. Server locations were discussed in the "ICA Client Server Location Configuration" section, earlier in this chapter. When a default server location has been defined, it applies to all custom ICA connections that are created and flagged to use the default setting.

I recommend that default server location information be defined only for network protocol types you will use in your implementation. If you are strictly using the Program Neighborhood application set component, there is no need to provide this information here. When using custom ICA connections, defining the proper server location defaults ensures that all created connections use the same server list and simplifies any upgrades or changes to the list if required.

The second tab in the Custom ICA Connections dialog box is the Default Options tab, shown in Figure 20.16. As the name implies, any options defined on this tab are the default options applied to all custom ICA connections, unless explicitly overridden. Table 20.6 summarizes the options available on this tab.

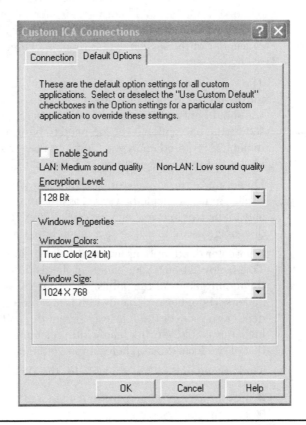

Figure 20.16 The Default Options tab of the Custom ICA Connections dialog box.

Table 20.6 Program Neighborhood Default Options for Custom ICA Connections

Setting	Description
Enable Sound	This enables client audio mapping support by default on custom connections. The default sound quality used depends on the type of connection being used. If the client connection has the LAN configuration, sound defaults to Medium quality. If the client connection is using either the WAN or dial-up networking option, sound quality is set to Low. This option can be overridden by explicitly setting the sound quality in the connection properties.
Encryption Level	MetaFrame employs the RSA RC5 encryption algorithm and supports 40-, 56-, or 128-bit keys. When using any encryption level other than basic, the authentication portion of the logon always uses 128-bit encryption, and the remainder of the session data is then encrypted using the desired cipher strength.
	The computational overhead of using strong encryption has a negligible impact on the MetaFrame server. Because of this there is little reason why you should not be using a strong encryption level, preferably 128-bit. When setting the encryption level you need to be sure it is not lower than the minimum required encryption level on the server, or you will be unable to log on and the message shown in Figure 20.17 will appear.
	Do not make the mistake of believing that Citrix's basic encryption level is secure. In fact it should be viewed as little more than plain text as far as being able to decrypt information, particularly user ID and password information. I discourage use of the basic encryption level even in test environments.
Window Colors Window Size	Four color-depth options are available: 16, 256, High Color (16-bit), and True Color (24-bit). Your choice in the default color depth will depend on the requirements of the published resources the users are accessing. In situations where network bandwidth is at a premium, reducing the color depth also reduces the ICA packet requirements. In implementations with higher available network bandwidth, selecting a color depth that matches that of the local desktop helps improve the user's computing experience.
	Three sizing options are available for the Window Size setting:
	■ Fixed Size (preset and custom) ■ Percentage of Screen Size ■ Full Screen
	Fixed Size lets you enter a custom value or select a preset size ranging from 640×480 all the way up to 1600×1200. If you select a window size greater than your current local desktop size, the Citrix session appears with horizontal and vertical screen bars you will need to use in order to view the entire screen.

Table 20.6   Program Neighborhood Default Options for Custom ICA Connections (continued)

Setting	Description
	Selecting the Percentage of Screen Size option (located near the bottom of the Window Size drop-down list) allows you to enter a percentage (50%, 75%, etc.); the ICA connection will display a window matching those dimensions.
	The Full Screen option, also located at the bottom of the Window Size drop-down list, sizes the ICA connection to completely fill the current screen size of the client, obscuring any local applications or files.

Once the default options for your custom ICA connections are defined, you are ready to continue configuring the individual connections to support your implementation scenario.

Figure 20.17   When the server enforces a higher encryption level than the client is attempting to use, an encryption level error message appears.

Creating a Custom ICA Connection

Double-clicking the Custom ICA Connections icon within the PN window opens a custom connection folder similar to the one shown in Figure 20.18. From here you create connections to servers and published resources that are specific to the client only. These connections have no relationship to application sets (described shortly).

A custom ICA connection is created as follows:

1. From within the Custom ICA Connections window, double-click the Add ICA Connection icon.
2. The first screen prompts you to select the type of network connection you want to create:

   - Local Area Network
   - Wide Area Network
   - Dial-Up Networking (PPP/RAS)
   - ICA Dial-In

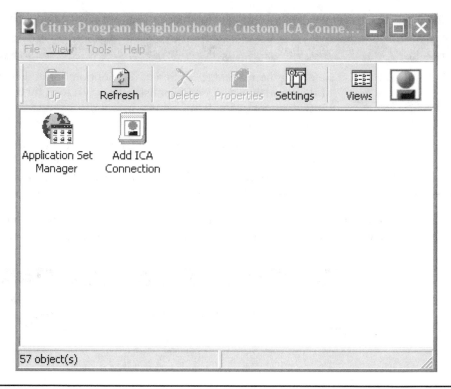

Figure 20.18 The main Custom ICA Connections window.

The PPP/RAS dial-up networking option initiates a Microsoft dial-up PPP or RAS connection prior to attempting to connect to the desired MetaFrame server. When selecting this option, you also are required to select an existing dial-up networking entry. If no dial-up networking entries exist, you must create one before proceeding. ICA dial-in establishes a direct dial-in connection to a MetaFrame server (running Windows 2000 only). When any of the three options other than Local Area Network is selected, the Bitmap Caching feature is automatically enabled. Caching allows for local storage of bitmap images and can speed up display of frequently used images over low-bandwidth connections.

Once you have selected the desired connection type, click Next to continue.

3. If you chose Local Area Network, Wide Area Network, or Dial-Up Networking, the next dialog box prompts you to provide information in the following fields (see Figure 20.19). If you chose ICA-Dial-In, skip ahead to Step 4; otherwise, provide the necessary information requested on this page:

■ **Provide a unique name for the connection**—This name cannot match an existing connection entry and or contain any of the following characters:

\ / ; : . * ? = < > | { } ( ) ' "

- **Select the network protocol to use (TCP/IP+HTTP, SSL/TLS+HTTPS, TCP/IP, IPX, SPX, NETBIOS)**—The appropriate protocol to use depends on how you configured your MetaFrame server environment. Details on MetaFrame server configuration were provided in Chapter 14. Depending on the protocol you chose, you may need to provide server location information if you have not already configured the proper default settings. Without server location information, you may be unable to access the desired server or published application. Use of the server location was discussed in the "Default Custom ICA Connec-tion Properties" section, earlier in this chapter.

- **Choose whether to connect directly to a server or to a published application**— When configuring a user's ICA connection, try to use published applications whenever possible instead of direct server connections. Using a published application eliminates the need to hard-code a specific server name on the client, making any changes to the server hosting the application transparent to the client and eliminating the need to revisit the client to modify this server reference at a later date. If the desired published application or server name does not appear in the drop-down list, you need to specify a server location. Refer to the section "Default Custom ICA Connection Properties," earlier in this chapter, for more information on configuring the server location.

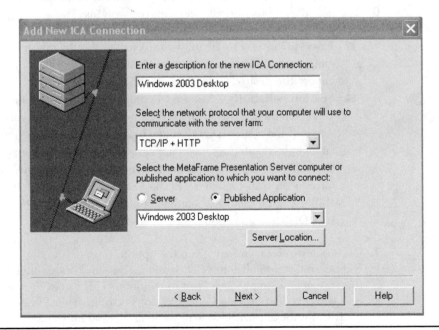

Figure 20.19 Providing custom ICA connection protocol and server/application information.

If you are connecting directly to a server, you can select the server from the drop-down list and then manually type in the name of the server or type in an IP address. If a name is entered, the server must be able to resolve it to an IP address; otherwise, the connection will fail.

After providing the necessary information, click Next to continue.

4. If you are configuring an ICA dial-in connection, the next screen asks you to provide a name for this connection along with choosing the device that will be used to dial into the remote MetaFrame server. Typically this device is a modem physically connected to the client device. Once this information is entered, the next dialog box prompts you to provide the phone number that will be used to establish the direct connection. Clicking Next takes you directly to Step 6.

5. If you are connecting to a published application, then the next dialog box prompts you to specify whether the application will run in a seamless window or in a remote desktop window. If you chose instead to connect directly to a specific MetaFrame server or you selected the ICA Dial-In option, this window does not appear. Direct server connections, including dial-in, support viewing only in a remote desktop window.

If your published application connection will be a full desktop scenario, you should select "View in a remote desktop window." If you are accessing an individual application, "View in a separate window (Seamless Window)" is likely the desired choice. For more information on seamless windows, see Chapter 2. Click Next once you have selected the desired window mode.

6. The next dialog box presents you with two options:

- **Encryption level**—If you wish to change the default option, which is set globally for all custom ICA connections, deselect Use Default and then choose the desired level from the drop-down list box.

- **Session reliability**—Choose whether this feature is enabled or disabled. When enabled, a user's application or desktop session remains visible on the screen if the connection is lost due to a network issue. The cursor is changed to an hourglass, and the session appears "busy" until the connection is reestablished. See Chapter 5 for more information on this feature, which was first introduced with version 8.0 of the Program Neighborhood client. Session reliability is not available when dialing directly into a MetaFrame server using the ICA Dial-In connection option.

7. On the next screen you are given the option to predefine the user credentials that will be used to establish the ICA session. You may choose none of the options on this screen and simply click Next to continue. This forces the user to provide the necessary credentials every time they log on to the MetaFrame server.

If you want to provide at least some credential information, by default you are allowed to provide the user ID and authenticating domain. Selecting the Save Password check box lets you also provide a password that will be stored with the connection. If you select the option "Use local User name and Password," the other options on this screen are disabled.

The "Use local User name and Password" option is grayed-out if any of the following has happened:

- You did not choose to allow passthrough authentication when installing the PN client.
- You have not enabled passthrough authentication in the global ICA settings for PN.
- You have not chosen to enable "Use local credentials to log on" in the global ICA settings for PN.

Once the desired authentication information has been provided, click Next.

8. Figure 20.20 shows the next screen in the Connection Setup wizard. If you chose the Seamless Window option earlier in the setup, only the Color Depth option is available. Otherwise, you can modify both the default window color depth and size if desired. Defaults for these options were discussed in the earlier section "Default Custom ICA Connection Properties."

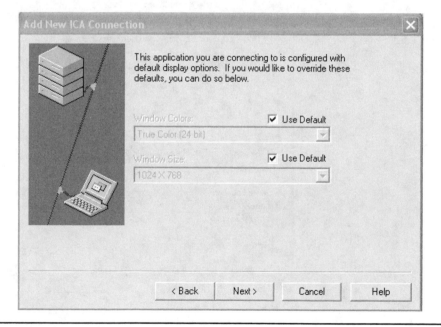

Figure 20.20 The window configuration choices when creating a new custom ICA connection.

9. If you are connecting directly to a MetaFrame server, the next dialog box prompts you to provide an application executable name and working directory. This information is used to automatically load the particular application when the user logs on. Alternatively these fields can be left blank, and a full desktop session on the target server is created. When you connect to a published application, this dialog box does not appear.

10. The final dialog box simply states that the new custom ICA connection was successfully set up. Clicking Finish creates the new connection within the Program Neighborhood.

Once the custom ICA connection is created, you should review the connection-specific properties to ensure it is properly configured for your desired implementation scenario.

Custom ICA Connection Properties

The properties for a custom ICA connection are retrieved by highlighting the desired icon, right-clicking or selecting the File menu, and then choosing Properties. When the Custom ICA Connection Properties window opens, the first tab that appears is the Connection tab (Figure 20.21).

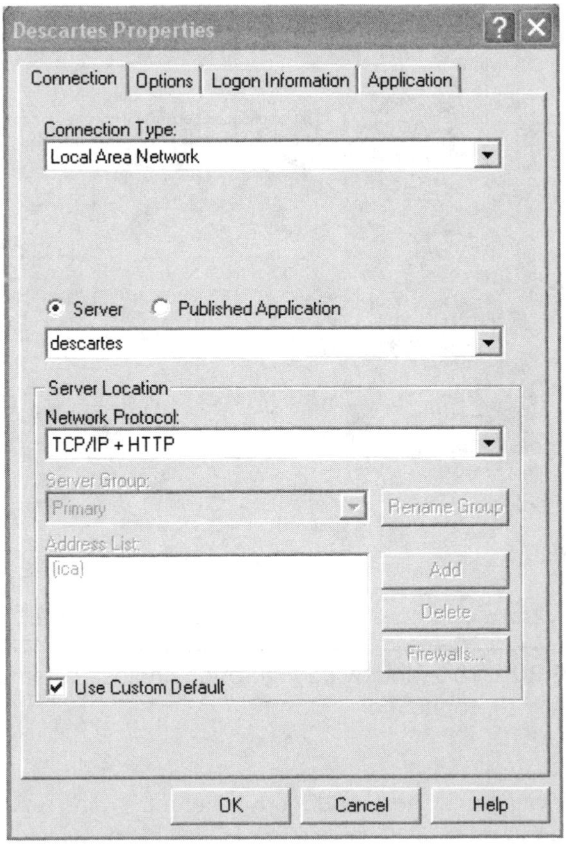

Figure 20.21   The Connection tab on the property page for a custom ICA connection.

All the options summarized on this tab are the same options you selected when configuring the new custom ICA connection. When the Use Custom Default option is enabled, the corresponding property uses the default you configured earlier when setting up the default custom ICA connection settings.

The next tab on the custom ICA connection property page is the Options tab (Figure 20.22). Table 20.7 summarizes the settings available on this tab.

Table 20.7 Custom ICA Connection Options

Setting	Description
Use data compression	Enables compression of ICA data before transmission between the client and the server. Compression reduces the size of the ICA data being transferred back and forth, is enabled by default for all connection types, and introduces only minimal processing overhead on the client and the server.
Use disk cache for bitmaps	Caches bitmaps and other graphic images locally to reduce duplication of traffic being transmitted between the client and the server. The actual disk cache settings are configured in the ICA settings portion of the PN client. This was discussed in the "Client-Wide Program Neighborhood Settings" section earlier in this chapter.
Queue mouse movements and keystrokes	Typically enabled only over low-bandwidth connections, this option reduces the frequency with which mouse and keyboard data are sent to the MetaFrame server. Instead multiple mouse movements and keystrokes are queued before being sent all at once.
Enable session reliability	Maintains the current state of the screen and the visible information in the event that network connectivity is momentarily lost. The mouse cursor is changed to an hourglass to signal a busy state until the connection is re-established.
Enable Sound	Enables client audio mapping support for this ICA connection. The default sound quality used is Medium, which is suitable in most situations. If sound is not required, it should be disabled to reduce bandwidth requirements.
Encryption Level	I recommend that you use the highest encryption level (128-bit) whenever possible to maximize security of the ICA session.
	When you select your own encryption level, it must be equal to or greater than the minimum level supported on the MetaFrame server; otherwise, the user cannot log on to the server or establish a connection to the published application.
SpeedScreen Latency	Lets you configure use of latency reduction features, which provide

Table 20.7 Custom ICA Connection Options (continued)

Setting	Description
Reduction	faster response to keyboard and mouse input over slow network connections. Unless you are accessing the custom ICA connection over a slow link, this option should not be modified. This setting is ignored if you are connecting to a MetaFrame server that does not support this feature. See Chapter 5 for details on SpeedScreen latency reduction features.
Window Colors Window Size	Four color-depth options are available: 16, 256, High Color (16-bit), and True Color (24-bit). Typically the server default should be used unless there is a reason to reduce the default color depth, such as in the situation where network bandwidth is at a premium. When accessing a published application, you can select the Seamless Window option, which is not available when connecting directly to a server. Seamless window support is discussed in Chapter 5.

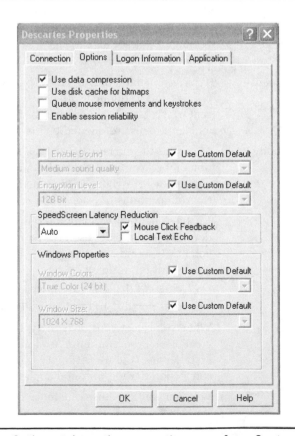

Figure 20.22 The Options tab on the properties page for a Custom ICA connection.

The next custom ICA connection properties tab is Logon Information (Figure 20.23), which is configured to use the logon credentials you specified when the connection was created. Table 20.8 lists the available options.

Table 20.8   Custom ICA Connection Logon Information Options

Setting	Description
Local user	Requests that the user authenticate when connecting to the target server or published application. When passthrough authentication is enabled, the local credentials are automatically used. Passthrough authentication is available only if the option was selected when the client was installed and if it is enabled under the general ICA settings for the client.
Smart card	Allows use of a smart card and corresponding PIN number to authenticate with. Passthrough authentication works exactly the same as it does when enabled under the Local User option.
User-specified credentials	You can specify a particular user name password and domain to use for authentication when accessing this custom ICA connection. If caching of password information has been disabled, the Save Password option is disabled.

The final properties tab for a custom ICA connection is the Application tab. If you provided an application executable and working directory when creating the custom ICA connection, the information is displayed here. While a specific application can be initiated automatically using this configuration, using a published application is the preferred method of access. You can also change the displayed icon for this particular custom ICA connection if desired.

Once the desired application set properties have been configured, the custom ICA connection is ready for use.

Application Sets

Unlike custom ICA connections, there are no default properties that apply to all application sets; instead, certain properties are defined when the application set itself is created while others must be configured once the application set exists. In this section I begin by explaining how a new application set is created and then follow up with a review of the properties that can be modified once the set exists.

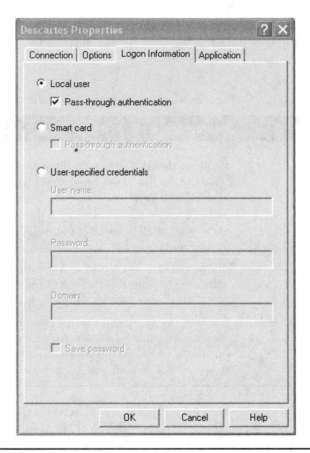

Figure 20.23   The Logon Information tab on the properties page for a Custom ICA connection.

Create a New Application Set

Application sets are created in one of two ways. The first way is performed automatically when you launch Program Neighborhood for the first time. As PN loads it attempts to locate an available server farm using the supported network protocols. If a server farm is located, a logon dialog box is displayed for the farm, prompting you to provide a user ID, password, and domain to use for authentication. Figure 20.24 shows an example of this the first time I load PN and it detects my NOISYRIVER farm.

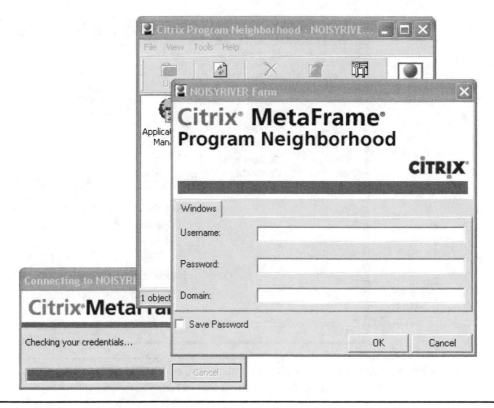

Figure 20.24   The first time PN loads, it automatically tries to detect an available server farm.

If you enter valid credentials, all available resources published in this farm are added to your PN desktop. If you decide to cancel entering your credentials, you are presented with an empty window showing only the Application Set Manager icon, which returns you to the main PN window. The next time you launch PN, you are once again presented with the logon dialog box for the farm.

As mentioned, you can define whether an application set initiates by default when the Program Neighborhood is opened simply by right-clicking the desired application set located in the Application Set Manager and selecting Set as Default, as shown in Figure 20.25. If you prefer having no application set launch by default but instead having PN open showing all available application sets and the Custom ICA Connections icon, deselect Set as Default on the current default application set.

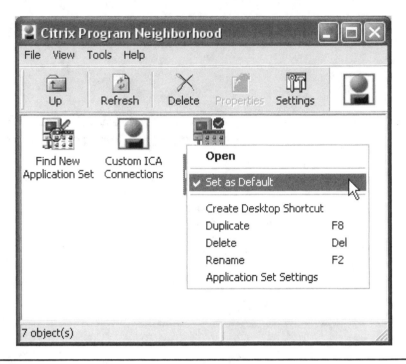

Figure 20.25   The default application set can be designated by right-clicking the set and selecting Set as Default.

You can also manually add application sets to Program Neighborhood as follows:

1. Open Program Neighborhood, and if necessary, click the Up toolbar icon until you see the Find New Application Set icon in the PN window. Double-click this icon to begin the process of adding a new application set.
2. The first screen prompts you to select the method of connecting to the application set. The only options you have are Local Area Network, Wide Area Network, and Dial-Up Networking (PPP/RAS). Logically, the direct Citrix Dial-In option that you have with custom ICA connections is not available for application sets, because this connection method establishes an ICA connection directly to a single target MetaFrame server; it would not allow you access to any other MetaFrame server in the farm.
3. After selecting the network configuration to use, you're prompted to enter a description for the application set and select an existing set from the drop-down list (see Figure 20.26). If no description is entered, the default matches the name of the selected application set.

Depending on where your MetaFrame servers are located in relation to your client device and what network protocol you are using, you may need to configure the server location information for this application set. Application sets *don't* use the default settings for custom ICA connections and also *don't* share server location information with any other existing application sets. Each server location list must be configured separately for each application set you create. See the section "ICA Client Server Location Configuration," earlier in this chapter, for more information on properly configuring the server location.

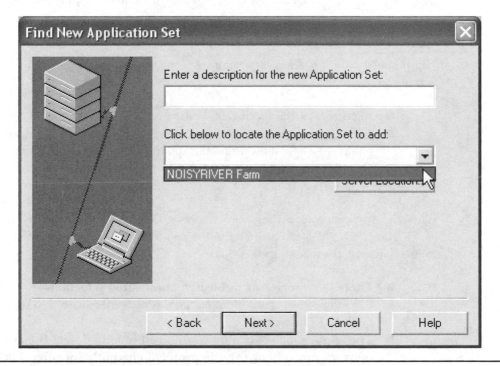

Figure 20.26 The desired application set should appear in the drop-down list.

4. On the next screen you are prompted to configure the following three options:

- **Enable sound for this Application Set**—If sound has been enabled on the host MetaFrame server, this option has been enabled, and the client device has a Sound Blaster 16–compatible sound card, then the published applications in this application set play sounds on the client device.
- **Window Colors**—You can choose an alternate color depth or use the default value provided by the MetaFrame server. I normally recommend leaving the check box Use Server Default selected.
- **Window Size**—You can also choose to override the server default and select a preferred window size. Again I suggest using the server default.

Once the desired settings are configured, click Next to complete configuration of the application set.

5. The final dialog box simply acknowledges that the new application set was created successfully. Click Finish, and the new set will now appear in Program Neighborhood.

Once the application set has been created, it is a good idea to go in, review the currently assigned properties, and make any changes you feel are necessary for your deployment.

Application Set Properties

The properties for a specific application set can be retrieved by choosing Application Set Settings in one of three ways:

- Right-clicking the specific application set's icon
- Right-clicking anywhere on the white space in the window showing the published applications within the application set
- Choosing the option from the File menu when the screen containing the published applications for the set is visible

When the Application Set Settings window opens, the first tab that appears is the Connection tab (Figure 20.27). This tab is similar to the one found in the properties for a custom ICA connection, with the following exceptions:

- **There is no server or published application selection**—Because these settings apply to an application set, there is obviously no need to specify a server or published application.
- **The application set can be configured to auto-detect the appropriate network protocol or use the protocol currently specified in the Server Location group box**—By default an application set attempts to auto-detect the correct network protocol to use. All protocols supported by the client are tested until an application set is successfully located. The TCP/IP+HTTP protocol attempts to contact the server farm by querying the "ica.<domain name>" server alias while the other protocols (TCP/IP, IPX, SPX, NETBIOS) all attempt a UDP broadcast looking for a server response. When a successful auto-detection has occurred, the detected protocol is the one displayed by default in the Network Protocol drop-down list box when you first open the Connection tab.

    You can specify the desired server location protocol by choosing the "Always use Server Location network protocol" option and then selecting the appropriate protocol from the drop-down list box. For more information on server location, refer to the earlier section "ICA Client Server Location Configuration."

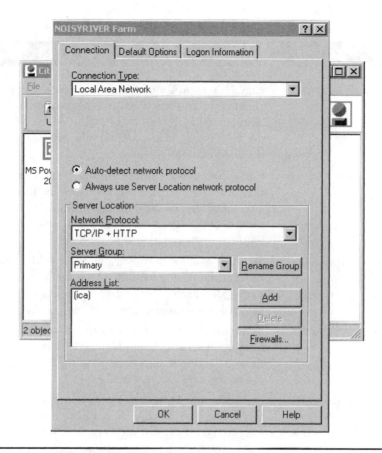

Figure 20.27 The Connection properties tab for a PN application set.

The next tab in the application set settings is the Default Options tab (Figure 20.28). The available settings on this tab are identical to the options available for a custom ICA connection, with the exception of the "Turn off desktop integration for this application set" option, which is not a custom ICA connection option. Table 20.9 summarizes the settings available on this tab. The options discussed earlier with custom ICA connections are repeated here for convenience.

Table 20.9   Program Neighborhood Application Set Default Options

Setting	Description
Use data compression	Enables compression of ICA data before transmission between the client and the server. Compression reduces the size of the ICA data being transferred back and forth, is enabled by default for all connection types, and introduces only minimal processing overhead on the client and the server.
Use disk cache for bitmaps	Caches bitmaps and other graphic images locally to reduce duplication of traffic being transmitted between the client and the server. The actual disk cache settings are configured in the ICA Settings portion of the PN client. This was discussed in the "Client-Wide Settings" section earlier in this chapter.
Queue mouse movements and keystrokes	Typically enabled only over low-bandwidth connections, this option reduces the frequency with which mouse and keyboard data are sent to the MetaFrame server. Instead, multiple mouse movements and keystrokes are queued before being sent all at once.
Enable session reliability	Maintains the current state of the screen and the visible information in the event that network connectivity is momentarily lost. The mouse cursor is changed to an hourglass to signal a busy state until the connection is re-established.
Turn off desktop integration for this application set	Available only when configuring an application set, when enabled this option prevents PN from adding application shortcuts automatically to the user's Start menu or desktop.
Enable Sound	Enables client audio mapping support for this application set. The default sound quality used is Medium, which is suitable in most situations. I recommend using the default option of Use Server Default. This ensures that the published applications in the set are executed using the settings desired by the administrator when the published application was created.
Encryption Level	While you can modify the default encryption level used, in most situations it is recommended that you enable Use Server Default. This ensures the application is executed using the encryption level required by the MetaFrame administrator.
	When you select your own encryption level, it must be equal to or greater than the minimum level supported on the MetaFrame server; otherwise, the user cannot connect to any published applications.

Table 20.9   Program Neighborhood Application Set Default Options (continued)

Setting	Description
SpeedScreen Latency Reduction	Lets you configure use of latency reduction features, which provide faster response to keyboard and mouse input over slow network connections. Unless you are accessing the application set over a slow link, this option should not be modified. This setting is ignored if you are connecting to a Meta-Frame server that does not support this feature.
	See Chapter 5 for details on SpeedScreen latency reduction features.
Window Colors Window Size	Four color-depth options are available: 16, 256, High Color (16-bit), and True Color (24-bit). Typically the server default should be used unless there is a reason to reduce the default color depth, such as in the situation where network bandwidth is at a premium.
	Usually, the preferred window size when using application sets is Seamless Window, which integrates the application with the local desktop environment. Seamless window support is discussed in Chapter 5.

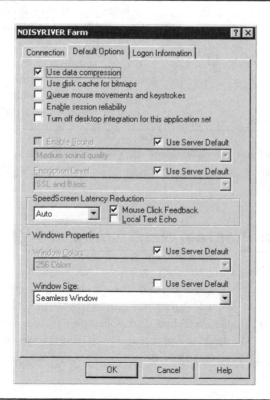

Figure 20.28   The Default Options tab for a PN application set.

The final PN application set property tab is Logon Information, which defaults to using user-specified credentials. This tab is identical to the Logon Information tab found in the properties for a custom ICA connection. The options described earlier are listed again in Table 20.10 for convenience.

Table 20.10 Program Neighborhood Logon Information Options

Setting	Description
Local user	Requests that the user authenticate when connecting to the application set. When passthrough authentication is enabled, the local credentials are automatically used. Passthrough authentication is available only if the option was selected when the client was installed and if it has been enabled under the general ICA settings for the client.
Smart card	Allows use of a smart card and corresponding PIN number to authenticate with. Passthrough authentication works exactly the same as when enabled under the Local User option.
User-specified credentials	You can specify a particular user name password and domain to use for authentication when accessing this application set. If caching of password information has been disabled, the Save Password option is disabled.

Once the desired application set properties are configured, the Program Neighborhood client is ready for use.

Configuring the Program Neighborhood Agent

After installation, when the user logs on to their local PC, the Program Neighborhood Agent (PN Agent) automatically starts and attempts to establish the connection with the target Web Interface server. The PN Agent application is automatically added to the All Users Startup folder during installation. When the application has successfully started, an icon appears on the system tray in the lower right-hand corner of the screen. If there is an issue connecting to the target Web Interface, an error message appears similar to the one shown in Figure 20.29.

NOTE: Linux Program Neighborhood Agent configuration is discussed in the "Configuring the Citrix ICA Client for Linux" section, later in this chapter.

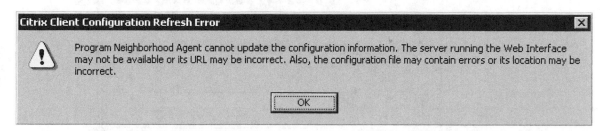

Figure 20.29   If the host Web Interface cannot be contacted, a message such as this appears.

To correct the problem you need to choose an alternate Web Interface server. This can be done by right-clicking the icon on the system tray and selecting Yes when prompted to provide an alternate URL. Remember to prefix the address with HTTP:// or HTTPS:// and use a fully qualified domain name.

When a connection is successfully established, the user is prompted for credentials unless passthrough authentication has been enabled. If a logon dialog box appears, it will look like the one shown in Figure 20.30. I prefer to implement passthrough authentication with the PN Agent whenever possible. This provides the most seamless integration of the PN Agent with the user's local desktop.

Once valid credentials are provided, the necessary shortcuts to the user's authorized applications are automatically added to the user's Start menu. Behavior of the PN Agent and the location of the application shortcuts can be configured through the PN Agent itself or centrally on the host Web Interface server using the Web-based Program Neighborhood Agent Console.

The ability of the user to locally modify the PN Agent's behavior is dictated by the settings in the PN Agent Console. Support issues can be minimized by limiting what settings are configurable directly from the PN Agent Console. Before looking briefly at the PN Agent Console, I begin by discussing the options available for configuration directly in the Program Neighborhood Agent.

Figure 20.30 The main Program Neighborhood Agent logon screen.

Local Program Neighborhood Agent Settings

The only access to the PN Agent user interface is through the PN Agent icon located on the system tray. Right-clicking this icon gives you access to a number of options (Figure 20.31):

- **Applications**—Provides a shortcut to the applications available based on the user credentials provided when logging on to the PN Agent.
- **Application Refresh**—Forces an immediate refresh of the available applications for the user.
- **Properties**—Opens the settings for the PN Agent.
- **Log off**—Logs the user off the farm if currently logged on.
- **Disconnect**—Immediately disconnects the user from all active published applications. Does not log the user off any server.
- **Reconnect**—Reconnects to all available disconnected applications for the user in the farm.
- **About**—Displays information about the PN Agent client.
- **Close**—Terminates the PN Agent client and removes it from the system tray.

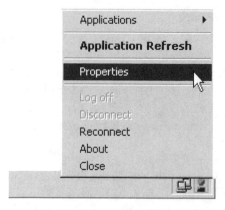

Figure 20.31   The PN Agent settings can be accessed through the icon located on the system tray.

The main properties dialog box for the Program Neighborhood Agent has five main tabs (Figure 20.32). Exactly what tabs are available and what options can be defined are based on the settings defined in the Web-based PN Agent Console. Through the PN Agent Console, some or all the option tabs shown in Figure 20.32 may not be available.

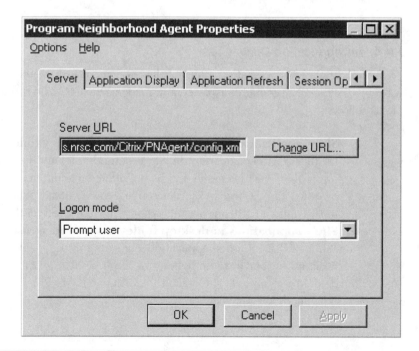

Figure 20.32   The local PN Agent properties have four main tabs that can be configured.

PN Agent Server Tab

The Server tab lets you modify the target Web Interface URL and the actual configuration file read by the PN Agent. The default XML file is called CONFIG.XML and is located in the default PN Agent folder on the Web Interface Web server. The URL can be changed by selecting the Change URL button and then providing the desired HTTP or HTTPS target URL.

The other option on this tab is Logon Mode, which has four possible options available in the drop-down list:

- **Prompt user**—This is the default and provides the user with the PN Agent logon window discussed earlier.
- **Single sign-on authentication**—The user's local desktop credentials are also used to authenticate with the Citrix server farm. Before this option takes effect, the PN Agent Console must also be configured to support this setting.
- **Smart card logon**—Allows use of smart cards for authentication. The MetaFrame environment must already be configured to support use of smart cards before enabling this option.
- **Smart card with single sign-on authentication**—Enables use of smart cards and also configures the PN Agent to use cached authentication information to log on to the server farm.

PN Agent Application Display Tab

The Application Display configuration tab lets you manage how the application shortcuts retrieved by the PN Agent are displayed and made accessible. The three options on this tab are as follows:

- **Show applications in Start menu**—Allows the application shortcuts retrieved for the user to be added to the Start menu. By default they appear directly under the Programs menu, but by providing an additional submenu in the field provided, the application shortcuts appear there instead. When changes are made to this option, the icons are moved or removed based on the desired settings.
- **Show applications in desktop folder**—By providing a subfolder name, you can have the published application icons directly accessible on the user's local desktop. As soon as these options are applied the target folder is created or deleted as required. The default folder name is My Program Neighborhood Applications.

- **Display applications in System Tray**—This option controls whether or not the Applications menu option for the PN Agent client displays the retrieved application shortcuts. When enabled the Applications menu still exists, but all subfolder icons are removed.

PN Agent Application Refresh Tab

The Application Refresh tab is where you can configure when and how often the PN Agent retrieves available published resource information from the Citrix server farm. The three available check boxes allow you to configure the following:

- Whether or not the application list is refreshed when the PN Agent starts
- If the list is refreshed whenever a published application is launched
- How often the list is refreshed based on a timed interval

By default this tab is hidden and is accessible to the end user only if the administrator modifies the PN Agent Console to re-enable this property tab feature.

Session Options

The fourth tab lets you control the display settings (window size and color depth) as well as the default audio settings. By default they are all configured with the Default option. Unless absolutely necessary you will likely not need to make any changes on this screen.

Reconnect Options

The Reconnect Options tab (Figure 20.33) controls how the PN Agent will handle the new Workspace Control feature available with the Web Interface for MetaFrame Presentation Server 3.0. If you are currently running an older version of the Web Interface, these options should be disabled; otherwise, the reconnect feature generates an error message when you attempt to reconnect. There are two main options on this screen:

- **Enable automatic reconnection at logon**—When this option is enabled, the user's sessions are automatically connected when the user logs on to the PN Agent. When this option is disabled, these connections can be reconnected only through the Reconnect PN Agent menu option.
- **Enable automatic reconnection from Reconnect menu**—When this option is enabled, the Reconnect menu choice found on the PN Agent icon allows you to manually reconnect to disconnected and/or active sessions. When disabled, this menu option is grayed out and not available.

For both options you have the choice of connecting to both existing active and disconnected sessions or only to disconnected sessions. When reconnecting to both active and disconnected sessions, the PN Agent communicates with the Web Interface 3.0 and requests that all active sessions initiated from this client be reconnected and that all existing disconnected sessions (initiated from this client or any other client) also be reconnected. There are situations where a user's session on the server is marked as active even though there is no active link between the session and a client device. This option allows for recovery of these sessions.

When only the reconnect to disconnected sessions is available, active sessions in the farm are ignored and all disconnected sessions (regardless of where they originally started) are reconnected.

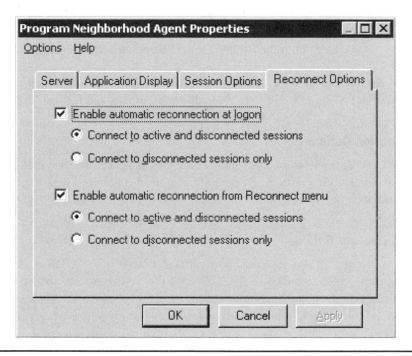

Figure 20.33   The local PN Agent properties have four main tabs that can be configured.

Program Neighborhood Agent Console Configuration

The Program Neighborhood Agent Console is a Web-based interface used to centrally configure the PN Agent. In this chapter I look at how this tool is used to configure the PN Agent. Details on the installation and configuration of the Web Interface and PN Agent Console were covered in Chapter 14.

The PN Agent Console is accessed on the Web Interface server using the following URL http://<server name>/Citrix/PNAgentAdmin/ where <server name> is the name of the Web server hosting the MetaFrame Web Interface component. When the Web page opens, it defaults to the configuration file management page shown in Figure 20.34. An XML configuration file is used to store the options that are set using the Program Neighborhood Agent Console. This file is then read by the PN Agent to determine what local options are available. Changes to the default file, config.xml, affect all PN Agent users unless alternate configuration files have been created and the PN Agent client has been updated to point to an alternate file.

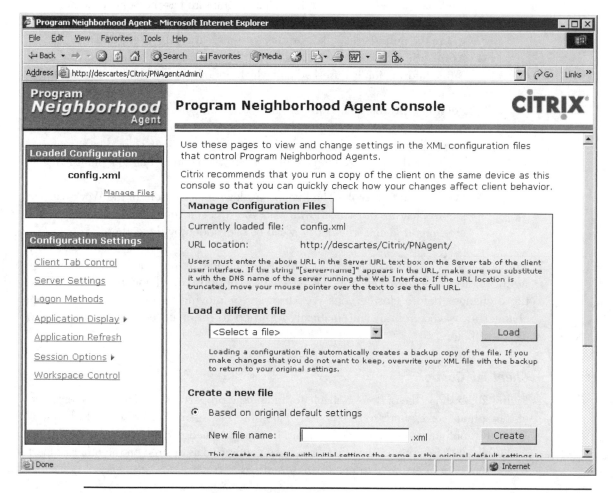

Figure 20.34   The XML configuration file stores the options that control the behavior of the PN Agent Console.

Once the PN Agent Console has loaded, you see seven menu options listed down the left-hand side. These settings control the behavior of the PN Agent:

- **Client Tab Control**—Options here let you control what property tabs are available for the PN Agent client under the Properties menu option.
- **Server Settings**—This page is where you configure how the PN Agent interacts with the target Web Interface server and how much control the user has over where the PN Agent can be directed to retrieve application information.
- **Logon Methods**—From here you define what authentication methods are available to the PN Agent and which are configured as the default method.
- **Application Display**—This page contains four submenus used to control where the published application shortcuts appear on the user's desktop.
- **Application Refresh**—This page controls how often the user's published application information is refreshed and which options, if any, can be customized by the user.
- **Session Options**—This page is where you configure some basic options pertaining to the ICA sessions established with one or more MetaFrame servers. Four submenus exist that let you dictate the window size, color depth, sound quality, and what ICA template file is used when connecting to a published resource.
- **Workspace Control**—The final page allows management of the Workspace Control feature introduced with MPS 3.0. You control what reconnect options are supported and whether they can be overridden by the end user.

When making changes to these properties, you can quickly test them by starting a PN Agent session on a client desktop and viewing the options you changed. Be sure to save these changes before closing your Web browser or moving to a different page. When changes are saved, you are automatically returned to the main configuration file management page.

Client Tab Control

Figure 20.35 shows the options available for hiding the property tabs on the PN Agent. Each of the options corresponds to the property tab in the PN Agent that I discussed when looking at the configurable options on the client. In most production deployments, you will want to disable all these options once they have been configured as desired on the other property pages. Rarely do users need to modify these settings.

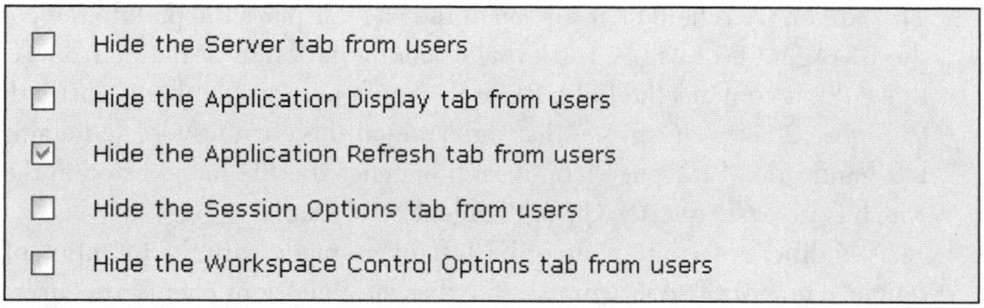

☐ Hide the Server tab from users

☐ Hide the Application Display tab from users

☑ Hide the Application Refresh tab from users

☐ Hide the Session Options tab from users

☐ Hide the Workspace Control Options tab from users

Figure 20.35   Client tab control for the PN Agent Console.

Server Settings

The Server Settings page is where you can manage the properties related to the redirection, modification, and refresh interval of the PN Agent configuration file as well as enable secure connectivity between the PN Agent client and the Web Interface server. Figure 20.36 shows the settings available on the Server Settings Web page.

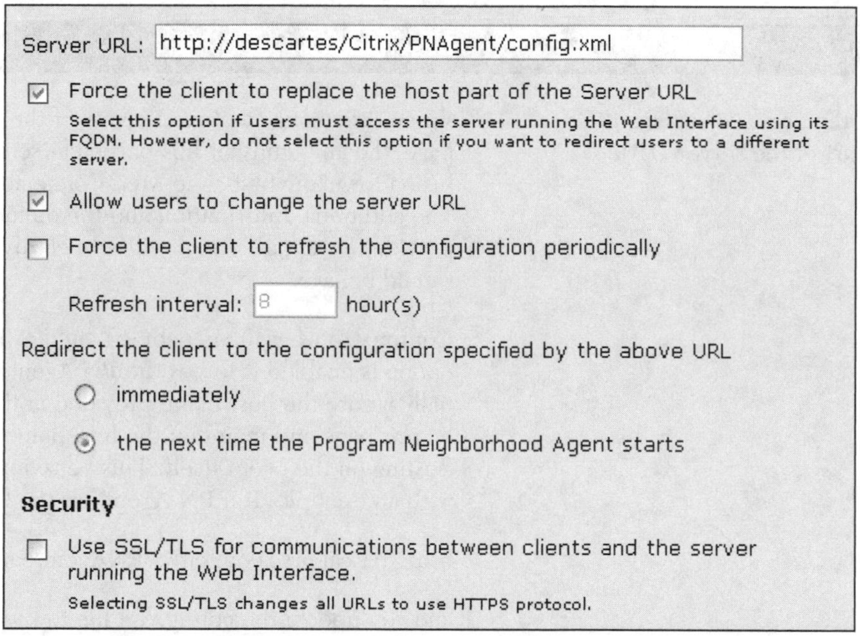

Server URL: http://descartes/Citrix/PNAgent/config.xml

☑ Force the client to replace the host part of the Server URL

Select this option if users must access the server running the Web Interface using its FQDN. However, do not select this option if you want to redirect users to a different server.

☑ Allow users to change the server URL

☐ Force the client to refresh the configuration periodically

Refresh interval: 8   hour(s)

Redirect the client to the configuration specified by the above URL

   ◯ immediately

   ◉ the next time the Program Neighborhood Agent starts

Security

☐ Use SSL/TLS for communications between clients and the server running the Web Interface.

Selecting SSL/TLS changes all URLs to use HTTPS protocol.

Figure 20.36   The Server Settings properties page for the PN Agent Console.

The Server URL field near the top of the page displays the path to the configuration file that the PN Agent is or will be retrieving its configuration information from. Unless you modified this field, it contains the full URL to the configuration file that is currently loaded. Referring to Figure 20.36 you can see that the name of the currently loaded configuration file on the left-hand side of the page (config.xml) matches the file name listed in the Server URL path, which is http://Descartes/Citrix/PNAgent/config.xml

Modifications to the Server URL field are made with the intention of changing the location or name of the configuration file that the PN Agent clients are currently pointed to. For example, if you had a new configuration file in the same location as the original called config2.xml, and you wanted all the PN Agent clients currently using the config.xml file to use this file instead, you would begin by updating the Server URL field to point to this new location as follows: http://Descartes/Citrix/PNAgent/config2.xml

Based on how the other settings on this page were configured, the PN Agent client at some point would replace its existing Server URL entry with the new setting you specified. The remaining settings on this page are summarized in Table 20.11.

Table 20.11   PN Agent Console Server Settings

Setting	Description
Force the client to replace the host part of the server URL.	When discussing the functionality of the Server Settings page, the ambiguity of this particular setting causes confusion for many first-time MetaFrame administrators. The additional information and the online documentation provide few details and do little to clarify how this feature should behave.
	Contrary to what many people would expect, when this option is enabled it forces the PN Agent client to essentially ignore the host name provided in the server URL on *this* page and maintain the host name setting currently existing on the client itself. This behavior can be clarified with an example. If a PN Agent has the local URL set to
	http://pascal.nrsc.com/citrix/PNAgent/config.xml
	and you update the config.xml file to specify that the client should be redirected to a new file with the following URL:
	http://descartes/citrix/PNAgent/config2.xml

Table 20.11   PN Agent Console Server Settings (continued)

Setting	Description
	then, if the "Force the client to replace the host part of the server URL" setting is enabled, the PN Agent client attempts to maintain its current host setting (ignoring the one specified in the configuration file) yet update its local reference to point to this configuration file:
	http//pascal.nrsc.com/citrix/PNAgent/config2.xml
	One of two things happens in this situation. Either the client starts up with an error stating the configuration could not be loaded, or it ends up pointing to the wrong configuration file and not the one on the intended target server.
	This option should be enabled only if you are updating the reference to a different file on the same host server. If the server hosting the configuration file has also changed, be sure to disable this option prior to saving the updated URL information.
Allow users to change the server URL.	When this option is enabled, a user can change the server URL through the local PN Agent graphical interface. If this option is disabled, the user can still view the current server URL (unless access to the Server tab has been disabled) but cannot modify it.
	In production, I recommend that users not be able to modify this setting.
Force the client to refresh the configuration periodically.	This option lets you configure the PN Agent to retrieve updated client information at regular intervals that you define. When enabled the default is to re-read configuration information every eight hours. The smallest accepted value is one hour, and only integer values (1, 2, 3, etc.) are valid. Any fractional values such as 1.5 generate an error message and are not saved.
	Once the desired options are properly configured and the deployment is in production, you usually do not need to force a periodic refresh of the configuration file. In newer implementations, where changes may occur more frequently, it may be necessary to enable this option to ensure that users are picking up the changes you made.

Table 20.11   PN Agent Console Server Settings (continued)

Setting	Description
Redirect the client to the configuration specified by the above URL.	This setting provides two possible options to choose from: ■ Immediately: The next time the client attempts to refresh configuration information, it immediately is redirected to the specified alternate server URL. ■ The next time the Program Neighborhood Agent starts: Choosing this option defers the update to the client's PN Agent configuration until it is restarted, either manually or after the client PC is rebooted.
Security: Use SSL/TLS for communications between the clients and the server running the Web Interface.	This option controls whether or not communications between the PN Agent and the Web Interface are secured using SSL/TLS. When you enable this option, you immediately notice that the HTTP reference in the server URL changes to HTTPS.

Logon Methods

Figure 20.37 shows the Logon Methods page, where you configure what logon methods are available to the PN Agent and what method appears as the default option in the logon mode presented in the PN Agent client interface. Define only the logon methods that your environment will actually support. All other methods should be disabled.

PN Agent supports five logon modes:

- **Anonymous logon**—Allows user logons through the PN Agent without requiring explicit user credentials. While the PN Agent can be used with anonymous logons to implement a kiosk-type workstation, if this type of login is desired, I instead recommend using the Web client and the Web Interface.
- **Smart card logon**—Select this option if users will authenticate using a smart card authentication system. To support this feature the underlying client operating system must be configured to use a Windows-compatible smart card reading device. With this authentication method, the PN Agent prompts the user for his or her personal smart card access PIN (personal identification number) each time a resource is requested from the Citrix farm. More information on use of the smart card in a Terminal Server/MetaFrame environment is provided in Chapter 1, "Microsoft Windows Terminal Services," and Chapter 2, "Citrix MetaFrame Presentation Server."

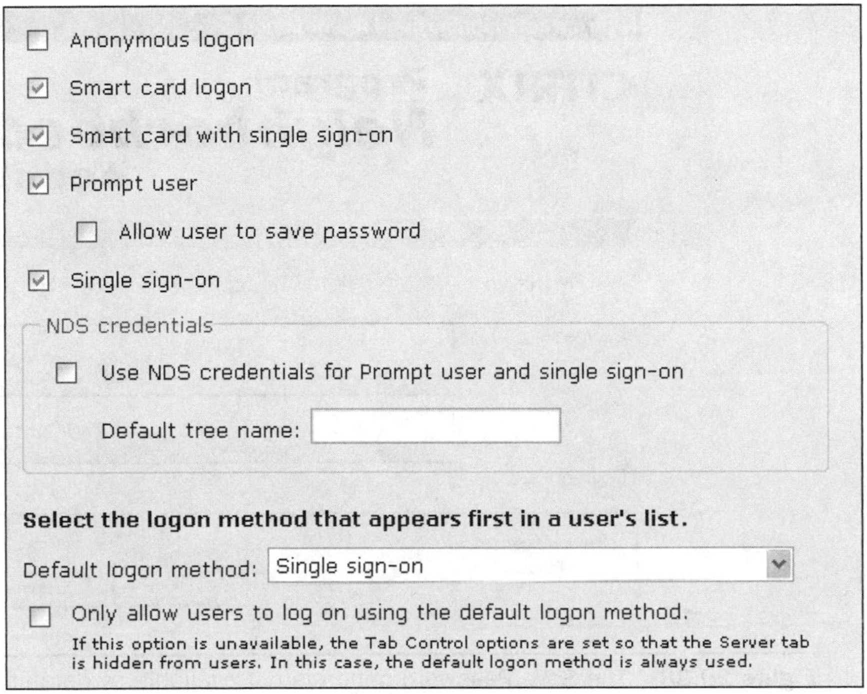

Figure 20.37   The Logon Methods properties page for the PN Agent Console.

- **Smart card with single sign-on**—This method performs the same authentication as the smart card logon method, except this method requests the PIN only when the initial connection is established. From that point on, the PIN information is cached by the client and re-sent automatically when requested.
- **Prompt user**—This is the standard logon method. The end user is prompted to provide their user ID and password in order to be authenticated by the farm. When the "Allow user to save password" option is enabled, the user has access to the Save Password option in the lower left-hand side of the PN Agent's authentication dialog box shown in Figure 20.38.
- **Single sign-on**—This option allows caching of local Windows credentials so they can be automatically passed when requested by the PN Agent for authentication. When logging on using this method, users are not prompted for credentials when accessing PN Agent applications. In order for single sign-on to function properly you must also enabled single sign-on from within the Web Interface for MetaFrame Presentation Server. The configuration of this component is discussed in the "Web Interface for MetaFrame Presentation Server" section later in this chapter.

Figure 20.38   The Save Password option is not available by default and can be seen only if enabled in the PN Agent Console.

If your users will be authenticating using Novell Directory Services (NDS) and the Single Sign-On or Prompt User options, you need to enable the "Use NDS credentials for Prompt user and single sign-on" option and then provide the name of the NDS tree that will be the default source for authentication information.

The final group of options on this page lets you to choose, from the list of enabled logon methods, which one is set as the client default and appears first in the Logon Mode drop-down list on the Server tab of the PN Agent client (see Figure 20.39). Once you have selected the default logon method, you can enforce this as the only allowed authentication method by enabling "Only allow users to log on using the default logon method"; when this option is enabled, the Logon Mode drop-down list box is grayed out and the method to be enforced is displayed.

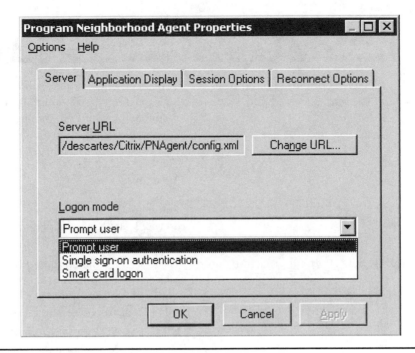

Figure 20.39   The logon mode appearing first in the list is dictated by the selection from the Logon Methods page in the PN Agent Console.

Application Display

The Application Display option controls all aspects of creation and placement of application shortcuts on the local client device. The location of these shortcuts and their behavior are controlled by options divided into four distinct subpages:

- **Shortcut Removal**—These settings dictate when shortcuts created by the PN Agent are removed.
- **Start Menu**—This page controls how the application shortcuts appear on the user's local Start menu.
- **Desktop**—This page controls how application shortcuts appear on the user's local desktop.
- **System Tray**—The final page is used to manage the display of shortcuts in the system tray.

Shortcut Removal   The properties for this page are listed in Table 20.12.

Table 20.12   Application Display's Shortcut Removal Properties

Setting	Description
Delete shortcuts created by Program Neighborhood.	Two check boxes are available for selection here, both of which are optional. If neither setting is desirable for your configuration, simply leave them unchecked.
	The first setting deletes shortcuts as soon as PN Agent exits.
	The second setting removes shortcuts when the user logs off PN Agent but does not necessarily close it.
Delete shortcuts created by users.	These settings dictate how PN Agent deals with user-created application shortcuts to published applications. Two options are provided here, but only one or the other can be selected:
	■ Always: When the user logs off or exits PN Agent, these shortcuts are deleted.
	■ Only when associated applications are not available: When this option is selected, PN Agent removes the user-created shortcuts only when the associated application itself is no longer available. You also need to provide the maximum depth to which PN Agent searches for shortcuts to delete. A value of zero (0) means to the maximum depth.

Start Menu and Desktop Options   Many options exist to configure how shortcuts are added and displayed in the user's local Start menu and/or their desktop. Figure 20.40 shows the contents of the Start menu property page, and Table 20.13 summarizes the purpose of these settings for both the Start menu and the desktop.

TIP: When testing how certain property changes can affect PN Agent, if you encounter a situation where it appears that changes to the client are being ignored, double-check to ensure the Allow User Customization option is at least temporarily disabled. When enabled, this option can cause PN Agent to ignore changes made from the PN Agent Console and continue to override them based on the current configuration settings of that client.

Table 20.13 Application Display's Start Menu and Desktop Properties

Setting	Description
Place Program Neighborhood shortcuts on the Start menu. Place Program Neighborhood shortcuts on the desktop.	Disabling this option prevents PN Agent from adding any shortcuts to the Start menu/desktop. When enabled there are one of two choices on how the icons will be added. Start Menu Only: ■ Have Program Neighborhood Agent create a folder for shortcuts: This setting creates a subfolder with the given name directly under the Start menu. For example, if the name "PN Agent Folder" is entered, a submenu is created directly on the main Start menu with that folder name. If the "Place the shortcut folder on the Programs submenu" is checked, the submenu is created under the Programs folder and not in the root of the Start menu. ■ Do not have Program Neighborhood Agent create a folder for shortcuts: In this case, the shortcuts to the applications are placed directly under the Start menu unless the "Place the shortcuts on the Programs submenu" is also checked; in that case, the shortcuts appear under the Programs folder. Desktop Only: ■ With customized folder name: When this option is enabled, the specified folder name is created on the user's desktop, and the published applications go into this folder. The default folder name is My Program Neighborhood Applications. ■ Using customized icon: The default icon for the custom Program Neighborhood folder is the same icon as the one used by the PN executable itself (the large black letter *i* with the red circle). You can specify an alternate icon by populating this field with the full URL to the icon file. Similarly to the server URL on the Server Settings page, you can force the client to ignore the host name provided and continue to use the host defined locally on the client PC by selecting the option "Force the client to replace the host part of the icon URL."

Table 20.13 Application Display's Start Menu and Desktop Properties (continued)

Setting	Description
Allow user customization.	This option controls whether the user can modify the Start menu settings under the Application Display tab of the PN Agent GUI interface. The check box "Allow users to change the shortcut folder name" controls whether the user can override the folder name if one was used for application shortcuts.
Display Program Neighborhood shortcuts on the Start menu. Display Program Neighborhood shortcuts on the desktop.	This setting controls from where PN Agent retrieves the information on how the shortcuts should be displayed on the Start menu/desktop. One of the three possible choices must be selected: ■ Use only Presentation Server Console settings if the published resource has Start menu/desktop placement settings: When an application is published using the Management Console for MPS, you can specify Start menu/desktop placement settings under the Program Neighborhood Settings tab. When this option is selected, only those settings specified in the Management Console are used if they exist. Any settings changed on this page are ignored. ■ Ignore Presentation Server Console settings: Regardless of whether or not Start menu or desktop settings have been defined in the Management Console, they are ignored and only the settings on this page are used for PN Agent clients. This setting does not override the option to add icons to the user's desktop or Start menu, whichever is the opposite of the setting currently being changed. For example, changes to the Start menu settings do not affect the desktop, and vice versa. ■ Use both Program Neighborhood Agent and Presentation Server Console settings: The Start menu and desktop settings from both locations are merged together. If different subfolders have been defined in the two locations, they both appear on the client's local desktop. I recommend that you decide during the planning phase whether you will have one set of common settings for all PN deployments, or whether you will maintain a unique set for the PN Agent. In most cases, enforcing a single set of Start menu and desktop options from the Management Console helps simplify the deployment and minimize the confusion for both the end user and the MetaFrame administrator.

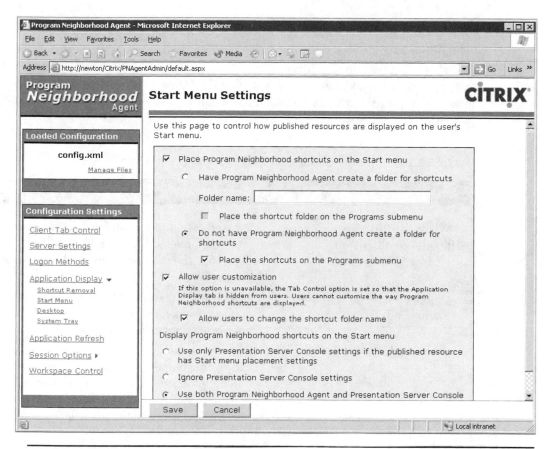

Figure 20.40   The Start menu settings in the PN Agent Console.

System Tray   The final submenu under Application Display controls placement of icons on the System Tray applet for PN Agent. There are only two options available on this page:

- **Place Program Neighborhood shortcuts on the system tray menu**— Controls whether the shortcuts to all available published applications appear under the Applications menu in the System Tray applet. When this option is disabled, the Application menu option still exists but the contents display only the word *Empty*.
- **Allow user customization**—Controls whether the user can override the previous setting under the properties for the PN Agent. The final setting on the Application Display tab for the applet lets the user select whether or not the shortcuts appear in the system tray menu. When this setting is disabled, that option is grayed out in the applet.

Application Refresh

The Application Refresh properties page is where you configure the frequency of the published application refresh performed by PN Agent. Three options are available on this tab and are summarized in Table 20.14. Note that the "Allow user customization" options on this page are displayed but cannot be modified at this time. These options will be available in a future release of PN Agent.

Table 20.14   Application Refresh Settings Properties Page

Setting	Description
When the Program Neighborhood Agent starts up.	When this option is enabled, the PN Agent first loads the updated list of applications from the farm once the user has supplied the proper user credentials.
When a published resource is launched.	If this option is enabled, an updated list of applications is retrieved whenever a user launches an existing application shortcut.
Periodically.	This option configures the PN Agent to periodically retrieve updated application information based on the specified interval. The default is six hours and can be changed to any integer value greater than or equal to one hour. You cannot specify a fraction of an hour.
	During the testing and piloting phases of your implementation, you may want to set this option to be one or two hours, but once you are in production, an interval of four, six, or even eight hours may be appropriate.

Session Options

On the Session Options page, you control all aspects of the user's computing experience when executing the published applications. Four subpages exist here:

- **Window Size**—This page dictates what session window size options are available to the user.
- **Color Depth**—This page lets you define what color-depth options are available to PN Agent.

■ **Audio Quality**—From here you can specify what audio quality (if any) is supported by the PN Agent client.

■ **Template File**—From this page you can select what ICA template file is used to establish the connection with the available published resources.

Window Size   The main option on the Window Size page is the "Allow users to select window size" setting. When this is disabled, the end user's ability to select an alternate window size from the Session Options tab in PN Agent is dependent on whether or not this option is enabled in the Web Interface for MPS. If it is also disabled in the Web Interface, the only available option in the drop-down list box is Default, as shown in Figure 20.41.

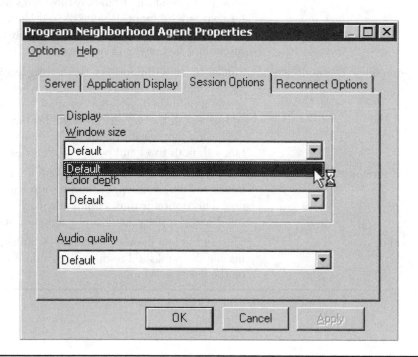

Figure 20.41   When users are not allowed to select an alternate window size, their only option is to select the Default setting.

When users are allowed to select a window size, there are four options that can be configured. These options are summarized in Table 20.15.

Table 20.15   ICA Session Window Size Options

Setting	Description
Enable fixed dimensions.	When fixed dimensions are enabled, you can build a custom list of fixed dimensions from which the user can select a desired window size for their application session. One or more standard and/or custom dimensions can be added to the dimension list, which is presented to the user in the drop-down list box on the Session Options tab in PN Agent.
	If you want to let users customize their own fixed window dimensions, limit the list to only those sizes that are reasonable for your environment. If none of your client devices support resolutions above 1024×768, you will likely not want to allow resolutions higher than this.
Enable percentage of the display.	Similar to fixed dimensions, this setting lets you add one or more percentage values representing what fixed portion of the screen a published resource occupies. Any percentages you add appear in the same drop-down list box that the fixed dimensions appear in. Figure 20.42 shows this drop-down list box with both fixed and percentage entries.
Enable full screen.	This setting adds the Full Screen option to the PN Agent list, letting the user run a published resource in a full screen window. This option is most commonly used in conjunction with a full desktop-replacement implementation scenario.
Enable seamless.	This setting lets the user select the Seamless Window option, making the published resource appear as if it is running locally on the user's desktop.

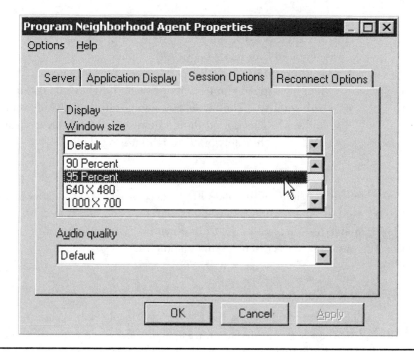

Figure 20.42   Both fixed dimensions and screen percentages appear in the same Window Size list box on the Session Options tab in PN Agent.

Color Depth   The Color Depth page is where you define the range of color depths available for selection by the end user. When users are given the ability to select an alternate color depth, the options selected on this page dictate what appears in the Color Depth drop-down list box on the Session property page of PN Agent. The four available color depths are 16 colors, 256 colors, High Color (16-bit), and True Color (24-bit). When users are prohibited from selecting colors on this page, the properties from the Web Interface are used.

Audio Quality   The Client Session Audio Quality property page lets you specify what audio options are available with PN Agent. As with the other Session Options settings, you define what alternate audio quality settings are available for selection in PN Agent. If none of these options are available, the only selection in PN Agent is Default. The available audio options are

- **Off**—Turns off all client-mapped audio.
- **Low quality**—Provides basic sound support, the preferred option when sound is required over a low-bandwidth connection.
- **Medium quality**—Delivers improved performance and should be used only when high-speed connectivity exists and higher quality audio is required.
- **High quality**—The highest available sound quality also consumes the most bandwidth. This option should be reserved for LAN environments only, where 10MB or higher network throughput is available.

Template File The ICA Template File page is where you can select an alternate .ICA file to be used when accessing published resources. Only files that exist in the specified folder are available for selection in the drop-down list. The purpose of the .ICA file and how it can be customized are discussed in Chapter 14.

Workspace Control

The final configuration page in the PN Agent Console is the Workspace Control page. Figure 20.43 lists the options available on this page. Workspace Control is one of the new features available with the Web Interface for MPS 3.0 and is also referred to in some Citrix literature as "follow-me roaming." Not only does Workspace Control let a user disconnect or log off all applications initiated from a device with one button click, but it also lets all currently active and/or disconnected applications be reconnected either manually or automatically when a user logs on to PN Agent or the Web Interface. Two main options are available on this screen:

- **Enable automatic reconnection at log in**—When this option is enabled, the user's sessions are automatically connected when the user logs on to PN Agent. When this option is disabled, these connections can be reconnected only through the Reconnect PN Agent menu option.
- **Enable automatic reconnection using the Reconnect menu**—When this option is enabled, the Reconnect menu choice found on the PN Agent icon lets you manually reconnect to disconnected and/or active sessions. When disabled, this menu option is grayed out and the reconnect option is not available.

Both of these options let you choose to connect either existing active and disconnected sessions or disconnected sessions only. If both active and disconnected sessions are chosen, PN Agent communicates with the Web Interface and requests that all active sessions initiated from this client be reconnected and that all existing disconnected sessions (initiated from this client or any other client) also be reconnected. Under certain circumstances, a user's session may be disconnected yet still appear active on the server. This option allows for recovery of these sessions.

When only the reconnect to disconnected sessions option is available, active sessions in the farm are ignored and only disconnected sessions (regardless of where they originated) are reconnected.

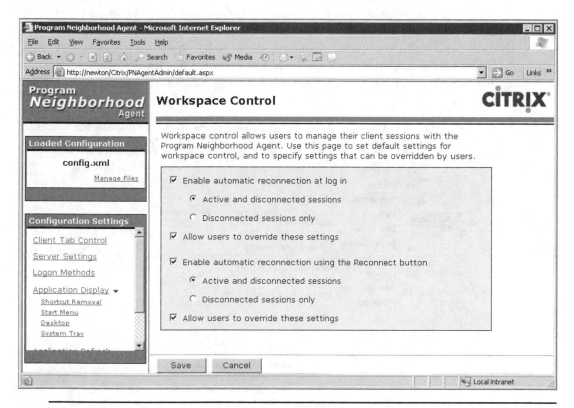

Figure 20.43 The Workspace Control property page.

When the user option to override these settings is enabled, the user has access to modify these settings under the Reconnect Options tab in PN Agent.

Configuring the Citrix ICA Client for Linux

Just as with the Program Neighborhood client for Windows, the Linux ICA client provides a set of client-wide settings that will affect all ICA connections created in the client and some of the functionality provided with the PN Agent component of this client, as well as settings specific to the individual connections and PN Agent. In this section I look first at the client-wide settings before looking more closely at the connection and PN Agent–specific options.

Client-Wide Linux Settings

The client-wide settings can be found by selecting the Settings option from under the Tools menu in the Citrix ICA client for Linux, as shown in Figure 20.44. Just as with the Win32 client, these settings apply to any connection defined within the Linux client, whether a custom connection or one retrieved by the Program Neighborhood Agent. Unlike with the Win32 client, this Settings dialog box contains global default settings specific to ICA connections, such as the default window size and server location. Both of these settings can be overridden within the properties of a specific connection or application set and are discussed shortly.

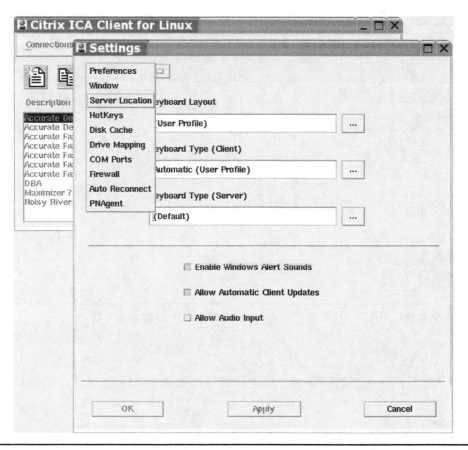

Figure 20.44   The Citrix ICA client for Linux has global settings that apply to all defined connections.

When looking at the global settings for the ICA client for Linux, you will immediately notice that not only does the interface differ from that of the PN client, but it also includes options not found with the 32-bit client.

The global settings for the ICA Linux client are divided into ten tabs:

- **Preferences**—Provides basic keyboard support options as well as the sound and client update features.
- **Window**—Where the default Window options are configured that are applied by default to all ICA connections.
- **Server Location**—Lets you configure the server location list used by all ICA connections.
- **Hotkeys**—Where the alternate hotkeys are defined to access the features not available due to standard Linux keyboard mappings.
- **Event Logging**—Where client-side event logging of information can be configured.
- **Disk Cache**—Where the caching feature for the client is configured.
- **Drive Mapping**—Lets client drives within the MetaFrame session be mapped back to directories in the Linux file system. This is a global setting available to all ICA connections.
- **COM Ports**—Lets COM port mapping be configured with the ICA Linux client.
- **Firewall**—Ensures connections are established properly when the ICA client must traverse a firewall or proxy server to access a MetaFrame server.
- **Auto Reconnect**—Lets you configure how the client should deal with disconnect scenario issues such as network availability causing a user's session to unexpectedly disconnect.
- **PNAgent**—Contains options specific to the PN Agent component of the Linux client. Accessibility of many of these settings is dictated by the PN Agent Console, basic configuration of which was discussed in the "Configuring the Program Neighborhood Agent" section.

Preferences   The Preferences tab in the Linux client contains only five items, most of them the same (or similar) to settings found in the Program Neighborhood Win32 client. Table 20.16 lists the general preferences for the Linux client.

Table 20.16   Linux Preferences Tab ICA Settings

Setting	Description
Keyboard Layout Keyboard Type (Client) Keyboard Type (Server)	Lets you define the keyboard layout and types used by the client device. The Keyboard Layout option determines what language you want to type in, while the two keyboard types represent the workstation keyboard type (client) and the physical keyboard type (server) being used. In most situations, the default options listed below are appropriate: ■ Keyboard Layout (User Profile) ■ Keyboard Type—Client (User Profile) ■ Keyboard Type—Server (Default)
Enable Windows alert sounds.	Passes Windows alert sounds through to the Linux workstation. This option does not control client audio redirection, which allows sounds originating from the MetaFrame session to play locally on the Linux workstation. This setting deals only with the "beep" style alerts that Windows sounds when there is an error. Client audio redirection is configured on a per-connection basis and is discussed shortly.
Allow automatic client updates.	Identical to the Program Neighborhood feature, this option controls whether the client will respond to a client update request issued from a MetaFrame server. For a client to be properly updated, this option must be enabled. Unfortunately this option can't currently be overridden by anything on the server side. This means that if a user has sufficient privileges on the desktop, he or she can disable this option and prevent client updates from occurring.

Window   The Window tab lets you configure the default window options for any newly created client connections. Unless overridden when you create a new connection, these settings are used. Figure 20.45 shows an example of how this dialog box might appear. Table 20.17 summarizes the options on this tab.

Table 20.17   Linux Window Tab Settings

Setting	Description
Default Window Colors	Four color-depth options are available: 16, 256, 32 thousand, or 16 million colors. Whenever possible select a color depth that most closely matches your Linux desktop configuration. When using the lower color settings, the color palettes in the Windows session and the local Linux session may differ, resulting in a flashing that occurs when you switch from an ICA session to a local Linux session. When you select 256 colors, Citrix enables the Default 256 Color Mapping option, which lets you determine whether the client uses a shared palette and approximates the colors in the Windows session using the local palette, or uses a private color palette and matches colors exactly. When the private palette is chosen, you will likely encounter this screen flashing phenomena. When you select 32 thousand or 16 million colors, you rarely encounter this screen-flashing issue.
Default Window Size	Three sizing options are available for selection: ■ Fixed Size ■ Percentage of Screen Size ■ Full Screen Fixed Size lets you enter a custom value or select a preset size ranging from 640×480 all the way up to 2048×1536. If you select a window size greater than your current local desktop size, the Citrix session appears with horizontal and vertical screen bars that you will need to use in order to view the entire screen. Selecting the Percentage of Screen Size option lets you enter a percentage (50%, 75%, etc.), and the ICA connection will display a window matching those dimensions. The Full Screen option sizes the ICA connection to completely fill the current screen size of the client, obscuring any local applications or files.

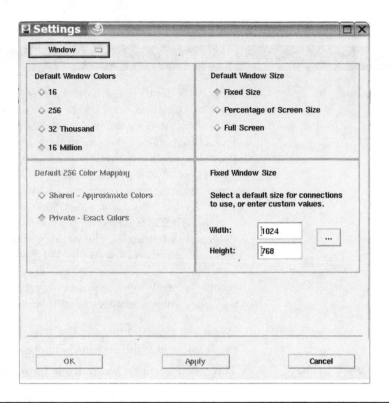

Figure 20.45 The Window dialog box for the ICA client for Linux is where default window options are configured.

Server Location   Server location information defined here is globally available to all of the user's ICA client connections unless overridden in the settings for an individual connection. As Figure 20.26 shows, the settings on this screen are very similar to those found in the Win32 Program Neighborhood client, exception for the IPX/SPX and NETBIOS protocols, which are not supported with the Linux client.

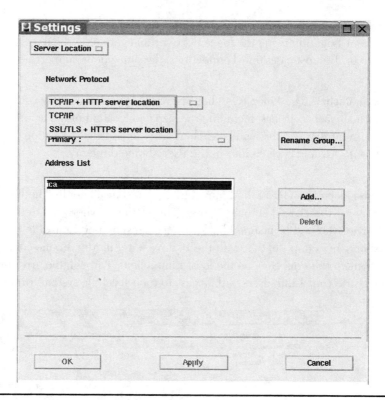

Figure 20.46   Providing multiple Start menus can be confusing to users with limited computer knowledge.

HotKeys   Similar to the Win32 hotkeys setting, the Linux client also provides a means of defining alternate keyboard combinations as substitutes for the standard keyboard shortcuts used in Windows. The traditional keystroke combinations are not available as they are being captured by Linux. One of the most common key combinations to be reported as a problem is the Alt + Tab combination. In Program Neighborhood, these keys are replaced with the Alt ++ (Plus) and Alt + - (Minus) keys. In Linux Alt + Tab is replaced by Alt + - (Alt + minus key).

When implementing a full desktop and alternate key combinations are going to be a factor, it is a good idea to be proactive and develop a one-page summary of what the different keyboard combinations are for the end user. This will help to make their life easier and hopefully reduce the call volume even a little.

Event Logging   When problems arise with a user accessing MetaFrame, event logging can be an effective tool in recording information about the user's session, which can later be reviewed and debugged. Event logging is identical between Linux and the Win32 client, so you will want to ensure that when gathering data, select the option to Append to Existing Event Log; otherwise, the log is overwritten every time the user logs on to a MetaFrame server. In most cases only connections, disconnections, and errors should be logged.

Disk Cache   The Linux ICA client provides the administrator with the ability to modify the bitmap cache settings, including the size and location of the actual cache files and the minimum bitmap size that will be cached. The default cache location for the Linux client is in the .ICAClient/cache folder in the user's home directory.

Drive Mapping   One of the Linux settings that you will not find in the Program Neighborhood client is the Drive Mapping setting. This setting is where you define what Windows-based drive letter will be mapped back to the corresponding Linux file directory. Figure 20.47 shows an example of this, with the P: drive letter in MetaFrame configured to point into the /home/toddm directory on the local Linux client. Through the drive mappings setting you can provide your Linux users with access to their local file system from within MetaFrame.

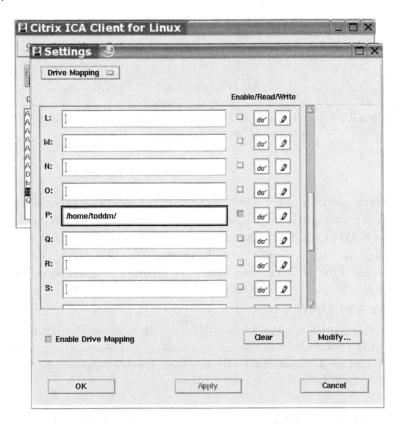

Figure 20.47   Providing multiple Start menus can be confusing to users with limited computer knowledge.

COM Port Mapping   Similar to the drive mapping component, Windows-based COM ports can be mapped to the desired Linux-based serial ports. In this way users are able to access serial devices locally connected to the Linux device from within the MetaFrame session.

Firewall Settings   The firewall settings for Linux were discussed along with Program Neighborhood client in the section "Server Location Configuration in the Program Neighborhood Client and ICA Client for Linux" earlier in the Chapter.

Auto-Reconnect   The Linux ICA client also supports the automatic session reconnect feature, allowing the client to detect an unintentional disconnect and attempt to automatically reconnect the users session. Credentials are cached and used to reestablish the connection. One difference between the Win32 Program Neighborhood client and the Linux client is that the Linux client provides an easily accessible means of adjusting the logic or disabling the feature all together. The Win32 client provides no GUI-based management and disabling the auto-reconnect feature requires a manual update to the user's personal APPSRV.INI file. Figure 20.48 shows the Linux Auto-Reconnect features.

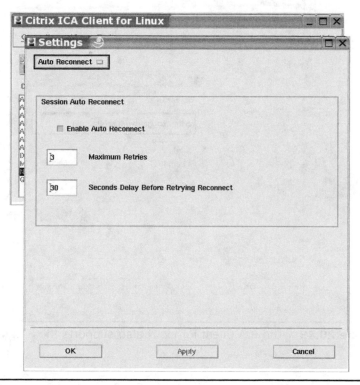

Figure 20.48   The Linux client provides an easy way to manage the settings for the auto client reconnect feature.

PNAgent   The last option in the settings list is the PNAgent Configuration tool (Figure 20.49). If you wish to retrieve your configuration information for the Linux client from a Program Neighborhood Agent Console, then you will need to setup the agent to communicate with the appropriate Web server. Clicking the Change button opens the dialog box shown in Figure 20.49, where you can enter the server URL that points to the source of the PNAgent XML configuration file. As with the Win32 PNAgent, the client-side options that are available for editing will depend on what access has been defined on the PNAgent server. The exact same configuration settings apply to both the Win32 and the Linux PNAgent, the details of which were discussed earlier in this chapter in the section entitled "Program Neighborhood Agent Console Configuration"

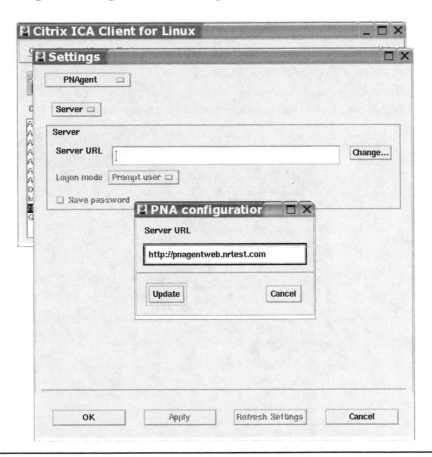

Figure 20.49   The ICA Client for Linux also supports the Program Neighborhood Agent.

Additional Linux Client Tools

In addition to the Settings that are accessible from under the Tools menu, the ICA Linux client has two additional tools. The first is the Connection Center, which is functionally identical to the Connection Center utility that runs on the Win32 platform. The Connection Center provides a single source where a user can see what connections are currently open between their client and one or more host MetaFrame servers. Active connections can be logged out or disconnected from this dialog box.

The other tool accessible from this menu is the xcapture utility. This utility is an ICA client helper application designed to assist in the exchange of graphical data between the MetaFrame server clipboard and Linux X Windows applications that are not ICCCM-complaint. ICCCM stands for Inter-Client Communication Conventions Manual, a standards document that outlines how X Windows applications must exist and interact on an X Server.

ICA Linux Connection Properties

The majority of the properties that are defined on a per-connection basis are identical to those that were just described in the "Client-Wide Linux Settings". In order to create a new connection simply select New from under the Connections menu. The Properties window then opens (Figure 20.50) to allow for the selection of the network protocol, server location and whether a specific server or published application link will be created. The network protocol and server location settings default to using the client-wide settings.

Once server or published application has been selected, clicking on the button to the right will browse and return a list of available resources. Once the desired server or application has been selected, clicking on Network in the top left corner will reveal a pull-down menu, and the next option to select should be the Connection settings (Figure 20.51). This is where you will define the characteristics of the session connection. You will want to enable sound only if required for your environment. Otherwise it should be disabled. I would recommend that you also enable the strongest encryption supported, which is typically RC5 (128-bit encryption).

Figure 20.50   Configuring an ICA connection in the Linux ICA client.

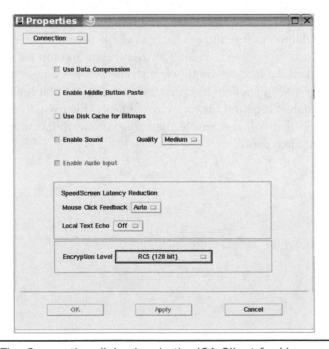

Figure 20.51   The Connection dialog box in the ICA Client for Linux.

The remainder of the options for this connection are:

- **Firewall**—Displays the same settings that were discussed in the "Client-Wide Linux Settings" section of this chapter.
- **Window**—Just as with the Firewall setting, the contents of the dialog box have already been discussed.
- **Application**—This option, consistent with a similar setting for Custom ICA Connections in the Program Neighborhood allows you to hard-code in the full path and working folder to an application hosted on the MetaFrame server.
- **Login**—Allows you to hard-code login credentials for the connection. I would highly recommend that this option not be used as it represents a significant security risk.
- **Auto Reconnect**—Provides you with the same settings that were defined early for the client-wide Linux settings.

The Linux ICA client from Citrix supports the majority of the features that are also available in the Win32 Program Neighborhod client, at least the Customer ICA Connections portion.

Citrix ICA Web Clients

In Chapter 14, I discussed the concept of Web-enabled applications, and detailed how the various server-side components (Web Interface for MPS and Program Neighborhood Agent Console) were installed. Of the four basic components that collaborate to deliver the Web-enabled MetaFrame environment, there remains only one that we have yet to touch on. The remaining pieces to this puzzle are the Citrix ICA Web clients. There are actually three different clients that collectivity are known as the ICA Web clients. They are:

- **32-bit ActiveX client**—This is the 32-bit ActiveX control for Microsoft Internet Explorer 5.0 or higher.
- **32-bit Netscape plug-in client**—This is the 32-bit Netscape plugin for Netscape Navigator or Communicator 4.78, 6.2 or later.
- **Java applet client—The Java applet is a 100 percent download and run client** that is designed specifically for those environments where installing a traditional ICA client on the client device is not possible.

Of the three, only the ActiveX and Netscape plugin clients actually require any kind of traditional installation process. The Java applet does not need to be installed on the client device. As long as the user is accessing the Web site with a Java-compatible Web browser the Java ICA client will download and execute. In order to utilize the Java client in your environment you will need to install and configure the client files on your Web server.

A common misconception is that in order to access a published application through a Web browser you *must* be running one of these Web clients. In actual fact, simply having an ICA client installed on the PC is usually sufficient to access the Web-based content.

Most of the existing ICA clients also ship with a "helper" application that can be used to access Web-enabled applications through a Web browser. What this means is that if you have one of the traditional ICA clients (Program Neighborhood for Win32, ICA Client for Linux, ICA Client for Macintosh, and so on) already installed on your PC, then you will be able to access published content available through a Web browser without having to explicitly download and use one of these Web clients.

Citrix has made these ICA Web clients available so that you, as the Citrix administrator, have another option at your disposal for delivering the necessary ICA client files to the end-user so that he or she can access the desired MetaFrame-based application.

Installing the 32-bit ActiveX or Netscape Plug-in Web Client

Either one of these clients can be installed using the 32-bit Windows installation files that I discussed in the "Installing the Citrix Program Neighborhood" section near the beginning of this chapter. Specifically these installation files can be used to acquire the desired 32-bit Web client:

- MetaFrame Presentation Server (MPS) Client Packager (Ica32Pkg.msi)
- Self-extracting executable (Ica32t.exe)
- A Microsoft cabinet (CAB) file (Wficat.cab – full client, Wficac.cab – minimal client)

The minimal installation client supports only the ActiveX control. A minimal installation version of the Netscape plug-in is not available.

Any one of the three installation files can be directly launched from a client PC in order to install the Web client. Once the client has been installed, it will remain available for use on the PC. In addition to manually installing the desired Web client on a PC, you can leverage the Web Interface for MetaFrame to detect and automatically make available the appropriate installation files for download and execution by the end user. Figure 20.52 demonstrates how the Web Interface can detect and recommend the necessary ICA installation files for the client. Details on this detection process are managed through the Web Interface for MetaFrame, which will be discussed in the "Web Interface for MetaFrame Presentation Server" later in this chapter.

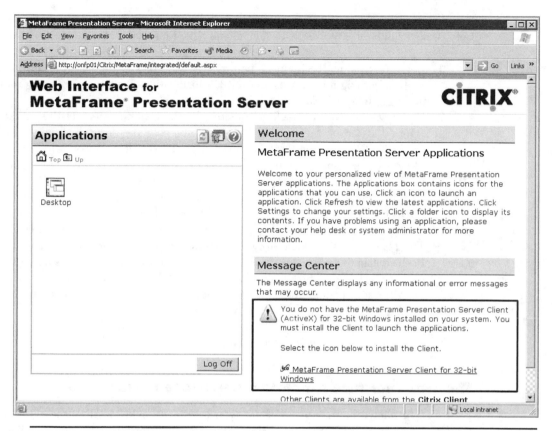

Figure 20.52   The Web Interface for MctaFrame Presentation Server can detect the client operating system and recommend the appropriate ICA client.

Installing the ICA Java Client

Unlike the 32-bit ActiveX and Netscape plug-in clients, the Java client is not installed on the client machine in the traditional sense. Instead, every time that the client is required it is downloaded and executed on the client device. Of course, certain caching features may retain the Java applet files locally, but this information cannot be considered permanent since the cache could be flushed at any given time.

Of course, before the end user can utilize the ICA Java client, it must be available on the Web site that is hosting the Web Interface for MetaFrame Presentation Server. If you chose to install these files when you installed the Web Interface, then everything you require is already on the server. It is now just a matter of configuring the Web Interface to make the Java client available. If the desired client files, in particular the ICA Java Client, were not copied over to the Web server during the Web Interface installation then you must manually add these before users will be able to use the desired client. Client installation files are added as follows:

1. Begin by creating the folder structure \Citrix\ICAWEB underneath the root of the Web publishing folder. Most default IIS installations have the publishing root under C:\Inetpub\wwwroot.
2. If you wish to deploy the client included on the Components CD-ROM that shipped as part of the installation media, then copy the desired subfolder under the ICAWEB folder on the CD-ROM to the ICAWEB folder on the Web server. Make sure that you keep the same directory structure, including the language prefix. For example, if the CD-ROM drive is E:, then the English Java client will be found under E:\icaweb\en\java. You will need to create the en folder under ICAWEB and then copy the java subfolder over to the Web server.

   You can also download the Java client from the Citrix Web site (www.citrix.com). The Java client is available in two different compression formats, .zip and .tar.gz. Both contain the exact same files and are provided to simplify processing on the corresponding target platform (Windows and UNIX/Linux respectively).

   After downloading the compressed Java file, extract the contents into the \Citrix\ICAWEB\<language>\icajava folder.
3. The necessary client files are now on the Web server and the only task remaining is to configure the Web Interface to use Java as the ICA client.

The Web Interface for MetaFrame Presentation Server

Figure 20.53 shows the main page of the Web Interface for MPS. All of the necessary configuration to manage the Web Interface is done through this console. The installation and basic setup of the Web Interface was discussed in Chapter 14. In this chapter we will focus on the client settings for the Web Interface. Specifically there are three components that make up the client settings for the Web Interface. They are:

- Client-side Proxy
- Client Deployment
- Client Customization

Client-side Proxy

If clients contacting your MetaFrame servers must do so through a client-side proxy server then the settings on this page can be used to ensure the ICA client is properly configured to use the proxy server. There are two categories of proxy settings that are managed from this page. The first is the default proxy setting that applies to all clients contacting the Web Interface, regardless of from where they originate. The second is the specific proxy setting, which allows you to define different proxy server configurations based on the client's subnet. After the desired settings have been added for a given subnet, you click the Add button to add the entry to the list of stored mappings, where it is retained and can be managed at a later date.

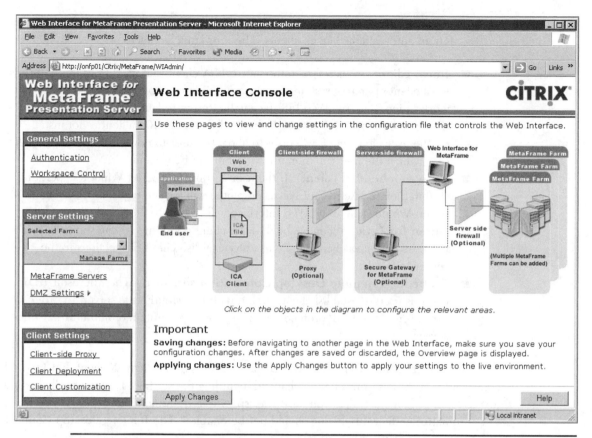

Figure 20.53 The Web Interface Console provides an intuitive tool for managing all aspects of the Web Interface environment.

Client Deployment

The client deployment settings page allows you to control:

- The default application launch client.
- What choices a user has for selecting his or her own launch client.
- Specific Web client settings, including what packages will be available with the Java client.
- Whether or not the client installation caption is always displayed or only shown when no client is present for the user.

Figure 20.54 shows the upper portion of the client deployment settings, where you select the default and available launch clients. The four launch choices are:

- **Local Client**—This refers to the native ICA client that would run on the user's local client operating system. For example, if a user connects from a Linux workstation, then the Web Interface will attempt to launch MetaFrame connections using the native Linux ICA client. If the Linux ICA client is not installed on the user's machine it will offer to allow the user to download the Linux client files, which the user can then use to install the ICA client.
- **Native embedded Client**—If the user is running a 32-bit Windows operating system then the ActiveX or Netscape plugin will try and be used. If the client OS is non-Windows then the Web Interface will default to the Local Client setting.
- **Client for Java**—When enabled, if the client operating system supports Java then the ICA Java client will be used to establish client connections to the server farm.
- **Embedded Remote Desktop Connection software**—The Microsoft RDP client is used to establish a connection with the MetaFrame server. In order to use this tool the RDP protocol must be properly configured on the MetaFrame server.

Under Web client settings you can modify certain features of the ActiveX client, but I would recommend that these settings not be changed including the setting to automatically deploy the Web Client at logon. Unless you have very specific requirements to deploy the ActiveX client automatically then this setting should not be enabled. The Remote Desktop Connect ActiveX settings are currently read-only.

The Client for Java Settings is where you will make the majority of your changes if you're implementing the ICA Java client. Figure 20.55 shows the settings that can be managed for the ICA Java client. The list of packages represents the various ICA features that the Java client supports. When a package is enabled, the corresponding feature is available to users of the Java client when accessing a MetaFrame server. Each selected package does consume additional overhead when downloading to the client device, so omitting any unnecessary components will help to reduce the download time of the ICA Java client. If the Allow user to choose packages option is enabled then the user will have access to this same list of packages and can choose which ones they wish to use. I normally suggest that this option be disabled and all necessary package management be performed through the Web Interface.

If you have also implemented the Secure Gateway for MetaFrame and have used certificates from a private certificate authority (from an internal Microsoft Certificate Services server for example), you will need to provide the name of the private root certificate that the Java client should process. The corresponding certificate file will also have to be placed in the same folder as the Java client files on the host Web server.

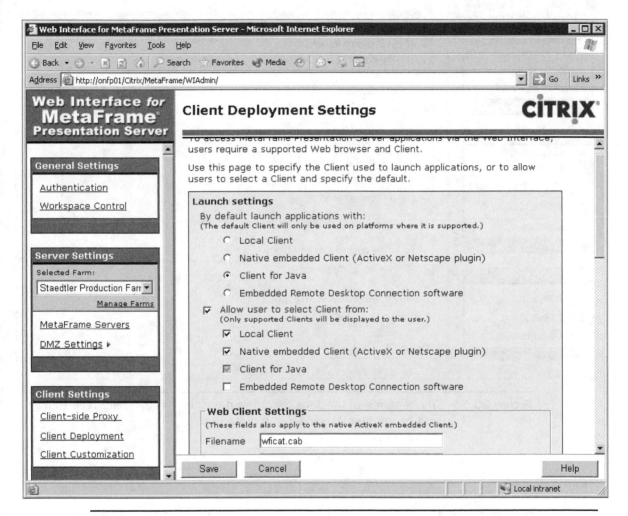

Figure 20.54   The upper portion of the client deployment settings is where you define the default launch client.

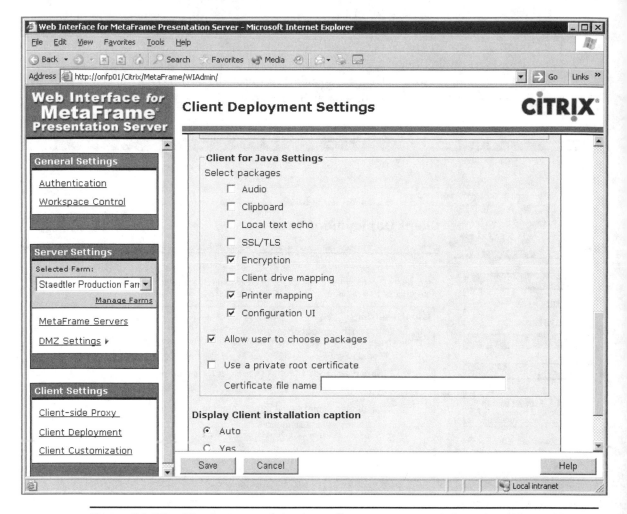

Figure 20.55   The features of the Java client are managed through packages that can be omitted if they're not required.

Citrix ICA Client Implementation Scenario Considerations

This section provides a brief summary of how the ICA Client can be configured to support the different implementation scenarios initially discussed in Chapter 5.

Desktop Replacement

When implementing a desktop-replacement scenario, there are a couple of things you need to consider during configuration of the client, regardless of whether you will use a custom ICA connection or an application set containing only the published desktop entry. Because users are running a full MetaFrame desktop session over the top of their existing local Windows desktop, there can be some confusion, particularly if they are seeing two Start menus, one positioned right on top of the other, as shown in Figure 20.56.

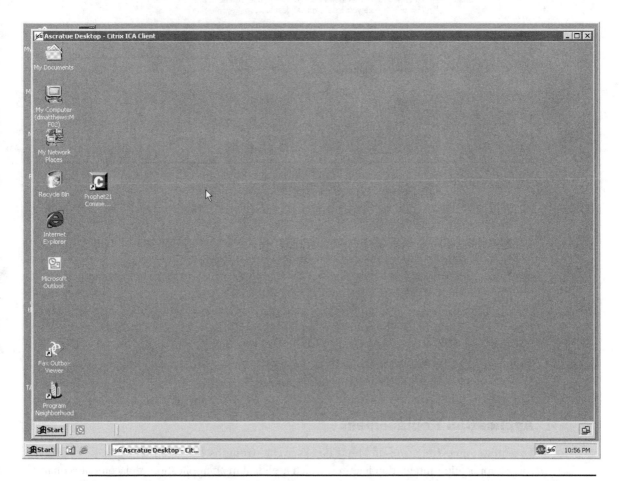

Figure 20.56 Providing multiple Start menus can be confusing to users with limited computer knowledge.

When possible, implement the desktop-replacement scenario using a full screen MetaFrame session instead of one contained in a remote desktop window. Do not attempt to configure the connection to use seamless windows; this would result in an error message appearing when you established the connection (Figure 20.57). Instead, select the full screen window size.

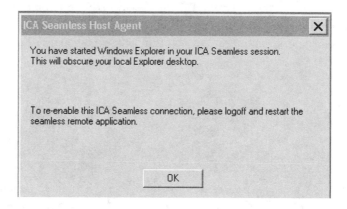

Figure 20.57   When accessing a published desktop, do not try to configure the session as a seamless window.

Pay particular attention to the hotkeys configured for the ICA session. Common key combinations such as Alt+Tab are not available to the user from within the MetaFrame desktop session, so they need to be educated before they go live so they can properly maneuver within their new desktop environment.

And finally, unless absolutely necessary to do otherwise, disable client drive and printer mapping support. Since the users are running everything from their MetaFrame sessions, they likely do not need access to any local printers or data on the hard drive. Both of these options are not configurable within the PN client but are configured on the MetaFrame server. See Chapter 14 for more information on this.

Application Replacement

For quite some time one of MetaFrame's great strengths has been its capacity to provide robust application-integration features, which are ideal in an application-replacement scenario

While the RDP client currently only supports configuring a specific application connection directly on the client, the ICA client supports the feature known as published applications, a superior method of delivering individual applications (as well as complete desktops) to the end user. Published applications provide centralized access control and management as well as transparent load balancing. Exactly how a published application is configured on the client will depend on how the user will access the application. If the user is running the Program Neighborhood Agent then there is no configuration done on the client at all and the published application is simply delivered to the user by the PN Agent. If on the other hand the user is running the ICA Client for Linux and wants to manually setup connections, then he or she will need to select the published application by name from a published application list. No other information such as executable location or working path needs to be stored on the client in order to be able to access and use the published application.

As I first mentioned in Chapter 5, whenever performing an application replacement project with MetaFrame, always implement published applications and never provide the executable name and working folder on the client. Specific servers should never be used.

Exactly how the published application will appear will depend on what ICA client is being used and the features that it supports. The three different configurations are:

- The published application is presented within a client window boundary, which is exactly the same as you would get with the RDP client.
- The published application displays without its own title bar but remains within a client window boundary. This is identical to the previous configuration except that the application's title bar is hidden. This helps to create the illusion that the application is actually running locally to the client. This property is configured when setting up the published application. The one complaint that I often hear from users working in this scenario is that they can't resize the application window. This is because it's actually the ICA session client window, which can't be resized. This can be particularly troublesome for applications such as Internet Explorer or Microsoft Word, which many users want to size to suite their personal preference.
- The third option has the published application presented within a seamless window. The seamless window overcomes the problems that exist with the previous two methods by eliminating the client window boundaries and allowing the application to visually function as if it were running locally. In fact, combining this with integration features such as printer and drive mappings results in an application that is nearly indistinguishable from a locally running application.

More information on published applications and seamless windows was discussed back in Chapter 2. Chapter 21 discusses the steps in configuring and publishing applications in a MetaFrame environment.

Desktop Integration

The wide support for heterogeneous computing environments provided by Citrix makes it still the leading solution for cross-platform access to a Terminal Server environment. The consistency in the user interface between different clients also means that it's very straightforward to configure a non-Windows client to access either a complete Windows desktop or an individual application, both using the published application feature of MetaFrame.

NOTE: The huge interest that I have from customers for the Linux and Macintosh-based ICA clients only seems to further underscore the interest in delivering Windows-based applications via MetaFrame to non-Windows desktop operating systems, the definition of the desktop integration scenario.

CHAPTER 21

Application Integration

The Challenge of Application Integration

It probably comes as no surprise that the greatest challenges you're likely to face during your Terminal Server project involve not the configuration and implementation of the servers but instead the installation, testing, and deployment of the applications you want to run on those servers. The purpose of implementing Terminal Server is to centralize the management and servicing of these applications, so it's vitally important that they be configured to work with as little loss of functionality as possible (or no loss).

In the role of an application integrator (AI), you're likely to face a combination of both technical and managerial challenges, such as these issues:

- **Release management**—One area where many AIs seem to have difficulty is in establishment and enforcement of release management procedures. One reason is simply that the PC computing environment has traditionally had poor release management control. For your Terminal Server environment to remain stable, you must adopt the release procedures common in more traditional multiuser environments, such as the mainframe and UNIX environments. As I state many times throughout this book, it's required that you put the proper release management procedures in place, regardless of whether you're deploying 2 or 20 applications. If there's no control over releasing of software into the Terminal Server environment, it's only a matter of time before a release causes your environment to fail. Please see Chapter 7, "Server and Application Software Planning," for more information on release management.

NOTE: Problems with implementing and enforcing release management can be very difficult in smaller implementations where two or three people are responsible for all aspects of the company's infrastructure. End users are generally accustomed to getting what they ask for quickly, so trying to enforce a release schedule that requires end users to wait for a specific time can be difficult to justify and implement. If you find yourself in such a situation, be diligent and ensure that you implement only the software changes you are certain will work properly.

- **Application stability**—Although application stability is not strictly an issue for the AI (it's more of a concern for Terminal Server operators), the AI must keep this requirement in mind when installing and configuring the application. On the desktop, an application failure affects only one person and usually results in no more than a few harsh words directed from the user to the computer. On a Terminal Server, however, an application failure could immediately affect 20, 50, 100, or more users. In this situation, the harsh words likely would be directed to the Terminal Server operators and administrators.

  As an AI, you must ensure that the installed application is configured to be as stable as possible. It must also interoperate with any other programs that users may be running on Terminal Server. Of course, you have little control over an application that's inherently buggy, but if this is the case, it's likely that these problems existed on the desktop.

  One thing you'll quickly learn is that whenever an issue comes up with any application running in the Terminal Server environment, the problem is immediately attributed to Terminal Server and not to the application.

- **Multiple simultaneous users**—The most obvious challenge you'll face is configuring applications to function properly when run simultaneously in multiuser sessions on the same computer. Although we're slowly starting to see the development of applications designed specifically to run in a Terminal Server environment (mostly to do with requirements for Windows 2000 and 2003 application certification), many applications on the market today were not developed with that purpose in mind. I've found that most apps still function properly, but in some situations additional work and "fiddling" are required to overcome specific problems. Typically, if an application was designed using proper Windows development techniques, such as storing program-specific information in HKEY_LOCAL_MACHINE while maintaining user-specific information in HKEY_CURRENT_USER, it should run on Terminal Server with few problems. I've encountered some very recent Windows applications that for some unknown reason require that the user have at least Power User permissions in order to run the application. I can understand elevated privileges being a requirement for the software installation, but requiring these privileges for normal operation really is completely unacceptable.

  A number of products available on the market support Terminal Server; Microsoft Office 2003 and WRQ Reflections, a host access application, are just two examples.

- **Enhanced security**—Very often the enhanced security requirements of Terminal Sever pose more of a problem to the AI than the multiuser requirements. Security issues can introduce unexpected problems, particularly when the AI has been testing with an administrative account instead of a regular user account. When you encounter a situation where the program runs for an administrator but not for a user, it's almost always a security-related problem.

NOTE: I can't count the number of times I've reviewed a Terminal Server implementation where the administrators have said, "We originally had the system locked down, but we couldn't get the application to run, so we gave everyone Full Control and now it works fine." Although this certainly fixes the immediate problem of getting the programs to function properly, it is not a solution. In fact, this is likely to cause more problems down the road. Every time you give a user elevated security access to the Terminal Server, you're introducing the potential for a problem. It is only a matter of time before the user installs or modifies something that causes an application to fail.

My goal in this chapter is to provide the information you need to become a successful application integrator in a Terminal Server environment. I discuss the application support features available in Terminal Server, the tools and techniques that will assist you, and the process I typically follow when installing an application. Although no amount of documentation can prepare you for every situation, I hope that, with the information in this chapter, you are able to resolve most application problems you encounter.

Here are the three rules I follow when performing application integration:

- **Have patience**—Although many applications can be installed on the first try, there are many that can't. You might need to try a few configurations to find the one right for your environment. Don't always settle for the first solution that comes along.
- **Automate as much as possible**—If you have the option of preconfiguring something or automating a process that would normally require user interaction, do so. The more the Terminal Server user must do before he or she can run an application, the more likely that the user won't do it properly. If a user must run a setup program before he or she can use the program for the first time, put it in a batch script and ensure that it runs before the application does.
- **Test, test, test**—Always test the applications with a restricted user account. Testing an application with an administrative account is useful only to ensure that it runs at all. Ninety-nine percent of the users in your environment are not administrators, so don't waste a lot of time testing with an admin account.

Terminal Server Application Support Features

To ensure that the majority of applications will function properly, Terminal Server incorporates a number of application support features that you must understand in order to be an effective application integrator. Before installing any applications, you should have a clear understanding of why these features are required and how you can use them to your advantage.

The User Home Folder

Chapter 1, "Microsoft Windows Terminal Services," talks about the management tools included with Terminal Services, including the special options available for configuring a user's account for operation on a Terminal Server. Active Directory Users and Computers for both Windows 2000 and 2003 provides these features. Figure 21.1 shows the Terminal Services Profile tab for a user's account properties. This is where the user's Terminal Server home and profile folders are defined.

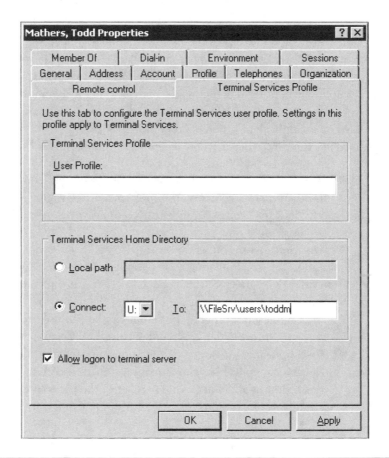

Figure 21.1   Populating the Terminal Services Home Folder field.

The home folder is of particular importance in a Terminal Services environment because it's where the user-specific application and environment data are stored. For example, a Terminal Server uses the home folder to store a *personal* copy of WINI.INI and SYSTEM.INI for each user who may be running a 16-bit application, instead of using the single copy normally found in the %SYSTEMROOT% folder.

The Terminal Server home folder and profile paths are referenced only when a user is logged on to a Terminal Server. When the user is logged on to a non–Terminal Server environment (such as a Windows 2000 or Windows XP Professional desktop), this information is ignored. Figure 21.2 shows the simple process flow used by Terminal Server to determine where the user's home folder is located.

If a Terminal Server home folder has been defined, it's used. If not, and a regular Windows home folder has been defined, that's used instead. If neither has been defined, Terminal Server defaults to using the user's local profile path:

%SystemDrive%\Documents and Settings\%Username%

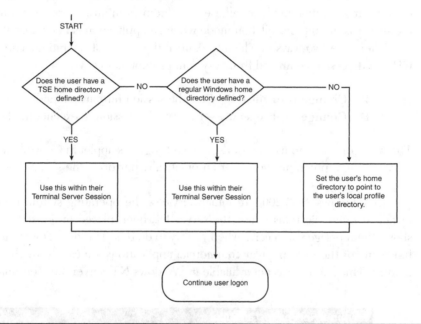

Figure 21.2   The process flow for determining the home folder path to use in a Terminal Services session.

You can view the current location of a user's home folder simply by opening a command prompt from within the session and running SET to view the current environment variables. The variables to look for are HOMEDRIVE, HOMEPATH, and HOMESHARE. Assuming that the share point is \\FileSrv\Users, a sample output of SET would look something like this:

```
HOMEDRIVE=U:
HOMEPATH=\
HOMESHARE=\\FileSrv\Users\twmathers
```

NOTE: Though I use the drive letter U: in my discussion of the home folder, you can use any drive letter you wish when defining the home folder of a user's account. Many environments I have worked with use the drive letter H:.

Installation and Execution Modes

Another application integration feature available with Terminal Server is having two special modes of operation: execution mode and installation mode. By default, the Terminal Server operates in execution mode for all users, including administrators. As you may have guessed, the server is put into installation mode when an application is being installed on the server.

There are two ways in which to control the mode of operation. The first is to use the CHANGE USER command from a system prompt as follows:

- **Change user /install**—Puts the session into install mode.
- **Change user /execute**—Returns the session to execute mode.

The other option is to use the Add/Remove Programs applet in Control Panel. When adding or removing a program, the server automatically performs the switch between execute and install modes.

In Windows 2003/2000 Terminal Services, the operating system itself doesn't let you install many applications unless the server has been placed into install mode. Figure 21.3 shows the message you receive when you try to do this. This doesn't work for all applications, but many of the most popular commercial applications are caught by this operating system feature. This feature was not available in Windows NT Server 4.0, Terminal Server Edition.

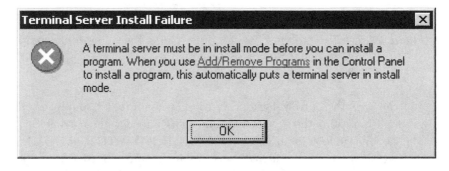

Figure 21.3 The warning message displayed on a Windows 2003 or Windows 2000 Terminal Server when you attempt to install an application while in execute mode.

Installation Mode Behavior

When the server is placed into installation mode, it performs the following tasks during an application installation:

- All registry entries created under HKEY_CURRENT_USER using the standard Windows APIs are copied into this registry key:
  HKLM\Software\Microsoft\Windows NT\CurrentVersion\
  Terminal Server\Install\Software
- Any changes to INI files are written to the appropriate INI in the %systemroot% directory.
- The times that the registry and files were last updated while in install mode are stored under this key:
  HKLM\Software\Microsoft\Windows NT\CurrentVersion\
  Terminal Server\Install\IniFile Times

NOTE: The key point to remember is that the Terminal Server captures changes made to the registry or INI files only if they have been made using the standard Windows API functions. Registry changes made using REGEDT32 while Terminal Server is in install mode are not captured and recorded under the Terminal Server registry key.

Execute Mode Behavior

When the Terminal Server is running in execution mode, the following may occur:

- If an application attempts to read an entry from HKEY_CURRENT_USER that doesn't exist, Terminal Server checks to see if a copy of the key exists under this registry entry:
  HKLM\Software\Microsoft\Windows NT\CurrentVersion\
  Terminal Server\Install\Software
  If it *does* exist, this key and all subkeys are copied to the corresponding area location under HKEY_CURRENT_USER.
- If an application tries to read from an INI file in the %SystemRoot% folder, Terminal Server transparently redirects the request to look in the user's personal Windows directory located under his or her home drive (for example, W:\Windows). If the INI file doesn't exist in the user's folder but does exist in %SystemRoot%, Terminal Server copies it into the user's Windows folder.
- Whenever a user logs on to the server, Terminal Server compares the last update time of the registry keys in Terminal Server\Install and the INI files with the user's last synchronization time. The user's registry synch time is stored in the value LastUserIniSyncTime in this registry key:

  HKCU\Software\Microsoft\CurrentVersion\Terminal Server

The synch times for the INI files are stored in the file INIFILE.UPD, located in the user's personal Windows folder on his or her home drive.

If any entries are out of date, they're updated for the user. By default, any out-of-date registry keys are deleted before the new registry keys are loaded into the current user's registry. The changes in the INI files are either merged with the existing ones or completely replaced. The default is to replace them. I talk about modifying the default behavior for both registry and INI files in the section "Program Compatibility Flags." The previous version of the INI file is renamed with the .CTX extension.

TIP: You can force an update of all existing INI files by deleting the INIFILE.UPD file from the user's Windows folder.

Exploiting the Installation Mode Behavior

Once you understand the behavior of a Terminal Server when operating in install mode, you can exploit this behavior to help preconfigure many applications with common settings that you want to have automatically picked up by the user the first time he or she runs the application. Install mode is not simply for performing the initial installation of the application. It can be used at any time to change configuration of many 32-bit or 16-bit applications. For example, you could run a Microsoft Office application such as Word while in install mode to set any defaults you want the users to have, such as turning off animation or modifying the default folder locations. This is an effective alternative to using the Office profile (.OPS) files.

NOTE: If you want to configure an application with a setting that you don't want your users to be able to modify afterward, you should investigate whether the application supports use of group policy objects (GPOs) in the active directory. For example, Microsoft Office XP and Office 2003 both support custom GPO templates that can be found in their respective Office Resource Kits. Whenever GPOs are available, I suggest using a GPO to configure an application, because it then can be locked down in most cases so the user is forced to run in a particular configuration.

The one caveat worth repeating is that changes are captured while in install mode only if the application is using standard Windows API calls to perform the registry/INI file updates. If an application directly manipulates an INI file through file system read and write operations, Terminal Server is not aware that the changes have occurred and does not update the last-modified date in the registry. This prevents the changes from being incorporated into an existing INI file in the user's home directory. Note that if the user didn't already have the INI file, it would still be copied to his or her home directory, even if the last update time had not been updated.

Program Compatibility Flags

Terminal Server provides the ability to modify the behavior of specific applications as well as the registry and INI file mappings that I discussed in the preceding section. This is done through use of program compatibility flags (PCFs). PCFs are a special set of registry values that tell Terminal Server what to do with a specific program, registry key, or INI file. These three registry keys are located under this key:

HKLM\Software\Microsoft\Windows NT\CurrentVersion\
Terminal Server\Compatibility

These are the specific keys:

- **Applications**—This key contains a list of subkeys corresponding to executable names, each containing specific values that dictate how the application should be handled when run. For example, the subkey EXCEL would contain options specific to EXCEL.EXE.
- **IniFiles**—This key contains a list of values, each corresponding to an INI file name in the %SystemRoot% folder. Each has an associated flag that determines how file replication should be handled. There are two entries by default: one for SYSTEM.INI and another for WINI.INI. The .INI extension is not included in the value name.
- **Registry entries**—This key contains a list of values corresponding to registry keys located under HKLM\Software. The value of each entry determines how registry replication is handled while the Terminal Server is in execute mode. Three entries usually exist: Classes, Microsoft\Windows NT, and Microsoft\Windows\CurrentVersion\Explorer\Shell Folders.

Depending on the key, certain compatibility flags are available to use in modifying the entries' behavior. All PCFs are REG_DWORD hexadecimal entries. If multiple entries are set for a particular value, you need to sum the individual hex values to determine the actual hex number to enter. If you're uncomfortable with performing hexadecimal arithmetic, use the Calculator application to perform hex calculations in scientific mode.

IniFiles and Registry Entries Registry Keys

Table 21.1 lists the valid flags for the IniFiles and registry entries keys.

Table 21.1 INI and Registry Compatibility Flags

Flag	Valid For	Action
0x00000004	INI files	Flags a 16-bit Windows app.
0x00000008	Registry entries	Flags a 32-bit Windows app.
0x00000040	INI files and registry entries	Synchronizes values to system version. For INI files this means that new entries from the system version of the INI file are merged with the user's version. Normally the user's version is deleted and replaced with the system version.
		For registry entries this flag means that new keys and values from the system registry are added, but existing keys and values are not deleted. The default is to delete any keys and values out of date with the system version.
0x00000080	INI files only	Do not substitute user's Windows directory for system directory. This means that the user's personal Windows directory is not substituted, and the %SystemRoot% directory is used instead.
0x00000100	Registry entries only	Disable registry mapping for the given key. This automatically includes all subkeys.

Multiple flags can be entered for a single value by summing them (in hex) to get the final flag value. The IniFiles folder on the Terminal Server contains the following two entries:

```
SYSTEM:REG_DWORD:0x44
WIN:REG_DWORD:0x44
```

As noted in Table 21.1, INI synchronization is on for the 16-bit files SYSTEM.INI and WIN.INI. Any changes made while you are in install mode are merged with any existing information in the user's SYSTEM.INI or WIN.INI. All other INI files are replaced.

Under the Registry Keys key is the following entry:

```
Microsoft\Windows NT:REG_DWORD:0x108
```

Referring again to Table 21.1, notice that registry mapping has been disabled for the 32-bit Windows NT key.

NOTE: Typically, you won't need to modify any of these entries. However, if there's a particular registry key or INI file that you don't want users to have in their personal area (registry or Windows folder), you can exclude it from synchronization. Default Permissions on the Windows folder prevents users from modifying the system version.

Application Registry Key

For a specific application, up to four registry values can be created that control the application's behavior while running on Terminal Server. Figure 21.4 shows the registry entries for the Microsoft Access application (MSACCESS.EXE). Notice that the .EXE extension is not included in the key name.

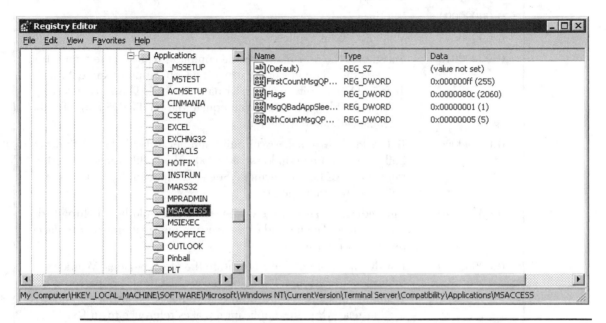

Figure 21.4   Program compatibility flags for Microsoft Access.

As the figure shows, there are four registry values for MSACCESS:

- FirstCountMsgQPeeksSleepBadApp
- MsgQBadAppSleepTimeInMillisec
- NthCountMsgQPeeksSleepBadApp
- Flags

The first three entries are used to tune an application to function optimally on Terminal Server. You shouldn't modify or set any of these values for an application unless you're experiencing a real performance issue. I talk more about these settings a little later in this section.

The fourth entry is the Flags value. It contains a hex value that provides Terminal Server with information about the application and indicates whether any special actions are required, such as disabling registry mapping. Table 21.2 lists the entries for the Flags value. As with the INI and registry settings, multiple values are set simply by summing the hex values to come up with the new hex value. For example, if you want to flag that the entry is for both the 16-bit and 32-bit applications, you sum 0x04 and 0x08, resulting in 0x0c in hex.

Table 21.2 Valid Flag Settings for an Application

Flag	Description
0x00000001	DOS application.
0x00000002	OS/2 application.
0x00000004	Windows 16-bit application.
0x00000008	Windows 32-bit application.
0x00000010	Substitutes the user name for the computer name. If the application requests the computer name using the GetComputerName API, Terminal Server returns the user name instead. This setting is typically used with applications that equate the NETBIOS name for the machine with an individual user.
0x00000020	Returns the Terminal Server build number instead of the Windows build number. For Windows 2003/2000, the build numbers are the same. On TSE4.0 the Terminal Server component has a different build number than the OS.
0x00000040	This indicates that INI file or registry data should be synchronized with any new data instead of the existing information being replaced by the new information.
0x00000080	For this application, don't substitute the user's personal Windows folder for the system folder. This means that the user's personal Windows folder is not substituted, and the %SystemRoot% folder is used instead when this application makes reference to an INI file.
0x00000100	Disables registry mapping for this application.
0x00000200	Enables per-object mapping for user and system global objects associated with this application.
0x00000400	Returns the %SystemRoot% folder to the application instead of the user's personal Windows directory. This overrides the server's default behavior when running in execute mode. This applies only to the specific application.
0x00000800	Limits the physical memory reported to the application. This flag is typically used when an application has problems running on a system with a large amount of physical memory. When specified, the default memory reported is 32MB. You can modify this value by including the PhysicalMemoryLimit value in the program compatibility key. This value should also be of type REG_DWORD.

Table 21.2   Valid Flag Settings for an Application (continued)

Flag	Description
0x00001000	Logs creation of named objects by the specified application. This flag is used to assist in debugging an application not running properly on Terminal Server. Normally, when an application runs, objects are created within the user's name space by appending the session ID to the object name. This can cause certain applications that expect to find a fixed object name to fail. Using the REGISTER command, you can tell the Windows Object Manager to not append the session ID to an object created by a specified DLL or EXE. Using this flag you can generate a list of the objects created by an application along with the associated DLL. From this, you can get a list of the DLLs that must be registered.
	For the logging to take place, you must create a system environment variable called CITRIX_COMPAT_LOGPATH and assign it a valid directory where the log will be created. The logfile "<app name>.log" will be created in the specified location.
	This flag should be set only while debugging because it will degrade the application's performance.
	For more information on the REGISTER command, see Appendix A, "Terminal Services Command Reference."
0x20000000	Indicates that the application should not be put to sleep when it polls the keyboard unsuccessfully. This option should normally not be set because it can cause significant performance degradation.

Notice in Figure 21.4 that the value for the Flags entry is 0x80c. Consulting Table 21.2, this equates to the following:

- For both 16-bit (0x008) and 32-bit (0x004) applications we get the following summed flag values: 0x008 + 0x004 = 0x00c
- Limiting the physical memory reported has the flag value 0x800.
- For both 16-bit and 32-bit applications: 0x008 + 0x004 = 0x00c.
- This value limits the physical memory reported (0x800).

This is easily validated by adding the results to get 0x80c.

Now that you're familiar with the various flags available for an application, the next thing to look at is the settings used for tuning a "badly behaved" application.

A "bad" application can exhibit unusually high or low processor utilization. If an application is run on a Terminal Server and a corresponding key does not exist for it under the Compatibility\Applications registry, it is automatically throttled by Terminal Server if it queries the message queue too often within a default time period. The result is an application that runs very slowly even though the system resource utilization (such as CPU and disk) is low. Software installation programs commonly fall into this category. A common solution is to add a registry key corresponding to the application's executable name with values that correspond to the MSACCESS key. The descriptions for these registry values are as follows:

- **FirstCountMsgQPeeksSleepBadApp**—This represents the number of times the application can query the message queue before Terminal Server initially flags it as "bad." Lowering this value causes the application to be flagged more quickly, decreasing its processor utilization.
- **MsgQBadAppSleepTimeInMillisec**—Once Terminal Server has decided that an application is "bad," this is the number of milliseconds that the application must "sleep" before it can query the message queue again. Increasing this value forces the application to sleep longer.
- **NthCountMsgQPeeksSleepBadApp**—Once Terminal Serer has flagged an application as "bad," this is the number of times the application can query the message queue before it is once again put to sleep. Typically, this value is less than the FirstCountMsgQPeeksSleepBadApp value.

Looking again at Figure 21.6 for the MSACCESS entry, the values for the three settings are as follows:

FirstCountMsgQPeeksSleepBadApp = 0xff (255 decimal)

MsgQBadAppSleepTimeInMillisec = 0x1 (1 decimal)

NthCountMsgQPeeksSleepBadApp = 0x5 (5 decimal)

So after 255 consecutive queries of the message queue, Access is put to sleep for one millisecond, and thereafter for every 5 queries.

NOTE: These tuning values apply only to 16-bit or 32-bit Windows applications. If they're set for a DOS application, they're simply ignored. No native Windows mechanism ships with Windows 2003 or Windows 2000 to tune a DOS application. Those of you familiar with using the DOSKBD command from NT 4.0, Terminal Server Edition, will find that this tool is no longer available with Windows 2003/2000 Terminal Services.

As mentioned, you shouldn't create or modify any of these program compatibility flags unless you have an application that's behaving "badly." If the application is running unusually slowly, even though the system utilization is low, then add an entry and assign values equal to those for the MSACCESS key. If an application exhibits unusually high processor utilization, I recommend performing the following steps to tune the application:

1. Launch PerfMon and monitor CPU utilization.
2. Start the offending application and record the baseline performance while running the application. Ideally, you should run it for 5 to 10 minutes or longer.

3. Exit the application and create the corresponding entry or entries in the registry under the Applications key. You can either type the entries or save the Setup key and then add it back in with the name of your application. The default values for Setup are as follows:

> FirstCountMsgQPeeksSleepBadApp = 0xf (15 decimal)
>
> MsgQBadAppSleepTimeInMillisec = 0x1 (1 decimal)
>
> NthCountMsgQPeeksSleepBadApp = 0x5 (5 decimal)
>
> Flags = 0xc (16-bit or 32-bit)

4. Rerun the application and compare the new PerfMon results with the baseline.
5. Exit the application and change the application settings to something like this:

> FirstCountMsgQPeeksSleepBadApp = 0xf (15 decimal)
>
> MsgQBadAppSleepTimeInMillisec = 0x64 (100 decimal)
>
> NthCountMsgQPeeksSleepBadApp = 0x5 (5 decimal)

6. Run the application again and compare the reduction in processor utilization to the responsiveness of the application. You may want to compare this to adjustments in the FirstCount value to see if one provides a larger improvement over the other. Unfortunately, this is not an exact science, so it might take some time to develop the ideal tuning values for a particular application. You'll likely have to settle for some excess utilization to ensure that the program is responsive enough that users will be able to use it.

Luckily, additional tuning isn't usually required with most applications that run on Terminal Server.

NOTE: Be careful with applications that are CPU-intensive. Many of these applications, even with use of program compatibility flags, are simply poor candidates for a Terminal Server environment. Compatibility flags won't always rein in a poorly behaved application.

Temporary Folders

The next application support feature I look at is Terminal Server's handling of each individual user's temporary folder location. Normally, every user who logs on to a Windows computer has a temporary directory defined with the environment variables TEMP and TMP, where temporary data can be stored that can be deleted when the user logs off.

The only difference on a Terminal Server is that multiple temporary folders exist at the same time and must be managed individually. The default temporary folder location for all users is the %UserProfile%\Temp folder. From Control Panel, open the system properties.

Select Advanced and then click the Environment Variables button to display the TEMP and TMP values set in the user variables (see Figure 21.5).

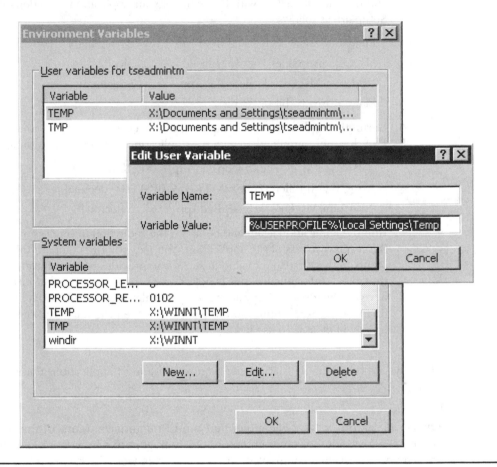

Figure 21.5   The default temporary folder settings on Windows 2003 Terminal Services.

To give multiple simultaneous users access to the temporary folder, Terminal Server provides a feature known as *per-session temporary folders*. Every time a user logs on, Terminal Server creates a subfolder corresponding to the user's session number underneath the TEMP folder. The user's TMP and TEMP variables are then updated automatically to point to this location. If you open a command prompt and type "SET", you see the modified values for these environment variables. For example, you might see this:

TEMP=C:\DOCUME~1\ADMINI~1\LOCALS~1\Temp\a5
TMP=C:\DOCUME~1\ADMINI~1\LOCALS~1\Temp\a5

The subfolder "a5" corresponds to the current session number, and the short name (eight-character maximum) is used to ensure that DOS and Win16 applications can use the same environment variable. If these were my temp folders and I did a QUSER from a command prompt, I would see something like this:

```
USERNAME        SESSIONNAME       ID   STATE     IDLE TIME    LOGON TIME
 nsamble        ica-tcp#390      143   Active        .        8/2/2004  9:47  AM
 jhayman        ica-tcp#391      148   Active        .        8/2/2004  9:49  AM
>twmathers      ica-tcp#392      165   Active        .        8/2/2004  9:50  AM
 gott           ica-tcp#393      169   Active        4        8/2/2004  9:53  AM
 bsmith         ica-tcp#394      170   Active        .        8/2/2004  9:59  AM
```

The hexadecimal number a5 in base-ten notation is 165, which corresponds to my session ID, not the session name shown in the list above.

The permissions set on the folder are set to allow access only by the specified user and SYSTEM. When the user logs off, Terminal Server automatically deletes the associated temporary folder.

Whenever you reference a user's temporary folder, be sure to use the TEMP or TMP environment variables. Never hard-code the complete path because it's very likely that the next time the user logs on, he or she will have a different temp folder.

The temporary folder mapping feature can be disabled using the FLATTEMP command or through Terminal Services configuration. When this feature is disabled, the special subfolder is not automatically created and the contents of the user's TEMP folder are not automatically deleted when the user logs off. I do not recommend disabling this feature.

Legacy Support Features

In order to ensure a smooth upgrade path from Windows NT 4.0, Terminal Server Edition (TSE) and Windows 2000 Terminal Services to Windows Server 2003 Terminal Services, certain legacy application support features had to be retained and supported. These are root drive mapping support and application compatibility scripts, both of which were well-used in the majority of the TSE implementations, saw diminished use in Windows 2000, and now are, for the most part, relegated to backwards compatibility status in a Windows Server 2003 environment.

While neither one of these features are necessary for the majority of new Windows 2000 or 2003 implementations, if you are tasked with supporting an environment that was upgraded from TSE, or are involved in a project to migrate an existing TSE environment, then I feel that it is important to have a clear understanding of how these two support features function so that you will better understand the roles that they serve and what requirements must be considered when migrating or supporting such an infrastructure.

NOTE: Those of you who are performing a clean Windows Server 2003 Terminal Server implementation and are not upgrading from an existing Windows NT 4.0, Terminal Server Edition or Windows 2000 Terminal Server environment should not be considering utilizing either of these legacy support features. Improved application support and Windows functionality negates the need for either feature except in the most limited of situations.

Root Drive Mapping

The first legacy support feature that we will look at is the Root Drive Mapping feature. If you have worked with Windows NT 4.0, Terminal Server Edition (TSE), or a Windows 2000 Terminal Services environment upgraded from NT 4.0 TSE, you likely are familiar with the Root Drive Mapping feature. If you are inheriting or planning on upgrading an existing TSE environment, you need to clearly understand this feature in order to plan your migration appropriately. This was one of the most common areas of confusion for administrators of an NT 4.0 TSE environment, and for those who need to work with it today, it seems to remain a bit of a mystery. To better understand how this feature works, it helps to understand why this functionality was created in the first place. A good place to start is with a simple example that demonstrates the underlying issue that existed in an NT 4.0 Terminal server environment.

TIP: Root drive mapping support exists in Windows 2000 Server and Windows Server 2003 in order to provide backwards compatibility for direct upgrades from NT 4.0, Terminal Server Edition to Windows 2000/2003. The root drive mapping is *not* intended for use in clean Windows 2000 or 2003 Terminal Server implementation. If you are considering using this feature in your new implementation, or it has been recommended to you by someone else, then I greatly encourage you to carefully review this section before make a decision.

If we refer to the example in the previous section of running the SET command, we have the following information returned from a Windows 2003/2000 Terminal Server.

```
HOMEDRIVE=U:
HOMEPATH=\
HOMESHARE=\\FileSrv\Users\twmathers
```

If the same SET command was run on an NT 4.0 Terminal Server, the results would appear slightly differently:

```
HOMEDRIVE=U:
HOMEPATH=\twmathers
```

The difference is that the HOMEPATH on Windows 2003/2000 is simply the root (\), while on NT 4.0 it's the path from the share point into the specific folder (\twmathers). This is because Windows 2003/2000 support a feature commonly called *map root*, which lets you map a drive letter to a specific folder located *below* a defined share point. This feature was not supported in NT 4.0. NT 4.0 would allow you to map a drive letter only to an explicitly defined share point.

So, on Windows 2003/2000, if I went to the U:\ location, I would still be within my personal home folder (\\FileSrv\Users\twmathers), but if I went to the same location on NT 4.0, I would actually be one folder above my home folder, in the root of the share (\\FileSrv\Users). Although the default file system security would prevent me from accessing any other user's home folder, I would still be able to generate a list of all of the other users. The shortcomings of not supporting the map root feature are personified when coupled with the multiuser Terminal Server environment.

Consider the following example:

> I'm installing an application on TSE 4.0. During the installation, the setup program asks me to provide a working folder where user information will be stored. What directory should I specify? Of course, I want to use the user's home folder. But how do I tell the installation program where this is, since I need the folder to change depending on the individual user? Ideally, I'd like to provide U:\%Username%, but most applications don't do variable expansion. Since TSE 4.0 doesn't support the map root feature, I don't have an easy solution to this problem.

> A common application that suits this example is Microsoft Word. Word lets you define custom folder locations where certain files are stored. For example, the default location for newly created documents or the location for personal template files can be defined within the Options dialog box for Word. The ability to use a constant drive letter would greatly simplify this configuration.

Microsoft's solution to this problem was to create a new drive mapping definition specific to Terminal Server called the *root drive* (this is not the same as %systemroot%), the purpose of which was to provide a means of defining a consistent drive letter that pointed directly to the user's home folder, regardless of what the user's home drive letter actually was and where their HOMEPATH was defined to be. Be aware that while the Terminal Server root drive is most often designated as W:, it can be assigned to any available drive letter.

TIP: Confusion can arise when a distinction is not made between *root drive* and the server's %SystemRoot%. Root drive mapping is not the same as %SystemRoot%. Root drive mapping points to the user's home directory, while %SystemRoot% points to the main Windows operating system folder.

The root drive normally is not defined until the first time an application compatibility script is run(discussed in the next section). You can create the root drive immediately by running this batch script:

```
%SystemRoot%\Application Compatibility Scripts\chkroot.cmd
```

When the script is run, Notepad opens, as shown in Figure 21.3. The root drive letter is set simply by entering the letter and colon immediately after the equal sign (=) and then saving and exiting the batch script. For example, if you want to use W:,as the Root drive then you would enter this:

```
Set RootDrive=W:
```

Once set, whenever a user logs onto the MetaFrame server, the user's home folder is automatically mapped to the root drive using the standard DOS command SUBST. For example, if my home directory was currently U:\users\twmathers, the SUBST command would be as follows:

```
Subst W: U:\users\twmathers
```

If the root drive letter ever needed to be changed, the only thing that had to be done was to edit this entry to contain the new drive letter to be used.

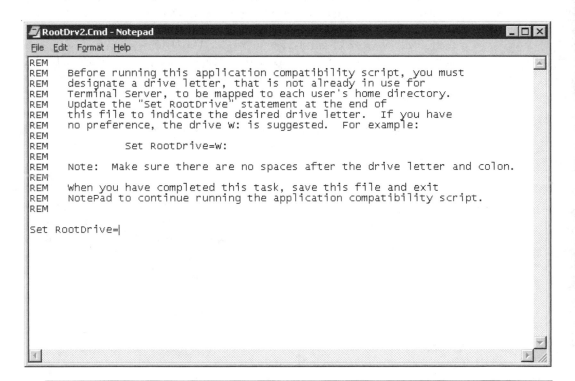

Figure 21.6 The root drive letter is entered and saved after running the chkroot.cmd batch file.

The actual drive letter substitution is done in the USRLOGON.CMD compatibility script. This script is automatically run for each user every time the user logs on to Terminal Server.

It appears momentarily as a minimized DOS window before the logon completes. I discuss application compatibility scripts in the next section.

As I mentioned at the beginning of this section, the root drive feature has been maintained in both Windows 2000 Server and Windows Server 2003 in order to ensure a smooth upgrade path from Windows NT 4.0, Terminal Server Edition. The usefulness of the root drive is really quite limited, considering that both Windows 2000 Server and Windows Server 2003 support the map root functionality, which was the limitation in TSE 4.0 that the root drive was created to overcome.

NOTE: When creating a new Windows 2000 or Windows Server 2003 Terminal Server you do not need to enable the root drive feature.

Application Compatibility Scripts

To help resolve issues that applications might have when trying to run on Terminal Server, particularly an NT 4.0 Terminal Server, Microsoft developed an intricate group of batch scripts called *application compatibility scripts* (ACSs). These scripts are used to perform any necessary file and registry modifications in order to allow an application to function properly on Terminal Server.

NOTE: The need to create and use application compatibility scripts has continued to diminish as the number of applications that recognize and support Terminal Services has increased. Many of the most popular products on the market today such as the Microsoft Office product suite will install and function with little or no issues.

Most often, the exceptions to this rule involve custom-developed or very specific vertical market software that changes very slowly over time and is developed for very specific industries. These types of applications may require some form of scripting to resolve the issues and so may still depend on application compatibility scripts.

Most of the files that collectively make up the ACS are located in the folder %SystemRoot%\Application Compatibility Scripts. The main batch script, which is called by every user who logs on to Terminal Server (whether remotely or from the console), is located in the System32 folder and is called USRLOGON.CMD.

The ACS has three main functions:

- **Configure the environment**—This includes defining the root drive (as described in the previous section), as well as setting any other environment variables that may be used in the compatibility scripts. The root drive feature does not have to be enabled in order to use application compatibility scripts.

■ **Run scripts immediately after an application has been installed**—These scripts run once in order to perform post-installation changes that must be made to an application. While all installation scripts do not require it, I recommend that you always have the server in install mode (discussed in the next section) prior to running an installation ACS. These scripts are located in the INSTALL subfolder under the ACS folder.

■ **Run scripts during a user's logon**—These scripts need to be run every time a user logs on in order to ensure that the necessary file and registry changes have been made to support any applications the user might run. Logon ACSs are located in the Logon subfolder, also under the ACS folder. One common use for these types of scripts is to copy a required file into a user's personal folder if it does not already exist so that the user is able to run an application properly.

TIP: The USRLOGON.CMD script that is invoked during every user's logon is launched from the AppSetup value located under this registry key:

HKLM\Software\Microsoft\Windows NT\CurrentVersion\Winlogon

Entries in this value are run during every user's logon. If you want to completely disable use of application compatibility scripts, you need only remove the USRLOGON.CMD entry from this registry value.

Typically, application compatibility scripts are invoked by an administrator the first time an application is installed on the Terminal Server. Not all applications require compatibility scripts, and Microsoft provides only a limited set of scripts for those that do. In certain situations, you may need to define your own compatibility scripts; I provide an example of how this can be done in the "Application Installation Examples" section of this chapter. Before you can develop your own scripts, you need a clear understanding of how the ACS environment operates, and you must know the exact functions of the files that comprise the ACS. Table 21.3 lists and describes the main scripts that make up the ACS environment. The scripts are identical on both Windows 2003 and Windows 2000.

Table 21.3 Components of Application Compatibility Scripts

Script Name	Location Under %SystemRoot%	Description
Usrlogon.cmd	System32	Called during every user's logon and by the ChkRoot script. It's responsible for calling all the other required scripts. It also performs the SUBST command to map the root drive.

Table 21.3   Components of Application Compatibility Scripts (continued)

Script Name	Location Under %SystemRoot%	Description
Usrlogn1.cmd	System32	Called by UsrLogon.cmd.Initially, this file doesn't exist. When it does exist (either by running a compatibility script or manually created), it contains calls to only those compatibility scripts that do not require the root drive to be defined.
Usrlogn2.cmd	System32	Called by UsrLogon.cmd. Initially, this file doesn't exist. When it does exist, it contains calls to any compatibility scripts that do require the root drive to be defined.
SetPaths.cmd	Application Compatibility Scripts	Called by UsrLogon.cmd. This script de-fines a number of environment variables used during running of the ACSs, such as the common and per-user startup folder locations.
RootDrv.cmd	Application Compatibility Scripts	Called by UsrLogon.cmd. This script simply calls RootDrv2.cmd if it exists.
RootDrv2.cmd	Application Compatibility Scripts	Called by RootDrv.cmd. This script sets the environment variable %RootDrive% to the desired drive letter so UsrLogon.cmd can perform the proper substitution. RootDrv2.cmd is created by the ChkRoot.cmd script.
ChkRoot.cmd	Application Compatibility Scripts	Called by the various application compatibility scripts to verify that the root drive has been set. If it hasn't been set, this creates the RootDrv2.cmd file and prompts the user to specify the drive letter to use as the root drive.
End.cmd	Application Compatibility Scripts	Called by UsrLogon.cmd. This script performs no function. It simply sets @ECHO OFF.

Terminal Server also comes with a set of three "helper" executables used by the compatibility scripts to retrieve and update registry and file information. These helper application names all begin with the *AC* (application compatibility) prefix. The helper applications are as follows:

- **ACINIUPD.EXE**—This tool is used to update INI files. Its usage is as follows:

```
Aciniupd.exe [/e] [/k] [/u] [/v] <ini filename> <section
name> <key name> <new value>
```

/e tells ACINIUPD to update the value for the given section and key name. An existing value is replaced by the new value given.

/k tells the tool to update the given key name in the section with the name specified in <new value>. This replaces the key name, not the key's value.

/u signals the tool to update the INI file in the user's Windows directory instead of in %SystemRoot%.

/v means to run in verbose mode. The default is to run silently.

- **ACREGL.EXE**—This utility searches the registry for the provided key and value and outputs them to a file as a SET statement with the provided environment variable name. This is primarily used to retrieve specific information from the registry and make it available as an environment variable that can then be used by the compatibility scripts. Its usage is as follows:

```
Acregl.exe <output filename> <set variable name> <registry
key> <registry value> <options>
```

The registry key must start with either HKCU (HKEY_CURRENT_USER) or HKLM (HKEY_LOCAL_MACHINE) and must be enclosed in a string, such as "HKLM\Software\Microsoft".

The <options> value can be an empty string (""), STRIPCHAR*cn*, or STRIPPATH. STRIPCHAR*cn*, starting from the right side of the string, strips *n* instances of the character *c*. Anything to the right of *c* is dropped. STRIPPATH removes the full path from a file name, so X:\Windows\System32\ UserLogon.cmd would become simply UserLogon.cmd.

- **ACSR.EXE**—This tool performs search-and-replace on the given input file, sending the results to the provided output file. The syntax is simple:

```
Acsr.exe <search string> <replace string> <input file> <output
file>
```

Every occurrence of <search string> is replaced with the <replace string> value and saved to the <output file> location.

NOTE: I've included the information regarding these helper programs more as a guide to reviewing the existing compatibility scripts than as a primer for using them to create your own scripts.

I prefer to use a scripting language such as VBScript or JavaScript when writing custom compatibility scripts. This allows much more flexibility and control over exactly what's happening than using these fairly limited tools.

Even with a list of all the components that make up the ACS, it's not necessarily clear how these pieces fit together. The flowchart in Figure 21.7 summarizes how the different application compatibility scripts interact from the main script, UsrLogon.cmd.

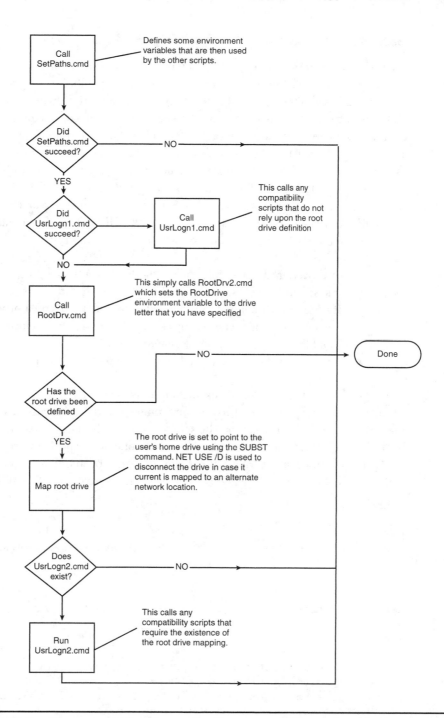

Figure 21.7 The process flow for application compatibility scripts during user logon.

Sample Application Compatibility Scripts

Each release of Terminal Server has included a number of application compatibility scripts created by Microsoft to assist in the installation and operation of applications on Terminal Server. Windows 2000 Server includes 31 compatibility scripts, while Windows Server 2003 includes only 3. When Windows 2000 Server was released, compatibility scripts were created for a number of legacy applications including Office 4.3 and Netscape Navigator 3.x. These applications had never been designed with the idea of a multi-user environment such as Terminal Services in mind, so some rather intricate scripting had to be done in order to enable these applications to function. Many of the scripts found in Windows 2000 were direct ports from scripts found in Windows NT Server 4.0, Terminal Server Edition.

With the release of Windows Server 2003, all of these legacy compatibility scripts were thankfully omitted with the exception of only 3. These 3 scripts are:

- **eudora4.cmd**—A script to allow the Eudora 4.0 mail program to function.
- **msvs6.cmd**—This script allows Visual Studio 6.0 to run on a Terminal Server. It is not recommended to run any development tools on a production Terminal Server, but certain circumstances may dictate that a development environment should run on a test or development server.
- **outlk98.cmd**—A script to allow Outlook 98 to function on Terminal Services.

A small portion of the Outlook 98 installation script is shown below. You will notice is that this script makes use of the %rootdrive% environment variable discussed in the "Root Drive Mapping" section of this chapter. The script begins by checking to see that %rootdrive% has been defined. This is done by calling the ChkRoot.cmd script. If the script fails, this script simply exits without any warning. If the root drive has been defined, the script next verifies that Outlook 98 has been installed by searching the registry using the ACRegL utility.

```
@Echo Off

Rem
###################################################################
#

Rem
Rem Verify that %RootDrive% has been configured and set it for this
script.
Rem

Call "%SystemRoot%\Application Compatibility Scripts\ChkRoot.Cmd"
If "%_CHKROOT%" == "FAIL" Goto Done
Call "%SystemRoot%\Application Compatibility Scripts\SetPaths.Cmd"
If "%_SETPATHS%" == "FAIL" Goto Done
```

```
Rem
####################################################################
#

Rem
Rem Get the installation location of Outlook 98 from the registry.
If
Rem not found, assume Outlook isn't installed and display an error
message.
Rem

..\ACRegL %Temp%\O98.Cmd O98INST
"HKLM\Software\Microsoft\Office\8.0\Common\InstallRoot" "OfficeBin"
"Stripchar\1"
If Not ErrorLevel 1 Goto Cont0
Echo.
Echo Unable to retrieve Outlook 98 installation location from the reg-
istry.
Echo Verify that Outlook 98 has already been installed and run this
script
Echo again.
Echo.
Pause
Goto Done
.
.
.


:SkipWarning

Pause

:done
```

Even though this script is dependent on the existence of the root drive, if you find that you must create an application compatibility script for an application that you are deploying, you are not required to enable the root drive feature. Instead I would recommend that you simply reference the proper drive letter that you have defined as the home folder for your Terminal Server users.

There is really no practical reason why the root drive functionality needs to be used in a Windows Server 2003 (or even a Windows 2000) Terminal Server environment.

NOTE: You may have noticed that there is an uninstall folder alongside the install and logon folders in the Application Compatibility Scripts folder. The scripts in this folder are run simply to remove the reference to the corresponding application compatibility script from either the usrlogn1.cmd or the usrlogn2.cmd script. This doesn't actually uninstall the software from the server. You still need to use Add/Remove Programs for this to work properly.

The Application Integrator Toolbox

In order to be an effective application integrator (AI) you need to have the proper tools for the job. While there is no question that a stable and reliable Terminal Server is key to a successful implementation, without the actual applications, the environment is of little use to the end user. Applications deployed on a Terminal Server must run properly, efficiently and reliably. If not, the end user will make their feelings known not only to yourself but most certainly to their superiors. The user's satisfaction is paramount to ensuring that the project is deemed to be a success.

One way to minimize the turnaround time required to resolve application issues is to familiarize yourself with some of the common tools and techniques available. Think of your AI toolbox as a combination of software utilities and a notebook of tips and techniques that can serve as a valuable reference source when dealing with any application issues that may come your way.

The following list summarizes the software utilities and integration techniques that I will discuss in more detail in this section of the chapter.

- **SysInternals RegMon**—Regmon allows you to monitor activity against the registry, providing an invaluable tool in resolving security-related registry issues.
- **SysInternals FileMon**—The sister tool to Regmon, Filemon allows you to monitor activity against the local file system. Security-related issues with the file system are quickly resolved using this tool.
- **Microsoft Windows Server Resource Kit**—The appropriate server resource kit (Windows Server 2003 or Windows 2000 Server) should be a staple of any Windows administrator's toolbox. The resource kit contains a wide assortment of tools developed by Microsoft and its partners to assist an administrator in a number of different tasks.
- **Microsoft Office Resource Kit**—The Office Resource Kit delivers a similar, Office-specific set of tools for deployment and administration.
- **Windows Scripting**—Having a basic knowledge of programming techniques and specifically, basic Windows scripting is an essential part of an application integrator's suite of talents. The ability to quickly develop simple scripts to assist in the configuration of an application can save hours of support and manual administration time.

In the next few sections of this chapter I will look more closely at each of these areas.

SysInternals Regmon and Filemon Utilities

If I had to choose only one utility to assist in the installation and configuration of applications on a Terminal Server, it would be an extremely difficult decision between these two excellent utilities. When it comes to troubleshooting security-related issues with applications running on a Terminal Server, no other utilities come close to SysInternal's Regmon and Filemon. Best of all, the basic versions of both of these tools are available free from the SysInternals Website (http://wwwsysinternals.com), where besides Regmon and Filemon, a plethora of other tools exist.

No proper installation is required for either product, simply download the appropriate Zip file and extract the single executable into the desired directory. My preference is to save these files into a folder that has been added to the system path so that the files can be launched by opening a command prompt and entering the desired executable name (regmon.exe or filemon.exe). Another option is to create a shortcut on the Windows desktop that points into a folder containing all of the tools that I commonly access. Figure 21.8 shows the main window of the Regmon utility, which is very similar in appearance to the main window of the Filemon utility.

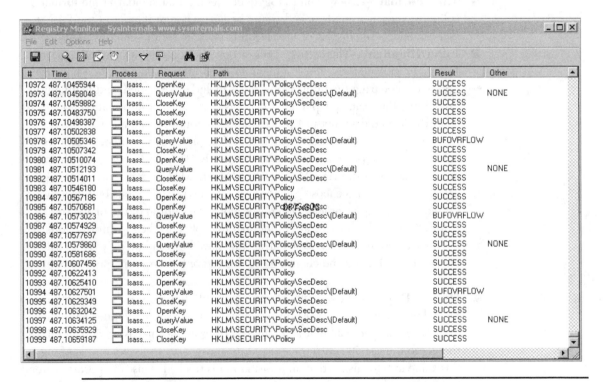

Figure 21.8   The main windows for the Regmon and Filemon utilities are nearly identical.

When either tool is first opened it will immediately begin to log all file or registry access and very quickly tracks thousands of log entries. Sifting through so much log data in an attempt to troubleshoot a problem is neither time-effective nor likely to be very successful.

Sysinternals provides some simple configuration options to help narrow down the scope of information being tracked and displayed. These settings are managed through a combination of toolbar (or hot-key) and menu selections. The options along the toolbar are:

- **Save**—Saves the current log contents to a text file, which can then be viewed using an application such as Excel or loaded back into Regmon or Filemon at a later date.
- **Capture**—Turns logging on and off. Capture defaults to being enabled when Regmon/Filemon is first opened.
- **Autoscroll**—When enabled the display will automatically scroll as new log entries are added, otherwise the display will remain static on the screen.
- **Clear**—Clears the current log display.
- **Time Format** — Allows you to toggle between either standard time format (hh:mm:ss) or in seconds since logging began. When in standard time format you can enable the display of milliseconds from under the Options menu.
- **Filter/Highlight**—This setting dictates how the logged information is filtered. Figure 21.9 shows the Filter/Highlight configuration dialog box. You have the option of specifying the information to be included, excluded, and highlighted. Something that many people don't know is that the filter information applies to all of the logged data, not just process information. For example you could choose to include Winword.°, which would display only information captured by Microsoft Word processes, or you could specify HKLM°, to capture only log data that accesses the HKLM (HKEY_LOCAL_MACHINE) portion of the registry. You can also choose to log only certain types of actions by selecting or deselecting the appropriate checkboxes along the bottom of the dialog box. After clicking OK, changes are immediately applied to the log information.

    You can also filter on specific entries that have been captured by right-clicking on the row in the log and choosing the desired option from the pop-up context menu.
- **History Depth**—The default value for this option is 0 (zero), meaning that all logged information is kept. Entering a value for this setting defines an upper limit on the logged data that is retained. For example, specifying 500 will limit the log to the last 500 entries captured. In most cases I recommend keeping this value at 0 to ensure that all information is tracked. This is important when trying to troubleshoot a problem since you rarely know the bounds that dictate where in the log the information you're looking for may be captured.
- **Find**—Allows you to search the log.
- **Regedit or Explorer Jump**—When a particular row is highlighted in the log, you can click this toolbar button to immediately open Regedit or Explorer and jump to that specific object reference. Double-clicking on a row will perform the equivalent action.

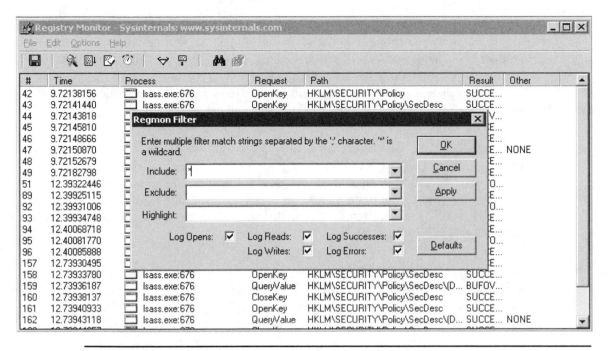

Figure 21.9   The Regmon Filter dialog box.

One option specific to Regmon is the Log Boot setting under the Options menu. When checked, this configure Regmon to log registry access during the system startup. This can provide valuable assistance in troubleshooting a problem during the startup of your Terminal Server.

Filemon also has some settings that are not found in Regmon. The Volume menu option in Filemon allows you to specify what drive volumes are monitored as well as alternate file sources such as mailslots and named pipes.

I will provide an example of the use of Regmon when discussing the installation of Infor Global Solutions' Invue product in the "Application Installation Examples" section of this chapter.

Microsoft Windows Server Resource Kit

Windows 2000 Server and Windows Server 2003 each have their respective set of resource kit tools available for download free from the Microsoft Website (www.microsoft.com). The resource kit tools were developed by Microsoft and their partners to assist in streamlining the support of a Windows server environment. Tools such as Lsview.exe, the Terminal Services License Server Viewer, have been designed specifically for Terminal Server environments, while other tools provide more generic functionality to an administrator.

After downloading the resource kit (or an individual tool), a very simple installation wizard will walk you through the actual installation steps. During installation, unless an alternate installation location is selected, the resource kit tools will go into the folder C:\Program Files\Windows Resource Kits\Tools.

The installation will then automatically update the system path to include a reference to this folder, allowing you or any authorized user the ability to execute a resource kit command from a command prompt without requiring the full path to where the tools reside.

TIP: Instead of allowing all of the resource kit tools to be accessible on a Terminal Server, you may want to consider placing only those executables that you will be implementing into an alternate folder that is referenced in the system path. This can provide a more secure environment by better controlling the tools directly accessible on your servers.

One resource kit tool that I use quite often when creating simple application-related scripts is the IfMember utility, which determines whether the current user is a member of one or more user groups. IfMember is commonly used to direct process flow in a batch script, and can be useful to an application integrator when scripting changes that must be applied to only certain users. The following code sample demonstrates how IfMember might be used to copy a folder of files into a user's personal U: drive, but only if a user belongs to a certain application group ("APPCustService"). Multiple user groups can be listed, allowing for a single test condition to be satisfied by more than one group membership. Multiple groups are separated by a space and logically OR'd together, so one positive membership match will satisfy the ifmember test.

The use of the IfMember utility as part of an application-specific script is also discussed in the "Application Installation Examples" section of this chapter.

```
@echo off
ifmember "APPCustService"
if not errorlevel 1 goto quit
xcopy "S:\CSConfig\*" "U:\CSConfig\." /s /I /R /Y /Z

:quit
```

Microsoft Office Resource Kit

Microsoft also makes available the Office Resource Kit (ORK), a collection of tools designed to aid an administering and deploying Microsoft Office. In particular, there are four components of the ORK that are of particular interest to a Terminal Server application integrator:

■ **Custom Installation Wizard**—This tool allows for the creation of a Microsoft Transform file (MST) that can be used to modify the default installation behavior of Microsoft Office. Options such as the default installation folder, the definition of default application settings or a customized default Outlook profile are just some of the settings that can be configured using this wizard. In order to create the MST file, the Custom Installation Wizard must be able to read the installation MSI file from the Microsoft Office installation media. An MST file viewer is also included in the ORK, allowing you to view the configuration of an existing MST file.

■ **Custom Maintenance Wizard**—The custom installation wizard can only be used to modify the installation behavior of Microsoft Office. It will not modify an existing installation. In order to apply certain changes to an existing installation of Office you need to use the Custom Maintenance Wizard (CMW). The CMW creates a CMW file that is then used to apply changes to a Terminal Server. Just as with the Custom Installation Wizard, the Custom Maintenance Wizard requires the original installation media in order to generate the corresponding CMW file. A CMW file viewer is also included in the ORK.

■ **Office Policy Template Files**—Probably the most important components of the ORK, at least from a Terminal Server application integrator's perspective are the Office Policy Template files. These files allow the AI to define application settings within group policy objects and have them apply to all Office users, in particular, those users running Office on one or more Terminal Servers. Figure 21.10 shows a sample of the configuration options available within these template files. When the Office Policy Template files are selected for installation as part of the ORK setup, they are automatically copied into the %WinDir%\INF folder.

If you wish to place these template files onto a domain controller I would recommend that you do not install the full ORK. Instead, select only the Office Policy Templates option during the installation. This will place the necessary files into the INF folder, where the Group Policy Management tool (or Active Directory Users and Computers) can be used to load the templates and use them in defining group policy objects. Details on the loading of template files and the creation of group policy objects were discussed in Chapter 15, "Group Policy Configuration."

■ **Profile Wizard and Removal Wizard**—The final two wizards included with the ORK are the Profile Wizard, a tool used primarily for capturing and migrating user settings from one computer to another, and the Removal Wizard, which is used to remove previous versions of Microsoft Office tools. The Profile Wizard is rarely used in a Terminal Server environment, but the Removal Wizard can be used if you'd like to ensure a clean removal of previous versions of Office from a Terminal Server.

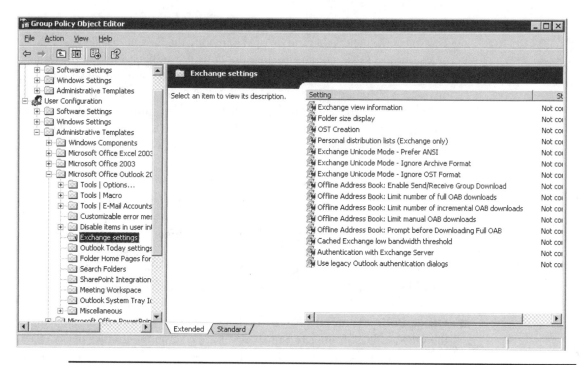

Figure 21.10   The Office administrative template policy files allow group policy objects to be created that contain Microsoft Office settings.

Windows Scripting

I've always felt that one of the most useful skills that an application integrator, (or a Windows administrator in general) can have is the ability to create basic Windows command line scripts. Whether it is copying files to a user's home folder or ensuring a required drive letter is mapped, not being able to automate these tasks with scripting can leave the administrator with few options other than manually making the necessary adjustments for each user or educating the users on how to do it themselves. While this type of solution does work, I find that it is neither very elegant, nor very time (and cost) effective to the user or the administrator.

Repetitive user intervention increases the likelihood of error and a subsequent support call. A basic understanding of scripting does not require an in depth knowledge of application development. A number of resources exist that provide excellent learning tools for those administrators that may need to brush up on their scripting. Many online resources exist including Microsoft's own scripting site, http://www.microsoft.com/script and the excellent scripting community site, the MSN Windows-Script group (http://groups.msn.com/windowsscript). Articles and information can be found to satisfy all skill levels, including webcasts that are put on periodically that are geared specifically to novice scripters.

Many of you will find that you can quickly get up to speed simply by investing a few hours in playing around with some basic scripting in a test environment. Once you understand the basics you will be able to perform many of the tasks commonly relegated to scripts, and you'll wonder how you ever managed to administer an environment without it.

Application Installation Examples

A discussion on application integration would not be complete without some examples of how to install applications on a Terminal Server. In this section I will provide a basic walkthrough on the installation of the following products:

- **Microsoft Office 2003**—I demonstrate the basic steps for installing a typical Windows-compliant application followed by some common configuration changes that can be made for a Terminal Server environment.
- **Invue 4.0**—A legacy application used to interact with a Trend, SHIMS, or WDS-II host system. This application is used to demonstrate some of the common issues encountered when deploying a legacy application in a Terminal Server environment. Some application integration techniques discussed in this section will include using RegMon to resolve a security issue and scripting to deliver personal session files to the application users.
- **Custom client-server application**—The final application is a customer-developed SQL Server application. This application is used to demonstrate the steps commonly involved when deploying an in-house developed application in a Terminal Server environment. We'll look at the application installation and the configuration of a required data source name on the server.

While I cannot hope to cover every scenario that may arise when deploying applications, these three applications do provide a broad summary of the different classification of applications that you're likely to encounter in the role of an application integrator.

Microsoft Office 2003

Since the release of Office 2000, Microsoft's flagship product has natively supported running in a Terminal Services environment, although it is only since Office XP that the product has seamlessly supported installation on a Terminal Server with no special configuration required by an administrator.

NOTE: When Microsoft Office 2000 was released, the default installation included features that were not recommended to run on a Terminal Server. Attempting to run the Setup program included on the installation CD would generate an error message saying that the product could not be installed on Terminal Server without using a special transform file. In order to perform the installation you were required to download the Office 2000 ORK and use the special TermSrv.mst transform file to complete the installation. This transform could be customized using the Office 2000 Custom Installation Wizard. Office XP and Office 2003 do not require such a transform file, although one can be used if you wish to customize the default installation of Office. Details on installing Office 2000 on a Terminal Server can be found in the Microsoft knowledgebase article 283675.

The installation of Office 2003 is very straightforward on a Terminal Server and is performed as follows:

1. Although not absolutely necessary, I suggest that you log onto the console (physically or using the remote console feature of the RDP client) to perform the Office 2003 installation. If you're performing the installation across the network, make sure you have the full UNC path to the installation files. I have had issues with Microsoft Installer packages (MSI) failing when launched from a mapped network drive on a Windows 2000 Terminal Server.

2. Open a command prompt and place the server into installation mode (change user /install). Alternatively you can initiate the installation through Add/Remove Programs by selecting Add New Program, selecting the CD or Floppy button and then browsing to find the setup program to initiate the installation.

3. Once setup has begun, follow the wizard until the end, selecting only the necessary components for your environment along the way. Whenever possible, remove any options that you know will not be required in your environment. For example, if users do not require Microsoft Access or FrontPage, then there is no need to install those products on the Terminal Server.

    One option that I recommend removing is access to the Office Assistant. This can be performed simply be setting the Office Assistant to Not Available. In order to see this option you will need to select "Choose advanced customization of applications" when selecting what components to install. The Office Assistant component is then found under Office Shared Features as shown in Figure 21.11.

4. Once the installation has completed, make sure to place the server back into execute mode using the change user /execute command. You will normally not be required to reboot the server in order to complete the installation.

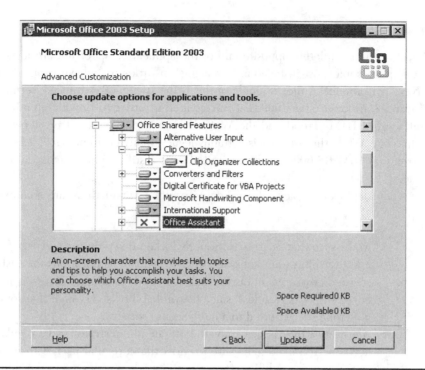

Figure 21.11   The Office Assistant is one component that should be disabled during the Office 2003 installation.

Before users begin to log onto your Terminal Server and work with Office, it is a good idea to configure the desired Office administrative policies in your Active Directory, establishing the desired default configuration from the very beginning. Details on the setup and creation of group policies were discussed in Chapter 15.

TIP: A common mistake made by many administrators is to create a group policy and proceed to define a number of different settings for the Office environment without clearly understanding what the setting is modifying or even testing to ensure the change is working as expected. The proper way to go about configuring group policy settings is to log onto the Terminal Server with a regular user account and run Office, looking for any settings that may cause issues on the Terminal Server. Modify the corresponding group policy, then log back in as the user and test to ensure the changes are applying properly. While potentially time consuming, it will ensure that you have configured the Office environment properly.

Invue 4.0 Advanced Terminal Emulator

Almost at the completely opposite end of the application spectrum are legacy applications that require some post-installation "tweaking" in order to behave properly in a Terminal Server environment. A nice example of this is the Invue 4.0 Advanced Terminal Emulation software. A product circa 1999 that was created in order to provide an advanced terminal interface to SHIM, Trend and the WDS-II host systems, are all products from NxTrend Technology. While the software is certainly legacy, many customers still access systems such as Trend on IBM RS/6000 hardware, and of course still require access via software such as Invue.

When deploying legacy software on a Terminal Server there are a couple of points to keep in mind:

■ Make sure that security is properly locked down on the server *before* you install and test this, or any software. Legacy software is notorious for misbehaving in a secured environment (as we shall see), and installing and testing on an unsecured server is pointless, since the probability is very high that something will go wrong when ported to a more secure server.

■ Always test the application with both an administrator and a regular user account. You need to be sure to verify that a regular user, with restricted access to the registry and file system can still work as expected in the software.

■ Test the application with multiple concurrent users. Another common issue with legacy applications is their inability to function with multiple simultaneous users accessing them. Typically this is caused by the application attempting to maintain some form of temporary log file in a centralized location where it cannot be created and/or accessed by more than one user at a time.

NOTE: Instead of viewing this as a detailed breakdown of how to install Invue, try to look at this as more of a generic training exercise in how to detect and resolve security and other common issues that arise from trying to deploy legacy applications on a Windows 2000 or Windows 2003 Terminal Server.

The installation steps for the Invue application, like most other Windows applications follow the standard installation wizard. After completing the installation some basic testing as an administrator indicates that everything is functioning normally, but as soon as an attempt is made to launch the application as a regular user, an error message appears stating that the application "Failed to update the system registry." Clicking OK terminates the message and the application starts but obviously such an error is not acceptable for the end-user.

Considering that the application functioned properly as an administrator but not as a regular user immediately raises the alert that it is permission related, and considering that the message states the registry, it is apparent that the Regmon tool is required.

Ideally you will want to run Regmon on a server that has no active users so that you can easily isolate the issue with only one instance of the offending application. For this test we will assume that there is only the test user running Invue.

I start by launching Regmon from within an administrator's session, immediately stop capturing data, and then configure the filter to capture data only originating from the Invue application. The executable is Invue40, so the Regmon filter would look as shown in Figure 21.12. As you can see I have entered "Invue40*". I've included the wildcard so that I capture all instances of the Invue executable running on the server. Because I don't know yet what the process ID is for the user when he or she runs the application, I can't narrow it down any further.

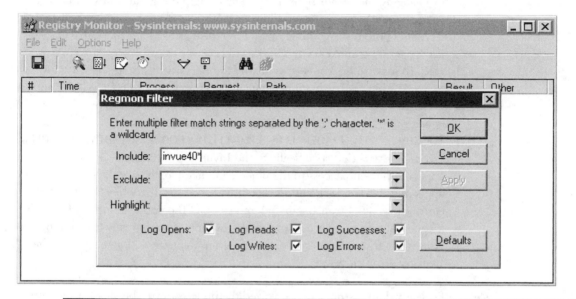

Figure 21.12   Regmon filtering allows you to specify a wildcard when filtering on an executable name.

Making sure that Regmon is once again capturing, I log on as the test user account and launch Invue. Immediately Regmon begins to capture all registry traffic from the Invue program. As soon as the registry error appears in the client session I halt capturing in the Regmon tool. There is no need to keep capturing data now. We already have what we need in the log.

From the top of the Regmon log file I perform a search for the text ACCDENIED, the telltale sign that the user did not have sufficient privileges to perform an action on the registry. Immediately I find three hits pertaining to the properties for a key called Joystick. This is a common ACCDENIED entry and can be ignored. This is not the source of the problem.

The next hit is for the subkey Pixel under HKLM\Software. This seems much more likely, since the About Window in Invue mentions Pixel Innovations. These entries are noted and I continue searching the log. The next entry is under HKCR\Session.Settings. This is also likely so it too is noted.

Another match is found pertaining to a CLSID entry. Security issues are common with legacy applications attempting to access CLSID entries, so this too is noted. This turns out to be the last match, so I find that there are 3 registry keys that are likely causing the error message in the application to appear. The registry entries are:

- **HKLM\Software\Pixel**—Users have only read access to this key. I will begin by changing the permissions on this key using the regedit utility and assigning users the Set Value property, allowing them to update an existing registry value. Rerunning the test we still fail with the registry error, but this particular key isn't generating an ACCDENIED anymore.
- **HKCR\Session.Settings**—Modifying the permissions on this key removes the ACCDENIED entry, but a new one appears now for the HKCR\.SES entry.
- **HKCR\.ses**—The permissions on this key are also corrected, but the error still appears. No new ACCDENIED entries are created.
- **HKCR\CLSID\ {DA0DBD41-8576-11D0-81C0-0080489EE34E}**—This CLSID entry is tied specifically to the Invue application and by default users appear to have no access to the object, and likely results in the error message appearing. I begin by granting users Read access to this object, but this of course still fails. From Regmon it appears that the application is trying to create a key. Granting users access to modify this entry immediately fixes the problem. Now when the user runs the Invue program they are no longer getting the Registry error message.

This example clearly demonstrates how involved the process of troubleshooting a permission issue can be, but also how helpful a tool such as Regmon is in tracking down and resolving these types of problems.

TIP: Instead of granting the Users group elevated access to these registry keys, a more secured approach would be to grant access to a special group containing only those users authorized to run this application. Always try and minimize the actual number of security permission changes required in order for an application to function.

Once these registry corrections were made, the pair of test users were able to log on and use this new application. Everything appears to be going well until it is determined that the users are unable to save the changes that they have made to their terminal sessions—changes such as font and background color changes, as well as customized macros. In some environments, administrators would not want their users modifying the default configuration, but in others the administrators may be less strict. Assuming that we're going to allow the users to save their Invue changes, we need to figure out a solution.

After some quick investigation it is determined that the default Invue configuration has all users accessing the same session file located in the folder containing the Invue executable. This introduces two problems. The first is that the file is located in a folder where users do not have write access; and second, even if they did, all users would share the same file, likely resulting some other kind of contention issue, or at the very least a situation were one user could easily overwrite changes made by another user.

A solution is devised where each user will keep their own personal copy of the default session file in their home folder. Invue is then configured to read that file using the home drive letter mapping. For example, if U: maps to each user's personal home folder, then we could configure Invue to read from the U:\InvueData folder.

The final piece to this puzzle is ensuring that each user has a copy of these default files in their personal U:\InvueData folder. The easiest way to do this is using a Windows script that checks for the existence of those files, and if they don't exist then copies them over to the user's U: drive. If they do exist, then we do nothing so that we don't accidentally overwrite any personal settings the user may have.

This script could be implemented as part of a logon script, but because it is required only on a Terminal Server, it actually makes more sense to configure it as an application compatibility script. The script in question looks as follows:

```
@ECHO OFF
REM This script configures Invue for everyone so that they can manage
their
REM own session files and save personal preferences
REM When users launch Invue they are accessing session files in their
own
REM personal home folder, in the "U:\InvueData" subfolder.

REM Begin by verifying group membership
IfMember "APP_Invue"
if not errorlevel 1 goto END

REM Now see if the folder already exists on the U: drive
U:
cd\
if exist "InvueData" goto END

REM Does not exist, so let's copy over the folder from the D: drive
xcopy "D:\InvueData\*" "U:\InvueData\." /s /I /R /Y /Z

:END
```

The actual script is copied into the %WINDIR%\ Application Compatibility Scripts\Logon folder, since we want this script to run for every user as they log onto the Terminal Server, but only if they belong to the group APP_Invue. You can see within this script that I have also used the IfMember script to verify group membership before attempting to copy the files.

In order for this script to run during the user's logon, we must configure it to do so. This requires adding an entry to the Usrlogn1.cmd batch script located in the %SystemRoot%\System32 folder. If the file does not exist it must be created. For a new file the contents would look as follows:

```
REM This batch script processes application compatibility scripts
that
REM do not require the existence of a RootDrive mapping. There should
be
REM no reason why the root drive feature should be enabled on a W2K3
Terminal Server.

REM Process the Invue application setup.
call Invue.cmd
```

When a user logs on, the Usrlogon.cmd file is run. This in turn launches the Usrlogn1.cmd file, which finally launches the custom Invue.cmd file, whose responsibility it is to ensure that the user's session is prepared to run Invue.

With the implementation of this script, the installation of the Invue application is complete.

Custom Client-Server Application

The final application that we will discuss involves the deployment of custom-developed client-server applications on Terminal Server. For the most part, the deployment of a custom application is somewhere between a typical legacy application and the most current Windows applications. Development environments such as Microsoft Visual Studio provide robust application packaging and deployment tools that allow a developer to create a self-contained set of installation files that can be used to deploy the application on Terminal Server.

While the number of issues is typically minor, there are some that I have encountered on more than one occasion. Issues such as:

- **Hard-coded to a specific installation folder**—Many custom applications that I have encountered have a tendency to assume that they will be installed and launched from a consistent location such as C:\Program Files\Application Name. While this assumption may be acceptable for most desktop deployments, in a Terminal Server environment, an administrator may want to force application deployments to all go to an alternate drive such as D:. If a MetaFrame Server has had its drives remapped as part of the MetaFrame installation, then there may not even be a valid C: drive to reference.

- **Elevated permissions requirements in the application folder**—This seems to fall into the realm of legacy issues, but for some reason many custom applications seem to expect elevated user privileges in the application folder, usually in order to access a log or configuration file of some kind that is remotely updated.
- **Packaged with installations of the Microsoft Data Access Component (MDAC)**—Some installation building programs may include the setup files for the latest MDAC version as part of the package. This could potentially cause an issue with existing programs on a Terminal Server that use a particular MDAC version. Before deploying a custom application make sure that either the existing MDAC is acceptable for the application, or the new MDAC version included will not affect existing programs on the Terminal Server.
- **Local application database use**—Applications developed around a desktop-based database system such as Access, Microsoft SQL Server 2000 Desktop Engine (MSDE) or Pervasive.SQL Workgroup can potentially cause problems for a Terminal Server deployment, depending on where the database is stored and how it is accessed. A locally running instance of a database can cause issues on Terminal Server, particularly if the same application is expected to run on multiple servers. Data on each Terminal Server will be different, and additional complexity is then introduced into the environment, because now volatile user data is being maintained on a Terminal Server.

All of these types of issues are preventable simply by properly educating the development team to the requirements of the environment that they are developing for. In my experience a brief phone call is not enough. Detailed boundaries within which the developers must comply is key to ensuring a successful application build the first time, eliminating the need for the development team to go back and correct the deficiencies.

NOTE: One installation note worth mentioning has to do with the configuration of a data source entry for accessing a database management system such as SQL Server or Sybase. A common question that I am asked is what type of database data source name (DSN) should be created? Should it be a User DSN, a System DSN, or a File DSN? When creating a DSN for a custom application, the appropriate type in most cases is a System DSN as shown in Figure 21.13. System DSNs are globally accessible by all users on a Terminal Server.

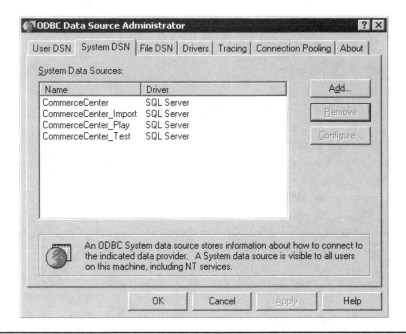

Figure 21.13 Custom applications that require a DSN entry, usually require a System DSN.

Application Publishing with MetaFrame Presentation Server

I will wrap up this chapter by looking briefly at the steps involved in publishing an application within MetaFrame Presentation Server. Throughout this book I have discussed published applications and how they provide a simple interface not only to making applications available to the end user but also for balancing the access load across multiple servers. The ease with which applications and full desktops are published within MPS makes the task almost anti-climactic. Most people expect the task to be much more complicated than it is, and more often than not when finished, I'm met with somewhat blank stares and the question "that's it?"

As with most management tasks in MPS, application publishing is driven from the Management Console, within the Applications folder (Figure 21.14). Any applications that have already been published will appear as icons under this folder.

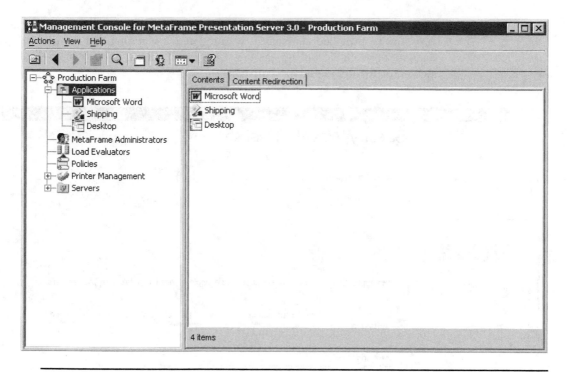

Figure 21.14   Application publishing is managed under the Applications folder in the Management Console.

The creation of a new published application is very straightforward and is performed as follows:

1. Begin by right-clicking on the Applications folder and selecting Publish Application. The Application Publishing Wizard starts and prompts you to provide a name and description for the application. The name entered here will be displayed when the application is published, and the description will appear if the user requests to see a description of the application when using a supported client.
2. In this example I will publish Microsoft Excel, so I enter the name Microsoft Excel and click Next to continue.
3. Now you are asked to specify what you would like to publish. An application, a desktop, or content. When publishing a full desktop you would select Desktop. Content allows you to publish a link to web-based content. The application used to open the content (local or Citrix-based) depends on how the content redirection has been configured. Details on this were discussed in Chapter 2.
4. Selecting Application will present you with space to provide the command line and working directory of the application (Figure 21.15). If you know this path information you can type this in, or you can click the Browse button and browse for the executable on one of the MetaFrame servers in the farm or another network-based

location. Network-mapped drives are not available for selection when browsing and must be provided manually. A warning message stating that the network path may not be available will appear, but you are still able to publish an application located on a network-mapped drive.

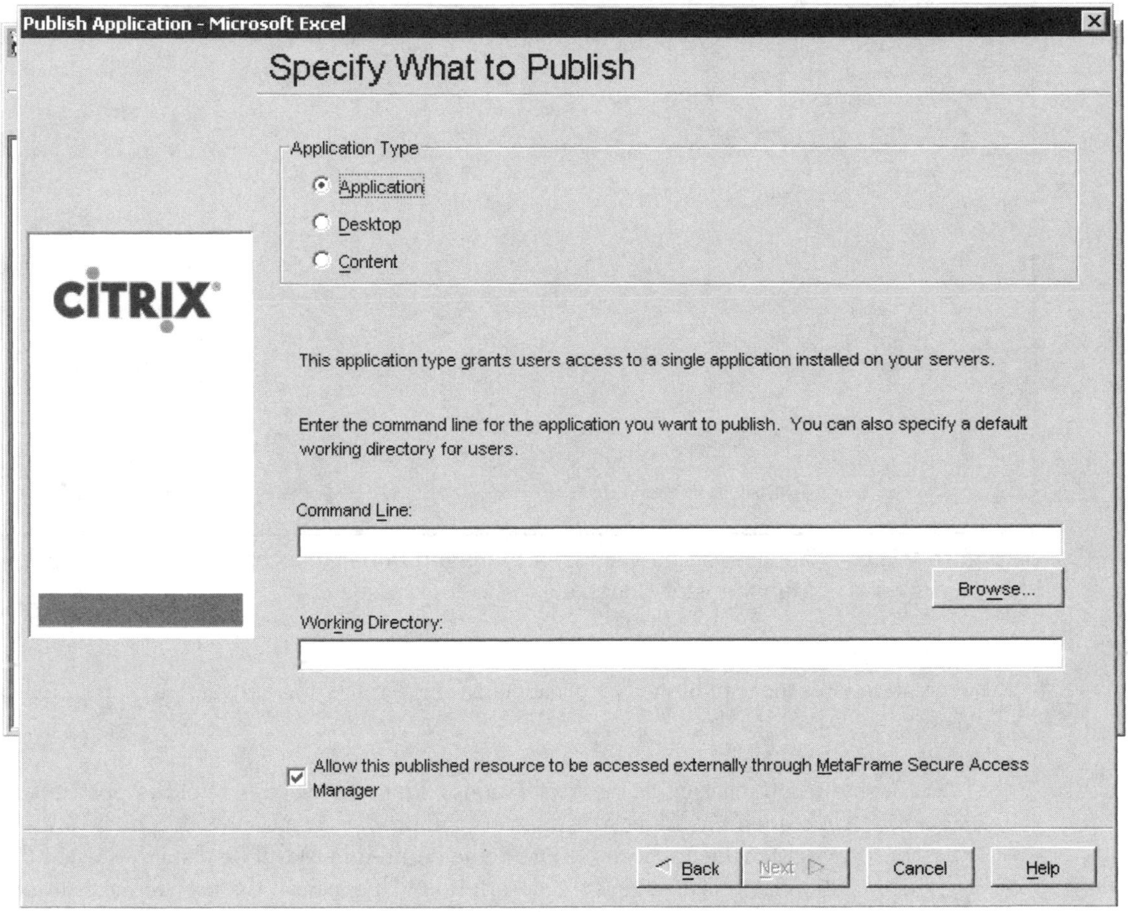

Figure 21.15 Selecting the desired application to be published.

Pay particular attention to the option at the bottom of this dialog box labeled Allow this published resource to be accessed externally through MetaFrame Secure Access Manager. If you have not implemented the Secure Access Manager (SAM) then you can ignore this setting, but if you are using SAM, then be certain that you want this application to be available outside your network, otherwise deselect this option before continuing.

5. The next dialog box is where you define the Program Neighborhood settings. These dictate where the icon for this application is displayed from either Program Neighborhood or the Program Neighborhood Agent. Certain options are available only when using the PNAgent client, and they are labeled as such. Click Next to continue.

6. The application's appearance is configured on the next screen. All of these options are ignored when an application is running in a seamless window on the user's desktop, otherwise these settings are applied unless overridden by the client. Specifics on how these options affect the appearance of an application on the client are discussed in Chapter 20, "ICA Client Installation and Configuration."

7. The Client Requirements dialog box is where you specify additional settings that are only applied when accessed by the PN or PNAgent clients. Unless necessary support for legacy audio should be disabled, encryption should be changed to 128-bit (RC5), and Start this application without waiting for printers to be created should be enabled in order to speed up the logon time and increase the perceived responsiveness for the end-user. This setting applies only to client-mapped printers.

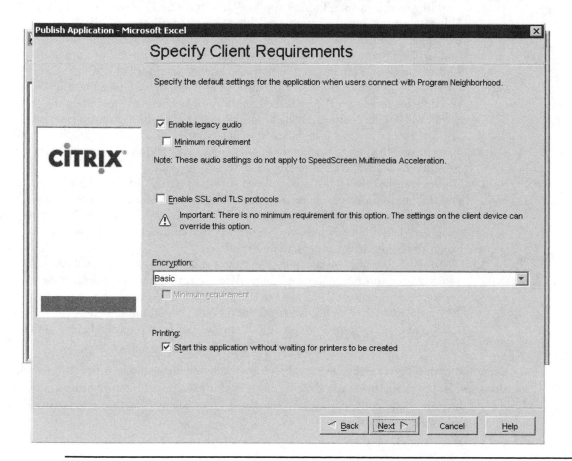

Figure 21.16 The Specify Client Requirements dialog box when configuring a published application.

8. Application Limits allows you to define restrictions on how many concurrent instances of an application may run and limit how many instances can be run by a single user. One reason to institute a maximum number of application instances that can run in a farm would be to ensure that a certain maximum license quota was being satisfied. Another reason might be to limit an ill-behaved program from consuming too many resources in a farm. Even though the option exists on this screen to adjust the CPU priority for the application, I highly recommend that this setting not be altered in any way. Setting an application to have a high priority can adversely affect other programs on the server.

9. The Specify Servers dialog box is where you decide what MetaFrame servers will simultaneously publish the same executable. If you are running Advanced or Enterprise Editions of MPS then you have the Load Management component, allowing you to publish the same application on multiple servers and automatically enabling load balancing.

   Simply by specifying more than one server to publish an application, you are enabling load balancing for that application. Figure 21.17 shows an example of this. If both servers are moved from Available to Configured, then they will automatically begin to load balance the published application between them. If the source and working folders differ between the two servers then the Edit Configuration button can be used to ensure the proper path was used for both.

   If a load evaluator is not specifically assigned to a published application, which can only be done after the published application has been created, then the application will default to using the load available assigned to the server. Unless modified, all servers that support load balancing will have the default load evaluator, which bases server load on the number of concurrent users and the maximum load is set when there are 100 concurrent users on the server.

10. The next-to-last dialog box is where you specify the users who will have access to run the published application. You can specify domain or local users or groups. Users not listed here will not see the published application in PN, PNAgent, or the Web Interface. Directly trying to connect to the published application will fail when the credentials are entered and validated.

11. The final dialog box is where you select the client file associations that can be redirected to this published application. This setting represents client-to-server redirection, meaning that a local file that is double-clicked will initiate the launching of the associated published application on the MetaFrame server. Associations can be modified at any time through the properties for a published application.

Once the application is published it will automatically appear with the other listed applications and is now ready to be accessed by authorized users. Any of the properties configured during the published application created can be modified at any time through the properties for the published application.

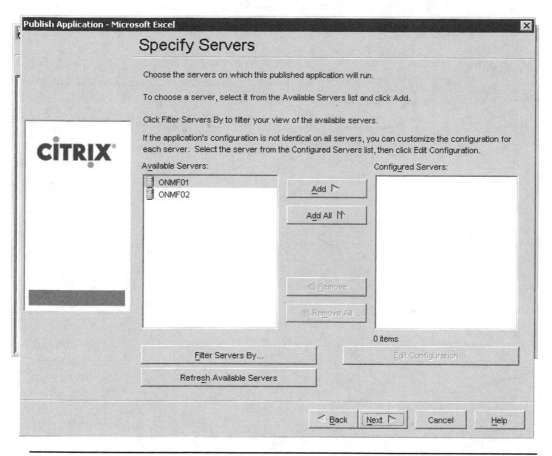

Figure 21.17 Assigning multiple servers to publish the same application implicitly enables load balancing between the selected servers.

CHAPTER 22

Server Operations and Support

Preparing for Terminal Server Operations and Support

Once you have completed all the implementation tasks discussed to this point in the book, the focus begins to shift away from planning and implementation to operations—ensuring that the environment is available and that users are able to work without difficulty. Although most Terminal Server environments continue to be managed by the same people involved in the implementation, this is not always the case, and a distinction should be made between the role of the operator and that of the administrator. Typically an administrator is responsible for security and for planning and coordinating updates to the environment, while an operator is responsible for monitoring the day-to-day stability of the environment, ensuring that the system runs smoothly and provides maximum uptime to the end user.

In most small to medium deployments, the roles of an administrator and an operator are one and the same, but in larger organizations, either the role of the operator is completely split off in a separate position, or the responsibilities of the operations role are divided between the administrators and the first-level help desk support staff.

NOTE: The role of an operator has its roots in the early mainframe days, when a system operator (sysop) was basically available 24×7 to ensure that the computer system remained operational. Routine tasks such as tape rotations for backups (these were large tapes), loading of punch-card code into the system, and print job collation and management were just some of the common duties an operator was required to perform. In addition, he or she was available in case of mainframe issues that required immediate attention.

Regardless of how the tasks are divided, someone is responsible for performing periodic maintenance and management of the environment in addition to planning and implementing the changes necessary for future growth requirements. The purpose of this chapter is to discuss some of the common tools and techniques used to manage an environment once it is in production. The chapter has been broken down into the following sections:

- **Load-Balancing Configuration**—On a number of occasions in the book I discuss use of software tools such as Microsoft's Network Load Balancing or Citrix Load Manager to provide load-balancing capabilities in your deployment. Load balancing not only provides a transparent way of distributing your user sessions across all the Terminal Servers in your environment, but it also can simplify maintenance by letting an administrator remove a server from the load-balancing cluster without having to change the client-side settings. Proper techniques can ensure that a server is taken offline with zero impact to the end users.
- **Server Cloning**—Besides load balancing, another method of providing redundancy in the environment and maximizing stability is to employ the technique of server cloning. When a Terminal Server/MetaFrame server has been properly configured and thoroughly tested, using server cloning to replicate that configuration can help ensure that the servers in the environment maintain a consistent configuration and minimize the chances of one configuration misbehaving due to differences in the installation and configuration.

NOTE: While some people argue that cloning can exaggerate issues by allowing a misconfigured server to be replicated across all hardware, I feel this is a concern only if the environment was not properly set up and tested in the first place. Proper testing helps ensure that the configuration deployed is correct and behaving as expected.

- **Server Health Monitoring**—Using integrated tools such as the Resource Manager, third-party tools or utilities from the Resource Kit, or even Performance Monitor, the operator takes on the role of proactively monitoring the status of all Terminal Servers so potential problems can be flagged early and resolved before they cause system degradation or unscheduled downtime. This task is extremely important for any organization that must guarantee a minimum level of service to its customers. Proactive server monitoring can also alert you to the need to plan for eventual expansion of the environment.

Load-Balancing Configuration

In Chapter 8, "Server Installation and Management Planning," I discussed Terminal Services load balancing using the Network Load Balancing functionality available in Windows 2000 (Advanced Server or Datacenter Server) and with all versions of Windows Server 2003. I also talked about the Load Manager component of MetaFrame Presentation Server, Advanced and Enterprise Editions. In this section I briefly discuss configuration and use of these tools.

Microsoft Network Load Balancing

In Chapter 8 I provided an overview of the features and functionality of the Microsoft Network Load Balancing (NLB) service and how it provides a means of introducing scalability to a Terminal Server environment. NLB is a component of Windows Clustering that allows multiple servers to provide TCP/IP-based services to users through one or more "clustered" IP addresses. The servers are "grouped" together and operate conceptually as a single entity. NLB was developed primarily to provide redundancy for Web-based services such as Web or FTP servers, but the same functionality can be used in a Terminal Server environment.

When configuring NLB to function with Terminal Services, there are three main tasks that must be performed:

- Verify the appropriate hardware configuration for your environment.
- Configure the Terminal Servers in the environment to operate using NLB.
- Configure the Terminal Services clients to connect to the cluster host name or IP address instead of a specific server name.

TIP: A network load-balancing cluster can contain a maximum of 32 nodes (servers).

Recommended Hardware Configuration

While Microsoft supports use of NLB on servers with only a single network adapter, the recommended configuration calls for two network adapters to be present. When a single network card is used it must handle both inbound cluster traffic and intra-host communications, while the same tasks can each be assigned to their own network card when two are present.

The number of network cards in the server dictate the operation mode of the cluster. The operation mode determines how the cluster interfaces with the network adapter(s) on the server and what type of MAC (media access control) addressing is assigned. Two modes are available:

- **Unicast mode**—This is the default configuration for an NLB cluster; selecting this option causes the MAC address for the cluster to overwrite the physical MAC address assigned to the network card on each server in the cluster. Because all hosts in the cluster share the same MAC address, in a single network interface card (NIC) deployment, no intra-host communications other than NLB-related communications are possible.
- **Multicast mode**—When this mode is selected the virtual MAC address of the cluster is assigned to each server's network card, but each card retains its own physical MAC address. In an NLB deployment with only single network cards, intra-host communications are still possible when multicast mode is enabled.

Multicast mode may not be supported in your network environment, depending on the router hardware in place. The router hardware must support mapping the single IP address of the cluster to the multicast MAC address, or the multicast mode cannot be used. Static address resolution protocol (ARP) entries may also be required on routers that do not accept ARP responses that give a multicast MAC address for a single IP address.

In a single network card configuration, the inability to support intra-host communications means that the NLB Manager tool provided with Windows Server 2003 cannot be used to manage operation of the cluster unless it is run from a host *outside* the cluster. This invariably causes confusion for administrators who are new to the operating behavior of NLB.

Restrictions on the management of one server from another are not limited to only the NLB Manager. Any type of management task attempted from one server to another within the cluster will not function properly, which can cause significant management issues, since a common practice for Terminal Server administrators is to connect to one Terminal Server in the environment and perform most of the management tasks remotely against all other Terminal Servers.

If you plan to employ NLB as the load-balancing solution for your Terminal Server deployment, I recommend using dual network cards. Most servers purchased today include dual network adapters in their base configuration, so I find this is rarely a cause for concern. In my installation and configuration example in this chapter, I assume you're deploying NLB in a dual network adapter configuration.

TIP: When using NLB, a user's Terminal Server session information is not simultaneously maintained across multiple servers, as the term *clustering* might suggest. If a user is active on a server that fails, their session and any information currently open within that session are lost. If the user reconnects, they are automatically directed to an alternate server still active in the cluster.

Installing and Configuring Network Load Balancing

No explicit installation steps are required to make NLB available. On a Windows server that supports NLB, the necessary NLB driver option is visible under the Local Area Connect properties, as shown in Figure 22.1. If an NLB option is not visible, you are not running a version of Windows that supports NLB. Enabling and configuring the properties for the driver dictate how the cluster behaves.

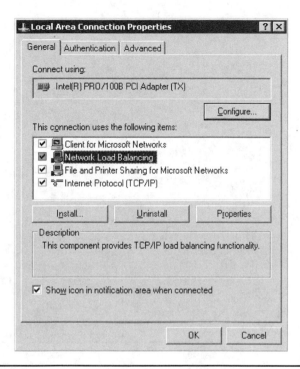

Figure 22.1   NLB is available as a special network service on all supported versions of Windows and is supported only with the TCP/IP protocol.

NLB is enabled and the settings configured in one of two ways:

- By selecting the properties for the NLB driver on each server participating in the cluster. This is the only configuration option supported by Windows 2000 Server.
- By using the Network Load Balancing Manager tool provided as part of Windows Server 2003.

In a Windows 2000 Server environment, you have little choice but to employ the manual method of configuration on a server-by-server basis; Figure 22.2 shows the main property page for NLB on a Windows 2000 Advanced Server. In this section I demonstrate configuring a cluster using the Windows Server 2003 NLB, but I include the associated position within properties of the NLB driver so you can find similar settings in a Windows 2000 deployment.

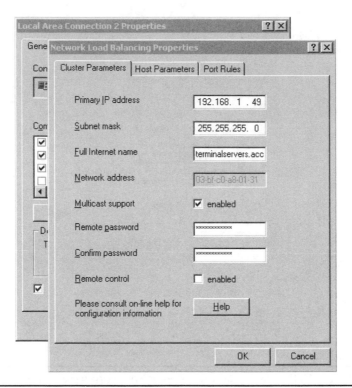

Figure 22.2   NLB in a Windows 2000 environment must be configured through the properties page for the NLB driver.

TIP: Always ensure that the network adapter to be used as the NLB cluster interface has a static IP address assigned. You cannot designate an adapter that was configured using DHCP for use in an NLB cluster.

Also, I do not recommend that you perform the NLB Manager installation and configuration when directly connected to the host via an RDP or ICA connection. If you do so, when the NLB component is configured you may be disconnected from the server. It is always preferable to perform configuration from a remote host using the NLB Manager or by running the NLB Manager from the physical console session directly on the host.

NLB is configured on a Windows 2003 Terminal Server as follows:

1. Begin by launching the NLB Manager from Administrative Tools on the Start menu.
2. If there are any existing clusters that have been managed from this host, they appear in the main program window; otherwise this window is empty.
3. Select New from the Cluster menu to bring up the first page of the configuration wizard, labeled Cluster Parameters (Figure 22.3).

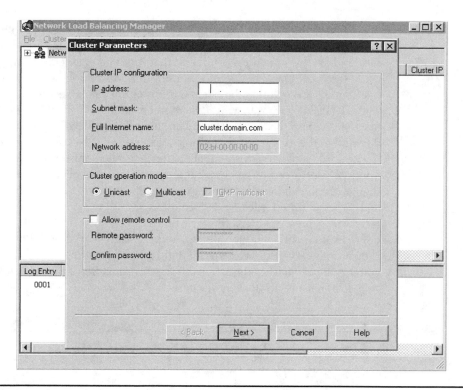

Figure 22.3   The Cluster Parameters screen is where you begin to create a new NLB cluster.

4. Begin by providing the IP address to be assigned to the cluster. Any Terminal Server client requests directed to this IP will be serviced by the cluster. Provide the IP address, the corresponding network mask, and the fully qualified domain name of the cluster. A name that I commonly use is terminalservers.<domain name>. For example, I might use terminalservers.nrtestdom.com within my Noisy River test domain. The network address (also known as the MAC address) cannot be manually modified, but if you change the cluster operation mode from unicast to multicast, you see the address change. When using a dual network adapter configuration, I recommend selecting the unicast mode.

Enabling the Allow Remote Control option allows the cluster to be remotely managed using the command line tool. Enabling this option can pose a security risk, and for this reason I recommend that it not be enabled. Managing the cluster using the NLB Manager does *not* require that this option be enabled. Once you have completed entering the desired information, click Next to continue.

5. The next dialog box prompts you to enter any additional IP addresses that you want to associate with this NLB cluster. This allows you to have multiple addresses all directed to the same cluster. Multiple addresses may be used if you're consolidating multiple separate environments under one NLB cluster. If you want to support multiple addresses, you can enter them now. To do so, click the Add button and then enter the address and subnet mask. Repeat this for each address you want to add. When finished, click Next to continue.

6. Next you're presented with the Port Rules dialog box, shown in Figure 22.4. The default rule is automatically applied, and the associated description for that rule is shown in the Port Rule Description field near the bottom of the dialog box. When you use this default configuration, all the Terminal Servers in the cluster automatically load-balance RDP client requests.

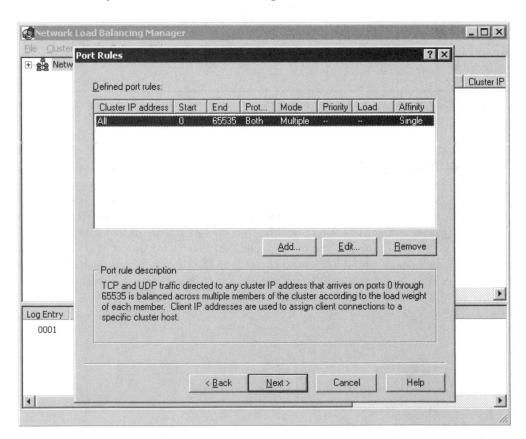

Figure 22.4 The Port Rules dialog box is where you configure what ports will be load balanced.

You can trim down the range of ports that are monitored to include only the RDP client port. By default this port number is TCP port 3389. You can modify the existing default port rule by clicking the Edit button; the Add/Edit Port Rule window appears. Figure 22.5 shows the settings to configure the cluster to monitor the RDP port 3389, and as a result load-balance Terminal Server client sessions across the cluster.

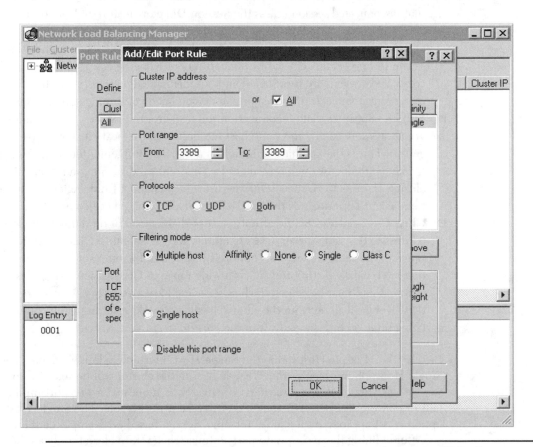

Figure 22.5 You can modify the default port rule to apply only to RDP client connections if desired.

The port range defines only the listening port for the hosts in the cluster, so only 3389 needs to be defined. TCP is also the only protocol that needs to be selected, since RDP connections are established using TCP, not UDP. The filtering mode has three options, with the default mode being Multiple Host. This specifies that multiple hosts in the cluster will service this port rule. This is the mode you choose when configuring load balancing for Terminal Services. With this selection, you have three client affinity options from which to choose. Affinity controls how servers in the cluster manage multiple connection requests from the same client. The details of each type are provided in Chapter 8 and in summary are as follows:

- **None**—Allows multiple connections from the same client to be serviced by different cluster members. If a user connects to the cluster, logs off, and then reconnects an hour later, he or she is not necessarily directed to the same server. This can pose a problem if a user has a disconnected session on a server in the cluster. With affinity None, there is no guarantee that the user will reconnect to that disconnected session unless the Session Directory feature of Windows Server 2003 is also used. Windows 2000 has no mechanism for automatically associating a client with a disconnected session in the cluster. Microsoft recommends that Terminal Servers in a cluster with an affinity of None be configured so that disconnected sessions are terminated and not maintained on the server, thus helping to prevent sessions from remaining unclaimed and consuming server resources.
- **Single**—Specifies that all connection requests from the same client IP address are always serviced by the same host (at least until the next cluster convergence). This is the default configuration and, when implemented, increases the likelihood that a user will reconnect to a disconnected session on a server in the cluster. For this to be successful, the user must connect from a client with the same client IP address as the one that originally initiated the connection.
- **Class C**—Similar to Single affinity, except that instead of directing a single IP address to the same server, Class C affinity directs an entire Class C address range to the same server. This option is best suited for Internet-based connects that are typically distributed across a wide range of Class C networks. Class C affinity should not be selected when servicing local area network users, because they likely will all be from the same Class C network, resulting in all connects being serviced by a single host in the cluster.

Besides the Multiple Host mode the Single Host filtering mode is available. The Single Host option specifies that a single host in the cluster will be selected to service this port rule. The same server manages all requests for this port until it fails or convergence selects a new server to take over this role. The Single Host option is not appropriate for most Terminal Server–based NLB implementations.

After defining the appropriate port settings, click OK to close the dialog box and return to the Port Rules window. Once you have defined the desired port rules, click Next to continue with the configuration

7. You now see the Connect dialog box, which prompts you to provide the name of a host in the cluster to which you will apply these configuration choices. You can provide the host name, a fully qualified domain name, or an IP address. After typing the desired server information, click the Connect button to establish the connection and return a list of all valid interfaces on the target server. Figure 22.6 lists the available interfaces on my first host server. Once I've selected the desired interface to be associated with the cluster, I can highlight it and click Next to continue. If you're connecting to a remote server, you cannot select the interface on which you are connected to be configured for load balancing. You also cannot select any interface that may have been configured using DHCP instead of static IP mapping. NLB requires static IP addresses to be set.

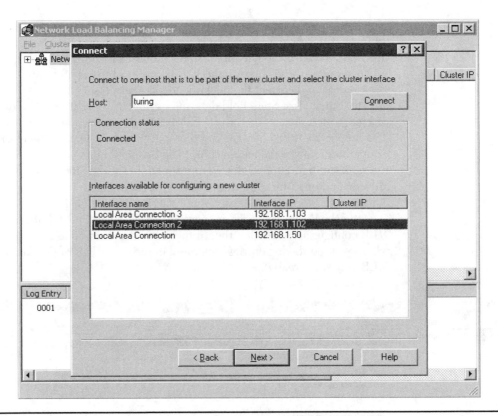

Figure 22.6   The Connect dialog box is where you select the host and an available interface on that host to configure the new cluster.

NOTE: If you select an interface enabled using DHCP, the NLB Manager does not always warn you that this is an issue, and as a result, lets you complete creation of the cluster. If this happens, the cluster node can enter what appears to be an undefined state where the interface is neither active nor accessible in the cluster. If this occurs, the most effective way I've found to recover is to reboot the host machine and run the NLB Manager from a console session to remove the offending host. You may have to remove the cluster and restart the process if the problem is not corrected by this method.

8. After highlighting the desired interface, click Next to continue to the Host Parameters dialog box. This is where you verify that the interface information is correct. Figure 22.7 shows an example of how this screen appears. The first option is the Priority identifier, which is used to uniquely tag the host servers in the cluster. Ensure that this number is unique for each host in the cluster.

The next field is Dedicated IP Configuration, which must contain a static IP address. If this field appears blank, either you chose an IP address that is configured via DHCP or the network adapter interface is somehow corrupted. Do not proceed under these circumstances. Either cancel the configuration or click the Back button and correct the network adapter selection.

The Initial Host State field determines how the host starts. The default is Started, which means when the server is booted it automatically joins the cluster. The Stopped setting boots the host computer without joining the cluster; the server operates as a standalone machine. The Suspend State setting starts the server in the same configuration as if it were stopped, but if the "Retain suspended state after computer restarts" setting is not selected, the next time the server boots, it comes up in Started mode instead of being suspended again.

After the desired settings are configured, click the Finish button to complete NLB configuration. You are then returned to the main NLB Manager window, where you see the log entries generated in the lower half of the window as the NLB cluster is created.

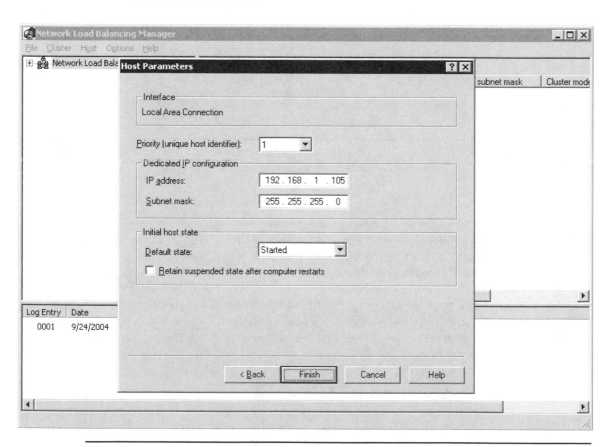

Figure 22.7   The Host Parameters dialog box is where you configure the final settings for the new NLB cluster.

Once the NLB cluster creation has completed, the host name appears in green under the cluster name and you can see a log entry stating that the update was successful. You can double-click this entry to see details of the log entry (Figure 22.8). At this point the cluster is operational, so you are ready to test connectivity to verify that the cluster is working properly.

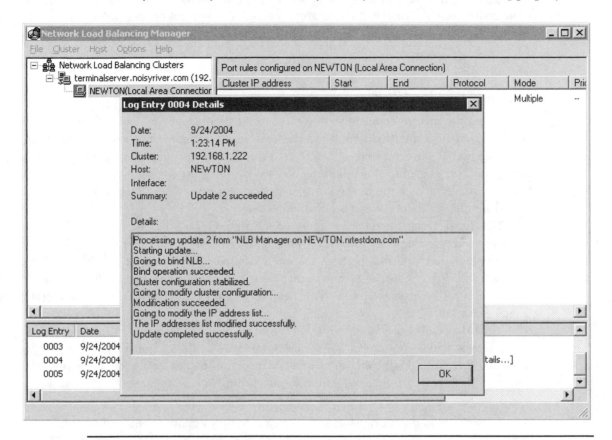

Figure 22.8   Log entry details are displayed by double-clicking on a log entry.

Testing RDP Client Connectivity to an NLB Cluster

Testing connectivity from an RDP client to a load-balanced Terminal Server cluster is straightforward. All you have to do is launch the Remote Desktop Connection client and then provide the host name or IP address of the cluster. You should then be presented with a logon screen for a server in the cluster. By testing two or three simultaneous connections from different clients, you can see the load balancing as it spreads users across the available servers.

TIP: Remember, if you configured your cluster to operate with Single affinity, the same client IP address automatically connects to the same host in the cluster until a condition within the cluster causes the convergence operation to initiate. Attempting to establish multiple connections from the same client machine to the cluster results in your continuously connecting to the same server. You are not divided among the available servers in the cluster.

Adjusting Host Load Weight

In your production environment you may have a situation where you have multiple servers available, but some are more powerful and so can handle a larger number of concurrent sessions than other servers in the cluster. Once a server has been added to a cluster, you can adjust the load weighting of that host in order to boost its responsiveness to new client connection requests. Using this method you can designate servers that will take a proportionally higher number of client connections than other servers.

The Load Weight options are accessed by right-clicking the host within the NLB Manager and selecting Host Properties. From here, click the Port Rules tab and then edit your defined port rule that pertains to your Terminal Server connections. New options appear in the Filtering Mode section of the dialog box, as shown in Figure 22.9. The Load Weight options are now available, and the default value of 50 can be changed by clicking the Equal check box.

The load weight is a relative factor that can be set to any value between 0 and 100. When set to 0, a host does not accept any connection requests. The default value is 50, and by adjusting this up or down, you can increase or decrease the percentage of connections the host accepts in comparison to other hosts in the cluster.

TIP: Network load balancing is based solely on network connections and not on heuristic calculations derived from processor utilization, memory utilization, or any other system factor. This means that if a server within the cluster is running in a degraded state, it can continue to attempt to process new client connections, even though another server in the cluster may have the capacity available to better handle the request.

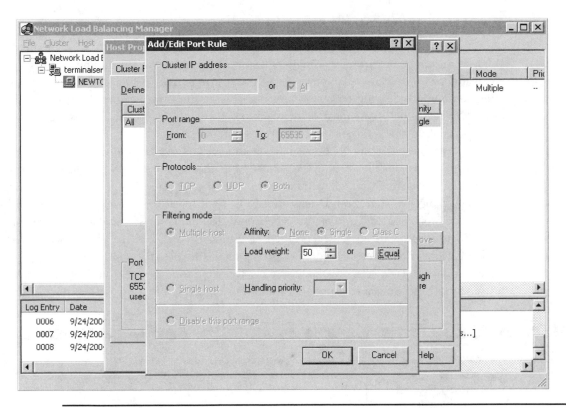

Figure 22.9   Load weights of the servers can be adjusted if necessary.

Adjusting Host Heartbeat Settings

When a connect request is made to the cluster, all Terminal Servers in the cluster receive the incoming request, and based on the distribution algorithm, one client accepts the connection request while all others discard it. Distribution is coordinated between the cluster members through the periodic exchange of heartbeat messages. When a new host is added or removed or fails to respond to a set number of heartbeat messages, the cluster enters a state known as *convergence*. During convergence, cluster membership is verified and the client load is redistributed accordingly. During this time, all cluster connections for the available hosts are serviced, but any requests destined for a failed host continue to fail until convergence is complete and an alternate host is selected to handle those requests. The default heartbeat interval is one second, and the threshold for missed heartbeats is five seconds. Both values can be modified by editing the following registry keys on all cluster members. Under the key **HKEY_LOCAL_MACHINE\SYSTEM\CurrentControlSet\Services\WLBS\Parameters** you find these values:

AliveMsgPeriod: The default value is 1,000 milliseconds (1 second).

AliveMsgTolerance: The default value is 5, for 5 missed heartbeats.

Taking an NLB Host Out of a Cluster

Often administrators find that they need to schedule taking a server offline for maintenance. While many environments have a single shift of workers and a window of time every evening when administrators can plan to make changes, some organizations have multiple shifts operating continuously, leaving no real time window when the server can be "forcefully" taken offline. Instead, the server must be configured so it continues to service existing requests while preventing new requests from being added to the server.

This is achieved within NLB using a technique called *drainstopping*. When this feature is enabled, hosts in the cluster stop accepting new connections but allow existing connections to function normally. Eventually all the active users log off, at which point the server automatically changes its state from Drainstop to Stop. You can stop connections immediately by issuing the Stop command, or you can cancel drainstop mode by issuing the Start command.

Drainstopping can be activated either at the host level or at the cluster level. When enabled at the cluster level, the drainstop rule applies to all servers in the cluster. You can enable drainstopping by clicking the host or cluster name and selecting the Control Host context menu. Five options are displayed, as shown in Figure 22.10.

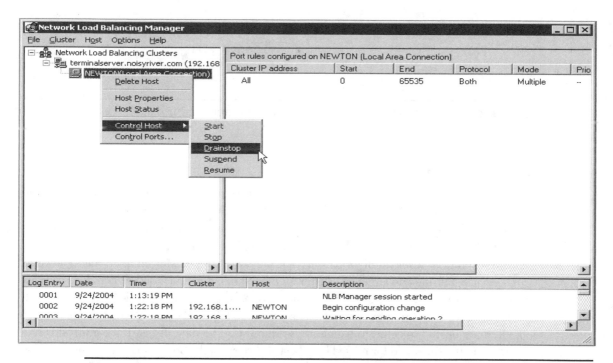

Figure 22.10 Drainstopping can be activated at the host or cluster level.

MetaFrame Presentation Server Load Manager

In Chapter 8, I also discussed the load management features of MetaFrame Presentation Server that are included with the Advanced and Enterprise editions of the product. Unlike Microsoft Network Load Balancing, which is an additional Windows service that must be installed and extensively configured before it can be used, Citrix Load Manager installs as part of the above-mentioned MPS editions and is preconfigured and ready to use with no special configuration by an administrator.

In Chapter 21, "Application Integration," I demonstrated how to publish an application and explained how the process of publishing an application on more than one MetaFrame server would automatically enable it for load balancing. Figure 22.11 illustrates how easy it is to load balance the published application Microsoft Word across multiple MetaFrame servers. In this figure, the published application is being configured to run on both the MF01 and MF02 servers. Any minor variations in the installation location of Microsoft Word would be adjusted from the Edit Configuration button, but otherwise adding the servers to the Configured Servers list and clicking OK are all that is required to enable basic load balancing.

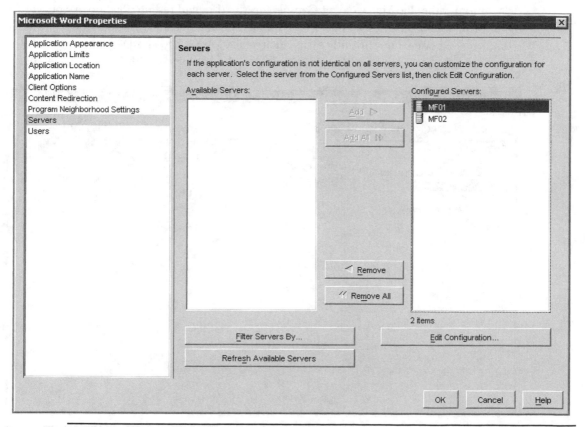

Figure 22.11 Load balancing applications or servers is very straightforward in MetaFrame.

Citrix Load Manager is an integrated part of the published application concept of MetaFrame. If an application is being published, then the application is automatically available for load balancing simply by publishing it on more than one MetaFrame server in a farm.

TIP: In order to load balance a published application across two or more servers, both must belong to the same server farm. Cross-farm load balancing is not supported.

Configuring Load Manager

MetaFrame's load manager comes preconfigured, and for most simple installations, will not even have to be adjusted. Administrators can simply publish the desired applications and watch users load balance across the available MetaFrame servers. In larger or more complicated application publishing scenarios, an administrator will likely want to make minor adjustments to the load manager's behavior to better reflect the desired load distribution in the environment. In order to do this you will need to understand the purpose of a load evaluator.

From within the Management Console for MetaFrame Presentation Server, you will see that there is an object for load management called Load Evaluators. Clicking this you will see that two load evaluators currently exist and are called Advanced and Default (Figure 22.12). These are the two evaluators that are included by default for use with Load Management.

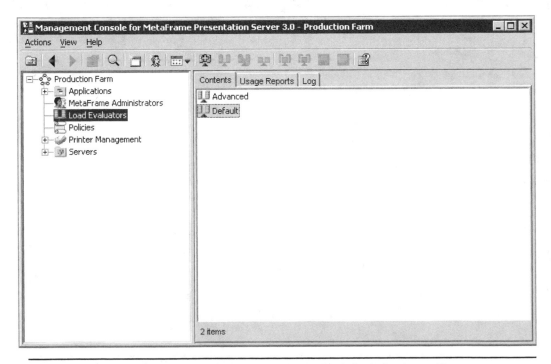

Figure 22.12   Two load evaluators are available by default for use with Load Management.

A load evaluator is simply a set of rules that dictates how a numeric load value is calculated for an object. The resulting numeric value for that object is then compared with the numeric values from other objects of the same type in order to determine which instance is "least loaded." When load balancing, the least-loaded object is chosen to satisfy the connection request. A simple example will help to illustrate this.

A user is attempting to connect to the Microsoft Word published application and has initiated the connection from her MPS client. The client contacts the farm and requests the IP address of the least-loaded server that is publishing Word. The farm then requests the current load from all servers publishing Word and determines based on the value returned, which server will satisfy that user's request. The IP address for that server is returned to the user, and she proceeds to log on. The actual load value that each server returns to the farm is determined by the load evaluator that is associated with the published application, in this case Microsoft Word.

In order for any object to load balance, it must have an associated load evaluator. When a MetaFrame server is installed, the server object is automatically assigned the Default load evaluator. This is the evaluator used by each application that is published on that server unless otherwise specified. A load evaluator is always assigned to a server, and can optionally be assigned to individual applications on a per server basis. If an application has an evaluator assigned, it will override any settings within the server's evaluator.

Returning to the two evaluators that are included with MetaFrame, Figure 22.13 shows the specific configuration settings for the Default evaluator. The Default load evaluator is configured so that it will return a load value of 100 percent when there are 100 users logged on to the server. Looking at the properties for this evaluator you see that the only assigned rule is the Server User Load, which generates a load value based solely on the number of active users on the server. Load evaluators are completely customizable, but you will notice that neither the Advanced nor the Default evaluators can be modified. This is because they are special MetaFrame application objects that cannot be changed. New copies of these objects can be created, which you can then modify as desired. New copies of these evaluators are created by right-clicking on the object name and selecting Duplicate Load Evaluator from the popup menu. You can also create a new evaluator by right-click and selecting New Load Evaluator.

Opening the properties for the Advanced evaluator you will see that it does not determine server load based on the number of concurrent users, but instead on real-time performance statistics from the server. Specifically it looks at CPU utilization, memory usage, and the number of page swaps. Click an individual rule to see the specific settings, which will be displayed in the lower section of the dialog box. Figure 22.14 demonstrates this. It shows the settings for the Memory Usage rule. Just as with the Default evaluator, the Advanced evaluator is read-only, but it can be duplicated and edited if desired.

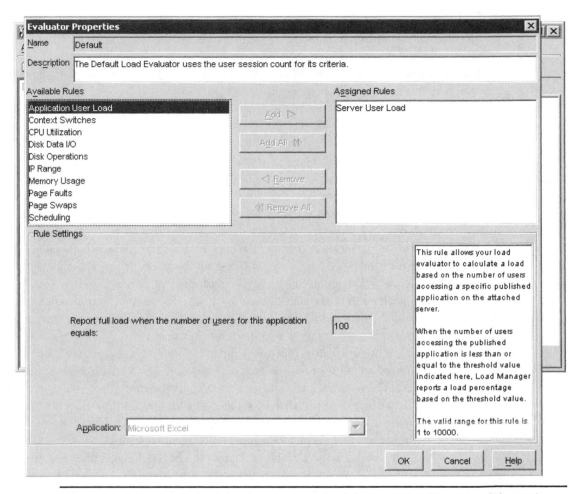

Figure 22.13   The Default load evaluator calculates user load based solely on the number of concurrent users.

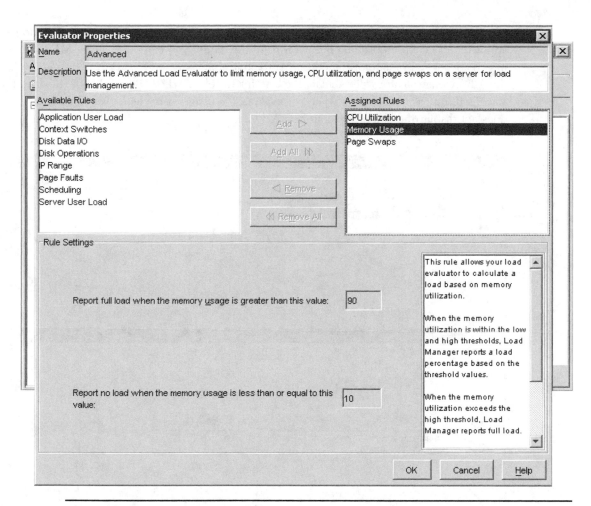

Figure 22.14 The individual properties for an assigned rule can be viewed and edited for a load evaluator.

Assigning Load Evaluators

Before a server or application can be assigned a custom load evaluator it must be created within the Load Evaluators object. Once evaluators exist, they are easily assigned by right-clicking on an application or server and selecting the Load Manage Server or Load Manage Application menu option. A dialog box then opens allowing you to choose from either the built-in evaluators or any evaluators that you may have created on your own.

Figure 22.15 shows the Load Manage Application dialog box for Microsoft Excel, another application that I'm publishing in my farm. In this figure you can see that the MF01 server has an advanced evaluator assigned for MF01, but none assigned for MF02. This means that the Advanced evaluator will calculate the load for Excel on MF01. But on MF02, the load for Excel will be calculated using whatever evaluator is assigned to the server. This dialog box does not display the default evaluator for MF02.

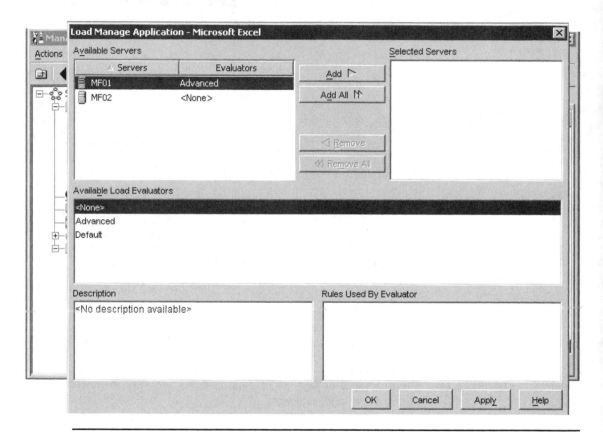

Figure 22.15   Load evaluators can be assigned to either the server or an individual application published on a server.

In order to see what the currently active evaluator is for a server or application, you need to return to the Load Evaluator component of the farm and select the Usage Reports tab from the right-hand pane. Figure 22.16 shows the By Evaluator report type, which lists all existing evaluators and what servers and/or applications they are assigned to. In this figure you will see that the Advanced evaluator is assigned to MF02, the Excel application runs on MF01, while MF01 is assigned the Default server evaluator.

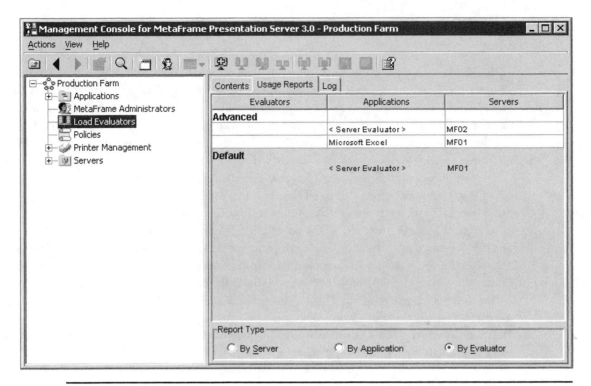

Figure 22.16   Load evaluator assignments allow you to easily see what evaluators are affecting which applications.

Testing Client Connectivity to a Load-Balanced Application

Testing connectivity to a load-balanced application is a trivial exercise. Simply configure a couple of MetaFrame Presentation Server clients to access a published application that is being load-balanced between two or more servers. You will see the user sessions balanced among the available servers.

If launching multiple sessions from the same client, make certain that you are logging on using a different user ID. If multiple applications are published off the same MetaFrame server and multiple connection attempts are made to the farm using the same user ID, the user will have to continuously go to the same server. This is because once a user has an active session, the load manager will direct that user to the same MetaFrame server if another application that they are attempting to run is also published on that server.

Server Cloning

In Chapter 7, "Server and Application Software Planning," I talked about the advantages of using server cloning in a Terminal Server implementation to quickly build up an environment from a single base image. Using cloning you can ensure that all your Terminal Servers have an identical configuration. The advantages of cloning quickly become apparent in a large server deployment scenario, since a single server can be used during installation and testing of the operating system and software. Then when it comes time to test the configuration on multiple servers, you simple place the cloned server's image onto the other hardware, and voilà, you have a multiserver environment. While alternatives such as scripted installations exist, I always select cloning if given the choice. Cloning can be ideal in a disaster recovery situation to get an environment back online as quickly as possible.

Figure 22.11 demonstrates how server imaging can be integrated into the build process for the Terminal Server environment. Of course, the environment could be created without the imaging step, but if a problem is encountered, it is highly likely that you would need to start all over again from the beginning to rebuild the server. If you have been maintaining server images, you can easily roll back to the point where you had a stable server configuration. For example, say that during the application installation phase you discovered a problem that left your Terminal Server unstable. You could quickly rebuild your server from the last image and re-evaluate the application installation process without having to completely rebuild the server from scratch. This process can be a valuable time-saver, even in a small Terminal Server implementation.

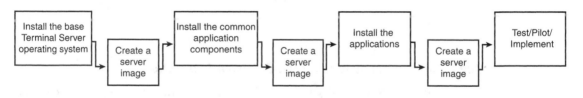

Figure 22.17   Server cloning in a Terminal Server implementation.

A key utility in the cloning process is the Microsoft SysPrep tool, the most recent version of which can be downloaded from the Microsoft Web site (http://www.microsoft.com). A version of SysPrep also can be found on the Windows installation CD, in the deploy.cab file. SysPrep is a tool specifically designed by Microsoft to prepare a server for cloning. Microsoft fully supports cloning of Windows Terminal Servers when this utility is used.

The first step in cloning a Terminal Server is to run SysPrep in order to prepare the server for cloning. SysPrep is run as follows:

1. First, create a directory called SysPrep off the root of %SystemDrive% and copy the files sysprep.exe and setupcl.exe into it. Both files are included with the SysPrep download file.

2. Next, remove the server from the domain and rename it if necessary. This way, when the cloned server is booted, it does not attempt to join the domain with a computer name already in use.

3. Now double-click on sysprep.exe to launch this tool. You will first see a warning message stating that the security configuration of the machine will be modified. After clicking OK to proceed you will be presented with the main System Preparation Tool setup dialog box (Figure 22.18).

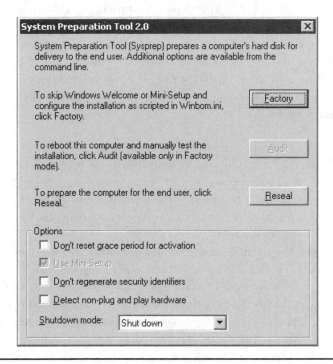

Figure 22.18   The SysPrep confirmation dialog box.

4. In order to clone a Terminal Server, you will want to leave the default options as shown in Figure 22.18 and click the Reseal button, after which SysPrep prepares the system for cloning, and once completed, automatically shuts down the server. At this point you are ready to capture the actual clone image using either a cloning software package or rebooting the server into a second OS and performing a traditional backup.

After you capture the image, the next time you reboot the server from which you took the image, or boot any server you clone from the image, SysPrep automatically initiates a mini installation of Windows 2000 or 2003. This mini install prompts you for a subset of the information you would provide when installing a fresh copy of Windows.

Some of the information you are asked to provide includes such things as the desired regional settings, the product license key, the computer name, the administrative password, the date and time, the desired network components to install, and whether or not you want to join a domain. After all the required information is provided, the server automatically reboots and the cloned server's setup is complete. The SysPrep directory of the %SystemDrive% is automatically deleted.

You can speed up configuration of a cloned server by using the Setupmgr.exe tool, which is included with the Windows deployment package for Sysprep. This tool can be used to create an answer file that is then used by SysPrep the first time a cloned server starts.

When you launch Setupmgr, it guides you through a wizard that generates an answer file called SysPrep.inf. Place this file into the %SystemDrive%\SysPrep folder along with the other two executables. When the cloned server is booted for the first time, SysPrep runs and uses the answer file to configure the server. You can configure all the desired options within Setupmgr, including

- The default server name to use.
- The administrative password to use.

    Unless you specify that you want this password to be encrypted, it will appear in plain text in the generated answer file. From a security perspective, I would recommend that you never store an administrative password in any form of answer file.

- The default console display resolution and color depth.
- Whether the server automatically joins a domain or workgroup.

    If you will be completely automating creation of the cloned image, you should configure the answer file so that the server remains in a workgroup. This way, you have the opportunity to rename the server and add it to the domain immediately after the first boot.

- The server's time zone.

A sample answer file looks as follows:

```
;SetupMgrTag

[Unattended]
    InstallFilesPath=C:\sysprep\i386

[GuiUnattended]
    AdminPassword=*
    EncryptedAdminPassword=NO
    OEMSkipRegional=1

[UserData]
    FullName="Noisy River"
    OrgName="Noisy River"
    ComputerName=*
```

```
[LicenseFilePrintData]
    AutoMode=PerSeat

[SetupMgr]
    DistFolder=C:\sysprep\i386
    DistShare=windist

[Identification]
    JoinWorkgroup=WORKGROUP

[Networking]
    InstallDefaultComponents=Yes
```

MetaFrame Cloning Considerations

When cloning a MetaFrame Presentation Server, there are some additional requirements that you will have to take into consideration. In particular, the type of data store that you have implemented will have an effect on exactly how you go about cloning the servers in your farm. The next two sections will discuss the basic imaging requirements depending on the type of data store that you have implemented.

When using the Access or Microsoft SQL Server 2000 Desktop Engine, the use of cloning is complicated slightly. Because the data store resides locally on the MetaFrame server, an image of the server hosting the data store cannot be used to build indirect servers for the farm. You will need to have an image of the first indirectly connected MetaFrame server in order to rapidly build additional servers for the farm.

Cloning the Access/MSDE Data Store Server

Even though you cannot simply take an image of the data store server and use it to build indirectly connected servers, this doesn't mean that you can't leverage any application installation or configuration work that you may have already done on the existing data store server. In order to clone the existing data store server for use in building the base image for indirectly connected servers, you should do the following:

1. Make sure a local administrator has full administrative privileges in the MetaFrame data store.
2. Create an image of the existing data store but do *not* run SysPrep on the server first. Running SysPrep can cause issues with the server. You simply want to take a snapshot of the existing server as-is.
3. Now restore this image onto the new hardware. Make sure not to connect the server to the network. Because we have not run SysPrep, it still has the same PC name, so we want to keep it completely separate from the real MetaFrame server.

4. Log on locally to the server and uninstall MPS. This will completely remove all MetaFrame components from our cloned machine. After the uninstall has completed, reboot the server, continuing to keep the server off of the network.

5. Without removing the server from the domain, run SysPrep on the server and reboot. Do not clone the image yet. Once the server has restarted, proceed through the mini-setup wizard for SysPrep. Once that has completed you should have a new server with all of the same applications that are on the Citrix server that was cloned, except that this machine is running only Terminal Services. Log on and verify that the applications are still functioning properly.

6. Now reinstall MetaFrame on this server with an indirect connection to the original server that houses the data store. Once the installation has completed you will have a basic MetaFrame system with all of the same applications as the original server.

Cloning the Direct or Indirect MetaFrame Server

Once you have verified that you have a server in your farm that is not housing the data store, you can use this server to create an image that is then used to rapidly build new servers for the farm. The following steps apply to both indirectly connected (Access and MSDE) and directly connected servers (SQL, Oracle, DB2).

This server image is built as follows:

1. Log on to the server to clone and delete the wfcname.ini file from the root of C:\.

2. Stop the IMA Server and configure its startup state to manual.

3. If the server is running Enterprise Edition with Resource Manager then the local Resource Manager database needs to be deleted. It can be found in the %Program Files%\Citrix\Citrix Resource Manager\LocalDB and is called RMLocalDatabase.

4. Run Sysprep and save an image of the server when complete. The core image is now saved.

5. Deploy the image onto the new server and proceed through the mini-setup wizard. Once it has booted successfully restart the IMA server and set it to automatic. The service should successfully start and the server should be automatically added to the server farm.

6. You will need to verify that the zone information for the new server is correct. By default, a newly imaged server will add itself to the default zone, which matches the subnet of the MetaFrame server. Zone information is found within the Management Console, under the properties for the server farm.

At this point the server build is complete. Validate that the software on the server is functioning properly and add it into any desired application publishing setups. When first creating servers from cloned images it is always a good idea to test the server before putting it into production.

Appendixes

Terminal Services Command Reference

Command Summary List

This appendix is a reference of the Terminal Server—specific commands available with a base Windows Server 2003 or Windows 2000 Server installation. For all Terminal Server commands, the /? parameter displays the usage for that command.

MetaFrame-specific commands are not listed in this appendix. Please see Appendix B, "MetaFrame Presentation Server Command Reference," for a complete list of the additional commands provided when MetaFrame Presentation Server is installed on a Terminal Server. Table A.1 summarizes the available Terminal Server commands referenced in this appendix.

Table A.1   Terminal Server Commands

Command	Description
Change Logon	Enables/disables all client session logons.
Change Port	Changes the COM port mappings.
Change User	Switches the server between install mode and execute mode.
Cprofile	Cleans user registry files (NTUSER.DAT) to reduce their size.
FlatTemp	Turns on and off Terminal Server's management of user temporary folders.
Logoff	Logs off a user session.
Msg	Sends a message to one or more user sessions.
MSTSC	Launches the Remote Desktop Connection RDP client.
Query Process	Lists running processes on a Terminal Server.
Query Session	Lists sessions on a Terminal Server.
Query Termserver	Lists Terminal Servers in your environment.

Table A.1 Terminal Server Commands (continued)

Command	Description
Query User	Lists the users logged on to a Terminal Server.
Query Winsta	Same command as Query Session.
Register	Registers a resource as system global or user global.
Reset Session	Performs a reset of a user's session.
Reset Winsta	Same command as Reset Session.
Shadow	Remotely views and controls another user's Terminal Server session.
TaskKill	Terminates processes running on the server by either user ID or process ID.
TSAdmin	Launches the Terminal Services Manager GUI tool.
TSCC.MSC	Launches the Terminal Services Configuration snap-in.
TSCon	Reconnects a user's session to a different user's session.
TSDisConn	Disconnects a user's session.
TSKill	Terminates a process on the Terminal Server.
TSMMC.MSC	Launches the Remote Desktop's snap-in.
TSProf	Views, copies, or edits certain Terminal Server user account information.
TSShutdn	Shuts down a Terminal Server.

CHANGE LOGON

Used mainly for system maintenance, this utility enables or disables logons for *all* client sessions on the Terminal Server. This includes administrators as well as regular users. This command will *not* disable logons at the Terminal Server console. When logons are disabled, a client connection attempt results in the message shown in Figure A.1, which appears even before a logon screen appears. This differs from disabling connections through Terminal Services Configuration, which results in a generic "The client could not connect to the remote computer" error message.

Figure A.1 Users see this message when logons have been disabled.

Disabled logons can be reset by using either the /ENABLE switch or by simply rebooting the server. A reboot automatically resets logons disabled through the CHANGE LOGON command.

Usage:

```
change logon {/enable | /disable | /query}
```

Option	Function
/enable	Allows clients to log on to the Terminal Server.
/disable	Prevents users from logging on to the Terminal Server. Users who are currently logged on are unaffected by this command. After the user logs off, however, he or she can't log on again until logons are enabled.
/query	Displays the current state of logons.

Examples:

```
C:\>change user /disable
Session logins are currently DISABLED
```

TIP: If the group policy "Allow users to connect remotely using Terminal Services" has been configured, it will override the CHANGE LOGON command and you will need to modify the policy in order to manipulate user logons. This policy is found under Computer Configuration\Administrative Templates\Windows Components\Terminal Services

CHANGE PORT

This command allows mapping of COM ports to other existing port numbers. This is most commonly used to provide COM port support to DOS-based applications, most of which support only COM ports 1 through 4. Conceptually this is similar to the SUBST command for assigning drive letters.

Note that changes made with the CHANGE PORT command will affect any applications on the server (Win32 or other) that utilize a COM port.

Usage:

```
change port [portx=porty | /d portx]
```

Options	Function
portx=porty	Maps COM port x to port y.
/d portx	Deletes the mapping for COM port x.

Examples:

```
C:\>change port COM3=COM1

C:\>change port
AUX = \DosDevices\COM1
COM1 = \Device\Serial0
COM2 = \Device\Serial1
COM3 = \Device\Serial0
```

CHANGE USER

This command switches the .INI mapping settings back and forth from execute mode to installation mode and is used when installing applications onto a Terminal Server. When in install mode, the following happens:

- Any INI files located in the system root (usually WINNT or WINDOWS) that are updated/created by the installation and that use the standard APIs for INI file manipulation will be "flagged" by Terminal Server as being changed and the update time recorded. This information will be used to synchronize with a user's personal INI file, explained shortly.
- The local registry on the server is monitored, and changes made in the HKEY_CURRENT_USER registry key are copied into the following key:

  HKEY_LOCAL_MACHINE\SOFTWARE\Microsoft\Windows NT\CurrentVersion\Terminal Server\Install

■ Any changes made to any other registry key outside of HKEY_CURRENT_USER are not replicated under the \INSTALL key.

When the server is placed back into execute mode, the following happens:

■ When an application attempts to access an INI file that doesn't exist in the user's personal system directory, Terminal Server looks in the system root of the server and then copies that file into the user's personal system directory. If a file on the server is newer, it's either recopied or the changes are merged. You can configure how Terminal Server processes individual files by adding the appropriate INI file name and configuration flag to the following registry key: HKEY_LOCAL_MACHINE\Software\Microsoft\Windows NT\CurrentVersion\Terminal Server\Compatibility\IniFiles

For details on how this is done, including the configuration flag options, see Chapter 21, "Application Integration."

TIP: A user's personal system directory is typically in the Windows folder under their home directory (%HOMEDRIVE%%HOMEPATH%). If you have defined the root drive on your Terminal Server (W:, for example), the Windows folder will be immediately accessible under the user's root drive.

■ When an application attempts to access the HKEY_CURRENT_USER key for a user and the requested registry entry doesn't exist, Terminal Server copies the existing key from the \Install key mentioned earlier and places it into the user's personal profile. Of course, if the user is using a mandatory profile, these changes won't be saved when he or she exits.

Detailed examples on use of the CHANGE USER command can be found in Chapter 21.

Usage:

```
change user {/install | /execute | /query}
```

Option	Function
/install	Switches the server from execution mode to installation mode.
/execute	Switches the server back to execution mode.
/query	Displays the current state of the file mapping, either install or execute.

Examples:

```
C:\>change user /install
User session is ready to install applications.

C:\>change user /execute
User session is ready to execute applications.
```

CPROFILE

The CPROFILE command cleans the registry file (NTUSER.DAT) of wasted space in one or more user profiles. If the profile is currently in use, it won't be modified. In Chapter 18, "User Profile and Account Configuration," I discuss using CPROFILE to help optimize the size of the users' registry files.

Usage:

```
cprofile [/l] [/i] [/v] [filelist]
```

Option	Function
/l	Cleans all local profiles, normally located under %SystemDrive%\ Documents and Settings. Additional profiles can be specified with the filelist parameter.
/i	Prompts for confirmation for each profile to be cleaned.
/v	Runs the command in verbose mode.
filelist	A list of files (separated by spaces) to be cleaned. You can also use wildcard characters.

This example shows how running the CPROFILE command can shrink the NTUSER.DAT file. It also demonstrates the errors generated when CPROFILE tries to modify a profile currently in use.

```
C:\>dir c:\documents and settings\toddm\NTUSER.DAT /a
Volume in drive C is System
Volume Serial Number is 5492-71B2

Directory of c:\documents and settings\toddm

01/17/2002   07:15 PM                 524,288 NTUSER.DAT
              1 File(s)         524,288 bytes
              0 Dirs(s) 4,653,066,041 bytes free

C:\>cprofile /l
Failed to load profile, error=2
```

```
Unable to open the profile
C:\WINNT\system32\config\systemprofile\NTUSER.DAT.  Profile skipped.
Profile is being used and cannot be processed
Unable to open the profile C:\Documents and
Settings\NetworkService\NTUSER.DAT.  Profile skipped.
Profile is being used and cannot be processed
Unable to open the profile C:\Documents and
Settings\Administrator\NTUSER.DAT.  Profile skipped.

C:\>dir c:\documents and settings\toddm\NTUSER.DAT /a
Volume in drive C is System
Volume Serial Number is 5492-71B2

Directory of c:\documents and settings\toddm

01/23/2002  09:21 AM               491,520 NTUSER.DAT
              1 File(s)         491,520 bytes
              0 Dirs(s) 4,653,098,809 bytes free
```

FLATTEMP

This command controls whether Terminal Server will automatically generate a user's temp folder when they log on (and delete it when they log out), or if each user will have a temporary folder whose name and contents are persistent between sessions.

By default, FLATTEMP is disabled, so Terminal Server automatically creates a user-specific temporary folder and assigns it a unique folder name. This folder will be created under the folder pointed to by the TEMP environment variable. The folder name corresponds to the user's current session ID on the Terminal Server.

For example, if I log on to a Terminal Server and end up with session ID 3, then my TEMP environment variable would point to

```
C:\DOCUME~1\TODD~1\LOCALS~1\Temp\3
```

This is the eight-character DOS-compatible path to

```
C:\Documents and Settings\TODD\Local Settings\Temp\3
```

Once I log off, the folder 3 is automatically deleted. The next time I log on, my new temporary folder corresponds to my current session ID.

If the FLATTEMP option is enabled, each user still has his or her own personal temporary folder but no session ID subfolder is created. Instead, all temporary data remains in the temp folder and is not deleted upon logout.

In this situation, my temporary folder would be

`C:\DOCUME~1\TODD~1\LOCALS~1\Temp`

I suggest leaving FLATTEMP disabled and allowing Terminal Server to automatically manage the user's temp folder location.

WARNING: I recommend that temp folders always remain local to the Terminal Server and not be moved to a folder located on a network share. Even short interruptions in communication could result in problems if an application doesn't have access to its temporary files.

The FLATTEMP option can also be managed through the Terminal Services Configuration application. It is the Use Temporary Folders Per Session option, shown in Figure A.2. Enabling FLATTEMP through a command prompt will *not* update the attribute in Terminal Services Configuration, or vice versa. I recommend that any changes be made through the GUI tool or through group policy objects. See Chapter 15, "Group Policy Configuration," for more information on GPOs. If temp folders are managed through a GPO, there is no need to use the FLATTEMP command.

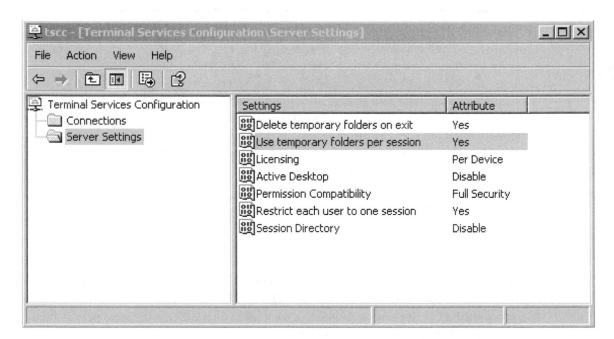

Figure A.2   Managing the temporary folder settings through Terminal Services Configuration.

Usage:

```
flattemp {/query | /enable | /disable}
```

Option	Function
/query	Displays the current setting for FlatTemp.
/enable	Configures all users to share the same temp folder by default.
/disable	Configures all users to have a unique temp folder by default.

Examples:

```
C:\>flattemp /enable
```

Temporary directories will be flat (users will share the temporary directory unless the temporary directory resides in the user's home directory).

LOGOFF

This command enables you to log off your own or, with sufficient privileges, another user's Terminal Server session.

WARNING: If you don't specify any parameters when running LOGOFF, it immediately logs you off your current session.

When a user who is running the RDP client version 5.1 or higher has their session forcibly logged off using a command such as this, they receive the error message shown in Figure A.3.

Figure A.3 Error message returned when a client is forcibly logged off.

Usage:

```
logoff [sessionname | sessionid] [/server:servername] [/v]
```

Option	Function
sessionid	ID of the session to log off.
sessionname	Name of the session to log off.
/server:servername	The Terminal Server on which the session to log off resides. The default is the current server.
/v	Runs the command in verbose mode.

Examples:

```
C:\>logoff 4 /v
Logging off session ID 4
```

MSG

Use MSG to send messages to one or more Terminal Server users in your environment. The user will receive the message in a dialog box similar to the one shown in Figure A.4. Unless the /time or /w parameters are included, MSG displays the message for 60 seconds and then automatically closes the dialog box.

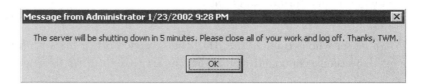

Message from Administrator 1/23/2002 9:28 PM   ✕

The server will be shutting down in 5 minutes. Please close all of your work and log off. Thanks, TWM.

OK

Figure A.4   MSG message dialog box on a Terminal Server user's session.

TIP: To send a message to other users, the sender must have the Message permission set for his or her connection. Connection permissions are discussed in Chapter 16, "Terminal Server Security."

Usage:

```
msg {username | sessionname | sessionid | @filename | *}
[/server:servername] [/time:seconds] [/v] [/w] [message]
```

Option	Function
username	Name of the user who will receive the message.
sessionname	Name of the session that will receive the message.
sessionid	ID of the session that will receive the message.
@filename	File that can contain a mixture of user names, session names, and session IDs to which you want to send the message. One entry should appear per line, separated by a carriage return and linefeed.
*	Sends the message to all users on the server.
/server:servername	Terminal Server where the message will be displayed.
/time:seconds	Length of time the message will display on the user's screen before automatically closing. The default is 60.
/v	Runs the command in verbose mode.
/w	Forces the dialog box to remain on the user's display until acknowledged. If the /time parameter is also used, this setting is ignored.
message	Message you want to send. If you specify no message, input is read from standard input (Stdin).

Examples:

```
C:\>msg rdp-tcp#6 /v "Please log off of the server now."
Sending message to session RDP-Tcp#6, display time 60
Async message sent to session RDP-Tcp#6
```

MSTSC

This command launches the Remote Desktop Connection RDP client.

Usage:

```
mstsc [[Client File] [/v:server[:port]] [/console] [/fullscreen] [/w:width
/h:height]] | /Edit "filename" | /migrate
```

Option	Function
Client File	The RDP file to read connection information from.
/v:server[:port]	Allows you to specify a server and an optional port to connect to.
/console	Establishes a connection with the console session on a server.
/fullscreen	Starts the connection in full-screen mode. You can use /f for short.

Option	Function
/w:width	The width of the RDP session.
/h:height	The height of the RDP session.
/edit "filename"	Opens the specified RDP file name for editing.
/migrate	Allows you to migrate a connection file created using the Client Connection Manager (CCM) on Windows 2000 to the new RDP format.

Examples:

```
C:\>mstsc /v:w2k3ts01.nrtestdom.com
```

QUERY PROCESS

This command displays the following information on processes running on a Terminal Server:

- The owner of the process
- The session name and ID that own the process
- The state of the process
- The process ID
- The image (executable) name of the process

TIP: The short form of this command is QPROCESS. All parameter options are identical.

Usage:

```
query process [processid | username | sessionname | /id:sessionid |
programname | *] [/server:servername] [/system]
```

TIP: Unless a user has the Query Process right, the user can view only his or her own processes.

Option	Function
Processed	ID of the process you want to display.
Username	Name of the user whose processes you want to display.
Sessionname	Name of the session containing the processes to display.
/id:sessionid	ID of the session containing the processes to display.
Programname	Name of the executable for which you want to display all processes. You must include the .EXE extension.
°	Shows information for all processes.
/server:servername	Name of the Terminal Server containing the processes to display. The default is the current server.
/system	Displays system process information. Windows 2000 only.

Examples:

```
C:\>qprocess *
USERNAME              SESSIONNAME        ID     PID    IMAGE
>network service      console            0      936    svchost.exe
>network service      console            0      1096   msdtc.exe
>administrator        console            0      1992   explorer.exe
>administrator        console            0      264    cmd.exe
 todd                 rdp-tcp#6          2      3772   rdpclip.exe
 todd                 rdp-tcp#6          2      3916   explorer.exe
>administrator        console            0      1816   qprocess.exe
```

QUERY SESSION

QUERY SESSION lets you view detailed information about sessions on any Terminal Server in your environment. Executing QUERY SESSION without any parameters lists all sessions configured on the Terminal Server. The following information is normally displayed:

- **Session name**—The name assigned when the connections were created.
- **User name**—If a user is connected to a session, his or her name is displayed.
- **Session ID**—The ID assigned to the session by the system.
- **State**—The state of the session, which is one of the following:
    - **active**—A user is currently logged on to the session.
    - **conn**—The session is connected, but no user is currently logged on.
    - **connq**—The session is currently in the process of connecting, and the logon screen has not yet appeared.

rctrl—The session is shadowing another session.

listen—The session is waiting to accept a client connection.

disc—The session has been disconnected.

idle—The session has been initialized.

down—The session has failed to initialize and is unavailable.

init—The session is currently initializing.

- **Type**—The session type, which is wdcon (console), wdica (ICA), or rdpwd (RDP).

- **Device**—The device name assigned to the session. It appears blank for console or network connections.

Usage:

```
query session [sessionname | username | sessionid] [/server:server-
name] [/mode] [/flow] [/connect] [/counter] [/sm]
```

Option	Function
sessionname	Name of the session you want to query.
username	Name of the user whose session information you want to query.
sessionid	ID of the session you want to query.
/server:servername	Name of the Terminal Server containing the sessions to query. The default is the current server.
/mode	Displays the current asynchronous line settings.
/flow	Displays the flow control settings.
/connect	Displays the connect settings.
/counter	Displays the total sessions created, disconnected, and reconnected.
/sm	Lists only the session name and the session's current state. This command is undocumented in both Windows 2000 and Windows 2003.

Examples:

```
C:\query session
 SESSIONNAME            USERNAME              ID   STATE   TYPE    DEVICE
>console                Administrator          0   Active  wdcon
 rdp-tcp                                    65536   Listen  rdpwd
 rdp-tcp#6             Todd                      2   Active  rdpwd
 rdp-tcp#8                                       1   Conn    rdpwd
                                                 3   ConnQ
                                                 4   Idle
```

QUERY TERMSERVER

This command lists the available Terminal Servers and provides some basic information about them. It returns the server name and the network and node address (if requested). This command should not be confused with the QUERY SERVER command, which displays information specific to ICA. See Appendix B for more information in this command.

TIP: An asterisk (*) appears in the output beside the name of the Terminal Server from which the command was run.

Usage:

```
query termserver [servername] [/domain:domainname] [/address] [/continue]
```

Option	Function
servername	The specific Terminal Server to query.
/domain:domainname	Provides Terminal Server information for the specified domain. The default is the current domain.
/address	Displays the network and node address for each server.
/continue	Suppresses stopping after each screen of data.

Examples:

```
C:\>query termserver
Known Terminal servers
_____

NOCTURNAL
TSTEST01
TSTEST02*
MFTEST01
MFTEST02
```

QUERY USER

QUERY USER displays information about the users currently logged on to a Terminal Server. It returns the following information:

- The username. A greater-than (>) character appears beside the name of the current user.
- The session name.
- The session ID.
- The session state, either active or disconnected.
- The amount of idle time since the last keyboard or mouse input was received. If the idle time is less than one minute, it appears as a dot (.)
- The logon time.

TIP: The short form of this command is QUSER. All parameter options are identical.

Usage:

```
query user [username | sessionname | sessionid] [/server:servername]
```

Option	Function
Username	Name of the user you want to query.
Sessionname	Name of the session you want to query.
Sessionid	ID of the session you want to query.
/server:servername	Name of the Terminal Server on which to perform the query. The default is the current server.

Examples:

```
C:\>query user
USERNAME          SESSIONNAME  ID   STATE    IDLE TIME   LOGON TIME
>administrator    console      0    Active         .     1/22/2002 7:32 PM
todd              rdp-tcp#6    2    Active         36     1/23/2002 9:21 PM
```

QUERY WINSTA

See the "QUERY SESSION" section. QUERY WINSTA and QWINSTA provide identical functionality, including parameter inputs and outputs.

REGISTER

The REGISTER command assigns special execution settings to an application on a Terminal Server. Most often the REGISTER program is used to assign system-global characteristics to an executable or one of its components, usually a DLL. By default, objects and resources run in a user-global state on a Terminal Server. This is how multiple instances of the same application can execute on the same Terminal Server without affecting each other.

At the simplest level, it works as follows. Assume you have an object called X running on your Windows desktop. An application accesses this information by the name X, and everything is fine. Now put this same object on a Terminal Server. When the object is referenced in the environment, it's no longer simply X but is now X:n, where n is the session ID belonging to the user who initiated the application. This way, two instances of the same object can exist on the server but are uniquely named and maintained independently of each other. X:9 and X:13 are considered distinct.

The most common purpose of the REGISTER command is to modify this behavior so an object is referenced by the same name for all users in the environment, thereby making the object globally available on the server. If you applied REGISTER to X, it would simply be X on the Terminal Server and not X:9 or X:13.

Fortunately, the need for the REGISTER command has always been quite small and unique to most situations. With the improved application support for Windows 2000/2003, and more specifically Terminal Server, the need for this tool will diminish even further. I talk more about use of the REGISTER command in Chapter 21.

TIP: For changes using REGISTER to take effect, the registered resource must be completely unloaded and reloaded. Either make sure no one is running an application that depends on the resource or restart the Terminal Server if necessary. Ideally this command should be run when there are no users on the system.

Usage:

```
register filename [/system | /user] [/v]
```

Option	Function
Filename	Name of the file to register.
/system	Registers file name as a system-global resource.
/user	Registers file name as a user-global resource.
/v	Runs the application in verbose mode.

Examples:

```
C:\>register atxxipl.dll /system
atxxipl.dll registered SYSTEM GLOBAL
```

RESET SESSION

This command performs a reset of a given Terminal Server session, causing the device to close and reopen and resetting the session to its startup state. If a session fails to reset properly, it usually ends up in a down state. If you need to close a user session, use the LOGOFF command instead, as it ensures the user's session terminates cleanly. Use the RESET SESSION command only when a session fails to respond to a LOGOFF request. Resetting an active session generates the same error on the client machine as a LOGOFF. Refer back to Figure A.3 for an example of this.

Usage:

```
reset session {sessionname | sessionid} [/server:servername] [/v]
```

Option	Function
Sessionname	The name of the session you want to reset.
Sessionid	The ID of the session you want to reset.
/server:servername	The Terminal Server where you intend to reset the connection.
/v	Runs the application in verbose mode.

Examples:

```
C:\>reset session rdp-tcp#6
Resetting session rdp-tcp#6
Session rdp-tcp#6 has been reset
```

RESET WINSTA

See the "RESET SESSION" section. RESET WINSTA provides identical functionality, including parameter inputs and outputs.

SHADOW

SHADOW enables you to establish a connection with another user's active session so you can view and interact with the other user's activities.

When using the ICA client, multiple people can shadow the same user session simultaneously, but you can't shadow a session that's currently busy shadowing someone else. With the RDP client, only one person can shadow a user at a time. See Chapter 22, "Server Operations and Support," for more information on shadowing functionality.

To be able to shadow, you must have the Shadow/Remote Control access permission. When notification is enabled, the user is warned and prompted for confirmation before you can establish the shadow session with that user (see Figure A.5). If the user does not respond within 30 seconds, the shadow request automatically terminates. The console can't be shadowed, nor can it directly shadow other sessions.

In order to terminate a shadow session initiated from the command prompt, the shadower must hit Ctrl+°, where ° is the one located on the numeric keypad on the right-hand side of the keyboard.

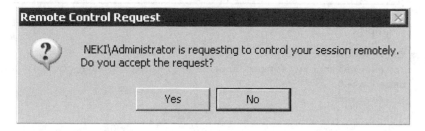

Figure A.5   User confirmation message before allowing shadowing.

NOTE: Shadowing is also known as *remote control* when referring to RDP 5.*x* shadow sessions, or when using the Terminal Services management tools.

If you are using the RDP 5.0 client that ships with Windows 2000, then in order to shadow a user, the following criteria must be met:

- The shadower's monitor resolution must be equal to or greater than that of the person to be shadowed.
- The shadower's session must have the same color depth as the person to be shadowed.

The RDP 5.1 client automatically matches the shadower's desktop resolution to that of the shadowed user. Scroll bars may be added if necessary to accommodate a target that has a higher resolution desktop.

Usage:

```
shadow {sessionname | sessionid} [/server:servername] [/v]
```

Option	Function
Sessionname	The name of the session you want to shadow
Sessionid	The ID of the session you want to shadow
/server:servername	The Terminal Server where the user you want to shadow is currently located
/v	Runs the application in verbose mode

Examples:

```
C:\>shadow 1
Your session may appear frozen while the remote control approval is being
negotiated.
Please wait...
```

TASKKILL (Windows Server 2003 Only)

TASKKILL is available only with Windows Server 2003 and Windows XP Professional or Home Edition. TASSKILL is a robust tool used to terminal processes either by process ID or by execution image name. The process ID or name is easily found using the QUERY PROCESS or the TASKLIST command.

Usage:

```
taskkill [/S system [/U username [/P [password]]]] { [/FI filter]
[/PID processid | /IM imagename] } [/F] [/T]
```

Option	Function
/S system	System specifies the name of the remote computer to connect to. The system name must resolve to an IP address. You do not require the double backslashes before the system name. For example, \\TODDPC.
/U username	If the user is not on the local computer, then prefix it with the domain name and a single backslash. You cannot specify the user name without also specifying the system name.
/P password	Allows you to provide the password for the specified user name. If omitted, you will be prompted to provide the password.
/FI	Filters the task list based on the specified criteria.
/PID process id	The process ID of the task to kill.
/IM imagename	The executable image name of the task to be terminated. The wildcard ° is a valid entry but only when used in conjunction with a filter.
/F	Performs a forceful termination. The process is not given the opportunity to respond to the shutdown request on its own.
/FI	Filters the task list based on the specified criteria. The valid filters are listed below, and the valid logical operators are as follows: eq = equal ne = not equal gt = greater than lt = less than ge = greater than or equal to le = less than or equal to

Filter Name	Operators	Supported Values
Status	eq, ne	Running Not Responding
ImageName	eq, ne	Image name to kill
PID	eq, ne, gt, le, ge, le	The process ID
Session	eq, ne, gt, le, ge, le	The session number
CPUTime	eq, ne, gt, le, ge, le	The CPU time for the process, formatted as hh:mm:ss, which is hours, minutes, and seconds

Option	Function		
	MemUsage	eq, ne, gt, le, ge, le	The current memory usage in KB
	UserName	eq, ne	The user name of the process owner
	Modules	eq, ne	The DLL name
	Services	eq, ne	The service name
	WindowTitle	eq, ne	The Windows title
/T	Kills the given process and all child processes that it created. /T is short for *tree*.		
?	Displays the usage for this command.		

Examples:

```
C:\>query process /ID:4
USERNAME                SESSIONNAME        ID     PID   IMAGE
todd test                                  4      196   rdpclip.exe
todd test                                  4      2612  explorer.exe
todd test                                  4      1967  notepad.exe

C:\>taskkill /FI "USERNAME eq todd test" /IM notepad.exe
SUCCESS: Sent termination signal to the process "notepad.exe" with the
PID 1967.
```

WARNING: Certain processes cannot be killed using the TASKKILL command, including some service and system processes. Other system processes can be killed but they can cause the server to halt with a Stop message. Use caution when terminating any running process on the server.

TSADMIN

TSADMIN launches the Terminal Services Manager application, which can also be found on the Start menu, under the Administrative Tools folder. Figure A.6 shows a screen shot of this tool.

Example:

```
C:\>tsadmin
```

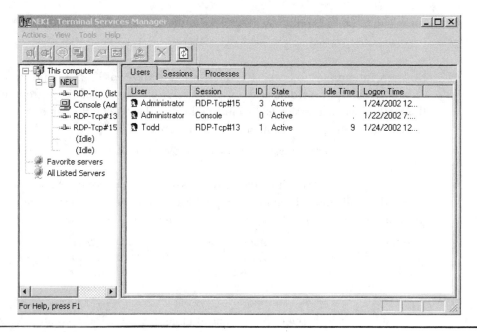

Figure A.6 Terminal Services Manager.

TSCC.MSC

TSCC.MSClaunches the Terminal Services Configuration snap-in. This tool can also be found on the Start menu, under Administrative Tools.

TSCON

This command allows a Terminal Server user session to be connected to another user session on the same server. The command differs from the SHADOW command in that if there is a user currently active on the target session, he or she will be immediately disconnected. When a user attempts to connect to another user's session, the *target* user's password is required, not the person who is trying to establish the connection. A couple of examples will make this clearer. Assume we have the following sessions on a server:

```
USERNAME              SESSIONNAME        ID   STATE
>administrator        console             0   Active
 todd                                     1   Disc
 administrator        rdp-tcp#17          3   Active
```

From the console I could issue the command

```
TSCON 1 /dest:rdp-tcp#17
```

Now, my intention is to connect Todd's session to rdp-tcp#17, but in this case I am required to have Todd's password since I am effectively returning his session from a "locked" state. Remember, when a session is disconnected it is still active on the server, just not visible from any client. So the proper command to run is actually

```
TSCON 1 /dest:rdp-tcp#17  /password:thisisplaintext
```

Notice that I must explicitly include the password in the command statement. There is no switch that will simply have me prompted for it, so instead it must be included as clear text from the command line. After I issue this command the sessions would look as follows:

```
USERNAME              SESSIONNAME        ID   STATE
>administrator        console             0   Active
 todd                 rdp-tcp#17          1   Active
 administrator                            3   Disc
```

Now, what actually happens is not what you might expect. Todd did not take over the administrator's session (ID=3), but instead Todd's original session was reloaded into the rdp-tcp#17 WinStation "slot" on the server and bumped the admin session that was previously connected into a disconnected state. Now let's return to our original scenario:

```
USERNAME              SESSIONNAME        ID   STATE
>administrator        console             0   Active
 todd                                     1   Disc
 administrator        rdp-tcp#17          3   Active
```

Except this time we are logged on as the remotely connected administrator (ID=3) and issue the command

```
TSCON 1
```

What happens is that an error is created saying that it was a bad user name or bad password. If the administrator in the above example knows the password for Todd, then he or she could issue the following command:

```
TSCON 1 /password:thisisplaintext
```

Now Todd's desktop will immediately receive the message that a remote user terminated his session. This is the same message that appears when using the LOGOFF or RESET SESSION commands. Next, the administrator's session on WinStation rdp-tcp#17 will be disconnected, and immediately Todd's session will be "hooked" into that WinStation to take its place. The administrator's client view on his or her desktop will immediately switch over to show Todd's session.

NOTE: When directly logged on to the console, you cannot use TSCON to connect to a remote user session. The reverse also holds true. You cannot use TSCON to connect from a remote user session directly to the console session.

Usage:

```
connect {<sessionid> | <sessionname>}[/dest:<sessionname>]
[/password:<password>] [/v]
```

Option	Function
<sessionid>	<sessionname>	Specifies either the ID or the name of the session. If the destination session name is included, this specifies the session that will connect to the destination. If no destination is specified, this is the target session that the current session will connect to. You can see the session ID or name using either Terminal Server Administration or the QUERY SESSION command.
/server:<servername>	Specifies the Terminal Server on which the sessions reside. If omitted, the current server is used.
/password:<password>	The password of the user who owns the target session. It's required only if the connecting user doesn't own the target session.
/v	Runs the command in verbose mode.

TSDISCON

TSDISCON is used to disconnect any non-console Terminal Server session in your environment. Just as with LOGOFF and RESET SESSION, a user receives a message stating that another user ended the first user's session.

WARNING: If you run TSDISCON without any parameters, it immediately disconnects your session. On Windows Server 2003, if you run TSDISCON from the console, doing so locks your desktop. On a Windows 2000 Server console, it generates an error message.

Usage:

```
tsdiscon [sessionid | sessionname] [/server:servername] [/v]
```

Option	Function
Sessionid	The ID of the session to disconnect. You can determine the ID by running Terminal Server Administration or the QUERY USER command. The default setting is the ID of the person running the command.
sessionname	The name of the session to disconnect, determined the same way you would find the session ID. The default setting is the session name of the person running the command.
/server:servername	The servername value represents the name of the Terminal Server on which you want to run the command. The default setting is the current Terminal Server.
/v	Runs the command in verbose mode.

Examples:

```
C:\>tsdiscon 4 /v
Disconnecting sessionID 4 from sessionname
```

TSKILL

TSKILL is used to terminate processes on a Terminal Server. You can kill only your own processes unless you have administrative privileges, in which case you can kill any process on the Terminal Server. The process ID or name is easily found using the QUERY PROCESS command.

Usage:

```
tskill {processid | processname} [/server:servername] [/id:sessionid |
/a] [/v]
```

Option	Function
Processed	ID of the process to terminate.
processname	Name of the process to terminate. You can use wildcards when specifying the name.
/server:servername	The Terminal Server on which the process to terminate resides. The default is the current server.
/id:sessionid	The Terminal Server session where the process to terminate resides.
/a	Specifies that the process should be killed under all sessions on the Terminal Server. This is used with the processname parameter.
/v	Runs the command in verbose mode.

Examples:

```
C:\>query process /ID:4
USERNAME                SESSIONNAME          ID    PID   IMAGE
todd test                                    4    196   rdpclip.exe
todd test                                    4   2612   explorer.exe
todd test                                    4   1952   notepad.exe

C:\>tskill 1952 /v
End Process(1952)
```

WARNING: Certain processes cannot be killed using the TSKILL command, including some service and system processes. Other system processes can be killed, but they can cause the server to halt with a Stop message. Use caution when terminating any running process on the server.

TSMMC.MSC

TSMMC.MSC launches the little-known Remote Desktops snap-in (see Figure A.7). This handy management tool lets you manage multiple server connections from within the snap-in. Each connection is displayed within the results pane. TSMMC is discussed in detail in Chapter 14.

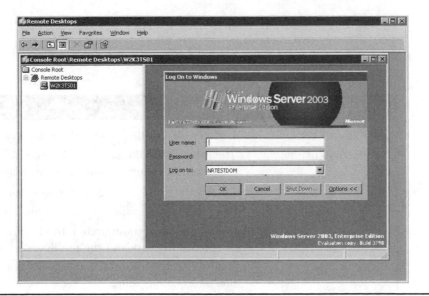

Figure A.7   Remote Desktops Microsoft Management Console snap-in.

Example:
```
C:\>tsmmc.msc
```

TSPROF

TSPROF allows you to view and copy the Terminal Server user configuration information from one user to another and to update the Terminal Server profile path for a user. Typically, this utility is used to script the migration or setup of user accounts for Terminal Server.

TIP: TSPROF doesn't let you edit the contents of the Terminal Services Home Folder field, although it copies this information from one user's configuration to another when using the /COPY command.

TSPROF does perform environment variable expansion, so if for example you have used %USERNAME% in the home directory or Terminal Server profile path for a user account, these variables are properly converted as the information in that profile is copied to the new account.

Upon successful completion, TSPROF doesn't return any status to the command prompt; only an error message, if there was a problem.

Usage:
```
tsprof /update {/domain:domainname | /local} /profile:profilepath
username
tsprof /copy {/domain:domainname | /local}[/profile:profilepath]
srcusername destusername
tsprof /q {/domain:domainname | /local} username
```

Option	Function
/update	Updates the profile path for the named user.
/domain:*domainname*	The name of the domain in which you will perform the operation. The current domain is the default.
/local	Applies the profile change to the local user accounts only.
/profile:*profilepath*	The path to the profiles on the Terminal Server.
/copy	Copies the user's configuration from *srcusername* to *destusername*. Also updates the profile path on the destination.
Srcusername	Name of the user from whom you will copy the configuration information (source).
Destusername	Name of the user to whom you will copy information (destination).

| /q | Displays the user's profile path, ensuring that it's valid. You must either specify the domain or use /local in conjunction with this command; otherwise an error is generated. |
| Username | Name of the person whose profile you want to update. |

TIP: If the user who is being queried doesn't have a profile path defined, or the user ID doesn't exist, you receive the following message:

```
Failed getting User Configuration, Error = 1332 (0x534)
```

or

```
Failed setting User Configuration, Error = 1332 (0x534)
```

Examples:

```
C:\>tsprof /update /domain:NRAD /profile:\\profserv\roaming\bob bob
```

```
C:\>tsprof /copy /local todd bob
Failed setting User Configuration, Error = 1332 (0x534)
```

TSSHUTDN

TSSHUTDN lets an administrator safely shut down a Terminal Server from the command prompt. Once the shutdown is initiated, every active session on the server receives a message similar to the one shown in Figure A.8.

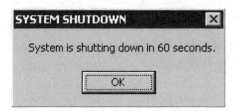

Figure A.8   Shutdown notification displayed after TSSHUTDN is called.

WARNING: Executing TSSHUTDN without any parameters initiates a shutdown of your server.

Usage:

```
tsshutdn [waittime] [/server:servername] [/reboot] [/powerdown]
[/delay:logoffdelay] [/v
```

Option	Function
waittime	Time (in seconds) that tsshutdn waits for users to log off the server. The default is 60 seconds.
/server:servername	Terminal Server to be shut down. If omitted, the server on which the command is run shuts down.
/reboot	Terminal Server shuts down and restarts.
/powerdown	Terminal Server shuts down and then initiates the actual power-down, if supported by the server hardware.
/delay:logoffdelay	Amount of time tsshutdn waits after all user sessions have been terminated before terminating all processes. The default is 30 seconds.
/v	Runs the application in verbose mode.

Examples:

```
C:\>tsshutdn 60 /reboot /v
Sending message to Session Console
Sending message to Session RDP-Tcp#31
Sending message to Session RDP-Tcp#39
Sending message to Session RDP-Tcp#43
Notifying Users, Type ^C to Cancel Shutdown.
System shutdown in progress ... Logging off all users ...
Sending message to Session Console
Notifying Users, Type ^C to Cancel Shutdown.

Shutdown is complete.
The system will now reboot.
```

MetaFrame Presentation Server Command Reference

Command Summary List

This appendix is a reference of the MetaFrame Presentation Server–specific commands available when installed on a Windows 2003/2000 Terminal Server. For most commands, the /? parameter displays the command's usage. In my examples, I assume that you have remapped the server drives starting at X:. If you used a different mapping or have not remapped the drives at all, simply substitute the X: drive for the desired drive letter and the examples will still work correctly.

Terminal Server–specific commands are not listed in this appendix. Please see Appendix A, "Terminal Services Command Reference," for a complete list of the basic commands provided with a Windows 2003 or 2000 Terminal Server installation. Table B.1 summarizes the available MetaFrame Presentation Server commands referenced in this appendix.

Table B.1 MetaFrame Presentation Server Commands

Command	Description
AcrCfg	Lets you configure the auto client reconnect settings.
AltAddr	Manages alternate IP addresses.
App	Simple, serial execution scripting tool.
AuditLog	Generates reports based on the contents of the security event log.
Change Client	Manages client device mappings.
ChFarm	Changes a server's farm membership.
ChgCdm	Same command as Change Client.
CltPrint	Adjusts the number of printer pipes for the client print spooler.

Table B.1 MetaFrame Presentation Server Commands (continued)

Command	Description
Ctxxmlss	Changes the listening port for the Citrix XML Service.
DSCheck	Performs an integrity check against the data store.
DSMaint Recover	Restores an Access data store from the system backup.
DSMaint Backup	Backs up an Access data store to a specified location.
DSMaint CompactDB	Compacts an Access data store.
DSMaint Compare	Compares the source data store with the migrated data store.
DSMaint Config	Modifies the data store connection parameters for the IMA service.
DSMaint FailOver	Changes the direct server pointed to by an indirect MetaFrame server.
DSMaint Migrate	Migrates a data store from one database to another.
DSMaint PublishSQLDS	Publishes SQL Server articles as part of SQL Server replication.
DSMaint RecreateLHC	Rebuilds the local host cache.
DSMaint VerifyLHC	Verifies the integrity of the local host cache.
ICAPort	Modifies the listening port for TCP/IP ICA connections.
IMAPort	Modifies the communication port for the IMA service, the management console, and the data store server port when running in indirect mode only.
Query Farm	Retrieves information about MetaFrame servers within an IMA server farm.
Query Server	Retrieves information from MetaFrame 1.x servers or XP servers in interoperability mode.
TWConfig	Configures the ICA display settings.

ACRCFG

This command lets you configure the auto client reconnect settings for an individual server or the farm-wide defaults.

Usage:

```
acrcfg [/query] {[/server:servername] | [/farm]}
acrcfg {[/server:servername] | [/farm]} [/inherit:on|off]
[/require:on|off] [/logging:on|off]
```

Option	Function
/query	Displays the current settings.
/server:servername	Specifies an alternate MetaFrame server to view or update. The default is the local server.
/farm	Specifies the farm to view or update.
/inherit:on|off	Turns on or off farm inheritance for this setting.
/require:on|off	Turns the requirement for user authentication on or off.
/logging:on|off	Turns logging on or off for client reconnections.

Examples:

```
X:\>acrcfg /query
Auto Client Reconnect Info for: Local Server

    INHERIT:      on
    REQUIRE:      off
    LOGGING:      off

X:\>acrcfg /query /farm
Auto Client Reconnect Info for: Farm-wide Settings

    REQUIRE:      off
    LOGGING:      off
```

ALTADDR

The ALTADDR command is used to manage the alternate IP address on a MetaFrame server. When requested, this alternate address is returned to an ICA client that is typically located on the external side of a firewall performing network address translation (NAT). Figure B.1 shows a simple example of this.

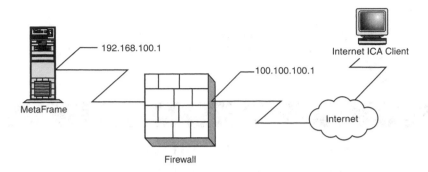

Figure B.1 A simple example of where ALTADDR could be used to provide connectivity.

As you can see, the MetaFrame server is located on the internal network and has address 192.168.100.1. The firewall is performing NAT from the external interface of 100.100.100.1 through to the MetaFrame server. When launching a published application (through Program Neighborhood, Program Neighborhood Agent, or Web Interface for MetaFrame, for example), normally the "true" IP address of the MetaFrame server is returned to the client, but in this case 192.168.100.1 would be of no use to an external client, since there is no valid route to that address.

Instead, the client actually wants to receive the *external* address (the one that will be translated). This is where the ALTADDR command comes in. ALTADDR lets you define the external address of the MetaFrame server that can then be returned to an ICA client if requested. The client must be configured to request the alternate address in order to receive it. Figure B.2 shows an example of where this would be set on a Win32 client. See Chapter 14, "MetaFrame Presentation Server Configuration," for a complete discussion on accessing a MetaFrame server through a firewall.

TIP: If external clients are connecting directly to a MetaFrame server through the external address, the ALTADDR setting does not need to be configured. It must be set up only if you will be connecting to published applications (directly, via Program Neighborhood or Web Interface for MetaFrame Presentation Server) and the MetaFrame servers in the farm are behind a firewall from the connecting clients.

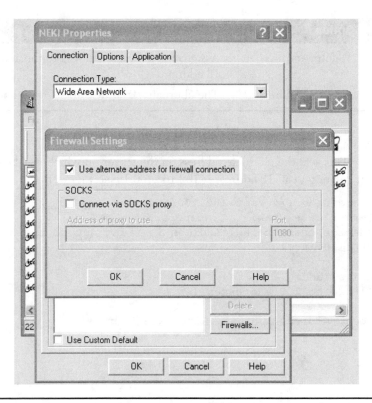

Figure B.2   Configuring use of an alternate address in the firewall settings of a Win32 client.

Usage:

```
altaddr [/v] [/server:name] [/set <AlternateAddress>]
altaddr [/v] [/server:name] [/delete [AdapterAddress]]
altaddr [/v] [/server:name] [/set <AdapterAddress>
<AlternateAddress>]
```

Option	Function
/v	For verbose display mode.
/server:name	Applies the configuration to the server specified by *name* instead of the current server.
/set	Sets the alternate TCP/IP address specified.
/delete	Deletes *only* the default alternate addresses on the server unless a specific adapter address (IP address) is given.

Option	Function
AdapterAddress	Assigns the alternate address to the adapter specified by this IP address.
AlternateAddress	The alternate IP address to set or delete.

Examples:

This sets the alternate address on the server on which it is being run. In this example, our server's "real" IP address is 192.168.100.1 (see Figure B.1).

```
X:\>altaddr /v /set 100.100.100.1
Server Name: neki    Transport Name: TCP
Adapter entry DefaultAddress is being set to the alternate address
100.100.100.1

X:\>altaddr
Alternate TCP addresses for neki

Local Address           Alternate Address
_____         _____

Default                 100.100.100.1
```

TIP: You must configure an alternate address for every server that will be accessed from across the firewall. If you have servers in your farm that will not be accessed externally, you will not be required to configure an alternate address.

APP

APP is a simple scripting tool you can use to fine-tune an application's behavior. It's often used to improve application security by letting you perform specific actions before and after execution of an application. APP differs from simply using a .CMD batch file because it ensures that the listed commands are processed sequentially and execution cannot be terminated by the user. If an application is started from within APP, the script waits until the application terminates before continuing. This can be very useful, particularly if you must perform an action only once the application has finished executing.

Any script files you create for APP must be located in the %SystemRoot%\Scripts folder. You may need to create this folder, as it does not exist by default. Because APP always looks in the same location for the script file, you can simply use the script file name regardless of where APP is actually called. For example:

```
X:\>app RunApp.txt
```

where `RunApp.txt` is the script file.

TIP: The APP scripting tool provides only limited functionality. Very often I use APP to control calling other scripts written using languages such as VBScript, which provide more robust functionality with such features as registry updates. After the application terminates, I can then use APP to call other scripts to perform additional cleanup.

Usage:

```
app <scriptfile>
```

Option	Function
Scriptfile	The name of the script file containing the APP commands. The commands are listed next. If scriptfile is omitted, APP terminates with an error. The script file must reside in %systemroot%\Scripts.

APP Command	Description
copy <source> <target>	Copies files from source to target. Wildcards (* or ?) are supported.
delete <file>	Deletes the specified file.
Deleteall <directory>\<file>	Deletes all files in the specified directory. A file name or wildcard must be included; otherwise, nothing gets deleted.
path <file>	Sets <file> to be executed by the execute command.
Workdir <directory>	Sets the working directory for the execute command.
Execute	Executes the file specified by the path command. The working directory is set with the workdir command.

Examples:

Begin by creating the folder %SystemRoot%\Scripts. Then create a command script called LISTIT.cmd that contains the following line:

```
Dir * /s > x:\temp\output.txt
```

You may need to create the X:\TEMP directory in order for this example to work properly. Next create an APP script in the same folder called RUNIT.TXT, which contains the following:

```
Path x:\windows\scripts\listit.cmd
Workdir x:\
Execute

Path x:\windows\notepad.exe output.txt
Workdir x:\temp
Execute

Deleteall x:\temp\*
```

And finally, from a command prompt, execute the following command:

```
X:\>app RUNIT.TXT
```

The APP script file pipes the directory listing for the entire X: drive into a temp folder. Once that has completed, Notepad opens the output file for editing. Only once you have closed Notepad are the contents of the temp folder deleted.

AUDITLOG

Citrix has made the AUDITLOG utility available to simplify review of logon/logoff activity on a MetaFrame server. AUDITLOG generates a report based on the Security portion of the event log.

NOTE: Logon/logoff auditing must be enabled for AUDITLOG to generate any output. Otherwise, you get the following message:

Unable to open security event log, make sure logon/logoff auditing is enabled.

See Chapter 16, "Terminal Server Security," for information on enabling and configuring auditing on your Terminal Server.

Usage:

```
auditlog [username | session] [/before:mm/dd/yy] [/after:mm/dd/yy]
[/write:filename | [/time | /fail | /all | /detail]] [/eventlog:file-
name]
auditlog /clear[:backup_log_filename]
```

Option	Function
Username	Generates the report for the specified user.
Session	Generates a report for the specified connection session. This will be the name assigned to the connection type, such as RDP-tcp#1, or CONSOLE. This option is most useful when reporting on the console usage.
/before:mm/dd/yy	Generates the report only for dates before the one entered.
/after:mm/dd/yy	Generates the report only for dates after the one entered.
/write:filename	Writes the output of Auditlog to the specified file. The data is comma-delimited so it can be imported easily into other applications, such as a spreadsheet or database, to produce reports or statistics. If the file already exists, the new data is appended to the end of the file.
/time	Generates a report that displays the logon/logoff times and total time online for each user. The output of this report differs from the standard report. It will list the user name and the logon computer, followed by a list of logon/logoff dates and times and finally the totals. This option in combination with the user name is an excellent way to create a summary of a user's system habits.
/fail	Generates a report for failed logon attempts only.
/all	Generates a report of all logon/logoff activity. This includes noninteractive logons such as drive mappings or the "logon" of system processes at startup.
/detail	Creates a detailed report of logon/logoff activity. This report reproduces the complete information displayed for each event in the security log pertaining to logon/logoff.
/eventlog:filename	Lets you run Auditlog against a file containing a backup of the security event log. The backup file can be created using the /clear option or from within the event viewer.
/clear[:backup_log_filename]	Clears the event log and saves the current contents to the backup file, if specified. If the file already exists, this command fails.

Examples:

```
X:\>auditlog
DOMAIN\USERNAME                EVENT        TIME
NEKI\Todd                      Logon OK     1/27/2002 22:41
NEKI\imevil                    Logon Fail   1/27/2002 22:40
   Reason: Unknown user name or bad password
NEKI\Administrator             Logon OK     1/27/2002 22:38
NEKI\Administrator             Logon OK     1/27/2002 22:28

X:\>auditlog /time
User: Todd
    Logon: 1/27/2002 22:41    CurTm: 1/27/2002 22:48    Total:
00:06:58
    Total logon time: 00:06:58

User: Administrator
    Logon: 1/27/2002 22:28    ShutDn: 1/27/2002 22:37    Total:
00:08:33
    Logon: 1/27/2002 22:38    CurTm: 1/27/2002 22:48    Total:
00:10:15
    Total logon time: 00:18:48

X:\>auditlog /fail
DOMAIN\USERNAME                EVENT        TIME
NEKI\imevil                    Logon Fail   1/27/2002 22:40
   Reason: Unknown user name or bad password
```

CHANGE CLIENT

The CHANGE CLIENT command is used to manage the settings for an active ICA client's *device* mappings (disk drive, LPT, and COM ports). Normally this tool updates the settings only for the session within which it is executed and cannot be used to configure other active sessions. The one exception to this is the *delete_client_printers* parameter, which will affect all users on the server. See the usage part of this section for more information on this option.

CHANGE CLIENT is most often used when certain client device mappings or options must be enforced, either during logon or possibly prior to launching an application.

TIP: Although you cannot explicitly view any mapped client network printers using the CHANGE CLIENT command, you still can manipulate their availability, including reconnecting default printers and deleting all client printer connections.

Usage:

```
change client [host_device client_device]
change client [/view | /flush | /current]
change client [{/default | /default_drives | /default_printers}
[/ascending]] [/noremap] [/persistent] [/force_prt_todef] [/delete
host_device]
change client [/delete_client_printers]
```

Option	Function
host_device client_device	This is common general usage of Change Client. host_device represents the target device on the server, and client_device is the device on the client to be mapped to host_device. For example, Change Client P: C: maps the P: drive on the server to the C: drive on the client computer.
/view	Displays the list of all connected client devices.
/flush	Forces the MetaFrame server and the client to resynchronize disk data. MetaFrame caches data from client disk drives to help improve access times. This is not a write cache but simply a cache of information about the client drives. A simple example demonstrates this: Open a client drive on a MetaFrame server through My Computer, go to the local drive on the client (not through MetaFrame) and delete a file, and then return to MetaFrame and close and reopen the client drive. The deleted file still appears in the list.
/current	Displays the current ICA client device mappings. Equivalent to typing Change Client only.
/default	Reconnects the drive and printer mappings to their defaults. Note: This command won't delete any existing drive mappings before re-creating the default ones. Running this command multiple times results in multiple client drive mappings pointing to the same client drives. You should use the /noremap parameter with this command to prevent extra mappings from appearing.

Option	Function
/default_drives	Reconnects the host drive mappings to their defaults. See the note in the /default row of this table regarding the actual behavior of this command.
/default_printers	Reconnects the host printer mappings to their defaults. Unlike the drive mappings, the printer mappings are reset to their defaults.
/ascending	Changes the drive order from descending to ascending when searching for available drivers and printers to map. This option is valid only with /default, /default_drives, or /default_printers. By default it searches backwards, starting at the highest available drive letter and working downwards towards A: to assign client drive mappings. When /ascending is used, it starts at the lowest available drive letter and works upwards towards Z:.
/noremap	Prevents any client drive that conflicts with the MetaFrame drive (either physical or mapped) from being mapped to an alternate drive letter. Using this option in combination with /default or /default_drives prevents duplicate mappings to the user's local drives from appearing.
/persistent	Makes the current client drive mappings persistent by saving them into the user's profile. These settings are lost if the user has a mandatory profile.
/force_prt_todef	Forces the default printer for the MetaFrame client to map to the default printer on the client's local desktop.
/delete host_device	Deletes the client device that's mapped to the device specified by host_device.
/delete_client_printers	Deletes all the client printers from the current user's session, or all sessions if run by an administrator.

Examples:

```
C:\>change client
Client Mappings on WinStation ICA-tcp#3

Host            Client
A:              \\Client\A$
C:              \\Client\C$
D:              \\Client\D$
F:              \\Client\F$
LPT1            \\Client\LPT1:
LPT2            \\Client\LPT2:
```

```
C:\change client /delete F:

C:\change client
Client Mappings on WinStation ICA-tcp#3

Host            Client
A:              \\Client\A$
C:              \\Client\C$
D:              \\Client\D$
LPT1            \\Client\LPT1:
LPT2            \\Client\LPT2:

C:\change client /default /noremap
Mapping Host Device A: To Client Device A:
Error Mapping Host Device A: to Client A:, The device is being
accessed by an active process.

Mapping Host Device F: To Client Device F:
Mapping Host Device LPT1: To Client Device LPT1:
Mapping Host Device LPT2: To Client Device LPT2:
Client Mappings on WinStation ICA-tcp#3

Host            Client
A:              \\Client\A$
C:              \\Client\C$
D:              \\Client\D$
F:              \\Client\F$
LPT1            \\Client\LPT1:
LPT2            \\Client\LPT2:
```

CHFARM

CHFARM lets you change the server farm membership of a MetaFrame server. Prior to MetaFrame XP FR2, this utility had to be run from the installation CD. All newer versions of MetaFrame now install this tool on the server by default and allow execution directly off the Terminal Server.

WARNING: CHFARM should *not* be used to change the farm membership of a MetaFrame server that contains the local data store for an active farm. Doing so would eliminate the current data store and any published applications or farm settings defined within it. See Chapter 14, "Server Operations and Support," for information on the proper way to decommission or migrate a server farm.

When you run CHFARM, you first are asked to confirm your desire to change the farm membership for the server. After you say yes, the IMA service is stopped and the Data Store Setup wizard launches. After you complete the wizard, the IMA service is once again started and your server is now a member of a different farm. There are no command line options for this tool.

Usage:

```
Chfarm
```

CHGCDM

See the "CHANGE CLIENT" section. CHGCDM provides identical functionality to the CHANGE CLIENT command, including parameter inputs and outputs.

CLTPRINT

This command sets the number of available printer pipes to the client print spooler. This setting has no effect on print jobs spooled on the Terminal Server itself. A *printer pipe* is used to send data from an application to the client print spooler. The number of available pipes represents the number of print jobs that can be simultaneously sent to a client printer. The default number of printer pipes is 10, which is also the minimum.

The value for the number of printer pipes is maintained in the registry key:

HKLM\System\CurrentControlSet\Control\Print\Monitors\
Client Printer Port\Parameters\NumClientPrinterPipes

TIP: If you change the number of available printer pipes, you must stop and restart the spooler service for the changes to take effect.

Usage:

```
cltprint [/q] [/pipes:nn]
```

Option	Function
/q	Displays the current number of printer pipes.
/pipes:*nn*	Sets the number of available printer pipes. nn must be between 10 and 63.

Examples:

```
X:\>cltprint /q
CLTPRINT No registry value found for Client Printer Pipes (error = 2)

        CLTPRINT /PIPES: <number> can be used to set the number of
        pipes

        use CLTPRINT /? for more information

X:\cltprint /pipes:12

CLTPRINT Spooler must be stopped and restarted
              to enable new Pipe Instances setting

X:\cltprint /q

The registry value for number of Client Printer Pipe Instances = 12
```

CTXXMLSS

CTXXMLSS lets you change the listening port for the Citrix XML Service.

TIP: If the XML service is not sharing port 80 with IIS, the running service will be visible on the Terminal Server when the NET START command is issued by an administrator. In this situation you must stop the Citrix XML Service before you can change the XML listening port. The easiest way to do this is to issue the following command from a command prompt:

```
net stop "Citrix XML Service"
```

When you are ready to restart the service, simply run

```
net start "Citrix XML Service"
```

If the XML service is sharing port 80 with IIS, it will not appear in the service list and is not required to be stopped in order for these changes to take effect.

For complete information on the Citrix XML Service, including sharing port 80 with IIS, refer to Chapter 13, "MetaFrame Presentation Server Installation."

Usage:

```
ctxxmlss [/Rnnn] | [/U] | [/Knnn]
```

Option	Function
/Rnnn	Specifies the new listening port as nnn. You must select a port that is not already in use on the server.
/U	Deletes the XML service information out of the registry. This command will not stop the service; you must do so manually.
/Knnn	Lets you change the keep-alive value for the XML connection in seconds. The default is nine seconds.

Examples:

```
X:\>net stop "Citrix XML Service"

The Citrix XML Service service was stopped successfully.

X:\>ctxxmlss /u

X:\>ctxxmlss /R83
Citrix XML Service: The service is now registered on port number 83.

X:\>net start "Citrix XML Service"
The Citrix XML Service service is starting.
The Citrix XML Service service was started successfully.

X:\>netstat -a p TCP

Active Connections

  Proto  Local Address          Foreign Address              State
  TCP    neki:83                neki.NR1.com:0   LISTENING
  TCP    neki:epmap             neki.NR1.com:0   LISTENING
  TCP    neki:microsoft-ds      neki.NR1.com:0   LISTENING
  TCP    neki:1494              neki.NR1.com:0   LISTENING
  TCP    neki:3389              neki.NR1.com:0   LISTENING
  TCP    neki:netbios-ssn       neki.NR1.com:0   LISTENING
  TCP    neki:1494              ICAClient1.NR1.com:1380   ESTABLISHED
```

DSCheck

This command performs an integrity check against the data store. If the integrity check fails, this command can be run with the /clean switch to fix any of the inconsistencies detected when DSCheck was first run.

Usage:

```
dscheck [/clean]
```

Option	Function
/clean	Deletes inconsistent records from the data store.

WARNING: It is recommended that you back up your data store prior to running the DSCHECK utility with the /clean option.

DSMAINT RECOVER

The DSMAINT RECOVER command is used to restore an Access data store from its back-up file. The backup file (mf20.bak) is located in the same folder as the data store (mf20.mdb), which is normally the following:

%ProgramFiles%\Citrix\Independent Management Architecture

Whenever the IMA service is safely shut down, it automatically creates a copy of mf20.mdb called mf20.unk. When the IMA service restarts, it deletes mf20.bak and renames mf20.unk to mf20.bak. This process exists as an attempt to ensure that a valid backup of the data store is always available.

Before DSMAINT RECOVER can be run, the IMA service must be stopped. When you run DSMAINT RECOVER, it renames the current mf20.mdb to mf20.sav and then renames mf20.bak to mf20.mdb. You must manually restart the IMA service to complete the recovery operation.

TIP: See Chapter 14 for an example of an automated recovery process that includes use of the DSMAINT RECOVER command.

Usage:

```
dsmaint recover
```

Examples:

```
X:\>dsmaint recover
ERROR: Cannot run this option while IMA service is running.
Please stop IMA service before continuing.
Recover local data store from last known good backup.
This option requires that the IMA Service be stopped, and is avail-
able
when using MS-Access or MSDE as your Data Store.

X:\>net stop "Independent Management Architecture"
The Independent Management Architecture service is stopping.
The Independent Management Architecture service was stopped success-
fully.

X:\>dsmaint recover
Attempting to connect to the data store with new configuration set-
tings.
Successfully connected to the data store.

X:\>net start "Independent Management Architecture"
The Independent Management Architecture service is starting..
The Independent Management Architecture service was started success-
fully.
```

DSMAINT BACKUP

This command is used to back up the Access data store to another location. The destination can be on either the MetaFrame Server or an alternate network location. This command *won't* back up a SQL or Oracle database.

Usage:

```
dsmaint backup <destination_path>
```

Option	Function
destination_path	The location where you want the data store copied. The target folder must already exist. You do not need to include a file name.

Examples:

```
X:\>dsmaint backup \\BackupServ\MFStore
Database file was copied to::\\BackupServ\MFStore\mf20.mdb
```

DSMAINT COMPACTDB

The DSMAINT COMPACTDB command is used to compact the Access data store. Compacting eliminates wasted space inside the Jet database and helps optimize performance. If the IMA service is running on the MetaFrame server housing the data store (the direct server), this command can be executed on any MetaFrame server in the farm. If the IMA service is not running, DSMAINT COMPACTDB can be executed only from the direct server.

Usage:

```
dsmaint compactdb [/ds] [/lhc]
```

Option	Function
/ds	Compacts the data store (mf20.mdb).
/lhc	Compacts the local host cache (imalhc.mdb).

Examples:

```
X:\>dsmaint compactdb /ds /lhc
Compact DB operation succeeded
```

DSMAINT CONFIG

This utility is used to change the connection parameters used by the IMA service to connect to a data store.

On an Access data store, this command resets the ID and/or password and updates the corresponding settings for the IMA service so it has access to the database. Once you have made the desired change to the Access data store, the IMA service must be restarted before the changes take effect.

When applying this command against a SQL or Oracle database, you must include a data source name with the /dsn option.

NOTE: The default user name and password on the Access data store (mf20.mdb) is citrix/citrix.

Usage:

```
dsmaint config [/user:username] [/pwd:password] [/dsn:filename]
```

Option	Function
/user:username	The new user name to use for database connectivity.
/pwd:password	The new password to use for database connectivity.
/dsn:filename	Lets you specify a file DSN to use to connect to the data store. If the DSN you provide differs from the current setting, the server points to the new data store.

Examples:

```
C:\>dsmaint config /user:todd /pwd:password
Attempting to connect to the data store with new configuration set-
tings.
Successfully connected to the data store.
Configuration successfully changed.
Please restart the IMA Service for changes to take effect.
```

DSMAINT FAILOVER

Changes the direct server location that a MetaFrame server uses to access the data store. Typically, this command is used when an alternate data store has been created and the existing MetaFrame servers need to be redirected to point to this new server.

This command is valid only on MetaFrame servers that make indirect connections to the server farm's data store.

Usage:

```
dsmaint failover direct_server
```

Option	Function
direct_server	The MetaFrame server that is directly connected to the data store.

Example:

```
X:\>dsmaint failover mfds01.nrtest.com
```

DSMAINT MIGRATE

This command is used to migrate the data store from one database to another. For example, you could use DSMAINT MIGRATE to migrate your data store from Access to Microsoft SQL Server.

TIP: See Chapter 14 for an example of migrating a data store from Access to SQL Server using the DSMAINT MIGRATE command.

Usage:

```
dsmaint migrate {/srcdsn:sdsn} [/srcuser:susername] {/srcpwd:spassword}
{/dstdsn:ddsn} [/dstuser:dusername] [/dstpwd:dpassword]
```

Option	Function
/srcdsn:sdsn	The DSN file for the existing data store that you wish to migrate. By default, the data store DSN called MF20.DSN is located in the folder "%ProgramFiles%\Citrix\ Independent Management Architecture".
/srcuser:susername	The user name used to authenticate against the source data store. The default user name for the Access data store is "citrix".
/srcpwd:spassword	The password used to authenticate against the source data store. The default password for the Access data store is "citrix".
/dstdsn:ddsn	The DSN file for the destination data store that you wish to migrate to.
/dstuser:dusername	The user name used to authenticate against the destination data store.
/dstpwd:dpassword	The password used to authenticate against the destination data store.

Examples:

```
X:\>dsmaint migrate /srcdsn:"x:\program files\citrix\independent man-
agement architecture\mf20.dsn" /srcuser:toddm /srcpwd:password /dstd-
sn:"y:\admin tools\SQL.dsn" /dstuser:toddm /dstpwd:password
```

DSMAINT PUBLISHSQLDS

This command is required only if you are currently using a Microsoft SQL Server data store and planning to create a distributed environment by making this SQL Server a *Publisher*.

The DSMAINT PUBLISHSQLDS command should be executed from the server that initially created the farm. Once executed, it runs the required SQL statements to create the published articles on the SQL Server. Remote SQL Servers can then be configured to "subscribe" to these published articles.

TIP: Please consult the Microsoft SQL Server 2000 documentation or the SQL Server 2000 Resource Kit for further information on SQL Server replication.

Usage:

```
dsmaint publishsqlds {/user:username /pwd:password}
```

Option	Function
/user:username	The username required to authenticate on the SQL Server data store.
/pwd:password	The password required to authenticate on the SQL Server data store.

DSMAINT RECREATELHC

DSMAINT RECREATELHC will re-create the local host cache on the server on which it is run. This command takes no parameters, but the IMA service must be stopped on the server where the local host cache will be recreated.

Usage:

```
dsmaint recreatelhc
```

Examples:

```
X:\>dsmaint recreatelhc
Recreating LHC database finished successfully.
```

DSMAINT VERIFYLHC

This command validates the integrity of the local host cache. If the /autorepair switch is provided, any inconsistencies will attempt to be corrected. In order for this command to run properly, the local host cache must be running.

Usage:

```
dsmaint verifylhc [/autorepair]
```

Option	Function
/autorepair	Will automatically repair any issues found during the integrity check.

Examples:

```
X:\>dsmaint verifylhc
The LHC integrity has been verified successfully.
```

ICAPORT

ICAPORT is used to set the TCP/IP listening port number used by a MetaFrame server for ICA connections. By default, MetaFrame listens for TCP/IP client connections on port 1494. You can use ICAPORT to change this port to any number in the range 0 to 65535. If you change the port number, you must restart the server for the changes to take effect. ICAPORT updates the following registry value: HKLM\System\CurrentControlSet\Control\Terminal Server\Winstations\ICAtcp\PortNumber

WARNING: When assigning an alternate port number, make sure it's not already in use. Avoid well-known TCP and UPD port numbers such as 80 (for HTTP or the Citrix XML Service) or 23 (for Telnet).

While ports 1 through 1024 are reserved for this purpose, some ports above this are also commonly used, such as many in the 6000 range that are used for X11 (a graphical UNIX interface). The following list shows some commonly assigned ports:

21: FTP

67: BOOTP/DHCP

110: POP3

177: X11 logons

2049: NFS

6667: IRC

After the port number has been changed, all clients that want to connect to the MetaFrame server will need their client updated as well. To assign an alternate port on the client, simply use the standard TCP/IP convention of assigning a port number by appending :<*port number*> immediately after the IP address or DNS name. For example, entering "ORCA:7832" as the MetaFrame server name would tell the client to attempt to establish an ICA connection with ORCA on port 7832. If you defined the wrong port or attempted to connect to a server that had had the default port changed, you would get a message stating that the MetaFrame server was not accepting connections.

TIP: You can also specify the port number by adding ICAPortNumber=*nnn* to the APPSRV.INI file on the client. This file contains the configuration information normally set using the Citrix ICA client. You can add this entry in one of two places. If you add it to the [WFCLIENT] section of the file, the defined port number will be used by all MetaFrame client entries. If you add this value to an individual server key, shown as [<*servername*>] in the file, the alternate port will be used for only that server entry.

Usage:

```
icaport {query | /port:nnn | /reset}
```

Option	Function
/query	Displays the current setting for ICAPORT.
/port:*nnn*	Reassigns the listening TCP/IP port number.
/reset	Resets the port number to the default of 1494.

Examples:

```
X:\>icaport /query
TCP/IP port for Winstation ICA-tcp is set to: 1494

X:\>icaport /port:7832
TCP/IP port for Winstation ICA-tcp is set to: 7832

X:\>icaport /reset
TCP/IP port for Winstation ICA-tcp is set to: 1494
```

IMAPORT

IMAPORT lets you modify the TCP/IP port for the IMA service, the management console, and the outbound communication port for an indirect data store connection. This command modifies these settings on the local server only. The following ports are used by default:

- **IMA service**—2512 (inbound)
- **Management console**—2513 (inbound)
- **Indirect data store**—2512 (outbound to direct data store server)

After modifying any of the port numbers, you must restart the IMA service for the changes to take effect. When two servers need to perform server-to-server communications, the appropriate ports to communicate on are retrieved from the data store for the farm.

If you modify the inbound management console port, when you launch the MetaFrame Presentation Server Management Console you will need to specify the port to communicate on. This can be done by modifying the shortcut for the application as follows: C:\Program Files\Citrix\Administration\ctxload.exe –port:<new port number> where <new port number> is the alternate port you specified.

WARNING: The same warning applies to the IMAPort as it did for the ICAPort. When assigning an alternate port number, make sure it's not already in use. Avoid well-known TCP and UPD port numbers such as 80 (for HTTP or the Citrix XML Service) or 23 (for Telnet).

Usage:

```
imaport {query} | {/set <IMA:port> | <DS:port> | <CMC:port>} |
{/reset IMA | DS | CMC | ALL}
```

Option	Function
/query	Displays the current setting for ImaPort.
/set IMA:port	Sets the specified port to the provided value.
DS:port	
CMC:port	
/reset IMA | DS | CMC | ALL	Resets the specified port to its default value.

Examples:

```
X:\>imaport /query
TCP/IP port for IMA communication is set to: 2512
TCP/IP port for CMC connection is set to:    2513

X:\>imaport /set ima:3000
For the new port setting to take effect, you must restart the
Independent
Management Architecture service.

X:\>imaport /query
TCP/IP port for IMA communication is set to: 3000
TCP/IP port for CMC connection is set to:    2513
```

QUERY FARM

QUERY FARM displays information about all available MetaFrame Presentation Servers in your server farm, using information gathered from the farm's data store. When the servers are listed, the current data store server is shown with the letter "D," situated to the right of the network address.

```
Usage:query farm [[servername] [/addr | /app [name] | /load |
/process]] [/tcp] [/ipx] [/netbios] [/app [name] | /disc | /load |
/process] [/zone [zonename]] [/zoneapp [appname]] [zoneload]
[/offline] [/online] [/continue]
```

Option	Function
Servername	Name of the server to query. The name is entered without the double backslash (\\) characters.
/addr	Displays network address data for the specified server.
/app [name]	Displays a list of published application names, the servers on which they are published, and their app and server loads. If the name is specified, only the information for that specific application is returned.
/load	Displays the load for either the specified server or all servers in the farm.
/tcp	Shows only TCP/IP information.
/ipx	Shows only IPX information.
/netbios	Shows only NetBIOS information.
/disc	Displays information on disconnected sessions.
/process	Lists all the active processes. If a server name is specified, only the processes on that server are listed; otherwise, all processes on all servers in the farm are listed.
/zone [zonename]	Displays all zones and their associated zone data collector. If zonename is included, only the data for that zone is displayed.
/zoneapp [appname]	Lists the published applications and their server load for the local zone. Including appname will display only that specific application name.
/zoneload	Displays the servers and their associated load for the current zone only.
/offline	Displays servers currently offline. Servers may be taken offline for maintenance or could be down because of a hardware failure.
/online	Displays servers that are online.
/continue	Suppresses pausing after each page of output.

Examples:

```
X:\>query farm

Server                 Transport   Network Address
_____            _____   _____

NEKI*                  TCP/IP          192.168.1.103 D
HILO                   TCP/IP          192.168.1.104
```

```
X:\> query farm /zone
Zone Name                    Data Collector
_____          _____

192.168.1.0                                  NEWTON
192.168.2.0                                  PASCAL
192.168.3.0                                  FOURIER
```

QUERY SERVER

QUERY SERVER is a legacy tool for use when run in a mixed-mode MetaFrame server farm (interoperability mode) or if you have MetaFrame 1.x servers in your environment that you would like to monitor from a MetaFrame Presentation Server. QUERY SERVER displays information about all available MetaFrame 1.x servers in your environment. QUERY SERVER uses information from the ICA master browser to gather the statistics that are displayed. This tool provides a quick way to view much of the information that would normally be available through the MetaFrame Administration tool.

TIP: QUERY SERVER queries the MetaFrame 1.x servers on only one network card at a time. If you have two or more network cards on your server, to access the MetaFrame 1.x servers on the other card's network you must specify the proper address of any MetaFrame server on that subnet.

Usage:

```
query server [[servername] [[/ping] [/count:n] [/size:n]]| [/stats |
/reset | /load | /addr | /debugnhwatch]] [/tcp] [/ipx]
[/netbios][/tcpserver:x] [/ipxserver:x] [/netbiosserver:x] [/license
| /app | /gateway | /serial | /disc | /serverfarm |/video | /update |
/election | /delete] [/continue] [/DEBUG:n]
```

Option	Function
servername	Name of the server to query. The name is entered without the double backslash (\\) characters.
/ping	Pings the named server.
/count:n	Number of times to ping. The default is 5.
/size:n	Byte size of the ping packet. The default is 256.
/stats	Displays the browser statistics.

Option	Function
/reset	Resets the browser statistics.
/load	Displays load-balancing data (valid only when the server has load balancing installed).
/addr	Displays network address data.
/debugnhwatch	Displays Program Neighborhood debugging information for the specified server. You must include the MetaFrame server name in order for this parameter to work properly. When run, it displays diagnostic information about what the server "knows" about the farm it belongs to and the applications available.
/tcp	Shows TCP/IP information.
/ipx	Shows IPX information.
/netbios	Shows NetBIOS information.
/tcpserver:x	Sets the default TCP/IP server address to x.
/ipxserver:x	Sets the default IPX server address to x.
/netbiosserver:x	Sets the default NetBIOS server address to x.
/license	Displays the user licenses.
/app	Displays published application names and corresponding servers.
/gateway	Shows the configured ICA gateway addresses.
/serial	Shows license serial numbers.
/disc	Displays information on disconnected sessions.
/serverfarm	Displays the known server farm names and their loads.
/video	Displays VideoFrame information.
/update	Forces the ICA browser update information to be sent to the master ICA browser immediately. If a server name exists in the server-name parameter, then only that server sends updated information; otherwise, all Citrix servers send their update information.
/election	Forces an ICA browser election.
/delete	Forces deletion of the ICA master browser data. The master browser eventually reconstructs its database as update information comes in from the other Citrix servers on the network.
/continue	Suppresses pausing after each page of output.
/DEBUG:*n*	Displays debug messages. After the nth message, the application halts automatically.

Examples:

```
X:\>query server
WARNING:  The MetaFrame server is not operating in interoperability
mode.
Please use the QUERY FARM command for reporting IMA based server
data.

Server                Transport Conns Free  Total  Network Address

MF18SRV               TCP/IP    0     15    15     10.10.10.10 M
```

TIP: When running this command, you see only those servers running the ICA browser service or running in interoperability mode. MPS servers running in native mode are not displayed.

TWCONFIG

TWCONFIG is the thinwire configuration utility you can use to adjust the ICA display options for your ICA clients. These settings can also be managed on a server-by-server basis or for the entire farm through the Citrix Management Console (CMC). Figure B.3 shows the ICA display properties for a server farm through the CMC. Using the TWCONFIG command, you can adjust only the settings for the server on which it is run.

NOTE: By default, MetaFrame Presentation Servers are configured to inherit their ICA display settings from the farm. If you run the TWCONFIG /q command while the inherit option is enabled, TWCONFIG displays the settings for the farm, not the settings for the individual computer.

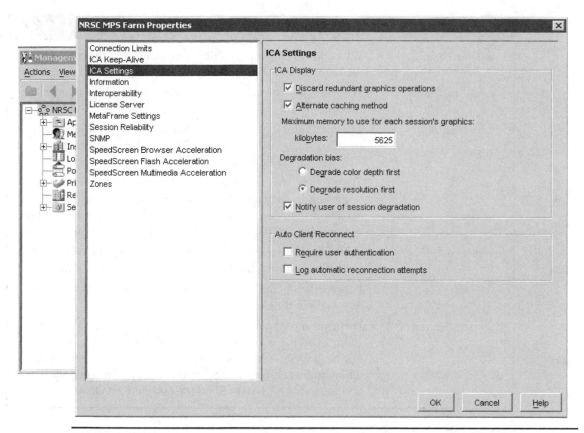

Figure B.3 Farm-wide ICA display settings within the Citrix Management Console.

Usage:

```
twconfig [/query] [/server:server] [/default] | [/inherit:on|off] |
[/discard:on|off] | [/supercache:on|off] | [/maxmem:nnn] |
[/degrade:res|color] | [notify:on|off] | [/Srvsrcpaint:on|off]
```

Option	Function
/query	Returns the current settings. If inherit is on, the returned information corresponds to the settings applied to the entire farm.
/server:server	You can provide the name of a remote server to configure.
/inherit:on|off	When set on, the ICA display settings for the farm are used. When off, the settings defined on the server are used. On is the default.

Option	Function
/discard:on|off	When on, redundant graphics operations are discarded. On is the default.
/supercache:on|off	When on, the alternate Citrix bitmap caching technique is used. On is the default.
/maxmem:nnn	The maximum memory in KB that can be used by each client session for graphics operations. The valid range is 150KB to 7500KB. The default value is 5625KB.
/degrade:res|color	Determines what factor is reduced first if the video mode requested by the client is unavailable. This occurs when the maxmem value has been reached. Either the screen resolution or the color depth can be degraded. The default is resolution.
/notify:on|off	When on, users are notified if the desired video mode is not available (maxmem has been reached). On is the default.
/default	Utilizes the default settings from the farm instead of the server-specific settings.
/srvsrcpaint:on|off	Performs the srcpaint method on the server instead of on the client. By default, this switch is off. This switch was added to resolve a specific srcpaint drawing issue. Do not enable this option unless absolutely necessary. See the Citrix documentation for hotfix XE103W2K040 for more information.

Examples:

```
X:\>twconfig /inherit:off
Update successful

X:\>twconfig /notify:off
Update successful

X:\>twconfig /q
INHERIT:     off
DISCARD:     on
SUPERCACHE:  on
SRVSRCPAINT: off
DEGRADE:     res
NOTIFY:      off
MAXMEM:      5625 kilobytes
```

Network Primer

The OSI Model

The sometimes-complicated interrelationship of components in a network can quickly become overwhelming without an understanding of the basic underlying theory that defines most networks. The most widely recognized model for understanding network communications is the OSI model. The Open Systems Interconnection (OSI) reference model was defined in 1978 by the International Standards Organization (ISO) to help define (and understand) how the different devices on a network interact with each other.

The OSI model consists of seven independent, functional layers, each providing and utilizing the services of the adjacent layers. The model represents a peer-to-peer communication relationship in which equivalent layers on different computers communicate with each other through a common protocol.

Figure C.1 demonstrates this peer-to-peer relationship between two computers. While the information travels down the layers on one computer and then up the layers on the other, conceptually, equivalent layers are talking directly to each other. This allows layers to work functionally independent of each other, with a change in one layer not requiring subsequent changes in the others. The only requirement is that each layer must be able to communicate with the adjacent layers immediately above and below. The figure also shows where RDP and ICA conceptually fit into the OSI model at the session layer. The data protocols responsible for transmitting data through the virtual channels supported in the RDP and ICA protocols would reside one layer up in the presentation layer. Citrix's thinwire protocol, which is responsible for transmitting presentation data from the server to the client, would reside in the presentation layer.

NOTE: The System Network Architecture (SNA) model, developed by IBM, was the basis for the OSI reference model.

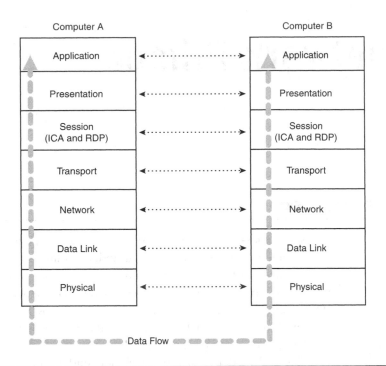

Figure C.1   The RDP and ICA protocols within the OSI reference model.

Following is a brief description of each of the OSI layers. Layers 5 through 7 are application-related; layers 1 through 4 are network-related:

- **Application layer (Layer 7)**—The uppermost layer provides services to user applications, letting them communicate with other applications that reside on other computers as if those applications were local. Examples include file copying and database access.
- **Presentation layer (Layer 6)**—This layer translates data into a standard format agreed upon by the computers involved in the data exchange.
- **Session layer (Layer 5)**—This layer provides synchronization between applications on different computers. RDP and ICA function at this layer, converting presentation information into the appropriate protocol data, which is then sent to the appropriate layer on the client machine to be decoded and displayed.
- **Transport layer (Layer 4)**—This layer provides for flow control and reliable data transfer between end nodes. This layer breaks up messages from the session layer into deliverable packets and reassembles these packets into messages to send to the session layer. Transmission Control Protocol (TCP) and User Datagram Protocol (UDP) exist at this layer.

- **Network layer (Layer 3)**—This layer handles routing of data packets through the network. It handles conversion of data from the transport layer into acceptable data packets if they're too large for the data link layer (Layer 2). Of course, it also handles reassembling the packets for the transport layer at the receiving end. Internet Protocol (IP) is a Layer 3 protocol.

- **Data link layer (Layer 2)**—The data link layer formats the packets from the network layer into groupings called *frames*, which are passed to the physical layer (Layer 1) for actual transmission. Error detection and recovery from physical errors are detected here. This layer also determines whether a broadcast is targeted for the current computer or not. Both switches and bridges are found at Layer 2.

- **Physical layer (Layer 1)**—The physical layer handles the encoding and decoding of data for the data link layer and is also responsible for sending bits to and receiving bits from the physical network. Repeaters function at this layer.

Figure C.2 shows the association of internetworking equipment (repeaters, switches, and so on) and the OSI layers within which they reside.

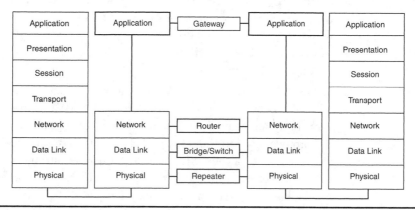

Figure C.2   Internetworking equipment and the OSI layers where they reside.

NOTE: Internetworking vendors are blurring the traditional boundaries of the OSI reference model with current product offerings and virtual LAN (VLAN) technology. Some Layer 3 switches now perform routing functions (found at Layer 3) as well as the switching/bridging functions of Layer 2. In general, the first packet is routed for path determination, and all subsequent packets are switched along the same path.

Communications Protocols

Terminal Server clients (and applications in general) require a means to navigate through the network and locate the intended destination. Similarly, the destination server must be able to recognize that the data on the wire is intended for it and be able to act on the packet accordingly. For two nodes to communicate, they must use the same set of well-defined rules. These rules are known as a *protocol*, and they govern the conversations between the nodes. Hosts that share a common protocol can communicate directly, whereas hosts that use different protocols for communication require an intermediary device, a *gateway*, to perform the necessary mapping and protocol conversions. For example, Microsoft's Host Integration Server performs the gateway function (amongst other things) that enables IP devices to communicate to SNA mainframes.

Three protocols (see the following list) are used by RDP/ICA clients to communicate with Terminal Server. Of these, RDP supports only TCP/IP, while ICA supports NetBIOS, IPX/SPX, and TCP/IP on Windows 2000 Server but only TCP/IP on Windows Server 2003. Even if the supporting protocol has been installed on Windows Server 2003, the Citrix Client Connection Manager will not allow selection of any transport other than TCP/IP.

- **NetBEUI**—The NetBIOS Extended User Interface (NetBEUI) is a non-routable Layer 2 protocol best suited for small LANs of between 2 and 200 workstations. Developed originally by IBM for OS/2 and LAN Manager networks, it is certainly the fastest protocol for small networks that do not require routing to other networks.

- **IPX/SPX**—Internetwork Packet Exchange/Sequenced Packet Exchange (IPX/SPX) was developed by Novell for the NetWare operating system in the early 1980s and is based on an early Xerox network called (XNS). IPX is actually the protocol used to transport packets and resides in the network and transport layers (3 and 4) of the OSI model. SPX operates at the transport layer and provides connection-oriented services to IPX, offering additional reliability. NWLink is Microsoft's implementation of IPX/SPX.

- **TCP/IP**—Transmission Control Protocol/Internet Protocol offers the most widely accepted means for interconnecting dissimilar network components. TCP/IP was born in conjunction with the Internet's predecessor, ARPAnet (Advanced Research Projects Agency network) in the early 1970s. IP is the protocol and is located at the network layer. TCP is the main transport layer protocol used in conjunction with IP and is connection-oriented, utilizing a connection ID, also known as a *port*, for each connection that is established. Another common transport layer protocol is User Datagram Protocol (UDP). This protocol is connectionless and does not attempt to acknowledge packet receipt. Although UDP may be more efficient than TCP, it is not as reliable.

Physical and Logical Networks

For most users, a local-area network (LAN) and a wide-area network (WAN) are nothing more than abstract terms used to describe how all the computers are connected to allow transfer of data. The graphical interface of Windows hides a well-structured cable plant and selection of networking components that interconnect heterogeneous systems using a set of predefined rules such as those discussed earlier. Although LANs and WANs both service the interconnection of networking devices, they are most often differentiated for geographical reasons.

LANs

Traditionally, a LAN has almost always been confined to a single building. Typically, LANs use higher-speed connections to link network segments together. Technologies such as Ethernet, Fast Ethernet, Gigabit Ethernet, and Fibre Distributed Data Interface (FDDI) dominate today's corporate LANs. Routers, bridges, and switches are devices used most often to link different LAN segments, technologies, and services together. Figure C.3 demonstrates a typical LAN configuration with multiple subnets. Subnets can be thought of as miniature LANs separated by a router. Traditionally, subnets have been created to isolate certain networks from others. A common example would be creation of a development subnet where application and server testing could be performed without fear of impacting a production environment.

TIP: A service known as a LAN extension can be used to establish a permanent connection between two locations, extending coverage of a LAN outside the boundaries of a single building. LAN extensions provide true LAN bandwidths (10Mbps, 100Mbps, 1000Mbps [1Gbps], and eventually 10Gbps) but are typically limited in range and can be cost prohibitive to implement between two locations separated by a large physical distance.

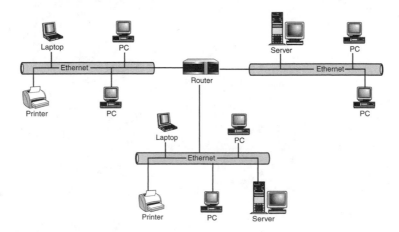

Figure C.3   A typical LAN configuration with multiple subnets.

WANs

A WAN is the interconnection of geographically dispersed LANs extending beyond a single metropolitan area. This usually means reliance on an outside source or vendor to provide the necessary bandwidth required to support your WAN. Service offerings range from regular analog dial-in modems (connecting anywhere between 15.4Kbps and 56Kbps) all the way up to Asynchronous Transfer Mode (ATM), reaching speeds of OC48 (2.4Gbps). The most common WAN service offerings today are T1/E1 (1.54Mbps/2.048Mbps), fractional T1/E1, and OC3 (155Mbps) with protocols such as Frame Relay, PPP, and ATM. The primary interconnection device for the WAN is the router. Figure C.4 illustrates the interconnection of three LANs located in different cities. While WAN is most often used to describe these types of interconnections, other terms exist that are sometimes used to describe specific WAN implementations:

- **MANs**—If an interconnection for a WAN is within a single metropolitan area, this network can also be referred to as a *metropolitan-area network* (MAN). Typically, MANs use an outside vendor for connectivity and also typically, although not always, operate as high-speed interconnections between locations.
- **CANs**—When interconnections of locations are geographically close but use private connectivity facilities instead of public services, they can be referred to as *campuses* or *campus-area networks* (CANs) instead of MANs. In many situations, a CAN is logically viewed as one large network, interconnected by using the LAN extensions described earlier.

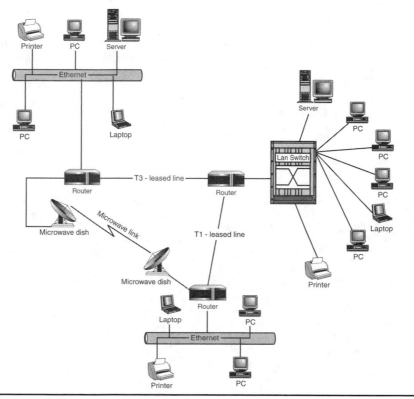

Figure C.4   A WAN configuration between three LANs.

Terminal Server Tuning and Configuration Checklist

Before You Begin

In response to feedback from readers of the previous edition of this book, I've included this summary checklist of all the changes discussed in Chapter 11, "Terminal Services Configuration and Tuning." In this list, you will find not only all options discussed but also a flag showing whether the change is recommended or optional and if it is specific to only Windows Server 2003 or Windows 2000 Server. Complete details on the listed change can be found in Chapter 11. Please review Chapter 11 completely before implementing any of the listed changes. An electronic version of this checklist is available on the Web site for this book at http://www.awprofessional .com/title/1578702763.

The abbreviations used in this checklist are as follows:

- **R/O**—Change is recommended or optional.

- **OS**—Operating system: B = both, W2K = Windows 2000 Server only, W2K3 = Windows Server 2003 only.

Stability and Availability Change Checklist

Change Description	R/O	OS	Implemented
Restrict Terminal Server connections	R	B	
Partition/format non-system drives	R	B	
Configure the pagefile	R	B	
Verify registry size	R	W2K	
Set server startup and recovery options	O	B	
Add recovery console to the startup menu	R	B	

Change Description	R/O	OS	Implemented
Configure the event log size	R	B	
Modify printer event logging	O	B	
Disable NIC auto-detection	R	B	
Disable automatic updates	R	B	
Modify the folder options' view	O	B	
Disable the Configure Your Server wizard	O	B	
Disable the Internet Connection wizard	O	W2K	
Disable Dr. Watson	R	B	
Suppress hard-error messages	O	B	
Customize the My Computer text	O	B	
Initialize the root drive	O	B	
Schedule automatic reboots	R	B	

Performance Considerations

Change Description	R/O	OS	Implemented
Disable Active Desktop	R	B	
Minimize Windows visual effects	R	B	
Optimize memory usage	R	B	
Optimize foreground thread timeslicing	R	B	
Disable error reporting	O	W2K3	
Stop unnecessary system services	R	B	
Remove unnecessary user startup applications	O	B	
Disable NT Executive paging	O	B	
Disable last access time update time on folder listings	O	B	
Adjust TCP/IP retransmission behavior	O	B	
Manage disk fragmentation	O	B	
Manage pagefile and registry fragmentation	O	B	

File System and Registry Security Primer

Access Control Lists and Entries

To successfully implement a secure Terminal Server, you must have a clear understanding of both the Windows NTFS and registry security. As with all objects in the
Windows 2003/2000 operating system, security is managed through the object's security descriptor. Access to view or manipulate the object is controlled through a special data structure in the security descriptor called the Discretionary Access Control
List (DACL). The entries in this list determine who has what type of access to the
object. Each entry in the DACL is known as an *access control entry* (ACE). Each
ACE contains the following information:

- **The security identifier (SID) of the person or group that this ACE
  refers to**—A SID uniquely identifies every user and group in a domain
  or on an individual computer.
- **Whether this ACE is an Allow or a Deny entry**—As the names
  imply, Allow entries refer to permissions granted to the SID, while
  Deny entries explicitly deny the SID the associated permission.
- **A list of permission attributes**—As you will see shortly, both the file
  system and registry security are built around the basic permission attribute. Permission attributes are normally grouped together into what are
  called *permission sets*, which make up the common security settings
  such as Read or Write.

TIP: See Chapter 16, "Terminal Server Security," for specific information on
securing your Terminal Server environment.

Figure E.1 shows a conceptual example of a simple folder/file structure with each
object's DACL and associated ACEs. For readability, I've used the common group
names such as Users instead of each group's SID.

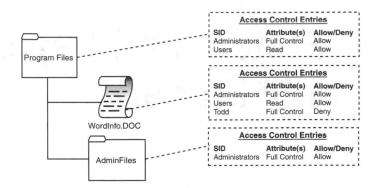

Figure E.1   File system DACL example with individual access control entries.

Whenever a user attempts to access an object, the user's SID and the SIDs of all groups the user belongs to are compared against the object's DACL. If after this comparison the system determines that the user has sufficient access then he or she is allowed to perform the requested action; otherwise, the user receives an Access Denied message.

TIP: The user's list of SIDs is maintained in the user's access token. Each time a user logs on to the system, an access token is generated for that user. This token is automatically requested whenever the user attempts to perform a privileged operation.

Note that this token is not dynamically updated, so if changes are made to the user's account they do not take effect until the next time the user logs off and back on to the system.

File System Permissions

As I mentioned earlier in this appendix when discussing DACLs, both the file system and registry security are built around the basic permission attribute. Windows 2003/2000 provide 13 file permission attributes, compared to the 6 previously available in Windows NT 4.0. Figure E.2 shows an example of the available permission attributes for a folder called TEMP on a 2003 server.

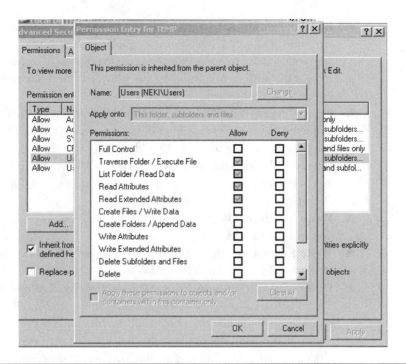

Figure E.2 Windows 2003 permission attributes.

Following is a list of descriptions for the 13 permission attributes. Full Control is not explicitly listed as an attribute since it actually implies selection of all 13 other attributes. Those of you familiar with NT 4.0 permission attributes will notice that the Windows 2003/2000 attributes have descriptive names that more clearly state what permissions each attribute grants when applied to a folder or a file. When the controlled action differs between a folder and a file, the description appears as <folder action>/<file action>. If the manageable action is identical for both objects, only a single description appears.

NOTE: The abbreviations listed in parentheses are *my* convention and not a Microsoft standard. I use these abbreviations to simplify my description of which permission attributes make up the different permissions sets, which I discuss shortly.

- **Traverse Folder/Execute File (TFEF)**—Lets you run an executable (.EXE, .COM, and so forth) or traverse into a folder.
- **List Folder/Read Data (LFRD)**—Allows viewing a folder's contents (file or subfolder names) or a file's contents. This doesn't grant access to view an object's permissions or its non-security attributes.
- **Read Attributes (RA)**—Allows viewing the basic non-security attributes of a file or directory. Some of the most common attributes are Read Only, Hidden, System, and Archive.

- **Read Extended Attributes (REA)**—Allows viewing extended non-security attributes. Extended attributes are usually specific to the type of file and the application that created it. For example, Microsoft Word stores information such as the author, title, subject, and keywords for a document in a document's extended attributes.

- **Create Files/Write Data (CFWD)**—Allows creation of files within a folder and writing data to a new file or changing data within an existing file. Doesn't let you append data to an existing file.

- **Create Folders/Append Data (CFAD)**—Allows creation of new folders within a folder and appending data to the end of an existing file. Doesn't allow changing data within an existing file.

- **Write Attributes (WA)**—Allows writing basic non-security attribute information to a file or folder.

- **Write Extended Attributes (WEA)**—Allows writing extended non-security attribute information to a file or folder.

- **Delete Subfolders and Files (DSF)**—This permission will undoubtedly introduce a fair amount of confusion to many administrators. Basically, it provides someone with the ability to delete all the files and subfolders within a folder—even if that person doesn't have explicit Delete permissions on any of the objects contained within that folder. This permission can be thought of as applying to a container (the folder) and allowing for the deletion of all objects within that container regardless of individual permissions. This permission is normally granted only to users with Full Control.

- **Delete (D)**—Allows you to delete a file or folder. If you also have the Delete Subfolders and Files permission (described in the preceding point) on a folder, you can simply delete the folder. If you have only the Delete permission, either the folder must be empty or you must also have Delete permission on all objects within the folder; otherwise, the delete operation will fail.

- **Read permissions (RP)**—Let you view the security attributes of a file or folder.

- **Change permissions (CP)**—Allow changing the security attributes of a file or folder. If you're the owner of a file or folder, you have the inherent right to change permissions on that object.

- **Take Ownership (O)**—Lets you take ownership of a file or folder. As owner, you can change permissions even if you have no other access to the object. By default, only the Administrators group has the right to take ownership of a file or folder. Taking ownership doesn't automatically grant you any rights to the object, but once you're the owner, you can assign yourself the necessary rights. The right to take ownership of a file or folder can be modified by assigning specific users or groups the user right "Take ownership of files or other objects."

This can be done within the local security policy of the server or defined within a domain group policy object. This policy is found in a GPO under

```
Computer Configuration\Windows Settings\Local Policies\User Rights
Assignment
```

Any combination of permission attributes can be assigned to both files and folders, granting or restricting access to individual users and/or groups of users.

File Object Permissions

Although the ability to assign individual attributes provides a large amount of flexibility, Microsoft also provides what are called *permission sets,* which combine the most common permission attributes into units that can be assigned collectively to an object. When you first open the Security tab for a file or folder you see the list of assigned groups and/or users, along with the associated permission sets, shown in Figure E.3.

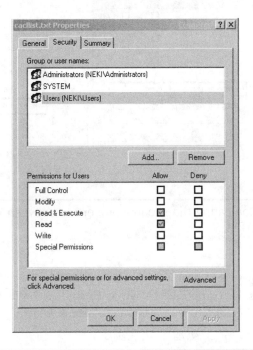

Figure E.3   A list of permission sets for a file on a Windows 2003 server.

TIP: The Security tab differs slightly between a Windows 2003 and a Windows 2000 server. Figure E.4 shows the properties listed in this dialog box for both Windows 2000 and Windows 2003. The 2003 dialog box has the additional permission set labeled Special Permissions. On a Windows 2000 server, this entry does not exist. Instead, if special permissions have been assigned, additional text appears next to the Advanced button saying, "Additional permissions are present but not viewable here. Press Advanced to see them."

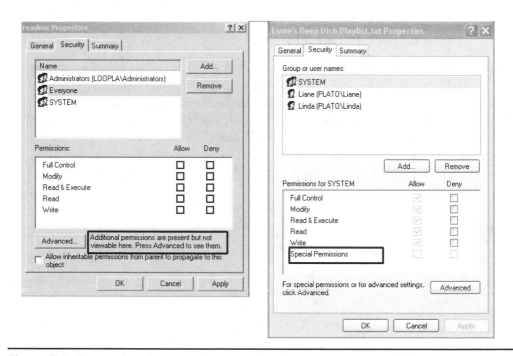

Figure E.4 Comparing the security properties between Windows 2000 and Windows 2003.

Table E.1 shows the default permission sets for Windows 2003/2000, along with the permission attributes that compose each set. As I mentioned, Windows 2003 includes the one additional permission set labeled Special Permissions, which is not found in Windows 2000.

Table E.1 Windows 2003/2000 File Permission Sets

Permission Sets	Permission Attributes	Description
Full Control	All	Provides full access to the file, including the ability to change security permissions and take ownership.
Modify	D, Read & Execute set, Write set	Combines the Read & Execute and the Write permission sets described in this table, in addition to the Delete permission attribute.
Read & Execute	TFEF, Read set	Identical to the Read permission described in this table but also includes the ability to launch executable files.
Read	LFRD, RA, REA, RP	Provides the basic ability to read the contents of a file, including data, security, and non-security attributes. This permission set doesn't grant access to launch an executable file.
Write	CFWD, CFAD, WA, WEA	Provides the basic ability to write data to a file. Note that you can't change a file unless you also have the Read permission set.
Special Permissions		Windows 2003 only. This permission set is merely a flag that indicates individual permission attributes have been assigned that do not fall within a standard permission set. You must click the Advanced button in order to view these special permission settings. You cannot directly allow or deny this permission set.

A common strategy for defining security on the file system is to assign certain permission sets to user groups and then use the Advanced option to fine-tune these permissions. Individual attributes can be added or removed to attain the desired security configuration. Clicking the Advanced button on a Windows 2003 server brings up the dialog box shown in Figure E.5. From here you can assign individual permission attributes, as well as configure auditing or take ownership of a file or folder.

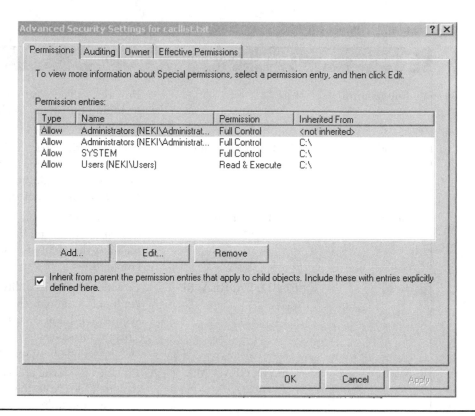

Figure E.5 Advanced access control settings on a 2003 server.

The Permissions tab includes an extra information feature in Windows 2003 that is not found in Windows 2000. The Inherit From column indicates whether or not the specified permission entry was inherited or explicitly defined for the object. See the "Permission Inheritance" section, later in this chapter, for more information on this.

Folder Object Permissions

Although it's not difficult to assign permissions to files, it obviously wouldn't be practical to set the permissions manually on every file on your Terminal Server. In reality, you'll assign permissions to individual files only in certain situations, and in most cases, you'll assign permissions at the folder level.

Windows 2003/2000 uses *permission inheritance* to assign rights to new files or subfolders created within a folder. What this means is that after you've set permissions on a folder and the files it contains, any new file or subfolder created in this directory automatically inherits the rights you assigned to the parent folder.

When a file or folder is copied into another folder, it inherits both the permissions and the ownership of the target folder. When copying, you're essentially creating a new object that's a duplicate of the original.

You're probably wondering how permissions are handled when a file or folder is *moved* into another folder. The behavior actually depends on whether the target folder is on the same disk partition as the source or on a different partition:

- **Source and target are on the same partition**—In this situation, permissions and ownership of the source object remain unchanged. For example, if you have a file that has only the administrator granted full control and you move it into a folder where everyone has read access, the file still only contains the administrator with full control. Windows does not actually move the file in this case but simply updates the file pointer to originate from the new folder location.
- **Source and target are on different partitions**—In this case, the move is actually treated as a copy-and-delete operation, and the permissions for the moved object *are* inherited from the target folder, as described earlier for a copy operation.

Folder permissions are built on the same permission attributes as file permissions and have nearly identical permission sets. Table E.2 shows the six permission sets for Windows 2003/2000 folders.

Table E.2   Windows 2003/2000 Folder Permission Sets

Permission Set	Permission Attributes	Description
Full Control	All	Provides full access to all files and folders, including the ability to change security permissions, take ownership, and delete subfolders and files.
Modify	D, Read & Execute set, Write set	Combines the Read & Execute and the Write permission sets described in this table, in addition to the Delete permission attribute.
Read & Execute	TFEF, Read set	Identical to the Read permission described in this table but also includes the ability to traverse into subfolders.

Table E.2   Windows 2003/2000 Folder Permission Sets (continued)

Permission Set	Permission Attributes	Description
List Folder Contents	Same as Read & Execute set	This security permission set enables you to perform the exact same operations as the Read & Execute permission set. The only difference between the two is in how the permission set is inherited when applied to a folder. A file can inherit *only* the Read & Execute permission, while a folder can inherit both.
		Take, for example, a folder with the List Folder Contents (LFC) permission assigned to the Users group.
		Now, if you copied a file into that folder, the Users group would be able to see it in the folder list but could not view its contents or execute it.
		If a subfolder was copied into this folder, the Users group *would* be able to list the contents of that subfolder.
		If the Users group had Read & Execute permissions on the parent folder instead of List Folder Contents, they could list all subfolders and read or execute the contents of all files in these folders, since the files would also inherit the Read & Execute permission.
Read	LFRD, RA, REA, RP	Provides the basic ability to read the contents of a folder, as well as security and non-security attributes. This permission set doesn't grant access to traverse into a folder.

Table E.2 Windows 2003/2000 Folder Permission Sets (continued)

Permission Set	Permission Attributes	Description
Write	CFWD, CFAD, WA, WEA	Provides the basic ability to create a file or subfolder within a folder.
Special Permissions		Windows 2003 only. This permission set is merely a flag that indicates individual permission attributes have been assigned that do not fall within a standard permission set. You must click the Advanced button in order to view these special permission attributes. You cannot directly allow or deny this permission set.

In most circumstances, you'll use the predefined folder permission sets to establish your file and folder security, although use of special file and folder access can be helpful in certain situations. The later section "Calculating Permissions" discusses how to determine what permissions a user has when he or she belongs to multiple groups with different permission settings.

Permission Inheritance

As I'm sure you've seen by now, there are many situations where the Allow/Deny option for a permission attribute or set is grayed out and cannot be edited, as shown in Figure E.6. A grayed-out permission indicates that the permission is being inherited by the parent object (which in turn may be inheriting its parent's permissions) and can't be edited here. When a child object is inheriting the permissions of its parent, any changes to the parent object's permissions are automatically reflected in the child.

If you wish to modify permissions of an object that is inheriting them from its parent, you have three options:

- **Augment the inherited permission**—Even though you cannot modify the grayed-out permissions, you are free to check any of the other permissions (either Allow or Deny) that are not grayed out. This lets you add additional permissions that are included when calculating the permissions for a user. In Figure E.7, I added the Modify and Write permissions for users to the TEMP folder.

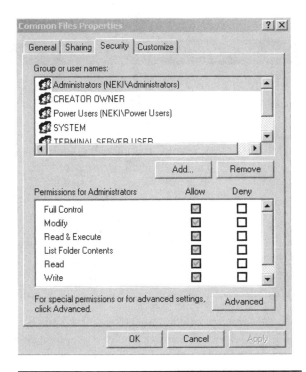

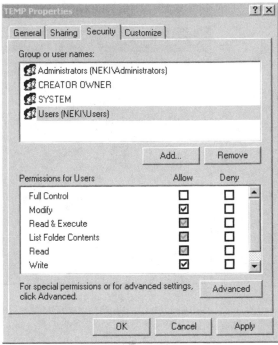

Figure E.6 A grayed-out permission, such as the Allow permission in this figure indicates it is actually inheriting permissions from a parent object.

Figure E.7 Augmenting inherited permissions.

■ **Modify the parent's permissions**—You can do this by first tracing back up through the object's lineage until you find the parent whose permissions are controlling the child's permissions and making the desired changes there. The downside to this, of course, is that your changes affect all other objects that may also be inheriting their permissions from the parent.

On a Windows 2000 server, you will need to examine the permissions of each successive parent object until you find the one no longer inheriting permissions. This will be the parent object controlling a child object's permissions. On a Windows 2003 server, the Permissions tab on the Advanced Security Settings dialog box includes the column Inherited From, which shows the uppermost parent object controlling this child's permissions. Figure E.8 shows that the inherited permissions for the PLUGINS folder are coming from the C:\Program Files parent folder.

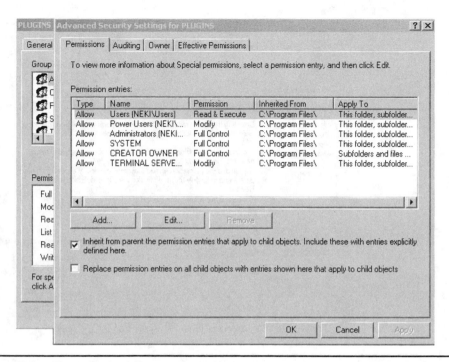

Figure E.8 The Inherited From column in the Permission entries table is a new feature in Windows 2003.

- **Break the inheritance and define your own permissions**—By deselecting the Inherit From Parent checkbox on the Advanced Security Settings dialog box, you break the inheritance link and define your own permissions. When you first deselect this option, the dialog box shown in Figure E.9 appears. As you can see, you are given the option to specify how you want security for the object configured now that you're breaking its inheritance with the parent object. You can make a copy of the inherited permissions, which you can then edit, or you can choose to remove all inherited permissions, keeping only those permissions explicitly defined on the object. In most cases, this results in an empty authentication list unless you have explicitly added additional permissions.

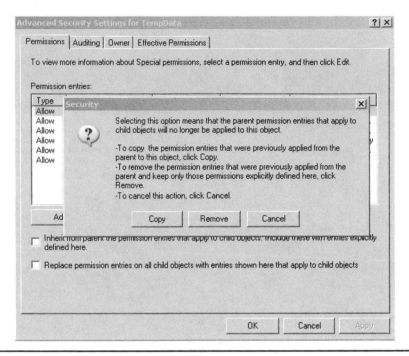

Figure E.9   Breaking permission inheritance.

If you are breaking the inheritance on a folder with subfolders, all subfolders retain their Inherit From Parent attribute, but if they were inheriting from the parent just severed, their reference now updates to point to the folder that broke the inheritance. Figure E.10 demonstrates this behavior. In Diagram 1, all subfolders of Program Data inherit its permissions. In Diagram 2, the inheritance between the Citrix folder and Program Data has been broken and the permissions for the Users group removed. The inheritance for the ICA subfolder will automatically update to point to Citrix, and its permissions will also change so that only administrators have Full Control access. The Microsoft and RDP folders remain unchanged.

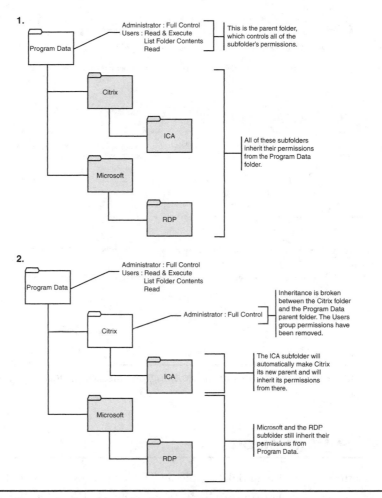

1.

Program Data

Administrator : Full Control
Users : Read & Execute
List Folder Contents
Read

This is the parent folder, which controls all of the subfolder's permissions.

Citrix

ICA

Microsoft

RDP

All of these subfolders inherit their permissions from the Program Data folder.

2.

Program Data

Administrator : Full Control
Users : Read & Execute
List Folder Contents
Read

Citrix

Administrator : Full Control

Inheritance is broken between the Citrix folder and the Program Data parent folder. The Users group permissions have been removed.

ICA

The ICA subfolder will automatically make Citrix its new parent and will inherit its permissions from there.

Microsoft

RDP

Microsoft and the RDP subfolder still inherit their permissions from Program Data.

Figure E.10   An example of breaking permission inheritance.

TIP: After deselecting the Allow Inheritable Permissions option, you're free to reselect it, but inheriting from the parent is not automatically re-enabled. If you want to reinstate inheritance, you need to do the following:

1. Select the Advanced option from the parent key and enable the checkbox for the option Replace Permission Entries on All Child Objects. On Windows 2000, this option is labeled Reset Permissions on All Child Objects.

2. Click Apply or OK. You are presented with a confirmation dialog box (Figure E.11). After you select Yes, any explicitly defined permissions that you or anyone else may have set on all subfolders are removed, and the permissions in the parent folder are automatically inherited by the children.

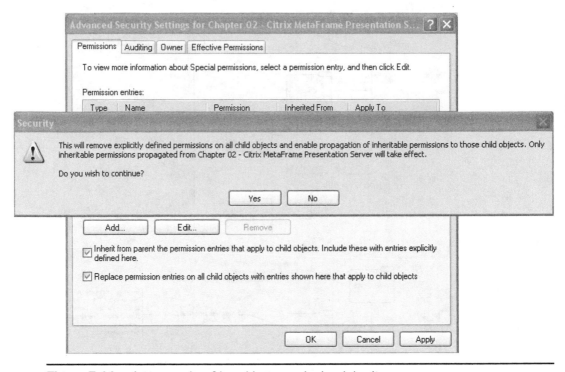

Figure E.11 An example of breaking permission inheritance.

Calculating Permissions

A critical part of manipulating file and folder permissions is understanding how Terminal Server collects and reviews these permissions to determine the effective permissions for a user.

Consider this simple scenario. Joe is a member of the groups Senior and Junior. These groups have the following permissions on the file KNOWITALL.TXT:

> Senior: Deny (Read & Execute)
> Junior: Allow Read

If Joe tries to access the file KNOWITALL.TXT, will he be able to read the file? The answer to this question depends on how Terminal Server handles calculation of Joe's permissions.

Terminal Server calculates file and directory permissions using the simple union $\cup$ of all permission sets assigned to the user as follows. If a user is assigned to the groups G1, G2, ..., Gn with permission sets S1, S2, ..., Sn (not necessarily different) on a file or folder, the user's permissions on that object will be the permission set resulting from the following calculation:

$$S1 \ldots \cup S2 \cup \ldots \cup Sn$$

The union of two or more permission sets is a new set consisting of all permission attributes that are in at least one of the sets being "unioned." This is made clear by the following simple example.

Linda is a member of two groups, Marketing and Sales, and these groups have the permissions Read and Modify, respectively, on the file PROFITS. Linda's final permissions on the PROFITS file are determined by taking the permission attributes for Read and Modify and calculating the union of those attributes:

```
Read   = {LFRD, RA, REA, RP}
Modify = {Read & Execute, Write, D}
       = {LFRD, RA, REA, RP, TFEF, CFWD, CFAD, WA, WEA, D}

Read [us] Modify
    = {LFRD, RA, REA, RP} [us] {LFRD, RA, REA, RP, TFEF, CFWD, CFAD, WA,
WEA, D}
    = {LFRD, RA, REA, RP, TFEF, CFWD, CFAD, WA, WEA, D}
    = Modify
```

Therefore, Linda will have Modify permissions on the file PROFITS.

After reviewing this somewhat trivial example, you may wonder why I bothered to go into such detail regarding union of permission sets when it appears that permissions are based on the group with the "greater" permissions. Taking the union of Read and Full Control would seem to back up this argument because

$$\text{Read} \cup \text{Full Control} = \text{Full Control}$$

If you're not convinced of this, simply work through the set union exercise as I did in the example.

The problem is that this simple view of "greater" permissions doesn't work when a user is assigned to multiple groups that may have special permissions assigned to them. Consider another example. Once again we have Linda, a member of Marketing and Sales. Marketing now has Read & Execute, while Sales has Read + Write + Delete (but not Execute). We take the union of these permission sets to calculate Linda's final permissions for the PROFITS file:

```
{Read & Execute} [us] {Read, Write, D}
    = {Read & Execute, Read, Write, D}
    = {Read & Execute, Write, D}
    = Modify
```

Therefore, Linda will have Modify permissions.

Notice this time that neither Marketing's nor Sales' group permissions could be considered "greater" when determining final access to the PROFITS file.

Until now, I purposely avoided the situation where a user is explicitly assigned Deny for a security set or attribute. Let's return to the example mentioned at the beginning of this section: Joe and the two groups Senior and Junior, with respective permissions Deny (Read & Execute) and Allow Read.

The logical solution is to apply the union of these two sets and determine the resulting values. In my calculation, I use the "not" symbol (a solid line) over an attribute to signify that it's a Deny permission instead of an Allow permission. For example, Deny Read appears as shown in Figure E.12.

$$\overline{\text{Read}}$$

Figure E.12   A solid line over the Read attribute indicates that Read permission is denied.

Before performing the calculation, we need to add one new rule to the union operation. You have both a Deny and an Allow permission in the same result set in this example. In these situations, the Deny permission *always* overrides the Allow permission, as shown in Figure E.13.

$$\text{Read U } \overline{\text{Read}} = \overline{\text{Read}}$$

Figure E.13   A Deny Read overrides an Allow Read.

We can now easily determine Joe's permissions, as shown in Figure E.14. Unfortunately for Joe, the Deny Read overrides the Allow Read and results in the Deny (Read & Execute) remaining in effect on the KNOWITALL.TXT file. Of course, this is a trivial example, and the result is as expected.

$$\text{Deny } \overline{(\text{Read \& Execute})} \text{ U Read}$$

$$= \overline{(\text{Read \& Execute}) \text{ U Read}}$$

$$= \overline{\text{Read}} \text{ U } \overline{\text{TFEF}} \text{ U Read}$$

$$= \overline{\text{Read} \text{ U } \overline{\text{TFEF}}} = \overline{\text{Read \& Execute}}$$

$$= \text{Deny (Read \& Execute)}$$

Figure E.14 Deny Read overrides Allow Read, resulting in Deny (Read & Execute).

Use of the Deny permission ensures that the user or group won't be able to exercise the denied permission, regardless of the other permissions assigned to that user or group. This is a very powerful security feature that ensures users cannot "accidentally" acquire more security rights than they should have.

To summarize, permissions on a file or folder are determined for a user by taking the union of all permission attributes assigned to that user, with Deny permissions automatically overriding any equivalent Allow permissions the user may have.

TIP: Windows 2003 provides an informational tool that automatically calculates permissions for a user or group and displays the results. On the Advanced Security Settings dialog box (accessed by clicking the Advanced button), there is a tab called Effective Permissions. Simply select the desired user or group by clicking the Select button, and Windows automatically calculates and displays the corresponding effective permissions. Figure E.15 shows an example of the effective permissions for the Users group on the file CACLLIST.TXT.

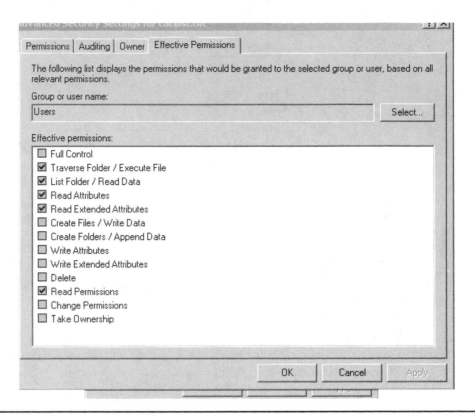

Figure E.15   Effective Permissions calculations on a 2003 server.

Registry Permissions

Since the initial release of Windows NT, application, operating system, and user-specific information has been maintained in a central repository known as the *registry*. The registry is a special database of information that is a critical component of the system, and as such requires proper protection, particularly in a Terminal Server environment, where users have local access to not only the registry but also by default to the tools used to manipulate the registry.

Fortunately, the default security configuration on the registry has continued to improve for Terminal Server since the release of Windows 2000. Both Windows 2000 and 2003 provide a much more secure default registry configuration than was present in NT 4.0, Terminal Server Edition. Even so, it is important as an administrator to have an understanding of how registry permissions are actually managed, so you can confidently make any changes that might be necessary to ensure a secure and stable configuration.

TIP: See Chapter 16 for more information on specific security changes that may be necessary.

Registry Editors

Windows 2000 ships with two registry-manipulation tools called REGEDT32 and REGED-IT. Both tools provide similar functionality, but there are certain situations where one tool provides a functional advantage over the other. The main differences between these tools are

- **REGEDT32**—Lets you manage the security configuration of the registry. Provides only limited registry key and value editing. No key value searching is available, and key entries cannot be renamed.
- **REGEDIT**—Provides no security-editing support. Provides robust registry key and value editing. Renaming and limited copying features are available. A search feature exists that allows searching of key names, value names, and data.

While Windows 2003 maintains both calling names (REGEDT32 and REGEDIT), the functionality of these two tools has actually been combined into a single application. So now, from within one tool, you can edit registry security as well as search and modify registry information (see Figure E.16). Both names have been maintained to ensure backwards compatibility with any scripts or operational processes that may depend on one name or the other.

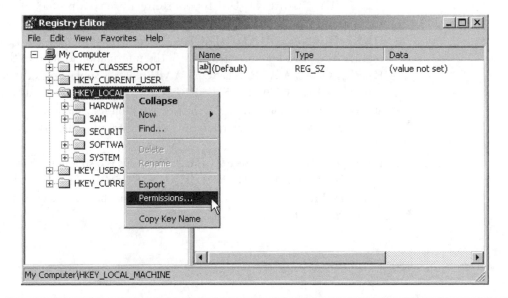

Figure E.16   The Permissions option within REGEDIT on Windows 2003.

TIP: Typing "REGEDT32" or "REGEDIT" from the Run option on the Start menu will launch the respective command.

Registry Hives

The registry consists of the following five components, commonly called *subtrees* or *hives*:

- **HKEY_LOCAL_MACHINE (HKLM)**—Contains all the information pertaining to configuration of the Terminal Server. This includes the hardware, software, and system configuration, as well as the local security account information.
- **HKEY_USERS (HKU)**—This registry hive contains profile data for all users currently logged on to the Terminal Server, listed by SID. In addition to USERS, the DEFAULT subkey is also always present. When a user logs off the server, his or her profile information is unloaded from this hive. When a user logs on, his or her profile information (either from a roaming profile or a local profile) is loaded into this hive.

  On a Windows 2003 server, there are two additional HKU SID entries corresponding to the special LOCAL SERVICE and NETWORK SERVICE system accounts. These keys are always present in HKEY_USERS on a 2003 server.
- **HKEY_CURRENT_USER (HKCU)**—This is simply a pointer into the HKEY_USERS hive for each individual user. Within your Terminal Server session, HKEY_CURRENT_USER points directly to your profile information subkey within the HKEY_USERS hive.
- **HKEY_CLASSES_ROOT (HKCR)**—In both Windows 2000 and 2003, this registry hive provides a merged view of the information located in the HKEY_LOCAL_MACHINE\SOFTWARE\Classes subkey plus the information stored in HKEY_CURRENT_USER\Software\Classes. These subkeys contain all the file-association and COM class registration information. Any settings in HKCU\Software\Classes override the defaults stored in the HKLM\Software\ Classes key.
- **HKEY_CURRENT_CONFIG (HKCC)**—This is also a pointer, this time to the subkey HKEY_LOCAL_MACHINE\SYSTEM\CurrentControlSet\ Hardware Profiles\Current. This subkey contains the server's current hardware configuration information.

The registry hives are stored in a set of files located in the folder %systemroot%\ System32\Config. Table E.3 lists the registry hives and associated files. In addition to the main file containing the registry information, two additional file types may be present:

- **.SAV**—These are copies of the corresponding files as they were at the end of the server installation.
- **.LOG**—This is a transaction log of the changes made within the associated hive and is used to ensure that the registry remains in a stable state even if a system failure occurs during a write operation.

Table E.3 Registry Hive Files

Registry Hive	Hive File Name
HKEY_LOCAL_MACHINE\SAM	SAM and SAM.LOG.
HKEY_LOCAL_MACHINE\SECURITY	SECURITY and SECURITY.LOG.
HKEY_LOCAL_MACHINE\SOFTWARE	SOFTWARE, SOFTWARE.SAV, and SOFTWARE.LOG.
HKEY_LOCAL_MACHINE\SYSTEM	SYSTEM, SYSTEM.SAV, and SYSTEM.LOG.
HKEY_USERS\.DEFAULT	DEFAULT, DEFAULT.SAV, and DEFAULT.LOG.
HKEY_CURRENT_USER	NTUSER.DAT. This file is *not* stored in the Config folder with the other files but instead resides wherever the user's profile is retained. This is normally in %systemdrive%\Documents and Settings\%UserName%. User profiles are discussed in Chapter 18, "User Profile and Account Configuration."

Registry Permission Attributes

Much like file system security, registry security is built upon permission attributes. There are 10 registry permission attributes, as shown in Table E.4. These permission attributes are the same for both Windows 2000 and Windows 2003.

Table E.4   Registry Permission Attributes

Permission Attribute	Abbreviation	Description
Query Value	(Q)	Grants access to read the value of a key. If you don't have this permission, the key appears grayed out and you can't view either the key values or any subkeys under that key, even if you have the Enumerate Subkeys permission.
Set Value	(S)	Allows access to set or modify the value of a key. This doesn't grant permission to add or delete keys.
Create Subkey	(C)	Allows creation of a new subkey under the selected key.
Enumerate Subkeys	(E)	Allows generation of a list of all subkeys under the selected key. To view subkeys under a given key, you must also have the Query Value permission.
Notify	(N)	Grants the right to monitor notification events from the key. This means that if a change occurs in the key, the user with this right automatically receives notification of the change. This notification is available through application programming interface (API) calls.
Create Link	(L)	Allows creation of a symbolic link from one key to another.
Delete Key	(D)	Grants access to delete the selected key. You can't delete a registry key unless you also have the Delete Key permission on all subkeys it may contain, because these subkeys must first be deleted before the parent key can be deleted.
Write DAC	(W)	Allows modification of the Access Control List (ACL) for the key. (DAC stands for Discretionary Access Control.)
Write Owner	(O)	Grants the right to take ownership of a key. If you're the owner of a key, you have inherent permission to modify the Access Control List (Write DAC permission).
Read Control	(R)	Grants the right to view the security data associated with the key.

Permission sets for the registry also exist. Just as with the file system, these permission sets are a predefined group of security attributes grouped together to provide a certain level of permissions. Unlike the file system, which has a robust list of permission sets, the registry provides only two, as listed in Table E.5.

NOTE: Windows 2003 provides a third permission set, called Special Permissions. This is identical to the file system permission set of the same name. It is merely a flag indicating that individual permission attributes have been assigned that do not fall within a standard permission set grouping. By clicking the Advanced button, you can view these special permissions. The Special Permissions set cannot be directly edited.

Table E.5   Default Registry Permission Sets

Permission Set	Set Attributes	Description
Read	(QENR)	This set defines the basic read access to keys and values, including viewing the existing security permissions.
Full Control	(All)	As the name suggests, this permission set provides full control over subkeys and values.

Unfortunately, no permission set exists that would grant only a "change" permission. For this, you have only the option of granting Read or Full Control. If you wish to grant a user or group anything other than Read, you must assign them individual permissions. You should never grant a non-administrator group full control to any registry key (with the exception of their own HKEY_CURRENT_USER key) unless absolutely necessary. In many situations, the Read permission set is appropriate.

TIP: The Advanced Security Settings tab for registry security provides the same information found in the Advanced Security Settings for the file system. Permission inheritance also applies to registry security and behaves exactly the same as file system security. See the section "Permission Inheritance," earlier in this chapter, for more information on this.

Index

THIS BOOK IS SAFARI ENABLED

INCLUDES FREE 45-DAY ACCESS TO THE ONLINE EDITION

The Safari® Enabled icon on the cover of your favorite technology book means the book is available through Safari Bookshelf. When you buy this book, you get free access to the online edition for 45 days.

Safari Bookshelf is an electronic reference library that lets you easily search thousands of technical books, find code samples, download chapters, and access technical information whenever and wherever you need it.

TO GAIN 45-DAY SAFARI ENABLED ACCESS TO THIS BOOK:

- Go to **http://www.awprofessional.com/safarienabled**
- Complete the brief registration form
- Enter the coupon code found in the front of this book on the "Copyright" page

If you have difficulty registering on Safari Bookshelf or accessing the online edition, please e-mail customer-service@safaribooksonline.com.